The *value of a common stock with growth apportunities* that has earnings of EPS_1 capitalized at k_s, plus future growth opportunities is

$$P_0 = (EPS_1/k_s) + \text{present value of growth opportuni}$$

The *return on a common stock* that pays dividends o
ending market price P_1, is

$$k = \frac{D_1 + (P_1 - P_0)}{P_0}$$

Risk and Return (4)

The *expected return (or mean)* when n states are involved, the probability of a state occurring is k_i, and the return per state is P_i, is

$$\bar{k} = \sum_{j=1}^{n} k_i P_i$$

The *standard deviation*, where the expected return is $\bar{k}$ and n states are involved, is

$$\sigma = \left[\sum_{j=1}^{n} (k_i - \bar{k}^2) P_i \right]^{0.5}$$

The *variance* is σ^2.

The *expected return on a portfolio* of Z stocks, where W indicates the proportion of the portfolio allocated to a stock, is

$$\bar{K}_p = W_A \bar{k}_A + W_B \bar{k}_B + \cdots + W_Z \bar{k}_Z$$

The *correlation* equals the *covariance* (or comovement), Cov_{AB}, between the returns for two assets divided by the two standard deviations, so

$$Corr_{AB} = Cov_{AB}/\sigma_A \sigma_B$$

The *total risk for a portfolio* consisting of assets A and B, with variances σ_A^2 and σ_B^2, proportions invested in assets of W_A and W_B, and a correlation between the returns on the assets of $Corr_{AB}$, is

$$\sigma_p = (W_A^2 \sigma_A^2 + W_B^2 \sigma_B^2 + 2W_A W_B \sigma_A \sigma_B Corr_{AB})^{0.5}$$

The *nondiversifiable risk (beta)* for asset j relative to market M is

$$\beta_j = Cov_{jM}/\sigma_M^2$$

Option Valuation (5)

The *value of a call option at expiration* when the market price of the underlying asset is P_0 and the exercise price is X, is

$$V_c = \text{Max}(0, P_0 - X)$$

The *value of a call option before expiration* (based on the Black-Scholes model) is

$$V_c = P_0 N(d_1) - \frac{X}{e^{k_{RF}t}} N(d_2)$$

(continued on next page)

where

$$d_1 = \frac{\ln(P_0/X) + (k_{RF} + 0.5\sigma^2)t}{\sigma(t)^{0.5}}$$

$$d_2 = d_1 - \sigma(t)^{0.5}$$

$N(d)$ = cumulative normal probability density function
P_0 = price of the underlying asset today
k_{RF} = continuously compounded risk-free rate
X = exercise price
t = time to expiration
σ^2 = continuously compounded variance of the rate of return of the underlying asset

The *value of a put option at expiration* is

$$V_p = \text{Max}(0, X - P_0)$$

The *value of a put option before expiration* is

$$V_p = V_c + \frac{X}{e^{k_{RF}t}} - P_0$$

Opportunity Cost of Capital (6)

A firm's *opportunity cost of capital* for projects as risky as the firm as a whole is a weighted average, where the weights W are of the after-tax costs of financing, so

$$k = k_i W_{\text{debt}} + k_s W_{\text{common equity}}$$

The *after-tax cost of debt*, where k_b is the before-tax cost and T is the firm's marginal tax rate, is

$$k_i = k_b(1 - T)$$

The *cost of common stock using the dividend valuation model*, k_s, is

$$P_0 = \frac{D_1}{(1 + k_s)} + \frac{D_2}{(1 + k_s)^2} + \cdots + \frac{D_\infty}{(1 + k_s)^\infty}$$

while using the *capital asset pricing model* it is

$$k_s = k_{RF} + \beta_j(k_M - k_{RF})$$

An *unlevered, or asset, beta* can be estimated by adjusting beta for a levered firm to account for the firm's tax rate, T, and its use of debt, B, and stock, S, so

$$\beta_{\text{asset}} = \beta_U = \frac{\beta_{\text{levered firm}}}{1 + (1 - T)(B/S)}$$

The *cost of equity capital for a division* of a firm is

$$k_{\text{division}} = k_{RF} + \beta_{\text{division}}(k_M - k_{RF})$$

(continued on inside end papers)

Financial Management

Financial Management

George E. Pinches
Wagnon Professor of Finance
University of Kansas

HarperCollins*CollegePublishers*

Acquisitions Editor: Kirsten D. Sandberg
Project Coordination and Text Design: York Production Services
Cover Design: Heather A. Ziegler
Cover Illustration: Rob Colvin
Production: Valerie Sawyer
Compositor: Interactive Composition Corporation
Printer and Binder: R. R. Donnelley & Sons Company
Cover Printer: Lehigh Press, Inc.

Financial Management

Library of Congress Cataloging-in-Publication Data

Pinches, George E.
    Financial management / George E. Pinches.
        p.   cm.
    Includes bibliographical references and index.
    ISBN 0-06-502470-2
    1. Business enterprises—Finance.   2. Corporations—Finance.
3. Investments.   I. Title.
    HG4026.P572   1994
    658.15—dc20
                                                                93–48504
                                                                CIP

94 95 96 9 8 7 6 5 4 3 2

To Carole, Susan,
Katharine, and Bill

Brief Contents

Detailed Contents

Preface

During the financially charged 1980s, the field of financial management changed tremendously: to maximize shareholder wealth and to provide managerial independence in a truly global and highly competitive environment, firms devised strategies including numerous mergers, friendly and hostile acquisitions, sometimes messy bankruptcies, vital recapitalizations, and privatizing public firms. Some companies were successful and others were not. American Airlines, for example, spent billions to expand its domestic market share only to find itself losing the fare wars to much smaller low-cost carriers, whereas Motorola invested in exclusive rights to radio frequencies to position itself as at the forefront of the industry. As markets for options and other derivative securities matured and grew complex, financial managers found new tools to manage corporate risk. Computer and telecommunications technology has fundamentally revolutionized—and will continue to improve—how financial managers do their jobs. Anticipating a good many more innovations as we approach the year 2000, I felt that M.B.A. students and advanced undergraduate finance and accounting majors, if they were to succeed in the 1990s, really needed a fresh text for understanding the financial management of corporations.

A daunting task lies ahead for those instructors who must teach the core M.B.A. financial management course that includes full- or part-time students who may or may not have business experience or even an undergraduate degree in business. This course—and this book—may be a student's first and only exposure to finance. Different students have different intellectual pursuits and needs: some want to understand how the Clinton administration's recent amendment to the tax code will affect a financial manager's capital structure decisions, while others want to master basic capital budgeting techniques for determining when to introduce new products. Undoubtedly, those concentrating primarily on finance want to understand the time value of money, the relationship between risk and return, market theories, valuation techniques, and the function of financial intermediation, and other key ideas that will make them more marketable job candidates. With such divergent customer needs, I have tried to provide a modern view of the fundamental concepts of finance and to demonstrate these concepts in contemporary examples.

There is, of course, more to know about finance than what falls between these two covers. But I hope that, after using my book, students who focus on finance will be able to apply the tools and techniques of finance in subsequent courses and throughout their careers, and students who concentrate in other areas of business will be able not only to appreciate the role of finance in making business decisions but also to communicate more effectively with the finance staff within the firm. Keeping this hope in mind, readers will find the following features in *Financial Management:*

DISTINGUISHING FEATURES

1. The text links financial decisions to seven fundamental concepts:
    a. *Maximization of the market value of the firm.* Market value refers to the price that someone will pay for the firm. For publicly traded firms, this value equals the total market price of the firm's stock plus the total market value of its debt.
    b. *Financial market efficiencies.* In efficient markets, the current price of the stock reflects all publicly avalable information about the firm. Students can truly fathom the implication of a financial manager's decisions only if they comprehend how the global financial system works and how financial markets operate within this global environment.
    c. *Agency theory.* Agency theory addresses the problem of the firm, that individuals may act in their own self interest rather than on behalf of the shareholders. Ongoing coverage of agency issues throughout the book adds a more human dimension to the study of finance.
    d. *Cash flows.* By emphasizing the incremental inflows and outflows of cash, essentially the financial lifeblood of the firm, the text turns student attention away from the firm's accounting earnings and toward a better measure of a firm's financial health.
    e. *Time value of money and net present value.* Simply put, the value of money differs over time; receiving a dollar today is worth more than getting a dollar tomorrow. Net present value enables us to weigh the economic costs against the benefits of a decision. This book stresses these two organizing principles so that students understand them as part of a paradigm rather than equations to memorize and to plug in numbers for a quick answer.
    f. *Risk and return.* Risk and return go hand in hand. Where appropriate, this book makes the point that all financial decisions involve risk for revenues: to increase an expected return, a firm or an individual must incur more risk.
    g. *Options and financial risk management.* Since financial managers now use options more extensively to hedge risk, this book introduces options earlier (Chapter 5) than most of its competitors and, as necessary thereafter, examines how to use options as a tool for risk management. Special tables in the book make valuing options fairly easy, and so the book focuses on applying options rather than on calculating their value. Due to time constraints, some instructors may choose to omit this material but might recommend it to finance majors for future reference.

By emphasizing these basic concepts, the book establishes a consistent and theo-retically sound framework that enables students to see (a) the relationships among all of the firm's financial decisions, (b) the larger economic picture rather than just the institutional detail, and (c) the importance of those areas of finance beyond the corporate walls.

2. Recent developments incorporated into the book include the following: the Fed-eral Reserve system's new Truth in Saving regulation, which requires depository institutions to determine the annual percentage yield on savings; the new income tax requirements due to the Budget Reconciliation Act of 1993; complete and up-to-date information on past security returns and their volatility; extensive and unique treatment of capital structure theory and application (Chapters 11 and 12); recent theoretical and empirical research; newer forms of financing including medium-term notes and hybrid securities; electronic payment systems and elec-tronic data interchange; and hedging techniques for managing interest rate risk and foreign exchange risk (Chapters 23 and 28).

3. Step-by-step examples illustrate each calculation so that students can see how to use the tools in the decision-making process. This learning aid particularly benefits those who are new to the business of solving financial problems.

4. Because of its rapidly expanding significance, international financial management appears in two separate chapters (Chapter 27 and 28) and in select chapters where appropriate. Chapter 28 is unique in that it looks at how firms hedge their foreign exchange risk.

5. To provide instructors with maximum flexibility in course design and to serve as a trusted reference for students throughout their business careers, the book in-cludes more material than any one course is apt to cover. Some chapters provide optional appendixes and detailed footnotes and source listings for further study; and the *Instructor's Manual* suggests alternatives for courses of varying lengths and emphasis.

6. Learning aids, all designed to help students make the most of their study time, include Executive Summaries, step-by-step calculations and numerical demon-strations of core concepts, Concept Review Questions for self-testing within each chapter, instructions for using financial calculators to solve problems more efficiently, end-of-chapter Concept Review Problems, references, glossary, and, for each chapter, a complete set of problems and a Mini Case for more in-depth analysis. At the beginning of each part, readers will find unique and highly moti-vating Executive Interviews which provide practical insights into the financial management of real companies. These part openers, and occasional in-chapter inserts, showcase industry leaders who explain in their own words the relevance of forthcoming material from a realistic point of view.

WHO'S WHO IN THE EXECUTIVE INTERVIEWS AND INSERTS

James M. Cornelius, Eli Lilly and Company . In 1986, Mr. Cornelius was elected to the Board of Directors and Executive Commttee of Eli Lilly. He has served as vice president of finance and chief financial officer of the Indianapolis-based firm since 1983. Born in Michigan, Mr. Cornelius earned an undergraduate degree in accounting and an M.B.A. degree from Michigan State University. After two years with the U.S. Army Finance Corps, he began his 25-year career with Lilly, first as a financial planning analyst, then as manager of corporate treasury, manager of economic studies for the Pharmaceutical Division, director of business planning for what is now the Medical Device and Diagnostics Division, president of IVAC Corporation (a Lilly subsidiary), and vice president and corporate treasurer.

James G. Duff, USL Capital USL CAPITAL. In 1988, Mr. Duff moved from the Ford Motor Credit Company to become chairman and chief executive officer of USL Capital, one of the country's largest leasing and commercial financing organizations founded in San Francisco in 1952 and now part of Ford Motor Company's financial Services Group *Ford* Ford Financial Services Group. An employee of Ford for 30 years, Mr. Duff has served the firm as director of finance with Ford of Europe and controller of the Ford division and Ford's Car Product Development Group. A native midwesterner, Mr. Duff holds bachelor's and master's degrees in finance from the University of Kansas.

David B. Ellis, Sara Lee Corporation SARA LEE CORPORATION. Presently assistant treasurer, Mr. Ellis joined the firm in 1984 and moved through positions in financial planning and treasury. For seven years before Sara Lee, he did quite a bit of environmental consuting, with an A.B. in earth sciences from the University of California at San Diego and a master's of science in oceanography from Oregon State University. He earned his master's of business administration from the University of Chicago.

Geoffrey M. Holczer, Design, Inc. DESIGNS Since 1988, Mr. Holczer has served the company as chief financial officer and, as of 1990, added the responsibilities of treasurer and vice president. Prior to that, he was associated with The Stop & Shop Companies, Inc., as controller of Bradlees Department Stores and as corporate controller. Mr. Holczer is a Certified Public Accountant as well.

Andrew J. Kalotay, Andrew Kalotay Associates. Prior to founding his own New York-based consulting firm, Dr. Kalotay directed research in the Bond Portfolio Analysis Group at Salomon Brothers, where his group supported the corporate liability management, the capital markets, and the investment banking desks. He has also served as senior research analyst at Dillon Read, worked in the treasury department of A.T.&T. and with Bell Laboratories in various managerial and technical positions. Dr. Kalotay earned his Ph.D. in mathematics from the University of Toronto, and his M.B.A. from Pace University.

James H. MacNaughton, Salomon Brothers Inc. **Salomon Brothers** . Currently managing director of the New York-based firm, Mr. MacNaughton is responsible for the company's global business with the insurance industry. During his nearly 15-year tenure at Salomon Brothers, he ran the Diversified Industrial Group in investment banking and also worked with assorted companies in the Financial Institutions Department. A native of Milwaukee, Mr. MacNaughton earned his B.A. degree in history and M.B.A. degree from Southern Methodist University. He is also a Certified Public Accountant in the state of Texas.

Mary J. Reilly, BancBoston Capital. Joining the Bank of Boston's Loan Review Department in 1978, Ms. Reilly taught the bank's lending officer trainees for a couple of years and then served as a lending officer for large key corporate accounts. In 1983, she moved into her current position in venture capital financing. Ms. Reilly holds a bachelor of arts degree in history from Connecticut College and a master's of business administration from Virginia Commonwealth University.

William J. Sinkula, Kroger Company . During his 15 years at Kroger, Mr. Sinkula has moved from vice president of finance to his current position, executive vice president and chief financial officer. Prior positions included vice president of administration for the Western Auto Supply Company, vice president of financial relations for F.W. Woolworth, and vice president and treasurer of the Montgomery Ward Company. Mr. Sinkula co-founded Hydro-Conduit Corporation and served as treasurer and executive vice president before Wards acquired Hydro-Conduit. He earned his B.S.B.A. from the University of Nebraska and his M.B.A. from the University of Denver, and is a Certified Public Accountant as well.

Fong Wan, Pacific Gas and Electric Company. Starting in 1988, Fong Wan advanced from financial analyst to director of financial analysis. Life before Pacific Gas included nearly three years as a business analyst for the Exxon Corporation. Fong Wan earned a bachelor's of science in chemical engineering from Columbia University, and a master's of business administration from the University of Michigan.

Alfred L. Williams Jr., United Gas Holding Corporation. As president and chief executive officer of this Houston-based corporation, Mr. Williams is charged with developing and executing acquisition strategy toward maximizing shareholder wealth. Concurrently, he serves as senior vice president and chief financial officer of the United Gas Pipe Line Company, an interstate natural gas transmission company. He holds a B.S. in accounting and an M.B.A. from Louisiana State University and is also a Certified Public Accountant in the state of Texas. His career includes 12 years at the Exxon Company and 10 years at Tenneco Gas, where he served as CFO, director of internal audit, and controller.

COURSE USE AND FLEXIBILITY

This book meets the learning objectives of two somewhat similar audiences: the core finance class in the standard M.B.A. curriculum *and* the second course in finance at the undergraduate level.

For the core finance class that all M.B.A. students must take, the book provides ample exposition to prepare readers for upcoming lectures as well as for case analysis. Also, since students who enter M.B.A. programs come from such diverse academic and practical backgrounds, the book thoroughly reviews the core theory of finance in Chapters 1 through 4. After reading these chapters, students should be familiar with the standard prerequisite knowledge of basic accounting concepts, financial theory, time value of money, valuation of stocks and bonds, returns from investing in financial assets, portfolio theory, and the relationship between risk and return.

In the second course in the undergraduate curriculum, usually taken by finance majors, instructors may cover the first four or five chapters of the book in the first class meeting as a more in-depth review of basic concepts. Beyond the basics, most intermediate level courses have various needs depending on what students really master in their introductory finance course. To accommodate these needs without compromising the quality of each course, the book contains several value-added chapters: "Options" (Chapter 5), "Value Creation from Capital Budgeting" (Chapter 10), "Interaction of Investment and Financing Decisions" (Chapter 14), "Warrants and Convertibles" (Chapter 17), "Leasing" (Chapter 18), "Hedging Interest Rate Risk" (Chapter 23), "Mergers and Corporate Restructuring" (Chapter 26), and "Hedging Foreign Exchange Risk" (Chapter 28). While these chapters fall outside the normal syllabi for a first M.B.A. course, they give instructors great flexibility in designing the second undergraduate course to expand upon and enrich what students learned in their first course regardless of the book used. No doubt, professors will want to recommend the book as a reference in subsequent case courses.

RELATIONSHIP TO *ESSENTIALS OF FINANCIAL MANAGEMENT*

For some time now, loyal Pinches customers—and my publisher—have been asking me to write an advanced text on financial management. And with good reason: at the University of Kansas, for example, the undergraduate and graduate business programs differ greatly in terms of student ability and expectations, the goals of the course, and the mix of theory and application. We really need two distinctive books. My widely used *Essentials of Financial Management* suits the first course in the undergraduate curriculum just fine. But, as I stated earlier in this Preface, the advanced undergraduate course and the first graduate course both begged for a fresh approach and prompted me to author this second book. How does this new book differ from *Essentials*? Instructors who assign both *Essentials of Financial Management* and *Financial Management* will undoubtedly notice some overlap. After all, there are only so many ways for one person to present material. While I strived to remove unnecessary overlays of content, those of my students who used drafts of *Financial Management* after using *Essentials* frequently commented that they appreciated the similarities between the texts for review and reinforcement. No contradiction in terms!

TEACHING AND LEARNING AIDS

FOR INSTRUCTORS

Instructor's Manual with Pinches Software, by George E. Pinches, with Ashish Arora and Mridu Vashist, University of Kansas

Customers have told me time and time again how much they appreciate the accuracy and consistency of the manuals that I prepare to accompany my books. This one is no exception. It contains the answers to all chapter questions as well as complete step-by-step solutions to all problems in the text. For those professors who would rather use the text in an intermediate-level undergraduate course, the manual suggests alternative syllabi for courses of varying lengths, levels, and emphasis. It also includes a copy of the *Pinches Software* for students to copy themselves or for instructors to copy and distribute. Designed exclusively to accompany *Financial Management*, the software contains Lotus 1-2-3 templates that enable students to solve in-test problems and conduct sensitivity analyses in areas usually demanding more extensive calculations.

Testing Materials, Prepared by Stephen E. Wilcox, Mankato State University

A citical part of the Pinches package, the test bank is consistent with the language, terms, notation, and conceptual framework of the main text; its solutions follow the problem-solving methodology used in the text. It includes true-false items and a good many rigorous conceptual and numerical types of objective and brief essay questions with solutions. Since the test bank is available in both printed and electronic formats (IBM-compatible TestMaster files), instructors really should contact their publisher's representative to find out which form best meets their testing needs. Users can also download the TestMaster version of the test bank into *QuizMaster*, an on-line testing program that enables users to conduct timed or untimed exams at computer workstations. Upon completing tests, students can see their scores and view or print a diagnostic report of those topics or objectives requiring more attention. When installed on a local area network, QuizMaster allows instructors to save the scores on disk, print study diagnoses, and monitor progress of students individually or by class section, and by all sections of the course.

Presentation Tools, Designed by Kathryn M. Kelm, Emporia State University

A combination of my lecture notes and Dr. Kelm's own work, this *Lecture Outline Transparency System (LOTS)* includes approximately 20 pages of notes per chapter, all three-hole punched, perforated, and formatted so that an instructor can copy them to acetates or integrate them into the instructor's own notes. To support the more quantitative and challenging course material, each chapter is typically comprised of a lecture outline and broad overview of chapter themes and plenty of examples and demonstrations. A set of *Transparency Acetates* includes key exhibits from the text.

FOR STUDENTS

Study Guide, Created by David C. Ketcham, Bryant College

The last few pages of the Preface showcase Chapter 2, "Value Creation and Time Value," from the study guide so that potential users can preview this superior study tool before making a purchase decision. More applied than most guides, this product provides a broad range of applications, from simple one-step exercises to sophisticated integrated problems, all with worked-out solutions. Since problem-solving in a realistic context in this market is more important than memorizing key terms, the guide goes beyond the standard fill-in-the-blank questions so that students not only recognize concepts but also relate them to each other. Each chapter features the following: a brief executive summary of the chapter contents relative to the rest of the text; a topical outline broken down by key points made in the parent text for quick review; list of notation and formulas applied in the chapter; completion questions of core financial relationships and simple calculations, also following the topical outline, with answers in an end-of-guide appendix; an Exercises section where each exercise involves a single calculation or application, roughly one for each first level head, where appropriate, so that students can work step-by-step toward solving problems, with answers in an end-of-guide appendix; a Problems section. Answers to Completion and Exercise items appear in an appendix; however, Solutions to Problems will appear at the end of each chapter for quick reference and incorporate selected Calculator Keystrokes where relevant.

ACKNOWLEDGEMENTS

Truly useful teaching and learning tools are never developed in isolation. My customers—teachers, colleagues, manuscript reviewers, supplements authors, and students—have all positively influenced how I approach the field of finance and how I teach the subject, and I owe each of these constituencies my sincerest gratitude. Individuals who have commented on the first four editions of *Essentials of Financial Management* have helped in clarifying my thoughts and presentation and in pointing out what I needed to move from *Essentials* to *Financial Management*. These individuals are:

J. Amanda Adkisson

Raj Aggarwal

Bruce D. Bagamery

Sheldon D. Balbirer

Earl S. Beecher

Thomas D. Berry

Mary Helen Blakeslee

Harold Blythe

Robert J. Boldin

John A. Boquist

Dallas Brozik

Mary Ellen Butcher

Philip L. Cooley

Thomas J. Coyne

Maryanne P. Cunningham

Wilfred L. Dellva

Benoit Deschamps

Arthur R. DeThomas

Peter DeVito

Norman S. Douglas

Eugene Drzycimski

David A. Dubofsky

Edward A. Dyl

John W. Ellis

Marjorie K. Evert

David C. Ewert

Thomas H. Eyssell

Alan W. Frankle

E. Bruce Fredrickson

Stephen Gardner

Lawrence J. Gitman

George L. Granger

Anita Ground

Manak C. Gupta

Lance Hart

Hal B. Heaton

Ronald Hennigar

J. Lawrence Hexter

Kendall P. Hill

Laura Hoisington

Ghassem Homaifar

Christine Hsu

Pearson Hunt

James F. Jackson

Stanley Jacobs

Michael D. Joehnk

Eldon C. Johnson

O. Maurice Joy

Ravindra R. Kamath

Narendra Khilnani

Shirly A. Kleiner

Christopher G. Lamoureux

David B. Lawrence

Dean R. Longmore

Richard L.B. LeCompte

Hyong J. Lee

John B. Legler

Laurian E. Lytle

Ginette M. McManus

Gerald A. McIntire

Leo P. Mahoney

Paul H. Malatesta

Herman Manakyan

Mary Kay Mans

Stephen G. Marks

Terry S. Maness

Edward M. Miller

Lalatendu Misra

Eric Moon

Steven P. Mooney

Scott Moore

Saeed Mortazavi

Tarun Mukherjee

Prafulla G. Nabar

Gary Noreiko

Robert A. Olsen

Larry G. Perry

Robert W. Phillips

Gary E. Powell

K. Ramakrishnan

Verlyn Richards

Lawrence C. Rose

Gary C. Sanger

Emmanuel S. Santiago

William L. Sartoris

Carl Schwendiman

David L. Scott

Jaye Smith

Carl Stern

George S. Swales

Gary D. Tallman

Martin Thomas

A. Frank Thompson	Nancy Wiebe
John Traynor	Jimmy B. Williams
Gary L. Trennepohl	Robert A. Wood
Keith Van Horn	B. J. Yang
James A. Verbrugge	Michael York
Jerry Viscione	J. Kenton Zumwalt
John B. White	

Manuscript reviewers, contributors, and supplements authors of *Financial Management* deserve special thanks for their helpful and insightful comments. They are

Raj Aggarwal, John Carroll University
Nasser Arshadi, University of Missouri at St. Louis
Carol J. Billingham, Central Michigan University
Helen M. Bowers, University of Notre Dame
Ka-Kung C. Chan, Ohio State University
George M. Coggins, Jr., High Point University
James M. Cornelius, Eli Lilly and Company
Charles J. Cuny, University of California at Irvine
Alfred H. R. Davis, Queen's University
James G. Duff, USL Capital
David B. Ellis, Sara Lee Corporation
R. Stevenson Hawkey, Golden Gate University
Jerry G. Hunt, Eastern Carolina University
Geoffrey M. Holczer, Design, Inc.
William P. Jennings, California State University at Northridge
Jarl G. Kallberg, New York University
Andrew J. Kalotay, Andrew Kalotay Associates
Kathryn M. Kelm, Emporia State University
David C. Ketcham, Bryant College
Robert T. Kleiman, Oakland University
Chan H. Lee, Mankato State University
David A. Louton, Bryant College
James H. MacNaughton, Salomon Brothers Inc.
Judy E. Maese, New Mexico State University
Stanley A. Martin, University of Wisconsin at Madison
Mary J. Reilly, BancBoston Capital
William J. Sinkula, Kroger Company
David A. Volkman, University of Nebraska - Omaha
Fong Wan, Pacific Gas and Electric Company

Daniel G. Weaver, Marquette University

Stephen E. Wilcox, Mankato State University

Alfred L. Williams Jr., United Gas Holding Corporation

Edward J. Zychowicz, Hofstra University

A number of other individuals added significant value to the book, and I am glad to have had this opportunity to work with them. Alfie Davis, my co-author of *Canadian Financial Management*, encouraged my thinking on numerous topics. Dave Volkman created the quite useful concept review questions, concept review problems, and solutions to them; Carol Billingham meticulously doublechecked the manuscript for accuracy and consistency; and Marlene Bellamy secured and crafted the insightful Executive Interviews for each part. I am proud also to have Kathryn Kelm, Dave Ketcham, and Steve Wilcox on the Pinches team, because each of them substantially increased the quality and utility of the supplements package. Ashish Arora and Mridu Vashist provided valuable research assistance; Ashish also helped me to complete the *Instructor's Manual*, and Mridu assisted me in upgrading the *Pinches Software*. I further appreciate the typing support of Karla Wallace and the constructive criticism of Kevin Bracker and Fraser Montgomery. The book team at HarperCollins deserves special thanks for its efforts on this project: my acquisitions editor Kirsten Sandberg labored long and hard to make this book a reality so that Kate Steinbacher in sales and marketing could make it a market success; Lisa Pinto, Arianne Weber, and Kathi Kuntz all moved the manuscript conscientiously through development so that Michael Weinstein could get it quickly into production. A last note of gratitude to Lynn Brown, Ann Torbert, Mike Roche, and York Production Services for the very professional manner in which they proceeded with this book.

Finally, I must acknowledge the continued love and support of my family. Without their understanding, I could not have completed *Essentials of Financial Management* or *Financial Management*.

To the extent that I have written an up-to-date, clear statement of the fundamental concepts, theoretical developments, and practical aspects of financial management, I owe a large debt of thanks to the help and criticism received from others. I encourage all users—instructors, students, and practitioners alike—to send me comments, suggestions, and criticisms for continually improving all I write for teaching and learning financial management.

George E. Pinches

SAMPLE FROM STUDY GUIDE SHOWN

Sample page from Study Guide: Each chapter opens with a brief paragraph executive summary of chapter content relative to the rest of the text, followed by a handy topical outline broken down by key points for quick review. (Note: Please see final published Study Guide for actual proofed pages from Chapter 2.)

CHAPTER 2

Net Present Value, Value Creation, and Time Value

EXECUTIVE SUMMARY OF CHAPTER

The time value of money is the first (and most important) basic financial concept discussed in this text. Since the goal of financial management is to maximize the value of the firm to its stockholders, an understanding of the concept of valuation is important to the practice of sound financial management. The net present value represents the incremental increase in value due to an investment. Time value is critical in determining the value of stocks and bonds (Chapter 3), capital budgeting (Chapters 7 - 10), leasing (Chapter 18), working capital management (Chapters 19 - 22) mergers and corporate restructuring (Chapter 26), and international financial management (Chapter 27).

TOPICAL OUTLINE

I.   The **present value** of a cash flow is the dollar equivalent today of a cash flow occurring in the future.

     A.   The **net present value** (NPV) is the present value of the cash flows from an investment , discounted at a rate of interest appropriate for the riskiness of the investment, less the cost.

          1.   Accept investments if the net present value is greater than $0.

          2.   If the investment has a negative NPV, the investor is better off finding alternate uses for the funds.

     B.   The **internal rate of return** (IRR) is the interest rate that equates the present values of the cash flows from the investment with investment's cost.

          1.   Choose investments with IRRs greater than the required return (or discount rate) on the investment.

          2.   The IRR is the discount rate that leads to a $0 NPV.

          3.   Generally, the NPV and IRR decision criteria lead to the same project choice. Conflicts may arise if projects have multiple cash flows.

     C.   Risk is incorporated into the discount rate used to calculate the investment's NPV. Projects with higher risks should earn higher rates of return.

B.   Under continuous compounding the number of compounding periods per year is infinitely large.

     1.   To calculate a future value,

$$FV_n = PV_0 e^{k \times n}$$

     2.   To calculate a present value,

$$PV_0 = FV_n e^{-kn}$$

C.   If there is more than one compounding interval per year, the **effective annual interest rate** will be different than the nominal rate.

$$k_{annual\ effective} = \left[1 + \frac{k_{nominal}}{m} \right]^m - 1$$

FORMULAS

<u>Notation</u>

FV_n $=$ Future value in period n of a cash flow or series of cash flows.

PV_0 $=$ Present value (today) of a cash flow or series of cash flows.

k $=$ Interest rate, sometimes called a discount rate, hurdle rate, or opportunity cost of capital.

n $=$ Number of years.

m $=$ Number of compounding periods per year.

PMT $=$ Annuity payment

$PV_{k,n}$ $=$ Present value interest factor for n years at k percent.

$FV_{k,n}$ $=$ Future value interest factor for n years at k percent.

$PVA_{k,n}$ $=$ Present value interest factor of an annuity for n years at k percent.

$FVA_{k,n}$ $=$ Future value interest factor of an annuity for n years at k percent.

e $=$ 2.71828...

<u>Future value of a single cash flow:</u>

$$FV_n = PV_0 (1 + k)^n = PV_0 (FV_{k,n})$$

*Sample page from Study Guide: Completion questions review core financial rela-
tionships, and exercises enable students to work step-by-step toward solving
more complex problems, with answers to both completion items and exercises in
an end-of-guide appendix.*

2.15   If the compounding interval is less than one year, the _____ interest rate will be greater than
        the _____ interest rate.

2.16   To calculate time values when the compounding interval is _____, use continuous
        compounding versions of the time value equations.

EXERCISES

2.1   What is the present value of $2,000 received one year from today if the interest rate is 6 percent?

2.2   Suppose an investment promises to pay $12,000 one year from today. If the investment costs $10,000
        and the required return is 8 percent, what is the investment's net present value?

2.3   Suppose that you pay $25,000 today for an investment that can be sold in one year for $27,250. What
        is the internal rate of return on the investment?

2.4   What is the future value of $10,000 in ten years if the interest rate is 12 percent?.

2.5   How much would you need to deposit in the bank today a 4 percent interest if you wish to have a
        balance of $1,000,000 in your account twenty-five years from today?

2.6   What is the future value of a fifteen year annuity of $2,000 per year at an interest rate of 7 percent if
        the first cash flow occurs one year from today?

2.7   Suppose you intend to make ten deposits of $6,000 in an account paying 6 percent interest with the first
        deposit made today. What will be the account balance ten years from today?

2.8   What is the present value of an ordinary annuity of $12,000 per year for 5 years if the interest rate is 9
        percent?

2.9   What is the present value of an annuity due of $6,500 per year for 7 years if the interest rate is 4
        percent?

2.10   What is the present value of the cash flows from an investment that promises to pay $1,000 in one
        year, $3,000 in two years, and $5,000 in three years if the required return is 12 percent?

2.11   Suppose an ordinary annuity of $3,200 per year for seven years has a present value of $17,862.40.
        What is the interest rate?

2.12   Suppose the bank quotes you a nominal rate of interest on your credit card of 18 percent per year, but
        applies interest charges monthly. What is the effective annual interest rate on your credit card?

2.13   Suppose you deposited $10,000 in a bank account ten years ago. If the bank paid 4 percent annual
        interest, compounded quarterly, what is the balance today?

2.14   Suppose you purchase a car for $15,000. The finance company is willing to lend you the money at 12
        percent interest and requires two years of monthly payments with the first payment made one month
        from today. How much will your car payments be?

2.15   What is the future value of $10,000 in ten years at 8 percent interest if interest is continuously
        compounded?

Sample page from Study Guide: The problems section allows students to apply the techniques and tools introduced throughout the chapter, with completely worked-out solutions at the end of each chapter for quick reviews.

PROBLEMS

2.1   Bob Richards is trying to determine what to do with an endowment of $100,000. The current market rate of interest is 10 percent and Bob faces five possible investments in real assets:

Investment	$Cost_0$	$Cash\ Flow_1$
1	$20,000	$24,000
2	$20,000	$23,500
3	$20,000	$22,800
4	$20,000	$21,700
5	$20,000	$21,000

Bob will receive no endowment next year, so these funds need to be sufficient for the next two years. Bob wishes to consume $60,000 this year (year 0), and maximize his consumption next year. What should Bob do to accomplish this objective? How much can he consume next year?

2.2   Suppose an investment promises cash flows of $500 per year for five years, starting next year, costs $2,000. Calculate the net present value of the investment if the required return is 10 percent.

2.3   Suppose you deposited $5,000 in a savings account 16 years ago. The balance today is $12,230. What rate of interest did the savings account pay?

2.4   Suppose you discover that your great-grandmother left you $5,000 when she died in 1945. The funds were invested in an account paying 8 percent interest. How much will you have in the account in 1995?

2.5   Suppose you wish to have $10,000,000 40 years from now. Your broker has suggested that you can expect your investments to earn 12 percent per year. How much do you need to invest today in order to meet your objective?

2.6   Suppose you put $10,000 in the bank 11 years ago. For the first 5 years your account earned 5 percent compounded annually; for the second 5 years, the account paid 8 percent compounded quarterly; for the last year, the account paid 12 percent compounded monthly. What is the balance in your account?

2.7   Suppose you've decided to supplement your parents' income. You wish to give them $25,000 per year for 20 years starting one year from today. If the bank pays 6 percent interest, how much would you need to deposit today to fully fund your parents' income supplement?

2.8   Suppose you save $10,000 per year for 30 years in an account paying 7 percent interest. What was the balance in your account immediately after your last deposit?

2.9   You've been offered an investment promising $100 per year for 20 years plus a $1,000 payment twenty years from now. If you think your investment should earn 8 percent, how much would you be willing to pay for the above?

2.10   Congratulations, you've just won the Printer's Clearinghouse sweepstakes grand prize. You've been offered **either** $1,000,000 today, **or** $125,000 per year for 10 years, with the first payment **made today**. If you can earn 6 percent on savings, which prize should you choose?

Sample page from Study Guide: Solutions to problems incorporate select calculator keystrokes where relevant for those students who prefer to use the financial calculator as a problem-solving tool.

Finally, solve for the balance after the last year. $n = 12$ months, k (12 percent)/(12 months) = 1 percent per month.

$$FV_{11} = FV_{10}(FV_{1\% \ per \ month, \ 12 \ months}) = \$18,961.36(1.127) = \$21,369.45$$

Keystrokes: PV = 18,984.87, n = 12, i=k = 1; solving, FV = $21,370.09

2.7 $PV_0 = PMT(PVA_{6\%, \ 20 \ years}) = \$25,000(11.470) = \$286,750$

Keystrokes: PMT = 25,000, n = 20, i=k = 6; solving, PV = $286,748.03

2.8 $FV_{30} = PMT(FVA_{7\%, \ 30 \ years}) = \$10,000(94.461) = \$944,610$

Keystrokes: PMT = 10,000, n = 30, i=k = 7; solving, FV = $944,607.86

2.9 The investment has two components; a twenty year ordinary annuity of $100, and a lump sum payment of $1,000 in 20 years. You would be willing to pay the present value of the investment at the required return of 8 percent, so

$$PV_0 = PMT(PVA_{8\%, \ 20 \ years}) + \$1,000(PV_{8\%, \ 20 \ years}) = \$100(9.818) + \$1,000(0.215)$$

$$= \$981.80 + \$215.00 = \$1,196.80$$

Keystrokes: For the annuity: PMT = 100, n = 20, i=k = 8; solving, PV = $981.81

For the lump sum: FV = 1,000, n = 20, i=k = 8; solving, PV = <u>$214.55</u>

Total: $1,196.36

2.10 You should choose the payment scheme with the highest present value. The present value of $1,000,000 today is simply $1,000,000. The second payment mechanism ($125,000 per year for 10 years with the first payment today) is an example of an annuity due. So,

$$PV_) = PMT(PVA_{6\%, \ 10 \ years})(1.06) = \$125,000(7.36)(1.06)$$

$$= \$125,000(7.8016) = \$975,200$$

Choose the $1 Million today; it has a higher present value.

Keystrokes: PMT = 125,000, n = 10, i=k = 6; solving, PV = $920,010.88

920,010.88 x 1.06 = $975,211.53

2.11 First, calculate the balance immediately after your last $15,000 deposit.

$$FV_{20} = \$15,000(FVA_{9\%, \ 20 \ years}) = \$15,000(51.160) = \$767,400$$

Keystrokes: PMT = 15,000, n = 20, i=k = 9; solving, FV = $767,401.79

Financial Management

PART 1

Foundations of Financial Management

EXECUTIVE INTERVIEW

J. G. Duff, Chairman and CEO, USL Capital

USL Capital is a financial services subsidiary of Ford Motor Company. It is one of the nation's largest and most diversified commercial financing organizations. We asked Mr. Duff to describe corporate financial management as he's seen it in practice.

What constitutes corporate financial management is, in essence, in the eye of the beholder. There is no right or wrong organizational definition of financial management. At Ford, we hold a very broad view of what financial management encompasses.

Financial management, in my view, has several essential components, which can be grouped and combined in various ways:

ACCOUNTING AND CONTROL   You must start with a set of books that provides you with accurate data. You also must have sound internal controls. And, you must support the operation of the business with cost-effective, reliable and customer-oriented accounts payable, accounts receivable, and tax functions.

TREASURY   You must raise the capital necessary to support the business, and it must be available at the right time and price. You also must effectively collect and manage the cash from operations.

SYSTEMS   You must have operating systems that provide the data necessary for planning and that support the day-to-day goal of turning out high-quality products and services.

FINANCIAL PLANNING AND ANALYSIS   You need operating plans that outline where the business is going and how it will get there. Equally important is the execution of the plan—reviewing the proposals for new products or facilities, allocating scarce capital among those wanting resources, divesting the firm of businesses no longer needed, acquiring new businesses, establishing the return to stockholders, and so on.

The perspectives of accounting and financial management differ. Let's assume you receive the following "good news" from the accounting department: Revenues are up 20 percent, costs are up only 12.5 percent, and profits are up 50 percent. This seems to be a good story for the CEO to present to security analysts and the stockholders. The accountants are happy that the books "foot" in accord with generally accepted accounting principles, the audit report is unqualified, and the "numbers are up."

Looking at these numbers, however, the financial analyst discovers that the high revenue reflects strong industry sales and somewhat higher pricing offset by a decline in the company's share of the market. That's not as good a story. And, the financial analyst may point out that the cost side doesn't look so good, either. Lower material and interest costs are more than offset by increased personnel expenses, at a time when the business world at large is downsizing. The analyst would conclude that a strong industry is making profits look good—and that management performance leaves a lot to be desired.

To be successful, financial analysis must be done *from the perspective of top-management*. This management considers sales, manufacturing, product development, marketing, personnel, customers, suppliers, and all other expected impacts. As a CEO, I shudder when I hear, "From a finance perspective, we recommend. . . . " I want to hear, "Based on all of the relevant factors, we recommend. . . . "

In the corporate world, financial analysis is the place to be. If you're doing it right, you get into everything—pricing, capital budgeting (you even get to use cost of capital, internal rate of return, net present value—the very things you'll learn in this book), cost analysis, new product decisions, long-range planning, assessing operating performance, buying and selling businesses, and so on. It's all real business—and, if your perspective is broad enough, it's looking at the various decisions as the CEO does.

To get the benefits of financial analysis as I've described it, you must go with a company that has (or wants) that type of analytical function. To get the broad perspective I've described—to be able to integrate the various financial aspects —requires a varied career in terms of jobs and functions. To get to the top of the finance function, you will have to work in a lot of different areas and be very good in several. You also must have the business judgment that allows you to make the right decisions with the right facts.

I've been asked a lot, "How do you get to the top?" Whether it's the top of a functional area, like finance, or the top of a company, my answer is the same: Be very good at what you do. Perform consistently. Get as broad a background as you can but make sure it's heavy in the most important areas to the company. Develop a bottom-line perspective. With these, you must also have a strong work ethic, be ready to show what you can do when the opportunity presents itelf, take some risks, and continue to grow, and consistently hit the long ball on the special (and generally few) opportunities you get to show what you can do.

*F*inancial management provides the rationale and tools for firms to make effective decisions. These decisions fall into three main categories—(1) the investments the firm makes in both long- and short-term assets, (2) how the firm is financed, and (3) how it makes its day-to-day operating decisions.

Chapter 1 examines seven key ideas that underlie financial decision making. Then Chapter 2 examines how firms create value and the importance of the timing of cash inflows and outflows. Chapter 3 discusses two primary vehicles employed by firms to raise funds—bonds and common stock. Risk and return are examined in detail in Chapter 4. Finally, Chapter 5 looks at options, which provide the right, but not the obligation, to buy or sell an asset (or undertake some opportunity). These five chapters provide the foundation for making decisions that assist in maximizing the long-run market value of the firm.

1

Why Financial Management Matters

EXECUTIVE SUMMARY

Financial management focuses on acquiring, managing, and financing a firm's resources by means of money, with due regard for prices in external economic markets. It is concerned with the efficient use of resources by firms and by the economy. The firm, however, does not operate in a vacuum; it is directly affected by its external environment in two primary ways. First, it has to pay the going market rates to obtain financing, purchase assets, and secure the services of employees and managers. Second, the ultimate success of the firm—which is measured by its total market value—is determined in the financial marketplace. The market value of the firm, which indicates the firm's economic worth, is the ultimate indicator of how effective the firm is. As firms maximize their value, the assets of firms and the entire economy are being employed in their most effective manner.

The seven key ideas you should understand, and remember, after reading this book are: (1) the goal of the firm is to maximize its market value; (2) financial markets in developed countries are efficient, and prices respond quickly to new information; (3) individuals act in their own self-interests, and the sometimes conflicting interests of the providers of capital, managers, employees, customers, and suppliers must be taken into account when firms make decisions; (4) in order to make value-maximizing decisions, firms focus on cash flows and their incremental effects; (5) the timing of the cash flows is important, so we use net present value to make investment decisions; (6) risk and return go hand-in-hand, so that higher returns cannot be achieved without higher risk; and (7) options, which provide the right, but not the obligation, to undertake some financial opportunity, are valuable.

By focusing on maximizing the long-run market value of the firm, and using these other ideas in the decision-making process, firms make decisions so that all assets—financial, real, and human—are used in their most effective manner.

3

WHAT IS FINANCIAL MANAGEMENT?

Finance is the word used to describe both the money resources available to governments, firms, or individuals, and the management of those resources. Our focus is on the second aspect, management. For our purposes, **financial management** is the acquisition, management, and financing of resources for firms by means of money, with due regard for prices in external economic markets. Let's look at this definition, part by part.

First, our focus is on the *acquisition, management, and financing of resources needed by firms.* Resources are generally physical, such as cash, inventory, accounts receivable, equipment and machinery, or manufacturing and distribution facilities. But they also include people—the managers and employees of the firm. The money for these resources comes from a variety of sources, such as the internal cash flow generated by the firm's activities, borrowing, leasing, and new stock issues. The firm's goal is to provide and manage all of these resources as efficiently as possible—that is, to balance needs against the risks and the returns expected from the use of the firm's resources.

Second, firms keep track of resources in terms of *money.* They could use production runs, tons, boxcar loads, or any other unit, but it is far simpler if all firms use a single standard. That standard is money, and the unit is dollars. The results of almost any activity considered by firms can be expressed in dollars. For example, one firm might consider using its stock to purchase another firm. The value of the transaction can still be expressed in dollars, even though stock is used to finance the deal.

The third part of the definition enlarges our focus to include the firm's *external environment.* Our primary concern is the firm and its operations, but no firm exists in a vacuum. Performance is affected by a variety of external factors, such as the health of the economy, taxes, interest rates, international tensions, and the prevailing political and regulatory moods. In fact, the performance of the firm is ultimately judged by the external **financial markets,** where stocks and bonds are traded.

The ideas, tools, and techniques of financial management apply to all kinds of firms and to individuals. Our focus in this book will be on corporations, rather than proprietorships or partnerships. A **proprietorship** is an unincorporated business owned by one individual. In a **partnership,** two or more individuals own the business. While a proprietorship or partnership is easy to set up, most successful ones are eventually converted into corporations. A **corporation** is a legal entity given the power to act as an individual and it has limited liability. **Limited liability** is a major advantage of the corporation; it means that if the firm goes bankrupt, the owners can lose no more than the money they have invested in the firm.

Corporations can raise funds by issuing and selling shares of their **common stock.** In return for investing in the firm the common stockholders become the owners of the firm. Corporations can also obtain funds by selling **bonds,** which are long-term debt instruments. Bonds are nothing more than IOUs that firms employ to obtain financing. The bondholders have a fixed, but limited, claim on the firm. In addition, firms obtain needed funds, and incur financial obligations, through bank loans and credit extended to the firm.

Concept Review Questions

■ What are the three major elements in the definition of financial management?

■ Describe the three major forms of ownership of a firm.

KEY IDEAS YOU NEED TO UNDERSTAND

As we proceed, new terms, ideas, and relationships will be introduced. While they are all important in one way or another, certain key ideas underlie the theory and practice of financial management. The seven key ideas that guide our discussions are: (1) the goal of the firm is to maximize its market value; (2) financial markets are efficient; (3) individuals act in their own self-interest; (4) firms focus on cash flows and incremental effects; (5) a dollar today is worth more than a dollar tomorrow; (6) risk and return go hand-in-hand; and (7) options are valuable. Before beginning to use these ideas in making financial decisions, let's briefly explore them one by one.

KEY IDEA #1: THE GOAL OF THE FIRM IS TO MAXIMIZE ITS MARKET VALUE

To achieve the goal of acquiring, managing, and financing resources efficiently, the firm must have an objective—a purpose. The fundamental objective of the firm is to maximize its market value.[1] To understand this objective, or purpose, it is helpful to think of the firm as a pie, as shown in Figure 1.1. The ingredients that go into the pie include the basic factors that financial management stresses—the acquisition of resources for the firm, and the financing and management of these resources. How effectively these resources are used, however, is determined by *how much someone else is willing to pay for a claim on them*. Thus, if the resources can be used more efficiently by another firm or in another part of the economy, market forces will operate so the firm can sell the assets to someone else for more than they are worth to the firm. For firms with publicly traded securities outstanding, the value of the firm is determined in the financial markets, where stocks and bonds trade.

Thus, the financial markets come into play. The value of any publicly owned firm is determined in the financial markets. As the firm makes decisions that maximize the usefulness of its assets, they create value for the firm. Alternatively, the firm will sell the assets if they are worth more to others. Firms that make value-maximizing decisions will be rewarded: The financial markets will recognize the value-maximizing decisions, and the market value of the firm will increase. Conversely, the financial markets will also notice if the firm does a poor job of making decisions, and the market value of the

---

[1] Value maximization is socially optimal as long as there are no externalities nor monopoly power. Externalities arise when a party benefits and does not bear any costs. An example of externalities is air and water pollution, without tax penalties on the parties causing the pollution or compensation to those affected.

Figure 1.1

The Firm as a Pie

Depending on how the investment community assesses a firm's decisions (via the financial markets), the size of the pie—the firm—can be enlarged or shrunk, often dramatically.

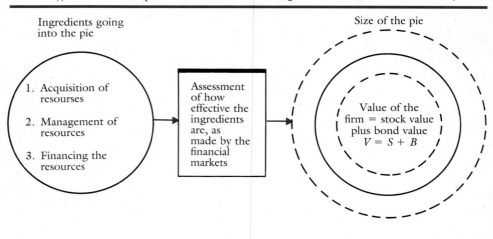

firm will decrease. The point to remember is this: Poor decisions within the firm will be recognized—you can't fool the financial markets very long.

We can express the value maximization goal mathematically. The total value of the firm, V, or size of the pie, is a function of the claims of both stockholders and bondholders on the firm,

market value of firm, $V = S + B$

where S is the market value of the stock and B is the market value of the firm's bonds (and other debt). The objective is to maximize the market value of the firm, V. For simplicity, we sometimes assume this can be accomplished by maximizing S—the market value of stockholder claims on the firm. This objective of **stockholder wealth maximization,** which typically assists in maximizing the total value of the firm, under-lies most financial decisions. As you will see, however, management may not always adhere to the objective of maximizing the value of the firm, and sometimes this objective puts stockholders into conflict with the firm's bondholders, creditors, and others who are interested in the firm.

One way to achieve the objective of maximizing the firm's market value is to maximize the value of stockholder and bondholder (or creditor) claims on the firm. An alternative way to think about these claims is to recognize the difference in the claims on the firm held by stockholders and bondholders. First, let's consider stock-holders. The value of the stockholder's claim, ignoring bondholders for a minute, is a function of the total value of the firm. Thus, the potential payoff for stockholders can be depicted as follows:

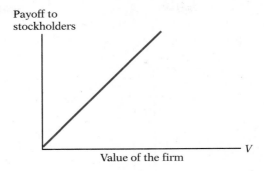

Next, consider the claims of bondholders (without considering the stockholder's claim). Suppose bondholders loan $100 to a firm, with the loan to be repaid in 1 year. Ignoring interest (for simplicity), we can depict this claim as follows:

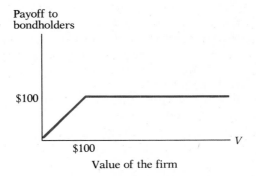

As long as the firm is healthy, and the total value of the firm exceeds the claims of the bondholders, then everything is fine. What happens, however, if the firm is not doing well? Stockholders, by law, have limited liability. Limited liability means that stockholders (with a few exceptions) are *not personally responsible* for seeing that the firm's debts are paid, if the value of the firm is not sufficient to pay the bondholders' claims.

If in 1 year the market value of the firm, V, is at least $100, the loan will be repaid, and the bondholders will get their $100. Even if the firm is worth a lot more than $100, the bondholders still receive only $100 (as depicted by the horizontal line above). As creditors, they have agreed to a fixed claim of $100, no matter how well the firm does.

If in 1 year the firm is not worth at least $100 the stockholders receive nothing, while the bondholders take over the firm. But, if the firm is worth more than $100, the bondholders receive their $100, and the stockholders claim the rest of the value of the firm. Putting both bondholder and stockholder claims together, we have:

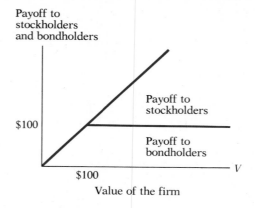

Value of the firm

where the total claims are depicted as a function of the total firm value, V. Viewed in this context, the bondholders have a fixed, but limited, claim on the value of the firm. The stockholders may receive nothing—if the firm is worth less than $100 in 1 year—or they may receive a lot—everything beyond the $100 claimed by the bond-holders. Whether viewed in this manner or in terms of a "pie," the goal of the firm remains the same—maximize market value.

The objective of maximizing the market value does not mean that stockholders are an especially deserving group, or that other parties who have an interest in the firm (such as employees, customers, suppliers, or the community in which the firm is located) should be ignored. Rather, value maximization means that all corporate resources should be allocated to the point where marginal costs equal marginal benefits among all parties having an interest in the firm and its well-being. Value-max-imizing decision making allocates resources to each important party to improve the terms on which they deal with the firm, to maintain and enhance the firm's reputation, and to reduce the threat of expensive (and restrictive) regulation on the firm.

One final point should be made in discussing market value and its maximization. Theoretically, maximizing the market value results in maximizing the value of the firm both in the short-run and in the long-run. If there ever is any conflict, it is the long-run market value in which we are interested.

KEY IDEA #2: FINANCIAL MARKETS ARE EFFICIENT

Another key idea is that in a developed country like the United States, the financial markets, where stocks and bonds trade, have been found to be "efficient." Let's see what is meant by a market being efficient. Think about what you already know about financial markets. Take a firm like British Petroleum, Coca-Cola, McDonald's, Toy-ota, or Wal-Mart, and ask yourself these questions: Is the firm well known? Is there plenty of information available about the firm? Is new information made readily available (in newspapers, on television, and the like) to anyone who is interested in the firm? Is this new information made available quickly? Are there many investors who may quickly place buy or sell orders for common stock in these firms when they receive important new information about the firm or the economic setting the firm operates in? The answer to all these questions is "yes!"

The preceding questions describe the characteristics of an efficient market. An **efficient market** is one in which market prices quickly reflect all available information about the firm. If the information about the economy, the firm, and the firm's prospects for the future are favorable, the price of the firm and its common stock will go up over time. Likewise, if the information about the firm indicates continued hard times, increased competition that is driving down profit margins, and the like, the market price of the firm and its common stock will also reflect that information. Hence, *in an efficient market, the best indication of what a firm is worth is to look at what someone is willing to pay for a claim on the firm.*

This simple idea may seem a little strange at first, but apply it to yourself. Let's say you are going to buy a used car. What is that car worth? One way to attempt to determine its worth is to calculate how much the steel, plastic, aluminum, glass, and rubber that make up the car are worth. A second way is to see what the separate parts of the car—such as the tires, engine, transmission, and so forth—would sell for if you dismantled the car. But neither of these ways of valuing the car is very direct, and both suffer from a variety of problems. What's the most direct way to determine the worth of the car? Simply to determine what you are willing to pay and what someone else is willing to sell the car for. If you are willing to pay $5,000, but the seller wants $8,000, and neither of you will budge, we don't know what the car is worth. Either you are a tightwad or the seller has an overly optimistic belief of the car's value. But, if after negotiation, you jointly arrive at a price of $6,700, then we know what the car is worth. It is worth the price that you, as a purchaser with other options (or cars) available, and the seller, with other individuals interested in the car, agree to.

When there is plenty of information, and many informed and active investors, markets tend to be efficient. The financial markets in developed countries have been found to be highly efficient. One of the key lessons from knowing that markets are efficient is the following: *If the market is efficient, trust market prices.* That is, if you want to know what an asset is worth, and it trades in an efficient market where there are many informed buyers and sellers, then look to the market price—the price at which knowledgeable parties to the transaction (sellers and buyers) are "willing to deal." A second key lesson from knowing markets are efficient is this: *Start from the market price, and then look for factors that if changed, could make the asset worth more or less.* For example, if your firm decides to purchase another publicly traded firm, the market value of that firm's assets is already known—it is given by the market value of the firm. If you are going to pay a premium (an amount over and above its current market value) to purchase the firm, you should ask yourself, "Why are the assets worth more to me than their current market value?"

The idea of market efficiency is both simple and important and is very well supported by the facts. You will see it underlying many of the financial decisions we consider. At the same time, there are some financial markets that are not efficient. These are most likely to occur in places where the government or other forces interfere with the markets, where information is not freely or readily available, where there are few informed buyers and sellers, or in third- and fourth-world countries. In such situations market values do not necessarily reflect the economic value of the assets.

KEY IDEA #3: INDIVIDUALS ACT IN THEIR OWN SELF-INTEREST

Underlying much of what you will study in this book is the idea that individuals usually act in their own self-interest. As a simple example, assume an individual chooses to go to the beach 4 days a week and lie in the sun. While you and I might question the decision, the individual is making what to him or her is a rational (and self-interest-based) decision. Say the individual's alternative is to spend those 4 days working for $150 per day (to keep things simple, let's ignore taxes). By going to the beach, the individual has implicitly placed a value on going to the beach of more than the $150 per day that could have been earned. We often speak of the **opportunity cost** associated with choosing one course of action instead of another. The opportunity cost associated with this action is the $150 per day bypassed by choosing to go to the beach.

The idea of self-interest comes up in many ways in finance. These are referred to as "agency problems" or "agency relationships." Narrowly defined, an **agency relationship** is a contract in which one or more parties [the principal(s)] engages another (the agent) to perform a service and delegates some decision-making authority to the agent. In the context of firms, think of the owners (the principals) engaging the managers (as their agents) to operate the firm on their behalf. In a slightly broader perspective, agency relationships emphasize that managers, stockholders, bondholders, and other interested parties act in their own self-interest, and that costly conflicts may arise due to these self-interests.

Think of a small business where you are owner and manager of the firm. You as the owner-manager will maximize your wealth by balancing the combination of wages, perquisites (or "perks") such as a company car, luxurious offices, and so on, and the market value of the firm's common stock. As long as a firm is owned and operated by a single owner-manager, no complication arises with the objective of maximizing stockholders' wealth. Because management and stockholders are the same person, actions taken in the stockholders' best interests also serve the self-interests of the manager.

In larger firms, however, management often owns only a small percentage of the firm's outstanding common stock. In this case managers may be "satisfiers" rather than maximizers. That is, their goal may be performance that ensures their own career security and advancement, rather than the goal of maximizing the value of the firm, because only a small proportion of one's wealth comes from changes in the value of the firm's common stock. This might cause them to bypass a risky but potentially beneficial new investment. Managers may prefer a safe project to a risky one which, if it fails, might cause them to lose their jobs.

In any agency relationship there are **agency costs**. These costs can be broken into three general classes:

Financial contracting costs:[2] the costs of structuring formal or informal contracts, opportunity costs that arise when firms make decisions or bypass opportunities that lower the value of the firm, and the costs of incentive plans designed to encourage the agent to act in the principal's best interests

---

[2] The examples of agency costs relate to those between managers and owners.

Costs of monitoring: the expenses incurred to check the performance of the agent, such as auditing the firm's accounting statements and performance

Loss of wealth when agents pursue their own interests: costs such as excessive expense accounts or other perks

All organizations in which there are divergent interests suffer some loss in value due to agency costs. *Agency costs are borne by the principals*—in this case the stockholders. Recently, firms such as Eastman Kodak and Chrysler have put in place restrictions that require top managers to purchase an amount of stock equal to at least 1 year's salary. These firms believe this requirement is the simplest and most effective way to align the interests of managers and stockholders.

Firms raise funds from **creditors** as well as from common stockholders. Creditors are parties that hold fixed-type financial claims against the firm: long-term debt (bonds, mortgages, leases), short-term debt (bank loans or commercial paper), accounts payable, wages and salaries, pension liabilities, and so forth. The creditors' claims against the firm create a second example of agency costs, this time because of potential conflicts between stockholders and creditors. Some of these agency costs relate to differences in which assets the firm should hold, in restrictive provisions (or covenants) written into bonds or loan agreements, in sinking fund provisions, and in restrictions on the payment of cash dividends.

Finally, in addition to stockholders, management, and creditors, the firm has to deal with other parties who are sometimes referred to as **stakeholders**. These include the firm's employees, customers, suppliers, and the community at large. Because of the possibility of conflicts of interest between the goal of maximizing the value of the firm and the self-interest of other parties, constraints exist. These constraints are reflected in the form of agency costs (related to managers or creditors) and requirements imposed by the government (for employees and communities) if stockholders attempt to expropriate wealth from the firm's stakeholders.

Agency problems arise when not all parties have the same information—that is, when there is **asymmetric information**. Throughout the book, we will explore a number of agency problems that involve parties having differing amounts of information. The important point to remember is that the self-interests of various groups must be taken into account as financial decisions are made. Also, because of differing self-interests and amounts of information, virtually all organizations incur agency costs. Firms seek to minimize total agency costs as they make financial decisions.

KEY IDEA #4: FIRMS FOCUS ON CASH FLOWS AND INCREMENTAL EFFECTS

How do firms go about maximizing the value of the firm? Our interest is in maximizing the value of the firm *in the financial marketplace*, not in its **book value** (assets minus liabilities in an accounting sense) or some other figure such as replacement value. We, as managers or investors, are interested in the highest market value of the firm. How do we go about valuing a firm? Theoretically, *the value of the firm is determined by the magnitude of the future cash flows to be received, the timing of these cash flows, and the risks involved.*

By **cash flows** we mean actual cash to be received or paid. This amount is not the same as earnings or net income in an accrual-based accounting sense. There is a fundamental difference between accounting and financial management: *The accountant looks at earnings; financial managers use cash flows.* Earnings are only a clue to the ability of the firm to generate cash flows. Earnings, in fact, are often misleading, because they are calculated by matching revenues and expenses in the proper time period based on historical costs. *The accounting system is not designed to report the inflow and outflow of cash.*

Accountants prepare the firm's statements in accordance with **generally accepted accounting principles, GAAP.** Although some exceptions exist, accounting's primary focus is on recording what has happened in the past and matching income and expense in the appropriate time period. In finance, our concern is with the future and with cash inflows and outflows.

While we are interested in cash flows, our primary focus is on the **incremental cash flows**—i.e., new minus existing cash flows. For example, if someone currently takes home $9,000 a year from a part-time job and due to a promotion, will take home a total of $11,000 in the future, the incremental amount by which he or she is better off is $2,000. Financial management is always concerned with these incremental cash flows.

We have emphasized that cash flows are important, but we have not really said why. They are important because *cash flow is theoretically correct, unambiguous, and essential to the well-being of the firm. Also, one cannot spend net income.* Financial theory has its roots in economics. Based on economic considerations, the value of the firm at any point in time is equal to the present value of the expected cash flows. Only by calculating cash flows will the firm and investors be able to determine if actions taken are consistent with the goal of maximizing the value of the firm.

By emphasizing cash flow, we have an unambiguous measure of the returns coming to the firm. This would not be true if we used net income as determined by generally accepted accounting principles. Under GAAP, different inventory, depreciation, or other generally accepted alternatives can result in differences in reported net income for two firms that are otherwise the same. Alternatively, two firms can report the same net income but have vast differences in actual cash flows for the period. Firms also employ different depreciation amounts for tax purposes (based on the Internal Revenue Service code) than they incorporate in their GAAP accounting statements. The use of cash flow instead of net income removes all of these accounting-induced ambiguities.

Finally, the flow of cash is essential to the well-being of the firm. Firms may have high profits but inadequate cash flow, or low profits but high cash flow. To see how this can be the case, consider the example in Table 1.1. The **balance sheet** for a firm reports the accounting-based value of the firm's assets, and the claims against those assets in the form of liabilities (held by creditors) and owners' equity. In addition to the balance sheet, firms also provide **income statements,** which show sales, cash and non-cash expenses, and other adjustments. Because interest on borrowing is important in financial management, **earnings before interest and taxes, EBIT,** can be determined. Then, when interest is deducted we arrive at **earnings before tax, EBT.** Subtracting taxes, we are left with **earnings after tax, EAT,** or net income.

Table 1.1 also shows that the firm is paying to its owners **cash dividends,** which are a direct cash outflow. For the next 3 months the firm is projecting its income and its cash needs. With net income of $280, the situation appears stable. However, looking closely, we realize that only half of the firm's sales of $2,000 will be for cash, and that

Table 1.1

Difference Between Net Income and Cash Flow

Cash flow and net income are never the same. In some situations, cash flows far exceed net income; in others, they fall short. For this reason, the emphasis in financial management must be on cash flow.

Balance Sheet as of December 31

Assets		Liabilities and Stockholders' Equity	
Cash	$ 200	Short-term debt*	$ 200
Other assets	800	Long-term debt	300
Total	$1,000	Equity	500
		Total	$1,000

Projected Income Statement for 3 Months Ending March 31

Sales (50% cash)	$2,000
Cash expenses except interest	1,480
Depreciation	100
Earnings before interest and taxes, EBIT	420
Interest	20
Earnings before tax, EBT	400
Taxes (30%)	120
Earnings after tax, EAT (or net income)	$ 280
Cash dividend to be paid in 2 months	$ 60

Cash Flows

For the next 3-month period, the projected cash inflows and outflows are as follows:

Cash Inflows		Cash Outflows	
Sales for cash	$1,000	Cash expenses	$1,480
Cash on hand	200	Interest	20
Total	$1,200	Taxes	120
		Cash dividend	60
		Repay short-term debt	200
		Total	$1,880

Resulting cash shortage = $1,880 − $1,200 = $680

* Due in 2 months

$1,480 in cash expenses must be paid, along with $20 in interest, taxes of $120, a cash dividend of $60, and repayment of a $200 short-term loan. Even after drawing its cash account down to zero, the firm has projected cash outflows that exceed projected inflows by $680. Over time, as the credit sales are collected, the firm's cash flow problem will probably be corrected. But it will suffer from a shortage of cash during the next quarter.

One additional point needs to be emphasized. Even though cash flow is the proper focus for financial decision making, in practice many firms concentrate on growth in sales, market share, or earnings. Too much attention is often given to these aspects and not enough to how they relate to cash flows. By focusing on cash flow, financial decision makers strive in the most direct manner possible to serve the interests of owners, creditors, managers, employees, customers, and suppliers of the firm. If cash flows are maximized, the accounting numbers (over time) will reflect this, and the value of the firm will be maximized. Inadequate cash flows will also be reflected in the firm's accounting statements and its market price. The firm pays a price if it ignores, or pays too little attention to, cash flows. That price is an opportunity cost equal to the attainable maximum market value of the firm minus the actual value of the firm.

KEY IDEA #5: A DOLLAR TODAY IS WORTH MORE THAN A DOLLAR TOMORROW

The next key idea in finance is easy. Simply put, a dollar today is worth more than a dollar tomorrow. That is, if I offer you $100 today, or the same $100 one year from now, you will be better off if you take the $100 today. In finance we formalize this idea when dealing with cash flows that occur at different points in time through the use of present value and future value techniques. But, *your basic instincts are correct: when in doubt, take the cash sooner rather than later.*

When dealing with timing problems, finance employs a standardized methodology to determine whether the cash flows associated with making an investment are worthwhile or not. Say you are offered an investment that promises a return of $150 in 1 year by investing $100 today. (Let's assume away risk for now, to keep things simple.) The question is, should you make the proposed investment? By investing $100 today you will receive $150 in 1 year. What should you do? If you are rational and act in your own self-interest, you would make the investment *unless* you had another opportunity that provided a better return. Let's say your next best opportunity would provide a return of $120 in 1 year based on the $100 investment. Faced with these alternatives you would make the investment that provides the return of $150 in 1 year. In financial management we deal with problems like this by determining the **net present value** of the proposed investment. The procedure is to discount the future cash inflows at a rate that reflects the opportunities bypassed and the risks involved, and then subtract the initial investment. Thus, the net present value of any proposed investment is:

$$\text{net present value} = \frac{\text{future value of cash inflows}}{1 + \text{discount rate based on forgone opportunities}} - \text{initial investment}$$

In this case the discount rate (or forgone return) on the next best investment is ($120/$100) − 1 = 1.20 − 1 = 0.20. The net present value of the proposed investment is, then, $150/(1 + 0.20) − $100 = $125 − $100 = $25. Because the net present value of $25 is positive, you would make the investment. By doing so you are making a value-maximizing decision.

KEY IDEA #6: RISK AND RETURN GO HAND-IN-HAND

The next important idea is the relationship of risk and return. By **risk,** we mean the uncertainty of something happening, or the possibility of a less-than-desirable outcome. Other things being equal, rational individuals require a higher return for exposing themselves to higher risk. Thus, if you believe investment B has more risk than investment A, investment B would have to offer you a higher return potential before you would invest in it.

The other side of this idea is that in order to increase the return expected from any kind of investment, we must increase our exposure to risk. Put more directly, we could say "there is no free lunch!" The key ideas are captured in the following diagram:

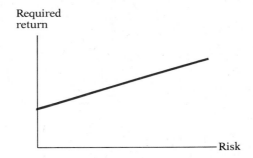

where, other things being equal, the **required return** demanded by an investor increases as one exposes oneself to more risk. If firms or individuals desire higher returns, then they must expose themselves to more risk. Likewise, if firms or individuals are exposed to more risk they have two basic choices. *The first choice is to price the risk*—that is, to see that the expected returns are high enough to justify undertaking that much risk. *The second choice is to do something to eliminate part or all of the risk*—in financial terms, to hedge. In most of what follows we will discuss "pricing the risk" by demanding a high enough return to compensate for the risk involved. In Chapters 23 and 28 we examine how firms can hedge specific kinds of risk—arising from fluctuations in market prices, interest rates, or foreign exchange rates.

In a practical sense, if someone promises you a "guaranteed" 25 percent return with no risk, my advice is simple—be extremely skeptical! Firms and individuals have lost billions by not understanding that risk and return go hand-in-hand.

KEY IDEA #7: OPTIONS ARE VALUABLE

The final key idea relates to **options**, which provide the opportunity, but not the requirement, to undertake some financial opportunity. Let's go back to the example where you received $100 and had the opportunity to make an investment that would return $150. Let's assume the opportunity to make the investment was available to you, and you alone, for 10 days. During those 10 days *you hold an option to make the investment, but you are not required to make the investment.* If something better comes along during that time period, you can elect to bypass this investment. If that happens, you have decided not to "exercise the option." If at the end of the 10 days you make the $100 investment, you have exercised the option.

During the last 30 years we have found that options exist in many different and unusual ways in financial management. And, we have also developed the ability to value both simple and very complex options. Any time a firm or individual has the opportunity, but not the requirement, to undertake some financial opportunity, an option exists. The flexibility provided by options, to either exercise them or let them expire, is what makes options so valuable. Options in financial management include the managerial flexibility associated with making capital investment decisions; they are present in various securities employed by firms; and they are part of any guarantee, loan, or insurance contract. Without the ability to incorporate and value options, we cannot properly evaluate the various courses of action available to firms and the costs or benefits associated with these alternatives. Financial management cannot be fully understood without understanding options.

Concept Review Questions

- What is the fundamental objective of any firm?
- Define an efficient market and how it affects the worth of a firm.
- What are the three general classes of agency costs?
- Define an agency relationship and describe how it affects financial decision making.
- How are risk and return related?

FINANCIAL MANAGEMENT AND THE FIRM

Financial management deals with the efficient allocation of resources—financial assets, such as stock and bonds; real assets, such as plant and equipment; and human assets, the managers and employees. Figure 1.2 depicts the interaction of the main factors that affect financial decisions as firms attempt to maximize their market value. First in importance are *external factors* such as the financial markets (where firms raise funds), government regulations, the tax structure, competition, and the state of the economy. The firm has only indirect influence over these—through lobbying the government and market positioning, for instance. Next are the *strategic policy decisions* directly under management control. These include the choice of products or services offered; marketing and production systems; investment, financing, and dividend policies; and employee practices.

Many of these strategic factors may appear fixed in the short run. Over the long run, though, all can be changed by the firm as it acquires assets, manages the assets, and secures the financing needed to support the firm's resources. These policies directly determine the magnitude, timing, and riskiness of the firms' future cash flows. In making all of these decisions the self-interests of the providers of capital, customers, managers, employees, and suppliers must be kept in mind. By doing so, and focusing on increasing and maximizing the long-run market value of the firm, all of the resources of the economy are allocated in their most efficient manner. At the same

Figure 1.2

Factors Affecting the Firm's Market Value

Firms cannot do much to affect the external environment, but their strategic and policy decisions have a direct impact on how the firm's resources are acquired, managed, and financed. These decisions, in turn, determine the magnitude, timing, and riskiness of the firm's expected cash flows. How the management of the firm's resources and its cash flows is assessed in the financial markets determines the market value of the firm.

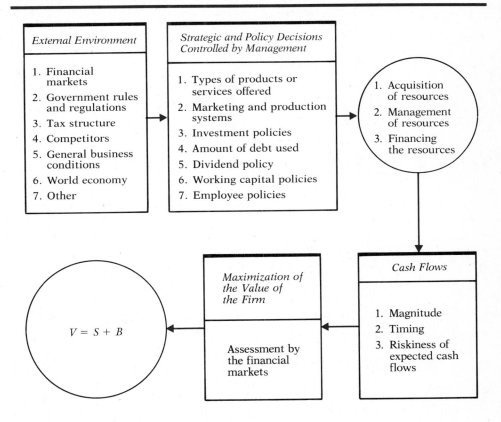

time, the needs of customers will be met, because if they are not met, the firm will wither away. Finally, the needs and desires of management and employees will be met; only if the firm prospers will the firm be in a position to reward individuals for their contributions to the success of the firm.

In practice, the objective of maximizing the value of the firm has three important messages. First, it is theoretically correct and leads to the most efficient use of all resources in the firm and economy. Second, because there are obviously some constraints on the objective, firms can maximize only subject to these constraints. Third, the objective provides a clear and precise frame of reference with which to make and judge decisions. In other words, it provides a standard of comparison and allows us to determine if the decisions are the best ones under the circumstances.

Business, and financial management, is increasingly conducted on a global basis. The fundamental ideas discussed in this chapter and the remainder of the book generally apply equally well in any country in the world. However, two important differences exist. First, some of the specifics assumed—such as efficient financial markets, details of the tax code, and so forth—often differ. Second, any time cash flows move between two countries the impact of exchange rates—that is, how much one currency is worth in terms of another currency—must be taken into consideration. While brief mention of some aspects of international financial management is made in a few of the chapters, Chapters 27 and 28 explore in detail financial management in an international context.

Concept Review Questions

- As firms attempt to maximize their market value, what are the main factors that affect their financial decisions?
- What messages are implied when the stated objective of management is the maximization of the value of the firm?

THE FINANCIAL MANAGER

In this book we use the term **financial manager** to refer to anyone directly engaged in making or implementing financial decisions. Except in the smallest firms, many individuals are responsible for financial activities. In most large firms the person ultimately responsible is the financial vice-president, who is the **chief financial officer, CFO,** of the firm. The chief financial officer is deeply involved in financial policy making, as well as in corporate or strategic planning.

Typically, at least two individuals report directly to the CFO. The **treasurer** is usually the person responsible for seeing that the firm obtains funds as needed, for making sure cash is collected and invested, for maintaining relations with banks and other financial institutions, and for seeing that bills are paid on time. In some organizations, the treasurer also oversees capital budgeting decisions and credit management. The **controller** (or comptroller) is responsible for preparing accounting statements, for cost accounting, for internal auditing, for budgeting, and for the firm's tax department.

Because of the importance of financial decisions to the long-run success of the firm, major decisions are often made by the board of directors or the executive committee. For example, major capital expenditures, proposed financing changes, and the firm's dividend policy are decided at the highest level of the firm. However, authority for less important decisions, such as small- or medium-sized investments, credit policies, and cash management changes, is often delegated to division managers or others at lower levels in the firm. Financial managers are all those individuals whose decision-making responsibility affects the financial health of the firm.

Concept Review Questions

- Who is a financial manager in a firm?
- What two individuals within a firm report directly to the chief financial officer?

KEY POINTS

1. Financial management focuses on the acquisition, management, and financing of resources. While the ideas are universal, we focus on applying them to firms organized as corporations.
2. The first key idea of financial management is that firms strive to maximize their long-run market value, as reflected by the market value of the owners' claims (through stock) and the creditors claims.
3. The second key idea is that in developed countries financial markets, where stocks and bonds trade, are efficient. Thus, the best indication of value is what someone else is willing to pay for an asset. When valuing assets in efficient markets, look first to market prices.
4. The third key idea is that individuals operate in their own self-interest. When differences in interests exist, agency costs are incurred in an attempt to ensure that joint interests are pursued. Differences in interests, and information, may exist between owners (stockholders) and management, between owners and creditors, and between any of them and other stakeholders like employees, customers, and suppliers.
5. The fourth key idea is to focus on cash flows and their incremental effects. Do not be mislead by accounting-induced influences; you can't spend net income.
6. The fifth key idea is that a dollar today is worth more than a dollar tomorrow.
7. The sixth key idea is that risk and return go hand-in-hand. The only way for individuals or firms to increase their expected return is to increase their risk exposure.
8. The last key idea is that options, which provide the right but not the requirement, to do something, are valuable.
9. By focusing on maximizing the long-run market value of the firm, financial management in a free enterprise economy leads to the most efficient allocation of all resources—financial, real, and human.
10. Financial managers are all the individuals in a firm who make decisions that have financial consequences. The chief financial officer, CFO, is ultimately responsible for the financial operations of a firm.

QUESTIONS

1.1 Explain what is meant by the statement, "Financial management is the acquisition, management, and financing of resources for firms by means of money, with due regard for prices in external economic markets."

1.2 How can the firm be viewed as a pie? Make sure to distinguish between the ingredients that go into the pie and the factors that determine the ultimate size of the pie.

1.3 The fixed nature of the bondholder's claim and the limited liability associated with common stock are important when considering the potential payoffs to bondholders and stockholders. Explain the potential payoffs as a function of the total value of the firm.

1.4 How do "agency relationships" and "agency costs" relate to the idea of constraints on the objective of maximizing the value of the firm?

1.5 There are agency costs related to both managers and creditors (among others). How do they differ from each other? What is their effect?

1.6 Explain why cash flow and net income are not, and cannot be, equal for firms.

1.7 Comment on the following statement made by Chris in the firm's executive suite: "I'm on the spot because I'm going to be judged by the common stockholders on the basis of market price, over which I have absolutely no control. In fact, I can't even control sales or earnings per share as well as I'd like, and they are the primary determinants of the market price."

1.8   Explain how cash flows, timing, and risk relate to the firm's objective of maximizing its market value.

1.9   What are the key ideas you should understand after reading this book?

CONCEPT REVIEW PROBLEMS

See Appendix A for solutions.

CR 1.1   Prepare a projected income statement for Johnstons & Associates from the following information: sales, $700,000; cost of goods sold, $100,000; administrative expenses, $300,000; depreciation, $50,000; interest paid, $60,000; and a tax rate of 40 percent.

CR 1.2   Assume Johnstons & Associates, from CR 1.1, operates on a cash budget—that is, all revenue and expenses are on a cash basis. In addition, the firm will pay a dividend of $100,000 at the end of the year.

a.   What is Johnstons & Associates' net cash flow?

Now assume Johnstons & Associates offers trade credit to its customers and the firm will receive only 60 percent of the projected sales in cash over the next year.

b.   How does the offering of trade credit affect the net cash flow for Johnstons & Associates?

CR 1.3   Whiz Kids, Inc., has the following balance sheet and projected income statement:

Balance Sheet as of December 31			
Assets		**Liabilities and Stockholders' Equity**	
Cash	$ 500	Short-term debt	$ 1,500
Other assets	80,000	Long-term debt	59,000
Total	$80,500	Equity	20,000
		Total	$80,500

Projected Income Statement for 6 Months Ending June 30	
Sales (70% cash)	$30,000
Expenses	15,000
Depreciation	1,000
Earnings before interest and taxes, EBIT	14,000
Interest	6,000
Earnings before tax, EBT	8,000
Taxes (38%)	3,040
Earnings after tax, EAT (or net income)	$ 4,960
Cash dividend to be paid in 5 months	$500

The following information also pertains to Whiz Kids:

1.   All of the short-term debt of $1,500 will become due within 6 months.
2.   Whiz Kids will receive $5,000 in cash from sales of the previous year.

3. Eighty percent of the estimated expenses will be paid in the first 6 months of the following year. The remaining 20 percent will be paid in the second half of the year.
4. Taxes and expenses will be paid in full during the first half of the year.

What are Whiz Kids' expected cash inflows and outflows for the next 6 months? Is there a cash shortage or a cash excess?

CR 1.4   Tom Moyers is considering investing in a new firm. Tom estimates his $10,000 investment will be worth $11,000 in 1 year.

a. What is the projected return on the investment?
b. Tom is considering another investment of similar risk with a return of 15 percent. What is the net present value of the investment in the new firm?

CR 1.5   Bill and Mary were discussing a problem assigned to them in their financial management course. They were to find the net cash flow for XYZ firm. The firm had sales of $80,000, expenses of $60,000, depreciation of $15,000, and interest expense of $10,000. The firm collected 80 percent of its sales in cash and paid 80 percent of its expenses in cash. In addition, the firm's marginal tax rate was 40 percent, and no dividends were paid. Bill and Mary calculated the firm had a negative net income of $5,000, but they were confused when they found net cash flow was positive $6,000.

Did Bill and Mary correctly calculate net income and net cash flow? Is it possible to have a negative net income and a positive net cash flow?

PROBLEMS

1.1   Mott's Transit has run into some cash flow problems due to rapid expansion. Kevin, the chief financial officer, is making plans for the next 6 months. Assume it is December 31. The balance sheet for the year just completed and the firm's projected income statement (for both accounting and tax purposes) for the first half of next year are as follows:

Balance Sheet as of December 31		Projected Income Statement for next 6 months	
Assets	$300	Sales	$500
Liabilities and equity		Expenses	360
Current debt	$100	Depreciation	30
Long-term debt	50	EBIT	110
Equity	150	Interest	25
Total	$300	EBT	85
		Taxes (40%)	34
		Net income	$ 51

In addition, Kevin notes the following:

a. Eighty dollars of the $100 in current debt comes due in the first half of next year, and the bank has indicated it will not renew the loan.
b. A long-term debt issue of $50 is planned for the first half of next year.

c. Seventy percent of the sales projected for the first half of next year will be received in cash by June 30; the remainder will not be collected until the second half of next year.

d. Forty dollars in cash will be received during the first half of next year from sales in the last half of this year. (Thus, this is an account receivable that will be collected.)

e. Ninety percent of the estimated expenses for the first half of next year will be paid in cash during the period; the remainder can be paid in the second half of next year.

f. Taxes and interest must be paid in full during the first half of next year. Also, cash dividends of $16 are payable during the first half of next year.

g. The cash account cannot be reduced from its present level.

Prepare an estimate of Mott's expected cash inflows and outflows for the next 6 months. Do you foresee any problems? What actions might Kevin take to secure the additional cash needed?

1.2 Parkwest Hotel has the following income statement for reporting purposes:

Income Statement	
Revenues	$180,000
All operating expenses except depreciation	142,000
Depreciation	15,000
EBIT	23,000
Interest	11,000
EBT	12,000
Taxes (30%)	3,600
Net income	$ 8,400

Assume that all revenues and expenses (except depreciation) are for cash. The firm uses accelerated depreciation for tax purposes, so the actual depreciation charged is $20,000, not $15,000. Given the difference between GAAP financial statements and those prepared for tax purposes, what is Parkwest's actual cash flow from operations?

1.3 Mini Case Four weeks into the current term you go home for the first time. While there you are asked to explain what you have learned so far in your finance course.

a. What is financial management? Why is the primary focus on corporations instead of proprietorships or partnerships?

b. What are the basic ideas in finance that should be understood? Explain why each is important.

c. How, instead of using the "pie" concept, can we visualize the claims of bondholders and stockholders? What role does the fixed claim held by bondholders play? Limited liability for stockholders?

d. What is an agency relationship? How does it influence the firm's goal?

e. Why are incremental cash flows so important?

f. During the conversation your uncle comes by. He does not understand balance sheets, income statements, and the difference between net income and cash flow. Using the following information, explain balance sheets, income statements, and the difference between net income and cash flow to him. Calculate the projected cash flow for the next 2 months, and then explain why the focus has to be on cash flow.

Balance Sheet

Assets		Liabilities and Stockholders' Equity	
Cash	$ 3,000	Short-term debt	$ 5,000*
Other	37,000	Long-term debt	15,000
Total	$40,000	Equity	20,000
		Total	$40,000

*$2,000 due this month

Projected Income Statement for Next 2 Months

Sales (90% cash)	$10,000
Cash expenses except interest	6,000
Depreciation	900
Earning before interest and taxes, EBIT	3,100
Interest	400
Earnings before tax, EBT	2,700
Taxes (40%)	1,080
Earnings after tax, EAT (or net income)	$ 1,620
Cash dividend to be paid next month	$ 200

g. During the conversation, an investment salesperson calls on the phone and offers a "guaranteed" 20 percent return with no risk on a $5,000 investment. If banks, savings and loans, and the like are paying 7 percent on current deposits, explain why individuals should be suspicious of a "guaranteed" 20 percent return with no risk.

REFERENCES

For more on financial theory, decision making, and its effect, see:

RAPPAPORT, ALFRED. *Creating Shareholder Value: The New Standard for Performance.* New York: Free Press, 1986.

SMITH, CLIFFORD W., JR. "The Theory of Corporate Finance: A Historical Overview." In *The Modern Theory of Corporate Finance,* 2nd ed., edited by Clifford W. Smith, Jr. New York: McGraw-Hill, 1984. pp. 3–24.

WENNER, DAVID L., AND RICHARD W. LEBER. "Managing for Shareholder Value—From Top to Bottom." *Harvard Business Review* 67 (November-December 1989): 52–54ff.

WILLIGAM, GERALDINE E. "The Value-Adding CFO: An Interview with Disney's Gary Wilson." *Harvard Business Review* 68 (January-February 1990): 85–93.

Information on agency issues and other stakeholders can be obtained in:

BARNEA, AMIR, ROBERT A. HAUGEN, AND LEMMA W. SENBET. *Agency Problems and Financial Contracting*. Englewood Cliffs, N.J.: Prentice-Hall, 1985.

CORNELL, BRADFORD, AND ALAN C. SHAPIRO. "Corporate Stakeholders and Corporate Finance." *Financial Management* 16 (Spring 1987): 5–14.

JENSEN, MICHAEL C., AND WILLIAM H. MECKLING. "Theory of the Firm: Managerial Behavior, Agency Costs, and Ownership Structure." *Journal of Financial Economics* 2 (October 1976): 305–60.

Other interesting reading about key concepts and what we know in finance, along with information about recent nobel laureates in financial economics, is contained in:

BERNSTEIN, PETER L. "The Vindication of the Professors." *Institutional Investor* 24 (November 1990): 81–87.

———— *Capital Ideas: The Improbable Origins of Modern Wall Street*. New York: The Free Press, 1992.

BREALEY, RICHARD A., AND STEWART C. MYERS. *Principles of Corporate Finance*. 4th ed. New York: McGraw-Hill, 1991, Ch. 36.

EMERY, DOUGLAS R., AND JOHN D. FINNERTY. *Principles of Finance: With Corporate Applications*. St. Paul, Mn: West Publishing, 1991, Ch. 2.

STEWART, G. BENNETT, III. "Market Myths." In *The New Corporate Finance: Where Theory Meets Practice*, edited by Donald H. Chew, pp. 3–20. New York: McGraw-Hill, 1993.

2 *Value Creation and Time Value*

EXECUTIVE SUMMARY

We know from Chapter 1 that financial managers use incremental cash flows for decision making and that a dollar today is worth more than a dollar tomorrow. To determine what tomorrow's dollars are worth today, we calculate their present value. Then we subtract the initial investment required from the present value of tomorrow's dollars. The result is the net present value of the proposed investment. The discount rate employed is the opportunity cost of the return forgone by making the investment, instead of investing in some equally risky alternative.

The presence of financial markets is important because it allows individuals and firms to trade between dollars today and dollars in the future. The "best" investments in real assets should provide higher returns than investing in financial assets. To maximize value, all positive net present value investments should be undertaken. Doing so maximizes value for both individuals and firms. Deciding what to invest in (the financing decision) and how to finance it (the investment decision) typically are separable decisions.

Knowing how to calculate present and future values, for both single amounts (or lump sums) and for streams of cash flows, requires an understanding of the time value of money. While annual cash flows and discounting are often employed in this book, financial practitioners often use more-frequent-than-yearly cash flows and discounting. This is especially true when determining the effective annual interest rate.

The messages from this chapter are clear: a dollar today is worth more than a dollar tomorrow; well-developed financial markets are important; maximize net present value; and, investment and financing decisions typically are separable.

INVESTMENT DECISION MAKING

Firms invest in many different assets. These include tangible assets like buildings and machinery as well as intangible assets such as patents, research and development programs, and training for employees. Firms need a frame of reference, or a decision-making process, that allows them to ask the right questions at the right time to make effective decisions so that the firm prospers. We start by focusing on cash flows and furthering our understanding of present value and the concept of net present value. Then we proceed by sketching out the basic elements of the theory of financial decision making. This is done from the standpoint of individuals, but the same ideas apply for firms. The latter portion of the chapter examines the important aspects of the time value of money, and how to proceed when cash flows occur over a number of time periods.

PRESENT VALUES

Suppose you were left with a tax-free gift of $250,000 and your current job brings in enough to take care of all of your (and your loved ones') current and anticipated future desires. The question, then, is what to do with the $250,000. You could bury it in the ground, give it away, or invest it. Let's rule out the first two possibilities and focus on investing the $250,000. Your financial advisor proposes that you invest the money in a new small office complex. The total cash outflow required to purchase the office complex is $250,000, and your financial advisor believes that due to the shortage of office space in that part of town, the office complex could be sold for a cash inflow of $325,000 in 1 year. The decision you face is simple—do you proceed with the office complex?

NET PRESENT VALUE AND INTERNAL RATE OF RETURN

To answer that question we have to compare the cash inflow of $325,000 to be received in one year with the $250,000 cash outflow to be made today. That comparison rests on understanding how to determine the **present value** of a set of future cash flows, or, alternatively, how to determine the rate of return you will earn on your investment. The present value of a cash flow that will occur in one year is found by discounting as follows:

$$\text{present value, } PV_0 = \frac{FV_1}{1 + k} \tag{2.1}$$

where

PV_0 = the present value today, at time $t = 0$, of a future cash flow
FV_1 = the cash flow occurring at time period 1
  k = the return demanded for accepting the delayed receipt of the funds

If we initially assume the investment is a sure thing, then what kind of return, k, would you demand on the investment? A completely safe alternative is to invest in U.S. government securities that mature in 1 year. Suppose that government securities are yielding 8 percent; that is, for every $1 invested today you can receive back $1.08 in one year with no risk. What is the present value *today* of $325,000 to be received in 1 year? It's simply:

$$PV_0 = \frac{FV_1}{1 + k} = \frac{\$325,000}{1 + 0.08} = \$300,926$$

where k is the **discount rate.** Alternatively, $300,926 is the amount that becomes $325,000 in 1 year when invested at 8 percent.

Should you make the investment? That's easy to answer: By making an investment of $250,000, you are acquiring something that is worth (in present value terms) $300,926. Because $300,926 is greater than $250,000, you are better off.

Another way to state this relationship is to determine the net present value of the investment, which is

net present value, NPV = present value − initial investment

$$NPV = \frac{FV_1}{1 + k} - PV_0 \tag{2.2}$$

$$= \frac{\$325,000}{1 + 0.08} - \$250,000$$

$$= \$300,926 - \$250,000 = \$50,926$$

Thus, you should invest in the office complex because it makes a net contribution to value of $50,926 after considering the timing of the expected cash flows and the alternative use of the funds.

Instead of calculating the net present value of the proposed office complex, we can make the same decision another way. This approach involves finding the *rate of return* on the project. To do this we compare the cash inflow from the project with the initial cash outflow. Thus, the incremental return is divided by the original investment, or ($325,000 − $250,000)/$250,000 = $75,000/$250,000 = 30 percent. More formally, the **internal rate of return, IRR,** is determined by solving for the unknown rate in the following equation:

$$\frac{FV_1}{1 + IRR} = PV_0 \tag{2.3}$$

$$\frac{\$325,000}{1 + IRR} = \$250,000$$

$$\$325,000 = \$250,000 + \$250,000\,IRR$$

$$IRR = \frac{(\$325,000 - \$250,000)}{\$250,000} = 30\%$$

By investing in the project you achieve a return of 30 percent. Because this return is greater than the 8 percent you could earn by investing in an equally risky alternative, you would accept the project.

Thus, we have two ways to make the capital investment decision[1]:

1.   NET PRESENT VALUE   Accept the proposed opportunity if the NPV is positive. The net present value is equal to the present value of the future cash flow minus the initial investment required.
2.   INTERNAL RATE OF RETURN   Accept the proposed opportunity if the return is greater than the discount rate, k. The return is the compound return earned based on the initial investment and the future cash inflows.

WHAT ABOUT RISK?

Until now we have assumed the investment in the small office complex was a sure thing. However, that assumption is unrealistic. In practice, not many investments in real estate or anything else (except short-term government securities) provide a risk-free return. You know the investment in the office complex is riskier than the investment in government securities. At the same time it is probably not as risky as investing in a professional soccer team or digging for gold. Let's say that based on your own knowledge and information you received from your financial advisor, you conclude the risk of the office complex is equal to that of the stock market. The financial advisor forecasts a 14 percent return from the stock market for the next year. Now the discount rate, k, employed to make the decision becomes 14 percent and the net present value is

$$NPV = \frac{\$325,000}{1 + 0.14} - \$250,000 = \$285,088 - \$250,000 = \$35,088$$

The investment is not as attractive now as it was before. However, you should still proceed, because the present value of next year's cash flow is greater than the initial cash outflow of $250,000. Using the internal rate of return, the comparison is now between a return of 30 percent and one of 14 percent from an equally risky alternative investment. Again you would make the investment. Later in the book we have a lot to say about risk and how it should be dealt with in capital investment decisions. For the present, just remember that *risk is one of the major items* that has to be considered in every financial decision.

THE OPPORTUNITY COST OF CAPITAL

Before leaving this section we need to explore another topic briefly: the rate k employed as the discount rate when calculating the net present value, or the rate that the internal rate of return is compared to. The terms discount rate, required return,

---

[1] When there are more than two cash flows, the two decision criteria may not produce the same decision. This topic is explored in Chapter 7. At that time we will discuss why net present value provides a better basis for decision making than internal rate of return.

hurdle rate, and **opportunity cost of capital** are used interchangeably. It is considered the *required rate of return* because it is what investors or firms seek as the reward for making an investment now and delaying consumption (or receiving payment) until some time in the future. It is a *hurdle rate* when it is employed as the standard against which the internal rate of return is compared. It is an *opportunity cost* because it is the return forgone by investing in a specific asset rather than investing in some equally risky investment, such as the stock market. In the above example, the required rate of return, hurdle rate, or opportunity cost of capital was 8 percent in the absence of risk; it was 14 percent once the risk of the office complex was considered. Determining the required rate of return, or opportunity cost of capital, is discussed in detail in Chapter 6.

Concept Review Questions

- Briefly describe the net present value, NPV, and internal rate of return, IRR, methods and their respective accept-or-reject criteria.
- Explain how the opportunity cost of capital affects the acceptance of an investment project.

VALUE CREATION

Present value and the net present value of an investment sound like common sense. They are. But, a greater understanding of current versus future decisions and the role played by the financial markets is needed; these ideas are key elements that underpin much of financial decision making.

CONSUMPTION AND INVESTMENT CHOICES

The problem of choosing between spending today versus spending in the future is illustrated in Figure 2.1. Assume you have a cash inflow of A dollars today and C dollars 1 period, or year, from now. If there is no way to save and borrow, you are forced to consume the A dollars today and then, 1 year from now, consume the C dollars. In some circumstances that may be fine. But what if you have a need for more consumption today (to purchase a car or house, for example) than provided for by the A dollars in cash flow? The answer is to go to financial markets and financial intermediaries, which enable you to transfer your cash flows across time.

A financial market is simply a market that provides the opportunity to trade between dollars (or cash flows) today and dollars in the future. The downward-sloping line DB in Figure 2.1 is the **interest rate line** which indicates the rate of exchange, called **interest,** between dollars today and dollars in 1 year.[2] The slope of line DB is $-(1 + k)$, where k is the 1-year rate of interest. For concreteness we refer throughout the book to the **risk-free rate** of interest as k_{RF}. In Figure 2.1 there is only one interest rate—you can borrow at the rate k_{RF} or you can lend (or invest in financial assets) at the same rate, k_{RF}.

---

[2] The interest rate line is sometimes referred to as the "capital market line."

Figure 2.1

Financial Market Effect

The interest rate line shows the cash flows from borrowing or lending. For example, by borrowing against future cash flow OC, an individual can consume an extra AB today.

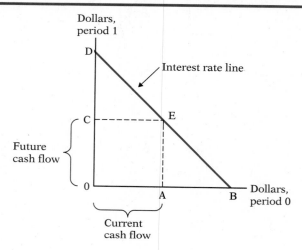

Assume your cash inflow today is $50,000, your inflow in one year is $60,000 and the risk-free rate of interest is 8 percent. If you invest all $50,000 of today's cash inflow at 8 percent, in one year you will have a **future value** of ($50,000)(1 + 0.08) = $54,000. This future value is composed of the original principal of $50,000 and the interest of $4,000. In 1 year you will also have another cash inflow of $60,000, for a *total* future value of $114,000. This total future value is shown on the vertical axis in Figure 2.2. Likewise, you could borrow against the $60,000 you will receive 1 year from now. The present value of the $60,000 discounted at 8 percent is $60,000/(1 + 0.08) = $55,556. Adding this amount to the current $50,000 cash inflow from time zero provides a *total* present value of $105,556. This amount is shown on the horizontal axis in Figure 2.2. Because of the existence of financial markets, opportunities to borrow or lend exist, as indicated in Figure 2.2.

Where on the interest rate line would you end up? It all depends on your needs and preferences for current consumption versus your desire and ability to save for the future. If you are a spendthrift, you will borrow against next year's cash inflows. On the other hand, if you are a tightwad, you will not spend all of this year's cash flows and will, instead, lend some of this year's cash flows. Even if you simply put your money in the bank, that is a lending decision. Assume you are a spendthrift and need $65,000 this year. You have $50,000 from current cash inflow and you will borrow $15,000 against next year's cash inflow. How much will be left for next year? It's simply the cash inflow next year of $60,000 − ($15,000)(1.08) = $43,800. The tradeoff of current versus future consumption for a spendthrift is illustrated in Figure 2.3 (a).

What if you are a tightwad? Say you need only $40,000 of this year's cash inflow and will invest (or lend) the rest at the risk-free rate of 8 percent. The amount available

Figure 2.2

Borrowing and Lending

If you consume $50,000 today and $60,000 in period 1, you neither borrow nor lend. But if you consume less than $50,000 today, you can lend; to consume more than $50,000 today, you must borrow.

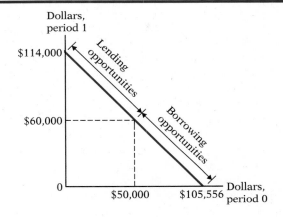

Figure 2.3

Spendthrift and Tightwad

By borrowing or lending, both the spendthrift and the tightwad can satisfy their desires for current versus future consumption.

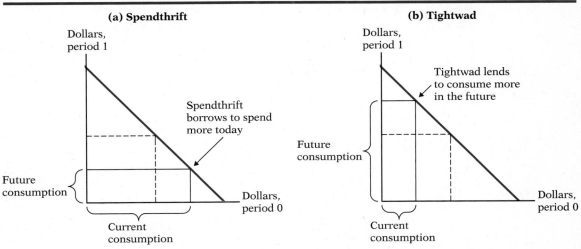

for consumption 1 year from now will be $60,000 + ($10,000)(1.08) = $70,800. This is shown in Figure 2.3 (b). By borrowing and lending in the financial markets, individuals can move anywhere they desire along the interest rate line. Thus, one of the crucial roles a well-developed financial market plays is to allow individuals the freedom to consume more or less than their current cash flow. Well-developed financial markets play a crucial role in financial decision making for both individuals and firms.

INVESTING IN REAL ASSETS

Not only can individuals invest in assets from the financial markets, they can also invest in real assets like buildings, machinery, and equipment. The return on the "best" real asset investments should be higher than the return on financial market investments; if it were otherwise, no one would invest in real assets. Therefore, the **investment opportunities line,** which shows the investment in and returns from investing in real assets, may at first have a steep slope, as shown in Figure 2.4. But, unless an inexhaustible supply of "good" investments in real assets exists, the anticipated returns decline, as shown by the progressively flatter investment opportunities line. Thus, the best investment (shown at the far right in Figure 2.4) produces the highest future cash flow, the next best (moving from right to left) has the second highest future cash flow, and so forth.

Now we need to consider what occurs when the opportunity for individuals to invest in both financial market assets and real (or capital) assets is available. This situation is shown in Figure 2.5. The line DB is simply the interest rate line from Figure 2.1; it indicates the opportunities available from investing or borrowing in the

---

Figure 2.4

Real Asset Investment Opportunities

The investment opporunities line indicates the investment in and returns from investing in real assets. Due to diminishing returns its slope becomes flatter with each additional project undertaken.

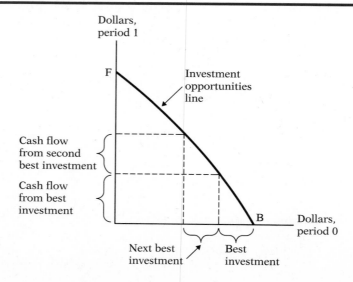

Figure 2.5

Specific Real Asset Investment Opportunities

The first investment in real assets of $20,000 produces a return of $45,000; clearly it should be undertaken. The second investment of $25,000 produces a return of $30,000 and should also be made.

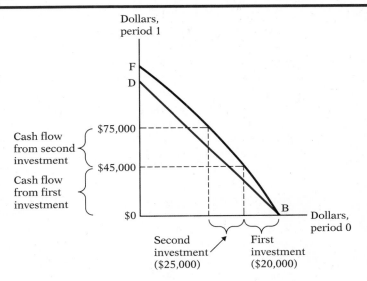

financial markets. The line FB is the investment opportunities line from Figure 2.4, which shows the investment in and return possibilities from investing in real assets. For simplicity, let's assume you are initially at point B. What should you do in the way of investing? If you invest in the financial markets (with returns as shown along the interest rate line DB), you will earn a return of 8 percent. But if you make an investment in real assets with part of your wealth, you will earn a higher return, as shown by the curved investment opportunities line FB.

Suppose the first investment in real assets requires an investment, or cash outflow, of $20,000 and has cash inflows of $45,000 one year from now. Should you make the investment? If you invest in financial market assets, instead of real assets, you would earn 8 percent; the future value in 1 year would be ($20,000)(1.08) = $21,600. However, if you invest in real assets, the future value is $45,000. Clearly, $45,000 is greater than $21,600, so you would invest in real assets with the first $20,000. The opportunities, investments, and returns available are shown in Figure 2.5.

An alternative way to make the same decision is to find the present value of the $45,000, discounted at 8 percent. The present value is $45,000/1.08 = $41,667. Because the present value of the inflow is greater than the initial investment of $20,000, the net present value of $41,667 − $20,000 = $21,667 is positive. Thus, the first investment in real assets should be made. Note what we accomplished by discounting at the opportunity cost of 8 percent. For the net present value to be positive, the project had to earn a return *greater* than the opportunity cost, or discount rate, of 8 percent. Hence, *discounting by the opportunity cost automatically compares the proposed investment in real assets to the next best alternative use of the funds,* in this case, investing in financial market assets with an 8 percent return.[3]

What about the proposed second investment of $25,000 shown in Figure 2.5? It promises to return $30,000 (i.e., $75,000 − $45,000, from Figure 2.5) in one year. Should the investment be made? The net present value is ($30,000/1.08) − $25,000 = $2,778. By making the second investment you earn a return that is also greater than the opportunity rate of 8 percent available from investing in financial assets. Make the second investment.

Should any more investments be made? The answer is "yes": *Invest in real assets as long as the net present value is positive.* Continue to invest in real assets as long as the return is greater than the opportunity cost, or opportunity rate of return. What happens when the net present value from making an investment in real assets becomes negative? The decision is clearcut: Do not invest; the incremental return earned on the investment in real assets is less than the incremental return of 8 percent from investing in financial assets.

While we haven't shown the net present value graphically, it is easy to do. Consider Figure 2.6, where it is assumed that the two investments of $20,000 and $25,000 in real assets from Figure 2.5 are optimal. That is, there are no other investments in real assets that have a positive net present value. We saw in Figure 2.5 that the future value of the cash inflows from investing a total of $45,000 in real assets was $75,000. The present value from making the investments is $75,000/1.08 = $69,444, and the net present value is $69,444 − $45,000 = $24,444. Investing in real assets produces a net present value of $24,444, so the *total* present value has increased from the original $105,556 to $130,000. This increase is shown as point G in Figure 2.6. Is the individual better off? Yes, wealth has increased by $24,444. This increase in wealth is due to accepting positive net present value investments in real assets that return more than the opportunity cost (or return) available from investing in financial market assets.

While we reached this conclusion for one specific individual, what about the spendthrift and the tightwad? Are they better off? Yes, because once the total present value has increased to $130,000 due to investing in real assets, individuals can move anywhere along the new interest rate line, HG, shown in Figure 2.6. (Note that point H is ($130,000)(1.08) = $140,400.) This is accomplished by borrowing or lending through the financial markets as we discussed previously. The important conclusion is that *no matter what the preferences of individuals, they are better off by accepting positive net present value investments.* Value creation through use of the net present value rule benefits all individuals, no matter what their preferences for consumption versus savings.

---

[3] The internal rate of return could also be used to make this decision. We have:

$$\frac{\$45,000}{1 + IRR} = \$20,000$$

$$\$45,000 = \$20,000 + \$20,000 IRR$$

$$IRR = \frac{(\$45,000 - \$20,000)}{\$20,000} = 1.25 \text{ or, } 125 \text{ percent.}$$

The return on financial assets is 8 percent; because the *IRR* is substantially greater than the opportunity cost, the decision to make the investment is the same as reached with net present value.

Figure 2.6

New Interest Rate Line and Net Present Value

By investing in real assets, individuals can attain any position on the new interest rate line, HG. The net present value equals the present value of the inflows minus the initial investment, or $69,444 − $45,000 = $24,444.

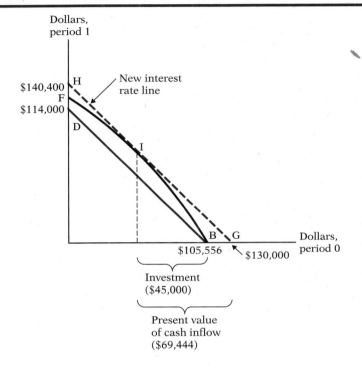

Note in Figure 2.6 that by accepting all positive net present value projects, we have made investments up to the point where the investment opportunities line FB just touches and is tangent to the new interest rate line HG. (The new interest rate line has exactly the same slope as the original interest rate line, DB. This has to be true unless the risk-free rate of interest changes.) The slope of the investment opportunities line represents the *return on the marginal investment* in real assets. The slope of the investment opportunities line is the internal rate of return on the investment. By moving up the investment opportunities line from B to I, we are accepting projects whose internal rate of return is greater than the opportunity cost of capital. When do we stop investing in real assets? When the investment opportunities line is just tangent to the new interest rate line, at point I. Before the point of tangency at I, the net present value is positive *and* the internal rate of return is greater than the opportunity cost of capital. Beyond the point of tangency (from I to F), the net present value is negative and the internal rate of return is less than the opportunity cost of capital.

Finally, one other item must be understood. The *presence of financial markets plays a major role* in what we have discussed. Without well-developed financial markets, individuals would not easily be able to borrow and lend. The presence of well-functioning financial markets effectively "uncouples" the individual's investment and saving decisions. Thus, in parts of the world that do not possess well-functioning financial markets, much of the above discussion does not hold nearly as well. Hence, be forewarned: Before you take your new-found knowledge to a third- or fourth-world country, ask yourself whether that country has anything resembling a well-developed financial market.

MOVING FROM INDIVIDUALS TO FIRMS

So far we have discussed the rationale for investing in real assets and the net present value rule from the standpoint of individuals. Moving from individuals to firms is straightforward. Think of a firm that is owned by one hundred individuals, each holding 1 percent of the firm's stock. For simplicity, assume that none of the owners is directly involved in running the firm, so they hire a management team to do so. What kinds of investments should the firm make? Exactly the same rule applies for the firm as for individuals: Take all positive net present value investment projects. By doing so, the value of the firm is maximized, no matter what the preferences of the owners for investment versus consumption. Taking positive net present value projects increases the value of the firm. All of the owners, as well as the firm's creditors, managers, and employees, benefit from the decision to make positive net present value investments.

This idea of making the same investment decisions in real assets no matter what the specific preferences of different individuals is called the Fisher **separation theorem.** In short, it says that the investment and financing decisions of the firm are separate. For the owners of the firm to maximize their value, the firm should take all positive net present value projects. How they are financed is a separate decision. We will discuss the separate investment and financing decisions in a number of later chapters. Then in Chapter 14 we will explore how to proceed when the investing and financing decisions are not separable. For now, remember four basic ideas of finance: a dollar today is worth more than a dollar tomorrow; well-developed financial markets are important; maximize the value of the firm by accepting positive net present value projects; and investment and financing decisions typically are separable.

SOME COMPLICATIONS

One complication is that in Figures 2.1 through 2.6 we have employed the risk-free interest rate as the opportunity cost of capital. That is fine in a world of certainty, but once the cash inflows are *forecasts*—i.e., not a sure thing—we have to deal with uncertainty. In general, dealing with uncertainty requires the use of higher discount rates for the opportunity cost of capital. Throughout our discussion of capital investment decision making in Chapters 7 through 10, and elsewhere in the book, we use the terms required rate of return, discount rate, hurdle rate, and opportunity cost of capital *assuming there is uncertainty*. Hence, a higher discount rate than the risk-free rate is appropriate.

Another complication is that in the discussion up to now we have assumed the interest rate for borrowing and for lending is the same. That is, any individual could borrow or lend at the same interest rate. For borrowing and lending rates to be the same, the following assumptions (implicitly or explicitly) are being made:

1. There is perfect competition; that is, no participants are large enough to have any material impact on prices.
2. There are no barriers to entry or frictions such as **transactions costs.** Transactions costs are the direct and indirect costs of issuing securities, or making a transaction.
3. Information is freely available to all financial market participants. When information is known to some, but not all of the participants, we have asymmetric information.
4. There are no **taxes,** or if there are any, all participants are taxed at the same rate so no distortions exist. The presence of taxes, or unequal tax rates, also affects financial prices and decisions.

In effect, the assumption of identical borrowing and lending rates is that perfectly competitive financial markets exist. Clearly this is not the case. Therefore, two questions arise: (1) How imperfect are the financial markets? and (2) what is the impact of less-than-perfectly-competitive financial markets? There have been many studies of the financial markets, the extent of frictions and other distortions, and the impact they have on the functioning of financial markets and on individuals and firms. As we proceed we will encounter situations in which transactions costs, asymmetric information, or taxes have important impacts on financial decisions.

The impact of less-than-perfectly-competitive financial markets means that individuals do not face the same borrowing and lending rates. This being the case, spendthrifts and tightwads would not select the previously indicated points on the investment opportunities line, because the slope of the interest rate line is different for borrowers than for lenders. How far apart are they? Probably not too far. How much impact do different borrowing and lending rates have on the decisions that individuals and firms make? Probably very little *at the margin*. Thus, although in some situations different borrowing and lending rates might change a decision, when considered *in total* the impact of different borrowing and lending rates does not appear to invalidate the major conclusions presented above.

The worst-case scenario is that the difference in borrowing and lending rates makes some decisions a little less precise. Should that worry financial decision makers? We don't think so, because finance is simply a way of structuring a common-sense approach to making financial decisions. If the prescription is "correct" in its direction and magnitude 98-plus percent of the time, why throw it out unless we have something better to offer? And, with each passing year we are learning still more about the theory, empirical aspects, and common sense of finance.

Concept Review Questions
■ Define the Fisher separation theorem.
■ How does the Fisher separation theory affect corporate and personal investment decisions?

TIME VALUE OF MONEY

We have introduced the basic ideas of present value and future value and have considered financial decision making using these techniques. So far, we have used present and future values only in situations where there were 2 time periods—today and 1 period (or year) from now. Before moving on, we need to learn how to deal with cash flows that are more than 1 period apart and cash flows that occur over multiple time periods.

WHEN CASH FLOWS ARE MORE THAN ONE PERIOD APART

Let's begin by considering cases where there are cash flows at 2 time periods, when these periods are not necessarily right next to each other. For example, the cash flows might occur today ($t = 0$) and 3 years from now ($t = 3$).

Present Value

We discussed present values when we presented Equation 2.1 and then used it to determine the net present value in Equation 2.2. To understand present values better, consider the following situation: What if you need $665.50 in 3 years? How much would you have to put aside today at a 10 percent annual compound interest rate to end up with the $665.50? We can use a timeline to show this graphically[4]:

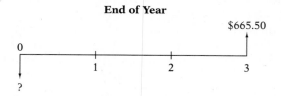

Let's define the variables we will consider:

PV_0 = the present, or today's, value of the amount

k = the annual interest rate, which is 10 percent, or 0.10

FV = the future, or ending, value of the amount, or $665.50

t = the number of periods or years, which can vary from zero to infinity, or 3 years

The general equation for the present value of a single amount to be received n periods in the future, discounted at k percent, is

$$\text{present value, } PV_0 = \frac{FV_n}{(1 + k)^n} \tag{2.4}$$

With a calculator it is easy to compute the present value of any amount for any period

---

[4] By convention, the present value is usually shown as an outflow (with the arrow going down), while the future value is shown as an inflow (with the arrow going up).

of time.[5] To determine the amount to put aside today, the present value, we have[6]

$$PV_0 = \frac{FV_3}{(1 + k)^3} = \frac{\$665.50}{(1 + 0.10)^3} = \$500$$

Equation 2.4 may also be written as follows: $PV_0 = FV_n[1/(1 + k)^n]$. The term in brackets is called the **present value factor, $PV_{k,n}$**. Table B.1, found at the end of the book, provides present value factors. Using PV factors, the basic present value equation (Equation 2.4) is

$$PV_0 = FV_n(PV_{k,n}) \qquad (2.5)$$

Thus,

$$PV_0 = FV_3(PV_{10\%,3yr}) = \$665.50(0.751) \approx \$500$$

While either Equation 2.4 or 2.5 can be used, we employ Equation 2.4 throughout the book.

Future Value

Finding the future value involves taking a cash flow today and determining what it will be worth sometime in the future if it earns a return of k percent interest per period. When compounding is employed, k is the **compound rate.** If you purchase a security worth $1,000 today that pays 8 percent interest compounded annually, how much will it be worth in 4 years? Graphically this is

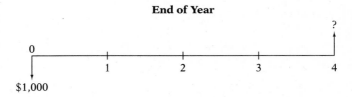

In general, the future value at the end of n periods is

future value, $FV_n = PV_0(1 + k)^n$ $\qquad (2.6)$

so[7]

$$FV_3 = \$1,000(1.08)^4 = \$1,360.49$$

---

[5] It is assumed all students have a basic calculator. However, many financial calculators are inexpensive, and they make financial calculations extremely simple. The footnotes in the rest of this chapter will assist you in using both basic and financial calculators.

[6] Using a basic calculator you divide $665.50 by $(1.10)^3$. With a financial calculator, you enter $n = 3$, $i = k = 10$, $FV = 665.50$, and then select PV to determine the answer of $500.

[7] To solve for the value $(1.08)^4$ using a basic calculator, it is necessary to use the exponential function, y^x. In this problem $y = 1.08$, $n = x = 4$, $y^x = 1.360. . .$, and $FV_4 = \$1,000 (1.360. . .) = \$1,360.49$. With a financial calculator, enter $n = 4$, $i = k = 8$, $PV = 1000$, and select FV to obtain $1,360.49.

Tables are also available that provide **future value factors, $FV_{k,n}$,** for the quantity $(1 + k)^n$ in Equation 2.6. Table B.3, given at the end of the book, provides future value factors for single amounts. In terms of future value factors, Equation 2.6 can be rewritten

$$FV_n = PV_0(FV_{k,n}) \qquad (2.7)$$

Using this equation, we find the future value is

$$FV_3 = PV_0(FV_{8\%,4yr}) = \$1,000(1.360) = \$1,360$$

which, except for a rounding difference of 49 cents, is the same as before. We employ Equation 2.6 throughout the book.

WHEN THERE ARE MULTIPLE CASH FLOWS

Up to now we have considered situations that involve only two cash flows and time periods. It is also necessary to deal with a series of cash flows. Let's begin by discussing the present value of a *perpetuity,* which is simply a series of cash flows of the same amount that continues indefinitely. Then we will consider the special case of an *annuity,* where the constant cash flows continue for only a finite period of time. Finally, we will examine the case of an uneven series of cash flows.

Perpetuities
Instead of single cash flows, let's go to the other extreme and consider how to value a series of cash flows of a constant amount that goes on forever—a **perpetuity.** The present value of a perpetuity with the first payment starting one period from now is equal to the constant cash flow stream, often called PMT (for payment), divided by the discount rate k, as follows:[8]

---

[8] We can verify Equation 2.8 by starting with the present value equation when there are many (an infinite number of) cash flows. Letting the individual future cash flows, the FVs, be PMT because they are the same amount in each future period,

$$PV_0 = \frac{PMT}{(1 + k)} + \frac{PMT}{(1 + k)^2} + \frac{PMT}{(1 + k)^3} + \ldots$$

Let $PMT/(1 + k) = a$ and $1/(1 + k) = x$. Then

$$PV_0 = a(1 + x + x^2 + \ldots) \qquad (1)$$

Multiplying both sides by x produces

$$xPV_0 = a(x + x^2 + \ldots) \qquad (2)$$

Subtracting (2) from (1) gives

$$PV_0(1 - x) = a$$

Substitution in for a and x, and rearranging gives

$$PV_0 = PMT/k$$

present value of a perpetuity, $PV_0 = \dfrac{\text{annual cash flow}}{\text{discount rate}} = \dfrac{PMT}{k}$ $\qquad$ (2.8)

Thus, if you have a benefactor who will provide a perpetuity of $140 per year *beginning 1 period (or year) from now,* discounted at 7 percent, so that

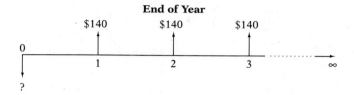

its present value is

$$PV_0 = \frac{PMT}{k} = \frac{\$140}{0.07} = \$2,000$$

Growing Perpetuities

Suppose that instead of a constant amount per year, the size of the payment provided by your benefactor is growing at a constant (percentage) rate of 3 percent per year, so the cash flow stream is:

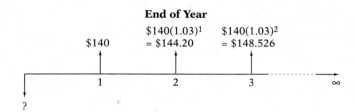

Given the **growth rate, g,** the present value of this stream of growing cash flows is

$$PV_0 = \frac{PMT}{(1+k)^1} + \frac{PMT(1+g)^1}{(1+k)^2} + \frac{PMT(1+g)^2}{(1+k)^3} + \dots$$

As long as the discount rate, k, is greater than the growth rate, g, this complicated-looking equation simplifies to[9]

present value of a growing perpetuity, $PV_0 = \dfrac{PMT}{k-g}$ $\qquad$ (2.9)

---

[9] As in footnote 8, we need to determine the sum of the infinite geometric series $PV_0 = a(1 + x + x^2 + \dots)$ where a is $PMT/(1+k)$ and x is now $(1+g)/(1+k)$. Substituting variables in and simplifying results in

$PV_0 = PMT/(k-g)$

With the size of the cash flow increasing by 3 percent per year, the value of your growing perpetuity is

$$PV_0 = \frac{PMT}{0.07 - 0.03} = \frac{\$140}{0.04} = \$3,500$$

As common sense tells us, the value of a growing perpetuity must be substantially greater than the value of a level perpetuity.

Present Value of an Ordinary Annuity

Once we understand how to value perpetuities, it is easy to value an **annuity,** which is just a limited-life perpetuity. That is, an annuity is a series of cash flows of the same amount that continues for a limited period of time, say, 4 years. Consider the case in which a promise is made to pay $600 at the *end* of each of 4 years as follows:

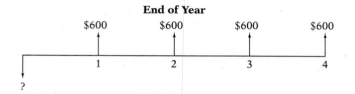

(When the cash flows occur at the end of each period, this is an **ordinary annuity.**) If the discount rate is 10 percent, what is the present value of this annuity?

Figure 2.7 indicates that there is an easy way to determine the present value of an annuity. For an typical perpetuity with the first cash flow starting 1 year from now, its value (as given by Equation 2.8) is

$$PV_0 = \frac{PMT}{k}$$

Now consider a second perpetuity that does not begin its cash flows until time period $n + 1$. That is, the second perpetuity is a *delayed perpetuity* whose constant cash flows start $n + 1$ periods in the future. The present value of this delayed perpetuity *at time* n is PMT/k, so its present value *today* (at $t = 0$) is

present value of delayed perpetuity, $PV_0 = \left(\dfrac{PMT}{k}\right)\dfrac{1}{(1 + k)^n}$

Both perpetuities provide payments from time period $n + 1$ onward. The first perpetuity also provides cash flows from period 1 to period n. Therefore, as shown in Figure 2.7, by taking the difference between the present value of the typical perpetuity and the present value of the delayed perpetuity we have the present value of an annuity of amount PMT for n periods, or years. This is

present value of an (ordinary) annuity, $PV_0 = PMT\left[\dfrac{1}{k} - \dfrac{1}{k(1 + k)^n}\right]$ (2.10)

Figure 2.7

The Present Value of an Annuity Equals the Difference in the Present Value of Two Perpetuities

An ordinary, or typical, perpetuity has constant cash flows that begin at time $t = 1$ and continue to infinity. A delayed perpetuity has constant cash flows that begin at time $n + 1$ and continue to infinity. By determining the present value at time $t = 0$ of the delayed perpetuity and subtracting it from the present value of the ordinary perpetuity, we determine the present value of an annuity that has constant cash flows from time $t = 1$ to time $t = n$.

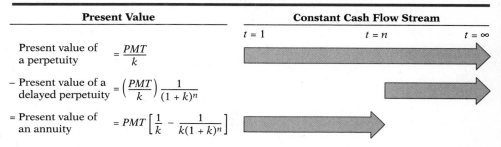

| **Present Value** | | **Constant Cash Flow Stream** |

Present value of a perpetuity $= \dfrac{PMT}{k}$

− Present value of a delayed perpetuity $= \left(\dfrac{PMT}{k}\right)\dfrac{1}{(1 + k)^n}$

= Present value of an annuity $= PMT\left[\dfrac{1}{k} - \dfrac{1}{k(1 + k)^n}\right]$

The present value of an annuity of \$600 to be received at the end of each of the next 4 years discounted at 10 percent is

$$PV_0 = \$600\left[\frac{1}{0.10} - \frac{1}{0.10(1 + 0.10)^4}\right] = \$600(3.1698\ldots) \approx \$1{,}902$$

Instead of using Equation 2.10, we can use tables that are available for the bracketed portion in the equation; these are called **present value factors for an annuity, $PVA_{k,n}$.** Using the value from Table B.2, the present value of this annuity is

$$PV_0 = PMT(PVA_{k,n}) \tag{2.11}$$
$$PV_0 = \$600(PVA_{10\%,4yr}) = \$600(3.170) = \$1{,}902$$

We use Equation 2.10 throughout.

Present Value of an Annuity Due

Although our primary concern is with ordinary annuities, what if the four cash inflows in the example above had occurred at the *beginning* of each period, not the end? This is the case of an **annuity due.** Each of the payments is shifted back one period, or year, on the timeline, so they now occur at $t = 0$, $t = 1$, $t = 2$, and $t = 3$:

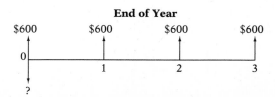

To calculate the present value of an annuity due, we multiply the present values determined before by the term $(1 + k)$. Equations 2.10 and 2.11 become

$$PV_0 \text{ (annuity due)} = PMT\left[\frac{1}{k} - \frac{1}{k(1 + k)^n}\right](1 + k) \qquad (2.10a)$$

and

$$PV_0(\text{annuity due}) = PMT(PVA_{k,n})(1 + k) \qquad (2.11a)$$

For our example, the present value in the case of an annuity due is

$$PV_0(\text{annuity due}) = \$600\left[\frac{1}{0.10} - \frac{1}{0.10(1 + 0.10)^4}\right](1 + 0.10) \approx \$2,092$$

Since the payments are made in advance, the present value of an annuity due is more valuable than if it is an ordinary annuity.

Future Value of an Ordinary Annuity

What if instead of finding the present value of an annuity, we need to find its future value? If you receive $600 at the end of each year and immediately invest it at 10 percent, how much will you have at the end of the 4 years? Graphically this is

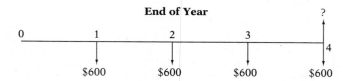

To find the future value of an annuity, we can make use of the knowledge developed previously. We know that the present value (at time $t = 0$) of an annuity, as given by Equation 2.10, is

$$PV_0 = PMT\left[\frac{1}{k} - \frac{1}{k(1 + k)^n}\right]$$

And we also know that we can move any single (or lump sum) present value to the future, using Equation 2.6 as follows:

$$FV_n = PV_0(1 + k)^n$$

Therefore, the future value of an annuity is equal to its present value at time $t = 0$ multiplied by the appropriate future value factor, so

$$FV_n = PMT\left[\frac{1}{k} - \frac{1}{k(1 + k)^n}\right](1 + k)^n$$

This simplifies to

future value of an (ordinary) annuity, $FV_n = PMT\left[\dfrac{(1 + k)^n - 1}{k}\right]$ (2.12)

The future value of an annuity of $600 to be received at the end of each of the next 4 years at 10 percent is[10]

$$FV_4 = \$600\left[\dfrac{(1 + 0.10)^4 - 1}{0.10}\right] = \$2,784.60$$

Alternatively, **future value factors for an annuity, $FVA_{k,n}$,** have been calculated for the bracketed portion of Equation 2.12. These are presented in Table B.4 at the end of the book. In terms of the table values, the future value of an ordinary annuity is

$FV_n = PMT(FVA_{k,n})$ (2.13)

$FV_4 = \$600(FVA_{10\%,4\,\text{yr}}) = \$600(4.641) = \$2,784.60$

We employ Equation 2.12 throughout the book.

Future Value of an Annuity Due

With the cash flows occurring at the beginning of the year, they must be compounded forward an extra year to determine the future value of an annuity due, so that

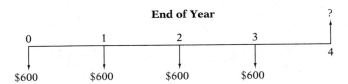

Because each cash flow is compounded for an extra year, Equations 2.12 and 2.13 are modified as follows:

FV_n (annuity due) $= PMT\left[\dfrac{(1 + k)^n - 1}{k}\right](1 + k)$ (2.12a)

and

FV_n (annuity due) $= PMT(FVA_{k,n})(1 + k)$ (2.13a)

Solving the earlier example as an annuity due, we have

$$FV_4 \text{ (annuity due)} = \$600\left[\dfrac{(1 + 0.10)^4 - 1}{0.10}\right](1 + 0.10) \approx \$3,063$$

[10] Using a financial calculator, enter $n = 4$, $i = k = 10$, $PMT = 600$, and then select FV to produce the same answer of $2,784.60.

The future value of an annuity due is larger than the future value of an ordinary annuity because of the extra year's compounding. Other things being equal, an annuity due is more valuable.

Present Value of an Uneven Cash Flow Series

It is also important to understand how to determine the present value when an uneven series of cash flows occurs. First, consider cash flows of $100 at year 1, $150 at year 2, $325 at year 3, and a discount rate of 12 percent. Graphically, this is

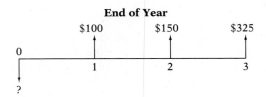

The general equation to find the present value of any series of cash flows is

$$\text{present value of any cash flow series, } PV_0 = \sum_{t=1}^{n} \frac{FV_t}{(1 + k)^t} \tag{2.14}$$

Using Equation 2.14, we have[11]:

$$PV_0 = \frac{\$100}{(1 + 0.12)^1} + \frac{\$150}{(1 + 0.12)^2} + \frac{\$325}{(1 + 0.12)^3} = \$89.29 + \$119.58 + \$231.33$$
$$= \$440.20$$

Now consider another example in which the cash flows are $100 at year 1, $150 at year 2, and then $325 for *each* of years 3 through 8, so that

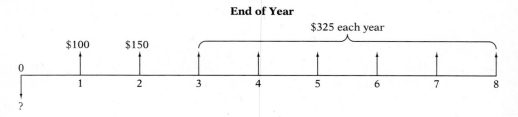

The discount rate remains 12 percent. This problem can be solved in eight separate steps using Equation 2.14, but time can be saved by using the techniques we have learned for annuities. To solve, proceed as follows:

STEP 1: Determine the present value at $t = 2$ of the annuity of $325 to be received

---

[11] With a financial calculator, you enter the three cash inflows, and $i = k = 12$. Selecting present value (typically called NPV, for net present value) produces the answer of $440.19. The 1 cent difference results from rounding.

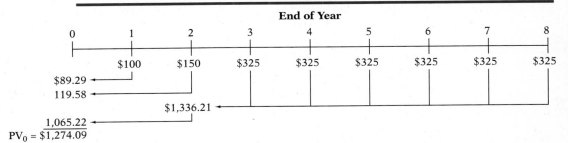

Figure 2.8

Present Value of an 8-Year Uneven Series Incorporating an Annuity, Discounted at 12 Percent

Instead of six separate steps, it is easier and faster to value the annuity at time $t = 2$ and then discount it to time $t = 0$. This step is unnecessary when using a financial calculator.

in years 3 through 8. Because this annuity is for 6 years (years 3, 4, 5, 6, 7, and 8), its present value at $t = 2$ is

$$PV_2 = \$325 \left[\frac{1}{0.12} - \frac{1}{0.12(1 + 0.12)^6} \right] = \$1,336.21$$

STEP 2: The lump sum of $1,336.21 is then discounted back to time $t = 0$, which is $1,065.22 [i.e., ($1,336.21)/(1 + 0.12)^2], as shown in Figure 2.8.

STEP 3: Discount the $100 to be received at the end of year 1 and the $150 to be received at the end of year 2 back to time $t = 0$. The amounts are $89.29 and $119.58, respectively.

STEP 4: Sum the values from steps 2 and 3. Thus, $89.29 + $119.58 + $1,065.22 = $1,274.09. This is the present value of the entire cash flow series discounted at 12 percent.[12]

DETERMINING INTERNAL RATES OF RETURN

In many cases both the present value (or cash outflow) at time $t = 0$ and the future cash flows and timing are known, but the interest or discount rate is not. (We know from before that the interest or discount rate is simply the internal rate of return.) We begin by determining examining individual cash flows, and then consider annuities and the case of a series of uneven cash flows.

Individual Cash Flows

Suppose you borrowed $1,000 today and agreed to pay the principal (of $1,000) and interest back in a lump sum in 5 years. The agreed payment at that time is $2,011.36. What compound annual rate of interest are you paying on the loan? While this

---

[12] Using a financial calculator, the present value is $1,274.08. The 1 cent difference results from rounding.

compound rate of interest may initially seem strange to you, it is nothing more than an internal rate of return. To determine the compound rate of interest, we need to solve for the unknown discount rate, k, where

$$PV_0 = \frac{FV_n}{(1 + k)^n}$$

$$\$1,000 = \frac{\$2,011.36}{(1 + k)^5}$$

You can get close to the correct answer using the present or future value tables (Tables B.1 or B.3) and interpolating. A far easier way involves using a financial calculator, which indicates that the interest rate, or internal rate of return, is 15 percent.[13]

Annuities

Precisely the same approach can be used when an (ordinary) annuity is being considered. Suppose you borrow $2,300 today and agree to repay $900 at the end of each of the next 3 years. What is the annual rate of interest you are paying on the loan? To determine this, we need to determine k, where

$$PV_0 = PMT\left[\frac{1}{k} - \frac{1}{k(1 + k)^n}\right]$$

$$\$2,300 = \$900\left[\frac{1}{k} - \frac{1}{k(1 + k)^3}\right]$$

Table B.2 and interpolation can be employed, but again the simpler way is to use a financial calculator. The compound interest rate is about 8.5 percent.[14]

Uneven Cash Flow Series

The internal rate of return can also be determined if the cash flow series is uneven. Suppose you invest $350 today and the series of payments promised is $80 at $t = 1$, $125 at $t = 2$, and $225 at $t = 3$. What is your expected annual compound percentage return? The problem becomes determining k in the following equation:

$$\$350 = \frac{\$80}{(1 + k)^1} + \frac{\$125}{(1 + k)^2} + \frac{\$225}{(1 + k)^3}$$

We need to determine what specific (single) rate *causes the present value of the cash inflows to exactly equal the initial present value,* which in this example is $350. Using a financial calculator, we find the interest rate, k, is about 9.3 percent.[15]

---

[13] Entering in $PV = 1000$, $FV = 2011.36$, and $n = 5$ and selecting $i = k$ produces an exact rate of 15.00003 percent.

[14] Enter $PV = 2300$, $PMT = 900$, and $n = 3$ and select $i = k$ to produce the exact interest rate of 8.46654 $\approx$ 8.5 percent.

[15] Enter the present value of $350 and the future values of 80, 125, and 225. Selecting $IRR = k$, the rate is 9.31927 $\approx$ 9.3 percent.

MORE FREQUENT CASH FLOWS

So far we have assumed that the compounding and discounting is done annually. That is, the period has been specified as "years." When compounding or discounting intervals of less than a year are employed, it is important to use the appropriate rate. The **nominal interest rate** is the quoted rate per year. The **effective interest rate** is the true rate *per time period*, and it depends on both the frequency of compounding and the nominal rate. Thus,

$$\text{effective rate per period} = \frac{\text{nominal interest rate, } k}{\text{number of compounding periods per year, } m} \qquad (2.15)$$

For example, if the nominal rate of interest is 8 percent per year, the effective *semiannual* rate is 8%/2 = 4%, and the effective *monthly* rate is 8%/12 = 0.66667%.

Discounting and Compounding

To illustrate more frequent periods, let's determine the present value of $10,000 to be received at the end of 2 years when the nominal interest rate is 8 percent and different discounting intervals are employed. Equation 2.4 becomes

$$\text{present value with more frequent discounting, } PV_0 = \frac{FV_n}{[1 + (k/m)]^{nm}} \qquad (2.16)$$

where

k = the annual nominal rate
m = the number of discounting intervals per year
k/m = the effective rate per period
n = the number of years

The present value, employing different discounting intervals, is

$$PV_0 \text{ (annual)} = \frac{\$10,000}{[1 + (0.08/1)]^{2(1)}} = \$8,573.39$$

$$PV_0 \text{ (semiannual)} = \frac{\$10,000}{[1 + (0.08/2)]^{2(2)}} = \$8,548.04$$

$$PV_0 \text{ (quarterly)} = \frac{\$10,000}{[1 + (0.08/4)]^{2(4)}} = \$8,534.90$$

$$PV_0 \text{ (monthly)} = \frac{\$10,000}{[1 + (0.08/12)]^{2(12)}} = \$8,525.96$$

Likewise, when continuous discounting is employed, Equation 2.4 becomes[16]

---

[16] Note that dividing FV_n by e^{kn} is the same mathematically as multiplying FV_n by e^{-kn}. All the minus sign in the exponent to e does is to indicate the inverse.

present value with continuous discounting, $PV_0 = FV_n/e^{kn} = FV_n e^{-kn}$ (2.17)

where e is the value 2.71828. The present value of $10,000 to be received 2 years from now if the nominal discount rate is 8 percent, employing continuous discounting, is[17]

$$PV_0 = \$10,000e^{-0.08(2)} = \$8,521.44$$

To determine future values, instead of present values, Equation 2.6 is modified to

future value with more frequent compounding $FV_n = PV_0\left(1 + \dfrac{k}{m}\right)^{nm}$ (2.18)

To illustrate, suppose we need to determine the future value in 4 years of $3,000 today, with a nominal interest rate of 9.5 percent, using daily compounding. It is

$$FV_4 = \$3,000\left(1 + \frac{0.095}{365}\right)^{4(365)} = \$4,386.64$$

Continuous compounding could be employed instead of daily compounding. The future value equation using continuous compounding is

future value with continuous compounding, $FV_n = PV_0 e^{kn}$ (2.19)

The future value at $t = 4$ of $3,000 today, when the nominal interest rate is 9.5 percent and continuous compounding is used, is[18]

$$FV_4 = \$3,000e^{0.095(4)} = \$4,386.85$$

Effective Annual Interest Rates

There is one other item to cover—how to determine an **effective annual interest rate.** The effective annual interest rate is

effective annual interest rate are, $k_{\text{effective annual}} = \left(1 + \dfrac{k_{\text{nominal}}}{m}\right)^m - 1$ (2.20)

Note that dividing k_{nominal} by m provides the effective rate per period as indicated by Equation 2.15. Then, Equation 2.20 converts this effective rate *per period* to an effective annual rate. For example, if the nominal rate is 12 percent per year, and the compounding period is quarterly, the effective annual rate is

---

[17] Enter -0.16 [i.e., $(0.08)(2) = 0.16$] followed by the e^x key. Then multiply by $10,000 to get $8,521.4379 \approx \$8,521.44$.

[18] Enter $(0.095)(4) = 0.38$ followed by the e^x key. Then multiply by 3000 to get $4,386.85.

$$k_{\text{effective annual}} = \left(1 + \frac{0.12}{4}\right)^4 - 1 = 0.1255 = 12.55 \text{ percent}$$

Effective June 21, 1993, all depository institutions (such as banks and savings & loan associations) have to comply with Regulation DD, the Truth in Savings Act, of the Board of Governors of the Federal Reserve System. Under the Truth in Savings Act, institutions have to calculate and report the **annual percentage yield, APY,** on all deposit accounts. Thus, if you have a savings account or purchase a certificate of deposit, the institution is required to report the annual percentage yield, which is calculated as follows:

$$\text{annual percentage yield, APY} = 100\left[\left(1 + \frac{\text{interest}}{\text{principal}}\right)^{(365/\text{days in term})} - 1\right] \quad (2.21)$$

To understand the APY, assume $1,000 is deposited for 1 year, with the interest to be paid at a nominal rate of 8 percent, compounded quarterly. The interest earned the first quarter is ($1,000)(0.08/4) = $20. For the second quarter the *total* principal on deposit is the original $1,000 *plus* the $20 in interest earned the first quarter, for $1,020. The interest earned for the second quarter is ($1,020)(0.08/4) = $20.40. Proceeding in the same manner, the interest earned in the third quarter (on the new principal of $1,040.40) is $20.808, while for the fourth quarter it is $21.224. The total interest earned for the year is $82.432 (i.e., $20 + $20.40 + $20.808 + $21.224). The annual percentage yield, given by Equation 2.21, is:

$$\text{annual percentage yield} = 100\left[\left(1 + \frac{\$82.432}{\$1,000}\right)^{(365/365)} - 1\right] = 8.243\% \approx 8.24\%$$

Instead of employing Equation 2.21, let us use the equation for the effective annual rate given by Equation 2.20 as follows:

$$k_{\text{effective annual}} = \left(1 + \frac{k_{\text{nominal}}}{m}\right)^m - 1$$

$$= \left(1 + \frac{0.08}{4}\right)^4 - 1 = 0.08243 \approx 8.24\%$$

The rate is 8.24 percent employing either Equation 2.20 or 2.21. Thus, we see that *the annual percentage yield required under the Truth in Savings Act is, in fact, an effective annual rate.* The advantage of Equation 2.21 is that it can be employed in more complex situations (such as accounts where different rates apply to specified balance levels) sometimes encountered by financial institutions.[19]

---

[19] Some financial institutions employ **simple interest.** In this situation the interest is received on the initial principal amount only; the interest is not compounded.

While financial institutions report the annual percentage yield on deposit accounts, for loans made by financial institutions they have to advise consumers of the **annual percentage rate, APR,** of the loan. As specified by Regulation Z of the Truth-in-Lending Act of the Federal Reserve System, the APR is determined by *multiplying* the periodic rate per period by the number of periods in a year. Hence, *the APR is a nominal interest rate, not an effective annual interest rate.*

Knowing how to deal with future values, present values, and finding the unknown interest rate or internal rate of return becomes important as we proceed in finance. The time value material just covered, while done fairly briefly, is comprehensive.

Concept Review Questions

- Explain how you would find the present and future values of a single cash flow and of multiple cash flows.
- What is the difference between an ordinary annuity and an annuity due?
- How do you modify the equations for the present value and future value of an ordinary annuity to determine the future and present value of an annuity due?
- What changes would you make to the future value and present value equations if the interest rate were compounded for less than a year?

KEY POINTS

1. Most financial decisions are made on the basis of expected incremental cash flows.
2. A dollar today is worth more than a dollar tomorrow. To determine the present value of tomorrow's dollars, you discount the future cash flows by the opportunity cost of capital.
3. The opportunity cost of capital is the forgone return that could have been earned by investing in a comparably risky asset.
4. The net present value is the present value of the expected cash inflows minus the initial cash outflow on an investment. Value is enhanced when positive net present value projects are accepted.
5. Well-developed financial markets allow individuals and firms to trade between dollars today and dollars tomorrow.
6. The investment decision of deciding what real (or capital) assets to invest in, and the financing decision of how to finance the investment, typically are separable. Because the returns on some real assets are higher than on financial assets, wealth enhancement occurs by allocating some investment to real assets.
7. The present value of some future cash flow is $PV_0 = FV_n/(1 + k)^n$. The future value is $FV_n = PV_0(1 + k)^n$.
8. The present value of a perpetuity is $PV_0 = PMT/k$. The present value of a perpetuity growing by a constant percentage rate per period is $PV_0 = PMT/(k - g)$.
9. The present value of an annuity is

$$PV_0 = PMT\left[\frac{1}{k} - \frac{1}{k(1 + k)^n}\right]$$

while the future value of an annuity is

$$FV_n = PMT\left[\frac{(1 + k)^n - 1}{k}\right]$$

10. With more-frequent-than-annual discounting, the present value is

$$PV_0 = \frac{FV_n}{[1 + (k/m)]^{nm}}$$

while with continuous discounting the present value is

$$PV_0 = FV_n/e^{kn} = FV_n e^{-kn}$$

11. In order to determine the effective annual interest rate, the yearly nominal rate is converted to an effective per period interest rate and then annualized, so that

$$k_{\text{effective annual}} = \left(1 + \frac{k_{\text{nominal}}}{m}\right)^m - 1$$

12. The annual percentage yield required for depository institutions is an effective annual interest rate.

QUESTIONS

2.1   Explain the relationship between net present value and internal rate of return. Is it true that the net present value can be positive only if the internal rate of return is greater than the opportunity cost of capital?

2.2   What is meant by the term "opportunity cost of capital"? What opportunities are we talking about?

2.3   Explain each of the following:

a. How individuals can consume more now or later.
b. Why well-developed financial markets are important.
c. What role is played by opportunities to invest in real assets.
d. Why both the spendthrift and the tightwad benefit from accepting positive net present value projects.

2.4   Graph an interest rate (or capital market) line, the investment opportunities line, and the new attainable interest rate line. Then, using your graph, explain what net present value is, how much investment in real assets should be made, and the relationship between net present value and internal rate of return.

2.5   What is the impact of the Fisher separation theorem for individuals and firms?

2.6   Present value and future value are the inverse, or mirror images, of each other. Explain why this is true. Then demonstrate how present value and future value relate to each other.

2.7   The following series of cash flows exists:

Time Period	Amount
t_1	$300
t_2	200
t_3	100
t_4	100

Find the present value of this stream. Show at least four different ways you could set up the cash flow stream to solve for this present value.

2.8   A firm's earnings are expected to increase by 50 percent, from $200,000 at the end of $t = 3$ to $300,000 at the end of $t = 8$. Show why the compound (or annual) growth rate is less than 10 percent per year.

2.9 Explain why you are not indifferent to having your money invested in a bank that may, at its discretion, compound annually, semiannually, quarterly, monthly, daily, or continuously. (*Note:* Assume everything else stays the same.)

CONCEPT REVIEW PROBLEMS

See Appendix A for solutions.

CR2.1 You are offered an investment in a local business for $500,000, and you are told that the business can be sold after 1 year. The after-tax cash flow from the sale of the business is estimated to be $600,000.

a. If the opportunity cost of capital is 14 percent, what is the net present value of the business venture?
b. What is the internal rate of return?

CR2.2 What will the following investments accumulate to?

a. $6,000 invested for 10 years at 10 percent compounded annually.
b. $8,000 invested for 5 years at 5 percent compounded annually.
c. $500 invested for 7 years at 8 percent compounded annually.
d. $10,000 invested for 3 years at 6 percent compounded annually.

CR2.3 What is the present value of the following investments?

a. $6,000 due in 10 years discounted at 10 percent annual rate.
b. $8,000 due in 5 years discounted at 5 percent annual rate.
c. $500 due in 7 years discounted at 8 percent annual rate.
d. $10,000 due in 3 years discounted at 6 percent annual rate.

CR2.4 What is the present value of the following perpetuities?

a. An $80 perpetuity beginning at time $t = 1$ discounted back to time $t = 0$ at 10 percent.
b. A perpetuity with an $80 payment at time $t = 1$ growing at 4 percent per year discounted back to the present at 10 percent.
c. A perpetuity with an $80 payment starting in 4 years discounted back to the present at 10 percent.

CR2.5 You recently sold your Porsche for $25,000. With this nest egg you place your funds in a savings account paying 8 percent compounded annually for 4 years and then move it into another savings account paying 10 percent interest compounded semiannually. How large will your nest egg be at the end of 7 years?

CR2.6 Susan is trying to save $5,000 for a vacation.

a. How much will she need to place in her account today if the rate of interest is 10 percent compounded monthly and she expects to make the trip in 3 years?
b. What is the effective annual interest rate paid on her savings account?

CR2.7   You recently won $1,000,000 from a national magazine firm. Upon announcing the winner, the entry officials notified you that you will be receiving the $1 million in equal payments over the next 20 years.

a.   If you receive the first payment after one year and all other payments at the end of the subsequent years, and the appropriate discount rate is 8 percent, what is the present value of your winnings?
b.   If you receive the first payment immediately and all other payments at the beginning of subsequent years, and the rate is still 8 percent, what is the present value of your winnings?

CR2.8   What is the future value of $500 deposited each year if:

a.   The interest rate is 10 percent, deposits are at the end of each year for 5 years, and interest is compounded annually?
b.   If the deposits are at the beginning of each year for 5 years?
c.   If the interest rate is 8 percent compounded quarterly and the deposit is at the end of the year?

CR2.9   Applied Communications is considering an investment with the following cash flows:

Year	Cash Flow
0	−$500,000
1	140,000
2	200,000
3	250,000

a.   If the firm's opportunity cost of capital is 12 percent, what is the project's net present value?
b.   What is the project's internal rate of return?

CR2.10   Mary is considering purchasing a new car costing $20,000. The car dealership is offering its customers one of two financing packages. Mary can either receive a $2,000 rebate or 2.9 percent financing with monthly financing for 2 years (24 payments). If she can obtain financing at her bank for 8 percent with monthly payments for 2 years, should she take the rebate or the 2.9 percent financing?

PROBLEMS

2.1   If the present value is $150 and the future value in 1 year is $180, what is the discount rate?

2.2   Suppose you pay $50,000 for an investment and it can be sold for $56,500 in 1 year.

a.   What is the internal rate of return on the investment?
b.   If the opportunity cost of capital is 11 percent, what is the present value of the investment? What is its net present value?
c.   Irrespective of (b), what if the internal rate of return is less than the opportunity cost? What can we say about the net present value of the investment?

2.3   FiFi makes $80,000 this year and $95,000 next year. If the interest rate is 10 percent, what will FiFi's consumption be next year if:

a. $100,000 is desired this year?
b. $45,000 is desired this year?

2.4   Answer based on the following figure:

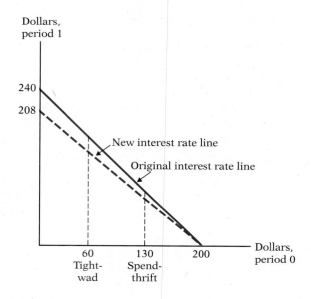

a.   What is the original interest rate?
b.   For the spendthrift, what is the future value of today's consumption? How much will be left for consumption tomorrow? What is the present value of tomorrow's consumption?
c.   For the tightwad, what is the future value of today's consumption? How much will be left for consumption tomorrow? What is the present value of tomorrow's consumption?

Now suppose that the interest rate falls and is now depicted by the line labeled "New interest rate line."

d.   What is the new interest rate?
e.   For the spendthrift at the new interest rate, what is the future value of today's consumption? How much will be left for consumption tomorrow? What is the present value of tomorrow's consumption?
f.   For the tightwad, what is the future value of today's consumption at the new interest rate? How much will be left for consumption tomorrow? What is the present value of tomorrow's consumption?

2.5   Suppose the market interest rate is 14 percent. An investment is available that will provide $125,000 *this* year in return for an investment of $150,000 *next* year. Should the investment be made?
2.6   Answer based on the following figure:

a.   What is the interest rate?
b.   How much should be invested in real assets?

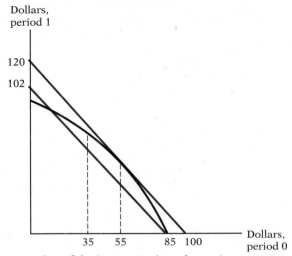

c. What is the present value of the investment in real assets?
d. What is the net present value of the investment?
e. What is the future value of the cash flow received from making the investment in real assets?
f. What is the internal rate of return on the investment in real assets?
g. How much will the individual consume today? How much tomorrow?

Now suppose the investment opportunities line remains as drawn in the figure but the investment in real assets is only $15 and the present value of the investment in real assets is $25.

h. What is the net present value?
i. What is the new total present value, or worth? What is the total future value?
j. If the individual continues to consume $35 today, how much can be consumed tomorrow?
k. What can we conclude about the real asset investment policy?

2.7   Answer based on the following figures:

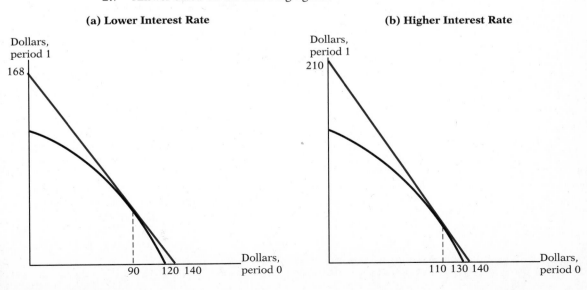

a. At the original interest rate given in (a) above, what is the interest rate?
b. How much is invested in real assets?
c. What is the present value of the investment in real assets?
d. What is the net present value?
e. What is the future value of the investment in real assets?
f. What is the internal rate of return?

Now suppose that the interest rate increases as show in (b) above.

g. What is the new interest rate?
h. How much is now invested in real assets?
i. What is the present value of the investment in real assets?
j. What is the net present value?
k. What is the new future value of the investment in real assets?
l. What is the internal rate of return?
m. Explain why an increase in the interest rate results in a decline in the investment in real assets.

2.8 Determine the future value of each of the following amounts:

a. An initial $325 compounded at 12 percent for 4 years.
b. An initial $650 compounded at 6 percent for 9 years.
c. An annuity of $150 per year for each of 6 years compounded at 10 percent.
d. An annuity of $480 per year for each of 3 years compounded at 17 percent.

2.9 Your firm has a retirement plan that matches all contributions on a one-to-two basis. That is, if you contribute $2,000 per year, the company will add $1,000 to make it $3,000. The firm guarantees an 8 percent return on the funds. Alternatively, you can "do it yourself," and you think you can earn 11 percent on your money by doing it this way. The first contribution will be made 1 year from today. At that time, and every year thereafter, you will put $2,000 into the retirement account. If you want to retire in 25 years, which way are you better off? (*Note:* Ignore any tax considerations.)

2.10 You plan to deposit $250 in a savings account for each of 5 years, starting 1 year from now. The interest rate is 9 percent compounded annually. What is the future value in each of the following cases?

a. At the end of 5 years?
b. At the end of 6 years if *no additional deposits* are made?
c. At the end of 5 years, as in (a), if an *additional* $250 is deposited today (i.e., at $t = 0$), so there are six deposits of $250 each?

2.11 Walt is planning for retirement. He plans to work for 25 more years. For the next 10 years, he can save $3,000 per year (with the first deposit being made 1 year from now), and at that time he wants to buy a weekend vacation home he estimates will cost $40,000. How much will he need to save in years 11 through 25 so that he has saved up exactly $300,000 when he retires? Assume he can earn 10 percent compounded annually for each of the next 25 years. (*Note:* Ignore any tax implications.)

2.12 Henderson is establishing a fund to pay off a $200,000 lump sum loan when it matures in 10 years. The funds will earn 8 percent interest per year. What is the size of the yearly payment in each case below?

a. The payment is made at the end of the year.
b. The payment is made at the beginning of the year.

2.13   Determine the present values (at $t = 0$) of the following:

a.   A single cash flow of $1,142 at time $t = 6$ discounted at 8 percent.
b.   An annuity of $300 per year to be received for each of 7 years discounted at 15 percent.
c.   An annuity of $400 per year to be received for each of 5 years, followed by a single cash flow of $1,000 at the end of year 6, discounted at 20 percent.
d.   An annuity of $200 for each of 6 years followed by an annuity of $800 for years 7 through 10, all discounted at 12 percent.

2.14   Olsen Electric has a line of small motors that no longer fits its corporate image. It is attempting to determine the minimum selling price for the small motors line. Olsen presently receives $250,000 per year after taxes in cash flows from the line. If the opportunity cost of capital is 16 percent, how much should Olsen ask if it thinks the life expectancy of the line is as follows?

a.   10 years.
b.   20 years.
c.   infinity.

2.15   Find the interest rates implied by the following:

a.   You lend $500 today and receive a promise for repayment 3 years from now of $595.
b.   You invest $500 today and have a promise of receiving $200 for each of the next 3 years.
c.   You invest $1,400 today and will receive $2,590 back at the end of 8 years.
d.   You lend $1,400 today and the repayments will be $282 for each of the next 8 years.

2.16   Richards Enterprises has decided to automate to increase efficiency. By purchasing word processing equipment costing $6,625, it can save $1,800 per year for each of 10 years in labor costs. What is the internal rate of return on the word processing equipment?

2.17   You are a lucky winner in the Big East Lottery. As a result, you have a choice between three alternative payment plans.

Plan I: A lifetime annuity of $60,425 annually, with the first payment 1 year from now.

Plan II: A $70,000 annual annuity for 20 years, with the first payment 1 year from now.

Plan III: $800,000 today.

Your life expectancy is 45 more years. Ignoring any tax effects, determine the following:

a.   At what interest rate would you be indifferent between plans I and III?
b.   At what interest rate would you be indifferent between plans II and III?
c.   At what interest rate (to the nearest whole number) would you be indifferent between plans I and II? (*Note:* It is easier to solve this by trial-and-error than algebraically.)
d.   What if (c) is now changed so you know the interest rate for both plans I and II is 12 percent for the first 20 years? What rate would you have to earn on the remaining 25 years of the $60,425 annuity to be indifferent between plans I and II?

2.18   Determine the internal rate of return for the following series of cash flows:

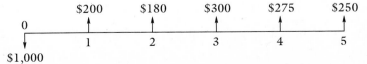

2.19   Consider the following set of annual cash flows: $t_1 = \$200$, $t_2 = \$200$, $t_3 = \$200$, $t_4 = \$500$, and $t_5 = \$500$.

a.   Find the present value of this series if the discount rate is 12 percent.
b.   If you could acquire the right to receive this series of cash inflows by paying $1,000 today, what would the compound percentage return be on your investment?

2.20   After graduating from college you make it big—all because of your success in financial management. You decide to endow a scholarship for needy finance students that will provide $3,000 per year indefinitely, beginning *1 year* from now. How much must be deposited *today* to fund the scholarship under the following conditions?

a.   The interest rate is 10 percent.
b.   The interest rate is 8 percent.
c.   For both 10 and 8 percent, if everything stays the same except that the first disbursement will not be made until *3 years* from now.

2.21   San Jose Winery needs $500,000 for expansion of its warehouse. The company plans to finance $100,000 with internally generated funds but wants to secure a loan for the remainder. The contracting firm's finance subsidiary has offered to provide the loan based on six annual payments of $97,300 each. Alternatively, San Jose Winery's bankers will lend the firm $400,000, to be repaid in six equal annual installments (covering both principal and interest) at a 15 percent interest rate. Finally, an insurance firm would also loan the money; it requires a lump sum payment of $750,000 at the end of 6 years.

a.   Based on the respective annual percentage costs of the three loans, which one should San Jose select?
b.   What other considerations might be important in addition to cost?

2.22   If $1,000 is invested today, how much will it be worth in (a) 5 years or (b) 10 years, if interest at a 12 percent nominal rate is compounded annually, semiannually, or quarterly?
2.23   How much would you have in the future in each of the following cases?

a. $2,500, invested today, if continuous compounding is employed, the nominal rate is 9 percent, and the period is 2-1/2 years.
b. $4.80, invested today, if the nominal rate is 12.6 percent continuously compounded, and the period is 15 years.
c. $100 invested today, if the nominal rate is 14 percent compounded annually, and the period is 10 years.
d.   same as in (c), except interest is compounded *continuously*.

2.24   Find the present value of each of the following:

a. $1,500 to be received in 8 years at a nominal rate of 6 percent discounted continuously.
b. $10 to be received in 4 years, and $50 to be received in 5 years, at a nominal rate of 15 percent discounted continuously.

2.25   What is the effective annual interest rate if the nominal rate is 9 percent per year, a 365-day year is used, and the compounding period is (a) yearly, (b) quarterly, (c) daily, or (d) hourly?
2.26   **Mini Case.**   Your best friend does not understand much about financial decision making and time value. To help him or her you have found the following questions from some old

financial management books. However, you don't have any answers to determine if his or her answers are correct. Thus, you need to answer the following:

a. Draw a graph to scale with an initial interest rate line, an investment opportunities line, and a new interest rate line.

   (1) What does the initial interest rate line rate line show?
   (2) Where would a spendthrift and a tightwad be?
   (3) Why does the investment opportunities line initially have a steeper slope than the interest rate line?
   (4) Label the net present value on your graph.
   (5) Where is the internal rate of return indicated on your graph?
   (6) What is the meaning of the new interest rate line?
   (7) Why are both the spendthrift and the tightwad better off?

b. What is the future value of $300 at the end of 4 years if the interest rate is 9 percent compounded annually? What would be the future value at the end of 6 years if for the last 2 years the interest rate decreased from 9 percent to 7 percent?

c. What is the present value today (at $t = 0$) of $600 to be received at $t = 6$ if the discount rate is 8.6 percent per year?

d. An annuity of $300 per year for 7 years exists. If the discount rate is 10 percent, what is the present value if it is an ordinary annuity? An annuity due? Explain the difference in values between the annuity and the annuity due.

e. You just won the Big Payoff. The payments are $350,000 for each of 13 years, with the first payment to be made at $t = 2$ and the last at $t = 14$. If the discount rate is 12 percent, what is the present value of your winnings?

f. What is the present value of a perpetuity of $200 per year if the discount rate is 16 percent? What if the first payment on the perpetuity does not occur until $t = 4$? Calculate the new present value of the perpetuity.

g. A cash flow stream exists as follows:

Year	Cash Flows
1	$100
2	300
3	−200
4	500

   (1) What is the future value at $t = 4$ if the interest rate is 11 percent?
   (2) What is the future value at $t = 6$ if the interest rate remains 11 percent?
   (3) What is the present value of the stream if the annual interest rate is 8 percent?

h. If an investment requires an outlay of $400 today, and promises to pay $50 at $t = 1$, $350 at $t = 2$, and $150 at $t = 3$, what compound percentage return would you earn if you made the investment?

i. What is the present value of $20,000 to be received 4 years from now if the discount rate is 10 percent and discounting is done:

   (1) annually?
   (2) quarterly?
   (3) monthly?
   (4) daily? (Assume all years have 365 days.)
   (5) continuously?

REFERENCES

For more information on consumption and savings decisions and on net present value, see:

COPELAND, THOMAS E., AND J. FRED WESTON. *Theory and Corporate Policy.* 3rd ed. Reading, Mass.: Addison-Wesley, 1988. Chap. 2.

FAMA, EUGENE F., AND MERTON H. MILLER. *The Theory of Finance.* New York: Holt, Rinehart and Winston, 1972. Chap. 1.

For more on future and present value and on using calculators, see:

BHANDARI, SHYAM B. "Compounding/Discounting of Intrayear Cash Flows: Principles, Pedagogy and Practices." *Financial Practice and Education* 1 (Spring 1991): 87–89.

CISSELL, ROBERT, HELEN CISSELL, and DAVID C. FLASPOHLER. *Mathematics of Finance,* 8th ed. Boston: Houghton Mifflin, 1990.

WHITE, MARK A. "Financial Problem-Solving with an Electronic Calculator." *Financial Practice and Education* 1 (Fall/Winter 1991): 73–88.

3
Valuation of Bonds and Stocks

EXECUTIVE SUMMARY

The financial system provides the framework within which managers operate to maximize the value of the firm. In developed countries sophisticated financial markets and institutions exist that provide an effective means of bringing together suppliers and demanders of capital.

Understanding how financial assets, such as stocks and bonds, are valued is important; effective financial decision making requires this knowledge. The required (or demanded) return for investing in financial assets equals the risk-free rate plus a risk premium.

Bonds are valued based on their expected interest payments and maturity values, discounted at the investor's required rate of return. A bond's yield to maturity is the compound rate of return that equates the present value of future interest payments plus the maturity value to the bond's current market value.

Theoretically, the market value of a common stock is determined in exactly the same manner as the market value of a bond. Thus, the market value of common stock is equal to the present value of all expected cash dividends, where the investor's required rate of return is employed as the discount rate. The magnitude and length of the expected growth in cash dividends has a major impact on stock prices.

The firm's stock price can be thought of as being composed of the capitalized value of the firm under a no-growth policy plus the present value of growth opportunities. Firms create value, as shown by increases in their market value, by accepting positive net present value projects. Investing in zero or negative net present value projects does not lead to value creation.

Expected *(ex ante)* returns and realized *(ex post)* returns are generally not equal. On an *ex ante* basis, risk and return are positively related. Thus, the greater the risk, the greater the return required by investors. Historically, the returns on stocks have exceeded those on corporate bonds, U. S. Treasury bills, and changes in the rate of inflation. Increased risk as perceived by investors leads to increased costs of financing for the firm.

THE FINANCIAL SYSTEM

As discussed in Chapter 2, the fundamental goal of the financial markets, and the purpose of the financial system that has developed to support the financial markets, is to allow individuals, firms, or governments to channel funds between consumption (or uses) today and consumption (or uses) in the future. An extensive financial system, such as that in developed countries, provides an effective means of bringing together suppliers and demanders of capital. The basic relationships are shown in Figure 3.1.

Figure 3.1

Relationship Among Suppliers and Demanders of Funds, Financial Institutions, and Financial Markets

Funds are supplied through the financial markets directly or by going through financial institutions. A well-developed network of financial institutions and financial markets is important for financial decision-making.

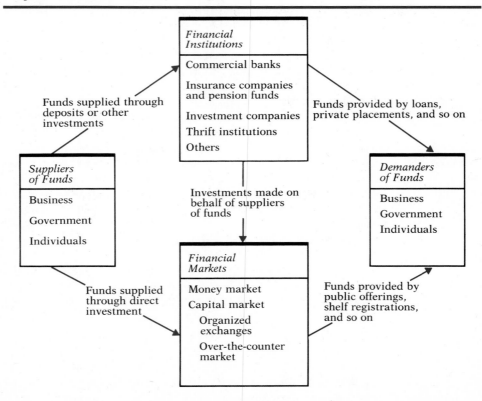

Note that not only are suppliers, demanders, and the financial markets part of the system, but so are the financial institutions that have evolved to increase the efficiency and smoothness of the system. Bonds and stocks are two of the major financial instruments that exist in a well-developed financial system. We need to understand how they are valued. But, before proceeding, it will help to understand more about the financial system.

FINANCIAL INSTITUTIONS

Financial institutions exist to facilitate bringing together suppliers and demanders of funds. These institutions, often referred to as **financial intermediaries,** accept savings; in return, the suppliers of funds acquire claims against the intermediaries. Then the intermediaries make loans or investments to the demanders of funds. As a reward for entrusting savings to a financial intermediary, the supplier expects some return in the form of interest or cash dividends. The major institutions in the financial system in the United States include:

1. Commercial banks, the traditional department stores of finance.
2. Insurance companies and pension funds, including life insurance companies, fire and casualty companies, and private and government retirement plans.
3. Investment companies, including various mutual funds in which investors pool their funds into a large fund managed by an investment advisor.
4. Thrift institutions, including savings and loan associations, mutual savings banks, and credit unions.
5. Other financial organizations including both "full-service" institutions as well as finance companies, mortgage companies, and real estate investment trusts.

Financial institutions provide a substantial portion of the funds available to corporations and other demanders of funds. Commercial banks have been the largest supplier of funds in recent years. Other financial institutions, such as insurance companies and pension funds, purchase stocks and bonds through the financial markets. Firms may also approach a financial institution to make a **private placement.** If Bristol-Myers Squibb, for example, needs to raise additional funds, it might approach the New York State retirement system directly for private placement of a new issue of bonds. **Investment banking firms,** such as First Boston, Klienwort Benson, Morgan Stanley, Nomura Securities, and Paine Webber, often provide assistance to firms needing funds. The investment banking firm may purchase a new stock or bond issue from the firm and then immediately resell it to investors—the suppliers of funds. Investment banking firms assist in bringing suppliers and demanders together by providing firms with expertise and marketing capabilities. Without investment banking firms, the worldwide financial system would not operate as smoothly as is does.[1]

---

[1] Investment banking firms, and the raising of long-term funds, are discussed in Chapter 15.

FINANCIAL MARKETS

A financial market exists whenever a financial transaction takes place. There are two general types of financial markets—the money market and the capital market. The **money market** is the market for short-term (1 year or less) debt. In contrast, the **capital market** is the market for long-term bonds or stocks. Included in the capital markets are (1) long-term government notes or bonds, (2) municipal bonds, (3) various forms of debt issued by firms, and (4) common and preferred stock issued by firms. The primary distinguishing feature of capital market securities is their life—they all have an anticipated life of longer than 1 year. They may range from a 5-year note issued by the government or some business, to common stock that has no specified maturity date.

All securities when they are originally offered—that is, when the proceeds of the sale go to the issuer of the securities—are issued in the **primary market.** (This applies to both money market and capital market securities.) By primary, we mean that the proceeds go to the issuer, which is typically a corporation or some government unit. After the securities begin to trade between individuals and/or institutional investors, they become part of the **secondary market.** In the primary market the firm and its lead investment banking firm generally work together to set the price at which securities are issued. However, in the secondary market, the original issuer has no part in the transaction. The secondary market exists to facilitate investor trading.

Transactions in the secondary market occur on both **organized security exchanges** and in the over-the-counter market. Among organized exchanges, the New York Stock Exchange, NYSE, is the largest secondary market for stocks in the world (in total dollar volume). (A few years ago the market value of stocks listed on the Tokyo Stock Exchange surpassed the market value of stocks listed on the NYSE. However, with the substantial decline in the value of Japanese stocks, the NYSE is again the largest stock exchange.) Approximately 1,500 common stocks and numerous preferred stocks are listed on the NYSE. It accounts for over 60 percent of the total dollar value of all stock outstanding in the United States. The next largest organized exchange in the United States is the American Stock Exchange, AMEX, which has more than 1,300 stocks listed. Information on the relative size of the secondary markets in the United States is provided in Table 3.1.

Other stocks are traded on various regional stock exchanges, or if they are unlisted, they trade in the **over-the-counter, OTC, market.** OTC is the term used to describe all buying and selling activity that does not take place on an organized exchange. The OTC market is made up of security dealers or brokers who, using telecommunications, interact to create a market for various securities. The total number of firms traded in the OTC market in the United States is around 10,000; however, many of those are not actively traded. In addition to the common stock of many smaller companies, most bonds are also traded in the OTC market. The one exception is that corporate bonds issued by large firms are sometimes traded on the New York Exchange. In addition, large institutional investors often trade among themselves in what is called the "fourth" market.[2]

Now that we've looked at the basics of the financial system, we focus our attention on understanding how bonds and stocks are valued. Then, later in the chapter, we

---

[2] There is also a "third" market; it involves over-the-counter trading of exchange-listed securities.

Table 3.1

Secondary Equity Markets in the United States

NASDAQ stands for the National Association of Security Dealers Automated Quotation System, used for trading in the over-the-counter market. Trading on the New York Stock Exchange has been diminishing; although it is still the largest equity market in the United States, the share volume in the over-the-counter market (NASDAQ) has gained substantial ground in recent years.

	Share Volume		Dollar Volume	
	(in millions)	Percent	(in millions)	Percent
New York Stock Exchange	39,665	46.6%	$1,325,332	63.7%
American Stock Exchange	3,329	3.9	37,715	1.8
Regional Stock Exchanges	6,208	7.3	178,139	8.5
NASDAQ	33,380	39.2	452,430	21.8
NASDAQ/Over-the-counter trading in listed securities	2,589	3.0	86,494	4.2
	85,171	100%	$2,080,110	100%

Source: NASDAQ 1991 Fact Book, NASDAQ, New York.

examine how firms create value by accepting positive net present value projects, and the returns and risk for some financial market securities.

Concept Review Questions

- How do financial institutions aid the transfer of funds between suppliers and demanders?
- How are primary and secondary markets different?

DETERMINING BOND VALUES AND YIELDS

A bond is simply a borrowing by a firm or government. Bonds carry a stated **par** (or **maturity**) **value**. This value is typically $1,000. Thus, the firm has borrowed $1,000 from investors with a promise to repay the principal of $1,000 in the future. The firm also pays interest on the borrowing as determined by the **coupon interest rate** stated in the bond.[3] On a borrowing of $1,000 and assuming a coupon interest rate of 9 percent, interest of ($1,000)(0.09) = $90 is paid by the firm to the owners of the bond each year. Although some bonds are relatively short-lived, most have an initial maturity of 10 to 30 years. At the maturity of the bond the firm pays back the principal of $1,000.

The bond is initially sold in the primary market, with the proceeds going to the issuer. At the time bonds are initially sold, they are typically priced so they sell close

---

[3] Another type of bond, the zero-coupon bond, does not have a stated coupon interest rate. These bonds are discussed in Chapter 16.

to their par value. *Outstanding bonds,* on the other hand, refer to all bonds that have previously been issued and are still held by investors. They may be bought or sold in the secondary market; their price may be close to or may be far from par value. [The term structure of interest rates, along with the expectations theory, the liquidity (maturity) preference theory, and the market segmentation theory of interest rates are covered in Appendix 3A.]

BOND VALUATION

The market price of a bond is equal to the present value of the series of interest payments to be received over the bond's life, plus the present value of the maturity value of $1,000, all discounted at the investor's required rate of return for the bond. Thus, a bond's price is equal to

$$\text{price, } B_0 = \sum_{t=1}^{n} \frac{I}{(1 + k_b)^t} + \frac{M}{(1 + k_b)^n} \tag{3.1}$$

where

B_0 = the current market price of the bond

I = the dollar amount of interest expected to be received each year (or par value times coupon interest rate)

n = the number of years to **maturity** for the bond

k_b = the required rate of return for the bond

M = the par or maturity value of the bond

Consider a $1,000 par bond that has a 10 percent coupon rate and a 25-year maturity. If investors demand (or require) a return of 10 percent on this bond and it pays interest annually, its value is

$$B_0 = \frac{\$100}{(1.10)^1} + \frac{\$100}{(1.10)^2} + \dots + \frac{\$100}{(1.10)^{25}} + \frac{\$1,000}{(1.10)^{25}}$$

$$B_0 = \$100 \left[\frac{1}{0.10} - \frac{1}{0.10(1 + 0.10)^{25}} \right] + \frac{\$1,000}{(1 + 0.10)^{25}}$$

$$= \$907.70 + \$92.30 = \$1,000$$

In this example, the bond has a current market value of $1,000, which is exactly equal to its par value. Thus, if the required rate of return demanded by investors is equal to the bond's coupon rate, the current market value of a bond is equal to its par value.[4]

---

[4] Bonds actually sell at their current market price plus accrued interest. For a new issue there is typically little or no accrued interest. However, if the bond were purchased one-fourth of the way through the year, then its actual purchase cost would be $1,000 + $\frac{1}{4}$($100), or $1,025.

INTEREST RATES AND BOND PRICES

Bonds generally do not sell for their par value. Instead, they sell for more or less than $1,000, depending on current economic conditions. To see why, remember what we learned in Chapter 2. In the absence of risk, the interest or discount rate required to satisfy borrowers and lenders is the risk-free rate. As a rough approximation, we can think of the risk-free rate as compensating investors for changes in expected inflation, where **inflation** refers to a change in purchasing power as reflected by changes in the price level.[5] The best proxy we have for the risk-free rate, k_{RF}, is short-term government borrowings called **Treasury bills** that typically mature in 90 or 180 days. The following data show the actual return from investing in U. S. Treasury bills, along with in changes in the rate of inflation, for different time periods:[6]

Time period	Treasury bills	Inflation
1960–1992	6.3%	4.9%
1970–1992	7.4	6.0
1980–1992	8.2	4.9

While investing in Treasury bills has provided returns that have been greater than inflation (especially for the 1980–1992 time period), these data support an important point: *On average, the return on short-term Treasury securities compensates investors only slightly better than changes in the rate of inflation.* While short-term Treasury securities are safe, investors won't get rich investing in them. The returns on Treasury bills, on average, have kept slightly ahead of changes in the rate of inflation.

When the world is not certain, the return required on a bond, k_b, is equal to the risk-free rate plus a **risk premium.** So,

required return on a bond, $k_b = k_{RF}$ + risk premium

We may think of the risk premium demanded by investors in bonds issued by firms as being composed of

$$\begin{matrix} \text{bond} \\ \text{risk} \\ \text{premium} \end{matrix} = \begin{matrix} \text{maturity} \\ \text{premium} \end{matrix} + \begin{matrix} \text{default} \\ \text{premium} \end{matrix} + \begin{matrix} \text{liquidity} \\ \text{premium} \end{matrix} + \begin{matrix} \text{other} \\ \text{premiums} \end{matrix}$$

The **maturity premium** arises because, as general interest rates change, longer-term bonds tend to fluctuate more in value than shorter-term bonds. The **default premium** arises because bonds issued by firms are more risky than government bonds and because firms differ in terms of their financial condition and likelihood of failing. The

---

[5] The **Fisher effect,** named after Irving Fisher, says that the nominal, or observed, risk-free interest rate ≈ the real rate of interest + expected inflation.
[6] Adapted from *Stocks, Bonds, Bills, and Inflation 1993 Yearbook*™, Ibbotson Associates, Chicago.

liquidity premium arises because investors in securities that are harder to sell, or less liquid, incur more transactions costs; they therefore demand additional compensation. Finally, individual bonds may contain many other features. Some are more or less attractive to investors; hence, difference features result in other premiums.[7]

Putting this all together, the return required by bond investors—which is the same as the cost to the bond issuers—is a function of the risk-free rate and premiums related to maturity, default, liquidity, and other characteristics of the bond.

BONDS ISSUED BY THE GOVERNMENT

For the moment, let's consider long-term bonds issued by the U.S. government. In this case we can ignore the last three types of premiums and say that

$$k_{\text{long-term Treasury securities}} = k_{RF} + \text{maturity premium}$$

Let's consider the two primary determinants of the return demanded by investors from long-term Treasury securities—expected inflation and the maturity premium.

Expected Inflation

Assume the 25-year bond discussed above is a U.S. Treasury bond. At the time it is issued, investors hold expectations as to future inflation. Suppose that after the bond is issued, due to changes in either worldwide or domestic economic conditions, expected inflation suddenly and unexpectedly jumps by 4 percent. Other thing being equal, this jump will cause the **market rate of interest** demanded by investors for new bonds of similar quality and maturity to increase from 10 to 14 percent. This change in market interest rates will also cause the required rate of return demanded by investors on *all outstanding bonds of similar quality and maturity* to increase—again, to 14 percent. This occurs because investors considering the 10 percent coupon rate bond will not be willing to settle for less than they can receive in newly issued securities of comparable quality but with a higher coupon rate. What would be the market value of these U.S. Treasury bonds? To determine this new market price, the interest payments and principal (or maturity value) are discounted at the new market rate of interest (or required rate of return) of 14 percent, so that

$$B_0 = \$100 \left[\frac{1}{0.14} - \frac{1}{0.14(1 + 0.14)^{25}} \right] + \frac{\$1,000}{(1 + 0.14)^{25}}$$

$$= \$687.29 + \$37.79 = \$725.08$$

An investor purchasing this 10 percent coupon rate bond for $725.08 and holding it for 25 years expects to receive a compound return of 14 percent.[8] This return is

---

[7] Other features of bonds are discussed in Chapter 16.

[8] This statement assumes the investor can reinvest the periodic interest payments at the promised return—14 percent in this case. If the interest received from this bond is reinvested at a rate lower than 14 percent, the actual return will be less than the promised return of 14 percent. This is the reinvestment rate risk discussed later.

composed of two parts—the 10 percent coupon, which is expected to provide $100 per year, plus the expected capital appreciation of $274.92 (i.e., $1,000 − $725.08) that occurs over the life of the bond. The difference between the $1,000 par value and the current market price of $725.08 is called the **discount** on the bond.

Bonds may also sell at a **premium.** To continue our example, what if economic conditions suddenly change, causing general market interest rates to unexpectedly drop to 6 percent on bonds of comparable quality and maturity? The current market price of the 25-year, 10 percent coupon rate Treasury bond becomes

$$B_0 = \$100 \left[\frac{1}{0.06} - \frac{1}{0.06(1 + 0.06)^{25}} \right] + \frac{\$1,000}{(1 + 0.06)^{25}}$$

$$= \$1,278.34 + \$233.00 = \$1,511.34$$

Because the coupon rate of 10 percent is greater than the new market interest rate of 6 percent, investors pay a premium of $511.34 (i.e., $1,511.34 − $1,000) for the bond. The relationship between the current market yield and the market price is graphed in Figure 3.2. The fundamental point to remember is this: *The price of a bond and general market interest rates move inversely.* If the market interest rate is less than a bond's coupon rate, the bond will sell at a premium. If market interest rates are greater than the coupon rate on a bond, the bond will sell at a discount. A second point to remember, as discussed previously, is: *The primary determinant of market interest rates is expected inflation.*

Figure 3.2

Relationship Among a Bond's Market Price and the Current Market Rate of Interest

As market interest rates fall, the bond price rises. Similarly, a rise in the market interest rates causes bond prices to decline.

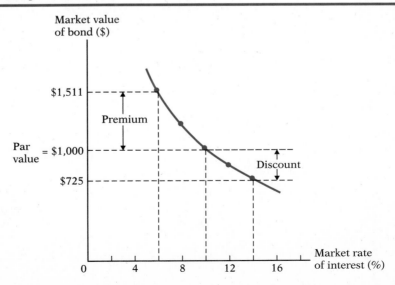

Interest Rate Risk and the Maturity Premium

Bond prices are influenced not only by market interest rates but also by the term (or length) to maturity of the bonds. To see this relationship, consider what happens to the current market price of the 10 percent U.S. Treasury bonds if they have only 3 years left until maturity, instead of 25. As Figure 3.3 shows, the market prices of the 3-year bonds adjust substantially less to changes in market interest rates than do the prices of 25-year bonds. This tendency for prices on short-term bonds to fluctuate less in response to market interest rate changes is called **interest rate risk.** It is because of interest rate risk that the return on long-term bonds typically incorporates a maturity premium (or requires a higher interest rate) over comparable short-term bonds. The liquidity (or maturity) preference theory of interest rates is discussed in Appendix 3A.

BONDS ISSUED BY FIRMS

Up to now, we have discussed the relationship between the prices on U.S. Treasury bonds, the returns required by investors, expected inflation, bond maturity, and bond prices. Corporate bonds are subject to additional risks arising from the possibility of default, liquidity, or other features. One impact of these other risks is to increase the whole structure of interest rates for corporate bonds versus U.S. Treasury bonds; investors demand a higher return to compensate them for the additional risks arising from investing in corporate bonds. Because investors demand more return, the cost to the firm for issuing bonds is higher than the cost to the government.

Figure 3.3

Relationship Among a Bond's Market Price, the Current Market Rate of Interest, and Bond Maturity

The market price of shorter-maturity bonds fluctuates substantially less than for longer-maturity bonds as the market interest rates change.

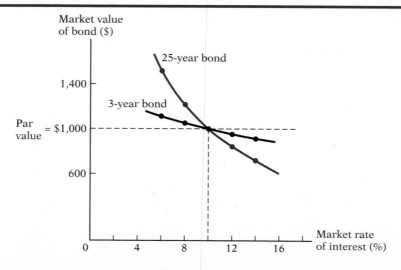

How might various factors affect the value of a firm's bonds? Consider what happens if Warehouse SuperStores is close to bankruptcy and files for protection under the federal bankruptcy laws. Because the risk of loss due to default is high, the required rate of return demanded by investors increases, leading to lower market prices for Warehouse SuperStores's outstanding bonds. The same effect occurs if the bond is not very liquid (i.e., if there is a "thin market" with few potential buyers). Similarly, if the bond differs in terms of some of its features, it may be seen as either more risky or less desirable than other bonds of comparable maturity. The result is higher returns demanded by investors, which translates into higher costs when firms issue new bonds with these features.

Two other sources of risk exist. One is **reinvestment rate risk,** which is the risk that an investor's income may fall if there is a need to reinvest in another bond issue. Suppose you purchased a bond a few years ago that has a 13 percent coupon rate. Due the changes in economic conditions, bonds of comparable maturity and risk now provide an 8 percent return. If your bond matures, or is called by the issuing firm, and you reinvest in a new 8 percent bond, you will now receive only $80 per year; in other words, you have lost $130 − $80 = $50 in interest per year.[9]

Another source of risk is **event risk,** where a drastic change in circumstances turns a "safe" bond into a "risky" one. This type of risk can be illustrated by looking at the leveraged buyout of RJR Nabisco that occurred in 1989. Before the buyout, RJR Nabisco had about $5 billion in bonds outstanding. To fund the leveraged buyout, another $16 billion in borrowing took place. Overnight, the possibility of default went up, and investors demanded a higher return to compensate themselves for the increased risk. The market value of already-outstanding RJR Nabisco bonds dropped 20 percent almost overnight. This is an example of a completely new kind of risk that most bondholders are not protected against. It also involves *risk shifting,* where part of the potential value created by the leveraged buyout was, in fact, due to the shift in risk from owners to bondholders.

Many factors can affect bond prices. The key point to remember is that as risk increases, market price decreases, and vice versa. Higher risk leads to higher returns demanded by investors and higher costs to the firm.

DETERMINING THE YIELD TO MATURITY

Instead of being given the required rate of return on a bond, suppose you are told that a 15-year maturity, $1,000 par bond with a 7 percent coupon rate sells for $915. What is the compound rate of return, called the **yield to maturity, YTM,** you would earn if you purchased the bond and held it for the entire 15 years? Answering this question involves finding the unknown discount rate, k_b, as follows:

$$\$915 = \sum_{t=1}^{15} \frac{\$70}{(1 + k_b)^t} + \frac{\$1,000}{(1 + k_b)^{15}}$$

[9] The topic of reinvestment rates is examined in end-of-chapter problems 3.6 and 3.7.

Before starting, note two points: First, the yield to maturity is simply an internal rate of return, as discussed in Chapter 2. Hence, we already know how to determine the unknown rate, k_b, which is the bond's yield to maturity. Second, because the market price of $915 is *less* than the par value of $1,000, the yield to maturity will be *greater* than the coupon interest rate of 7percent. Using a financial calculator, we find that k_b is 7.99 percent. Thus, the yield to maturity, which represents the investor's expected compound return by buying the bond at $915 and holding it to maturity, is 7.99 percent.

If the bonds can be called by the firm and retired prior to maturity, it is often helpful to compute the **yield to call, YTC,** which is the unknown k_b such that

$$B_0 = \sum_{t=1}^{n} \frac{I}{(1 + k_b)^t} + \frac{\text{call price}}{(1 + k_b)^n}$$

where n is the number of years until call. The call price is typically greater than (or occasionally equal to) the bond's par value.

BONDS WITH SEMIANNUAL INTEREST

Most bonds pay interest semiannually. Valuing bonds with semiannual interest payments is easy *if* we remember the discussion from Chapter 2 on discounting and compounding when it is done more frequently than yearly. Our basic bond valuation equation (Equation 3.1) is modified as follows:

price with
semiannual, $B_0 = \sum_{t=1}^{2n} \frac{I/2}{(1 + k)^t} + \frac{M}{(1 + k)^{2n}}$ (3.2)
interest

Note that the yearly interest, I, is divided by 2 in order to determine the semiannual interest payments. Also, the number of periods, n, is doubled to $2n$. A potential stumbling block is the rate k in Equation 3.2. If k_b is a nominal annual rate as discussed in Chapter 2, then k in Equation 3.2 is

k (if k_b is a nominal annual rate) $= k_b/2$

However, if k_b is intended to be an effective annual interest rate, then

k (if k_b is an effective annual rate) $= (1 + k_b)^{0.5} - 1$

For example, if k_b is 10 percent, then assuming it is a nominal rate produces a rate, k, of $10/2 = 5$ percent; assuming it is an effective annual rate means that k is $(1 + 0.10)^{0.5} - 1 = 4.881$ percent. We follow convention and assume k_b is a nominal rate.

To illustrate bond valuation with semiannual interest payments, consider the earlier example of a 25-year, 10 percent coupon rate bond. With semiannual interest and a rate of 14 percent per year or 7 percent per semiannual period, the value of the bond is

$$B_0 = \$50 \left[\frac{1}{0.07} - \frac{1}{0.07(1 + 0.07)^{50}} \right] + \frac{\$1,000}{(1 + 0.07)^{50}}$$

$$= \$690.04 + \$33.95 = \$723.99$$

What if we want to determine the yield to maturity when interest is paid semiannually? Assume the current market value of a bond, B_0, is $1,060, the coupon interest rate is 11 percent per year, interest is paid semiannually, and the bond has a maturity of 8 years. We divide the coupon interest rate in half, so it becomes 5.5 percent per 6 months, and double the maturity to 16 periods. The yield to maturity is found by solving for the unknown discount rate, where

$$\$1,060 = \sum_{t=1}^{16} \frac{\$55}{(1 + k_b)^t} + \frac{\$1,000}{(1 + k_b)^{16}}$$

By financial calculator, the yield is 4.95 per semiannual period, so the YTM on an annual basis is (4.95 percent)(2) = 9.90 percent. At a purchase price of $1,060 for the bond, with interest paid semiannually, the bond's expected yield to maturity is 9.90 percent per year.

CONSOLS AND PREFERRED STOCK

A **consol** is a perpetual coupon rate bond. These bonds got their name from British consols, issued to help finance the Napoleonic wars in the early nineteenth century. In Chapter 2 we determined how to find the present value of a perpetuity. Using that same idea, the market price of a perpetual bond is

$$\text{price of perpetual bond, } B_0 = \frac{I}{k_b} \qquad\qquad (3.3)$$

where I is the interest to be received at time $t = 1$ and every subsequent t, and k_b is the required return demanded by investors. If the return demanded by investors is 9 percent, and the coupon interest rate is 4 percent, then a $1,000 par value perpetual bond would be worth $40/0.09 = $444.44.

Preferred stock has a prior, but limited, claim on the firm. This claim takes precedence over the claim of the firm's common stockholders. The valuation of preferred stock that is not expected to be retired (either ever, or at least not for a long time) is similar to consols. As such, the same approach can be employed using dividends, instead of interest, in Equation 3.3. If the preferred stock has an $80 par value,[10] and the dividend is 9 percent per year, the yearly dividend is ($80)(0.09) = $7.20. If

---

[10] While most bonds have a par value of $1,000, the par value on preferred stock can be almost anything; often it is $100 or less.

the required rate of return is 12 percent, the value of the preferred stock is $7.20/ 0.12 = $60.

Bonds trade every day in the financial markets based on their discounted present value. Thus, for bonds their actual market price and yield to maturity are a direct function of the cash flow expected, the time value of money, and the returns demanded by investors.

Concept Review Questions

■ What series of payments determines a bond's market price?

■ What are the different risk premiums that compose the bond risk premium required by investors?

■ Explain what happens to the price of a bond if (1) interest rates increase or (2) interest rates decrease.

■ How are consols and perpetual preferred stocks priced?

DETERMINING COMMON STOCK VALUES

The valuation of common stocks, although conceptually similar to bond valuation, has some additional complications because neither the cash dividends nor the ending values are constant (as the interest and maturity value are for bonds). Also, with bonds the interest and maturity value are a legal liability of the firm; they have to be paid or the firm can be forced into bankruptcy. With common stock, the cash dividends and any anticipated future price of the stock can be predicted only with a great deal of uncertainty. And, there is no legal requirement that forces firms to pay cash dividends.

Common stock represents the primary ownership in firms. The following definitions are helpful for understanding common stock valuation:

D_t = the amount of cash dividends expected to be received at the end of the tth period (or year)

D_0 = the current dividend *just* paid

D_1 = the cash dividend expected 1 period from now.[11] For one share of stock this is simply the **dividend per share.**

k_s = the rate of return required by investors on the stock

n = the number of time periods, or years

P_t = the expected market price of the stock at the end of period t

P_0 = the price today *right after* the receipt of the cash dividend, D_0

P_1 = the expected price 1 period from now *right after* receiving the dividend, D_1

g = the expected (compound) growth rate, in the cash dividends. We also assume this is the rate of growth in the market price.

[11] In practice, most firms pay cash dividends on a quarterly basis (see Chapter 13). However, for simplicity we assume they are all paid at one time—the end of the year.

If financial markets are efficient, then the actual market price of a share of common stock is a direct function of the cash flow expected, the time value of money, and the returns required by investors. Like investors in bonds, the return demanded by common stock investors, k_s, is equal to the risk-free rate plus a risk premium, or

required return on a stock, $k_s = k_{RF} +$ risk premium

We can think of the risk premium demanded by common stock investors as being composed of

$$\text{stock risk premium} = \text{default premium} + \text{liquidity premium} + \text{other premiums}$$

The maturity premium that bond investors demand is not relevant when considering common stock because common stock has an infinite life. Common stock investors have a residual (or the last) claim on the firm; that is, the government and creditors have a prior claim that must be met before anything can be distributed to common stockholders. Therefore the size of the default premium demanded by common stock investors will be larger than that demanded by investors in the same firm's bonds. Similarly, common stock investors will demand a liquidity premium if it is hard to sell the stock or if when they sell, the market price has a tendency to drop significantly because there is a small, or "thin," market for the stock. Finally, other characteristics of common stock may also affect their risk.[12]

Due to the risks involved, the risk premium on stocks is typically higher than the risk premium on bonds. With rare exceptions, the required return demanded for investing in stocks is higher than the required return demanded for investing in bonds.

DIVIDEND VALUATION

To start, think of common stock valuation as being exactly like bond valuation. The current market price of a share of common stock is theoretically equal to the present value of the expected cash dividends and future market price, where

$$\text{price, } P_0 = \sum_{t=1}^{n} \frac{D_t}{(1 + k_s)^t} + \frac{P_n}{(1 + k_s)^n} \tag{3.4}$$

The current market price of a stock that is expected to pay cash dividends of $1.00 at $t = 1$, $1.50 at $t = 2$, and $2.00 at $t = 3$ and have an expected market value of $40.00 at $t = 3$ can be determined in a straightforward manner. If the return de-

---

[12] Some other features, such as different classes of stock, are discussed in Chapter 15.

manded by investors is 14 percent, the price of this stock is[13]

$$P_0 = \frac{D_1}{(1 + k_s)^1} + \frac{D_2}{(1 + k_s)^2} + \frac{D_3}{(1 + k_s)^3} + \frac{P_3}{(1 + k_s)^3}$$

$$= \frac{\$1.00}{(1.14)^1} + \frac{\$1.50}{(1.14)^2} + \frac{\$2.00}{(1.14)^3} + \frac{\$40.00}{(1.14)^3}$$

$$= \$0.88 + \$1.15 + \$1.35 + \$27.00 = \$30.38$$

If an investor pays $30.38 for the stock, and the stream of dividends and ending market price occurs as projected, the compound rate of return realized on the stock will be 14 percent.[14]

What if we keep adding more years of dividends to Equation 3.4, so that we can think of the cash dividends going on forever? In that case, we have the fundamental common stock model—the **dividend valuation model**—which states that the market price of a share of common stock is equal to the present value of all future dividends:

$$\text{price, } P_0 = \frac{D_1}{(1 + k_s)^1} + \frac{D_2}{(1 + k_s)^2} + \cdots + \frac{D_\infty}{(1 + k_s)^\infty} \tag{3.5}$$

$$= \sum_{t=1}^{\infty} \frac{D_t}{(1 + k_s)^t}$$

In Equation 3.4, the second term is $P_n/(1 + k_s)^n$, where P_n represents the market price at time $t = n$. But what determines the market price at time n? It is simply the present value of all cash dividends expected to be received *from period n + 1 to infinity,* discounted at the investor's required rate of return of k_s. Equation 3.4 is simply a special case of the more general Equation 3.5. This relationship will prove useful when we consider valuing stocks that are expected to have nonconstant growth in future cash dividends. However, before doing that, we want to consider the simpler cases of no growth in cash dividends and constant growth in cash dividends.

NO GROWTH IN CASH DIVIDENDS

In the special case of no future expected growth in cash dividends, assume that the stock will pay a constant dividend of, say, $2 per year from now until infinity. Although the **no-growth model** is obviously unrealistic, it often provides a convenient benchmark. In such a case, the dividend valuation equation (Equation 3.5) is simply a perpetuity. For a common stock with a constant expected cash dividend from $t = 1$

[13] We could add together the $2 cash dividend at $t = 3$ and the market price of $40; however, for clarity they are kept separate.
[14] This assumes, similar to the interest received on bonds, as noted in footnote 8, that the cash dividends received at $t = 1$ and $t = 2$ can be reinvested for 2 years and 1 year, respectively, at 14 percent.

to infinity, its current market price is given by

price with no growth, $P_0 = \dfrac{D_1}{k_s}$ (3.6)

If we have a no-growth stock that is expected to pay a cash dividend of $2 per year from time $t = 1$ until infinity, and the investor's required rate of return is 16 percent (or 0.16), then its current price, P_0, is $2/0.16 = $12.50. A rational investor would pay no more than $12.50 for this stock if his or her required rate of return is 16 percent.

CONSTANT GROWTH IN CASH DIVIDENDS

In another special case, consider what happens if cash dividends are expected to increase at a constant (percentage) rate each year. This situation is just a growing perpetuity, so we can use our knowledge from Chapter 2 (Equation 2.9) to value this stream of constantly growing dividends. The **constant-growth model** is

price with constant growth, $P_0 = \dfrac{D_1}{k_s - g}$ (3.7)

In valuing a stock with constantly growing cash dividends, we must use *the cash dividends expected 1 year hence,* or D_1. If we have a stock whose current cash dividend (at time $t = 0$) is $2, the constant compound growth rate in dividends is 10 percent per year, and the return demanded by investors is 16 percent, the value of this stock is

$$P_0 = \frac{D_1}{k_s - g} = \frac{D_0(1 + g)}{k_s - g} = \frac{\$2(1.10)}{0.16 - 0.10} = \frac{\$2.20}{0.06} = \$36.67$$

Note that this price of $36.67 is substantially higher than the $12.50 when no growth in future cash dividends was assumed. This makes common sense because, other things being equal, an investor would value a growing cash flow stream at a higher rate than a nongrowing stream.

NONCONSTANT GROWTH IN CASH DIVIDENDS

The next situation we consider is when a firm grows at a fast rate for a few years and then reverts to a constant- or no-growth situation. This might occur because a firm made previous positive net present value investments that produced high cash flows and increases in value, but increasing competition is expected to reduce the future growth rate. For example, if the required rate of return demanded by investors remains at 16 percent, consider how we would value this stock: (1) Dividends at time $t = 0$ are $2; (2) followed by 10 percent growth in dividends for each of years 1, 2, and 3;

(3) followed by 3 percent compound growth thereafter until infinity. This set of cash flows is graphed in Figure 3.4.

The following four-step procedure can be used to solve this problem:

STEP 1:   Determine the cash dividends until the series reverts to either constant growth to infinity or no growth. Thus,

$D_1 = \$2.00(1 + 0.10)^1 = \$2.20$
$D_2 = \$2.00(1 + 0.10)^2 = \$2.42$
$D_3 = \$2.00(1 + 0.10)^3 = \$2.66$

STEP 2:   Determine the first year's dividend *after* the growth rate changes to either constant growth to infinity or no growth.

$D_4 = D_3(1 + 0.03) = \$2.66(1 + 0.03) = \$2.74$

Because the growth rate changed to 3 percent (from 10 percent), the new growth rate of 3 percent must be used in this step.

STEP 3:   Determine the market price of the stock as of time $t = 3$ for the constant-

---

Figure 3.4

Cash Dividend Series Growing at 10 Percent for 3 Years Followed by 3 Percent Growth to Infinity

Due to the compounding effect, the lines between years 0 and 3 and between years 3 and 6 are not quite straight.

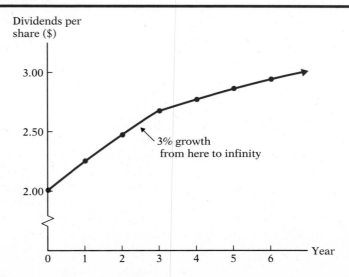

or no-growth period. Thus

$$P_3 = \frac{D_4}{k_s - g} = \frac{\$2.74}{0.16 - 0.03} = \frac{\$2.74}{0.13} = \$21.08$$

Note that (1) the growth rate used is the constant one expected from time $t = 3$ until infinity, and (2) the market price is as of time $t = 3$.

STEP 4:   Using Equation 3.4 and the required rate of return of 16 percent, discount both the expected cash dividends from step 1 and the expected market price from step 3 back to the present. As shown in Figure 3.5, the present value of this stream of expected cash flows is $18.91. Thus, the current market value of the stock should be $18.91.

To see the relationship between growth opportunities, the growth rate in expected cash dividends, and the current market price of a stock, consider Table 3.2, which summarizes our calculations. In the case of no future growth, the market price is $12.50, whereas it is $36.67 at a 10 percent compound rate to infinity. Finally, growth at 10 percent for 3 years followed by low or no growth[15] thereafter produces market prices of $18.91 and $16.05, respectively. Clearly, *the rate and duration of the expected growth opportunities leading to growth in cash dividends have a major impact on the market price of a common stock.* Accurate estimation of growth opportunities and expected growth rates is the most important aspect of common stock valuation using the dividend valuation approach. It is also one of the most difficult.

Figure 3.5

Timeline and Solution for Nonconstant Dividend Series

The dividend in year 4 equals $2.66(1 + 0.03). The market price determined using D_4 is the price at time $t = 3$. This market price must be brought back to time $t = 0$, as are the cash dividends for years 1, 2, and 3, by discounting at 16 percent.

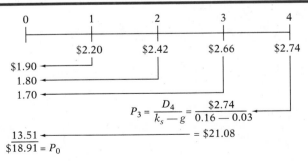

[15] If there was no growth in cash dividends expected after year 3, $P_3 = D_4/k_s = \$2.66/0.16 = \$16.625$. Discounting this back to time zero at 16 percent and adding it to the discounted value of the cash dividends to be received for periods 1, 2, and 3 produces a market price of $16.05.

Table 3.2

Relationship Between Expected Growth and Market Price

There is a direct relationship between the amount and length of expected growth in cash dividends and a stock's market price.

Condition*	Resulting Market Price (P_0)
No future growth in expected cash dividends	$12.50
10 percent compound growth in expected cash dividends for $t = 1$, $t = 2$, and $t = 3$, followed by no future growth†	16.05
10 percent compound growth in expected cash dividends for $t = 1$, $t = 2$, and $t = 3$, followed by 3 percent compound growth to infinity	18.91
10 percent compound growth in expected cash dividends to infinity	36.67

* $D_0 = \$2$ and $k_s = 16$ percent for all conditions.
† From footnote 15.

NON-DIVIDEND-PAYING STOCKS

We have discussed stock valuation when the firm pays cash dividends, but not all firms do so. How should we value non-dividend-paying stocks? There are three ways. The first is to estimate *when* the firm will start paying dividends, their size, growth rate, and so forth; then simply proceed as we have discussed. The second is a variation of the first, except you must estimate some future market price and then discount it back to the present, as we have done previously. The final approach employs earnings and multiplies (or capitalizes) them by some factor (based on perceived growth, risk, and/or estimates derived by looking at "similar" firms) to arrive at an estimated value.

VOLATILITY, LIQUIDITY, AND STOCK PRICES

Recently many empirical studies have examined the volatility of stock prices and returns. In doing so they have often focused on one or more of the three basic variables that can lead to stock price volatility. These are (1) shocks (or unexpected changes) in a firm's cash flows and, therefore, cash dividends; (2) changes in the discount rate (k_s) due to predictable changes in macro forces such as gross domestic product (GDP), industrial production, and investment, which are important determinants of the cash flows for firms; and (3) unexpected shocks (or changes) in the discount rate employed. At the same time, there is some evidence that investors demand additional compensation for investing in less-liquid stocks. Given the apparent acceleration in the research in these areas, it is safe to say that a lot more will be known in the future about the causes and impact of volatility and liquidity on stock prices.

Most investors, amateur or professional, do not employ the dividend valuation model exactly as we have described it. However, their decision making does have some characteristics in common with the model: They (1) focus on cash flows and dividends; (2) they consider the returns needed to compensate them for the risks incurred (given their alternatives and economic conditions); and (3) they look for growth opportunities. As such, the intuition behind the dividend valuation model underlies much of what drives the decisions made by investors.

Concept Review Questions

- What are the risk premiums that affect a stock's price?
- What are the cash flows that determine a stock's price?
- Describe how you would price a stock with non-constant growth and cash dividends.
- What are the three basic variables that lead to stock price volatility?

EXECUTIVE INTERVIEW

Mary Reilly
Vice President
BancBoston Capital

Mary Reilly is Vice President of BancBoston Capital, a firm that makes a specialized type of venture capital investment: buyouts and recapitalizations of mature manufacturing, media, and distribution companies. We asked Ms. Reilly to describe how BancBoston values the firms it considers as investment candidates.

Our investment targets are mostly private companies or subsidiaries of public firms, with track records of profitable operations—a large corporation spinning off a division, a company whose owner wishes to retire, or a public company going private. We make different types of investments depending on the situation. In some cases, we provide equity financing. In others, we provide mezzanine capital, which is the layer of financing between equity and debt, with features of both.

Although we may provide more than one form of capital, we make one basic investment decision: Should we invest x to receive y dollars and z% return? We *recover* 90 to 100 percent of our investment dollars from debt repayment. But our *return* comes from interest payments on debt and from capital gains on equity. So, obviously, our ability to value the equity of these companies is critical. Our valuation is based on our judgment about the appropriate return for the company's risk as well as the perceived risk of the security. For example, preferred stock is a riskier—and therefore more expensive—investment than subordinated debt, so a company pays more if it needs preferred stock on its balance sheet.

It's a challenge to value a privately held company. Public companies have an earnings record, maybe a dividend stream, and comparable public companies to point you to a range of equity values. Valuing private companies requires all the same judgments as valuing public companies, but we don't have as much published information. And, because private companies tend to be smaller—usually under $100 million in revenues—they often aren't comparable to public companies. Also, we can't sell our investment easily if we make a mistake; there's not much liquidity.

Therefore, we must perform a very rigorous analysis, including valuation, as part of the investment process. This "due diligence" includes meeting management; looking at the facilities, operations, products, and markets; studying the industry research for competition and technological change; talking to company suppliers and customers; and making environmental assessments. Our objective is to understand the firm's cash flow and to develop valid projections for the company, so we can predict what it will be worth in 5 years when we harvest our capital gains.

We use a multiple of *current* cash flow to value companies. We talk in terms of the value of the company—not simply the value of the equity—because our transactions are buyouts of the whole company, and leverage is a major factor in our deals. Using current cash flow focuses our analysis on current operations, not on expectations of future improvements which may or may not be realized. In any event, discounting *future* cash flows to calculate net present value gives the same answer, theoretically, *if* you correctly project the future and *if* you choose the correct discount rate.

Calculating cash flow for valuation purposes isn't straightforward. As a start, it can be earnings before interest, taxes, depreciation, and amortization. We adjust up or down for such factors as capital expenditures, working capital, non-recurring items, excess expenses by previous management, or expenditures required to create a stand-alone company if it was previously a division. Then we apply a multiple to that cash flow and come up with the firm's value. Most of our companies trade at five or six times cash flow. For example, if the 1993 cash flow after adjustments is $25 million and similar companies sell for six times cash flow, the company is worth $150 million. We'll use a higher multiple if there are favorable circumstances, such as a hot new product or a valuable brand or franchise, or a lower multiple if negative factors exist. While we're deciding what we think the company is worth, we're negotiating with the seller to see if we have a deal. It's a dynamic process.

We value companies because we're buying them. But *all* financial managers should be able to perform valuation analysis, whether they're valuing the firm's assets or evaluating a proposed investment, acquisition, or divestiture. The financial manager needs to know more than just finance to do this. A thorough understanding of the risks of the business is essential to evaluate historical financials or accurately project future results.

THE PRESENT VALUE OF GROWTH OPPORTUNITIES

Based on what we have just learned, a number of important observations can be made about stocks and the creation of value for the firm. First, let's go back to determining the stock price when the firm and its cash dividends are expected to grow at a constant compound rate g until infinity. As given by Equation 3.7, the stock price is

$$P_0 = \frac{D_1}{k_s - g}$$

Assume you are looking at two firms, Growth and Nongrowth. For simplicity, assume both will pay dividends of $1 at time $t = 1$ and the required rate of return is (for illustration purposes) the same in each case—15 percent. What should their market prices be if g is 10 percent for Growth and 0 percent for Nongrowth? The prices are:

$$P_0(\text{Growth}) = \frac{\$1}{0.15 - 0.10} = \$20$$

$$P_0(\text{Nongrowth}) = \frac{\$1}{0.15 - 0} = \$6.67$$

Other things being equal, we see that the market price of a firm which is expected to grow is higher than the market price of a firm that is not expected to grow. Although firms do not grow at a constant percentage compound rate forever, and the return required by investors might not be the same for both Growth and Nongrowth, the basic conclusion from this example holds: *Expected growth is valuable.*

PRICE/EARNINGS RATIOS

The term **price/earnings (P/E) ratio** is often heard when common stocks are analyzed. The price/earnings ratio is simply the market price per share of common stock divided by the **earnings per share, EPS,** where earnings per share equal (total earnings available for common stockholders)/(number of shares of common stock outstanding). Likewise, the **dividend payout ratio** is simply (cash dividends paid per share of common stock)/(earnings per share of common stock). For example, if a firm has earnings of $5 per share and pays a cash dividend of $2 per share, the dividend payout ratio is $2/$5 = 40 percent. Let's go back to the constant-growth model given by Equation 3.7 and define the dividend next year, D_1, as being equal to the earnings per share, EPS_1, times the dividend payout ratio. Thus, $D_1 = EPS_1$(dividend payout ratio). Therefore, Equation 3.7 becomes

$$P_0 = \frac{EPS_1(\text{dividend payout ratio})}{k_s - g} \tag{3.8}$$

Rearranging Equation 3.8, we find the price/earnings ratio is

$$\frac{P_0}{EPS_1} = \frac{\text{dividend payout ratio}}{k_s - g}$$

Looked at in this manner, *the price/earnings ratio is a function of the firm's dividend payout ratio, the return demanded by investors, k_s, and the expected future growth, g, for the firm.*

Should a firm and investors be happy if a stock has a "high" price/earnings ratio? That all depends! One way a firm can have a high P/E ratio is if it has little or no earnings. For example, if the market price for a stock is $15 and the firm had a very bad year and expects earnings will be only $0.20, its P/E would be 75 times (i.e., $15/$0.20 = 75). In this instance the high price/earnings ratio is due to the depressed level of earnings.

But, another possibility that leads to high P/E ratios is for the expected growth, g, to be high. As we saw in the previous example of Growth and Nongrowth, other things being equal, higher expected growth and higher stock prices go hand-in-hand. Thus, a second and more favorable meaning of a high P/E ratio is that the expected growth for the firm is "high." The message is simple and straightforward: High P/E ratios may be "good news" or "bad news." Don't automatically assume a high P/E ratio signals good news in the form of high expected growth.

GROWTH OPPORTUNITIES AND VALUE CREATION

Now let's consider growth opportunities and how firms create value. Assume Everyday Supply is not growing at all. The earnings are $100 per year and the required return demanded by Everyday's investors is 10 percent. Because the firm is not growing, the earnings can be distributed to the common stockholders; thus, the dividend payout ratio is 100 percent, or 1.0. The market value of Everyday, using Equation 3.8 is

$$P_0 = \frac{EPS_1(\text{dividend payout ratio})}{k_s - g} = \frac{\$100(1.00)}{0.10 - 0} = \$1,000$$

and the firm pays all of the earnings of $100 out in cash dividends each year.

What if Everyday has the opportunity to make a $100 investment next year in a project that promises to return $10 forever? In order to make the capital investment, Everyday will forgo paying cash dividends at time $t = 1$, but from $t = 2$ on the dividends will be $110. This project is as risky as the firm, so the required return on it is 10 percent. What is the net present value of the proposed project? With the returns going on forever, this investment is a perpetuity. The net present value is equal to the present value of the future cash flows minus the initial investment, so

$$\text{net present value}_1 = \frac{\$10}{0.10} - \$100 = 0$$

What about the market price of Everyday after it makes this investment? Earnings (i.e., dividends) will not be paid out to investors at time $t = 1$, but from time $t = 2$ until infinity they will be $110. What is the new market price of Everyday? Because the cash inflow stream is still a perpetuity, the price at $t = 1$ is EPS_2/k_s, so its price at $t = 0$ is,

$$P_0 = \frac{P_1}{1 + k_s} = \frac{EPS_2/k_s}{1 + k_s} = \frac{\$110/0.10}{1 + 0.10} = \frac{\$1,100}{1.10} = \$1,000$$

This example indicates a simple and important fact: *The value of a firm does not increase or decrease when it accepts zero net present value projects.*

What if there is another project to consider? Suppose this project requires Everyday to invest $100 at $t = 1$, promises a return of $20 from $t = 2$ on, and the investor's required return remains 10 percent? The net present value at $t = 1$ is $100, where

$$\text{net present value}_1 = \frac{\$20}{0.10} - \$100 = \$100$$

and the new market price of Everyday at $t = 0$, after making this positive net present value investment, is $1,091, or

$$P_0 = \frac{\$120/0.10}{1 + 0.10} = \frac{\$1,200}{1.10} = \$1,091$$

By investing in a positive net present value project, Everyday has increased its market value.

What if Everyday could invest the $100 in another project that promised a return of $30 forever, or alternatively one that promised a return of only $5 forever? The figures for these alternative investments along with the two already considered are as follows:

Return from $t=2$ on	Investment at $t=1$	Net Present Value	Market Price
$30	$100	$200	$1,182
20	100	100	1,091
10	100	0	1,000
5	100	−50	955

In looking at these figures, the message is clear: *To increase the value of the firm, positive net present value projects—which promise to return above average returns—are necessary. Simply investing in projects that provide the return demanded by investors, which is also the firm's opportunity cost of capital, does not create value. Likewise, when firms accept projects that have a negative net present value, the firm and its investors suffer a loss in value.*

The above discussion can be summarized as follows: The stock price can be thought of as being composed of the capitalized value of the assets in place under a no-growth policy plus the **present value of growth opportunities, PVGO,**

$$\text{stock price, } P_0 = \frac{EPS_1}{k_s} + PVGO \tag{3.9}$$

$$= \begin{array}{c} \text{Present value of} \\ \text{assets in place} \end{array} + \begin{array}{c} \text{present value of} \\ \text{growth opportunities} \end{array}$$

For a firm to prosper, it must find and exploit investment opportunities that allow it to grow. *Investing in a project that provides an average rate of return is not growth!* Likewise, investing in projects that can be easily replicated by others invites immediate competition, price cutting and, therefore, limits the opportunity of the firm to increase its value. The message is simple and direct: The way for firms to create value is to find and exploit investment projects that have positive net present values. *Positive net present value projects and value creation are synonymous with one another.* This finding is one of the central ideas of finance. We examine net present value, and how to make wealth-maximizing capital investment decisions, in Chapters 6 through 10.

Concept Review Questions

- Is it true that investors prefer high P/E ratio stocks? Explain.
- How does the growth rate affect a firm's value?
- How does the present value of growth opportunities affect a firm's market value?

RETURNS AND RISK

Before leaving this chapter, let's take a look at returns and risk. We'll define how returns are measured and then examine returns and risk from investing in various financial market securities.

EXPECTED VERSUS REALIZED RETURNS

The **return** from investing in any financial asset comes from one of two sources: (1) income from interest, dividends, and so forth; and (2) capital gains or losses—that is, the difference between the asset's beginning and ending market values. For common stocks these returns are cash dividends received during the period, and capital appreciation or loss. For any period (e.g., month, year) we can define the return on a stock as

$$\text{return, } k = \frac{D_1 + (P_1 - P_0)}{P_0} \tag{3.10}$$

If a firm expects to pay cash dividends of $3.50 per share at time $t = 1$, the market price today is $40, and the expected price at time $t = 1$ is $42, then the return is

$$k = \frac{\$3.50 + (\$42 - \$40)}{\$40} = \frac{\$5.50}{\$40} = 0.1375 = 13.75\%$$

In the example, this is an *ex ante* (**expected or required**) **rate of return;** it is what investors anticipate receiving *before* the fact. Their *ex post* (**realized**) **rate of return** over the period (calculated using Equation 3.10, but with historical data) may differ from the expected return if cash dividends are more or less than the expected $3.50, or if the ending market price is different from the $42 projected.

Returns from bonds or from any other financial asset can be computed in exactly the same way, using appropriately specified values in Equation 3.10. In practice, we can measure returns over any time period, but a year is typical. Also, note that we can calculate realized returns whether or not we actually sell the financial asset. To illustrate this, suppose an investor purchased a stock and plans to hold it for 3 years. If the actual cash dividend received at the end of the first year was $3.50 and the actual ending market price was $42, then the return over the first year was 13.75 percent—whether or not the investor actually sold the security. For the second year $42 represents the initial price; any capital gain or loss for the year is measured against the $42 figure. This process is repeated over and over again, and a series of realized, or *ex post*, returns exists as long as the stock is owned by the investor.

RETURNS AND RISK FOR FINANCIAL ASSETS

We will explore the topic of returns and risk in detail in Chapter 4; here, it is important to establish the fundamental relationship. The relationship between returns and risk is also the relationship between risk and cost to the issuer. Looking at it from the investor's viewpoint, if you expose yourself to more risk, you require a higher return. *Higher returns demanded by investors have to come from somewhere: they come from the higher costs of raising capital borne by the firm.*

To understand more about returns and risk, let's examine realized returns for the 1960–1992 period. Figure 3.6 shows graphically the growth of a dollar invested in small-firm common stocks, common stocks in general, and long-term corporate bonds. All results assume reinvestment of dividends or interest, and no taxes. Each of the indexes is initiated at $1.00 at the beginning of 1960. The figure shows that the return from small-firm common stocks over this time period was far greater than from the other securities shown. If $1.00 had been invested in small common stocks at the beginning of 1960, it would have grown to $76.47 by the end of 1992. Likewise, for common stocks $1.00 would have grown to $25.68, while a dollar invested in long-term corporate bonds would have grown to only $10.30. Finally, $1.00 invested in risk-free U.S. Treasury bills would have grown to only $7.45. For comparison, inflation is also graphed. What we purchased for $1.00 at the beginning of 1960 required an expenditure of $4.83 by the end of 1992. While all three long-term securities outperformed inflation, small-firm common stocks were the big winner over this time period.

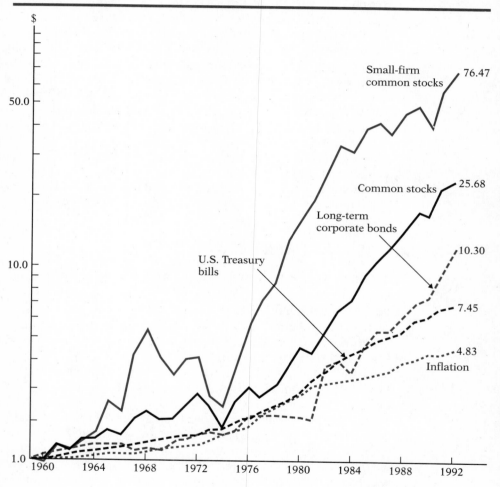

Figure 3.6

Return Indices, 1960–1992

The vertical scale is logarithmic; equal distances represent equal percentage changes any place along the scale. Small-firm stocks were the big winners over this time period. [*Source: Stocks, Bonds, Bills, and Inflation 1993 Yearbook*™, Ibbotson Associates, Chicago (annually updated work by Roger G. Ibbotson and Rex A. Sinquefield). Used with permission. All rights reserved.]

This return is not without substantial risk, however. In Figure 3.7 the annual percentage realized returns for common stocks, small-firm common stocks, and corporate bonds are presented. Note that the variability of returns for small-firm common stocks is much greater than for common stocks in general. Likewise, the variability of returns for long-term corporate bonds is less than for common stocks. Finally, while not shown in Figure 3.7, it should be noted that the direction and magnitude of the returns are not consistent across the three securities, or over time. For example, in 1968 the returns for common stocks was 11.06 percent, for small-firm common stocks

Figure 3.7

Histograms of Annual Percentage Returns, 1960–1992

Common stocks, especially small-firm stocks, exhibit much more volatility in their returns than do bonds. [*Source: Stocks, Bonds, Bills, and Inflation 1993 Yearbook*™, Ibbotson Associates, Chicago (annually updated work by Roger G. Ibbotson and Rex A. Sinquefield). Used with permission. All rights reserved.]

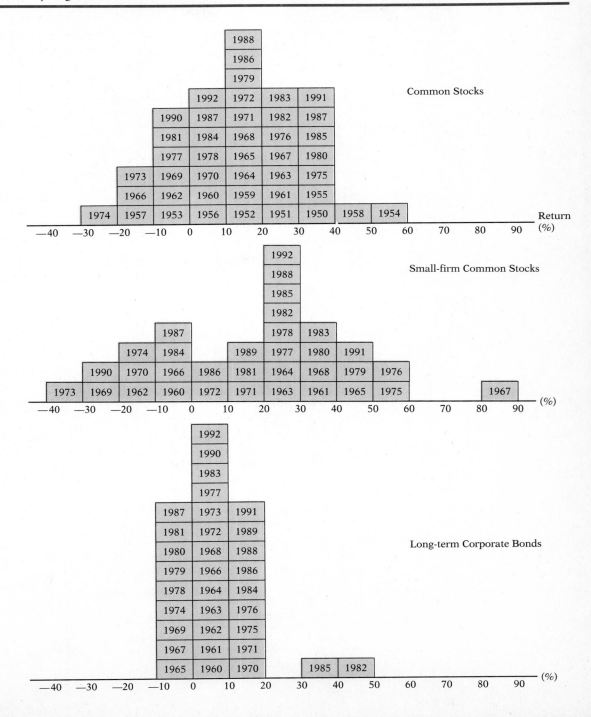

Figure 3.8

Total Returns, Dividend Income, and Capital Appreciation for Common Stocks, 1960–1992

Returns from dividends are much more dependable than those attributed to price appreciation or loss. [*Source: Stocks, Bonds, Bills, and Inflation 1993 Yearbook*™, Ibbotson Associates, Chicago (annually updated work by Roger G. Ibbotson and Rex A. Sinquefield). Used with permission. All rights reserved.]

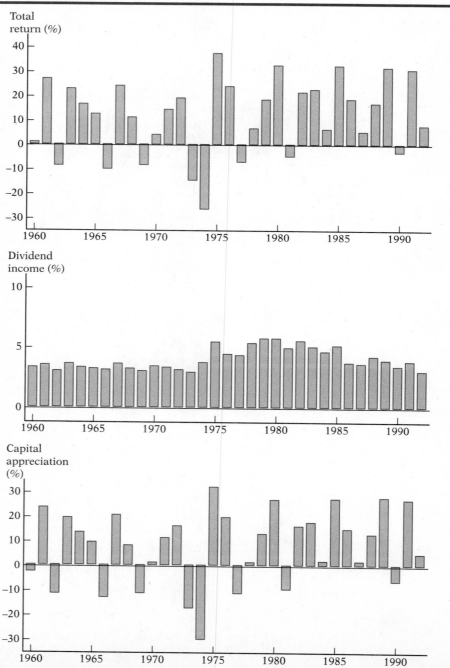

Figure 3.9

Relationship Between Required Return (or Cost to the Issuer) and Risk

U.S. Treasury bills provide a risk-free return. As risk increases (as evidenced by default, liquidity, or other premiums), the returns demanded by investors increase; so do the costs to the issuer.

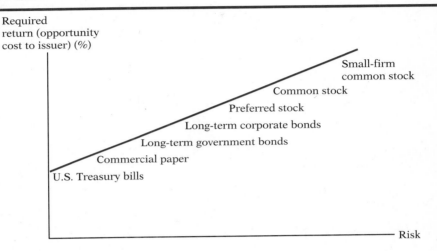

it was 35.97 percent, and for corporate bonds it was 2.57 percent. In 1992 the returns on the three securities were 7.67 percent, 23.35 percent, and 9.39 percent, respectively.

An investor's realized return may differ from his or her expected return. In theory, expected (or required) returns are always positive, because investors will not expose themselves to risk without the prospect of appropriate returns over and above the risk-free rate. But an examination of Figure 3.8 shows that realized common stock returns have not always been positive. While the dividend component is relatively stable, the capital (or price) appreciation or loss is not. Over the 1960–1992 time period, between 35 and 40 percent of the total return on common stocks came from dividend income; the remainder was due to changes in the market price of common stocks.

Figures 3.6 through 3.8 visually demonstrate that higher return and higher risk go hand-in-hand. As risk increases for different types of securities, so does the return demanded by investors, and therefore the cost to the issuer. This relationship is depicted in Figure 3.9. The relationship between return (or the cost to the firm) and risk is another of the fundamental ideas of finance; it will be pursued throughout the book. For now, all you need to remember is this: If a firm increases its risk exposure, it increases the return demanded by investors, and hence its costs. *There is no free lunch; increases in risk cause increases in costs.*

Return, risk, bond prices, stock prices, and managerial decisions are closely related, as Figure 3.10 shows. Beginning at the top left, we start with financial management decisions. These affect the magnitude, timing, and riskiness of the firm's expected cash flow. Next, based on all the information coming to them about the firm, the economy,

---

Figure 3.10

Relationship Between the Firm's Financial Management Decisions and Investors' Actions

Because of the interrelated and circular nature of the decision-making process, investors' actions, and the value of the firm, managers must understand the importance of financial markets and financial assets in the decision-making process.

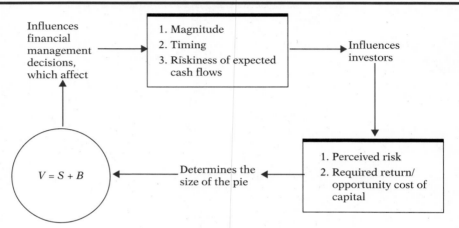

Influences financial management decisions, which affect

1. Magnitude
2. Timing
3. Riskiness of expected cash flows

Influences investors

$V = S + B$

Determines the size of the pie

1. Perceived risk
2. Required return/ opportunity cost of capital

---

and so forth, investors assess the perceived risk for the firm—which directly affects the returns they demand. These actions determine the market value of the firm. Based on the performance of the firm's stock and bonds and the firm's opportunity cost of capital, additional financial management decisions are made: The relationship between financial management decisions, the market value of the firm, and its opportunity cost of capital is continuous and ongoing.

Concept Review Questions

- Explain the difference between *ex ante* and *ex post* rates of return.
- What is the relationship between return and risk for financial assets?

KEY POINTS

1. The role of the financial system is to provide an effective and efficient way to bring together suppliers and demanders of capital.
2. Secondary markets allow investors to buy and sell financial securities, such as bonds and stocks, after they have been issued.
3. Based on cash flows, the market price of any financial asset, like a bond or stock, is equal to the expected cash flows coming from the asset, discounted at the investor's required rate of return.
4. On average, the return from risk-free Treasury bills have provided returns slightly in excess of changes in inflation.
5. The return required, or demanded, by an investor is equal to the risk-free rate of interest plus a risk premium. For a bond the risk premium may include a maturity premium, a

default premium, a liquidity premium, and other premiums. For a stock the risk premium may include a default premium, a liquidity premium, and other premiums. Due to greater risk, the risk premium for stocks is generally larger than the risk premium for bonds. Consequently, the return demanded by investors in stocks is generally higher than the return demanded by investors in bonds.

6. As general market interest rates increase, the market price of a bond decreases. Alternatively, as general market interest rates decrease, the market price of a bond increases.

7. The yield to maturity is the compound rate of return expected to be earned by purchasing a bond at the current market price and holding it to maturity.

8. The rate and duration of the expected growth in cash dividends have a major impact on the market price of common stock. Other things being equal, higher expected growth and higher stock prices go hand-in-hand.

9. The firm's stock price is composed of the present value of the assets in place plus the present value of growth opportunities. The firm can create value, as shown by increases in the market price, only by accepting positive net present value projects.

10. *Ex post* (or realized) returns will not necessarily equal *ex ante* (expected) returns.

11. The *ex post* returns on common stocks, especially small-firm common stocks, has exceeded the returns on long-term corporate bonds, Treasury bills, and inflation.

12. Higher returns demanded by investors lead to higher costs of debt and equity financing for the firm.

13. Returns and risk go hand-in-hand. To increase expected returns, it is necessary to increase the exposure to risk.

QUESTIONS

3.1 How do financial institutions and financial markets interact to bring together suppliers and demanders of funds? Why are financial institutions so important in this process?

3.2 Using both stocks and bonds, explain why their current market price is equal to the present value of the future cash flows expected by investors, discounted at their required rate of return.

3.3 Why is it that bonds do not typically sell at face value? How do fluctuations in market interest rates and the time to maturity influence bond price fluctuations?

3.4 The rate of return you will receive on a bond if you buy it today and hold it until maturity is its yield to maturity, YTM. (*Note:* In answering these questions, ignore any reinvestment problem associated with the future interest to be received.)

a. What happens to the YTM as market interest rates change?

b. Will you receive any more, or any less, if interest rates change as long as you hold the bond to maturity? Why?

c. Will you receive any more, or any less, as interest rates change if you are forced to sell before maturity? Why?

3.5 Explain the difference in determining either the value of a bond or its yield to maturity, employing annual versus semiannual discounting. With semiannual discounting, why do we adjust for the number of periods not only for the coupon interest but also for the maturity value?

3.6 The following formula is used when dividends have been estimated for a few years, at which time the estimated future market price is then employed:

$$P_0 = \sum_{t=1}^{n} \frac{D_t}{(1 + k_s)^t} + \frac{P_n}{(1 + k_s)^n}$$

Explain where the term P_n comes from.

3.7   Carl is in the process of valuing a common stock under various circumstances, as follows:

Conditions	Estimated Stock Price
Required return = 15%; D_0 = $1.00; g = 0; period = ∞	$ 6.67
Required return = 15%; D_0 = $1.00; g = 10%; period = ∞	22.00
Required return = 15%; D_0 = $1.00; g = 10% for each of 5 years followed by 5% from there to infinity; period = ∞	10.00
Required return = 15%; D_0 = $1.00; g = 5%; period = ∞	10.50

Which one of his answers does not make sense? Why?

3.8   Does a high price/earnings ratio mean a firm is a "growth firm?" Explain.

3.9   Under what conditions does the P/E ratio equal $1/k_s$?

3.10   The market price of a firm can be thought of as:

$$P_0 = \frac{EPS_1}{k_s} + PVGO$$

Explain the ideas behind this formula. How does it relate to value creation and accepting positive, zero, or negative net present value projects?

CONCEPT REVIEW PROBLEMS

See Appendix A for solutions.

CR3.1   Arkansas Corporation has a bond with a 10 percent coupon rate and a $1,000 face value. Interest is paid semiannually, and the bond has 15 years to maturity.

a.   If investors require an 8 percent yield, what is the bond's value?
b.   If the bond is expected to be called in 5 years at $1,100, what is the bond's value?

CR3.2   Tyco bonds are selling for $945. These 20-year $1,000 par value bonds pay 6 percent interest semiannually. If they are purchased at the market price, what is the yield to maturity?

CR3.3   You are thinking of buying 300 shares of Texaco preferred stock which currently sells for $70 per share and pays annual dividends of $6.50 per share.

a.   What is the expected return?
b.   If you require a 10 percent return, what would you pay for Texaco's preferred stock?

CR3.4   Dwyer's common stock paid $1.65 in dividends last year and is expected to grow indefinitely at an annual rate of 6 percent. What is the value of the stock if you require a 14 percent return?

CR3.5   In CR3.4, what would the stock sell for today if the dividend is expected to grow at 20 percent for the next 4 years and then grow at 6 percent per year thereafter? (*Note*: The required return remains 14 percent.)

CR3.6   Now assume that Dwyer's in CR3.4 has an expected growth rate of 20 percent for 20 years and then settles down to a 6 percent per year growth rate. What would the stock sell for today if the required return remains 14 percent?

CR3.7   Homestake recently paid a dividend of $2.00 per share and is expected to have a growth rate of –15 percent infinitely. If you require a 20 percent return what is the current value of Homestake?

CR3.8   The common stock of NBDC is selling for $35. The stock recently paid dividends of $2.50 per share and has a projected growth rate of 6 percent. If you purchase this stock at the market price and hold it for one year, what is your expected rate of return?

PROBLEMS

3.1   Yang Computer bonds pay $80 annual interest, mature in 10 years, and pay $1,000 at maturity. What will their price be if the market rate of interest is (**a**) 6 percent, or (**b**) 10 percent, and interest is paid (**1**) annually, (**2**) semiannually?

3.2   Find the current market price of a 20-year, 9 percent coupon rate bond with a par value of $1,000, if interest is paid annually and if current market rates are (**a**) 11 percent, or (**b**) 7 percent. What are the current market prices if everything is the same except the bond has only (**1**) 10 years to maturity, or (**2**) 2 years to maturity? What can we say about the relative influence of changing market interest rates on the market prices of short-term versus long-term bonds? Can you speculate on why this is so?

3.3   Greenman Engineering has some 15-year, $1,000 par bonds outstanding, which have a coupon interest rate of 9 percent and pay interest annually. What is the yield to maturity on the bonds if their current market price is

a. $1,180?
b. $800?
c.   Would you be willing to pay $800 if your minimum required rate of return was 11 percent? Why or why not?

3.4   Zepher's has some 12-year, $1,000 par bonds outstanding. The bonds have a coupon interest rate of 10.4 percent and pay interest semiannually. What is the yield to maturity on the bonds if their current market price is

a. $960?
b. $1,125?

3.5   A $1,000 par value bond has a 12 percent coupon rate, pays interest annually, and has 15 years remaining until it matures.

a.   If $B_0 = \$1,160$, what is its yield to maturity, YTM?
b.   If the bond can be called in 6 years at $1,030, what is the bond's yield to call, YTC? Why is the YTC in this problem lower than the YTM? Would this always be true?

3.6 Three years ago, Jack purchased a 3-year, $1,000 par, 16 percent coupon rate bond issued by Swales Manufacturing at par. The bond pays interest annually. Immediately after purchasing the bond, market interest rates fell to 6 percent and remained there throughout the 3 years.

a. What was Jack's expected yield to maturity, YTM?
b. What was his actual (or realized) compounded percentage return? (*Note:* The interest received at $t = 1$ and $t = 2$ must be reinvested at 6 percent and compounded forward to $t = 3$. You can then solve for the percentage return.)

3.7 Five years ago, Karen purchased $20,000 of 15-year, 14 percent coupon rate bonds at par. The bonds pay interest annually. At the end of 5 years the issuing firm called the bonds at a call price of 105, so that Karen received $1,050 per bond, or a total of $21,000.

a. What was Karen's original expected yield to maturity, YTM?
b. If interest rates remained at 14 percent over the 5-year period, what was Karen's actual compound percentage return? (*Note:* You do *not* have to compound the intermediate interest payments forward to $t = 5$ to answer this part. Simply calculate the yield to call, YTC.)
c. If interest rates immediately dropped to 10 percent and remained there for the 5 years, what was Karen's actual compound percentage return? (*Note:* Now you *must* compound the intermediate interest payments forward to $t = 5$.)

3.8 You are interested in buying 100 shares of a $60 par value preferred stock that has an $8\frac{1}{2}$ percent dividend rate.

a. If your required return is 11 percent, how much would you be willing to pay to acquire the 100 shares?
b. Assume no dividends will be paid until $t = 3$. At the same required return, how much would you now be willing to pay?

3.9 Smith Supermarkets' common stock is selling at $54, the cash dividend expected next year (at time $t = 1$) is $3.78 per share, and the required rate of return is 15 percent. What is the implied compound growth rate (to infinity) in cash dividends?

3.10 A stock currently pays cash dividends of $4 per share ($D_0 = \$4$), and the required rate of return is 12 percent. What is its market price in the following cases?

a. There is no future growth in dividends.
b. Dividends grow at 8 percent per year to infinity.
c. Dividends grow at 5 percent for each of 2 years, and there is no growth expected after D_2.

3.11 Siegel Mines' ore reserves are depleted. Hence, the expected future rate of growth in the firm's cash dividends is –5 percent. (That is, the cash dividends will decline 5 percent per year.) The cash dividend at time $t = 0$ is $4.40, and the required rate of return is 11 percent. What is the current market price of the stock if we assume dividends decline at 5 percent per year until infinity?

3.12 Steve is contemplating the purchase of a small, one-island service station. After-tax cash flows are presently $20,000 per year, and his required rate of return is 14 percent.

a. What is the maximum price Steve should pay for the service station if he expects cash flows to grow at 4 percent per year to infinity?

b. If Steve decides he needs a 15 percent return, and there will be no growth in after-tax cash flows for 3 years, followed by 10 percent per year for years 4 and 5, followed by 3 percent growth to infinity, what is the maximum amount he should pay?

3.13 Dubofsky Energy is a new enterprise that is not expected to pay any cash dividends for the next 5 years. Its first dividend (D_6) is expected to be $2, and the cash dividends are expected to grow for the next 4 years (through $t = 10$) at 25 percent per year. After that, cash dividends are expected to grow at a more normal 5 percent per year to infinity. If $k_s = 18$ percent, what is P_0?

3.14 Jane is considering purchasing stock and holding it for 3 years. The projected dividends (at a 5 percent growth rate) and market price are: $D_1 = \$4.20$; $D_2 = \$4.41$; $D_3 = \$4.63$; and $P_3 = \$97.23$. Her required rate of return, given the risk involved, is 10 percent.

a. What is the maximum price Jane should pay for the stock?

b. If the dividends for years 1 and 2 remain at $4.20 and $4.41, respectively, and are expected to grow at 5 percent per year to infinity, what would the market price have to be at the end of the second year if Jane sold the stock but still demanded a 10 percent return?

c. What is the current price, which is composed of the dividends from years 1 and 2, and the market price you determined in (b) above?

d. Why are your answers the same for (a) and (c), aside from any rounding errors?

e. Does the price of the stock today depend on how long Jane plans to hold it? That is, does its price today depend on whether Jane plans to hold the stock for 2 years, 3 years, or any other period of time?

3.15 Suppose you believe that Legler Products common stock will be worth $144 per share 2 years from now. What is the maximum you would be willing to pay per share if it pays no cash dividends and your required rate of return is 16 percent?

3.16 Nelson's Enterprises is a no-growth firm that pays cash dividends of $8 per year. Its current required rate of return is 12 percent.

a. What is Nelson's current market price?

b. Management is considering an investment that will convert the firm into a constant-growth firm, but it requires stockholders to forgo cash dividends for the next 6 years. When cash dividends are resumed in year 7, they will be $8.88 [i.e., ($8)(1.11)]; the expected constant growth is 11 percent from year 6 to infinity. If its new required return is 16 percent, will the stockholders be better off? (*Note:* Calculate the current price, P_0.)

c. What happens if everything is the same as in (b), except that the growth rate is only 10 percent?

3.17 Alfred's is able to generate an EPS of $4 on its existing assets. If the firm does not invest except to maintain the existing assets, its EPS is expected to remain at $4 per year. A new investment opportunity has come up that requires an investment of $4 per share at time $t = 1$. The return required by investors is 10 percent.

a. What is the net present value of the project, and the market price of Alfred's if:

(1) The project provides a return of $1 per year forever?

(2) The project provides a return of $1 per year for only 10 years (that is, for $t = 2$ through $t = 11$)?

b. How much did the market price increase in each case in (a) from what the market price was before the investment?

3.18 Consider three firms with market prices, earnings per share, and returns required (or expected) by investors as follows:

Firm	Market Price, P_0	Earnings per Share, EPS	Required Return, k_s
A	$40	$2.00	0.18
B	90	8.50	0.10
C	76	7.00	0.17

a. Determine the price/earning ratio, the implied present value of growth opportunities, PVGO, and the ratio of PVGO to P_0 for each of the firms.
b. Do each of the firms look as if they are valued properly by investors?

3.19 Mini Case As a junior analyst for Walden and Sons, your boss just gave you the following group of securities to analyze:

Securities	Today's Market Value
7% coupon rate, $1,000 par, 20-year bond, paying interest annually	$ 900
10 shares of 7½ percent, $100 par, preferred stock	900
18 shares of a low-growth common stock	900
30 shares of a high-growth common stock	900
Total value	$3,600

a. What is the yield to maturity on the 20-year bond?
b. What is the required return on the preferred stock?
c. Your boss is afraid that due to worldwide economic and political problems, expected inflation will increase. If that happens, she predicts the required rates of return demanded for all securities will increase. Her specific projections for the securities are as follows:

Security	New Required Return
Bond	11%
Preferred stock	11½
Low-growth common stock	17
High-growth common stock	20

The details for the two common stocks are as follows:

Low-growth	$D_0 = 4.00, growth at 6 percent per year for 3 years, followed by a decline from 6 percent to 4 percent forever.
High-growth	$D_0 = 1.00, growth for the next 4 years at 40 percent per year, followed by a decline from 40 percent to 5 percent forever.

(1) Do you agree that required rates of return would increase if expected inflation increases? Why or why not? Explain.

(2) What would be the new market price for the bond, the preferred stock, and the two common stocks if your boss is correct?

(3) What is the new total market value of the group of securities?

(4) How much, in terms of percentage, does the value of the group of securities fall? Which security suffers the most loss in value? The least loss in value? Why does this occur?

d. Explain, in terms of the low-growth and high-growth stocks, the present value of growth opportunities. Other things being equal, does a high price/earnings ratio mean the stock is a high-growth stock and a low price/earnings ratio mean the stock is low-growth? Explain.

REFERENCES

For a comprehensive analysis of returns on stocks, bonds, and inflation, see:
Stocks, Bonds, Bills and Inflation. Chicago: Ibbotson Associates, published yearly.

The valuation and other aspects of bonds are covered in:

CRABBE, LELAND. "Event Risk: An Analysis of Losses to Bondholders and 'Super Poison Put' Bond Covenants." *Journal of Finance* 46 (June 1991): 689–706.

FONS, JEROME S. "The Default Premium and Corporate Bond Experience." *Journal of Finance* 42 (March 1987): 81–97.

RICH, STEVEN P., and JOHN T. ROSE. "A Note on Finance Principles, Bond Valuation, and the Appropriate Discount Rate." *Financial Practice and Education* 1 (Fall/Winter 1991): 99–101.

The dividend discount model is considered in:

DONNELLY, BARBARA. "The Dividend Discount Model Comes into Its Own." *Institutional Investor* 19 (March 1985): 1977ff.

GEHR, ADAM K., JR. "A Bias in Dividend Discount Models." *Financial Analysts Journal* 48 (January/February 1992): 75–80.

HICKMAN, KENT, and GLENN H. PETRY. "A Comparison of Stock Price Predictions Using Court Accepted Formulas, Dividend Discount, and P/E Models." *Financial Management* 19 (Summer 1990): 76–87.

Information on the role of volatility and liquidity on prices and returns, along with some other topics of interest, is contained in:

AFFLECK-GRAVES, JOHN, and RICHARD R. MENDENHALL. "The Relation Between the Value Line Enigma and the Post-Earnings-Announcement Effect." *Journal of Financial Economics* 31 (February 1992): 75–96.

FAMA, EUGENE F. "Stock Returns, Expected Returns, and Real Activity." *Journal of Finance* 45 (September 1990): 1089–1108.

HAUGEN, ROBERT A., ELI TALMOR, and WALTER N. TOROUS. "The Effect of Volatility Changes on the Level of Stock Prices and Subsequent Expected Returns." *Journal of Finance* 46 (July 1991): 985–1007.

"Volatility in U.S. and Japanese Stock Markets: A Symposium." *Journal of Applied Corporate Finance* 5 (Spring 1992): 4–35.

Some recent evidence on the term structure of interest rates is contained in:

COX, JOHN C., JONATHAN E. INGERSOLL, JR., and STEPHEN A. ROSS. "A Theory of the Term Structure of Interest Rates." *Econometrica* 53 (March 1985): 385–408.

FROOT, KENNETH A. "New Hope for the Expectations Hypothesis of the Term Structure of Interest Rates." *Journal of Finance* 44 (June 1989): 283–305.

RICHARDSON, MATTHEW, PAUL RICHARDSON, and TOM SMITH. "The Monotonicity of the Term Structure." *Journal of Financial Economics* 31 (February 1992): 97–105.

APPENDIX

3A
The Term Structure of Interest Rates

YIELD CURVES

U.S. Treasury securities are free of any default risk. There is virtual certainty that the government will pay interest on the bonds and will redeem them in full and on time when they mature. Thus, the return on any government security is equal to the risk-free return, k_{RF}, and a maturity premium. The return for Treasury securities as of December 1980 and June 1992 are plotted in Figure 3A.1. The lines are called **yield curves,** and the graphs depict the **term structure** of interest rates for a given risk class of securities. A downward-sloping yield curve, such as that in December 1980, indicates lower expected rates of inflation. An upward-sloping yield curve, like that in June 1992, indicates higher inflation expected in the future. Some observations concerning yield curves are:

1. They fluctuate depending on the general supply and demand for funds and the rate of inflation.
2. Their shapes change—from downward-sloping, to being flat, to upward-sloping—depending on the future rate of inflation expected by investors.
3. Yield curves for firms will be above those of the government. The more risky the firm is perceived to be, the higher the yield curve.

The yield curves plotted in Figure 3A.1 also embody the maturity premium. This maturity premium increases with the length to maturity of any bond. The effect can be seen in Figure 3A.2, where the solid lines depict the yield curves, which encompass both expected inflation and the maturity premium. The dashed lines, which lie below the yield curves, indicate what the yield curves would look like if no maturity premium existed.

Figure 3A.1

The Term Structure as of December 1980 and June 1992

A downward-sloping yield curve occurs when inflation is expected to decrease. An upward-sloping yield curve occurs when inflation is expected to increase. (*Source*: Federal Reserve Bulletin, various issues.)

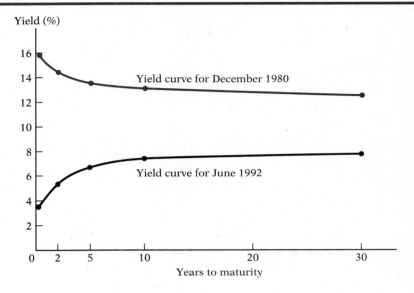

Figure 3A.2

Effect of the Maturity Premium on Yield Curves

Maturity premiums, which arise due to the heightened interest-rate sensitivity of longer-term bonds, increase with the maturity of the bond.

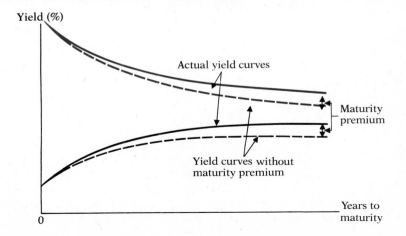

TERM STRUCTURE THEORIES

The term structure of interest rates depicts the yield-maturity relationships for securities of equivalent risk. Figure 3A.1 shows that at times the term structure is upward-sloping, with long-term rates of interest higher than short-term rates; at other times it slopes down, with short-term rates higher than long-term rates. This leads to the question: Why do we observe these different shapes and levels of the term structure over time? A great deal of theoretical and empirical work has focused on this question. Three of the theories offered in explanation are the expectations theory, the liquidity (maturity) preference theory, and the market segmentation theory.

THE EXPECTATIONS THEORY

The **expectations theory** argues that the shape of the term structure can be explained *solely* on the basis of investors' expectations about the course of future interest rates. If investors expect future rates to be higher than current rates, then the term structure will be upward-sloping, and vice versa. Specifically, the theory leads to the conclusion that long-term rates are the geometric average of the current short-term rate and other **forward interest rates** expected to occur between the current period and the maturity date of the long-term bonds.

To understand the expectations theory and the concept of forward rates, assume that the current yield to maturity, often called the **spot interest rate,** on a 2-year Treasury security is 9 percent. In terms of the return to be received on this security, with annual compounding we have

```
0              1              2
|   Year 1   |   Year 2   |
|—— 9% ——→|←—— 9% ——→|
```

The total return earned over the 2 years will be $(1 + 0.09)(1 + 0.09) = (1.09)^2$. Now consider a second Treasury security bond, this time a 1-year security with a return of 7 percent. Graphically, we can depict both securities as follows:

```
0              1              2
|   Year 1   |   Year 2   |
|—— 7% ——→|←—— ?% ——→|
|——————— 9% ———————→|
```

The expectations theory says that an individual investing in either the 1-year bond or the 2-year bond will be exactly as well off at the end of year 2. The question then becomes: What is the rate that would have to be earned in year 2 so an investor originally investing in the 1-year, 7 percent bond is equally well off? More formally, we require that

$$(1 + k_2)^2 = (1 + k_1)(1 + f_2) \tag{3A.1}$$

where k_2 is the current 2-year spot rate of interest, k_1 is the current 1-year spot rate of interest, and f_2 is the implied 1-year forward rate of interest occurring 1 period from now.

For the expectations theory to hold, Equation 3A.1 must be true. Rearranging Equation 3A.1 to solve for the implied forward rate, f_2, we have

$$\text{implied forward rate}_2, f_2 = \frac{(1 + k_2)^2}{1 + k_1} - 1 \qquad (3A.2)$$

$$= \frac{(1.09)^2}{1.07} - 1 = 1.1104 - 1 = 11.04\%$$

Thus, we can think of investment in the 2-year bond which earns 9 percent compounded annually as being equivalent to getting the 1-year spot rate of 7 percent and locking in a forward rate of return of 11.04 percent over the second year.

From this simple example we can develop a general equation for the expectations theory. That is, the long-term spot rate for an n-year bond, k_n, can be expressed as a series made up of the product of the current 1-year spot rate, k_1, and $n - 1$ one-period forward rates expected to occur between the current period and the maturity date of the long-term security:

$$(1 + k_n)^n = (1 + k_1)(1 + f_2)(1 + f_3) \cdots (1 + f_n) \qquad (3A.3)$$

The rate f_2 is the one-period forward rate for a bond bought at the end of year 1 and held until the end of year 2; f_3 is the one-period forward rate for a bond bought at the end of year 2 and held until the end of year 3; and so forth. By rearranging Equation 3A.3, we find the return on a bond with n years to maturity to be

$$k_n = [(1 + k_1)(1 + f_2)(1 + f_3) \cdots (1 + f_n)]^{1/n} - 1 \qquad (3A.4)$$

Likewise, the implied forward rate over any single period can be calculated via

$$\text{implied forward rate}_n, f_n = \frac{(1 + k_n)^n}{(1 + k_{n-1})^{n-1}} - 1 \qquad (3A.5)$$

where

f_n = the 1-year forward rate over the nth year
k_n = the n-year spot rate
k_{n-1} = the spot rate for $n - 1$ years

To illustrate this, assume that the following current spot rates for U.S. Treasury securities exist, indicating an upward-sloping yield curve:

Years to Maturity	Current Spot Rate
1	6%
2	7
3	7.5%
4	8

We can calculate the implied forward rates for years 2, 3, and 4 using Equation 3A.5 as follows:

$$f_2 = \frac{(1 + k_2)^2}{(1 + k_1)} - 1 = \frac{(1.07)^2}{1.06} - 1 = 1.0801 - 1 = 8.01\%$$

$$f_3 = \frac{(1 + k_3)^3}{(1 + k_2)^2} - 1 = \frac{(1.075)^3}{(1.07)^2} - 1 = 1.0851 - 1 = 8.51\%$$

$$f_4 = \frac{(1 + k_4)^4}{(1 + k_3)^3} - 1 = \frac{(1.08)^4}{(1.075)^3} - 1 = 1.0951 - 1 = 9.51\%$$

The relationship between the spot yield to maturity for 1, 2, 3, and 4 years and the implied forward rates is shown in Figure 3A.3.

This discussion indicates that investing in a 4-year bond with a current spot rate of return (or yield to maturity) of 8 percent is exactly the same as investing in a 1-year bond with a spot rate of 6 percent, followed by investing in a series of 1-year forward-rate securities with interest rates of 8.01, 8.51, and 9.51 percent, respectively. This is easy to see using Equation 3A.4 as follows:

$$\begin{aligned} k_4 &= [(1 + k_1)(1 + f_2)(1 + f_3)(1 + f_4)]^{0.25} - 1 \\ &= [(1.0600)(1.0801)(1.0851)(1.0951)]^{0.25} - 1 \\ &= (1.3605)^{0.25} - 1 = 1.0800 - 1 = 8.00\% \end{aligned}$$

If the yield on the 4-year bond were anything other than 8 percent, there would be an opportunity for wealth-maximizing investors to choose the security or combination of securities

Figure 3A.3

Yield to Maturity and Implied Forward Rates

Under the expectations theory, the n-year spot rate of interest (i.e., the yield to maturity) is equal to the current 1-year spot rate and the series of $n - 1$ implied 1-year forward rates of interest between the 1-year spot rate and the maturity of the bond.

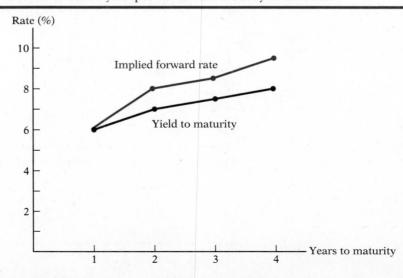

that maximizes their return over the 4-year period. For example, if the yield on the 4-year bond were only 7.75 percent, then all investors would prefer to hold the combination of 1-year bonds because it promises a higher return. Consequently, investors would sell the 4-year bond, thereby driving down its price and driving up its yield. This process would continue until any difference in yields between the two investment strategies was eliminated.

THE LIQUIDITY (MATURITY) PREFERENCE THEORY

The **liquidity preference theory** states that investors find short-term securities more desirable than long-term securities and, therefore, that long-term securities must offer a premium in order to attract investors away from short-term securities. Consequently, *yields on long-term securities are greater than those indicated by the expectations theory*. Note that the theory's name is somewhat misleading, because it actually explains "maturity premiums," or "giving up liquidity" premiums.

The crux of this theory is that future interest rates are not certain, as implied by the expectations theory; rather, unexpected changes may occur. Long-term bond prices fluctuate more as market interest rates change than do short-term bond prices. Because investors prefer less risk, they will prefer to invest in short-term rather than long-term bonds with the same expected rate of return. On the other hand, to reduce the uncertainty of financing long-term projects, firms will prefer to borrow with long-term bonds. As a result, the maturity preferences of borrowers and lenders do not coincide. For firms to raise long-term funds they must offer a (maturity) premium to investors to compensate them for the greater potential price volatility of long-term bonds compared with short-term bonds. As shown in Figure 3A.2, the actual yield curve will be above the one obtained from the expectations theory.

THE MARKET SEGMENTATION THEORY

The **market segmentation theory** holds that the short- and long-term markets are independent of each other and that rates of return (or yields) are determined by supply and demand in each market. The theory argues that different groups of investors have different maturity needs, which lead them to restrict their security purchases to specific portions of the maturity spectrum. Similarly, borrowers are believed to tailor the maturity of their securities to the type of assets they wish to finance or the length of time over which they need funds. For example, banks, with primarily short-term liabilities, prefer short-term investments, while pension funds or insurance companies, with long-term liabilities, prefer long-term investments. On the other side of the market, firms that need funds to finance seasonal increases in current assets (such as inventory or accounts receivable) would borrow on a short-term basis, while firms that want to finance long-term projects would prefer to borrow on a long-term basis.

If these borrowing and lending requirements were strictly adhered to, long-term and short-term securities would not be perfect substitutes for each other. Consequently, the rates of return in the short and long segments of the market would be determined solely by the interaction of supply and demand for funds in the particular segment. If the demand for funds were stronger than the supply of funds in the long-term market, relative to the demand-supply relationship in the short-term market, then long-term rates would be higher than short-term rates. In such a situation, not only would the term structure be upward-sloping, it also would lie above the levels indicated by the expectations and liquidity preference theories.

THEORY, TESTING, AND VOLATILITY

Over time an impressive amount of research has examined various alternative term structure theories. Unfortunately, there is an amazing lack of agreement about which, if any of the three theories discussed, is the most descriptive of the term structure of interest rates. In the last few years a number of new approaches have been suggested. One of the most important is the Cox, Ingersoll, and Ross equilibirum model. At the same time more attention is being given to the role that volatility may play in explaining the observed term structure of interest rates. Although all of the theories have both some logical elements and empirical support, we lean slightly towards the liquidity (maturity) premium argument.

PROBLEMS

3A.1 Current spot rates exist as follows:

Years to Maturity	Spot Rate
1	6.95%
2	7.86
3	8.43

a. Assume the expectations theory holds. What are the implied 1-year forward interest rates for years 2 and 3?

b. Verify that your answers in (a) are correct by using the 1-year spot rate and your two implied forward rates of interest to obtain the 3-year spot rate of 8.43 percent.

3A.2 The following series of spot interest rates exist:

Years to Maturity	Spot Rate
1	8.62%
2	7.78
3	7.49
4	7.40
5	7.38

a. Under the expectations theory, what are the implied 1-year forward rates of interest?

b. Verify that your answers in (a) are correct by using the 1-year spot rate and your four implied forward interest rates to obtain the 5-year spot interest rate of 7.38 percent.

3A.3 Suppose that the 3-year spot rate of interest at time $t = 0$ is 9 percent while the 4-year spot interest rate at time $t = 0$ is 10 percent.

a. What is the implied forward rate of interest for year 4?

b. What does the expectations theory of interest rates say about the implied forward interest rate for year 4 and the 1-year spot rate at year 3?

c. Over a long period of time, the term structure has been, on average, upward-sloping. Does this support the expectations theory?

d. Under the liquidity preference theory, what is the relationship between the implied forward interest rate for year 4 and the 1-year spot interest rate at year 3?

e. Assuming inflation is predictable and you need to plan on meeting long-term liabilities, should you invest in long- or short-term bonds if you accept the liquidity preference theory? Why?

f. If the market segmentation theory holds, and the demand for funds is stronger than the supply of funds in the long-term market relative to the short-term market, what can we say about the term structure of interest rates?

4 *Risk and* Return

EXECUTIVE SUMMARY

Investors are risk-averse. To induce investors to buy the firm's securities—in other words, to raise capital—the firm must offer investors a rate of return that compensates them for the risk they bear. This brings us to two important tasks: first, to define and measure the risk of the firm's securities; and, second, to establish a quantifiable relationship between risk and the required rate of return.

An asset's total risk is measured by the standard deviation of its expected future returns. When an asset is held in isolation, or as part of a nondiversified portfolio, the standard deviation is a good measure of an asset's risk. In a diversified portfolio, however, risk can be divided into two components: diversifiable risk and nondiversifiable risk. Because diversifiable risk can be eliminated in a portfolio, the appropriate measure of the remaining nondiversifiable risk, is beta, β_j.

The capital asset pricing model relates risk and the returns required by investors via the security market line, which says that the required rate of return on any asset in equilibrium is equal to the risk-free rate, plus a risk premium based on the asset's nondiversifiable risk. Increases in expected returns require an increase in nondiversifiable risk as measured by beta. Although assets are occasionally out of equilibrium, this is not generally the case; the expected rate of return and the required rate of return are typically equal.

Financial markets in developed countries are reasonably efficient. Due to the widespread availability of information that many potential buyers and sellers have access to, the current price of a financial asset reflects all available information about the asset, including its risk. The best estimate of the value of any widely traded asset is its market price.

MEASURING RISK

Whenever you are in a situation in which the outcome is unknown, you are exposed to risk, or **uncertainty.** We use these terms interchangeably to mean that the outcome is subject to chance and not definitely known, or to describe a situation in which there is exposure to possible loss. If you gamble in the casinos in Atlantic City or in Nevada, you bear risk. Investing in stocks, bonds, real estate, or gold bullion also exposes you to risk. Most of the decisions a business makes—to raise prices, to expand production, or to bring out a new product—expose the firm, its owners, its creditors, and other stakeholders to risk. Thus, although the firm's managers make the decision, it is the firm's securities holders, along with the firm's managers, employees, suppliers, and other stakeholders, who experience the risk. Risk arises from many different sources and has a number of different meanings in practice. The important point to remember is this: *As firms face risk, so do their owners, creditors, and other interested parties.* To understand risk we focus on it from an investor's standpoint. The ideas developed, however, enable us to understand the risks that financial managers must consider in order to make wealth-maximizing decisions.

To measure risk, we begin with individual assets and then move to **portfolios,** which are just groups of assets. To start, suppose we are interested in measuring the risk associated with two common stocks—Houston International and American Chemical. Although we employ common stock throughout this chapter, the concepts and ideas apply to all financial assets.

Table 4.1

Probability Distributions for Houston International and American Chemical

The rates of return are those expected to occur under various states of the economy. These rates could be given in decimal form, but we employ percentages throughout.

State of the Economy (1)	Probability of State Occurring (2)	×	Associated Rate of Return (3)	=	Mean or Expected Rate of Return (4)
Houston International					
Boom	0.30		60%		18.0%
Normal	0.40		20		8.0
Recession	0.30		−20		−6.0
	1.00		expected rate of return =	$\bar{k}$ =	20.0%
American Chemical					
Boom	0.30		25%		7.5%
Normal	0.40		15		6.0
Recession	0.30		5		1.5
	1.00		expected rate of return =	$\bar{k}$ =	15.0%

PROBABILITY DISTRIBUTIONS

The **probability** associated with an event is the chance the event will occur. Because we are interested in future events, we focus on *ex ante*, or expected, states of the economy and returns. In column 1 of Table 4.1 the possible states of the economy are given,[1] followed by the estimated probabilities associated with the various states in column 2. The probability of a boom during the next period is 0.30, the probability of a normal state of the economy is 0.40, and the probability of a recession is 0.30. Note that the probabilities must sum to 1.00.[2] Column 3 shows the estimated returns associated with the three states of the economy. One point should be stressed: *Finance has a future orientation; our interest is in the expected rate of return*. Because the future is uncertain, there is risk associated with owning either Houston International or American Chemical common stock.

The probability distributions presented in Table 4.1 and graphed in Figure 4.1 are called *discrete* probability distributions. By discrete, we simply mean that the probabilities are assigned to specific outcomes. Another type of probability distribution is continuous. Except when dealing with options in Chapter 5 and elsewhere, we primarily emphasize discrete distributions.

Figure 4.1

Discrete Probability Distributions for Houston International and American Chemical

A discrete probability distribution means that a spike occurs at each specific outcome. A continuous probability distribution would show a smooth curve.

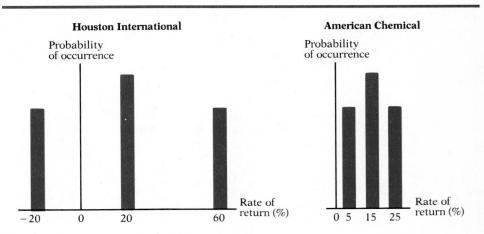

---

[1] In this example we deal with only three states of the economy—boom, normal, and recession—although more could be used if desired.
[2] More formally, the following three conditions hold: First, all outcomes must be accounted for. Second, each individual probability must be greater than or equal to zero. Third, the probabilities must sum to 1.00.

THE MEAN OR EXPECTED RATE OF RETURN

Two measures are typically employed to summarize information contained in probability distributions. The first is the **mean** or **expected value.** For *ex ante*, or expected outcomes, this value is calculated by multiplying the probabilities of occurrence by their associated outcome values, so that

$$\text{expected value, } \bar{k} = \sum_{i=1}^{n} k_i P_i \tag{4.1}$$

where

$\bar{k}$ = the expected value or expected return
n = the number of possible states
k_i = the rate of return associated with the ith possible state
P_i = the probability of the ith state occurring

Thus, the expected value (or expected return) is the weighted average of the possible outcomes (k_i values), with the weights being determined by the probability of occurrence (P_i values).

The expected returns for both firms are presented in Table 4.1. Houston International's expected return is 20 percent; American Chemical's is 15 percent. As noted in Chapter 3, these expected (or *ex ante*) rates of return will generally not be equal to the actual (or *ex post*) rate of return. The actual rate of return depends on which specific state of the economy occurs.

STANDARD DEVIATION

The second summary measure arising from probability distributions is a measure of risk or variability in the possible outcomes. Risk is a difficult concept; one measure that is helpful is the **standard deviation, σ,** which is a measure of **total risk.** It measures how "tightly" the probability distribution is centered around the expected value. Looking back at Figure 4.1, we can easily see that American Chemical's possible rates of return are much more tightly bunched than Houston International's. However, it is hard to say much else about the riskiness of the two stocks without some measure that allows us to determine the spread of the distribution. The standard deviation is such a measure. Using *ex ante* (or expected) outcomes, it is defined as

$$\text{standard deviation, } \sigma = \left[\sum_{i=1}^{n} (k_i - \bar{k})^2 P_i \right]^{0.5} \tag{4.2}$$

where

σ = sigma or the standard deviation (the bigger the spread of the distribution, the larger the standard deviation)
k_i = the outcome associated with the ith state
$\bar{k}$ = the expected value or expected return
P_i = the probability associated with the ith outcome

Table 4.2

Calculation of Variances and Standard Deviations for Houston International and American Chemical

Calculating standard deviations based on discrete returns is easy, following this procedure, as long as there are not too many possible outcomes.

$(k_i - \overline{k})$	$(k_i - \overline{k})^2$	$\times$	P_i	$=$	$(k_i - \overline{k})^2 P_i$
Houston International					
$(60 - 20)$	1,600		0.30		480
$(20 - 20)$	0		0.40		0
$(-20 - 20)$	1,600		0.30		480
			variance $= \sigma^2 =$		960

standard deviation $= \sigma = (\sigma^2)^{0.5} = (960)^{0.5} = 30.98\%$

American Chemical					
$(25 - 15)$	100		0.30		30
$(15 - 15)$	0		0.40		0
$(5 - 15)$	100		0.30		30
			variance $= \sigma^2 =$		60

standard deviation $= \sigma = (\sigma^2)^{0.5} = (60)^{0.5} = 7.75\%$

Note that the standard deviation is the square root of the **variance, σ^2,** of a distribution.

To calculate the standard deviation, we use the steps shown in Table 4.2.[3] We see that the standard deviation for Houston International is 30.98 percent, and for American Chemical it is 7.75 percent. These results confirm our observation from looking at Figure 4.1. There is more total risk associated with Houston International because it has a larger standard deviation.

Two additional points should be made concerning standard deviations. First, the scale of measurement for the standard deviation is exactly the same as the original data and the expected value. In our example, the original unit of measure was the percentage rate of return per unit of time. Both the expected value and the standard deviation are expressed in exactly the same unit of measure. Thus, we can summarize the information contained in a probability distribution simply by reporting its expected value and standard deviation.[4]

[3] Although our concern is primarily with the chance of a loss, indicating that only downside risk is important, the standard deviation measures risk on both sides of the expected value. Because standard deviations are relatively easy to calculate, and because of the developments to follow, we use the standard deviation. If the distribution is skewed, with a long tail in one direction or the other, both the expected value and the standard deviation may be deficient. In those cases, some other measure is often needed. These complications are ignored.

Sometimes it is useful to calculate the **coefficient of variation, CV,** which is the standard deviation divided by the mean. This is a measure of risk *relative* to the mean and is useful for examining the relative variability when two or more means are not the same.

[4] This statement assumes that the probability distributions are relatively normal. This assumption, although not strictly true for securities, allows considerable simplification. Also, for groups of securities in a portfolio, the portfolio returns tend to be approximately normal.

The second point is that as long as we are talking about single assets, the standard deviation, which measures total risk, *is* the appropriate measure of risk. If that asset is part of a nondiversified portfolio, then the standard deviation is still a valid measure of risk. (A nondiversified portfolio might contain two assets, with 95 percent represented by one asset, or security, and only 5 percent of the portfolio invested in the second asset.) However, *when we consider an asset in a diversified portfolio with a number of other assets, the standard deviation is not the most appropriate measure.* Before developing this idea further, let's focus on understanding portfolios and portfolio theory.

Concept Review Questions

- What two measures are typically employed to summarize information contained in probability distributions?
- What is a standard deviation?
- What type of risk does the standard deviation measure?
- Describe how to calculate a variance.

PORTFOLIO RISK AND DIVERSIFICATION

Up to now we have been examining risk for single assets. However, most individuals do not hold just one asset; they hold a portfolio of assets. If you hold only one asset, you suffer a loss if the return turns out to be very low. If you hold two assets, the chance of suffering a loss is reduced: returns on both assets must be low for you to suffer a loss. By **diversifying,** or investing in multiple assets that do not move proportionally in the same direction at the same time, you reduce your risk. The important point to remember is this: *It is the total portfolio risk and return that is important. The risk and return of individual assets should not be analyzed in isolation; rather, they should be analyzed in terms of how they affect the risk and return of the portfolio in which they are included.* Much of what follows is based on the work of Harry Markowitz, a recent Nobel Laureate in economics for his pioneering work in portfolio theory.

PORTFOLIO RETURNS

Measures of risk and return for a portfolio are exactly the same as for individual assets—the expected return, or mean, and the total risk as measured by the standard deviation. The **expected return on a portfolio, $\overline{K}_p$,** is simply the average of the returns for the assets weighted by the proportion of the portfolio devoted to each asset. We can write this as

expected return on a portfolio, $\overline{K}_p = W_A \overline{k}_A + W_B \overline{k}_B + \ldots + W_Z \overline{k}_Z$ (4.3)

where

$\overline{K}_p$ = the expected rate of return on a portfolio

$W_A \ldots W_Z$ = the proportion of the portfolio devoted to asset A through asset Z
(the sum of the W's = 1.00, or 100%)

$\bar{k}_A \ldots \bar{k}_Z$ = the expected rates of return on assets A through Z

To illustrate, consider a portfolio of three stocks, A, B, and C, with expected returns of 16 percent, 12 percent, and 20 percent, respectively. The portfolio consists of 50 percent stock A, 25 percent stock B, and 25 percent stock C. The expected return on this portfolio is

$$\bar{K}_p = W_A\bar{k}_A + W_B\bar{k}_B + W_C\bar{k}_C$$
$$= 0.50(16\%) + 0.25(12\%) + 0.25(20\%) = 8\% + 3\% + 5\% = 16\%$$

PORTFOLIO RISK

Unlike the expected return, the portfolio risk, as measured by its standard deviation, is (with the exception of one special case) *not* a weighted average of the standard deviations of the assets making up the portfolio. To understand why, we must consider the concept of **correlation.** Correlation (Corr) measures the degree of linear relationship to which two variables, such as the returns on two assets, move together. Corr takes on numerical values that range from +1.0 to –1.0. The sign (either + or –) indicates whether the returns move together or inversely. If the sign is positive, the returns on the two assets tend to move up and down together. If it is negative, the assets move inversely; that is, when the return for one asset (or stock, in our example) decreases, the return on the other increases.

The magnitude of the correlation coefficient indicates the strength (or degree) of relationship between the returns on the two assets. If the correlation is +1.0, the returns on the two assets move up and down together, meaning that the relative magnitude of the movements is exactly the same. If Corr is between 0.0 and +1.0, the returns usually move up and down together, but not all the time. The closer the Corr is to 0.0, the less the two sets of returns move together. When the correlation is exactly 0.0, there is no relationship between the returns. Similarly, when the Corr is negative, the closer it is to –1.0, the more the returns on the two assets tend to move *exactly opposite* to each other. These general relationships are shown in Figure 4.2.

TWO-SECURITY PORTFOLIOS

A portfolio's standard deviation depends not only on the risk of the individual securities, or assets, but also on the correlations between their returns. We calculate portfolio risk, σ_p, for a two-security portfolio as follows:

standard deviation
(two-security portfolio),
$$\sigma_p = (W_A^2\sigma_A^2 + W_B^2\sigma_B^2 + 2 W_A W_B \sigma_A \sigma_B \text{Corr}_{AB})^{0.5} \qquad (4.4)$$

where

W_A, W_B = the proportion of the total portfolio devoted to asset A and to asset B, respectively

Figure 4.2

Correlation Coefficient Under Three Different Conditions

If the correlation were perfectly positive (+1.0), all the points in (a) would lie on a straight line with an upward (to the right) slant. Likewise, perfectly negative correlation (−1.0) would result in all points in (b) plotted on a straight line with a downward slant.

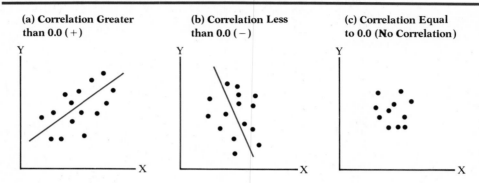

(a) Correlation Greater than 0.0 (+)

(b) Correlation Less than 0.0 (−)

(c) Correlation Equal to 0.0 (No Correlation)

σ_A^2, σ_B^2 = the variances for securities A and B, respectively

Corr_{AB} = the degree of correlation between the returns on assets A and B

σ_A, σ_B = the standard deviations for assets A and B, respectively

$\sigma_A \sigma_B \text{Corr}_{AB}$ = the **covariance,** or comovement, between assets A and B[5]

To see the impact of different degrees of correlation on portfolio standard deviation, consider a portfolio made up of 20 percent Houston International and 80 percent American Chemical. Any portfolio's expected rate of return, no matter what the correlation is between the two assets, will always be determined by Equation 4.3. Recalling that Houston International had an expected return of 20 percent and American Chemical had an expected return of 15 percent, we find our portfolio's expected return to be

$$\overline{K}_p = W_{HI}\overline{k}_{HI} + W_{AC}\overline{k}_{AC}$$
$$= 0.20(20\%) + 0.80(15\%) = 4\% + 12\% = 16\%$$

Let's assume for the moment that the correlation between the returns for the two stocks is perfectly positive, or +1.0 (i.e., $\text{Corr}_{HI:AC} = +1.0$). Also, recall that Houston had a standard deviation, σ_{HI}, of 30.98 percent, while American's standard deviation, σ_{AC}, was 7.75 percent. With this information, we can now use Equation 4.4 to calculate the portfolio's standard deviation as follows:

$$\sigma_p = (W_{HI}^2\sigma_{HI}^2 + W_{AC}^2\sigma_{AC}^2 + 2W_{HI}W_{AC}\sigma_{HI}\sigma_{AC}\text{Corr}_{HI:AC})^{0.5}$$
$$= [(0.20)^2(30.98\%)^2 + (0.80)^2(7.75\%)^2$$
$$+ 2(0.20)(0.80)(30.98\%)(7.75\%)(1.00)]^{0.5}$$
$$= (38.39\% + 38.44\% + 76.83\%)^{0.5} = (153.66\%)^{0.5} \approx 12.40\%$$

[5] Calculation of covariances is discussed in Appendix 4A.

This same result can be obtained more directly by recognizing that when the returns on two assets are perfectly positively correlated, the portfolio standard deviation is simply the weighted average of the standard deviations of the two individual assets. Thus,

$$\sigma_p \text{ (when Corr} = +1.0), = W_A\sigma_A + W_B\sigma_B \tag{4.5}$$

$$= 0.20(30.98\%) + 0.80(7.75\%)$$

$$= 6.196\% + 6.200\% \approx 12.40\%$$

The important implication is that when two assets' returns are *perfectly positively correlated, there are no diversification benefits* to be achieved and consequently no reduction in the portfolio standard deviation. *This is the only situation in which forming portfolios does not provide risk reduction to an investor.*

Now consider the other extreme case—the returns on the two assets have a perfect negative correlation, $\text{Corr}_{\text{HI:AC}} = -1.0$. What happens to the portfolio standard deviation in this case? Using Equation 4.4, we find that the standard deviation in this example is now zero:

$$\sigma_p = [(0.20)^2(30.98\%)^2 + (0.80)^2(7.75\%)^2$$

$$+ 2(0.20)(0.80)(30.98\%)(7.75\%)(-1.00)]^{0.5}$$

$$= (38.39\% + 38.44\% - 76.83\%)^{0.5} = 0.00\%$$

Because the returns for these two assets move exactly opposite to one another in both sign and magnitude, when one goes up the other goes down—with the result that the portfolio standard deviation is zero. Obviously, this is the best of all worlds: We have maintained our 16 percent portfolio expected return but eliminated the risk. Why? Because the correlation between the two assets was perfectly negative. (*Note that the total elimination of risk in this example is a direct result of how it was constructed.* More generally, when the returns on two assets are perfectly negatively correlated, the standard deviation is reduced, but not all the way to zero.)

What happens to the portfolio risk when we have positive, but less than perfectly positive, correlation between the returns? To answer this, let's calculate the portfolio standard deviation when the correlation between the returns for the two assets is $+0.50$. The portfolio standard deviation is

$$\sigma_p = [(0.20)^2(30.98\%)^2 + (0.80)^2(7.75\%)^2$$

$$+ 2(0.20)(0.80)(30.98\%)(7.75\%)(+0.50)]^{0.5}$$

$$= (38.39\% + 38.44\% - 38.42\%)^{0.5} = (115.25\%)^{0.5} \approx 10.74\%$$

Remember that when we had perfectly positive correlation, the portfolio standard deviation was 12.40 percent. We see that *with positive but less than perfectly positive correlation in the returns, some risk reduction has occurred. The primary finding is that, because the portfolio standard deviation is less than the weighted average of the individual asset standard deviations, portfolio diversification led to a reduction in total portfolio risk.* We conclude that part of the total risk can be eliminated, or diversified away. Table 4.3 presents the portfolio standard deviation for various correlations between

Table 4.3

Standard Deviation for a Two-Security Portfolio Made Up of 20 Percent Houston International and 80 Percent American Chemical as the Degree of Correlation Changes

With perfect positive correlation, the portfolio standard deviation is a weighted average of the two assets' standard deviations. In all other cases, the portfolio standard deviation is less.

Data

Houston International: $W_{HI} = 20\%$ $\bar{k}_{HI} = 20\%$ $\sigma_{HI} = 30.98\%$
American Chemical: $W_{AC} = 80\%$ $k_{AC} = 15\%$ $\sigma_{AC} = 7.75\%$

$\bar{K}_p = W_{HI}\bar{k}_{HI} + W_{AC}\bar{k}_{AC} = 0.20(20\%) + 0.80(15\%) = 16\%$

$\sigma_p = (W^2_{HI}\sigma^2_{HI} + W^2_{AC}\sigma^2_{AC} + 2W_{HI}W_{AC}\sigma_{HI}\sigma_{AC}Corr_{HI:AC})^{0.5}$

$Corr_{HI:AC}$	Portfolio Return, $\bar{K}_p$	Portfolio Standard Deviation, σ_p
+1.00	16.00%	12.40%
+0.50	16.00	10.74
+0.00	16.00	8.77
−0.50	16.00	6.20
−1.00	16.00	0.00

the two stocks when 20 percent of the portfolio is invested in Houston International and 80 percent is invested in American Chemical. We see that the portfolio standard deviation declines as the degree of correlation goes from +1.0 to −1.0.

In addition, it is important to recognize that in a two-security case with perfect negative correlation, *some* set of weights will cause the portfolio standard deviation to be zero. For our two stocks the weights are 20 percent and 80 percent, respectively. *However,* the weights that drive a portfolio's standard deviation to zero may be anything and depend on the specific standard deviation of returns for the two assets in question. Therefore, *do not* assume that a 20/80 weighting always results in a portfolio standard deviation of zero.

THE EFFICIENT FRONTIER

The foregoing shows that, given any particular pair of weights, the standard deviation of the portfolio's returns decreases as the correlation between the assets' returns decreases. An investor is not restricted, however, to investing only one fixed amount in each asset. Table 4.4 shows a sample of the many portfolios of Houston International and American Chemical that can be formed, and their expected return and standard deviation for various correlations.

Figure 4.3 graphs the set of all possible portfolios that can be formed from these two stocks when the correlation between their returns is +1.0, 0.0, and −1.0, respectively. The set of all possible portfolios for a given correlation is called the **feasible set,** which for a two-security portfolio is either a straight line or a curve. For example, if

Table 4.4

Portfolio Expected Returns and Standard Deviations for Various Correlations and Weights

With perfect positive correlation there is no benefit to diversification, because the portfolio standard deviation is a weighted average of the two assets' standard deviations. With perfect negative correlation there is one portfolio that has a standard deviation of zero. Most assets, or securities, are positively, but not perfectly positively, correlated; therefore, forming portfolios of these assets can reduce, but not eliminate, risk.

Weight		Portfolio Expected Return, $\overline{K}_p$	Portfolio Standard Deviation, σ_p Given Corr$_{HI:AC}$				
HI	AC		1.00	0.50	0.00	−0.50	−1.00
0.00	1.00	15.0%	7.75%	7.75%	7.75%	7.75%	7.75%
0.10	0.90	15.5	10.07	8.93	7.63	6.05	3.87
0.20	0.80	16.0	12.40	10.74	8.77	6.20	0.00
0.30	0.70	16.5	14.72	12.89	10.76	8.09	3.87
0.40	0.60	17.0	17.04	15.26	13.24	10.84	7.75
0.50	0.50	17.5	19.36	17.75	15.97	13.96	11.62
0.60	0.40	18.0	21.69	20.32	18.85	17.25	15.49
0.70	0.30	18.5	24.01	22.94	21.81	20.62	19.36
0.80	0.20	19.0	26.34	25.60	24.84	24.05	23.24
0.90	0.10	19.5	28.66	28.28	27.90	27.51	27.11
1.00	0.00	20.0	30.98	30.98	30.98	30.98	30.98

Figure 4.3

The Feasible Sets of Portfolios That Can Be Formed from Houston International and American Chemical if the Correlation Between Them Is −1.0, 0.0, or +1.0

The feasible set for a two-security portfolio is a straight or a curved line.

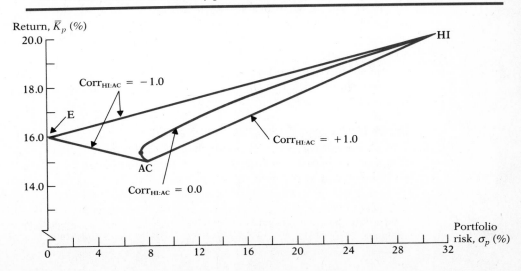

the correlation is +1.0, the feasible set is a straight line from AC, where 100 percent of the portfolio is invested in American, to HI, where 100 percent is invested in Houston. If the correlation is −1.0, the feasible set is made up of two straight line segments, and there is one portfolio in the set (in this case, portfolio E) for which the risk of the portfolio is zero. If the correlation is anything other than +1.0 or −1.0, we have a feasible set that is a curve. This situation is representative of most portfolios, because risk can be reduced but not eliminated.[6]

The objective behind forming portfolios is not simply to reduce risk but, rather, to select efficient portfolios. An **efficient portfolio** is one that provides the highest possible expected return for a given level of risk, and the lowest possible risk for a given level of expected return. Not all portions of the feasible sets in Figure 4.3 represent efficient portfolios. If the correlation between Houston and American is −1.0, then the portion of the set from E to HI dominates the portion from AC to E because it offers a higher return for risk levels between zero and 7.75 percent. Thus, E to HI represents the **efficient frontier** of portfolios when the correlation is −1.0. Similarly, E to HI is the efficient frontier of portfolios when the correlation is zero. A rational investor will choose the portfolio from the efficient frontier that best suits his or her personal risk-return preferences.

Returns on most securities are positively (but not perfectly positively) correlated. This occurs because the returns on most assets tend to move, to a greater or lesser degree, with the general movements in the economy. For stocks issued by United States-based firms, the correlation tends to be between +0.40 and +0.75.

An Example: Diversifying Internationally

An efficient frontier can also be generated when two individual assets are portfolios. Say one asset is the Standard & Poor's 500 Index of U.S. stocks and the other is Morgan Stanley's Europe, Australia, and Far East (EAFE) Index. From 1983 through 1992, the mean of the yearly returns were 16.7 and 19.1 percent, respectively; the standard deviations were 12.4 and 28.2 percent, respectively. Security returns in different countries do not move exactly together; that is, the returns are less than perfectly positively correlated. The correlation between these two indices (or markets) was +0.50 over the 1983–1992 time period. Graphically, the efficient frontier for these two sets of securities is shown in Figure 4.4. Both the returns and risks for foreign stocks were higher than for U.S. stocks.

Investors wanting to increase their expected return from that available with U.S. stocks, and take advantage of the less than perfectly positive correlation between the returns in different countries, needed to diversify internationally. The minimum-risk portfolio should have had about 20 percent of its assets in foreign stocks and the other 80 percent in United States stocks.

When There Are More than Two Assets

When we move beyond two assets, the same relationships discussed previously exist; however, the feasible set is no longer a line or a curve but a space, as represented by the shaded area in Figure 4.5. The two-security portfolio case can be generalized to

[6] For simplicity, we are assuming no short selling is allowed. Short selling involves the sale of a security that is not owned but, instead, has been borrowed. It can be shown that under certain conditions, risk reduction can be accomplished even when the correlation between the two sets of returns is +1.0.

Figure 4.4

Efficient Frontier Attainable from Investing in U.S. and Foreign Securities

Due to the correlation of +0.50, there were substantial benefits from diversifying among U.S. and foreign securities.

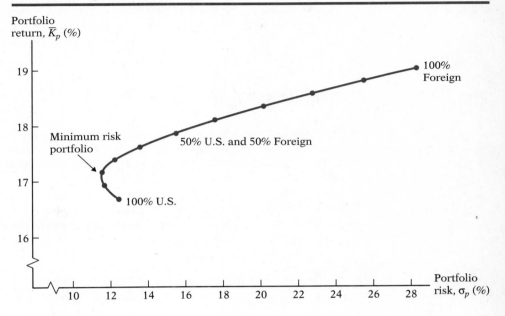

Figure 4.5

The Efficient Frontier for an N-Security Portfolio

The feasible set for a many-security portfolio is a space, not a straight or curved line. All portfolios to the left of the space are unattainable.

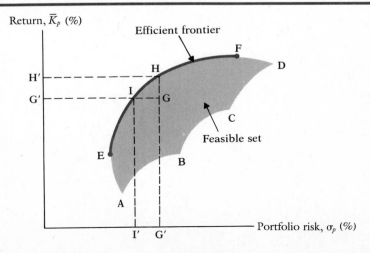

the N-security case, and the feasible set is the infinite number of portfolios (and their respective risks and returns) into which the N securities can be formed. The curve EF is the efficient frontier. All portfolios on this curve dominate the rest of the feasible set because they offer the highest expected return for a given level of risk, and the lowest risk for a given level of expected return. To see this, consider portfolio H on the efficient frontier and portfolio G in the feasible set. Although they both provide the same level of risk, H has the higher expected return; therefore, portfolio H dominates portfolio G. *Because portfolios on the efficient frontier dominate all others by providing a higher return for a given amount of risk, and a lower level of risk for a given expected return, they are preferred.*

DIVERSIFIABLE AND NONDIVERSIFIABLE RISK

Risk can be reduced by forming portfolios. But just how much risk reduction can we achieve? The answer has been provided by a number of studies, as shown in Figure 4.6. The total portfolio risk, measured by its standard deviation, declines as more stocks are added to the portfolio. Adding more stocks to the portfolio can eliminate some of the risk, but not all of it.

The total risk can thus be divided into two parts: diversifiable risk (sometimes called *company-specific* or *unsystematic* risk) and nondiversifiable (sometimes called *systematic*

Figure 4.6

The Impact of the Number of Securities on Portfolio Risk

By the time 20 to 30 securities are in a portfolio, most of the diversifiable risk has been eliminated, leaving only nondiversifiable (i.e., systematic or market) risk. The benefits of diversification arise from reducing the exposure to diversifiable risk.

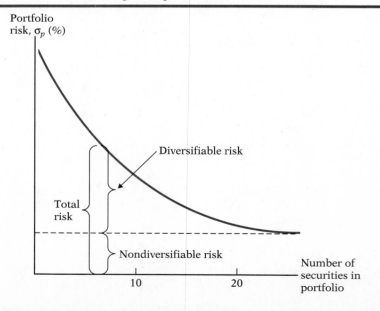

or *market*) risk, so that

total risk = diversifiable risk + nondiversifiable risk   (4.6)

Diversifiable risk relates to events that affect individual companies, such as strikes, product development, new patents, and other activities unique to an individual firm. Because these events occur somewhat independently, they can be largely diversified away, so that negative events affecting one firm can be offset by positive events for other firms. The second type, **nondiversifiable risk,** includes general economic conditions, the impact of monetary and fiscal policies, inflation, and other events that affect all firms (to a greater or lesser extent) simultaneously. Because these risks remain, whether or not a portfolio is formed,

relevant risk = nondiversifiable risk

The only risk a well-diversified portfolio has is the nondiversifiable or systematic portion. Therefore, the *contribution of any one asset to the riskiness of a portfolio is its nondiversifiable or systematic risk.*

Concept Review Questions

- Describe how diversifying your assets will help lower the risk of your portfolio.
- If the expected return on a portfolio, $\overline{K}_p$, is simply the average of the returns for the assets weighted by the proportion of the portfolio devoted to each asset, then is the portfolio standard deviation of the portfolio, σ_p, simply a weighted average of the standard deviations of the assets making up the portfolio? Explain why or why not.
- Explain what an efficient portfolio is and how it is related to the efficient frontier.
- Describe the two types of risks comprising an individual stock's total risk.

RISKLESS BORROWING AND LENDING

So far, we have concentrated on the ideas of portfolio theory. Portfolio theory, as articulated by Harry Markowitz, deals with portfolios of risky assets. By "risky assets" we mean that in order to invest in an asset with an expected return greater than zero, some exposure to risk, as measured by a standard deviation of greater than zero, is required. William Sharpe, who also is a recent Nobel Laureate in economics, carried these ideas further by noting that individuals also have the ability to invest in (or, alternatively, to lend) a risk-free asset. By *adding the idea of risk-free borrowing and lending to portfolio theory,* Sharpe makes it possible to examine investment not only in a portfolio of risky assets but also in a risk-free asset (e.g., Treasury bills). The inclusion of this risk-free asset alters the shape of the efficient frontier from that shown in Figure 4.5 for the N-security case.

Figure 4.7 shows the efficient frontier of risky assets, EF, from Figure 4.5, and also the risk-free asset, k_{RF}. Because a risk-free asset is defined as one that has a known return and a standard deviation of zero, its return plots on the vertical axis. Investors can now combine investing in this riskless asset with investing in portfolios on the

---

Figure 4.7

The Efficient Frontier When Borrowing and Lending Are Allowed

The inclusion of borrowing and lending possibilities changes the efficient frontier from the curve (arc) EF to the straight line k_{RF}ML.

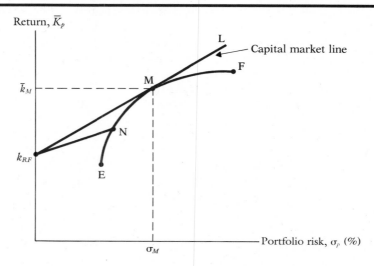

efficient frontier of risky portfolios to obtain combinations of risk-return payoffs that did not exist before. The specific portfolio selected on the efficient frontier is portfolio M; it is the only portfolio on the efficient frontier that is tangent to a straight line starting at k_{RF}. The new set of risk-return opportunities is given by the line k_{RF}ML in Figure 4.7. All portfolios on the line segment between k_{RF} and M represent lending portfolios, because when an investor buys a Treasury bill, he or she is lending to the government at the risk-free rate. Investors are also assumed to be able to borrow at the risk-free rate. Consequently, any investor who is willing to accept higher risk (than σ_M) to obtain a higher return (than $\bar{k}_M$) may borrow at k_{RF} and invest the borrowings plus their initial funds in the risky portfolio, M. These borrowing portfolios are represented by the line segment that extends from M to L in Figure 4.7.

As shown in Figure 4.7, all investors are better off by holding portfolios that are linear combinations of the risk-free asset (either lending or borrowing) and one risky portfolio, M. They are better off because they can obtain a higher return (represented by the straight line k_{RF}ML) for the same amount of risk than at their original position (given by the efficient frontier represented by the curved line EF). The portfolio M is called the **market portfolio** and is a value-weighted portfolio of all risky assets. In equilibrium[7] it must contain all risky assets in proportion of their market value to the total value of the portfolio. Accordingly, if the market value of Walt Disney Company represents 1 percent of the market value of all risky assets, then Walt Disney would constitute 1 percent of the market portfolio.

---

[7] The theory calls for the market portfolio to contain all risky financial assets (e.g., stocks, bonds, options) and all risky real assets (e.g., precious metals, jewelry, real estate, stamp collections). Such a market, however, is not observable. Therefore, in practice, a broad-based stock index is often used as a proxy for the market portfolio.

Because investors can borrow and lend at the risk-free rate, they are able to attain portfolios that were previously unattainable. As shown in Figure 4.7, the *new* efficient frontier represents linear combinations of the risk-free asset and the market portfolio. As depicted by the line designated $k_{RF}ML$, this new efficient frontier is called the **capital market line**, CML. This line has an intercept of k_{RF}, which represents the return on the risk-free asset. If investors are to invest in risky assets, they must receive a risk premium to compensate for the added risk. We see from Figure 4.7 that for an investor to invest in the market portfolio, he or she must receive a return of k_M. The amount $(k_M - k_{RF})$ represents the risk premium, or excess return over the risk-free rate, expected for incurring the risk, σ_M, associated with the market portfolio. Therefore

$$\text{slope of the CML} = \frac{k_M - k_{RF}}{\sigma_M} \tag{4.7}$$

The slope of the CML is called the **market price of risk.** It can be thought of as the equilibrium expected reward per unit of risk. Because the capital market line shows the trade-off between return and risk for efficient portfolios, the unit of risk must be the portfolio standard deviation. Therefore, the equation for the CML is written as

$$\text{capital market line, } \overline{K}_p = k_{RF} + \left(\frac{k_M - k_{RF}}{\sigma_M}\right)\sigma_p \tag{4.8}$$

where

$\overline{K}_p$ = the required rate of return for any efficient portfolio on the CML
k_{RF} = the risk-free rate of return, which is generally measured by the return on Treasury bills
k_M = the expected rate of return on the market portfolio
σ_M = the standard deviation of returns on the market portfolio
σ_p = the standard deviation of the returns on the efficient portfolio being considered

Because all efficient portfolios must lie on the capital market line, Equation 4.8 states that the required return on an efficient portfolio *in equilibrium* is equal to the risk-free rate plus the market price of risk multiplied by the amount of risk on the portfolio being considered. It is important to remember that *only efficient portfolios made up of various linear combinations of the risk-free asset and the market portfolio, M, lie on the* CML. Also, remember that the benefits of diversification, which allows us to diversify away part of the total risk, underlies our present discussion.

BETA AS THE MEASURE OF NONDIVERSIFIABLE, OR SYSTEMATIC, RISK

The capital market line applies to portfolios. We need to extend the analysis to individual assets. Individual assets bear the same direct relationship between risk and return as that observed for portfolios. Therefore, the fundamental question is: How do we measure risk for an individual asset?

For assets held in a diversified portfolio, the contribution of any one asset to the riskiness of a particular portfolio is its nondiversifiable, or systematic, risk. Therefore, for assets in a diversified portfolio, risk can best be measured by how their returns move, or are correlated, with the returns of the portfolio as a whole. If the portfolio is reasonably well diversified, we can, for simplicity, talk about the returns for assets in general as measured by the market portfolio, not just for the portfolio in question.

This market portfolio is often measured by some broad-based stock index, like the New York Stock Exchange Index or the Standard & Poor's 500 Stock Index. The important point is that *for individuals holding diversified portfolios of assets, the appropriate measure of risk is how the return on an individual asset moves relative to the returns for the market portfolio.* This nondiversifiable risk is measured by **beta, β_j,** where the subscript j refers to the jth asset. Thus, beta reflects the nondiversifiable risk remaining for asset j after a portion of its total risk has been diversified away by forming a portfolio. The beta coefficient, β_j, is the measure of the asset's volatility in relation to the riskiness of the market portfolio as a whole. In other words, it measures what the returns on the asset are expected to be, relative to the returns on the market.

Generally the stock market as a whole is our frame of reference; it has a beta of 1.0. The beta for an individual stock indicates the expected volatility of that stock in relation to the volatility of the market portfolio. Any stock whose returns fluctuate over time exactly as the market does has average systematic risk and thus a beta of 1.0. Risky stocks (see Figure 4.8), such as airlines and high-technology firms, whose returns tend to move up and down faster than the general market's returns, are more volatile and have betas greater than 1.0.

We can be even more specific: The returns on a stock with a beta of 1.40 will, on average, increase 40 percent faster than the market in up markets; likewise, they will decrease 40 percent faster in down markets. Lastly, as also shown in Figure 4.8,

Figure 4.8

Beta, Volatility, and Returns

High-beta stocks have much greater volatility in their returns relative to market portfolio returns than do low-beta stocks.

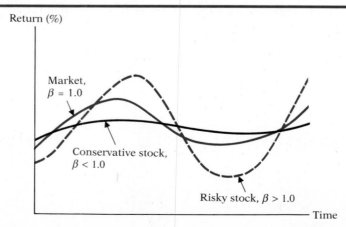

Table 4.5

Beta Coefficients for Selected Firms

Beta is a measure of the volatility of the firm's returns versus the market's returns. It measures risk for individual stocks, or assets, in well-diversified portfolios.

Amdahl	1.35	Kellogg	1.00
American Express	1.50	Limited	1.50
Biogen	1.80	McDonald's	1.05
Consumers Water	0.55	Monsanto	1.10
Exxon	0.75	Paine Webber Group	1.65
General Motors	1.10	Telefones de Mexico	1.10
Glaxo Holdings	1.00	Texas Utilities	0.65
IBM	0.95	Xerox	1.15

Source: Value Line Investment Survey, February 19, 1993, various pages.

conservative firms with very stable cash flows and returns, such as public utilities, fluctuate less than the market and therefore have betas of less than 1.0.

Betas for a select group of stocks are listed in Table 4.5. The range of beta values in the table, from 0.55 to 1.80, indicates the general range of betas in practice. Examining this table we see that IBM, Kellogg, and McDonald's had betas close to 1.00. Their returns were of average volatility. On the other hand, Biogen, with a beta of 1.80, had very volatile returns, while returns for Consumers Water were very stable, as indicated by its beta of 0.55.

THE CAPITAL ASSET PRICING MODEL

We have seen that the capital market line, as depicted in Figure 4.7, represents the risk-return trade-off for efficient portfolios and that the standard deviation of portfolio returns, σ_p, represents the total risk of a portfolio. We also have seen that the best measure of an asset's relevant or nondiversifiable risk is its beta and that betas are distributed around 1.0, the beta of the market. The final step is to formulate the risk-return relationship for an individual asset. This can be done by recognizing that *individual assets bear the same direct relationship between risk and return as portfolios do. The only fundamental difference is that the standard deviation of portfolio returns, σ_p, represents the risk of the portfolio, whereas the relevant measure of risk for individual assets is beta, β_j.* To obtain the return relationship for an individual asset, we reformulate the trade-off of Figure 4.7, now using beta on the horizontal axis, as shown in Figure 4.9. This relationship is the **capital asset pricing model, CAPM.**[8] This figure

---

[8] The major assumptions of the CAPM are (1) all investors are expected wealth-maximizers who evaluate portfolios on the basis of means and standard deviations; (2) all investors can borrow or lend an unlimited amount at the risk-free rate, k_{RF}, and there is no restriction on short sales; (3) all investors have homogeneous expectations concerning expected returns and risks on securities; (4) the market is frictionless, and there are no taxes (or taxes do not affect investment decisions); and (5) all investors are price takers and cannot, based on their buying or selling, influence the market price. Even though these assumptions may appear to be very limiting, all of them can be relaxed without seriously affecting the basic conclusions derived from the model.

Figure 4.9

The Security Market Line, SML

The security market line is a graphic representation of the capital asset pricing model, CAPM.

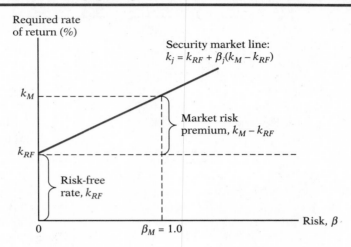

shows that if a higher return is desired, more risk must be incurred.[9] The line shown in Figure 4.9 is called the **security market line, SML.** It shows the risk-return trade-off for individual assets, securities, and portfolios.

The SML relationship depicted in Figure 4.9 is specified as

$$\text{security market line, } k_j = k_{RF} + \beta_j(k_M - k_{RF}) \tag{4.9}$$

where

k_j = the required (or expected) rate of return on any risky asset j held in a diversified portfolio

k_{RF} = the risk-free rate of return, which is generally measured by the return on Treasury bills[10]

β_j = the beta coefficient for the asset

k_M = the expected rate of return on the market portfolio

$(k_M - k_{RF})$ = the market risk premium required to encourage investment in the market portfolio as opposed to investing in some risk-free asset

$\beta_j(k_M - k_{RF})$ = the risk premium for the asset or security in question. This premium is greater than or less than the market risk premium depending on the size of β_j, which measures how the returns on asset j move in relation to the returns for the market portfolio.

---

[9] This assumes that the beta is positive, as it is for the vast majority of assets. Only occasionally are there assets whose returns move counter to the returns on the market. An example of a negative beta stock might be a gold mining company.

[10] If the term structure of interest rates is essentially flat, then the use of Treasury bills as the risk-free rate is justified. However, if the term structure is upward-sloping, so that the interest rate on long-term government bonds is substantially higher than the rate on Treasury bills, then the long-term government bond rate is a better proxy for the risk-free rate.

The security market line, Equation 4.9, when graphed as in Figure 4.9, shows that the rate of return required, or demanded, by an investor is equal to the return on a risk-free asset, k_{RF}, plus a risk premium $\beta_j(k_M - k_{RF})$. In a risk-free world, only the risk-free rate would be relevant. Because the world is not risk-free, the risk premium is added to the risk-free rate to determine the required return an investor demands for investing in a risky asset.

USING THE CAPITAL ASSET PRICING MODEL

In order to use the capital asset pricing model to estimate the rate of return required, or demanded, on an investment, it is necessary to have three elements: the expected risk-free rate, k_{RF}; the expected return on the market portfolio, k_M; and the asset's (in this instance, the stock's) beta, β_j. At any point in time, these might be estimated as follows:

RISK-FREE RATE, k_{RF}
1. The risk-free rate is primarily a function of expected inflation and economic conditions. Typically the rate on Treasury bills is employed as a proxy for k_{RF}. By looking at *The Wall Street Journal*, or some other source of current financial market information, we can determine the return on 1-year Treasury bills. Let's assume it is 7 percent.[11]

EXPECTED RETURN ON THE MARKET PORTFOLIO, k_M
2. The expected return on the market portfolio can be estimated by relying on econometric forecasts, or by viewing the expected return on the market as a function of three items:

$$k_M = \frac{\text{expected}}{\text{inflation}} + \frac{\text{real growth in}}{\text{the economy}} + \frac{\text{risk premium of}}{\text{stocks over bonds}} \qquad (4.10)$$

Thus, if the expected (not historical) rate of inflation is 6.5 percent, real growth (in constant dollars) in gross domestic product (GDP) is expected to be 2.5 percent, and the risk premium (or return) of stocks over bonds is 4 percent, then we would estimate $k_M = 13$ percent.

BETA, β_j
3. We could estimate a stock's riskiness by relying on published betas by *Value Line,* Merrill Lynch, or other investment advisory services. Alternatively, employing the techniques discussed subsequently, we could estimate β_j based on historical returns for the asset and the market. Assume we estimate beta to be 1.40.

To find the required return on the asset, we use Equation 4.9 as follows:

$$k_j = k_{RF} + \beta_j(k_M - k_{RF})$$
$$= 7\% + 1.40(13\% - 7\%) = 7\% + 8.4\% = 15.4\%$$

This approach can be used to find the required rate of return for any asset, or a portfolio of assets.

---

[11] This assumes, in line with the discussion in footnote 10, that the term structure is essentially flat.

Historical Risk Premiums

An alternative approach to estimating the returns on the market portfolio, k_M, is to use the market-risk premium. The market-risk premium is simply the difference between the returns on the market portfolio, k_M, and the risk-free rate, k_{RF}. Thus, this alternative way of estimating the return on the market portfolio is:

$$k_M \text{ (based on market-risk premium)} = k_{RF} + \text{market-risk premium} \qquad (4.11)$$

Data for three different time periods, all ending with 1992, for historical returns on common stocks and Treasury bills are as follows:[12]

	1960–1992	1970–1992	1980–1992
Common stock returns	11.5%	12.7%	16.7%
− Treasury bill returns	6.3	7.4	8.2
Market-risk premium	5.2%	5.3%	8.5%

An examination of these figures indicates that historical market-risk premiums have fluctuated depending on the specific time period employed. Hence, *the use of historical market-risk premiums to estimate the expected return on the market portfolio using Equation 4.11 invites trouble.* Remember, the returns on the market portfolio when using the capital asset pricing model *must be the expected returns, not historical returns.*

The same problem of using historical data exists with the premium that common stocks have earned relative to long-term corporate bonds, as required in Equation 4.10. The historical risk premium of stocks over bonds is[13]

	1960–1992	1970–1992	1980–1992
Common stock returns	11.5%	12.7%	16.7%
− Corporate bond returns	7.8	10.4	13.4
Risk premium of stocks over bonds	3.7%	2.3%	3.3%

Just like the market-risk premium, the risk premium of stocks over bonds has fluctuated, although not as widely, over time. The message from looking at all of these historical returns is simple: No matter what method is used to estimate the expected return on the market portfolio, remember that *it is the future returns in Equation 4.9 that are important.* Any past returns provide, at best, only a rough guideline to the expected returns in the future.

Calculating Beta

We also need to measure the nondiversifiable or systematic risk needed in the capital asset pricing model. To calculate beta directly, we might begin with the *ex post,*

[12] Adapted from *Stocks, Bonds, Bills, and Inflation 1993 Yearbook*™, Ibbotson Associates, Chicago.
[13] Adapted from *Stocks, Bonds, Bills, and Inflation 1993 Yearbook*™, Ibbotson Associates, Chicago.

historical or realized, returns for the asset in question, k_j, and the market portfolio, k_M. Consider the returns presented in Table 4.6. To determine beta for asset j, we can begin by plotting the data as in Figure 4.10. Note that there is a relationship between the returns on the market and the returns on asset j, such that when the returns on the market are high, the returns on asset j tend to be high, and vice versa. This relationship

Table 4.6

Historical Rates of Return on Stock j and the Market Portfolio

The returns encompass both cash dividends and any capital gain or loss for the year and were calculated using Equation 3.10.

Year	Stock j, k_j	Market, k_M
−4	22.51%	8.78%
−3	14.96	4.06
−2	−10.05	−3.99
−1	26.46	20.70
0	5.12	7.45
Mean	11.80%	7.40%
Standard deviation	14.68%	8.94%
Correlation$_{jM}$	0.85	

Figure 4.10

Plot and Fitted Regression of the Returns on Stock j and the Market

The least-squares regression line is called the characteristic line. The slope coefficient from this regression is beta.

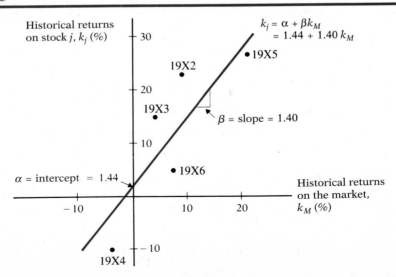

can be expressed as a least-squares regression of the form $Y = \alpha + \beta X$, where α is the intercept on the vertical axis, and β is the slope of the fitted line. The fitted regression, which is called the **characteristic line**, is[14]:

$$\text{characteristic line, } k_j = \alpha + \beta k_M \tag{4.12}$$
$$= 1.44 + 1.40 k_M$$

where

$\alpha = 1.44 = $ alpha, the intercept on the vertical axis
$\beta = 1.40 = $ beta, the sensitivity of the returns on asset j relative to the returns on the market portfolio

Beta for asset, or stock, j is 1.40, meaning that its nondiversifiable risk is 40 percent more than the average nondiversifiable risk. Therefore, asset j is more risky than the market.

Instead of fitting a least-squares regression, beta may also be determined if we know the standard deviation of the assets's returns, the standard deviation of the market's returns, and the correlation between the two returns. Employing this approach, we find that beta equals the covariance (or comovement) between the asset's and market's returns divided by the variance of the market's returns, or

$$\text{beta, } \beta_j = \frac{\text{covariance}_{jM}}{\text{variance}_M} = \frac{\text{Cov}_{jM}}{\sigma_M^2} \tag{4.13}$$

The covariance of the returns between asset j and the market is equal to the standard deviation of asset j, σ_j, times the standard deviation of the market, σ_M, times the correlation between asset j and the market M, Corr_{jM}, so

$$\text{Cov}_{jM} = \sigma_j \sigma_M \text{Corr}_{jM} \tag{4.14}$$

Inserting Equation 4.14 into Equation 4.13 and simplifying, we have

$$\beta_j = \frac{\text{Cov}_{jM}}{\sigma_M^2} = \frac{\sigma_j \sigma_M \text{Corr}_{jM}}{\sigma_M^2} = \frac{\sigma_j \text{Corr}_{jM}}{\sigma_M} \tag{4.15}$$

Note that the standard deviation, σ_M, of the market returns appeared in the numerator of Equation 4.15 before simplifying, while the variance of the market returns, σ_M^2, appeared in the denominator. By dividing through, we are left with the result that beta is equal to the standard deviation of the asset's returns times the correlation between the returns on the asset and the market's returns, divided by the standard deviation of the market's returns. Returning to the data given in Table 4.6, beta could be calculated as follows:

---

[14] Most financial calculators have a built-in regression function. Alternatively, the procedure for calculating a least-squares regression is illustrated in Chapter 25.

$$\beta_j = \frac{\sigma_j \text{Corr}_{jM}}{\sigma_M} = \frac{(14.68)(0.85)}{8.94} = \frac{12.478}{8.94} \approx 1.40$$

Hence, employing either a linear regression approach or Equation 4.15, we calculate the beta to be 1.40. In practice, adjustments are made when deriving expected, as opposed to historical, betas.

Portfolio Betas

We have been discussing the capital asset pricing model and examining betas for individual assets. A *portfolio* of assets also has a beta. This **portfolio beta** is a weighted average of the betas of individual assets:

$$\text{portfolio beta, } \beta_p = \sum_{j=1}^{n} W_j \beta_j \qquad (4.16)$$

where

β_p = the portfolio beta or volatility of the entire portfolio relative to the market
n = the number of assets in the portfolio
W_j = the percent of the total value of the portfolio in asset j
β_j = the beta for asset j

Depending on the composition of the portfolio, the beta can be more than 1.0, equal to 1.0, or less than 1.0.

Suppose you have $10,000 invested in each of 10 stocks, so that your total investment is $100,000; the amount invested in each stock is 10 percent, or 0.10. If all the stocks have a beta of 1.20, then the portfolio beta is also 1.20. What happens if you sell one of the stocks and reinvest in another stock with a different beta? If the new stock has a beta of 0.60, then the new portfolio beta will be

$$\text{new portfolio beta} = \beta_p = \sum_{j=1}^{n} W_j \beta_j$$
$$= 0.90(1.20) + 0.10(0.60) = 1.14$$

Similarly, if the new stock has a beta of 2.00, then the portfolio's new beta will be 1.28 [i.e., $0.90(1.20) + 0.10(2.00)$]. The required return on the portfolio of stocks can then be estimated using the CAPM, based on the portfolio beta, and the expected returns on risk-free assets and on the market portfolio.

Concept Review Questions

■ Describe how the capital market line, CML, is formed and how it affects investors' portfolio decisions.

■ What type of risk does β measure?

■ Verbally describe the capital asset pricing model and how it is used to determine a stock's required rate of return.

■ What three elements are necessary to employ the capital asset pricing model when estimating an investment's required rate of return?

MORE ON THE CAPITAL ASSET PRICING MODEL

There are three other points related to the capital asset pricing model that we need to discuss. These relate to changes in risk and prices, the equilibrium nature of the capital asset pricing model, and some cautions about applying the CAPM.

CHANGES IN RISK AND PRICES

The CAPM can assist us to see what happens to the required rate of return, and to the market price of a firm's stock, as risk changes. To illustrate the price impact, let's suppose that a firm is expecting a constant growth in dividends of 8 percent per year, the current cash dividend (at $t = 0$) is $3, and the required rate of return, which is the return demanded by investors, is 16 percent. Employing the constant growth formula (Equation 3.7) for valuing stocks, we find that the current market price of the stock is

$$P_0 = \frac{D_0(1 + g)}{k_s - g} = \frac{\$3.00(1 + 0.08)}{0.16 - 0.08} = \frac{\$3.24}{0.08} = \$40.50$$

What happens if, because of changes in risk, the investor's required rate of return increases to 18 percent or if it decreases to 13 percent, while everything else remains unchanged? With an increase in risk and required return, the new market value falls to $P_0 = \$3.24/(0.18 - 0.08) = \$32.40$. Likewise, a decrease in risk and required return results in an increase in market value to $P_0 = \$3.24/(0.13 - 0.08) = \$64.80$. Other things being equal, *increased risk lowers the market value of the firm's stock, and reduced risk increases its value.* This result shows that risk, as perceived by investors, has a major impact on the value of the firm. Managers must always be aware of the impact of their actions on the perceived riskiness of the firm, for this is how they influence the firm's market value.

THE EQUILIBRIUM NATURE OF THE CAPM

The capital asset pricing model specifies what the required rate of return on any asset should be. In **equilibrium,** the rate of return required, or demanded, as specified by the CAPM, equals its expected return, which is the best estimate of the return expected from making the investment. What happens if this is not the case? Consider Figure 4.11, which shows a security market line based on investor beliefs about the relationship between required rates of return and nondiversifiable risk. For some reason, suppose the two stocks from earlier in the chapter, Houston International and American Chemical, are improperly priced: Houston is underpriced; American Chemical is overpriced. This mispricing occurs because Houston International's expected rate of return is greater than its required rate of return (as specified by the SML); therefore the stock is **underpriced.** Likewise, American Chemical's expected rate of return is less than the required return; consequently, it is **overpriced.**

Figure 4.11

Process When Securities Are Not in Equilibrium

Houston International is underpriced and therefore is providing an excess (risk-adjusted) return; the opposite is true for American Chemical. The price of Houston will increase and that of American Chemical will decrease until their expected and required returns are equal.

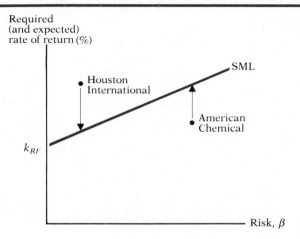

To solidify our understanding, let's use an example. Assume Houston does not pay cash dividends, its current market price, P_0, is $20, and its expected market price, P_1, is $28. Using Equation 3.10 to calculate the expected return, we have

$$k = \frac{D_1 + (P_1 - P_0)}{P_0} = \frac{0 + (\$28 - \$20)}{\$20} = \frac{\$8}{\$20} = 0.40 = 40\%$$

If Houston's required return, as given by the security market line, SML, is 25 percent, what will happen to the current market price? It will increase as investors see that Houston is undervalued and begin to buy it. To what level will the price rise? We can determine that by setting k equal to 25 percent and solving for the new equilibrium price as follows:

$$k = \frac{P_1 - P_0}{P_0}$$

$$0.25 = \frac{\$28 - P_0}{P_0}$$

$$1.25(P_0) = \$28$$

$$P_0 = \frac{\$28}{1.25} = \$22.40$$

We see that if the price increases from $20 to $22.40, the expected and required rates of return for Houston will be equal, at 25 percent.

Exactly the opposite will happen to American Chemical. Because its expected return is below its required return, investors will sell American Chemical, driving the market price down. This will continue until the expected and required rates of return are equal; that is, until they are in equilibrium.

SOME WORDS OF CAUTION

The capital asset pricing model is simple and logical; its assumptions can be relaxed without invalidating the model; and it describes in a formal manner how non-diversifiable risk and return are related. Even so, caution needs to be employed when using it.

1.   The model is based on *ex ante,* or expected, conditions; yet we have only *ex post,* or realized, data. To use historical data without adjustment for future expectations invites trouble. Future, not past, risk and return are the items of concern.
2.   The capital asset pricing model explains, on average, only about 30 percent of the fluctuations in firms' returns as a function of the fluctuations in the returns on the market portfolio. Thus, there are many other factors that affect the returns on common stocks.
3.   Evidence exists that certain stocks provide *ex post* returns greater than could be expected based on the CAPM. Three of these "anomalies" relate to stocks of smaller firms, stocks with low price/earning ratios, and certain seasonal effects. The seasonal, or January, effect relates to the fact that a large part of the total returns for stocks historically has occurred in January.
4.   Recently, Fama and French argued that (1) the market value of equity (or size of the firm) and (2) the ratio of the book value of equity divided by the market value of equity " . . . provide a simple and powerful characterization of the cross-section of average stock returns for the 1963–1990 period." In addition, they show that average stock returns are weakly, if at all, positively related to beta. In effect, they are saying that beta doesn't matter. Given the Fama and French results, we can confidently say that the next few years will produce much more empirical and theoretical work on risk and return.

The capital asset pricing model is the simplest model available at present that depicts the relationship between risk and return. Although other models are available (such as arbitrage pricing theory, discussed briefly later in the chapter, or option pricing models developed in Chapter 5), the CAPM is still the general frame of reference.

Concept Review Question
■ Describe what will happen to the security market line, SML, if investors become more risk adverse and require higher market risk premiums.

THE EFFICIENT MARKET HYPOTHESIS

Extensive empirical evidence suggests that the prices of stocks and other financial assets in developed countries adjust rapidly to disequilibrium situations. Consequently, equilibrium ordinarily exists, and, in general, required and expected returns are equal. Stock prices certainly change, sometimes violently or rapidly, but these changes simply reflect changing economic or firm-specific conditions and expectations. Stock prices may also continue to react over longer periods of time to favorable or unfavorable information. This is to be expected because as new information becomes available, the market adjusts to the new information.

An efficient market, as discussed in Chapter 1, is one in which information is widely and cheaply available to all investors, and in which all relevant and ascertainable information is already reflected in security prices. The notion that financial markets are efficient has been around for about 25 years. The **efficient market hypothesis** states that market participants react quickly to events that convey useful information; therefore, prices of financial assets adjust quickly and unambiguously to new information. By unambiguously, we mean that although sometimes the price may overreact and other times it may underreact, on net the magnitude of the reaction will be "on target."

There are three main streams of research that have focused on the efficient market hypothesis.[15]

1. TESTS FOR RETURN PREDICTABILITY   This research is based on the past record of stock or bond prices and on other historical information such as dividend yields, earnings/price (the inverse of price/earnings) ratios, and interest rates. The results of these tests suggest that future returns are, to some extent, predictable from past returns, dividend yields, and various term-structure variables. With respect to returns on stocks, the research points to certain factors (i.e., size, earnings/price ratios, the amount of debt to equity employed, and book-to-market effects) that are not adequately explained by the capital asset pricing model. However, at the present time we have no better model that explains these anomalous results.

2. TESTS FOR RETURN MOVEMENT (embodied in event studies)   This research takes all publicly available information as the information base. Thus, information about earnings, dividends, new products, mergers, and so forth, has been examined, to see how prices react to the release of this information by firms. The results of a wide range of empirical studies indicate that, with respect to firm-specific events, stock prices react quickly; that is, the markets are efficient.

3. TESTS FOR PRIVATE INFORMATION   This research focuses on assessing whether there is an ability to earn excess returns (i.e., returns that are greater than expected based on the amount of risk incurred) from insider trading, security analysis, and professional portfolio management. The results of these studies suggest that informed investors do not appear to earn excess returns after taking account of transactions costs and the costs of generating the unique, or informed, information.

In recent years a number of studies have challenged the efficient market hypothesis. Although the upshot of this trend is not completely clear, it may be summarized as follows:

> Though evidence of market inefficiency has soared in recent years, that does not mean markets have become less efficient. More likely, it means academics have got better comput-

---

[15] Instead of the three categories of weak-form, semistrong-form, and strong-form efficiency used in finance for many years, we will use Fama's (1991) more recent descriptive titles.

ers and bigger databases, and that there are more of them data-crunching. In fact, most economists believe financial markets are more efficient now than ever before, thanks not least to shrinking official intervention.[16]

There is a very important lesson we need to understand because of market efficiency: *You can trust market prices because they impound available information about the value of a security.* For the average investor, this means that there is no way to achieve *consistently* superior rates of return. To do so you have to know *more* than is publicly available; you have to have access to (or generate) unique private information beyond that available to other investors. Does that mean you should despair? Not at all. *What is important in an efficient market is to determine the amount of risk you are willing to bear.* The most important decision is to determine how comfortable you are with a higher versus a lower risk exposure. If you can't tolerate much risk, that decision dictates the type of investments you will make, and the returns you can expect (or require).

The efficient market hypothesis also has a number of very important messages for managers:

1. Because markets are efficient, the best indication of the worth of the firm and the actions of managers is obtained by looking at market prices. Thus, the best estimate of the value of the firm is the market value of its stock and bonds.
2. When estimating value, start first with market prices, if they exist, and then consider what impact subsequent actions undertaken by the firm might have on the value.
3. In making investment decisions, the only way to increase the value of the firm is to find superior investments whose expected return is greater than the required return. Actions of the firm that have been anticipated by the financial markets are already incorporated in the prices of its financial assets.
4. In an efficient market you should expect to pay an equilibrium rate (or price) for the financing obtained, commensurate with the riskiness of the firm as perceived by investors.

Throughout this book we will make use of the findings and implications of the efficient market hypothesis when making wealth-maximizing financial management decisions.

Concept Review Questions

- Describe the three main streams of research that are focused on the efficient market hypothesis.
- Why is the efficient market hypothesis important to corporate managers?

ARBITRAGE PRICING THEORY

An alternative to the CAPM, the **arbitrage pricing theory**, APT, has received considerable attention. The APT requires fewer assumptions than the CAPM; likewise, the market portfolio does not play a special role in the theory. The return for an individual

[16] "Yes, It Can be Done," *The Economist* (December 5, 1992): 21–23.

asset, j, in the APT is assumed to be a linear function of a number of factors common to all assets

return on asset under APT, $k_j = a_j + b_{j1}F_1 + b_{j2}F_2 + \cdots + b_{jN}F_N + e_j$ (4.17)

where

k_j = actual return on asset j
a_j = the expected return on asset j if unaffected by all factors
$b_j's$ = the sensitivity of asset j to factors $1, \ldots, N$
$F's$ = factors common to the returns of all assets being considered
e_j = unique effects on the return of asset j

Like the CAPM, the APT is interested only in nondiversifiable risk. The APT theorizes, however, that the risk premium associated with this nondiversifiable risk is a function of a number of factors rather than solely the expected returns on the market portfolio. This means that the risk premium is actually the sum of a set of risk premiums. Thus, the required rate of return on asset j is written as

$$k_j = k_{RF} + \sum_{n=1}^{N} b_{jn}(k_n - k_{RF})$$ (4.18)

where

k_n = the required rate of return on the nth factor
$(k_n - k_{RF})$ = the market price of risk for the nth factor
$\sum_{n=1}^{N} b_{jn}(k_n - k_{RF})$ = the risk premium for asset j

The APT is more general than the CAPM. One problem with the APT is that the underlying factors are not known *ex ante*. Some research on the APT includes factors for short-term inflation, long-term inflation, the spread of long- vs. short-term interest rates, default risk, and industrial activity. If only one factor affects an asset's return, and that factor is the market portfolio, then Equation 4.18 reduces to Equation 4.9, the SML equation of the CAPM. Empirical testing indicates that the return on the market portfolio appears to be the most important risk variable for the majority of firms. That being the case, the CAPM continues to be a useful model for representing the relationship between risk and required rates of return for large, actively traded firms.

Concept Review Question

■ How do the capital asset pricing model and the arbitrage pricing theory differ?

KEY POINTS

1. Financial management deals with the future; hence, it is future returns and actions that are important.
2. The mean, or expected value, and the standard deviation are used to capture the information contained in probability distributions.

3. When the correlation between the returns on two or more assets is less than $+1.0$, there are benefits to be gained by diversifying in terms of lower risk, as shown by a lower portfolio standard deviation.
4. Efficient portfolios provide the highest return for a given amount of risk, and the least risk for a given level of returns.
5. Because part of the total risk can be diversified away, the relevant risk for assets in a diversified portfolio is the nondiversifiable, or systematic, risk measured by beta, β_j.
6. The consideration of risk-free borrowing and lending, along with the essential results from portfolio theory, changes the efficient frontier to a straight line called the capital market line. All individuals are better off with the new efficient frontier specified by the capital market line than they were without the addition of the risk-free asset.
7. The capital asset pricing model, CAPM, describes the return required, or demanded, on an asset as a function of the return on a risk-free asset plus a risk premium that incorporates beta. Thus, increases in expected returns require increases in risk.
8. In estimating the capital asset pricing model, it is the future risk-free rate, the future return on the market portfolio, and the future beta that are relevant.
9. Other thing being equal, increases in risk lead to decreases in the prices of financial assets.
10. The expected returns and required return for financial assets are generally equal; that is, they are in equilibrium.
11. Financial markets in developed countries are reasonably efficient. Consequently, security prices react quickly and unambiguously to new information.
12. Efficient financial markets mean that:

   a. The best estimate of the value of the firm is provided by the market prices of the firm's stock and bonds.
   b. When estimating the value of financial assets, look first to their current market value; then consider any incremental value that might be created.
   c. To increase its value, the firm has to make investment decisions that provide returns above those already incorporated in the prices of its financial assets.
   d. Expect to pay an equilibrium rate for any new financing provided from the financial markets.

QUESTIONS

4.1   In what situation is an asset's standard deviation an appropriate measure of risk? Why is this so?

4.2   Security A has a mean of 25 and a standard deviation of 15; security B has a mean of 40 and a standard deviation of 10.

a. Which security is more risky? Why?
b. What if the standard deviation on security B was 15? 20? (*Note:* In answering this part, you must consider whether it is absolute risk, as measured by the standard deviation, or relative risk, as measured by the coefficient of variation, that is important.)

4.3   Explain how forming a portfolio may result in a reduction in risk. What is the necessary condition for this risk reduction to occur?

4.4   Explain the ideas behind the efficient frontier concept. What does the efficient frontier look like if we are considering (**a**) only risky assets and (**b**) a risk-free asset and the market portfolio of risky assets?

4.5   The interest rate line from Figure 2.1 in Chapter 2 is sometimes referred to as the capital market line. What similarities exist between it and the capital market line illustrated in Figure

4.7? What differences exist between the two capital market lines? (*Note:* In answering this question it may be helpful to consider the assumptions that underlie the two different figures.)

4.6 The primary outcome of the capital asset pricing model, CAPM, is the security market line, SML, which is $k_j = k_{RF} + \beta_j(k_M - k_{RF})$. What do all these terms mean? How can they be estimated?

4.7 Why is it that most stocks have positive betas? What would be the required rate of return, relative to the risk-free rate, on a stock that had a negative beta?

4.8 Security *j* has a beta of 0.90, the risk-free rate is 8 percent, and the expected return on the market portfolio is 16 percent. What will happen to the required rate of return on security *j* under the following conditions (assume each part is independent)?

a. Inflation is expected to increase by 3 percent over the next number of years.
b. Due to stringent monetary and fiscal controls, the government is shrinking its deficits and encouraging additional optimism for industry, consumers, and investors.
c. The company just won an unexpected victory in a major lawsuit concerning patent infringement.
d. International competition is increasing rapidly in the firm's market areas, leading to increased risk.
e. The government has decided to place an excess profits tax, amounting to 50 percent, on all corporate profits.

4.9 The capital asset pricing model indicates the relationship between risk and the required return. However, occasionally securities get out of equilibrium, and their expected rate of return is greater or less than their required rate of return.

a. What process occurs to bring the expected rate of return back into equilibrium so it equals the required rate of return?
b. How does the idea of market efficiency relate to this process?

4.10 Explain the efficient market hypotheses, being sure to distinguish between the three streams of research that have evolved in assessing market efficiency. What important implications does market efficiency have for investors and for managers?

4.11 Two securities exist as follows: security A has an expected return of 10 percent and a standard deviation of 15 percent; while security B has an expected return of 8 percent and a standard deviation of 20 percent. Explain in detail whether this information supports or refutes the notion that risk and return are related.

CONCEPT REVIEW PROBLEMS

See Appendix A for solutions.

CR4.1 Jay is considering investing in one of two stocks, IBM or Discount Computers (DC). Given the following probability distribution of returns, what is the expected rate of return for each stock? What is the expected rate of return for the market?

State	Probability	IBM	DC	Market
1	0.2	-15%	42%	-8%
2	0.6	10	12	10
3	0.2	35	-30	25

CR4.2 Given the probability distributions in CR4.1, what is the standard deviation for each of the investments? What is the coefficient of variation for each of the investments?

CR4.3 Assume that Jay is holding a well-diversified portfolio in which the expected returns on his portfolio resemble the expected market returns as in CR4.1. If Jay adds IBM to his investment portfolio, in which the new portfolio is comprised of 20 percent of IBM and 80 percent of the old portfolio, what is the new portfolio's expected return? If Jay added Discount Computers, instead of IBM, to his new portfolio in the same proportion, what would be the expected return on his new portfolio?

CR4.4 Cris has been asked by her employer to estimate the systematic risk of two different investment opportunities, Bram Inc., and Itel Labs. She estimates the standard deviation for Bram is 10.56 percent and its correlation coefficient with the market is +0.45. Itel has a standard deviation of 12.15 percent and a correlation coefficient with the market of +0.85. If the standard deviation of the market is 8.67 percent, what are the beta estimates for both Bram and Itel?

CR4.5 Cris obtained information about the risk-free rate of return and the market rate of return from a local brokerage firm. The brokerage firm estimates the expected risk-free rate of return is 6 percent and that investors require a return from the market of 11 percent. Using her beta estimates from CR4.4, what is the required rate of return for both Bram and Itel?

CR4.6 After estimating the required rate of return for both Bram and Itel Labs in CR4.5, Cris was interested in what would happen to the required rates of return of both corporations if inflation expectations increased the risk-free rate to 8 percent. What are the required returns? (*Note:* Other things being equal, does k_M stay at 11 percent, or change?)

CR4.7 Bram recently paid a dividend of $2.00 per share and is expected to grow at 3 percent per year indefinitely. Itel Labs just paid a dividend of $4.00 per share and has an anticipated growth rate of 6 percent.

a. Using the required rates of returns estimated in CR4.5, what is the stock price for each of the firms?

b. Now assume that inflation increased by 2 percent as stated in CR4.6. What is the stock price for both Bram and Itel after the increase in inflation?

PROBLEMS

4.1 A firm is considering investing in one of two projects, which have the following returns and probabilities of occurrence:

Probability	Project A	Project B
0.10	40%	50%
0.20	20	20
0.40	10	5
0.20	0	−20
0.10	−20	−40

a. Calculate the expected return for each project. Which is more profitable?
b. Calculate the standard deviation for each project. Which is more risky?
c. Which project is preferable?

4.2 Securities A, B, and C have rates of return and probabilities of occurrence as follows:

	Security Return (%)		
Probability	A	B	C
0.30	60	50	10
0.40	40	30	50
0.30	20	10	90

a. Calculate the probability distribution of expected rates of return for a portfolio composed 50 percent of security A and 50 percent of security B. [*Note:* First convert the individual security returns for securities A and B to a single series of returns via 0.50(60) + 0.50(50) = 55, which has a 0.30 probability of occurrence. Do the same for A and B for the other two probabilities.] Now do the same for a portfolio composed of 50 percent security A and 50 percent security C.

b. Calculate the expected value (or mean) and standard deviation for portfolios AB and AC from (a). [*Note:* Once you have the probability distributions in (a), then you can treat the returns like that of a single security.]

c. Which portfolio has the highest expected return? The lowest risk? Which portfolio is preferable?

d. Assume that the standard deviation calculated for portfolio AC is 21 percent, but that everything else remains the same. Which portfolio would now be preferable? Why?

4.3   Securities D, E, and F have the following characteristics with respect to expected return, standard deviation, and correlation among them:

Security	Expected Return, $\bar{k}$	Standard Deviation, σ	Correlation
D	8%	2%	$\text{Corr}_{DE} = +0.40$
E	16	16	$\text{Corr}_{DF} = +0.60$
F	12	8	$\text{Corr}_{EF} = +0.80$

What are the expected return and standard deviation of a portfolio comprised of 50 percent of security D, 25 percent of security E, and 25 percent of security F? [*Note:* For three securities, Equation 4.4 becomes:

$$\sigma_P = (W_D^2\sigma_D^2 + W_E^2\sigma_E^2 + W_F^2\sigma_F^2 + 2W_DW_E\sigma_D\sigma_E\text{Corr}_{DE} + 2W_DW_F\sigma_D\sigma_F\text{Corr}_{DF} + 2W_EW_F\sigma_E\sigma_F\text{Corr}_{EF})^{0.5}.]$$

4.4   Consider two stocks, A and B, with their expected returns and standard deviations, as follows:

	A	B
Expected return, $\bar{k}$	15%	10%
Standard deviation, σ	10	8

a. What is the expected return if the portfolio contains equal amounts (0.50) of each security?

b. What is the standard deviation for the equally weighted portfolio in (a) if the correlation between the security returns is **(1)** $Corr_{AB} = +1.00$, **(2)** $Corr_{AB} = +0.50$, and **(3)** $Corr_{AB} = -0.50$?

c. How does the decrease in the portfolio standard deviation (as the correlation between the security returns drops) relate to diversifiable and nondiversifiable risk?

4.5 You have estimated the following probability distribution of returns for two stocks:

Stock N		Stock 0	
Probability	**Return**	**Probability**	**Return**
0.20	8%	0.20	26%
0.30	4	0.30	12
0.30	0	0.30	0
0.20	−4	0.20	−4

a. Calculate the expected rate of return and standard deviation for each stock.

b. If the correlation between the returns on the two stocks is −0.40, calculate the portfolio return and the standard deviation for portfolios containing 100 percent, 75 percent, 50 percent, 25 percent, and 0 percent of security N, respectively.

c. Plot the results from (b). Which portfolios lie on the efficient frontier?

d. If there is no risk-free asset, which portfolio would *you* prefer? Why? Would other individuals necessarily choose the same portfolio?

4.6 The following portfolios are available for selection:

Portfolio	Return, K_p	Risk, σ_p
1	16%	16%
2	14	10
3	8	4
4	12	14
5	9	8
6	10	12
7	7	11
8	5	7
9	11	6
10	3	3

a. By plotting the data, determine which portfolios lie on the efficient frontier.

b. Which portfolio would *you* prefer? Why? Would other individuals necessarily choose the same portfolio?

c. Independent of (b), now assume a risk-free asset exists that returns 10 percent. What is the market portfolio of all risky assets? Which portfolio would *you* now prefer? Why?

4.7 The risk-free rate is 8 percent, and the expected return on the market portfolio is 14 percent. What are the required rates of return for the four stocks listed below?

Stock	R	S	T	U
Beta	2.0	0.6	1.0	−0.2

What can we say about the volatility of each stock relative to the market's volatility?

4.8   Returns for the next period for two stocks, A and B, and for the market, M, are given by the following probability distribution:

State of the Economy	Probability of State Occurring	Associated Rate of Return		
		A	B	M
Boom	0.20	40%	50%	40%
Normal	0.50	0	5	15
Recession	0.30	−10	−5	−15

a. Calculate the expected rate of return for stocks A and B individually. Then calculate (**1**) the associated rates of return for a portfolio comprising 50 percent stock A and 50 percent stock B and (**2**) the expected rate of return for the portfolio AB.
b. Calculate the standard deviation for stock A, stock B, and the portfolio AB. (Carry to two decimal points.) Comparing the average of the individual stock's standard deviations with the portfolio's standard deviation, what can we say about the correlation between the two stocks?
c. Calculate the expected return on the market.
d. If the risk-free rate is 5 percent and the market is efficient so that the expected and required returns for portfolio AB are equal, what is the beta for portfolio AB?

4.9   Larry is attempting to estimate the required rate of return for Davidson Steel. The risk-free rate is 7 percent. Based on the analysis provided by a number of investment advisory firms, Larry estimates the expected return on the market portfolio is 15 percent and the beta for Davidson Steel is 1.25.

a. What is the required rate of return for Davidson Steel?
b. Larry decides to estimate the expected return on the market himself. He believes expected inflation is 6 percent, the real rate of growth in the economy is 3 percent, and the risk premium of stocks over bonds is 4 percent. The risk-free rate remains at 7 percent, and beta is still 1.25. What impact does this have on Larry's estimate of Davidson's required rate of return?

4.10   Haber Fund has a total investment in five stocks as follows:

Stock	Investment (Market Value)	Beta
1	$3.0 million	0.50
2	2.5 million	1.00
3	1.5 million	2.00
4	2.0 million	1.25
5	1.0 million	1.50

The risk-free rate, k_{RF}, is 7 percent, and the returns on the market portfolio are given by the following probability distribution:

Probability	k_M
0.10	8%
0.20	10
0.30	13
0.30	15
0.10	17

What is Haber Fund's required rate of return?

4.11 Suppose that two securities lie exactly on the security market line, SML, with the following characteristics:

Security	k_j	β_j
A	19.6%	2.25
B	16.8	1.75

What are k_{RF} and k_M? (*Note:* The solution involves solving simultaneous equations.) What does the graph of the SML look like?

4.12 The returns and probabilities for a stock and the market are as follows:

Probability of Occurrence	Stock Returns	Market Returns
0.20	45%	50%
0.30	0	20
0.30	−5	10
0.20	−15	−10

a. What is the expected rate of return for each?
b. What is the standard deviation of each?
c. If the correlation between the stock's and the market's returns is +0.95, what is the beta for the stock?

4.13 If a security's required rate of return is 18 percent, the return on the market portfolio is 15 percent, the risk-free rate is 9 percent, the correlation between the security's and the market's returns is +0.50, and the standard deviation of the security's return is 16 percent, what is the variance about the expected market return?

4.14 Assume that you hold the following two securities, A and B:

Security A		Security B	
Probability, P_i	Return, k_i	Probability, P_i	Return, k_i
0.40	40%	0.30	65%
0.40	10	0.40	15
0.20	−10	0.30	−15

The correlation between security A and the market, M, is +0.50.

a. Calculate the expected return and standard deviation for each security.
b. What must the value of Corr$_{BM}$ be to make the two securities equally risky in terms of their beta coefficients? (*Note:* You are not given the standard deviation of the market, σ_M, but it is the same for each security and therefore does not affect your answer.)

4.15 Year-end stock prices and dividends for J.C. Penney and the S&P 500 stock index for some recent years are as follows:

	J. C. Penney		S&P 500
Year	Dividend	Ending Price	Ending Value
−8	—	$14.312	122.55
−7	$1.00	24.188	140.64
−6	1.08	28.312	164.93
−5	1.18	23.188	167.24
−4	1.18	27.750	211.28
−3	1.24	36.125	242.17
−2	1.48	43.375	247.08
−1	2.00	50.625	277.72
0	2.18	72.750	348.81

a. Using the formula, return = $(D_1 + P_1 - P_0)/P_0$, calculate the returns for each year for Penney and the S&P 500. (*Note:* Ignore dividends for the index.)
b. What is the beta for Penney? (Either use a calculator with a linear regression function, or see Chapter 25, which shows how to calculate a least-squares regression.)

4.16 Hoisington Investments has the following portfolio:

Stock	Investment	Stock's Beta
A	$20 million	0.90
B	40 million	1.40
C	10 million	2.00
D	30 million	1.20

a. What is the portfolio's beta coefficient?
b. If the risk-free rate is 8 percent and the return on the market portfolio is 15 percent: (1) What is the SML? (2) What is the (percentage) return Hoisington should be earning on the portfolio if its risk-return pattern puts it right on the SML?
c. Hoisington has just received $25 million in additional funds and is considering investing it in security E, which has a beta of 1.80 and an expected return of 19 percent. (1) Should stock E be purchased? (2) If not, at what rate of return would it be suitable for purchase (if its beta remains at 1.80)?

4.17 Brad has the following investments:

Stock	Required Return, k_j	Portfolio Weight, W_j	β_j
Chicago Power & Light	7.5%	0.40	0.60
Uptown	12.7	0.30	1.40
Summit Industries	10.3	0.30	1.10

a. What is the required return on the portfolio?

b. What is the portfolio beta?

c. Brad has decided to take on some more risk in order to increase his return. He sold some of the Chicago Power & Light stock and invested the proceeds into the other two stocks already held. If the new portfolio's required return is 11.06 percent, and the new portfolio beta is 1.165, how much is now invested in each of the three stocks? (*Note:* The solution involves solving simultaneous equations. Let X equal the proportion of the portfolio invested in Chicago Power & Light, and Y equal the proportion of the portfolio invested in Uptown. Because the sum of all three proportions equals 100 percent, or 1.0, then $1 - X - Y$ equals the proportion of the portfolio invested in Summit Industries.)

4.18   Zumwalt Products has dividends today, D_0, of $2 per share, an expected growth rate of 9 percent per year to infinity, a beta of 1.40, $k_M = 13\%$, and $k_{RF} = 8\%$.

a. What is the required rate of return?

b. What is the current market price of Zumwalt's common stock?

c. Zumwalt is contemplating the divestiture of an unprofitable but stable revenue-producing division. The effect will be to increase the growth rate in cash dividends to 11 percent, and also increase beta to 1.60. What will be the new market value?

d. Instead of (c), Zumwalt could merge with another firm that is a steady cash producer but is less risky. The effect would be to lower beta to 1.20 and reduce the growth rate in dividends to 8 percent. What would be the market value in that case?

e. Instead of either (c) or (d), a new, aggressive management could be brought in. Beta would go to 2.00, and the growth rate in dividends would be 13 percent. Now what would be the stock price?

f. Is Zumwalt better off staying where it is, or moving to one of the plans outlined in (c), (d), or (e)? Which plan should the firm choose? Why is this the best plan?

4.19   Ohio Electronics' common stock is expected to pay a dividend of $3.15 next year, D_1; the growth rate is 5 percent; its beta is 1.50; $k_M = 15$ percent; and $k_{RF} = 7$ percent.

a. What is the current market value of Ohio Electronics' common stock?

b. The combined actions of the Federal Reserve system and the U.S. Treasury cause the risk-free rate to drop to 5 percent. (*Note:* At every beta, the SML is 2 percent less than before.) What is the new market price?

c. *In addition to the change in (b),* risk aversion has decreased, so the return on the market is now 11 percent. What is the current market price?

d. Finally, *in addition to the changes in (b) and (c),* the firm closes some of its marginal operations. Beta decreases to 1.333, while D_1 is $3.12 and g decreases to 4 percent. What is the current market value for Ohio Electronics?

4.20   Landmark Industries is in the process of evaluating the effect of different factors on its market value. Landmark expects to pay dividends of $3 a year from now ($D_1 = \$3$), and the growth rate in its dividends is 4 percent per year until infinity. Landmark estimates the following: $k_{RF} = 6\%$, $k_M = 11\%$, $\sigma_j = 16\%$, $\sigma_M = 10\%$, and $Corr_{jM} = 0.50$.

a. What is the required rate of return for Landmark and the current market value of its stock?

b. What is Landmark's required rate of return and stock market value if everything stays the same, except that its correlation with the market increases to 0.75?

c. If all the conditions are as in (a) except that σ_j increases to 64 percent and σ_M increases to 20 percent, what is the required rate of return and market price for Landmark?

d. If all the conditions are as in (a) except that σ_j decreases to 8 percent, what is the required rate of return and market price for Landmark?

4.21 The risk-free rate is 5 percent, and the expected return on the market portfolio, k_M, is 10 percent. The expected returns and betas for four stocks are listed below:

Stock	Expected Return	Beta
Steelman Zinc	12.0%	1.3
Rose Paint	9.5	0.8
Ramakrishnan Automotive	10.5	1.1
Blythe Electronics	13.0	1.7

a. Which stocks are over- or undervalued?
b. In an efficient market, what occurs to bring expected and required rates of return back into equilibrium?
c. Which stocks are over- or undervalued if the risk-free rate increases to 7 percent and the expected return on the market portfolio goes to 11 percent?

4.22 The stock of Lewis Hardware is currently selling for $25. You have evaluated the future prospects of both the firm and the market and have come up with the following estimates. Lewis is expected to pay a dividend of $2.00 at $t = 1$, and this dividend is expected to grow indefinitely at 6 percent a year. The standard deviation for Lewis and the market are 10 percent and 6.25 percent, respectively. The correlation between the returns for Lewis and for the market is +0.80. If the return on the market is 14 percent and the risk-free rate is 8 percent, is Lewis a good buy?

4.23 **Mini Case** Answer the following questions that deal with portfolios and the capital asset pricing model.

a. Total risk for a stock is measured by its standard deviation. What do we mean by total risk?
b. Two stocks, Cyclical and Stable, exist with probability distributions and associated possible rates of return as follows:

State of the Economy	Probability of State Occurring	Rate of Return Cyclical	Rate of Return Stable
Boom	0.30	50%	25%
Normal	0.50	15	10
Recession	0.20	−20	5

Calculate the mean, or expected value, for each stock, and its standard deviation.

c. The correlation between the returns on Cyclical and Stable is estimated to be +0.20. What are the expected portfolio return and standard deviation for a portfolio of these two securities if the following portfolio weights are employed?

Weight Cyclical	Stable
0.00	1.00
0.25	0.75
0.50	0.50
0.75	0.25
1.00	0.00

Plot the results. What does the efficient frontier tell us?

d. Do the same as in (c) except now assume the correlation between the returns on the two securities is −0.75. What happens to the efficient frontier compared with the efficient frontier determined in (c)? What would the efficient frontier be if the correlation between Cyclical and Stable were +1.0? If it were −1.0?

e. What is the primary lesson to be learned from portfolio theory?

f. Distinguish between diversifiable and nondiversifiable risk. Why is nondiversifiable risk, as measured by beta, the relevant measure of risk?

g. What are the differences between the capital market line and the security market line? The similarities?

h. Assume the two stocks in (b) have prices and betas as follows: $P_{Cyclical} = \$50$ while $\beta_{Cyclical} = 1.58$, and $P_{Stable} = \$25$ while $\beta_{Stable} = 0.75$. A portfolio with 20 percent invested in Cyclical and 80 percent invested in Stable has been formed. What is the beta of the portfolio? If the stock market as a whole increases by 30 percent, by approximately what percent should the value of the portfolio increase? What should be the new market price of the two stocks after the 30 percent increase in the stock market?

i. Independent of (h) assume the risk-free rate is 9 percent and the expected return on the market, k_M, is 15 percent. What is the required return on the two stocks, Cyclical and Stable? What do we know about the two stocks?

j. Assume the risk-free rate increases to 10 percent while the expected return on the market portfolio increases to 18 percent. What are the new required returns for Cyclical and Stable?

REFERENCES

The seminal work of Markowitz and Sharpe and publications after they were awarded the Nobel Prize in economics include:

MARKOWITZ, HARRY M. "Foundations of Portfolio Theory." *Journal of Finance* 46 (June 1991): 469-78.

MARKOWITZ, HARRY M. "Portfolio Selection." *Journal of Finance* 7 (March 1952): 77–91.

SHARPE, WILLIAM F. "Capital Asset Prices: A Theory of Market Equilibrium under Conditions of Risk." *Journal of Finance* 19 (September 1964): 425–42.

SHARPE, WILLIAM F. "Capital Asset Prices With and Without Negative Holdings." *Journal of Finance* 46 (June 1991): 489–509.

Other information on portfolio theory, the CAPM, the arbitrage pricing theory, and efficient markets is contained in:

BODURTHA, JAMES N., JR., and NELSON C. MARK. "Testing the CAPM with Time-Varying Risks and Returns." *Journal of Finance* 46 (September 1991): 1485–1505.

ELTON, EDWIN J., and MARTIN J. GRUBER. *Modern Portfolio Theory and Investment Analysis*, 4th ed. New York: Wiley, 1991.

FAMA, EUGENE F. "Efficient Capital Markets: II." *Journal of Finance* 46 (December 1991): 1575–1617.

GREEN, RICHARD C., and BURTON HOLLIFIELD. "When Will Mean-Variance Efficient Portfolios Be Well Diversified?" *Journal of Finance* 47 (December 1992): 1785–1809.

HAUGEN, ROBERT A. *Modern Investment Theory*, 3rd ed. Englewood Cliffs, N.J.: Prentice–Hall, 1993.

ROSS, STEPHEN A. "The Arbitrage Theory of Capital Asset Pricing." *Journal of Economic Theory* 13 (December 1976): 341–60.

There is a tremendous amount of material on risk and return. Some recent items include:

ARIEL, ROBERT A. "High Stock Returns before Holidays: Existence and Evidence on Possible Causes." *Journal of Finance* 45 (December 1990): 1611–26.

BHARDWAJ, RAVINDER K., and LEROY D. BROOKS. "The January Anomaly: Effects of Low Share Price, Transaction Costs, and Bid-Ask Bias." *Journal of Finance* 47 (June 1992): 553–75.

BROWN, KEITH C., W. V. HARLOW, and SEHA M. TINIC. "Risk Aversion, Uncertain Information, and Market Efficiency." *Journal of Financial Economics* 22 (December 1988): 355–85.

CLARKSON, PETER M., and REX THOMPSON. "Empirical Estimates of Beta When Investors Face Estimation Risk." *Journal of Finance* 45 (June 1990): 431–53.

FAMA, EUGENE F., and KENNETH R. FRENCH. "The Cross-Section of Expected Stock Returns." *Journal of Finance* 47 (June 1992): 427–65.

HUBERMAN, GUR, and SHMUEL KANDEL. "Market Efficiency and the Value Line Record." *Journal of Business* 63 (April 1990): 187–216.

For information on historical rates of return see, for example:

CARLETON, WILLARD, and JOSEF LAKONISHOK. "Risk and Return on Equity: The Use and Misuse of Historical Estimates." *Financial Analysts Journal* 41 (January-February 1985): 38–47.

CHAN, K. C., G. ANDREW KAROLYI, and RENE M. STULZ. "Global Financial Markets and the Risk Premium on U.S. Equity." *Journal of Financial Economics* 32 (October 1992): 135–67.

IBBOTSON, ROGER G., and REX A. SINQUEFIELD. *Stocks, Bonds, Bills, and Inflation: Yearbook.* Chicago: Ibbotson Associates, updated yearly.

APPENDIX

4A *Calculating Covariances and Correlations*

The covariance is

$$\text{covariance, Cov}_{AB} = \sigma_A \sigma_B \text{Corr}_{AB} \tag{4A.1}$$

where

σ_A, σ_B = the standard deviations for assets A and B, respectively

Corr_{AB} = the degree of correlation between the respective returns on assets A and B

Like the correlation coefficient, the covariance is a measure of the degree of linear relationship between two variables. However, the covariance may take on any value (positive or negative), whereas the correlation coefficient can take on values only from +1.0 through zero to –1.0.

USING *EX ANTE* (EXPECTED) RETURNS

The formula for calculating the covariance from expected returns is

$$\text{Cov}_{AB} = \sum_{t=1}^{n} (k_{Ai} - \bar{k}_A)(k_{Bi} - \bar{k}_B)P_i \qquad (4A.2)$$

where

k_{Ai}, k_{Bi} = the outcome associated with the ith state for assets A and B, respectively
$\bar{k}_A, \bar{k}_B$ = the expected value for assets A and B, respectively
P_i = the probability associated with the ith state
n = the number of possible states

To illustrate the calculation of the covariance, let's continue with the two stocks from Figure 4.1, Houston International and American Chemical. The mean, or expected rate of return, is 20 percent for Houston International and 15 percent for American Chemical. To determine the covariance, we need to perform the following calculations:

State of the Economy (1)	Houston International's Deviations from the Mean $(k_{HI} - \bar{k}_{HI})$ (2)	×	American Chemical's Deviations from the Mean $(k_{AC} - \bar{k}_{AC})$ (3)	×	Probability of State Occurring P_i (4)	=	Product of Probability × Deviations (5)
Boom	(60−20)		(25−15)		0.30		120
Normal	(20−20)		(15−15)		0.40		0
Recession	(−20−20)		(5−15)		0.30		120
						$\text{Cov}_{HI:AC} =$	$+\overline{240}$

Once we know the covariance is +240, we can calculate the correlation between Houston International's and American Chemical's returns using Equation 4A.1. Because Houston International's standard deviation is 30.98 percent, whereas American Chemical's is 7.75 percent, we have

$$\text{Cov}_{HI:AC} = \sigma_{HI}\sigma_{AC}\text{Corr}_{HI:AC}$$

$$+240 = (30.98)(7.75)\text{Corr}_{HI:AC}$$

$$\text{Corr}_{HI:AC} = \frac{+240}{(30.98)(7.75)} = \frac{+240}{240.095} \approx +1.00$$

Hence, the correlation between the expected returns on Houston International and American Chemical is +1.00. As we should have expected by inspecting Figure 4.1, their returns tend to move together (even though those of Houston International have wider fluctuations than those for American Chemical).

USING *EX POST* (HISTORICAL OR REALIZED) RETURNS

Instead of having discrete probabilities of occurrence, we might want to calculate the covariance between the returns for two assets using historical returns. The formula for calculating the covariance in that case is

$$\text{covariance, Cov}_{FG} = \frac{\sum_{t=1}^{n} (k_{Ft} - \bar{k}_F)(k_{Gt} - \bar{k}_G)}{n - 1} \tag{4A.3}$$

where

k_{Ft}, k_{Gt} = the outcome associated with the tth time period for assets F and G, respectively
$\bar{k}_F$, $\bar{k}_G$ = the expected value for assets F and G, respectively
n = the total number of time periods

To illustrate this, let's calculate the covariance between the historical returns for stocks F and G with the data below:

Year	Stock F k_{Ft}	Stock G k_{Gt}
−3	5%	25%
−2	30	15
−1	−10	0
0	15	40
Average return	10%	20%
Standard deviation	16.83%	16.83%

From these data we see that the average return for stock F is 10 percent, and its standard deviation is 16.83 percent.[1] For stock G its return is 20 percent, even though its standard

---

[1] To calculate the standard deviation when historical returns are available, the following formula is employed:

$$\sigma = \left[\frac{\sum_{t=1}^{n} (k_t - \bar{k})^2}{n - 1} \right]^{0.5}$$

For stock F we proceed as follows:

$$\bar{k} = \frac{\sum_{t=1}^{n} k_t}{n} = \frac{5 + 30 - 10 + 15}{4} = 10\%$$

$$\sigma = \left[\frac{(5 - 10)^2 + (30 - 10)^2 + (-10 - 10)^2 + (15 - 10)^2}{4 - 1} \right]^{0.5}$$

$$= \left(\frac{25 + 400 + 400 + 25}{3} \right)^{0.5} = \left(\frac{850}{3} \right)^{0.5} = (283.3333)^{0.5} = 16.8325 \approx 16.83$$

Note that we use 4, because there are 4 years in figuring the mean, but only 3 ($n - 1$) in calculating the standard deviation.

deviation is also 16.83 percent. Given these data the calculations necessary to determine the covariance are as follows:

Year	Stock F's Deviations from the Mean, $(k_{Ft} - \bar{k}_F)$ (1)	×	Stock G's Deviations from the Mean, $(k_{Gt} - \bar{k}_G)$ (2)	=	Product of the Deviations, $(k_{Ft} - \bar{k}_F)(k_{Gt} - \bar{k}_G)$ (3)
−3	(5−10)		(25−20)		−25
−2	(30−10)		(15−20)		−100
−1	(−10−10)		(0−20)		400
0	(15−10)		(40−20)		100
			$\sum_{t=1}^{n} (k_{Ft} - \bar{k}_F)(k_{Gt} - \bar{k}_G) = +375$		

From Equation 4A.3, the covariance is:

$$\text{Cov}_{FG} = \frac{+375}{4 - 1} = \frac{+375}{3} = +125$$

Knowing the covariance between the historical returns on stocks F and G, we can calculate the correlation between them using Equation 4A.1 as follows:

$$\text{Cov}_{FG} = \sigma_F \sigma_G \text{Corr}_{FG}$$
$$+125 = (16.83\%)(16.83\%)\text{Corr}_{FG}$$
$$\text{Corr}_{FG} = \frac{+125}{283.2489} \approx +0.44$$

PROBLEMS

4A.1   Two securities have probability distributions of returns as follows:

Security A		Security B	
Probability	Return	Probability	Return
0.10	40%	0.10	30%
0.40	25	0.40	60
0.40	10	0.40	20
0.10	0	0.10	−10

a.   Calculate the mean and the standard deviation of the returns for both securities.
b.   What are their covariance and their correlation?

4A.2   Hull Brothers and Tubbs Trucking have returns as follows:

Year	Hull Brothers	Tubbs Trucking
-4	3%	15%
-3	-8	10
-2	15	-3
-1	22	16
0	-2	7

a. Calculate the mean and the standard deviation of the returns for both securities.
b. What are their covariance and their correlation?

4A.3   Irene currently has 100 percent of her funds invested in stock A. She is contemplating forming a portfolio consisting of 75 percent of stock A and 25 percent of stock B. She asks for your advice in making her decision. You have been able to determine the following returns and probabilities for the two stocks:

Probability of Occurrence	Stock A Returns	Stock B Returns
0.20	60%	30%
0.30	10	20
0.30	-5	0
0.20	-15	-10

In doing your analysis, answer the following questions:

a. What is the expected return for each stock?
b. What is the standard deviation for each stock?
c. What are the expected return and the standard deviation of returns on her proposed portfolio?
d. Is Irene better or worse off by holding her proposed portfolio than investing only in stock A, or is it impossible to say?

4A.4   Stocks A and B have the following historical cash dividend and price data:

	Stock A		Stock B	
Year	Cash Dividend, D_t	Year-End Price, P_t	Cash Dividend, D_t	Year-End Price, P_t
-4	$—	$40.00	$—	$15.00
-3	2.00	43.00	—	22.00
-2	2.50	38.50	0.50	18.50
-1	2.50	48.00	0.50	14.00
0	3.00	44.00	0.50	28.50

a. Calculate the yearly returns for stock A, stock B, and a portfolio comprised of 50 percent A and 50 percent B. (*Note:* Carry the calculations to four decimal places; then convert the returns to percentages with two decimal places for use in the rest of the problem.)

b. Calculate the means for stock A, stock B, and the portfolio AB. Do the same for the standard deviation. (*Note:* Use the equations for the mean and standard deviation given in footnote 1 in this appendix.)

c. Take the average of the two individual stocks' standard deviations [i.e., (standard deviation A + standard deviation B)/2] and compare this with the portfolio standard deviation AB. Based on the extent to which the portfolio has a lower risk than the average of the two stocks' standard deviations, what would you estimate the correlation to be between the returns on stock A and stock B? More specifically, if you were told the correlation was either +0.85 or −0.65, which one would you choose? Why?

5

Options

EXECUTIVE SUMMARY

In recent years one of the biggest changes in finance, and in financial markets, is the development and widespread use of options. An option provides the right, but not the obligation, to buy or sell a particular asset for a limited time at a specified price. Options on common stock were first traded on the Chicago Board Options Exchange in 1973. Since then, the importance of options has grown phenomenally.

The value of European options (which can be exercised only at maturity) on nondividend-paying stocks is determined by: (1) the price of the underlying asset, (2) the exercise price, (3) the time to expiration, (4) the risk-free rate, and (5) the variability of the underlying assets' returns. The binomial option pricing model deals with a world in which there are only two possible outcomes per period. The Black-Scholes option pricing model assumes there are many possible outcomes.

The value of a call option, which is an option to buy, is equal to the current market value of the underlying asset times the hedge ratio, minus the present value of the exercise price. The hedge ratio is simply the number of units of the underlying asset that are needed to replicate one option. The value of European call options can readily be determined using either the binomial option pricing model or the Black-Scholes option pricing model. Likewise, the value of an option to sell, called a put option, can also be easily determined.

The joint claims of stockholders and bondholders on the firm can be analyzed in an option context. The stockholders' claim is simply a call option. In essence, stockholders have bought the firm's assets, borrowed the present value of the bondholders' claims on the firm, and bought a put (or default) option that allows them to walk away from the firm and give it to the bondholders. The default option arises from the limited liability aspect of stock ownership; that is, stockholders are liable for only what they invest directly.

Firms create value by making positive net present value investment decisions. Viewing the firm in an option pricing context clearly indicates that conflicts may arise between stockholders and bondholders. The option pricing context also shows that restructuring or simply reacting to changing economic conditions is likely to shift value from stockholders to bondholders, or vice versa, but not create value.

THE BASICS OF OPTIONS

Option trading is a specialized business, and its participants speak a language all their own. Why, then, should we be interested in options? The answer is that managers routinely come in contact with decisions or securities that have options embedded in them. Only by understanding options will we be in a position to recognize and value these often-hidden options. Our objective in this chapter is threefold: first, to develop an understanding of what options are all about; second, to learn how to value options; third, to apply this knowledge and see that owning equity in a firm is just like owning a call option on the assets of the firm. Later in the book we will see other uses of options and the concepts learned in this chapter.

An option provides its owner with the right, but not the obligation, to buy or sell a particular good for a limited time at a specified price. The most familiar options are stock options—options to buy or sell shares of common stock. The development of options has been a major financial success story. Since they were first developed and traded on the Chicago Board Options Exchange, CBOE, in 1973, options have become one of the biggest financial markets in the world. Option trading now takes place on a number of exchanges, both in the United States and around the world. In addition to options on common stock, there are also options on stock indexes, bonds, commodities, futures, and foreign exchange rates.

Some of the major U.S. options exchanges and the options traded on them are the following:

Chicago Board Options Exchange
  Individual stocks
  General stock market indexes
  Treasury bonds
American Exchange
  Individual stocks
  General stock market indices
  Oil and gas index
  Transportation index
  Treasury bills
  Treasury notes

Philadelphia Exchange
  Individual stocks
  Foreign currencies
  Gold and silver indexes

New options are introduced over time. At the same time, some options cease to exist if demand for them wanes. When options on stocks were first introduced, they were relatively short-term in nature. Thus, the longest maturity was less than 6 months. That market still exists, but in the last few years longer-term options, with maturities of up to 3 years, have begun being traded on major option exchanges.[1]

In order to discuss options we need to understand certain basic terms. These include:

1. CALL OPTION VERSUS PUT OPTION   A **call option** provides the owner of the option with the right, but not the obligation, to buy the underlying asset. Conversely, a **put option** provides the owner with the right, but not the obligation, to sell the asset.
2. EXERCISE PRICE (OR STRIKE PRICE)   The fixed price, stated in the option contract, at which the underlying asset may be purchased or sold is the **exercise (or strike) price.**
3. EXPIRATION DATE OR MATURITY   The maturity date is when the option expires. After this date the option is worthless.
4. EXERCISING AN OPTION   The act of buying or selling the underlying asset via an option contract is called *exercising the option.*
5. AMERICAN OPTION VERSUS EUROPEAN OPTION   An **American option** may be exercised any time up to and including the expiration date. On the other hand, a **European option** can be exercised only at the expiration date.

A LOOK AT OPTIONS ON STOCKS

If you picked up *The Wall Street Journal* and looked at the option quotations for Ford Motor Company, you might see something similar to:

Option/Strike			Vol	Exch	Last	Net Chg	a-close	Open Int
Ford	Jun 35	p	52	CB	1/4	. . .	47 1/4	166
Ford	Mar 40	p	55	CB	1/16	−1/8	47 1/4	1,128
Ford	Feb 45		45	CB	2 5/8	+7/8	47 1/4	3,037
Ford	Mar 45	p	67	CB	3/8	−1/4	47 1/4	825
Ford	Mar 45		45	CB	3 1/8	+9/16	47 1/4	5,562
Ford	Mar 45	p	134	CB	15/16	−1/4	47 1/4	1,244
Ford	Jun 45	p	62	CB	2	−1/2	47 1/4	782
Ford	Feb 50		54	CB	5/16	+1/8	47 1/4	1,759
Ford	Mar 50		366	CB	3/4	+3/16	47 1/4	3,562
Ford	Jun 50		120	CB	2	+3/8	47 1/4	2,000

The first column lists the firm, Ford. The second column lists the exercise (or strike) prices available and the month in which the option expires. These exercise prices are

[1] These long-term options are referred to as "leaps" in *The Wall Street Journal.*

set fairly close to the prevailing market price of the stock. For volatile stocks, more exercise prices will be available; likewise, as the stock price changes, new exercise prices are opened for trading, at $5 intervals. Each contract is written for 100 shares, but the option prices are quoted per share. Upon purchase of an option, an investor would have the right, but not the obligation, to purchase (a call option) or sell (a put option) 100 shares of Ford at the exercise (or strike) price.

The letter "p" in the third column indicates the option is a put; those without a "p" are call options. The fourth column shows the number of contracts traded that day. The fifth column indicates the exchange the option is listed on. For example, the Ford options trade on the Chicago Board of Exchange (CB). The sixth column shows the last price of the option, while the seventh indicates the net change in the price from the previous day. The "a-close" column shows the closing price of the underlying asset; Ford Motor common stock closed at 47 1/4th this day. The final column gives the total number of options outstanding.

If you purchased the June call option on Ford with a strike price of $50, you would pay (100 shares)($2) = $200, plus any commission fee. Once you own the call option, you can exercise it by paying (100 shares)($50) = $5,000. The writer of the option is obligated to sell you 100 shares at $50 per share, providing you exercise the option.

Before proceeding it is helpful to consider a few other terms often used when options are discussed. The buyer of an option contract has purchased the option and has a **long** position, or *holds the contract long*. On the other hand, the seller, or writer, of an option contract has a **short** position, or has sold the option. It should be noted that *investors* create, or "write," stock options. Thus, the options on Ford common stock were created by investors, not by Ford.

One often hears that an option is **in-the-money.** An option is in-the-money if it would produce a gain if exercised. A call option is in-the-money if the market price of the stock, P_0, is *greater* than the exercise price, X. Conversely, a put option is in-the-money if the market price of the stock, P_0, is *less* than the exercise price, X.

On the other hand, an option can be **out-of-the-money.** An option is out-of-the-money if it would produce a loss if exercised. A call option is out-of-the-money if the market price of the stock, P_0, is less than the exercise price, X. A put option is out-of-the-money if P_0 is greater than X.

VALUE OF A CALL OPTION AT EXPIRATION

The right to buy Ford Motor common stock at a specific exercise price as indicated in the call option is valuable. How valuable the option is depends on five specific factors to be discussed shortly. Before moving into the formal valuation of options, though, let's examine the value of a call option at one specific point in time—*at the date of expiration.*

For simplicity, we will restrict our discussion to European options—that is, options that can be exercised only at their maturity date.[2] The value of a call option on the

---

[2] Much of what follows applies equally well to American call options. For non-dividend-pay stocks the market price of an American call option is always greater than its value if exercised immediately. Rational investors will not exercise American call option early; hence, its value is the same (on non-dividend-paying stocks) as that of a European option. But more complications exist when valuing American put options. These topics are beyond the scope of our treatment.

Figure 5.1

The Value of a Call Option at Expiration

If the market price of the stock, P_0, is greater than the exercise price, X, then at expiration the value of the option (as given by the 45° line) is $P_0 - X$. Otherwise, the call option at expiration is worthless.

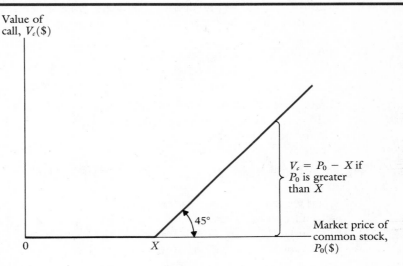

expiration date can be summarized as follows:

Condition	Value of Call Option
Market price of stock is greater than the exercise price	market price − exercise price of the stock
Market price is less than the exercise price	0

This relationship is shown graphically in Figure 5.1. We see that as long as the market price of the stock *at the expiration date* is below the exercise price, the call option is worthless. But, if the market price of the common stock is greater than the exercise price, the value of the call option is equal to $P_0 - X$. The colored line in Figure 5.1 indicates the lower limit on the call option's value. The value of a call option at expiration is often written as

value of call option at expiration, $V_c = \text{Max}(0, P_0 - X)$

For example, assume you paid $200 [i.e., (100 shares)($2)] to purchase a June call option on 100 shares of Ford with an exercise price of $50. The expiration date has now arrived. If the market price of Ford common stock has increased and is now $55, while the exercise price is $50, you can exercise the option—purchase 100 shares at $50 per share—and immediately sell the shares at $55. The value of the option is (100 shares)($55 − $50) = $500. Your profit is equal to the value of the option of $500, less the $200 you paid for the option. Ignoring any commissions and taxes, your profit is $500 − $200 = $300. Alternatively, if the market price of Ford common stock at the expiration date is $50 or below per share, you will throw the option away and incur a loss of $200.[3] The value of the call option on Ford, V_c, at expiration is

$$100(P_0 − X) \quad \text{if } P_0 \text{ is greater than } X$$
$$0 \quad \text{if } P_0 \text{ is less than } X$$

Thus, we see that the relationship of the stock price to the exercise price determines whether an option has any value *at the expiration date of the option*. This condition is true for both call options and put options.

THE BUYER'S POSITION VERSUS THE SELLER'S POSITION

So far we have said that you can purchase an option, or alternatively, you can write (sell) an option. There is a minor addition that needs to be made to what we said previously; this is to formally recognize the *option premium*. Although the potential benefit to the purchaser of a call option may be evident, why would anyone want to write or sell the option? (Remember, individuals write or sell options; the firm the option is on is *not* involved in creating the option.) The answer is that *on net* the seller expects to earn a profit. In the Ford example above, the purchaser profits if at expiration the market price of Ford is sufficiently above the exercise price to more than cover the cost, or premium paid, of the option. This position is shown graphically in Figure 5.2 (a), where the price (or premium) paid per share for the option is $2.

How about the seller's position? For simplicity, assume the original writer, or seller, of the call option on Ford common stock sold it for its current secondary market price of $2 per share. In this case the per share profit to the seller is shown in Figure 5.2 (b). The writer of the call option receives the premium and realizes a gain as long as the value of the stock at the expiration date is less than the exercise price *plus* the premium. Thus, the expiration date gain or loss to the buyer and to the writer are mirror images of each other. It is a zero-sum game, in which one can gain only at the expense of the other. Because only 10 to 15 percent of all stock options written end up being in-the-money at expiration, there are sufficient incentives for some individuals or investment banking firms to write options.

Concept Review Questions
- Define an option.
- How do call options differ from put options?
- Define an in-the-money option and an out-of-the-money option.

---

[3] Thus, in order for the option holder to profit, the price of Ford common stock has to be enough above the exercise price to cover the purchase price paid by the holder of the option; in this case, that price is $52.

Figure 5.2

Profit Opportunities for a Buyer and a Seller of a Ford Call Option

With a premium of $2, the buyer profits if at expiration the price of Ford common stock is above $52; otherwise the seller profits.

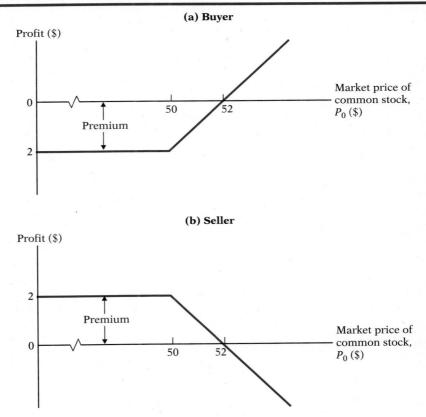

(a) Buyer

(b) Seller

VALUING EUROPEAN CALL OPTIONS

In the last section we discussed the value of the option on the expiration date. Now we need to determine how options are valued at times other than the expiration date. At these times the value of the option will be greater than the lower limit of their value. This occurs because there is risk: We don't know whether *at expiration* the value, or stock price in the case of options on stocks, will be above or below the exercise price. The probability of expiring in-the-money is one of the primary forces that keeps the price of the option before expiration above the lower limit of its value. Thus, the actual value of a call option *prior to the expiration date* will lie above the lower limit (given by $P_0 - X$, if P_0 is greater than X; or 0, if P_0 is less than X) shown previously in Figure 5.1. This is illustrated in Figure 5.3.

Figure 5.3

The Value of a Call Option Before Expiration

The lower bound on the value is given by the solid colored line. But, other things being equal, (a) the higher the price of the asset, P_0, (b) the longer the time to expiration, t, (c) the higher the risk-free rate, k_{RF}, or (d) the greater the variability, σ, the higher will be the value of the option, V_c, as indicated by the dashed line.

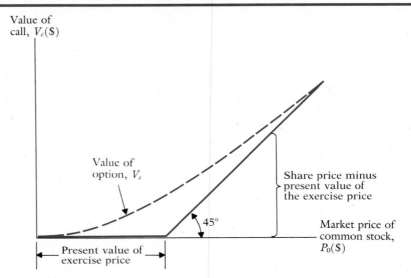

BASIC DETERMINANTS OF OPTION VALUES

The factors that determine an option's value can be broken down into two basic sets. The first are those that relate to the option contract itself, while the second relate to the underlying asset (or stock). The three factors related to the option contract that affect the option's value are the exercise price, the expiration date, and the level of interest rates, as indicated by the risk-free rate.

1. EXERCISE PRICE   Other things being equal, the higher the exercise price, the lower will be the value of a call option. This makes sense because the higher the exercise price, the less likely it is that the market price of the underlying asset will be above the exercise price at the expiration date. As long as there is some probability that the price of the underlying asset will exceed the exercise price, however, the call option will have value.

2. EXPIRATION DATE   The longer the time until expiration, the higher the value of the call option. Thus, other things being equal, if you hold a 6-month option, and also a 1-year option, the 1-year option is more valuable because there is more time for the market price of the underlying asset to fluctuate. This increase in time provides greater opportunity for the price of the underlying asset to move, and hence increases the value of the option.

3. RISK-FREE RATE   The level of interest rates also affects the value of call options. The reason is that the market price of the asset, P_0, is in today's dollars, while the exercise price is in future dollars. These must be stated at the same time, which is today, at time $t = 0$. Based on the time value of money, the present value of the exercise price is less when the risk-free rate is high, and the present value of the exercise price is more when the risk-free rate is low. Because the value of the call option is equal to at least the stock price, P_0, minus the *present value of the exercise price*, a call option is more valuable the higher the risk-free rate. Thus, the value of a call option is positively related to the level of interest rates, as measured by the risk-free rate.

In addition, two other factors related to the underlying asset also affect the value of call options. These are the price of the underlying asset and the variability (or riskiness) of the underlying asset.

1. ASSET PRICE   Other things being equal, the higher the price of the underlying asset, the more valuable the call option. This occurs because at maturity the owner of the option will reap a larger return the higher the asset price is above the exercise price.

2. VARIABILITY OF THE ASSET PRICE   Finally, the greater the variability of the underlying asset, the more valuable a call option will be. To see this, it is important to remember that a call option is valuable only when the market price of the underlying asset is greater than the exercise price. Call options on assets with greater price volatility will therefore be worth more, other things being equal. Consider two 6-month call options, both with an exercise price, X, of $60, and a current market price, P_0, of $55. Let's assume the volatility of asset A is more than that of asset B. The call option on asset A will be more valuable, because with more volatility, there is more likelihood for A than for B that the value of the underlying asset will be above the exercise price. As a consequence, *no matter what the degree of risk aversion of an individual investor, we find high variability in the underlying asset desirable when valuing options.*

To summarize, the value of a call option is a function of five variables:

1. Price of the underlying asset, P_0
2. Exercise price, X
3. Time to expiration, t
4. Risk-free rate, k_{RF}
5. Variability[4] of the underlying asset, σ

Thus, the value of a call option, V_c, on a nondividend-paying stock, or asset, is

value of call option, $V_c = \int (P_0,\ X,\ t,\ k_{RF},\ \sigma)$ (5.1)

---

[4] In the Black-Scholes model considered shortly, the variability is reflected by the standard deviation of the returns for the underlying asset, σ. For simplicity, we refer to the variability as the standard deviation, although in the binomial model considered in the next section the standard deviation is not directly calculated.

where the plus (minus) sign by the variable indicates the effect of an increase in that variable on the price of the call option:

Variable	Effect of an Increase of Each Factor on V_c
Asset price, P_0	+
Exercise price, X	−
Time to expiration, t	+
Risk-free rate, k_{RF}	+
Variability of asset's return, σ	+

As long as it is before the expiration date, an increase in any of the following will cause the value of the call option to go up: the price of the asset, P_0; the time to expiration, t; the risk-free rate, k_{RF}; or the variability of the underlying asset, σ. Thus, increases in any of these four variables will cause the actual option value to be farther above the lower limit, as shown previously in Figure 5.3.

Likewise, decreases in the price of the underlying asset, the time to expiration, the risk-free rate, or the variability of the asset's return cause the dashed option value line in Figure 5.3 to snuggle closer to the solid lower-limit value line. For example, if a 1-year option and a 3-month option exist on the same asset and both have the same exercise price, their general relationship is shown in Figure 5.4.[5]

VALUING CALL OPTIONS THAT HAVE ONLY TWO POSSIBLE OUTCOMES

To understand how options are valued, we start with a situation in which there are only two possible outcomes. Then we will extend the discussion to value options that have many possible outcomes.

A Replicating Portfolio of Stock and Borrowing

Assume you want to value a call option that is good for 1 year to buy a share of stock of Xelab, Inc. The current price of Xelab is $50, the exercise price is $60, and the risk-free rate is 10 percent. To keep things simple, there are only two possible outcomes—the price of Xelab will increase to $80 at the end of the year or it will decrease to $40—and the probability of each of the two outcomes is identical. If the price increases to $80, the call option is worth $80 − $60 = $20. On the other hand, if the price falls to $40, the call is worthless. Therefore, the possible payoffs are:

	Stock Price = $80	Stock Price = $40
One call is worth	$20	$0

---

[5] The intercept of the diagonal 45° line in Figures 5.3 and 5.4 is equal to the present value of the exercise price. While not shown in either of these figures, as time elapses and the option moves closer to its maturity, or expiration, date, the present value of the exercise price increases. Therefore, the diagonal 45° line actually shifts slightly to the right (while keeping its same slope).

Figure 5.4

The Value of a Call Option as The Time to Maturity Decreases

As the maturity date of the option draws nearer, the value of the option, other things being equal, snuggles closer and closer to the lower bound given by the solid colored line.

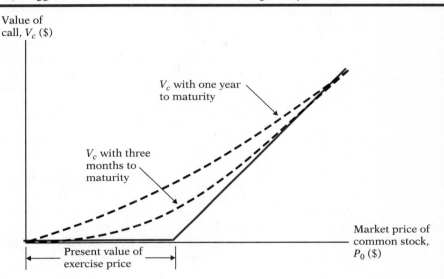

Now consider what would have occurred if instead of buying the option you had purchased the stock directly and borrowed against it at 10 percent. The *amount of the borrowing is based on the lowest stock price outcome*, in this case, $40. The size of the loan would have been $40/(1 + 0.10) = $36.36. Thus, you borrowed $36.36 (the principal) and will repay $40 (the principal plus interest) in 1 year. The possible payoffs from this strategy are:

	Stock Price = $80	Stock Price = $40
One share of stock is worth	$80	$40
Repay loan	−40	−40
Total payoff	$40	0

Note that when the stock price is $80, the payoff is $40 with the stock-and-loan transaction, but it is only $20 if the call is purchased. When the stock price is $40, the payoff is zero in both cases. The payoff by purchasing stock and taking out the loan is twice that of the payoff if the call is purchased. Therefore,

Value of two calls = original stock price − loan

$$= \$50 - \$36.36 = \$13.64$$

If the value of two calls is equal to $13.64, then the value of a single call, V_c, is

$13.64/2 = 6.82. For the case with only two outcomes, it is easy to value a call option! Along the way, we learned how to use the **binomial option pricing model.**

In order to value the call, we borrowed money and purchased stock in such a manner that we exactly replicated the payoff from the call option. This procedure creates a **replicating portfolio** whose payoff *exactly* matches the payoff from purchasing the call option directly. The number of shares of stock that are needed to replicate one option is called the **hedge ratio** (or **delta**). For Xelab, the hedge ratio is 1/2, because it took a half a share of stock to replicate the levered position indicated by the call option. If the total payoff with the stock-and-loan portfolio had been $60, instead of $40, the hedge ratio would then have been 1/3.

In this two-payoff case, the hedge ratio can be determined by comparing the possible spread of option prices with the possible spread of stock prices, so that

$$\text{hedge ratio} = \frac{\text{spread of option prices}}{\text{spread of stock prices}} = \frac{\$20 - \$0}{\$80 - \$40} = \frac{\$20}{\$40} = \frac{1}{2}$$

Let's stop a minute and consider how we valued the call option on Xelab. Instead of valuing it directly, we saw that the value of the call option was equivalent to purchasing the underlying asset and borrowing against the asset. The only requirement in determining this replicating portfolio was that we employ the proper hedge ratio to make sure the position in the levered asset exactly matches the call option. This approach can be expressed as follows:

value of call option, $V_c = (\text{stock price})(\text{hedge ratio}) - \text{present value of loan}$ (5.2)

where the present value of the loan in Equation 5.2 is the present value of the loan from before adjusted by the hedge ratio. In the case of Xelab, the present value of the total loan is $36.36, and because we need only half a share of stock for the replicating portfolio, the appropriate value for the loan is ($36.36)(1/2) = $18.18. Using Equation 5.2, the value of the call option in this binomial, or two-outcome, world is

$$V_c = \$50(1/2) - \$18.18 = \$25 - \$18.18 = \$6.82$$

which is the same result we got before.

Likewise, if a call option does not exist on an asset, we now have the knowledge necessary to create a homemade call option. All you do is purchase the asset and borrow against it to replicate the position that would exist if a call option actually existed on the asset.

An Alternative Way to Value Options

Consider one other aspect of our new-found knowledge about options. The value of the call option on Xelab is $6.82. What if the option did not sell for $6.82? Suppose, for example, it sold for $8? Then you can make a guaranteed profit with no risk simply by purchasing the stock, selling two call options, and borrowing $36.36. Likewise, if the call option sells for less than $6.82, you can make a guaranteed profit with no risk by selling the stock, buying two call options, and lending the balance of $36.36. This ability to profit is independent of your preference for risk. Remember the point we made earlier: No matter what your risk preferences, more volatility in the underlying asset is preferred because it leads to a higher option value. *The valuation of options does not depend on the risk preferences of individuals;* therefore, the simple assumption that all investors are risk-neutral can be made.

This last insight leads to an alternative way to value call options; this is the **risk-neutral** approach to option valuation. In our example, if the price of the option is either greater or less than $6.82, you can profit. The reason you profit is that if investors are risk-neutral, the expected return from investing in Xelab stock is equal to the risk-free rate of interest, k_{RF}. Thus, the expected return from investing in Xelab is 10 percent. If we know the expected return is 10 percent, we can determine the probability of an upward or downward movement in the price of the stock. An increase to $80 is a 60 percent increase in value [i.e., ($80/$50) − 1 = 0.60 = 60 percent] from the current market price of $50; a fall in price to $40 is a decrease of 20 percent [i.e., ($40/$50) − 1 = −0.20 = −20 percent]. Therefore, the expected return from investing in Xelab is

$$\text{Expected return} = \begin{pmatrix}\text{probability} \\ \text{of upward} \\ \text{movement}\end{pmatrix}\begin{pmatrix}\text{return from} \\ \text{an upward} \\ \text{movement}\end{pmatrix} + \begin{pmatrix}\text{probability} \\ \text{of downward} \\ \text{movement}\end{pmatrix}\begin{pmatrix}\text{return from} \\ \text{a downward} \\ \text{movement}\end{pmatrix}$$

$$10\% = (W)(60\%) + (1 - W)(-20\%)$$

Solving for W, the probability of an upward movement in the price of Xelab, we have

$$W = 30\%/80\% = 0.375$$

Thus, the probability of an upward movement in the price of Xelab to $80 is 0.375, while the probability of a downward movement to $40 is 1 − 0.375 = 0.625.[6]

Now that we know the probabilities of an upward movement, W, in the stock price, we can calculate the expected value of the call option on Xelab in this risk-neutral world. The expected value of the call option 1 year from now is

$$\text{expected value}_1 = (W)\begin{pmatrix}\text{call value if} \\ \text{stock price is } \$80\end{pmatrix} + (1 - W)\begin{pmatrix}\text{call value if} \\ \text{stock price is } \$40\end{pmatrix}$$

$$= (0.375)(\$20) + (0.625)(\$0) = \$7.50$$

This expected option value is 1 year hence. Therefore, it must be discounted back at 10 percent to determine the value of the call option today, which is

$$\text{value of call option, } V_c = \text{expected value}_1/(1 + k_{RF})$$
$$= \$7.50/(1 + 0.10) = \$6.82$$

which is exactly the value we determined previously.

[6] The general formula for determining the probability of an upward movement, W, is

$$\text{probability of upward movement, } W = \frac{\text{interest rate} - \% \text{ downward change}}{\% \text{ upward change} - \% \text{ downward change}}$$
$$= \frac{0.10 - (-0.20)}{0.60 - (-0.20)} = 0.375$$

The previous discussion indicates there are two equivalent methods for valuing a call option. These are:

1. Determine the combination of the asset and borrowing that replicates the call option. Because the call option and the levered position in the asset must produce the same return, the call option and the replicating portfolio sell for the same price.
2. Determine the expected future value of the option and then discount it back to the present.

While this binomial, or two-possible-outcome, case appears simple, it contains virtually all of the underlying ideas needed in order to understand options and their valuation.[7]

VALUING OPTIONS THAT HAVE MANY POSSIBLE OUTCOMES

The previous example of Xelab assumed there were only two possible outcomes, or stock prices, and they occurred 1 year from now. What if we looked at 6-month instead of 1-year intervals? Then there would be more outcomes; those for the second 6 months would be contingent on what happened in the first 6 months. There is no reason to stop at 6-month intervals—we could go to 3-month intervals, 1-month intervals, daily intervals, and even hourly intervals. Eventually we reach the place where prices change continuously and generate a continuous probability distribution of possible stock prices.

The Black-Scholes Option Pricing Model

Although it seems like a major task to value options when prices change continuously, it really is straightforward. The **Black-Scholes option pricing model** gives the correct expression for the value of European options on nondividend-paying stocks assuming continuous compounding. It consists of three equations. The primary one for valuing call options is

$$\text{value of call option, } V_c = P_0 N(d_1) - \frac{X}{e^{k_{RF}t}} N(d_2) \tag{5.3}$$

where

V_c = the value of the call option
P_0 = the current price of the stock
X = the exercise (or strike) price
t = time remaining before expiration of the option (expressed in decimal form as a portion of a year)
k_{RF} = continuously compounded risk-free rate of interest (in decimal form)

---

[7] The binomial model can be extended to more possible outcomes, with those in successive periods being contingent on what occurs in the earlier periods. The basic approach is similar to what we have shown. See, for example, Cox and Rubinstein, or Hull.

e = natural antilog of 1.00 or 2.71828

$N(d)$ = the probability that a standardized, normally distributed random variable will have a value less than or equal to d

The two subsidiary equations are

$$d_1 = \frac{\ln(P_0/X) + (k_{RF} + 0.5\sigma^2)t}{\sigma(t)^{0.5}}$$ (5.4)

$$d_2 = d_1 - \sigma(t)^{0.5}$$ (5.5)

where

$\ln(\ )$ = the natural logarithm of the number in parentheses[8]

σ = the standard deviation of the continuously compounded annual rate of return on the asset

Although Equation 5.3 looks complicated, it is simply a restated version of our replicating portfolio approach to valuing a two-outcome call option. Thus,

$$V_c = P_0\, N(d_1) - \frac{X}{e^{k_{RF}t}}\, N(d_2)$$

stock hedge | present value
price ratio | of loan

Equation 5.3 employs exactly the same ideas we used to value a call option when only two outcomes existed. To determine the value of a call option, Black and Scholes simply employed the knowledge that the value of a call option has to be equal to an equivalent portfolio where $N(d_1)$ shares of stock are purchased and then borrowed against. As we saw previously in Equation 5.2, the value of the call option and the value of the equivalent replicating portfolio are one-and-the-same.

Using the Black-Scholes Model

To understand how to use the Black-Scholes model, it is best to start with an example. Assume the data are as follows:

P_0 = $100 (current price of the stock)

X = $90 (exercise price)

t = 6 months, or 0.50 of a year (maturity of the option)

k_{RF} = 10 percent, or 0.10 continuously compounded (annual risk-free rate)

e = 2.71828 (natural antilog of 1.00)

σ = 28 percent, or 0.28 (risk on a continuously compounded annual basis)

[8] When using your calculator to determine option values, be sure to note that ln means the LN key, as opposed to e, which means the e^x key.

STEP 1:   Calculate d_1 and d_2, rounding the answers to three decimal places:

$$d_1 = \frac{\ln(P_0/X) + (k_{RF} + 0.5\sigma^2)t}{\sigma(t)^{0.5}}$$

$$= \frac{\ln(100/90) + [0.10 + 0.5(0.28)^2]0.50}{(0.28)(0.50)^{0.5}}$$

$$= \frac{0.1054 + 0.0696}{0.1980} = \frac{0.1750}{0.1980} = 0.884$$

$$d_2 = d_1 - \sigma(t)^{0.5} = 0.884 - 0.198 = 0.686$$

STEP 2:   Compute $N(d_1)$ and $N(d_2)$ using a cumulative normal distribution function table (Table B.5, at the end of the book). To use this table, locate the number closest to the value of d in the appropriate d column. In our case $d_1 = 0.884$, and the closest tabled value is for 0.88, which gives a value for $N(d_1)$ of 0.811. Similarly, $d_2 = 0.686$, and the closest tabled $N(d)$ value (for 0.69) is 0.755.

STEP 3:   Determine the value of the call option, V_c. This is done using the main equation (Equation 5.3) as follows:

$$V_c = P_0 N(d_1) - \frac{X}{e^{k_{RF}t}} N(d_2) = \$100(0.811) - \frac{\$90}{e^{(0.10)(0.50)}}(0.755)$$

$$= \$81.10 - \$64.64 = \$16.46$$

The value of this call option with 6 months to maturity is approximately $16.46.

In the Black-Scholes option pricing model, the value of an option on a nondividend-paying stock, or asset, is determined by the five variables discussed earlier: the current price of the asset, P_0; the stated exercise price, X; the current risk-free rate, k_{RF}; the time to expiration of the option, t; and the standard deviation of the asset, σ. When calculating options on stocks, we know the price, stated exercise price, and time to maturity. The current risk-free rate can be estimated based on the yield on U.S. Treasury bills with the same time to maturity as the option. The only unknown is the standard deviation of the stock price, for which a starting value is typically estimated by determining the past variability in the stock's return.[9]

The most difficult part of the option pricing model to understand is given by Equations 5.4 and 5.5. Once these calculations are made, they are then used to estimate probabilities of occurrence. This is exactly the part of the Black-Scholes model that takes account of risk.

The Black-Scholes model indicates that

$$V_c = P_0 N(d_1) - \frac{X}{e^{k_{RF}t}} N(d_2)$$

[9] An alternative approach is to determine the *implied* standard deviation. By taking the actual market price on a call option, say yesterday's quoted price, and inserting it into Equation 5.3, we know every variable except the standard deviation. The implied standard deviation necessary to produce the actual option price yesterday can then be determined. This procedure could be employed using data for some previous time period, or periods, to estimate the implied standard deviation. Then this implied standard deviation could be used to calculate today's market price for the call option.

The term $X/e^{k_{RF}t}$ is simply the present value of the exercise price when continuous discounting is employed. This means that the value of a call option is

$$V_c = P_0 N(d_1) - (\text{present value of } X) N(d_2)$$

The terms involving cumulative probabilities are the terms that take account of risk. If the stock had little or no risk (i.e., a very small standard deviation, σ), the calculated values for d_1 and d_2 would be large, and the probabilities would both approach the value of 1. If $N(d_1)$ and $N(d_2)$ both equal 1, then the option pricing model can be simplified to

$$V_c = P_0 - \text{present value of } X$$

which, as shown in Figures 5.3 and 5.4, is the lower bound on the value of a call option before the expiration date. (As always, if P_0 is less than the present value of X, then the option has a value of zero.) Thus, the expressions $N(d_1)$ and $N(d_2)$ capture the risk involved in the option. They are what cause the actual value of the option (as shown previously by the dashed lines in Figures 5.3 and 5.4) to be greater than the lower bound (i.e., the solid colored line).

To derive their model, Black and Scholes made a number of assumptions:

1. There are no transactions costs or taxes.
2. The risk-free rate is constant over the life of the option.
3. The stock market operates continuously (both day and night).
4. The stock price is continuous; that is, there are no sudden jumps in price.
5. The stock pays no cash dividends.
6. The option can be exercised only at the expiration date (i.e., it is a European option).
7. The underlying stock can be sold short without penalty.
8. The distribution of returns on the underlying stock is lognormal.

Although some evidence exists that indicates the Black-Scholes model tends to undervalue in-the-money options and overvalue out-of-the-money options, is it still a good predictor of actual option prices. Upon first acquaintance with the Black-Scholes option pricing model, many think it is too complicated to be useful. Nothing could be farther from the truth. The Black-Scholes option pricing model, and the binomial option pricing model, have gained wide acceptance for valuing all kinds of options.[10]

Shortcuts for Valuing Call Options

The Black-Scholes formula is precise, but it requires considerable calculation, as shown in the three-step procedure discussed earlier. However, if our objective is to determine an *approximate* value of an option, it is simpler to use tables. Consider the same example used earlier in which

$P_0 = \$100$ $k_{RF} = 0.10$

$X = \$90$ $\sigma = 0.28$

$t = 0.50$

---

[10] Other option pricing models exist. In practice, options that cannot be valued using the Black-Scholes model can often be valued by a more elaborate formulation of the binomial approach considered earlier.

A simple procedure can be employed to find the approximate value of this call option:

STEP 1: Calculate the standard deviation times the square root of time:

$$\sigma(t)^{0.5} = (0.28)(0.50)^{0.5} = 0.198$$

STEP 2: Calculate the market price divided by the present value of the exercise price:

$$\frac{P_0}{X/e^{k_{RF}t}} = \frac{\$100}{\$90/e^{(0.10)(0.50)}} = 1.168$$

STEP 3: Using the two values from steps 1 and 2, determine the tabled factor and multiply it by the share price.

Rounding to 0.20 for the standard deviation times the square root of time and to 1.16 for the market price divided by the present value of the exercise price, Table B.6 (in the back of the book) provides a value of 0.163. Multiplying the stock price of $100 by 0.163, we have the price of the call option, V_c, which is $16.30. This corresponds to the value of $16.46 determined earlier. Although use of these tables is not completely precise, it is close enough, because our emphasis is on understanding option pricing and valuation.

Concept Review Questions

- Describe the three factors related to the option contract and the two factors related to the underlying asset that affect the value of an option.
- Describe how to use the binomial option pricing model to price a call option.
- How are the Black-Scholes option pricing model and the binomial option pricing model similar?
- Describe the three steps used when pricing an option using the Black-Scholes option pricing model.

PUT OPTIONS

Up to now we have focused on call options, which are options to purchase. We also know that put options, which are the right, but not the obligation, to sell an underlying asset at a specific price for a predetermined period of time, also exist. The same five factors discussed previously for call options—the market price of the underlying asset, P; exercise (or strike) price, X; time to expiration, t; risk-free rate, k_{RF}; and standard deviation of the underlying asset's returns, σ—also affect the value of a put. The value of a put, V_p, *at maturity* is shown in Figure 5.5. As can be seen, the value of the put option at expiration is:

0   if P_0 is greater than X

$X - P_0$ if P_0 is less than X

Figure 5.5

The Value of a Put Option at Expiration

If the market price of the asset, P_0, is less than the exercise price, X, then the value of the option at expiration (as given by the 45° line) is $X - P_0$. Otherwise, the put is worthless.

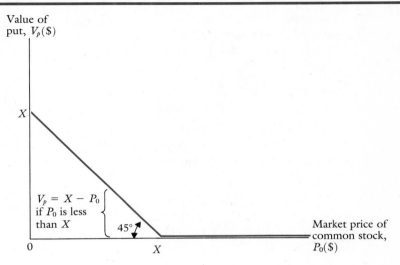

This is often written as

value of put option at expiration, $V_p = \text{Max}(0, X - P_0)$

Hence, for a put option the relationship is just the reverse of a call option. The put option has value only at its expiration date if the market price of the stock is *less* than the exercise price.

Although a put option is affected by the same five factors as a call option, the impact of an increase of each variable on the value of the put is somewhat different, as follows:

Variable	Effect of an Increase of Each Factor on V_P
Asset price, P_0	−
Exercise price, X	+
Time to expiration, t	either[11]
Risk-free rate, k_{RF}	−
Variability of asset's return, σ	+

[11] As t increases, normally V_p increases; but if the price of the underlying asset, P_0, is a good deal below the exercise price, X, then as t increases, V_p actually decreases.

Just like a call option, the actual value of a put option, V_p, will be above the lower limit depicted in Figure 5.5, except at its expiration date.

VALUING EUROPEAN PUT OPTIONS

European put options, like European call options, can be exercised only at maturity. Once you know the value of a call option with a specific exercise price, determining the value of a put option is easy.[12] It is given by

$$\text{value of put option, } V_p = V_c + \frac{X}{e^{kRFt}} - P_0 \tag{5.6}$$

where V_p is the value of the European put option, and the rest of the terms are as defined before. For our example, with a call option value of \$16.46, the value of a put option (with everything else the same) is

$$V_p = V_c + \frac{X}{e^{kRFt}} - P_0$$

$$= \$16.46 + \frac{\$90}{e^{(0.10)(0.50)}} - \$100 = \$16.46 + \$85.61 - \$100 = \$2.07$$

The reason for the relatively low value of the put option is the relationship of the market price of the stock to the exercise price. The call option can be exercised (i.e., has value) as long as the market price remains above the exercise price of \$90. However, this put option becomes valuable only if the current market price drops by more than \$10, so it is less than the exercise price of \$90. In our example, the market price of the common stock is above the exercise price; consequently, the put option is not very valuable.

SHORTCUTS FOR VALUING PUT OPTIONS

Instead of employing Equation 5.6 to value the put option, we can use Table B.7 (in the back of the book). From our earlier calculations, $\sigma(t)^{0.5} = 0.198$ while $P_0/(X \div e^{kRFt}) = 1.168$. Going to Table B.7, we find the tabled value is 0.025.

---

[12] The principle of the put-call parity states that the value of a call option, plus the present value of the exercise price, equals the value of the put option plus the market price of the underlying asset, or

$$V_c + \frac{X}{e^{kRFt}} = V_p + P_0$$

Therefore,

$$V_p = V_c + \frac{X}{e^{kRFt}} - P_0$$

Multiplying by the market price of $100 produces $2.50, which compares closely with the $2.07 calculated earlier.[13]

Throughout our discussion of options and their valuation, we have considered options that are written on the common stock of a firm. However, options exist in many forms; often the underlying asset is not common stock. Thus, the underlying asset could be crude oil, gold, the German mark, or one of many other assets. Hence, the ideas and application are general and are applied in many different settings. We will explore a number of these applications as we proceed. Now, though, we want to show how the claim held by the owners of a firm, in the form of owning common stock in the firm, is nothing more than a call option written on the assets of the firm.

Concept Review Questions

- What is a put option, and when is it valuable upon expiration?
- Describe how the value of a put option and the value of a call option are related.

STOCK IS JUST A CALL OPTION

In Chapter 3 we considered how to value both bonds and stock based on the present value of their future cash flows. Although this approach is widely used, it has one major shortcoming—it fails to consider the simultaneous interaction between the value of a firm's stock and its bonds. Using the knowledge we just acquired about valuing options, we can value the financial claims on a firm *and* take account of the interaction between the value of the firm's stock and its debt.

In a very informal way in Chapter 1 we employed option concepts to depict the value of the claims of both stockholders and bondholders on the firm. This representation is shown in Figure 5.6. The claim, or payoff, for the stockholders at the maturity of the debt is simply a call option, as shown in Figure 5.6 (a). The bondholders, on

---

[13] We can also value European options on dividend-paying stocks. If only one known cash dividend is expected to be paid before the expiration of the option, the equations are

$$V_c^\star = \left(P_0 - \frac{D}{e^{k_{RF}t^\star}} \right) N(d_1) - \frac{X}{e^{k_{RF}t}} N(d_2)$$

and

$$V_p^\star = V_c^\star + \frac{X}{e^{k_{RF}t}} - P_0 + \frac{D}{e^{k_{RF}t^\star}}$$

where

D = the cash dividend that will be paid before the expiration date

$t^\star$ = the time (in decimal form) in years until the dividend is expected to be paid

and the other terms are as defined before. If more than one cash dividend is expected before the expiration of the option, then the expression $D/e^{k_{RF}t^\star}$ must be modified to reflect the present value of all known dividends to be paid before expiration of the option. Cash dividends tend to reduce the value of call options and to increase the value of put options.

Figure 5.6

The Payoff to Stockholders and Bondholders

Stockholders have a call option on the assets of the firm. At the maturity of the debt, if the value of the assets is greater than the bondholder claims, stockholders will pay off the bondholders and claim the remaining value of the firm.

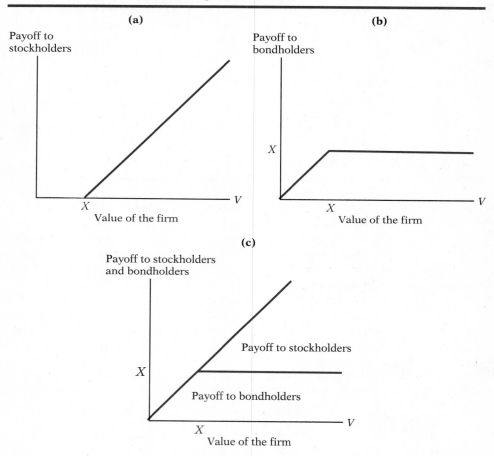

the other hand, provide long-term debt financing for the firm. Suppose the bondholders lend the firm money that *at its maturity date* is worth X amount of dollars. As shown in Figure 5.6 (b), the bondholders have a fixed, but limited, claim on the assets and value of the firm. If the value of the firm, V, is greater than the bondholders' claim when the debt matures, the debt will be paid off and the stockholders gain control of the remaining assets of the firm. The dual claims of both stockholders and bondholders on the firm are shown in Figure 5.6 (c). The total value of the firm, V, is simply the sum of stockholders' claims, S, and bondholders' claims, B, or

total value of firm = stockholders' claims + bondholders' claims (5.7)

$$V = S + B$$

Let's now develop these ideas in a more formal way, using the Black-Scholes option pricing model. To keep things clear, it helps to restate what calls, the current stock price, puts, and the exercise price are, once we consider valuing the joint claims of stockholders and bondholders on the firm. Thus,

Value of Calls and Puts	→ Becomes Value of Equity and Debt
V_c	S: the market value of the equity claims on the firm
P_0	V: value of the firm's assets
V_p	Default option: the value of the limited liability of stockholders; that is, the value of the stockholders' right to walk away from the debt of the firm and hand the firm over to the creditors.
$\dfrac{X}{e^{k_{RF}t}}$	B (riskless): the present value of the promised payments to zero-coupon[14] bondholders, discounted at the risk-free rate; the value of the bonds if there is no risk of default.

When we are valuing the claims of both stockholders and bondholders, the stockholders' claim, S, is simply a call option on the value of the firm, V, so

stockholders' claim, S = call option on firm value

$$= \text{total value of firm} - \text{bondholders' claim}$$

$$= V - B$$

So far this is just a restatement of Equation 5.7. However, in an option pricing context, two separate items exist in place of the single risky claim of the bondholders, B. The first is equivalent to the risk-free present value of the exercise price. This value is what the bondholders' claim is worth *if* there were no risk that the stockholders might default and turn the firm over to the bondholders. The second is the default, or put option, held by the stockholders. Due to limited liability, if the firm gets into serious financial difficulties, the stockholders have the option to walk away from the firm and turn it and all of its remaining assets and liabilities over to the creditors. Thus, the risky bondholders' claim, B, is equal to their riskless claim minus the default option which lowers the value of their riskless bonds, so that

bondholders' risky claim, B = bondholders' riskless claim − default option

$$B = B(\text{riskless}) - \text{default option} \tag{5.8}$$

[14] Zero-coupon bonds do not pay periodic interest. Instead they are issued at a discount (from the par value, which is typically $1,000 per bond). The total interest is simply the difference between their issuance price and their par, or maturity, value. Zero-coupon bonds are considered in more detail in Chapter 16.

Putting this all together, we see that the stockholders' claim is simply

stockholders' claim, $S = V - B(\text{riskless}) + \text{default option}$ \hfill (5.9)

In effect, the stockholders have bought the firm's assets, borrowed the present value of the bondholders' riskless claims on the firm, and bought a put (or default) option that allows them to walk away from the firm and give it to the bondholders. The default option can be thought of as a loan guarantee that eliminates default risk for the stockholders.

Similarly, the market value of the risky bondholders' claim on the firm, B, may be determined by using either Equation 5.7:

bondholders' risky claim, $B = V - S$

or Equation 5.8:

bondholders' risky claim, $B = B(\text{riskless}) - \text{default option}$

From the bondholders' standpoint, the value of the put (default) option can be thought of as a *default risk discount* that bondholders apply to the current market value of the firm's riskless debt.

JOINT VALUATION OF EQUITY AND DEBT

An example might be helpful at this point. Zeffers, a well-known chemical firm, has a total market value, V, of $500; it has $400 face value of 8-year zero-coupon bonds; the risk-free rate is 0.12; and the annual standard deviation of Zeffers' assets is 0.40. What is the value of the stockholders' claim on Zeffers? What is the value of the bondholders' risky claim on Zeffers? And what is the value of the default option held by the stockholders?

To determine the value of the stockholders' claim we first need[15] d_1 and d_2. They are

$$d_1 = \frac{\ln(V/\text{face value of bonds}) + (k_{RF} + 0.5\sigma^2)t}{\sigma(t)^{0.5}}$$

$$= \frac{\ln(500/400) + [0.12 + 0.5(0.40)^2]8}{0.40(8)^{0.5}}$$

$$= \frac{0.2231 + 1.600}{1.1314} = \frac{1.8231}{1.1314} = 1.611$$

$$d_2 = d_1 - \sigma(t)^{0.5} = 1.611 - 1.131 = 0.480$$

[15] Although Table B.6 could be employed, in this example we use Table B.5 for slightly greater precision.

From Table B.5, the cumulative distribution table, $N(d_1)$ is 0.946 and $N(d_2)$ is 0.684. The value of the stock is

$$S = VN(d_1) - \frac{\text{face value of debt}}{e^{kRFt}} N(d_2)$$

$$= \$500(0.946) - \frac{\$400}{e^{(0.12)(8)}}(0.684)$$

$$= \$473.00 - \$104.76 = \$368.24$$

Because the total value of Zeffers is $500, the stockholders' claim of $368.24 is equal to about 74 percent of the total value of the firm.

Once we know the total value of the firm, which is $500, and the value of the stockholders' claim, which is $368.24, we can determine the value of Zeffers' bondholders' risky claim. This is,

$$B = V - S = \$500 - \$368.24 = \$131.76$$

In order to determine the value of the default (or put) option, we need to determine the value of the riskless claim held by bondholders on the firm. Assuming continuous discounting, the present value of the zero-coupon bonds is equal to

$$B(\text{riskless}) = \frac{\$400}{e^{kRFt}} = \frac{\$400}{e^{(0.12)(8)}} = \$153.16$$

Thus, if there was no risk of the stockholders defaulting and not paying off the bonds when they mature, the zero-coupon bonds would be worth $153.16. Using Equation 5.8, we find that the default option is

$$B = B(\text{riskless}) - \text{default option}$$
$$\$131.76 = \$153.16 - \text{default option}$$
$$\text{default option} = \$153.16 - \$131.76 = \$21.40$$

The default, or put, option held by Zeffers' stockholders has some value, but because the likelihood of severe financial difficulty (as shown by a large standard deviation) is not great, the option's value is limited.

Viewing the claims of stockholders and bondholders in an option context provides a number of important insights. Because stock is simply a call option on the firm's assets, we know that, other things being equal, the equity will become *more* valuable as:

1. The value of the firm's assets increases.
2. The size of the debt claim (i.e., the exercise price) decreases.
3. The maturity of the debt increases.
4. Interest rates increase.
5. The volatility of the firm's assets increases.

Similarly, viewing the value of a bond in an option pricing framework indicates that, other things again being equal, the value of the bondholders' risky holding (i.e., B) will become *less* valuable when:

1. The value of the firm's assets decreases.
2. The promised payment (or size of the claim) decreases.[16]
3. The maturity of the debt grows longer.[17]
4. Interest rates increase.[18]
5. The volatility of the firm's assets increases.

To understand the effect on the claims of both stockholders and bondholders, consider a change in one of the variables that affects the value of call and put options—the volatility of the underlying asset.

WHAT IF RISK CHANGES?

With the sudden and unexpected death of Zeffers' founder, control has passed to the heirs, Sabestin and Dorothy. Being tired of the chemical business, they have just sold off over half of the existing firm and acquired two biotech firms. Although the value of the firm's assets and the amount and maturity of its debt remain the same, the restructuring has resulted in more risk, as reflected in the more-than-doubling of the standard deviation of the firm's assets. Whereas it was 0.40, it is now 0.85. Who wins and who loses with this restructuring?

Without making any calculations, we know that the stock of Zeffers is just a call option. Like any call option, more risk is desirable; that is, increases in risk result in a higher value for the owner of a call option. Thus, the stockholders should benefit from this restructuring. Who loses? Because the total value of the firm is unchanged (at least for the present), Zeffers' bondholders must lose. With no change in the value of the firm, the only way stockholders can benefit is if there is a transfer of value from Zeffers' bondholders to its stockholders.

To make sure our intuition is correct, let's determine the effect of the restructuring. Again, we need d_1 and d_2, which are now:

$$d_1 = \frac{\ln(500/400) + [0.12 + 0.5(0.85)^2]8}{0.85(8)^{0.5}}$$

$$= \frac{0.2231 + 3.8500}{2.4042} = \frac{4.0731}{2.4042} = 1.694$$

$$d_2 = 1.694 - 2.404 = -0.710$$

---

[16] If the promised payment (or exercise price) decreases, the present value of the zero-coupon bond, B(riskless), decreases. This effect has to be considered along with the change in the value of the put option when the value of the risky bond claim, B, is valued.

[17] Similar to reducing the exercise price, lengthening the maturity decreases the present value of the zero-coupon bond.

[18] Like reducing the exercise price and lengthening the maturity, raising the interest rate reduces the present value of the zero-coupon bond.

From Table B.5, $N(d_1)$ is 0.954 and $N(d_2)$ is 0.239. The value of Zeffers' stock is now

$$S = \$500(0.954) - \frac{\$400}{e^{(0.12)(8)}}(0.239)$$

$$= \$477.00 - \$36.60 = \$440.40$$

The new value of Zeffers bondholders' risky claim is

$$B = V - S = \$500 - \$440.40 = \$59.60$$

and the default option held by the stockholders is

$$\text{default option} = \$153.16 - \$59.60 = \$93.56$$

The effects are as follows:

Party/Claim	Value when $\sigma = 0.40$	Value when $\sigma = 0.85$	Who wins/loses?
Stockholders	$368.24	$440.40	Gain of $72.16
Bondholders	131.76	59.60	Loss of $72.16
Default option	21.40	93.56	Gain of $72.16

The restructuring clearly benefited the stockholders, while the bondholders lost; value flowed away from the bondholders and toward the stockholders. The default, or put, option is also much more valuable. With the much higher level of risk, the likelihood of default has increased. If things take a turn for the worse, the limited liability feature of stock ownership is now more valuable than it was previously.

The message from viewing the stockholders' and bondholders' claims in an option framework is clear: *Unless additional value is created, the gains to one party (owners or creditors) come from losses incurred by the other party (creditors or owners).* A corollary to this conclusion is: *Value creation comes from making positive net present value investment decisions; restructuring or simply reacting to changing economic conditions is likely to shift value from one party to the other but not create value.*

STOCKHOLDER-BONDHOLDER AGENCY ISSUES

Agency problems (i.e., conflicts between individuals acting in their own self-interests) arise between bondholders and stockholders, just as they do between stockholders and managers as discussed in Chapter 1. In the previous example, Zeffers' stockholders benefited at the expense of the firms' bondholders due to the *unanticipated* change in the composition of the firm's assets. Conflicts may also arise due to underinvestment in positive net present value projects, if firms issue new bonds that have a prior claim over already outstanding debt issued by the firm, or if a large increase in cash dividends paid to stockholders occurs.

To protect themselves, bond investors normally recognize these possible occurrences and demand higher compensation (in the form of a higher interest rate) before investing in bonds. In addition, as discussed in Chapters 12 and 16, covenants are included in bonds to constrain firms from engaging in some activities that would be detrimental to the bondholders. The option pricing approach, by allowing us to examine the simultaneous impact on the claims of both stockholders and bondholders, facilitates our ability to examine possible sources of conflict between a firm's providers of capital. These conflicts will be discussed in more detail as we proceed.

ONE FINAL POINT

Those of you who have been reading very carefully might have noticed a possible inconsistency between our earlier discussion in Chapter 4 and the discussion in this chapter. In Chapter 4, when viewed in the context of the dividend valuation model and the capital asset pricing model (see the section entitled "Changes in Risk and Prices"), we said that, other things being equal, as risk increases the market price of common stock decreases. Yet in the Zeffers example just discussed, when viewed in the option pricing model context, *increases in risk increased the value of the stockholders' claim, and hence the price of common stock.* Which is correct?

In answering this question, it is important to keep two points in mind. First, the option pricing model simultaneously values both the stockholder and the bondholder claims, whereas the dividend valuation/CAPM approach focuses solely on the equity of the firm. Second, and more important to the current discussion, is the statement "other things being equal." Zeffers sold off half of its existing assets and used the proceeds to acquire two biotech firms. While risk (in the form of the standard deviation of the firm's assets) more than doubled, Zeffers' expected growth would also be expected to increase due to the nature of the biotech industry. To illustrate why there may be no inconsistency, assume that the following conditions existed for Zeffers before the acquisition of the biotech firms:

$$k_{RF} = 8\% \qquad g = 3\%$$
$$k_M = 15\% \qquad D_1 = \$2$$
$$\beta = 0.90$$

Given this information, we can use the captal asset pricing model to estimate the stockholders' required return, k_s, as

$$k_s = k_{RF} + \beta(k_M - k_{RF}) = 8\% + 0.90(15\% - 8\%) = 14.3\%$$

The price of Zeffers' stock before the acquisition of the biotech firms was

$$P_0 = \frac{D_1}{k_s - g} = \frac{\$2}{0.143 - 0.03} \approx \$17.70$$

What might have happened with the asset change? Suppose that β increased to 1.20 and the growth rate increased to 6 percent. Then the new required return would be

$$k_s \text{ (new)} = 8\% + 1.20(15\% - 8\%) = 16.4\%$$

and the new market price would be

$$P_0 \text{ (new)} = \frac{\$2}{0.164 - 0.06} \approx \$19.23$$

Because *other things did not stay constant* (i.e., the growth rate, g, increased), there is no conflict between the prediction from the option pricing model and the dividend valuation/CAPM approach from Chapter 4. The lesson is simple: Use common sense, and make sure you don't miss something obvious by blindly applying financial models. The models we present throughout the book are just a convenient means of organizing our thought processes—and encouraging us to ask the right questions at the right time when making financial decisions. As such, financial models are a means to an end, rather than an end in themselves.

Concept Review Questions

- Using the concept of options, describe the pricing of a firm's stock and bonds.
- Using an option pricing context describe what would happen to the value of stockholders' and bondholders' claims if the overall risk of a firm decreases.
- Comment on the following statement: The value of a firm can be increased by simply restructuring the firm.
- Does an inconsistency exist between the capital asset pricing model and the option pricing model when analyzing the relationship between a stock price and the risk of a firm?

KEY POINTS

1. Options provide the right, but not the obligation, to buy (a call option) or sell (a put option) a particular asset for a limited time at a specified price.
2. An in-the-money option has value if exercised at maturity; an out-of-the-money option has no value if exercised.
3. Options are created, or sold, by investors, investment banking firms, and the like. Other things being equal, the seller and the buyer are playing a zero-sum game; the profit (loss) to one party equals the loss (profit) to the other.
4. The value of an option on a nondividend-paying stock, or asset, is a function of: (a) the price of the underlying asset, (b) the exercise price, (c) the time to expiration, (d) the risk-free rate, and (e) the variability of the underlying asset.
5. Risk preferences are not important in valuing options. Any increase in the variability of the returns on the underlying asset leads to an increase in the price of the option.
6. Both the binomial and the Black-Scholes models can be employed to value options. In either case the value of a call option = (the asset's price)(hedge ratio) − the present value of a loan (on the underlying asset).
7. The value of stockholder claims and bondholder claims on the firm may be considered simultaneously using option pricing techniques.
8. Option concepts show that, in effect, the stockholders have bought the firm's assets, borrowed the present value of the bondholders' claims on the firm, and also bought a put (or default) option that allows them to walk away from the firm and give it to the bondholders. This default option arises because stockholders have limited liability.

9. Viewing the firm in an option pricing context indicates that unless actions are undertaken that create additional value for the firm, gains to one party (owners or creditors) come from losses incurred by the other party (creditors or owners).
10. Firms create value by making positive net present value investment decisions; restructuring or simply reacting to changing economic conditions is likely to shift value from stockholders to bondholders, or vice versa, but not create value.
11. Agency problems arise between stockholders and bondholders primarily due to (a) asset-substitution issues (in which high-risk projects are substituted for low-risk projects), (b) underinvestment in capital investments, (c) issuing additional debt, which results in claim dilution, and (d) substantial changes in the firm's cash dividend policy. To protect themselves, bondholders require higher interest rates and expect covenants to be placed in bond agreements that limit the firm's ability to undertake actions detrimental to bondholders.

QUESTIONS

5.1   What determines the lower limit on the value of a call option at expiration? Before expiration?

5.2   What incentives are there for buyers to purchase options and for writers to sell options? How does the premium enter into their decision process?

5.3   What five factors affect the value of a call option? How would a decrease in their level, other things being equal, affect the value of a call option?

5.4   Explain why risk is desirable when investing in options. How do the terms $N(d_1)$ and $N(d_2)$ capture this risk?

5.5   Discuss replicating portfolios and the hedge ratio. How do they enter into the valuation of call options when there are two possible outcomes? When there are many possible outcomes?

5.6   How do puts differ from calls? Why is a decrease in the market price of the underlying asset desirable if you hold a put option, but not desirable if you hold a call option?

5.7   Explain how an increase in any of the five factors determining a put option's value affects the value of the put option.

5.8   How do cash dividends affect the value of a call option? A put option?

5.9   Jerome argues that options on stocks can and do exist but that stock cannot be viewed as an option. Set Jerome straight. Be sure to mention limited liability and its impact.

5.10   Strous Brothers has both common stock and zero-coupon debt outstanding. What impact will each of the follow have on the market value of Strous' common stock and its debt? (Assume each part is independent of other parts and that "other things remain unchanged.")

a. Interest rates fall.
b. Strous retires its existing debt and issues an equal amount of longer-term debt.
c. It uses cash to acquire assets that are more risky than the firm's existing assets.
d. Strous issues more stock to retire some of its debt.
e. Unexpectedly, Strous received patent protection on two of its major products.

5.11   Agency issues exist between stockholders and bondholders. Explain the major causes of agency problems, and what bondholders (and other creditors) do in the presence of agency issues.

CONCEPT REVIEW PROBLEMS

See Appendix A for solutions.

CR5.1   Attempting to make a quick profit, Jana paid $300 for a call option on 100 shares of Texas stock with an exercise price of $55.00; she also paid $200 for a put option on 100 shares of BM stock with an exercise price of $60.00 per share. What is Jana's total dollar profit if at the expiration date Texas stock closed at $54 per share and BM stock closed at $49 per share?

CR5.2   Tyco Company has a current stock price of $60 per share. Because of potentially profitable but risky capital budgeting decisions, the company's stock price will (with equal probability) either increase to $90 per share or drop to $50 per share at the end of one year. The cost of borrowing is 8 percent. Using the replicating portfolio approach, find the price of a call option for 100 shares of Tyco stock.

CR5.3   Using the risk-neutral approach to option valuation, value the option in CR5.2.

CR5.4   Xerox's current stock price is $85 with a 0.30 instantaneous standard deviation of returns. The current 9-month risk-free rate is 6 percent. Using the Black-Scholes model, what is the value of a 9-month call option with an exercise price of $90?

CR5.5   Using the information in CR5.4, what is the price of a put option with an exercise price of $90 and 9 months to expiration?

CR5.6   The Fisher-Myron Corp. has a total market value of $20 million. The firm has $12 million in face value of zero-coupon debt with a maturity of 10 years. The annual standard deviation is 0.36. If the risk-free rate of return is 8 percent, what is:

a.   The value of stockholders' claim on Fisher-Myron?
b.   The value of the bondholders' risky claim?
c.   The value of the default option?

CR5.7   Fisher-Myron Corporation from CR5.6, is considering restructuring. The firm will issue $32 billion in 15-year zero-coupon bonds, buy back the $12 billion in 10-year zero-coupon bonds, and use the approximately $3 billion difference to repurchase stock. The standard deviation of the firm's assets is unchanged at 0.36, while the yield to maturity on the 10- and 15-year zero-coupon bonds is 10 percent. After this restructuring, what is the stockholders' value and the bondholders' value?

PROBLEMS

5.1   Prices for Digital Equipment's options (which are traded on the American Stock Exchange) appeared as follows in *The Wall Street Journal*:

Option/Strike			Vol	Exch	Last	Net Chg	a-close	Open Int
DigEq	Feb 40		73	AM	3 5/8	+1/2	43 5/8	2,613
DigEq	Feb 40	p	96	AM	5/16	−1/4	43 5/8	2,579
DigEq	Mar 40	p	354	AM	13/16	−3/8	43 5/8	905
DigEq	Apr 40		97	AM	5	+3/4	43 5/8	2,803
DigEq	Apr 40	p	162	AM	1 3/8	−1/2	43 5/8	3,121
DigEq	Jul 40	p	45	AM	2 3/8	−1/2	43 5/8	800
DigEq	Feb 45		207	AM	13/16	+1/8	43 5/8	3,780
DigEq	Mar 45		112	AM	1 3/4	+3/8	43 5/8	1,767
DigEq	Apr 45		74	AM	2 5/16	+5/16	43 5/8	3,051

a. For April calls, explain why the call price decreases as the exercise price increases. Would you expect the price of a put option to increase or decrease as the exercise price increases? Why?
b. For both calls and puts, explain why the option price increases as the maturity increases.
c. What other factors influence option values? In what direction?

5.2   A 1-year option exists with an exercise price of $100. The current price of the stock is $80, and the two possible equally likely outcomes for the stock price at the end of the year are $120 or $60. The risk-free rate is 8 percent.

a. Using the replicating portfolio approach, determine the value of the option. What is the hedge ratio? What does the hedge ratio signify?
b. Now using the risk-neutral approach, determine the probability that the stock will increase in price (or decrease in price). Now determine the value of the option using the risk-neutral approach.
c. Why is the value of the option the same using either the replicating portfolio approach or the risk-neutral approach?

5.3   You just purchased a call option on a stock. The two possible equally likely outcomes in 1 year are $150 and $75, the exercise price is $100, and the current market price is $90. What is the value of the call option if the risk-free rate is

a. 12 percent?
b. 6 percent?

5.4   An option exists that has two equally likely outcomes in 1 year of $98 and $44. The current market price is $65, and the risk-free rate is 7 percent. What is the value of the call option, assuming everything else is equal, if the exercise price is

a. $70?
b. $60?

5.5   The current market price of Erie Trucking is $60, the exercise price is $65, the risk-free rate is 10 percent, and the two possible equally likely stock prices of Erie's common stock in 1 year are $95 and $35. What is the value of a call option on Erie's stock if

a. The prices are at $t = 1$?
b. The prices are at $t = 2$?

5.6   The common stock of Martin is selling at $80.

a. If the exercise price is $70, $k_{RF} = 0.12$, and $\sigma = 0.26$, what is the value of (1) a 3-month call option and (2) a 6-month call option?
b. If the common stock price remains at $80, k_{RF} at 0.12, and σ at 0.26, what is the value of a *3-month* call option on Martin if the exercise price is (1) $60 or (2) $80?

5.7   The current market price of a share of stock is $50. A 3-month call option exists on the stock with an exercise price of $55; the standard deviation is 0.40.

a. What is the value of the call option if the risk-free rate is (1) 0.15 or (2) 0.05? Why does the value of the call option decline as interest rate fall?
b. What is the value of the call if the risk-free rate is 0.15 and everything is the same as before except the standard deviation increases to 0.60?

5.8   The base case for Hercules Ground is as follows:

$P_0 = \$34 \qquad t = 0.60$

$X = \$30 \qquad \sigma = 0.20$

$k_{RF} = 0.10$

a.   Calculate the base case value of a call option on Hercules Ground.

b.   Calculate the value of a call option on Hercules Ground if the price increases by 50 percent. Do the same if each variable (i.e., X, k_{RF}, t, and σ) increases by 50 percent *while the rest* of the variables remain as in (a). To which variable is the call price of Hercules Ground most sensitive to a 50 percent increase? Least sensitive?

c.   What is the value of the call option if all the variables in (a) *simultaneously* increase by 50 percent?

5.9   The common stock of Michelson Mutual is selling at $50.

a.   What is the value of a 3-month put option on Michelson if the risk-free rate is 0.08, a similar call option is valued at $2, and the exercise price is $60?

b.   What is the value of the put option if everything remains the same as in (a), except the risk-free rate increases to 0.16, causing the call option's value to become $2.27?

c.   What if everything is the same as in (a), except the current stock price is $45, causing the call option's value to become $0.86?

5.10   The following applies for a call option:

$P_0 = \$35 \qquad t = 0.65$

$X = \$40 \qquad \sigma = 0.20$

$k_{RF} = 0.11$

a.   Determine the value of a call option on the stock.

b.   What is the value of a put option?

c.   What is the value of the call option if the time to maturity drops to 0.30?

5.11   A stock sells for $70, the exercise price is $80, the time to maturity is 0.40, the risk-free rate is 0.09, and the standard deviation is 0.30.

a.   What is the value of a call option on the stock?

b.   What is the value of a put option?

c.   If the market price of the stock increases to $85, what is the value of **(1)** the call option? **(2)** Of the put option?

5.12   Jordan Enterprises common stock has a current market value of $55. An option that will expire in 150 days exists. The risk-free rate is 8 percent, the exercise price is $75, and the standard deviation of Jordan's common stock returns is 0.90. (*Note:* Assume a 365-day year.)

a.   What is the value of a call option on the stock?

b.   What is the value of a put option?

c.   The Federal Reserve system just took action that unexpectedly increased interest rates to 15 percent. What is the new value of the call option? Of the put option?

5.13 In celebration of your birthday, your best friend gave you an option that expires in 6 months on 100 shares of Westerfield's common stock. Westerfield's, a very stable firm, is selling for $32, the exercise price is $25, the risk-free rate is 7 percent, and the standard deviation of Westerfield's stock returns is 0.25.

a. Do you have a strong preference whether the option is a call or a put? Why? What is the value of the call? The put?

b. Now assume that Westerfield's pays cash dividends. Without working it out, indicate why you are better off when cash dividends are paid in one case (the call or the put) whereas you are not better off in the other (i.e., the put or the call).

5.14 Hyper is a risky stock that just started paying cash dividends. The stock's price is $60, the exercise price is $55, the risk-free rate is 0.14, σ is 0.80, and the maturity of the option is 0.40 of a year. The next cash dividend will be $1 and will be paid in 0.20 of a year.

a. What is the value of a call option on Hyper (**1**) without cash dividends and (**2**) with cash dividends? (*Note:* See footnote 13 for the proper equations when cash dividends are present.)

b. What is the value of a put option on Hyper (**1**) without and (**2**) with cash dividends?

5.15 A firm has $40 million in outstanding zero-coupon debt that matures in 4 years. The market value of the firm's assets is $60 million, the standard deviation is 0.60, and the risk-free rate is 0.14.

a. What is the value of the firm's stock? Of its debt?

b. What is the value of the default option?

5.16 Bagamery has $1,000 in zero-coupon bonds outstanding that mature in 5 years. The market value of Bagamery's assets is $1,400, the standard deviation is 0.40, and the risk-free rate is 0.08.

a. What is the value of Bagamery's stock, debt, and the default option held by the stock-holders?

b. Now assume that everything stays the same as in (a) except that unexpected inflation increases the risk-free rate to 0.13. What is the new value of Bagamery's stock, debt, and the default option? Explain your results.

c. Finally, assume that everything is the same as in (a) except that the standard deviation of the assets is reduced to 0.25 from 0.40. What is the new value of Bagamery's stock, debt, and the default option? Explain your results.

5.17 Silversheet has a market value of assets of $100. It has $90 in 6-year zero-coupon bonds outstanding, the risk-free rate is 10 percent, and the standard deviation of the firm's assets is 0.45.

a. What is the value of the stockholders' claim? Of the bondholders' claim?

b. In order to finance a new project that will raise the market value of Silversheet's assets to $150, the firm plans to issue *an additional* $91.10 in 6-year zero-coupon debt. What is the new value of the stockholders' claim? Of the bondholders' claim?

c. Comparing your answers to (a) and (b), how much of the total gain was claimed by the stockholders? By the bondholders? Explain.

5.18   Your firm is considering two new product lines. Product 1 is fairly certain and may result in a market value of the firm's assets as high as $80 million or as low as $60 million in 2 years. Product 2 is much more risky and may result in a market value for the firm of either $200 million or $0. Assume the outcomes for each product are equally likely and the firm's $40 million zero-coupon bonds mature in 2 years.

a.   What are the possible outcomes for the stockholders from the two products?
b.   What are the possible outcomes for the bondholders?
c.   Which product would the stockholders favor? The bondholders? Explain.

5.19   Mini Case   You have been hired by Century Resources to conduct a seminar on options. In order to do so you have been told to assume that they know little or nothing about options. Therefore some combination of discussion and problems is appropriate.

a.   Explain what options are. Be sure to differentiate between call and put options and between American and European options. Also, what do in-the-money and out-of-the-money mean with respect to call options and put options?
b.   Discuss the factors that determine the value of any option. What specific effect do they have on the value of a call option? Of a put option? What about cash dividends on the stock if an option exists on that stock?
c.   To introduce options you will employ the binomial option pricing model. Suppose a stock has a current market price of $40 and at the end on one year its price may with equal likelihood increase to $65 or decrease to $25. The exercise price is $45, and the risk-free rate of interest is 9 percent. Show how the value of the option can be determined, using first the replicating portfolio approach and then the risk-neutral approach. Be sure to indicate to the seminar participants the hedge ratio and its importance in the replicating portfolio approach.
d.   Explain how the Black-Scholes option pricing model is similar to the replicating portfolio approach employed to value the stock in (c). What variables are known, and what variables have to be estimated to employ the Black-Scholes model? What about an individual's attitude toward risk?
e.   The following information has been gathered about a stock: The current market price is $65, the exercise price is $75, the time to maturity is 6 months (or 0.50 of a year), the risk-free rate is 9 percent, and the standard deviation is 0.55. What is the value of a call option on the stock? Of a put option?
f.   What is the value of the call option from (e) if everything remains the same except: (*Note:* Consider each part separately).

   (1)   The current market price is $55?
   (2)   The exercise price is $65?
   (3)   The maturity is 3 months?
   (4)   The risk-free rate is 5 percent?
   (5)   The standard deviation is 0.30?

g.   Explain what is meant by the statement "Stock is just a call option." What role does limited liability play? What is the value of the debt of a firm?
h.   Show how to value the stock and bonds of a firm if the value of the firm's assets is $2,000, the firm has $1,500 of 4-year zero-coupon bonds outstanding, the risk-free rate is 7 percent, and the standard deviation of the firm's assets is 0.45. What is the value of the default, or put, option?

REFERENCES

For a discussion of option pricing models, see:

BLACK, FISCHER, and MYRON SCHOLES. "The Pricing of Options and Corporate Liabilities." *Journal of Political Economy* 83 (May-June 1973): 637–54.

BUNCH, DAVID S., and HERB JOHNSON. "A Simple and Numerically Efficient Valuation Method for American Puts Using a Modified Geske-Johnson Approach." *Journal of Finance* 47 (June 1992): 809–16.

COX, JOHN, and MARK RUBINSTEIN. *Options Markets.* Englewood Cliffs, N.J.: Prentice-Hall, 1985.

HULL, JOHN C. *Options, Futures, and Other Derivative Securities.* 2nd. ed. Englewood Cliffs, NJ: Prentice-Hall, 1993.

JOHNSON, HERB, and DAVID SHANNO. "Option Pricing When the Variance Is Changing." *Journal of Financial and Quantitative Analysis* 22 (June 1987): 143–51.

Some discussion of the use of option pricing model in financial management is contained in:

KESTER, W. CARL. "An Options Approach to Corporate Finance." In *Handbook of Corporate Finance.* Edited by E. Altman. New York: Wiley, 1986. Pp. 5.1–5.35.

MASON, SCOTT, P., and ROBERT C. MERTON. "The Role of Contingent Claims in Corporate Finance." In *Recent Advances in Corporate Finance.* Edited by Edward I. Altman and Marti G. Subrahmanyam. Homewood, Il.: Richard D. Irwin, 1985. Pp. 7–54.

SMITH, CLIFFORD W., JR. "Applications of Option Pricing Analysis." In *The Modern Theory of Corporate Finance,* 2nd ed. Edited by Clifford W. Smith, Jr. New York: McGraw-Hill, 1990. Pp. 345–87.

Long-Term Investment Decisions

EXECUTIVE INTERVIEW

James M. Cornelius
Vice President, Chief
Financial Officer,
and Treasurer
Eli Lilly and Company

Eli Lilly is a research-based pharmaceutical and health care products corporation. We asked Mr. Cornelius to discuss the long-term investment practices used at Eli Lilly.

I have seen major changes both in our industry and at this firm over the past decade. Nowhere are these changes more evident—or more important—than in the long-term investment area. To remain competitive, we must commit ever-larger amounts of capital, placing a high premium on making good investment decisions.

At Eli Lilly, our largest long-term investment category is research and development (R&D). Although R&D finds its way into the expense side of the income statement, it is indeed a long-term investment, and we analyze R&D cash outflows just as we do plant and capital, using the same cost of capital and discounted cash flow tools.

Calculating the Cost of Capital

To evaluate long-term investment projects, Lilly uses a firmwide cost of capital as the hurdle rate. Although we make other medical products, we consider ourselves primarily a pharmaceutical firm, and so we calculate one cost of capital for the whole company. Currently it's 15 percent—and has been for about 20 years. The relatively high rate reflects our industry's high risk.

We are now facing a very different business climate. The political issues surrounding health care costs require that we take a hard look at our calculations and the assumptions on which they are based. I predict that we'll probably lower the cost of capital to reflect the next—rather than the past—decade's investment opportunities.

A major change at Eli Lilly is the addition of more debt to our capital structure. Our longstanding philosophy was that the pharmaceutical business has enough operating risk that we shouldn't add financial risk to it. Like most major pharmaceutical firms, we borrowed very little. In late March 1993, we issued $200 million of 10-year bonds with a before-tax interest rate of 6.35 percent, which is relatively inexpensive capital. We're rated AAA, so we can borrow at favorable rates. With more lower-cost debt in our financing mix, I expect our revised cost of capital will drop below 15 percent.

In terms of actually calculating cost of capital, the easiest part is the after-tax cost of debt. When it comes to valuing our common stock, we use the capital asset pricing model (CAPM). The difficult part is the required premium for equity capital. Data for the past 10 to 15 years suggest equity premiums of 4 to 6 percent. Our beta has been about 1. It will probably become more volatile. I expect new calculations will give us a beta of 1.05 to 1.1.

A lower equity premium and the addition of more debt will lower our weighted average cost of capital. I don't know whether the new cost of capital will be closer to 13 or to 10 percent. But the new rate is probably more realistic; it will reflect possible government price constraints and lower profitability levels.

Capital Budgeting at Eli Lilly

Our capital budgeting process works from the top down. First, we make companywide estimates of the coming year's sales, income, and cash flow. Then we divide the company into seven or eight strategic business units (SBUs). We look at each SBU as if it were an independent company. We pull together sales, unit costs, R&D expenses, and allocation of common manufacturing costs, to get the SBU income and profit contribution. Usually the SBU capital budgets total more than the corporate allocation. So the SBUs rank projects, defer some, speed up others. It's a process that results in an acceptable operating plan for the next year.

In our capital budgeting, we use both net present value (NPV) and internal rates of return (IRR), complementing that with a graphic analysis of the payback. Of two projects with similar NPVs or IRRs, the one that pays back more quickly would be ranked higher. We graph the cash flows to see how deep the curve is. You may have a project that requires $300 million and pays back in 3 years, compared to another that may cost $30 million and also pays back in 3 years. The depth of the investment obviously makes the $300 million project riskier than the $30 million one. And, even though the $300 million project may have a terrific return, we can do only so many big-risk projects. We need to balance risk across the whole portfolio each year, with one large project, a few at $100 million and several smaller ones in the $20 to $50 million range.

We use scenario analysis to adjust for risk. We keep the 15 percent cost of capital but run sensitivity analyses changing cash flow assumptions: What if we can charge only 50 cents rather than a dollar per day for the new therapy? What if the product launch is delayed 6 months, costs are different, or competitive entry is sooner/later?

The international factor is another dimension we incorporate into our capital budgeting analysis. We may prepare domestic versus international cost and revenue forecasts, but they are combined in the total analysis to make a global decision. Every country in the world right now wants jobs, and that presents a strategic dilemma. Pricing negotiations are quasi-political; elements like job creation, employment, and balance of trade enter into those discussions. So Lilly manufacturing facilities are distributed around the world, even though we'd probably prefer fewer plants and larger economies of scale.

Historically, we relied almost exclusively on products developed in-house. Now there is an explosion in life sciences research in academic settings and the biotechnology industry. We have terrific opportunities for new product acquisitions and strategic alliances but typically don't have as much data on them as on in-house projects. This makes the analysis more difficult, and sometimes we invest in a product that fails. You can have a good analysis on the front end, but the marketplace or science can turn it into a bad decision. That's the nature of doing business in a industry with a high rate of innovation and risk.

*I*n Chapter 6 we examine how firms determine firmwide, divisional, and project-specific opportunity costs of capital. Chapter 7 discusses capital budgeting techniques, and Chapter 8 examines the issues that arise when these techniques are applied. In Chapter 9 we consider how risk is handled in capital investment decision making. Then in Chapter 10 we consider how firm's operate in order to make value-creating capital investment decisions, which are the cornerstone of maximizing the value of the firm.

6

The Opportunity Cost of Capital

EXECUTIVE SUMMARY

Calculating an appropriate opportunity cost, or required rate of return—whether it is a firmwide, divisional, or project-specific rate—is an integral part of the investment decision process. As discussed previously, to maximize the market value of the firm, the firm uses the net present value decision criterion and accepts any project that returns more that it costs. The costs to the firm are captured by the discount rate, or opportunity cost of capital employed. Because financial markets are efficient, they provide reliable and up-to-date information about the returns demanded by investors, which are the costs to the firm.

In determining the opportunity cost of capital, the cost of debt is typically the cheapest source, and common equity is the most expensive. By using the costs of new financing and the market value proportions, a firm can calculate its opportunity cost of capital. This is the *minimum* market-determined required rate of return for new projects of average risk undertaken by the firm. By investing in these projects, a firm assists in maximizing its market value.

If a project's risk differs significantly from the average risk of projects undertaken, an opportunity cost that reflects that degree of risk must be employed as the discount rate. A frequently used method in practice is to calculate divisional opportunity costs. In doing this, the assumption is that risk is homogeneous within a division but differs between divisions. Project-specific opportunity costs can also be employed.

WHAT IS THE FIRM'S OPPORTUNITY COST OF CAPITAL?

The most important determinant of the value of the firm is its investment decisions. To maximize the market value of the firm, V, a thorough understanding of capital budgeting techniques is required. An important part of the decision involves the use of the proper opportunity cost as the discount rate for net present value decisions.

199

To keep things simple, we start with projects that can be viewed as being equal in risk to the firm as a whole. The proper rate to employ can be viewed in one of two ways:

1.   THE OPPORTUNITY COST OF CAPITAL   When viewed as the opportunity cost of capital, the discount rate is what the funds could earn in an alternative investment of similar risk. If a firm has a million dollars that could be invested externally to yield 15 percent, then an internal (i.e., capital investment) project with equal risk should return more that 15 percent. Otherwise, the value of the firm will not be maximized.
2.   THE WEIGHTED AVERAGE COST OF CAPITAL, WACC   The **weighted average cost of capital** is simply the average after-tax cost of new funds available for investment by the firm. For example, if the firm's average after-tax cost of the last dollar of new funds is 15 percent, then it must earn more than 15 percent (after taxes) on new investments in order to maximize the value of the firm.

When talking about the appropriate discount rate for average-risk projects, *we use the terms opportunity cost of capital, required rate of return, or weighted average cost of capital interchangeably.* Whatever it is called, it is the minimum rate the firm must earn to ensure that the value of the firm does not fall. In addition, it is important to recognize that the feasibility of a project depends on how much it will cost the firm to raise *new* funds. Therefore, the opportunity cost of capital represents the cost of *new funds* needed to finance the project and *not* the cost of funds raised in the past.

Accurate estimation of the firm's opportunity cost of capital (when dealing with projects whose risk is equal to the firm's risk) is important. We begin by determining how to calculate the firm's opportunity cost of capital—first for a hypothetical example and then for PepsiCo. Remember, if a project returns less than it costs, then the net present value, NPV, will be negative and the value of the firm will decrease if the project is accepted. So, *the opportunity cost of capital represents the minimum return a firm must earn.* Accepting projects whose expected returns are higher than their costs, as evidenced by positive NPVs, assists in maximizing the value of the firm. Later in the chapter we also consider how to proceed when the risk of proposed capital budgeting projects differs from the firm's average risk.

DEFINITIONS AND CALCULATIONS

Before calculating the firm's opportunity cost of capital, we begin by defining some terms we will use throughout:

opportunity cost of capital = the weighted average of the cost of the last dollar of capital expected to be raised by the firm.

k_b = the before-tax cost of new debt issued by the firm. Ignoring flotation costs, this is equal to the yield to maturity, YTM, expected by investors, as defined in Chapter 3.

$k_i = k_b(1 - T)$, the after-tax cost of new debt issued by the firm, where T equals the firm's effective marginal tax rate.

k_{ps} = the after-tax cost of new preferred stock issued by the firm.

k_s = the after-tax cost of equity capital. This k_s is identical to the k_s defined in Chapter 3, where it was called the investor's required return on common stock.

W_i = the weights that indicate the future financing proportions to be employed by the firm.

The firm's opportunity cost of capital is a weighted average of the various sources of new capital. Note that the costs are expressed on an after-tax basis. This is to ensure consistency for decision-making purposes with the cash flows that are also calculated on an after-tax basis. If a firm raises capital with debt, preferred stock, and internally generated common equity, the opportunity cost of capital would be

$$\frac{\text{opportunity}}{\text{cost of capital}} = k_i W_{\text{debt}} + k_{ps} W_{\text{preferred stock}} + k_s W_{\text{common equity}} \qquad (6.1)$$

where the W's *indicate the proportions of future funding to be raised from each specific source.*

BASIC ASSUMPTIONS

In order to determine a firm's opportunity cost of capital, we begin by going back to the notion that financial markets in developed countries are efficient. As informed investors in efficient financial markets process all available information and make decisions to invest in various financial assets (like stocks and bonds), their actions reflect all that is known about the firm, the economy, and the future. Hence, to determine what a financial asset is worth, we "look to market values." In addition, to determine how the firm is expected to finance itself in the future, we also "look to market values." Efficient financial markets play an important role in many of the firm's decisions; one of them is determining the firm's opportunity cost of capital. The returns demanded by the firm's investors, and the possible returns that could be earned on comparable risky investments, can best be determined by examining the firm's existing financial assets. As returns demanded by investors increase or decrease, the costs to the firm must also increase or decrease.

To use the firmwide opportunity cost of capital for decision-making purposes, two basic conditions must be met. First, the risk of the project under examination must be approximately equal to the risk of all new projects being undertaken by the firm. Although, as we discuss in Chapter 9, the precise estimation of project risk is not easy, our concern is that the risk not be substantially above or below that of the other projects being undertaken. When risk differs significantly, a divisional or project-specific opportunity cost of capital (as discussed later in the chapter) should be employed. Second, it is important that the firm not materially change its financing policies as a result of the investments it undertakes. Because these proportions directly affect the opportunity cost, the cost of capital will change as the financing mix and the firm's **capital structure** (which reflects the mix of debt and equity employed) change.

At this point, we are assuming that the firm's **target capital structure** (or desired debt/market value of equity ratio) will be constant. The reason for making this assumption is that different capital structures may influence the firm's cost of capital.[1] Our concern here is with determining the opportunity cost of capital, assuming a firm is at the appropriate target capital structure. In Chapters 11 and 12 we examine the impact the firm's capital structure may have on the value of the firm.

Before proceeding, it is important to emphasize that *the opportunity cost of capital is a marginal cost.* What is meant by the term "marginal"? We are using "marginal" in the economic sense—as the cost of raising the last dollar of funds. For each of the components—debt, preferred stock, and common equity—we are interested in the cost of the last dollar of additional funds. If the cost of the last dollar of additional funds increases, so does the firm's required return. *Calculation of the firm's cost of capital has a future orientation.* The opportunity cost of capital is a weighted average of the after-tax costs of various future sources of capital; *any past or historical costs are irrelevant.* The only reason to consider historical costs when calculating an opportunity cost is to obtain some idea of the future-oriented estimates that must be made. But, in general, it is best to ignore them; considering historical costs or proportions often leads to incorrect conclusions.

Concept Review Questions

- What does a firm's opportunity cost of capital measure?
- What two basic conditions must be met to use the firmwide opportunity cost of capital for decision-making purposes?
- What is meant by the term marginal cost of capital when describing the opportunity cost of capital?

CALCULATING COSTS AND FINANCING PROPORTIONS

First we will consider the explicit costs of three types of financing—debt, preferred stock, and common equity—and then the specific financing proportions.

COST OF DEBT

The cost of debt to be used for cost of capital purposes is the before-tax cost, k_b, adjusted for the tax "subsidy" provided by the government to profitable firms (because interest is a tax-deductible expense). The after-tax cost of debt, k_i, is

$$\text{after-tax cost of debt} = k_i = k_b(1 - T) \tag{6.2}$$

[1] In addition, we are assuming that risk does not change and that the firm's cash dividend policy is constant. If either of these changes, some of the costs might change, affecting the whole decision making process.

where

k_b = the before-tax cost of debt
T = the firm's marginal corporate tax rate

To calculate the before-tax cost for long-term debt, we solve for the expected yield to maturity, YTM. Thus, the before-tax cost to the firm, k_b, is found by solving for the unknown discount rate:

$$B_0 = \sum_{t=1}^{n} \frac{I}{(1 + k_b)^t} + \frac{M}{(1 + k_b)^n} \qquad (6.3)$$

where

B_0 = the net proceeds from the bond
I = dollar amount of interest paid on a bond each year
M = the par or maturity value of the bond (typically \$1,000)
n = the number of years to maturity for the bond
k_b = the before-tax cost to the firm

This is no different from solving for the yield to maturity as discussed in Chapter 3.

Consider the example of Ambassador Corporation, which plans to issue a new 20-year bond that has a \$1,000 par value, carries a 12.75 percent coupon rate, and pays interest annually. The firm expects to receive \$980. The before-tax cost to Ambassador is

$$\$980 = \sum_{t=1}^{20} \frac{\$127.50}{(1 + k_b)^{20}} + \frac{\$1,000}{(1 + k_b)^{20}}$$

so, $k_b = 0.13035 \approx 13\%$.[2]

The before-tax cost is 13 percent. The after-tax cost, calculated using Equation 6.2 and assuming a marginal tax rate of 40 percent, is

$$k_i = k_b(1 - T) = 13\%(1 - 0.40) = 7.8\%$$

The after-tax cost of debt is used because it is, in fact, the cost to the firm. Although the before-tax cost is 13 percent, as long as the firm is profitable, interest is a deductible expense for tax purposes. So, the after-tax cost with a 40 percent effective marginal tax rate is only 7.8 percent.

Remember that we are interested in the cost of new debt financing. The coupon rate on existing debt is not relevant, nor are any costs connected with existing debt. The explicit cost of debt tends to be the *least expensive* of the three sources we consider, for two reasons: First, from the investor's standpoint, it is a fixed legal claim; bondholders have greater security than preferred or common stockholders. On a risk-return basis, we would expect bond investors to demand less return than stockholders—which they do. Second, the tax status of interest also makes debt cheaper

---

[2] Using a financial calculator, k_b is 13.035 percent.

than other sources, as long as the firm is profitable (and it does not use so much debt that it becomes as or more expensive than equity).[3]

Determining the cost of debt financing for a firm becomes more complicated in practice because most firms employ many different kinds of debt. Some of these include short-term debt, zero-coupon bonds, convertible securities, and leases. The cost of some of these alternative sources of debt financing may differ from the cost of debt financing given by Equation 6.3.

For short-term debt, the shape of the term structure of interest rates (as discussed in Appendix 3A) will determine whether its before-tax cost is higher or lower than k_b from Equation 6.3. The before-tax cost of zero-coupon bonds can be determined using the approach discussed in Chapter 16. Convertible securities (Chapter 17) have a before-tax cost that is between that of debt and common equity (discussed shortly). Finally, as discussed in Chapter 18, the before-tax cost of lease financing is approximately equal to the cost of long-term debt financing given by Equation 6.3.

COST OF PREFERRED STOCK

The cost of preferred stock is calculated in much the same manner as the cost of debt, except for one basic difference. Because dividends on preferred stock are paid out of after-tax earnings, no tax adjustment is required. Thus, the cost of preferred stock, k_{ps}, is[4]

$$\text{cost of preferred stock} = k_{ps} = \frac{D_{ps}}{P_0} \qquad (6.4)$$

where

D_{ps} = the cash dividends paid on the preferred stock each year
P_0 = the proceeds from the sale of the preferred stock

If Ambassador is planning to issue a $50 par preferred stock that pays $6 in dividends per year and the firm expects to realize $48 per share, the after-tax cost of the preferred stock is

$$k_{ps} = \frac{D_{ps}}{P_0} = \frac{\$6}{\$48} = 0.125 = 12.5\%$$

Compared with the 7.8 percent cost of debt calculated above, the cost of preferred stock is higher. This occurs primarily because the dividends on preferred stock are not tax-deductible.

---

[3] If a firm is operating at a loss, its marginal tax rate is zero. For a firm that does not expect to pay taxes for a long time, there is no tax subsidy for using debt, and $k_i = k_b$.
[4] Equation 6.4 assumes the preferred stock is a perpetuity. If it is expected to be called or retired in a specific number of years, the cost of preferred stock should be obtained by using Equation 6.3 after adjusting to reflect preferred stock instead of debt.

COST OF COMMON EQUITY

The final cost to be considered is that of common equity. Actually, there are two possible costs here—one if the firm uses internally generated funds, and the other if it expects to issue additional shares of common stock. **Internally generated funds** are those cash flows that arise as a function of the firm's ongoing activities and that can be reinvested in the business. Because internally generated funds typically supply most of the common equity, we focus primarily on their cost.

Like the cost of debt and preferred stock, the cost of equity capital is also a function of the returns expected by investors. To estimate the cost of equity, k_s, it is necessary to estimate the returns demanded by investors. As with preferred stock, there is no need to adjust for taxes, because cash dividends on common stock are paid out of after-tax earnings. The difficulty in estimating the cost of equity capital arises because, unlike debt or preferred stock, there is no stated interest or dividend rate. In addition, due to the ability to share in both the good and bad fortunes of the firm, common stock may incur substantial price changes. So, estimating the cost of equity capital is more difficult than estimating the cost of debt or preferred stock. We examine three approaches for estimating the cost of common equity—the dividend valuation approach, the capital asset pricing model, CAPM, and an ad hoc method using bond yield plus a risk premium.

The logic behind assigning a cost to internally generated funds involves the opportunity cost concept. Management faces a choice with the funds generated by the firm: It can distribute them to the firm's owners (its common stockholders) in the form of cash dividends, or it can reinvest them in the firm on behalf of the same common stockholders. The decision to reinvest funds instead of paying them out involves an opportunity cost. Stockholders could have taken the funds and reinvested them in something else. Therefore, the firm must earn a return on the reinvested funds equal to what common stockholders could have earned in alternative investments of comparable risk.

What return is this? It's simply k_s, which is the return investors require on investments with comparable risk. If the firm cannot earn a return of at least k_s on the reinvested internally generated funds, it should distribute the funds to investors so they can invest them in other assets that provide an expected return equal to k_s.

Dividend Valuation Approach

In Chapter 3, we saw that one way to determine the value of a share of stock was the dividend valuation model. This model states that the market value, P_0, is equal to the present value of the future dividends, $D_1, \ldots, D_\infty$, where the discount rate, k_s, is the investor's required rate of return. Thus,

$$P_0 = \frac{D_1}{(1 + k_s)} + \frac{D_2}{(1 + k_s)^2} + \cdots + \frac{D_\infty}{(1 + k_s)^\infty} \qquad (6.5)$$

If the growth rate in dividends, g, is expected to be constant and less than k_s, Equation 6.5 reduces to

$$P_0 = \frac{D_1}{k_s - g} \qquad (6.6)$$

where D_1 is the cash dividend expected 1 year from now, k_s is the investor's required rate of return, and g is the constant percentage growth rate in cash dividends. Solving Equation 6.6 for k_s, we have one way of estimating the investor's required rate of return (which is the firm's cost of common equity). Thus:

$$\begin{matrix} \text{dividend} & & \text{expected} \\ \text{valuation} = k_s = & \text{dividend} + \text{expected growth} \\ \text{approach} & & \text{yield} \end{matrix} \tag{6.7}$$

$$k_s = \frac{D_1}{P_0} + g$$

Investors expect to receive a **dividend yield,** D_1/P_0, plus growth of g, for a total return of k_s.

To illustrate, assume the present market price on Ambassador's common stock is \$25, dividends to be paid in 1 year, D_1, are \$1.75, and the expected growth in dividends is 9 percent per year. The dividend valuation approach[5] to estimating the cost of equity capital yields

$$k_s = \frac{D_1}{P_0} + g = \frac{\$1.75}{\$25} + 9\% = 0.07 + 9\% = 7\% + 9\% = 16\%$$

The estimation of the expected growth rate in cash dividends is the most difficult aspect of applying the dividend valuation approach. We could start by analyzing past growth rates. That information is generally supplemented, however, by projections made by the firm itself or by security analysts. And it is the future growth rate that is important.

Capital Asset Pricing Model Approach

The second approach to estimating the cost of common equity employs the capital asset pricing model, CAPM. As described in Chapter 4, the CAPM states that the investors' required rate of return is equal to the risk-free rate plus a risk premium, so that

$$\text{CAPM approach} = k_s = \text{risk-free rate} + \text{expected risk premium}$$

$$k_s = k_{RF} + \beta_j(k_M - k_{RF}) \tag{6.8}$$

where

k_{RF} = the risk-free rate of return
β_j = the beta of security j
k_M = the expected rate of return on the market portfolio

---

[5] If the expected growth rate in cash dividends is not constant, the nonconstant growth valuation approach discussed in Chapter 3 will have to be employed. Also, be careful if the expected growth rate in cash dividends is "high." In such a case, blind usage of the constant dividend valuation approach often leads to a "high" estimate of the cost of equity capital.

The risk-free rate is generally measured by the yield on U.S. Treasury bills. Betas can be obtained by referring to *Value Line Investment Survey,* Merrill Lynch, or many other investment advisory services. Although the expected rate of return on the market cannot be measured directly, it can be approximated. One approach to estimating the expected return on the market, k_M, involves focusing on three components: (1) expected inflation, (2) expected real growth in the economy, and (3) an expected risk premium commanded by stocks relative to bonds.[6]

To illustrate the CAPM approach, assume Ambassador's beta is 0.95, the yield on Treasury bills is 10 percent, expected growth in the economy (as measured by projected GDP growth in constant dollars) is 3 percent, and the expected risk premium of stocks over bonds is 5 percent. Adding the last three components together provides an estimate of the future returns on the market of $10 + 3 + 5 = 18$ percent. The investor's required rate of return, which is the cost of common equity, is

$$k_s = 11\% + 0.95(18\% - 11\%) = 11\% + 6.65\% = 17.65\%$$

This second approach to estimating the cost of common equity provides a figure of 17.65 percent versus the earlier figure of 16 percent estimated by the dividend valuation approach. The dividend valuation and CAPM approaches should provide approximately the same answer, unless some drastic differences in assumptions are made. Our difference is not too large and should give us some confidence in the reliability of the estimates.

Bond Yield Plus Expected Risk Premium Approach

The third approach to estimating the cost of common equity is an ad hoc method that states the investor's required rate of return is equal to what he or she could get on the bonds of the firm plus a premium for risk, so that

bond yield plus expected risk premium approach $= k_s =$ bond yield $+$ expected risk premium of common stock over corporate bonds   (6.9)

This method is useful when the firm does not pay any cash dividends (so that the dividend valuation approach is not applicable) or when the common stock is not traded (so that neither the dividend valuation nor CAPM approaches can be employed). To continue our earlier example, the before-tax bond yield of Ambassador was 13 percent, and the risk premium of stocks over corporate bonds was expected to be 5 percent.[7] The required rate of return is then

$$k_s = \text{bond yield} + \text{expected risk premium} = 13\% + 5\% = 18\%$$

[6] Another way would be to add the expected market-risk premium ($k_M - k_{RF}$) to the risk-free rate. Research indicates that risk premiums are not constant over time. See the discussion later in the chapter under "Estimating the Expected Return on the Market Portfolio and Risk Premiums Using Historical Data."
[7] This risk premium is firm-specific and may be more or less than the market-risk premium employed in estimating k_M. For simplicity, we assume the two risk premiums are equal.

Putting It All Together

For Ambassador, we have three estimates of its cost of common equity, as follows:

Approach	Estimated k_s
Dividend valuation	16%
CAPM	17.65
Bond yield plus expected risk premium	18

All differ slightly, but they are close. Taking everything into account, we would estimate Ambassador's cost of common equity is between 16 and 18 percent. A simple average of these estimates is 17.22 percent [i.e., (16% + 17.65% + 18%)/3]. We will round this to 17.25 percent for use below when calculating Ambassador's opportunity cost of capital.

Although the use of three different approaches may seem unduly complicated, it is very useful in practice. By using several alternative approaches to estimating the cost of common equity, managers are forced to consider which estimates are most useful. Estimating the cost of equity capital requires both judgment and an understanding of what the firm's common stockholders expect.

The cost of common equity is higher than the cost of debt or preferred stock. This occurs because from the investor's standpoint, there is more risk with common stock than with debt or preferred stock. Investors therefore have a higher required rate of return for common stock. But because the investor's required rate of return is the firm's cost, we see that the cost of common equity is the *most expensive* form of financing to the firm. Even though it is the most expensive source of financing, firms routinely use extensive common equity financing. They do so from the desire to retain ownership of the firm (especially for smaller firms), and balancing the benefits of debt financing versus the increased risks that go along with it, as discussed in Chapters 11 and 12.

NEW COMMON STOCK AND FLOTATION COSTS

If a firm must issue common stock to raise additional equity capital, it will have to sell the stock at a price below its current market price. This means that P_0 in Equation 6.7 would have to be replaced by some lower price, to reflect the underpricing required to sell the stock. The effect is to raise the cost of equity capital when the dividend valuation approach is employed. To illustrate this idea, assume Ambassador has used up its internally generated common equity funds and must issue new common stock. The dividends next year are still $1.75, but in order to sell the new shares, a discount (or underpricing) of $4 per share is necessary. Thus, P_0 for new external common equity capital is $25 − $4 = $21. Also, the growth rate is still 9 percent. Using Equation 6.7 we have

$$k_s(\text{external common equity}) = \frac{\$1.75}{\$21} + 9\% = 8.3\% + 9\% = 17.3\%$$

This is higher than the 16 percent we estimated earlier for internally generated common equity.

While this underpricing adjustment is straightforward for the dividend valuation approach, it is not so simple for either the CAPM or bond yield plus expected risk premium approaches. The reason is that the price of common stock does not appear directly in Equations 6.8 or 6.9. The best one can do using Equations 6.8 or 6.9 is to make a slight subjective adjustment if new common stock is to be issued.

Another possible concern involves flotation costs that are incurred when securities are sold. Some finance experts argue that the dollar amount of flotation costs should be incorporated as an additional cash outflow when estimating the initial investment for capital budgeting purposes. (Estimation of the initial investment is discussed in Chapter 8.) Conceptually, there are some points in favor of this argument, but the problem is that the firm is *estimating the cost of a pool of funds raised over time* and invested in numerous capital projects. Also, as discussed in Chapter 2, the Fisher separation theorem says that the investment (or capital budgeting) decision and the financing (or fund-raising) decision are separate and distinct activities. Therefore, it is often impractical to ascribe specific flotation costs to specific projects, and it is also unnecessary (if we are to separate the investment and financing decisions). If flotation costs are small, our preference is to ignore them. If they are larger, we typically reduce the proceeds received from the specific financing employed. It can be shown that this latter treatment produces a biased low estimate of a project's NPV. We prefer that result, however, to trying to tie specific financing to specific projects, so that the investment and financing decisions are not kept separate. The joint interaction of investment and financing decisions is discussed in Chapter 14.

THE FINANCING PROPORTIONS

Now that we know how to calculate the specific after-tax costs of debt, preferred stock, and common equity, we are almost ready to calculate the firm's after-tax opportunity cost of capital. Before doing that, however, we need to determine the financing proportions, or amount of **financial leverage,** to be employed by the firm. These proportions are a function of the firm's target capital structure, which is its desired mix of debt to total market value. The target capital structure should be the long-run desired mix of financing the firm intends to employ for meeting all of its financing needs, *measured in market value terms.* To calculate the financing mix, we again employ current market value information, assuming that financial markets are efficient and incorporate all that is known about the firm.

Thus, if the firm intends to finance with 50 percent debt and 50 percent equity, the target capital structure should reflect that mix. Although many things influence a firm's target capital structure, it can be approximated by determining the current market value of the firm's outstanding securities. *These current market values provide the best estimate of the firm's future financing mix.*[8] However, temporary deviations from the target capital structure should be taken into account if the firm knows its current market-value-based capital structure does not provide a valid indication of the

---

[8] An alternative would be to employ a cash budget that provides an estimate of the expected sources of funds over the next three to five years.

future target capital structure. Proper estimation of the future financing proportions is essential when estimating the firm's opportunity cost of capital.

Concept Review Questions

- What are the three primary component costs used when estimating the opportunity cost of capital?
- Is a tax adjustment required when estimating the cost of either preferred or common stock? Why?
- Describe three methods used to estimate the cost of common equity.

ESTIMATING THE OPPORTUNITY COST OF CAPITAL

Once we have the specific market costs and proportions, calculating the firm's opportunity cost of capital is straightforward. Let's return to the Ambassador example, and then we'll briefly discuss what happens if Ambassador decides to increase its capital substantially. Finally, before proceeding to estimate PepsiCo's opportunity cost of capital, we'll consider the question of how often firms should estimate their cost of capital.

THE OPPORTUNITY COST FOR AMBASSADOR

Earlier we calculated the specific costs of debt, preferred stock, and common equity for Ambassador Corporation. In addition to these after-tax costs, let's assume the market value proportions of financing to be employed are 30 percent debt, 10 percent preferred stock, and 60 percent common equity. Given these market value costs and proportions, Ambassador's opportunity cost of capital is 13.94 percent, as shown below:

Component	After Tax Cost	×	Market Value Weight	=	Opportunity Cost of Capital
Debt	7.8%		0.30		2.34%
Preferred stock	12.5		0.10		1.25
Common equity	17.25		0.60		10.35
			Opportunity cost of capital =		13.94%

By using this as the minimum discount rate for net present value calculations, Ambassador can make investment decisions for projects of average risk that assist in maximizing the long-run market value of the firm.[9]

---

[9] We are assuming Ambassador is at its target (or optimal) capital structure.

WHAT IF THE AMOUNT OF FINANCING INCREASES?

So far we have considered a firm raising a given amount of financing at a specific period in time. What if one or a number of new investment opportunities come along that require an additional amount of financing? The general rule in such a case requires us to recognize that not only are there new investment opportunities, but also the total amount of capital to be raised has increased substantially. In such a case, the risks involved, and therefore the costs of financing, may increase substantially. If that happens, the firm's opportunity cost of capital should be recalculated, and the new higher discount rate should be used in making all investment decisions faced by the firm.

HOW OFTEN SHOULD THE COST OF CAPITAL BE CALCULATED?

How often does the firm's cost of capital need to be recalculated? There is no hard-and-fast rule—we know firms that do it yearly and others that estimated their opportunity cost 5 years ago and have not really looked at it since. The best guide is to reexamine it periodically, especially when the financing proportions have changed (or are expected to change) or when economic conditions, such as interest rates, have changed substantially. In these rapidly changing economic times, firms would be wise to review their cost of capital at least every year. Given the rapid rise in actual and expected inflation in the late 1970s and early 1980s, firms that did not reestimate their cost of capital ended up underestimating their real cost of funds. Likewise, when inflation decreased, as it did in the early 1990s, a downward revision was necessary.

Concept Review Questions
- What is the formula for a firm's opportunity cost of capital?
- Comment on why a firm should recalculate its opportunity cost of capital when considering a number of new investment opportunities requiring substantial amounts of financing.

ESTIMATING PEPSICO'S OPPORTUNITY COST OF CAPITAL

In practice, calculating a firm's opportunity cost of capital follows the same process we have described. We will use PepsiCo, Inc.; *our calculations are made as of December 1991.* This is an example of how to make the calculations, but obviously they would have to be reestimated to calculate today's opportunity cost of capital, or required return, for PepsiCo.

MARKET VALUE PROPORTIONS

The book value balance sheet for PepsiCo as of December 28, 1991, in millions, was as follows:

Assets		Liabilities and Stockholders' Equity	
Current	$ 4,566	Payables, accruals, and other	$ 4,126
Long-term	14,209	Deferred taxes	1,070
Total	$18,775	Interest-bearing debt	
		and lease obligations	8,034
		Stockholders' equity	5,545
		Total	$18,775

Note that we have grouped the liabilities in a somewhat different manner than is used by accountants. All accounts payable, accruals (for taxes, cash dividends, and so forth), and other are lumped together. These are typically ignored for cost of capital purposes. The reason is that for capital budgeting purposes, we will net out increases in current liabilities against increases in the current assets and will deal only with incremental net working capital needs. Because of this netting-out process (and assuming the firm pays these on time so their direct cost is zero), accounts payable and accruals are typically ignored. Deferred taxes are also excluded, because this is an accounting phenomenon that arises from using different depreciation methods for tax and accounting purposes. However, short-term debt is typically included when firms calculate their cost of capital. We will also follow this procedure. Also, lease obligations are included, because they represent a form of long-term financing.

PepsiCo's interest-bearing debt and lease obligations are listed in Table 6.1. Its commercial paper and other short-term notes payable are not listed on any exchange, but we'll assume their current market value is approximately equal to their book value of $228 million. Then the notes and bonds are listed along with their market prices. Market prices were not available for a number of PepsiCo's long-term debt securities, so we used book values. Looking again at Table 6.1, we see that although the par value of PepsiCo's debt is $8,034 million, its estimated market value as of December 1991 was $8,101 million.[10]

Looking farther down Table 6.1, we see that the book value (the sum of the common stock, additional paid-in capital, retained earnings, and any other common equity accounts on the balance sheet) of PepsiCo's common equity is $5,545 million, whereas the market value of the firm's common stock is $26,731 million. As is typical of most firms, the book value and market value for PepsiCo's common equity are not very similar. Using these market value proportions, we estimate that PepsiCo will raise approximately 24 percent of its new financing with debt; the other 76 percent will be raised through common equity financing. This common equity financing for most firms is largely funded through the retention of cash in the firm, instead of paying it out to the shareholders in the form of cash dividends. An examination of the 1991 annual report and the statement of cash flows for PepsiCo indicates that in 1991 PepsiCo generated $2.4 billion from its ongoing operations and borrowed a net amount of $439 million. Thus, our projected financing proportions appear to be reasonable.

---

[10] As is fairly typical, the book value and market value of PepsiCo's debt are close. This is especially true when current market interest rates are close to the coupon interest rates on the firm's debt.

Table 6.1

Calculation of Market Value Weights for PepsiCo, as of December 28, 1991

Where market prices are not available, judgment has to be employed to determine the estimated market value. For both short-term and other debt and lease obligations, the par (or book) value was employed.

Interest-Bearing Debt and Lease Obligations	Par (or Book) Value (in millions)	Market Price	Market Value (in millions)
Short-term debt	$228	—	$228
8.10% notes of '92	200	$101\frac{7}{8}$*	204
$7\frac{3}{8}$% notes of '93	250	102	255
$7\frac{7}{8}$% notes of '94	200	$104\frac{1}{4}$	208
$5\frac{7}{8}$% notes of '94	200	$100\frac{1}{4}$	200
$7\frac{7}{8}$% notes of '96	350	$105\frac{1}{2}$	369
7% notes of '96	200	102	204
$7\frac{3}{4}$% notes of '98	250	$103\frac{7}{8}$	260
$7\frac{5}{8}$% notes of '98	300	$103\frac{3}{8}$	310
$7\frac{5}{8}$% notes of '98	165	104	172
Zero-coupon notes of 1992–2012	366	—	366†
Swiss franc perpetual foreign interest payment bonds	211	—	211
$7\frac{3}{8}$% European Currency Units notes of '92	134	—	134
$9\frac{1}{8}$% Pound sterling notes of '93	112	—	112
$5\frac{1}{4}$% Swiss franc bearer bonds of '95	100	—	100
$7\frac{1}{8}$% Swiss franc notes of '94	74	—	74
Other long-term debt and lease obligations	4,694	—	4,694
Total debt	$8,034		$8,101
Common equity	$5,545	$33\frac{7}{8}$	$26,731††

Market Value	Dollars	Proportions
Short-term debt	$ 228	0.007
Long-term debt and lease obligations	7,873	0.226
Common equity	26,731	0.767
Total	$34,832	1.000

* Bond price as a percent of par.
† Book value employed because market information was not available.
†† 789,101,000 shares($33\frac{7}{8}$) = $26,730,790,000.

These are the proportions to use in calculating PepsiCo's opportunity cost of capital. Obviously, PepsiCo plans to rely on its internal cash-generation capability to finance about three-quarters of its financing needs.

COST OF DEBT

The before-tax cost of debt for PepsiCo is the amount the firm has to pay to raise additional debt. PepsiCo had a number of intermediate term notes outstanding, and all had an A rating according to Moody's Investment Service. We can assume that any new long-term debt will have a 10-year or longer maturity. What rate of return would the market require on a new issue with this risk? One approach is to calculate the yield to maturity on PepsiCo's existing long-term debt. However, a more straightforward approach is to determine what the market rate of return (or interest) was on comparable debt in December 1991. At that point in time, the yield to maturity on bonds rated A was about 8.9 percent. In our judgment, if PepsiCo had decided to issue new intermediate- to long-term debt in December 1991, the firm would have had to pay approximately 8.9 percent. This is their before-tax cost, k_b. We estimate that PepsiCo's effective marginal tax rate is about 30 percent.[11] Therefore, our estimate of the after-tax cost of debt is

$$k_i = k_b(1 - T) = 8.90\%(1 - 0.30) = 6.23\%$$

PepsiCo also had short-term debt and lease obligations in its capital structure. What should we do about them? The term structure of interest rates was upward-sloping in December 1991, so short-term debt was cheaper than intermediate- or long-term debt. We will use 6.10 percent for the approximate before-tax cost of short-term debt, or 4.27 percent on an after-tax basis. Finally, as we discuss in Chapter 18, the cost of both debt and lease financing should be the same for the firm. We will use 8.90 percent for the before-tax cost of leasing for PepsiCo.

COST OF COMMON EQUITY

In recent years PepsiCo has financed almost all its common equity needs through internally generated funds, so our approach is to ignore any possible sale of common stock. The first step is to estimate the growth rate in future dividends, as required by the dividend valuation approach. As Table 6.2 shows, the 10-year and 5-year historical growth rates in dividends per share are 11 and 17 percent, respectively. *Value Line* was projecting a 15 percent expected growth rate in dividends over the next 3 to 5 years. Note also that the historical and projected growth rates in earnings are 14 to 21 percent and 15 percent, respectively. We believe the *Value Line* estimate of 15 percent is a reasonable estimate of the expected compound growth rate in cash dividends as of December 1991.

[11] Be careful in estimating a firm's effective marginal tax rate. From its income statement, PepsiCo's tax rate is about 35 percent for both 1990 and 1991. But the actual taxes paid (per the statement of cash flows) indicates a tax rate of 23 percent of earnings before taxes in both 1990 and 1991. We averaged these and employ an effective tax rate of 30 percent.

Table 6.2

Growth Rates of Earnings per Share and Dividends per Share for PepsiCo

The historical growth rates are useful only as guides for the future. In this case there are some differences between historical and expected growth rates for both earnings and cash dividends.

Year	Dividends per Share	Earnings per Share
1981	$0.16	$0.40
1982	0.18	0.36
1983	0.18	0.33
1984	0.19	0.38
1985	0.20	0.50
1986	0.21	0.58
1987	0.22	0.74
1988	0.27	0.91
1989	0.32	1.12
1990	0.38	1.31
1991	0.46	1.50
10-year growth rate	$0.16(1 + g)^{10} = \$0.46$	$0.40(1 + g)^{10} = \$1.50$
	$g \approx 11\%$	$g \approx 14\%$
5-year growth rate	$0.21(1 + g)^{5} = \$0.46$	$0.58(1 + g)^{5} = \$1.50$
	$g \approx 17\%$	$g \approx 21\%$
Projected by *Value Line* for 1995–1997	15%	15%

All three approaches discussed earlier were employed to estimate the cost of equity capital for PepsiCo. First, using the dividend valuation approach (shown in Table 6.3), the cost of equity capital is estimated to be 16.56 percent. Then, employing PepsiCo's beta of 1.05 (from *Value Line*), a risk-free rate of 7 percent,[12] and an expected return on the market portfolio of 15.00 percent, the CAPM approach produces an estimated cost of common equity of 15.40 percent. Finally, the bond yield plus expected risk premium approach produces an estimated cost of 13.90 percent.

The three approaches produce somewhat similar estimates of PepsiCo's cost of equity capital. For simplicity, we averaged the three estimates to provide an estimate

---

[12] As noted in Table 6.3, the term structure of interest rates was fairly steeply upward-sloping as of December 1991. The yield to maturity of short-term U.S. Treasury bills was about 4.10 percent, while the yield on 10-year U.S. government bonds was 7.00 percent, and the yield on longer-term U.S. government bonds was about 7.75 percent. In such a situation we recommend employing the intermediate- or long-term bond rate. We employed the intermediate-term bond rate of 7.00 percent.

Table 6.3

Calculation of PepsiCo's Cost of Equity Capital, as of December 1991

These three estimates provide some measures of the "reasonableness" of the final k_s figure.

Assumptions
current market price, $P_0 = \$33\frac{7}{8}$
expected growth rate in dividends, $g = 15\%$
next year's cash dividends, $D_1 = \$0.46(1.15) = \$0.53$
risk-free rate*, $k_{RF} = 7.00\%$
market risk for PepsiCo, $\beta_j = 1.05$
expected return on market portfolio, k_M = expected inflation + expected real
    growth in economy + expected risk premium = 7% + 3% + 5% = 15.00%
expected bond yield = 8.90%
expected long-term risk premium of stocks over bonds = 5%

Dividend Valuation Approach
$$k_s = \frac{D_1}{P_0} + g = \frac{\$0.53}{\$33.875} + 15\% = 0.0156 + 15\% = 1.56\% + 15\% = 16.56\%$$

CAPM Approach
$$k_s = k_{RF} + \beta_j(k_M - k_{RF})$$
$$= 7.00\% + 1.05(15\% - 7\%) = 7.00\% + 8.40\% = 15.40\%$$

Bond Yield Plus Expected Risk Premium
$$k_s = \text{bond yield plus expected risk premium} = 8.90\% + 5\% = 13.90\%$$

* As of December 1991 the term structure of interest rates was fairly steeply upward-sloping. The yield on 6-month Treasury bills was about 4.10 percent, the yield on 10-year Treasury bonds was about 7 percent, and the yield on longer-term Treasury bonds was about 7.75 percent. When the yield curve is upward-sloping, as it was then, we recommend employing the intermediate- or long-term Treasury bond rate for the risk-free rate when estimating the opportunity cost of capital.

of PepsiCo's cost of equity capital of 15.29 percent [i.e., (16.56% + 15.40% + 13.90%)/3]. (If the three approaches had produced very divergent estimates of the cost of equity capital, we would have gone back and investigated the assumptions going into the various calculations in an attempt to reconcile any major differences in the estimates.)

PEPSICO'S OPPORTUNITY COST OF CAPITAL

Now that we have estimates of PepsiCo's after-tax cost of short-term debt of 4.27 percent, long-term debt of 6.23 percent, and an estimated cost of equity of 15.29 percent, we can calculate the opportunity cost of capital as of December 1991. As shown below, we estimate that PepsiCo's opportunity cost of capital is 13.17 percent.

Component	After-Tax Cost	×	Market Value Weight	=	Opportunity Cost of Capital
Short-term debt	4.27%		0.007		0.03%
Long-term debt	6.23		0.226		1.41
Common equity	15.29		0.767		11.73
			Opportunity cost of capital =		13.17%

Given all the estimates that go into calculating an opportunity cost of capital, we would round this up to 13.50 percent. This is the minimum discount rate PepsiCo should use as of December 1991 for projects of average risk; accepting projects with less than a 13.50 percent expected return is not consistent with the goal of maximizing the long-run market value of the firm.

This opportunity cost of capital can be used for making capital budgeting decisions (for projects of average risk) *as long as PepsiCo does not attempt to increase its level of financing substantially.* If it seeks to secure a large increase in financing, then the cost of some or all of its capital sources would increase, and consequently PepsiCo's opportunity cost of capital would also increase. Also, PepsiCo has three primary divisions—soft drinks (featuring Pepsi, Mountain Dew, 7-Up, etc.), snack foods (Doritos, Lays, Ruffles, Tostitos, etc.), and restaurants (Pizza Hut, Taco Bell, and KFC). Due to differences in risk between divisions, it may not be reasonable to use 13.50 percent as the opportunity cost of capital for each of the three divisions.

ESTIMATING THE EXPECTED RETURN ON THE MARKET PORTFOLIO AND RISK PREMIUMS USING HISTORICAL DATA

In order to estimate a firm's opportunity cost of equity capital, certain assumptions have to be made. These assumptions depend on the approach that is employed. If the capital asset pricing model is used, assumptions must be made about the expected return on the market portfolio, k_M. If the ad hoc bond yield plus expected risk premium approach is employed, assumptions must be made about the expected risk premium commanded by stocks over corporate bonds. For PepsiCo, we employed 15 percent as the expected return on the market portfolio, k_M, and 5 percent for the risk premium commanded by common stocks over corporate bonds. As discussed in Chapter 4, care must be taken in estimating these amounts, especially if historical data is employed. The annual compound rates of return on common stocks, corporate bonds, long-term U.S. government bonds, and U.S. treasury bills for various periods are as follows:[13]

[13] Adapted from *Stocks, Bonds, Bills, and Inflation 1993 Yearbook*™, Ibbotson Associates, Chicago.

	1926–1991	1960–1991	1975–1991
Common stocks	12.4%	11.6%	16.9%
Corporate bonds	5.7	7.8	11.5
Long-term government bonds	5.1	7.3	10.8
Treasury bills	3.8	6.4	8.0

Let's see what happens if we use this historical data to estimate the expected return on the market portfolio, k_M, for use with PepsiCo as of December 31, 1991. One way to estimate k_M would simply be to take the historical return on common stocks as our expected return on the market portfolio. If we use the 1926–1991 data, the expected return on the market is 12.4 percent; however, if we decide to use the more recent 1975–1991 period, the expected return on the market is 16.9 percent. It's easy to see that depending on what specific prior time period is employed, the expected return on the market portfolio differs substantially.

To alleviate some of this problem, we could estimate the expected return on the market portfolio to be:

expected return on k_M = risk-free rate + expected risk premium

As of December 1991, the yield to maturity on Treasury bills was about 4.10 percent, and the yield to maturity on long-term government bonds was about 7.75 percent. First, we might estimate the return on the market portfolio using the Treasury bill rate. The historical difference in the return on common stocks and Treasury bills for the three time periods is:

$$
\begin{array}{ll}
1926\text{–}1991 & 12.4\% - 3.8\% = 8.6\% \\
1960\text{–}1991 & 11.6\% - 6.4\% = 5.2\% \\
1975\text{–}1991 & 16.9\% - 8.0\% = 8.9\%
\end{array}
$$

Therefore, the expected return on the market portfolio, k_M, using the 4.10 percent return on Treasury bills and the historical risk premiums could be anything from 9.3 percent to 13 percent as follows:

4.1% + 8.6% = 12.7% (using 1926–1991 data)

4.1% + 5.2% = 9.3% (using 1960–1991 data)

4.1% + 8.9% = 13.0% (using 1975–1991 data)

An alternative approach is to employ a longer-term government bond rate as the risk-free rate. (This is what we did by using 7 percent as the expected risk-free rate when estimating the expected return on the market portfolio for PepsiCo. We chose this rate due to the fairly steeply upward-sloping term structure of interest rates at that point in time.) If the long-term bond rate of 7.75 percent is employed, along with the historical risk premium of stocks over long-term government bonds, then the expected return on the market portfolio would be anything from 12.05 percent to 15.05 percent:

7.75% + (12.4% − 5.1%) = 15.05% (using 1926–1991 data)

7.75% + (11.6% − 7.3%) = 12.05% (using 1960–1991 data)

7.75% + (16.9% − 10.8%) = 13.85% (using 1975–1991 data)

As can be seen, these estimates of the expected returns on the market portfolio are much higher than the earlier ones. The major reason is the upward-sloping term structure of interest rates at the end of 1991. The moral of this discussion is straightforward: Although it may be tempting simply to use historical data, estimation of the expected return on the market portfolio requires judgment based on an understanding of what has gone on in the past, current economic conditions, and expected economic and financial market conditions.

There is one other topic that we need to mention; it concerns the ad hoc bond yield plus risk premium of stocks over corporate bonds approach. What is the appropriate expected risk premium to employ is this case? Using historical data, the risk premium of common stocks over corporate bonds could be anything from 3.8 percent to 6.7 percent:

1926–1991	12.4% − 5.7% = 6.7%
1960–1991	11.6% − 7.8% = 3.8%
1975–1991	16.9% − 11.5% = 5.4%

Again, we see the sizable differences in historical risk premiums, this time between the returns on common stocks and those on corporate bonds. When estimating the opportunity cost of capital, don't be lulled into an easy (and often incorrect) decision by using historical information on returns without questioning the wisdom of the approach.

Concept Review Questions

- When estimating PepsiCo's opportunity cost of capital, accounts payable, accruals, and deferred taxes were excluded. Why?
- Describe the steps used to estimate PepsiCo's opportunity cost of capital.
- Describe some of the complications that may arise when using historical data to estimate the cost of capital.

DIVISIONAL AND PROJECT-SPECIFIC OPPORTUNITY COSTS

Up to now we have determined how to calculate the firm's opportunity cost of capital, which can be employed if new projects have a risk approximately equal to the firm's overall risk. We know, however, that each project must stand on its own legs if the firm is going to maximize its value. Firms must expect to receive a return sufficient to compensate them for the risk involved—that is, what they could get by investing in an equally risky project outside the firm. To deal with differences in risk, many medium- and large-size firms employ an approach that calculates the divisional cost of capital.

DIVISIONAL OPPORTUNITY COSTS OF CAPITAL

The essence of this approach is shown in Figure 6.1, where different discount rates will be employed depending on the riskiness of the division. If a firm employs a firmwide opportunity cost of capital when differences in risk exist, it makes the mistake of setting too high a required return for low-risk projects and too low a return for high-risk projects. The result is to underallocate capital to low-risk divisions and to overallocate funds to high-risk divisions.

The most widely used method in practice to implement risk adjustment is based on the assumption that project risks within divisions are somewhat similar but that risk between divisions differs. To estimate **divisional opportunity costs of capital,** we proceed as follows:

STEP 1:   Determine the firm's after-tax cost of debt, k_i, and use this as the cost of debt for each division. (Slightly more precision can be obtained by using separate after-tax costs for each division, but our approach is simpler and generally provides approximately the same answer.)

STEP 2:   Because we don't have any market-based estimate of the risk of the division and its cost of equity capital, identify one or more publicly traded firms that are similar in terms of product line to each separate division. These should be **pure-play firms**—publicly traded firms that are engaged solely in the same line of business as the division with the same operating risks. If the publicly traded firm has

---

Figure 6.1

Relating Risk to Divisional Opportunity Costs of Capital for Capital Budgeting Purposes

Use of a firmwide opportunity cost of capital when risk differs results in underallocation of resources to low-risk divisions and overallocation to high-risk divisions.

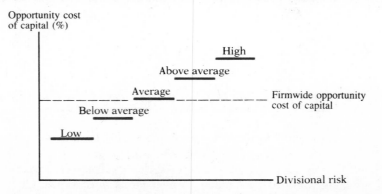

a different capital structure (or amount of financial risk) than the division, an adjustment will be required because this difference will affect beta. Also, the effective tax rate of the pure-play firm and the division are often different. One way to estimate an **asset** (or unlevered) **beta** is as follows:[14]

$$\beta_{\text{asset}} = \beta_U = \frac{\beta_{\text{levered firm}}}{1 + (1 - T)(B/S)} \qquad (6.10)$$

where

$\beta_{\text{asset}} = \beta_U$ = the beta for an unlevered firm or unlevered set of assets
$\beta_{\text{levered firm}}$ = the observed market beta for the publicly traded pure-play firm
T = the pure-play firm's effective marginal tax rate
B = the market value of the pure-play firm's debt (this includes bonds, loans from banks, leases, and short-term debt)
S = the market value of pure-play firm's equity

After calculating the unlevered asset beta, we can estimate the divisional beta by substituting in the β_{asset}, marginal tax rate for the division, T, and target capital structure proportions, S and B, and then solving for the levered β for the division.

STEP 3:   Employing the beta of the pure-play firm (with or without adjustment for differences in financial risk and taxes, as explained in Step 2), calculate each division's cost of equity capital as if each were a separate firm. Thus, each division's estimated cost of common equity is

$$\text{divisional cost of equity} = k_{RF} + \beta_{\text{division}}(k_M - k_{RF}) \qquad (6.11)$$

STEP 4:   Estimate the division's target or appropriate capital structure as if it were a freestanding firm. Due to differences in the basic risk and business conditions between divisions, some may be able to employ substantially more debt than others.

STEP 5:   Calculate the division's opportunity cost of capital using the costs and financing proportions estimated in steps 1, 3, and 4 above.

To illustrate step 2 above (how to calculate a division's appropriate beta), assume that we have identified a pure-play firm similar to the division in question.[15] Its beta (which is a levered beta because the pure-play firm uses debt), is 1.50; its ratio of debt to stock in market value terms, B/S, is 0.667; and its effective marginal tax rate, T, is 40 percent. For the division in question, its target ratio of debt to stock, B/S, is 0.40, and its effective marginal tax rate is 30 percent. To determine the appropriate beta for the division, we first "unlever" the pure-play firm's beta using Equation 6.10 as follows:

$$\beta_U = \frac{\beta_{\text{levered firm}}}{1 + (1 - T)(B/S)} = \frac{1.50}{1 + (1 - 0.40)(0.667)} \approx 1.07$$

[14] Equation 6.10 is discussed in more detail in Chapter 14.

[15] In practice, considerable work and a good deal of knowledge and judgment is required to identify appropriate pure-play firms. There is no substitute for a thorough understanding of possible pure-play firms.

Now that we have an unlevered or asset beta, we can "relever" it to determine the division's systematic risk after adjusting for its effective marginal tax rate and capital structure. Rearranging Equation 6.10, we have

$$\beta_{\text{levered division}} = \beta_U[1 + (1 - T)(B/S)]$$
$$= 1.07[1 + (1 - 0.30)(0.40)] \approx 1.37$$

Thus, based on using a pure-play firm, the appropriate beta for estimating the division's cost of equity capital is 1.37.

To illustrate the calculation of divisional opportunity costs of capital, consider the example of Wagner Industries. As shown in Table 6.4, with a beta of 1.25, k_{RF} of 10 percent, $k_M = 18$ percent, $k_i = 8$ percent, and using 40 percent debt and 60 percent common equity, we would estimate Wagner's firmwide opportunity cost of capital to be 15.20 percent. This would be the appropriate rate for capital budgeting purposes if all of Wagner's divisions were equally risky.

But what if Wagner has three very different divisions? The furniture division is in a very mature industry with low risk; the paper division has a risk that is close to the average risk of the firm; the data systems division is very risky. Due to the differences in risk, the divisions have different betas, which range from 0.75 for furniture to 1.25 for paper and 2.0 for data systems (as determined by examining publicly traded pure-play firms with similar product lines). The financing proportions also differ, with the more risky divisions being less able to employ as much debt financing. As shown in Table 6.5, these differences produce very different divisional opportunity costs of

---

Table 6.4

Calculation of Opportunity Cost of Capital for Wagner Industries

This firmwide opportunity cost is appropriate for divisions or projects whose risk is approximately equal to the average risk of new projects undertaken by the firm.

Assumptions
after-tax cost of debt, $k_i = 8\%$
market risk, $\beta_j = 1.25$
risk-free rate, $k_{RF} = 10\%$
expected return on the market portfolio, $k_M = 18\%$

Cost of Common Equity
$$k_s = k_{RF} + \beta_j(k_M - k_{RF})$$
$$= 10\% + 1.25(18\% - 10\%) = 10\% + 10\% = 20\%$$

Opportunity Cost of Capital

Component	After-Tax Cost	×	Market Value Weight	=	Opportunity Cost of Capital
Debt	8%		0.40		3.20%
Common equity	20		0.60		12.00
			Opportunity cost of capital =		15.20%

Table 6.5

Calculation of Divisional Opportunity Costs of Capital for Wagner Industries

Using divisional opportunity costs improves resource allocation decisions if risk differs substantially between a firm's divisions.

Furniture Division

$\beta_{\text{furniture}} = 0.75$

$k_{\text{furniture}} = k_{RF} + \beta_{\text{furniture}}(k_M - k_{RF})$
$= 10\% + 0.75(18\% - 10\%) = 10\% + 6\% = 16\%$

Divisional Opportunity Cost of Capital

Component	After-Tax Cost	×	Division's Financing Proportions	=	Opportunity Cost of Capital
Debt	8%		0.50		4.00%
Common equity	16		0.50		8.00
			Furniture Division's opportunity cost of capital =		12.00%

Paper Division

$\beta_{\text{paper}} = 1.25$

$k_{\text{paper}} = 10\% + 1.25(18\% - 10\%) = 10\% + 10\% = 20\%$

Debt	8%		0.40		3.20%
Common equity	20		0.60		12.00
			Paper Division's opportunity cost of capital =		15.20%

Data Services Division

$\beta_{\text{data services}} = 2.00$

$k_{\text{data services}} = 10\% + 2.00(18\% - 10\%) = 10\% + 16\% = 26\%$

Debt	8%		0.20		1.60%
Common equity	26		0.80		20.80
			Data Services Division's opportunity cost of capital =		22.40%

capital. The furniture division's opportunity cost is 12 percent, while 15.20 percent is appropriate for the paper division. The data services division's opportunity cost of capital is 22.40 percent, indicating that projects originating from that division must have a substantially higher expected return to compensate for the increased risk.[16]

[16] When calculating firm-wide and divisional opportunity costs of capital, certain relationships should hold. For example, the firm-wide equity beta should equal the average of the divisional betas. Thus, for a firm with two divisions,

$$\beta_{\text{firm-wide}} = \beta_{\text{Division A}} W_{\text{Division A}} + \beta_{\text{Division B}} W_{\text{Division B}}$$

where the weights reflect the respective sizes of the two divisions. Likewise, when firm-wide and divisional opportunity costs of capital are calculated, the following relationship should hold:

opportunity cost of capital$_{\text{firm-wide}}$ = opportunity cost$_A$ $W_{\text{Division A}}$ + opportunity cost$_B$ $W_{\text{Division B}}$

Keeping these relationships in mind is important to ensure that the estimates for the divisions are compatible with what we know about the firm as a whole.

Estimating divisional opportunity costs of capital in practice requires a thorough understanding of the firm's divisions and identification of appropriate publicly traded firms that are similar to the divisions, following the steps as given here. The most difficult part of the process is coming up with "good" pure-play firms.[17]

PROJECT-SPECIFIC OPPORTUNITY COSTS OF CAPITAL

The same basic steps used to determine divisional opportunity costs of capital can be applied for specific projects. That is, we estimate the risk of the project, estimate an appropriate cost of equity capital, determine the amount of debt financing (and hence the debt/market value of equity ratio) to be employed, and then calculate a project-specific opportunity cost, or required rate of return. If the project is really a major undertaking, we may be able to employ the pure-play approach involving some other publicly traded firm in the same line. For smaller projects, however, we will have to estimate the project's beta. It is often difficult to come up with a good means of estimating project betas. Finance theory doesn't help us much in terms of providing a simple procedure for estimating project-specific betas if the pure-play approach doesn't work. Even subjective estimates by knowledgeable parties, however, are far better than no adjustment for risk. Generally, their estimates will provide a good idea of the direction of the adjustment required, even if the magnitude of the adjustment is subject to some unknown amount of error.

Concept Review Questions

- Why is it important to use divisional opportunity costs of capital rather than a firmwide opportunity cost of capital?
- Describe the steps used to estimate a divisional opportunity cost of capital.

WAS THE COST OF CAPITAL LOWER IN JAPAN?

During much of the 1970s and 1980s Japanese firms became world leaders in industries such as automobiles and electronics. One point often raised, in addition to productivity differences and the Japanese emphasis on quality, is that the cost of capital was cheaper in Japan than in the United States and other developed countries. A lower cost of capital would provide more positive net present value projects. Equally important, it would allow and encourage Japanese firms to invest in projects that had much longer lives while still providing positive returns to the firm.

The opportunity cost of capital (ignoring preferred stock) is

$$\text{opportunity cost of capital} = k_b(1 - T)W_{\text{debt}} + k_s W_{\text{common equity}}$$

---

[17] Recently some modified approaches using industry data to estimate the "pure-play" firms have been suggested. See Harris, O'Brien and Wakeman, and Ehrardt and Bhagwat.

where

k_b = the before-tax cost of debt

T = the marginal tax rate

k_s = the cost of equity

the W's = the financing proportions

For the cost of capital to be lower in Japan than in the United States, one of four explanations, or some combination of the four, had to apply: (1) the before-tax cost of debt was lower; (2) the cost of equity was lower; (3) the Japanese used more debt; or (4) the marginal tax rate was higher in Japan (thereby driving down the after-tax cost of debt).

Many studies have examined this question. Although some disagreements exist, the primary findings suggest that: (1) the before-tax cost of debt was lower in Japan;[18] (2) the cost of equity, particularly in the mid- and late-1980s, was lower in Japan; (3) the use of debt financing may have been more pervasive in Japan; and (4) the tax rate was not significantly higher in Japan. One of the most interesting aspects of this question relates to the different structural arrangement of firms in Japan, where they are often members of an industrial grouping known as *keiretsu*. There are indications that both the cost of financing and the risk of bankruptcy may have been less for firms that were members of a *keiretsu* than for those that were not. Most of the borrowing during this period of time was done from the firms' main banks (during the 1970s and 1980s corporate bond markets were very small in Japan), and all loans were backed by collateral. Studies suggest that banks and other members of the *keiretsu* went out of their way to buffer firms from financial distress and/or bankruptcy. Accordingly, Japanese firms may have been able to use more debt than firms in the United States and other developed countries.

In the 1990s any advantage Japanese firms might have received due to a lower cost of capital appears to have disappeared. This is due to an increase in the cost of debt, the over 50 percent decline in Japanese stock prices, and a move to more of a market-based financing system, in which the former benefits of the *keiretsu* are less important. Thus, while differences in the cost of capital many have existed in the past, that does not appear to be the case in the 1990s.

Concept Review Question

■ What are the primary findings of the studies examining the cost of capital in Japan?

KEY POINTS

1. The opportunity cost of capital is a future-oriented marginal cost which is used as the discount rate in net present value calculations when average-risk projects are being evaluated. It is the forgone return that could have been earned by investing in a similar-risk project.

---

[18] Japanese firms also employed substantial amounts of convertible bonds (discussed in Chapter 17) in the 1980s. With soaring stock prices, the effective cost of the convertible debt was lower than would otherwise be expected.

2. In order to determine the firm's opportunity cost of capital, we employ the knowledge that financial markets are efficient and, therefore, fully reflect the returns demanded by the firm's providers of capital and the risks faced by the firm.
3. By accepting all investment projects with positive net present values, in which the returns are more than the costs involved, the firm is making wealth-maximizing decisions that assist in maximizing the long-run market value of the firm.
4. Debt is typically the least expensive source of financing, whereas common equity capital is the most expensive. This is because of tax considerations and the risk and return requirements of investors.
5. The opportunity cost of capital is a weighted average of the expected future costs of funds. The weights are given by the market-value proportions of the firm's capital structure.
6. The use of historical data to estimate the expected returns on the market portfolio, or the risk premium of stocks over corporate bonds, without considering current conditions, can lead to estimation errors.
7. When risk differs substantially across various divisions of the firm, the use of a firmwide opportunity cost of capital overallocates capital to safer divisions and projects and underallocates capital to more risky divisions and projects. The misallocation serves to reduce the value of the firm.
8. The most important part of estimating divisional costs of capital involves determining the division's cost of equity capital. Identifying publicly traded pure-play firms similar to the divisions is the most difficult step in the process.

QUESTIONS

6.1   Explain the concept of a firm's opportunity cost of capital. What two ways can we approach this return?

6.2   Why is the cost of debt typically the lowest, and the cost of common equity the highest, of the specific costs?

6.3   "Internally generated funds are costless. Accordingly, the cost of new common stock is the only relevant cost of common equity for cost of capital purposes." Evaluate this statement.

6.4   Compare and contrast the dividend valuation, CAPM, and bond yield plus expected risk premium approaches to estimating the cost of common equity.Which do you believe is theoretically the best? Which is best in a practical sense?

6.5   Discuss the practical aspects of estimating a firm's opportunity cost of capital. Under what circumstances can you ignore payables and accruals? What about leases?

6.6   What problems exist when employing historical data to provide any of the estimates needed for determining a firm's cost of capital?

6.7   Explain how you might use the dividend valuation or bond yield plus expected risk premium approach to estimate the cost of common equity when calculating a divisional opportunity cost of capital. Does either of these approaches have any advantages or disadvantages compared to the CAPM approach for estimating a division's cost of common equity?

6.8   How would each of the following affect the firm's after-tax cost of debt, k_i; cost of equity, k_s; and opportunity cost of capital? Use a plus sign ($+$) to indicate an increase, a minus sign ($-$) to indicate a decrease, and a zero to indicate either no effect or an indeterminate effect. (*Note:* Treat only the direct effect, not any secondary effects.)

	k_i	k_s	Opportunity Cost of Capital
a. The corporate tax rate is decreased.	—	—	—
b. The firm begins to make substantial new investments in assets that are less risky than its present assets.	—	—	—
c. The firm is selling more bonds. Because Standard & Poor's decides the firm is more risky, it lowers the bond rating.	—	—	—
d. The firm decides to triple its financing.	—	—	—
e. Investors become less risk-averse.	—	—	—

CONCEPT REVIEW PROBLEMS

See Appendix A for solutions.

CR6.1 Armstrong Inc. is planning to issue new debt. Armstrong's outstanding debt has an annual coupon interest rate of 10 percent, pays interest semiannually, has 20 years to maturity, and is currently trading at $1,198 per bond. If Armstrong's tax rate is 35 percent, what is the after-tax cost of debt?

CR6.2 In addition, Armstrong is planning on issuing $100 par value preferred stock with an $8.50 dividend payment. The firm expects to receive $93 per share. What is the cost of preferred stock?

CR6.3 Armstrong's stock is currently selling at $40 per share, has an expected EPS at $t = 1$ of $7.20, a dividend payout ratio of 50 percent, and an expected growth rate of 4 percent. *Value Line* has estimated Armstrong's beta at 1.5. If the risk-free rate of return is 6 percent, the return on the market is 14 percent, and the average return on corporate bonds is 8 percent, what is Armstrong's cost of equity? (*Note:* Use all three methods and then take an average of them.)

CR6.4 If Armstrong's target capital structure is 20 percent debt, 10 percent preferred stock, and 70 percent equity, what is Armstrong's opportunity cost of capital?

The following facts given for National Products are needed for CR6.5 through CR6.9.

National Products Company (in millions)			
Assets		**Liabilities and Stockholders' Equity**	
Cash	$5	Accounts payable	$ 5
Accounts receivable	5	Short-term debt	10
Inventories	10	Long-term debt	30
Long-term assets	55	Preferred stock	10
Total assets	$75	Common stock (2 million shares outstanding)	5
		Retained earnings	15
		Total liabilities and stockholders' equity	$75

1. Short-term debt consists of bank loans that currently cost 6 percent.
2. Long-term debt consists of 20-year semiannual payment bonds with a coupon rate of 12 percent. Currently these bonds provide a yield to investors of 9 percent.
3. National Products' perpetual preferred stock has a $100 par value, pays a dividend of $12, and has a yield to investors of 10 percent.
4. The current stock price is $37.50. The firm expects to pay a dividend of $4.00 next year, the growth rate is 6 percent, beta is 1.2, the required return on the market is 15 percent, the marginal tax rate is 35 percent, and the risk-free rate is 6 percent.

CR6.5   What are the market value proportions of debt, preferred stock, and common equity for National Products? (*Note:* Carry to 3 decimal places.)

CR6.6   What is the cost of short-term debt, long-term debt, preferred stock, and common equity for National Products? (*Note:* Calculate all 3 costs of common equity and then average them.)

CR6.7   What is National Products' opportunity cost of capital?

CR6.8   Now assume all equity financing for National Products will have to be obtained from external sources. If the underpricing is $3.50 per share of common stock, what is the firm's new opportunity cost of capital? (*Note:* Use only the dividend valuation approach to determine the cost of common equity.)

CR6.9   The CEO of National Products wants to expand. The new division is expected to be riskier than the firm as a whole. Therefore, the capital structure of the division will contain no short-term financing, no preferred stock financing, 20 percent long-term debt, and 80 percent common equity financing. Similar firms have an average beta of 1.5, a debt-to-equity ratio of 50 percent, and a tax rate of 40 percent. What is the opportunity cost of capital for the division?

PROBLEMS

6.1   Calculate the after-tax cost of debt under the following conditions if the maturity value of the debt is $1,000, interest is paid annually, and the corporate tax rate is 35 percent.

a. Coupon interest rate is 8 percent, proceeds are $900, and the life is 20 years.
b. Bond pays $100 per year in interest, proceeds are $960, and the life is 10 years.
c. Coupon interest rate is 14 percent, proceeds are $1,120, and the bond has a 30-year life.
d. Proceeds are $1,000, coupon interest rate is 12 percent, and the life is 5 years.

6.2   What is the after-tax cost of preferred stock under the following circumstances?

a. Par is $80, dividend is $8 per year, and the proceeds are $76.
b. Proceeds are $46, and dividends are $7.
c. Par is $60, dividend is 9 percent (of par), and proceeds are $55.
d. Par is $40, dividend is 11 percent (of par), and proceeds are $40.

6.3   Given the following information, calculate the cost of common equity, k_s, under each of the following conditions.

a. $P_0 = \$80$, $g = 8$ percent, and $D_1 = \$5$.
b. It is now January 1, 19X7; cash dividends in 19X2 were $2.05; they were $3 in 19X6. $P_0 = \$47$.

c.   Historical growth in dividends is 4 percent, expected growth is 7 percent, $D_0 = \$4$, and $P_0 = \$73$.

d. $P_0 = \$50$, and the past dividends have been

Year	Dividends per Share
−5	$2.50
−4	2.80
−3	2.80
−2	3.10
−1	3.67
0	3.67

6.4   Calculate the cost of common equity, k_s, under the following conditions:

a.   Expected return on the market portfolio is 16 percent, risk-free rate is 6 percent, and beta is 1.50.

b. $k_M = 18$ percent, $k_{RF} = 12$ percent, σ_M (standard deviation of the market) $= 14$ percent, σ_s (standard deviation of stock s) $= 35$ percent, and Corr_{sM} (correlation between returns on stock s and returns on the market) $= +0.80$. (From Chapter 4, remember that $\beta_s = \sigma_s \text{Corr}_{sM} / \sigma_M$.)

c.   The current market interest rate on comparable long-term debt is 9 percent, and the expected risk premium differential of stocks over bonds is 4 percent.

d.   The coupon rate on the firm's existing debt is 9 percent; current market yield on short-term debt is 10 percent; current market yield on long-term debt is 12 percent; and the expected risk premium differential of stocks over bonds is 5 percent.

6.5   Chesapeake Motors has called you in as a consultant to estimate its cost of common equity. After talking with its chief financial officer and consulting an econometric forecasting firm, you have come up with the following facts and estimates:

Estimates	Year	Dividends per Share
$P_0 = \$85$	−5	$1.21
$\beta_{\text{Chesapeake Motors}} = 1.50$	−4	1.21
U.S. Treasury bill rate = 10%	−3	1.30
market yield on comparable quality long-term debt = 13%	−2	1.40
expected return on the market portfolio = 16%	−1	1.71
expected risk premium of stocks over bonds = 4%	0	1.86
current earnings per share, EPS = $5.75		

Chesapeake plans to use 30 percent debt and 70 percent equity for its incremental financing. Also, the firm's marginal tax rate is 33 percent.

a.   What do you estimate the past growth rate in cash dividends per share has been? Employ this as your estimate of g (round to the nearest whole number).

   b. What is the estimated cost of common equity employing the following approaches: (1) dividend valuation, (2) CAPM, and (3) bond yield plus expected risk premium?

   c. Explain why one of the estimates from (b) is substantially lower than the other two.

   d. Take an average of all three answers from (b) for your estimate of Chesapeake's cost of common equity.

   e. What is your estimate of Chesapeake's opportunity cost of capital? How confident of it are you?

6.6 Schwendiman Tire plans to raise $20 million this year for expansion. The firm's current market value capital structure, shown below, is considered to be optimal.

Debt	$ 40,000,000
Common equity	60,000,000
	$100,000,000

New debt will have a market interest rate of 10 percent. Common stock is currently selling at $40 per share, expected growth in dividends is 7 percent, and $D_1 = \$3.60$. If new common stock is sold, the proceeds are expected to be $36 per share. Internally generated funds available for capital budgeting purposes are expected to be $6 million, and Schwendiman's marginal tax rate is 30 percent.

   a. Calculate the market value proportions of debt and common equity.

   b. Calculate the cost of the two relevant sources of capital. (*Note:* Remember it is the cost of the last dollar of each feasible source that is important. Firms tend to use internally generated funds before they issue additional common stock.)

   c. What is Schwendiman's opportunity cost of capital?

6.7 The chief financial officer of Portland Oil has given you the assignment of determining the firm's cost of capital. The present capital structure, which is considered optimal, is as follows:

	Book Value	Market Value
Debt	$50 million	$40 million
Preferred stock	10 million	5 million
Common equity	30 million	55 million
	$90 million	$100 million

The anticipated financing opportunities are these: Debt can be issued with a 15 percent before-tax cost. Preferred stock will be $100 par, carry a dividend of 13 percent, and can be sold to net the firm $96 per share. Common equity has a beta of 1.20, $k_M = 17$ percent, and $k_{RF} = 12$ percent.

   a. If the firm's tax rate is 40 percent, what is its opportunity cost of capital?

   b. What happens to its opportunity cost of capital if Portland's marginal tax rate is zero?

6.8 The management of Lincoln Hotel is considering further expansion. To evaluate the various alternatives, management needs to estimate Lincoln's cost of capital. Various financial data are given, as follows:

Balance Sheet (in millions)			
Total assets	$500	Accounts payable and accruals	$ 50
		Short-term debt	100
		Bonds ($1,000 par)	100
		Common stock (50 million shares)	50
		Retained earnings	200
		Total liabilities and	
		stockholders' equity	$500

Estimates	Year	Dividends per Share
P_0 = $15.50	−7	$1.00
expected return on the market portfolio = 12%	−6	1.00
risk-free rate (U.S. Treasury bills) = 7%	−5	1.05
market interest rate on comparable bonds = 9%	−4	1.05
beta for Lincoln Hotel = 0.80	−3	1.10
	−2	1.10
	−1	1.18
	0	1.23

a. Calculate the historical growth rate in cash dividends per share. Estimate the dividends to be paid in year +1.
b. Estimate the cost of common equity using both the dividend valuation and CAPM approaches. Average the two estimates and then round to the nearest whole number.
c. Calculate Lincoln Hotel's after-tax cost of long-term debt if the firm's marginal tax rate is 35 percent.
d. The short-term debt will carry a different cost. Using the U.S. Treasury bill rate and adding 1 percent to estimate Lincoln's before-tax cost of short-term debt, calculate the after-tax cost of Lincoln's short-term debt.
e. Determine the market value proportions if all of the following hold simultaneously:

(1) Accounts payable and accruals are ignored.
(2) Short-term debt is taken at face value.
(3) The current market value of long-term debt is $125 million.
(4) Common equity is determined by multiplying the number of shares times the stock price.

f. What is Lincoln's opportunity cost of capital?

6.9 Mendelson Markets is in the process of estimating its cost of capital. Financial data for the firm are as follows:

Balance Sheet			
Total assets	$100,000	Accounts payables and accruals	$ 15,000
		Short-term debt	15,000
		Bonds ($1,000 par)	25,000
		Common stock (12,000 shares)	20,000
		Retained earnings	25,000
		Total liabilities and stockholders' equity	$100,000

Estimates	Year	Dividends per Share
$P_0 = \$8.00$	−5	$0.25
expected return on the market portfolio = 17%	−4	0.25
risk-free rate (U.S. Treasury bills) = 10%	−3	0.28
market interest rate on comparable bonds = 13%	−2	0.28
beta for Mendelson = 1.30	−1	0.36
	0	0.40

a. Calculate the historical growth rate in cash dividends per share. (*Note:* Round the growth rate to the nearest whole number.) Estimate the dividends to be paid in year +1.

b. Estimate the cost of equity capital using the dividend valuation, CAPM, and bond yield plus expected risk premium approaches. Assume the expected risk premium is 6 percent. Average the three estimates and then round to the nearest whole number.

c. Calculate Mendelson's after-tax cost of long-term debt if the firm's marginal tax rate is 40 percent.

d. For short-term debt, the before-tax cost is the U.S. Treasury bill rate plus 1 percent. Calculate Mendelson's after-tax cost of short-term debt.

e. Determine the market value proportions if all of the following hold simultaneously:

(1) Accounts payable and accruals are ignored.
(2) Short-term debt is taken at face value.
(3) The current market value of long-term debt is $21,000.
(4) Common equity is determined by multiplying the number of shares times the stock price.

f. What is Mendelson's opportunity cost of capital?

6.10 Jefferson requires $15 million to fund its current year's capital projects. Jefferson will finance part of its needs with $9 million in internally generated funds. The firm's common stock market price is $120 per share. Dividends of $5 per share at $t = 0$ are expected to grow at a rate of 11 percent per year for the foreseeable future. Another part will be funded with the proceeds (at $96 per share) from an issue of 9,375 shares of 12 percent $100 par preferred stock that will be privately placed. The remainder will be financed with debt. Five thousand 10-year $1,000 par bonds with a coupon rate of 15 percent will be issued to net the firm $1,020 each. Interest is paid annually on the bonds. The firm's tax rate is 30 percent.

a. What is Jefferson's opportunity cost of capital?

b. Jefferson has now decided to double its funding requirements. The financing proportions will remain as in (a). No additional internally generated funds are available. New common stock can be sold at $100 per share. Additional preferred stock and debt can be sold with all of the same conditions as in (a) *except* the dividend rate on preferred stock is 13.5 percent and the coupon interest rate on bonds will be 17 percent. What is Jefferson's opportunity cost of capital for this second increment of financing?

6.11 Honeycutt is calculating its opportunity cost of capital. The following has been determined:

Debt. $1,000 par value, 20-year, 9 percent coupon-rate bond can be sold at a discount of $50 per bond. Interest is paid annually, and the marginal corporate tax rate is 40 percent.

Preferred Stock. $100 par value, 8.5 percent preferred stock can be sold at a discount of $9 per share.

Common Equity. The present market price is $75 per share. The cash dividend next year is expected to be $5, and the growth rate is expected to be 7 percent for the foreseeable future.

Internally Generated Financing. All the common equity needs will be funded by internally generated funds.

Honeycutt's current market value capital structure is as follows:

Debt	30%
Preferred stock	20
Common equity	50
	100%

a. What is Honeycutt's opportunity cost of capital?

b. Assume now that instead of (a), Honeycutt decides to increase its financing substantially. Everything is the same as in (a) except:

    Debt. 11 percent coupon interest rate.

    Preferred Stock. 10 percent dividend rate.

    Common Stock. Underpricing is $12 per share.

    Internally Generated Financing. All used up, so none available.

    What is Honeycutt's new opportunity cost of capital?

6.12 Khilnani Products has three different divisions—A, B, and C. In estimating divisional opportunity costs of capital, management has determined that $\beta_A = 1.20$, $\beta_B = 0.60$, and $\beta_C = 2.00$. Also, $k_{RF} = 8$ percent and $k_M = 13$ percent. If the after-tax cost of debt is 5 percent, and the appropriate capital structures for the divisions are given below, what are the three divisional opportunity costs of capital?

	Target Financing Proportions		
	Division A	**Division B**	**Division C**
Debt	0.50	0.20	0.60
Common equity	0.50	0.80	0.40

6.13 Gage Equipment has traditionally employed a firmwide opportunity cost of capital for capital budgeting purposes. However, its two divisions—machinery and farm implements—have different degrees of risk. Data on the firm and the divisions are as follows:

	Gage Equipment	**Machinery Division**	**Farm Implement Division**
Beta	1.4	1.0	2.0
Appropriate percentage of debt	40%	50%	20%
Appropriate percentage of common equity	60	50	80

The following estimates have been made: $k_i = 7$ percent, $k_{RF} = 10$ percent, and $k_M = 15$ percent. The firm is considering the following capital expenditures:

	Proposed Capital Projects	**Initial Investment (in millions)**	**IRR**
Machinery	M-1	$1	15%
	M-2	3	12
	M-3	2	9
Farm implements	F-1	4	16
	F-2	6	20
	F-3	5	12

a. Calculate Gage Equipment's firmwide opportunity cost of capital.
b. Based on your answer in (a), which projects should Gage select? What is the size of the capital budget?
c. Calculate the opportunity costs of capital for the two divisions.
d. Which projects should now be selected? What is the size of the resulting capital budget?
e. What happens if a firm uses a firmwide opportunity cost for capital budgeting purposes when it should be using divisional opportunity costs?

6.14 In order to estimate the equity cost of capital for their electronics division, Li Industries has identified a pure-play firm. Data for the electronics division and the pure-play firm are

	Electronics Division	**Pure-Play Firm**
Marginal tax rate, T	0.45	0.35
B/S	0.50	0.60

If the pure-play firm's levered β is 1.20, the risk-free rate, k_{RF}, is 11 percent, and the expected return on the market, k_M, is 20 percent, what is the electronics division's cost of equity capital?

6.15   Gene's Suprs has two divisions, wholesale and retail. Data are as follows:

marginal tax rate for Gene's, $T = 0.40$

after-tax cost of debt, $k_i = 9\%$

B/S for the wholesale division $= 0.65$

B/S for the retail division $= 0.50$; risk-free rate, $k_{RF} = 10\%$; expected return on the market, $k_M = 18\%$

Two pure-play firms for each division and pertinent data for them include

	Firm	
Pure Play for Wholesale Division	**A**	**B**
market risk, β_j	1.20	1.40
marginal tax rate, T	0.30	0.40
B/S	0.60	0.40

	Firm	
Pure-Play for Retail Division	**C**	**D**
market risk, β_j	1.50	1.40
marginal tax rate	0.35	0.40
B/S	0.45	0.50

a.   Calculate the asset beta for each of the four pure-play firms. Then take a simple average for each pair to determine an unlevered pure-play asset beta for each division.
b.   Calculate the levered betas for both divisions, and then determine the opportunity cost of capital for the wholesale division and for the retail division. {*Note*: $B/V = (B/S)/[1 + (B/S)]$.}

6.16   **Mini Case**   Alliance Consolidated's new CFO is undertaking a thorough review of how the firm makes its capital investment decisions. A major component of this review is to examine how the firm determines its opportunity cost of capital.

a.   What is meant by "opportunity cost of capital"? What assumptions are employed in arriving at a firm's opportunity cost of capital? What role do efficient financial markets play?
b.   What sources are the least expensive? The most expensive? Why? What role do corporate taxes play?
c.   Debt can be issued at par and will carry a 13.5 percent coupon interest rate, and preferred stock can also be issued at par and will carry a 13 percent dividend. Information on common stock is as follows:

	Year	Dividends per share
$P_0 = \$40$	-4	$\$2.00$
$\beta = 1.25$	-3	2.00
$k_{RF} = 11\%$	-2	2.40
expected return on the market portfolio $= 16\%$	-1	2.75
expected risk premium of stocks over bonds $= 5\%$	0	2.93

The market value capital structure for Alliance is 40 percent debt, 50 percent common equity, and 10 percent preferred stock. The firm's marginal tax rate is 35 percent.

(1) Determine the cost of common equity using the three different approaches. (*Note*: For the dividend valuation approach, round g to the nearest whole percent.) Take an average of the three estimates for Alliance's cost of equity.
(2) What is Alliance's opportunity cost of capital?

d. What is the impact of flotation costs on the firm's cost of capital? Also, short-term debt financing?
e. After further investigation it is determined that Alliance's three divisions have vastly different risks. Hence, divisional opportunity costs of capital are required. What occurs if a firmwide opportunity cost is employed when risk differs significantly among divisions?
f. Three pure-play firms have been identified as follows:

	Pure-Play Firms		
	A	B	C
Levered beta, β	1.83	1.35	0.70
Marginal tax rate, T	0.40	0.30	0.40
B/S	0.30	0.90	1.00

For Alliance Consolidated the appropriate B/S ratios for the three divisions are: division A, 0.20; division B, 0.70; and division C, 1.10. What are the appropriate opportunity costs of capital for the three divisions if $k_{RF} = 11\%$, $k_M = 16\%$, $T = 0.35$, and the following are the appropriate percentages of debt and stock for the three divisions?

	Division A	Division B	Division C
Debt	0.167	0.412	0.524
Equity	0.833	0.588	0.476

(*Note:* The percentages have been determined from the B/S ratios given above. Only debt and common equity need to be considered.)

REFERENCES

Further information on the cost of capital is contained in:

ARDITTI, FRED D., and HAIM LEVY. "The Weighted Average Cost of Capital as a Cutoff Rate: A Critical Analysis of the Classical Textbook Weighted Average." *Financial Management* 6 (Fall 1977): 24–34.

BEY, ROGER P., and J. MARKHAM COLLINS. "The Relationship Between Before- and After-Tax Yields on Financial Assets." *Financial Review* 23 (August 1988): 313–31.

FRANKEL, JEFFRY A. "The Japanese Cost of Finance: A Survey." *Financial Management* 20 (Spring 1991): 95–127.

HARRIS, ROBERT S., and JOHN J. PRINGLE. "Risk-Adjusted Discount Rates—Extensions from the Average-Risk Case." *Journal of Financial Research* 8 (Fall 1985): 237–44.

Divisional costs of capital are examined in:

EHRARDT, MICHAEL, and YATIN N. BHAGWAT. "A Full-Information Approach for Estimating Divisional Betas." *Financial Management* 21 (Summer 1991): 60–69.

FULLER, RUSSELL J., and HALBERT S. KERR. "Estimating the Divisional Cost of Capital: An Analysis of the Pure-Play Technique." *Journal of Finance* 36 (December 1981): 997–1009.

HARRIS, ROBERT S., THOMAS J. O'BRIEN, and DOUG WAKEMAN. "Divisional Cost-of-Capital Estimation for Multi-Industry Firms." *Financial Management* 18 (Summer 1989): 74–84.

7

Capital Budgeting Techniques

EXECUTIVE SUMMARY

The analysis of proposed capital expenditures is probably the most important topic in financial management. As discussed previously, net present value, NPV, is the decision criterion to employ in making investment decisions that assist in maximizing the long-run market value of the firm. In practice, the capital budgeting process has four phases: search and identification; estimation of the magnitude, timing, and riskiness of cash flows; selection or rejection; and control and postcompletion audit.

Although net present value is the preferred decision criterion, the internal rate of return is often employed in practice. In most circumstances the two techniques will lead to the same accept or reject decision. The two methods may rank mutually exclusive projects differently, however, because they implicitly assume different reinvestment rates. Because of the possibility of multiple internal rates of return and ranking problems, the net present value criterion is preferred; it always leads to wealth-maximizing decisions. In mutually exclusive situations where the assets will be replaced, unequal lives must also be considered in the analysis.

Without an effective capital budgeting process it is difficult to consistently make decisions, and select the growth opportunities, that maximize the long-run market value of the firm. Capital budgeting is one of the most important topics in finance.

CAPITAL BUDGETING AND THE VALUE OF THE FIRM

The primary goal of the firm is to maximize its long-run market value, or, in the analogy of Chapter 1, to maximize the size of the pie. Although many things contribute to maximizing the value of the firm, the most important single factor is the investments the firm makes. These investments determine the direction of the firm,

239

because, over time, how the firm has positioned itself (in terms of its products or services, its position in its industries, and so forth) is a direct function of its past, present, and future investment decisions. Good investment decisions build on the firm's growth opportunities and take advantage of the unique aspects and advantages a firm has vis-a-vis its competitors.

Capital budgeting techniques are used to evaluate proposed investments in long-term assets. *Long-term* is taken to mean any investment for which returns are expected to extend beyond 1 year. An investment can be as small as the purchase of some office furniture or as large as a complete new plant. The **capital budget** contains estimates of cash flows for long-term projects. **Capital budgeting** is the process by which long-term investments are generated, analyzed, and placed in the capital budget.

PROJECT CLASSIFICATION

Capital budgeting projects can be categorized into three broad categories: expansion, replacement, and regulatory. **Expansion projects** are those designed to improve the firm's ability to produce or market its products. If a firm decides to add a new line of machine tools, the plant necessary to produce the tools is an expansion project. A **replacement project** is one designed to take the place of existing assets that have become physically or economically obsolete. Finally, there are **regulatory projects.** These provide no direct cash benefits to the firm but must be completed for the firm's operations to continue. For example, the federal Occupational Safety and Health Administration (OSHA) and the Environmental Protection Agency (EPA) can require firms to spend billions of dollars to improve the health and safety of the workplace or to prevent harm to the environment.

Another method of classifying projects is to view them as **mutually exclusive projects** or, alternatively, **independent projects.** When two projects are mutually exclusive, the acceptance of one precludes the acceptance of the other. A proposal to purchase one computer network system precludes a proposal to acquire another computer network system, if only one system is needed. The two proposals are mutually exclusive. However, a proposal to acquire a computer network system and another proposal to build a new warehouse are independent. The cash flows are unrelated, and the firm may choose one, both, or neither.

VALUE MAXIMIZATION

In capital budgeting, we calculate the net present value, NPV, which is equal to the present value of the expected after-tax cash flows, discounted at the opportunity cost of capital, or minimum required rate of return, minus the initial cash investment required. Accepting positive-NPV projects has a direct impact on the value of the firm. Consider an all-equity firm that has a current market value of $6 million. That amount includes $2 million in cash that can be invested in new long-term investment projects. You have to decide whether to invest the $2 million in a proposed capital investment or keep it in cash. The choice is as follows:

	Market Value (in millions)	
Asset	Reject New Project	Accept New Project
Cash	$2	$0
Other	4	4
New project	0	PV
	$6	$4 + PV

Clearly, the new project is worthwhile if its present value, PV, is greater than the $2 million required investment. This occurs only if the NPV is greater than zero; when the NPV is zero, the discounted cash inflows from the project would *just equal* the initial investment of $2 million.

What happens, for example, if the proposed project has a net present value of $3.5 million? The firm will receive back its $2 million investment plus an additional $1.5 million (both after discounting). What will happen to the value of the firm? It will increase by $1.5 million as investors recognize the impact of the capital investment decision. *Only by accepting positive-NPV projects can a firm increase its long-run market value; accepting projects with negative NPVs leads to a decrease in the value of the firm.*

Concept Review Questions

- Describe three different types of capital budgeting projects.
- How is the long-run market value of a firm related to a project's net present value?

THE CAPITAL BUDGETING PROCESS

While the ideas behind capital budgeting using net present value are simple and straightforward, complications develop when we put our knowledge to work. To see why, it is important to understand that capital budgeting is a process involving a number of somewhat separate but interrelated activities. The **capital budgeting process** can be broken down into four steps:

1. Search and identification of growth opportunities
2. Estimation of the magnitude, timing, and riskiness of cash flows
3. Selection or rejection
4. Control and postcompletion audit

The relationships among these steps are shown in Figure 7.1.

Figure 7.1

The Capital Budgeting Process

Capital budgeting is an ongoing process in which effective feedback should assist in improving decision making for subsequent capital investments.

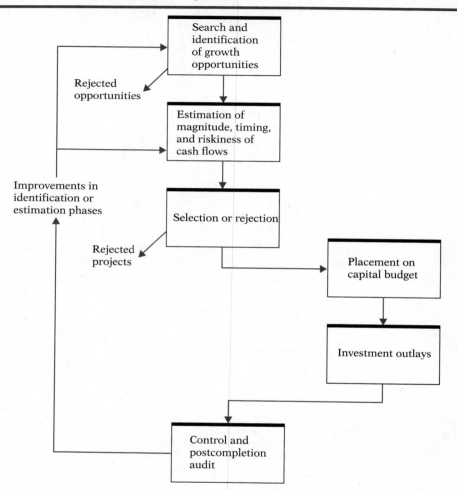

SEARCH AND IDENTIFICATION OF GROWTH OPPORTUNITIES

The search and identification stage involves actively searching for new growth opportunities within the firm's expertise *or* identifying problems that need attention. It is a triggering process: The thrust of this phase is not to analyze and solve well-defined problems, but to identify growth opportunities for possible capital investment.

In the broadest sense, there is a direct connection between the search and identification stage and the firm's overall strategic objectives. The relationship between long-term strategic objectives and the capital budgeting process must be fully integrated and consistent. Too often, this is not the case. The decision to grow by entering a new market or adopting a new production technology is often just the first in a long series of investment decisions. Then either additional investments are made because they "are necessary" given the previous decision, or the capital budgeting decision-making process is employed only *within* the previously defined strategic plan.

Either way, the firm has the cart before the horse. It should be the firm's capital budgeting techniques that determine the firm's long-run strategic decisions—not the other way around!

ESTIMATING THE MAGNITUDE, TIMING, AND RISKINESS OF CASH FLOWS

Once growth opportunities have been searched for and identified, the next step is to develop alternative courses of action and to estimate the magnitude, timing, and riskiness of the cash flows associated with each one. This is often the most difficult part of the entire process. It requires extensive knowledge, hard work, and an understanding of how possible competitor actions will affect cash flow projections. The estimation phase tends to become narrower in focus than the search and identification phase. The reason is that the desired outcome is detailed and specific: a set of alternative capital budgeting projects and associated cash flows, with risk estimates and specification of the key assumptions incorporated into the forecasts. This topic is examined in detail in Chapter 8.

SELECTION OR REJECTION

After the estimates have been made, the firm will select the most promising projects. The important points to remember about this phase are these:

1. The methods used to select or reject projects must be consistent with the objective of maximizing the value of the firm.
2. The key underlying assumptions (concerning the techniques employed and the data used) must be understood by the firm's capital budgeting experts as well as by senior management.
3. Alternative courses of action (including the possibility of delaying a project and the follow-on nature of many capital investment growth opportunities), changes in risk, and possible actions of competitors must be considered.

CONTROL AND POSTCOMPLETION AUDIT

The final phase is that of control and postcompletion audit. Control can be thought of as the process by which the actual cash flows are compared with the projections. In addition, this phase should involve the subsequent reevaluation of the economic merits of ongoing projects—in order to determine whether to continue them. Evaluating the performance of ongoing capital investments is important for any complete capital budgeting process. A successful feedback program suggests needed revisions in the identification procedure, provides information to improve future estimates of cash flows and risk, and indicates projects that should be abandoned. Effective control and postcompletion audits are vital to maximizing the long-run market value of the firm.

All four steps are important. In our study of financial management, we will focus on the second and third—estimation of the magnitude, timing, and riskiness of cash flows, and project selection. *Throughout this chapter and the next, we assume that all projects being considered are equally risky.* That is, their risk is equal to the firm's overall level of risk. Although this assumption is obviously unrealistic, it allows us to focus on the essential elements of the capital budgeting process. Assuming all projects are equally risky means we can use a single hurdle (or discount) rate throughout. This rate is the firm's opportunity cost of capital. In Chapter 9 we will consider situations when the risk of the project is not equal to the firm's overall risk level.

Concept Review Questions

- Describe the four steps of the capital budgeting process.
- Why is estimating the magnitude, timing, and riskiness of cash flows important in capital budgeting decisions?

SELECTING CAPITAL BUDGETING PROJECTS

Firms use a variety of techniques to determine whether to accept proposed projects. The payback period is a simple but naive (unsophisticated) technique that does not employ discounting. The net present value, NPV, and internal rate of return, IRR, techniques both employ discounting to deal with the magnitude, timing, and riskiness of the cash flow stream.[1] The relevant cash flow stream, as discussed in Chapter 8, is the *incremental after-tax* cash flow stream related to the project. This stream is referred to as cash flow, CF.

PAYBACK PERIOD

The **payback period** is the number of years it takes for the firm to recover its initial investment in a project. Payback occurs when the cumulative net cash inflows minus the initial investment equals zero, or

$$\text{payback is the time, } T, \text{ such that } \sum_{t=1}^{T} CF_t = CF_0 \qquad (7.1)$$

---

[1] Two other techniques are the average (or accounting) rate of return and the profitability index. Given the deficiencies of accounting data for effective decision making, we should be wary of any attempt to make capital investment decisions with the average rate of return. The profitability index is discussed in Chapter 8 (footnote 10).

The decision rule for the payback period is as follows:

1. If T is less than the maximum T, accept.
2. If T is greater than the maximum T, reject.
3. If T is equal to the maximum T, you are indifferent.

Consider the two projects in Table 7.1. Project A has an initial investment of $442 and cash inflows of $200 for each of 3 years. Project B requires an initial investment of $718 followed by cash inflows of $250, $575, and $100, respectively, for the 3 years. For project A, which is an annuity, the payback period can be found simply by dividing the initial investment by the annual CF. Thus, $442 divided by $200 yields a payback period, T, of 2.21 years. For project B, the payback is found by determining how many years are needed to recoup the initial investment of $718. In the first year, $250 is recovered; by the end of the second year, a total of $825 is recovered. So, the payback period is between 1 and 2 years. Table 7.1 shows that the payback period is about 1.8 years. Thus, project B has the shorter payback period. If a firm's maximum acceptable payback period is 2 years, it would accept project B and reject project A.

The payback period has some advantages. First, it is simple to calculate. Second, it is easy to understand and can be explained easily. Third, it provides a rough indicator of the riskiness of the project, because projects that pay back sooner are often viewed as being more liquid and hence less risky than those with longer payback periods.

At the same time, the payback period has three significant disadvantages. The first is that the maximum acceptable payback period is arbitrary; that is, it is set without any economic justification. Second, it does not take into account the timing of the cash flows, because discounting is not employed. Third, it does not deal with any cash flows

---

Table 7.1

Calculation of the Payback Period for Projects A and B

When the cash inflows are unequal, as in project B, interpolation can be employed to determine the exact payback period.

Cash Flow Streams

		$200	$200	$200
Project A (an annuity)	0	1	2	3
	$442			

		$250	$575	$100
Project B (nonconstant series)	0	1	2	3
	$718			

Payback Period

Project A: $T = \$442/\$200 = 2.21$ years

Project B: $T = 1 \text{ year} + \dfrac{\$718 - \$250}{\$825 - \$250} = 1 \text{ year} + \dfrac{\$468}{\$575} = 1.81$ years

that occur beyond the payback period. To illustrate, suppose that we had two projects with cash flows as follows:

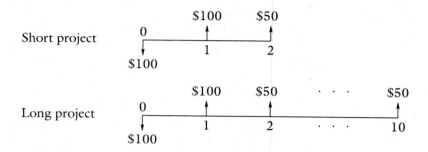

It is obvious that the longer project is better than the shorter one. However, both projects have the same payback of 1 year. Because of these disadvantages, the payback period is not normally considered an appropriate decision-making criterion.[2]

Although the payback period does not appear to be a viable decision criterion, it is widely employed in practice. Why might this be so? One possible explanation[3] is due to agency-related issues that exist between the firm's managers (the agents) and the firm's stockholders (the principals). **Moral hazard** is said to exist when the information available to the firm's managers is superior to that available to outside investors (a case of asymmetric information). In such a case the agent (or managers) can take unobserved self-interested actions that are detrimental to the principals. For risk-averse managers, three important areas in which they can take self-interested actions relate to (1) the amount of effort they expend, (2) the amount of risk (or total variability in firm value) they expose the firm to, and (3) the time horizon adopted for decision making (i.e., will they be with the firm for 6 months, 5 years, or 20 years?). Because of self-interest, managers may prefer shorter-payback capital investment projects, especially when the risk (or total possible variability) in a project's cash flows is high.

NET PRESENT VALUE

The appropriate selection technique is our familiar net present value, NPV. The NPV is determined by discounting the cash inflows back to the present ($t = 0$) at the opportunity cost, k, and then subtracting the initial investment, so that

$$\text{net present value, } NPV = \sum_{t=1}^{n} \frac{CF_t}{(1 + k)^t} - CF_0 \tag{7.2}$$

[2] Some firms calculate a discounted payback period to overcome the timing disadvantage, but the other problems remain.

[3] See Chaney in the end-of-chapter references.

The decision rule for net present value is as follows:

1. If NPV is greater than zero, accept.
2. If NPV is less than zero, reject.
3. If NPV is equal to zero, you are indifferent.

When the NPV is greater than zero, the firm is in the position where it is generating funds above and beyond those necessary to (1) repay the initial investment and (2) provide it with a return of k percent on its investment. This incremental return represents the funds generated by the project that can be used for other purposes by the firm. Assuming the opportunity cost for projects A and B is 12 percent, their net present values are calculated in Table 7.2. Because both projects have positive NPVs, both should be accepted. Notice that the net present value criterion says project A is preferable (because it has a larger NPV), whereas the payback criterion (from Table 7.1) indicates project B is preferred. If we were choosing between the two projects, the net present value would lead us to make the correct decision; the payback period would lead to an erroneous decision.

In addition to solving for a project's NPV, we can depict the capital budgeting decision graphically. When a variety of rates are used to discount a project's cash flows,

Table 7.2

Calculation of the Net Present Value for Projects A and B
The opportunity cost employed was 12 percent. Because both NPVs are positive, both projects assist in maximizing the value of the firm.

Cash Flows Streams

Project A (an annuity)

Project B (nonconstant series)

Net Present Value
Project A

$$NPV = \$200\left[\frac{1}{0.12} - \frac{1}{0.12(1 + 0.12)^3}\right] - \$442 = \$38$$

Project B

$$NPV = \frac{\$250}{(1 + 0.12)^1} + \frac{\$575}{(1 + 0.12)^2} + \frac{\$100}{(1 + 0.12)^3} - \$718$$

$$= \$223 + \$458 + \$71 - \$718 = \$34$$

a **present value profile** can be constructed. For project A, employing various discount rates results in the following net present values:

Discount Rate	Net Present Value
0%	$158
5	103
10	55
15	15
20	−21
25	−52

Plotting these values produces the present value profile shown in Figure 7.2. The present value profile provides a pictorial representation of the sensitivity of NPV to the discount rate employed. The steeper the slope of the present value profile, the more sensitive the NPV is to the opportunity cost of capital employed.

INTERNAL RATE OF RETURN

A third decision criterion is the internal rate of return, IRR; it is the discount rate that equates the present value of the cash inflows with the initial investment. Stated differently, the IRR is the rate that causes the net present value to equal zero. The internal rate of return is found by solving for the unknown IRR in Equation 7.3:

$$\sum_{t=1}^{n} \frac{CF_t}{(1 + IRR)^t} - CF_0 = 0, \text{ or } \sum_{t=1}^{n} \frac{CF_t}{(1 + IRR)^t} = CF_0 \qquad (7.3)$$

This internal rate of return for a project is then compared with the hurdle rate, k, which is the opportunity cost of capital. The internal rate of return decision rule is as follows:

1. If IRR is greater than k, accept.
2. If IRR is less than k, reject.
3. If IRR is equal to k, you are indifferent.

We discussed determining the internal rate of return in Chapter 2. As shown in Table 7.3, the calculated IRR for project A is 17 percent, whereas for project B it is 15 percent. Because the hurdle rate is 12 percent, both projects would be accepted by this criterion.

Figure 7.2

Present Value Profile for Project A

A present value profile shows what happens to the NPV as the discount rate changes. The internal rate of return is the point at which the present value profile line intersects the horizontal axis (or discount rate).

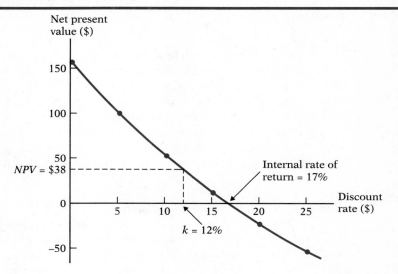

Table 7.3

Calculation of the Internal Rate of Return for Projects A and B

Because both projects have internal rates of return that exceed the hurdle rate, or opportunity cost of capital, of 12 percent, both would be selected.

Cash Flow Streams
Project A (an annuity)   Project B (nonconstant series)

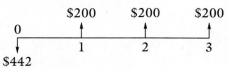

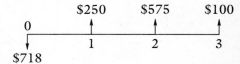

Internal Rate of Return
Project A

$$\sum_{t=1}^{n} \frac{CF_t}{(1 + IRR)} - CF_0 = 0 \qquad \sum_{t=1}^{3} \frac{\$200}{(1 + IRR)} - \$442 = 0$$

The IRR is $16.988 \approx 17$ percent.

Project B

$$\frac{\$250}{(1 + IRR)^1} + \frac{\$575}{(1 + IRR)^2} + \frac{\$100}{(1 + IRR)^3} - \$718 = 0$$

The IRR is $14.993 \approx 15$ percent.

Another way to think about the IRR can be seen by going back to the present value profile in Figure 7.2. The point where the present value profile intersects the horizontal axis is the internal rate of return on a project. As shown in Figure 7.2, the profile line for project A intersects the horizontal axis at 17 percent.

WHY NPV IS PREFERRED

Surveys and discussions with firms indicate that the internal rate of return tends to be widely employed in practice, presumably because it is easier to understand than the NPV technique. For example, an NPV of $25 may not have the same intuitive appeal as an IRR of 18 percent. However, there are circumstances when employing the internal rate of return may lead to incorrect decisions that do not maximize the value of the firm. For this reason, net present value is the preferred capital investment decision criterion. To understand why this is so, it is necessary to consider two additional topics—multiple internal rates of return and ranking problems.

Multiple Internal Rates of Return

One problem that occasionally occurs when the IRR is calculated is that there may be more than one return. **Multiple internal rates of return** may occur when a nonsimple cash flow series occurs. A **simple cash flow** sequence is one in which there is an initial investment (which is negative) followed by a series of positive cash inflows:

Because there is only one change of sign, from negative to positive, there can be only one IRR.[4] A **nonsimple cash flow** series, however, has more than one change in the cash flow sign:

In this case, there are three changes in sign, and there may be three internal rates of return. *None is meaningful for decision making.* Graphically, a present value profile of this multiple-IRR problem with three sign changes might appear as follows:[5]

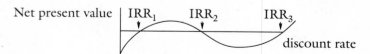

---

[4] Mathematically this is a result of Descartes' rule of signs, which implies that every time the sign of the cash flows change, there will be a maximum of one new real root.
[5] The present value profile could have other shapes and still be consistent with three sign changes. For example, the profile could be just the opposite and still have three intersections with the discount rate line.

Under circumstances such as these, the IRR criterion is inappropriate for decision making, and the net present value approach should be used. Examples of projects producing nonsimple cash flows are strip mining or forest harvesting, where after a section of land has been mined or harvested an after-tax cash outlay is required to return the land to its original condition.

Ranking Problems

The net present value and internal rate of return always make the same accept-reject decision for independent projects.[6] However, when two (or more) mutually exclusive projects are considered, the firm can select only one. That one should be the project that contributes most to the value of the firm. Unfortunately, IRR and NPV do not always rank projects in the same order in terms of their economic desirability. Consider two projects, F and G, with cash flows as follows:

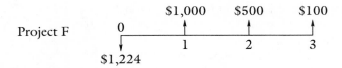

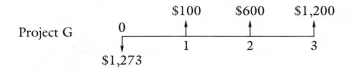

The net present values for these two projects at 11 percent are $156 for project F and $181 for project G. According to the NPV criterion, we should select project G. This is easy to see with NPV because if we select project F, we give up the opportunity to take project G. The opportunity cost associated with taking F instead of G is

$$NPV_{F-G} = \$156 - \$181 = -\$25$$

The internal rate of return for project F is 21 percent, whereas it is 17 percent for project G. According to the IRR criterion, we should select project F. Obviously, a conflict exists.

Alternatively, it could also be tangent to (just touch) the discount rate line and then go back up (or down). Finally, it could turn back up (or down) before reaching the discount rate line, in which case the roots are imaginary.

[6] Excluding the possibility of multiple internal rates of return.

We can calculate the net present values at various discount rates, as follows:

Discount Rate	Project F	Project G
0%	$376	$627
5	268	403
10	173	215
15	89	57
20	14	−79
25	−53	−195

We now have the data necessary to plot the projects' present value profiles in Figure 7.3. As shown in the figure, up to the crossover discount rate of 12.67 percent, the net present value of project G will be higher than the NPV of project F. Above 12.67 percent, the net present value of project F is greater than that of project G.

Conflicting rankings can occur with mutually exclusive projects under two conditions: (1) when the *size of the initial investment* for one project is considerably different from the initial investment for the other, and (2) when the *timing of the two projects'*

Figure 7.3

Conflicting Rankings Between Net Present Value and Internal Rate of Return

Using NPV, the firm would select project G: however, project F has a higher IRR.

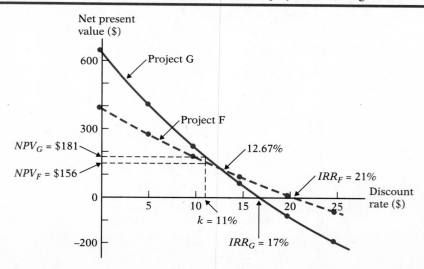

cash inflows differs significantly. Looking at the cash flow streams for projects F and G, we see that the timing of their cash inflows does differ significantly.

The ultimate factor that causes the difference in rankings is the implicit reinvestment rate assumptions incorporated into the NPV and IRR formulas. The NPV method assumes that intermediate cash flows (those from years 1 and 2 for projects F and G) are reinvested at a rate equal to the discount rate employed. In our example the implicit reinvestment rate for the NPV method is the opportunity cost of capital of 11 percent for both projects. The IRR method assumes that these same intermediate cash flows can be reinvested at the project's internal rate of return. Under the IRR method, the implicit reinvestment rate assumption is 21 percent for project F and 17 percent for project G.

Which reinvestment rate assumption is better—the opportunity cost of capital in the NPV approach or the project's IRR in the internal rate of return method? The opportunity cost of capital is, because (1) it is a market-based rate that is the same across all projects of similar risk; (2) any project that returns more than it costs is contributing to the maximization of the long-run market value of the firm; and (3) it allows us to maximize dollars, not percentages.

Modified Internal Rate of Return

An attempt to "save" the internal rate of return has been proposed. This method computes an IRR with an *explicit* reinvestment rate assumption. It assumes that the intermediate cash inflows are reinvested at the opportunity cost of capital, k, not at the project's internal rate of return. This **modified internal rate of return, MIRR,** calls for the project's cash inflows to be compounded out to the end of the project's useful life at k to obtain their future value, FV. Then the discount rate that equates this future value to the initial investment is determined. The modified internal rate of return is found by solving for the unknown MIRR in Equation 7.4:

$$\frac{\sum_{t=1}^{n} CF_t(1 + k)^{n-t}}{(1 + MIRR)^n} - CF_0 = 0, \text{ or } \frac{\sum_{t=1}^{n} CF_t(1 + k)^{n-t}}{(1 + MIRR)^n} = CF_0 \tag{7.4}$$

The calculations of MIRR for projects F and G are shown in Table 7.4. With the required rate of return of 11 percent used as the explicit reinvestment rate, we see that project F has an MIRR of 15.52 percent whereas for project G it is 16.04 percent. Because these projects are mutually exclusive, we would choose the project with the higher MIRR—project G. This choice is the same choice as that made when these projects are evaluated by the NPV criterion.

Does this mean the MIRR will *always* give the same result as NPV? The answer is "no." The MIRR will select the same project as NPV *if* the initial investments are of equal size. In addition, MIRR also overcomes the problem of multiple rates of return.[7]

---

[7] This is accomplished because the MIRR approach allows any negative cash flow that occurs after $t = 0$ to retain its negative value when calculating the future value of the flows. If the sum of the individual future values is greater than zero, there will be only one MIRR for the project; however, if the future sum is less than zero, there is no real MIRR for the project.

Table 7.4

Calculation of the Modified Internal Rate of Return for Projects F and G

With an opportunity cost of 11 percent, project G is chosen. For these two projects, this is the same project that was selected using NPV.

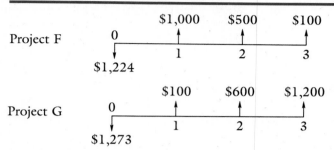

Modified Internal Rate of Return

Project F
Future value of inflows:
$FV_3 = \$1,000(1 + 0.11)^2 + \$500(1 + 0.11)^1 + \$100(1 + 0.11)^0$
$= \$1,232 + \$555 + \$100 = \$1,887$
Calculation of MIRR:
$$\frac{\$1,887}{(1 + MIRR)^3} - \$1,224 = 0$$
The MIRR is 15.52 percent.

Project G
Future value of inflows:
$FV_3 = \$100(1 + 0.11)^2 + \$600(1 + 0.11)^1 + \$1,200(1 + 0.11)^0$
$= \$123 + \$666 + \$1,200 = \$1,989$
Calculation of MIRR:
$$\frac{\$1,989}{(1 + MIRR)^3} - \$1,273 = 0$$
The MIRR is 16.04 percent.

If the initial investments differ significantly in size, however, MIRR may not rank the projects in the same order as NPV. For example, assume we are considering the following two mutually exclusive projects, D and E:

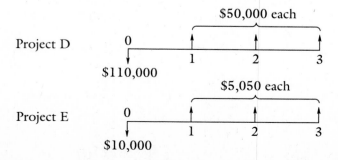

If the minimum opportunity cost of capital, k, is 14 percent, then

	Project	
	D	**E**
NPV (at 14%)	$6,082	$1,724
IRR	17.27%	24.04%

Using the net present value, we would select project D, whereas using the internal rate of return criterion, we would select project E.

If a modified internal rate of return is calculated using 14 percent as the reinvestment rate, then we have

Project D	Future value at $t = 3$ is $171,980
	MIRR = 16.06%
Project E	Future value at $t = 3$ is $17,370
	MIRR = 20.21%

Based on MIRR, project E is still preferred to project *D*—the same conclusion reached with the IRR criterion and exactly opposite to the ranking provided by the NPV criterion. Thus, incorporation of an explicit reinvestment rate assumption for the IRR criterion *does not overcome the ranking problem associated with significant size disparities between projects.* Hence, the MIRR criterion only partially solves the ranking problem and may not lead a firm to select those projects with the highest net present value. The message is clear: Attempts to "save" the internal rate of return by modifying it create more trouble than they are worth. Why not simply stick with net present value? It is easy to calculate and always provides the correct wealth-maximizing investment decision.

Reconciliation of IRR and NPV

From the previous examples we see that choosing the mutually exclusive project with the higher IRR or MIRR may lead to a choice that is inconsistent with the NPV criterion. We can show how the internal rate of return could be used correctly, if you had to use it, so that the selection from both criteria is the same.

The IRR method will rank mutually exclusive projects such as F and G in the same order as the NPV method if we apply the **incremental IRR approach.** This approach is used to make choices between two projects by carrying out the following steps:

STEP 1:   Calculate the IRR for both of the projects under consideration. Using projects F and G, these are 21 percent and 17 percent, respectively.

STEP 2:   If both projects have IRRs that are lower than the opportunity cost of capital, both are rejected. If only one project has an IRR that is above the opportunity cost of capital, select it and reject the other project. If both projects have IRRs that are above the opportunity cost of capital, then the one with the smaller initial investment is set up as the "defender," the project presumed preferable for the time being.[8] In our example, project F, with an outlay of $1,224, has the smaller initial investment. Therefore, F is our defender.

STEP 3:   Calculate the incremental cash flows for the "challenger," project G, minus those for the defender. The incremental cash flows in our example are

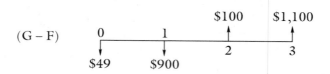

STEP 4:   Calculate the IRR for these incremental cash flows. In our example the IRR for (G − F) is 12.67 percent.[9]

STEP 5:   Compare the IRR for the incremental cash flows to the opportunity cost of capital, k. If it is less than k, the defender should be chosen; if it is greater than k, the challenger should be chosen. In our example, the IRR of 12.67 percent is greater than 11 percent; therefore, project G, the challenger, should be picked. This is the same choice that the NPV criterion provides.

This five-step procedure has reconciled the IRR and NPV methodologies. It shows us how we can properly apply the IRR methodology to mutually exclusive projects. In effect, the procedure has broken project G into two parts. One is equivalent to project F and has an IRR of 21 percent, and the other is project (G − F) with an IRR of 12.67 percent. Thus, the firm has undertaken a package of projects, consisting of F and (G − F), that provides the highest total NPV of the two projects under consideration.

The procedure as outlined above using the incremental IRR may not solve the multiple rate of return problem. It will solve the problem *if* there is a size disparity in the initial investments and the cash flows are such that all of the incremental cash flows are positive. The same cannot be said for the time disparity problem, because a meaningful IRR cannot be calculated for the first step of the procedure. But why go to all of this trouble? The net present value always makes the correct decision and without all of this hassle.

ARE THERE REDEEMING QUALITIES OF INTERNAL RATE OF RETURN?

As indicated before, the internal rate of return is widely used. The primary redeeming quality of the internal rate of return is that the expected return on a project, such as a new plant, can be communicated to executives and the board of directors in percent-

---

[8] If both projects require the same initial investment at time period $t = 0$, then move to time period $t = 1$ and select the project with the most outflow (or, more likely, the least inflow) as the defender.
[9] Note that the IRR for (G − F) of 12.67 percent is the same as the crossover rate of return in Figure 7.3. The reason is that the crossover rate of return, known as the Fisher rate, is the rate of return that makes the NPV of the two projects equal to each other. Thus, this must be the same rate of return that makes the NPV of the difference between the projects equal to zero.

age terms, such as "it provides an expected return of greater than 30 percent." In practice, firms often require that the initial investment be negative and that all subsequent inflows be positive. Therefore, any possibility of multiple internal rates of return is avoided. Hence, firms act as if they understand some of the problems with internal rate of return. Over time there appears to have been some movement away from internal rate of return in practice. Our best guess is that its demise will be slow but continual, as the problems with internal rate of return are more widely known.

Concept Review Questions

- What are some of the advantages and disadvantages of using the payback period?
- Describe how you would use a project's internal rate of return when evaluating whether to accept or reject a project.
- What are some problems with the internal rate of return?
- Describe the steps performed when calculating the modified internal rate of return.
- When do the net present value, the internal rate of return, and the modified internal rate of return all lead to the same accept/reject decision?
- Describe how one would calculate the incremental internal rate of return.

SOME COMPLICATIONS

A number of complications exist when making wealth maximizing capital budgeting decisions. Two of them are how to deal with unequal lives, and how to proceed when only cash outflows exist.

UNEQUAL LIVES

Firms must often make a decision between two or more mutually exclusive projects that have unequal lives. Consider the choice between purchasing two different sanding machines. Model A-3 is semi-automated, requires an initial investment of $320,000, and produces after-tax cash flows of $160,000 for each of 3 years, at which time it will have to be replaced. Model B-6 is an automated machine with a 6-year life, requires an initial investment of $420,000, and produces annual after-tax cash flows of $120,000. As Table 7.5 shows, at a 10 percent discount rate the net present value of the automated machine is greater. With an NPV of $102,631, it appears that model B-6 should be chosen.

But the net present value is a function of the life of the project. Although this does not matter when projects are independent, it does matter when they are mutually exclusive and future replacement is expected (i.e., it is *not* a one-shot investment). To make a valid comparison, it is necessary to equalize the lives of the two projects. There are a number of ways to do this. One is the **replacement chain** approach in which the lives are physically equalized. Under this procedure, the life of Model A-3 would have

Table 7.5

Net Present Value for Two Mutually Exclusive Projects, Ignoring Their Unequal Lives

Other things being equal, model B-6 would be chosen because it has the higher NPV. However, because NPV is a function of the life of the project, it is necessary in mutually exclusive cases to adjust for differences in lives.

Cash Flow Streams

Model A-3

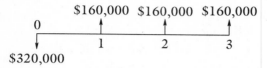

Model B-6

$420,000

Net Present Value
Model A-3

$$NPV = \$160,000\left[\frac{1}{0.10} - \frac{1}{0.10(1 + 0.10)^3}\right] - \$320,000$$
$$= \$397,896 - \$320,000 = \$77,896$$

Model B-6

$$NPV = \$120,000\left[\frac{1}{0.10} - \frac{1}{0.10(1 + 0.10)^6}\right] - \$420,000$$
$$= \$522,631 - \$420,000 = \$102,631$$

to be extended to equal that of Model B-6 as follows:

NPV for Model A-3 over 6 years = original 3-year *NPV* + second 3-year *NPV*

$$= \$77,896 + \frac{\$77,896}{(1.10)^3} = \$136,420$$

Comparing this 6-year NPV for Model A-3 of $136,420 with the NPV of $102,631 for Model B-6, we see that the wealth-maximizing decision is to invest in Model A-3 and then reinvest in another Model A-3 in 3 more years. The replacement chain procedure works fine in this case, but what happens if the lives of the two projects are 7 years and 9 years? Then the analysis has to be taken out to 63 years, because that is the least common denominator of the lives of the two projects.

   Due to potential problems of this type, we use the equivalent annual NPV method.[10] The **equivalent annual NPV** approach to the unequal-life problem converts the original NPVs to yearly net present value figures. The effect is to assume the existing projects will be replicated over and over, with the result that the NPV can be stated as a yearly figure. The equivalent annual NPV is

$$\text{equivalent annual } NPV = \frac{NPV_n}{\left[\dfrac{1}{k} - \dfrac{1}{k(1 + k)^n} \right]} \tag{7.5}$$

where

$$NPV_n = \text{the project's net present value over its original life}$$

$$\left[\frac{1}{k} - \frac{1}{k(1 + k)^n} \right] = \text{the present value of an annuity based on the opportunity cost}$$
of capital and original life of the project

The equivalent annual NPVs for the two models are

$$\text{Model A-3} \quad \frac{\$77,896}{\left[\dfrac{1}{0.10} - \dfrac{1}{0.10(1 + 0.10)^3} \right]} = \$31,323$$

$$\text{Model B-6} \quad \frac{\$102,631}{\left[\dfrac{1}{0.10} - \dfrac{1}{0.10(1 + 0.10)^6} \right]} = \$23,565$$

Because Model A-3 has the higher equivalent annual NPV, *it contributes more to the firm's goal of maximizing the value of the firm per year.* Therefore, Model A-3 is preferable.

Two points should be stressed. First, managers and students sometimes get the impression that different lives have to be taken into account for *all* projects. This is not true: *Unequal lives must be dealt with only for mutually exclusive projects.* For all independent projects, the NPV criterion already takes into account timing differences. By selecting independent projects with the largest NPV, we are making the correct decision without having to adjust for unequal lives. Second, neither the replacement chain nor the equivalent annual NPV approaches allows for differing rates of inflation or other changes (such as new technology). The best way to handle complications such as these is to build the effects of expected inflation, new technology, and so forth, into the cash flow estimates. Then the lives of the two projects will have to be equalized—perhaps by assuming some common termination point and considering the resale value at that point in time for each project. The NPVs for the two projects can then be calculated and compared.

---

[10] There are other methods. One is the infinite replication approach, which converts both projects to perpetuities.

WHEN ONLY CASH OUTFLOWS EXIST

Occasionally you will run into capital investment decisions when only the cash outflows are relevant. This may occur when a firm argues it has to have the machine (perhaps to stay in business) and the only issue is to choose the best machine from a number of mutually exclusive alternatives.

Three points should immediately be recognized in such a situation. First, are the inflows really irrelevant? As we discuss in Chapter 10, often firms don't consider the abandonment decision or ask the question, "Should we continue in this business?" Second, *with only cash outflows the objective becomes that of minimizing the value of the discounted cash outflows.* Thus, you need to determine the **equivalent annual cost** of the alternatives. Third, the goal is to select the alternative with the *lowest* equivalent annual cost. The procedures are exactly the same as for NPV and equivalent annual NPV, but there are only cash outflows to consider.

Thus far we have examined the basic procedures by which most medium and large firms make capital investment decisions. We have examined what selection technique to employ, and we have considered unequal lives between mutually exclusive projects. However, capital budgeting is a complex subject. Other important issues are discussed in Chapters 8–10 and 14.

Concept Review Questions

- What are two methods used to evaluate capital budgeting projects with unequal lives?
- When using either the replacement chain or the equivalent annual NPV to compare projects of unequal lives, what assumptions are being made?
- How are accept/reject decisions applied to capital budgeting projects that have only cash outflows?

KEY POINTS

1. Only by accepting positive net present value investment projects can the firm maximize its long-run market value.
2. Expansion projects result in the net addition of assets as the firm makes decisions that expand the scope of its activities; replacement decisions involve the consideration of retaining existing assets or replacing them with other assets. When projects are independent of one another, all positive NPV projects should be taken, in order to maximize the market value of the firm. However, when projects are mutually exclusive, accepting one automatically leads to the rejection of the other project(s).
3. In practice, the capital budgeting process has four phases: search and identification of growth opportunities; estimation of the magnitude, timing, and riskiness of cash flows; selection or rejection; and control and postcompletion audit. While all are important, we focus on the second and third steps.
4. Although the payback period is widely employed in practice, it is not economically justifiable, it does not take the timing of the cash flows into account, and it does not account for expected cash flows that occur beyond the payback period.
5. Net present value, NPV, is the only decision criterion that always produces decisions

consistent with the goal of maximizing the value of the firm. Despite its widespread use, the internal rate of return suffers from possible multiple internal rates of return and ranking problems.

6. The modified internal rate of return may provide an incorrect ranking of which mutually exclusive project to accept when projects require different initial investments.
7. When the lives of mutually exclusive projects are unequal, they must be equalized. The easiest way to accomplish this is by employing equivalent annual NPVs.
8. If only cash outflows exist, the objective becomes one of minimizing the discounted cash outflows.

QUESTIONS

7.1 A firm is considering the construction of two projects. Project A is a new receiving dock for supply trucks. Project B is a rail car receiving dock that will accept supplies by rail. Are projects A and B mutually exclusive, independent, or interdependent? Why?

7.2 Trace the important relationships among the four phases of the capital budgeting process. Irrespective of Figure 7.1, indicate how all four phases could be related to one another.

7.3 Three decision criteria examined in this chapter were payback period, net present value, and internal rate of return. Why is the NPV an appropriate technique, whereas the payback period and IRR are not?

7.4 What does it mean when the NPV is zero? What decision should be made? What is the IRR when the NPV is zero?

7.5 What causes the internal rate of return occasionally to have multiple rates? Are any of these rates useful for decision making?

7.6 Under what conditions do the NPV and IRR methods provide different rankings? Explain the cause of the difference between the two.

7.7 Explain how the modified internal rate of return, MIRR, is similar to or different from both IRR and NPV. What problem does it overcome? What problem doesn't it overcome?

7.8 Many firms calculate the equivalent annual NPV of mutually exclusive projects when making capital budgeting decisions. In what circumstances does or doesn't this approach lead to sensible investment decisions?

CONCEPT REVIEW PROBLEMS

See Appendix A for solutions.

CR7.1 Monford Partnership is considering two projects with the following cash flows:

	CF_0	CF_1	CF_2	CF_3
A	−$500	$200	$200	$300
B	− 500	400	500	−1,000

Using the payback period, which project should Monford accept?

CR7.2 Using net present value and a cost of capital of 10 percent, evaluate the two projects in CR7.1.

CR7.3   United Railroad is considering purchasing one of two different types of locomotives. Both cost $500,000 and are expected to last for 3 years. Cash inflows from each of the locomotives are as follows:

Locomotive	CF$_1$	CF$_2$	CF$_3$
A	$350,000	$250,000	$80,000
B	0	0	800,000

What is the internal rate of return for each of the locomotives?

CR7.4   If United Railroad's opportunity cost of capital is 10 percent, what is the net present value of the two projects considered in CR7.3?

CR7.5   United Railroad is also considering a third project, Project C, with the following cash flows:

CF$_0$	CF$_1$	CF$_2$	CF$_3$
−$500,000	$8,000,000	$8,000,000	−$20,000,000

What is the internal rate of return and the net present value of Project C? Should the project be accepted?

CR7.6   Calculate the modified internal rate of return for A and B being considered by United Railroad in CR7.3.

CR7.7   Jed is planning to plant one of two types of alfalfa seed. The more expensive of the two will produce higher yields over a 3-year period. The projects are mutually exclusive and the opportunity cost of capital is 12 percent. He has calculated the following after-tax net cash flows:

Year	Select Seed	Cheap Seed
0	−$4,000	−$840
1	3,000	630
2	2,000	630
3	1,000	420

Calculate each project's net present value, internal rate of return, and modified internal rate of return. Which type of alfalfa seed should Jed plant?

CR7.8   Calculate the incremental internal rate of return of the two seed projects in CR7.7. Which seed should be planted?

CR7.9   ConCOR is considering two mutually exclusive pieces of machinery. One piece of machinery, A, has a 3-year life, and the other piece of machinery, B, has a 9-year life. The two alternatives provide the following after-tax cash flows:

Year	Machine A	Machine B
0	−$40,000	−$40,000
1	25,000	13,200
2	25,000	13,200
3	25,000	13,200
4		13,200
5		13,200
6		13,200
7		13,200
8		13,200
9		13,200

Using the replacement chain approach, which project should be accepted? Assume ConCOR's opportunity cost of capital is 15 percent.

CR7.10   Using the equivalent annual net present value approach, evaluate both of the machines considered by ConCOR in CR7.9.

PROBLEMS

7.1   Cash flow streams for two mutually exclusive projects are given below.

	After-Tax Cash Inflows	
Year	Project A	Project B
1	$300	$600
2	400	200
3	50	100
4	50	700

Project A requires an initial investment of $600, and project B requires an initial investment of $1,000.

a.   Use the payback period to determine which project should be selected.
b.   If the opportunity cost is 8 percent, determine the net present value for both projects.
c.   Which project should be chosen? What are the drawbacks of the payback period method?

7.2   Trennepohl Production is contemplating the acquisition of a new multiperson word processing system for $90,000. The system is expected to produce after-tax cash inflows of $25,800 for each of 5 years.

a.   What is the net present value of the system if the discount rate is 0, 5, 10, 15, or 20 percent?
b.   Graph the project's present value profile. What is the project's approximate IRR?

7.3   The initial cash outlay for a machine is $300,000. The expected after-tax cash inflows from the machine are $90,000, $104,400, $88,800, $84,000 and $82,800 in years 1 through 5, respectively. The machine has no anticipated resale value in 5 years. What is the project's internal rate of return, IRR?

7.4   Each of two mutually exclusive projects involves an investment of $120,000. The estimated CFs are as follows:

Year	Project X	Project Y
1	$70,000	$10,000
2	40,000	20,000
3	30,000	30,000
4	10,000	50,000
5	10,000	90,000

The opportunity cost is 11 percent. Calculate the NPV and IRR for both projects. Which project should be chosen? Why?

7.5   The projected cash flows from a project are as follows:

Year	After-Tax Cash Inflows
1	$1,000
2	1,300
3	2,000
4	2,500
5	1,400

a.   If the opportunity cost is 16 percent, what is the maximum the firm can afford to invest in the project?

b.   If the firm can actually implement the project by making an initial investment of $4,200, what is the project's internal rate of return?

7.6   Projects A and B both require a $20,000 initial investment and have projected cash inflows as follows:

	After-Tax Cash Inflows	
Year	Project A	Project B
1	$10,000	$7,000
2	8,000	7,000
3	6,000	7,000
4	4,000	7,000

a. Calculate each project's net present value if the opportunity cost is 12 percent.
b. Calculate the internal rate of return for each project.
c. Should either project be rejected if they are independent?
d. Which project should be selected if they are mutually exclusive?

7.7 A mining company can open a new strip mine for an initial investment of $24 million (at $t = 0$). In year 1, the mine produces a net cash inflow of $78 million. In year 2, the land must be returned to its original state, which requires an outflow of $60 million.

a. Find the net present values not calculated below.

Rate (%)	NPV (in millions)
0	$ ____
25	
50	____
75	0.980
100	0
125	−1.185

b. Construct a present value profile with the data from (a).
c. Should the mine be built if the hurdle rate is 20 percent?

7.8 Richardson Products is analyzing two mutually exclusive projects. Both require an initial investment of $65,000 and provide cash inflows as follows:

	After-Tax Cash Inflows	
Year	Project C	Project D
1	$40,000	0
2	30,000	0
3	20,000	$104,200

a. If the opportunity cost is 10 percent, which project would Richardson choose if NPV is employed?
b. Calculate the internal rate of return for both projects. Which project should be selected according to IRR? Why does the difference in rankings occur?

7.9 Miles Equipment is considering two mutually exclusive projects, each with a 5-year life. Project P requires an initial investment, CF_0, of $20,000 and has CFs of $6,541.00 for each of 5 years. Project Q has an initial investment of $100,000 and CFs of $29,831.56 for each of 5 years.

a. Calculate the IRR for each project, and select the preferred project.
b. Assuming the projects are of equal risk and the opportunity cost is 13 percent, which project is preferable? Defend your answer.

c. At what specific discount rate would the firm be indifferent between the two projects?

d. Calculate the MIRR for each project, and select the preferred project. Has the use of MIRR given the same choice as NPV? Explain.

7.10 Two mutually exclusive projects have after-tax cash flows as follows:

Time	Project X	Project Y
$t = 0$	−$50	−$30
$t = 1$	15	35
$t = 2$	85	15

a. If the discount rate is 10 percent, what are the NPVs for the two projects? What are their IRRs? Which project should be chosen?

b. Using the incremental IRR approach, determine which project should be chosen.

c. Why does the incremental IRR approach provide the same ranking as NPV for mutually exclusive projects?

7.11   Consider a firm in need of a stamping machine. It can buy a one-speed machine that requires an initial investment of $350 and produces after-tax cash inflows of $300 for each of 2 years, or it can purchase a three-speed machine that costs $1,200 and produces cash inflows of $500 for each of 4 years. Neither machine has any resale value, and the opportunity cost is 16 percent. Which machine should be purchased?

7.12   Either of two new molding machines that makes drinking glasses requires an initial investment of $2,000. Model 3SR produces short glasses and has a 5-year life. Model 3TR produces tall glasses and has a 9-year life. CFs expected from the purchase of model 3SR and model 3TR are $700 and $500 per year, respectively. If the opportunity cost is 13 percent and there is no resale value, which model should be purchased?

7.13   Constantia is contemplating replacing its existing boiler, which is worn out and has no resale value. One of two boilers will be chosen; both offer increased operating efficiency. The after-tax cash flows are as follows:

Year	Short-Life Boiler	Long-Life Boiler
Initial investment	$5,000	$8,000
1	2,500	2,750
2	2,500	2,750
3	2,500	2,750
4		2,750
5		2,750

a. Calculate the internal rate of return and net present value for both boilers over their original lives. The appropriate opportunity cost is 18 percent.

b. Which boiler should be chosen? Why?

7.14 A new truck is needed to replace an existing one. Three alternatives exist as follows:

Year		A	B	C
Initial investment		$30,000	$45,500	$42,000
After-tax cash flow:	1	600	1,240	2,160
	2	600	1,240	1,560
	3	0	1,240	1,560
	4	−1,200	640	1,560
	5	−1,200	640	960
	6	−5,400	−3,000	
	7		−3,000	

If the opportunity cost of capital 15 percent, which truck should be selected?

7.15 **Mini Case**   Gullett Manufacturing is expanding into producing see-through bottle caps. The relevant data has been estimated as follows: The initial cash outlay is $44,000, and the after-tax cash inflows are $14,800, $16,480, $14,660, $14,100 and $25,960 in years 1 through 5, respectively.

a. What is the purpose of capital budgeting? How does it relate to the firm's objective?
b. Assuming the opportunity cost of capital is 15 percent, calculate the payback period, net present value, and internal rate of return. Should the project be accepted?
c. Instead of the machine outlined above, a second machine that requires substantially less investment but has higher operating cash outflows could be employed to produce the see-through bottle caps. The estimated after-tax cash flows for the second machine are as follows: CF_0, −$11,000$; CF_1, $7,000$; CF_{2-5}, $5,000$ each. Calculate the payback period, net present value, and internal rate of return for this second alternative. Which machine— the first or second—should be selected? Does a ranking problem exist?
d. Why is the net present value the preferred decision criterion for making capital investment decisions while the internal rate of return is not?
e. If we did not know the net present values for the two machines, how could we use the incremental IRR to make the correct decision? What is the incremental IRR between these two machines?
f. One of the firm's managers has heard of the modified IRR criterion, but does not understand it completely. Explain it to the manager. Then calculate modified IRRs for the two alternatives. Does the modified IRR lead to the correct decision in this case? In all cases?

REFERENCES

For general information on capital budgeting, see, for example, the following:

BIERMAN, HAROLD, JR., and SEYMOUR SMIDT. *The Capital Budgeting Decision.* 7th ed. New York: Macmillan, 1988.

GORDON, LAWRENCE A., and GEORGE E. PINCHES. *Improving Capital Budgeting: A Decision Support System Approach.* Reading, Mass.: Addison-Wesley, 1984.

PINCHES, GEORGE E. "Myopia, Capital Budgeting and Decision Making." *Financial Management* 11 (Autumn 1982): 6–19.

Some articles on relevant topics include these:

CHANEY, PAUL K. "Moral Hazard and Capital Budgeting." *Journal of Financial Research* 12 (Summer 1989): 113–28.

DORFMAN, ROBERT. "The Meaning of Internal Rates of Return." *Journal of Finance* 36 (December 1981): 1011–21.

HOWE, KEITH M. "Perpetuity Rate of Return Analysis." *Engineering Economist* 36 (Spring 1991): 248–57.

NARAYANAN, M. P. "Observability and the Payback Criterion." *Journal of Business* 58 (July 1985): 309–23.

Two studies on the impact of capital budgeting on a firm's market value are:

HAKA, SUSAN F., LAWRENCE A. GORDON, and GEORGE E. PINCHES. "Sophisticated Capital Budgeting Selection Techniques and Firm Performance." *Accounting Review* 60 (October 1985): 651–69.

McCONNELL, JOHN J., and CHRIS J. MUSCARELLA. "Corporate Capital Expenditure Decisions and the Market Value of the Firm." *Journal of Financial Economics* 14 (September 1985): 399–422.

8 Capital Budgeting Applications

EXECUTIVE SUMMARY

Wealth-maximizing capital investment decisions require a well-designed capital budgeting process, knowledge of the proper selection techniques, a thorough understanding of the nature of the projects under consideration (including interactions with other projects), and determination of the relevant cash flows. Understanding depreciation and tax factors based on the Internal Revenue Service Code, not as recorded by accountants under GAAP, is essential to determining the relevant cash flows.

For all three parts of the cash flow stream—initial, operating, and terminal—it is necessary to determine the incremental (new minus old) after-tax cash flows. Failure to do so results in an incomplete and faulty analysis. This same approach of focusing on incremental cash flows is required when evaluating interrelated projects. Only by considering all possible combinations of projects can the proper decision be made.

The opportunity cost of capital already takes into account expected inflation. Failure to incorporate the effect of inflation in the cash flow stream therefore leads to biased figures, and possibly wrong decisions. Financing costs are not incorporated into the cash flow stream; the investment, or capital budgeting, decision and the financing decision are normally made separately. If that is impossible, then techniques discussed in Chapter 14 should be employed.

ESTIMATING CASH FLOWS

To accurately estimate the relevant cash flows, we must understand how corporations treat **depreciation** and taxes under the Internal Revenue Service Code. The first and most important point to remember is that what matters is the actual depreciation and tax provisions built into the tax code. Do not be led astray by what is used for generally accepted accounting principle, GAAP, purposes. Only what firms do as required by the Internal Revenue Service, IRS, is important—because it directly affects the taxes paid, and hence, the cash flows of the firm.

DEPRECIATION FOR TAX PURPOSES

The Tax Reform Act of 1986 introduced the **Modified Accelerated Cost Recovery System, MACRS,** of depreciation. The essence of MACRS was to divide all assets (excluding real estate) into six classes, as shown in Table 8.1. Firms and individuals have no choice in determining the asset class. Thus, all assets of a certain type, such as light trucks, have a class life of 5 years for tax purposes. Firms must depreciate all assets within a class over the **normal recovery period** for that class of assets.

One complication is that the Internal Revenue Service assumes all assets (excluding real estate) are purchased halfway through the year; hence the first year's depreciation is one-half of the "normal" rate. Likewise, all assets are assumed to have a useful tax life of one-half year *longer* then their class life. For example, light trucks and other 5-year class-life assets have a tax life of $5\frac{1}{2}$ years. Firms can employ accelerated percentages,[1] as specified in Table 8.2, or they can employ straight-line depreciation over the class life. For 5-year-class-life assets, the relevant depreciation percentages per year are

Year	MACRS	Straight-Line
1	20.00%	10.00%
2	32.00	20.00
3	19.20	20.00
4	11.52	20.00
5	11.52	20.00
6	5.76	10.00

Thus, even though the assets are in a 5-year class, they are depreciated over 6 years. The same procedure is required by the IRS for all other asset classes.

In addition, there is another difference between depreciation for tax purposes and GAAP accounting depreciation. In accounting the firm often takes the original cost of the equipment and then subtracts the estimated salvage value before determining the per year depreciation. But, *under the tax code any estimated salvage value is irrelevant when determining depreciation; the original value of any asset is not reduced by the estimated salvage value, and all assets are depreciated to zero.* Thus, for a light truck that costs $15,000, the relevant depreciation for tax purposes—and the only depreciation

---

[1] For 3-, 5-, 7-, and 10-year assets, the 200 percent (or double) declining balance method is used, whereas the 150 percent declining balance method is used for 15- and 20-year assets. Switching to straight-line depreciation is incorporated in the MACRS percentages.

Table 8.1

Normal Recovery Period and Property Classes

Instead of MACRS, straight-line depreciation may be used over the normal recovery period.

Normal Recovery Period (Years)	Property
3	Certain short-lived property and special-purpose tools
5	Automobiles; light trucks; buses; technological equipment; information systems; construction equipment; electronic and semiconductor manufacturing equipment
7	Most manufacturing equipment; office furniture and equipment; railroad cars and locomotives; amusement parks
10	Some manufacturing equipment; cement plants; petroleum refineries; barges and tugs
15	Industrial steam and electric-generation equipment; sewage treatment plants; telephone distribution plants; pipelines
20	Most public utility property; railroad structures

Table 8.2

MACRS Depreciation Factors by Normal Recovery Period and Year

The first year's factors are lower because a half-year convention is employed—that is, all assets are assumed to be purchased halfway through the fiscal year. Likewise, all assets are depreciated for one-half year longer than their normal recovery period.

Year	3-Year	5-Year	7-Year	10-Year	15-Year	20-Year
1	0.3333	0.2000	0.1429	0.1000	0.0500	0.0375
2	0.4445	0.3200	0.2449	0.1800	0.0950	0.0722
3	0.1481	0.1920	0.1749	0.1440	0.0855	0.0668
4	0.0741	0.1152	0.1249	0.1152	0.0770	0.0618
5		0.1152	0.0893	0.0922	0.0693	0.0571
6		0.0576	0.0893	0.0737	0.0623	0.0528
7			0.0893	0.0655	0.0590	0.0489
8			0.0445	0.0655	0.0590	0.0452
9				0.0655	0.0590	0.0446
10				0.0655	0.0590	0.0446
11				0.0329	0.0590	0.0446
12–15					0.0590	0.0446
16					0.0299	0.0446
17–20						0.0446
21						0.0225

that is relevant—is as follows:

Year	MACRS	Straight-line
1	(0.2000) ($15,000) = $3,000	(0.10) ($15,000) = $1,500
2	(0.3200) (15,000) = 4,800	(0.20) (15,000) = 3,000
3	(0.1920) (15,000) = 2,880	(0.20) (15,000) = 3,000
4	(0.1152) (15,000) = 1,728	(0.20) (15,000) = 3,000
5	(0.1152) (15,000) = 1,728	(0.20) (15,000) = 3,000
6	(0.0576) (15,000) = 864	(0.10) (15,000) = 1,500
	Total depreciation $15,000	$15,000

As you can see, either MACRS or straight-line depreciation results in the same total amount of depreciation being allowed for tax purposes. The difference is that due to the greater depreciation charged off in the early years under MACRS, the firm actually pays less taxes in the early years, thereby reducing the present value of the cash outflows for taxes. Other things being equal, profitable firms prefer to pay the taxes later rather than sooner; hence, firms have a strong incentive to use MACRS rather than straight-line depreciation for income tax purposes.

Due to the differing depreciation rates over the years under MACRS, it is often simpler to use tables to reduce the calculation time needed in determining the present value of the depreciation tax shield. Suppose we had a $30,000 asset in the 7-year class and the discount rate employed is 12 percent. Applying the appropriate factor of 0.681 from Table 8.3, we find that the present value of the depreciation is ($30,000)(0.681) = $20,430. We will use this knowledge later in the chapter.

Likewise, if the firm elects to employ straight-line depreciation over the asset's normal recovery period, similar to MACRS, the half-year convention applies to both the first and last year's depreciation (i.e., one year longer than the class life). A table (see Table 8.4) can also be used to save time when straight-line depreciation is employed. *Some of the problems at the end of this chapter will employ Tables 8.3 and 8.4 when determining the present value of the depreciation. Others, for simplicity, ignore the half-year convention and with straight-line depreciation and a 5-year asset, for example, simply depreciate 20 percent per year.*

For the previous $30,000 asset in the 7-year class, the present value of the depreciation at 12 percent when straight-line depreciation is employed is ($30,000)(0.617) = $18,510. We see that the present value of the depreciation is $20,430 with MACRS, while it is only $18,510 with straight-line depreciation. This difference illustrates the benefits to the firm of employing MACRS instead of the alternative straight-line depreciation allowed under the tax code.

Real estate is covered by two special depreciation classes: The $27\frac{1}{2}$-year class includes residential rental property, defined as buildings or structures with 80 percent or more of their rental income from dwelling units. The $31\frac{1}{2}$-year class includes nonresidential real estate. For both classes the straight-line method of depreciation is required. We ignore real estate throughout the text.

Table 8.3

Present Value of Depreciation Charges Under MACRS

The tabled factors are per dollar of depreciable base. Thus, if a 5-year-class-life asset has a depreciable base of $40,000 and the discount rate is 14 percent, the present value of the MACRS depreciation is ($40,000)(0.706) = $28,240.

Interest Rate (%)	3-year	5-year	7-year	10-year	15-year	20-year
1	0.981	0.973	0.965	0.953	0.926	0.905
2	0.962	0.946	0.932	0.910	0.860	0.823
3	0.944	0.921	0.900	0.870	0.800	0.752
4	0.926	0.898	0.870	0.832	0.747	0.690
5	0.910	0.875	0.842	0.797	0.698	0.635
6	0.893	0.853	0.816	0.765	0.655	0.587
7	0.877	0.832	0.790	0.734	0.615	0.544
8	0.862	0.811	0.766	0.706	0.580	0.506
9	0.847	0.792	0.743	0.679	0.547	0.473
10	0.832	0.773	0.721	0.654	0.517	0.442
11	0.818	0.755	0.701	0.631	0.490	0.415
12	0.804	0.738	0.681	0.608	0.465	0.391
13	0.791	0.722	0.662	0.588	0.442	0.369
14	0.778	0.706	0.644	0.568	0.421	0.349
15	0.766	0.690	0.627	0.549	0.402	0.331
16	0.753	0.675	0.611	0.532	0.384	0.315
17	0.742	0.661	0.595	0.515	0.367	0.299
18	0.730	0.647	0.580	0.499	0.352	0.286
19	0.719	0.634	0.565	0.484	0.338	0.273
20	0.708	0.621	0.552	0.470	0.324	0.261
21	0.697	0.609	0.538	0.457	0.312	0.250
22	0.687	0.597	0.526	0.444	0.300	0.240
23	0.677	0.585	0.514	0.432	0.289	0.231
24	0.667	0.574	0.502	0.420	0.279	0.222
25	0.657	0.563	0.491	0.409	0.270	0.214
26	0.648	0.553	0.480	0.398	0.261	0.207
27	0.639	0.542	0.469	0.388	0.252	0.200
28	0.630	0.533	0.459	0.379	0.244	0.193
29	0.621	0.523	0.450	0.369	0.237	0.187
30	0.613	0.514	0.440	0.361	0.229	0.181
32	0.596	0.496	0.423	0.344	0.216	0.170
34	0.581	0.480	0.406	0.329	0.205	0.160
36	0.566	0.464	0.391	0.315	0.194	0.152
38	0.552	0.449	0.377	0.302	0.184	0.144
40	0.538	0.435	0.363	0.290	0.175	0.137

Table 8.4

Present Value of Depreciation Charges Under Straight-Line Depreciation as Required under the Tax Reform Act of 1986

The tabled factors are per dollar of depreciable base. Thus, if a 5-year-class-life asset has a depreciable base of $40,000 and the discount rate is 14 percent, the present value of the straight-line depreciation is ($40,000)(0.644) = $25,760.

Interest Rate (%)	3-year	5-year	7-year	10-year	15-year	20-year
1	0.975	0.966	0.956	0.942	0.920	0.898
2	0.952	0.933	0.916	0.889	0.848	0.810
3	0.929	0.903	0.877	0.841	0.784	0.733
4	0.907	0.873	0.841	0.795	0.727	0.666
5	0.886	0.845	0.807	0.754	0.676	0.608
6	0.866	0.819	0.775	0.715	0.629	0.557
7	0.846	0.793	0.745	0.679	0.587	0.512
8	0.827	0.769	0.716	0.646	0.549	0.473
9	0.809	0.746	0.689	0.615	0.515	0.438
10	0.791	0.724	0.664	0.587	0.484	0.406
11	0.774	0.703	0.640	0.560	0.456	0.378
12	0.758	0.682	0.617	0.535	0.430	0.353
13	0.742	0.663	0.595	0.511	0.406	0.331
14	0.726	0.644	0.575	0.490	0.384	0.311
15	0.711	0.627	0.556	0.469	0.364	0.293
16	0.697	0.610	0.537	0.450	0.346	0.276
17	0.683	0.593	0.520	0.432	0.329	0.261
18	0.669	0.578	0.503	0.415	0.314	0.247
19	0.656	0.563	0.487	0.399	0.299	0.235
20	0.644	0.548	0.472	0.384	0.286	0.223
21	0.631	0.534	0.458	0.370	0.273	0.213
22	0.619	0.521	0.444	0.357	0.262	0.203
23	0.608	0.508	0.431	0.344	0.251	0.194
24	0.597	0.496	0.418	0.333	0.241	0.186
25	0.586	0.484	0.406	0.321	0.232	0.178
26	0.575	0.473	0.395	0.311	0.223	0.171
27	0.565	0.462	0.384	0.301	0.215	0.164
28	0.555	0.451	0.374	0.291	0.207	0.158
29	0.545	0.441	0.364	0.282	0.200	0.152
30	0.536	0.431	0.354	0.273	0.193	0.147
32	0.517	0.412	0.336	0.258	0.180	0.137
34	0.500	0.395	0.320	0.243	0.169	0.128
36	0.484	0.378	0.304	0.230	0.159	0.120
38	0.469	0.363	0.290	0.218	0.150	0.113
40	0.454	0.349	0.277	0.207	0.142	0.107

OTHER IMPORTANT PROVISIONS OF THE TAX CODE

Corporate Taxes

Aside from a progressive feature at very low levels of taxable income, the top marginal corporate tax rate, as specified by the Budget Reconciliation Act of 1993, is 35 percent; the alternative minimum tax is 20 percent. Earlier tax changes did away with different rates for ordinary income versus capital gains for firms, as well as the investment tax credit. The investment tax credit is a provision that has been in and out of the tax code over the years; its purpose is to spur capital investment by allowing firms a credit against their income tax for making capital investments.

Sale of Assets

Depreciable assets acquired by the firm are generally subject to taxes when they are sold. No matter how long the asset is held, any gain is treated as an ordinary, or operating, gain; likewise, any loss on the sale of assets is treated as an ordinary loss.

To illustrate this, suppose Metroplex Distributors acquired some equipment 4 years ago for $20,000 that has now been depreciated down to $6,000 for tax purposes. It plans to sell the equipment and wants to determine its tax liability and net cash proceeds (after paying taxes) from the sale. First, let us consider the simplest case: It sells the equipment for its IRS-depreciated value of $6,000. In this case there is no tax liability, and the net cash proceeds are simply the $6,000 received from the sale.

Next, consider the sale of the equipment for more, or less, than its depreciated tax value. As shown below, two different situations are presented.

	Sold at a Gain (1)	Sold at a Loss (2)
Selling price	$11,000	$2,000
Depreciated value	6,000	6,000
Gain (loss) on sale	$ 5,000	($4,000)
Tax at 35%	$1,750	($1,400)
Net proceeds	$11,000 − $1,750 = $9,250	$2,000 + $1,400 = $3,400

In column (1), the equipment is sold for $11,000. Note that because the selling price is greater than the depreciated value, the IRS says Metroplex overdepreciated the asset, and thus underreported its taxable income and underpaid its taxes. The difference between the $11,000 selling price and the depreciated value of $6,000 is subject to recapture. At a 35 percent marginal corporate tax rate, Metroplex's additional tax is $1,750, resulting in net proceeds from the sale of $9,250. Now consider column (2), when the asset is sold for $2,000 while its value for tax purposes is $6,000. In this case, the firm underdepreciated the asset, with the result that it realizes a tax savings *if the firm as a whole is profitable*. At a 35 percent marginal tax rate, the tax loss of $4,000 results in a $1,400 reduction in the firm's tax liability. The net cash flow due to selling the asset is the $2,000 plus the $1,400 reduction in cash outflow for taxes, for a total of $3,400.

Operating Losses

An operating loss refers to the situation in which the firm has a negative taxable income. In this case, the firm has no income tax liability. These losses will first be carried back for a maximum of 3 years and then are carried forward for up to 15 years.[2] For simplicity, in this book we ignore carryback and carryforward.

THE RELEVANT CASH FLOWS

Three points should be mentioned in connection with estimating cash flows: First, we are interested in cash flows (both inflows and outflows) as stated on an after-tax basis. Because taxes are an important determinant of cash flows, we are interested in looking at cash flows after all taxes have been taken into account. These are called cash flows after tax, CF, to distinguish them from cash flows before tax, CFBT. Second, we must guard against carelessly counting costs or benefits that should not be considered. A classic example is the treatment by accountants of certain overhead costs. If these overhead costs are fixed and their total amount does not change as a result of implementing a project, they do not affect the cash flows and are irrelevant for decision-making purposes. Finally, it is helpful to divide the cash flow stream into three segments:

1. The initial investment is the net after-tax cash outflow that typically occurs at the start (i.e., at time $t = 0$) of the project under consideration.
2. The operating cash flows are the relevant net after-tax cash flows expected over the economic life of the project.
3. The terminal cash flow is the net after-tax inflow or outflow that occurs when the project is terminated.

Concept Review Questions

■ Why would a firm prefer MACRS over the straight-line method of depreciation?
■ What affect does the sale of a depreciable asset have on a firm's cash flows?
■ What three major segments should be considered when estimating a firm's cash flows?

EXPANSION PROJECTS

First we will consider the cash flow stream for a simple decision in which the firm is expanding, not replacing, existing assets. Then we will consider the relevant incremental cash flows for replacement decisions.

---

[2] Firms can "irrevocably" give up the carryback option and elect to use the carryforward provision.

THE INITIAL INVESTMENT

The **initial investment, CF₀,** is the net after-tax cash flow that occurs at time zero. For an expansion project, it is calculated as follows:

1. Cost of equipment, facilities, and land purchased.
2. All other costs related to the investment (transportation, installation, additional personnel, training expenses, and so forth, net of taxes).
3. Additional **net working capital** required.[3]
4. Opportunity costs, net of taxes (e.g., land used for this project that could have been sold).

Although the initial investment in many complex projects is spread over a number of years, for simplicity we treat it as occurring at the present ($t = 0$). When after-tax cash outflows occur beyond $t = 0$, they are treated like other CFs, except that the negative sign is retained.

OPERATING CASH FLOWS

The second part of the cash flow stream, **operating cash flows, CFs,** are the net cash flows that occur while the asset is in operation. They begin in year 1 and continue throughout the project's useful life. These operating cash flows are typically positive, although there may be occasional years when the outflows are greater than the inflows. Operating cash flows are calculated by taking the difference in the cash inflows minus the cash outflows, to provide the cash flow before tax, CFBT, attributable to the proposed project. IRS depreciation then enters into the picture, because it is a deductible expense for tax purposes and serves to reduce taxes.

To illustrate the calculation of operating cash flows for an expansion project, consider Warner Manufacturing, a firm that is in the process of evaluating a new project. The firm estimates the project's annual before-tax cash inflows and outflows will be $5,000,000 and $4,000,000 respectively, for each of 4 years. Furthermore, the equipment costs $1,800,000, straight-line depreciation is employed, and it falls in the 3-year class. Given the half-year convention employed by the IRS, the depreciation amounts are $300,000 in years 1 and 4, and $600,000 in years 2 and 3. The firm's marginal tax rate is 40 percent. Consequently, the firm will incur $280,000 [i.e., ($5,000,000 − $4,000,000 − $300,000)(0.40)] in taxes directly attributable to the project in years 1 and 4, and $160,000 [i.e., ($5,000,000 − $4,000,000 − $600,000)(0.40)] in each of years 2 and 3. One method of calculating the annual

---

[3] Net working capital is the difference between current assets and current liabilities such as accounts payable and accruals. Often a project requires an increase in accounts receivable or inventory, say by $300,000, while at the same time causing a spontaneous increase in accounts payable of, perhaps, $100,000. The additional net working capital attributable to the project would be $200,000. At the end of the project's life the additional net working capital is no longer needed, and current assets and current liabilities may return to normal levels.

after-tax operating cash flows for the project is

$$\text{operating } CF_t = (\text{cash inflows}_t - \text{cash outflows}_t) - \text{taxes}_t$$
$$= CFBT_t - \text{taxes}_t \qquad (8.1)$$

where $CFBT_t$ is the **cash flow before tax, CFBT.** Applying this to Warner's project for the first year we have

$$\text{operating } CF_1 = (\$5,000,000 - \$4,000,000) - \$280,000 = \$720,000$$

Another calculation that highlights the impact of taxes and the tax shield arising from depreciation recognizes that

$$\text{taxes}_t = (CFBT_t - Dep_t)T \qquad (8.2)$$

where T is the firm's marginal tax rate. Substituting Equation 8.2 into Equation 8.1 we get

$$\text{operating } CF_t = CFBT_t - (CFBT_t - Dep_t)T$$
$$= CFBT_t - CFBT_t(T) + Dep_t(T)$$
$$= CFBT_t(1 - T) + Dep_t(T) \qquad (8.3)$$

The second part of Equation 8.3—that is, $Dep_t(T)$—is the depreciation tax shield. Because depreciation is a tax-deductible expense, even though no cash outflow occurs at the time of the depreciation charge, the presence of depreciation allows firms to reduce their income taxes. That is, they receive a "tax shield" due to depreciation. Equation 8.3 can be employed directly to calculate the **cash flows after tax, CF.** Applying it to Warner for the first year we have

$$\text{operating } CF_1 = (\$5,000,000 - \$4,000,000)(1 - 0.40) + \$300,000(0.40)$$
$$= \$1,000,000(0.60) + \$300,000(0.40)$$
$$= \$600,000 + \$120,000 = \$720,000$$

For the second and third years the figures are

$$\text{operating } CF_{2-3} = \$1,000,000(0.60) + \$600,000(0.40)$$
$$= \$600,000 + \$240,000 = \$840,000$$

For year 4 the figure is the same as for year one, or

$$\text{operating } CF_4 = \$600,000 + \$120,000 = \$720,000$$

In calculating depreciation, remember that land cannot be depreciated and that all other assets are depreciated to zero for tax purposes under the Internal Revenue Service Code. Finally, sometimes there are opportunity costs that have to be considered as part of the operating cash flows.

Depreciable Life Versus Economic Life

Under MACRS depreciation, the **depreciable lives** (as specified by the normal recovery period) have been shortened for virtually all assets. The result is that the normal recovery period is often less than the asset's useful **economic life.** In such a case, cash inflows and outflows may occur every year, while the effects on the operating CF from depreciation will occur only in the early years of the project's life.

Consider the example of Sunbelt Industries, which is contemplating the purchase of a new machine with a 5-year tax life, or normal recovery period, but with a 10-year economic life. If the machine costs $200,000, cash flow before tax, CFBT, is $25,000 for each of 10 years, and the tax rate is 35 percent, then the MACRS depreciation and operating cash flow stream are as shown in Table 8.5. Notice that because depreciation occurs in only the first 6 years, the cash flows in the early years are greater than in the later years.

Opportunity Costs

Opportunity costs also have to be taken into consideration. For example, suppose a firm is analyzing a project that would employ warehouse space currently being rented out for $4,800 a year. If the company decides to expand, it loses the benefit of $4,800 per year in rental income. If the firm has a marginal tax rate of 40 percent, the loss in

Table 8.5

Depreciation and Operating Cash Flows for Sunbelt Industries

The approach used to calculate the operating cash flows highlights the importance of the depreciation tax shield.

		Depreciation		
Year	Original Cost	× MACRS Factors	=	Depreciation
1	$200,000	0.2000		$40,000
2	200,000	0.3200		64,000
3	200,000	0.1920		38,400
4	200,000	0.1152		23,040
5	200,000	0.1152		23,040
6	200,000	0.0576		11,520

		Operating Cash Flows		
Year	CFBT	$CFBT(1 - T)$* +	$Dep(T)$* =	CF
1	$25,000	$16,250	$14,000	$30,250
2	25,000	16,250	22,400	38,650
3	25,000	16,250	13,440	29,690
4–5	25,000	16,250	8,064	24,314
6	25,000	16,250	4,032	20,282
7-10	25,000	16,250	0	16,250

*The tax rate equals 35 percent.

after-tax cash inflows of $2,880 [i.e., $4,800(1 − 0.40)] is an opportunity cost and must be deducted from each year's operating cash flows. Similarly, if a car manufacturer decides to market a new model, sales of the firm's other models may decline. The decline in after-tax cash inflows due to reduced sales of the other models is an opportunity cost of the new model.

Sunk Costs

Equally important is the notion of **sunk costs,** that is, cash outflows that have already been incurred and therefore do not affect the decision. For example, suppose a firm spent $200,000 two years ago for a detailed feasibility study by some consultants about the possibility of doubling the size of their present physical plant. No action was taken then, but now the firm is reassessing the project. Should the $200,000 be included as a cash outflow of the project for capital budgeting purposes? The answer is "no!" Sunk costs should be ignored; they are not incremental cash flows that are relevant for decision making.

TERMINAL CASH FLOW

Terminal cash flows are the net after-tax cash flows other than the operating cash flows that occur in the last year of the project's life. For an expansion project, they are calculated as

1. Funds realized from the sale of the asset plus a tax benefit if it is expected to be sold at a loss, or minus a tax liability if it is expected to be sold at a gain.[4]
2. Release of net working capital
                minus
3. Disposal costs (net of taxes)

The terminal cash flow typically is positive, but it may be negative.

AN EXPANSION PROJECT EXAMPLE

To refine our understanding of the capital budgeting process, consider an expansion project. Ideal Industries is contemplating the purchase of some special equipment with a total cost of $120,000 to increase the efficiency of its production force. Although it will be depreciated via MACRS to zero over its 3-year normal recovery period, the benefits of the machine will last for 4 years. Ideal estimates the equipment will have a resale value of $15,000 in 4 years. The cash inflows and cash outflows are $75,000 and $25,000 per year, respectively. The firm's marginal tax rate is 30 percent, and the opportunity cost of capital is 14 percent.

The initial cash outflow is $120,000 as shown in Table 8.6. One way to determine the operating cash flows, employing Equation 8.3, is shown in Table 8.6. The terminal after-tax cash flow of $10,500 is also shown in Table 8.6. Because all equipment is

---

[4] Assuming the firm is profitable.

Table 8.6

Calculation of the After-Tax Cash Flow Stream and Net Present Value for an Expansion Project

This approach emphasizes the operating cash flows as being equal to the $CFBT(1 - T) + Dep(T)$. Use of the present value depreciation factors given by Tables 8.3 and 8.4 often speeds the calculation process.

Initial Investment
Cost of equipment, $CF_0 = \$120,000$

Operating Cash Flows

Year	Cash Inflows	−	Cash Outflows	CFBT	CFBT × (1 − T)*	+	Dep(T)*	=	CF
1	$75,000		$25,000	$50,000	$35,000		($120,000)(0.3333)(0.30) = $12,000		$47,000
2	75,000		25,000	50,000	35,000		(120,000)(0.4445)(0.30) = 16,000		51,000
3	75,000		25,000	50,000	35,000		(120,000)(0.1481)(0.30) = 5,332		40,332
4	75,000		25,000	50,000	35,000		(120,000)(0.0741)(0.30) = 2,668		37,668

Terminal Cash Flow

Estimated resale value	$15,000
Less: Tax on sale	4,500
Net terminal cash inflow	$10,500

Net Present Value

$$NPV = \frac{\$47,000}{(1 + 0.14)^1} + \frac{\$51,000}{(1 + 0.14)^2} + \frac{\$40,332}{(1 + 0.14)^3} + \frac{\$37,668 + \$10,500}{(1 + 0.14)^4} - \$120,000$$

$$= \$41,228 + \$39,243 + \$27,223 + \$28,519 - \$120,000 = \$16,213$$

*The tax rate is 30 percent.

depreciated to zero for tax purposes and the estimated resale value in 4 years is $15,000, Ideal must pay taxes on the $15,000. At a rate of 30 percent the taxes are $4,500, resulting in a net terminal cash inflow of $10,500.

Finally, the net present value is calculated. As shown in Table 8.6 it is $16,213.[5] Ideal Industries should proceed with the acquisition of the special equipment, because the NPV is greater than zero. By doing so Ideal is contributing to an increase in its value. You can think of a firm as a portfolio of projects. The value of the firm is equal to the sum of the project NPVs. Acceptance of positive NPV projects increases the value of the firm; hence, Ideal is contributing to the maximization of its value by accepting the project.

[5] There is a good deal of discussion about the appropriate discount rate to use when finding the present value of the depreciation tax shield. Some argue that once the asset is purchased, there is no uncertainty about the depreciation, and hence, the depreciation tax shield is riskless. Accordingly, a risk-free discount rate should be employed. Two issues are important. First, firms are not always profitable and hence, may not always be certain of receiving the benefits of the depreciation tax shield. Second, Congress can and does change the tax code and depreciation allowances from time to time. We treat all cash flows and tax shields as risky; accordingly we employ the opportunity cost of capital as the appropriate discount rate. The effect, compared to treating the depreciation tax shield as risk-free, is a slightly lower net present value.

TAKING A SHORTCUT

Although the procedure described above works fine, an easier way to determine the net present value is to employ the MACRS depreciation present value table, Table 8.3. The initial investment remains the same, and the after-tax operating cash flows (ignoring depreciation which for simplicity we will treat separately) are still $35,000 per year. The present value of the depreciation tax shield can be found employing the MACRS (or straight-line) depreciation present value factors from Table 8.3 (or Table 8.4) as follows:

$$\begin{array}{l}\text{Present value} \\ \text{of depreciation} \\ \text{tax shield}\end{array} = \left(\begin{array}{c}\text{Amount to be} \\ \text{depreciated}\end{array}\right)\left(\begin{array}{c}\text{Tax} \\ \text{rate}\end{array}\right)\left(\begin{array}{c}\text{Depreciation present} \\ \text{value factor}\end{array}\right) \qquad (8.4)$$

Employing MACRS depreciation, the present value of the depreciation tax shield is ($120,000)(0.30)(0.778) = $28,008. The terminal cash inflow of $10,500 is the same as before. Now the net present value is determined as follows:

$$NPV = \$35,000\left[\frac{1}{0.14} - \frac{1}{0.14(1+0.14)^4}\right] + \$28,008 + \frac{\$10,500}{(1+0.14)^4}$$
$$- \$120,000$$
$$= \$101,980 + \$28,008 + \$6,217 - \$120,000 = \$16,205$$

Aside from a minor rounding difference, the two net present values are the same. This second approach to calculating the net present value is easier because we avoided having to determine the *per year* MACRS depreciation. Tables 8.3 and 8.4 are employed in the remainder of the chapter and in some of the end-of-chapter problems.

Concept Review Questions

- Briefly describe how to calculate a project's initial investment.
- How are "operating cash flows" calculated?
- Explain how opportunity costs and sunk costs affect a firm's cash flows.

REPLACEMENT DECISIONS

Replacing assets is often necessary. Determining the cash flows for a replacement project can be complicated. These are incremental cash flows—that is, the cash flows related to the new equipment less the cash flows related to the old equipment. While the idea seems straightforward, it is fundamental to effective capital investment decision making.

INCREMENTAL CASH FLOWS

Consider Bits & Bytes, a computer software firm that produces a popular computer game called Spacelords. The firm estimated after-tax operating cash flows, CFs, over a 3-year period as follows:

$600,000 $500,000 $300,000

Spacelords initial CF estimate

1   2   3

The estimated cash flows decline due to an anticipated increase in competition and the development of more complicated and challenging games. Bits & Bytes planned, therefore, to withdraw Spacelords from the market after 3 years.

Recently, Bits & Bytes came up with a new computer game called Rampagers. Although similar to Spacelords, Rampagers has many features that make it more challenging. The estimated initial investment and subsequent cash inflows were estimated as follows:

$700,000 $1,000,000 $600,000

Rampagers initial CF estimate   0

$500,000

1   2   3

Given the favorable cash flow estimates, Bits & Bytes developed and is now marketing Rampagers. All indications are that the projected CFs appear accurate, but a strange thing is happening—Spacelords sales have fallen off dramatically. What did Bits & Bytes forget to consider when it developed the after-tax CF estimates for Rampagers?

The answer should not surprise you. The two games have overlapping markets, with the result that the products are viewed as being partial *substitutes* for each other. Instead of buying Spacelords, many would-be purchasers are now acquiring Rampagers, so the cash flows from Spacelords have declined sharply. The newly revised cash flows for Spacelords are

$100,000 $100,000   0

Spacelords revised CF estimate

1   2   3

The problem arose because in making the initial estimate of the CFs attributed to Rampagers, Bits & Bytes did not properly evaluate the incremental cash flows. *It is the incremental (denoted by a delta, Δ) cash flows that are important.* The relevant incremental operating cash flow stream, ΔCF, that Bits & Bytes should have considered before introducing Rampagers is calculated as follows:

	Year		
Original CFs, Rampagers	$700,000	$1,000,000	$600,000
Less: Decrease in CFs, Spacelords	500,000	400,000	300,000
Incremental (Δ) operating CFs	$200,000	$ 600,000	$300,000

Based on this more complete analysis, the incremental cash flow stream for the new product should have been estimated as follows:

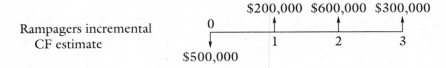

Rampagers incremental CF estimate

Even with this revised set of after-tax CFs, the NPV (at any reasonable discount rate) is positive, so Bits & Bytes should still come out ahead on its investment. But the message is clear: To make effective investment decisions, managers must focus on the incremental cash flow stream. This involves an analysis of the cash inflows and outflows related to the new investment, minus the anticipated inflows and outflows associated with an existing investment.

Often it is important to ask, "What will happen to the existing (or anticipated) cash flows if we do not make the investment?" In today's highly competitive and rapidly changing environment, managers cannot simply assume that existing cash flows will continue. Price cutting, product or marketing innovations, and the like can undermine a profitable investment. For this reason, managers need to know what to look for when calculating incremental cash flows.

ESTIMATING INCREMENTAL CASH FLOWS FOR REPLACEMENT DECISIONS

To calculate incremental after-tax cash flows, we proceed by breaking them into three parts—initial investment, operating cash flow, and terminal cash flow. We make our capital budgeting decision by focusing on the difference between the new and the existing cash flows. Any other cash flow stream is erroneous and may lead to incorrect replacement decisions.

The Initial Investment

The incremental initial investment, ΔCF_0, is calculated as follows[6]:

---

[6] In calculating the initial, operating, and terminal incremental cash flows, we assume that the firm is profitable and, therefore, taxes are relevant.

1. Cost of new equipment, facilities, and land purchased.
2. All other costs related to the investment (transportation, installation, additional personnel, and so forth, net of taxes).
3. Additional net working capital required.
4. Opportunity costs, net of taxes

   minus
5. Funds realized from the sale of replaced assets plus tax benefit if it is expected to be sold at a loss, or minus tax liability if it is expected to be sold at a gain.

As with expansion projects, we assume the initial investment occurs at time $t = 0$; in practice, however, it may be spread out over a number of time periods.

Operating Cash Flows

The incremental operating after-tax cash flow, ΔCF, must take into consideration the difference in the cash flows before tax, CFBT, for the new and the old projects, as well as the depreciation for tax purposes on both the new and the old assets. To calculate the incremental operating cash flows, we have the following:

$$\text{incremental operating } CF_t = (CFBT_{t\text{new}} - CFBT_{t\text{old}})(1 - T)$$
$$+ (Dep_{t\text{new}} - Dep_{t\text{old}})(T)$$
$$\Delta CF_t = \Delta CFBT_t(1 - T) + \Delta Dep_t(T) \tag{8.5}$$

The first term, $\Delta CFBT(1 - T)$, is the change in the cash flows expected, ignoring the tax shield due to depreciation. The net effect on the tax shield is captured in the second term, $\Delta Dep(T)$. As we saw in the Bits & Bytes example, it is especially important to consider the exact nature of the cash flow before tax, CFBT, stream expected from the old (or existing) asset. Often a good deal of interchange between the marketing department, the production department, and the capital budgeting group will be required to arrive at reasonable estimates of both the new and the old CFBT streams. In addition, opportunity costs must also be taken into consideration.

Terminal Cash Flow

Finally, we need to estimate the incremental after-tax terminal cash flow that occurs in the last year of the replacement project's life. The incremental terminal after-tax cash flow, ΔCF_n, is calculated as follows:

1. Funds realized from the sale of the new asset plus tax benefit if it is expected to be sold at a loss, or minus tax liability if it is expected to be sold at a gain.
2. Release of net working capital (assuming the project will be terminated at time period n)

   minus
3. Disposal costs for new asset (less disposal costs on old asset, if any, net of taxes).
4. Funds realized from the sale of the replaced asset plus tax benefit if it is expected to be sold at a loss, or minus tax liability if it is expected to be sold at a gain.

A REPLACEMENT PROJECT EXAMPLE

Consider Phoenix Industries, which is investigating replacing an existing assembly line with a new, automated one. The existing assembly line was installed 3 years ago at a cost of $500,000. It is being depreciated for tax purposes via straight line to a zero value over its normal recovery period of 5 years. The straight-line depreciation is $50,000 in the first and sixth years, and $100,000 in years 2, 3, 4 and 5. Because 3 years have already elapsed, $250,000 has already been depreciated. Depreciation will continue for 2 more years at $100,000 per year and for a third year at $50,000 on the old machine. The old equipment will last 6 more years, at which time its resale value will be $10,000, but it could be sold now for $40,000.

The main benefit of the project would be to reduce yearly expenses from $450,000 on the existing line to $200,000 for the newer, automated line. However, the new line would require a $20,000 increase in inventory. The new line would cost $1 million and be depreciated via straight-line over its 5-year normal recovery period.[7] The estimated resale value of the new assembly line in 6 years is $80,000. Phoenix's tax rate is 40 percent, and the opportunity cost of capital for this project is 16 percent.

In solving this replacement problem, it is useful to begin by calculating the present value of the depreciation on the new assembly line equipment, less the present value of the depreciation on the old assembly line. Employing Equation 8.4 and the straight-line present value factor at 16 percent and 5 years of 0.610 from Table 8.4, the present value of the new depreciation tax shield is

$$PV \text{ depreciation tax shield}_{new} = (\$1,000,000)(0.40)(0.610) = \$244,000$$

The present value of the remaining depreciation on the existing machine is

$$\frac{\$100,000}{(1 + 0.16)^1} + \frac{\$100,000}{(1 + 0.16)^2} + \frac{\$50,000}{(1 + 0.16)^3} = \$192,556$$

Multiplying by the tax rate of 40 percent produces $77,022, which is the present value of the depreciation tax shield remaining on the old machine. Taking the difference in the two present values, we have the present value of the incremental depreciation tax shield from making the replacement, which is $244,000 − $77,022 = $166,978.

Now we can proceed to calculate the incremental initial investment and operating cash flows. As shown in Table 8.7, the incremental initial investment is the $1 million for the new assembly line, less $40,000 to be received from selling the old assembly line, less $84,000 due to the tax consequences of selling the existing equipment at a loss. This last item arises because the old assembly line has a depreciated value of $250,000, but it could be sold for only $40,000, producing a $210,000 tax loss. Because the equipment was underdepreciated, we can write off the full $210,000 in the year of replacement and reduce taxes by $84,000 [i.e., ($210,000)(0.40)], provided that the firm is profitable. Finally, the additional net working capital (due to the

[7] For simplicity, the lives of the old and new assembly lines are both 6 years. If the lives were unequal, then the techniques discussed in Chapter 7 for unequal-lived projects would have to be employed.

Table 8.7

Calculation of Incremental After-Tax Cash Flow Stream and Net Present Value for a Replacement Project

For replacement projects the incremental cash flow must be calculated for all portions of the cash flow stream. The comparison is between keeping the existing equipment versus selling the existing equipment at time $t = 0$ and purchasing the replacement equipment.

Initial Investment

Cost of new assembly line	$1,000,000
Plus: Additional net working capital	20,000
Less: Sale of old assembly line	−40,000
Tax savings on sale of old assembly line*	−84,000
Incremental initial investment, $\Delta CF_0 =$	$896,000

Operating Cash Flows

Year	Cash Outflows (Old)	−	Cash Outflows (New)	=	Incremental CFBT	Incremental $CFBT \times (1 - T)$[†]
1	$450,000		$200,000		$250,000	$150,000
2	450,000		200,000		250,000	150,000
3	450,000		200,000		250,000	150,000
4	450,000		200,000		250,000	150,000
5	450,000		200,000		250,000	150,000
6	450,000		200,000		250,000	150,000

Present Value of Incremental Depreciation Tax Shield

PV depreciation tax shield$_{new}$ = ($1,000,000)(0.40)(0.610) = $244,000

$$PV \text{ depreciation tax shield}_{existing} = \left[\frac{\$100,000}{(1.16)^1} + \frac{\$100,000}{(1.16)^2} + \frac{\$50,000}{(1.16)^3}\right](0.40) = \$77,022$$

PV Δdepreciation tax shield = $244,000 − $77,022 = $166,978

Terminal Cash Flow

After-tax proceeds from sale of new assembly line, $80,000(1 − 0.40)		$48,000
After-tax proceeds from sale of old assembly line, $10,000(1 − 0.40)	*Less:*	6,000
Incremental after-tax proceeds		$42,000
Release of net working capital		20,000
Incremental terminal cash flow		$62,000

Net Present Value

$$NPV = \$150,000\left[\frac{1}{0.16} - \frac{1}{0.16(1.16)^6}\right] + \$166,978 + \frac{\$62,000}{(1.16)^6} - \$896,000$$
$$= \$552,710 + \$166,978 + \$25,447 - \$896,000 = -\$150,865$$

*(IRS depreciated value of old asset − selling price)(tax rate), or ($250,000 − $40,000)(0.40) = $84,000.

† The tax rate is 40 percent.

increase in inventory required) must be treated as part of the initial investment. So, the net incremental investment needed to replace the existing assembly line is $896,000.

Next, we calculate the incremental operating cash flows, except for depreciation. The old assembly line had cash outflows of $450,000 a year, whereas the new one has cash outflows of $200,000 per year. The incremental savings (or $\Delta CFBT$) from the replacement is $250,000 per year. Finally, the difference in the after-tax expected resale values in 6 years and the release of the $20,000 of additional net working capital are treated as terminal cash inflows in year 6.[8] Given the incremental after-tax CF stream shown in Table 8.7 and the 16 percent opportunity cost of capital, the NPV is $-$150,865$. The decision is to reject the new line and to continue to use the existing one in order to maximize the value of the firm.[9]

Replacement decisions are an important part of the capital budgeting process. Following the steps outlined, and making sure we understand incremental cash flows, we can make the proper decisions needed to maintain the firm's competitive advantage and maximize its value.

Concept Review Questions

- What are the incremental cash flows in a replacement decision?
- What are the differences in the cash flows for an expansion project compared to a replacement project?

MORE ON CASH FLOW ESTIMATION

So far in Chapters 7 and 8 we have focused on three primary topics—the capital budgeting process, gaining a fuller understanding of net present value and internal rate of return, and estimating the incremental cash flows. Now we need to consider inflation, why financing costs are excluded, and how to proceed when cash flows between projects are interrelated.

INFLATION

Often cash flows are estimated on the basis that they are not expected to change much over the life of the project. If inflation is low, the cash flows may not change too much. But, if inflation is high, or if it changes during the life of the project, then we have to specifically consider any impacts on the estimated cash flows. In only one special case do the effects of inflation cancel each other out and not affect the decision—when both the CFs and the opportunity cost of capital properly anticipate and adjust for the

---

[8] This assumes that the project terminates at this point in time. In reality, net working capital often is an ongoing commitment and cannot be assumed to be released.

[9] Some additional tax complications arise if presently owned equipment is traded in on new equipment. For simplicity, these complications are ignored.

same percentage rate of inflation. *If this special case occurs, then inflation does not have to be considered as a separate issue.*

A more likely occurrence, however, is for the opportunity cost of capital to reflect expected inflation while the cash flows do not. Investors incorporate expectations of inflation into their required rates of return. Because this is the case, the firm's opportunity cost of capital also reflects expected inflation. But what about the estimated cash flows? If inflation is taken into account in the discount rate but not in the after-tax CFs, then the calculated NPV will be biased downward. Alternatively, if low expected inflation is reflected in the discount rate used but a higher inflation estimate is built into the CFs, then the NPV will be biased upward.

To see the importance of adjusting for inflation, consider Sullivan Paper. Table 8.8 shows that the firm calculated the net present value of a proposed capital expenditure to be $3,467 at its opportunity cost of capital of 15 percent. The project should be selected, because it returns more than the 15 percent required. But what happens if expected inflation was ignored in estimating the cash outflows in Table 8.8? Once inflation is taken into account the cash outflows are projected to increase by $1,500 per year. As Table 8.9 shows, the project's NPV is now −$508, which changes Sullivan's decision. Now the firm should reject the project.

Table 8.8

Cash Flows and Net Present Value for Sullivan Paper Project, Without Adjusting for Inflation

The $21,000 investment was depreciated to zero over 4 years by straight-line depreciation under the tax code. Hence, the depreciation is $3,500 for the first and fourth years and $7,000 for the second and third years.

Initial Investment
$21,000

Operating Cash Flows

Year	Cash Inflows	− Cash Outflows	= CFBT	CFBT × $(1 − T)^*$	+ $Dep(T)^*$	= CF
1	$20,000	$10,000	$10,000	$7,000	$1,050	$8,050
2	20,000	10,000	10,000	7,000	2,100	9,100
3	20,000	10,000	10,000	7,000	2,100	9,100
4	20,000	10,000	10,000	7,000	1,050	8,050

Terminal Cash Flow
None

Net Present Value

$$NPV = \frac{\$8,050}{(1 + 0.15)^1} + \frac{\$9,100}{(1 + 0.15)^2} + \frac{\$9,100}{(1 + 0.15)^3} + \frac{\$8,050}{(1 + 0.15)^4} - \$21,000$$

$$= \$7,000 + \$6,881 + \$5,983 + \$4,603 - \$21,000 = \$3,467$$

*The tax rate is 30 percent.

TABLE 8.9

Cash Flows and Net Present Value for Sullivan Paper Project, Taking Account of Inflation

With the substantial increase in the estimated cash outflows once inflation is taken into account, the project should be rejected.

Initial Investment

$21,000

Operating Cash Flows

Year	Cash Inflows	−	Cash Outflows	=	CFBT	CFBT × $(1 - T)^*$	+	$Dep(T)^*$	=	CF
1	$20,000		$10,000		$10,000	$7,000		$1,050		$8,050
2	20,000		11,500		8,500	5,950		2,100		8,050
3	20,000		13,000		7,000	4,900		2,100		7,000
4	20,000		14,500		5,500	3,850		1,050		4,900

Terminal Cash Flow

None

Net Present Value

$$NPV = \frac{\$8,050}{(1 + 0.15)^1} + \frac{\$8,050}{(1 + 0.15)^2} + \frac{\$7,000}{(1 + 0.15)^3} + \frac{\$4,900}{(1 + 0.15)^4} - \$21,000$$

$$= \$7,000 + \$6,087 + \$4,603 + \$2,802 - \$21,000 = -\$508$$

*The tax rate is 30 percent.

Anticipating inflation is not easy, but it is important if the proper capital budgeting decisions are to be made. Managers should remember the following:

1. Be consistent—make sure the inflation consequences are built into the cash flows, because they are already incorporated in the discount rate (unless a real instead of a nominal discount rate is employed).
2. Even if cash inflows and regular cash outflows change in line with the general rate of inflation, CFs generally do not change because of the tax structure. Taxes tend to increase more than proportionately as cash inflows rise. Also, inflation often requires an increased working capital investment above and beyond that required with little or no inflation.
3. Inflation is not constant across different sections of the economy. Therefore, it may *not* be reasonable to use a general price index to incorporate the effects of changing rates of inflation on expected CFs for a project.
4. Differential price changes may occur due to supply and demand considerations. These effects, which are due to factors other than the rate of inflation, can also have a significant impact on the CFs and must be taken into account.

WHY ARE FINANCING COSTS EXCLUDED?

We have ignored one cash flow that a firm incurs when undertaking a capital budgeting project—the financing costs. Suppose that a firm is evaluating whether to build a new plant. If the firm decides to use debt financing, should we recognize the after-tax interest and principal repayments as ongoing cash outflows? Similarly, if equity is employed, should any costs related to it be treated as part of the ongoing cash outflow stream? *In both cases, the answer is "no!"* As discussed in Chapter 2, the Fisher separation theorem indicates that the investment, or capital budgeting, decision should be separated from the financing decision. The investment decision is based on the economic desirability of the project, irrespective of how it is financed; the financing costs are built into the opportunity cost of capital. If financing costs were to be deducted from the after-tax cash flows, they would be double-counted (once in the numerator of the NPV and again in the denominator, as part of the opportunity cost of capital, k) and the project's net present value would be underestimated. *However,* there are some decisions in which the investment and financing cash flows are interrelated. Approaches for handling such situations are considered in Chapter 14.

INTERRELATED PROJECTS

In Chapter 7 we classified projects as either mutually exclusive or independent. A more accurate picture would show a continuum of relationships among projects, as in Figure 8.1. At one end stand **complementary projects.** If one of several complementary projects is undertaken, the cash flows of all related projects also increase. An example is a combination self-service gasoline station and convenience store; combining both in one operation generally produces incremental business beyond the simple sum of what each would generate separately. In the extreme case, the cash flows and success or failure of the projects are so closely related that a decision has to be made to accept or reject a **systemwide project.** The entire system must be evaluated, because accepting only part of it produces nothing of value.

Figure 8.1

Degree of Dependence Among Capital Budgeting Projects

A continuum of projects exists from those that are perfect complements to those that are perfect substitutes. Knowing the degree of dependence is necessary for effective decision making.

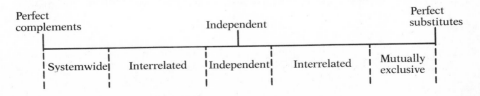

At the other end of the continuum are **substitute projects.** In this case acceptance of one project reduces the cash flows from another. If the effect is pronounced enough, the projects are said to be mutually exclusive; that is, accepting one precludes accepting others. A special case, lying between systemwide and mutually exclusive projects, is that of independent projects. In this case acceptance of one has no appreciable impact on the cash flows of other independent projects.

Finally, as shown in Figure 8.1, we have a broad spectrum of **interrelated projects,** where the acceptance of one project can partially affect—either positively or negatively—the cash flows of other possible projects. *The joint cash flows for two (or more) interrelated projects must be analyzed together.* Suppose that Wilson Paint, which as part of its activities manufactures paint sprayers, is evaluating the desirability of producing two new models—the Quik Painter and the Quik Painter II. The firm has the choice of producing and selling either or both paint sprayers. The initial investment, cash inflows, and NPVs for both are as follows:

	Producing and Selling Only Quik Painter	Producing and Selling Only Quik Painter II	Producing and Selling Both
Initial investment	$200,000	$250,000	$ 400,000
After-tax cash flows for each of 10 years	50,000	60,000	70,000
Net present value at 13%	$ 71,312	$ 75,575	$−20,163

At the opportunity cost of capital of 13 percent, both projects considered independently have positive net present values and should be selected.

But look what happens if Wilson decides to introduce both sprayers. Wilson's combined initial investment is slightly less than the sum of the two separate outlays, so there are some economies from producing both. The total after-tax cash flows, however, increase only slightly when both sprayers are introduced. Why? Because the two paint sprayers are really substitutes. A customer needs only one of the sprayers, and two different models provide very little in the way of incremental sales. The cash inflows are interrelated, so the total NPV from producing both paint sprayers is negative. Obviously, Wilson shouldn't introduce both sprayers—and because the Quik Painter II has the higher NPV, it should be produced and sold.

This example suggests a basic procedure to be followed when interrelated projects exist:

STEP 1:   Identify all possible combinations of interrelated projects. Assume three projects, A, B, and C, are interrelated. In addition to analyzing A, B, and C separately, the combinations of A and B, A and C, B and C, and A and B and C must also be evaluated.

STEP 2:   Determine the initial investment and after-tax cash flow stream for each project and combination, along with the total NPV of each project and combination.

STEP 3: Choose the individual project or combination of projects that has the highest total NPV.

One could argue that all projects within a firm are somewhat related. If this is the case, then the analysis of any project is a tremendous chore, because all possible combinations have to be considered. However, many projects are mutually exclusive, independent, or systemwide. The key, then, is to make sure that proper analysis has been done to determine the appropriate relationship, if any, between proposed capital budgeting projects. When the analysis has been done correctly, the proper projects are considered, the proper cash flows are identified, and the proper decisions will result.

Concept Review Questions

- Why is it important to adjust a firm's cash flows for inflation?
- Comment on the statement: "A firm's cash flows will be biased downward if financing costs are included."
- What are complementary projects and substitute projects?

CAPITAL RATIONING

Unfortunately, all acceptable projects cannot always be undertaken. This is the case of **capital rationing:** A limit is placed on the size of the capital budget. It generally arises because of *internally imposed constraints* on the amount of external funds a firm will raise or because of dollar limits imposed on the capital expenditures various divisions of firms can undertake. These can be thought of as **soft capital rationing** constraints; they are limits adopted by management. There exists another type of capital rationing—**hard capital rationing,** in which the firm cannot raise any more funds in the capital markets. Theoretically, hard capital rationing rarely, if ever, exists if the proposed project has a positive NPV because additional funds should be available (at some cost) to finance the project.

To see the effect of capital rationing, consider the following information on 4 independent proposed projects:

Project	CF$_0$	NPV
L	$10	$5
M	20	5
N	30	8
P	30	4

Without any capital rationing constraint, the value-maximizing decision is to accept all 4 projects. The initial cash outlay is $90, and the total NPV is $22. But, what occurs if a capital rationing constraint exists and only $30 is available? The objective is to maximize the total NPV up to the constraint. This can be accomplished by accepting projects L and M; the outlay is $30, and the total NPV is $10.

Capital rationing leads to suboptimal decisions because it does not allow the firm to attain its maximum value. It is another opportunity cost that reduces the value of the firm if positive NPV projects are bypassed. In the face of capital rationing, the goal is to *maximize the total net present value over all projects accepted*. If there are not too many projects, this can be accomplished by listing all feasible combinations (within the budget constraint) and then determining which combination has the largest total NPV.[10] If the number of projects becomes too large, and/or capital is expected to be rationed over a number of years, integer programming can be used.

If capital rationing, especially soft capital rationing, is an opportunity cost and tends to reduce the value of the firm, why does it exist? One possibility is that in large firms the use of fixed (or relatively fixed) divisional allocations of capital is simply a means of imposing control on the activities of subordinates. One of the key ideas in finance is that individuals act in their own self-interest. Subordinates have a vested interest in proposing capital expenditure projects and having them accepted. Employees look good by doing so, and being a self-starter who produces results is one of the keys to promotion and financial well-being in many firms. Imposing capital limits on divisions may simply be one means of dealing with the tendency of employees to be overly optimistic or aggressive in proposing capital projects for inclusion on the capital budget.[11]

A second possibility is that soft capital rationing is simply a reflection of the fact that managers have large amounts of firm-specific human capital. That is, managers have both their reputation and their chances for advancement, as well as their financial livelihood, invested in the firm. With a great deal of their own wealth tied up in the firm, managers have incentives to manage the firm "conservatively" and, therefore, to reduce the firm's riskiness and any possibility of financial distress. Risk reduction can be accomplished by practicing asset substitution—that is, by accepting projects that have less total risk (or variability in their cash flows) than might be desirable. Managers may also have incentives to retain more cash in the firm and to employ less debt than might be optimal. These actions are simply another form of agency costs which arise due to differential interests between the firm's managers and its owners. Whatever the reasons, capital rationing tends to be practiced by many firms. As such, we need to be aware of possible reasons for and the consequences of capital rationing.

---

[10] An alternative selection criterion, the **profitability index,** is often recommended when a 1-period capital rationing constraint is considered. The profitability index is

$$\text{profitability index} = \frac{\sum_{t=1}^{n} \dfrac{CF_t}{(1 + k)^t}}{CF_0}$$

Because the discounted after-tax operating and terminal cash flows are divided by the initial investment, CF_0, the profitability index is a *relative* measure of economic desirability. Projects are ranked from highest to lowest, and all those with PIs greater than 1.0 are selected up to the dollar limit. With a 1-period capital rationing constraint, this approach selects the best set of projects *only if all the funds available for investment (up to the capital constraint) are expended*. Because the total NPV approach is not affected by this problem, it is a more appropriate selection criterion.

[11] For further discussion of this point see the end-of-chapter references.

Concept Review Questions

■ Define the terms "soft capital rationing" and "hard capital rationing."

■ Why does capital rationing exist?

KEY POINTS

1. For effective capital budgeting to occur, the relevant incremental after-tax cash flows must be determined. This determination requires an understanding of depreciation as specified by the Internal Revenue Service and certain other aspects of the tax code.

2. Opportunity costs are an important component of the costs; they must be considered. Sunk costs are just that; they should be ignored in determining the proper cash flows, which are the incremental (new minus old) CFs.

3. The cash flows must be determined at three times: at the initiation of the project; over the expected economic life of the project, using the operating cash flows (including incremental depreciation tax shields); and at the termination of the project.

4. For replacement-type decisions, the focus is on the incremental cash flows.

5. Proper decision making requires that inflation, but not financing costs, be considered in the after-tax cash flow stream.

6. When projects are interrelated, the net after-tax cash flow stream over all of the projects must be employed in order to make wealth-maximizing decisions.

7. Under capital rationing, the firm should select the set of positive NPV projects that maximizes total NPV and stays within the budget constraint.

QUESTIONS

8.1 Explain the differences between the initial investment, operating cash flows, and the terminal cash flow.

8.2 Explain the idea of opportunity costs. How do they relate to the notion of the operating CF stream?

8.3 Which of the following should be considered when calculating the incremental CFs associated with a new warehouse? Assume the firm owns the land but that existing buildings would have to be demolished.

a. Demolition costs and site clearance.
b. The cost of an access road built a year ago.
c. New forklifts and conveyer equipment for the warehouse.
d. The market value of the land and existing buildings.
e. A portion of the firm's overhead.
f. Lost earnings on other products due to managerial time spent during the construction and stocking of the new warehouse.
g. Future IRS depreciation on the old buildings and equipment.
h. Landscaping for the warehouse.
i. Financing costs related to the bonds issued to build the new warehouse.
j. The effects of inflation on future labor costs.

8.4 By comparing the calculations necessary for determining ΔCFs of replacement decisions with the calculations for determining CFs for expansion decisions, identify the *specific* differences that exist for the initial, operating, and terminal cash flows.

8.5   Explain the difference between complementary and substitute projects. How are they related to (a) systemwide projects, (b) interrelated projects, (c) independent projects, and (d) mutually exclusive projects?

8.6   How does inflation affect the capital budgeting process?

8.7   Differentiate between financing and investment decisions. Why are financing costs excluded when calculating the CFs necessary for capital investment decision making?

8.8   Define capital rationing, and explain why it does not lead to the maximization of the value of the firm.

Concept Review Problems

See Appendix A for solutions.

CR8.1   Myers Inc. purchased an asset costing $200,000, with installation and shipping costs (which will be capitalized and depreciated) of $50,000. The equipment has a 7-year normal recovery period.

a.   Using MACRS compute the annual depreciation.

b.   Does it matter if the office equipment was purchased in the first half of the year or the second half of the year?

CR8.2   Paymore Rent-a-Car just purchased a new fleet of cars with an average cost of $18,000 per car.

a.   The normal recovery period for automobiles is 5 years. Using MACRS, what is the depreciation per year?

b.   The firm plans to sell each car after 3 years at 50 percent of the purchase price. Determine Paymore's tax liability and net cash proceeds, after paying taxes, from the sale of each car. Paymore's tax rate is 30 percent.

c.   What is the tax liability and net cash proceeds if the cars are sold at only 25 percent of the purchase price?

The following information is used in CR8.3 through CR8.7.

King Corp. has spent $500,000 on research to develop a lowfat imitation wine. The firm is planning to spend $200,000 on a machine to produce the new wine. Shipping and installation costs will be capitalized and depreciated; they are $100,000. The machine has an expected life of 6 years, a $10,000 estimated resale value, and falls in the 5-year MACRS recovery period. Revenue from the lowfat wine is expected to be $650,000 per year, with costs of $400,000 per year. The firm has a tax rate of 35 percent, an opportunity cost of capital of 14 percent, and it expects net working capital to increase by $40,000.

CR8.3   What is the initial investment, CF_0, for the lowfat wine project?

CR8.4   What are the operating cash flows for years 1 through 6?

CR8.5   What are the terminal cash flows of the project?

CR8.6   What is the net present value of the project? Should King expand into the wine market?

CR8.7   John, who is in charge of King's premium wine division, estimates that the lowfat wine would lower premium wine CFBT by approximately $125,000 per year. Now what is the NPV?

CR8.8   Zio's Pizzeria is considering replacing its old pizza ovens with new ovens. The old ovens have a current resale value of $100,000, a book value of $80,000, and are being depreciated at $20,000 per year. It is estimated that if the machines are held for 4 years, the old machines will have a resale value of $20,000.

The new pizza ovens will cost $335,000, and be depreciated using straight-line over 3 years as required by the IRS. Sales using the old pizza ovens were 75,000 pizzas at $t = 0$, with an average selling price of $10 per pizza. Sales have been growing at a rate of 1 percent per year. The selling price with the new pizza ovens remains $10 per pizza; the units sold at $t = 1$ are 81,600 and are expected to grow at 2 percent per year.

Operating costs using the old pizza ovens are 80 percent of total revenue, while operating costs using the new pizza ovens are expected to be 75 percent of total revenue. Management estimates the new ovens will have a resale value of $50,000 in 4 years. The tax rate is 40 percent, and the opportunity cost of capital is 12 percent. Should Zio's replace the ovens?

CR8.9   Roper is considering 6 capital investment proposals, as follows:

Project	CF_0	CF_n	Years
A	$500	$175	4
B	1,000	350	4
C	200	50	6
D	150	40	7
E	200	100	3
F	150	42	6

Under a capital rationing constraint of $1,200, and assuming an opportunity cost of capital of 13 percent, in which projects should Roper invest?

PROBLEMS

8.1   An asset has a remaining depreciable value for tax purposes of $48,000. The marginal tax rate is 34 percent. Find the tax liability (or credit) if the asset is sold for (a) $60,000 or (b) $20,000. (Assume the firm is profitable.)

8.2   Roberts Stores is considering opening a new store in Seattle. Gross cash inflows are expected to be $1,000,000 per year, and cash outflows are predicted to be $800,000 per year. In addition, Roberts' cost accounting department estimates that overhead costs of $75,000 per year should be charged to the new store. These costs include the store's share of the firm's management salaries, general administrative expenses, and so forth. Finally, the new store is expected to reduce CFBTs by $50,000 per year from one of the firm's existing stores. Roberts' marginal tax rate is 30 percent. (*Note:* For simplicity, ignore any impact of depreciation.)

a.   If all the overhead consists of fixed costs that will be incurred whether or not the new store is opened, what is the relevant operating CF?

b.   What if $50,000 of the overhead consists of variable costs related to the new store, and $25,000 consists of fixed overhead costs? What is the relevant operating CF now?

8.3   A firm is considering an investment requiring the purchase of a machine that will cost $800,000 and be depreciated via straight-line depreciation over its 5-year normal recovery period. The firm's marginal tax rate is 35 percent. The cash inflows expected over the 6-year life of the project are $240,000 per year, cash expenses are $80,000 per year, and the reduction in the before-tax cash inflows from other machines currently owned will be $20,000 per year if this new machine is purchased. Finally, the new machine will require a one-time increase both in accounts receivable of $15,000 and in inventory of $25,000. At the end of 6 years the machine will be worthless, and the firm will not replace it because it will be emphasizing other products by then. What is the relevant CF stream? (*Note:* Use the half-year convention when calculating depreciation.)

8.4 A $32,000 machine with a 5-year normal recovery period was purchased 2 years ago. The machine will now be sold for $24,000 and replaced with a new machine costing $40,000, with a 5-year normal recovery period. Straight-line depreciation is employed for both machines, and the marginal corporate tax rate is 30 percent. (*Note:* Use the half-year convention when calculating depreciation.)

a. What is the depreciated value for tax purposes on the old machine?
b. What is the tax liability from selling the old machine and the net proceeds, considering both the selling price and the tax?
c.. What is the gross outlay for the new machine by itself?
d. What is the incremental initial investment that is determined by subtracting the net proceeds on the old machine (calculated in b) from the gross outlay on the new machine (calculated in c)?

8.5 Los Vegas Hospital is a private hospital that has an opportunity to purchase a generator. The generator costs $98,000 and will be depreciated to zero under straight-line depreciation over its 7-year normal recovery period. The tax rate is 30 percent, and the cash flows before taxes over its 9-year economic life follow:

	Years				
	1	2	3	4–5	6–9
CFBT	$10,000	$12,000	$16,000	$20,000 each	$30,000 each

If the opportunity cost of capital is 17 percent, should the generator be purchased? (*Note:* Use the half-year convention when calculating depreciation.)

8.6 Evert Fashions is contemplating bringing out a new line of sweaters to add to its existing lines. The projected initial investment is $100,000, CF is expected to be $40,000 per year for each of 5 years, and the cost of capital is 15 percent.

a. Should the new line of sweaters be produced?
b. What happens if you discover that introducing the new line of sweaters will reduce CFs from existing sweater lines by $12,000 per year?
c. Why must the possibility of opportunity costs always be considered when the cash flow stream is being estimated?

8.7 New equipment costs $40,000, freight is $1,000, and site preparation costs are $5,000. Both the freight and site preparation costs occur at $t = 0$, but they are tax-deductible. Cash inflows are $21,000 per year for each of 6 years, and cash outflows are $6,000 per year. Straight-line depreciation (based on the cost of $40,000) to a value of zero at the end of its normal recovery period of 5 years will be employed. However, in 6 years it is estimated that the equipment can be sold for $10,000, less $2,000 in dismantling costs. (*Note:* Take the tax on the

$8,000, because the dismantling costs are tax-deductible.) The firm's tax rate is 30 percent, and the opportunity cost of capital is 15 percent. Should the equipment be acquired? (*Note:* Use the half-year convention when calculating depreciation.)

8.8   Norris is a manufacturer of electronic devices. Sales have recently been lost because of the inability to store sufficient finished goods inventory, even though Norris has the capability of increasing production. The solution under discussion is to increase production to create a larger finished goods inventory so that lost sales will not occur in the future. To increase the inventory, Norris estimates the following will be required:

1. The finished goods inventory needs to be expanded by $150,000.
2. Existing vacant warehouse space is available for storing the additional inventory. However, new equipment costing $80,000 with a 5-year normal recovery period is required. Straight-line depreciation will be employed, and Norris's marginal tax rate is 40 percent. Additional wages will be $40,000 per year. (*Note:* Ignore the half-year convention when calculating depreciation.)
3. The sales and production people estimate that the increased sales will result in a net cash inflow to the firm (after all production costs, but before considering the additional ware-house expense and taxes) of $100,000 per year.
4. In 5 years the equipment will have a resale value of zero. The $150,000 buildup in inventory is no longer required.

a.   If the opportunity cost of capital is 13 percent, should the expansion take place?
b.   What decision should be made if everything remains the same as in (a), except that the warehouse space is currently rented out for $50,000 (before taxes) per year?

8.9   Best Products has a proposed project for $200,000 of research and development equipment that falls under the 3-year category. MACRS depreciation will be employed, and a $40,000 addition to net working capital will be required. The estimated benefits, CFBT, are $80,000 per year for each of 4 years; the equipment has an estimated resale value of $50,000 in 4 years; the firm's tax rate is 35 percent; and Best Products estimates that a 20 percent return is required for this project. Should the new equipment be acquired? (*Note:* Use the half-year convention when calculating depreciation.)

8.10   A firm is considering a major expansion of its operations. If it expands, the firm antici-pates an initial investment in equipment of $500,000 that will be depreciated via straight-line depreciation over 5 years. The projected cash inflows are $200,000, $250,000, $200,000, $200,000 and $150,000, respectively, over the 5 years. At that time the resale value of the equipment is estimated to be $125,000. The marginal tax rate is 35 percent, and the opportu-nity cost of capital is 15 percent.

a.   Should the investment be made? (*Note*: Ignore the half-year convention when calculating depreciation.)
b.   After running the analysis in (a) you remember that if the investment is made the firm will have to use a building that is presently rented out for $70,000 per year (before taxes) *payable in advance* (i.e., at $t = 0, t = 1, \ldots, t = 4$). Does this new information affect the decision you reached in (a)?

8.11   SafteFirst has moved into new quarters and wants to replace its office equipment. The existing equipment is fully depreciated, but it can be sold today for $40,000. In another 6 years it will have a resale value of zero. The new equipment costs $250,000, has a 5-year life, and has zero resale value in 6 years. Straight-line depreciation will be employed, the tax rate is 35 percent, and the opportunity cost of capital is 12 percent. Due to increased worker productivity and morale, the estimated benefits before tax, ΔCFBT, are $55,000 per year. (*Note:* Use the half-year convention when calculating depreciation.)

a.   Determine the relevant cash flows.
b.   Should the equipment be replaced?

8.12   Mackey Electronics bought a $145,000 piece of equipment 2 years ago; its present depreciated value is $101,500. Because of substantial increases in the demand for used equipment, it can be sold today for $140,000 (before taxes). If kept, however, it will last 6 more years and produce expected cash flows, CFBTs, of $13,000 for each of 6 years. A replacement machine costs $180,000, and it is expected to produce CFBTs of $28,000 for each of 6 years. Assume neither machine has any resale value in 6 years. If the marginal tax rate is 40 percent, and the discount rate is 10 percent, should the equipment be replaced, assuming straight-line depreciation is employed for both pieces of equipment? (*Note:* Use the half-year convention when calculating depreciation for both pieces of equipment.)

8.13   Marshall Interiors is considering replacing its two delivery trucks. The models being used have been fully depreciated to zero, but can be sold today for $3,000 *each*. In 5 years these two trucks can be sold for $500 *each*. The two new trucks will cost $20,000 *each* and have a 5-year normal recovery period. Straight-line depreciation will be employed, the firm's marginal tax rate is 35 percent, and the trucks are expected to have a resale value of $3,500 *each* (before taxes) 5 years from now. Because of the efficiency of the new trucks, the total benefit will be a reduction in after-tax operating costs [i.e., ($CFBT$)(0.65)] of $9,000 per year. Should these new trucks be purchased if the opportunity cost of capital is 12 percent? (*Note:* Ignore the half-year convention when calculating depreciation.)

8.14   YourToys is contemplating the replacement of one of its machines. The new machine costs $1,400,000, has a 10-year economic life, and is expected to save $250,000 (before taxes) in operating expenses each year. It will be depreciated under straight-line over its 7-year normal recovery period. The old machine cost $980,000, has a 10-year economic life remaining, but is being depreciated for tax purposes with the 7-year straight-line method. It was purchased 2 years ago, so there are still 5 years of depreciation remaining on the existing machine. The incremental initial investment, ΔCF, is $1,100,000, but the incremental operating cash inflows have yet to be calculated. At the end of 10 years, neither machine will have any resale value. The discount rate is 14 percent, and the marginal tax rate is 40 percent. Should the old machine be replaced? (*Note:* Ignore the half-year convention when calculating depreciation.)

8.15   West Coast Developers has designed an apartment building that will cost $7 million and produce after-tax cash inflows of $1.5 million for each year of its 10-year life. The firm also has plans for a recreation center that would cost $3.2 million and produce after-tax cash flows of $600,000 per year for 10 years. The firm owns land near Los Angeles and must decide which project to build. The land is large enough to accommodate both projects. West Coast Developers believes that if both projects are built next to each other, the residents of the apartment building will use the recreation center and increase its expected cash inflows to $700,000 per year. If the opportunity cost of capital is 14 percent, what should the company do?

8.16   Pisano Industries is considering two possible capital projects. Project I has the following CFs:

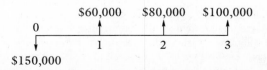

Project II can be undertaken only if the $150,000 initial investment for project I has been made. The *additional* CFs for project II are as follows:

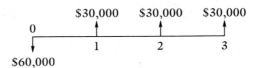

However, because projects I and II are partial substitutes, the CFs from project I will decrease by $10,000 in each of years 1, 2, and 3 if project II is also undertaken. If the discount rate is 14 percent, what should the company do?

8.17 A project has an initial investment of $30,000, CFBT of $16,000 for each of 3 years, and an opportunity cost of capital of 13 percent. Straight-line depreciation will be employed, and the firm's marginal tax rate is 40 percent. (*Note:* Ignore the half-year convention when calculating depreciation.)

a. What is the project's NPV? Should it be accepted?
b. Due to inflation, the CFBT in years 2 and 3 was overstated. It should be $14,000 in year 2 and $12,000 in year 3. Does this information cause you to change the decision made in (a)?

8.18 Aqua-Products has the following independent investments under examination:

Project	Initial Investment	After-Tax Cash Flows per Year	Life of the Project (in years)
A	$100,000	$39,000	4
B	50,000	12,000	6
C	80,000	39,000	3
D	60,000	15,000	7
E	75,000	25,000	5
F	90,000	25,000	6

Aqua-Products' opportunity cost of capital is 14 percent.

a. In the absence of capital rationing, which projects should be selected? What is the size (in total dollars) of the capital budget? The total NPV of all of the projects selected?
b. Now suppose that a limit of $250,000 (maximum) is placed on new capital projects. Which projects should be selected?
c. What is the total NPV determined in (b)? What is the loss to Aqua-Products due to the capital rationing constraint?

8.19 A project requires an initial investment of $300,000 and is expected to produce CFBTs of $95,000 for each of 5 years. Straight-line depreciation will be used over the 5-year normal recovery period. No-Tax Company has substantial tax losses and does not expect to pay any taxes in the foreseeable future. Tax Company has a marginal tax rate of 35 percent. (*Note:* Ignore the half-year convention when calculating depreciation.)

a. If both companies have an opportunity cost of capital of 14 percent, to which company is the investment worth more? (*Note:* No carryback or carryforward of the tax credit is feasible.)

b. Is it reasonable to use the same cost of capital for both companies? Why or why not?

8.20 Mini Case Service Systems is considering the replacement of a piece of equipment that was purchased 3 years ago for $60,000 and is generating CFBT of $15,000 per year. The equipment is being depreciated by the straight-line method over its 5-year tax life. If sold today it would bring $18,000; its estimated resale value if kept for 5 more years is $10,000. The new piece of equipment costs $75,000 and will require installation-related expenses of $8,000, which will be expensed. The CFBT for the new equipment is $30,000 per year, and straight-line depreciation over 5 years is being used. At the end of 5 years the new equipment's estimated resale value is $20,000. The marginal tax rate is 40 percent, and the opportunity cost of capital is 14 percent. (*Note:* Ignore the half-year convention when calculating depreciation for both pieces of equipment.)

a. You, as chief financial analyst for the firm, have been assigned the responsibility of deciding whether Service Systems should keep or replace the existing system. What is your recommendation?

b. In presenting your recommendation, you mention that a replacement capital budgeting decision can be broken down into its separate components. These components are: (1) Should the new project be accepted? and (2) should the existing project be keep or abandoned? Thus,

$$NPV_{replacement} = NPV_{new} - NPV_{keep\ or\ abandon}$$

Your boss does not believe you and challenges you to prove it. In order to do so, proceed as follows: First, take *only those cash flows* that would exist for the new equipment in (a). This is simply an expansion project. Calculate the NPV for the new equipment. Then take the remaining cash flows that involve keeping the old equipment for 5 more years versus abandoning it today. Calculate the NPV for the keep-versus-abandon decision. Now, use these figures to prove the point to your boss.

c. In further conversation with your boss you mention that the two projects considered in (a) and (b) are mutually exclusive. What is meant by the term "mutually exclusive"? How would you have to proceed if the two projects were either partial complements or partial substitutes, not mutually exclusive?

d. Two other projects exist with after-tax cash flows as follows, where the required return is now 16 percent:

Year	Project A	Project B
0	−$20,000	−$30,000
1	5,000	18,000
2	7,000	15,000
3	9,000	13,000
4	9,000	10,000
5	9,000	
6	16,000	

(1) Calculate the internal rate of return for each project.
(2) If the projects are independent, what decision should be made? Why?

(3)   If the projects are mutually exclusive, what decision should be made? Why?

What assumptions are you making in answering (3)? How comfortable are you with the assumptions?

e.   In estimating the CFs for the two projects in (d), you inadvertently ignored the effects of inflation on the operating cash flows. The net after-tax cash flows for project A will decline at 6 percent each year, and those for project B will decline at 8 percent each year. [*Note:* The cash flow for project A in year 1 will be $5,000(1 − 0.06). For year 2 it will be $7,000(1 − 0.06)^2, etc.] If the projects are independent, does this new information change the decisions made in (d)?

f.   Your boss is continually lamenting that many profitable capital budgeting projects have to be turned down because funds are not available. How would you make your boss understand that from a financial standpoint funds are not limited and can always be secured for good projects? What causes your boss, and many managers, to argue that funds are limited?

8.21   Mini Case   Kaw Resources is a diversified firm that raises capital in the following proportions: debt, 30 percent; preferred stock, 15 percent; and common equity, 55 percent. Kaw estimates that new debt financing can be secured at 12 percent and additional preferred stock financing at 11.5 percent. It has come up with the following estimates of the expected returns on its common stock and the market portfolio:

State	Probability of State Occurring	Return Kaw Resources	Return Market Portfolio
Boom	0.30	50%	35%
Average	0.50	20	15
Recession	0.20	−20	−10

The risk-free rate is 10 percent, Kaw's marginal tax rate is 40 percent, and the correlation between Kaw's returns and the market returns is +0.70.

a.   What is beta for Kaw's stock? Its required return on equity?
b.   What is the opportunity cost of capital for Kaw Resources? (*Note:* Round to the nearest whole number.)
c.   Two sizable investments Kaw is considering have after-tax cash flows as follows:

Time Periods	Project A	Project B
0	−$20,000,000	−$20,000,000
1	− 3,000,000	6,000,000
2	− 1,000,000	6,000,000
3	2,000,000	6,000,000
4–10	5,000,000	2,700,000
11–15	10,000,000	

(1)   Calculate the internal rates of return for the projects. If the two projects are independent, what decision should be made?
(2)   What decision should be made if the two projects are mutually exclusive?

REFERENCES

For more on cash flow estimation and the effects of inflation, see:

DEO, PRAKASH S. "Practical Approach to Fixed-Asset Policy." *Financial Practice and Education* 2 (Spring/Summer 1992): 83–88.

HOWE, KEITH M. "Capital Budgeting Discount Rates Under Inflation: A Caveat." *Financial Practice and Education* 2 (Spring/Summer 1992): 31–35.

POHLMAN, RANDOLPH A., EMMANUEL S. SANTIAGO, and F. LYNN MARKEL. "Cash Flow Estimation Practices of Large Firms." *Financial Management* 17 (Summer 1988): 71–79.

Capital rationing and related issues are covered in:

PRUITT, STEPHEN W., and LAWRENCE J. GITMAN. "Capital Budgeting Forecast Biases: Evidence from the Fortune 500." *Financial Management* 16 (Spring 1987): 46–51.

TAGGART, ROBERT A., JR. "Allocating Capital Among a Firm's Divisions: Hurdle Rates vs. Budgets." *Journal of Financial Research* 10 (Fall 1987): 177–89.

9 *Risk and Capital Budgeting*

EXECUTIVE SUMMARY

The effective treatment of risk is both difficult and important in capital budgeting decisions. Some firms have employed a strategic planning approach without fully understanding the use of present values in making wealth-maximizing capital budgeting decisions. Failure to do so is dysfunctional and can lead to a decline in the value of the firm.

First and foremost, the cash flows should reflect all possible sources of risk. For projects of average risk, a firmwide opportunity cost of capital is appropriate. For other projects, a project-specific or divisional cost of capital should be employed to account for the above- or below-average risk. These approaches assume implicitly that risk is above or below the average risk of the project for its entire economic life. For projects for which risk differs over time, the use of sequential analysis is appropriate. Thus, later cash flows are not inappropriately penalized as they would be by using a single discount rate.

Sensitivity analysis, in which one input variable is changed at a time, is often employed in analyzing capital budgeting projects. A specific case in point is the use of break-even analysis. It is inappropriate from a wealth-maximizing standpoint to conduct a break-even analysis based on GAAP net income. Simulation, in which all of the relevant variables are allowed to change, may also be employed in order to deal with risk when capital budgeting decisions are made.

RISK AND STRATEGIC DECISIONS

We know that risk and return are positively related. To improve expected return, investors must expose themselves to more risk. Exactly the same relationship holds for capital budgeting decisions: For a firm to increase its expected return, it must increase its exposure to risk. Yet many questions remain. We shall find that managers must still use judgment whenever there is risk.

STRATEGIC DECISIONS

All sources of risk are important for the capital budgeting process because of their effect on cash flows. But cash flows are not the only source of uncertainty; managers must also consider the firm's strategic position in its segment of the industry and market. Unfortunately, when considering strategic and risky decisions, firms may find reasons to ignore the capital budgeting techniques described in Chapters 7 and 8. One reason is the inherent complexity of some projects—especially when future invest- ments may be an option that can be exercised in the future. (The topic of options in capital investments is considered in Chapter 10.) Another reason is the difficulty, both in practice and in theory, of effectively identifying and quantifying which of the risks should be considered in analyzing prospective capital budgeting projects. Taking risk into account is one of the most difficult tasks in the capital budgeting process, but it cannot be ignored. To do so is simply to invite further problems.

Risk Can Be Beneficial

Risk can also be a positive factor in project selection. That idea may seem strange, but remember that higher expected returns are possible only from exposure to additional risk. "If you know everything there is to know about a new product," said an executive of a major firm, "it's not going to be good business. There have to be some major uncertainties to be resolved. This is the only way to get a product with a major profit opportunity." This manager has learned an important lesson: If the firm is to prosper, it must find new product areas that have the potential to increase the value of the firm significantly. That is, it must find positive net present value projects from which the firm can earn excess returns due to its competitive advantages. To find these areas, the firm may expose itself to risks above and beyond the average risks it faces. Is that additional risk exposure bad? No—not unless the firm does a poor job of evaluating and considering the risks.

Most significant, profitable investments and innovations have faced high risks. But higher expected returns accompanied those higher risks. Of course, not all high-risk capital investments pan out. But managers must foster an environment within the firm that does two things: (1) encourages the development and consideration of high risk-high expected return projects, and (2) provides a proper format for adequately considering and evaluating these projects. Otherwise, the environment either will not encourage risk-taking or will lead to making high-risk, complex capital investment decisions based on seat-of-the-pants analysis. Either result can have serious—and perhaps fatal—long-run consequences for the firm.

A Common Mistake

Many managers believe they must increase the opportunity cost of capital to account for the greater risk of the more distant cash flows. This is wrong. *The use of any discount rate (above the risk-free rate) automatically recognizes that more distant cash flows are proportionally more risky.* One way to think about the opportunity cost of capital for a project, or its required return, is to view it as a function of both the risk-free rate and a risk premium. That is,

$$\text{opportunity cost of capital} = \text{risk-free rate} + \text{risk premium based on project risk} \tag{9.1}$$

If the risk-free rate is 6 percent and the risk premium for the project is 8 percent, for a total of 14 percent, both the 6 percent and the 8 percent compound over time. The compounding of the 6 percent adjusts solely for differences in the timing of the cash flows—in the absence of risk. The compounding of the 8 percent risk premium recognizes that more distant cash flows for the project are more risky. Thus, if cash flow distributions become more risky over time (as shown in Figure 9.1), then discounting implicitly takes account of some or all of this increase in risk.

The use of a discount rate that embodies a built-in risk premium compensates for the *risk borne per period*. The more distant the cash flows, the greater the number of periods and, hence, the greater the adjustment for risk. The only question is how much more risky the more distant cash flows are. If they are highly risky, then a higher discount rate, embodying a higher risk premium, may be needed. The point to remember is this: Some, and perhaps all, of the increase in riskiness of more distant cash flows is already accounted for simply by using the opportunity cost of capital.

Figure 9.1

Increasing Risk over Time

As the dispersion increases, risk increases. Using any rate above the risk-free rate in the discounting process implicitly compensates for some increases in risk.

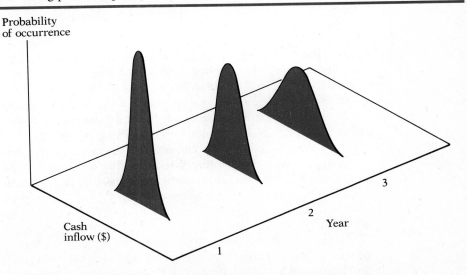

FACTORS TO CONSIDER WHEN ESTIMATING RISK

Risk relates to variability in returns, particularly returns that are less than those expected. Although the assessment of the risk associated with capital budgeting decisions is not easy, executives make such judgments every day. Some of the things they need to take into consideration are fudge factors, cyclicality, operating leverage, and financial leverage.

Make the Adjustment in the Cash Flows

In working with firms, we have encountered situations in which the firm felt that some projects were more risky than the average risk of the firm. Their "solution" was to add a fudge factor to the opportunity cost of capital to compensate for the additional risk. Although that may be the correct procedure in some cases, too often the impact of potential bad outcomes is not fully reflected in the cash flow forecasts. Thus, mistakes in estimating cash flows are compensated for by adding a fudge factor to the discount rate.

Consider a project that requires a $5 million outflow and is expected to produce after-tax inflows of $2.25 million for each of 3 years. If the discount rate is 13 percent, the net present value of the project is

$$NPV = \$2,250,000\left[\frac{1}{0.13} - \frac{1}{0.13(1 + 0.13)^3}\right] - \$5,000,000$$

$$= \$5,312,593 - \$5,000,000 = \$312,593$$

It looks as if the project should be accepted. However, upon investigation you find out that due to problems getting government clearance there is a strong possibility that no cash inflow will occur in the first year. If that happens, and assuming that $2.25 million in cash inflow will occur in each of years 2 through 4, the revised NPV is

$$NPV_{revised} = \frac{\$5,312,593}{(1 + 0.13)^1} - \$5,000,000 = -\$298,590$$

Clearly, this revised NPV is a lot different from the first NPV. In this case, there is *some* discount rate that when applied to the original set of cash inflows of $2.25 million for years 1 through 3 will produce the revised NPV of −$298,590. That discount rate is about 20.52 percent; but how do you know beforehand to add a risk premium of 20.52 − 13.00 = 7.52 percent to account for the probability that no cash flows will occur until year 2? The answer is you generally don't have any idea! Hence, the preferable approach in *all* capital investment decisions is to spend a lot of time, ask a lot of questions, and make sure that all possible assumptions and contingencies have been built into the cash flows. *Many of the problems in dealing with risk can be solved by first and foremost focusing on the cash flows.*

Cyclicality

The revenues and cash flows of some firms and projects are tied very closely to the state of the economy. Thus, firms and projects in high-tech industries, automobile firms, and retailers tend to be affected by the stage of the business cycle much more than firms in utilities or foods. Due to this greater risk, which typically cannot be diversified away, higher returns and discount rates are needed on investments whose performance is strongly tied to the stage of the business cycle.

Operating Leverage

The concept of **operating leverage** refers to the commitment of the firm to incur fixed cash outflows for production and administration, no matter what the level of sales. Other things being equal, firms that have more operating leverage (that is, relatively more fixed cash outflows for operations) will see their cash flows fluctuate much more in response to a change in sales.

Consider two firms as follows:

	Low-fixed-cost Firm	High-fixed-cost Firm
Sales	$1,000,000	$1,000,000
Variable operating costs	600,000	200,000
Fixed operating costs	100,000	500,000
EBIT	$ 300,000	$ 300,000

Operating leverage can be determined by

$$\text{Operating leverage} = \frac{(\text{sales} - \text{variable costs})}{EBIT} \tag{9.2}$$

where EBIT is the earnings before interest and taxes.[1] Using Equation 9.2, we find that the operating leverage for the low-fixed-cost firm is 1.33, while it is 2.67 for the high-fixed-cost firm. As sales fluctuate, the low-fixed-cost firm's EBIT will fluctuate 1.33 times as much. Thus, if sales go up by 20 percent, then due to the lower use of fixed operating costs, EBIT will go up by about 27 percent [i.e., (20 percent) (1.33) = 26.60 percent ≈ 27 percent]. For the high-fixed-cost firm, the higher operating leverage indicates that for a 20 percent increase in sales, EBIT will increase by about 53 percent (i.e., (20 percent)(2.67) = 53.40 ≈ 53 percent).

Firms or projects that have mostly high fixed operating costs have more operating leverage. Other things being equal, higher operating leverage means that the firm's or project's cash flows vary much more over the stage of the business cycle. These higher-risk projects require higher returns and discount rates.

Financial Leverage

Financial leverage refers to the presence or absence of high fixed costs of financing. It is a concept that is analogous to operating leverage, except that now the fixed costs relate to financing, not operations. Firms or projects that employ a lot of debt or other

---

[1] Operating leverage can also be measured by:

$$\text{operating leverage} = \frac{\text{percentage change in EBIT}}{\text{percentage change in sales}}$$

Operating leverage, as given by Equation 9.2, is simply the linear approximation for the elasticity measured at a given level of output.

fixed-financing-cost sources of financing (such as leases or preferred stock) have more financial leverage. As EBIT fluctuates, high financial leverage means that more cash flows go to the fixed-cost providers of capital and less goes to the firm and its owners. The impact of financial leverage on the value of the firm is examined in detail in Chapters 11 and 12.

Since many factors affect the riskiness of projects, estimating the specific amount of risk is not an easy task. By first focusing on the cash flows, financial managers can avoid many of the problems related to adjusting the opportunity cost of capital to reflect the project's riskiness. Then, the key is to focus on the major uncertainties facing the economy and how they will affect the proposed project and to consider the action (and/or reaction) of competitors.

Concept Review Questions

- Why is consideration of a project's risk important for capital budgeting decisions?
- How can risk benefit the firm?
- Describe the factors that should be considered when estimating risk.
- What is the difference between operating leverage and financial leverage?

OPPORTUNITY COST OF CAPITAL FOR CAPITAL BUDGETING DECISIONS

Once we start considering risk adjustment, we need to distinguish between two different situations. The first is those for which *both initially and over time* the risks are above or below the average risk of the projects considered by the firm. The second involves projects for which *initially the risks are above the average risk of the firm, but after some initial period the risks decrease*. Because different approaches are needed to deal with these two cases, we examine them separately. In this section we first consider opportunity costs of capital for capital budgeting projects, then we examine possible portfolio effects, and, finally, we consider situations in which risk is expected to decrease after an initial start-up period.

FIRM, DIVISIONAL, AND PROJECT-SPECIFIC OPPORTUNITY COSTS

In Chapters 7 and 8 we assumed, for simplicity, that risk was the same for all projects faced by the firm. But, we know this cannot be true. Some projects must be more risky, while others are probably viewed as being very safe. In cases in which risk differs significantly from the firm's overall level of risk, the use of a firmwide opportunity cost of capital results in the misallocation of resources.

Consider Figure 9.2, which depicts the effect of using a single firmwide opportunity cost of capital when risk is not uniform across projects. If the firm's opportunity cost is employed, project A will be rejected and project B will be accepted. However, if project A is less risky than the average project faced by the firm, then a lower discount rate (as given by the sloped project-specific opportunity cost of capital line) should be employed. All projects whose return and risk fall on the solid line whose intercept is

Figure 9.2

Firmwide and Project-Specific Opportunity Costs of Capital

Use of a firmwide cost of capital will overallocate funds to risky projects (like project B) and underallocate them to safe projects (project A).

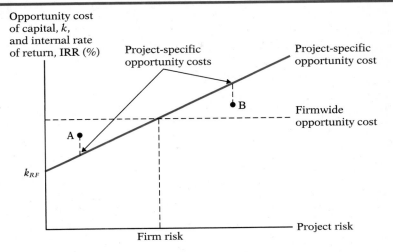

k_{RF} are zero net present value projects. Those above the line are positive NPV projects; those below the line are negative NPV projects. Because project A has an IRR greater than its appropriate opportunity cost of capital, it should be accepted. Conversely, project B is more risky; accordingly, an opportunity cost higher than the firm's overall opportunity cost of capital should be employed. Because the anticipated return on project B is less than its project-specific opportunity cost, it should be rejected. It is easy to see the effect of using a single rate for discounting all capital budgeting proposals: We overallocate resources to risky projects, while we underallocate resources to safer projects. The impact of such a mistake is to reduce the value of the firm.

As noted previously, the opportunity cost of capital appropriate for evaluating any capital budgeting project can be thought of as:

$$\text{opportunity cost of capital} = \text{risk-free rate} + \text{risk premium based on project risk}$$

There are, in fact, three different approaches (as discussed in Chapter 6) to specifying what this opportunity cost should be. The first, based on the firm's weighted average cost of capital, provides a single firmwide opportunity cost of capital. This rate is appropriate for use when considering most replacement projects for a firm, or when the firm is homogeneous in terms of its projects and is not investing in any high- (or low-) risk projects.

The second approach is embodied in the form of divisional costs of capital. For example, an integrated oil company may have four divisions—domestic exploration, international exploration, refining, and marketing. Based on perceived risks in the different areas, the firm may establish divisional opportunity costs of capital as follows:

Domestic exploration	20%
International exploration	30
Refining	16
Marketing	12

These are the discount rates used in each division with net present value. The use of divisional rates may be thought of as a way station between the use of a single firmwide opportunity cost of capital and, alternatively, different opportunity costs of capital for each project. In practice many firms employ some type of divisional cost of capital for capital budgeting purposes.

Finally, a project-specific opportunity cost of capital can be used based on the risk associated with an individual project. Often the capital asset pricing model, CAPM, is employed to estimate these project-specific rates of return. Based on nondiversifiable risk, *for an all-equity-financed firm* a project's opportunity cost of capital using the CAPM would be

$$k_{\text{project}} = k_{RF} + \beta_{\text{project}}(k_M - k_{RF}) \qquad (9.3)$$

where

k_{project} = the project's opportunity cost of capital
k_{RF} = the risk-free rate of interest
β_{project} = the project's nondiversifiable risk as measured by its beta coefficient
k_M = the expected rate of return on the market portfolio

Thus, if the firm is all equity financed, the project-specific discount rate based on the CAPM is given by the security market line, SML, introduced in Chapter 4. These three approaches to estimating the opportunity cost of capital are depicted in Figure 9.3.

Two points should be emphasized with the use of alternative opportunity costs of capital that consider the risk of capital budgeting projects. First is the **stand-alone principle.** This principle says that a proposed project should be accepted or rejected by comparing it with the returns that could be secured based on investing in a similar-risk project. The forgone returns from the bypassed investment are captured by using the appropriate opportunity cost of the forgone alternative for the project. For example, if an equally risky investment involves investing in securities that would provide an expected return of 20 percent, then the proposed capital investment must return at least 20 percent. Otherwise the firm should reject the proposed capital project and invest in the securities. This stand-alone principle is important for all capital investment decisions made by the firm.

Second, estimation of the appropriate opportunity cost of capital in the face of risk is part science and part judgment. Although no method of dealing with risk is entirely precise, it is an important step that managers must take if they want to maximize the value of the firm. Failure to do so results in the same effect the ostrich achieves by

Figure 9.3

Alternative Opportunity Costs of Capital

Use of appropriate opportunity costs of capital, based on the risks and forgone opportunities, is essential for effective capital budgeting decision making.

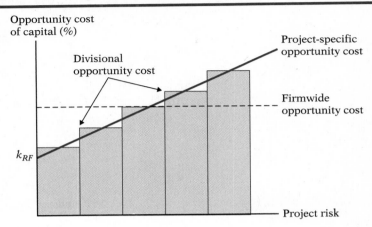

burying its head in the ground—the world continues to spin and change while the ostrich (or firm) maintains its naive view that all is well.

WHAT ABOUT PORTFOLIO EFFECTS?

Should firms concern themselves about the possible interaction between the cash flows expected from a new project and those from existing projects? The answer to that question is generally "no," but it is more complicated than that. *First and foremost,* if a new project is expected to have any positive or negative effect on cash flows associated with existing projects, then these must (as noted in Chapter 8) be treated as opportunity costs or benefits and incorporated into the cash flows estimated for the new project.

The bigger question is this: Are there risk-reducing benefits that arise when a firm undertakes a project whose returns are less than perfectly positively correlated with those of the firm? That is, should the firm consider itself a portfolio and attempt to accept projects that reduce the risk (or standard deviation) of the portfolio returns? If financial markets are efficient, the answer is "no." The reason is that investors are able to diversify on their own; they do not receive any incremental benefits from having the firm diversify. In effect, the firm is performing a redundant service.

In countries where financial markets are not completely efficient, there may be some risk reduction (in terms of the volatility of the firm's cash flows, probability of bankruptcy, and so forth) that can be achieved. It is very hard, however, to measure this benefit, and very easy to overestimate its impact. For this reason, projects should be considered on their individual merits, without attempting to quantify any benefits from risk reduction. Then, if (and only if) it appears to be very important, possible portfolio effects can be introduced into the decision-making process.

WHEN A SINGLE DISCOUNT RATE CANNOT BE USED

Up to now we have considered how to deal with risk that is above or below the firm's risk over the entire economic life of the project. But what about the situation in which risk is high at first but then decreases? Consider the proposed development and marketing of "Clean-Ez," a portable electric car washer. In making its capital budgeting decision, the firm estimated that the preliminary phase, involving a small pilot plant and test marketing, would require a $7 million initial investment at time $t = 0$. If the preliminary phase is successful, a $40 million cash investment will be required to build the plant at time $t = 1$; then for the next 9 years ($t = 2$ through $t = 10$), the after-tax cash inflows will be $12 million per year. Thus, the estimated cash flow stream is as follows:

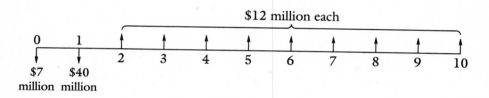

Because of the high risk of the project, a 20 percent return (versus the firm's opportunity cost of capital of 12 percent) was used. Based on a 20 percent discount rate, the NPV was

$$NPV = \frac{\$12,000,000 \left[\dfrac{1}{0.20} - \dfrac{1}{0.20\,(1 + 0.20)^9} \right]}{(1 + 0.20)^1} - \frac{\$40,000,000}{(1 + 0.20)^1} - \$7,000,000$$

$$= \$40,309,665 - \$33,333,333 - \$7,000,000 = -\$23,668$$

Because the NPV is negative, the initial decision was to reject Clean-Ez.

However, Kay, one of the finance staff, asked: "Have we accurately considered the riskiness of Clean-Ez? If risk decreases after the preliminary phase, then the use of a 20 percent discount rate over the entire life of Clean-Ez unnecessarily penalizes more distant cash flows." After some discussion, it was determined that there was only a 50-50 probability the second investment (of $40 million) would be made at $t = 1$. If the test marketing in the preliminary phase was below expectations, then the additional funds would not be spent. On the other hand, if the preliminary phase was a success, then Clean-Ez would be of average risk, and a 12 percent discount rate would be appropriate over its remaining life.

Based on this additional information, Kay proceeded to employ **sequential analysis** as follows. First, she pointed out that there are two separate parts to the proposed project. The $7 million for the preliminary phase will be spent regardless. Depending on the results of that phase, there is a 50 percent chance that a $40 million cash investment will be made in 1 year for a project of average risk. Likewise, there is a 50 percent chance that no additional investment will be made. So,

Success
(50%)

$$NPV = \$12,000,000 \left[\frac{1}{0.12} - \frac{1}{0.12(1 + 0.12)^9} \right] - \$40,000,000$$

Preliminary phase

$$= \$63,938,998 - \$40,000,000 = \$23,938,998$$

Failure
(50%)

$$NPV = 0$$

The **expected NPV** in year 1 is simply $0.50(\$23,938,998) + 0.50(0) = \$11,969,499$. But this NPV is for a project starting at $t = 1$, and we have not considered the $7 million initial investment. Looking at the NPV of the total project from its inception, it is

$$NPV = \frac{\$11,969,499}{(1 + 0.20)^1} - \$7,000,000$$

$$= \$9,974,582 - \$7,000,000 = \$2,974,582$$

Based on this analysis, Kay concluded (correctly, we might add) that the Clean-Ez project has a positive NPV and should be funded.[2]

One often hears executives or other critics of the present value approach say it unnecessarily penalizes long-term projects. As we have just seen, that does not have to be the case. By treating the decision as a sequential investment, we can handle the risk adjustment question. However, if we simply use a high discount rate, we *will* be guilty of penalizing long-term projects if risk is not consistently at the higher level.

Concept Review Questions

- What are the effects of using the firm's opportunity cost of capital when evaluating projects with different risks?
- What are the three different approaches to estimating an opportunity cost of capital?
- Describe how to adjust a project's opportunity cost of capital if you anticipate a decrease of risk in future years.

---

[2] An alternative approach to this problem involves the use of option concepts. The subsequent investment is an option that will be exercised only if the pilot plant and test marketing phase are successful. This topic is discussed further in Chapter 10.

Information About the Riskiness of Projects

Up to now we have discussed risk in general as it relates to capital budgeting projects, and then considered how differences in risk can be dealt with through the use of a firmwide opportunity cost of capital, divisional opportunity costs, or project-specific opportunity costs of capital. Before making capital budgeting decisions, it is important to examine the critical variables and assumptions that are expected to affect the project's success or failure. To do so we can employ sensitivity analysis, break-even analysis, and simulation.

Sensitivity Analysis

Sensitivity analysis does not formally attempt to quantify risk. Rather, it focuses on determining how sensitive the net present value is to changes in any of the input variables. To understand sensitivity analysis, let's consider the following example:

Year	CF
0	−$55,000
1	20,000
2	20,000
3	20,000
4	20,000
5	20,000

At a discount rate of 13 percent, the base-case NPV is

$$NPV = \$20,000\left[\frac{1}{0.13} - \frac{1}{0.13(1 + 0.13)^5}\right] - \$55,000$$

$$= \$70,345 - \$55,000 = \$15,345$$

To conduct a sensitivity analysis, we need to change one of the input variables to determine how sensitive the NPV is to changes in that particular variable. The input data can be changed by a certain percentage, or by a given dollar amount.

To see how sensitive the NPV is to changes in the initial investment and number of years, we changed them each by 20 percent.[3] This results in an NPV of $4,345 for

---

[3] For simplicity we assume the per year depreciation remains constant, although the initial investment changes.

a 20 percent increase or $26,345 for the same size decrease in the initial investment. Likewise, the NPV is $24,951 if the number of years increases by 20 percent (to 6 years) or $4,489 if it decreases by 20 percent (to 4 years). In Figure 9.4, this information is plotted against the base-case NPV. The steeper the slope, the more sensitive the project's NPV is to a change in the input variable. We see that this project's NPV is slightly more sensitive to a 20 percent change in the initial investment than to a 20 percent change in its life. Sensitivity analysis is widely employed in practice. This is especially true with the increasing use of spreadsheet programs and on-line capital budgeting computer systems.

BREAK-EVEN ANALYSIS

When undertaking a sensitivity analysis of a project, we are asking how serious it would be if some factor (i.e., cash inflows, life of the project, and so forth) turns out far worse than expected. Managers sometimes prefer to rephrase this question and ask how bad sales (and therefore, cash inflows) could get before the project loses money. This approach is known as **break-even analysis.** The break-even point occurs where the present value of the inflows equals the present value of the outflows, so the net present value is zero.

To illustrate break-even analysis, assume that Whiz-Bang Motors is projecting net income and cash flows for its new product line as shown in Table 9.1. Under simplifying assumptions, where sales equal gross cash inflows, there are no accruals, and tax

---

Figure 9.4

Sensitivity Analysis of 10 Percent Change in Initial Investment and Years

The steeper the slope, the more sensitive the NPV is to a change in the input variable.

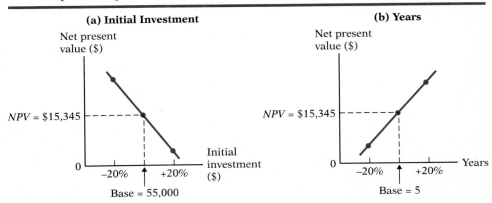

and GAAP depreciation are the same, Whiz-Bang estimates that when sales are $300, net income will be $54. Based on an initial cash investment of $1,000, a 10-year life, and a discount rate of 15 percent, the per year cash flows after tax, CF_t, are $154, and the net present value is equal to $-$227.11. With the same assumptions, if sales are zero, or, alternatively, $600, the net income, cash flows, and net present values are as follows:

	Sales of 0 Per Year	Sales of $600 Per Year
Net income	−$90	$198
Cash flow per year, CF_t	10	298
NPV	−949.81	495.59

We see that the NPV is highly negative when sales are zero, moderately negative when sales equal $300, and positive when sales equal $600 per year. Clearly, the zero NPV point occurs between $300 and $600 in sales.

Table 9.1

GAAP Net Income and Cash Flow for Whiz-Bang

For simplicity, we assume that the equipment costs $1,000 and is depreciated to zero over 10 years via straight-line for both accounting and tax purposes. (The half-year convention built into straight-line depreciation for IRS purposes is ignored in this example.) Also, we assume that there are no accruals and that sales and costs are all collected (or incurred) so they are equal to cash inflows and outflows.

	GAAP Income	Cash Flow
Sales	$300	$300
Variable costs (20% of sales)	60	60
Fixed costs	50	50
Depreciation	100	
Earnings before tax (EBT)	90	
Taxes (40%)	36	36
Net income	$ 54	
Cash flow		$154

$$NPV = \$154\left[\frac{1}{0.15} - \frac{1}{0.15(1 + 0.15)^{10}}\right] - \$1,000$$

$$= \$772.89 - \$1,000 = -\$227.11$$

To solve for the zero NPV level we proceed as follows:

zero $NPV = PV$ of inflows $- PV$ of outflows $= 0$

$$CF_t\left[\frac{1}{0.15} - \frac{1}{0.15(1+0.15)^{10}}\right] - \$1,000 = 0$$

$$CF_t(5.0188) = \$1,000$$

$$CF_t = \$1,000/5.0188 = \$199.25$$

The sales volume (before variable cost, fixed cost, and tax cash inflow) needed to generate after-tax cash inflows of \$199.25 for each of 10 years is obtained as follows, where W is the unknown sales level:

$$\text{Sales} - (\text{variable} + \text{fixed costs}) - \text{taxes} = \$199.25$$

$$W - (0.20W + \$50) - (W - 0.20W - \$50 - \$100)(0.40) = \$199.25$$

$$W - 0.20W - \$50 - 0.40W + 0.08W + \$20 + \$40 = \$199.25$$

$$0.48W + \$10 = \$199.25$$

$$W = \$189.25/0.48$$

$$= \$394.27$$

This relationship is plotted in Figure 9.5. The present value of the cash inflows and the present value of the cash outflows cross at sales of \$394.27. This is the point where

Figure 9.5

Break-Even Chart Based on Total Present Values

This is a form of sensitivity analysis, allowing sales (or the present value of the cash inflows) to change.

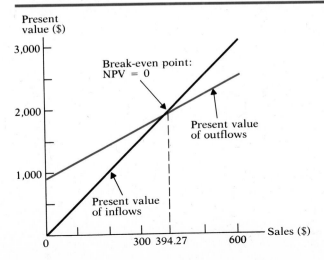

the project has a zero NPV. As long as sales are greater than $394.27 per year, the project has a positive NPV.

Instead of working with the present value of the cash inflows and outflows, we can work equally well with the equivalent annual inflows and outflows.[4] The annual cost of the project includes the recurring costs (i.e., variable costs, fixed costs, and taxes) *plus* the equivalent annual cost of the initial investment of $1,000. This equivalent annual cost is determined by dividing the initial cash investment of $1,000 by the 10-year present value factor:

$$\text{equivalent annual cost} = \frac{\text{initial investment}}{\left[\frac{1}{k} - \frac{1}{k(1+k)^n}\right]} \tag{9.4}$$

$$= \frac{\$1,000}{\left[\frac{1}{0.15} - \frac{1}{0.15(1+0.15)^{10}}\right]} = \$199.25$$

In Table 9.2 we show the equivalent annual cash inflows and outflows for our three levels of sales; the difference between the equivalent annual inflows and outflows is shown in column 7. As long as the difference is positive, the project has a positive NPV.

This relationship is graphed in Figure 9.6. As you would expect, except for the change from the present value of the total inflows and outflows to the equivalent annual inflows and outflows, the results are exactly the same as shown in Figure 9.5.

Table 9.2

Equivalent Annual Cash Inflows and Outflows for Whiz-Bang Motors

We assume that if the project operates at a loss, the firm can use the loss to reduce its tax bill. Thus, when sales are zero, the project produces a tax saving.

			Cash Outflows			
Sales; Gross Cash Inflow (1)	Variable Costs (2)	+ Fixed Costs + (3)	Taxes + (4)	Equivalent Annual Cost (5)	= Total (6)	Net Equivalent Annual Flow (1) − (6) (7)
$ 0	$ 0	$50	−$ 60	$199.25	$189.25	−$189.25
300	60	50	36	199.25	345.25	− 45.25
600	120	50	132	199.25	501.25	98.75

[4] This is exactly the same concept used in Chapter 7 when we determined the equivalent annual NPV, so that mutually exclusive projects with different lives could be compared.

Figure 9.6

Break-Even Chart Based on Equivalent Annual Cash Flows

We can redraw Figure 9.5, but it is now based on the equivalent annual inflows and outflows. The break-even NPV remains at the same level of sales of $394.27.

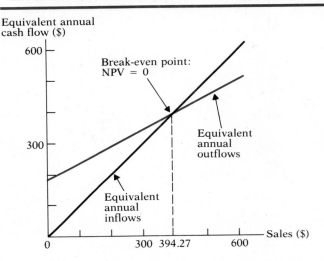

The zero NPV still occurs when sales are $394.27 per year. It makes no difference whether we work with the total present values or the equivalent annual inflows and outflows in order to determine the financial break-even point. Whiz-Bang does not want to introduce the project unless sales are expected to be at least $394.27 per year. To do so will lower the value of the firm.

Instead of employing present values, many firms still calculate their break-even point based on GAAP net income. In Figure 9.7, we have plotted this relationship; it shows that the accounting-based break-even point is at a sales level of only $187.50 per year. Remember that Figures 9.5 and 9.6, based on present values, showed a financial break-even point of $394.27. The difference in the two approaches hinges on the depreciation of $100 per year that is deducted for GAAP accounting purposes and the required rate of return of 15 percent for the project. *By treating break-even analysis in an accounting manner, managers are ignoring the opportunity cost of the $1,000 investment.* We must allow for the fact that the $1,000 could have been invested elsewhere to earn a return of 15 percent. Depreciation thus understates the true cost by ignoring the forgone opportunity to earn a return on the $1,000 initial investment. Companies that break even on an accounting basis are really losing money—they are losing the opportunity cost of their investment.

SIMULATION

Sensitivity analysis allows you to consider the effect of changing one variable at a time. A more refined approach, **scenario analysis,** is based on changing a limited number of possible combinations. A further refinement is **simulation,** which is a technique for

Figure 9.7

Break-Even Chart Based on GAAP Net Income

By ignoring the opportunity costs associated with capital investments, net-income-based break-even analysis seriously understates the financial break-even point.

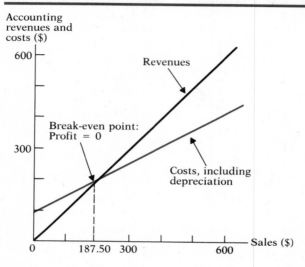

considering the effect of changing *all* of the relevant variables in an analysis. While simulation used to require relatively sophisticated computer programming, recent developments in computer software make it easy to use within a **spreadsheet program** like Enable or Lotus 1-2-3®.

The first step in a computer simulation is to specify the relevant variables and the probability distributions associated with each variable. In our Whiz-Bang example, the relevant variables (at a minimum) are sales, the relationship of variable costs to sales, the initial investment, and the economic (as opposed to tax) life of the project. In fact, as any executive will testify, this is a very short list of relevant variables. To illustrate simulation, let's suppose that the probabilities of Whiz-Bang's sales associated with this new project have been estimated as follows:

Sales (1)	Probability (2)	Associated Random Number (3)
$ 0	0.05	0–4
150	0.25	5–29
300	0.40	30–69
450	0.25	70–94
600	0.05	95–99

The sales may be between $0 and $600, with the probabilities as indicated in column 2. Also, the associated random variables, as shown in column 3, are recorded.[5] Once this probability distribution of possible outcomes is estimated for sales, we then proceed to estimate probability distributions for all of the other relevant variables that are likely to change. While specifying the variables and their probabilities is not easy, it is often easier than the next step.

The second step involves specifying the interdependencies between variables and across time. Specifying the interdependencies is the hardest, and also the most important, part of a simulation. If all of the components of a project's cash flows are unrelated, then the simulation is easy.

Once the variables, probabilities, and interdependencies have been specified, the simulation proceeds as follows:

STEP 1:   Computers, through random number generations, will select a possible outcome for each variable. For sales, let us assume the random number 73 comes up.

STEP 2:   For each variable, the random number selected determines the value to be employed for that variable. The 73 associated with sales means that the appropriate sales level for the first run of the simulation is $450. Values for all of the other variables are set in a similar manner.

STEP 3:   Once a value has been established for each of the variables, the computer generates an NPV for the first run of the simulation.

STEP 4:   This NPV is then stored, and the computer runs the second analysis. Here a different set of random numbers, and therefore a different set of values for the variables, is selected. The NPV is then computed and stored. This procedure goes on for 250 to 500 (or more) runs.

STEP 5:   Once the 250 or 500 runs are completed, the frequency distribution of NPVs, the expected value, and the standard deviation are all printed out. Often a graph is presented much like that shown in Figure 9.8.

Simulation, though complicated, has the obvious merit of compelling the decision maker to face up to uncertainty and interdependency. Once the model is constructed, it is simple to analyze what would happen if the probability distribution changed for any one variable, or if the degree of interdependency increased or decreased from that specified. Thus, simulation has the potential to enable us to ascertain many facets of the risk associated with proposed capital budgeting projects. Before we jump on the bandwagon, however, and conclude that simulation solves all of our ills, we need to consider a few of the problems with simulation.

The main problems are as follows:

1.   COST AND TIME   Until recently it was very difficult to do realistic computer simulations on PCs. Although new computer software is changing that, it must be

---

[5] For simplicity, we assume sales are a discrete variable that takes on only five values. This is solely for illustrative purposes; computer simulations routinely deal with continuous distributions.

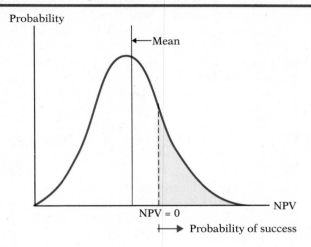

Figure 9.8

Probability Distribution of NPVs

By calculating the probability of success, information is provided about the likelihood of accepting a project that has the potential to increase the value of the firm.

recognized that big, complex projects still require significant amounts of time to set up and run. Equally important, unless the end users have been instrumental in setting up the simulation, they may not have confidence in the results and/or the specific assumptions underlying the simulation.

2. INTERDEPENDENCIES   As indicated previously, specifying the interdependencies between variables, and over time, is the most difficult part of any simulation. Here, it is crucial for managers to pool their resources and knowledge and to come up with reasonable educated guesses as to interdependencies. Then these assumptions should be tested in the simulation, and communicated to the final decision makers.

3. INTERPRETATION   In capital budgeting techniques considered up to now, the outcome has been a single NPV. This simplifies the analysis and decision making, even though it may be unrealistic. But simulation may go to the other extreme: It provides a whole distribution of possible outcomes that can be converted into the probability of success. This **probability of success,** as shown in Figure 9.8, indicates what the chances are that the project will have a positive NPV. Not all managers are comfortable, however, with this additional information. They may have too much information or too little guidance as to what are acceptable probabilities of success or risk levels.

4. PROBLEMS RELATED TO NPV   Finally, there are some peculiar problems related to probability distributions of NPVs. If the NPV approach is employed, then the appropriate discount rate may not be the project's opportunity cost of capital. Rather, all of the risk may be captured by specifying the probability distributions of the relevant variables. If all the risk is incorporated into the probability distribution, the NPV is calculated by *discounting at the risk-free rate,*

k_{RF}. Once this step is taken, however, the resulting probability distribution of NPVs is very different from what is typically encountered. This is because we normally discount at the opportunity cost of capital, not at the risk-free rate. Hence, calculating NPVs in a simulation may lead to as many problems as it solves.[6]

Where do we stand on using simulation for dealing with risk in capital budgeting decisions? Although many theoretical and empirical advances have been made in using probability distribution approaches to make capital budgeting decisions, their use by firms has been very limited until recently. The recent developments in terms of more powerful PCs and good simulation software are, however, refocusing attention on using simulation to help get a better handle on risk. Used wisely, with a knowledge of both its strengths and limitations, simulation can aid effective decision making. While no panacea, it has progressed to the point where it can help decision makers gain a better understanding of the importance different variables, assumptions, and interactions have for capital budgeting decisions. As such, we view it as a reasonable addition to a good capital budgeting program.

In this chapter we have identified a number of different ways of handling risk. Because risk comes from many sources, it is difficult to generalize about it. One thing is certain, however: Effective managers make a determined effort to probe for possible risks associated with capital budgeting projects. By proceeding in the manner described in this chapter, *they are ensuring that the right questions about risk are asked at the right time and that reasonable methods of dealing with it are being employed.*

Concept Review Questions

- What is the purpose of employing sensitivity analysis, break-even analysis, and simulation?
- What are some of the advantages and disadvantages of using simulation to evaluate a capital budgeting project?

KEY POINTS

1. Risk may be beneficial; only by searching out its competitive advantages and accepting risks can firms expect to earn above-average returns.
2. First and foremost, build all risk impacts into a project's cash flows if possible.
3. Using any discount rate above the risk-free rate assumes implicitly that risk increases over time. The only questions are these: Is too much (too little) risk adjustment built into the discount rate employed? Does risk change over time more (or less) than accounted for by the discount rate employed?
4. "High" cyclicality, operating leverage, and financial leverage can all lead to greater risk.
5. Project-specific or divisional opportunity costs of capital should be employed for more- or less-risky projects.
6. The stand-alone principle is important: A project should be accepted or rejected by comparing it with the returns that could be secured based on investing in a similar-risk project.

---

[6] See the references at the end of the chapter for more on this problem.

7. Sequential analysis can be employed when risk changes over the economic life of a project. Sensitivity analysis is also widely used. Break-even analysis should be conducted based on discounted cash flows, not GAAP accounting numbers. Firms that break even on the basis of GAAP accounting numbers are really losing money—they are losing the opportunity cost of their investment.

8. Simulation can provide a great deal of information to decision makers by allowing all of the input variables to change simultaneously. At the same time, it has some peculiar quirks that must be recognized when using it in capital budgeting decision making.

QUESTIONS

9.1   Mike, the CEO of Larson Enterprises, believes that the risk of a proposed capital budgeting project increases over time. As a result, a project-specific or divisional opportunity cost of capital must be chosen. As Larson's chief financial officer, explain to Mike when this strategy may not be appropriate.

9.2   The divisional opportunity cost of capital approach to capital budgeting, employing categories of projects with different risks, might be graphed as follows:

Explain how divisional opportunity costs capture many of the risk and return ideas of the capital asset pricing model. In what significant ways do the two differ?

9.3   Explain the importance of the stand-alone principle. Why are opportunity costs (or the forgone returns from bypassed investments) so important in making wealth-maximizing capital budgeting decisions?

9.4   Should the firm be concerned primarily with diversifying its investment (or asset) portfolio? Why or why not?

9.5   How should you proceed when risk changes over time substantially faster or slower than accounted for by using a single discount rate? Explain.

9.6   Adam believes that sensitivity analysis is a viable way to deal with risk. Do you agree with him? Why or why not?

9.7   Why does break-even analysis, when conducted employing GAAP accounting numbers, result in understating the financial break-even point? Can you see any redeeming features of an accounting-based break-even analysis?

9.8   Explain both the strengths and the weaknesses of simulation.

CONCEPT REVIEW PROBLEMS

See Appendix A for solutions.

CR9.1   Campbell's is considering purchasing a new dehydration facility. The facility will cost $500,000 and has a beta of 1.4. The risk-free rate of return is 6 percent, and the expected return on the market portfolio is 12 percent. After-tax cash flows from the project are expected to be $100,000 for each of 10 years.

a. What is the project's risk premium? Its required return?

b. Should Campbell's accept the project?

CR9.2 Volkman Inc. is considering purchasing a coal mine in Wyoming. Cost of the coal mine is $8 million, and the opportunity cost of capital is 15 percent. Volkman's engineers believe (with 50 percent probability) there is enough coal to produce $2 million in after-tax cash flows for the next 5 years. On the other hand, there may be (with 50 percent probability) enough coal to produce $2 million in after-tax cash flows for 10 years. What is the expected net present value of the project?

CR9.3 Mary, owner of Flowers Forever, is considering expanding into the silk floral market. She estimates the expansion will cost $60,000 and that she will sell approximately 600 different silk floral arrangements per year over the next 4 years, at an average price of $100 per arrangement. Her operating costs are estimated to be approximately 50 percent of revenue.

a. If Flowers Forever's tax rate is 28 percent and the opportunity cost of capital is 10 percent, what is the net present value of this project? (For simplicity, assume no depreciation will be taken on the $60,000 expenditure.)

b. Mary is concerned about the risk of the silk floral arrangement project. She is concerned that sales may not be 600 floral arrangements per year. Perform a sensitivity analysis on the number of silk floral arrangements sold per year in which the floral arrangements drop by 10 percent, 20 percent, or 30 percent or increase by 10 percent, 20 percent, or 30 percent.

CR9.4 Using the information for Flowers Forever given in CR9.3, what is the break-even for the number of units of floral arrangements sold per year?

CR9.5 Mary is concerned about the effects of a fluctuating economy on the profitability of the silk flower expansion in CR9.3. If a downturn in the economy occurs, she will be able to sell only 500 units at $80 per unit. However, if the economy is better than anticipated, she will be able to sell 700 units at $120 per unit. (*Note:* The operating costs remain 50 percent of revenue.)

a. If the probabilities are 30 percent for a downturn in the economy, 40 percent for the base-case economy with 600 units sold at $100 per unit, and 30 percent for an improved economy, what is the expected net present value of the three scenarios?

b. What is the standard deviation about the expected net present value?

PROBLEMS

9.1 Norton Industries employs the capital asset pricing model to estimate project-specific costs of capital for capital budgeting decisions. The risk-free rate is 7 percent, the expected return on the market portfolio is 15 percent, and the project's beta is 1.50. The cash flow stream is as follows:

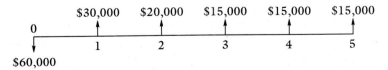

a. Should Norton undertake the proposed project?

b. Can you see any problems associated with using the capital asset pricing model to estimate project-specific costs of capital for capital budgeting decision making?

9.2 Hexter is considering the investment in some new equipment. The CFs are as follows:

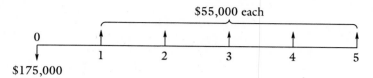

The CAPM approach will be used to estimate the appropriate project-specific opportunity cost of capital; $k_{RF} = 7$ percent, $\sigma_{project}$ (standard deviation of the project's returns) $= 32.20$ percent, $Corr_{project,M} = +0.60$, and the distribution of the market's return is:

Probability, P_i	Market Return, k_M
0.20	30%
0.20	20
0.30	15
0.30	-5

a. What is the project's beta? (*Note:* Carry to two decimal places. From Chapter 4, $\beta_{project} = \sigma_{project} Corr_{project,M}/\sigma_M$.)
b. Should Hexter purchase the equipment?

9.3 Manakyan Bar-B-Q plans to open two new fast-food stores, one in Dallas and one in Oklahoma City. The Dallas operation is estimated to be a riskier project and is assigned a risk premium of 3 percent above the firm's opportunity cost of capital compared with the 1 percent risk premium assigned to the Oklahoma City store. Expected after-tax cash flows for each store are estimated below:

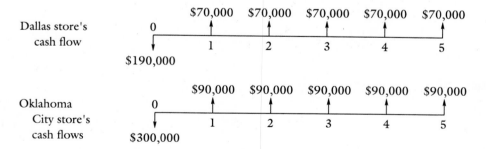

If the firmwide opportunity cost is 15 percent, should the Dallas store be opened? The Oklahoma City store?

9.4 The following equation is employed to estimate the project-specific opportunity cost of capital:

$$opportunity\ cost\ of\ capital = risk\text{-}free\ rate + 10\%(coefficient\ of\ variation)$$
$$= 11\% + 10\%CV_{project}$$

Your firm is considering two mutually exclusive projects with the following CFs:

	Project A		Project B	
Initial investment	$120,000		$150,000	
CFs and probabilities	0.30	$35,000	0.30	$60,000
of occurrence	0.40	30,000	0.40	40,000
for *each of 6 years*	0.30	20,000	0.40	30,000

a. Which project is riskier, based on its coefficient of variation? (*Note:* The coefficient of variation is standard deviation/mean.)
b. Which, if either, of the projects should be selected? (*Note:* Round the opportunity cost of capital to the nearest whole percent.)

9.5   White Enterprises is evaluating whether to build an exclusive resort on the island of St. Vincent in the Caribbean. The CFs are estimated to be $23 million for each of 15 years, the initial after-tax investment is $150 million, and the appropriate discount rate is 10 percent.

a. Should White proceed with the project?
b. Upon further investigation, it is decided that the CFs could be better characterized by the following probability distribution:

Condition	Probability	CFs Per Year
Economy great	0.2	$30 million
Economy average	0.7	23 million
Hurricane: resort demolished	0.1	0

Does this new information affect the decision?

9.6   Berry Foods has developed chocolate marbles. The product will be test marketed in the southeastern United States for 2 years, requires an initial investment of $2 million, and because of heavy promotional expenses is not expected to generate any positive CFs during the first 2 years. There is a 60 percent chance that demand for the chocolate marbles will be satisfactory; if that is so, an $8 million after-tax cash investment will be incurred at $t = 2$ to market the chocolate marbles in the eastern half of the United States. Subsequent CFs are as follows:

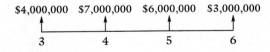

$4,000,000 $7,000,000 $6,000,000 $3,000,000

3	4	5	6

If the test-market results are unfavorable (a 40 percent chance), then the chocolate marbles will be withdrawn from the market. Once consumer preferences are known, Berry Foods considers chocolate marbles an average-risk project requiring a 14 percent return. During the test-marketing phase a 25 percent return is required. What decision should Berry make?

9.7   Greentree Products is considering investing in a capital budgeting project with the following CFs:

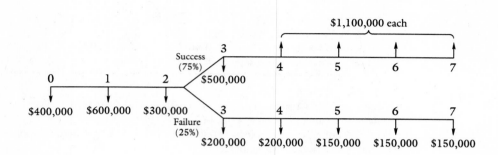

For the first 3 years, the appropriate opportunity cost of capital is 30 percent; after that, it drops to 10 percent. What decision should Greentree make?

9.8   Rainbow Painters would like to purchase a mixing machine for an initial investment of $11,000. It would last 5 years and produce after-tax operating cash flows of $3,900 per year. The discount rate is 16 percent.

a.   If each of the following conditions is considered independently, decide whether the company should purchase the mixer if:

1.   The estimates are correct.
2.   The machine lasts only 4 years.
3.   After-tax operating cash flows, which are constant over time, decrease by 10 percent for years 1 through 4.
4.   The discount rate is 3 percent too low.

To which variable is the accept-reject decision most sensitive?

b.   Should the company invest in the mixer if all of the following conditions exist simultaneously?

1.   Machine cost = $13,000.
2.   Discount rate = 15 percent.
3.   Marginal tax rate = 33 percent.
4.   Terminal resale value (before tax) = $2,000.
5.   Machine will last 10 years.
6.   After-tax operating cash flows, which are constant over time, increase by 25 percent for years 1 through 10.

9.9   The board of directors of Peninsula Industries has just received a proposal that requires an initial investment of $1 million and is expected to produce cash flows before tax, CFBT, of $300,000 for each year of its life. As presented, the project has a 7-year economic life, but the initial investment will be depreciated by straight-line over its 5-year normal recovery period. The discount rate is 15 percent, and the firm's tax rate is 35 percent. (*Note:* Ignore the half-year convention when calculating depreciation.)

a. Should Peninsula's board recommend acceptance of the project?
b. After discussing the project, certain members of the board feel the economic life will be only (1) 5 years or (2) 6 years, not 7. Does this new information change the previous decision?

9.10 Lloyds is considering the extension of an existing product line. The incremental initial investment is $1.4 million, and the rest of the assumptions are as follows:

1. Depreciation for tax purposes to zero will occur over 7 years via straight-line; the economic life is also 7 years. (*Note:* Ignore the half-year convention when calculating depreciation.)
2. Variable costs are 30 percent of estimated sales.
3. Fixed costs are $100,000.
4. The tax rate is 40 percent and the discount rate is 20 percent.

What is the per year financial break-even level of sales?

9.11 A proposed project has the following characteristics:

Units sold per year	110,000
Price per unit	$600
Variable cost per unit	$460
Fixed cost	$4 million per year
Initial investment, CF_0	$21 million
Depreciation	straight-line over 7 years
Economic life	7 years
Opportunity cost of capital, k	0.20
Marginal tax rate, T	0.35

a. What is the NPV for the proposed project? (*Note:* Ignore the half-year convention when calculating depreciation.)
b. By increasing the initial investment *to* $28 million, variable costs will be cut *to* $420 per unit and fixed costs will be cut *to* $3 million per year. What is the financial break-even number of units between the two alternatives?

9.12 McManus Systems has developed a whole new concept for distributing "gee-whizs." Excluding land costs, the new outlets require an initial investment of $4 million per location. The following conditions apply:

1. Depreciation for both GAAP accounting and for tax purposes will be to a value of zero over 10 years using straight-line. (*Note:* Ignore the half-year convention when calculating depreciation.)
2. Variable costs are 50 percent of sales.
3. Fixed costs are $300,000 per year.
4. The firm's marginal tax rate is 30 percent, and the discount rate is 18 percent.

Excluding land costs, what is the accounting break-even point? What is the financial break-even point (also excluding land costs)? Why does the accounting break-even point underestimate the volume of sales necessary to produce a zero NPV project?

9.13   Costs have decreased, and Indiana National is considering replacing its existing refrigeration system. To help in negotiating the final purchase price, it has hired you as a consultant. The relevant facts are:

Existing System

Purchased 5 years ago for $800,000.

Being depreciated to zero employing straight-line over 10 years. (*Note:* Five years have already elapsed; ignore the half-year convention when calculating depreciation.)

Will last 10 more years if retained.

Resale value if sold today is $150,000; resale value in 10 more years is $20,000.

New System

Will be depreciated to zero employing straight-line over 10 years. (*Note:* Ignore the half-year convention when calculating depreciation.)

Will last 10 years.

Resale value in 10 years is $50,000.

Benefits are a before-tax reduction in operating cash outflows of $75,000 per year.

a.   If the tax rate is 35 percent and the opportunity cost of capital is 15 percent, what is the initial purchase price on the new system so that the NPV equals zero? (*Note:* Assume the firm is profitable, so it receives the tax benefit from selling the existing system at a loss.)

b.   Explain why the information calculated in (a) is important for effective decision making.

9.14   Hart's employs simulation analysis when evaluating major capital budgeting projects. After running a recent analysis it arrived at a probability distribution of possible outcomes as follows:

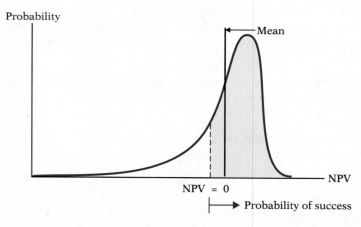

a.   Based on this probability distribution, what do we know about the project?

b.   What are the strengths and the limitations of simulation when making capital budgeting decisions?

9.15   Mini Case You were recently hired by Dutton Products to head up its capital and strategic decisions group. Dutton has three major divisions as follows: a farm implements division that continues to experience intense competition and weak demand, a high-tech metal and materials division, and a financial services division. The financial services division originally provided financing only to dealers and farmers, but over the last 15 years it has undergone tremendous changes. Now it provides many different financial services to firms worldwide. At present Dutton employs a firmwide opportunity cost of capital of 15 percent and does little to consider risk when making capital expenditure decisions.

a. One of your first jobs is to educate the board of directors and upper management on the basic ideas concerning the importance of risk-taking when making capital budgeting decisions, and the negative impact that the reliance on a firmwide opportunity cost of capital may have on project selection. What should the firm be doing in terms of the opportunity costs of capital employed? How would you respond when one of the top executives challenges you by saying, "As long as we are discounting future cash flows we are considering risk, because future cash flows are treated as being inherently risky."

b. The metals and materials division is evaluating a new project. The division's projections for the after-tax cash flows associated with the proposed project are as follows:

Year	CF
0	$-2,500,000
1	-3,000,000
2	-4,000,000
3	5,000,000
4	6,000,000
5	6,000,000
6	3,000,000

(1) At the firm's opportunity cost of capital, what decision should be made?

(2) After listening to your presentation in (a), the board adopts a new divisional cost of capital structure. The new discount rate for the metals and materials division is 20 percent. Does this change the decision?

(3) After talking with individuals in the metals and materials division, you find that the proposed project is actually more complicated. Specifically, you find out that there are two phases to the proposed project. The preliminary phase requires the investments at times $t = 0$, $t = 1$, and $t = 2$. Depending on the outcome of the preliminary phase the following might happen:

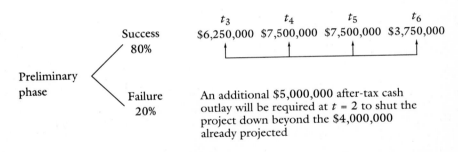

	t_3	t_4	t_5	t_6
Success 80%	$6,250,000	$7,500,000	$7,500,000	$3,750,000

Failure 20% — An additional $5,000,000 after-tax cash outlay will be required at $t = 2$ to shut the project down beyond the $4,000,000 already projected

The preliminary phase is viewed as being very risky; a 40 percent discount rate is appropriate. After the preliminary phase, the 20 percent discount rate is viable. Does this new information affect the decision to accept or reject the project?

c.   Now the financial services division comes to you with a project that has cash flows as follows:

Year	Cash Inflow	Cash Outflow
0	$ 0	$80,000
1	30,000	5,000
2	30,000	5,000
3	50,000	10,000
4	50,000	10,000
5	50,000	10,000
6	40,000	25,000
7	40,000	25,000
8	40,000	25,000

Depreciation will be straight-line over 5 years, the appropriate tax rate is 30 percent, and the discount rate is 15 percent.

1.   What is the base-case NPV? (*Note:* Ignore the half-year convention when calculating depreciation.)

2.   What is the NPV if each of the following occurs? (*Note:* Each part is separate and distinct from the other parts.)

   a.   Cash inflows decrease by 20 percent each year.
   b.   Cash outflows in time periods $t = 1$ through $t = 8$ increase by 20 percent each year.
   c.   The tax rate increases by 20 percent.
   d.   The initial investment increases by 20 percent. (*Note:* This also changes the per year depreciation.)
   e.   The discount rate increases by 20 percent.
   f.   The life of the project decreases to 6 years.

   To which variable is the NPV most sensitive?

3.   How is break-even analysis just another form of sensitivity analysis?

d.   The farm implements division has been considering using simulation to assess the riskiness of its projects. What are the strengths and weaknesses of simulation?

REFERENCES

More information on risk and capital budgeting can be found in:

BUTLER, J. S., and BARRY SCHACHTER. "The Investment Decision: Estimation Risk and Risk Adjusted Discount Rates." *Financial Management* 18 (Winter 1989): 13–22.

DAY, GEORGE S., and LIAM FAHEY. "Putting Strategy into Shareholder Value Analysis," *Harvard Business Review* 68 (March–April 1990): 156–62.

HODDER, JAMES E., and HENRY E. RIGGS. "Pitfalls in Evaluating Risky Projects." *Harvard Business Review* 63 (January–February 1985): 128–35.

LEVARY, REUVEN R., and NEIL E. SEITZ. *Quantitative Methods for Capital Budgeting.* Cincinnati: South-Western Publishers, 1990.

More on simulation and other related approaches is contained in:

CHEN, SON-NAN, and WILLIAM T. MOORE. "Investment Decisions Under Uncertainty: Application of Estimation Risk in the Hillier Approach." *Journal of Financial and Quantitative Analysis* 17 (September 1982): 425–40.

GIACCOTTO, CARMELO. "A Simplified Approach to Risk Analysis in Capital Budgeting with Serially Correlated Cash Flows." *Engineering Economist* 29 (Summer 1984): 273–86.

ROBICHEK, ALEXANDER A. "Interpreting the Results of Risk Analysis." *Journal of Finance* 30 (December 1975): 1384–86.

10

Value Creation from Capital Budgeting

EXECUTIVE SUMMARY

Merely conducting the capital investment decision-making process in a mechanical manner, in line with the material discussed in the last four chapters, in no way guarantees that firms will be pleased with the results. Capital budgeting is a complex process that (1) attempts to help firms formulate the right questions to ask at the right times and (2) focuses on the important topics to consider before making long-term capital investments. Successful implementation requires great understanding and attention to numerous items ignored so far.

Value-enhancing investment projects rely on the unique abilities of firms or projects. Due to competitive markets, virtually all positive-NPV projects have limited lives. Successful firms find niches they can exploit while keeping ahead of the competition. Market values should always be examined when they are available. Failure to do so often results in poorer capital investment decisions.

Numerous options are hidden in all capital investments. The initial decision to proceed or not is an option. Likewise, the decision to continue with an ongoing project as opposed to terminating it is also an option. The contingent purchase of an asset, the ability to expand in the future, and the ability to delay making an investment are all call options that have value. Likewise, any abandonment opportunity, guarantee, loan, or insurance policy contains elements of put options. Knowing and understanding these options is an essential element in making value-enhancing investment decisions.

Although there are no secrets of successful capital investment decisions, 10 important points to remember are:

1. The discount rate is an opportunity cost.
2. Don't confuse short-run profits or cash-flows with value creation.
3. Question the cash flows and assumptions.

4. Unique ideas and strengths are valuable, and they have limited lives.
5. Use market values.
6. Options are important.
7. Ask *why* the firm should continue with this project (or business).
8. Provide top management with the information it needs.
9. Tie the measurement and reward system to long-run value creation.
10. Conduct effective postaudits.

Incorporating these 10 points into a carefully designed capital budgeting system provides firms with the opportunity to create value and see that the needs of all the firm's constituencies are enhanced.

WHAT LEADS TO POSITIVE NPVS?

We have concluded that long-term investments having a positive net present value should be accepted. By doing so, the firm is maximizing its value. As discussed in Chapter 3, the value of the firm is equal to the present value of the assets in place (that is, a nongrowing firm that is simply reinvesting enough to maintain its value) plus the present value of growth opportunities, PVGO. While we have discussed some of the most important aspects of capital budgeting in the last four chapters, is that all of the story? The answer is that *a lot remains to be said*. Let's start by considering the characteristics of projects with positive net present values.

UNIQUE ATTRIBUTES OF THE FIRM OR PROJECTS

If product and labor markets are completely efficient, competition will quickly bid prices down or costs up to a level at which the NPVs are equal to zero. That is, competitors will continue to enter the market until prices allow no more than the minimum acceptable return on capital, k. Hence, for a capital budgeting project to have a positive net present value, one of two situations must exist:

1. There are unique attributes of the firm or project.
2. We have estimated the data incorrectly—overstating the magnitude or timing of the cash inflows, understating the outflows, or employing too low a discount rate.

Let's examine these one by one. First, although we know that financial markets are reasonably efficient in developed countries, there is evidence that the labor and product markets are not as efficient. Less efficient product and labor markets may result from numerous causes—such as unique advantages in quality or cost (perhaps due in part to the special abilities of the firm's management and employees, or the use of nonunion employees), and legally imposed barriers to competition (such as patents). Other possible sources include consistent technological leadership, econo-mies of scale that provide a continuing cost advantage, an established distribution and marketing system, or brand loyalty and trusted product warranties. All these barriers serve to accomplish one important goal: They delay the effective response of competi-tors and provide opportunities for firms to capture positive net present values before they erode away. But unless there are legal or other effective barriers to entry, others will become aware of the excess returns (evidenced by positive NPVs) and devote the resources necessary to become effective competitors. Hence, *effective capital budget-ing procedures must recognize the limited life potential of virtually all projects for producing positive NPVs,* and they should include an analysis of market imperfections, unique capabilities of the firm, and barriers to entry that form the keystone of positive NPV projects.

In less developed countries, simply producing and selling goods may provide unique advantages and the ability to earn excess returns. Within the last few years the author spent some time in India. While there I visited with numerous executives about their capital budgeting decision-making process and the value-creating opportunities in India. A number of executives indicated that due to the tremendous demand for certain types of goods, simply having the goods available for sale, irrespective of their quality or price (within some limits), provided the opportunity to earn substantial returns. In an environment such as this, the combination of high demand and lack of effective competition means firms may enjoy the substantial returns that go along with positive NPV projects. In fact, it is not even necessary to do a very sophisticated capital budgeting analysis; back-of-the-envelope calculations may be sufficient. Over time, however, as the country's economy develops and competition enters, the ability to earn excess returns will be eroded away, just as in any other competitive market.

The second possible reason for positive NPVs is due to estimation problems. Several studies, along with discussions with numerous managers, suggest that in practice capital investment plans tend to be overly optimistic in formulating cash flow and risk estimates. Depending on the approach taken, this tendency can be traced to many different factors—the inherent optimism of managers, statistical problems, peer pressure, or ineffective performance and measurement systems. Whatever the cause, the result is that the input data used in the capital budgeting process may be deficient. The old saying "garbage in, garbage out" clearly applies to the capital budgeting process. No matter how sophisticated the selection technique, if the estimated cash flows or discount rate is incorrectly specified, the resulting net present value will also be incorrect.

Although there is no simple "cure" for measurement problems, there is one impor-tant ingredient of any successful capital investment program: a process and atmosphere which ensure that all assumptions are articulated and challenged, and that the unique strengths of the firm and project, and the potential reactions of competitors, are incorporated into the analysis. As I have told numerous firms, "If you don't quiz me too hard or look at the assumptions very closely, I can make the numbers in almost any investment project look good." But, that in no way ensures success for the project; poor analysis and making the numbers *look* good may be worse than seat-of-the-pants capital investment decision-making by informed and demanding executives.

THE TALE OF TWO FIRMS: IBM AND MOTOROLA

To understand some of the elements of effective capital budgeting decision making, let's look at the experiences of two firms. The first is IBM. In 1987 the market price of IBM stock peaked at $175 per share; by 1993 its price had fallen to under $50 per share. During approximately the same time period, IBM slashed its workforce from 407,000 to 300,000 and reduced its manufacturing capacity by 40 percent. What happened to IBM? During the 1970s and into the 1980s, IBM had a near stranglehold on the market for large, mainframe computers that enabled it to earn oligopoly profits. But, a drastic transformation of the computer industry took place, driven by the soaring power of personal computers, and drastically falling prices. IBM's size made it unable to make quick decisions (even if it had industry-leading technology), yet the firm was committed to compete in every segment of the computer industry. Hence, IBM found its markets and leadership attacked on all sides—by firms that had lower costs, reacted quickly to change, and targeted specific segments of the industry.

Motorola, on the other hand, became a nimble giant, committed to getting the most out its employees in terms of new ideas and having the highest-quality production and the lowest costs. Recognizing these accomplishments, the price of Motorola's stock surged from the high $30s in 1987 to $125 in 1993. To foster innovation and even encourage dissent about ideas, Motorola allows every employee to file a "minority report" if he or she feels ideas are not being heard. And retribution for filing a minority report is rare; dissent and dispute at open meetings is encouraged. At the same time, Motorola has taken total quality management to levels almost unheard of by American firms—it had to in order to compete with and beat Japanese firms. In the past 5 years Motorola claims to have reduced its defect rate in manufacturing by 99 percent, while generating cost savings estimated at $3.1 billion. Today, Motorola is the global market leader in cellular phones, two-way radios, and microprocessors used to control devices other than computers.

To illustrate how Motorola operates, consider how the firm reacted when it discovered that a small Oregon firm, In Focus Systems, had developed a revolutionary type of video screen that Motorola badly needed. Within three months the two firms worked out a joint venture to manufacture the screens, and a month later they launched the venture. The plant to produce the screens cost $70 million. Likewise, in 1985, a small group of engineers built a cellular phone that had 70 percent fewer components, was two-thirds smaller and lighter, and could be assembled by robots. The phones took one-tenth the time to assemble, and defects were reduced by 90 percent. When the phones were introduced in 1987, sales soared and Motorola leapfrogged Japanese manufacturers, even in Japan.

To succeed, firms must regularly ask themselves: *"Why is our firm able to beat the competition?"* and, *"Why are the various bits of the organization better off as part of the firm, rather than as independent businesses?"* Although these questions sound deceptively simple, they have to be asked—not once, but on a repeated basis. In the case of IBM, the ability to beat the competition eroded as the computer industry changed. And, by attempting to compete in too many segments of the market, IBM managed to get beat in many of them. For Motorola, its ability to beat the competition is a result of its commitment to dissent, its total quality manufacturing orientation, and being a low-cost producer. Also, by focusing its attention on specific market segments, Motorola has become a leader in those industries. But, past success is no guarantee of future success. That is why firms have to continually ask themselves the two questions posed at the start of this paragraph.

RELYING ON MARKET VALUES

The capital budgeting approach discussed in the preceding four chapters involves a detailed analysis of the magnitude and timing of expected cash flows, along with their riskiness, associated with any project. Assuming that a good job of analysis has been done, the estimated NPV provides an indication of the potential outcome and wealth creation associated with the capital investment. But, the actual outcome may be more or less than the expected outcome—due to unforeseen occurrences and/or forecasting errors. How should managers proceed in order to limit the potential for less-than-desired outcomes?

In many instances there is market value information that helps assess the economic desirability of making the proposed investment. As an example, suppose a firm produces the "farmhelper," which promises to provide substantial time savings for most farmers. To ship "farmhelper" to various retailers, the firm can employ either commercial trucking services or purchase their own trucks. The trucks require an initial investment of $3 million, while using the commercial trucking services requires after-tax cash outflows of $1.25 million per year. This market information, on the rates charged by commercial trucking services, is important. Alternatively, if the firm purchases the trucks, its after-tax cash outflows on the trucks will be $750,000 each year. In 4 years the trucks will be replaced. Ignoring any subsequent replacement, the net present value problem faced by the firm if it purchases the trucks, as opposed to contracting with the commercial carriers at going market rates, is as follows:

$$NPV = \sum_{t=1}^{4} \frac{(\$1{,}250{,}000 - \$750{,}000)}{(1 + k)^4} - \$3{,}000{,}000 + \frac{\text{resale value}}{(1 + k)^4} + \begin{array}{c}\text{extra gains} \\ \text{from} \\ \text{owning trucks}\end{array}$$

Clearly, this net present value is negative unless the resale value is very large or there are substantial benefits associated with owning the trucks. Let's assume the after-tax resale value is $400,000, and the opportunity cost of capital is 14 percent. Then,

$$NPV = \sum_{t=1}^{4} \frac{(\$500{,}000)}{(1.14)^4} - \$3{,}000{,}000 + \frac{\$400{,}000}{(1.14)^4} + \begin{array}{c}\text{extra gains from} \\ \text{owning trucks}\end{array}$$

$$= \$1{,}456{,}856 - \$3{,}000{,}000 + \$236{,}832 + \begin{array}{c}\text{extra gains from} \\ \text{owning trucks}\end{array}$$

$$= -\$1{,}306{,}312 + \text{extra gains from owning trucks}$$

For the investment in the trucks to be beneficial, substantial extra gains must be associated with owning the trucks. What might those benefits be? Perhaps better and more reliable delivery times. Or, the firm might have additional uses for the trucks.

The important point is that by using existing market values of what it would cost to contract with private shippers, the firm has an immediate idea of what the magnitude of the benefits have to be before investing in the trucks. Unless the benefits are substantial, the decision is straightforward: Contract with commercial trucking firms for their services and concentrate the firm's attention on improvements in "farm-helper" that (1) increase its value, (2) keep ahead of competition, and/or (3) drive costs down and quality up.

Consider another example, in which MacroProducts has decided to acquire another firm through a merger.[1] If the other firm is reasonably large, its stock will be traded and a market value already exists. How much will MacroProducts pay for the firm? Based on numerous studies and observation of ongoing mergers, we know that the typical premium paid is 30 to 50 percent above the going market value of the target firm. Say the target firm has a market value of $500 million and MacroProducts pays a premium of 40 percent for a total of $700 million. Where is the value creation going to come from? The $500 million market value of the target firm reflects the investment community's best estimate of the fair (i.e., risk-adjusted) value of the firm's future cash flows. By paying 40 percent above the fair market value of the firm, MarcoProducts has to achieve a lot of efficiencies just to recoup its investment. Will it be able to earn enough to more than cover the 40 percent premium paid? Many empirical studies indicate that, on average, mergers are zero-NPV projects from the standpoint of the acquiring firm. The price paid is simply too great to allow them to earn any more than a normal return on their investment. Will such investments add value to the purchasing firm? Often the answer is emphatically "no!" Again, market values tell us much about what a group of assets is worth, and how much and where we have to look for value-enhancing benefits from the investment.

A key lesson to be carried away from this discussion is that when market values exist, you need to ask yourself the following question: *"Why are these assets worth more to me than their fair market value?" If a simple and direct answer to that question is not forthcoming, the acquisition of the assets is immediately suspect, no matter what a detailed capital investment analysis indicates.*

Although reliable market values don't exist for many assets, often they crop up in unexpected ways. For assets such as trucks, ships, real estate, crude oil and other minerals, some machine tools, and any financial assets such as stocks and bonds, reasonably competitive markets exist. When they exist, market values should always be employed as either the starting point, to simplify the analysis, or to provide straightforward direction concerning the general magnitude of the benefits needed and where they might come from. Although using existing market values does not solve all of the problems associated with capital budgeting, ignoring them results in valuable information being lost.

Now that we understand more about where positive-NPV projects come from and the importance of using existing market values whenever possible, we need to consider other aspects of the capital investment process that have been ignored in the previous chapters. The implicit assumption has been that firms and managements held assets

---

[1] Mergers are considered in detail in Chapter 26.

passively. But, by doing so, *traditional capital budgeting analysis based on discounted cash flows ignores the options that are embedded in most capital investments. You could say that the value of flexibility and management's ongoing decision-making ability is ignored.*

Concept Review Questions

- What are the two situations that may exist in order for a capital budgeting project to have a positive net present value?

- Why should effective capital budgeting procedures recognize the limited life potential of projects producing positive net present values?

- Why are market values important when evaluating capital budgeting projects?

ABANDONING NOW VERSUS CONTINUING TO OWN

A series of options exists in virtually every capital investment. Too often in the traditional capital budgeting decision-making process these options are not explicitly considered. We will consider immediate options to abandon in this section. Then later we examine a number of other options that are embedded in many capital investments.

HAS ABANDONMENT BEEN CONSIDERED?

One of the most difficult problems in estimating cash flows is to make sure all the options are examined. Consider a manufacturing firm reevaluating an ongoing machine line. Assume the machine line has a 3-year life and the expected after-tax cash inflows are as follows:

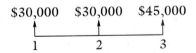

Looking at this cash flow stream, we might be tempted to conclude the machine line has a positive NPV. But what happens if you discover the machine line could be sold today for $85,000 after taxes? This $85,000 is an opportunity cost that must be considered. The choice now is between $85,000 today or the stream of expected after-tax cash flows, as follows:

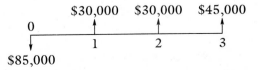

Assuming a discount rate of 14 percent, the NPV is

$$NPV = \frac{\$30,000}{(1 + 0.14)^1} + \frac{\$30,000}{(1 + 0.14)^2} + \frac{\$45,000}{(1 + 0.14)^3} - \$85,000$$

$$= \$26,316 + \$23,084 + \$30,374 - \$85,000 = -\$5,226$$

With this additional knowledge, the machine line has a negative NPV.

In the absence of any further information, the proper decision would be to abandon the project. This **abandonment decision** would maximize the value of the firm. Let's assume, however, the option to modernize the machine line exists. The cash flows associated *solely* with the modernization are as follows:

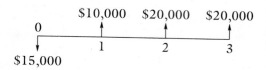

The relevant set of cash flows for decision making is now the combination of the existing and the new cash flows. Assuming the cash flows are additive (i.e., not complements or substitutes), the relevant cash flows for this abandon versus modernization decision are

	$t = 0$	$t = 1$	$t = 2$	$t = 3$
Existing machine line	−$ 85,000	$30,000	$30,000	$45,000
Plus: Modernization	− 15,000	10,000	20,000	20,000
Relevant CFs	−$100,000	$40,000	$50,000	$65,000

At a discount rate of 14 percent, the NPV is

$$NPV = \frac{\$40,000}{(1 + 0.14)^1} + \frac{\$50,000}{(1 + 0.14)^2} + \frac{\$65,000}{(1 + 0.14)^3} - \$100,000$$

$$= \$35,088 + \$38,473 + \$43,873 - \$100,000 = \$17,434$$

Based on the relevant set of cash flows, the firm should keep and modernize the machine line. The second best alternative is to abandon the present line. The worst path is to continue operating the machine line as it is. By doing so, the firm passes up the opportunity of modernizing or abandoning—both of which are preferable.

In any abandonment-type decision it is important to recognize that some assets are much easier to bail out of than others. It is typically easier to bail out of tangible assets when a good secondary market exists. For very specialized or unique tangible assets, and for many intangible assets, good secondary markets do not exist, and their abandonment value may be almost nonexistent.

DIVESTITURES

In addition to abandoning a single piece of equipment, firms also sell off whole lines of business. The basic question is, "Should we continue to be in this business?" Too often in the past, divestitures carried with them negative connotations about how well the firm had done in managing the unit. But a **divestiture** should properly be viewed as the product of good management, which is harvesting the fruits of past successful investments. The only question remaining should be, "Can the firm create more value holding on to the unit due to some unique competitive advantage that a buyer does not have?"

The steps to be used in making the decision to keep or divest a division (or any group of assets) are as follows (see Figure 10.1):

STEP 1:   Estimate the operating after-tax cash flow stream associated with the division. Be sure to consider any impacts on the cash flows arising from complementary or substitute effects with other aspects of the firm's operations, as well as any future cash investments required in the division.

STEP 2:   Determine the opportunity cost of capital, k, that reflects the risk associated with the division.

STEP 3:   Calculate the present value of the CFs expected to accrue to the firm by keeping the division.

STEP 4:   Subtract the current market value of the division's associated liabilities.[2] This produces the NPV to the firm of keeping the division, which is

$$NPV = \sum_{t=1}^{n} \frac{CF_t}{(1 + k)^t} - B \qquad (10.1)$$

where

CF_t = the after-tax cash flows expected in year t from retention of the division
k = the opportunity cost of capital appropriate for the division
B = the current market value of the liabilities associated with the division

STEP 5:   Compare the NPV of keeping the division with the net after-tax divestiture proceeds, DP, to be received if the division is sold. The decision rule is as follows:

1.   If NPV is greater than DP, keep the division.
2.   If NPV is less than DP, sell the division.
3.   If NPV is equal to DP, you are indifferent.

In calculating the after-tax divestiture proceeds, two situations may exist. If the purchaser *acquires both the division's assets and associated liabilities,* then the net after-tax amount received by the seller represents the divestiture proceeds, DP. But if

---

[2] Debt should be valued at today's market value, because that is the present value of the firm's future obligation, discounted at the appropriate discount rate.

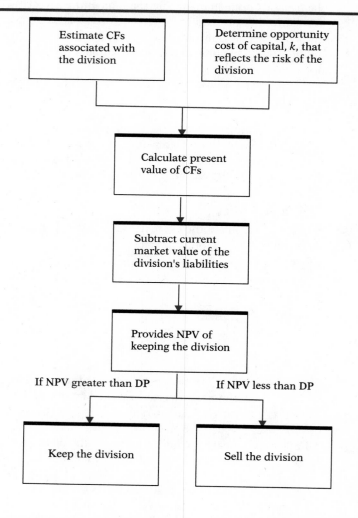

Figure 10.1

Steps in Making the Divestiture Decision

These steps are similar to those employed when calculating the NPV of a proposed product, except now the market value of the liabilities supported by the division must be formally considered.

the purchaser acquires only the division's assets, then the seller retains the division's liabilities, which must—sooner or later—be paid off.[3] To make a consistent comparison *when the seller retains the division's liabilities,* the net divestiture proceeds are

---

[3] As discussed previously, we want to keep the investment and financing cash flows separate (at least until Chapter 14 where their interrelated nature is considered). The indicated adjustment keeps the proportion of debt in the firm's capital structure constant, thereby separating the investment and financing decisions.

calculated as follows:

$$DP\begin{pmatrix}\text{if seller retains}\\\text{division's liabilities}\end{pmatrix} = \begin{array}{c}\text{after-tax divestiture}\\\text{proceeds offered}\\\text{for the division}\end{array} - B \qquad (10.2)$$

To understand the divestiture decision, consider General Communications. General is evaluating whether it should keep or divest a small movie theater operation. American Enterprises has offered to buy the theater division for $7 million after taxes; it will not acquire any of the division's liabilities. To determine if General should sell the division, we need to estimate the after-tax cash flows, CFs, expected if General holds on to it. These cash flows should reflect (or be net of) any additional investments General will have to make in the future. The after-tax cash flows are shown in Table 10.1. Note that we have estimated year-by-year cash flows for the first 5 years, and then assumed they grow at a constant percentage growth rate to infinity.

Table 10.1

Net Present Value of Theater Division if Retained

Because the NPV of $9.953 million is greater than the net divestiture proceeds of $6 million, General should retain its theater division.

Cash Flow Stream

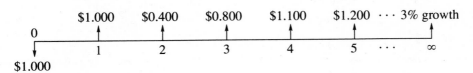

Present Value of Expected Cash Flows

Year	Cash Flow (in millions) −	Additional Investment (in millions) =	CF (in millions) ÷	$(1 + k)^n$ =	Present Value (in millions)
1	$1.000	0	$1.000	$(1.12)^1$	$ 0.893
2	1.000	0.600	0.400	$(1.12)^2$	0.319
3	1.000	0.200	0.800	$(1.12)^3$	0.569
4	1.100	0	1.100	$(1.12)^4$	0.699
5	1.200	0	1.200	$(1.12)^5$	0.681
Beyond 5	3% per year	0	13.733*	$(1.12)^5$	7.792

Present value of future cash inflows = 10.953

Less: Present market value of associated debt, B = 1.000

NPV = $ 9.953

$$^*V_5 = \frac{D_5(1 + g)}{k - g} = \frac{\$1.200(1.03)}{0.12 - 0.03} = \frac{\$1.236}{0.09} = \$13.733$$

In addition, General has determined that the opportunity cost of capital is 12 percent and that the division's associated debt is $1 million. In years 2 and 3, additional investment is required if General keeps the theater division. Based on its projected cash flows, the NPV of keeping the theater division (after taking into account the division's debt) is $9.953 million, as shown in Table 10.1. Because this value far exceeds the after-tax divestiture proceeds of $6 million ($7 million from American Enterprises minus $1 million in the division's debt), General should retain the theater division. By doing so, it maximizes the value of the firm.

In considering whether to keep or liquidate assets, the decision facing the firm is exactly the opposite of the capital investment decision. It calculates the NPV of retaining the assets and continuing to operate them versus the after-tax cash proceeds from selling. If the benefits from keeping the assets are greater than the forgone opportunity cost arising from divesting, then the assets are retained. Otherwise, they are disposed of.

This type of analysis can also be used to assess the financial desirability of voluntarily liquidating a firm. In the case of a voluntary liquidation, the NPV of continuing to operate is estimated with Equation 10.1. The liquidation proceeds represent the net after-tax proceeds available for distribution to the firm's stockholders, after all the firm's liabilities have been met.

Concept Review Questions

- Describe how the ability to abandon a project is of value in making capital budgeting decisions.
- What are the steps used in making divestiture decisions?

CALL OPTIONS IN CAPITAL INVESTMENT DECISIONS

Options exist in many of the investment and financing decisions a firm makes. We will now examine some of the uses of option pricing theory in helping to make capital investment decisions; however, we do so in a simplified (i.e., Black-Scholes or simple binomial model) world. The same basic ideas, but with more complications than we illustrate, can be employed to more accurately determine the value of more complex options faced by firms. The whole thrust is an understanding that *today's decision may depend on what options are available tomorrow.*

OPTIONS TO INVEST

An example of a call option is an option to buy another firm. Assume your firm is privately held and is embarking on some exciting new developments. If these developments are successful, you will need extensive marketing experience you do not presently have. The outcome of the current developments should be known within a year. To protect yourself, you enter into an option to purchase Associated Wholesalers. The current market price of Associated is $56 per share, the risk-free rate is 0.11, the estimated standard deviation of Associated's stock is 0.20, and the exercise price (or contingent purchase price in 1 year) is $66. The first thing is to recognize that this option has all of the elements of any other option. In addition, it is a call option because you have the opportunity, but not the obligation, to buy Associated Wholesalers in 1 year.

What is the value per share of this call option? To find out, we can employ our three-step procedure from Chapter 5:

$$\sigma(t)^{0.5} = (0.20)(1)^{0.5} = 0.2000$$

$$\frac{P_0}{X/e^{k_{RF}t}} = \frac{\$56}{\$66/e^{(0.11)(1)}} = 0.9471$$

The tabled value from Table B.6 is 0.054, so the value of the option to invest is $56(0.054) = $3.02 per share. That is the price you should pay per share in order to have the option of buying Associated Wholesalers in 1 year.

Another option exists in many of the traditional capital investments undertaken by a firm. These investments can often be expanded upon, modernized, replaced, or abandoned. Decisions such as these are contingent on the present values of the future cash flows that result if the options are exercised. Thus, *if capital expenditures are made now, they often create opportunities to make additional capital expenditures in the future.* These future opportunities are, in effect, options that exist only if the current capital project is undertaken. As such, they are sometimes referred to as **growth options.** Previously we have discussed the idea of the present value of growth opportunities, PVGO. Figure 10.2 depicts the option-like aspects of these follow-on growth opportunities that exist in many capital investment projects, where the horizontal axis is the present value of the expected cash inflows and X is the initial investment in the follow-on opportunity.

To deal with these follow-on opportunities we need what many, especially in industry, refer to as the **strategic NPV,** which is

$$\begin{matrix} \text{strategic} \\ NPV \end{matrix} = \begin{matrix} \text{original} \\ NPV \end{matrix} + \begin{matrix} \text{value of} \\ \text{follow-on opportunity} \end{matrix} \qquad (10.3)$$

For an option to make additional capital expenditures, the strategic NPV is

$$\text{strategic } NPV = \text{original } NPV + \text{follow-on call option}$$

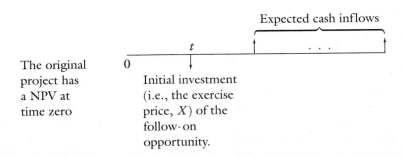

Figure 10.2

Option Value of Follow-On Opportunity

The ability in the future to accept or reject the follow-on investment is a call option. Ignoring this option understates the value creation potential of the original capital investment.

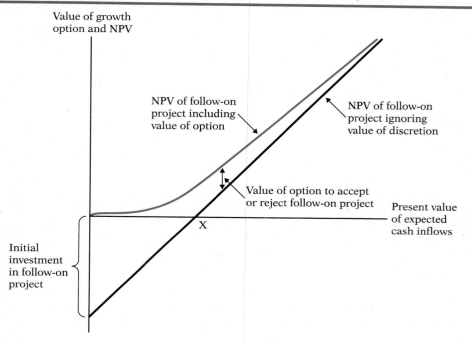

By undertaking the original project, the firm gains the right, but not the obligation, to make a follow-on investment at time t in the future. The follow-on opportunity is simply a call option. The exercise price, X, for this follow-on option is the initial investment required at time t to undertake the follow-on project. The present market price, P_0, of the follow-on opportunity (needed in order to value the call option) is determined in a two-step procedure. First, the expected cash *inflows* from the follow-on project are discounted back to time t at the appropriate opportunity cost of capital. (Note that if we subtracted the present value of the follow-on project's cash inflows from the follow-on project's initial investment at time t, we would have the NPV of the follow-on project. *But the NPV of the follow-on project is not directly needed.*) Second, we then further discount the expected cash inflows back to time zero, to determine the current market value, P_0, of the expected cash inflows of the follow-on investment.

Consider Sanders Electronics, which is eyeing the rapid developments in automated receders. If it invests now the NPV of a 2-year project at the appropriate discount rate is −$45 million. Hence, Sanders' initial decision is to reject the move into automated receders. However, you point out that if Sanders does not make the present investment, expertise and opportunity may be lost—due to competitors getting the jump on

Sanders. You project that in 2 years a new generation of automated receders can go on-stream. The NPV of this additional, or contingent, project that could be undertaken in 2 years is $60 million, based on discounted cash inflows at time $t = 2$ of $800 million and an initial investment at $t = 2$ of $740 million. In this light, the initial investment in the original negative NPV project creates a call option. If the results from the first 2 years are great, then Sanders exercises the follow-on investment option and proceeds; otherwise, it walks away from automated receders. If Sanders doesn't act now, however, then the costs and time delays may be prohibitive in the future.

The key to the decision turns out to be the accuracy of the second NPV (in 2 years) of $60 million. Because automated receders may be risky, the actual NPV realized could be substantially more or less than $60 million. First, let's assume that the risk of automated receders is low, with a standard deviation of 0.10. Also, the risk-free rate is 0.09. The decision is then based on the following analysis.

First, we estimate the value of the call option. The time is 2 years; the value of the follow-on investment *today* (i.e., P_0) is the cash inflow of $800 million (expected in 2 years) discounted back to the present at the opportunity cost of capital of 0.20, or $\$800/e^{(0.20)(2)} = \$536.26$ million.[4] The exercise price is the investment required in 2 years, which is $740 million. Thus, we see that

$P_0 = \$536.26$ million	$k_{RF} = 0.09$
$X = \$740$ million	$\sigma = 0.10$
$t = 2$ years	

Using the three-step option valuation procedure, the value today of this call option to invest 2 years from now is

$$\sigma(t)^{0.5} = (0.10)(2)^{0.5} = 0.1414$$

$$\frac{P_0}{X/e^{k_{RF}t}} = \frac{\$536.26}{\$740/e^{(0.09)(2)}} = 0.8676$$

From Table B.6, the tabled value is 0.013, and the value of the call option (to expand in 2 years) is $536.26 million (0.013) = $6.97 million.

The total value of the opportunity to invest in automated receders is its strategic NPV, which is equal to the sum of the first NPV that exists today plus the option to make the second investment in 2 years, or

strategic NPV $= -\$45.00$ million $+ \$6.97$ million $= -\$38.03$ million

If the variability of the returns from the second investment in automated receders is expected to be low, then Sanders should not enter this field.

---

[4] For consistency we will use continuous discounting to move the cash inflows and cash outflows around when the Black-Scholes option pricing model is employed.

Consider what happens, however, if the variability of expected returns from the second investment has a standard deviation of 0.32 (instead of 0.10 assumed previously). Using our three-step procedure, we have

$$\sigma(t)^{0.5} = (0.32)(2)^{0.5} = 0.4525$$

$$\frac{P_0}{X/e^{k_{RF}t}} = \frac{\$536.26}{\$740/e^{(0.09)(2)}} = 0.8676$$

From Table B.6, the tabled value is 0.122, and the value of the option to expand is ($536.26 million)(0.122) = $65.42 million. The strategic NPV = −$45 million + $65.42 million = $20.42 million. In this case, Sanders should proceed with the investment in automated receders.

What should you finally recommend? It all depends on how valuable the follow-on growth opportunities are expected to be. The key variable, and one that is hard to determine, is just how risky the follow-on opportunity is. Other things being equal, the more the variability in the follow-on opportunity's returns, the more valuable the call option becomes. Thus, as we noted in Chapter 9, risk may be beneficial in many capital budgeting decisions. Once an option pricing framework is employed, we see that greater risk (as shown by a larger standard deviation in the contingent project's returns) leads to a higher option value. While there may be more risk, there is also the potential for substantially higher NPV projects.

OPTIONS TO DEFER

In addition to options to make follow-on investments, other situations exist in which the firm has the option of investing now or waiting until some time in the future to make the investment. Previously, our decision rule was simple: If the project has a positive NPV it should be accepted. However, life is more complicated, and many times more information is gained by waiting (perhaps for additional test marketing, technological developments, changes in economic conditions, or to see what competition does). In such cases the option to delay is valuable. The option-like aspects of this option to delay starting a project are shown in Figure 10.3.

Consider the example of Electroanalysis, which is investigating the launching of a new product. The product can be introduced today, or it can be delayed for 1 year. If it is introduced today, the initial investment is $90; the present value of the expected after-tax cash inflows of $10 per year in perpetuity at an opportunity cost of capital of 10 percent is $100. Hence, the product has an NPV of $10 as follows:

$$NPV = \frac{\$10}{0.10} - \$90 = \$100 - \$90 = \$10$$

The value of the option to invest in the project today is simply $10. Thus, by investing $90 the firm immediately exercises the option to undertake the project today. But, Electroanalysis knows there are major uncertainties about the product that should be resolved within the next year. To analyze this option to delay making the investment (which involves an intermediate cash flow that is similar to a cash dividend), we employ

Figure 10.3

Option Value of Delaying

Some capital investments are now-or-never projects. But those that can be delayed contain a call option, which has value.

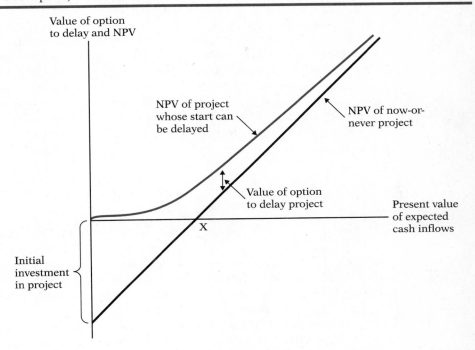

the binomial option pricing model from Chapter 5. The intermediate cash inflow is the after-tax cash inflow (or opportunity cost) from the project during the first year.

If the questions about the new product are resolved positively, the after-tax cash flow at $t = 1$ will be \$20, and the present value of the project's after-tax cash inflows will be \$20/0.10 = \$200. The incremental return *above the total present value* of the cash flows of \$100 if the investment is made right now is [(\$20 + \$200)/\$100] − 1 = 120 percent. Thus, if things turn out well, the incremental return is substantial.

But, there is also a strong chance that the potential of the new product will not be realized. If things don't go well, the after-tax cash flow at $t = 1$ will be \$6, and the present value of the project's cash inflows will be \$6/0.10 = \$60. The incremental return in this case will be [(\$6 + \$60)/\$100] − 1 = −34 percent. So far we haven't said anything about the probabilities associated with the two different possible outcomes. If the risk-free interest rate is 6 percent, and assuming risk neutrality (as discussed in Chapter 5), the expected return from this investment is equal to the risk-free rate of 6 percent. So,

$$\begin{pmatrix} \text{Expected} \\ \text{return} \end{pmatrix} = \begin{pmatrix} \text{probability} \\ \text{of good} \\ \text{outcome} \end{pmatrix}\begin{pmatrix} \text{return from} \\ \text{a good} \\ \text{outcome} \end{pmatrix} + \begin{pmatrix} \text{probability} \\ \text{of bad} \\ \text{outcome} \end{pmatrix}\begin{pmatrix} \text{return from} \\ \text{a bad} \\ \text{outcome} \end{pmatrix}$$

$$6\% = (W)(120\%) + (1 - W)(-34\%)$$

Solving for W, the probability of a good outcome, we have

$$W = 40\%/154\% = 0.2597 \approx 0.26$$

Thus, the probability of a good outcome is about 26 percent, while the probability of a bad outcome is $1 - 0.26 = 0.74$, or 74 percent.

What is the value of the option at time $t = 1$ if the good outcome occurs? The returns are $200 versus the investment of $90, so the value of the option is $110 (i.e., $200 − $90). What if the bad outcome occurs? In that case, the option has no value because the return of $60 is less than the investment required, or exercise price, of $90. To calculate the expected value of the option at time $t = 0$, we take the probability of occurrence times the possible outcomes, and discount then from time $t = 1$ back to $t = 0$ at the risk-free rate of 6 percent. Thus, the value of the option to defer for 1 year is

$$\text{Value of option to defer} = \frac{(\$110)(0.26) + (\$0)(0.74)}{1 + 0.06} = \$26.98 \approx \$27$$

If Electroanalysis defers investing in the product for 1 year, the value of the option to defer is $27. This is compared to the value of the option to invest right now, which is $100 − $90 = $10. What should Electroanalysis do? The decision is simple. Even though the proposed product has a positive NPV today, that is not a sufficient reason for investing. The firm should wait 1 year and then either invest or exercise the option not to invest in the product.

Numerous other illustrations of call options exist in capital investments. Thus, an option to purchase land or any other asset is simply a call option. The opportunity cost of diverting excess capacity to some other use can be determined using option ideas. A series of operating decisions—to increase or reduce production, to expand the existing plant, to temporally shut down a line or a plant—are all options that require managerial attention. Likewise, compound options exist—like research and development projects—that may lead to new investment opportunities and affect the value of existing growth opportunities.

Viewed from an option standpoint, the greater the proportion of the firm's value that is dependent on the value of future discretional investments, the higher the risk of the firm's stock, other things being equal. Thus, a high-tech firm (such as one in the biotech industry), which has a large portion of its value accounted for by the present value of growth opportunities, PVGO, has higher stock risk than a mature firm whose value is largely dependent on the present value of the assets in place.

Concept Review Questions

- Describe some options available to management when making capital budgeting decisions.
- What is a strategic NPV, and how is it calculated?
- How would you proceed in analyzing an option to defer?

PUT OPTIONS IN CAPITAL INVESTMENT DECISIONS

In addition to call options, there are also put options in capital investments. We will consider two—options to abandon in the future and guarantees.

FUTURE ABANDONMENT DECISIONS

When a firm has the option to abandon a capital investment some time in the future, this is simply a put option. Assume your firm is making the investment in a new division (at time $t = 0$) that is expected to have a positive net present value of $1,000,000. But if cash inflows are low at the end of the first year, the firm plans to abandon (i.e., sell) the project for an after-tax cash inflow of $5 million. The present value at time $t = 0$ of the cash flows expected after year 1 is $6.5 million; the risk-free rate is 0.12, and the standard deviation of the project, assuming no abandonment, is 0.55. Thus,

$P_0 = \$6.5$ million	$k_{RF} = 0.12$
$X = \$5$ million	$\sigma = 0.55$
$t = 1$ year	

Using the three-step procedure, the value of the option to abandon (i.e., a put option) is

$$\sigma(t)^{0.5} = (0.55)(1)^{0.5} = 0.5500$$

$$\frac{P_0}{X/e^{k_{RF}t}} = \frac{\$6.5}{\$5/e^{(0.12)(1)}} = 1.4657$$

From Table B.7, the tabled value is 0.067, and the value of the option to abandon is $6.5 million $(0.067) = \$435,500$. The ability to get out of the proposed project has value. This has to be taken into consideration when calculating the project's net present value.[5] The strategic NPV including this option to abandon the project in the future is

$$\text{strategic } NPV = \$1,000,000 + \$435,500 = \$1,435,500$$

---

[5] In general, the valuation of abandonment options becomes more complicated because they may be exercised at the end of year 1, year 2, and so forth. This more general approach views the option to abandon as an American put on a dividend-paying stock, in which both the dividend payments and exercise price are uncertain. Numerical approximation techniques are required to value the general abandonment option.

Earlier in the chapter we discussed how to proceed when the issue was that of abandoning *today*, versus continuing to operate. In that case the value of the option to abandon today is simply the difference between the present value of the cash flows from continuing to operate and the after-tax proceeds from selling the assets. Now we can add to that calculation because we know how to proceed when abandonment in the future is also a possibility. In general, the option of abandoning is always available to firms. Too often this option is implicitly or explicitly ignored. Firms, however, should "cut and run" when the value of the firm is greater without the assets than it is with the assets.

Other examples of put options exist for firms. A common one is insurance coverage that is taken out on physical or human assets of the firm; this is simply a put option that can be exercised by the firm under certain conditions.

GUARANTEES

The final put option we'll consider is more difficult, but the general issue involved is widespread because it deals with the topic of guarantees. A guarantee—whether granted by a firm, a financial institution, or a government—provides a floor, or exercise price, under which the cash flows cannot fall. There are many examples of guarantees that creep into financial transactions. Consider Megamarkets, which is planning to divest its textiles division to Modern Fabrics. To facilitate the sale, Megamarkets guarantees that the cash flows from the textiles division will not fall below $6 million for each of the next 3 years. The question is, how much extra should Megamarkets charge for this cash flow guarantee?

To determine the value of this guarantee, two items need to be considered. First, we need the actual forecasted cash flows and related information. Second, we need to recognize that the cash flow guarantees are simply a *series* of put options for which $6 million is the exercise price. If the forecasted cash flows are as follows, and the appropriate discount rate for the guarantees is 25 percent, then the present value, P_0, for each of the forecasted cash flows is

Year	Forecasted Cash Flow (in millions)	Present Value (at 25 percent) of Forecasted Cash Flows Employing Continuous Discounting (in millions)
1	$4.50	$4.50/e^{(0.25)(1)} = $3.50
2	5.50	$5.50/e^{(0.25)(2)} = 3.34
3	8.00	$8.00/e^{(0.25)(3)} = 3.78

If the standard deviation of the annual cash flow changes is 0.40 per year and the risk-free rate is 0.09, then

Year	Standard Deviation Times the Square Root of Time	Price (or Asset Value) Divided by the Present Value of the Exercise Price	Value of Guarantee (in millions)
1	$(0.40)(1)^{0.5} = 0.4000$	$\dfrac{\$3.50}{\$6/e^{(0.09)(1)}} = 0.6383$	$(0.691)(\$3.50) = \$2.42$
2	$(0.40)(2)^{0.5} = 0.5657$	$\dfrac{\$3.34}{\$6/e^{(0.09)(2)}} = 0.6665$	$(0.529)(3.34) = \ \ 1.77$
3	$(0.40)(3)^{0.5} = 0.6928$	$\dfrac{\$3.78}{\$6/e^{(0.09)(3)}} = 0.8253$	$(0.404)(3.78) = \ \ \underline{1.53}$
			Value of guarantee $= \$5.72$

Using Table B.7 for valuing put options, the tabled values are entered in the last column to the right above and multiplied by the present value (or current market value) of the cash flow guarantees. In pricing the textile division, Megamarkets should add $5.72 million to the price quoted because of the cash flow guarantees provided to Modern Fabrics. Failure to do so results in an underpricing of the worth of the textiles division and associated guarantees.

Numerous other examples of guarantees exist for firms. Any loan made by firms to subsidiaries or other parties (other than the government, where there should be no risk) can be decomposed into a default-free loan and a loan guarantee, as follows:

risky loan = default free loan − loan guarantee

Thus, any time a firm offers a loan, or guarantees debt issued by a subsidiary, an option exists. In addition, many firms employ swap contracts (as discussed in Chapters 23 and 28) to hedge some of the firm's risk. Guarantees exist in swap contracts. Thus, we see that many different guarantees exist that firms must understand. Keep looking, and you will find many more options, both in decisions that firms make and in everyday life.

Concept Review Questions

- What are some capital investment decisions that can be modelled as put options?
- Explain what a guarantee is and how it can be valued.

SOME FINAL THOUGHTS

Before leaving capital investment decision making, we need to consider some complications and provide some guidelines to facilitate the effectiveness of the capital budgeting decision making process.

THE OPPORTUNITY COST OF CAPITAL, CAPITAL RATIONING, AND CAPITAL INVESTMENT OPTIONS

In Chapter 6 we discussed the opportunity cost of capital. Based on both agency considerations and the possibility that there may be more "bad" than "good" investments projects in a competitive world, some arguments have been made for increasing the firm's discount rate (for average-risk projects) above its opportunity cost of capital.[6] In Chapter 8 we also found out that many firms apparently practice soft capital rationing. That is, they constrain the amount of funds available for capital investments such that not all positive net present value projects are accepted. Other things being equal, soft capital rationing decreases the value of the firm from what it would be in the absence of capital rationing.

Viewed from an option pricing perspective, we see that one of the shortcomings of the traditional capital investment analysis based on discounted cash flows is that it fails to adequately deal with the wide variety of options inherent in many capital investments. While we have examined options that may increase the strategic NPV, many of the investments a firm makes are at least partially irreversible. By making investments that are irreversible, the firm may "kill" another option—the option to productively invest in the same opportunity but at a later time, or to employ the same resources (physical, financial, and human) to make other investments. In such a case, the value of the lost option must be included as part of the cost of investment. In such a case, it has to be argued *that the present value of the cash inflows should be increased, and might be at least double the initial investment.*[7]

How might this major increase in the present value of the inflows be accomplished? One way is to substantially increase the discount rate employed, so that it is substantially above the opportunity cost of capital that would normally be used. A second way might be to ration capital and require that the net present value of accepted projects be substantially in excess of zero. Thus, although we can't say for sure that firms are rational if they increase the opportunity cost of capital or practice capital rationing, perhaps ". . . managers use the wrong method to get close to the right answer."[8]

Our understanding of how to evaluate capital investments by considering their option aspects has advanced a long way in the last decade; that trend is surely to continue as we attempt to understand the options embedded in capital investments.

---

[6] For some suggestive readings see, for example, Ang and Dukas; Miller; Mills; and Smidt, cited at the end of the chapter.

[7] See, for example, McDonald and Siegel, or Majd and Pindyck.

[8] Robert S. Pindyck, "Irreversible Investment, Capacity Choice, and the Value of the Firm," *American Economic Review*, 78 (December 1988): 983.

As we learn even more, we are better able to add to the traditional capital budgeting analysis by valuing the flexibility firms have and management's ongoing decision-making ability.

SOME GUIDELINES FOR STRUCTURING AND EVALUATING CAPITAL INVESTMENTS

The fact that there is a large body of capital budgeting theory, such as that covered in the last five chapters, does not mean that firms and managers can expect their capital expenditures to lead automatically to increases in the value of the firm. Too often there are gaps between capital budgeting knowledge held by firms and managers and truly superior capital investment decision-making. We will highlight a number of these areas and suggest some guidelines for improving the capital investment performance of the firm.

1. THE DISCOUNT RATE IS AN OPPORTUNITY COST   It is vitally important to remember that the discount rate for any project is an opportunity cost. Thus, if you can earn 20 percent on a comparable-risk project, the opportunity cost of capital for that project has to be 20 percent; otherwise, the value of the firm will not be maximized.

2. DON'T CONFUSE SHORT-RUN PROFITS OR CASH FLOWS WITH VALUE CREATION   In visiting with managers we are always amazed at the overwhelming emphasis given to short-run goals and returns. Recently we visited a firm where if the capital investment couldn't pay for itself within *less than a year*, it was unacceptable. Clearly, for that firm short-run concerns are impeding the ability to make investments that create long-run value. Also, you need to recognize that some types of projects are necessarily much harder to quantify. Many firms that are emphasizing total quality management have more difficulty relating cash flow figures to the hoped-for improved quality. But, remember, some studies have suggested that up to 50 percent of the effort in some businesses is spent in correcting something that was not done right the first time. Cash flow benefits often exist in a total quality management environment; it's just that we have to work a little harder to recognize and quantify them.

3. QUESTION THE CASH FLOWS AND ASSUMPTIONS   Remember, anyone with a good understanding of the capital budgeting process can "make the numbers look good" if not too many questions are asked about the sources or assumptions underlying the numbers. *A good capital investment process forces the right questions to be asked at the right time about the project, and assesses the unique strengths of the firm and project, and possible competitor action or reaction.*

4. UNIQUE IDEAS AND STRENGTHS ARE VALUABLE AND HAVE LIMITED LIVES   The cornerstone of value-enhancing NPV projects is the unique strengths and ideas that firms or projects possess. What are they? What type of steps can be taken to limit or impede the response of competitors from eroding the value-enhancing opportunities from the project? Attention to these areas must be incorporated into the capital budgeting process.

5. USE MARKET VALUES   When market values exist, it is foolish to begin the capital expenditure decision-making process by first doing a detailed cash flow analysis. Make use of the existing market data; if you can't convince yourself that the project has a positive NPV using the market value data, then it probably doesn't have one, no matter what a detailed cash flow analysis might indicate. Also, ask yourself why you think the asset is worth more to you than its going market value. What uniquely can the firm add that will result in the creation of a positive NPV project?

6. OPTIONS ARE IMPORTANT   Often we hear of major investment decisions that are negative-NPV projects but are undertaken by firms because of "strategic considerations." The key ingredient missing is often a thorough assessment and valuation of the options imbedded in the project. Numerous options exist—to abandon, expand on, defer, and so forth. Making capital investment decisions without explicitly recognizing and attempting to value these options provides incomplete and potentially fatal information voids. At the same time, when irreversible investments are made, there may be justification for firms employing discount rates above the opportunity cost of capital, or for rationing capital.

7. QUESTION WHY THE FIRM SHOULD CONTINUE WITH THIS PROJECT (OR BUSINESS)   Simply asking the question of what incremental value can be created by continuing with the project or business, versus putting the assets to alternative uses within the firm or selling them, is done all too infrequently by many firms. The implicit assumption is, "We are in this business, and to stay competitive we have to make this investment." But, that attitude often begs the real question: What is the most valuable usage that can be made of the assets and resources—physical, financial and human—of the firm?

8. PROVIDE TOP MANAGEMENT WITH THE INFORMATION IT NEEDS This seems like a simple idea; top management can make good decisions only if it has good information. But, individuals preparing capital expenditure proposals have vested interests in getting them accepted. Both personal pride and prestige are involved, along with financial remuneration and future promotions within the firm. Normally when top management doesn't get the information it needs, there are informational, behavioral, or financial remuneration factors impeding the process.

9. TIE THE MEASUREMENT AND REWARD SYSTEM TO LONG-RUN VALUE CREATION   Increasingly, newspapers and magazines report the financial remuneration for top executives. Often, they are rewarded for short-term accounting profits or rewarded if the firm's stock price gets above a certain value and stays there for some minimum time, such as 30 days. But, such actions are not in line with long-run value creation. Likewise, if the firm has a compensation system that rewards project initiators for short-run performance and or accounting returns, it should expect the capital investment decisions that are made to be ones that maximize the wrong set of goals.

10. CONDUCT EFFECTIVE POSTAUDITS   In theory it makes sense to conduct postaudits on some, but probably not all, of the capital investments the firm makes. The goal is simple—to learn from past mistakes so that future decisions are improved. Just having a postaudit program in place may accomplish this goal, but often the exercise is seen as unnecessary or is used to point the finger and assess blame. Effective postaudit plans avoid some or all of these tendencies.

We haven't covered all of the possible guidelines for improving the capital investment decision-making process. Others exist, and we encourage you to add to our list. *The key is to view the capital budgeting process, which is the primary source of value creation in firms, as a triggering and questioning form of structured decision-making.* Merely doing things "by the numbers" and ignoring market values, options, managerial discretion, and the impact of the firm's decision-making process on the quality of the outcome invites disappointment and criticism of the entire capital budgeting process. It is not a panacea, but done properly, capital investment decision-making forces the right questions to be asked at the right time. That is the value of an effective capital investment decision-making process and environment as the firm strives to create value and serve the needs of all of its constituencies, which include its management and employees, its customers and suppliers, and the providers of capital.

Concept Review Questions

■ Describe how option theory may explain or justify the practice of soft capital rationing.

■ Discuss the guidelines suggested for improving the capital investment performance of a firm.

KEY POINTS

1. Positive NPV projects build on the unique strengths of the firm or project and have limited lives.
2. Market values provide the basis for assessing many of the costs or benefits of proposed capital investments. Ignoring market values is a primary source of problems in effective capital budgeting decision making.
3. Abandonment, either now or in the future, is an option that should always be recognized and built into capital budgeting decision making.
4. Traditional capital budgeting analysis, based on discounted cash flows, ignores the value of flexibility and management's ongoing decision-making ability. Guarantees and options to make further investments in the future, to defer, or to abandon abound in capital investments; they must be recognized and valued.
5. By making irreversible capital investments, firms use some of their physical, financial, and human capital; in so doing, they may preclude the option of undertaking future investment opportunities. In this light, increasing the discount rate above the opportunity cost of capital, or using soft capital rationing, may be an indirect means of considering the forgone option that the bypassed future investment opportunities contain.
6. Effective capital budgeting procedures encourage decision makers to ask the right questions at the right time, as the firm strives to maximize its long-run value creation opportunities.

QUESTIONS

10.1   How are positive NPVs, the unique attributes of firms and projects, and good data related?

10.2   Explain the importance of market value information in the capital budgeting process.

10.3 Evaluate the following: "For a firm to remain in business, it must keep and update its equipment and processes. Hence, abandonment decisions are not relevant in practice."

10.4 Why are capital budgeting projects and the opportunity to abandon a project closely related to call and put options?

10.5 How should a firm go about deciding whether to divest one of its divisions? What role does the division's debt play in the decision?

10.6 How is a liquidation (voluntary or involuntary) like a divestiture? How should the analysis proceed?

10.7 The opportunity to expand or to delay is simply an option. What similarities and differences exist between these two options?

10.8 Compare the option to abandon today versus the option to abandon in the future. What major differences, if any, are there between these options?

10.9 Explain how to value guarantees and why guarantees—whether provided by firms or governments—are valuable.

CONCEPT REVIEW PROBLEMS

See Appendix A for solutions.

CR10.1 Jack's Rentall is considering selling the company's supply of side-discharge lawn-mowers. Because of the increased customer demand for mulching mowers, income from rental fees on the side-discharge mowers has declined. The mowers are expected to last 3 more years with an after-tax cash flow from the mowers of $5,000 for each year.

a. Jack estimates the mowers could be sold for $10,000 after taxes, and the opportunity cost of capital is 15 percent. Should the side-discharge mowers be sold?

b. Jack also has the option to increase the demand for his mowers by installing a conversion kit that easily allows the switch from a side-discharge mower to a mulching mower. Conversion kits will cost $3,000 to purchase and install. Cash flows will increase to $7,000 per year for the next 3 years. Should Jack purchase the conversion kits?

CR10.2 AutoHelp is considering selling the firm's small shock absorber division. Firmwheel has offered $45 million (after taxes) for the division, provided that AutoHelp retains the division's liabilities of $6 million. The estimated after-tax cash flows for years 1 through 4 for the division are $3 million, $3.5 million, $3.5 million, and $4 million, respectively. After the fourth year, the divisions CF's are expected to grow at a 4 percent rate. If the appropriate opportunity cost of capital is 14 percent, should AutoHelp sell the division?

CR10.3 Waterhouse is considering expanding into the Russian market. Cost of a new production plant today will be $200 million, with expected after-tax cash flows of $35 million for each of 10 years. The firm's opportunity cost of capital is 15 percent.

a. Based on the project's NPV, should Waterhouse expand into the Russian market?

b. Rob, the CFO, notes that one purpose of the new plant is to "get a jump on the competition." He commented that after a 3-year period, if the Russian market is stronger than anticipated, the firm could make an investment of $50 million in a follow-on project that has a net present value of $40 million. The risk-free rate is 7 percent. If the standard deviation is 0.55, what is the strategic NPV of the project?

CR10.4 Sharon, assistant CFO of Waterhouse, noted that another option available is to abandon the Russian project if cash flows are less than expected. Assume the present value (at

$t = 0$) of the cash flows after 3 years is $60 million, the project can be sold for an after-tax cash inflow of $45 million, and the standard deviation and k_{RF} are the same as in CR10.3. Taking the results from CR10.3 and CR10.4 together, what is the project's strategic NPV?

CR10.5   Jim is considering purchasing a franchise license from Hot Dog Haven and opening a hot dog stand on campus. For a franchising fee, Hot Dog Haven will supply management training, advertising, and specialty products. In addition, the Hot Dog Haven franchisor will guarantee a minimum after-tax cash flow of $10,000 each year for 2 years. Jim expects an after-tax cash flow of $15,000 in 1 year and $25,000 in 2 years. If the risk-free rate is 8 percent, Jim's required return is 18 percent, and the expected standard deviation of future cash flows is 0.45, what is the value of the guarantee?

PROBLEMS

10.1   Noreiko Instruments sells a number of specialized product lines. Due to increasing competition, the CFs for its Gamma product line are estimated as follows:

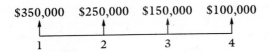

$350,000 $250,000 $150,000 $100,000

A competitor has approached Noreiko and offered $650,000, after taxes, for the product line. If Noreiko Instruments' opportunity cost for this product line is 17 percent, what should it do?

10.2   Hill's Products is considering abandoning a product line. The line could be sold for $50,000 after taxes, or it could be kept and it will produce after-tax cash flows of $17,500 for each of 4 years. In addition, the possibility of modernizing the line with after-tax cash flow consequences solely for the modernization is as follows:

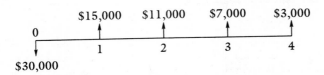

$15,000 $11,000 $7,000 $3,000

$30,000

Should Hill's abandon, keep, or modernize if the discount rate is 14 percent?

10.3   A machine belonging to Homaifar, Inc., is worn out. It can be sold today for scrap for $300 (after taxes). Alternatively, it can be overhauled completely for $900 and will produce the following stream of CFs:

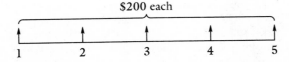

$200 each

Finally, if the machine is replaced, the *incremental* initial investment will be $2,500. The economic life of the machine is 5 years if it is overhauled or replaced; the resale value at the end of 5 years is zero. If it is overhauled, the $900 is a tax-deductible expense that cannot be depreciated. If it is replaced, however, the new machine will be depreciated via the straight-line method over 5 years. (*Note:* Ignore the half-year convention.) If it is replaced, the operating cash flows for each year will equal $600 + Dep(T)$. If the marginal tax rate is 40 percent, and the opportunity cost of capital is 15 percent, what should Homaifar do?

10.4 LEM is evaluating the possibility of divesting its African division. It estimates the division's after-tax flows for the next 4 years as follows: $CF_1 = 200, $CF_2 = 215, $CF_3 = 230, and $CF_4 = 240. After year 4, the cash flows are estimated to grow at 2 percent per year to infinity. The appropriate discount rate is 13 percent, the division's debt is $500, and the division can be divested for $2,200 (after taxes), but LEM retains the division's liabilities. Should LEM divest or keep the division?

10.5 Automation Industries has an offer of $8 million after taxes for its plastics machine division. The cash flows from the division presently are constant at $2 million per year and are expected to remain that way. The division's present debt is $11 million; it will be assumed by the buyer. However, Automation has been considering modernizing the division, with the following expected consequences:

Year	After-Tax Cash Flows Without Modernization (in millions)	− Additional Investment (in millions)	+ Additional After-Tax Cash Flows (in millions)	= Postmodernization CFs (in millions)
1	$2.0	$3.0	$ 0	_____
2	2.0	2.0	0	_____
3	2.0	1.0	1.0	_____
4	2.0	0	1.5	_____
5	2.0	0	2.0	_____
Beyond year 5	2.0	0	2.0	8% growth to infinity

If the modernization is done, then the division's debt will increase to $15 million. The appropriate opportunity cost of capital is 14 percent either way. The proposed purchaser will offer $24 million after-tax, contingent on the modernization being done and the purchaser assuming the $15 million in debt.

a. If Automation does not modernize, should it divest or keep the plastics machine division?
b. What if the division is modernized?
c. Based on your answers to (a) and (b), what course of action should Automation take?

10.6 Delores and Anita are trying to decide whether to liquidate their catering business or to continue with it. They can agree on the following estimated cash flows: $CF_1 = 680, $CF_2 = 680, $CF_3 = 740, and $CF_4 = 760. They think growth will continue at 4 percent per year after year 4. The market value of the firm's debt is $1,500, and they estimate the firm's liquidation value is $5,200 after subtracting the $1,500. They cannot agree, however, on the proper discount rate to employ. Delores thinks 12 percent is relevant; Anita believes it should be 15 percent. Does the difference in discount rates have any impact on their decision? What course of action should they take?

10.7 Kleiner Designs is considering a number of acquisitions. On three of them, Kleiner wants to take out an option, pending further evaluation and developments. The three are as follows:

Firm	Current Market Price	Purchase (Exercise) Price	Terms of Option	Volatility of Stock
Green and Sons	$74	$72	30 days	0.15
Feldman	41	45	100	0.40
Longmore	67	80	182	0.85

If the risk-free rate is 0.12, what is the cost (or value) per share of each of the options? (*Note:* Use a 365-day year.)

10.8 Coopertronics must decide whether to purchase Megatron, a high-tech firm with a potential breakthrough in microsize motors. The funds required to complete testing and bring the motors to market can be as high as $100 million or as low as $50 million. The potential payoff is also uncertain because the present value of the cash inflows at $t = 0$ could be as high as $175 million or as low as $60 million. The risk-free rate is 0.11, the standard deviation is 0.60, and the time period is 2 years.

a. How much should Coopertronics pay to purchase Megatron in a best-case scenario?
b. In a worst-case scenario?

10.9 A project has an NPV of −$80,000. By accepting this project, however, in 2 more years you could make a subsequent investment of $250,000 and receive a present value (at $t = 2$) of $300,000. The standard deviation of the subsequent project is 0.25, $k_{RF} = 0.08$, and the appropriate discount rate for bringing the cash inflows of $300,000 back to time $t = 0$ is 0.20.

a. Should you make the investment?
b. What would the standard deviation have to be so that you would be indifferent between accepting and rejecting the project?

10.10 NextSource is at the forefront of the developments in using lasers as a cost-effective alternative source of energy. To proceed farther requires an investment of $200 million today; the results will not be known until sometime in the future. NextSource estimates that under the most optimistic circumstances (with a probability of 0.20) the results will be known in 2 years. But a more realistic estimate (with a probability of 0.40) is that it will take 3 years for the results to be known. Finally, under the worst case (with a probability of 0.40) the results will not be known for 4 years. Their best estimates of the timing and cash flows are as follows:

Year	PV of Inflows (in millions)	−	Outlay (in millions)	=	NPV (in millions)	Standard Deviation
2	$1,500		$700		$800	0.50
3	1,200		800		400	0.50
4	800		900		−100	0.50

NextSource has determined that the appropriate opportunity cost of capital to discount the future inflows back to time $t = 0$ is 0.25. The risk-free rate is 0.10. Should NextSource proceed? (*Note:* All three outcomes are independent of one another. Also, do *not* take a weighted average of the input variables and then calculate a single option value. Instead, calculate one option value for each year and then weight them by the probability of occurrence.)

10.11   Wolfers had the opportunity to build a plant to produce snowgos. The investment required is $150, and the plant is expected to return $20 in perpetuity. The discount rate is 10 percent. It has just come to the attention of Wolfers management that they can delay the plant for 1 year. The possible returns, if delayed, are $22 per year in perpetuity or $10 per year in perpetuity. The risk-free rate is 7 percent. Which should Wolfers do—invest now or delay making the decision for 1 year?

10.12   A firm has a capital investment that requires an expenditure of $500 and promises to return $52 per year in perpetuity. The discount rate is 10 percent. Alternatively, it can defer the investment for 1 year. The two possible outcomes are $56 per year in perpetuity or $44 in perpetuity. The risk-free rate is 4 percent.

a.   Should the firm undertake the capital investment now, or should it delay making the decision for 1 year?
b.   What decision should be made if the risk-free rate is 10 percent, instead of 4 percent? Does your answer make sense in terms of what happens to the value of a call option as the risk-free rate increases?
c.   Finally, independent of (b), what decision should be made if everything is the same as in (a) except the two possible outcomes are $56 in perpetuity or $48 in perpetuity? Explain why this occurs.

10.13   A project can be abandoned at the end of 1 year; the proceeds would be $100,000. If the project continues, the present value (at $t = 0$) of the future proceeds past year 1 would equal $160,000. The risk-free rate is 0.10, and the volatility (standard deviation) of the project's cash flows, assuming no abandonment, is 1.30.

a.   What is the value of the option to abandon?
b.   If everything stays the same as in (a) except the standard deviation drops to 0.20, what is the value of the option to abandon? Why does this occur?

10.14   Without considering the opportunity to abandon, a project has an NPV of −$25. The project can be abandoned, however, at the end of *either* 1 or 2 years as follows:

Year Abandoned	Abandonment Value	Present Value (at $t = 0$) of Future Cash Inflows if Project Is Not Abandoned
1	$150	$200
2	140	160

The risk-free rate is 0.09, and the volatility (standard deviation) of the project's cash flows is 0.70. Should the project be undertaken? Why or why not?

10.15   Santiago, Inc., is attempting to sell its electronics division to its current management in a leveraged buyout. To effect the sale, Santiago will guarantee that the free cash flows (i.e., cash flows over and above those required to meet normal outflows and make certain capital investments) of the electronics division will be a minimum of $6 million the first year, $7 million the second year, and $8 million the third year. Santiago estimates the free cash flow will actually be $5.5 million, $9.5 million, and $12 million, respectively, and that 25 percent is an appropriate discount rate for the estimated cash flows. If the standard deviation of the annual free cash flow changes is 0.32 per year, and the risk-free rate is 0.11, how much should Santiago ask over and above the "normal" price for the division due to the cash flow guarantees?

10.16 The government provides guarantees to certain groups, like farmers, depositors in banks, and so forth. Assume that the forecasted cash flows are $100 for year 1 and $125 for year 2, while the guarantee is $115 each year. The appropriate discount rate for the forecasted cash flows is 0.25, the risk-free rate is 0.10, and the volatility of the cash flows is 0.35.

a. How much is this guarantee worth?
b. Who benefits from the guarantee? Who subsidizes the guarantee?

10.17 Your firm is buying the chemical division of Savewest Chemical. Two alternative 4-year guarantees of the cash flows from the chemical division are being offered as follows:

Year	Guarantee One	Guarantee Two
1	$8.0	$4.50
2	9.0	7.00
3	9.0	11.00
4	10.0	13.00

The forecasted cash flows for the 4 years are as follows: year 1 = $10, year 2 = $13, year 3 = $15, and year 4 = $20. The appropriate discount rate for the cash flows is 0.20, the risk-free rate is 0.11, and the volatility of the cash flows is 0.50. If it does not affect the price you pay, which guarantee should you accept—one or two?

10.18 **Mini Case** Kelly just finished attending a seminar on advanced capital budgeting issues offered by the business school at the local university. During the seminar the option-like characteristics of many investment decisions were repeatedly stressed. The concept of "strategic NPV," which incorporates both the base-case NPV plus any option-like aspects, is particularly appealing to Kelly. Also, Kelly has heard some chief financial officers at competing companies discussing strategic NPVs. To implement this at Kirkwood International, Kelly decides to start applying these ideas when reviewing all capital budgeting proposals.

a. During the course of a conversation with some of the staff, Kelly is questioned: "What is a call option?" "What is a put option?" "What factors determine the value of call or put options?" "Why does any of this apply to the evaluation of proposed capital expenditures?" "What do you mean by strategic NPV?" How would you answer these questions?
b. At times in the past Kirkwood International has employed the sequential analysis approach discussed in Chapter 9. How, conceptually, could option techniques be employed instead of the sequential analysis approach?
c. To illustrate the use of option techniques, Kelly provides the following data on a proposed project

Preliminary phase

Follow on project at $t = 4$

Initial investment at t_4 = $1,000,000
Present value at t_4 of
   follow-on projects
   cash inflows   = $2,500,000
         $\sigma = 0.45$
         $k_{RF} = 9\%$

What is the strategic NPV of the project if the discount rate is 18 percent? (*Note:* Use continuous discounting.)

d. Kelly notes that option ideas also apply to future abandonment decisions. One of Kirkwood International divisions just brought forth the following proposed project:

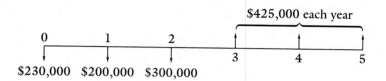

$$\$425,000 \text{ each year}$$

```
0         1         2         3         4         5
|         |         |         |         |         |
$230,000  $200,000  $300,000
```

Due to the fact that the project is slightly more risky than Kirkwood's typical project, the discount rate is 20 percent.

(1) What is the NPV of the project? Should it be accepted? (*Note:* Use continuous discounting.)

(2) After questioning the division, Kelly finds that the cash outflows at $t = 0$ and $t = 1$ have to be made no matter what. However, if the prospects look good, the project could be a real money winner. The problem is that the cash flows in years 3, 4, and 5 have a high degree of uncertainty. The standard deviation is 0.60, and the risk-free rate is 9 percent. No matter what occurs later on, the cash outflows at $t = 0$ and $t = 1$ have to be made. But the $200,000 outflow in year 2 is an option that will be exercised only if subsequent prospects look favorable. Given this new information, what is the project's strategic NPV? What decision should be made? {*Note:* Continue using continuous discounting [as in (1)] to determine the price, P_0, of the option at $t = 0$.}

(3) In (2), the option to abandon was not considered. Now Kelly finds out that not only can the project be expanded upon as in (2), but if the project is abandoned at $t = 2$ the firm will receive $250,000 after-tax from the sale of assets invested in the project. What is the value of the option to abandon? (*Note:* Continue using continuous discounting.) What is the final strategic NPV [which includes the NPV of the original project, the option to expand in (2), and the option to abandon]? Should the firm proceed with the project?

e. To illustrate the use of options further, Kelly presents the following information, in which Kirkwood is proposing to sell a division for $10,000,000. In order to facilitate the sale, Kirkwood is preparing to guarantee the following net cash flows from the division for its first 3 years. The forecasted and guaranteed cash flows are projected to be equal as follows:

Year	Guaranteed Cash Flow	Forecasted Cash Flow
1	$2,000,000	$2,000,000
2	4,000,000	4,000,000
3	5,000,000	5,000,000

But there is uncertainty associated with the forecasted cash flows; hence their standard deviation is 0.35. The discount rate is 18 percent, and the risk-free rate is 9 percent. Kelly argues that the cash flow guarantees are valuable to the purchaser of the division. Why is this so? How much should be added to the $10,000,000 sale price to compensate Kirkwood for the guarantee it is providing?

REFERENCES

For information on strategic decisions and the impact of capital budgeting announcements and R & D expenditures on the value of the firm, see:

BIERMAN, HAROLD, JR. *Strategic Financial Planning*. New York: Free Press, 1980.

CHAN, SU HAN, JOHN D. MARTIN, and JOHN W. KENSINGER. "Corporate Research and Development Expenditures and Share Value." *Journal of Financial Economics* 26 (August 1990): 255–76.

CLARKE, ROGER G., BRENT WILSON, ROBERT H. DAINES, and STEPHEN D. NADAULD. *Strategic Financial Management*. Homewood, Ill.: Irwin, 1988.

Information on investment decisions in an option pricing framework, and guarantees, is contained in:

MCDONALD, ROBERT, and DANIEL R. SIEGEL. "The Value of Waiting to Invest." *Quarterly Journal of Economics*, 101 (November 1986): 707–28.

MCLAUGHLIN, ROBYN, and ROBERT A. TAGGART, JR. "The Opportunity Cost of Using Excess Capacity." *Financial Management* 21 (Summer 1992): 12–23.

MAJD, SAMAN, and ROBERT S. PINDYCK. "Time to Build, Option Value, and Investment Decision." *Journal of Financial Economics* 18 (March 1987): 7–27.

MERTON, ROBERT C., and ZVI BODIE. "On the Management of Financial Guarantees." *Financial Management* 21 (Winter 1992): 87–109.

MYERS, STEWART C. "Finance Theory and Financial Strategy." *Midland Corporate Finance Journal* 5 (Spring 1987): 6–13.

PINDYCK, ROBERT S. "Irreversible Investment, Capacity Choice, and the Value of the Firm." *American Economic Review*, 78 (December 1988): 969–85.

TRIGEORGIS, LENOS, and SCOTT P. MASON. "Valuing Managerial Flexibility." *Midland Corporate Finance Journal* 5 (Spring 1987): 14–21.

Information on uncertainty and competition, and its potential impact on the decision rules employed, is contained in:

ANG, JAMES S., and STEPHEN P. DUKAS. "Some Implications of Competition for Capital Investment." In *Capital Budgeting Under Uncertainty*, edited by Raj Aggarwal. Englewood Cliffs, NJ: Prentice-Hall, 1993. Pp.169–86.

MILLER, E. M. "Uncertainty Induced Bias in Capital Budgeting." *Financial Management*, 7 (Autumn 1978): 12–18.

MILLS, D. E. "Preemptive Investment Timing." *Rand Journal of Economics*, 19 (Spring 1988): 114–22.

SMIDT, SEYMOUR. "A Bayesian Analysis of Project Selection and of Post Audit Evaluations." *Journal of Finance*, 34 (June 1979): 675–88.

Capital Structure and Dividend Decisions

EXECUTIVE INTERVIEW

James MacNaughton
Managing Director
Salomon Brothers

Salomon Brothers is one of the largest and best-known investment bankers in the world. We asked Mr. MacNaughton to discuss capital structure and dividend decisions in the financial institutions industry.

During my 14 years with Salomon Brothers, I've worked with both industrial companies and financial institutions. From a capital structure standpoint, it is the *type* of assets that the capital supports that distinguishes a financial institution from a nonfinancial institution— "hard" assets such as plants and inventory versus financial assets such as bank deposits, insurance policies, and consumer loans.

Capital Structure Issues

Significant changes have taken place in the capital structure of financial institutions since 1980. Many companies had a low percentage of debt and a high percentage of equity. As business activity expanded in the 1980s, they learned to use leverage. Adding debt to their capital structure was a new development for most corporations. Today, companies are more comfortable with and likely to use debt in their financing mix. They will take advantage of low interest rate environments like the one we have now (Fall 1993) to borrow money in anticipation of future needs.

A firm's capital structure has a tremendous impact on its overall market value. The amount of debt is a key factor in its debt rating. The debt rating affects borrowing cost, and borrowing cost affects market value. Assuming that a group of similar companies typically trades in a similar P/E range, a company with more debt is riskier and might trade at the lower end of that P/E spectrum. Another company with debt and equity in more balanced proportions and an A or AA credit rating could trade at the higher end of the range.

However, companies must balance the risk with the return offered to shareholders. A capital structure with all equity and no debt doesn't take advantage of leverage to improve return on equity. Too much debt and less equity creates more risk than desired. Finding the right balance is the key, and that also depends on your industry and competitors. Almost all companies today use leverage to raise return on equity and, therefore, maximize the total worth of the company.

There's an ongoing debate about whether a company can afford to be rated AA versus A. The lower-rated company is almost by definition more highly leveraged. But that extra leverage increases the return on equity. So, companies look for an equilibrium point—and that equilibrium may not be at the highest credit rating.

I can't overemphasize the importance of credit ratings for this industry. Dropping below an A rating signals that an institution has a financial and maybe even an operating disadvantage compared to its competitors. Industrial companies are concerned about credit ratings, but less so than financial institutions. If you are a widget manufacturer and have an investment-grade rating (BBB/Baa and above), lenders will lend you money in both good and bad markets. In general, an industrial company's sales are not affected by its credit rating. Consumers don't buy cars—or any product—because the manufacturer is rated AA or BBB; they care more that the manufacturer will be around to service the warranty. But consumers of financial services often won't put money in a double B bank or buy an insurance policy from a double B company, because failure could mean loss. Ratings are also the imprimatur of a financial institution's safety.

Dividend Policy

Dividend policies of financial institutions have also changed over time. The more mature public financial institutions typically allowed their dividends to increase at a small growth rate. In some cases the dividend growth rate kept edging higher; today dividends at some financial institutions represent a high percentage of stock price. This is not necessarily good. Most financial institutions are capital-intensive, and dividends are counterproductive to a capital-intensive business, which should use the capital to grow its business rather than to pay dividends.

In my opinion, a company is better off retaining earnings than paying dividends. The additional equity helps the company grow faster, and investors benefit in the long run from a higher stock price. But many investors want the 5 percent dividend yield *plus* 5 percent a year in price appreciation. These two scenarios are in conflict in capital-intensive businesses.

I would advise companies to view their dividend policy in the same capital planning mode as other capital needs that support current operations and growth. Are dividends a good use of excess cash, or is there a better use? Companies should consider the cushion they want for liquidity and then choose a dividend that, over a business cycle, will show some consistency.

In recent years, many companies have managed their capital using nominal or smaller dividends together with stock repurchase programs. That policy allows greater flexibility than common dividends to manage capital ratios or capital position. Buying back stock may be a better investment than an acquisition, another plant, or cash dividends. Basically it's another capital investment decision for analysis: What is the best use of my capital given these different options?

Today, institutional investors have a dramatic effect on markets because they set values and can also dictate terms of bond and stock offerings as well as debt covenants. Big companies who borrow large amounts through bonds and sell large amounts of stock have to deal with institutions in the end. So they gear some of their capital structure and dividend policies to institutional investors' needs. For example, many recent initial public offerings have had nominal dividends. Why offer any dividend at all? Who cares about 1/2 of 1 percent or even 1 percent? Pension funds do. The nominal dividend is necessary because some pension funds cannot buy a non-yielding stock. The small dividend is manageable, and the company broadens the market for its stock.

*T*he primary way in which a firm maximizes its value is through the investment, or capital budgeting, decisions it makes. However, other decisions may also affect the value of the firm. In Chapters 11 and 12 we explore the impact of the firm's debt/equity, or capital structure, decision on the value of the firm. In Chapter 13 we consider dividend policy. Finally, in Chapter 14, we discuss how to make decisions when the investment and financing aspects are intertwined.

11 *Capital Structure Theory*

EXECUTIVE SUMMARY

In the absence of taxes and other imperfections, the firm's capital structure does not influence the value of the firm. The value of the firm is determined solely by its investment decisions, not by its financing decisions. However, once corporate taxes, personal taxes and other tax issues, financial distress costs, agency costs, signaling, and the impact of capital structure decisions on the firm's capital investment decisions are considered, the value of the firm is not completely independent of its capital structure. The amount of debt relative to the amount of equity employed may have an impact on the value of the firm.

In making the financing decision, the firm must consider two issues. First, does the firm's capital structure *directly* affect the value of the firm? The best answer finance can provide is that we think so, but the impact on firm value is much less than that provided by the investment decisions the firm makes. Second, do the firm's financing decisions preclude it from making value-enhancing investment decisions? The answer here is clearcut: If the financing decisions preclude a firm from undertaking positive-NPV investment projects, the total value of the firm is clearly diminished.

CAPITAL STRUCTURE AND THE VALUE OF THE FIRM

Until now we have not questioned the firm's debt/equity ratio, which signifies the amount of financial leverage being employed. We have taken it as a "given." For managers, however, it is not a given; it is one of the decisions firms have to make. The issue can be visualized as follows, where we have two different ways of slicing up the pie between stockholders and bondholders:

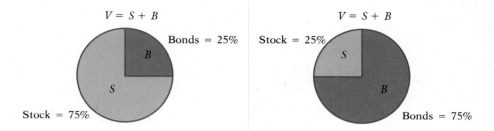

The question is this: Holding everything else constant, does how we slice the pie affect its size? *By holding everything else constant, we are assuming that the firm's investments remain the same, as well as its underlying cash flows and everything else.* If everything remains the same, then should the value of the firm be affected by how it is financed?

The answer to this simple question is not simple. In fact, a tremendous amount of controversy and discussion swirls around this question. In this chapter we examine capital structure theory. Then in Chapter 12 we examine factors that lead to capital structure differences and the practical considerations firms face in setting their debt/equity ratio.

Determining a firm's financial structure means answering two basic questions: First, how should the firm's total sources of funds be divided among long-term and short-term financing? Second, what proportion of funds should be financed by debt and what proportion by equity? The first question, the maturity composition of the total sources of funds, requires focusing on the nature of the assets owned. We address short-term sources of funds in Chapter 19, where we see that the matching principle provides some guidance.

Now, however, we focus our attention on the long-term sources of funds—debt, leases, preferred stock, internally generated funds, and common stock. The proportions of these long-term sources describe the capital structure of the firm. Our focus is therefore on the second of the questions: What does theory say about the impact of the firm's capital structure on its value? For simplicity, we focus on the two main sources of capital—equity capital and debt capital.

THE DEVELOPMENT OF CAPITAL STRUCTURE THEORY

To highlight the issues involved, we start with a simplified example. The assumptions are as follows:

1.   Only two types of securities are employed—long-term debt and common stock.
2.   The firm is not expected to grow. Thus, the value of a share of stock can be determined by employing the basic no-growth dividend valuation approach (from Chapter 3) which capitalizes the perpetual cash dividend stream as follows:

$$P_0 = \frac{D_1}{k_s}$$

(11.1)

where

P_0 = the current stock price
D_1 = the expected constant amount of cash dividends in perpetuity
k_s = the equity investor's required rate of return, or opportunity cost of equity capital

3. All earnings are assumed to be paid out in the form of cash dividends, so dividends equal earnings in each future time period. Accordingly, Equation 11.1 can be rewritten as

$$P_0 = \frac{EPS_1}{k_s} \tag{11.2}$$

or for the firm as a whole

$$S = \frac{E_1}{k_s} \tag{11.3}$$

where E is now the expected constant cash dividends (or earnings in perpetuity) and S is the total market value of the firm's stock.[1] In line with the discussion in Chapter 3, when there is no growth, the present value of growth opportunities, PVGO, is zero. Equation 11.3 is, therefore, a straightforward statement of the present value of the firm's assets in place when no growth is expected.

4. There are no costs or penalties (such as legal fees or the disruption of operations resulting from default) if the firm does not pay interest on the debt, although the bondholders may take over the firm.

We are now in a position to investigate what impact, if any, the firm's capital structure can have on the value of the firm. We begin with the celebrated no-tax case presented by Modigliani and Miller (1958).

THE MODIGLIANI AND MILLER MODEL WITHOUT CORPORATE TAXES

In its simplest situation, a firm has only common stock and debt financing.[2] For the moment, we also assume that *there are no corporate taxes*. Under these conditions, how does the firm's financing decision affect the value of the firm? To understand this question, consider NewWest Industries, which is an all-equity-financed firm. NewWest has an opportunity to receive $100,000 in cash flow from both its existing operations and a new investment. To receive the $100,000 in cash flow (or earnings

---

[1] As we will see in Chapter 13, the impact of cash dividends on the value of the firm's common stock is also a subject of debate. To avoid complicating this discussion, it is easier to assume that all earnings are paid out in the form of cash dividends.
[2] The following analysis could be presented in the context of the capital asset pricing model, CAPM, but it is less complicated to present it without introducing the CAPM. Also, growth can be incorporated, but it only further complicates the discussion.

before interest and taxes, EBIT), NewWest needs to make an additional $400,000 investment.[3] The equity investor's required rate of return is 10 percent.

If only common stock financing is used to raise the additional $400,000, the total market value of NewWest will be the present value of the dividends to the firm's stockholders. With EBIT of $100,000, no interest, and no corporate taxes, EBIT = earnings after tax, EAT; and, with all cash flows paid out as cash dividends, the dividends are a perpetual stream of $100,000. Using Equation 11.3, we find that the value of NewWest is

$$\text{value of NewWest's stock} = S = \frac{\$100,000}{0.10} = \$1 \text{ million}$$

When only common stock is employed, the total value of the firm, V, is equal to the value of the firm's common stock, S, which is $1 million.

What happens if NewWest decides to raise the $400,000 by issuing debt instead of common stock? The debt has an interest rate, k_b, of 6 percent, so that the earnings (and dividends) now available to NewWest's common stockholders are

EBIT	$100,000
Interest ($400,000)(0.06)	24,000
EBT	76,000
Taxes	zero for now
EAT	$ 76,000

If the earnings for common stockholders of $76,000 are *mistakenly divided by the previous all-equity required rate of return* of 10 percent, then the *apparent* value of NewWest's common stock (which is now the "levered" value of the equity, designated by the subscript L) is

$$\text{apparent value of NewWest's stock} = S_L = \frac{\$76,000}{0.10} = \$760,000$$

Finally, with the value of NewWest's debt equal to $400,000, the *apparent* total value of the levered firm, V_L, would be

total firm value = apparent market value of levered common stock
          + market value of debt

$$V_L = S_L + B \tag{11.4}$$
$$= \$760,000 + \$400,000 = \$1,160,000$$

---

[3] The firm is not expected to grow; therefore, all cash flows are perpetuities. This implies that annual investment must equal the annual (economic) depreciation in order to maintain the assets in place. Accordingly, EBIT will equal cash flow.

If the equity investor's required return remains 10 percent, simply using debt instead of equity financing has apparently allowed NewWest to raise the value of the firm from $1 million to $1,160,000. At this point, Franco Modigliani and Merton Miller, both recent Nobel prize winners in financial economics, raised an important question: "Is it reasonable for the required rate of return demanded by equity investors to be the same when debt, as opposed to common stock, is employed?" Their answer was "no!" *Equity risk has increased because the use of debt places a drain on the cash flow stream before anything goes to the common stockholders.* This risk is composed of (1) the possibility of not receiving any earnings or cash flow, and (2) increased variability in earnings and cash flows due to the increased amount of debt employed.

Modigliani and Miller (MM) developed their model given the following assumptions *in addition to those already mentioned:*

1. PERFECT CAPITAL MARKETS   In perfect capital markets, buying and selling securities involves no brokerage fees. All investors have equal and costless access to information, and there are a large number of individual buyers and sellers, none of whom individually can affect market prices.
2. DEBT IS RISK-FREE   Any debt issued by investors and firms is always riskless debt, no matter how much is issued. Therefore, the interest rate on all debt is the risk-free rate.
3. RISK CLASSES   All firms can be grouped into risk classes based on the variance of their earnings before interest and taxes, EBIT.[4]
4. HOMOGENEOUS EXPECTATIONS   Individual investors agree on the expected value of the future income of firms, that is, on each firm's earnings before interest and taxes, EBIT.

Using these assumptions, MM derived two propositions concerning the valuation of securities for firms with different capital structures: *The first says that the value of the firm is determined by its capital investment decisions, not by its financing decisions. The second says that as a firm adds more debt to its capital structure, its opportunity cost of equity capital increases.* Let's explore these two propositions more formally.

Proposition I

The equilibrium *market value of any firm when there are no corporate taxes is independent of its capital structure* and is found by capitalizing its expected EBIT by the appropriate cost of capital for an all-equity firm, k_s^U, in its risk class

$$V_L = S_L + B = \frac{EBIT}{k_s^U} = V_U \tag{11.5}$$

---

[4] At the time Modigliani and Miller developed their model, no complete model of risk and return (such as the capital asset pricing model) existed. Risk classes were used by MM to allow for differences in risk among firms.

where

V_L = the market value of a levered firm

S_L = the market value of stock for a levered firm

k_s^U = the equity investor's required rate of return for an all-equity-financed firm; the cost of equity capital for an all-equity-financed firm

V_U = the market value of an unlevered firm

(Note that the unlevered value is denoted by the subscript U.)

Another way to state proposition I is this: The value of any firm when there are no taxes is determined by its capital investment decisions, not by its financing decisions. Other things being equal, various proportions of equity or debt may be employed, but the total market value of the firm is unaffected.

Proposition II

The cost of equity for a levered firm, k_s^L, is equal to the appropriate cost of capital for an all-equity firm, k_s^U, plus a risk premium equal to the debt/equity ratio times the spread between k_s^U and the cost of debt, k_b, as follows:

$$k_s^L = k_s^U + (k_s^U - k_b)(B/S_L)$$

(11.6)

Thus, as the firm adds more debt to its capital structure, equity investors demand a higher return to compensate for the additional debt, and the opportunity cost of equity capital increases.

Taking the two propositions together, MM conclude in the no-tax case that there is no advantage or disadvantage to financing with common stock. *Any "savings" from debt financing are immediately offset by a higher return required by common stockholders (due to greater financial risk), leaving the firm and its stockholders in the same position as before.*

Now that we have presented the two propositions of MM, let us go back to the example of NewWest. According to MM, the total market value of NewWest must remain at $1 million (i.e., $V_L = V_U$), because nothing of value has been created. *In the no-tax case we can think of debt being a zero-NPV project;* that is why $V_L = V_U$. Subtracting the $400,000 in debt, we see that the value of the stock, S_L, in the MM no-tax case is $600,000. Because the earnings before taxes, EBT, going to NewWest's common stockholders are $76,000, Equation 11.3 can be rearranged and solved for the levered cost of equity capital:

$$\text{levered cost of equity capital} = k_s^L = \frac{\text{earnings to stockholders}}{\text{market value of stock}}$$

$$= \frac{\$76,000}{\$600,000} = 0.1267 = 12.67 \text{ percent}$$

Alternatively, we can use MM's proposition II (Equation 11.6) directly to determine the cost of equity funds to the firm and the return demanded by equity investors, once debt is added to the firm's financing mix. This is

$$k_s^L = k_s^U + (k_s^U - k_b)\,(B/S_L)$$
$$= 10\% + (10\% - 6\%)(\$400{,}000/\$600{,}000) = 12.67 \text{ percent}$$

MM concluded that common equity investors neither gained nor lost from the use of debt in the no-tax case. Thus, *the value of the firm does not change; rather, increased financial risk causes the stockholders' required rate of return to increase. Accordingly, the opportunity cost of equity capital increases so that any apparent gain from using cheaper debt financing is completely offset.*

Because the market value of the firm does not change with financial leverage, in the no-tax case the firm's opportunity cost of capital is also constant as financial leverage changes. When NewWest was all-equity-financed, its opportunity cost of capital was equal to its unlevered cost of equity capital, k_s^U, which was 10 percent. In the no-tax case its opportunity cost of capital must remain at 10 percent after it shifts to any amount of debt financing. Using Equation 11.7 (which is just Equation 1 from Chapter 6) to determine the firm's opportunity cost of capital, and with corporate taxes equal to zero, we have

$$\begin{aligned}\text{opportunity cost} \atop \text{of capital} &= k_b(1 - T)\ W_{\text{debt}} + k_s^L\ W_{\text{common equity}} &(11.7)\\[6pt]
&= k_b(1 - T)\left(\frac{B}{B + S}\right) + k_s^L\left(\frac{S}{B + S}\right)\\[6pt]
&= 6\%(1 - 0.00)\left(\frac{\$400{,}000}{\$1{,}000{,}000}\right) + 12.67\%\left(\frac{\$600{,}000}{\$1{,}000{,}000}\right)\\[6pt]
&= 6.00\%(0.40) + 12.67\%(0.60) = 10.00\%\end{aligned}$$

Modigliani and Miller's no-tax position is graphed in Figure 11.1. As the firm increases its financial leverage (by moving to the right), we see in Figure 11.1(a) that the value of the firm remains constant. In Figure 11.1(b) we see that the firm's opportunity cost of capital is constant regardless of the amount of financial leverage employed. Both the value of the firm and its cost of capital are independent of financial leverage in the absence of taxes.

WHERE TO LOOK FOR CAPITAL STRUCTURE IMPACTS ON FIRM VALUE

The importance of the Modigliani and Miller no-tax model is that (1) it presents a theoretical, rigorous statement of the value of the firm, where none existed before, and (2) it tells us where to look to determine whether the firm's capital structure affects the value of the firm. In effect, the MM no-tax case says:

If there are no taxes,

if there are no transactions costs, and

if the investment (or capital budgeting) policies of the firm are fixed,

then capital structure does not affect a firm's value.

Figure 11.1

Value of the Firm and Opportunity Cost of Capital with No Taxes, According to Modigliani and Miller

As the firm moves to the right, it substitutes cheaper debt for more expensive equity capital. Because financial risk increases as you move to the right, the opportunity cost of equity capital increases, exactly offsetting any benefits from using more cheap debt financing.

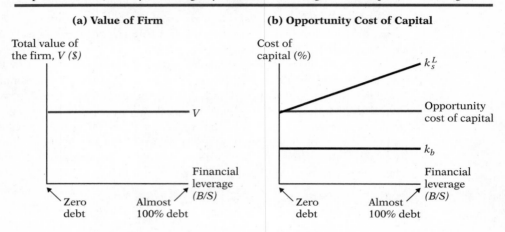

(a) Value of Firm

Total value of the firm, V ($)

V

Financial leverage (B/S)

Zero debt   Almost 100% debt

(b) Opportunity Cost of Capital

Cost of capital (%)

k_s^L

Opportunity cost of capital

k_b

Financial leverage (B/S)

Zero debt   Almost 100% debt

To determine whether capital structure affects firm value, we will look at the impact of taxes, both corporate and personal, the impact of transactions costs, and the capital investment policies of the firm. Along the way we will see that a tremendous amount of attention has been devoted to answering the simple question, "Does the firm's capital structure affect its value?"

Concept Review Questions

- What assumptions did Modigliani and Miller make when they developed their capital structure model?
- Describe Miller and Modigliani's proposition I and proposition II.
- Briefly explain Modigliani and Miller's capital structure model.

CORPORATE TAXES AND THE DEDUCTIBILITY OF INTEREST

Almost immediately after Modigliani and Miller published their no-tax article they were reminded that corporate taxes are a fact of life for firms. Accordingly, they incorporated corporate taxes into their capital structure model.

THE MODIGLIANI AND MILLER MODEL WITH CORPORATE TAXES

Suppose we introduce corporate taxes into the NewWest example. We will assume that the marginal corporate tax rate, T, is 30 percent and that to obtain the $100,000 EBIT, NewWest still needs to raise the additional $400,000. Once corporate taxes are introduced the earnings after taxes are

EBIT	$100,000
Interest	0
EBT	100,000
Taxes (30%)	30,000
EAT	$ 70,000

Because all earnings are paid out as cash dividends, the payment to *all* the investors of the unlevered firm is

$$\text{payments to all investors}_U = EBIT(1 - T) \tag{11.8}$$

With only common stock being employed, the return demanded by investors is still 10 percent, that is, $k_s^U = 10$ percent, and the total value of NewWest, V_U, is equal to its unlevered stock value, which is

$$V_U = S_U = \frac{EBIT(1 - T)}{k_s^U} \tag{11.9}$$

$$= \frac{\$70,000}{0.10} = \$700,000$$

What happens when NewWest uses $400,000 of debt financing instead of equity financing? With $400,000 of debt at 6 percent, interest is $24,000. Therefore, with debt financing and corporate taxes, the earnings are

EBIT	$100,000
Interest $(k_b B)$	24,000
EBT	76,000
Taxes (30%)	22,800
EAT	$ 53,200

It is important to consider the impact that interest has on the taxes paid by the firm. *Because of interest, the firm actually pays less taxes.* If no interest is present, the taxes are $100,000(0.30) = $30,000. With the interest of $24,000, the taxes drop to $22,800—a savings of $7,200 in taxes. The impact of interest on the amount of taxes actually paid by the firm is referred to as the *interest tax shield*. Other things being equal, the payment of interest by the firm shields (or reduces) the amount of corporate taxes paid by the firm.

Although earnings have declined due to the use of debt financing, the *debt financing has value because on an after-tax basis it costs the firm less than equity.* According to MM, the value of the levered firm, V_L, once corporate taxes are introduced, is equal to the unlevered value of the firm, V_U, plus the present value of the interest tax shield. The amount of interest per period is given by $k_b B$, and the interest tax shield is simply $T k_b B$. Because debt is a perpetuity in the case being considered, the *present value of the interest tax shield* is given by capitalizing the interest tax shield at the appropriate discount rate, k_b, so that $T k_b B / k_b = TB$. Once corporate taxes are introduced, while everything else remains as before, MM conclude that the value of the levered firm is[5]

$$V_L = V_U + TB \qquad (11.10)$$

Thus, the total value of NewWest once corporate taxes are introduced and the firm has $400,000 of debt outstanding is

$$V_L = \$700,000 + (0.30)(\$400,000) = \$820,000$$

Because the total value of the firm, V_L, is also equal to the sum of its levered stock, S_L, and bonds, B, the value of the stock of the levered firm is $S_L = V_L - B$. For NewWest, its stock will now be valued at $S_L = \$820,000 - \$400,000 = \$420,000$.

If the debt/equity ratio, B/S_L, is specified at ($400,000/$420,000), then proposition II (Equation 11.6) can be adjusted for taxes to determine the firm's levered cost of equity capital. Thus,

$$
\begin{aligned}
k_s^L &= k_s^U + (k_s^U - k_b)(1 - T)(B/S_L) \qquad (11.11)\\
&= 10\% + (10\% - 6\%)(1 - 0.30)(\$400,000/\$420,000)\\
&= 10\% + 2.8\%(0.952) = 10\% + 2.67\% = 12.67\%
\end{aligned}
$$

Note that the opportunity cost of equity capital of 12.67 percent is the same as it was in the no-tax case. Now that we know NewWest's levered cost of equity, k_s^L, we can use a modified version of Equation 11.9, which now reflects both corporate taxes and the interest paid on the debt financing, to solve directly for S_L:

$$S_L = \frac{(EBIT - k_b B)(1 - T)}{k_s^L} \qquad (11.12)$$

$$= \frac{\$53,200}{0.1267} \approx \$420,000$$

Once the tax subsidy provided by the government is recognized, we see that by using debt, NewWest has increased the total value of the firm from $700,000 to $820,000. This is composed of the levered stock, S_L, valued at $420,000 and debt, B, valued at $400,000.

---

[5] Equation 11.10 is derived in Appendix 11A.

Let's now see what happens to NewWest's overall opportunity cost of capital. With all-common stock financing, NewWest's opportunity cost of capital is still equal to its unlevered cost of equity capital, k_s^U, which is 10 percent. Once debt is introduced, we can use Equation 11.7 to determine NewWest's new opportunity cost of capital:

$$\begin{aligned}
\text{opportunity cost} \atop \text{of capital} &= k_b(1 - T)\left(\frac{B}{B + S}\right) + k_s^L\left(\frac{S}{B + S}\right) \\
&= 6\%(1 - 0.30)\left(\frac{\$400,000}{\$820,000}\right) + 12.67\%\left(\frac{\$420,000}{\$820,000}\right) \\
&= 2.05\% + 6.49\% = 8.54\%
\end{aligned}$$

Figure 11.2 shows the MM results once corporate taxes are introduced. Note that *financial risk increases as debt is employed, as signified by the rising cost of common stock, k_s^L. Even with this increase in financial risk, the presence of corporate taxes has the effect of subsidizing the use of debt; the result is that increases in financial leverage lead to increases in the total value of the firm and decreases in the firm's overall opportunity cost of capital.* As long as firms are profitable, and the government provides an incentive for using debt through allowing interest to be tax-deductible, there is an advantage to using debt financing. This advantage leads to an increase in the value of the firm, providing that the investment decisions of the firm are unaffected.

Figure 11.2

Value of the Firm and Opportunity Cost of Capital with Corporate Taxes, According to Modigliani and Miller

When corporate taxes are introduced, the government, in effect, supplies a subsidy for the use of debt as long as firms are profitable. This is so because interest is a tax-deductible expense. By using debt, the firm can increase its total value and decrease its opportunity cost of capital.

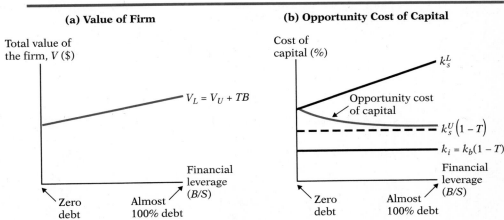

THE NO-TAX CASE AND THE TAX CASE

Comparing the stock- versus the stock-and-debt-financing plans for both the no-tax and the corporate tax case, Modigliani and Miller conclude that

	No-Tax Case		Tax Case	
	All Stock Financing	**Combination Stock and Debt Financing**	**All Stock Financing**	**Combination Stock and Debt Financing**
Total stock value	$1,000,000	$600,000	$700,000	$420,000
Total debt value	0	$400,000	0	$400,000
Total value of firm	$1,000,000	$1,000,000	$700,000	$820,000
Cost of equity capital	10%	12.67%	10%	12.67%
After-tax cost of debt capital	6%	6%	4.2%	4.2%
Overall opportunity cost of capital	10%	10%	10%	8.54%

Thus, the overall conclusions are that (1) with no corporate taxes, the capital structure decision is irrelevant, and (2) once corporate taxes are considered, firms maximize their value and lower their opportunity cost of capital by employing debt. In fact, the more debt used, the greater the value of the firm.

Before going any further, let's stop and summarize the important conclusions and equations presented by the MM no-tax and tax cases. Table 11.1 summarizes this information. In part I for the no-tax case, the value of the firm, that is, $V_L = S_L + B$, is shown to be independent of the amount of financial leverage employed. Once corporate taxes are introduced, the value of the firm can be found via either $V_L = S_L + B$ or $V_L = V_U + TB$, and the value increases as the firm replaces equity with debt in its capital structure. Table 11.1, in parts II, III and IV, also summarizes the value of the unlevered equity, S_U, and the levered equity, S_L, for both the no-tax and the tax cases, along with the levered cost of equity capital, k_s^L, in both cases. From an applications standpoint, *always use the equations for the tax case; if no taxes exist, the equations employing taxes simply collapse into the no-tax equations.*

We used Equation 11.7 to determine the firm's opportunity cost of capital as follows:

$$\text{opportunity cost of capital} = k_b(1 - T)\, W_{\text{debt}} + k_s^L W_{\text{common equity}}$$

Two other approaches can also be employed to determine the firm's opportunity cost of capital when the MM tax case is being considered. The first says that the firm's opportunity cost of capital is equal to the unlevered cost of capital, which is just k_s^U,

Table 11.1

Summary of the Fundamental Relationships for the MM No-Tax Case and the MM Corporate Tax Case

For simplicity, the tax-case equations should always be employed. If there are no corporate taxes, the tax-case equations collapse into the no-tax equations.

No-Tax Case	Tax Case

I. The Total Value of the Firm, V_L

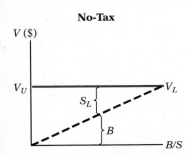

$V_L = V_U$
$V_L = V_U = S_L + B$
[*Note:* The second equation is Equation 11.5.]

$V_L = S_L + B$, or
$V_L = V_U + TB$
[*Note:* The second equation is Equation 11.10.]

II. Value of the Equity If There Is No Debt, S_U

$$S_U = \frac{E}{k_s^U}$$
[*Note:* This is Equation 11.3. Because there is no debt or taxes, $EBIT = E$.]

$$S_U = \frac{EBIT(1 - T)}{k_s^U}$$
[*Note:* This is Equation 11.9. Because there is no debt, $EBIT = EBT$.]

III. Value of the Equity If There Is Debt, S_L

$$S_L = \frac{(EBIT - I)}{k_s^L}$$
[*Note:* This is a modification of Equation 11.3. $EBIT = E$ and $I = k_b B$.]

$$S_L = \frac{(EBIT - I)(1 - T)}{k_s^L}$$
[*Note:* This is Equation 11.12. $I = k_b B$.]

IV. Levered Cost of Equity Capital, k_s^L

$k_s^L = k_s^U + (k_s^U - k_b)(B/S_L)$
[*Note:* This is Equation 11.6.]

$k_s^L = k_s^U + (k_s^U - k_b)(1 - T)(B/S_L)$
[*Note:* This is Equation 11.11.]

adjusted for taxes and the amount of debt employed, so that

$$\text{opportunity cost of capital} = k_s^U \left\{ 1 - \left[T \left(\frac{B}{S + B} \right) \right] \right\} \tag{11.13}$$

$$= 10\% \left\{ 1 - \left[0.30 \left(\frac{\$400,000}{\$820,000} \right) \right] \right\} = 8.54\%$$

The second approach says that the opportunity cost of capital is equal to the after-tax operating cash flows to the firm if there is no debt, divided by the total market value of the firm, so

$$\begin{matrix} \text{opportunity cost} \\ \text{of capital} \end{matrix} = \frac{EBIT_{\text{at a zero debt level}} \ (1 - T)}{S_L + B} \tag{11.14}$$

$$= \frac{\$100,000(1 - 0.30)}{\$820,000} = 8.54\%$$

Equations 11.13 and 11.14 work just as well as Equation 11.7 when the MM tax case is considered. However, *remember that Equations 11.13 and 11.14 assume an MM corporate tax world; do not employ them to determine a firm's opportunity cost of capital unless the world you and the firm are operating in is the MM corporate tax world.*

When MM presented their capital structure theory in the late 1950s and early 1960s, many individuals, both in the business and the academic communities, immediately took issue with them. The arguments, in simple form, were: "Of course, capital structure is important. That is why we see firms purposefully select different capital structures—because they know it is important and, accordingly, select the one most appropriate for their firm." An alternative reaction was: "If capital structure and the debt tax shield are important, why aren't all firms almost 100 percent debt financed, because that is the point at which the value of their firm would be maximized? All we have to do is examine a few firms and see that they are not 100 percent, or even close to 100 percent, debt financed. Therefore, MM, your theory is incorrect."

Don't fall into the trap of rejecting MM as irrelevant without considering the full meaning of their position. In the simplest terms, *MM's argument was that the value of the firm is determined solely by the capital investments it makes.* Thus, the underlying message delivered by MM was simply to restate that the primary means of creating value is by focusing on the left-hand side of the balance sheet and make "good" capital investment decisions. According to MM, any other decisions, such as the capital structure decision or the dividend decision, *are irrelevant as long as there are no taxes and they don't affect the capital investment decisions made by the firm.*

Concept Review Questions

■ Describe the effect of corporate taxes on Modigliani and Miller's model.

■ Briefly summarize the difference in the conclusions and equations of the MM no-tax case and the MM tax case.

PERSONAL TAXES AND OTHER TAX RELATED IMPACTS

Many more tax impacts on the value of the firm have been investigated in the last thirty years. First, we will examine the impact of personal taxes on the firm. Then we will consider other possible tax impacts on the firm's value.

PERSONAL TAXES AND THE VALUE OF THE FIRM

When MM developed their tax model, they included corporate taxes but not the personal taxes on any income investors received from holding stocks or bonds. As a result, MM concluded, as shown in Equation 11.10, that the value of the levered firm is $V_L = V_U + TB$. Consequently, the gain from leverage, G_L, is simply the difference between the value of the levered and unlevered firms (which is the present value of the interest tax shield).

$$G_L = V_L - V_U = TB \tag{11.15}$$

This gain from leverage, and consequently the value of the levered firm, increases as a firm uses more debt. Thus, the optimal capital structure employs almost 100 percent debt.

What happens to the gain from leverage and the value of a firm that uses debt when both corporate and personal taxes exist? *With the inclusion of personal taxes, the objective is to maximize income after all taxes (both corporate and personal).* Thus, the focus shifts from the firm's viewpoint, to the viewpoint of investors and what they receive from investing in stocks and bonds after both corporate and personal taxes are paid. About fifteen years after the original MM article, Merton Miller (1977) introduced personal taxes into the model and developed the following equation:[6]

$$V_L = V_U + \left[1 - \frac{(1 - T)(1 - T_{ps})}{(1 - T_{pb})}\right]B \tag{11.16}$$

where

T = the corporate tax rate
T_{ps} = the personal tax rate on stock income (cash dividends and capital appreciation or loss)
T_{pb} = the personal tax rate on bond income (interest)

With this more complete and realistic tax structure, the gain from leverage is now[7]

$$G_L = \left[1 - \frac{(1 - T)(1 - T_{ps})}{(1 - T_{pb})}\right]B \tag{11.17}$$

---

[6] Equation 11.16 is derived in Appendix 11A.
[7] The marginal personal tax rate on stock income, and on bond income, is assumed to be the same for all investors in Miller's model.

If the *personal tax rates are zero* ($T_{ps} = 0$ and $T_{pb} = 0$) *or if they are equal to one another for both stock income and bond income* ($T_{ps} = T_{pb}$), *the gain from leverage reduces to TB.* Thus, in either of these instances the benefits from the interest tax shield, once both corporate and personal taxes are considered, are the same as those provided by the MM corporate tax model.

What happens, however, if the effective personal tax rate on stock income is less than the effective tax rate on bond income? If T_{ps} is less than T_{pb}, then, other things being equal, the before-tax return on bonds must be high enough to compensate for the additional taxes that must be paid on bond income. If this were not true, investors would never hold bonds. Although the firm receives a subsidy because of the tax-deductibility of the interest payment, this benefit may be offset because the interest payment has to be "grossed up" to compensate for the higher personal taxes that must be paid on the interest income. By grossing up, we mean that the interest paid by the firm is higher than it would be if personal taxes did not exist. Consequently, the gain from leverage diminishes and, in fact, will disappear completely if $(1 - T_{pb}) = (1 - T)(1 - T_{ps})$. If this happens, the results are the same as the MM model with no taxes: G_L will be zero, $V_U = V_L$, and, accordingly, the amount of debt used by a firm will not have any effect on its value. These relationships are illustrated in Figure 11.3.

Under the Budget Reconciliation Act of 1993, $T = 35$ percent, $T_{ps} = 39.6$ percent, and $T_{pb} = 39.6$ percent. If the *effective* personal tax rates on stock income and bond income are equal, then the gain from using debt is

$$G_L = \left[1 - \frac{(1 - 0.35)(1 - 0.396)}{(1 - 0.396)} \right] B = 0.35B$$

Figure 11.3

Gains from Financial Leverage: MM Models (With and Without Taxes) and Miller's Model

Depending on the effective rate of personal taxes on stock versus bond income, Miller's model may indicate an intermediate value for the firm.

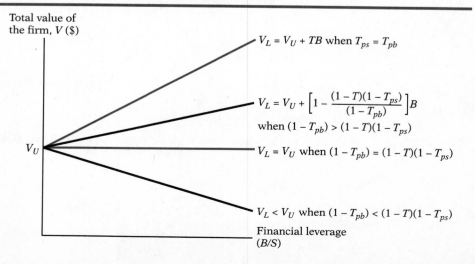

which is the same as that given by the MM model with only corporate taxes. We would conclude that there are substantial gains from using debt.

On the other hand, even with the stated marginal personal tax rate on stock income and bond income at 39.6 percent, there is one big tax advantage for investors who invest in stocks as opposed to bonds. It arises because over 50 percent of the return from investing in stock comes from capital gains, and an investor does not have to realize the capital gain (and pay taxes on it) immediately.[8] This *option to delay realizing capital gains* means the effective tax rate on stock income is probably less than that for bond income. What if the effective tax rate on stock income, T_{ps}, is 20 percent? Then the gain from using debt is

$$G = \left[1 - \frac{(1 - 0.35)(1 - 0.20)}{(1 - 0.396)}\right]B = 0.139B$$

While still substantial, there is less subsidy than when the effective personal rates on stock and bond income are equal. Under the most likely scenario, the Miller model indicates that the value of the tax benefits to the firm is a compromise between the MM model with no taxes and the MM tax model. This effect is also illustrated in Figure 11.3.

OTHER TAX IMPACTS AND THE FIRM'S CAPITAL STRUCTURE DECISION

When arriving at his result, Miller traded off the corporate benefits of debt against the personal tax disadvantage of the resulting interest income; he did not consider any corporate disadvantages to debt, or the impact of different marginal tax rates between firms or individuals. As we will see, things become more complicated as we introduce more realistic aspects of the tax code into the discussion.

Non-Debt Tax Shields

In the MM cases and in Miller's personal tax argument, interest is the only relevant deduction for tax purposes. However, firms also can, and do, shield themselves from paying taxes by using depreciation and depletion. DeAngelo and Masulis (1980) recognized this and extended Miller's work by including the effects of these tax shields other than interest. DeAngelo and Masulis refer to tax shields arising from depreciation and depletion as "non-debt tax shields." *The existence of non-debt tax shields serves to decrease a firm's taxable income, thus causing a decline in the probability of being able to use all of the interest tax shield.* Consequently, as more debt is used, the expected value of the interest tax shield declines. The impact of non-debt tax shields reduces the incentive for the firm to use debt financing. Therefore, the firm is forced to balance the use of debt substitutes (such as depreciation and depletion) against the use of additional debt in order to be able to use all its tax deductions. Without considering any other factors, DeAngelo and Masulis demonstrated that this balancing procedure

---

[8] The tax rate on capital gains is 28 percent.

will lead to a capital structure that entails less than 100 percent debt (and more than zero debt).

Bond Clienteles and Different Effective Marginal Tax Rates

In Miller's personal tax model all individual investors are assumed to have the same effective marginal tax rate. However, once uncertainty is introduced and the asymmetric nature of the tax code for bond income is recognized, Park and Williams (1985) and Zechner (1990) both show how bondholder clienteles, based on differential personal marginal tax rates, exist for bonds that pay different effective rates of interest. The impact is that different firms will employ different amounts of debt depending on how risky the firms are and how much they have to pay at the margin for debt capital.

The Maturity Structure of Debt

Firms can also issue debt that matures at different times in the future. Thus, we could have two firms that are essentially the same except that they issue debt with different maturities. In practice, we see this happening all the time; firms that borrow from banks, for example, end up with shorter average maturities than similar firms who issue long-term bonds in the capital markets. In a multiperiod context, Lewis (1990) has shown that the firm's capital structure decision—that is, its debt/equity ratio—and its debt maturity structure—that is, the length of maturity of the debt—are intertwined. In such an environment firms can have a variety of different mixes of capital structures and debt maturities that are consistent with maximizing the value of the firm. In addition, due to differences in the interest costs (if the term structure of interest rates is either upward- or downward-sloping), the tax implications for different debt financing strategies may not be equivalent.

With only corporate taxes we saw that the value of the firm should rise as firms substitute debt for equity financing. With personal taxes, firm value should still increase, but probably not as much, when debt is added to the capital structure. However, as more and more debt is added to the capital structure, the tax-deductibility of interest is less likely, due to the presence of depreciation, depletion, and other non-debt tax shields. In addition, different effective personal tax rates and different debt maturities lead firms to reach the point where the probability of the tax-deductibility of debt is low enough that there are no more benefits from adding additional debt. Thus, as shown in Figure 11.4, tax considerations by themself suggest that firms will issue more than zero debt but will use less than 100 percent debt. The presence of taxes suggests there is some optimal level, or amount of debt, B^*, that leads to the maximization of the total market value of the firm.

Concept Review Questions

- What is the difference between the Miller model and the Modigliani and Miller model?
- Briefly describe how personal taxes affect the MM tax case and the MM no-tax case.
- How does the use of tax shields and long-term debt affect corporate capital structure?

Figure 11.4

Gains from Financial Leverage: MM and Miller Models and the Impact of Non-debt Tax Shields

Once personal taxes and non-debt tax shields (such as depreciation and depletion) are considered, the gains from using financial leverage may be less than suggested by the MM tax case. An optimal capital structure, $B*/S$, may exist at which the marginal benefits of additional debt are exactly offset by tax consequences of additional debt.

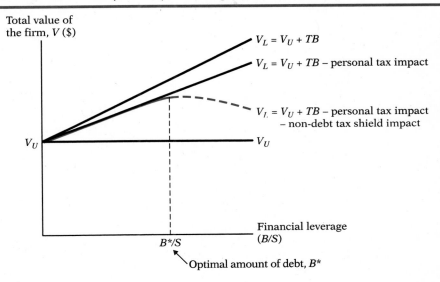

TRANSACTIONS COSTS AND CAPITAL STRUCTURE DECISIONS

Earlier we indicated three places to look in order to determine if a firm's capital structure affected its total market value. The first was taxes. The second is transactions costs. The two primary transactions costs relate to financial distress and agency costs. In looking at the impact of transactions costs, we will ignore taxes, for the time being.

FINANCIAL DISTRESS COSTS

Not all firms succeed; some experience periods of **financial distress,** when they do not have enough cash on hand or readily available to meet their current financial obligations; some may even fail. Think of the firm in an option sense as we discussed briefly in Chapter 1 and in more detail in Chapter 5. The owners of the firm (or its stockholders) have a call option on the firm, as shown in Figure 11.5. If at the maturity of the firm's debt, the value of the firm's assets is greater than the value of the debt, the stockholders exercise the call option, pay off the bondholders, and claim the rest of the value of the firm for themselves. But, in the event of a loss in value of the firm's

Figure 11.5

The Payoff to Stockholders and Bondholders

If the value of the firm is greater than the bondholders' claim, stockholders pay off the bonds when they mature and claim the rest of the value of the firm. Otherwise, they exercise their option and walk away, turning the firm over to the bondholders.

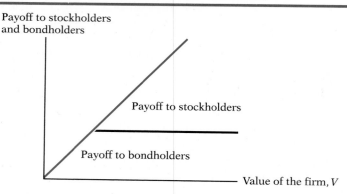

assets, the stockholders will exercise the put option, which arises due to limited liability, and walk away from the firm, turning it over to the creditors. Note that the loss in value is what triggered exercising the option. Many individuals think that bankruptcy leads to a loss in value. In fact it is just the reverse: *The loss in value is what leads to bankruptcy.*

Bankruptcy Costs

If stockholders exercise their option and walk away from the firm, there are direct costs associated with the transaction. These are **bankruptcy costs**, which include legal and other costs associated with the bankruptcy or reorganization proceedings. These are the "dead weight" costs of failing; only the accountants and lawyers benefit from them. How big are these costs? Studies of the direct costs of bankruptcy do not indicate they are large—they may be anything from less than 1 percent to a maximum of 4 or 5 percent of the firm's value.[9] Although not trivial, bankruptcy costs per se are not large enough to make a material difference in the thrust of the Modigliani and Miller arguments.

In addition to the direct bankruptcy costs, there are other indirect costs associated with financial difficulties. These include risk shifting, failing to invest, and operational and managerial inefficiencies.

Risk Shifting

Firms maximize their value by accepting positive net present value projects and rejecting negative net present value projects. But, faced with severe financial difficulties, some perverse incentives may exist. Consider, Waste Masters, whose current market-

[9] See, for example, Weiss in the end-of-chapter references.

value-based balance sheet is:

Cash	$100	Debt	$115
Other assets	25	Equity	10

The debt matures in one year at $200, but because of the high risk of Waste Masters, its current market value is only $115.

Two investment projects are available for Waste Masters—a low-risk project and a high-risk one.

	Low-Risk			**High-Risk**	
Today	**Possible Payoffs Next Year**		**Today**	**Possible Payoffs Next Year**	
	$160 (probability of 0.40)			$400 (probability of 0.20)	
$100			$100		
	$90 (probability of 0.60)			$0 (probability of 0.80)	

At a discount rate of 10 percent, the net present value of the low-risk project is $7.27, while the NPV of the high-risk project is -27.27. Clearly, any ordinary firm would accept the low-risk project and reject the high-risk project.

But, from the stockholders' standpoint there is no benefit from accepting the low-risk project because it doesn't provide enough cash inflow even to pay off the debt, let alone benefit the stockholders. The stockholders conclude that the low-risk project should be rejected and the high-risk project accepted. By accepting the high-risk project, if the project hits and produces the payoff of $400, the bondholders can be paid off and the stockholders walk away with the rest. Financial managers who act solely in the interest of the firm's stockholders (and, therefore not in the interests of *all* of the firm's providers of capital) would clearly favor the high-risk project. In fact, they may even invest in negative net present value projects. This type of problem is typically referred to as the **asset substitution problem;** it was originated by Jensen and Meckling (1976).

Failing To Invest
Conflicts of interest between stockholders and bondholders can also lead to firms' failing to raise additional equity capital. Say a firm has a "sure" winner that will produce an NPV of $25 in one year on a $50 investment. As in our Waste Masters example, the bondholders' claim is substantial, and bondholders do not want to invest any more in the firm. Unlike Waste Masters, this firm does not have enough cash on hand to fund the project; the only way to undertake this sure winner is to issue equity capital. Why would the stockholders (either the existing or new stockholders) ever make the investment? All, or virtually all, of the NPV will be claimed by the bondhold-

ers when the stockholders walk away from the firm in one year. The answer is, they won't make the investment.

The general point is this: Holding other things constant, any increase in the value of a firm making positive-NPV investments is shared between stockholders and bondholders. When the debt claims are substantial relative to the equity claims, virtually all of the gains from making positive-NPV investments are captured by the bondholders. Thus, it may not be in the stockholders' best interests to contribute additional capital even if "sure" NPV projects are forgone. This **underinvestment** problem was first examined by Myers (1977). In fact, faced with the foregoing situation, stockholders would favor distributing the assets of the firm to them in the form of a massive cash dividend. That way, they claim part of the assets. Of course, their gain comes at the expense of the bondholders.[10]

Operational and Managerial Inefficiencies

There are other possible consequences of impending financial distress. There may be increased inefficiency caused by key employees leaving or having their attention diverted from managing the firm as an ongoing entity. Customers may cancel orders if they are worried about the ability of the firm to deliver the product or service. Or, there may be a tendency of the firm to skimp on employee training, product quality, research and development, or even pay less attention to the safety of the work environment. Whatever form they take, increased inefficiencies do affect firms that are undergoing periods of high financial distress. In order to survive, the firm sacrifices some important activities that it normally undertakes, even though by doing so it may simply be buying a little more time.

The sum of the direct and indirect costs associated with bankruptcy and financial difficulties are called **financial distress costs.** Financial distress costs can affect the firm directly and also lead to increased returns being demanded by both bondholders and stockholders. As bondholders perceive the probability of financial distress increasing, they may require a higher expected return. Likewise, stockholders face the same concerns; accordingly, they will also require a higher expected return before investing additional capital.

How high are the total direct and indirect costs of financial distress? Direct costs, as we mentioned earlier, are not very large. But when indirect costs are included, some estimates place the financial distress costs at 10 to 20 percent of a firm's value.[11] At that level, they are large enough to have an impact on the value of the firm. Although analysis of the costs of financial distress does not tell us what the firm's capital structure should be, it does suggest that firms with a greater probability of experiencing financial distress will borrow less.

AGENCY COSTS

Other transactions costs, as discussed originally in Chapter 1, may arise because of the presence of stockholders, managers, and bondholders. First, consider stockholders and managers. As long as the firm is owned and operated by a single entrepreneur, no

[10] This finding is exactly what we illustrated in Chapter 5 when we viewed the claims of both stockholders and bondholders on the firm in an option pricing context.
[11] See Altman or Cutler and Summers in the end-of-chapter references.

complications arise because management and the owner are the same person. In this situation, the entrepreneur maximizes his or her wealth by balancing the combination of wages, perquisites (or "perks") such as a company car, company jet, luxurious office, and so on, and the market value of the firm's common stock.

As the firm grows, however, the entrepreneur may meet financing needs by raising external funds, either by sharing ownership with others (issuing common stock) or by incurring debt financing. Furthermore, as the firm grows the providers of new capital (the principals) delegate decision-making authority to a separate management group (the agent). This delegation of decision-making authority may result in an agency problem if a conflict of interest arises between the agent and principal, or among the principals, that affects the firm's operations. Such conflicts can be resolved only by incurring agency costs.

As sole owner, the entrepreneur obtains part of his or her wealth through perks. In this situation, the owner not only receives all of the benefits of these perks but also bears all of their costs. However, if the entrepreneur sells part ownership of the firm to outsiders while retaining the management capacity, he or she has an incentive to increase perks. Now the entrepreneur will receive all of the benefits of these perks but will pay only his or her ownership fraction of their costs. If the new co-owners realize this agency problem before they buy into the firm, they will not be willing to pay as much for each share. The difference between the price of the share without and with the agency problem represents an agency cost that serves to reduce the value of the firm. On the other hand, the entrepreneur and the new co-owners may enter into a monitoring agreement to ensure that the entrepreneur acts in the best interest of *all* stockholders. In either case agency costs are incurred.[12] As the firm uses less equity and more debt, the agency costs of equity decrease.

Another form of an agency problem occurs between stockholders and bondholders. The fact that the bondholders' claims on the firm's income are fixed creates an incentive for stockholders to engage in riskier projects that transfer wealth from bondholders to stockholders, no matter what the possibility of financial distress. To prevent such expropriation of their wealth, bondholders will demand various types of restrictive covenants and monitoring devices (as discussed in Chapter 12). The cost of these instruments is another agency cost. As the use of debt increases, the agency costs of debt increase.

The impact of agency costs and their implication for the capital structure of the firm are shown in Figure 11.6. Note that the unlevered firm has agency costs—these are the agency costs of equity. For example, if the value of a firm with no debt and *in the absence of any agency costs* would be $500, and equity agency costs are $100 when the firm is unlevered (i.e., with no debt), then the observed value of the firm, V_U, is $500 − $100 = $400. As the firm adds debt, it reduces the agency costs of equity but increases the agency costs of debt. In the context of agency costs, the value of the firm is maximized at the point where total agency costs are minimized.

The analysis so far—which includes the tax subsidy associated with debt, personal taxes and other tax-related impacts, financial distress costs, and agency costs—is illus-

---

[12] The impact of executive compensation plans, which serve to align the interests of managers and owners, has also been examined as they relate to capital structure decisions. See, for example, Mehran or Smith and Watts in the end-of-chapter references.

Agency Costs and Financial Leverage

While the agency costs of equity decrease with increasing financial leverage, the agency costs of debt increase. The optimal capital structure, in the absence of other considerations, minimizes total agency costs.

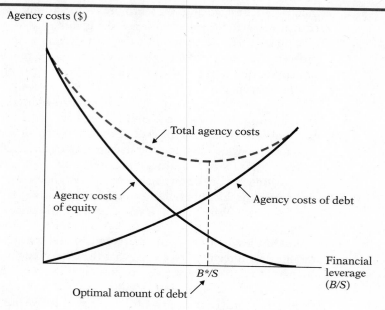

trated in Figure 11.7. In the MM tax model, once corporate taxes are considered, the value of the firm increases continuously as more debt is used. The value-maximizing firm would issue 100 percent debt. The introduction of personal taxes reduces the benefit of the interest tax shield somewhat, but firms still have an incentive to use more debt. However, once other tax-deductible items, such as depreciation and depletion, and the costs of financial distress and the agency costs are included, the total value of the firm becomes

$$V_L'' = V_U + \begin{matrix}\text{present value}\\ \text{of tax}\\ \text{savings}\end{matrix} - \left(\begin{matrix}\text{present value}\\ \text{of financial}\\ \text{distress costs}\end{matrix} + \begin{matrix}\text{present value}\\ \text{of}\\ \text{agency costs}\end{matrix} \right) \quad (11.18)$$

where

$$V_U = \text{the unlevered value of the firm}$$
$$\text{tax savings} = TB - \text{non-debt tax shields}$$
$$\text{financial distress costs} = \text{costs which depend on the probability and costs}$$
$$\text{associated with financial distress}$$
$$\text{agency costs} = \text{agency costs of equity} + \text{agency costs of debt}$$

The tax impacts are shown in Figure 11.7(a), and the additional impact of transactions costs, in the form of financial distress and agency costs, is shown in part (b) of Figure

Figure 11.7

Gains from Leverage, Tax Aspects, and Transactions Costs

Part (a) indicates the gains from leverage considering taxes (as previously shown in Figure 11.4). Part (b) introduces the additional impact of transactions costs, in the form of financial distress and agency costs. Based on all of these factors, an optimal capital structure may exist.

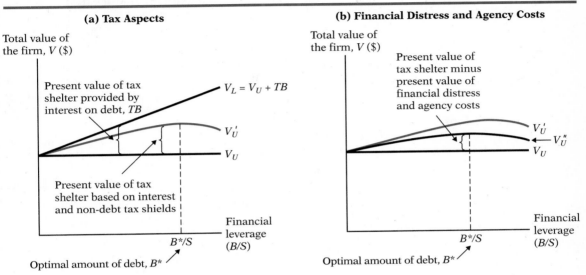

11.7. Under this scenario there may be an optimal debt/equity ratio, B^*/S, where the value of the firm is maximized. This optimum ratio, or more likely a range of alternative, almost equally desirable levels of financial leverage, would be such that substituting one more dollar of debt for equity would raise the costs more than the benefits. Similarly, cutting back would lower the costs by less than the benefits are reduced.

Concept Review Questions

- Describe some types of bankruptcy costs.
- Give an example of why stockholders might prefer to accept a negative net present value project over a positive net present value project.
- Give some examples of financial distress costs.
- How is Miller and Modigliani's tax model affected by the presence of financial distress and agency costs?

IMPACT ON CAPITAL INVESTMENT DECISIONS

In the last section we examined transactions costs in the form of financial distress and agency issues. One topic that crept in was incentives either to overinvest or underinvest that exist under certain conditions. A related argument on the interrelations between the capital structure and capital investment decisions arises when we consider a signaling approach to capital structure decisions.

SIGNALING

An alternative approach to examining the capital structure issue is based on the premise that managers as insiders have information—often called asymmetric information—that outside investors do not have access to. When financial markets react to the actions of firms as signs of insider information, **signaling** occurs. Thus, the choice of a capital structure can convey information about the firm to investors and cause a change in the value of the firm.

Ross (1977) developed a model in which the capital structure decision signals the firm's future prospects. Suppose there are two identical firms that investors see no difference between. Managers for both firms have information that has not been revealed to the financial markets. Suppose one firm has substantially better prospects than the other firm. By issuing debt, the firm with the better prospects signals this information to the financial markets. Under the Ross signaling model, increases in firm value (due to the previously unrevealed prospects) would be associated with increased debt issuance.

An alternative signaling model by Leland and Pyle (1977) is based on the idea that firms with "great" NPV projects will want to keep the proceeds of such projects to themselves, rather than share them with either new equity investors or debt investors. Under the Leland and Pyle model, the percentage of owner financing (as represented by the amount of the firm owned by insiders and the financing they provide) may be a credible signal of the future prospects of the firm.

These ideas have been further developed by Myers and Majluf (1984). They presented a model in which the current market value of the firm is considered along with new investment projects. Let's think first about the impact of the firm's current market value on its financing decisions. If the current shareholders of the firm perceive it as being overvalued at its present price, they would like some additional equity partners to share in the decline in the value of the firm. In that case, they would prefer to see additional common stock issued to finance any needs. On the other hand, if they consider the firm to be undervalued, existing common shareholders do not want additional equity partners to share in the expected increase in the market value of the firm.

What happens if we add new investment projects in our consideration of the current market value of the firm? Suppose a firm is undervalued by the market and the firm has a "good" investment project but can finance it only by issuing equity. The cost of the new financing may be so much that the new investors capture more than the NPV of the new project, resulting in a net loss to existing stockholders. Hence, the firm would bypass this "good" investment project. This underinvestment can be avoided if the firm finances the project with debt (that is not too risky) or internally generated funds. The ideas of Myers and Majluf have been carried forward by various researchers.[13]

While many different models and conclusions have been suggested, the important point to remember is that *with a signaling approach, capital structure becomes more of*

---

[13] Krasker (1986), Narayanan (1988), and Heinkel and Zechner (1990) all obtain results similar to Myers and Majluf. However, Brennan and Kraus (1987), Noe (1988), and Constantinides and Grundy (1989) show that by allowing a wider range of financing choices, some of the results suggested by Myers and Majluf can be invalidated.

a dynamic, ongoing, evolving decision. There is not a single optimal level of debt, because managers continually have access to information before it is available to outside investors. And, depending on the nature of the information, managers may choose to issue debt or equity in amounts that will at one time push the firm toward an optimal debt/equity ratio or range while at another time may push the firm away from an optimal debt/equity ratio or range.

CAPITAL STRUCTURE IMPACTS ON FIRM VALUE

Earlier we indicated that the importance of the Modigliani and Miller no-tax model is that (1) it presented a theoretical, rigorous statement of the value of the firm, where none existed before, and (2) it tells us where to look to determine if the firm's capital structure affects the value of the firm. The MM no-tax case says that:

If there are no taxes,

if there are no transactions costs, and

if the investment (or capital budgeting) policies of the firm are fixed,

then capital structure does not affect a firm's value.

We have examined each of these three possibilities and concluded that arguments can and have been made about possible relationships between a firm's capital structure and its market value. Although neither executives nor academicians agree on all of the details, the bottom line on the impact of capital structure on the value of the firm is simple and straightforward: Due to tax impacts, transactions costs in the form of financial distress or agency costs, and interactions between capital structure and capital investment decisions, firms choose capital structures with more than zero debt and less than 100 percent debt. With this in mind, we will explore capital structure differences and applications in Chapter 12.

Concept Review Questions

■ What is signaling and how it is related to corporate capital structure?

■ What factors lead to capital structure impacting the market value of the firm?

KEY POINTS

1. In the absence of taxes and other financial market imperfections, the choice of a capital structure is "a mere detail." The value of the firm is a function of the investment decisions it makes, not its financing decisions.
2. There are three places to look when examining the possible impact of capital structure decisions on the value of the firm: taxes, transactions costs, and interrelationships between the firm's financing decisions and its capital investment decisions.
3. Once corporate taxes are introduced, the firm can increase its total value and reduce its opportunity cost of capital by replacing equity financing with debt financing.
4. If the effective personal tax rate on stock income is less than the effective personal tax rate on bond income, there is less advantage to the firm from using debt financing than implied by the MM tax case.

5. The presence of non-debt tax shields, bond clienteles with different effective tax rates, and different maturity structures of debt suggests that firms will not employ as much debt as indicated by the MM tax case.
6. Transactions costs include financial distress costs and agency costs. The direct costs of bankruptcy are "small" (relatively speaking); however, once risk shifting, failure to invest, and other operational and managerial inefficiencies are considered, the costs of financial distress may be as high as 10 to 20 percent of firm value. At that level they may affect a firm's capital structure decisions. Agency costs can also lead to firms' using less than 100 percent debt.
7. Both signaling and financial distress arguments indicate there may be interactions between a firm's financing decisions and its capital structure decisions.
8. Because of taxes, transactions costs, and interactions between financing and investment decisions, firms choose capital structures that have more than zero debt and less than 100 percent debt.

QUESTIONS

11.1   In a world of no corporate taxes, the capital structure is a "mere detail." Explain why and under what conditions this is so.

11.2   "Investment decisions are all that are relevant; financing decisions have no significant impact on the value of the firm." Evaluate this statement.

11.3   Assume the MM no-tax model holds. A firm exists that has 20 percent of its capital structure in the form of debt which has a cost of 6 percent. Now the firm moves to 60 percent debt in its capital structure, again with a cost of 6 percent. What two effects occur as the firm moves from 20 percent debt to 60 percent debt? How do these effects counterbalance each other?

11.4   What happens when corporate taxes are introduced into the capital structure decision? Other things being equal, what should the firm do?

11.5   Compare the Modigliani and Miller no-tax case with the MM tax case. What similarities and differences are there between the two cases? What happens to the overall cost of capital under the no-tax case? Under the tax case? What limit does it approach in the tax case? What are the unlevered and levered costs of equity capital under the no-tax case? Under the tax case?

11.6   Taxes come in many shapes and forms. Explain how corporate taxes affect the capital structure decision. Then incorporate personal taxes into the discussion. What is the impact of non-debt tax shields on the interest tax shield? What other tax-based considerations also may come into play that affect a firm's capital structure decision?

11.7   Explain Miller's personal tax model. Under what circumstances does it lead to the same conclusion as MM without corporate taxes? With corporate taxes?

11.8   What risk shifting, failure to invest, or other problems may arise when the probability of financial distress is high?

11.9   What are agency costs? What two types are evident? How do they affect the capital structure decision of the firm?

11.10   Firms may signal their intentions (or the state of the firm) to the investment community through their actions. What kinds of signals exist when capital structure decisions are considered?

11.11   Explain how financial decisions and capital structure decisions may be related to one another.

11.12   The Modigliani and Miller no-tax model tells us that (1) if there are no taxes, (2) if there are no transactions costs, and (3) if the investment (or capital budgeting) policies of the firm are fixed, then capital structure does not affect a firm's value. Provide a complete discussion of the theoretical aspects of capital structure and its possible impact on the value of the firm.

CONCEPT REVIEW PROBLEMS

See Appendix A for solutions.

CR11.1   Bristol Brush operates without debt, has EBIT of $4.5 million, and an opportunity cost of capital of 15 percent.

a.   If the firm's earnings have a zero growth rate and all the MM assumptions are met, including no corporate taxes, what is the market value of the firm?

b.   Now assume Bristol issues $15 million in perpetual 10 percent bonds and uses the $15 million to retire equity in the firm. What are the cost of equity, the opportunity cost of capital, and the total value of the newly leveraged firm? Was Bristol's management able to increase the value of the firm by financing with cheaper debt?

Now assume that all the facts given in CR11.1 continue to hold, except Bristol Brush now has a corporate tax rate of 40 percent. What are the value of the firm, the cost of equity, and the opportunity cost of capital for the firm: (a) before issuing debt, and (b) after issuing debt under the MM tax case?

CR11.3   Sandra is analyzing two firms —Unleveraged Partners and Leveraged Partners. Unleveraged Partners is totally financed with equity, whereas Leveraged Partners believes the value of the firm can be increased with the use of debt and has $60 million of 8 percent bonds outstanding. The cost of equity for Unleveraged Partners is 12 percent. Both firms have EBIT of $30 million and a corporate tax rate of 32 percent. The marginal personal tax rate for all individuals is 28 percent on debt income and 20 percent on equity income.

a.   Employing the Miller model, what is the value of each firm? Is there a gain from the use of debt?

b.   Now assume Congress passes a law instituting a flat tax rate of 30 percent for all corporate and individual income. What is the value of each firm? Is there a change in the gain from the use of debt?

CR11.4   High Stakes Industries has had a long string of bad luck. All the firm's assets have been wiped out except for $100,000 in cash. On the liability side, the firm has debt of $150,000 due in 1 year. Two investment opportunities requiring an investment of $100,000 each and having a 1 year payoff are available. The first project has a 20 percent probability of having a $200,000 cash flow and an 80 percent probability of having an $80,000 cash flow in 1 year. The second project has a 50 percent chance of receiving $130,000 and a 50 percent chance of receiving $110,000 in 1 year. The opportunity cost of capital is 15 percent.

a.   What are the expected cash flows and standard deviation of the cash flows for each project?
b.   What is the NPV of each project?
c.   If you are a stockholder, which project would you prefer? If you are a bondholder which project would you prefer?

CR11.5   Edgar Ltd. is an unlevered firm with a constant EBIT of $10 million per year. The corporate tax rate is 40 percent, and the cost of equity is 15 percent. Management is considering the use of debt that would cost the firm 10 percent regardless of the amount used. The firm's management asked a consulting firm to estimate the cost of financial distress and the probability of these costs for each level of debt. The estimated present value of future financial distress is

$10 million and the probability of financial distress would increase with leverage as follows:

Value of Debt (in millions)	Probability of Distress
$ 0	0%
20	5
25	10
30	15
35	30
40	60
45	90

Using the MM model with corporate taxes, what is the optimal amount of debt for Edgar (without and with financial distress)?

PROBLEMS

11.1   Paul will invest $50,000 in a stock by borrowing (B) $30,000 and putting up $20,000 ($S$) himself. The cost of debt, k_b, is 8 percent, and there are no taxes. Paul expects a return, k_s^L, of 17 percent. What would Paul's return be without the use of financial leverage?

11.2   Scott Power is an electric utility that operates in a taxless world. It currently has $50 million in EBIT, $200 million in 5 percent coupon-rate bonds outstanding, and $400 million in stock outstanding.

a.   Determine the firm's yearly interest and earnings, and the firm's cost of equity capital, k_s^L. What is the opportunity cost of capital?

b.   Scott has decided to issue $100 million in stock and use the proceeds to buy back $100 million in bonds. What must the new cost of equity capital be according to Modigliani and Miller? What is the firm's overall opportunity cost of capital?

11.3   Assume that the MM tax case holds. The market value of a firm that has $300,000 in debt is $1,200,000. The interest rate on debt is 12 percent, and the marginal corporate tax rate is 30 percent. If the firm was all-equity-financed, the required return (or cost of equity capital) would be 18 percent.

a.   What is the firm's EBIT?

b.   What would the market value be if the firm is all-equity-financed?

11.4   Rollins International is an all-equity firm that generates earnings before interest and taxes, EBIT, of $3 million per year. The cost of equity capital, k_s^U, is 16 percent, and its marginal tax rate, T, is 35 percent.

a.   What is the market value of Rollins International?

b.   If Rollins now issues $4 million of debt, what is the market value of the firm? The market value of the firm's stock?

c.   What assumptions are you making in order to come up with your answers in (b)?

11.5 Assume that the MM tax case holds. A firm with EBIT of $2 million is in the 40 percent tax bracket. Its cost of debt is 10 percent, it pays $500,000 per year in interest, and its unlevered cost of equity capital is 15 percent.

a. What is the market value of the firm?
b. What is its levered cost of equity?

11.6 Goering Brothers is an unlevered firm with an EBIT of $4 million. Its tax rate is 40 percent, and the opportunity cost of equity capital is 15 percent. Assume that the MM tax case holds and that Goering is fairly valued.

a. What is the market value of Goering?
b. Suppose that Goering now issues $10 million of 8 percent bonds. What is the new market value of Goering?
c. Assume that there are two firms, Y and Z, that are identical in all respects to the unlevered Goering and the levered Goering, respectively. Explain what will happen if the current market value of Y is $14 million, while that of Z is $23 million.

11.7 Appalachian Industries is presently an all-common-stock-financed firm, with 8,000 shares of common stock outstanding and a tax rate of 35 percent. Assume the MM tax case holds. The firm is evaluating two different financing plans, as follows:

Common Stock	Debt
2,000 additional shares	$60,000 at an 8% coupon rate
$k_s^U = 10\%$	$k_s^L = 10.2727\%$
EBIT = $50,000	EBIT = $50,000

a. If common stock is employed, what is (**1**) the total stock value, S, (**2**) earnings per share, EPS, (**3**) the market price per share, P_0, (**4**) total value of the firm, V, and (**5**) its overall opportunity cost of capital?
b. Rework (a) if debt financing is employed.
c. Explain why, in the absence of financial distress and agency costs, the firm may be able to lower its opportunity cost of capital and raise the total value of the firm by employing debt financing.

11.8 Debt-Free Co. is an unlevered firm that has an equilibrium market value of $7 million. The firm is contemplating issuing $4 million of 10 percent coupon bonds. The firm has a corporate tax rate of 30 percent and has estimated that the tax rates for its investors are 20 percent on stock income and 25 percent on bond income. Assume that Miller's personal tax case holds.

a. If only corporate taxes exist, what is the new total value of the firm and the gain from leverage?
b. With both corporate and personal taxes, what is the gain from leverage and the total value of the firm?
c. Why is the gain from leverage (or, alternatively, the total value of the firm) less in (b) than in (a)?

11.9   A firm has long-term debt outstanding with a market value of $100,000. The corporate tax rate is 40 percent. Assume that Miller's personal tax case holds.

a.   If there are no personal taxes, what is the value of the interest tax shield?

b.   Now assume that personal taxes exist and the tax rate on bond income is twice the tax rate on stock income. At what personal tax rate on stock income does the advantage of debt financing vanish?

c.   If the actual personal tax rate on stock income is 25 percent, and the relationship between personal taxes on stock and bond income from (b) still exists, what does this imply about the optional level of debt for the firm?

11.10   Benefit Mutual has $20 million of debt outstanding. The firm has a corporate tax rate of 40 percent. A survey by its investment banker has revealed that the marginal tax rate of the firm's common stockholders (average of dividends and capital gains) is 15 percent, whereas the marginal tax rate on bond income is 30 percent.

a.   What is the firm's gain from using the $20 million of debt?

b.   What would the gain to the firm be if all of its investors paid no taxes?

11.11   Mini Case   Port Howard Products is presently an all-equity firm. It needs to raise $2,500,000 in additional funds. After raising the funds it expects EBIT to be $600,000. The firm's unlevered cost of equity capital, k_s^U, is 12 percent, and its before-tax cost of debt, k_b, is 8 percent.

a.   If there are no corporate taxes, under MM what is the value of Port Howard Products if it employs common stock to raise the needed funds? Alternatively, what happens to k_s and the value of the firm if it employs debt to raise the needed funds? What happens to its opportunity cost of capital? What is the fundamental determinant of the value of the firm in the MM no-tax case?

b.   Now assume that the corporate tax rate is 35 percent.

(1)   What is the all-equity value of Port Howard Products?
(2)   What is its value if $2,500,000 in debt is employed? What is the new k_s^L? The new opportunity cost of capital?
(3)   What if everything is as in (2) except that now $4,000,000 in debt is employed?

c.   So far the impact of personal tax has been ignored.

(1)   What is Miller's argument concerning the impact of personal taxes?
(2)   If everything is as in (b2), and the personal tax rates on debt and equity are both 40 percent, what is the value of Port Howard Products?
(3)   What if everything is as in (c2) except now the personal tax rate on stock is 20 percent?
(4)   Under what conditions, even after considering personal taxes, do we arrive at the same conclusion implied by the MM no-tax case? If T is 25 percent, and T_{pb} is 40 percent, what would the personal tax rate on stock, T_{ps}, have to be for the value of the firm to be independent of the firm's capital structure?

d.   In addition to the MM and Miller arguments, a number of other factors have been cited as affecting the firm's capital structure decision. Provide a complete discussion of other possible factors and how they affect the capital structure decision. Then indicate what conclusions can be reached from capital structure theory.

REFERENCES

Some of the key articles in this area are:

DEANGELO, HARRY, and RONALD W. MASULIS. "Optimal Capital Structure Under Corporate and Personal Taxation." *Journal of Financial Economics* 8 (March 1980): 3–30.

JENSEN, MICHAEL C., and WILLIAM H. MECKLING. "Theory of the Firm: Managerial Behavior, Agency Costs and Ownership Structure." *Journal of Financial Economics* 3 (October 1976): 305–60.

MILLER, MERTON H. "Debt and Taxes." *Journal of Finance* 32 (May 1977): 261–75.

MODIGLIANI, FRANCO, and MERTON H. MILLER. "Corporate Income Taxes and the Cost of Capital: A Correction." *American Economic Review* 53 (June 1963): 433–43.

_____ "The Cost of Capital, Corporation Finance, and the Theory of Investment." *American Economic Review* 48 (June 1958): 261–97.

MYERS, STEWART C., and NICHOLAS S. MAJLUF. "Corporate Financing and Investment Decisions When Firms Have Information That Investors Do Not Have." *Journal of Financial Economics* 13 (June 1984): 187.

Three sources that provide an overview of capital structure theory are:

BARNEA, AMIR, ROBERT A. HAUGEN, and LEMMA W. SENBET. *Agency Problems and Financial Contracting.* Englewood Cliffs, NJ: Prentice-Hall, 1985.

HARRIS, MILTON, and ARTHUR RAVIV. "The Theory of Capital Structure." *Journal of Finance* 46 (March 1991): 297–355.

MASULIS, RONALD W. *The Debt/Equity Choice.* Cambridge, Mass.: Ballinger, 1988.

Of the many articles on capital structure, some key or recent ones include:

ALTMAN, EDWARD I. "A Further Empirical Investigation of the Bankruptcy Cost Question." *Journal of Finance* 39 (September 1984): 1067–89.

BERKOVITCH, ELAZAR, and E. HAN KIM. "Financial Contracting and Leverage Induced Over- and Under-Investment Incentives." *Journal of Finance* 45 (July 1990): 765–94.

BRENNAN, MICHAEL, and ALAN KRAUS. "Efficient Financing Under Asymmetric Information." *Journal of Finance* 42 (December 1987): 1225–43.

CHANG, CHUN. "Capital Structure as an Optimal Contract Between Employees and Investors." *Journal of Finance* 47 (July 1992): 1141–58.

CONSTANTINIDES, GEORGE M., and BRUCE D. GRUNDY. "Optimal Investment with Stock Repurchases and Financing as Signals." *Review of Financial Studies* 2 (1989): 445–65.

CUTLER, DAVID M., and LAWRENCE H. SUMMERS. "The Costs of Conflict Resolution and Financial Distress: Evidence from the Texaco-Pennzoil Litigation." *Rand Journal of Economics* 19 (Summer 1988): 157–72.

EMERY, DOUGLAS R., and ADAM K. GEHR, JR. "Tax Options, Capital Structure, and Miller Equilibrium: A Numerical Illustration." *Financial Management* 17 (Summer 1988): 30–40.

HEINKEL, ROBERT, and JOSEF ZECHNER. "The Role of Debt and Preferred Stock as a Solution to Adverse Investment Incentives." *Journal of Financial and Quantitative Analysis* 25 (March 1990): 1–24.

KRASKER, WILLIAM. "Stock Price Movements in Response to Stock Issues Under Asymmetric Information." *Journal of Finance* 41 (March 1986): 93–105.

LELAND, HAYNE, and DAVID PYLE. "Information Asymmetries, Financial Structure, and Financial Intermediation." *Journal of Finance* 32 (May 1977): 371–88.

LEWIS, CRAIG M. "A Multiperiod Theory of Corporate Financial Policy under Taxation." *Journal of Financial and Quantitative Analysis* 25 (March 1990): 25–43.

MEHRAN, HAMID. "Executive Incentive Plans, Corporate Control, and Capital Structure." *Journal of Financial and Quantitative Analysis* 27 (December 1992): 539–60.

MYERS, STEWART C. "Determinants of Corporate Borrowing." *Journal of Financial Economics* 5 (November 1977): 147–75.

NARAYANAN, M. P. "Debt Versus Equity Under Asymmetric Information." *Journal of Financial and Quantitative Analysis* 23 (March 1988): 39–51.

NOE, THOMAS H. "Capital Structure and Signaling Game Equilibria." *Review of Financial Studies* 1 (Winter 1988): 331–55.

PARK, SANG YONG, and JOSEPH WILLIAMS. "Taxes, Capital Structure, and Bondholder Clienteles." *Journal of Business* 58 (April 1985): 203–24.

PINEGAR, J. MICHAEL, and LISA WILBRICHT. "What Managers Think of Capital Structure Theory: A Survey." *Financial Management* 18 (Winter 1989): 82–91.

ROSS, STEPHEN. "The Determination of Financial Structure: The Incentive-Signalling Approach." *Bell Journal of Economics* 8 (Spring 1977): 23–40.

SMITH, CLIFFORD W., JR., and ROSS L. WATTS. "The Investment Opportunity Set and Corporate Financing, Dividend, and Compensation Policies." *Journal of Financial Economics* 32 (December 1992): 263–92.

WEISS, LAWRENCE A. "Bankruptcy Dissolution: Direct Costs and Violation of Priority and Claims." *Journal of Financial Economics* 27 (October 1990): 285–314.

ZECHNER, JOSEF. "Tax Clienteles and Optimal Capital Structure under Uncertainty." *Journal of Business* 63 (October 1990): 465–91.

APPENDIX

Value of the Levered Firm

In the chapter we saw how to value the levered firm: first, for the MM model where only corporate taxes are considered, and second for Miller's model where both corporate and personal taxes are included. In this appendix, we will see how two of the equations necessary for those calculations are derived.

VALUE OF THE LEVERED FIRM WITH CORPORATE TAXES

To understand how Equation 11.10 comes about, we return to the example of NewWest Industries. NewWest has a tax rate of 30 percent, EBIT of $100,000, and $400,000 of

6 percent coupon rate bonds outstanding. Its condensed income statement is

EBIT	$100,000
Interest ($k_b B$)	24,000
EBT	76,000
Taxes (30%)	22,800
EAT	$ 53,200

In this situation the payment to *all* investors of the levered firm is made up of two components: the $53,200 paid to stockholders, which may be represented as $(EBIT - k_b B)(1 - T)$, and the $24,000 [i.e., ($400,000)(0.06)] in interest, $k_b B$, paid to bondholders. Therefore, the payment to all investors of the levered firm is

$$\text{payment to all investors}_L = (EBIT - k_b B)(1 - T) + k_b B$$

which may be rearranged to read

$$\text{payment to all investors}_L = (EBIT)(1 - T) + Tk_b B \tag{11A.1}$$

To find the value of the levered firm, V_L, we determine the present value of Equation 11A.1. Note that the first term on the right-hand side of Equation 11A.1, $(EBIT)(1 - T)$, is identical to Equation 11.8. This is the payment made to the investors of the unlevered firm and, therefore, is discounted at the required return for the unlevered firm, k_s^U, as we did in Equation 11.9. The second term on the right-hand side of Equation 11A.1 represents the tax shield, or subsidy, provided by the interest payment on debt. Because all debt is assumed to be riskless in the Modigliani-Miller model, and assuming it is perpetual, the present value of the debt tax shield can be found by dividing it by k_b. The value of the levered firm is

$$V_L = \frac{EBIT(1 - T)}{k_s^U} + \frac{Tk_b B}{k_b} \tag{11A.2}$$

Because the first term on the right-hand side is identical to Equation 11.9, which is the value of the unlevered firm, and the k_b's cancel in the second term, Equation 11A.2 can be rewritten as

$$V_L = V_U + TB \tag{11A.3}$$

which is Equation 11.10, the value of the levered firm according to the MM corporate tax model.

VALUE OF THE LEVERED FIRM WITH CORPORATE AND PERSONAL TAXES

A similar approach can be used to find the value of the levered firm for Miller's model. In addition to a corporate tax rate, T, Miller's model also includes a personal tax rate on stock income, T_{ps}, and a personal tax rate on bond income, T_{pb}.

The payments to all investors in the levered firm are made up of two parts, and may be written as follows:

$$\text{payment to all investors}_L = (EBIT - k_b B)(1 - T)(1 - T_{ps}) + k_b B(1 - T_{pb}) \qquad (11A.4)$$

where the first term is equal to the payment received by stockholders after both corporate and personal taxes have been deducted, and the second term is the after-personal-tax interest payment that the bondholders receive. Equation 11A.4 can be rearranged as follows:

$$\begin{matrix}\text{payment to} \\ \text{all investors}_L\end{matrix} = EBIT(1 - T)(1 - T_{ps}) - k_b B(1 - T)(1 - T_{ps}) + k_b B(1 - T_{pb}) \qquad (11A.5)$$

The first term of Equation 11A.5 is identical to the after-tax payment that the stockholders of an unlevered firm would receive. The present value of this term is found by discounting it by k_s^U, as we did in Equation 11.9. The second term represents the payment that stockholders forgo by having debt outstanding, and the third term is the after-personal-tax payment received by bondholders. Because debt is assumed to be risk-free and perpetual, the present value of these two terms is obtained by dividing them by k_b. The value of the levered firm is

$$V_L = \frac{EBIT(1 - T)(1 - T_{ps})}{k_s^U} - \frac{k_b B(1 - T)(1 - T_{ps})}{k_b} + \frac{k_b B(1 - T_{pb})}{k_b} \qquad (11A.6)$$

The first term in Equation 11A.6 represents the value of an unlevered firm, V_U; therefore, after we cancel k_b's in the second and third terms, Equation 11A.6 may be written as

$$V_L = V_U - B(1 - T)(1 - T_{ps}) + B(1 - T_{ps}) \qquad (11A.7)$$

which in turn, may be rearranged to

$$V_L = V_U + [(1 - T_{pb}) - (1 - T)(1 - T_{ps})]B$$

If we divide both terms in the squared bracket by $(1 - T_{pb})$, we obtain

$$V_L = V_U + \left[1 - \frac{(1 - T)(1 - T_{ps})}{(1 - T_{pb})}\right]B \qquad (11A.8)$$

which is Equation 11.16, the value of the levered firm for Miller's model.

12

Capital Structure Applications

EXECUTIVE SUMMARY

Firms do not employ almost 100 percent debt financing as suggested by the MM corporate tax model. The pecking order theory and observation of financial practice both suggest the capital structure decision is dynamic, sometimes involving equity and sometimes debt, as firms act as if they have a target capital structure.

The amount of financial leverage employed by firms is not constant, but varies over time. Likewise, there are substantial differences in the amount of debt employed among different industries and, often, between firms within industries. The ability to use tax shields and asset uniqueness are important considerations in determining a firm's debt/equity ratio. The interests of stockholders and bondholders can be better aligned by using financing that has elements of both types of financing. In addition, protective covenants are important in dealing with agency problems. Capital structure decisions and the future fortunes of the firm in terms of free cash flow may interact. Additional factors, such as growth options, product or input effects, economic conditions, and corporate control, also affect the amount of debt used by firms.

In assessing the firm's capital structure, we have available a number of tools that come in handy. These include an analysis of the impact that changes in earnings before interest and taxes, EBIT, have on earnings per share, EPS; examination of coverage ratios; consideration of lender and bond rating standards; and an analysis of the firm's cash flow under different scenarios. Ultimately, the capital structure decision depends on the ability of the firm to take advantage of tax shields, the risk the firm is exposed to, and the necessity for financial slack.

CAPITAL STRUCTURE THEORY AND PRACTICE

In Chapter 11 we explored capital structure theory. We started with the Modigliani and Miller model, which argues that *the value of the firm is solely a function of its investment decisions.* As long as financing decisions (including the cash dividend decision, as discussed in Chapter 13) do not affect the investment decision, MM argue that in the absence of taxes and transactions costs the value of the firm is independent of its capital structure. We saw, once corporate taxes are introduced, that the government provides a subsidy to the firm in the form of an interest tax shield. That is, the direct costs of debt financing are tax-deductible, whereas the costs of equity financing are not. Smart firms would then employ almost 100 percent debt financing in order to take maximum advantage of the subsidy provided by the government. However, if Miller's personal tax argument is reasonable, the benefits of the interest tax shield are not as great as indicated by the MM corporate tax analysis.

In practice we do not see firms financing with virtually 100 percent debt. Why not? Capital structure theory suggests a number of reasons. First, interest is not the only deduction that firms have for tax purposes; they also have non-debt tax shields in the form of depreciation and depletion. If firms are not likely to take full advantage of the interest tax subsidy, they are less likely to employ as much debt. In addition, there are other tax-related factors that suggest limits exist on the amount of debt employed. Second, the sum of the direct and indirect costs of financial distress appear to be substantial enough to encourage firms to use less than 100 percent debt. Third, there are agency costs attached to ensuring that management acts in the interests of stockholders, and bondholders protect themselves from having their wealth expropriated by imposing protective covenants and monitoring devices. These agency costs also indicate that firms will be less than 100 percent debt-financed.

Signaling arguments also suggest that issuing equity provides a negative signal about the future prospects of the firm. If the prospects are so rosy, why share the anticipated benefits with new equity participants? In addition, there are indications that the firm's capital structure decision and its capital investment decisions are not always independent. In a dynamic context capital structure becomes an ongoing, evolving decision. These relationships are incorporated in the **pecking order theory**, which was developed by Myers (1984). The pecking order theory suggests that:

1. Firms prefer internal (equity) financing first because: (a) the total costs of obtaining new external financing are substantial and can be minimized by avoiding going to the financial markets more often than is absolutely necessary; and (b) by not going to the financial markets, specific attention is not drawn to the firm and its financial performance. (As discussed in Chapter 15, internal financing accounts for 75–80 percent of total financing for firms.) Poorly performing firms do not want to draw attention to themselves by having to sell a very expensive stock or bond issue which substantiates the lack of performance and/or weakness of the firm.

2. Firms prefer to pay cash dividends; hence some amount of cash flows out of the firm instead of funding capital investments. Under normal circumstances, reductions in the level of cash dividends are not viewed favorably by firms and their

common stockholders. In fact, firms favor a "sticky" dividend policy: they increase cash dividends only when they think the higher level of dividends can be maintained but are reluctant to cut dividends when times get tough.

3. Given sticky cash dividend policies, uncertainty about future cash inflows from operations, and uncertainty concerning the cash outflow needs for capital investments, *firms want some financial flexibility in terms of a cash reserve.* When times are flush they will pay down debt, repurchase stock, or make acquisitions. When times aren't so good, firms reduce the level of cash.

4. If external financing is needed, firms issue debt first. New equity financing is a last resort; both theoretical and empirical evidence indicates that by issuing equity the firm is signaling that its present and future prospects are not that strong.

The pecking order theory attempts to pull together what we know from financial theory and what we observe in practice. Firms appear to act much as described by the pecking order theory. They also act as if they have a target capital structure; that is, there is some target debt/equity ratio or range they attempt to stay close to over time.

In this chapter we focus first on *the effects* of capital structure decisions by examining actual debt/equity ratios. Then we turn our attention to *the factors* firms take into consideration in making capital structure decisions. We examine a number of factors consistent with differences in capital structures across industries and firms, along with certain actions taken to protect various interested parties. Finally, we discuss some tools for analysis. All of this leads to some simple and straightforward guidelines about what firms should look for when setting debt/equity ratios.

Concept Review Questions

■ Give some reasons why firms would not adopt a 100 percent debt level as hypothesized by Modigliani and Miller.

■ Explain the pecking order theory and how it affects corporate capital structure.

DEBT/EQUITY RATIOS IN PRACTICE

Before considering factors that are consistent with observed differences in capital structures, let's examine some actual debt/equity ratios. We know it is the market value of the firm that is important in finance; therefore, the ratio of debt to the *market value* of equity is of primary interest. However, many publications report the ratio of debt to the book value of equity. We examine both ratios.

AGGREGATE DEBT/EQUITY RATIOS

Figure 12.1 shows the two ratios—debt/book value of equity and debt/market value of equity for nonfarm, nonfinancial U.S. corporations for the 1960–1991 time period. Up to about 1972 the two ratios were about the same; after 1972 we see that the ratio of debt to the market value of equity was greater than the ratio of debt to book value

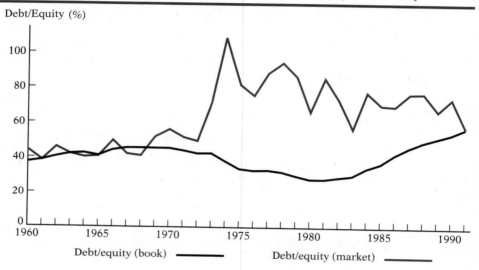

Figure 12.1

Ratio of Total Debt to Book Value Equity and Market Value Equity for U.S. Nonfarm, Nonfinancial Corporations, 1960–1991

From 1973 to 1991 there was substantial divergence between debt/equity ratios using the book value of equity versus using the market value of equity. [*Source*: Board of Governors of the Federal Reserve System. *Balance Sheets for the U.S. Economy, 1960–1991.*]

of equity. One important reason for the divergence between the ratio of debt/book value of equity and the ratio of debt/market value of equity is the fall in relative stock prices after the 1960s. Think of it this way: If the amount of debt remains constant, say at \$4, but the market value of equity falls from \$10 to \$5, the ratio of debt/market value of equity increases from \$4/\$10 = 40 percent to \$4/\$5 = 80 percent.

One way to gauge the level of relative stock prices is to look at average price/earnings (P/E) ratios, during various time periods. Using the Standard & Poor's 500 stock index, the average per year earnings and P/E ratios for three time periods selected to correspond with the time periods (from Figure 12.1) when debt/book value of equity and debt/market value of equity were closer together (or further apart) are as follows:

Time Period	Earnings	Average P/E Ratio
1960–1972	$ 4.89	17.9 times
1973–1982	11.57	9.4
1983–1991	18.35	14.4

Although earnings rose over the 1960–1991 time period, we see that for the 1960–1972 time period the average price/earnings ratio of 17.9 was much higher than that for the 1973–1982 period when it was 9.4 times earnings. Since 1983 the price/earnings ratio increased and averaged 14.4. Taking into account the decrease in relative stock prices, as reflected in lower P/E ratios during the 1973–1982 time period, we see that an important reason for the sharp increase in the ratio of debt/market value of equity (relative to debt ÷ book value of equity) was due to lower relative stock prices.

What accounts for the convergence of the debt/market value of equity and debt/book value of equity ratios in the late 1980s and early 1990s? One factor is the increase in the relative price of stocks as reflected by the higher P/E ratios; other things being equal, higher stock prices result in a lower ratio of debt/market value of equity. A second factor is that during the 1980s U.S. firms issued substantial amounts of net new debt financing (both short- and long-term), while they actually *retired more stock than they issued*. Three factors contributed to the net retirement of stock: numerous mergers which were often financed in large part with debt; leveraged buyouts in which publicly traded firms were taken private and often ended up with debt/book value of equity ratios consisting of up to $9 of debt for every $1 of equity; and swaps or exchanges of debt for outstanding common stock. The net result of these activities was to rely more heavily on debt in the late 1980s and the 1990s (as shown in Figure 12.1 by the increase in the debt/book value of equity ratio). We see that one of the important points to remember from Figure 12.1 is that over time the amount of debt relative to equity financing changes; that is, *firms do not always employ the same amount of financial leverage*.

INDUSTRY DEBT/EQUITY RATIOS

While it is important to understand overall debt/equity ratios, it is also important to examine debt/equity ratios for different types of firms. For simplicity we group firms based on their dominant industry, and we look at industry groupings of firms.[1] Table 12.1 shows the 3-year (1989–1991) average ratios of debt/book value of equity and debt/market value of equity for a number of different industries. An examination of this table indicates that: *(1) debt/book value of equity and debt/market value of equity figures are not the same, and (2) there are substantial differences in the use of debt among the industries examined (whether measured in book value or market value terms)*. For example, firms in metal mining, drugs and cosmetics, machinery, electronics, and instruments use substantially less debt in their capital structures than do firms in the construction, metal working, motor vehicle parts, trucking, and airline industries.

It is helpful to compare the results presented in Table 12.1 with the results of studies that examined the amount of debt employed by firms in different industries. Table 12.2 presents a summary of findings of some previous studies that examined the amount of financial leverage employed by firms in different industries. In Table 12.2 the designations of *low*, *medium*, and *high* were supplied on an *ad hoc* basis by the authors of the study from which the table is drawn.

---

[1] Although any "industry" grouping is by necessity arbitrary, such groupings are employed in both practice and empirical research. We employ 2-digit SIC (Standard Industrial Classification) codes in Table 12.1; however, other sources, like *Value Line Investment Service*, use ad hoc groupings of firms.

Table 12.1

Debt/Equity Ratios for Selected Industries, 1989–1991

The debt/equity ratios were computed from the Compustat data tapes based on firms that had a reasonable amount of equity and also had data available for all 3 years. Debt is defined as the total of short-term credit debt (i.e., bank loans, commercial paper, and the current portion of long-term debt) and long-term debt.

2-Digit SIC Code	Industry	Number of Observations	Mean (Debt/ Book Equity)	Mean (Debt/ Market Equity)
10	Metal mining	73	0.48	0.34
13	Petroleum exploration	149	0.59	0.40
15, 16, 17	Construction	43	1.03	1.10
20	Food	82	0.97	0.56
22	Textile mill products	36	0.93	0.94
23	Apparel	30	0.71	0.68
26	Paper	49	0.84	0.83
27	Publishing	66	0.78	0.62
28	Chemicals	68	0.73	0.46
2830 and 2840	Drugs and cosmetics	139	0.46	0.20
29	Petroleum refining	37	0.83	0.50
30	Rubber	55	0.75	0.76
33	Steel	63	0.76	0.85
34	Metal working	83	1.31	1.41
35	Machinery	275	0.64	0.57
36	Electronics	254	0.69	0.60
37	Motor vehicle parts	86	1.09	1.15
38	Instruments	243	0.57	0.40
42	Trucking	23	1.27	1.54
45	Airlines	15	1.57	1.05
49	Electric and gas utilities	233	1.20	0.86
53	Retail department stores	37	0.77	0.80
54	Retail grocery stores	24	1.22	0.84

Comparing the results for 1989–1991 from Table 12.1 and the results of the studies given in Table 12.2, we see that the general rankings of low, medium, and high from Table 12.2 apply fairly well to the findings for the 1989–1991 period presented in Table 12.1. However, there are some differences. In 1989–91 (Table 12.1) firms in both the rubber and retail department store industries look much more like medium-leverage firms, whereas in Table 12.2 these two industries were designated high-leverage industries. These and other differences might be due to differences in terms of the actual firms examined, how the debt ratios were calculated, or they might reflect fundamental shifts in capital structures over time. The important points are these: *(1) There are differences among industries in terms of the amount of debt em-*

Table 12.2

Industry Financial Leverage Rankings

A number of studies have examined the amount of debt used by firms in different industries. The low, medium, and high designations were arbitrarily made by Harris and Raviv. Some of the differences in ranking may be due to different time periods analyzed.

Industry	Bradley, Jarrell, and Kim[a]	Bowen, Daly, and Huber[b]	Long and Malitz[c]	Kester[d]
Drugs and cosmetics	Low		Low	Low
Instruments	Low		Low	Low
Metal mining	Low			
Publishing	Low			
Electronics	Low		Low	Low
Machinery	Low			Medium
Food	Low			Low
Petroleum exploration	Medium			
Construction	Medium			
Petroleum refining	Medium	Low	High	High
Metal working	Medium			
Chemicals	Medium	Medium		High
Apparel	Medium			Medium
Motor vehicle parts	Medium		Low	High
Paper	Medium		High	High
Textile mill products	High	Medium	High	Medium
Rubber	High			
Retail department stores	High	Medium		
Retail grocery stores	High	Medium		
Trucking	High			
Steel	High	Low	High	High
Telephone	High			
Electric and gas utilities	High			
Airlines	High	High		

Source: Adapted from Table III in Milton Harris and Arthur Raviv, "The Theory of Capital Structure," *Journal of Finance*, 46 (March 1991): 297–355. Footnotes from the original table are omitted.
[a] Michael Bradley, Gregg Jarrell, and E. Han Kim, "On the Existence of an Optimal Capital Structure: Theory and Evidence," *Journal of Finance* 39 (July 1984): 857–78.
[b] Robert M. Bowen, Lane A. Daly, and Charles C. Huber, Jr., "Evidence on the Existence and Determinants of Interindustry Differences in Leverage," *Financial Management* 11 (Winter 1982): 10–20.
[c] Michael Long and Ileen Malitz, "The Investment-Financing Nexus: Some Empirical Evidence," *Midland Corporate Finance Journal* 3 (Fall 1985): 53–59.
[d] Carl W. Kester, "Capital and Ownership Structure: A Comparison of United States and Japanese Manufacturing Operations," *Financial Management* 15 (Spring 1986): 5–16.

ployed, and (2) although shifts may occur, there is a good deal of consistency in terms of which industries use more or less debt over time.

DEBT/EQUITY RATIOS WITHIN AN INDUSTRY

It is also important to recognize that substantial differences in debt/equity ratios may exist between firms within the same industry. Table 12.3 presents debt/equity ratios for some firms in the chemical industry for 1989–1991. From Table 12.1 the average debt/book value of equity ratio for the 68 firms in the chemical industry is 0.73, whereas the debt/market value of equity ratio is 0.46. Looking at individual chemical firms in Table 12.3, we see that the following firms have less debt than the industry: Air Products & Chemicals, American Cyanamid, du Pont, Ethyl, Great Lakes Chemical, Hercules, Monsanto, Rohn & Haas, Sterling Chemicals, and Witco. At the other end of the spectrum, the following firms are using substantially more debt than the

Table 12.3

Debt/Equity Ratios for Selected Firms in the Chemical Industry, 1989–1991

These firms were selected from the 68 observations that were in the chemical group from Table 12.1. Therefore, these debt/equity ratios are directly comparable to those presented in Table 12.1.

Firm	Debt/Book Equity	Debt/Market Equity
Air Products & Chemicals	0.56	0.36
American Vanguard	1.03	0.73
American Cyanamid	0.33	0.15
Cabot	1.32	0.82
Dow Chemical	0.78	0.45
du Pont	0.54	0.31
Ethyl	0.63	0.22
W. R. Grace	1.16	0.82
Great Lakes Chemical	0.22	0.07
Grow Group	1.66	0.79
Hercules	0.42	0.44
ICN Biomedicals	1.25	0.70
IMC Fertilizer	0.71	0.57
Monsanto	0.55	0.30
Olin	1.10	0.76
PPG Industries	0.65	0.33
Rohm & Haas	0.54	0.27
Sterling Chemicals	0.66	0.21
Union Carbide	1.20	1.12
Witco	0.40	0.30

industry: American Vanguard, Cabot, W. R. Grace, Grow Group, ICN Biomedicals, Olin, and Union Carbide. Finally, Dow Chemical, IMC Fertilizer, and PPG Industries have capital structures close to the industry averages given in Table 12.1. The important point from Table 12.3, and it is the same for other industries, is that *although firms in different industries employ more or less debt, there are also substantial differences within an industry.*

Firms have different debt/equity ratios over time, between industries, and among firms in the same industry. These differences are the result of decisions made by financial managers. Thus, we know something about the *effects* of the capital structure decisions. But, how do we explain the differences—why, for example, do American Cyanamid and Great Lakes Chemical employ so much less debt than W. R. Grace and Olin? Our next task is to examine the *factors* that cause differences, and some of the items taken into consideration as firms make their capital structure decisions.

Concept Review Questions

- Give some examples of industries that make substantial use of debt and some that use little debt.
- Why might firms in the same industry use different amounts of debt?

USING MODIGLIANI AND MILLER TO IDENTIFY FACTORS AFFECTING CAPITAL STRUCTURE DECISIONS

In Chapter 11 we used Modigliani and Miller as a means of guiding our search for factors that may lead firms to adopt one capital structure as opposed to another. We will use the same structure to assist in understanding differences in actual capital structures by first looking at tax impacts, then financial distress and agency issues, and finally signaling and impacts on the firm's capital investment decisions.

TAXES

The ability to utilize tax shields to the fullest extent possible is one factor that explains differences in the amount of debt employed. Whereas Modigliani and Miller stressed the interest tax shield, DeAngelo and Masulis showed that non-debt tax shields in the form of depreciation and depletion are also important. The ability to take full advantage of all the tax shields provided by the government is one of the primary factors affecting capital structure differences. Although the tax code allows operating losses to be carried back for 3 years and then forward for up to 15 years, eventually firms may not be able to use the tax shields due to the lack of profitability. Thus, for a firm like American Ship Building, which has been unprofitable since 1987 and is not expected to recover soon (if ever), any additional tax shields quickly become meaningless. Likewise, XOMA, a biotech company, has been unprofitable since it went public in 1986. Tax shields are almost meaningless for firms such as these. Thus, it is not surprising XOMA has a debt/equity ratio of about 0.01.

FINANCIAL DISTRESS AND AGENCY CONSIDERATIONS

One of the continuing problems faced by firms is the divergent interests of stockholders, bondholders, and managers. These differences in terms of orientation can lead to a variety of activities that reduce the value of the firm. In discussing these activities as they affect capital structure decisions, we examine asset uniqueness, the use of convertible and subordinated debt, and protective covenants.

Asset Uniqueness

Firms whose principal assets are intangible in nature, such as those that rely on brain power (or human capital), research and development, product quality, brand name and advertising, and the like, have higher costs of financial distress. If the firm gets into financial difficulty, these intangible assets can dissipate quickly, due to individuals leaving the firm or simply due to neglect. Such firms include those in the computer, computer software, and drug industries. For this reason we see much less use of debt by firms such as Dell Computer, Hewlett-Packard, Bantec, Microsoft, Merck, and Syntex.

On the other hand, firms that have substantial physical assets which have a ready secondary market can carry more debt. If you are in the hotel business and fail, there is a ready secondary market for hotel rooms. Likewise, there is a market for grocery stores (people have to eat), airplanes, and numerous other physical assets. Thus, we see higher debt usage by firms such as Circus Circus, Marriott, Safeway, AMR (American Airlines), Federal Express, and Black & Decker.

The key issue is the potential loss in value if trouble comes. Some assets have a much better secondary market than others, which are likely to lose their value quickly. *It's not simply the probability of financial distress that is important; rather it's the potential loss in value of the assets.* Firms that would suffer a sizable loss in value of the assets tend to use less debt than those whose assets retain value.

Convertible and Subordinated Debt

One of the problems faced by firms is that the interests of stockholders and bondholders often diverge. Thus, as we discussed in Chapter 11, asset substitution or underinvestment problems may occur. One way to align the interests of the parties is to use financing that combines elements of both debt and equity. Convertible debt, which may be exchanged for common stock of the issuing firm, mitigates some of the divergent interests by combining elements of both debt and equity.[2] If the capital projects are a "success," the bondholders share in the upside benefits from investing in the capital projects. This is precisely why we often see smaller, younger firms, such as AZLA, GenRad, Michaels Stores, and Schuler Homes using convertible securities. Subordinated debt (i.e., debt that has a lower claim on assets in case of financial distress than other debt) has much the same effect, and it also tends to alleviate some of the divergent interests between bondholders and stockholders.

---

[2] Convertible bonds are discussed in Chapter 17.

Protection

Another important means of dealing with some of the divergent interests between bondholders and stockholders is the incorporation of **protective covenants** as part of the bond (or loan agreement).[3] These covenants are important because a violation of them can lead to the default of the issue. Four major sources of conflict between bondholders and stockholders are:

1. ASSET SUBSTITUTION   If firms sell bonds for a stated purpose and then use the funds from the bond offering to finance other, more risky projects, the value of the bondholder's claim is reduced. This is called asset substitution.
2. UNDERINVESTMENT   If all, or virtually all, of the benefits from a new capital investment accrue to the bondholders, firms (and the firm's stockholders) have an incentive to bypass positive net present value projects. This is referred to as the underinvestment problem.
3. CLAIM DILUTION   If the firm sells bonds under the assumption that no additional bonds will be issued, the value of the existing bondholders' claim is reduced by then issuing additional debt of the same or higher priority.
4. DIVIDEND PAYMENT   If the firm sells bonds with the assumption that the same level of dividends will be maintained, the value of the existing bondholders' claim is reduced by increasing the percentage of cash paid out as dividends.

In order to reduce these problems, all bonds and loan agreements have protective covenants written into them. While protective covenants cannot eliminate all sources of conflict between bondholders and stockholders, they can reduce financial distress and agency costs. Table 12.4 lists typical bond covenants, divided into four categories. First are those that deal with the firm's production and investing policies. These are followed by financing covenants, dividend covenants and, finally, bonding (or monitoring) covenants. Smith and Warner (1979) examined public issues of debt issued in 1974 and 1975 and found that 91 percent of them included covenants that restricted the issuance of additional debt, 23 percent restricted dividends, 39 percent restricted mergers, and 36 percent limited the sale of assets. Malitz (1986) studied senior nonconvertible debentures sold between 1960 and 1980 in terms of sinking fund provisions, limitations on future debt, and limitations on dividend payments. All of the bonds examined by Malitz had sinking fund provisions. Likewise, firms using more debt benefitted to a greater extent than firms using less debt from provisions limiting additional debt and dividend payments. Also, smaller firms, for which information asymmetry is more likely, were more inclined to include restrictions of debt and dividends. These covenants appear less important for larger firms, due to the larger number of financing options available to them, the greater availability of public information about the firms, and the constant scrutiny they face from the financial markets, security regulators, underwriters, and bond-rating agencies.

Although financial distress and agency problems cannot be alleviated entirely, the amount and types of financing employed by firms make more sense once we consider

---

[3] Bonds and loans are discussed in detail in Chapter 16.

Table 12.4

Some Typical Bond Covenants

Bond covenants are designed to address both financial distress and agency considerations.

I. Production/Investment Covenants

Restrictions on common stock investments, loans, extensions of credit, and advances

Restrictions on the disposition of assets

Secured debt that gives bondholders title to pledged assets until the bonds are paid in full

Restrictions on mergers

Requirements on the maintenance of assets

II. Covenants That Restrict Subsequent Financing Policy

Limitations on the issuance of any additional debt or on the priority of claim of new debt

Limitations on leases or sale-and-leasebacks

Inclusion of a sinking fund so the bondholders are paid off over time, rather than all at once at the maturity of the bond

Call provisions

III. Covenants That Restrict Payment of Dividends

Restrictions specifying the amount or source of funds that can be employed to pay dividends

Outright restrictions under certain circumstances

IV. Covenants That Reduce the Cost of Monitoring the Firm

Specification of required reports, such as annual and quarterly financial statements, having the reports audited, etc.

Specification of how certain restrictions will be computed

Certificates of compliance stating that the firm is fulfilling all of its obligations under the indenture

Required purchase of insurance

---

asset uniqueness, the alignment benefits of convertible securities, and the role played by protective covenants in terms of controlling some of the financial distress and agency costs.

SIGNALING, CAPITAL STRUCTURE, AND CASH FLOW

From a signaling standpoint, as well as from a financial distress/agency standpoint, we learned in Chapter 11 that there may be interactions between a firm's capital structure decisions and its capital investment decisions. Although our primary interest in this chapter is the firm's capital structure decision, our coverage would not be complete unless we consider some broader issues. First, we will look at the results of a number of studies that have examined how financial markets respond as firms take actions to either increase or decrease the amount of debt in their capital structure. Then we will examine how financial markets respond to actions that signal increased prospects for the firm (in the form of increased future cash flows) or diminished prospects (and reductions in expected cash flows).

Holding everything else constant, a firm could increase its reliance on debt either by issuing additional debt or by exchanging new debt for some of its outstanding common stock. Likewise, it could reduce its reliance on debt financing by issuing additional common stock or by exchanging new common stock for some of its outstanding debt. The first type of transaction is a leverage-increasing transaction, whereas the second is a leverage-reducing transaction. Table 12.5 summarizes the empirical results of a number of studies that examined leverage-increasing, leverage-

Table 12.5

Impact of Capital Structure Changes on the Value of Common Stock

The 2-day announcement period return indicates the increase (or decrease) in the stock price (or return) associated with the transaction. These transactions represent almost pure capital structure changes.

Type of Transaction	Security Issued	Security Retired	Average Sample Size	2-Day Announcement Period Return
Transactions that Increase Leverage				
Stock repurchase	Debt	Common	45	21.9%
Exchange offer	Debt	Common	52	14.0
Exchange offer	Preferred	Common	9	8.3
Exchange offer	Debt	Preferred	24	2.2
Exchange offer	Income bonds	Preferred	24	2.2
Transactions with No Change in Leverage				
Exchange offer	Debt	Debt	36	1.6*
Security sale	Debt	Debt	83	0.2*
Transactions that Reduce Leverage				
Conversion-forcing call	Common	Convertible preferred	57	−0.4*
Conversion-forcing call	Common	Convertible bond	113	−2.1
Security sale	Convertible debt	Debt	15	−2.4
Exchange offer	Common	Preferred	30	−2.6
Exchange offer	Preferred	Debt	9	−7.7
Security sale	Common	Debt	12	−4.2
Exchange offer	Common	Debt	20	−9.9

Source: Adapted from Table 3 in Clifford W. Smith, Jr. "Investment Banking and the Capital Acquisition Process," *Journal of Financial Economics* 15 (January/February 1986): 3–29. Footnotes from the original table are omitted.
*Not statistically different from zero.

neutral, and leverage-reducing transactions. The results presented in Table 12.5 (and other research on similar transactions) indicates the following: *(1) The stock market reacts positively to leverage-increasing transactions and negatively to leverage-reducing transactions, and (2) the larger the change in financial leverage, the greater the price reaction.*

Because of asymmetric information (that is, differences in information available to

---

Table 12.6

Impact of Implied Changes in Corporate Cash Flow on the Value of Common Stock

As in Table 12.5, the 2-day announcement period return indicates the increase (or decrease) in value. Changes in financing, investment policy, and cash dividend decisions are examined.

Type of Announcement	Average Sample Size	2-Day Announcement Period Return
Implied Increase in Expected Corporate Cash Flow		
Common stock repurchases:		
intra-firm tender offer	148	16.2%
open market repurchase	182	3.6
targeted small holding	15	1.6
Calls of non-convertible bonds	133	−0.1*
Dividend increases:		
dividend initiation	160	3.7
dividend increase	180	0.9
specially designated dividend	164	2.1
Investment increases	510	1.0
Implied Decrease in Expected Corporate Cash Flow		
Security sales:		
common stock	262	−1.6
preferred stock	102	0.1*
convertible preferred	30	−1.4
straight debt	221	−0.2*
convertible debt	80	−2.1
Dividend decreases	48	−3.6
Investment decreases	111	−1.1

Source: Adapted from Table 2 in Clifford W. Smith, Jr. "Investment Banking and the Capital Acquisition Process," *Journal of Financial Economics* 15 (January/February 1986): 3–29. Footnotes from the original table are omitted.

*Not significantly different from zero.

the parties involved), we see that the impact on value is the most acute for transactions in which common stock is exchanged for debt, or debt for common stock. Because debt and preferred stock have claims that are senior to that held by common stockholders, their values are less sensitive to changes in capital structure when common stock is not involved. Also, the use of convertible debt results in smaller changes in value than when nonconvertible debt is used.

Up to now we have been concerned only with changes in capital structure. We now will widen the argument by considering Jensen's (1986) suggestion that agency conflicts over the payout of free cash flow (that is, cash flow above that needed to fund all positive net present value projects) also must be taken into consideration. The **free cash flow theory** predicts that for firms with positive cash flow, stock prices will increase with unexpected increases in the payout to corporate claimholders and will decrease with unexpected increases in the demand for funds via new issues. In addition, the theory predicts that stock prices will increase with increasing tightness of the constraints binding the payout of future cash flow to claimants and will decrease with reductions in the tightness of these constraints. Table 12.6 summarizes the empirical results from a number of studies examining changes in financing, investment, and dividend policy that signify implied increases or decreases in corporate cash flow. In general, the results presented in the table agree with the predictions of the free cash flow theory.

The joint impact of both capital structure decisions and changes in implied cash flow are summarized in Figure 12.2. Empirical results (from Tables 12.5, 12.6, and other studies) generally support the predictions summarized in Figure 12.2. Thus, whereas our concern is to assess the impact of capital structure on the value of the firm holding everything else constant, *in practice other things are not constant.* Many factors—some related directly to capital structure decisions, but others related to the firm's investment decisions or its cash dividend decisions—can have a positive, neutral, or negative impact on the value of the firm as the financial leverage of the firm changes. As shown in Figure 12.2, the predicted impact of actions undertaken by the firm may have two impacts—and these impacts may complement or contradict one another. For example, by issuing more common stock, the firm reduces the amount of financial leverage, indicating a decrease in value, and at the same time signals lower free cash flows in the future, also indicating a decrease in the value of the firm. Alternatively, by selling debt the firm increases its use of debt, which should lead to an increase in value, while it also signals lower free cash flows in the future. The predictions incorporated in Figure 12.2 suggest that the firm's capital structure decision is not independent of its investment and dividend decisions.

Concept Review Questions

- Explain why firms whose principal assets are intangible in nature would prefer lower debt levels than do firms with tangible assets.
- Give some examples of conflicts of interest between bondholders and stockholders that protective covenants may reduce.
- Describe the free cash flow theory and the relationship between a firm's cash flow and its capital structure.

Figure 12.2

Predicted Impact on Firm Value Associated with Various Capital Structure, Investment, and Dividend Decisions

Capital structure decisions and their impact on the value of the firm may not be independent of implied changes in corporate cash flow on the value of the firm.

		Implied Cash Flow Change		
		Negative	Zero	Positive
Capital Structure Change	Decreasing financial leverage	Common sale Dividend decrease	Common sale to retire debt Convertible bond sale to retire debt Common/preferred exchange offer Preferred/bond exchange offer Common/bond exchange offer Call of convertible bonds Call of convertible preferred	Calls of nonconvertible bonds
	Zero	Convertible preferred sale Convertible bond sale Investment decrease	Bond/bond exchange offer Bond sale to retire debt	Investment increase
	Increasing financial leverage	Preferred sale Debt sale	Common repurchase financed with debt Bond/common exchange offer Preferred/common exchange offer Bond/preferred exchange offer Income bond/preferred exchange offer	Common repurchase Dividend increase Dividend initiations Specially designed dividends

Predicted negative abnormal returns

Predicted insignificant abnormal returns

Predicted positive abnormal returns

OTHER CONSIDERATIONS

In addition to the factors identified by the MM model, numerous other factors have been suggested as factors potentially affecting capital structure decisions. These include growth options, product or input market factors, economic conditions, and corporate control motives.[4]

GROWTH OPTIONS

One of the most important factors affecting capital structure decisions, and one we have not yet looked at, is the ability to take advantage of growth options. Where high future growth is possible (i.e., where there are many positive net present value projects that the competition will not immediately erode away), firms want financial slack. They do not want to be so loaded with debt that they hamper their flexibility or future opportunity to secure additional capital as needed to make the necessary investments. Smith and Watts (1992), among others, find that firms that have more growth options have lower financial leverage. The existence of growth options is one reason that specialty retailers have a lower level of debt than general retailers; they have better growth prospects. Best Buy, 50-Off Stores, and The Gap have much better growth prospects than Dayton Hudson or Sears, for example; thus, they have less debt in their capital structures. Likewise, Home Depot, Mylan Labs, and U.S. Surgical all have high expected growth rates and many potential growth opportunities, and they use less debt.

PRODUCT OR INPUT MARKET FACTORS

In recent years a number of studies have identified possible relationships between product or input markets and the amount of financial leverage employed by the firm. Titman (1984) postulated that leverage increases to the extent to which a firm's products are not unique and do not require specialized service. Maksimovic and Zechner (1991) developed a model that suggests why firms within the same industry have different debt/equity ratios. They suggested that firms that adopt the technology chosen by the majority of the firms in the industry are partially hedged against shocks in production costs, since changes in production costs will be reflected in the price of the goods for all firms using the same technology. At the same time, firms that use the same technology are less levered than firms that adopt a technology chosen by fewer firms.

In another vein, Kim and Maksimovic (1990) turn the analysis around and analyze the impact the firm's financial structure has on its production decisions. That is, they are concerned with whether using a large amount of debt, as evidenced by a high debt/equity ratio, affects a firm's production decisions. Using the passenger air trans-

---

[4] When we look at firms domiciled in different countries, there are additional factors that we must consider. Some of these are briefly discussed in Chapter 27.

port industry (which has a high debt/equity ratio), they conclude that high debt levels are associated with suboptimal investment in capacity and inefficient combinations of variable production inputs. They also suggest that the air transport industry's high level of debt created a loss in efficiency which was large enough to dissipate a substantial fraction of the potential tax benefits of debt financing. These ideas suggest that factors not traditionally considered in finance may also affect a firm's capital structure decision.

ECONOMIC CONDITIONS

In a recent article Berkovitch and Narayanan (1993) propose that the proportion of equity financing relative to debt financing is higher when economic conditions are improving. This follows because the average quality of the projects developed is lower in a time of economic expansion, and lower-quality projects are more likely to be financed with equity.

In a different vein, Shleifer and Vishny (1992) examine the ability of firms to sell assets in the face of financial distress. They argue that general economic conditions affect the ability of firms to employ more or less debt. Thus, when a firm in financial distress needs to sell assets, because of economic conditions its industry peers are likely to be experiencing financial difficulties themselves. This limits the potential buyers of the firm's assets; the result is to make assets cheap in times of weak economic conditions. The overall impact is that asset liquidity is not constant over time, and therefore the amount of debt that can be effectively supported varies with economic conditions.

While our understanding of the impact of economic conditions on capital structure is in its infancy, these studies indicate possible relationships that may exist between overall economic conditions and a firm's capital structure.

EXECUTIVE INTERVIEW

Fong Wan, Director of Finance Pacific Gas & Electric Company

Fong Wan is Director of Finance of Pacific Gas & Electric Company, the largest combined gas and electric utility in the United States. From company headquarters in San Francisco, California, Mr. Wan discusses the challenges of managing the financial affairs of a public utility.

Financial management can be more challenging for utilities than for most industrial corporations. Although every business must comply with some regulation, the regulatory environment is of paramount importance to how utilities operate.

Each year, Pacific Gas and Electric (PG&E) files a Cost of Capital Testimony with the California Public Utility Commission. This filing represents the company's position for the capital structure that best supports our utility assets and the business environment within which we operate for the coming year. In addition, the filing also details the company's proposed cost of capital, given our position on capital structure. The cost of debt and preferred equity are weighted averages of the existing and prospective issuances. The cost of common equity, on the other hand, involves extensive analyses of comparable utility studies and theoretical tools such as the capital asset pricing model.

In 1992, PG&E requested a capital structure of about 49.5 percent common equity, 5.5 percent preferred equity, and 45 percent long-term debt. The Commission, instead, authorized PG&E to collect revenues based on a capital structure of 46.75 percent common equity, 5.75 percent preferred equity, and 47.5 percent long-term debt.

The difference in the capital structures was mainly attributed to the extent to which purchase-power contracts limit PG&E's financial flexibility. Let me explain: Utilities that are in need of additional power but elect to purchase from others have to make long-term financial commitments for the power. This additional power can be purchased from other utilities or from independent power generators. Such financial commitments or required payments are viewed by rating agencies as debt equivalents. For example, one rating agency considers one-third of the required payments as a debt equivalent, similar to a lease treatment. This debt equivalent is added on to the actual debt outstanding, thereby increasing the company's leverage from a debt-rating perspective. Knowing that the Commission currently has a different view on purchase power contracts, PG&E elected to finance the company more conservatively with additional equity. In our 1993 Cost of Capital filing, PG&E will continue to attempt to convince the Commission that these required payments can have a detrimental impact on our credit rating and cannot be neglected.

We may elect to deviate from the Commission's authorized capital structure in the short run, but in the long run the company and the Commission have to see eye-to-eye in the best interest of customers as well as shareholders. In our opinion, we believe we can achieve our lowest cost of capital at bond ratings of either A or BBB. Our studies show that this is our optimal capital structure that properly balances risk and return. Currently, we are targeting an overall corporate capital structure with a single A rating to allow for unforeseeable events. This additional cushion also provides inexpensive, timely access to the market for financing our extensive capital expenditure programs.

PG&E's capital structure policy is reviewed every two years. We carefully evaluate each piece of our business during the review process. In addition to the utility business, the company also has investments in nonregulated industries. Our goal is to ensure that the creditworthiness of the utility is not adversely affected by our diversification effort. Therefore, the risk of each of those nonregulated subsidiaries is thoroughly analyzed, and financing is set up as appropriate. If a subsidiary is of substantial size, we further require that subsidiary to be within one bond rating of the utility's for the industry it is in. This will ensure that the utility will always be "well-financed" to provide reliable service to our customers for the long run.

CORPORATE CONTROL

Finally let's consider another factor that affects a firm's capital structure decision. Assume a firm exists that is a tempting takeover candidate. What kind of capital structure action might it take to make it either less attractive to a potential acquiring firm or more expensive?[5] Harris and Raviv (1988), Israel (1991) and Stulz (1988) have developed models that predict potential takeover targets will increase their debt levels.[6] This increase in debt should be accompanied by a positive stock price reaction; at the same time, it should reduce the probability of being successfully taken over by another firm. We should stress that capital structure arguments based on corporate control motivations focus on short-run changes in capital structure taken in response to possible takeover threats. *Corporate control considerations say nothing about the long-run capital structure of firms.*

FACTORS TO LOOK FOR WHEN MAKING CAPITAL STRUCTURE DECISIONS

In Chapters 11 and 12 we have examined capital structure theory and actual debt/equity ratios and then considered numerous factors that may have an impact on a firm's capital structure decision. In order to summarize this material, it is helpful to consider the findings of a number of studies that have examined factors associated with different amounts of financial leverage. These findings are presented in Table 12.7. *These studies generally agree that leverage increases with non-debt tax shields, growth opportunities, fixed assets, and firm size, and that it decreases with volatility, advertising expenditures, research and development expenditures, bankruptcy probability, profitability, and uniqueness of the product.* It is safe to conclude that a firm's capital structure is affected by many factors. And, depending on the nature of the firm, the economy, and competition, firms may at various points in time add to or reduce the amount of debt in their capital structure. Thus, available theory and empirical evidence support the notion that capital structure is a dynamic, ongoing, evolving decision.

Concept Review Questions

- Explain how a firm's growth potential and capital structure are interrelated.
- Several researchers have hypothesized that product/input considerations and economic conditions can affect a firm's capital structure. Briefly explain these theories and their conclusions.

---

[5] One question of importance is, "Whose interests are we trying to maximize by making the firm more difficult to take over?" We refer you to articles in the end-of-chapter references, as well as Chapter 26, where mergers and defensive tactics are discussed.

[6] As discussed in Chapter 26, there are a number of other actions firms undertake to make themselves less attractive merger candidates.

Table 12.7

Some Potential Determinants of Financial Leverage

Many studies have examined the relationship between firm-level capital structure and observable factors that may affect capital structure decisions.

Characteristic	Bradley, Jerrell and Kim[a]	Chaplinsky and Niehaus[b]	Friend, Hasbrouch, and Long[c]	Gonedes, Long and Chikaonda[d]	Long and Malitz[e]	Kester[f]	Kim and Sorensen[g]	March[h]	Titman and Wessels[i]
Volatility	−		−			−			−
Bankruptcy probability							+	−	
Fixed assets	+	+	+					+	+
Non-debt tax shields				+	+		−		−
Advertising	−				−				
R&D expenditures	−				−				
Profitability		−	−	−		−			−
Growth opportunities					+	+	−		
Size		−	+			−	−	+	−
Free cash flow		−						+	
Uniqueness									−

Source: Adapted from Table IV in Milton Harris and Arthur Raviv, "The Theory of Capital Structure," *Journal of Finance,* 46 (March 1991): 297–355. Footnotes from the original table are omitted.

[a] Michael Bradley, Gregg Jarrell, and E. Han Kim, "On the Existence of an Optimal Capital Structure: Theory and Evidence," *Journal of Finance* 39 (July 1984): 857–78.

[b] Susan Chaplinsky and Greg Niehaus, "The Determinants of Inside Ownership and Leverage," working paper, University of Michigan, 1990.

[c] Irwin Friend and Joel Hasbrouch, "Determinants of Capital Structure," in Andy Chen, ed., *Research in Finance,* Volume 7 New York: JAI Press, 1988, pp. 1–19; and ——, and Larry Long, "An Empirical Test of the Impact and Managerial Self-Interest on Corporate Capital Structure," *Journal of Finance* 43 (June 1988): 271–81.

[d] Nicholas J. Gonedes, Larry Long, and Mathias Chikaonda, "Empirical Results on Managerial Incentives and Capital Structure," working paper, University of Pennsylvania, 1988.

[e] Michael Long and Ileen Malitz, "The Investment-Financing Nexus: Some Empirical Evidence," *Midland Corporate Finance Journal* 3 (Fall 1985): 53–59.

[f] Carl W. Kester, "Capital and Ownership Structure: A Comparison of United States and Japanese Manufacturing Operations," *Financial Management* 15 (Spring 1986): 5–16.

[g] Wi Saeng Kim and Eric H. Sorensen, "Evidence on the Impact of the Agency Costs of Debt in Corporate Debt Policy," *Journal of Financial and Qualitative Analysis* 21 (June 1986): 131–44.

[h] Paul March, "The Choice Between Equity and Debt: An Empirical Study," *Journal of Finance* 37 (March 1982): 121–44.

[i] Sheridan Titman and Roberto Wessels, "The Determinants of Capital Structure Choices," *Journal of Finance* 43 (March 1988): 1–19.

SETTING A FIRM'S DEBT/EQUITY RATIO

It should be clear by now that there is no single answer to why we see different capital structures among industries and firms. We can't make a blanket statement that firms should have a debt/equity ratio of 0.50 or 1.00, for example. But we can provide tools, guidelines, and some thoughts on planning ahead. The goal of the firm when determining its debt/equity ratio is to determine the firm's **debt capacity.** Knowing this will assist in maximizing the firm's value. By debt capacity, we mean the amount of debt, preferred stock, and leases a firm can effectively carry and service.

TOOLS FOR DIGGING

Some tools that can be employed to explore the capital structure issue include the following:

1. EPS-EBIT ANALYSIS   To employ **EPS-EBIT analysis,** we begin with the firm's estimated EBIT.[7] Consider the example of Seaboard Industries, which currently has $2 million of 10 percent debt outstanding and 1 million shares of common stock with a market price of $20 each. Seaboard needs to raise $10 million in new capital and has two options. The first involves issuing 500,000 shares of additional common stock at $20 per share. The second would use debt financing to raise the $10 million. The debt would carry a coupon interest rate of 12 percent. After the new investment, Seaboard's EBIT is $6 million. As shown below, at the $6 million EBIT, Seaboard's EPS would be $2.32 with common stock financing or $2.76 with the debt financing.

	Common Stock Financing (in millions)	Debt Financing (in millions)
EBIT	$6.00	$6.00
Interest	0.20	1.40*
EBT	5.80	4.60
Taxes (40%)	2.32	$1.84
EAT	$3.48	$2.76
Number of shares of common stock (millions of shares)	1.50	1.00
EPS	$2.32	$2.76

*$200,000 on existing debt plus $1,200,000 interest on new debt.

Instead of simply calculating EPS, it is generally helpful to consider what happens to EPS at various EBIT levels. We can also calculate the crossover EBIT,

[7] More on earnings per share, EPS, and earnings before interest and taxes, EBIT, is presented in Appendix 12A.

EBIT*, which is the EBIT level that causes both financing alternatives to produce the same EPS, as follows:

$$\frac{(EBIT^* - I_1)(1 - T) - D_{ps1}}{N_1} = \frac{(EBIT^* - I_2)(1 - T) - D_{ps2}}{N_2} \qquad (12.1)$$

where

$$EBIT^* = \text{the unknown crossover point in EBIT}$$
$$I_1,\ I_2 = \text{the annual total interest charges under the two financing plans}$$
$$T = \text{the firm's marginal tax rate}$$
$$N_1,\ N_2 = \text{the number of shares of common stock outstanding under the two plans}$$
$$D_{ps1},\ D_{ps2} = \text{the dollar amount of cash dividends on preferred stock under the two plans}$$

EPS-EBIT analysis, although ignoring risk and the value of the firm, does provide some information on the impact of alternative financing plans on the firm's EPS.

2. COVERAGE RATIOS Most firms and analysts calculate various coverage ratios to ascertain how the firm's EBIT relates to the cash outflows resulting from the use of fixed-cost[8] financing. These ratios range from the times interest earned and fixed charges coverage ratios discussed in Chapter 24 to more complicated ratios that take into account principal repayments, sinking fund payments, and/or cash dividends on preferred stock. The basic intent of all these ratios is to ascertain how safe the firm is in terms of meeting its fixed-cost financing charges.

3. LENDER STANDARDS Often a firm's lenders impose certain standards of financial performance. A bank loan or debt issue may contain financial performance standards that have to be met before assets can be sold, cash dividends paid, and so on. In addition, many larger firms tie their target capital structure decision to the bond rating the firm desires to maintain. For example, a firm may decide it always wants to be able to issue reasonable amounts of new debt with an A bond rating. (Bond ratings are considered in Chapter 16.) Accordingly, the capital structure and other financial affairs are maintained at a level that achieves this result.

4. CASH FLOW ANALYSIS A final approach is to investigate what happens to the ability of the firm to survive a severe recession. This involves a scenario analysis, in which the firm focuses on the cash flow consequences under alternative, assumed future states of the economy.

All these tools assist managers in determining the firm's appropriate, or target, capital structure.

---

[8] Although some long-term bonds and leases have floating or variable rates, they are still a fixed-cost type of financing, because there are periodic payments required and they have a prior but limited claim before common stockholders receive anything. In addition, adjustable-rate preferred stock also exists; however, it still has the essential elements of a fixed-cost security.

GUIDELINES FOR SETTING DEBT/EQUITY RATIOS

Although we have examined a wide variety of issues and factors related to a firm's capital structure decision, the primary results can be stated in a very straightforward way: *In making the capital structure decision, focus first and foremost on taxes, risk, and financial slack.*

1. TAXES   For firms in a taxpaying position, an increase in the amount of debt reduces the taxes paid by the firm. Of course, it's not just whether the firm is in a taxpaying position that is important; it's also whether it is expected to remain in a taxpaying position. Firms with less assurance of being able to benefit from the various tax shields will use less debt.
2. RISK   With or without bankruptcy, financial distress is costly. Although many factors affect risk, financial distress is most likely in firms that have high business risk. Business risk is often related to the type of assets employed. Where intangible assets play a major role, the value of the assets may erode quickly. Typically, firms that employ a lot of "brain power" or other intangible assets use less debt than do those whose assets have a ready secondary market. Also, competition and the nature of the industry often affect the firm's risk.
3. FINANCIAL SLACK   In the long run, a firm's value depends first and foremost on the investment and operating decisions its managers make. These have the potential to add more value to the firm than its financing decisions. Therefore, firms want a certain amount of financial slack so they can react to new positive-NPV opportunities. This is one of the reasons that high-growth firms tend to use less debt, because that posture provides greater financial slack.

PLANNING AHEAD

The firm's capital structure decisions cannot be made in a vacuum. They have to be part of the firm's complete financial plan, which takes into account its investment opportunities, operating strategy, dividend policy, and so forth.

In Chapter 25 we examine cash budgets and pro forma accounting statements. Although they don't tell you where to raise funds, they do provide insight into the anticipated amount and timing of the needs or surpluses. The use of sensitivity or scenario analysis is just as helpful when planning a firm's capital structure as it is for analyzing long-term investment decisions or the firm's cash budget. In addition, simulation is also useful because it allows the whole probability distribution of financial consequences to be examined. Remember that planning ahead, and having some financial slack, is important when considering how much debt the firm should have.

Concept Review Questions
- Briefly describe some methods used to determine a firm's debt capacity.
- What are three key variables that affect a firm's capital structure?

KEY POINTS

1. The pecking order theory and the observed behavior of firms suggest that the capital structure decision is a dynamic, evolving process.
2. In practice, capital structures vary widely over time and among firms and industries.
3. Based on the MM model, taxes are one of the important determinants of capital structures. Asset uniqueness is another important factor because it is closely related to the potential loss in value if financial distress occurs.
4. Convertible debt serves to combine the interests of both debt and equity, thereby lessening any conflicts of interest. Protective covenants are widely used in bonds and loan agreements in order to deal with possible conflicts of interest—especially between stockholders and bondholders.
5. Capital structure decisions, investment decisions, and cash dividend decisions appear to be interrelated. One possible approach to considering the potential interactions is to combine the impact of leverage-changing decisions and the free cash flow theory.
6. Other factors that need to be considered in making capital structure decisions are the presence of growth options, product or input effects, economic conditions, and implications provided by corporate control actions.
7. The key variables that effect the capital structure choice are the ability to take advantage of tax shields, risk differences related to the assets employed by the firm and its competition, and the need to maintain financial slack due to growth opportunities.

QUESTIONS

12.1 Explain the pecking order theory. How does it relate to what we observe in practice and to the idea of a target capital structure?

12.2 How would you go about explaining why we see so many different capital structures in practice, both between and within industries?

12.3 Why don't we see continually profitable firms financing with almost 100 percent debt in their capital structures?

12.4 Explain in detail how taxes and asset uniqueness assist in explaining some of the capital structures we see in practice.

12.5 The interests of stockholders and bondholders often diverge. What specific bond (or loan) covenants address each of the four sources of conflict between stockholders and bondholders discussed in the book?

12.6 How could changes in capital structure and changes in a firm's free cash flow interact? What types of actions indicate increases under both capital structure impacts and under the free cash flow theory? Which actions cause a positive/negative impact under one theory, but a negative/positive impact under the other?

12.7 Explain how other factors, in addition to those indicated by the MM model, may affect a firm's capital structure.

12.8 What key points should guide the firm when it plans its capital structure?

12.9 Explain what causes business risk. What do you believe the relative business risk of the following would be: grocery stores, jewelers, farm equipment manufacturers, airlines? Why?

12.10 Financial leverage generally has two effects on earnings per share. Identify these two effects and then explain why they occur.

12.11 Why can firms with low business risk have high financial risk, and vice versa? From your observation, is this generally the case?

CONCEPT REVIEW PROBLEMS

See Appendix A for solutions.

CR12.1 Molin Industries has EBIT of $500,000, a tax rate of 30 percent, a market value of debt of $1,000,000, a cost of debt, k_b, of 8 percent, and a cost of equity, k_s^L, of 12 percent. The firm anticipates no future growth and a 100 percent dividend payout ratio.

a. What is the total market value of the firm?
b. What is the firm's opportunity cost of capital?
c. The firm is planning to increase its debt by $500,000 and use the proceeds to repurchase equity. The cost of all debt, k_b, will increase to 10 percent, and the cost of equity will increase to 14 percent. Should the firm proceed with the capital restructuring?

CR12.2 Logan Logging currently has no debt, an EBT of $400,000, a cost of equity of 15 percent, and 100,000 shares of common stock outstanding. The firm's tax rate is 40 percent. Logan is considering restructuring by selling debt and repurchasing equity. If the firm sells $800,000 in debt, the cost of debt, k_b, will be 10 percent and the cost of equity, k_s^L, will increase to 17 percent.

a. What effect will the increase in debt have on the value of the firm?
b. If the stock is repurchased at $16 per share, what is the per share price after the restructuring?
c. What is the per share price if stock is repurchased at $20 per share, instead of $16 as in part (b)?

CR12.3 Mega Corporation is comparing two different capital structures. Under the all-equity capital structure Mega would have 100,000 shares of common stock outstanding. Under the levered capital structure, Mega would have 50,000 shares of stock outstanding and $400,000 in debt. The cost of debt is 12 percent, EBIT is $500,000, and the firm's tax rate is 40 percent.

a. What is EPS under each capital structure?
b. If the P/E ratio is 12 for all-equity and 8 for levered, what is the stock price under each capital structure?

CR12.4 Wafer Board Industries currently has $10 million of 8 percent debt outstanding and 500,000 shares of common stock. The firm needs $1 million to finance an expansion project and can raise the funds by issuing debt at 8 percent or selling stock at $25 per share. The tax rate is 36 percent and after the expansion EBIT will be $3,750,000.

a. What is the EPS under each financing option?
b. What is the crossover EBIT at which the decision to finance with debt or equity will not affect the firm's EPS?

CR12.5 Bell Towers has EBIT of $3 million, a zero growth rate, a tax rate of 40 percent, and $20 million of 9 percent debt outstanding. The firm has 288,000 shares of common stock outstanding and a P/E ratio of 15. Bell Towers' opportunity cost of capital is 10 percent.

a. What is Bell Tower's stock price?

b. Recently management investigated an expansion project that would cost $6 million and would return $800,000 (in both after-tax cash flow and after-tax earnings) per year indefinitely. What is the NPV of the project?

c. If the firm issues debt to pay for the project, the cost of all debt becomes 10 percent, and the firm's P/E ratio drops to 13. What is the firm's stock price if it accepts the project from part (b)? Should the project be accepted?

PROBLEMS

12.1   Traynor Enterprises currently has $100 million of 13 percent (coupon rate) debt outstanding, its EBIT is $80 million, and its cost of equity capital, k_s^L, is 12 percent. Due to a decrease in interest rates, Traynor has decided to call the bond issue. (The bonds will be called at par.) Because Traynor is not at its target capital structure, it will issue either $150 million or $200 million of new debt at par. In either case, $100 million will be used to refund the existing bond issue. The remainder will be used to buy back outstanding shares of Traynor's common stock. If the $150 million bond issue is employed, then the coupon interest rate will be 10 percent and k_s^L will increase to 12.5 percent. If the $200 million issue is employed, then the coupon interest rate is 11 percent and k_s^L will be 14 percent. The marginal corporate tax rate is 30 percent, and all earnings are paid out as cash dividends.

a. If the bonds are selling at 115 percent of par, what is the current total value, V, of the firm (before any refinancing)?

b. What is the total value, V, of the firm if the $150 million bond issue is sold? If the $200 million issue is sold? (Assume the market value of the bonds is equal to their par value.)

c. What action should Traynor take?

12.2   Howell Graphics is doing some capital structure planning. Its investment bankers have estimated after-tax costs of debt and equity at various levels of debt as follows:

Proportion of Debt	k_i	k_s
0	5.4%	12.0%
0.10	5.4	12.2
0.20	5.8	12.7
0.30	6.3	13.2
0.40	6.9	14.1
0.50	7.9	15.6
0.60	9.0	17.4

Based on this information, at what ratio of total debt to total equity is Howell's target capital structure?

12.3   Big Three Enterprises is in the process of determining its target capital structure. The firm is currently all-equity-financed but is thinking about issuing debt and using the proceeds to retire some of its common stock. The risk-free rate is 6 percent, there is no growth, and all earnings are paid out as cash dividends. Based on a good deal of internal discussion and on some projections made by its investment bankers, Big Three has come up with the following schedule:

Proportion of Debt (1)	EPS (2)	Beta (3)	$k_s^L = k_{RF} + \beta(k_M - k_{RF})$ (4)	Market Price, P_0 (2)/(4) (5)
0.00	$2.00	0.80	10.8	$_____
0.10	2.20	____	11.4	19.30
0.20	2.38	1.00	____	19.83
0.30	2.55	1.10	____	____
0.40	2.68	____	13.5	____
0.50	2.80	1.40	____	____
0.60	2.90	____	____	17.90

a. Fill in the schedule above. At what proportion of debt is the market price maximized?
b. After you complete (a), your boss asks, "What will be the impact on the firm's overall opportunity cost of capital?" To provide an answer, you have begun preparing the following schedule:

Proportion of Debt (1)	After-Tax Cost of Debt (2)	Weighted Debt Cost (1) × (2) (3)	Proportion of Equity (4)	k_s^L[from (a)] (5)	Weighted Equity Cost (4) × (5) (6)	Opportunity Cost of Capital (3) + (6) (7)
0.00	4.8%	0	1.0	10.8%	10.8%	10.8%
0.10	4.8	____	____	____	____	____
0.20	5.1	____	____	____	____	____
0.30	5.4	____	____	____	____	____
0.40	6.0	____	____	____	____	____
0.50	6.9	____	____	____	____	____
0.60	7.8	____	____	____	____	____

Complete the schedule. Does the minimum opportunity cost of capital occur at the same proportion to equity where the market price of Big Three's stock is maximized? Explain.

12.4 Harrison Appliances is considering raising $5 million by selling 200,000 shares of stock or by issuing 8 percent coupon rate bonds at par. There are presently 100,000 shares of common stock outstanding, the tax rate is 35 percent, and Harrison already pays $100,000 in interest before any new financing.

a. What is the crossover point where the EPS will be the same for either financing plan? (*Note:* Don't forget the existing interest.)
b. If you are told there is a 50 percent chance EBIT will be $600,000, and a 50 percent chance it will be $1,000,000, which plan would you recommend? Why?

12.5 Outboard Equipment is an all-equity-financed firm with the following financial statements:

Balance Sheet		Income Statement	
Total assets	$1,000,000	Sales	$2,500,000
		Operating costs	2,100,000
Common stock ($5 par)	$ 250,000	EBIT=EBT (16%	
Retained earnings	750,000	of sales)	400,000
Total equity	$1,000,000	Taxes (40%)	160,000
		EAT	$ 240,000

Outboard Equipment is planning to raise $400,000 through the sale of common stock at $50 per share or through the issuance of debt with a 10 percent coupon rate. Once the expansion is completed, sales are expected to increase to $3 million; EBIT should be the same percentage of sales at this new level.

a. Determine the present number of shares of stock outstanding, and Outboard Equipment's present EPS.
b. What is the crossover EBIT between the two financing plans?
c. Determine the EPS under the two plans.

12.6 A firm is considering two different financing plans. Under plan I the interest is $8,000 and there are 1,000 shares of common stock outstanding. Under plan II the interest is $2,000. If the crossover EBIT (i.e., EBIT*) is $20,000 and the marginal tax rate is 30 percent, how many shares of common stock are outstanding for plan II?

12.7 Joy Regulator currently has 100,000 shares of common stock outstanding with a market price of $60 per share. It also has $2 million (par value) in 6 percent coupon rate bonds outstanding. The firm is considering a $3 million expansion program that can be financed employing either (1) preferred stock sold at par with a 7 percent cash dividend, or (2) half common stock (sold at $60 per share) and half 8 percent coupon rate bonds (sold at par). The tax rate is 40 percent.

a. What is the indifferent EBIT between the two plans? (*Note:* Don't forget the existing interest.)
b. If EBIT is expected to be $1 million after the financing, what is the EPS under the two plans?
c. If the marginal tax rate is 20 percent, what are your answers to (a) and (b)?

12.8 Louisiana General is an all-equity firm. The firm has 200,000 shares of common stock outstanding, the EPS is $2, and all earnings are paid out to the stockholders as dividends. The current market value of the stock is $20 per share, and the opportunity cost of equity capital is 10 percent. Louisiana General is considering two alternative plans to raise $3 million for a new and highly promising investment project, as follows:

Plan A: issue 150,000 more shares of common stock at $20 per share,

Plan B: issue $3 million of 9 percent coupon rate bonds.

After the new investment, Louisiana General expects EBIT to be $1,400,000. The tax rate is 35 percent.

a. Calculate the EPS (and dividends per share) under each plan after the expansion.
b. If the opportunity cost of equity stays at 10 percent when common stock is employed, what is the new market price per share?
c. If bonds are used, the opportunity cost of equity capital increases to 12 percent. What is the new market price per share under that plan?
d. Explain why the market price calculated in (b) is higher than the beginning market price of $20. Then explain why the market price calculated in (c) is greater than that calculated in (b). How does this relate to the basic business of the firm, and the financing employed?
e. Which financing plan do you recommend? Why?

12.9 Armour Motors is undertaking a thorough cash flow analysis. At present the firm has no debt or preferred stock outstanding. Although Armour is profitable and expects substantial long-run positive cash flows, it is experiencing a temporary problem. The forecasted financial information for next year, before any financing, is as follows:

Cash inflows from sales	$6 million
Cash wages and salaries	$2.2 million
Cash payments for materials used in production process	$2.8 million
Other cash outflows *including taxes*	$700,000

Even though the year is expected to be a poor one, Armour is considering expanding through a $5 million bond issue with a 13 percent coupon interest rate. Armour's current cash position is $600,000. Under no circumstances does it want to lower its cash balance to less than $300,000. The tax rate is 30 percent.

a. Based on the forecasted information, what is the projected addition to Armour's cash level?
b. What is the amount of cash outflow for interest on the new bond issue before and after taxes?
c. Based on your analysis, should Armour issue the bond?

12.10 Mini Case You have just been hired as the Chief Financial Officer of Harrison Chemicals, a relatively young firm that has developed specialty chemical products to serve a number of "niche" markets. Until recently Harrison was a family-run business, but with the retirement of "Bull" Harrison, the founder of Harrison Chemicals, nonfamily professional management has been brought into the firm. Harrison has grown rapidly in recent years and expects to continue growing at a compound rate of 18 percent per year for the next 4 years. In planning for the future, you begin by examining Harrison's balance sheet:

Current assets	$150,000	Current liabilities	$275,000
Long-term assets	450,000	Long-term liabilities	25,000
Total assets	$600,000	Common stock	200,000
		Retained earnings	100,000
		Total liabilities and stockholder's equity	$600,000

Of the current liabilities, only $25,000 is bank debt; the rest are accounts payable and accrued liabilities. In visiting with others in the firm, you find out that in the past Harrison financed its expansion almost entirely with internally generated funds, and it has never paid any cash dividends.

a. What does the pecking order theory say about the capital structure decision? Based on what you know about Harrison Chemicals, does the pecking order theory appear to describe the firm?

b. Calculate Harrison Chemicals debt/book equity ratio. How does it correspond with that of other firms in the chemical industry? What if you also find out that Harrison's earnings are $45,000, and its P/E ratio is about 7 times earnings, while the average P/E ratio for chemical firms is about 10 times earnings? (*Note:* Calculate debt/market equity and debt/industry-based market equity ratios.) What conclusion do you reach about Harrison's capital structure?

c. The new President and CEO of Harrison wants to understand more about factors that affect capital structure decisions in practice. You need to provide that information by, first, discussing the factors suggested, using Modigliani and Miller to frame the discussion. (Be sure to discuss in some detail possible agency issues as well as possible interrelationships between a firm's capital structure and its free cash flow.) Second, discuss other possible factors that may affect a firm's capital structure decision.

d. Harrison Chemical has employed very little debt relative to other chemical firms. Which of the factors discussed in (c) appear to be the most important ones that apply to Harrison? Why?

e. Based on the 18 percent growth expected for Harrison Chemicals, you have been estimating possible financing needs. Your conclusion is that Harrison will not be able to undertake all of the positive net present value capital investment projects necessary to achieve this level of growth without obtaining external financing. Harrison currently has 30,000 shares of common stock outstanding. You estimate they will need $200,000 in additional capital immediately; this will last for $1\frac{1}{2}$ to 2 years. The funds can be raised by selling 20,000 shares of common stock at $10 each; by selling 10,000 shares at $10 each and issuing $100,000 of 11 percent coupon rate bonds at their par value of $100,000; or by selling $200,000 of 11 percent bonds at their par value of $200,000. Harrison currently has $50,000 in total interest-bearing debt; the average interest rate on the existing debt is 10.5 percent. Earnings before interest and taxes, EBIT, for next year are estimated to be $80,000, and Harrison's tax rate is 40 percent. Determine the following:

1. The debt/equity ratio under the three alternatives.
2. Earnings after taxes and earnings per share under the three plans.
3. The interest coverage (times interest earned = EBIT/interest) under the three plans.
4. The crossover EBIT, EBIT*, between the all-common-stock financing plan and the all-debt financing plan.

f. In part (e) the emphasis was on the impact on the debt/equity ratio, earnings, and interest coverage for next year. What other factors need to be considered in determining the financing used and the resulting capital structure for Harrison? Given the data available, which financing plan do you want to recommend to the President and CEO of Harrison? Why is this plan superior to the other two?

REFERENCES

There is an enormous amount of theoretical and empirical research related to the capital structure decision. A sampling of some key articles, along with some other additional recent articles, includes (in addition to those listed in the Chapter 11 references):

BERKOVITCH, ELAZAR, and M. P. NARAYANAN. "Timing of Investment and Financing Decisions in Imperfectly Competitive Financial Markets." *Journal of Business* 66 (April 1993): 219–48.

DONALDSON, GORDON. *Strategy for Financial Mobility.* Homewood, Il.: Irwin, 1971.

FISCHER, EDWIN O., ROBERT HEINKEL, and JOSEPH ZECHNER. "Dynamic Capital Structure Choice: Theory and Tests." *Journal of Finance* 44 (March 1989): 19–40.

HARRIS, MILTON, and ARTHUR RAVIV. "Corporate Control Contests and Capital Structure." *Journal of Financial Economics* 20 (January/March 1988): 55–86.

——— "The Theory of Capital Structure." *Journal of Finance* 46 (March 1991): 297–355.

ISRAEL, RONEN. "Capital Structure and the Market for Corporate Control: The Defensive Role of Debt Financing." *Journal of Finance* 46 (September 1991): 1391–1409.

JENSEN, MICHAEL C. "Agency Costs of Free Cash Flow, Corporate Finance and Takeovers." *American Economic Review* 76 (May 1986): 323–39.

KALE, JAYANT R., THOMAS H. NOE, and GABRIEL G. RAMIREZ. "The Effect of Business Risk on Corporate Capital Structure: Theory and Evidence." *Journal of Finance* 46 (December 1991): 1693–1715.

KIM, MOSHE, and VOJISLAV MAKSIMOVIC. "Technology, Debt and the Exploitation of Growth Options." *Journal of Banking and Finance* 14 (December 1990): 1113–31.

MAKSIMOVIC, VOJISLAV, and JOSEF ZECHNER. "Debt, Agency Costs, and Industry Equilibrium." *Journal of Finance* 46 (December 1991): 1619–43.

MALITZ, ILEEN. "On Financial Contracting: The Determinants of Bond Covenants." *Financial Management* 15 (Summer 1986): 18–25.

MYERS, STEWART C. "The Capital Structure Puzzle." *Journal of Finance* 39 (July 1984): 575–92.

SHLEIFER, ANDREI, and ROBERT W. VISHNY. "Liquidation Values and Debt Capacity: A Market Equilibrium Approach." *Journal of Finance* 47 (September 1992): 1343–66.

SMITH, CLIFFORD W., JR., and JEROLD B. WARNER. On Financial Contracting: An Analysis of Bond Covenants." *Journal of Financial Economics* 7 (June 1979): 117–61.

SMITH, CLIFFORD W., JR., and ROSS L. WATTS. "The Investment Opportunity Set and "Corporate Financing, Dividend, and Compensation Policies." *Journal of Financial Economics* 32 (December 1992): 263–92.

STULZ, RENE. "Managerial Control of Voting Rights: Financing Policies and the Market for Corporate Control." *Journal of Financial Economics* 20 (January/February 1988): 25–54.

TITMAN, SHERIDAN. "The Effect of Capital Structure on a Firm's Liquidation Decision." *Journal of Financial Economics* 13 (March 1984): 137–151.

——— and ROBERTO WESSELS. "The Determinants of Capital Structure Choice." *Journal of Finance* 43 (March 1988): 1–19.

APPENDIX

12A *Business Risk, Financial Risk, and EPS*

Although the goal of the firm is to maximize the total market value of the firm, it is sometimes instructive to understand the impact that both the basic investment decisions made by the firm as well as the financing decisions have on the firm's earnings. One way to accomplish this is to examine earnings per share, and its variability, for an all-equity-financed firm, and then to consider what occurs when debt financing is employed.

BUSINESS RISK

One way to look at **business risk** is to quantify it as the relative dispersion (or variability) in the firm's earnings before interest and taxes, EBIT. Consider Table 12A.1, which presents the expected sales and resulting EBIT in three different states of the economy for one firm, Consolidated National. The expected EBIT for Consolidated is $10,000, and the standard deviation is $3,098. The coefficient of variation (i.e., standard deviation/mean), which measures the relative variability of Consolidated's EBIT, is 0.31. If we were comparing it to another firm with an EBIT coefficient of variation of 0.80, we would conclude that Consolidated National has less business risk.

Table 12A.1

Probabilities, Sales, and EBIT for Consolidated National

Business risk is measured by the coefficient of variation of EBIT. The higher the coefficient of variation, the more business risk exists.

Probability	0.30	0.40	0.30
Sales	$24,000	$32,000	$40,000
Costs	18,000	22,000	26,000
Earnings before interest and taxes, EBIT	$ 6,000	$10,000	$14,000

expected EBIT = 0.30($6,000) + 0.40($10,000) + 0.30($14,000) = $10,000

standard deviation = $[0.30(\$6,000 - \$10,000)^2 + 0.40(\$10,000 - \$10,000)^2 + 0.30(\$14,000 - \$10,000)^2]^{0.5}$
= $(\$9,600,000)^{0.5}$ = $3,098

coefficient of variation = standard deviation/expected EBIT
= $3,098/$10,000 ≈ 0.31

Figure 12A.1

Probability Distributions of EBIT for Low and High Business Risk Firms

For simplicity, the same expected EBIT is assumed. Other things being equal, low business risk firms will experience much smaller fluctuations in EBIT than will high business risk firms.

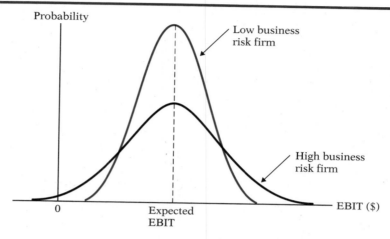

Another way of thinking about the impact of business risk is presented in Figure 12A.1. If two firms have the same expected EBIT, then the one with more business risk will experience much wider fluctuations in EBIT as its sales fluctuate. Both Consolidated National and the other firm might experience a 10 percent change in sales in a given year. But if the second firm has higher business risk, its EBIT might change by 25 percent from last year's, while Consolidated National's EBIT changes by only, say, 15 percent. This greater fluctuation in EBIT for the second firm is directly attributable to its greater business risk.

Business risk is caused primarily by the nature of the firm's operations. As a first approximation, we can think about business risk as a function of the industry in which the firm operates. But business risk is more complex than that. Other primary determinants of business risk are the following:

1. SENSITIVITY OF SALES TO GENERAL ECONOMIC FLUCTUATIONS   Firms whose sales fluctuate more when general economic conditions change have more business risk.
2. DEGREE OF COMPETITION AND SIZE   The smaller the firm and its share of the market, the greater its business risk.
3. OPERATING LEVERAGE   The higher the proportion of fixed to variable operating costs, the more operating leverage exists and, hence, the more business risk. Firms in service industries often have low fixed operating costs and therefore a low amount of operating leverage. Steel firms, on the other hand, have high fixed operating costs and more operating leverage and business risk.
4. INPUT PRICE VARIABILITY   The more uncertain the input prices for the firm's products, the more business risk.
5. ABILITY TO ADJUST OUTPUT PRICES   Firms that are in a monopolistic or oligopolistic situation, or that face an inelastic demand curve for their products, may have greater ability to adjust output prices and so be exposed to less business risk.

Business risk is a direct function of the firm's accumulated investment (capital budgeting) decisions. As these decisions are made, they affect both the nature of the firm's business and the composition of its assets. Firms with low business risk often exist in such industries as food processing and grocery retailing. Cyclical manufacturing industries and steel, copper, or aluminum firms are generally regarded as having high business risk.

An old adage is that business risk and financial risk are interrelated, so that "The more business risk, the less financial risk." Although the adage is not always true in practice, it is important to remember that business risk appears to have a major impact on the amount of debt a firm is willing or able to undertake.

FINANCIAL RISK

Financial risk is a result of the firm's long-term financing decisions. **Financial risk** refers to (1) the increased variability of earnings available to the firm's common stockholders, and (2) the increased probability of financial distress borne by the firm's owners if financial leverage is employed by the firm. Financial leverage refers to the use of fixed-cost types of financing. Although what we have to say applies equally to leases or preferred stock, we restrict our analysis to the major source of financial leverage—debt.

To see the impact of different amounts of debt on the firm, let's return to our example of Consolidated National. Assume it can employ three different capital structures, as follows:

Capital Structure A (zero debt)	
Debt	$ 0
Common stock	30,000
Total liabilities and stockholders' equity	$30,000
Capital Structure B (30% debt at a 10% coupon rate)	
Debt	$ 9,000
Common stock	21,000
Total liabilities and stockholders' equity	$30,000
Capital Structure C (60% debt at a 10% coupon rate)	
Debt	$18,000
Common stock	12,000
Total liabilities and stockholders' equity	$30,000

Capital structure A has no debt. Capital structure B has 30 percent of the firm's capital structure in debt; capital structure C has 60 percent of the firm's capital structure in debt.

Table 12A.2 shows the impact of the three different capital structures on Consolidated's earnings per share. (The three EBITs and associated probabilities are from Table 12A.1.) For capital structure A, earnings per share range from $0.72 to $1.68. Under both B and C, the variation of the EPS is larger, ranging from $0.87 to $2.25 with 30 percent debt, and from $1.26 to $3.66 with 60 percent debt.

To determine the impact of financial risk, we can calculate the coefficient of variation of Consolidated's EPS for the three different capital structures. The expected EPS and standard deviation of EPS are calculated from the data in Table 12A.2 (just as we calculated the expected

Table 12A.2

Earnings per Share for Three Capital Structures for Consolidated National

If there was preferred stock, those dividends would be subtracted from EAT to arrive at earnings available for common stockholders, EAC. Then EAC would be divided by the number of shares of common stock outstanding to arrive at the firm's EPS.

Probability	0.30	0.40	0.30
Capital Structure A (zero debt)			
EBIT	$6,000	$10,000	$14,000
Interest	0	0	0
EBT	6,000	10,000	14,000
Taxes (40%)	2,400	4,000	5,600
EAT	$3,600	$ 6,000	$ 8,400
EPS (based on 5,000 shares)	$0.72	$1.20	$1.68
Capital Structure B (30% debt)			
EBIT	$6,000	$10,000	$14,000
Interest	900	900	900
EBT	5,100	9,100	13,100
Taxes (40%)	2,040	3,640	5,240
EAT	$3,060	$ 5,460	$ 7,860
EPS (based on 3,500 shares)	$0.87	$1.56	$2.25
Capital Structure C (60% debt)			
EBIT	$6,000	$10,000	$14,000
Interest	1,800	1,800	1,800
EBT	4,200	8,200	12,200
Taxes (40%)	1,680	3,280	4,880
EAT	$2,520	$ 4,920	$ 7,320
EPS (based on 2,000 shares)	$1.26	$2.46	$3.66

EBIT and its standard deviation in Table 12A.1). These are as follows:

	Expected EPS (1)	Standard Deviation of EPS (2)	Coefficient of Variation of EPS (2) ÷ (1) (3)
Capital structure A (zero debt)	$1.20	$0.37	0.31
Capital structure B (30% debt)	1.56	0.53	0.34
Capital structure C (60% debt)	2.46	0.93	0.38

Probability Distributions of EPS for Different Capital Structures

Favorable financial leverage results in an increase in the expected EPS and also in the dispersion of the possible EPSs.

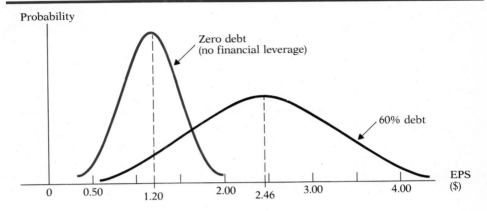

Examining these data, we see that the EPS coefficient of variation when there is no debt (capital structure A) is 0.31, whereas it is 0.34 with 30 percent debt and 0.38 with 60 percent debt. Because an increase in the coefficient of variation signifies an increase in relative variability, we see that *financial risk increases as the firm adds more debt* to its capital structure. This increased riskiness is graphed in Figure 12A.2. There we see that the dispersion of possible EPS outcomes increases substantially when 60 percent debt is employed, compared with no debt.

In Table 12A.1 we calculated the coefficient of variation of Consolidated's EBIT to be 0.31. Note that the coefficient of variation of Consolidated's EPS under capital structure A is also 0.31. Is this just a coincidence? No! The reason these two are exactly the same is that they both represent the basic business risk of the firm. *Because capital structure A has no debt, it has no financial risk. Thus, the riskiness of the EPS under capital structure A reflects only business risk.* The coefficients of variation for capital structures B and C, however, reflect the effects of *both* business and financial risk. That part *attributable only to financial risk* is measured by the difference between the coefficient of variation of 0.31 and either 0.34 for capital structure B or 0.38 for C.

This example confirms our earlier observation: Fluctuations in a firm's EPS are first and foremost a function of the firm's accumulated capital investment decisions. Once that is accounted for, the effects of the firm's capital structure on both the magnitude and fluctuations in earning per share can be seen. In the Consolidated National example, note that a large part of the fluctuation in EPS was due to the impact of the past investment decisions. Then the impact of the mix of debt and equity employed can be seen.

Although we are concerned with maximizing market value, not earnings per share, we have just seen that financing decisions have two impacts on earnings. First, the financing decision can lead to higher (or lower) earnings per share when compared to the no-financial-leverage case. Second, as EBIT fluctuates, the use of financial leverage leads to larger movements in earning per share when compared with the no-financial-leverage case.

PROBLEMS

12A.1   Two firms, A and B, have the following probability distributions of EBIT:

Probabilities	0.30	0.40	0.30
A's EBIT	$ 20,000	$ 40,000	$ 60,000
B's EBIT	$200,000	$280,000	$360,000

Which firm has more business risk? Why?

12A.2   State Systems is currently in the process of a substantial expansion program. The $3.5 million program will be financed by a stock issue (of 100,000 shares) or with a new 10 percent coupon rate bond issue. The firm's preexpansion income statement (in millions of dollars) is

Sales	$5.00
Operating costs	3.50
EBIT	1.50
Interest	0.25
EBT	1.25
Taxes (36%)	0.45
EAT	$0.80
EPS (200,000 shares)	$4.00 per share

After the expansion, the EBIT is expected to be $1.5, $2.5, or $3.5 million, with associated probabilities of 0.30, 0.40, and 0.30.

a. Determine the EPS for both plans with each different probability.
b. Calculate the expected EPS, the standard deviation, and the coefficient of variation of EPS for each plan. (*Note:* The coefficient of variation = standard deviation/mean.)
c. Which plan has more risk? Explain.

13 *Dividend Policy*

EXECUTIVE SUMMARY

The firm's cash dividend decision involves determining how much of internally generated funds to pay out in the form of dividends and how much to use for other corporate purposes. Under both the MM and residual dividend arguments, the value of the firm is independent of the firm's cash dividend policy. On the other hand, items related to taxes, cash flow and growth options, and signaling have been suggested as factors that influence dividend policy. Most firms follow a policy consistent with the smoothed residual dividend approach and the pecking order theory. They establish both a dollar amount per share they plan to maintain and a target dividend payout ratio around which they attempt to fluctuate. Then the firm finances its corporate needs with internally generated funds and debt while fluctuating around both its target payout ratio and target capital structure.

Some firms elect to repurchase shares of their own outstanding common stock. The primary reasons are to use excess cash, provide a form of dividend to stockholders, and sometimes "leverage up" the firm. Both stock splits and stock dividends provide additional shares to the firm's current stockholders on a pro rata basis. The firm's cash dividend policy, along with repurchases and stock splits or stock dividends, appears to be used by firms to signal information about the firm's future cash flows.

DIVIDENDS AND FINANCING

In order to maximize the value of the firm, we need to understand a firm's cash dividend policy. The question is, does a high or a low (or no) cash dividend policy maximize the value of the firm? Or should the firm simply repurchase shares of its common stock—which can be an alternative approach for distributing cash flows back to the owners? We will see that the answers to these questions are somewhat messy, and we are not completely sure if a firm's dividend policy directly affects the value of the firm.

The decision to pay cash dividends is simultaneously a decision not to reinvest this same cash in the firm. To see this, consider the relationship between cash flow and possible uses, shown in Figure 13.1. A firm's available cash comes from two sources—internally generated financing and new external financing. Once cash is on hand, it has three general uses. First, ongoing operations must be maintained. These include

Figure 13.1

Relationship Between Cash Flow and Potential Uses of Cash

The more cash distributed to stockholders, the less available for maintaining ongoing operations and expansion or the more new external financing that must be obtained.

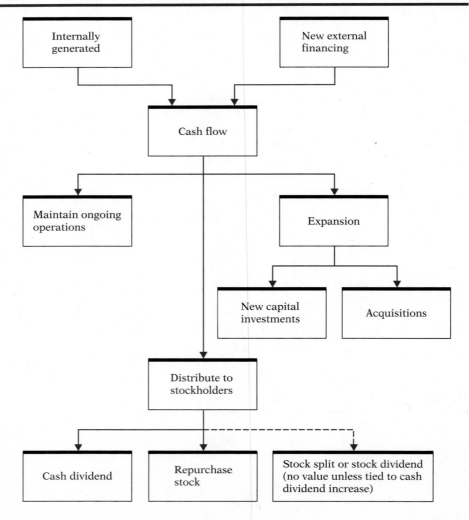

paying salaries, the cost of materials, marketing expenses, taxes, financing charges and debt repayments, maintaining and updating equipment, and so forth. The remaining funds are then available for one of two other purposes: expansion—through new capital investments or the acquisition of other firms—or distribution to the firm's stockholders. Other things being equal, the more cash distributed to stockholders, the less internally generated equity capital is available (which affects the firm's capital structure) and the smaller the firm's capital budget. Thus, the firm's cash dividend decision simultaneously affects its capital structure and capital budgeting decisions. For analytical purposes we often separate the three decision areas—investment decisions, financing decisions, and dividend policy—but their interrelationships must be kept in mind.

Once the firm decides to make a distribution to investors, it has two primary means of doing so. These also appear in Figure 13.1. The first and most direct is through cash dividends. The second is through stock repurchases. Many firms also declare stock splits and stock dividends that they would like investors to consider valuable. As we shall see, however, neither a stock split nor a stock dividend by itself alters the value of the firm.

Before we discuss these topics, it is useful to understand the magnitude of cash dividends. Table 13.1 shows total earnings, taxes, and cash dividends for firms during the 1983–1992 period. As we can see, taxes rose to over 45 percent of earnings before falling in recent years. The total amount of cash dividends increased every year until

Table 13.1

Total Earnings, Taxes, and Cash Dividends for Firms (in billions)

Dividend payout ratios have increased due to continued increases in total cash dividends being paid, coupled with slower growth in earnings.

	Taxes			Dividends		
Year	Taxes (1)	Earnings Before Taxes (2)	Taxes as a Percentage of Before-Tax Earnings (1)/(2) (3)	Cash Dividends Paid (4)	Earnings After Taxes (5)	Dividend Payout Ratio (4)/(5) (6)
1983	$75.8	$203.2	37.3%	$ 72.9	$127.4	57.2%
1984	93.9	239.9	39.1	79.0	146.1	54.1
1985	96.4	224.2	43.0	83.2	127.8	65.1
1986	106.6	236.3	45.1	88.2	129.8	68.0
1987	124.7	266.7	46.8	98.7	142.0	69.5
1988	137.9	306.8	44.9	110.4	168.9	65.4
1989	129.7	290.6	44.6	122.1	160.9	75.9
1990	136.7	335.4	40.8	149.3	218.7	68.3
1991	124.0	334.7	37.0	146.5	210.7	69.5
1992	140.2	371.6	37.7	149.4	231.4	64.5

Source: Federal Reserve Bulletin, various issues.

1991—from $72.9 billion in 1983 to $149.4 billion in 1992. Over this period the percentage increase in cash dividends was substantially in excess of the increase in earnings (before or after taxes); this was accomplished by increasing the dividend payout ratio (cash dividends divided by earnings after taxes).

Also, consider the following data, which show the percentage increase in both cash dividends and inflation:

Year	Total Cash Dividends (percent change)	Consumer Price Index (percent change)
1983	5.4%	3.2%
1984	8.4	4.0
1985	5.3	3.6
1986	6.0	1.9
1987	8.3	3.6
1988	11.9	4.1
1989	10.6	4.8
1990	22.3	6.1
1991	(1.9)	3.1
1992	2.0	2.9
Mean	7.8	3.7

Source: Federal Reserve Bulletin, various issues.

Many firms have expressly stated that one of their goals is to increase cash dividends at a rate at least equal to inflation. An examination of this data indicates that total cash dividends increased faster than inflation in all but the last 2 years shown—1991 and 1992.

Although there are many differences among firms, in general they pay out a sizable portion of their cash flows in the form of cash dividends. This understanding is important given the many factors that influence dividend policy and the tremendous differences of opinion concerning the importance of dividend policy. We now turn to a discussion of these topics.

Concept Review Questions

- What are two primary means a firm can use to distribute excess cash to the firm's stockholders?
- Briefly describe the general change in dividends paid over the period 1983 to 1992.

DOES DIVIDEND POLICY MATTER? THE IRRELEVANCE ARGUMENTS

Next to the firm's appropriate capital structure and capital budgeting techniques, the dividend decision has probably generated the most discussion in financial management. The controversy centers around this question: Does the firm's cash dividend policy influence the value of its common stock? To address this question, we begin by discussing the arguments of those who say that cash dividends don't matter.

MILLER AND MODIGLIANI'S IRRELEVANCE ARGUMENT

As a follow-on to their capital structure irrelevance argument, which we encountered in Chapters 11 and 12, Miller and Modigliani (1961) also concluded that the firm's cash dividend policy does not affect the value of the firm. To understand this position it is important to note three items: First, they assumed that capital markets are perfect in that no taxes, brokerage fees, or flotation costs exist. Second, the firm's capital structure is fixed so that we do not mix dividend policy with the firm's capital structure policy. Third, the firm's investment policy is fixed in that the firm follows a value-maximizing policy of accepting all positive-NPV projects.

To understand the reasoning behind the Miller and Modigliani argument, let's consider AMT Research. Its current market-value-based balance sheet is as follows:

Cash	$ 5,000	Debt	$20,000
Long-term assets	45,000	Equity	30,000 + NPV
Investment opportunity ($5,000 investment required)	$\dfrac{\text{NPV}}{\$50,000 + \text{NPV}}$		$\overline{\$50,000 + \text{NPV}}$

The firm has $5,000 in cash that can be paid out to the firm's shareholders in the form of cash dividends or be invested in the new positive NPV investment opportunity. It seems that the firm has a dilemma—it can pay the cash dividend and return some of the firm to its owners, or it can take the investment opportunity and maximize its value. But, it also has the ability to do both—that is, to pay the dividends and also make the wealth-maximizing investment. All it has to do is to raise more funds so that it has $5,000 to make the investment. The firm can't issue debt, because that would change the capital structure proportions, so the firm sells more stock. How much does it need to sell? That's easy, it needs to sell $5,000 worth of stock to replace the $5,000 paid out in dividends.

What happens to the value of the original shareholders' stock during the process of paying the cash dividend, selling more stock, and making the investment? Their original claim on the firm was for $30,000 + NPV. Because the investment and capital structure policies of AMT Research are unaffected, the total equity value of $30,000 + NPV must be unchanged. The value of the stock held by the original shareholders is now

$$\begin{aligned}
\text{value of original} \\
\text{shareholder's shares}
\end{aligned} \begin{aligned}
&= \text{equity value of firm} - \text{value of new shares} \\
&= (\$30,000 + \text{NPV}) - \$5,000 \\
&= \$25,000 + \text{NPV}
\end{aligned}$$

But, the original shareholders have also received a cash dividend of $5,000. Hence, their value is unaffected, and we can conclude that dividend policy does not matter to the original shareholders, nor does it affect the value of the firm.

Providing that AMT Research takes all positive-NPV investment opportunities, the value of the firm is maximized. All that has happened is that cash is being recycled. AMT Research pays it out with one hand to the original shareholders, while with the other hand it sells new stock to raise additional cash.[1]

While the MM argument ignores taxes, flotation costs, and some other complications that exist in practice, it provides *the* frame of reference for considering what factors might cause cash dividends to affect the value of the firm. Before considering these issues, let's consider another version of the dividend irrelevance argument.

THE RESIDUAL THEORY OF DIVIDENDS

The basis of the **residual theory of dividends** is that investors are as well or better off if the firm retains and reinvests internally generated funds as if it pays them out, *provided* the investment opportunities facing the firm are at least as good as those facing investors. Under the residual theory, the firm's dividend policy would be the following:

1.   Establish the optimum capital budget—that is, accept all projects with positive net present values.
2.   Determine the amount of common equity needed to finance the new investments while maintaining the firm's target capital structure.
3.   Use internally generated funds to supply this equity whenever possible.
4.   Pay cash dividends only to the extent that internally generated funds remain after taking all appropriate capital investment opportunities.

The residual theory of dividends is concerned with the "leftover" internally generated funds. Under this theory, cash dividends should be paid only if there is cash left over after making the investment decision.

Consider Pacific Industries, which finances 40 percent of its investments via debt and the remaining 60 percent with common equity. The firm's internally generated funds are $12 million which, in part or total, can be distributed to the stockholders or reinvested in the firm. The investment opportunities facing Pacific are as follows:[2]

---

[1] Note that the original shareholders get the benefit of the positive-NPV investment opportunity. All that the new shareholders receive is a fair return on their investment, provided that markets are efficient and the stock was sold at a fair price.

[2] For simplicity the internal rate of return criterion is employed to measure project desirability, and it is assumed that the ranking of project desirability is the same with internal rate of return as with net present value. The same results can be obtained using net present value, but the presentation is slightly more complex.

Project	Initial Investment (in millions)	IRR
A	$5	25%
B	3	21
C	6	18
D	6	16
E	4	13
F	5	10

These opportunities are graphed in Figure 13.2, along with the opportunity cost of capital of 14 percent. As indicated, projects A, B, C, and D, requiring an initial investment of $20 million, should be undertaken. Out of this $20 million, $12 million [i.e., ($20 million)(0.60)] in equity financing would be used. Because the $12 million needed is exactly equal to the internally generated funds, Pacific would use these funds for capital investment and thus pay no cash dividends. The other $8 million required to finance the capital investments would be secured via debt financing.

If, on the other hand, Pacific's opportunity cost of capital had been higher, so that only projects A, B, and C had been undertaken, a total of $14 million would be needed for capital investment. Sixty percent of this, or $8.4 million [i.e., ($14 million)(0.60)], would be provided via internally generated funds. The remainder, $12 million minus

Figure 13.2

Investment Opportunities and Opportunity Cost of Capital Schedules for Pacific Industries

Pacific would accept all projects providing a return equal to or greater than its opportunity cost of capital of 14 percent. Thus, A, B, C, and D would be accepted, and E and F rejected.

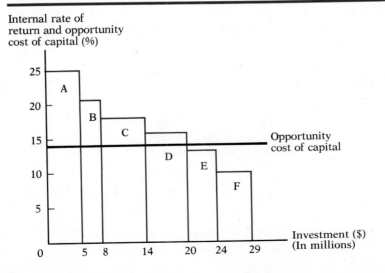

$8.4 million, or $3.6 million, would be distributed to the firm's common stockholders as a cash dividend.

Under the residual dividend theory, cash dividends are paid only if funds are left over after accepting all profitable capital budgeting projects. *The value of the firm is a function of its investment decisions. Thus, like the MM argument, the residual theory suggests that dividend policy is a passive variable and has no influence on the value of the firm.*

We should pause here and clarify one point before going on. In Chapter 3, we said that cash dividends are the foundation for the valuation of common stock. Thus, the market value of a share of stock is equal to the present value of all future cash dividends. While this is true, the *timing* of the dividends can vary. When we say that dividend policy does not matter, we are simply saying that the present value of the future cash dividends remains unchanged even though dividend policy may influence their timing. Dividends, including liquidating dividends, can still be paid, but it is a matter of indifference when they are paid, as long as their present value remains unchanged.

Concept Review Questions

- Briefly describe the Miller and Modigliani dividend irrelevance argument.
- What is the firm's dividend payout policy under the residual theory of dividends?

WHY DO FIRMS PAY CASH DIVIDENDS?

Under the irrelevance argument, dividend policy does not affect the value of the firm. However, that is not all of the story. As we saw in Table 13.1, firms pay out over 60 percent of total earnings in the form of cash dividends. In addition, firms appear to value some stability in terms of their dividend payout. To understand dividend policy better, we first examine taxes and their possible impact on the firm's dividend decision. Then we examine interrelationships among dividends, cash flow, and growth options. Third, we look at some signaling arguments related to the firm's cash dividend policy. Finally, we consider some other factors potentially related to the dividend decision.

TAXES AND THE FIRM'S CASH DIVIDEND POLICY

As we have discussed previously, taxes affect many financial decisions. They also come into play in the dividend decision. Firms that pay cash dividends do not get to deduct the dividends as an expense of doing business. Hence, cash dividends are paid out of the firm's after-tax cash flows. For the recipients of cash dividends, however, there are tax consequences.

Under the Budget Reconcilliation Act of 1993 the top marginal tax rate for corporations is 35 percent. For individuals the ordinary marginal tax rates are as follows based on taxable income:[3]

---

[3] Taxable income = adjusted gross income − (exemptions and itemized deductions, or the standard deduction).

Single Individual	Married Couple Filing Joint Return	Marginal Tax Rate
Up to $22,100	Up to $36,900	15%
22,101 to 53,500	36,901 to 89,150	28
53,501 to 115,000	89,151 to 140,000	31
115,001 to 250,000	140,001 to 250,000	36
over 250,000	over 250,000	39.6

On assets like common stock held for investment purposes and then sold, the capital gains tax (if the stock is held for a year or longer) is 28 percent; if it is held for less than a year, the ordinary marginal tax rate applies.

There are tax aspects for both corporations and individuals who receive cash dividends. First let's look at firms who own shares of common stock in another firm. For corporations, 70 percent of the cash dividends received from the investment in another firm are excluded from the firm's income.[4] For a firm in the 35 percent marginal tax bracket, the tax rate on cash dividend income is only 10.5 percent [i.e., $(1 - 0.70)(0.35)$]. This is lower than the effective tax rate of 35 percent that the same firm would pay on any gain realized from selling the stock. Thus, there is a minor tax issue for corporations receiving cash dividends. However, the major tax issue relates to individuals.

Prior to the Tax Reform Act of 1986, capital gains were taxed at a substantially lower rate than ordinary income—one half of the ordinary income tax rate. If an individual was in a 30 percent marginal tax bracket, the tax rate on capital gains was only 15 percent. The argument was often made that because of different tax rates on ordinary income versus capital gains, individuals would benefit from firms *not* paying cash dividends. To illustrate, assume a firm has a positive-NPV project that requires an investment of $100. The firm also has free cash flow of $100. To make the investment the firm has two alternatives. The first is to pay no cash dividends, and simply take the $100 in free cash flow and make the investment. The value of the firm will increase by $100, so stockholders obtain the full benefit of the $100. The second alternative is to pay a cash dividend of $100, and turn around and sell $100 of new common equity to fund the positive-NPV project. Considering the differential impact of taxes and that investors have an option of when they will pay the taxes if the return is in the form of capital gains, there was a tax deferral advantage to not paying cash dividends.

From 1986 to 1993 the effective personal rates were 31 percent for ordinary income and 28 percent for capital gains. During this period the tax code effectively wiped out the difference between the tax rate on ordinary income versus capital gains. However, *there was still an option held by common stockholders on when they would pay taxes if the returns came from capital gains instead of cash dividends*. With the new tax code of 1993 the difference between the tax rates on ordinary income and capital gains have widened somewhat for individuals with substantial income. Thus, it appears that (1) tax rate differences between ordinary income and capital gains, and (2) deferral motives provide a rationale for why firms pay cash dividends and, at the same time,

---

[4] If the firm owns 20 percent or more of the firm, it may exclude 80 percent of the dividends.

continue to issue additional equity to replace the equity drained out through the dividend process.

In examining the tax impacts on dividend policy, Miller and Scholes (1978) argue that the tax disadvantage of dividends can be reduced by the investors' ability to offset dividend income by interest deductions on borrowing, combined with investment of the proceeds from borrowing in tax-sheltered investments such as insurance contracts and retirement funds. Whether this strategy has ever been employed on a widespread basis is unknown. Numerous studies have attempted to determine if taxes directly affect dividend policy; the results are mixed, and the answer is unclear.

Recently, Brennan and Thakor (1990) developed a model dealing with alternative procedures for distributing cash from corporations to stockholders. They show that even with the preferential tax treatment of capital gains, the majority of a firm's shareholders may support the receipt of cash dividends for small distributions. If the distribution is large, a repurchase of stock by the firm (which, others things being equal, drives up the value of the stock) is preferred. In another recent article DeAngelo (1991) builds on logic similar to Miller's personal tax argument (see Chapter 11) and argues that even with the tax and deferral implications firms will pay cash dividends. The logic is as follows: (1) If all firms decided to adopt a low or zero payout policy there would be less present consumption in the economy and an excess of future consumption; and (2) in equilibrium, adjustments must occur to override the tax benefits of deferral, so that firms *in aggregate* supply the appropriate mix of taxable cash dividends and capital gains. In conclusion, although the tax differential and deferral arguments may make intuitive sense, both theory and empirical evidence cast doubt on whether these factors affect dividend policy in any consistent manner.

DIVIDENDS, CASH FLOW, AND GROWTH OPTIONS

In Chapter 12 we examined the free cash flow theory developed by Jensen (1986); this theory also has relevance for interrelationships between a firm's investment decision and its dividend decision. The greater the amount of new investment undertaken by the firm, the smaller the cash dividend that can be paid, or the more new equity that needs to be issued. Firms with more growth opportunities channel cash to fund the growth options; accordingly, they have lower free cash flow and pay lower dividends. This cash flow argument by Jensen is also supported by two agency cost arguments.

From the standpoint of the firm's bondholders, any time the firm pays cash dividends without issuing new equity, the value of the bondholders' claim decreases. Smith and Warner (1979) and Kalay (1982), by evaluating dividend covenants contained in bonds, conclude that restrictions on dividend payout effectively impose a minimum investment requirement on the firm, thereby lowering the underinvestment problem. (The underinvestment problem was discussed in Chapters 11 and 12 when we examined the firm's capital structure decision.) Firms with more growth options can tolerate more restrictions on dividends; hence, firms with more growth options should pay out less in the form of cash dividends.

Finally, Rozeff (1982) and Easterbrook (1984) note that, other things being equal, paying dividends increases the frequency with which firms go to the equity markets to raise additional equity capital. By going to the equity markets, the firm is more frequently subjected to the intensive capital market monitoring and discipline that occurs at the time new funds are raised, thereby lowering agency costs. At the same time, establishing a dividend policy may also reduce agency costs. Firms will adopt policies that minimize total agency costs. Those firms with high growth rates and growth options and a high demand for capital have less reason to pay dividends, and they minimize agency costs by going periodically to the capital markets. Firms with lower growth options pay higher dividends, thus minimizing agency costs via their cash dividend policy. The important point is that firms that have more growth options are expected to pay lower cash dividends. From a free cash flow standpoint, we see that a firm's growth options and its dividend policy are linked together.

SIGNALING

Another way to examine the cash dividend decision is from a signaling perspective. These ideas have been developed by Bhattacharya (1979), Miller and Rock (1985), Ambarish, John, and Williams (1987), and Ofer and Thakor (1987), among others. The underlying thrust of these arguments is that in a risky world with heterogeneous expectations and less-than-perfect markets, the cash dividend policy communicates information—provides a signal—about the firm's future cash flows over and above any existing information. An increase in the payout ratio would be seen to indicate an increase in the future cash flows of the firm, and the market price of the firm's common stock would increase simply as a result of the increased cash dividends.

This viewpoint has been strengthened in recent years by empirical evidence.[5] Thus, the initiation of a dividend (that is, when a firm first starts to pay cash dividends) or an unexpected increase in cash dividends leads to an increase in the value of the firm's stock. Additionally, dividend initiations may also be associated with future increases in the firm's earnings (and hence, its cash flow).[6] This line of theory and empirical support suggests that dividends may signal unique information about the future prospects of the firm.

SOME FURTHER ARGUMENTS FOR THE INFLUENCE OF DIVIDEND POLICY

In addition to the factors discussed previously, other less theoretical arguments have been made that either a high or a low dividend payout ratio may affect the value of the firm. Some of these arguments are as follows.

Resolution of Uncertainty

One argument presented in favor of a price effect is that by paying dividends, the firm resolves investor uncertainty. Because the retention of funds and promise of future dividends is uncertain, investors may prefer higher current dividends. Accordingly, they would bid up the market price for firms with higher payout ratios. Although the

---

[5] Some of this evidence is summarized in Asquith and Mullins (1983) and Eades, Hess, and Kim (1985).
[6] See, for example, Healy and Palepu (1988).

risk and return of the firm is not influenced, it is argued that investor perception of riskiness may decrease, thereby causing the market price to increase.

The basic valuation framework we have employed is $P_0 = D_1/(k_s - g)$, where P_0 is the current market price, D_1 is the cash dividend expected at time $t = 1$, k_s is the equity investors' required return, and g is the expected growth rate in cash dividends. If the investors' perception of risk decreases, their required return, k_s, will decrease. If the cash dividend, D_1, is \$3, k_s is 16 percent, and g is 8 percent, the initial price is

$$\text{price with no uncertainty resolution} = P_0 = \frac{\$3.00}{0.16 - 0.08} = \$37.50$$

If a higher payout ratio resolves investor uncertainty, and everything else remains the same, the required return might decrease to 15 percent. In that case, the market price would be

$$\text{price with uncertainty resolution} = P_0 = \frac{\$3.00}{0.15 - 0.08} = \$42.86$$

Thus, if a high payout ratio reduces investor uncertainty, the market price of the firm's common stock increases.

Desire for Current Income

Another factor might be investor preferences for current income. In Chapter 3 (Figure 3.8), we examined the total returns on common stock investment between 1960 and 1992. Cash dividends provided almost 40 percent of the total returns from investing in common stock during this period. In addition, there is much less risk associated with cash dividends than with capital appreciation or loss, as evidenced by the much lower variability for the dividends. Investors with a preference for current income would favor a high-payout firm and thus might bid its price up.

Flotation Costs

As we discussed in Chapter 6, the presence of flotation costs makes the cost of internally generated common equity cheaper than the cost of issuing new common stock. If a firm's cost of internal common equity is 16 percent, then its cost of issuing new common stock may be 18 or 19 percent. This is due to the transaction costs and underpricing that occur when additional common stock is sold. Flotation costs may cause firms to favor retaining more funds, via a low dividend payout policy, because doing so reduces their cost of equity capital.

Brokerage Costs

In the absence of brokerage costs, investors could always buy or sell securities to create their own cash "dividend" stream if they did not like the policy followed by the firm. The presence of brokerage costs, however, means that investors receive less than 100 percent on the dollar when they buy or sell securities. Investors preferring high current income cannot sell stock without incurring additional costs. Likewise, those preferring a low level of current income also incur additional costs on reinvesting the cash dividends. The net effect may be to cut both ways—brokerage costs may create a preference for either a high or a low level of cash dividends.

Concept Review Questions

- Why would investors prefer a return in the form of capital gains rather than cash dividends?
- How are a firm's growth options and its dividend policy related?
- Describe how the dividend policy can "signal" a firm's financial position.

IS THERE AN OPTIMAL DIVIDEND POLICY?

We see that firms and individuals may have a preference for different kinds of dividend policies due to various factors and considerations. From the firm's standpoint, firms with substantial growth options may prefer a low payout policy. Likewise, from an investor's standpoint, we see that certain investors might have a preference for high- or low-payout firms. Investors with low incomes and high current needs would favor high-payout firms. Investors in high income brackets would favor low-payout firms. This has often been called the **clientele effect.** That is, depending on the cash dividend policy that a firm establishes, it attracts a certain clientele of investors. Once that clientele is established, it may be that dividend policy does not directly influence the value of the firm's stock. A significant shift in the firm's cash dividend policy, however, would disrupt the firm's clientele, causing price effects until a new investor clientele owns the firm's common stock.

Although there has been both extensive debate and substantial empirical testing, there is no consensus on the primary issue: whether or not the firm's cash dividend policy *by itself* influences the value of the common stock. Litzenberger and Ramaswamy (1979 and 1982) concluded that higher dividend yields are associated with higher expected returns; this would imply that dividend policy does affect the value of the firm. However, Miller and Scholes (1982) argue that the procedures employed by Litzenberger and Ramaswamy introduced bias into the estimation procedure, which led to an overstatement in the effect of dividends. The best we can say right now is that the firm's cash dividend policy *may* influence the market value of the firm's stock—but then again it may not. Our personal view is that Miller and Modigliani, Black and Scholes (1974), Miller and Scholes, and Miller (1986) are essentially correct: A firm's cash dividend policy does not affect the value of the firm *providing* the policy does not affect its investment decisions. Most managers look at a number of other factors that come into play when the cash dividend decision is made.

OTHER FACTORS IN THE DIVIDEND DECISION

In addition to growth options and possible price effects, other factors appear to influence dividend policy in practice. These include liquidity and profitability, earnings stability, access to equity markets, and control.

Liquidity and Profitability

The cash position of the firm can influence cash dividends. Firms with a shortage of cash often restrict or discontinue cash dividends. Highly profitable firms with substantial cash positions often increase their cash dividends (or repurchase some of their outstanding common stock). One reason cash-rich firms pay more dividends is to provide greater protection against a possible takeover by another firm. By paying higher dividends, the cash-rich firm accomplishes two things—it makes its current stockholders happy, and it reduces its cash position, thus becoming a less tempting takeover target.

Earnings Stability

Another factor often considered in practice is the stability of the firm's earnings. Other things being equal, more stable firms are often in a better position to pay larger cash dividends than less stable firms. The reason is that they can plan for the future with much more certainty than can highly cyclical firms. Public utility firms, for example, pay high cash dividends. They can do this, in part, because of their relatively stable operating environment.

Access to Equity Markets

Smaller firms generally have much more difficulty or incur substantially higher costs when they attempt to raise external equity capital than do larger firms. Because their access to equity markets is limited, small firms tend to pay lower cash dividends.

Control

For many small- and medium-sized firms, ownership control is an important issue. They may be reluctant to sell more common stock, opening ownership to "outsiders." They also will prefer to retain more internally generated funds to provide the equity capital needed for growth. By using internally generated common equity plus any borrowing required, they may be able simultaneously to maintain control *and* to meet the firm's capital needs.

CONSTRAINTS ON DIVIDENDS

Finally, certain constraints may inhibit the firm's ability to pay cash dividends. These involve contractual restrictions, legal restrictions, and taxes on improperly accumulated earnings.

Contractual Restrictions

Bond indentures, term loan agreements, and even preferred stock provisions may often impose restrictions on the payment of cash dividends. For example, a firm may be required to maintain a certain level of working capital or a minimum current or times interest earned ratio. Another common restriction states that common stockholders may not be paid cash dividends until the preferred stockholders have received their dividends. Although these (and similar) restrictions typically do not inhibit the firm's ability to pay dividends, they may do so when a firm is experiencing financial difficulties. From the creditors' or preferred stockholders' points of view, that is exactly what restrictions of this type are intended to do.

Legal Restrictions

Most state laws governing the incorporation of a firm provide statutory restrictions prohibiting the firm from paying cash dividends under certain conditions. These vary from state to state, but they usually include a restriction on the firm's dividend-paying ability when the firm's liabilities exceed its assets, when the anticipated dividend exceeds the retained earnings, or when the dividend would be paid from the firm's invested capital.

Taxes on Improperly Accumulated Earnings

Firms do not have to pay cash dividends as long as the funds are used to purchase productive assets. But if the firm does not pay cash dividends and instead elects to keep increasing its level of cash and marketable securities, problems may arise. If the Internal Revenue Service finds the level of cash and marketable securities to be beyond that deemed reasonable to meet liquidity needs, a special surtax is imposed on the improper accumulation. Although infrequently used, this requirement is designed to ensure that smaller firms do not avoid paying taxes through an excessive accumulation of cash.

Concept Review Questions

- Briefly describe the results of empirical studies on the relationship between dividend policy and the value of common stock.
- Describe how a firm's dividend policy is influenced by the firm's liquidity, profitability, earnings stability, access to equity markets, and control of the firm.

DIVIDEND POLICY IN PRACTICE

Neither theory nor empirical testing provides a complete answer to the question of whether dividend policy influences the market value of the firm's common stock. But, in practice, firms (and their boards of directors) act as though dividend policy *is* an important decision. They view it as being important both in and of itself and because of its signaling content. Stability of dividends is perceived as being important; firms prefer to maintain a steady and increasing level of cash dividends per share over time. Equally important, there is an extreme reluctance to reduce cash dividends. Most firms in practice follow a **smoothed residual dividend policy.** After taking into account many of the items discussed previously, they set the cash dividend policy based on the following considerations:

1. The dividend is set at a constant dollar amount per share.
2. A target dividend payout ratio, which the firm plans to maintain over time, is established.
3. Dividends will be increased when and if it appears the increased dollar amount per share can be maintained.
4. The dollar amount of cash dividends paid per share will be decreased only with great reluctance.

5. Over the long run, the firm attempts to finance capital expenditures with internally generated funds and debt (supplemented only occasionally, if at all, by new common stock), while fluctuating around its target capital structure.

This smoothed residual dividend policy is consistent with some early work done by Lintner (1956). In addition, it is consistent with the pecking order theory suggested by Myers (as discussed in Chapter 12). A firm's dividend policy is determined simultaneously with its investment and financing decisions.

INTERFIRM DIFFERENCES

In assessing the firm's dividend policy in practice, it is useful to look at what firms actually do. In Table 13.2, the earnings per share, dividends per share, and dividend payout ratios are presented for Alcan Aluminum, Baltimore Gas & Electric, and Union Pacific. Alcan Aluminum has had widely fluctuating dividends and payout ratios as its earnings fluctuated dramatically over the 1983–1992 period. Baltimore Gas & Electric has had a very stable dividend policy that up to 1990 involved paying out 50 to 70 percent of earnings in the form of cash dividends. Since 1990 lower earnings for Baltimore Gas & Electric, along with roughly the same cash dividends per share, resulted in a much higher dividend payout ratio. Union Pacific has had stable and increasing cash dividends in line with its increasing earnings per share. These patterns are typical of some of the interfirm differences in cash dividends.

Table 13.2

Dividend Payouts of Three Firms

Alcan Aluminum's cash dividends and dividend payout ratio have fluctuated widely due to wide swings in earnings. Both Baltimore Gas & Electric and Union Pacific have had more consistent payout ratios.

Year	Alcan Aluminum Limited			Baltimore Gas & Electric Company			Union Pacific Corporation		
	Dividends per Share	EPS	Dividend Payout	Dividends per Share	EPS	Dividend Payout	Dividends per Share	EPS	Dividend Payout
1983	$0.40	$0.29	138%	$0.97	$1.65	59%	$0.90	$1.79	50%
1984	0.53	1.15	46	1.03	1.85	56	0.90	2.01	45
1985	0.49	(0.81)	*	1.12	1.87	60	0.90	2.09	43
1986	0.35	0.97	36	1.19	2.10	57	0.93	2.10	44
1987	0.39	1.68	23	1.25	2.31	54	1.00	2.45	41
1988	0.59	3.85	15	1.32	2.31	57	1.05	2.45	43
1989	1.12	3.58	31	1.39	2.03	68	1.12	2.81	40
1990	1.12	1.46	77	1.40	1.40	100	1.19	3.09	39
1991	0.86	(0.25)	*	1.40	1.52	92	1.31	3.16	41
1992	0.45	(0.60)	*	1.42	1.63	87	1.45	3.57	41

* Not a meaningful figure.
Source: Annual reports for each of the firms cited.

Table 13.3

Selected Industry Dividend Payout Ratios for 1992

Notice the differences, from low payout ratios for firms in the machinery, medical supply, restaurant, and steel industries to high ones for firms in the chemical and electric utility industries.

Industry	Payout Ratio
Chemical	86%
Computer	54
Drug	45
Electric utility	84
Food processing	35
Machinery	30
Medical supply	33
Newspaper	65
Restaurant	20
Steel	30

INDUSTRY DIFFERENCES

Dividend payout policies also vary, to an extent, depending on the primary industry in which the firm is involved. This variation results from different amounts of risk, profitability, growth opportunities, and regulation among industries. In Table 13.3 we see a wide range of dividend payout ratios. The machinery, medical supply, restaurant, and steel industries paid out less than 35 percent of earnings in the form of cash dividends in 1992. On the other hand, the chemical and electric utility industries paid out over 80 percent of their earnings in the form of cash dividends.

Not only do dividend payout ratios vary considerably among industries, they also vary among firms within a single industry. Consider the following data, which show the 1992 dividend payout ratios for firms in the machine tool industry.

Firm	Dividends per Share	Payout Ratio
Acme-Cleveland	$0.40	75%
Cincinnati Milacron	0.36	62
Giddings & Lewis	0.11	9
Gleason	0.40	*
Monarch Machine Tool	0.20	*
Snap-on Tools	1.08	69
Stanley Works	1.28	60

*Not a meaningful figure.

We see that both Gleason and Monarch Machine Tool paid cash dividends even though they suffered losses, while Giddings & Lewis paid out only 9 percent of its earnings in the form of cash dividends. On the other hand, Acme-Cleveland, Cincinnati Milacron, Snap-on-Tools, and Stanley Works all paid out between 60 and 75 percent of earnings in the form of cash dividends. These vastly different policies within an industry reflect the substantial differences among firms. Thus, although there do appear to be industry differences that influence cash dividend policies, we must not let these differences obscure the sizable interfirm differences that exist as well.

DIVIDEND CHANGES

We can also examine the actions taken by firms with respect to increasing or decreasing cash dividends. Table 13.4 presents the number of firms increasing, resuming, decreasing, or omitting cash dividends for the 1983–1992 period. In the last few years we see that the number of firms increasing their cash dividends has fallen compared to earlier years. This is the result of the slowness in parts of the economy, with the attendant impact on earnings and internally generated funds. The extreme reluctance of firms to decrease or eliminate cash dividends, however, is highlighted by the relatively small number of decreases or omissions, although they have risen some in recent years.

One other aspect of Table 13.4 deserves attention—the "extra" column. Many firms follow the practice of paying a regular cash dividend and then in good years declaring a **dividend extra**. This practice allows them to have a stated amount of cash dividends per share that can be supplemented, if desired, without raising the stated rate to a new higher level. In this way, the basic per share rate will not have to be cut in bad years.

Table 13.4

Number of Firms Taking Action on Cash Dividends

These data are based on over 10,000 publicly traded stocks. Note the increases relative to decreases, and the number of extras.

Year		Action			
	Increased	Resumed	Decreased	Omitted	Extra
1983	2,006	183	137	172	630
1984	2,085	162	95	199	630
1985	1,898	88	104	231	627
1986	1,685	93	148	257	462
1987	1,822	114	84	186	533
1988	1,858	62	83	175	579
1989	1,869	65	89	218	625
1990	1,433	52	195	328	491
1991	1,129	44	205	387	388
1992	1,364	73	133	294	399

Source: Moody's Annual Dividend Record.

Concept Review Questions

■ How is a firm's dividend policy established?

■ Do dividend payout ratios vary among industries, among firms within an industry, or both?

DIVIDEND PAYMENT PROCEDURES

Cash dividends are normally paid quarterly. Assume that a firm has decided to pay a cash dividend of 75 cents each quarter. The relevant dates that stockholders would be concerned about if they owned or contemplated purchasing the stock, and the payment procedure, might be as follows:

Amount	Date Declared	Ex-Dividend Date	Date of Record	Date Payable
$0.75	January 21	February 8	February 14	March 12
0.75	April 15	May 4	May 10	June 11
0.75	July 15	August 4	August 10	September 9
0.75	October 14	November 4	November 10	December 10

1. DECLARATION (OR ANNOUNCEMENT) DATE This is the date the board of directors meets and issues a statement declaring the next quarter's cash dividends. For our example, this is January 21 in the first quarter, April 15 in the second quarter, and so on. Once the dividends are declared, they become a legal liability of the firm. For example, the first announcement would indicate that a dividend of 75 cents a share will be paid on March 12 to stockholders of record as of February 14.

2. EX-DIVIDEND DATE The **ex-dividend date** is an arbitrary date established for the convenience of the securities industry. The ex-dividend date is the fourth business day (i.e., Monday through Friday) preceding the record date as fixed by the firm. Establishing this date enables the firm (or its registrar, which is usually a bank) to obtain an accurate determination of all stockholders by the record date. All shares owned before the ex-dividend date receive the cash dividend. Stock purchased on or after the ex day will not be entitled to the next cash dividend, because they will not be listed as an owner of record on the record date. For the firm in our example, the first quarter's record date was February 14; accordingly, the ex day is February 8.[7] If you purchased the stock on or before February 7, you would receive the dividend of 75 cents per share when it was paid on March 12. If you bought the stock on February 8, or any time thereafter, the former owner is entitled to the cash dividend paid on March 12.

---

[7] Note that in most cases a weekend will be involved, so the ex-dividend day is typically 6 calendar days preceding the record date.

3. RECORD DATE   The **record date** is the date the stockholder books are closed, to determine who the current stockholders are.
4. PAYMENT DATE   The **payment date** is the date when the firm actually mails the dividend checks to its common stockholders.

The record date is important, but the ex-dividend date is actually more important in terms of deciding who is the owner of the stock for dividend purposes. Because of its importance for determining who is entitled to the next cash dividend, we would expect to see an adjustment in the firm's common stock market price on the ex-dividend date. If you owned the stock in our example on the day before the ex date, you would receive 75 cents on the next pay date. But because you will be 75 cents better off and the firm will be 75 cents worse off, what should happen to the market price of the firm's common stock on the ex day? Other things being equal, it should decrease by an amount approximately equal to the value of the cash dividend to be received.

DIVIDEND REINVESTMENT PLANS

In recent years, many firms have instituted **dividend reinvestment plans.** Under these plans, stockholders can reinvest their cash dividends in additional shares of common stock. The stock can be existing or newly issued shares. Under the first type of plan, a bank acting as trustee accumulates funds from all stockholders electing this option and then purchases shares in the open market. Costs are borne on a pro rata basis but are generally small because of the volume of purchases.

In the second type of plan, the cash dividends go to buy newly issued shares of stock. In this plan, there may be a 3 to 5 percent reduction in the purchase price from the stock's current market price. Often no other fees are charged to the stockholders. A new-issue dividend reinvestment plan enables firms gradually to raise substantial amounts of new common stock capital. It has been estimated that in recent years about 25 percent of all new common stock issued has been through dividend reinvestment plans. Due to their advantages, these plans have continued to grow in popularity.

Despite their growth in popularity, dividend reinvestment plans have one drawback from the stockholder's standpoint. Stockholders must pay taxes on the cash dividends each year, even though they never receive any cash. This factor, more than any other, has probably prevented more investors from signing up for dividend reinvestment plans.

REPURCHASING STOCK

In addition to paying cash dividends, firms sometimes repurchase their stock and hold it as treasury stock. Repurchasing may be accomplished by a tender offer to all the firm's stockholders, by purchasing stock in the secondary market, or by agreeing with one or a small group of the firm's major investors to buy their shares. Many repurchases are small in amount; others are very large. With fewer shares outstanding after a repurchase, other things being equal, the earnings per share of the remaining shares will increase. This increase should result in a higher per share market price.

For example, consider Northern Airlines, which has earnings after taxes of $10 million and plans to use 40 percent ($4 million) of it for cash dividends or for repurchasing some of the firm's common stock. Remember that neither usage affects the firm's reported net income or the total market value of the firm. There are 4 million shares outstanding, and the market price of the stock is $15 per share. Northern can use the $4 million to repurchase 250,000 shares of common stock at $16 per share,[8] or it can pay a cash dividend of $1 per share. The net effect of the repurchase would be as follows:

$$\text{current EPS} = \frac{\text{total earnings}}{\text{number of shares outstanding}} = \frac{\$10\ \text{million}}{4\ \text{million}} = \$2.50\ \text{per share}$$

$$\text{current P/E} = \frac{\text{market price per share}}{\text{earnings per share}} = \frac{\$15}{\$2.50} = 6\ \text{times}$$

$$\begin{matrix}\text{EPS after} \\ \text{repurchasing} \\ \text{250,000 shares}\end{matrix} = \frac{\$10\ \text{million}}{3.75\ \text{million}} = \$2.667\ \text{per share}$$

$$\begin{matrix}\text{expected market} \\ \text{price after} \\ \text{repurchasing}\end{matrix} = (\text{P/E})\,(\text{EPS}) = (6)(\$2.667) = \$16\ \text{per share}$$

From this example, we see that investors receive a $1 benefit either way. If cash dividends are paid, they receive the dollar directly; with the repurchase, the market price of the common stock increases by $1 to $16 per share. This occurs because we assumed that the shares would be repurchased at exactly $16 per share, and the P/E ratio remained constant. *If the firm pays less than $16, the remaining (or nonselling) investors are better off; if more than $16 is paid, the remaining investors are worse off.*

Although this is a purely mechanical exercise so far, it serves to highlight some aspects of repurchasing. In fact, firms that repurchase their common stock *almost always repurchase shares while maintaining their current cash dividend policy.* With this background, it is now possible to consider some of the advantages and disadvantages of repurchasing.

Advantages of Stock Repurchases

From the firm's standpoint, there are a number of possible advantages to stock repurchases:

1. If a firm had a temporary excess of cash being generated but did not want to adjust its stated cash dividend policy, it might decide to repurchase some of its stock. This provides nonselling stockholders with an alternative form of a dividend.
2. By repurchasing, a firm may reduce its future cash dividend requirements or, alternatively, may raise the dividends per share paid to its remaining stockholders without increasing the total cash flow drain on the firm.
3. Repurchases can be used to effect an immediate and often large-scale change in the firm's capital structure. For example, if a firm previously had no debt and

---

[8] The $16 figure is chosen because it is the price at which nonselling investors are neither better nor worse off than selling investors.

decided its target capital structure should include 20 percent debt, it could issue a bond and use the proceeds to repurchase common stock, thereby effecting the capital structure realignment.

4. Repurchasing can also be used to signal information about the firm's future cash flows.

Disadvantages of Stock Repurchases

From the firm's standpoint, some disadvantages may result from repurchasing its own shares:

1. In the past, firms that repurchased substantial amounts of stock often had poorer growth and investment opportunities than firms that did not. Announcing a repurchase program might signal to investors that good investment opportunities did not exist. This negative impact appears to have lessened in recent years as different types of firms started viewing repurchases as an alternative to increasing their dividend payout ratio.

2. From a legal standpoint, the SEC may raise some questions for smaller or family-held firms if it appears the firm is using the repurchases to manipulate the price of its common stock. The Internal Revenue Service also may become interested, if it appears the repurchases are primarily for the avoidance of taxes on cash dividends. If this occurs, the IRS can impose penalties, because the firm's activities fall under Section 531 of the tax code, which deals with improper accumulation of earnings.

On net, it appears that firms will continue to repurchase shares of their common stock. This is particularly true because repurchasing has gained favor as a means of attempting to fend off unwanted corporate suitors and as a means of "leveraging up" the firm's capital structure. Note, however, that by reducing the proportion of cash or marketable securities in a firm's asset structure, the risk composition of the firm may increase. This increased risk, if it occurs, must be balanced against the benefits expected to be derived from the repurchase.

Concept Review Questions

- Describe the dividend payment procedures of a firm.
- Explain what a dividend reinvestment plan is.
- What are some advantages and disadvantages of a stock repurchase?

STOCK SPLITS AND DIVIDENDS

In addition to paying cash dividends, and sometimes repurchasing their own outstanding common stock, firms often issue more shares via a stock split or a stock dividend. Stock splits and stock dividends have exactly the same effect from a financial standpoint. For accounting purposes, however, there are differences between a stock split and a stock dividend.

STOCK SPLIT

The accounting treatment for a **stock split** is straightforward. First, the stockholders must approve increasing the number of shares of common stock. Then, for a 2-for-1 split, for example, the number of shares of common stock is doubled and the par value is halved. For example, as shown in Table 13.5, Wilbur Industries had 1 million shares at a **par value** of $2 per share before the split. After the split, Wilbur had 2 million shares at a par of $1 per share.

STOCK DIVIDEND

With a **stock dividend,** the par value is not reduced, but an accounting entry is made to transfer capital from the retained earnings account to the common stock and additional paid-in capital accounts. The amount to be transferred is determined by the

---

Table 13.5

Effect of Stock Split or Stock Dividend on Wilbur Industries' Stockholders' Equity Accounts

In both cases, the total stockholders' equity remains $7,000,000. However, a stock dividend involves capitalizing some of the firm's retained earnings by a transfer to the common stock and additional paid-in capital accounts.

Before Stock Split or Stock Dividend

Common stock (1 million shares outstanding, ($2 par)	$2,000,000
Additional paid-in capital	550,000
Retained earnings	4,450,000
Total stockholders' equity	$7,000,000

After 2-for-1 Stock Split

Common stock (2 million shares outstanding, $1 par)	$2,000,000
Additional paid-in capital	550,000
Retained earnings	4,450,000
Total stockholders' equity	$7,000,000

After 10 Percent Stock Dividend

Common stock (1.1 million shares outstanding, $2 par)*[†]	$2,200,000
Additional paid-in capital[†]	1,350,000
Retained earnings[†]	3,450,000
Total stockholders' equity	$7,000,000

---

* 100,000 shares are issued.
[†] Based on a market price of $10, ($2)(100,000 shares) = $200,000 which is added to the common stock. Likewise, ($10 − $2)(100,000 shares) = $800,000 which is added to the additional paid-in capital account. Retained earnings is reduced by $1,000,000 (i.e., $200,000 + $800,000).

size of the stock dividend and the current market price of the firm's common stock. In our example, if Wilbur declares a 10 percent stock dividend, it will issue 100,000 (10 percent of 1,000,000 shares) more shares of stock. With a current market price of $10 per share, the transfer out of retained earnings will be $1,000,000. Finally, as also shown in Table 13.5, the common stock account will be increased by $200,000 [i.e., ($2 par)(100,000 shares)], and the remaining $800,000 will be added to the additional paid-in capital account. Note that for both a stock split and a stock dividend, Wilbur's total stockholders' equity is $7 million both before and after the transaction.

BEWARE OF FALSE GIFTS

In the absence of any other simultaneous occurrence, the effects of a stock split or dividend can be summarized as follows:

1. There is no change in the firm's *total* assets, liabilities, stockholders' equity, earnings, cash dividends, or market value.
2. There is a drop in the *per share* earnings, cash dividends, and common stock market price, and a corresponding increase in the number of shares of common stock outstanding.

The consequence of a stock split or stock dividend is to increase the number of shares held by each investor. But each share is worth less, because nothing of value has been created. *The net effect would seem neither to increase nor to decrease* the total market value of the firm. To see this, consider the example of Wilbur Industries again. In Table 13.6, we see that before the split Wilbur had total earnings of $1,150,000, total cash dividends of $460,000, and with a stock price of $10 per share, a total market value of $10,000,000. After the 2-for-1 split, Wilbur still has earnings of $1,150,000, cash dividends of $460,000, and a total market value of $10,000,000. Likewise, as also shown in Table 13.6, an investor owning 1 percent of Wilbur stock does not benefit directly from the stock split.[9]

WHY DECLARE A STOCK SPLIT OR STOCK DIVIDEND?

In the absence of any value-creating activities, it would seem that not many companies would want to declare stock splits or stock dividends. As Table 13.7 shows, however, from 1983 until 1991 and 1992 over 1,000 companies every year declared one or the other.[10] Why is this so? Some possible explanations are:

[9] If a stockholder is entitled to a fractional share, then the firm will pay cash in lieu of the fractional share. For example, if an investor held 25 shares and a 10 percent stock dividend was declared, the stockholder would be entitled to 2.5 shares. If the market price of the stock was $30 per share, the stockholder would receive 2 full shares and $15 cash in lieu of the fractional share.
[10] A **reverse split** is just the opposite of a stock split. If a firm had 10,000 shares of stock outstanding selling at $5 per share, a 1-for-5 reverse split would reduce the number of shares to 2,000 and increase the market price to $25 per share.

Table 13.6

Effect of 2-for-1 Stock Split on both Wilbur Industries and an Individual Investor

There can be no benefit from a stock split unless it causes the total market value of the firm to increase. Stock dividends are similar.

Wilbur Industries	Investor

Before Stock Split

Total earnings $1,150,000
Total cash dividends $460,000
Total shares outstanding 1,000,000

$$\text{EPS} = \frac{\$1,150,000}{1,000,000} = \$1.15$$

$$\text{DPS} = \frac{\$460,000}{1,000,000} = \$0.46$$

$$\text{Dividend payout ratio} = \frac{\$0.46}{\$1.15} = 40\%$$

Market price per share = $10
Total market value, $S = (\$10)(1,000,000)$
$\qquad\qquad = \$10$ million

Owns 10,000 shares, which is equal to 1 percent of total shares outstanding

Cash dividends received
$= (10,000 \text{ shares})(\$0.46)$
$= \$4,600$

Market value of stock
$= (10,000 \text{ shares})(\$10)$
$= \$100,000$

After Stock Split

Total earnings $1,150,000
Total cash dividends $460,000
Total shares outstanding 2,000,000

$$\text{EPS} = \frac{\$1,150,000}{2,000,000} = \$0.575$$

$$\text{DPS} = \frac{\$460,000}{2,000,000} = \$0.23$$

$$\text{Dividend payout ratio} = \frac{\$0.23}{\$0.575} = 40\%$$

Market price per share = $5
Total market value, $S = (\$5)(2,000,000)$
$\qquad\qquad = \$10$ million

Owns 20,000 shares, which is equal to 1 percent of total shares outstanding

Cash dividends received
$= (20,000 \text{ shares})(\$0.23)$
$= \$4,600$

Market value of stock
$= (20,000 \text{ shares})(\$5)$
$= \$100,000$

1. Some firms declare a stock split or stock dividend at the same time as a cash dividend. They view this action as an extension of the firm's cash dividend policy. If the firm actually increases its total cash dividend payout, then stockholders are receiving more total cash dividends. Note, however, that the firm's dividend payout ratio could be increased without simultaneously declaring a stock split or stock dividend.

Table 13.7

Stock Splits, Reverse Splits and Stock Dividends

These data are based on over 10,000 firms. Except for 1991 and 1992, 10 to 15 percent of the firms were involved in a stock split or stock dividend each year. A reverse split decreases the number of shares of common stock outstanding.

Year	Stock Splits	Reverse Stock Splits	Stock Dividends	Total
1983	705	55	903	1,663
1984	392	58	783	1,233
1985	516	84	763	1,363
1986	736	84	854	1,674
1987	602	128	791	1,521
1988	295	114	627	1,036
1989	408	182	610	1,200
1990	315	242	470	1,027
1991	285	267	344	896
1992	148	243	244	635

Source: Moody's Annual Dividend Record, various years.

2. Many firms apparently believe their stock has an optimal trading range. Perhaps this is between $20 and $50 per share. If the market price of the firm's common stock increases to, say, $70, the firm may declare a 2-for-1 split to drive the price down to about $35 per share. Implicit in this idea is that the total value of the firm will be more when it is in its "trading range" than when it is outside it.

3. A third possible reason for declaring stock splits or stock dividends involves the signaling idea discussed when we considered cash dividend policies. The essence of the argument is that firms declaring stock splits or dividends communicate information about the firm's future cash flows over and above any existing information. Theoretical and empirical evidence provided by Grinblatt, Masulis, and Titman (1984) and by McNichols and Dravid (1990), among others, lends support to this idea because the market value of a firm's stock tends, other things being equal, to increase when the firm has a stock split.

4. A final possible reason sometimes given is "to conserve the firm's cash." Firms in financial difficulty fairly frequently say they will declare the dividend in the form of stock *rather* than cash. By doing so the firms conserve cash, but stockholders are worse off. Stockholders suffer the loss of the cash dividend, and because the market value of each share of stock decreases proportionately as more shares are issued, the stockholders' total market value remains, at best, unchanged.

So why do firms continue to declare both stock dividends and stock splits? The answer appears to involve some elements of all the above. Although issuing additional shares of stock is much more expensive than issuing cash dividends, firms often use both stock splits and stock dividends to supplement their cash dividend policy and to signal positive information about the future cash flows of the firm.

Concept Review Questions

■ Describe the differences in accounting procedures between a stock split and a stock dividend.

■ Why do firms declare stock splits or stock dividends?

KEY POINTS

1. Firms pay out over 60 percent of earnings as cash dividends. The rate of increase in cash dividend payout exceeds the rate of inflation.

2. Under both the MM and residual dividend theories, the value of the firm is independent of the firm's cash dividend policy.

3. Tax impacts, in terms of differential tax rates on ordinary income versus capital gains, and the deferral option available with capital gains, do not appear to have much impact on a firm's dividend policy.

4. Firms with substantial growth options appear to adopt lower dividend payout ratios. Also, firms appear to signal future cash flows via their dividend policy.

5. In practice, firms act as if cash dividends are important. Most adopt a smoothed residual dividend policy. This policy includes maintaining a target payout ratio and a target capital structure.

6. Other things being equal, stock repurchases increase the earnings per share and market price of the remaining shares. It is an alternative way for the firm to pay "dividends" to its investors.

7. Neither stock splits nor stock dividends by themselves benefit stockholders. However, firms may signal future cash flow prospects with stock splits and stock dividends similar to signals given by cash dividends and stock repurchases.

QUESTIONS

13.1 Explain the trade-off between paying cash dividends and retaining internally generated funds.

13.2 Discuss the Miller and Modigliani and the residual dividend theories and how they relate to the value of the firm.

13.3 Discuss factors related to taxes, growth options, and signaling that may affect a firm's cash dividend policy.

13.4 Describe what other factors and constraints may also influence the firm's cash dividend decision.

13.5 How do you think the following conditions would affect dividend payout ratios, in general? (*Note:* For some, the direction may not be clear.) Explain your answer.

a. Interest rates fall.

b. A reduction in the corporate tax rate is coupled with increased depreciation allowances for tax purposes.

c. Taxes decrease for individuals.

d.   The firm is in a mature industry and faces intense foreign competition. It decides to meet the competition head on.

e.   The firm is repositioning itself into a new, young, growing industry.

13.6   Explain the smoothed residual dividend policy. How does this policy incorporate many of the observed practices of firms?

13.7   Discuss the relationship among the dividend declaration day, the ex-dividend date, the record day, and the payment date. What should the market price do on the ex-dividend date? Why?

13.8   When a firm repurchases shares of stock to hold as treasury stock, the shares are not viewed as an asset, because they never show up on the left-hand (or asset) side of the firm's balance sheet. Why do firms pay money for them if they are not an asset? Are nonselling stockholders better or worse off after the firm repurchases shares? Explain.

13.9   Explain the main differences between a stock split and a stock dividend from (a) an accounting viewpoint and (b) an investor's standpoint.

13.10   Theoretically, investors should not benefit directly from a stock split or stock dividend.

a.   Explain fully why this is so.

b.   How would you react if an investor said her investment had a price of $50 before a 2-for-1 split, and a price of $28 after the split? Is the market still efficient?

Concept Review Problems

See Appendix A for solutions.

CR13.1   The Eberg Company has EBT of $50 million, a tax rate of 35 percent, and a debt ÷ total asset ratio of 60 percent. The firm is interested in investing $25 million in profitable projects. If the firm wants to maintain its existing debt ratio, how large should Eberg's dividend payout ratio be if its dividend policy is based on the residual dividend policy?

CR13.2   The equity accounts of AVR Corporation are as follows:

Common stock ($1 par value)	$ 1,000
Additional paid-in capital	30,000
Retained earnings	50,000
Total equity	$81,000

a.   If AVR's common stock is currently selling for $30 per share, what affect would a 10 percent stock dividend have on the firm's capital accounts?

b.   If the board of directors of AVR declares a 4-for-1 stock split, what would happen to AVR's capital accounts?

CR13.3   Wise Holdings has the following market-value-based balance sheet:

(in millions)	
Current assets	$25
Long-term assets	75
Total assets	$100
Equity	$100

The company has 5 million shares of common stock outstanding, an EPS of $4, and it has declared a cash dividend of $1 per share. What are the firm's stock price and P/E ratio before the ex dividend date? What are the stock price, P/E ratio, and total market value of equity after the ex dividend date?

CR13.4 Assume Wise Holdings, in CR13.3, decides to repurchase $5 million of common stock (at $20 per share) rather than pay the $1 per share dividend. What would be the effect of the repurchase on the firm's market value of equity, stock price, and P/E ratio?

CR13.5 Andrew Entertainment Ltd. follows a residual dividend policy and has a debt/equity ratio of 2.

a. If the firm has earnings and free cash flow of $900,000 and does not want to issue equity or change the firm's debt/equity ratio, what is the maximum amount of capital spending the firm can participate in?

b. Assume Andrew is not concerned with small fluctuations in its debt/equity ratio, does not want to issue debt, and has $700,000 in investment opportunities. The firm has a cost of equity of 16 percent, a growth rate of 5 percent, and 100,000 shares of common stock outstanding. What is the firm's dividend per share and stock price?

c. Andrew's management is concerned that the residual dividend policy causes too much fluctuation in the firm's dividends per share. The firm's management believes a dividend of $1.75(1.05) at $t = 1$ will signal to the market the strength of Andrew's future earnings, thereby resulting in a lower cost of equity of 13 percent. What will Andrew's stock price be if management is correct?

PROBLEMS

13.1 Husky Manufacturing follows a residual cash dividend policy. For the next year, the firm expects to have internally generated funds of $1 million, profitable investment opportunities are $2 million, and the firm's target capital structure is 40 percent equity and 60 percent debt.

a. How much should Husky pay out to its stockholders in cash dividends?

b. What if profitable investment opportunities are $3 million? If they are $1.5 million?

13.2 Alexander International is considering seven average-risk capital expenditures as follows:

Capital Investment	CF_0	Internal Rate of Return
A	$200	25%
B	300	22
C	150	17
D	450	16
E	350	14
F	250	12
G	100	9

The firm's target capital structure is 30 percent debt and 70 percent equity. Alexander's opportunity cost of capital is 15 percent, and there is $1,200 available in internally generated funds that can be reinvested in the firm or paid out in the form of cash dividends.

a. Which capital budgeting projects should be accepted? If the firm follows a residual dividend policy, how much is available to be paid out in the form of cash dividends?

b. How does your answer change if Alexander's cost of capital is only 11 percent?

13.3 Kyle just invested the same amount of money in two stocks, A and B, which have returns as follows:

	Dividends Expected, D_1,	Dividends Expected, D_2	Capital Gain Expected When Sold at End of Year 2 (after receiving any cash dividend)
Stock A	$100	$100	$400
Stock B	0	0	600

Kyle's required return is 10 percent, and he is in the 28 percent tax bracket for ordinary income.

a. Calculate the present value of his expected returns. Which stock provides higher returns? Why?

b. How much more would Kyle have to receive from stock B to be indifferent between the two stocks?

13.4 Viscione Industries is planning to liquidate in 2 years; that is, at time $t = 2$. At $t = 0$, the management was considering two alternative dividend policies. The first would be to pay a cash dividend of $2 at $t = 1$, followed by a liquidating dividend of $29.34 at $t = 2$. The second plan calls for a cash dividend of $10 at $t = 1$ and a liquidating dividend of $19.83 at $t = 2$.

a. If the cost of equity capital for Viscione Industries is 19 percent, which plan (if either) should *management* favor? (*Note:* Ignore any tax aspects and assume there is no uncertainty concerning whether the firm will actually have the cash to pay the dividends as indicated.)

b. Are there any practical considerations that need to be taken into account that might favor one over the other? Explain.

13.5 McCormick Steel has a current stock market value of $4 million. It has 1 million shares of stock outstanding and currently pays no cash dividends. Two dividend policies are under consideration: Plan I is to continue paying no cash dividends. Plan II involves selling $500,000 of new stock (with no flotation costs) and immediately paying the $500,000 to the existing (but not the new) stockholders. Because there are presently 1 million shares of common stock outstanding, every current stockholder would receive 50 cents per share in cash dividends. The new stock would have to be sold at $3.50 per share (the current market value of $4 million divided by the current 1 million shares, less the cash dividend of 50 cents).

a. How many shares will have to be issued to raise the $500,000? Compare the per share value of the current stockholders' holdings, taking into account both market price and dividends under plan I versus plan II. (*Note:* Ignore taxes.)

b. Now assume that McCormick also has to incur flotation costs of 20 cents per share, so the new stock will sell at $3.30 per share. How many shares will now have to be issued to raise the $500,000? Compare the total per share value of the current stockholders' holdings for both plans now.

c. Comparing your answers to (a) and (b), what can you say about the impact of flotation costs on the dividend (and valuation) decision?

13.6 Westwood Corporation and Mayfair Company are in the same industry, are both publicly traded, and both have a large number of stockholders. Their characteristics are as follows:

	Westwood	Mayfair
Expected annual net cash flows (in thousands)	$75,000	$100,000
Standard deviation of cash flows (in thousands)	40,000	50,000
Annual capital expenditures (in thousands)	60,000	65,000
Existing long-term debt (in thousands)	80,000	100,000
Cash, marketable securities, and unused line of credit (in thousands)	40,000	50,000
Flotation costs and underpricing on common stock issue as a percentage of the gross proceeds	7%	4%

Which company is likely to have the higher dividend payout ratio? Why?

13.7 A firm has adopted a smoothed residual dividend policy. This is supplemented by declaring a dividend extra as follows:

1. Regular dividends paid out are presently 30 percent of earnings. The firm wants to keep its regular dividend payout at 30 percent and will increase the regular payout only when net income increases for 2 consecutive years. (*Note:* For the data given below, this means that the regular cash dividend will not increase until time $t = .4$.)
2. Once the regular dividend is increased, it remains at that level until it can be raised again (based on 2 consecutive years' increases in net income).
3. Each year the firm pays out a total of 40 percent of earnings by declaring an extra dividend. The size of the extra dividend is then the difference between the 30 percent payout policy and the 40 percent payout policy.

If the firm has earnings as follows, what are its regular and extra dividends per year?

t_1	t_2	t_3	t_4	t_5	t_6	t_7	t_8
$100	$100	$110	$140	$120	$160	$180	$220

13.8 On March 1 (a Thursday), the board of directors of Save-More Enterprises met and declared a cash dividend of 50 cents per share, payable April 18 (a Wednesday) to stockholders of record March 22 (a Thursday).

a. If you were going to purchase some stock in Save-More and wanted to receive this cash dividend, by what date would the purchase have to be made?
b. Approximately how much should the market price of Save-More drop on the ex-dividend day?
c. What happens to the cash dividend if you already own the stock and the firm declares bankruptcy on March 12?

13.9 A firm has 1,000,000 shares of common stock outstanding, selling at $90 per share. Its earnings after tax, EAT, is $6,000,000. Because it has excess cash, the firm has decided to buy back 200,000 shares of its common stock. However, because the excess cash has been invested in short-term marketable securities, the EAT will decrease to $5,000,000 once the repurchase is completed. If we assume the P/E ratio remains the same after the repurchase as it is now, what is the price per share that should be offered so that both selling and nonselling stockholders are indifferent to the repurchase?

13.10   Nelson Drug has 50,000 shares of stock outstanding, total earnings of $600,000, and a market price per share of $96. It pays a cash dividend of $4 per share.

a.   Determine the (1) total market value, (2) EPS, (3) P/E ratio, and (4) dividend payout ratio.

b.   Gary, who owns 2,000 shares, has expressed great displeasure with the management policies of Nelson Drug. Management has approached him with the idea of buying back his shares.

(1)   If the firm offers Gary $100 per share instead of paying a cash dividend of $4 per share, are the remaining stockholders better off, worse off, or the same? Assume that the P/E ratio remains the same.

(2)   If after the repurchase the firm elects to pay the same *total* dollar amount out in the form of cash dividends, what happens to the dividends per share? What, if anything, happens to the dividend payout ratio?

(3)   Discuss, but do not work out, what the general effect would be on the remaining stockholders if Nelson Drug had to pay $125 per share to repurchase the shares from Gary. (Assume that the firm spends more than $200,000, so it purchases all of Gary's shares.)

13.11   Markham Brothers has decided to go public. It has retained the services of an investment banker who has indicated that a P/E ratio for Markham of about 8 times earnings would be reasonable for a new offering of this type. In addition, the investment banker figured an offering price of $40 per share would be appropriate. Markham Brothers has earnings after taxes, EAT, of $7.5 million and presently has 500,000 shares of common stock. How large a stock split would you recommend for Markham before the firm goes public?

13.12   Van Horn Distributors lists the following on its annual report (dollars in thousands):

Common stock, $2.50 par; authorized, 6,000,000	
shares; issued and outstanding, 3,589,970 shares	$ 8,975
Additional paid-in capital	2,239
Retained earnings	49,496
Total	$60,710

a.   What changes would occur if Van Horn declared a 2-for-1 stock split? (*Note:* Assume that the authorized shares double to 12,000,000.)

b.   Independent of (a), what if Van Horn declared a 20 percent stock dividend and the market price was $25 per share?

13.13   Horizon Enterprises has 600,000 shares of common stock outstanding, and its EPS is $6. The firm has a dividend payout ratio of 20 percent and a current market price of $90 per share.

a.   Before the split, what are Horizon's (1) total earnings; (2) total cash dividends; (3) cash dividends per share; (4) total market value; and (5) P/E ratio?

b.   Jim owns 50 shares of Horizon. What are his (1) total cash dividends and (2) total market value?

c. Horizon declares a 3-for-1 stock split. What are the new **(1)** total earnings; **(2)** EPS; **(3)** total cash dividends; **(4)** dividends per share; **(5)** dividend payout ratio; **(6)** P/E ratio; and **(7)** total market value? [*Note:* Assume that there are no signaling effects in (c) or (d).]

d. After the split, what are Jim's total cash dividends and total market value?

e. Under what circumstances (if any) might an investor be better off after a stock split?

13.14 The SLP Corporation had a market price of $60 per share on September 1. On September 5, the firm announced a 20 percent stock dividend, payable October 20 to stockholders of record on September 30. You own 90 shares of SLP.

a. What is the ex-dividend date?

b. If you sold your stock on September 20, what price would you receive? (Assume other things are equal and no brokerage costs.)

c. After the stock dividend, how many shares will you own?

d. What should be the market price per share, other things being equal, on September 28 if there are no signaling effects?

e. What is the total market value of your holdings both before and after the 20 percent stock dividend?

13.15 Mini Case Healthcare Plus is a 6-year-old firm that serves the fast-growing need for quality health care for those older than 50. Its target debt to total value ratio is $33\frac{1}{3}$ percent [that is, for every $1 of debt the firm employs $2 of equity, so the debt/total value ratio is $1/($1 + $2)]. Up to this point in time, no cash dividends have been paid out. However, Healthcare Plus "went public" 3 years ago and now some investors are asking when the company will start paying cash dividends. There are 1 million shares of common stock outstanding.

a. What factors argue for the irrelevance of dividend policy? What factors argue for the relevance of dividend policy? That is, explain why you believe cash dividends do or do not affect the market price for the firm's common stock.

b. Healthcare Plus estimates that free cash flow available to be paid out in the form of cash dividends, to pay down debt, or to fund new capital investments, is $2,000,000. It has the following set of independent capital investment opportunities available:

Project	Initial Investment	IRR
A	$ 200,000	50%
B	500,000	30
C	300,000	17
D	800,000	16
E	600,000	18
F	1,400,000	25
G	700,000	14
H	400,000	21

(1) If the firm's opportunity cost of capital is 20 percent and it follows a residual dividend policy, what should the firm do? (*Note:* With a target capital structure of $33\frac{1}{3}$ percent debt, to fund any new investment project the firm uses $\frac{1}{3}$rd debt and $\frac{2}{3}$rds equity financing. The $2,000,000 in free cash flow can, therefore, support $3,000,000 in new capital projects.)

(2)   What happens if everything is as in (1) except that Healthcare Plus initiates a policy of paying a cash dividend of $1.00 per share per year? (*Note:* Assume Healthcare Plus still takes all wealth-maximizing projects and that it will not increase its debt/total value ratio. Also, the capital investment projects are not divisible; that is, partial projects may not be undertaken. Finally, any remaining funds can be invested at 10 percent.)

(3)   What if in addition to the requirement in (2) the firm has a policy of not issuing any more debt?

c.   Assume now that the situation is as in (b2), except that the opportunity cost of capital is 15 percent and wealth-maximizing capital investments can be carried forward one year to time $t = 1$. If the free cash flow at $t = 1$ is estimated to be $2,400,000, the cash dividends are still $1.00 per share (and will be paid in each year), and the following additional capital projects exist (in addition to those carried forward), what decisions should be made?

Project	Initial Investment	IRR
I	$ 500,000	18%
J	300,000	35
K	1,000,000	22
L	800,000	12

d.   If Healthcare Plus proceeds to start paying cash dividends, what sequence of events occurs? If investors are buying or selling the stock, how do they know whether they are entitled to receive a cash dividend or not?

e.   What is a dividend reinvestment plan? What are the benefits to the firm? To shareholders? What tax consequences exist for shareholders?

f.   One of the members of Healthcare Plus's board of directors recommends that the firm repurchase stock instead of paying cash dividends. Does this proposal make sense? Why or why not?

g.   The same board member then suggests that instead of paying cash dividends, the firm pay the dividend in the form of additional shares of stock. Does this proposal make sense? Why or why not?

REFERENCES

Some of the important articles on dividend policy are:

BLACK, FISCHER, and MYRON SCHOLES. "The Effects of Dividend Yield and Dividend Policy on Common Stock Prices and Returns." *Journal of Financial Economics* 1 (May 1974): 1–22.

LINTNER, JOHN. "Distribution of Incomes of Corporations Among Dividends, Retained Earnings, and Taxes." *American Economic Review* 46 (May 1956): 97–113.

LITZENBERGER, ROBERT, and KRISHNA RAMASWAMY. "The Effect of Personal Taxes and Dividends on Capital Asset Prices: Theory and Empirical Evidence." *Journal of Financial Economics* 7 (June 1979): 163–95.

MILLER, MERTON H., and FRANCO MODIGLIANI. "Dividend Policy, Growth, and the Valuation of Shares." *Journal of Business* 34 (October 1961): 411–33.

MILLER, MERTON H., and MYRON S. SCHOLES. "Dividends and Taxes." *Journal of Financial Economics* 6 (December 1978): 333–64.

Recent articles on external financing and the relevance or impact of a firm's cash dividend policy include:

AMBARISH, RAMASASTRY, KOSE JOHN, and JOSEPH WILLIAMS. "Efficient Signaling with Dividends and Investment." *Journal of Finance* 42 (June 1987): 321–44.

ASQUITH, PAUL, and DAVID W. MULLINS, JR. "The Impact of Initiating Dividend Payments on Shareholders' Wealth." *Journal of Business* 56 (January 1983): 77–96.

BHATTACHARYA, SUDIPTO. "Imperfect Information, Dividend Policy, and the 'Bird-in-the-Hand' Fallacy." *Bell Journal of Economics* 10 (Spring 1979): 259–70.

BRENNAN, MICHAEL J., and ANJAN V. THAKOR. "Shareholder Preferences and Dividend Policy." *Journal of Finance* 45 (September 1990): 993–1018.

DEANGELO, HARRY. "Payout Policy and Tax Deferral." *Journal of Finance* 46 (March 1991): 357–82.

EADES, KENNETH M., PATRICK J. HESS, and E. HAN KIM. "Market Rationality and Dividend Announcements." *Journal of Financial Economics* 14 (December 1985): 581–604.

EASTERBROOK, FRANK H. "Two Agency-Cost Explanations of Dividends." *American Economic Review* 74 (September 1984): 650–59.

HEALY, PAUL M., and KRISHNA G. PALEPU. "Earning's Information Conveyed by Dividend Initiations and Omissions." *Journal of Financial Economics* 21 (September 1988): 149–75.

KALAY, AVNER. "Stockholder-Bondholder Conflict and Dividend Constraints." *Journal of Financial Economics* 10 (June 1982): 211–33.

LANG, LARRY H. P., and ROBERT H. LITZENBERGER. "Dividend Announcement: Cash Flow Signalling vs. Free Cash Flow Hypotheses." *Journal of Financial Economics* 24 (September 1989): 181–92.

LITZENBERGER, ROBERT H., and KRISHNA RAMASWAMY. "The Effects of Dividends on Common Stock Prices: Tax Effects or Information Effects." *Journal of Finance* 37 (May 1982): 429–43.

MILLER, MERTON H. "Behavioral Rationality in Finance: The Case of Dividends." *Journal of Business* 59 (October 1986): S451–68.

————, and KEVIN ROCK. "Dividend Policy and Asymmetric Information." *Journal of Finance* 40 (September 1985): 1031–51.

MILLER, MERTON H., and MYRON S. SCHOLES. "Dividends and Taxes: Some Empirical Evidence." *Journal of Political Economy* 90 (December 1982): 1118–41.

OFER, AHARON R., and ANJAN V. THAKOR. "A Theory of Stock Price Responses to Alternative Cash Disbursement Methods: Stock Repurchases and Dividends." *Journal of Finance* 42 (June 1987): 365–94.

ROZEFF, MICHAEL S. "Growth, Beta and Agency Costs as Determinants of Dividend Payout Ratios." *Journal of Financial Research* 5 (Fall 1982): 249–59.

SMITH, CLIFFORD W., JR., and JEROLD B. WARNER. "On Financial Contracting: An Analysis of Bond Covenants." *Journal of Financial Economics* 7 (June 1979): 117–61.

Special dividends and stock splits are examined in:

BRENNAN, MICHAEL J., and THOMAS E. COPELAND. "Stock Splits, Stock Prices, and Transaction Costs." *Journal of Financial Economics* 22 (October 1988): 83–101.

GRINBLATT, MARK S., RONALD W. MASULIS, and SHERIDAN TITMAN. "The Valuation Effects of Splits and Stock Dividends." *Journal of Financial Economics* 13 (December 1984): 461–490.

MCNICHOLS, MAUREEN, and AJAY DRAVID. "Stock Dividends, Stock Splits, and Signaling." *Journal of Finance* 45 (July 1990): 857–880.

14

The Interaction of Investment and Financing Decisions

EXECUTIVE SUMMARY

In most cases net present value based on the opportunity cost of capital works well when firms make value-enhancing capital investment decisions. However, it occasionally runs into difficulties because if the discount rate is a weighted average of the costs of equity and debt, two specific, but implicit, assumptions are made. The first assumption it that in every future time period the firm is profitable so that the benefit of the interest tax shield is realized. The second is that the project's debt capacity is a constant proportion of the project's remaining present value. Some investment decisions, or the financing employed in them, violate these assumptions.

The way to proceed when net present value based on the opportunity cost of capital—called adjusted discount rate NPV in this chapter—doesn't work is to divide and conquer. This can be done by employing adjusted present value, APV. With adjusted present value the base-case net present value of the after-tax operating cash flows, CF, from an all-equity-financed project are determined. Then the present value of the financing benefits (or costs) related to the specific financing employed is determined and added to (or subtracted from) the base-case NPV. Using adjusted present value, unusual financing arrangements can be considered, the financing proportions of debt and equity can deviate substantially from those the firm generally uses, and other issues, such as flotation costs and subsidized financing, can be readily incorporated into the analysis. An alternative to adjusted present value is the flows-to-equity, FTE, method.

Generally the adjusted discount rate NPV, adjusted present value, and flows-to-equity will yield different answers to the same capital investment. Adjusted discount rate NPV can and normally is employed when the firm is involved in "scale-enhancing" projects that do not deviate too far from its normal business, and when the target debt to total value ratio is expected to be constant. But, when clearly "out of the ordinary" situations occur, such as when subsidized financing is available or when project financing is employed, adjusted present value or flows-to-equity may be more appropriate.

WHY NOT JUST EMPLOY NPV AS BEFORE?

In previous chapters we have discussed how firms determine their opportunity cost of capital, based on the firm's weighted average cost of capital, divisional costs of capital, or some project-specific cost of capital (Chapter 6), how they make capital expenditure decisions (Chapters 2 and 7–10), and how they consider the impact of the firm's capital structure on its value (Chapters 11–12). The primary decision criterion we have employed has been net present value, NPV, with a weighted cost of capital used as the discount rate. Net present value—whether using the firm's weighted average cost of capital, some divisional cost of capital, or any other proportion of debt and equity costs as the discount rate—incorporates the benefits of the after-tax operating cash flows of the project along with the benefits of the financing employed for the project. As we know, *the financing costs and benefits are typically captured by the discount rate employed in net present value. That is why no financing costs or benefits (as discussed in Chapter 8) are incorporated in the cash flow stream when a project's net present value is determined.*

For clarity, in this chapter we will employ the term **adjusted discount rate NPV** when discussing the net present value decision criterion with a discount rate that is a weighted average opportunity cost of capital. Implicitly, two important assumptions are generally made when employing adjusted discount rate NPV. The first is that the firm is currently paying taxes (so it gets the benefit of the interest tax shield).[1] The second assumption is that the project's debt capacity is a constant proportion of the project's present value. By **project debt capacity** we mean the incremental contribution a project makes to the firm's ability to borrow. As a firm adds more projects, it increases the cash flows and consequently increases its ability to borrow. Similarly, as the project continues over time toward termination, the amount of debt the project and firm can support normally diminishes.

Thus, the adjusted discount rate NPV decision criterion employing the firm's weighted average cost of capital (or any combination of debt and equity financing costs as the discount rate) generally assumes that the *financing proportions employed are constant over time* and that the amount of debt the project can support diminishes as the project's economic value declines. Another way to say this is that *the adjusted discount rate NPV assumes the debt to total value ratio is constant* over the life of the project. This implicit financing assumption—which separates the investment decision from the financing decision—is the result of incorporating the after-tax costs of both debt and equity financing into the discount rate.

Think about it this way: Let's say you have an almost insatiable craving for red gum balls. In a bowl there are 40 red gum balls and 60 black licorice gum balls. The gum balls, which all have the same size and feel, are mixed together. You are blindfolded before you reach into the bowl. The first time you reach in you take out 5 balls. You continue doing this until you have found and eaten 30 balls. Because they are mixed together (like the financing employed when both debt and equity are incorporated into the discount rate), you have selected some red balls—which make you happy—

---

[1] If the firm is not profitable for a period of time, the before- and after-tax costs of debt capital are the same. One way to handle different tax rates with net present value is to employ different opportunity costs (or discount rates) for different years.

and some black licorice balls, which you will eat anyway. By the laws of chance, you will have selected about 12 red balls and 18 black balls.

What still remains in the bowl? The total number of balls is now only 70 because you have eaten 30 of them. Likewise, as a capital budgeting project moves through its life, its remaining value becomes less and less. Of the 70 balls still remaining in the bowl, about 28 [i.e., (70)(0.40)] of them should be red balls and about 42 [i.e., (70)(0.60)] should be black balls. How about the ability of the remaining balls to satisfy your insatiable craving for red gum balls? Because there are now only about 28 balls remaining, the ability of the remaining red balls to satisfy your craving is less than before. Likewise, as a capital investment project moves forward and the economic value of the remaining part of the project is reduced, its ability to support debt diminishes. Any time the adjusted discount rate NPV is employed, the implicit assumption is that as the economic value of the project is reduced (that is, as you eat the gum balls), the project can carry less and less debt (there are fewer and fewer red gum balls).

There are, in fact, a number of alternative decision criteria that can be employed for making capital expenditure decisions. We investigate two of them—adjusted present value, APV, and flows-to-equity, FTE.[2] To understand the differences among adjusted discount rate NPV, adjusted present value, and flows-to-equity, we must consider which discount rates to employ, what kind of financing will be used, the levered and unlevered costs of equity capital, and the size of the loan that is implied when the adjusted discount rate NPV is employed. All of this adds complications to the decision-making process. At the same time, there are cases in which the adjusted discount rate NPV does not do a good job because of the interrelated nature of the investment and financing decisions.

Before proceeding, however, it is important to reemphasize the point made in Chapters 1, 2, 7, 10 and throughout. That is, *although many things affect the value of the firm, the most important single factor is the investments the firm makes.* Thus, to maximize the value of the firm, V, the firm's most important activity is to make good investment decisions. The financing benefits discussed in this chapter, though still important, lead to substantially less value creation than investment decisions. And, *to make good investment decisions, the most important factors are those discussed earlier: the proper estimation of the expected cash flows, CFs, and assessment of risk.*

Concept Review Questions

- What two assumptions are implicitly made when employing the adjusted discount rate NPV?

- When making capital expenditure decisions, what are some alternatives to the adjusted discount rate NPV?

- Although there are a number of alternative decision criteria for making capital expenditure decisions, what is the most important factor for maximizing the value of the firm?

---

[2] The flows-to-equity approach is sometimes called the equity residual method. For another alternative investment decision criterion, see Arditti and Levy (1977).

ADJUSTED PRESENT VALUE

The essence of the **adjusted present value** decision criterion is to separate the effects of the investment (or capital budgeting) decision from the effects of the financing decision.[3] This is accomplished by first estimating the project's base-case NPV as if the project is fully equity financed. The financing effects are then considered in a separate present value calculation. There are generally three effects of financing that may need to be considered:

1. Tax shield from debt.
2. Flotation costs.
3. Effects of subsidized financing.

The opportunity cost of capital, divisional costs of capital, or any other combination of debt and equity costs, incorporates the tax shield because the after-tax cost of debt capital is $k_b(1 - T)$, where k_b is the before-tax cost of debt and T is the firm's marginal tax rate. Although the debt tax shield is easy to include, it is not always that simple to incorporate flotation costs and the effects of subsidized financing into the discount rate employed in adjusted discount rate NPV. That is why adjusted present value and flows-to-equity sometimes come in handy.

To keep the discussion simple, we make the following assumptions:

1. The capital asset pricing model, CAPM, is a reasonable description of the relationship between risk and return.
2. An appropriate all-equity, or unlevered, beta for the firm can be determined as follows:

$$\beta_s^U = \beta_{\text{debt}}\left(\frac{B}{B + S}\right) + \beta_s^L\left(\frac{S}{B + S}\right) \tag{14.1}$$

where

$$\beta_s^U = \text{the unobserved, unlevered equity beta}$$
$$\beta_{\text{debt}} = \text{the nondiversifiable risk of the firm's debt}$$
$$B = \text{the market value of the firm's debt}$$
$$S = \text{the market value of the firm's equity}$$
$$\beta_s^L = \text{the firm's observed, or levered, equity beta}$$

With the assumption that the beta of debt is zero,[4] the first part of Equation 14.1

---

[3] The adjusted present value was developed by Myers (1974).
[4] Bond betas can be estimated just like stock betas by determining their returns and then regressing them on the market's returns. While the average stock beta is 1.0, bond betas are generally below 0.20. For simplicity, we assume they are zero. Problem 14.6 examines the impact when a bond's beta is greater than zero.

drops out and we can estimate the unlevered equity beta[5] to be:

$$\beta_s^U = \beta_s^L \left(\frac{S}{B + S} \right) \tag{14.2}$$

An alternative way to state Equation 14.2 is

$$\beta_s^U = \beta_s^L / \left(1 + \frac{B}{S} \right) \tag{14.3}$$

3. There are no personal taxes, or the effective tax rates on debt and equity are equal. Thus, for simplicity, we are assuming away Miller's "debt and taxes" world discussed in Chapter 11.[6]
4. All debt tax shields are uncertain in terms of whether the firm will actually receive them.

The adjusted present value is equal to the base-case NPV of the project's after-tax operating cash flows, CF, discounted at the all-equity, or unlevered, cost of capital plus the present value of the financing benefits. Thus,

$$\begin{matrix} \text{adjusted} \\ \text{present} \\ \text{value, APV} \end{matrix} = \begin{matrix} \text{base-case NPV of} \\ \text{project's operating} \\ \text{cash flow discounted at } k_s^U \end{matrix} + \begin{matrix} \text{present value of} \\ \text{financing benefits} \end{matrix} \tag{14.4}$$

To illustrate the adjusted present value decision criteria, Vitacom has provided information on a proposed capital budgeting project for developing, manufacturing, and marketing its new creation, winged liperts. The expected after-tax cash flows, CF, are as follows:

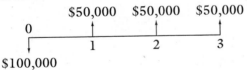

We know that the risk-free rate, k_{RF}, is 10 percent; the expected return on the market portfolio, k_M, is 16 percent; Vitacom's levered equity beta, β_s^L, is 0.80; and Vitacom has determined its target market value ratio of total debt to total value is 0.40, or 40 percent. (Note that β_s^L *is the observed beta* for Vitacom, because it has debt and/or preferred stock outstanding.)

---

[5] The unlevered beta can also be estimated by

$$\beta_s^U = \frac{(k_s^U - k_{RF})}{(k_M - k_{RF})}$$

where k_s^U is the firm's unlevered cost of equity, k_{RF} is the risk-free rate, and k_M is the return on the market portfolio.

[6] For a complete discussion dealing with the impact of personal taxes see Taggart (1991). Cordes and Sheffrin (1983) and Masulis (1983) provide some evidence that the benefit of the interest tax shield is less than the firm's marginal tax rate. If that is so, then personal taxes, or some other factors, may need to be considered.

To calculate the base-case NPV of the winged lipert project's after-tax operating cash flows, CF, we must use Vitacom's unlevered cost of equity capital, which signifies the operating or business risk of the project. (We are also assuming the winged lipert project is no more nor less risky than Vitacom itself.) The levered cost of equity capital, k_s^L, using the capital asset pricing model, CAPM, is

$$k_s^L = k_{RF} + \beta_s^L(k_M - k_{RF}) \qquad (14.5)$$
$$= 10\% + 0.80(16\% - 10\%) = 14.80\%$$

To calculate the unobservable unlevered cost of equity capital, k_s^U, we first estimate the unlevered beta for Vitacom's equity, employing Equation 14.2, as follows:

$$\beta_s^U = \beta_s^L\left(\frac{S}{B+S}\right) = 0.80\left(\frac{0.60}{0.40 + 0.60}\right) = 0.48$$

The unlevered cost of equity capital, which measures the underlying business risk of Vitacom, can now be estimated:

$$k_s^U = k_{RF} + \beta_s^U(k_M - k_{RF}) \qquad (14.6)$$
$$= 10\% + 0.48(6\%) = 12.88\%$$

Once the unlevered cost of equity capital has been estimated, we can determine the base-case NPV of the winged lipert's operating cash flows as follows:

$$\text{base-case } NPV = \frac{\$50,000}{(1 + k_s^U)^1} + \frac{\$50,000}{(1 + k_s^U)^2} + \frac{\$50,000}{(1 + k_s^U)^3} - \$100,000$$

$$= \frac{\$50,000}{(1 + 0.1288)^1} + \frac{\$50,000}{(1 + 0.1288)^2} + \frac{\$50,000}{(1 + 0.1288)^3} - \$100,000$$

$$= \$44,295 + \$39,241 + \$34,763 - \$100,000 = \$18,299$$

The all-equity value of the winged lipert capital investment is $18,299. As such, even without considering the financing benefits of the project, the winged lipert project is a value-enhancing capital investment.

VALUE OF THE ADDITIONAL DEBT CAPACITY

The financing benefits of the new project, which are equal to the present value of the interest tax shield, must now be determined. To calculate the interest tax shield, *we must specify the exact form of the financing to be employed* and the discount rate to be used in determining the present value of the interest tax shield. Specifying the exact form of the debt financing is unnecessary if Vitacom uses the adjusted discount rate NPV decision criterion and some combination of debt and equity financing costs as the discount rate (because an implicit assumption about the amount and form of borrowing employed has already been made).

Although we know that the present value of the interest tax shield needs to be calculated, considerable debate exists about the proper discount rate to employ. Modigliani and Miller (1963) use the before-tax cost of debt for all interest cash flows. Miles and Ezzell (1980) use the before-tax cost of debt for the first period and then use the unlevered cost of equity for the remainder, whereas Harris and Pringle (1985) use the unlevered cost of equity throughout. Modigliani and Miller assume that interest tax shields are certain (i.e., they assume the firm will be profitable in all future periods); Miles and Ezzell assume the interest tax shields are uncertain after the first period, because the future value of the firm is uncertain; and Harris and Pringle assume the value of the firm, and hence the interest tax shield, is uncertain throughout. We follow Harris and Pringle and assume the interest tax shield is risky in the first and all future time periods; therefore, the discount rate to employ is the unlevered cost of equity capital.

To see the effect of different debt-financing alternatives on the adjusted present value, let's examine two alternative debt-financing plans being considered by Vitacom. The first requires Vitacom to borrow 40 percent of the value of the winged lipert project, or $40,000, under a bullet loan and pay only interest on the loan until the end of the project at $t = 3$; the principal is repaid at the end of the loan. Thus, with a bullet loan, no principal repayments are made until the loan matures. The before-tax cost of debt is 10 percent.[7] With a marginal corporate tax rate of 35 percent, the present value of the uncertain interest tax shield (discounted at Vitacom's risky unlevered equity rate of 12.88 percent) is

Year	Borrowing (1)	Interest (1)(0.10) (2)	Interest Tax Shield (2)(0.35) (3)	Present Value of Interest Tax Shield at 12.88% (4)
1	$40,000	$4,000	$1,400	$1,240
2	40,000	4,000	1,400	1,099
3	40,000	4,000	1,400	973
				Total $3,312

With the bullet loan form of debt financing, the adjusted present value is

$$APV \text{ (bullet loan)} = \text{base-case } NPV + \text{present value of financing benefits}$$
$$= \$18,299 + \$3,312 = \$21,611$$

After taking account of the financing benefits, which further enhance the value-creation aspects of the winged lipert project, Vitacom decides it should proceed with the proposed capital expenditure. The APV decision criterion first captures the economic benefits of the proposed project as if it is all-equity-financed; then the financing benefits of the interest tax shield are taken into account in a separate step. For the

---

[7] Because we assumed $\beta_{\text{debt}} = 0$, the risk-free rate, k_{RF}, can be employed as the before-tax cost of debt. Other (higher) costs of debt may be employed without changing the basic analysis and implications.

winged lipert project the specific form of the debt financing required to fund 40 percent of the project must be specified; the rest of the financing will be equity financing.

Alternatively, what happens to the adjusted present value if Vitacom employs an alternative debt financing plan that involves paying off the borrowing in equal increments over time? In this case less total interest is paid, so the present value of the financing benefits is less:

Year	Borrowing at the Start of the Year (1)	Interest (1)(0.10) (2)	Interest Tax Shield (2)(0.35) (3)	Pesent Value of Interest Tax Shield at 12.88% (4)
1	$40,000	$4,000	$1,400	$1,240
2	26,667	2,667	933	733
3	13,334	1,333	467	324
				Total $2,297

The APV with the equal principal payment debt financing is

$$APV \text{ (equal principal payment)} = \$18,299 + \$2,297 = \$20,596$$

as opposed to $21,611 when the bullet loan was employed and no principal payments are made until the end of the project's life. Although Vitacom should accept the project no matter which debt financing plan is chosen, this example illustrates a very important point: *With adjusted present value the specific form of financing directly affects the subsequent APV.* Thus, depending on the specific interest and principal repayment pattern associated with the debt financing, the adjusted present value differs.[8]

FLOTATION COSTS

Vitacom proposes to finance the project based on the proportions specified by its target capital structure, so 60 percent of the financing, or $60,000 in common equity, is needed. What if no internally generated common equity exists and Vitacom has to sell additional common stock to finance the equity portion of the project? Suppose the flotation costs (to underwriters, lawyers, and others) amount to an after-tax cost of 5.5 percent of the gross proceeds of the issue. This means Vitacom has to issue $63,492 [i.e., $60,000/(1 − 0.055)] in stock to obtain the $60,000 in cash. The $3,492 difference (which occurs at time $t = 0$) is a direct cost of the equity financing. The flotation costs must now be subtracted, to arrive at the project's adjusted present value. Therefore, the adjusted present value when the bullet loan is employed and new common stock is required is

$$APV = \text{base-case } NPV + \begin{matrix}\text{present value of}\\\text{financing benefits}\end{matrix} - \begin{matrix}\text{present value of}\\\text{the cost of new}\\\text{equity financing}\end{matrix}$$

$$= \$18,299 + \$3,312 - \$3,492 = \$18,119$$

[8] Appendix 14A considers the adjusted present value in an MM world.

We see that once financing costs are considered, the adjusted present value of the proposed project declines. Although these financing costs relate to equity, financing costs related to debt financing could be treated in the same manner.

Based on the analysis for Vitacom, we see that to determine the adjusted present value, the present value of the financing benefits and any financing or flotation costs are calculated separately and then combined with the base-case NPV of the project's operating cash flows. Different financing amounts or arrangements will influence the present value of the financing benefits (or costs), and hence will affect the adjusted present value.

SUBSIDIZED LOANS

In order to attract Vitacom to locate in their community, Centralia has agreed to provide low-cost debt financing to help Vitacom finance the project. The interest rate on the subsidized debt financing is 4 percent, whereas the market interest rate for Vitacom is 10 percent. This subsidy results in Vitacom paying less interest over the life of the loan; accordingly, the discounted present value of the loan (which includes both its interest and principal) is less. *To determine the present value of the financing benefits, two separate calculations are now required.* The first is just the present value of the interest tax shield, calculated as before, but using the 4 percent interest rate. In effect, owing to the subsidy, Vitacom has a smaller interest tax shield than at the higher 10 percent market interest rate. The second calculation takes into account that Vitacom (in present value terms) actually pays back less with the subsidized loan than with the nonsubsidized loan.

To illustrate the calculations needed, let's go back to the bullet loan debt financing for $40,000 that Vitacom was originally considering. At the subsidized interest rate of 4 percent, the present value of the interest tax shield (discounted at Vitacom's un-levered cost of equity capital of 12.88 percent) is less than it was before:[9]

Year	Borrowing (1)	Interest (1)(0.04) (2)	Interest Tax Shield (2)(0.35) (3)	Present Value of Interest Tax Shield at 12.88% (4)
1	$40,000	$1,600	$560	$ 496
2	40,000	1,600	560	439
3	40,000	1,600	560	389
				Total $1,324

[9] The question might be asked, "Why do we continue to discount the tax shield at the unlevered equity rate of 12.88 percent?" The answer is that the tax shield in the first and every future period is still uncertain, and therefore, following Harris and Pringle, the unlevered equity rate that reflects this uncertainty must be employed. If a set of cash flows is determined to be completely riskless, Ruback (1986) indicates that the after-tax borrowing rate is employed. For example, some financial experts treat depreciation cash flows as riskless and propose discounting them at either the before- or after-tax risk-free rate. Such treatment assumes that in every future period the firm will be profitable, and therefore, there is no uncertainty. In practice there are few, if any, completely riskless cash flow streams.

This is the first part of the benefit that Vitacom receives from the subsidized loan financing. Vitacom also benefits from having to pay back less (in present value terms) with the subsidized loan.

How much less? The cash outflows experienced by the firm with the subsidized loan—and its present value discounted at the after-tax borrowing rate[10] on the unsubsidized loan of $(10\%)(1 - 0.35) = 6.5\%$—are

Year	Principal repayment (1)	Interest ($40,000)(0.04) (2)	After-Tax Interest Outflow (2)(1 − 0.35) (3)	Principal plus After-Tax Interest (1) + (3) (4)	Present Value at 6.50% (5)
1	—	$1,600	$1,040	$ 1,040	$ 977
2	—	1,600	1,040	1,040	917
3	$40,000	1,600	1,040	41,040	33,975
				Total	$35,869

Because of the subsidized loan, the present value of the debt financing is only $35,869 instead of $40,000; hence, Vitacom saved an additional $4,131 with the subsidized loan. The adjusted present value, ignoring any flotation costs, is therefore

$$APV = \text{base-case } NPV + \begin{array}{c}\text{present value}\\ \text{of interest}\\ \text{tax shield}\end{array} + \begin{array}{c}\text{present value of}\\ \text{savings due to}\\ \text{subsidized financing}\end{array}$$

$$= \$18,299 + \$1,324 + \$4,131 = \$23,754$$

Comparing this with the APV of $21,611 for the unsubsidized loan, we see that Vitacom is better off by $2,143 (i.e., $23,754 − $21,611) in present value terms because of the cut-rate financing obtained. Although Vitacom should proceed with the project no matter what debt financing plan is employed, the value of the firm is enhanced the most by accepting the subsidized financing.

Compared with the adjusted discount rate NPV decision criterion, the adjusted present value sometimes appears more difficult to employ. However, there are times when it may be the only way to proceed, due to the complications involved or the interrelated nature of the investment and financing decisions. Two cases in which adjusted present value comes in handy are (1) when flotation costs are substantial and (2) when subsidized financing is present. Other situations also exist, but before examining them let's consider the flows-to-equity criterion for making capital investment decisions.

Concept Review Questions

- What is the main principle of the adjusted present value decision criterion?
- Describe how to calculate a project's adjusted present value.

[10] The 6.50 percent rate is employed to discount these cash flows because that is the after-tax rate at which the firm could borrow without the benefits of subsidization.

FLOWS-TO-EQUITY

Both the adjusted discount rate NPV and adjusted present value employ a project's after-tax operating cash flows. However, another decision criterion—the **flows-to-equity**—values the cash flows that accrue directly to the firm's stockholders. That is, flows-to-equity focus on the cash flows that go to the firm's owners *after* deducting the after-tax interest payments and the principal part of the loan payments. The flows-to-equity criterion, which is used extensively in valuing real estate investments, is

$$
\begin{array}{l}
\text{flows to} \\
\text{equity, } FTE
\end{array} =
\begin{array}{c}
\text{present value of} \\
\text{after-tax cash flow} \\
\text{accruing to the} \\
\text{stockholders discounted at } k_s^L
\end{array} -
\begin{array}{c}
\text{net outlay by} \\
\text{stockholders}
\end{array}
\qquad (14.7)
$$

where the discount rate employed is the levered cost of equity capital, k_s^L. The levered cost of equity is the appropriate discount rate because it is what the equity participants demand in the way of a return, *given* both the firm's and project's risk and the financing employed.

Instead of using adjusted present value, Vitacom is now going to employ the flows-to-equity decision criterion to evaluate the economic benefits of winged liperts under the two different debt financing plans considered earlier. The actual cash flows that go to the stockholders when Vitacom borrows $40,000 with the bullet loan and pays only interest on the loan until the end of the project are given in Table 14.1. Note that the only additional calculations relate to the interest outflow, the tax benefits of

Table 14.1

Cash Flows to Stockholders with the Bullet Loan Financing

To calculate the flows-to-equity value, we must calculate the cash flows to stockholders. With the bullet loan, only interest is paid for the first 2 years and then the principal is repaid in year 3.

	Year			
	0	**1**	**2**	**3**
1. Operating cash flows, CF		$50,000	$50,000	$50,000
2. Initial investment	−$100,000			
3. Borrow 40 percent of the value of the project (row 2)(0.40)	40,000			
4. Principal repayment				−40,000
5. Interest at 10 percent (lagged 1 year)		−4,000	−4,000	−4,000
6. Tax benefit of the interest: (row 5)(0.35)		1,400	1,400	1,400
7. Cash flow to stockholders (row 1 + row 4 + row 5 + row 6)	−$ 60,000	$47,400	$47,400	$ 7,400

the interest, and the repayment of principal. As indicated, the stockholders must invest $60,000 at time $t = 0$ and will receive net cash flows (after the firm pays interest and principal and takes advantage of the tax deductibility of interest) of $47,400 at both $t = 1$ and $t = 2$, followed by $7,400 at $t = 3$. Based on the levered cost of equity capital of 14.80 percent, which is what Vitacom's stockholders require to compensate them for the risks involved in the firm and in the winged lipert project, the flows-to-equity value is

$$FTE \text{ (bullet loan)} = \frac{\$47,400}{(1 + 0.1480)^1} + \frac{\$47,400}{(1 + 0.1480)^2} + \frac{\$7,400}{(1 + 0.1480)^3}$$
$$- \$60,000$$
$$= \$41,289 + \$35,966 + \$4,891 - \$60,000 = \$22,146$$

Although Vitacom stockholders would still accept the proposed project because it helps maximize their value, the flows-to-equity value of $22,146 is different from the adjusted present value of $21,611 when the same bullet loan is employed to provide the debt financing.

Consider now the second debt financing plan, in which the $40,000 is paid off in equal installments over 3 years. The cash flows going to the stockholders are now shown in Table 14.2. With this new set of net cash flows going to the stockholders, the flows-to-equity value is

$$FTE \text{ (equal principal payment)} = \frac{\$34,067}{(1.1480)^1} + \frac{\$34,933}{(1.1480)^2} + \frac{\$35,799}{(1.1480)^3} - \$60,000$$
$$= \$29,675 + \$26,506 + \$23,662 - \$60,000 = \$19,843$$

Table 14.2

Cash Flows to Stockholders with the Equal Principal Payment Loan

With the equal principal payment loan, both principal and interest are paid in each of the 3 years of the loan. Because less interest is paid with this loan, the total cash flow to stockholders is higher than with a bullet loan, but the timing of the cash flows differs.

	Year			
	0	**1**	**2**	**3**
1. Operating cash flows, CF		$50,000	$50,000	$50,000
2. Initial investment	−$100,000			
3. Borrow 40 percent of the value of the project: (row 2)(0.40)	40,000			
4. Principal repayment		−13,333	−13,333	−13,334
5. Interest at 10 percent (lagged 1 year)		−4,000	−2,667	−1,334
6. Tax benefit of the interest: (row 5)(0.35)		1,400	933	467
7. Cash flow to stock-holders (row 1 + row 4 + row 5 + row 6)	−$ 60,000	$34,067	$34,933	$35,799

As before, the flows-to-equity method produces a value for this plan different from the adjusted present value, which was $20,596. With one exception (to be discussed next), adjusted discount rate NPV, adjusted present value, and flows-to-equity always provide different answers and, hence, may result in different decisions for any proposed capital investment.

Concept Review Questions

- What discount rate is employed when calculating the adjusted present value and the flows-to-equity? Why?
- Describe the steps performed when calculating a project's FTE.

WHEN ARE ADJUSTED DISCOUNT RATE NPV, APV, AND FTE THE SAME?

If exactly the same assumptions are employed, the adjusted discount rate NPV (based on the firm's weighted average cost of capital, or any other combination of debt and equity costs of financing, as the discount rate), the adjusted present value, and the flows-to-equity decision criteria will provide the same value. The basic assumptions that must be made for the three decision criteria to produce the same value are these:

1. The project's debt capacity is determined by the present value of both the project's operating and financing cash flows.
2. Tax impacts from interest, both inflows and outflows, are reflected immediately.

USING ADJUSTED DISCOUNT RATE NPV

To show how we can arrive at exactly the same value with the three decision criteria, let's go back to the decision faced by Vitacom. The operating cash flows are

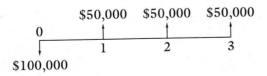

The rest of the assumptions are again

$\beta_s^L = 0.80$, so $k_s^L = 14.80\%$
k_b (the before-tax cost of debt) = 10%
$T = 0.35$, so k_i (the after-tax cost) = 10%(1 − 0.35) = 6.50%
W_B (or B, the proportion of debt) = 0.40
W_S (or S, the proportion of equity) = 0.60

The opportunity cost of capital, as given by Vitacom's weighted average cost of capital, is[11]

$$\text{opportunity cost of capital} = k_s^L W_S + k_i W_B \tag{14.8}$$
$$= 14.80\%(0.60) + 6.50\%(0.40)$$
$$= 8.88\% + 2.60\% = 11.48\%$$

The project's adjusted discount rate NPV at 11.48 percent is

$$NPV = \frac{\$50,000}{(1 + 0.1148)^1} + \frac{\$50,000}{(1 + 0.1148)^2} + \frac{\$50,000}{(1 + 0.1148)^3} - \$100,000$$
$$= \$44,851 + \$40,232 + \$36,089 - \$100,000 = \$21,172$$

USING ADJUSTED PRESENT VALUE

As mentioned previously, adjusted discount rate NPV makes a very specific (although not explicitly stated) assumption about the debt financing used when the discount rate is some average of the after-tax costs of debt and equity financing. We employ the firm's weighted average cost of capital in this example, but the same conclusions hold for any other discount rate employed with NPV that is a combination of the after-tax costs of debt and equity. To get the figure of $21,172 provided by adjusted discount rate NPV, we must make sure the loan implied by the adjusted discount rate NPV decision criterion is actually calculated and then employed in the determining the project's adjusted present value. The base-case NPV at the unlevered equity discount rate of 12.88 percent is just what we determined earlier—that is, $18,298.60. Now the *exact loan implied by the adjusted discount rate NPV criterion must be determined.* This loan is equal to 40 percent of the present value of both the after-tax operating cash flows, CF, and the financing tax benefits provided by the project. Note that the value of the implied loan decreases over time as the present (or economic) value of the remaining operating cash flows and financing benefits decline.

To calculate the implied loan incorporated in the net present value, we first discount the after-tax cash flows, employing the unlevered cost of equity capital, because we are examining the financing benefits as a separate part of the process. The implied loan is determined as follows:

---

[11] An alternative equation for determining the opportunity cost of capital once the unlevered equity rate is known, and assuming the debt tax shield is uncertain, is

$$\text{opportunity cost of capital} = k_s^U - (k_{RF})(T)(B/V)$$

With the unlevered cost of equity of 12.88 percent determined previously, the opportunity cost of capital is

$$\text{opportunity cost of capital} = 12.88\% - (10.00\%)(0.35)(0.4/1.0)$$
$$= 11.48\%$$

Table 14.3

Loan Implied by Adjusted Discount Rate NPV: Tax Shield Benefit from the First Layer of Financing

To obtain the same value from adjusted present value as from adjusted discount rate NPV, the exact loan implied by adjusted discount rate NPV must be calculated. This loan financing provides an interest tax shield that is incorporated in the adjusted present value calculation.

		Year		
	0	1	2	3
1. Operating cash flows, CF		$50,000.00	$50,000.00	$50,000.00
2. Present value of the remaining cash flows (row 1 from previous year + row 2 from previous year)/(1 + 0.1288)	$118,298.60	83,535.46	44,294.83	
3. Borrow 40 percent of the value of the project: (row 2)(0.40)	47,319.44	33,414.18	17,717.93	
4. Interest at 10 percent (lagged 1 year)		4,731.94	3,341.42	1,771.79
5. Tax benefit of the interest: (row 4)(0.35)		1,656.18	1,169.50	620.13
6. Present value of the tax benefit [(row 5 from previous year + row 6 from previous year)/(1 + 0.1288)]	2,816.20	1,522.74	549.37	

$$PV_2 = \frac{\$50,000}{(1.1288)^1} = \$44,294.83$$

$$PV_1 = \frac{\$50,000}{(1.1288)^1} + \frac{\$50,000}{(1.1288)^2} = \$83,535.46$$

$$PV_0 = \frac{\$50,000}{(1.1288)^1} + \frac{\$50,000}{(1.1288)^2} + \frac{\$50,000}{(1.1288)^3} = \$118,298.60$$

These cash flows are summarized in row 2 of Table 14.3. Then, the borrowing of 40 percent of the present value of the cash flows is calculated in row 3, followed by the interest at 10 percent in row 4, the tax shield (at 35 percent) in row 5, and the present value of the interest tax shield in row 6. The present value (at time $t = 0$) of the interest tax benefits is $2,816.20. Thus, as discussed earlier, *there is a financing benefit to the project, in addition to its operating benefit* of $18,299 determined earlier.

Can we stop there? No, we cannot, because the present value of the $2,816.20 financing benefit permits another layer of borrowing. This second layer of borrowing and the present value of the interest tax shield of $2,873.20 are shown in Table 14.4. When we add the present value of the interest tax shield of approximately $2,873 to

Table 14.4

Loan Implied by Adjusted Discount Rate NPV: Tax Shield Benefit from the Second Layer of Financing

Due to the first layer of financing shown in Table 14.3, the firm obtains an interest tax shield and therefore can obtain more financing.

	Year			
	0	**1**	**2**	**3**
1. Present value of the operating cash flows (row 2 from Table 14.3) at 12.88 percent	$118,298.60	$83,535.46	$44,294.83	
2. Present value of the first layer of tax benefits (row 6 from Table 14.3) at 12.88 percent	2,816.20	1,522.74	549.37	
3. Total present value of operating cash flows and the first layer of tax benefits: (row 1 + row 2)	121,114.80	85,058.20	44,844.20	
4. Borrow 40 percent of the value of the project: (row 3)(0.40)	48,445.92	34,023.28	17,937.68	
5. Interest at 10 percent (lagged 1 year)		4,844.59	3,402.33	1,793.77
6. Tax benefit of the interest: (row 5)(0.35)		1,695.61	1,190.81	627.82
7. Present value of the tax benefit [(row 5 from previous year + row 6 from previous year)/ (1 + 0.1228)]	2,873.20	1,547.66	556.18	

the base-case NPV of $18,299, we get an adjusted present value that includes the second layer of financing benefits of

APV = base-case NPV + present value of financing benefits

= $18,299 + $2,873 = $21,172

We can carry this one step further. The $2,873.20 now permits another layer of borrowing, as shown in Table 14.5. Adding the present value of the "total" interest tax shield of approximately $2,874 to the base-case NPV of $18,299, we get an adjusted present value of

APV = $18,299 + $2,874 = $21,173

which, except for a rounding difference of $1, is equal to the adjusted discount rate NPV calculated earlier. Thus, when we specify the loan consistently (i.e., as implicitly assumed by adjusted discount rate NPV), adjusted present value and adjusted discount rate NPV give exactly the same answer.

The loan and principal repayments implied by adjusted discount rate NPV (calculated from line 4 in Table 14.5) are as follows:

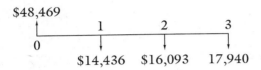

$48,469

| 0 | 1 | 2 | 3 |

$14,436 $16,093   17,940

Table 14.5

Loan Implied by Adjusted Discount Rate NPV: Tax Shield Benefit from the Third Layer of Financing

Due to the second layer of financing shown in Table 14.4, the firm obtains another small interest tax shield and therefore can obtain a little more financing. After three layers of financing, the adjusted present value and the adjusted discount rate NPV are almost exactly equal.

	Year			
	0	**1**	**2**	**3**
1. Present value of the operating cash flows (row 1 from Table 14.4) at 12.88 percent	$118,298.60	$83,535.46	$44,294.83	
2. Present value of the second layer of tax benefits (row 7 from Table 14.4) at 12.88 percent	2,873.20	1,547.66	556.18	
3. Total present value of the operating cash flows and the second layer of benefits: (row 1 + row 2)	121,171.80	85,083.12	44,851.01	
4. Borrow 40 percent of the value of the project: (row 3)(0.40)	48,468.72	34,033.25	17,940.40	
5. Interest at 10 percent (lagged 1 year)		4,846.87	3,403.32	1,794.04
6. Tax benefit of the interest (row 5)(0.35)		1,696.41	1,191.16	627.91
7. Present value of the tax benefit [(row 5 from previous year + row 6 from previous year)/ (1 + 0.1288)]	2,874.24	1,548.04	556.26	

This loan must be calculated, and then the principal repayments must be paid off in exactly the manner determined, if we are to get the same figure from adjusted present value and adjusted discount rate NPV. Using any other borrowing pattern with APV will result in a figure different from that reached using adjusted discount rate NPV.

USING FLOWS-TO-EQUITY

For flows-to-equity we must use the same loan implied by adjusted discount rate NPV determined above. The cash flow stream to the stockholders under the flows-to-equity method is shown in Table 14.6. The flows-to-equity value, based on the appropriate (i.e., levered) equity discount rate of 14.80 percent, is

$$FTE = \frac{\$32,413}{(1.1480)^1} + \frac{\$31,695}{(1.1480)^2} + \frac{\$30,893}{(1.1480)^3} - \$51,531$$
$$= \$28,234 + \$24,050 + \$20,419 - \$51,531 = \$21,172$$

which is the same as the adjusted discount rate NPV calculated earlier. Thus, *as long as we make exactly the same assumptions,* the adjusted discount rate NPV, adjusted present value, and flows-to-equity decision criteria provide exactly the same answer.

Table 14.6

Cash Flows to Stockholders Based on the Loan Implied by Adjusted Discount Rate NPV

For flows-to-equity to produce the same answer as adjusted discount rate NPV, the exact loan implied under the adjusted discount rate NPV must be employed. Then the cash flows to stockholders can be determined.

		Year		
	0	**1**	**2**	**3**
1. Operating cash flows, CF		$50,000	$50,000	$50,000
2. Initial investment	−$100,000			
3. Borrow 40 percent of the present value of the operating and tax benefits	48,469			
4. Principal repayment		−14,436	−16,093	−17,940
5. Interest at 10 percent (lagged 1 year)		−4,847	−3,403	−1,794
6. Tax benefit of the interest: (row 5)(0.35)		1,696	1,191	627
7. Cash flow to stockholders (row 1 + row 4 + row 5 + row 6)	−$ 51,531	$32,413	$31,695	$30,893

WHEN ADJUSTED PRESENT VALUE AND FLOWS-TO-EQUITY COME IN HANDY

We have already examined two situations in which the adjusted present value approach is useful. The first is when there are large flotation costs that cannot readily be taken into account with the adjusted discount rate NPV approach. In practice this situation rarely causes such severe problems that we have to throw adjusted discount rate NPV out the window. In the second situation, the project contains some type of specialized financing that cannot be readily incorporated into the discount rate. Note that the risk of the project does not have to equal the firm's average risk for adjusted present value to be useful. Adjusted present value is also useful when the firm has a temporary loss and there are no benefits due to interest tax shields. The interest tax shield benefits can then be built into the adjusted present value if and when they are expected to occur.

Adjusted present value can be employed in other circumstances as well. Most of these involve situations in which the financing employed over the life of the project changes, so that a constant target debt to total value ratio is not a reasonable assumption. Such a situation occurs when firms are involved in major **project financing** activities. Under project financing, a variety of different financing arrangements may exist for large, individual capital investments. An early example of project financing occurred in the early 1970s when Sohio (subsequently merged into British Petroleum) obtained direct project financing for developing its Alaskan oil fields. More recently, in 1988 General Electric Capital Corporation arranged $105 million in limited recourse project financing for construction of the BevPak beverage container plant in Monticello, Indiana. This plant makes both tin-plated steel and aluminum beverage cans, yet it is independent of any beverage producer. Independent ownership enables BevPak to reduce the risks of operating at less than full capacity by allowing it to enter into contracts to supply competing beverage makers, such as Coca-Cola and Pepsi. When a project financing enterprise is being considered and analyzed, adjusted discount rate NPV may not provide the most appropriate decision criterion because the ratio of debt to total value is generally not constant.

As a general rule, net present value using an adjusted discount rate can be employed in all capital investment decisions that are extensions of the basic activities of the firm that do not result in the consideration of completely new types of endeavors. Such activities might be thought of as "scale-enhancing" investments, in that they emphasize enlarging (or shrinking) the firm's primary business activities. However, if the firm is evaluating decisions that are totally outside of its normal business activities, or if the financing is of a very different nature from that assumed under adjusted discount rate NPV, adjusted present value may be more appropriate. In practice, very few firms employ adjusted present value on an ongoing basis. Rather, for the vast majority of their capital investment decisions they use net present value employing an adjusted discount rate, assuming a constant target debt to total value ratio.

The flows-to-equity method is often used with highly levered projects, typical of many real estate investments and leveraged buyouts (LBOs). In these cases the main concern is the magnitude and timing of the after-corporate-tax and debt-financing charges that the owners can expect to recognize. The ownership and financing arrangements often make it hard to incorporate the proper adjustments directly into the discount rate employed under adjusted discount rate NPV. In these situations flows-to-equity is much easier to employ than adjusted discount rate NPV.

Concept Review Questions

■ What basic assumptions must be made for the adjusted discount rate NPV, APV, and FTE to produce the same accept or reject decisions?

■ When making capital budgeting decisions, what are the benefits to using APV or FTE?

KEY POINTS

1. Adjusted discount rate NPV, based on the firm's weighted average cost of capital, divisional costs of capital, or any other combination of debt and equity costs of financing as the discount rate, implicitly assumes a very specific loan is employed to provide the debt-financed portion of a proposed project's financing. This loan keeps the debt to total value ratio constant over the life of the project.

2. The adjusted present value is equal to the base-case NPV of the after-tax operating cash flows discounted at the unlevered cost of equity capital plus the present value of the financing benefits, or

$$\begin{matrix} \text{adjusted} \\ \text{present} \\ \text{value, APV} \end{matrix} = \begin{matrix} \text{base-case NPV of} \\ \text{project's operating} \\ \text{cash flow discounted at } k_s^U \end{matrix} + \begin{matrix} \text{present value of} \\ \text{financing benefits} \end{matrix}$$

3. Different types of financing, floatation costs, and subsidized financing can be incorporated into adjusted present value.

4. Flows-to-equity is equal to the operating cash flow minus after-tax interest and principal repayments discounted at the levered cost of equity capital, less the equity cash outflows, or

$$\begin{matrix} \text{flows to} \\ \text{equity, FTE} \end{matrix} = \begin{matrix} \text{present value of} \\ \text{after-tax cash flow} \\ \text{accruing to the} \\ \text{stockholders discounted at } k_s^L \end{matrix} - \begin{matrix} \text{net outlay by} \\ \text{stockholders} \end{matrix}$$

5. Adjusted discount rate NPV, adjusted present value, and flows-to-equity provide the same numerical answer when the project's debt capacity is equal to the present value of the operating and financing cash flows (so the debt to total value ratio is constant) and when tax impacts are reflected immediately.

6. Some of the situations in which investment and financing cash flows are intertwined include subsidized financing, project financing, and those in which firms are operating at a loss and cannot use the interest tax shield. Adjusted present value or flows-to-equity is more appropriate in these instances.

7. Although the financing benefits discussed in this chapter are important, the most important elements of successful capital investment decisions are estimation of the project's cash flows and assessment of risk.

QUESTIONS

14.1   Net present value using the weighted average cost of capital (or any other proportion of the after-tax costs of debt and equity financing) as the discount rate, implicitly assumes the firm is and will remain profitable, and that the project's debt capacity is a constant proportion of the project's present value. Explain these assumptions.

14.2   There are generally three effects of financing that the firm may need to consider. What are they? How do, or could, we incorporate them into the adjusted discount rate NPV? (*Note: Reference to Chapter 6 and careful thought on your part may be needed to answer this question.*)

14.3   When adjusted present value is employed, the present value of the interest tax shield must be determined. Explain the different discount rates that could be employed and the assumptions behind the different rates.

14.4   You have just been employed by a well-established firm that, along with its other divisions, has a division that develops and owns shopping centers. The firm's market-value-based capital structure is 40 percent equity and 60 percent debt. In order to understand more about the firm and its activities, you obtain the firm's pre-opening estimates of the after-tax operating cash flows for a shopping center that just opened. You decide to calculate the shopping center's adjusted discount rate NPV. To your great surprise, the adjusted discount rate NPV is highly negative. In rechecking your figures, you conclude they are all correct. Did the firm make a big mistake, or have you forgotten something? Explain.

14.5   Under what conditions do adjusted discount rate NPV, adjusted present value, and flows-to-equity provide the same solution to a capital investment? Do those conditions normally apply? Why or why not?

14.6   Tracy understands net present value but has no clue as to what you mean when you assert that there is a loan implied by adjusted discount rate NPV when the discount rate employed is the firm's weighted average cost of capital (or any other proportion of the after-tax costs of debt and equity financing). In clear and simple terms, explain the implied loan.

14.7   When should adjusted discount rate NPV be employed? Adjusted present value? Flows-to-equity?

CONCEPT REVIEW PROBLEMS

See Appendix A for solutions.

CR14.1   During the 1920s, on three different occasions Coca-Cola had the option to purchase a small company experiencing financial problems. It was called Pepsi-Cola. On all three occasions Coca-Cola management refused.

a.   Assume that Coca-Cola could have purchased Pepsi-Cola for $1 million and would have received after-tax cash flows of $135,000 each year for 10 years after the purchase. If Coca-Cola's opportunity cost of capital was 7 percent, what was the net present value of this purchase?

b.   Now assume some of Coca-Cola's middle managers planned to purchase Pepsi-Cola. Assume the risk-free rate is 3 percent, the expected return on the market portfolio is 7 percent, Pepsi-Cola's levered beta is 1.3, and Pepsi has 30 percent debt in its market-value-based capital structure. A bullet loan with a maturity of 4 years at an interest rate of 6 percent could be obtained for $800,000 of the purchase price of $1 million. If the tax rate is 25 percent, what is the project's APV?

CR14.2   If the loan to purchase Pepsi-Cola in CR14.1 was a 4-year amortized loan in place of a bullet loan, what would the APV be?

CR14.3   XYZ Corporation is planning to build an auto manufacturing plant in either North Carolina or Nebraska. The plant will cost $300 million to build and have after-tax cash flows of $45 million per year for 20 years, no matter which location is selected. XYZ's levered beta is 1.2 and it has a capital structure of 35 percent debt and 65 percent equity. The risk-free rate is 8 percent, and the expected return on the market portfolio is 15 percent. XYZ will borrow $200 million at 10 percent interest in the form of a bullet loan with a 10-year maturity.

a.   If XYZ's corporate tax rate is 40 percent, what is the adjusted present value of either location?

b.   If representatives from the state of North Carolina offer to subsidize the construction of the plant by granting XYZ a 10-year $200 million bullet loan at 5 percent, what is the APV of the North Carolina plant?

CR14.4   Assume that, because of an IRS tax ruling against XYZ in CR14.3, XYZ would not be able to take advantage of *any* interest tax benefits for the next 3 years. After the third year, tax benefits from debt financing would then start accruing to the firm. What is the APV of the North Carolina plant with the subsidized loan if tax benefits cannot be taken for the first 3 years?

CR14.5   Morgan and Associates is purchasing a small office complex for $250,000. The firm plans to borrow $150,000 on a 3-year bullet loan at 10 percent. Operating cash flows from the property are expected to be $30,000 each year for 3 years, with an after-tax resale value of $275,000 from the property at the end of the third year. If the levered cost of equity is 20 percent and the tax rate is 36 percent, what is the FTE for the purchase?

PROBLEMS

14.1   Sandberg Medical is evaluating whether to undertake a $10,000,000 modernization of some of its facilities. The after-tax cash flows from the project are estimated to be $1,750,000 for each of 10 years. The firm's target market value debt to total value ratio is 30 percent, the after-tax cost of debt is 8 percent, and the cost of equity is 18 percent. The project is no more nor less risky than the firm's average project. John, the assistant CFO, has evaluated the project and recommends that it be accepted and, because debt is so much cheaper than equity, the entire $10,000,000 be raised by issuing debt.

a.   Do you agree with John's reasoning concerning the financing for the project? Why or why not?

b.   Should the project be accepted?

14.2   A firm employs 45 percent equity and 55 percent debt in its market-value-based capital structure. The opportunity (or weighted average) cost of capital is 13.20 percent, the before-tax cost of debt is 10 percent, the firm's marginal tax rate is 40 percent, the risk-free rate is 8 percent, and the returns on the market portfolio are 16 percent. What is the firm's *unlevered* cost of equity capital?

14.3   Minnesota Industries follows a policy of financing 55 percent with debt and 45 percent with equity. It plans to pay a cash dividend of $4.00 next year, and the expected growth rate in dividends is forecasted to be 6 percent per year. The firm's current stock price is $25, its marginal tax rate is 34 percent, the before-tax cost of debt capital is 11.50 percent, the risk-free rate is 8.50 percent, and the expected return on the market portfolio is 15.50 percent.

a.   What is the cost of equity capital for Minnesota Industries?

b.   Determine the firm's opportunity (or weighted average) cost of capital.

c.   What is the implied unlevered equity beta and unlevered cost of equity capital for Minnesota?

d.   What would you conclude about your answers to (a) through (c) if Minnesota's investment bankers informed you that the firm's levered beta is 1.25?

14.4   Johnson's Textiles has evaluated a proposed project that is all debt financed and has determined its adjusted present value is $69,688, of which the base-case NPV is $29,942 and the present value of the interest tax shield is $39,746. The project requires an initial outlay of $500,000 and is expected to produce after-tax operating cash inflows of $160,000 for each of 4 years. Johnson's marginal tax rate is 40 percent, the expected returns on the market are 10 percent, and Johnson's typically finances with 40 percent equity and 60 percent debt.

a.   What is Johnson's unlevered cost of equity?
b.   Assume the firm's debt is no more risky then required by the risk-free rate. What is the before-tax cost of debt in percentage terms (which is also k_{RF})?
c.   What is the firm's opportunity (or weighted average) cost of capital and the adjusted discount rate NPV of the project? Why aren't the APV and adjusted discount rate NPV figures equal?

14.5   Jason's Technology is considering the development of a new plant in Indonesia. The initial after-tax cash outflow to fund the project (all cash flows in U.S. dollars) is $5,000,000, and Jason's expects the after-tax cash inflows to be $900,000 for each of the 7 years of the project's expected life. Due to the nature of the project, Jason's expects to fund most of the project by issuing $4,000,000 of 10 percent 7-year bonds that pay interest annually. Jason's unlevered equity cost of capital is 15 percent and the firm is in the 40 percent tax bracket.

a.   Determine the adjusted present value for the project. Should Jason's proceed?
b.   Before the final decision was made, the government of Indonesia indicated they will provide $3,000,000 in a 7-year bullet loan at 5 percent interest. Interest will be paid each year, but the principal will not be repaid until the end of the loan. The rest of the project (of $2,000,000) will be funded with a 7-year 10 percent coupon rate bond issued by Jason's. What decision should Jason's make now?

14.6   Eastman Products has been evaluating putting a new plant in one of three towns. The new plant will require an initial investment of $40,000,000 and is projected to provide after-tax cash inflows of $6,000,000 for each of 10 years. The firm's levered beta is 1.15 at its market-value-based capital structure which is 40 percent debt and 60 percent equity. The marginal tax rate is 35 percent, the risk-free rate is 7.5 percent, the before-tax cost of debt is 9 percent, and the expected return on the market portfolio is 14 percent. Because of the unique nature of the plant, Eastman Products is treating it as a separate subsidiary and, therefore, will finance the plant with 80 percent debt and 20 percent equity. The debt will be financed by a 10-year bond that pays interest annually.

a.   What is the adjusted present value of the proposed plant?
b.   Assume now that Eastman's bond beta is 0.25. Employing Equation 14.1, recalculate the unlevered cost of equity and determine the new adjusted present value. Does this alternative calculation change the decision?
c.   Going back to (a), assume now that Eastman finds out that flotation costs will be $1\frac{1}{2}$ percent of the bond issue and that common stock will have to be issued for the equity portion. Equity flotation costs will be 11 percent of the size of the equity issue. What is the new adjusted present value?
d.   In determining where to locate the plant, Eastman has indicated that a determining factor will be the economic incentives provided. Laramie, which is one of the locations, has offered a tax abatement of $200,000 for each of the 10 years. This will provide a direct increase in the plant's after-tax cash flows. In addition, Laramie is willing to provide long-term debt financing at the rate of 6 percent. Going back to (a), what is the new adjusted present value?

What decision should Eastman make if the other two locations under consideration provide smaller adjusted present values? What other factors might come into play in making the decision?

14.7 Savile Investors is evaluating the purchase of an apartment complex which will require a total outlay of $4,000,000. Ninety percent of the outlay will be financed by a 5-year loan at 12 percent that requires annual interest payments. The principal will be paid off in five equal increments beginning at time $t = 1$. The net after-tax operating cash flows are estimated to be $900,000 in the first year and $1,100,000 in each of the next 4 years. Savile estimates it needs a 20 percent return on the investment; its tax rate is 40 percent. Using flows-to-equity, should Savile make the investment?

14.8 A firm has a proposed capital investment project that requires an initial after-tax investment of $750 and should produce after-tax inflows of $250, $300, $350, and $400 in years 1 through 4, respectively. The firm's investment advisor, Dattan and Sons, has provided the following estimates: $k_{RF} = k_b = 9$ percent, $\beta_s^L = 1.30$, $k_M = 17$ percent, $T = 40$ percent, and the market value proportion of the capital structure in equity is 75 percent.

a. What is the firm's opportunity cost of capital and the adjusted discount rate NPV of the proposed project?
b. Now determine the loan implied by adjusted discount rate NPV and the adjusted present value. (For the adjusted present value, carry through three layers of financing benefits.)
c. Using the loan implied by adjusted discount rate NPV from (b), calculate the cash flows to the stockholders and the flows-to-equity. Why are the adjusted discount rate NPV, APV, and FTE given by (a), (b), and (c) the same (except for any rounding differences)? Is this always the case when these three decision criteria are employed? Explain.

14.9 UtilityAnalysis is examining a major new venture. The firm has provided you with the following estimates: the risk-free rate is 7.50 percent, which is also the cost of debt for Utility-Analysis; T is 40 percent; the levered beta is 1.00; the expected return on the market portfolio is 16 percent; and the proportion of debt in their capital structure is 10 percent. The new venture requires an outlay of $1,800 and will produce after-tax operating cash inflows of $550 for each of 5 years.

a. Determine the adjusted discount rate NPV for the new venture.
b. Now determine the adjusted present value and flows-to-equity value using the loan implied by adjusted discount rate NPV. Why do the three answers agree with one another? Is this always the case?
c. Determine the adjusted discount rate NPV, the adjusted present value, and the flows-to-equity value using the loan implied by net present value if all of the following conditions occur simultaneously:

1. The risk-free rate increases by 20 percent.
2. The tax rate increases by 20 percent.
3. The levered beta increases by 20 percent.
4. The return on the market increases by 20 percent.
5. The percent of debt increases *to* 30 percent.
6. The initial outlay increases by 20 percent.
7. The operating cash inflows increase by 20 percent (to $660) in each year.
8. The number of years of the operating cash flows increases to 6.

14.10 Mini Case Park Ridge, Ltd., is in the process of deciding whether to set up a plant that will produce easyglides. Park Ridge plans to use some of the easyglides itself but will also supply easyglides to a number of other firms. Initial research suggests the market exists, but a number of the other firms that might purchase easyglides do not want to purchase them directly from Park Ridge. Therefore, Park Ridge is exploring a number of alternatives, including building the plant itself and treating it like any other capital investment, setting up a separate subsidiary for easyglides, or simply building and leasing the plant to others. As chief of planning and analysis, your job is to complete the economic analysis and provide recommendations to the board of directors. After considerable study, your staff came up with the following estimated after-tax cash flows for easyglide:

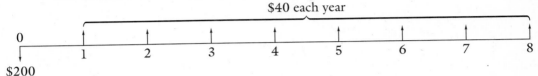

Your staff has also concluded that Park Ridge's beta is 1.35, the market-value-based target amount of debt is 40 percent, k_{RF} is 8.80 percent, k_M is 18.00 percent, Park Ridge's before-tax cost of debt is 12.50 percent, and the marginal tax rate is 35 percent.

a. What is Park Ridge's opportunity (or weighted average) cost of capital? Should the project be undertaken if the project has the same risk as the average project undertaken by the firm?
b. What specific (but implied) financing assumption did you make in answering (a)?
c. One of the alternatives being considered is to set easyglide up as a separate division and obtain project financing for the plant. Preliminary discussion with investment bankers indicates the firm should be able to borrow 75 percent of the financing of $200 at a cost of 13.5 percent. An 8-year bond that pays interest annually will be employed. Flotation expenses will equal 3 percent of the amount of the debt financing obtained. What decision should now be made?
d. A third alternative exists: for Park Ridge simply to build the plant and lease it to other firms. Under this plan there are no flotation costs as in (c); Park Ridge will borrow 90 percent of the initial investment; the cost of the bond financing is 14 percent; and Park Ridge has determined it would require a 25 percent return on its equity investment. What decision should now be made?
e. Athens wants Park Ridge to build the plant in their city. Athens will provide a tax abatement of $2 per year for the first 4 years and will also provide bond financing at a rate of 7 percent. In addition, Athens will take care of any flotation costs Park Ridge incurs. If everything else is the same as in (c), what decision should Park Ridge now make?
f. Explain why adjusted discount rate NPV, adjusted present value, and flows-to-equity do not normally provide the same answer. How can we obtain the same answer from all three methods?

REFERENCES

Net present value (based on some weighted opportunity cost of capital), adjusted present value, and flows-to-equity are discussed in:

CHAMBERS, DONALD R., ROBERT S. HARRIS, and JOHN J. PRINGLE. "Treatment of Financing Mix in Analyzing Investment Opportunities." *Financial Management* 11 (Summer 1982): 24–41.

HARRIS, ROBERT S., and JOHN J. PRINGLE. "Risk-Adjusted Discount Rates: Extensions from the Average Risk Case." *Journal of Financial Research* 8 (Fall 1985): 237–44.

MILES, JAMES A. and JOHN R. EZZELL. "The Weighted Average Cost of Capital, Perfect Capital Markets, and Project Life: A Clarification." *Journal of Financial and Quantitative Analysis* 15 (September 1980): 719–30.

————. "Reformulating Tax Shield Valuation: A Note." *Journal of Finance* 40 (December 1985): 1485–92.

MYERS, STEWART C. "Interactions of Corporate Financing and Investment Decisions—Implications for Capital Budgeting." *Journal of Finance* 29 (March 1974): 1–25.

TAGGART, ROBERT A., JR. "Consistent Valuation and Cost of Capital Expressions with Corporate and Personal Taxes." *Financial Management* 20 (Autumn 1991): 8–20.

Coverage of related topics is provided in:

ARDITTI, FRED D., and HIAM LEVY. "The Weighted Average Cost of Capital as a Cutoff Rate: A Critical Examination of the Classical Textbook Weighted Average." *Financial Management* 6 (Fall 1977): 24–34.

CORDES, JOSEPH J., and STEVEN M. SHEFFRIN. "Estimating the Tax Advantage of Corporate Debt." *Journal of Finance* 38 (March 1983): 95–105.

MASULIS, RONALD W. "The Impact of Capital Structure Change on Firm Value: Some Estimates." *Journal of Finance* 38 (March 1983): 107–26.

MILLER, MERTON H. "Debt and Taxes." *Journal of Finance* 32 (May 1977): 261–75.

MODIGLIANI, FRANCO, and MERTON H. MILLER. "Corporate Income Taxes and the Cost of Capital: A Correction." *American Economic Review* 53 (June 1963): 433–43.

RUBACK, RICHARD S. "Calculating the Market Value of Riskless Cash Flows." *Journal of Financial Economics* 15 (March 1986): 323–40.

Project financing and related topics are covered in:

BARRY, CHRISTOPHER B., CHRIS J. MUSCARELLA, JOHN W. PEAVY III, and MICHAIL R. VETSUYPENS. "The Role of Venture Capital in the Creation of Public Companies." *Journal of Financial Economics* 27 (October 1990): 447–71.

COOPER, KERRY, and R. MALCOLM RICHARDS. "Investing the Alaskan Project Cash Flows: The Sohio Experience." *Financial Management* 17 (Summer 1988): 58–70.

KENSINGER, JOHN W., and JOHN D. MARTIN. "Financing Network Organizations." *Journal of Applied Corporate Finance* 4 (Spring 1991): 66–76.

PHILLIPS, PAUL D., JOHN C. GROTH, and R. MALCOLM RICHARDS. "Financing the Alaskan Project: The Experience at Sohio." *Financial Management* 8 (Autumn 1979): 7–16.

APPENDIX

14A
Adjusted Present Value in an MM World

The adjusted present value decision criterion is a direct result of the Modigliani and Miller proposition, originally given in Chapter 11, that the value of the levered firm is equal to the value of the unlevered firm plus the debt tax shield, so

$$V_L = V_U + TB \tag{14A.1}$$

where V_L is the value of the levered firm, V_U is the value of the unlevered firm, T is the firm's marginal tax rate, and B is the market value of the firm's debt. In an MM world there is no uncertainty about the firm receiving the full benefit of the interest tax shield, and the value of the firm is maximized by employing almost 100 percent debt. To calculate the adjusted present value in an MM world, we have to make two adjustments to what we have presented so far:

1. Equation 14A.2 must be employed to determine the unlevered beta of the firm (retaining, for simplicity, the assumption that the bond beta is zero).

$$\beta_s^U = \beta_s^L \left[\frac{S}{B(1 - T) + S} \right] \tag{14A.2}$$

   Then the unlevered equity cost of capital is determined using Equation 14.6 with this new unlevered beta.

2. The discount rate employed to determine the present value of the interest tax shield (or the financing benefits) is the before-tax cost of debt. If the interest tax shield is certain, the before-tax cost of debt should be employed as the discount rate.

Let's see what happens to the adjusted present value if we assume the firm receives the full benefit of the interest tax shield and there is no uncertainty. To do so we employ the same example with the bullet loan analyzed in the chapter. Using Equation 14A.2, we find that the unlevered beta in an MM world is

$$\beta_s^U = \beta_s^L \left[\frac{S}{B(1 - T) + S} \right] = 0.80 \left[\frac{0.60}{0.40(1 - 0.35) + 0.60} \right] = 0.558$$

which is higher than the unlevered beta of 0.48 we previously estimated in Chapter 14 using Equation 14.2. The unlevered cost of equity capital in an MM world is

$$k_s^U = k_{RF} + \beta_s^U(k_M - k_{RF}) = 10\% + 0.558(6\%) \approx 13.35\%$$

The base-case NPV is then

$$\text{base-case } NPV = \frac{\$50,000}{(1 + 0.1335)^1} + \frac{\$50,000}{(1 + 0.1335)^2} + \frac{\$50,000}{(1 + 0.1335)^3} - \$100,000$$

$$= \$44,111 + \$38,916 + \$34,333 - \$100,000 = \$17,360$$

With the bullet loan, the interest is $1,400 per year, and the interest tax shield, now discounted at the before-tax cost of debt of 10 percent, is

$$\frac{\text{interest}}{\text{tax shield}} = \frac{\$1,400}{(1 + 0.10)^1} + \frac{\$1,400}{(1 + 0.10)^2} + \frac{\$1,400}{(1 + 0.10)^3}$$

$$= \$1,273 + \$1,157 + \$1,052 = \$3,482$$

The adjusted present value is

$$APV \text{ (MM bullet loan)} = \$17,360 + \$3,482 = \$20,842$$

which is less than the adjusted present value of $21,611 calculated in Chapter 14. Comparing the figures, we see that in an MM world the unlevered equity value of the project is lower than indicated in Chapter 14, whereas the value of the interest tax shield is higher. Chambers, Harris, and Pringle (1982) show that adjusted present value using the MM assumptions provides more conservative estimates of the value of a project than adjusted discount rate NPV, adjusted present value using other assumptions, or flows-to-equity. Hence, if a project has a positive value using adjusted present value in an MM world, it should be positive if other capital investment decision criteria are employed.

There is one other item to be mentioned. What if firms receive less than the maximum possible tax advantage from corporate borrowing than MM assume? Based on the discussion in Chapter 11 and from empirical studies, evidence suggests that the effective tax shield is less than the maximum corporate tax rate that exists in an MM world. The primary reasons the effective tax shield is less than the statutory rate are (1) the firm has to be profitable in all future periods to claim the tax shield and (2) both corporate and personal taxes exist. Let's call this effective tax rate T^* and assume it is 25 percent. Then the present value of the interest tax shield for the bullet loan is

$$\frac{\text{interest}}{\text{tax shield}} = \frac{\$4,000(0.25)}{(1 + 0.10)^1} + \frac{\$4,000(0.25)}{(1 + 0.10)^2} + \frac{\$4,000(0.25)}{(1 + 0.10)^3}$$

$$= \$909 + \$826 + \$751 = \$2,486$$

and the adjusted present value is only

$$APV \text{ (bullet loan)} = \$17,360 + \$2,486 = \$19,846$$

As we see, the assumptions made influence the resulting figures. Substantial disagreement exists even among financial experts regarding many of these issues. A saving grace is to remember that the firm benefits most from making good investment decisions. If minor changes in financing assumptions change the decision from selection to rejection, or vice versa, then you should be especially careful when making investment decisions. Accurately estimating the cash flows and assessing risk are more important than minor differences caused by employing different decision criteria or different tax or financing assumptions.

PART 4

Managing Long-Term Financing

EXECUTIVE INTERVIEW

Alfred L. Williams, Jr. President and Chief Executive Officer United Gas Holding Corporation

United Gas is an energy holding company that purchased financially ailing United Gas Pipeline and turned its fortunes around. We asked Mr. Williams about long-term financing strategies used in the energy industry.

The decision to go to the market for financing begins with the company's overall strategic plan—including cost of capital, capital structure, and targeted debt and equity ratios. That decision is followed by consideration of more specific factors like the average maturity of existing long-term debt and the mix of floating versus fixed rate debt. The financing environment is also important: financing trends and market conditions, and market demand for both your industry and the specific securities you wish to issue, also affect whether you can raise money efficiently.

Long-Term Financing Strategies

Energy companies continually require large amounts of long-term financing. However, today we have fewer financing sources, since many lenders—especially the banks, a traditional source of medium-term financing—have moved out of energy financing. Therefore, we use a variety of financing instruments and work with investment bankers to create innovative ways to raise money. One technique that we use extensively is project financing, in which lenders focus not on the credit of the sponsoring company but on the revenues from the project itself. These revenues depend on the strength of both the companies that contract to purchase gas and the contracts themselves. Maturities on these financings are tied to the life of the assets they finance—about 15 to 20 years in the case of pipelines. Project financings can be used only for projects that have discrete, revenue-generating capabilities. The sponsoring company gives the lender a mortgage on the assets and first call on the revenues.

Additions to existing infrastructure or capital assets are financed with more standard types of financing based on the firm's credit. On the whole, debt maturities have shortened in recent years. In the energy business these days, we see mostly intermediate-term note financings—7 years or so.

Few major pipeline companies have an investment grade credit rating (Baa/BBB) at the moment. That makes it difficult to raise money without using high-yield debentures or convertible securities. High-yield debentures—what used to be known as junk bonds—have been quite popular with both investors and issuers, because they yield anywhere from 9 to 13 percent at a time when many other securities yield around 3 percent.

Convertible securities are also used to finance energy-related companies. If the issuing company is solid and has a good story to tell about its future prospects, a financing instrument that converts to equity offers the investor the potential for attractive returns from the equity. The issuer benefits from a lower interest rate cost compared to straight bond financing. In addition, a company may not want to sell equity due to the condition of the equity markets or its capital structure, or because its stock is not performing well and there would be too much dilution. Convertibles provide a way to convert the debt into an equity component in the future.

Financing under Adverse Circumstances

Managing long-term financing involves more than obtaining debt and equity capital. Another critical aspect is working with lenders to keep them well informed about the company's operations and to alert them to any potential problems. They don't like surprises. When a company gets into financial difficulties, it must work closely with its lenders to develop a financing strategy to work through the problems. This strategy may include obtaining waivers of financial covenants contained in loan agreements or renegotiating the loan.

United Gas Pipeline's situation is an interesting case study of what happens when financing plans do not go according to plan. In 1987 the company went through a leveraged buyout (LBO). As was often the case with LBOs, the amount of debt put on the balance sheet was greater than the company's ability to service it. That, coupled with operational problems, led to the company's filing bankruptcy under Chapter 11 in 1990. The debt was held by a syndicate of banks and an insurance company, all of whom had been part of the LBO. Because of the bankruptcy, the lenders had a lien on all our assets.

We were in a tough situation in terms of renegotiating the loan—and at the same time, we were trying to negotiate the sale of the company. However, a company must try to retain as much financial flexibility as possible, and as part of our strategy we had also filed a high-yield debt offering with the Securities and Exchange Commission. This offering provided an alternative to renegotiating the existing note and strengthened our bargaining position with buyers. As a result, we were able to get a good price for our shareholders.

The holding company's objective in buying the pipeline was the acquisition of an industrial company with good management and sufficient taxable income and growth potential to utilize the significant ($300 million) net operating loss carryforwards that resulted from the pipeline's sale.

My financing strategy for this company is pretty straightforward: I believe in maintaining a conservative debt-equity ratio and locking in fixed-rate debt. Also, any financing we do will have maturities closely tied to asset lives. I don't agree with the trend today of using very large amounts of short-term, floating rate debt to finance long-term assets. Although some may say our approach doesn't provide the capital for rapid growth, over the long term it provides the safety valve to ride the ups and downs in the economy and achieve moderate growth. You have a lot of flexibility when you have little or no debt. Few companies have gone out of business because they had too little debt.

Firms have two primary sources of funds: They can generate funds internally from continuing operations, or they can secure them externally from creditors or investors. It is these external, long-term sources we focus on now. Our attention in Chapters 15 and 16 will be primarily on the two main vehicles used by firms to raise external long-term capital—common stocks and bonds. Then in Chapter 17 we discuss warrants and convertibles, followed by leasing in Chapter 18.

15 *Raising Long-Term Funds*

EXECUTIVE SUMMARY

Firms acquire the majority of their financing from internally generated funds. Bonds are the most important source of long-term *external* financing. Public offerings involve either cash offerings or, to a far lesser extent, rights offerings. Bond and stock issues can be underwritten by investment banking firms on either a firm commitment basis or through a best efforts offering. Underwriting transfers the risk from the issuing firm to the underwriting syndicate formed to sell the issue.

An alternative to the public offering is private placement. The major advantages of private placements are the speed with which they may be effected and elimination of the registration procedure. In addition, terms can be tailored to meet the needs of both issuer and investor. Shelf registration, adopted by the SEC in 1982, allows large firms to lower their issuing costs; it also increases the speed and flexibility of the issuing process.

Common stockholders are the residual owners of the firm; as such, they have last claim on earnings in the form of cash dividends and assets in case of liquidation. Empirical evidence indicates that the value of the firm's stock falls as common stock is publicly issued. The sum of cash expenses and the fall in the price of stock accompanying a new issue of common stock are substantial; they range from 15 to 30 percent of the total financing.

RAISING EXTERNAL LONG-TERM FUNDS

Firms raise long-term funds from two sources: internally generated funds that are reinvested in the firm and external funds obtained by selling stock or debt. Table 15.1 indicates the funds raised by nonfarm, nonfinancial U.S. firms between 1981 and 1992

Table 15.1

Internal and External Financing for Nonfarm, Nonfinancial U.S. Firms

In recent years firms have raised 80 percent and more of their funds from internally generated sources. The net use of equity financing dropped substantially in the 1980s, as more equity was retired than issued.

| | Financing in Dollars (billions) | | | | | Financing in Percentages | | | |
| | | External | | | | | External | | |
Year	Internal	Net Equity	Net Debt	Total	Total Financing	Internal	Net Equity	Net Debt	Total
1981	$250	−$ 14	$104	$ 90	$340	74%	−4%	30%	26%
1982	246	2	49	51	297	83	1	16	17
1983	282	20	61	81	363	78	5	17	22
1984	321	−79	172	93	414	78	−19	41	22
1985	332	−85	137	52	384	86	−22	36	14
1986	311	−85	215	130	441	70	−19	49	30
1987	366	−76	143	67	433	84	−17	33	16
1988	412	−130	199	69	481	86	−27	41	14
1989	385	−125	174	49	434	89	−29	40	11
1990	376	−63	86	23	399	94	−16	22	6
1991	365	18	4	22	387	94	5	1	6
1992	423	27	54	81	504	84	5	11	16

Source: Board of Governors of the Federal Reserve System, *Flow of Funds Accounts*, various issues.

both from internally generated funds and from issuing stock and debt. As the data clearly indicate, over this time period firms raised over 80 percent of their total needs for funds from internally generated sources. Thus, *the primary source of financing is from the retention of cash flows generated by the firm.* The data also show that during the last few years firms, in total, retired more stock than they issued. That is, although some firms issued new common stock, the amount of stock retired was greater than the amount of newly issued common stock. This net retirement of stock was due to mergers and acquisitions, leveraged buyouts in which firms were taken private, debt-for-stock swaps, voluntary retirement of stock, and a "leveraging up" of firms in the United States. One other important point illustrated in Table 15.1 is the cyclical nature of new debt and equity financing.

MEANS OF RAISING EXTERNAL FUNDS

Firms have a number of means of securing financing. These are shown in Figure 15.1. Once the firm decides it has to raise funds externally,[1] it has three basic alternatives. First, it can use a **public offering.** The two main types available are (1) a cash offering,

[1] This determination is made based on cash budgets or pro forma statements as discussed in Chapter 25.

Figure 15.1

Methods of Securing Financing

Since its introduction, shelf registration has become important for most large firms.

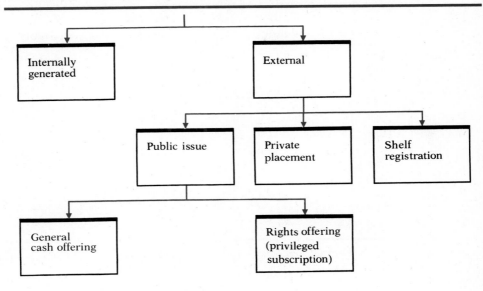

which is made to investors at large, or (2) a rights offering (or privileged subscription), which is available only to the firm's current stockholders. Second, if the securities are not offered to the general public, then a private placement is made. The securities are sold to one or more institutional investors such as insurance companies, banks, or pension funds. Finally, large, creditworthy firms can take advantage of the shelf registration form of financing. We will look at the basic features of all three methods and at the role played by investment banking firms.

CASH OFFERINGS

Firms can issue common stock, preferred stock, or long-term debt through a **cash offering.** Table 15.2 indicates the amount of funds raised via cash offerings between 1981 and 1992. Note that the vast majority of funds raised in cash offerings involve long-term debt. This is not surprising, because firms can generate substantial equity capital internally but can secure debt financing only by going to the public markets or through private placements.

THE ROLE OF INVESTMENT BANKING FIRMS

Most firms making a cash offering of securities use the services of an investment banking firm, which does the actual selling. Investment banking firms serve as an intermediary between the financial markets and firms needing capital. Firms generally

Table 15.2

New Publicly Issued Long-Term Securities (in billions)
Bonds typically have dominated the new-issue market.

Year	Common Stock	Preferred Stock	Debt	Total
1981	$14.2	$ 1.7	$ 39.0	$ 54.9
1982	13.4	5.0	44.8	63.2
1983	29.7	7.7	49.3	86.7
1984	8.6	4.2	59.6	72.4
1985	18.4	7.0	89.7	115.1
1986	34.2	12.2	177.5	223.9
1987	37.6	11.7	191.3	240.6
1988	22.2	6.5	172.5	201.2
1989	26.0	6.2	181.4	213.6
1990	19.4	4.0	188.8	212.2
1991	47.9	17.4	287.1	352.4
1992	55.1	21.3	377.5	453.9

Source: *Federal Reserve Bulletin*, various issues; and *Monthly Statistical Review*, Securities and Exchange Commission, for data prior to 1989.

prefer to have the new issue **underwritten.** This is generally called a **firm commitment offering**: The investment banking firm purchases the issue from the firm *at a fixed price* and then resells it. When an issue is underwritten, the risk of its not selling is borne by the investment banking firm—that is, the selling firm is guaranteed a fixed dollar amount.[2] Another approach is for the investment banking firm to take the issue on a **best efforts** basis, under which the securities are sold for a fixed commission but any unsold securities are the responsibility of the selling firm, not the investment banking firm. This method is often used by large, well-known firms who feel the issue will sell easily or by very small firms when the risks and costs are too great for underwriting. Finally, some firms sell securities via **direct placement** without using the services of investment bankers.

Investment banking firms, through the underwriting syndicate, provide marketing services, risk-bearing, certification, and monitoring of the firm's managers and its affairs. Marketing services include searching the primary market for buyers and compensating participants for their costs of providing funds. Risk-bearing involves the underwriters taking the risk of the issue not selling. Certification involves bearing the liability imposed by the federal Securities Act of 1933 for the "fairness" of the offer price. Finally, by engaging the services of well-known investment banking firms, the issuing firm is seeking additional monitoring in the hopes of adding value to the offering and firm.[3]

[2] The firm has, in effect, purchased a put option by engaging the services of the investment banking firm.
[3] For more on the role played by investment banking firms see, for example, Booth and Smith (1986), Carter and Manaster (1990), and Hansen and Torregrosa (1992).

The Underwriting Process

To understand the investment banking process, it is helpful to trace the steps required. Our focus is on the negotiated underwritten process and the role played by the lead investment banking firm or firms.

Preunderwriting Conference.   Members of the issuing firm and the investment banking firm hold preunderwriting conferences in which they discuss how much capital to raise, the type (or types) of security to employ, and the terms of the agreement. The investment banking firm then begins the underwriting investigation. In addition to its own investigation of the issuing firm, the investment banking firm calls in a public accounting firm to audit the firm's financial condition and to assist in preparing the registration statement submitted to the Securities and Exchange Commission, SEC. Lawyers are also required to rule on the legal aspects of the proposed issue.

After the investigation is completed, an underwriting agreement is drawn up. This agreement, which may be changed by subsequent approval of the parties, contains all the details of the issue except its price.

Registration and Pricing.   The **registration statement,** or prospectus, is then filed with the SEC. This statement presents all the pertinent facts concerning the firm and the proposed issue. During a waiting period, the factual adequacy of the information is judged. The SEC assesses only the accuracy of the information; *it does not judge the investment quality of the security.* The preliminary registration statement—often called a **red herring** because of the statement printed on it that the securities have not been approved or disapproved by the SEC—can, however, be distributed.

Once the issue has cleared registration and an offering price has been determined, a "tombstone" advertisement listing the names of the underwriting firms from whom the prospectus may be obtained is often made. Figure 15.2 shows an example of a tombstone for a Starter Corporation common stock issue that involved over 60 underwriters.

Underwriting Syndication and Selling.   The primary investment banking firm that the issuing firm has dealt with does not typically handle the purchase and distribution of an issue by itself. Instead, a **syndicate** is formed for the purpose of underwriting (buying and then reselling) the issue. Syndicates often have between 10 and 60 underwriters in addition to the managing investment banking firm. The primary reasons for underwriting syndicates are to spread the risk and to ensure national or international marketing capability.

Costs.   The **flotation cost** to the issuing firm of selling securities includes the underwriting fee and all the other expenses related to the offering. These other expenses include accounting and legal fees, an SEC registration fee, and printing costs. Total flotation costs are the difference between what the securities are sold to investors for (the gross proceeds) and what the issuing firm actually receives (the net proceeds). Thus, if a $50 million par bond issue is sold to the public for $50.5 million and the issuing firm receives only $49.5 million, the flotation costs are $1 million, or slightly under 2 percent ($1 million/$50.50 million = 0.0198 = 1.98 percent).

Figure 15.2

Tombstone for Starter Corporation Common Stock Issue

Advertisements like this one appear in many financial sources, such as *The Wall Street Journal* and *Institutional Investor*.

For common stock, flotation costs range from 3 to 10 percent for large, well-known firms to over 20 percent for smaller firms. This high direct cost for small issues is a function of the risks involved and the higher actual distribution expenses, because more effort is required to sell small common stock issues. For bonds and preferred stocks, the costs to large issuers are often less than 2 percent. This is due to the lower degree of risk involved compared to common stocks. Their lower flotation costs are also due to the fact that bonds and preferred stock are usually sold in large blocks to institutional investors, whereas thousands of investors may purchase common stock.

SHELF REGISTRATION

In 1982 the Securities and Exchange Commission modified its registration procedure for some types of offerings by adopting Rule 415, or what is called **shelf registration.** To register under this rule, a firm must file a relatively short form describing its financing needs and the securities it intends to issue over the next 2 years. When it thinks market conditions are favorable, the firm can take part of the issue "off the shelf" in a matter of minutes, without further disclosure being necessary, and offer the securities to investors.

The increased flexibility provided by shelf registration has been welcomed by chief financial officers at large corporations. In recent years, about half of all securities registered with the SEC were marketed through the shelf registration method. The rapid acceptance of shelf registration is due to its reduced cost and increased convenience—both of which are important when firms raise external capital. The reduced costs associated with shelf registrations primarily benefit firms that are considered less risky, as opposed to firms with more risk.[4] In 1992 the Securities and Exchange Commission liberalized the rules, allowing more firms to qualify for shelf registrations. In another move, this time designed to assist smaller firms, the SEC also increased to $1 million the amount of securities that could be issued in a year without any SEC registration.

PRIVATE PLACEMENTS AND RULE 144A

The private placement of securities has always been a means of financing. In recent years it has accounted for as much as 35 percent of total corporate financing in the United States. But even that is not as much as it may be in the future. In early 1990, the Securities and Exchange Commission approved Rule 144a, which is transforming the way many firms, both domestic and foreign, raise capital.

Before Rule 144a, buyers of private placement securities could not easily resell them without registering them with the SEC or holding them for at least 2 years. This regulation reduced the liquidity of the investments, and in turn sent many U.S. companies overseas to raise capital. In addition, many foreign firms could not easily enter the U.S. capital markets, even via private placement, without disclosing much more information than they were required to reveal in their home countries.

[4] See Blackwell, Marr, and Spivey (1990) and Allen, Lamy, and Thompson (1990).

Rule 144a created a new private placement secondary market in which large investors can trade among themselves without going back to the registration and disclosure process. To limit the market to sophisticated investors who should be able to do their own homework about the merits of the securities, the SEC allows only institutions that own $100 million or more in securities to participate in the new private placement secondary market. In addition, stocks or bonds that are traded on any public exchange, such as the NYSE, will not be allowed in the 144a market.

The SEC disclosure requirements, which provide for full and complete disclosure and therefore promote market efficiency in our public secondary markets, are relaxed in the 144a market. The trade-off is full disclosure versus helping both domestic and foreign firms raise capital in the cheapest, most effective manner. In designing Rule 144a, the SEC attempted to balance its role of providing for full disclosure for investors against helping firms with their financing needs.

GLOBAL FINANCING

Increasingly, financing is being acquired on a global basis. For example, in 1991 British Telephone sold $10 billion and Telefonos de Mexico sold $2 billion in equity internationally. This was followed in 1992 by firms like Britain's Wellcome ($4 billion) and General Motors ($2 billion) who also raised funds through international equity issues. Non-U.S. firms who want to sell stock in the United States and have it listed on an exchange (such as the New York Stock Exchange) have to register with the SEC and meet all of the reporting requirements that U.S.-domiciled firms meet. During recent years there have been some discussions about relaxing the reporting rule for non-U.S.-based firms who want to have their stock listed on an exchange; however, no important changes have been made by the SEC to relax the reporting requirements for such firms.

One of the biggest changes in the international financing arena is the growing presence of non-U.S. companies raising private funds in the U.S. through 144a offerings. Deals involving non-U.S. firms now comprise about 30 percent of all private placements in the United States. The big attraction of 144a is the speed with which the financing can be arranged and the minimal disclosure nature of the financing. In addition, Rule 144a does not require foreign firms to conform to U.S. accounting standards; however, it does require all 144a issues to secure a credit rating from either Moody's Investors Service or Standard & Poor's Corporation. In addition, the volume of financing in the Eurobond market, after being relatively flat for many years, is moving upward. Increasingly, whether it is equity or debt, larger firms look globally when seeking financing.

Concept Review Questions

■ What is the primary source of financing for nonfarm, nonfinancial U.S. firms?

■ What are the three basic alternatives available to firms to raise external funds?

■ Describe the process firms employ for raising external funds. What role do investment banking firms play?

■ How has the SEC's Rule 144a affected private placements?

COMMON STOCK: RIGHTS AND PRIVILEGES

Now that we understand some of the issues related to raising external funds, let's turn our attention to one of the sources of funds for firms—common stock. The common stockholders are both the owners of the firm and one of its suppliers of long-term capital. This capital may be in the form of funds invested in the firm directly in exchange for new shares of common stock, or it may occur through the action of the firm's board of directors by retaining funds rather than authorizing them to be paid out in the form of cash dividends.

INCOME

Common stockholders have a residual right to the income of the firm in that the claims of creditors, lessors, the government, and preferred stockholders must be met before common stockholders receive cash dividends. Thus, if a firm has earnings before interest and taxes, EBIT, of $200,000, interest payments of $50,000, and taxes (at 35 percent) of $52,500, earnings after taxes, EAT, are $97,500. Assuming that cash flows are sufficient, firms typically pay out some proportion of their earnings in the form of cash dividends. They are not obligated to do so, and some firms, such as Genentech, Microsoft, and Toys 'R' Us, do not currently pay dividends.

The risk and potential returns are greater for common stock investors than for others with financial interests in the firm. To see why, consider our example: If EBIT drops to $50,000, with interest payments of $50,000, earnings after taxes are zero, and no funds are left for distribution to common stockholders. On the other hand, if EBIT increases to $600,000, with interest of $50,000 and taxes of $192,500, EAT is $357,500, and larger cash dividends may be paid out. The cash not paid out to common stockholders can be reinvested in the firm.

CONTROL

The firm's stockholders elect the members of the board of directors each year. Sometimes an outside or dissident group may challenge management by proposing its own slate of directors. These challenges, or **proxy fights,** represent one of the more effective means of attempting to turn around the fortunes of a firm. In the past, they have been rare; however, recently, more proxy fights have been initiated, including some involving major firms. Obviously, it is only in firms that are providing lackluster performance (in terms of market price, dividends, and/or earnings) that successful proxy fights are possible.

Depending on the corporate charter or the law of the state in which the firm is incorporated, the board of directors is selected under a majority voting or a cumulative voting system. Under the **majority voting** system, each stockholder has one vote per director for each share of stock owned. Directors are elected if they secure one more vote than 50 percent of the votes cast. Instead of majority voting, the firm's charter or the state of incorporation may require **cumulative voting,** which permits multiple votes for a single director. Each share is entitled to one vote, so a stockholder who owns 100 shares has 100 votes. The purpose of cumulative voting is to allow minority groups representation on the board of directors.

In order to determine how many shares are needed to elect any given number of directors under cumulative voting, we can use the following formula:

$$\begin{matrix} \text{minimum number} \\ \text{of shares required} \\ \text{to elect a desired} \\ \text{number of directors} \end{matrix} = \frac{\left(\begin{matrix} \text{total shares outstanding} \\ \text{and entitled} \\ \text{to vote} \end{matrix}\right)\left(\begin{matrix} \text{number of} \\ \text{directors} \\ \text{desired} \end{matrix}\right)}{\begin{matrix} \text{total number of directors} \\ \text{to be elected} + 1 \end{matrix}} + 1 \qquad (15.1)$$

For example, if a firm has 195,000 shares of stock authorized to vote and 12 directors are to be elected, a group wanting to elect 3 directors would have to control

$$\frac{(195,000)(3)}{12 + 1} + 1 = 45,001 \text{ shares}$$

On the other hand, if the minority group controls a given number of shares and wants to find out how many directors it can elect, Equation 15.1 can be modified to:

$$\begin{matrix} \text{number of directors} \\ \text{that can be elected} \\ \text{with shares owned} \end{matrix} = \frac{\left(\begin{matrix} \text{number of shares} \\ \text{owned} - 1 \end{matrix}\right)\left(\begin{matrix} \text{total number of directors} \\ \text{to be elected} + 1 \end{matrix}\right)}{\text{total shares outstanding and entitled to vote}} \qquad (15.2)$$

To continue our example, suppose that the minority group controls 70,000 shares. How many directors can it elect? Employing Equation 15.2, the answer is

$$\frac{(70,000 - 1)(12 + 1)}{195,000} = 4.67, \text{ or 4 directors}$$

Actually, the group may be able to do better than that if not all the shares outstanding are voted. For example, what happens if only 180,000 shares in total will be voted? In this case, the minority can elect

$$\frac{(70,000 - 1)(12 + 1)}{180,000} = 5.06, \text{ or 5 directors}$$

A firm can partially thwart the intent of cumulative voting procedures by reducing the size of its board or by electing only a portion of the board each year. To see this, suppose the firm decides to only elect 6 instead of 12 directors each year, and they each hold office for 2 years. If our minority group still controls 70,000 shares and assuming only 180,000 votes will be cast, then the number of directors the group can elect in any given year is

$$\frac{(70,000 - 1)(6 + 1)}{180,000} = 2.72, \text{ or 2 directors}$$

By electing 2 directors this year and 2 directors next year, the minority group ends up with only 4 directors instead of 5, as when all directors are elected each year.

In addition to voting on the board of directors, stockholders are frequently asked to approve the selection of the firm's accounting auditor for the next year, and to vote on issues such as authorizing additional shares of common stock, approval of a merger financed by common stock, antitakeover amendments, and various other corporate governance issues.[5]

CLAIM ON ASSETS

As in the case of income, common stockholders have a residual claim with regard to the firm's assets in case of liquidation. Although some changes have occurred because of the bankruptcy code that went into effect in 1979, creditors, bondholders, and preferred stockholders all have a prior claim on assets and will be paid something before common stockholders receive anything in liquidation. This residual claim increases the risk to common stockholders.

LIMITED LIABILITY

Under our legal system stockholders have limited liability. Because corporations are distinct entities under the law, stockholders are not personally responsible for the firm's debts. The impact of limited versus unlimited liability on stockholders is illustrated in Figure 15.3. Say a firm has $1,000 in debt. With limited liability, if the value of the firm's assets falls below $1,000, stockholders can default and walk away from the firm. But if unlimited liability existed, when the value of the firm's assets fell below $1,000, stockholders would have to use their personal resources to pay off the bondholders.

With either limited or unlimited liability, stockholders may be disappointed if a firm's operating performance is poor. But the right to default and walk away from the firm—which is a put option—is a valuable privilege that exists due to limited liability.

PREEMPTIVE RIGHT

The **preemptive right** is a provision that grants stockholders the right to purchase new shares of common stock in the same proportion as their current ownership. This right may exist in the corporate charter or may be required by state statute. The raising of funds through use of a preemptive right is called a **rights offering.** Although this right used to be widespread, it is less so now because *many firms have amended their charters to eliminate the preemptive right.* One of the primary reasons for doing away with it is to provide the firm with more freedom to use common stock for mergers and acquisitions or other corporate purposes.

---

[5] For a summary of the impact of voting on antitakeover amendments and corporate governance items on the value of the firm see, for example, Brickley, Lease and Smith (1988) and Gordon and Pound (1993).

Figure 15.3

Effect of Limited Versus Unlimited Liability on Stockholders

For a firm with $1,000 in debt, if the value of the firm at the maturity of the debt is below $1,000, with limited liability, as in (a), the stockholders default and bondholders own the firm. But with unlimited liability, as in (b), stockholders must reach into their own pockets to pay off the bondholders.

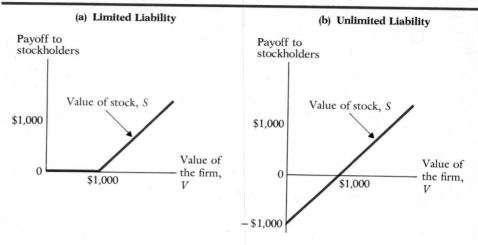

When the preemptive right exists, current stockholders have first claim on any new shares to be issued.[6] For example, if a firm had 100,000 shares of stock outstanding and decided to issue 25,000 new shares, a stockholder owning 1,000 shares would have the opportunity to purchase 250 new shares. By doing so, the stockholder would maintain his or her current percentage ownership of 1 percent of the firm's outstanding shares.

RIGHT OF TRANSFER

Common stockholders generally have the right to transfer ownership to another investor. All that is required is for an investor to sell the stock to another person and sign the stock (endorse it on the back of the stock certificate) over to the buyer. If the stock is traded publicly, the stockholder may use the services of a securities broker to sell the stock. The purchaser of the stock (or the broker) sends the stock certificate to a transfer agent representing the firm. The transfer agent then issues a new certificate under the purchaser's name and records the transaction in the firm's records. At this point, the new owner is entitled to receive cash dividends and has any other rights or privileges associated with owning the common stock.

---

[6] Rights are simply a call option, as discussed in Chapter 5.

Concept Review Questions

- Define the terms *residual right*, *residual claim*, *preemptive right*, and *right of transfer* when applied to common stockholders.

- Describe the difference between majority voting and cumulative voting when electing a firm's board of directors.

FEATURES OF COMMON STOCK

AUTHORIZED, OUTSTANDING, AND TREASURY SHARES

The firm's charter specifies the number of authorized shares—that is, the maximum number of shares that can be issued without amending the charter. Additional shares can be authorized by a vote of the common stockholders. For convenience, most firms have more authorized shares than they currently have issued. For example, in Table 15.3, Philip Morris, at the end of 1992, is shown to have 4 billion shares authorized, but "only" 935 million have been issued. The outstanding shares are those held by the public; the firm can buy back issued stock and hold it as treasury stock. The number of shares outstanding for Philip Morris is 935,320,439 − 42,563,254 = 892,757,185. The number of shares of stock outstanding is employed when calculating per shares figures, such as earnings per share, or dividends per share.

PAR AND BOOK VALUE

Common stock can be issued with or without a par value. The par value of a share of common stock is stated in the firm's charter but is of no financial significance. Firms with a specific par value for their common stock try to issue new stock at prices higher than par, because the stockholders are liable as creditors for the difference between the issuance price, if below par, and the par value of the stock. For this reason, most par values are very low. Philip Morris, for example, has a par value of $1.00 per share of common stock.

From Table 15.3 we can see that Philip Morris has **retained earnings**, which it refers to as "earnings reinvested in the business," of almost $14.9 billion. Retained earnings represent the total residual amount that has been transferred from the firm's income statements over the years. In recent years firms have also had to report the impact of foreign currency translation adjustments in their stockholder's equity accounts; Philip Morris has a small foreign currency adjustment. The total of the common stock, preferred stock (if any), additional paid-in capital (which Philip Morris does not report separately), retained earnings, and currency translation adjustment, less the treasury stock, is equal to total stockholders' equity. For Philip Morris, this is $12.6 billion.

Book value per share of common stock reflects the "accounting-recorded" worth of the firm. It is calculated by dividing the common stockholders' equity (or, equiva-

Table 15.3

Common Stockholders' Accounts and Related Information for Philip Morris Companies, Inc., as of December 31, 1992 (in millions)

The "earnings reinvested in the business" account is often called "retained earnings" at other firms. Also, some firms will report an additional paid-in capital account. When a firm sells common stock, the difference between the selling price and the par value is often record in the addition paid-in capital account.

Common stock, $1.00 par; 4,000,000,000 shares authorized, 935,320,439 shares issued	$ 935
Earnings reinvested in the business	14,867
Currency translation adjustments	(34)
	15,768
Less: Treasury stock (42,563,254 shares at cost)	3,205
Total common equity	$12,563

earnings per share = net income minus dividends on preferred stock (millions)/shares of common stock outstanding (millions)

$$= (\$4{,}939 - 0)/(935.3 - 42.6) = \$5.54$$

dividends per share on common stock = $2.35

book value per share = total stockholders' equity minus book value of preferred stock (millions)/shares outstanding (millions)

$$= \$12{,}563 - 0/(935.3 - 42.6) = \$14.07$$

market price per share = $86 5/8 to $69 1/2 (range for the year)

Source: Philip Morris Companies, Inc., 1992 Annual Report.

lently, total assets minus total liabilities minus the book value of preferred stock) by the number of shares of common stock outstanding. Philip Morris had a book value of $14.07 per share at the end of 1992, but its stock traded between 86\frac{5}{8}$ and 69\frac{1}{2}$ during that year.

CLASSES OF COMMON STOCK

Most firms have only one class of common stock, but some have more than one class. Where two classes exist, one is often sold to the general public and the other is retained by the founders, with all or part of the voting rights reserved for the founder's group. Three examples will help to illustrate the use of different classes of stock. Ford has two classes of stock, both of which have voting privileges. As of December 31, 1992, the issued shares (in millions) were as follows:

	Shares Issued
Common	452.1
Class B	35.4
	487.5

Class B stock is owned by members of the Ford family and constitutes 40 percent of the voting power of the firm.[7] The common stock is held by the general public and has 60 percent of the total voting power. Each share of common stock is entitled to one vote. To maintain their 40 percent voting power, owners of class B shares have more than one vote per share. As of December 31, 1992, each class B share had

$$\left(\frac{452.1}{35.4}\right)\left(\frac{0.40}{0.60}\right) = 8.51 \text{ votes}$$

Although each share of both classes participates equally in cash dividends or in liquidation if it were to occur, each class B share has more voting power than a similar share of common stock.

A second example is that of Adolph Coors. Coors has two classes of stock: class A, which is held by the founders and has voting power; and class B, which is held by the general public and, except for certain situations, has no voting power. Shares of both classes participate equally in dividends or liquidation.

A third, and somewhat different, example of stock classes occurs when a firm ties different classes of stock to distinct parts of its total business. For example, General Motors has three different classes of stock: General Motors common, GM class H, and GM class E. The class H shares are pegged to the auto maker's Hughes Aircraft Company, and the class E shares are tied to its Electronic Data Systems business. In 1991 USX separated its energy and steel businesses into two parts, with separate classes of common stock for each. RJR Nabisco also considered two classes of stock, one primarily tied to its food business and another structured more for its tobacco operations.

Concept Review Questions

- Why is the par value of most firms significantly less than the market value of common stock?
- Explain why some companies have several classes of common stock.

[7] If the number of class B shares is below 30,374,940 but equal to or greater than 16,874,966, then the voting power drops to 30 percent.

COMMON STOCK FINANCING

Although not the major external source of financing, common stock is often employed to raise external capital, especially for smaller, growing firms. So it is important to understand more about the use of common stock as a means of raising long-term capital.

ISSUING EQUITY AND THE VALUE OF THE FIRM

In recent years a number of studies have examined the market impact of common stock issuance. The results, at first glance, have been surprising: When firms sell common stock publicly, their stock price declines. For industrial firms in the United States the decline amounts to 2 to 3 percent. Although that may not sound overwhelming, the fall in the market value represents a dollar amount equal to 10 to 20 percent of the money raised by the issue. Thus, the net increase in the value of the firm, ΔS, due to issuing new common stock for cash is equal to the net proceeds from the issue *minus* the decrease in the value of the outstanding stock. Stated another way, the cost of issuing common stock includes the direct flotation costs plus the indirect costs captured by the loss in value of the firm's outstanding stock.

How can we account for this result? In an efficient market, investor expectations are built into the share price. These expectations may change as the firm issues new common stock. Consider two reasons why the price of the firm's stock may fall:

1. INFORMATION ASYMMETRY   Management always has some information about the firm that is not available to shareholders. What if this information allows management to determine when the firm is overvalued in the marketplace, and when it is undervalued? Management will then attempt to issue new shares only when the firm is overvalued. This move benefits existing stockholders, but potential new stockholders are not stupid. They will anticipate this situation and discount it by offering to pay less for the stock at the new issue date. Dierkens (1991), for example, finds that firms in which there is more information asymmetry have larger losses in value when equity issues are sold.
2. INVESTMENT PROSPECTS   Investment demands exist for most firms, sometimes due to growth options with high NPVs, while other times for not so great projects. What if informed investors interpret the issuance of new common stock as a negative signal about the firm's investment projects? After all, if the new projects are really great, why should the firm let new stockholders in on them? In that case it could simply issue debt and let existing stockholders capture all the gain. Again, new investors are not stupid and will offer a lower price for the common stock on the new issue date. In a recent study Pilotte (1992) used the dividend status of the issuing firms as a proxy for growth opportunities. Non-dividend-paying firms were considered to have more growth options, or opportunities, than firms that had either high and stable dividends or firms that had suspended their cash dividends. Pilotte found that firms that did not pay dividends

suffered smaller losses in value when they issued securities than did those with either high/stable dividends or suspended dividends.

Although we don't know which, if either, of these explanations accounts for the decline in stock prices when common stock is publicly sold, we do know the decline occurs. Instead of a public offering of stock, what about the private placement of common stock? Studies by Wruck (1989) and Hertzel and Smith (1993) show that when firms sell stock through a private placement they actually experience *an increase* in the value of the firm. How can these findings of an increase in value be accounted for? Firms that engage in private equity issues are typically smaller and sell a larger percentage of ownership (relative to the already outstanding shares) than firms that sell stock through a public offering. Cooney and Kalay (1993) argue that for such firms the uncertainty surrounding new capital investment projects is large, and by securing the private financing, some of this uncertainty is resolved. Alternatively, Hertzel and Smith (1993) present results consistent with private equity placements providing more efficient transmission of information, so that firms with undervalued assets are encouraged to seek private capital.

When firms issue common stock publicly, they suffer a loss in value; when done privately, they have a gain in value. What occurs when they issue other securities? As we discuss in Chapter 16, stock prices decline little, if at all, when the firm issues new debt. Effective managers must keep these findings in mind when contemplating how to raise long-term financing.

IPOs AND UNDERPRICING

When a firm first goes public with its common stock, the offering is referred to as an **initial public offering, IPO.** A number of studies have examined initial public offerings. By calculating the difference between the offering price and the price shortly after offering, these studies have examined the issue of **underpricing.** Underpricing is a real, but hidden, cost incurred by any firm when it first goes public. These studies have estimated that the magnitude of underpricing with IPOs is high—as much as 10 to 20 percent. As such, the cost of underpricing and the direct cash costs of financing must both be considered when raising equity capital. Table 15.4 shows cash expenses and total costs (which include underpricing) for over 1,000 equity offerings that occurred between 1977 and 1982. The highest cash expenses and total costs occur for small offerings. But, even for the average firm, cash expenses are about 15 percent of gross financing, and the total costs, including underpricing, are about 25 percent of the value of the gross financing. Thus, issuance costs are significant.

Why does underpricing occur? Probably for at least two reasons. The first is that both the investment banking firm and the issuing firm have some vested interest in seeing that the issue is fully sold. One way—but an expensive one—to ensure that the issue is sold is to underprice it. The second is that determining the market worth of a firm that has never been traded is more an art than a science.[8]

---

[8] Another possibility is that underpricing is a signal of the quality of the issue. Garfinkel (1993) considered this proposition but did not find any support for it.

Table 15.4

Cash Expenses and Total Costs for Common Stock Offerings, 1977-1982

This table includes both firm commitment and best efforts offers. Cash expenses equal the underwriter's discount (or commission) and other expenses like legal, printing, and auditing fees. Total costs equal 100 percent - (net proceeds/market value of proceeds).

Gross Proceeds	Number of Offers	Cash Expenses	Total Costs
$100,000–$1,999,999	243	19.96%	31.85%
2,000,000–3,999,999	311	16.86	30.26
4,000,000–5,999,999	156	14.59	19.95
6,000,000–9,999,999	137	12.44	18.74
10,000,000 and over	181	9.37	15.82
Total	1,028	15.34%	24.99%

Source: Adapted from Table 4 in Jay R. Ritter, "The Costs of Going Public," *Journal of Financial Economics* 19 (September 1987): 269–81. Footnotes from the original table are omitted.

PRICING A NEW ISSUE

When a firm already has stock outstanding and is issuing additional shares, they are typically priced a few dollars below the closing price the day before the stock is sold. If the firm is making an initial public offering, however, the pricing decision is much more difficult.

One way to go about establishing the initial selling price is to determine what the total value of the firm should be after the issue, and then divide this value by the number of shares of common stock to be issued. For example, if we assume that United Transport is estimated to be worth $3.5 million and 350,000 shares of common stock will be issued, the estimated selling price is $3,500,000/350,000, or $10 per share. Note that we are interested in the total number of shares to be issued, including any privately held or founder's shares not issued to the public. If United Transport decides to sell 150,000 shares, the offering would consist of 150,000 shares priced at $10 each, for gross proceeds (before flotation costs and other direct issuance expenses) of $1,500,000. To use this approach, however, we must answer the following question: How do we determine the firm's total value—in this case, $3,500,000?

One way to do this is to use the valuation approach described in Chapter 3. For the constant dividend growth situation, the value of the total firm can be estimated by[9]

$$S = \frac{D_1}{k_s - g} \tag{15.3}$$

[9] It is assumed no debt exists.

where

S = the value of an all-equity firm

D_1 = total cash dividends expected to be paid to stockholders next year (at $t = 1$)

k_s = the equity investors' required return

g = the expected (compound) growth rate in cash dividends

Suppose that United expects earnings after taxes of $700,000 and plans to pay 50 percent out in the form of cash dividends, so that D_1 = $350,000. Also, the firm expects its earnings and dividends to grow at approximately 7 percent per year for the foreseeable future. We have estimated D_1 and g in Equation 15.3; all that is needed now is an estimate of k_s. Estimating k_s, however, is not easy, especially for a firm that has never been traded publicly. United's investment banking firm can supply an estimate of k_s, we can use the k_s for some comparable publicly traded firm, or we can use some approach like adding a risk premium to the expected interest rate on long-term corporate bonds. If the rate on long-term bonds is expected to be 9 percent and the risk premium is determined to be 8 percent, then our estimate of k_s is 17 percent. With this we can estimate the value of United Transport to be

$$S = \frac{\$350,000}{0.17 - 0.07} = \frac{\$350,000}{0.10} = \$3,500,000$$

In practice, an ad hoc approach based on comparative price/earnings ratios is often employed. The price/earnings, P/E, ratio is calculated by dividing the market price for a share of common stock by the earnings per share. To use this approach, United's investment banker might examine P/E ratios for publicly traded firms in the same industry, as well as the P/E ratios of firms that have recently gone public. Other pertinent information—such as United's financial condition, growth prospects, quality and stability of management, and size—is also compared. Once a P/E ratio for the firm is estimated, the total market value is determined by

$$S = \text{(net income)}\text{(estimated P/E of stock)} \tag{15.4}$$

Continuing with United Transport, let's assume that United's investment banking firm determines the stock's estimated P/E ratio is 5. The total value of United would be ($700,000)(5) = $3,500,000. Once the total value of the firm is determined, the pricing of the new shares to be issued proceeds as described previously. With either the dividend valuation or comparative P/E approach, the pricing of new issues is an imperfect and subjective process.

RECORDING A STOCK ISSUE

Once stock is issued, it must be recorded on the firm's balance sheet. To see how this occurs, let's continue with United Transport. It currently has 200,000 shares of $2 par value common stock outstanding. The value recorded in United's common stock account is $400,000 [i.e., (200,000 shares)($2 per share)]. United now sells 150,000

Table 15.5

Balance Sheet of United Transport Before and After Stock Issue

The $1,500,000 is split between the common stock and additional paid-in capital accounts on the basis of the par value and the issuance price. An offsetting entry is made indicating that the firm's cash account has increased by $1,500,000.

	Before the Issue	After the Issue
Assets		
Cash	$ 200,000	$1,700,000
Other	1,800,000	1,800,000
Total assets	$2,000,000	$3,500,000
Liabilities and Stockholders' Equity		
Liabilities	$1,000,000	$1,000,000
Stockholders' equity:		
Common stock ($2 par)	400,000	700,000*
Additional paid-in capital	200,000	1,400,000
Retained earnings	400,000	400,000
Total liabilities and stockholders' equity	$2,000,000	$3,500,000

* 350,000 shares at $2 par.

additional shares of common stock and receives $10 per share (ignoring flotation and other issuance costs). The entries are an increase in the common stock account of $300,000 [i.e., (150,000 new shares)($2 per share par value)]; an increase in the additional paid-in capital account of $1,200,000 (150,000 shares times the difference between the issuance price of $10 per share and the par value of $2 per share); and an offsetting entry indicating that the cash account has increased by $1,500,000. The "before" and "after" balance sheets for United Transport are presented in Table 15.5.

LISTING THE STOCK

In addition to selling stock to raise additional capital, publicly held firms must also decide whether the stock should be listed on an organized stock exchange. Small firms are typically traded in the over-the-counter market because there is simply not enough activity to justify listing. As a firm gets bigger, it may decide to apply for listing on one of the regional stock exchanges. A West Coast firm might apply to the Pacific Coast Stock Exchange; one located in Milwaukee might apply to the Midwest Stock Exchange. With continued growth, the firm may decide to apply for listing on the American Stock Exchange, or if it is one of the nation's largest firms, it may apply to the "Big Board"—the New York Stock Exchange.[10]

[10] For a summary of research findings on listing, see Baker and Meeks (1991).

To apply for listing on an organized exchange, the firm must meet certain conditions, file a listing application with both the exchange and the SEC, and pay a fee. The minimum characteristics a firm must possess if it wants a listing on the NYSE are presented in Table 15.6. After a firm is listed, it must meet certain exchange requirements in order to continue its listing. The SEC also requires that both quarterly and annual financial reports be published by listed firms.

In recent years, off-board trading of NYSE-listed stocks has grown. In 1992, for example, the NYSE handled only 65 percent of the trades in its listed stocks. More and more NYSE stocks are being traded on regional exchanges such as the Midwest Stock Exchange; on overseas exchanges, such as the London exchange, where disclosure and trading rules are looser; and in the United States' "third" or "fourth" markets of private dealers and electronic systems. Although many reasons exist for off-board trading of NYSE stocks, a primary reason relates to the NYSE's inability to execute trades of big blocks of stocks for institutional investors without moving prices sharply. Critics of the NYSE argue that its auction-based system relying on specialists simply doesn't provide the necessary infrastructure to deal with very large buy and sell orders. With the movements toward global equity markets and 24-hour trading, some question whether the NYSE will retain its status as one of the world's dominant secondary markets.

Concept Review Questions

- Why does a company's stock price decline with a public common stock offering but increase with a private common stock offering?

- Explain how an investment banking firm can estimate the stock price of a company that has never been traded publicly.

Table 15.6

New York Stock Exchange Listing Requirements for Common Stock

Other considerations include the degree of national interest in the firm, position in the industry, and prospects for both the firm and the industry.

Profitability
Earnings before taxes, EBT, for the most recent year must be at least $2.5 million. For the two preceding years, EBT must have been at least $2 million.

Assets
Net tangible assets of at least $16 million, but greater emphasis is placed on the aggregate market value.

Market Value
The market value of the publicly held stock must be at least $16 million.*

Public Ownership
At least 1 million shares must be publicly held, and there must be at least 2,000 stockholders, each of whom owns at least 100 shares.

Source: New York Stock Exchange Fact Book, 1992.

*This requirement might conceivably be as low as $8 million depending on the level of the NYSE Index of Common Stock prices.

REGULATION OF PUBLIC ISSUES

Until 1933, regulation of the securities markets was done entirely by the individual states. One of the earliest state security laws was enacted by Kansas in 1911. A member of the Kansas legislature remarked that the new law would prevent sellers from promising the "blue sky" to unsophisticated investors; hence, state regulations are referred to as **blue sky laws.** But state regulation was spotty, and when the security markets collapsed in 1929, it became evident that many securities had been misrepresented. Today, state laws continue to exist, but the primary laws governing the securities markets have been enacted at the federal level.

PRIMARY MARKET REGULATION

The new issues, or primary, market is governed by the Securities Act of 1933. The basic objective of this act is to provide *full disclosure* of all pertinent information; it does not attempt to prevent a firm from issuing highly questionable or risky securities. To accomplish this objective, the act includes the following provisions:

1. The act applies to all interstate offerings to the public except for very small issues ($1 million to $5 million, depending on the circumstances); short-term issues (maturing in 270 days or less); or those regulated by other federal agencies (such as railroads, banks, and public utilities).
2. Securities must be registered for a minimum number of days before a public offering. The registration statement supplies financial, technical, and legal information about the issue and the firm. Any misleading or incomplete information may cause a delay in the registration.
3. After the registration has become effective, the securities can be offered for public sale if accompanied by the prospectus.
4. Under shelf registration, however, a firm may register all securities needed over a 2-year period and then issue them as desired during that period.

SECONDARY MARKET REGULATION

Once securities have been issued, they are traded between investors in the secondary market. This market is regulated by the Securities Exchange Act of 1934. The primary provisions of this legislation are as follows:

1. The act created the Securities and Exchange Commission. (For one year, the Federal Trade Commission administered the Securities Act of 1933.)
2. Major securities exchanges, such as the New York Stock Exchange and the American Stock Exchange, must register with the SEC. In addition, firms whose securities are listed on these exchanges must file periodic reports with both the exchange and the SEC.
3. Corporate insiders who are officers, directors, or major stockholders must file

monthly reports. Any short-term profits from holding the firm's stock less than 6 months are payable to the firm.

4. Manipulative practices are prohibited.
5. Margin requirements[11] are set, and may be changed as desired, by the Federal Reserve System.

Regulation of the securities market has important consequences for managers. Because they are regulated, both the primary and the secondary markets are viewed as being both orderly and efficient. Firms can issue securities with full confidence that the issue will be sold in a manner that secures the needed capital and provides investors a ready market for resale. Without the development of an extensive investment banking community and efficient and orderly security markets, the costs and risks involved in issuing long-term securities would rise, increasing the firm's opportunity cost of capital and, through the capital budgeting process, influencing its investment decisions.

Concept Review Questions
- Explain the goal and the requirements of the Securities Act of 1933.
- What are the primary provisions of the Securities and Exchange Act of 1934?

VENTURE CAPITAL

In the discussion so far in this chapter we have implicitly assumed the firm was big enough to be able to secure financing from the public markets or through "traditional" private placements. However, for very small firms this is not the case. For small businesses, finding **venture capital** (that is, new high-risk capital) is one of the major problems it faces. One way to look at the initial financing stages is to break them into phases, as follows:

1. SEED MONEY FINANCING   A small amount of financing is needed to prove a concept or develop a product.
2. START-UP AND FIRST-LEVEL FINANCING   Financing for firms that need money for research and development, initial production, marketing, and the like.
3. SECOND-LEVEL FINANCING   Financing for firms that are producing and selling a product but are not breaking even yet.
4. THIRD-LEVEL OR MEZZANINE FINANCING   Financing for a firm that is producing a product, breaking even, and considering an expansion.
5. FOURTH-LEVEL OR BRIDGE FINANCING   Financing provided for firms that are likely to go public within the next year.

Seed money almost always comes from personal savings or loans and from investments by family and friends. Start-up and first-level financing is needed to get the firm off and

[11] Instead of paying the full amount initially, an investor can buy on margin and borrow the remainder from a securities dealer.

running and to help it meet production quality and quantity standards so that it may begin to break even. Although some firms provide start-up and first-level financing, many venture capital firms avoid this type of financing. Second-level financing is designed to help firms reach an economic break-even point. Third-level, or mezzanine, financing is often provided by venture capital firms. Some large industrial or financial firms (such as Citicorp Venture Capital) have venture capital operations, but most of this type of financing is provided by smaller firms specializing in providing venture capital. Some of these same firms also provide fourth-level, or bridge, financing.[12] Other venture capital financing is provided by pension funds, foreign investors, insurance companies, individual investors and families, and endowments and foundations.

For every ten first-level venture capital investments, only two or three may make it beyond a few years. In fact, some estimates are that 15 percent of new firms don't make it beyond the first year and 50 percent don't make it beyond the fifth year. Because of the very high risk in first- and second-level financing, and the long time before the firm is successful (if it ever is), we see why venture capital firms are reluctant to invest in these stages. They believe, probably rightly so, that the risk/reward prospects are better for later-level investments.

Concept Review Question

■ What are the five phases of initial financing a small firm typically experiences?

KEY POINTS

1. Internally generated funds supply the vast majority of long-term financing needed by firms. However, about 20 percent is provided by new long-term issues, of which bonds play the largest part.
2. Investment banking firms provide marketing services, risk-bearing, certification, and monitoring to issuing firms.
3. Shelf registration lowers the cost to the firm and increases the speed and flexibility of obtaining long-term financing. Rule 144a has provided benefits to both U.S. and non-U.S. firms who use the private placement market.
4. Outstanding shares equal issued shares minus treasury shares. Par value, book value, and market value are all quoted on a per share basis for common stock. Only market value has any financial meaning.
5. Firms issue new common stock only infrequently; studies indicate they suffer a loss in market value when they do issue common stock publicly. Cash expenses average 15 percent and total costs average 25 percent of the total value of new public common stock issues.

QUESTIONS

15.1   Because large firms often have extensive and well-trained finance staffs, they appear to be incurring extra costs by employing the services of investment banking firms. What reasons can you give for engaging the services of investment bankers?

[12] For more on venture capital, see Pratt's *Guide to Venture Capital* or the *Journal of Business Venturing*.

15.2 Before entering into an underwriting agreement, investment banking firms make a careful investigation of the firm, especially if it is making its initial public offering. Since investment banking firms quickly resell the securities, why the extensive investigation?

15.3 What changes have been brought about by shelf registration and Rule 144a?

15.4 Explain the difference between majority and cumulative voting. What are the advantages or disadvantages of the two plans from (a) the firm's standpoint, and (b) the viewpoint of minority stockholders?

15.5 Discuss how stock with limited liability is like a call option.

15.6 The primary purpose of the preemptive right is to allow stockholders to maintain their proportionate ownership and control of a firm. How important do you believe this right is for the following:

a. The average stockholder of a firm listed on the New York Stock Exchange?
b. An institutional investor such as a mutual fund or a pension fund?
c. The stockholders of a closely held firm? Explain.

15.7 Differentiate among par value, book value, and market value per share. Why is market value generally the only important figure? Under what limited circumstances may par value or book value be of some importance? Explain.

15.8 The market price of a firm's common stock falls by 2 to 3 percent when it issues additional shares of common stock through a public offering. What possible reasons can we advance for this rather surprising finding? What happens when firms have a private placement of common stock? What possible reasons exist for this effect?

15.9 Explain the direct cash expenses and the total costs of issuing common stock. Why do you believe the costs are so high?

15.10 For underwritten common stock issues of about $5 million in size, issuance costs average about 20 percent. Does this mean the cost of external common equity is roughly 20 percent higher than the cost of internally generated funds for these firms?

15.11 How might firms proceed when pricing a new issue of common stock? What makes this decision important?

15.12 What advantages (either real or imagined) exist when a firm decides to list its common stock? Which are real, and which imagined?

15.13 How do the Securities Act of 1933 and the Securities Exchange Act of 1934 attempt to regulate activities in the primary and secondary capital markets?

15.14 Each month, the Securities and Exchange Commission publishes a report of corporate insider purchases and sales in their own firms' equity securities. Why is such a report issued?

Concept Review Problems

See Appendix A for solutions.

CR15.1 Seattle Publishers is raising $500,000 in new equity. If direct floatation costs are estimated to be 15 percent of gross proceeds, how large does the offering need to be? How much will Seattle Publishers pay in flotation costs?

CR15.2 Cooper Corporation has a current stock price of $35 per share and needs to raise $10 million. The investment banking firm underwriting Cooper's common stock offering stated the offering price will have to be $32 per share because of indirect costs such as investors' concerns about information asymmetry and the firm's investment prospects. Direct flotation costs charged by the investment banking firm are 5 percent of the issue price. How many shares must the firm sell to net $10 million after indirect and direct flotation costs?

CR15.3 Cambridge Management has minority ownership in Silverado Gold Mines. Silverado has 10 members on its board of directors and 550,000 shares of stock outstanding.

a. How many shares of common stock must Cambridge own if all 10 seats of Silverado's board are to be elected and Cambridge wants to control 4 of the seats?
b. If Cambridge owns 130,000 shares, how many directors will it be able to elect?
c. Silverado changed its election policy so that each director will hold office for 2 years and only half the board will be elected each year. Does this change affect the number of directors that can be elected by Cambridge?

CR15.4 ACI is going public and would like to issue 700,000 shares of common stock. Earnings for the year just completed were $700,000.

a. Assume ACI has a growth rate of 8 percent, a required return on equity, k_s, of 12 percent, and it plans to have a dividend payout ratio of 70 percent. What should be ACI's initial offering price?
b. Other firms similar to ACI have a P/E ratio of 18. If we apply this P/E ratio to ACI, what should be ACI's initial offering price?

CR15.5 BGI Corp. has the following balance sheet:

Cash	$ 50,000	Liabilities	$400,000
Other	750,000	Common stock ($1 par)	50,000
Total assets	$800,000	Additional paid-in capital	200,000
		Retained earnings	150,000
		Total liabilities and	
		stockholders' equity	$800,000

Assume BGI sells 10,000 additional shares of stock at $20 per share. What its BGI's balance sheet after the stock issue?

PROBLEMS

15.1 Welker Products recently sold a $30 million bond issue at par. The underwriting fees were 1.2 percent, and additional issuance costs were $125,000.

a. How many dollars did Welker net from the sale?
b. What were the fees (including both underwriting and other issuance costs) as a percentage of the gross proceeds of the bond issue?

15.2 In an $80 million bond issue by Consumers Power, the bonds were purchased by the underwriting group at 99.125 percent of par and sold to the public at par, which was $1,000 per bond.

a. What was the total amount Consumers Power received from the issue?
b. What were the total underwriting costs? What were the underwriting costs as a percentage of the gross proceeds? What were the underwriting costs per $1,000 bond?

c. If an underwriting firm was also the seller, it received all the commission. Otherwise, other security dealers (not in the underwriting group) could buy the bonds and sell them for a commission of $2.50 per bond. If a dealer bought 50 bonds, how much in total did the dealer make, and how much did the dealer pay to the underwriter for the bonds?

15.3 Precision Computers, a new and rather speculative firm, wishes to raise additional capital by selling stock and going public. The firm's investment banker has suggested two alternatives. Plan I is a firm commitment offering of 1 million shares at $7.50 per share, with an underwriting fee of 8 percent of the gross proceeds. Plan II is a best efforts offering at $7.75 per share, subject to an underwriting commission of 3 percent of the expected gross proceeds sold, plus a $150,000 fee. The "best guess" is that 95 percent of the issue would be sold under plan II.

a. Based on the net proceeds to the firm, which plan should Precision choose?
b. Does your answer change if only 90 percent of the issue can be sold under the best efforts plan?
c. All things considered, which plan would you recommend? Why?

15.4 Thomas, Inc., is planning a private placement of 60,000 new shares to an institutional investor at a 10 percent discount from the present market price of $40. There are presently 300,000 shares outstanding. If the current book value of the stockholders' equity is $6,000,000, calculate (a) book value per share both before and after the private placement, and (b) the market price per share after the private placement. Are existing stockholders better or worse off after the new shares are sold? Defend your answer, given your calculations.

15.5 Phyllis and her associates control 152,000 shares of Champion, Inc., and they desire representation on the firm's board. Champion has 500,000 shares outstanding, 8 directors are to be elected, and cumulative voting is used. How many board members can Phyllis and her associates elect in each of the cases below?

a. All 500,000 shares vote.
b. Only 90 percent of the total shares vote.

15.6 Ken and George plan to pool their shares so they can both be elected to the board of directors. The firm has 1,000,000 shares of stock outstanding and plans to elect ten directors. How many shares do Ken and George jointly need to control to obtain two seats on the board in each of the cases below?

a. Majority voting is employed.
b. Cumulative voting is employed.
c. The size of the board is reduced to five and cumulative voting is employed.

15.7 FMW Corp. is incorporated in a state that requires cumulative voting. The firm has 12,000 shares of common stock outstanding and a board of directors composed of 5 members. Monica, a dissident stockholder, has accumulated 2,001 shares of stock, which gives her just enough votes to elect herself to the board.

FMW knows it cannot block Monica from joining the board, but it wants to dilute her influence by adding more members to the board of directors. Assuming that (1) the number of total shares remains at 12,000 and (2) Monica does not acquire any more shares, how many additional directors should be added to the board so that Monica can still elect only herself with the shares she controls?

15.8 J. B. Eagen is a new firm that needs to raise $16,560,000 to begin operations. No debt will be used. Eagen's common stock is expected to pay a $4 cash dividend next year, and dividends and earnings are expected to grow at 9 percent per year for the foreseeable future. If k_s is 19 percent and the cost of issuing the stock is 8 percent of the gross proceeds from the sale, how many shares must be issued and sold?

15.9 Kletzin Enterprises is planning its first public offering of common stock. The CFO estimates that the equity investor's required return is between 11 and 14 percent. Earnings and cash dividends are expected to grow at 6 to 9 percent per year for the foreseeable future, and cash dividends to be paid next year, D_1, are $800,000.

a. What is the range of possible total current market values for the stock of Kletzin Enterprises?

b. If 500,000 shares of stock are authorized and outstanding, but 300,000 will be held by the founders, what are the maximum and minimum selling prices per share and the maximum and minimum total proceeds from the issue?

15.10 Granbe Enterprises is a new firm that needs to raise $6,412,500 through the issuance of 1 million shares of stock. No debt will be employed. Next year's cash dividends are expected to be $0.60 per share, and cash dividends and earnings are expected to grow at 8 percent per year for the foreseeable future. If k_s is 16 percent and the cost of issuing the stock is 10 percent of the gross proceeds, what percentage of the issue must be sold in order for Granbe to obtain the net amount of $6,412,500? (*Note:* Any unsold shares will be distributed among the firm's owners, so a total of 1 million shares will be outstanding.)

15.11 Spartan Energy is planning its first public offering. Its past growth in cash dividends and earnings has averaged 10 percent per year. Based on the number of shares Spartan is planning to issue, cash dividends and earnings per share for next year ($t = 1$) are expected to be $0.90 and $2, respectively. The firm's investment banking firm, Lindsay & Sons, has recommended that the stock be issued at a price of $15 per share. (Ignore any flotation or issuance costs.)

a. What is the P/E ratio implied by the recommended market price?

b. Two firms similar to Spartan Energy have the following characteristics:

	Firm Y	Firm Z
Expected EPS	$ 1.50	$ 3.00
Expected DPS	0.80	1.25
Expected growth rate per year	7%	9%
Market price	$15.00	$45.00

For firm Y and firm Z, determine (1) their P/E ratios and (2) their implied k_s. Then calculate an estimated market price for Spartan Energy using first the separate P/Es and k_s's, and then an average of them. Based on these comparable firms, what range of prices is implied for Spartan?

c. What required return, or cost of equity capital, k_s, is implied by the price of $15 if investors' expectations of the future are consistent with the past?

d. You believe the rate calculated in (c) is high; it should be between 11.5 and 13 percent. The expected growth rate of 10 percent is okay. What issue price is implied, given these estimates?

e. Based on your analysis in (a) through (d), how would you respond to the Lindsay & Sons proposal?

15.12   Ellis Paper is planning to issue 500,000 additional shares of common stock at an offering price of $12 each. Show the net effect of the transaction on the firm's balance sheet. (Ignore any underwriting or other issuance expenses.)

Assets		Liabilities and Stockholders' Equity	
Cash	$ 3,000,000	Liabilities	$25,000,000
Other	62,000,000	Common stock ($2 par)	4,000,000
Total	$65,000,000	Additional paid-in capital	10,000,000
		Retained earnings	26,000,000
		Total	$65,000,000

15.13   Mans & Sons has 200,000 shares of common stock authorized. Its common equity shown on the firm's balance sheet is as follows:

Common stock ($2 par)	$300,000
Additional paid-in capital	95,000
Retained earnings	600,000
	995,000
Less: Treasury stock (3,000 shares)	25,000
Common stockholders' equity	$970,000

a.   How many shares are issued?

b.   How many are outstanding? Explain the difference between (a) and (b).

c.   How many additional shares can be issued without the approval of Mans & Sons stockholders?

d.   If the firm issues 5,000 more shares at $15 each, prepare the new common stockholders' equity accounts.

15.14   Mini Case   Office Supplies, Inc., is a fast-growing privately held firm. In order to continue expanding into new markets, it needs additional common stock financing.

a.   What different methods are available for selling common stock? What are the advantages and disadvantages of each?

b.   If Office Supplies decides to have the issue underwritten through a firm commitment offering, what sequence of events will occur?

c.   If the current owners are concerned about giving up too much control of the firm in terms of voting rights, how might they proceed?

d.   To determine the selling price of the new issue, Office Supplies has made the following estimates. The firm does not presently pay cash dividends, nor are there any plans to start paying them in the near future. Based on internal projections, the rate of growth is expected to be 40 percent per year for each of the next 5 years, after which it will be 10 percent per year to infinity. Because no dividends are paid, a variation of the dividend valuation model will be employed as one way to estimate the total value of Office Supplies. Under this approach the firm's free cash flow available after necessary expenses will be projected into the future, discounted at the opportunity cost of equity capital of 18 percent, and then the firm's liabilities will be subtracted. The free cash flow at time $t = 0$ is \$3,000,000, and the liabilities are \$25,000,000.

The second way that will be used to estimate the value of the firm is based on comparable P/E ratios. The firm's current earnings are \$2,500,000 and due to its high growth, a P/E ratio of 35 times earnings is believed to be appropriate.

(1) Estimate Office Supplies' total equity value, S, using both the discounted cash flow approach and the comparable P/E approach.

(2) Then average them together to determine the estimated equity value of Office Supplies.

e. Office Supplies has 5,000,000 shares of common stock authorized. It will sell 2,000,000 to the public (with 3,000,000 being retained by the original owners), and the cash expenses of the sale will be 7 percent of the issue price.

(1) What market price per share will the stock sell for? How much per share will Office Supplies receive after expenses? How much in total will it receive?

(2) Why are issuance expenses higher with common stock, especially for a smaller firm, than for bonds?

f. In what market will Office Supplies stock trade? What are the advantages if in the future it decides to have its stock listed on one of the stock exchanges? What are the disadvantages?

REFERENCES

For more on investment banking, equity financing, and shelf registrations, see:

ALLEN, DAVID S., ROBERT E. LAMY, and G. RODNEY THOMPSON. "The Shelf Registration of Debt and Self Selection Bias." *Journal of Finance* (March 1990): 275–87.

BLACKWELL, DAVID W., M. WAYNE MARR, and MICHAEL F. SPIVEY. "Shelf Registration and the Reduced Due Diligence Argument: Implications of the Underwriter Certification and the Implicit Insurance Hypothesis." *Journal of Financial and Quantitative Analysis* 25 (June 1990): 245–59.

BOOTH, JAMES R., and RALPH L. SMITH, II. "Capital Raising, Underwriting and the Certification Hypothesis." *Journal of Financial Economics*, 15 (January/February 1986): 262–81.

CARTER, RICHARD, and STEVEN MANASTER. "Initial Public Offerings and Underwriter Reputation." *Journal of Finance* 45 (September 1990): 1045–67.

COONEY, JOHN W., JR., and AVNER KALAY. "Positive Information from Equity Issue Announcements." *Journal of Financial Economics* 33 (April 1993): 149–72.

DIERKENS, NATHALIE. "Information Asymmetry and Equity Issues." *Journal of Financial and Quantitative Analysis* 26 (June 1991): 181–99.

ECKBO, B. ESPEN, and RONALD W. MASULIS. "Adverse Selection and the Rights Offer Paradox." *Journal of Financial Economics* 32 (December 1992): 293–332.

GARFINKEL, JON A. "IPO Underpricing, Insider Selling and Subsequent Equity Offerings: Is Underpricing a Signal of Quality?" *Financial Management* 22 (Spring 1993): 74–83.

HANSEN, ROBERT S., and PAUL TORREGROSA. "Underwriting Compensation and Corporate Monitoring." *Journal of Finance* 47 (September 1992): 1537–55.

HERTZEL, MICHAEL, and RICHARD L. SMITH. "Market Discounts and Shareholder Gains for Placing Equity Privately." *Journal of Finance* 47 (June 1993): 459–85.

PILOTTE, EUGENE. "Growth Opportunities and the Stock Price Response to New Financing." *Journal of Business* 65 (July 1992): 371–94.

RITTER JAY R. "The Long-Run Performance of Initial Public Offerings." *Journal of Finance* 46 (March 1991): 3–27.

WRUCK, KAREN H. "Equity Ownership Concentration and Firm Value: Evidence from Private Equity Financings." *Journal of Financial Economics* 23 (June 1989): 3–28.

Voting rights, listings, and other topics of interest are discussed in:

BAKER, H. KENT, and SUE E. MEEKS. "Research on Exchange Listings and Delistings: A Review and Synthesis." *Financial Practice and Education* 1 (Spring 1991): 57–71.

BRICKLEY, JAMES A., RONALD C. LEASE, and CLIFFORD W. SMITH, JR. "Ownership Structure and Voting on Antitakeover Amendments." *Journal of Financial Economics* 20 (January/March 1988): 267–93.

COWAN, ARNOLD D., RICHARD B. CARTER, FREDERICK H. DARK, and AJAI K. SINGH. "Explaining the NYSE Listing Choices of NASDAQ Firms." *Financial Management* 21 (Winter 1992): 73–86.

GORDON, LILLI A., and JOHN POUND. "Information, Ownership Structure, and Shareholder Voting: Evidence from Shareholder-Sponsored Corporate Governance Proposals." *Journal of Finance* 48 (June 1993): 697–718.

MEGGINSON, WILLIAM L., and KATHLEEN A. WEISS. "Venture Capitalist Certification in Initial Public Offerings." *Journal of Finance* 46 (July 1991): 879–903.

PARTCH, M. MEGAN. "The Creation of a Class of Limited Voting Common Stock and Shareholder Wealth." *Journal of Financial Economics* 18 (June 1987): 313–39.

16 *Liability Management*

EXECUTIVE SUMMARY

Long-term debt and preferred stock are fixed-income-type securities, because both obligate the issuing firm to a series of payments over time. (The one exception is zero-coupon bonds, which obligate the firm to a lump-sum payment when the bond matures.) A primary measure of the riskiness of bonds is the bond rating. Other things being equal, the higher (lower) the rating, the lower (higher) the yield to maturity on the bond.

Zero-coupon bonds are sold at a discount and do not provide cash interest payments; rather, the interest provided is the difference between the original discounted selling price and the maturity value of the bond. As market interest rates fluctuate, the market price of zero-coupon bonds fluctuates more than the market price of similar coupon bonds.

Increasingly, firms have begun to practice long-term liability management with tactics such as bond refunding, buybacks, and interest rate swaps. Preferred stock, due to its higher cost to the issuing firm, has been less frequently used. The creation of adjustable rate preferred stock, however, has lowered the cost and broadened the appeal of preferred stock.

Conflicts of interest exist between bondholders and stockholders because what benefits one may cause the other to suffer a loss. These conflicts are intensified during periods of financial distress.

LONG-TERM DEBT

Long-term debt and preferred stock obligate the firm to pay a fixed annual return—interest on debt or cash dividends on preferred stock. To secure funds, managers choose from among the various kinds of long-term securities depending on world markets, what investors are currently interested in, and the firm's financial position. This chapter focuses primarily on the two main types of long-term securities—bonds and preferred stock.

BOND TERMS

When a firm borrows with bonds, it issues a long-term promissory note to a lender. The contract between the firm and the lender is called a bond **indenture.** For cash offerings a copy of the indenture is included in the registration statement filed with the Securities and Exchange Commission. It is a legal document specifying all the provisions attached to the bond. One specific provision states that the lenders will receive regular interest payments, generally semiannually, during the term of the bond, and will receive the par or maturity value of the bond upon maturity. For example, if IBM issues a 20-year, $100 million bond with a coupon rate of 10.3 percent, it will pay $10.3 million per year in interest each year until maturity. The interest will be paid in two semiannual installments of $5.15 million each. On the maturity date in 20 years, IBM would then repay the $100 million. While long-term corporate bonds typically have a 20 to 30 year maturity when issued, in 1992 and 1993 Boeing, Consolidated Rail (Conrail), Ford Motor, and Texaco all issued bonds with a 50-year maturity, while Walt Disney and Coca Cola both issued 100-year bonds.

TRUSTEE

Bonds are not only long-term in nature, they are typically of substantial size. Issues of $50 to $500 million are not uncommon, and some are even larger. To ease communication between the issuing firm and the lenders, a trustee is appointed for all public issues of long-term debt. The primary responsibilities of the trustee (typically a bank) are as follows:

1. To see that all the legal requirements for drawing up the bond indenture are met before issuance.
2. To monitor the action of the issuing firm to see that its performance is in agreement with the conditions specified by the indenture.
3. To take appropriate action on behalf of bondholders if the firm defaults on interest or principal payments.

SECURITY AND SENIORITY

Bonds come with many types of provisions. As Figure 16.1 shows, one primary distinction is between secured and unsecured bonds. We will discuss the provisions in order.

Forms of Secured Debt

The vast majority of secured debt consists of **mortgage bonds,** which may be *first mortgage bonds* if they have a primary claim on assets in the event of default, or *second mortgage bonds,* whose claim is subordinate to that of the first mortgage bondholders.

Figure 16.1

Types of Bonds

Many other variations exist, but the ones shown here represent the primary types. Note that other features, such as adjustable rates or zero coupons, can be incorporated with any of these bonds.

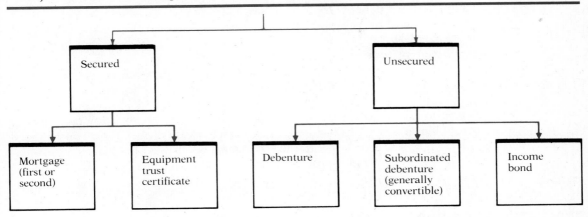

Bonds come with many different types of restrictions, or protective covenants. Some mortgage bonds have a "closed-end provision" that prohibits the firm from issuing additional debt with equal priority against the pledged assets. With an "open-end provision," no specific limit on the amount of debt secured by the firm's assets exists. In between these two is a "limited open-end" mortgage, in which some limited amount of additional debt may be issued. To strengthen the position of the bond-holder, the indenture also may contain an "after-acquired property" clause. This provision specifies that any property acquired by the firm in the future will also serve as collateral for the bonds.

A second form of secured debt is the **equipment trust certificate.** These frequently are used to finance railroad cars and airplanes. Here, the trustee acquires formal ownership of the asset in question. The issuing firm arranges to purchase the equipment and provides a down payment of 10 to 25 percent; the remainder is provided by the purchasers of the equipment trust certificates. The certificates are issued with varying maturities, often ranging from 1 to 15 years. After the entire issue is paid off, title to the equipment passes to the firm. Because the trustee holds title to the pledged equipment, equipment trust certificates provide good security to their purchasers.

Unsecured Debt

Unsecured bonds, called **debentures,** have no specific assets pledged as collateral. Instead, they are backed by the full faith and credit of the issuing corporation. Large firms with excellent credit ratings, such as Procter & Gamble, Exxon, and Shell, use debentures almost exclusively. Most debentures have a claim on assets in the event of default that comes after that held by bank loans, short-term debt, the government, and any mortgage bonds.

Although asset security is sometimes important, in the final analysis it is the firm's cash flow that determines the attractiveness of a bond issue. Debentures frequently contain a "negative pledge clause," which prohibits issuing new debt with a priority over the debentures' claim on assets. This provision generally applies to assets acquired in the future as well as to those already owned by the issuing firm.

Subordinated debentures, which have a claim on assets inferior to that of other debentures in the case of liquidation, are widely used in raising long-term debt capital. Subordinated debt allows the issuing firm to increase its borrowing without jeopardizing the security position of its other long-term debt.

One last form of unsecured bond is the **income bond,** which requires interest to be paid only to the extent that it is earned by the firm. Income bonds typically arise out of reorganizations. They are somewhat like preferred stock in that the firm is not required to pay interest if it is not earned. Income bonds have the advantage that any interest, if paid, is a tax-deductible expense, whereas cash dividends paid on preferred stock are not. The provisions attached to income bonds vary, but many are **cumulative;** that is, if interest is not paid in a given period, it must be paid in the future if it is earned.

ADDITIONAL BOND PROVISIONS

Many different types of provisions and protective covenants occur in bonds. Some of these were discussed in Chapter 12; others were considered in the last section. There are three provisions that warrant additional consideration; these are the call provision, sinking funds, and convertibility.

Call Provision

A **call provision** gives the issuing firm the option to call the bond for redemption before it matures. This provision states that if it calls the bond, the firm must pay an amount greater than the par or maturity value of the bond; the additional amount is the **call premium.** For most long-term bonds, the call premium starts out close to the coupon rate on the bond. Thus, if the firm wants to call the bonds soon after issuance, it pays a penalty of about 1 year's additional interest. This rate declines over time.

The call provision, which is simply a call option held by the issuing firm, has value to the firm but is potentially detrimental to investors. The problem for investors is that the call provision enables the issuing firm to substitute bonds with a lower coupon rate for bonds with a higher rate, or bonds with less protective covenants for ones with more stringent covenants.[1] To make them more attractive investments, many bonds now carry a 5- to 10-year "nonrefundable provision" if the coupon rate on the new bonds will be below the current coupon rate on the bond to be refunded.

Sinking Fund

A **sinking fund** provision requires the firm to retire a given number of bonds over a specified time period. The logic behind sinking funds is to encourage firms to adopt a systematic pattern for retiring the largest portion of the debt before the maturity

---

[1] Refunding a bond issue involves calling one issue and replacing it with another. Refunding is considered later in the chapter and in Appendix 16A.

date. Generally bonds are redeemed for the sinking fund at par. Although it is called a sinking fund, we should emphasize that a separate fund is *not* set up and accumulated over the life of the bonds. Rather, a given number of bonds *are actually retired each year.*

In most cases, the firm can decide how to meet the sinking fund provision. If market interest rates have increased, causing the price of the bonds to fall below the par or sinking fund price, the firm can buy sufficient bonds on the open market to meet the requirement. But if market interest rates are low (and therefore bond prices are high), the firm will call the bonds by lottery at par. This flexibility obviously benefits the issuing firm.

If the bonds are privately placed, the sinking fund provision is omitted because the bonds must be redeemed at par. In that case, instead of sinking funds, firms use **serial bonds**, which is a package of bonds that mature in different years. A package of serial bonds is similar to a bond with a sinking fund provision, because both provide for the periodic repayment of the firm's debt. But the serial bond does not give the issuing firm an alternative—the bonds must be redeemed at par.

Convertibility

Some bonds and an even smaller percentage of preferred stock contain another feature—convertibility. **Convertible securities** are convertible bonds or convertible preferred stock, originally issued as debt or preferred stock, that can be exchanged for common stock of the issuing firm at the discretion of the investor. By combining elements of both debt and equity, convertible bonds assist in minimizing agency problems and conflicts between bondholders and stockholders. Convertibles are considered in Chapter 17.

Bond Features, Asymmetric Information, and Damage Containment

Firms wanting to finance new capital budgeting projects which require external financing can issue either equity or debt. Substantial empirical evidence has been presented (see Chapters 12 and 15) that when firms issue equity they suffer a loss in value. One reason suggested for this loss in value is that the issuing firm is transmitting information about the future prospects of the firm: If prospects for the firm and its capital projects are "good," the firm will use debt, but if the prospects are "poor," it will use equity. In addition, Flannery (1986) and Robbins and Schatzberg (1986) present a "signaling view": Firms with high-quality projects can signal that information through the features of the bond issue. In this context high-quality projects can be signaled by issuing short maturity bonds, bonds that are callable, and bonds that do not have sinking funds.

Another view, articulated by Barnea, Haugen, and Senbet (1980, 1981) is that of "damage containment," where bond features are designed to minimize possible loss of shareholder wealth by making the bonds easy to retire early. Under the damage containment view, an optimal bond contract has either a short maturity or is callable. Ogden (1988) notes that although the sinking fund feature is inferior to a bond being callable, it does allow some of the bond to be retired at the lower par value as opposed to the higher call price.

In an empirical study Mitchell (1991) found that firms facing information asymmetries tend to finance with bonds that have shorter maturities and are callable (with or without sinking fund provisions). On the other hand, where there are fewer information asymmetries, firms tend to finance with long-term, callable, sinking fund bonds. Although more research is needed, Mitchell notes that these findings are slightly more consistent with the damage containment view than with the signaling view.

Concept Review Questions

- What is the purpose of appointing a trustee for all long-term issuances?
- Give some examples of secured debentures and unsecured debentures.
- How do a callable bond and a convertible bond differ?

FINANCING WITH LONG-TERM AND MEDIUM-TERM DEBT

The frequency with which firms issue long-term debt varies considerably. At one extreme are large public utility firms, which may issue debt every few years. Other firms issue long-term debt only infrequently. But however often they employ it, managers must be aware of special considerations when they use long-term debt.

PRICING AND SELLING THE BOND ISSUE

Many large bond issues are underwritten through a firm commitment offering, although an increasing number are being offered through shelf registration and private placement. The coupon interest rate is determined shortly before the bonds come to market, so that they may be sold at a price close to par. Most bonds are issued in denominations of $1,000 in **fully registered** form. This means that the registration agent for the issuing firm (often a bank) will record the ownership of each bond, so that both interest and principal are paid directly to the owner of the bond. Until the last few decades, most bonds were issued in **bearer form.** When bearer bonds are employed, the certificate is the primary evidence of ownership. The owner must send coupons in for payment of interest, and the bond itself must be returned upon maturity for repayment of principal. Because of the risk of loss and the time and inconvenience involved in "clipping" coupons, and because of actions by the U.S. Congress in 1982, most bonds are now issued in fully registered form.

The price of a bond is expressed as a percentage of its par value. Thus, a price of 99.5 means 99.5 percent of its $1,000 par value, or $995. When a bond is sold, the price is quoted net of accrued interest. This means the purchaser pays not only the purchase price, but also any interest that may have accrued between interest payment dates. Finally, the major secondary market for bonds is the over-the-counter, OTC, market.

BOND RATINGS

The most widely employed method for examining the relative quality of bonds is **bond ratings,** which reflect the probability of payment of both interest and principal. Two bonds with similar ratings and the same maturity have approximately the same yield

Table 16.1

Bond Rating Classifications

Generally, both Moody's and Standard & Poor's rate a bond similarly, although differences in ratings can and do exist. Bonds in the top four classifications (AAA-BBB or Aaa-Baa, respectively) are considered "investment grade." All of the rest, in contrast, are non-investment grade, or "junk" bonds.

	Standard & Poor's		**Moody's**
AAA	Highest rating	Aaa	Best quality, "gilt edge"
AA	Very strong	Aa	High quality
A	Strong	A	Upper medium grade
BBB	Adequate	Baa	Medium grade
BB	Least speculative of the BB to CCC bonds	Ba	Have speculative elements
B	More speculative	B	Lack characteristics of a desirable investment
		Caa	Poor standing; may be in default
CC	Still more speculative	Ca	High degree of speculation; often in default
CCC	Most speculative	C	Extremely poor prospect of ever attaining any real investment standing
D	Income bonds in default		

Source: Standard & Poor's *Creditweek* and Moody's *Bond Record*.
Note: AA to BB bonds may be modified by the addition of a plus or minus sign to show relative standing, which Aa to B bonds carry a 1, 2, or 3 to designate the top, middle, and bottom range of the rating.

to maturity.[2] The two major rating agencies are Moody's Investors Service and Standard & Poor's Corporation. Their ratings are described in Table 16.1.

The AAA/Aaa and AA/Aa bonds are of high quality; A and BBB/Baa bonds are also viewed as being of "investment grade." Bonds with these four top grades may be held by banks and other institutional investors. BB/Ba and B bonds are more speculative with respect to payment of interest and principal; bonds rated below B are either in default or have other characteristics that make them highly speculative. Bonds rated below BBB/Baa are collectively referred to as junk, or high-yield, bonds.

Many factors influence the determination of bond ratings, but some of the most important are these:

1. Accounting ratios such as the debt/equity ratio, times interest earned, and various profitability ratios (as discussed in Chapter 24), which provide some evidence of the strength and riskiness of the firm.
2. The current status of the firm in terms of its competitiveness and management. In addition, the industry or industries in which the firm is engaged often is a factor.

---

[2] Exceptions occur when we compare bonds issued by industrial firms and those issued by public utilities. Because of different provisions and demand, the yields on utilities are typically higher than those of similarly rated corporate bonds.

3. If the firm is in a regulated industry, such as public utilities, the attitude of the appropriate regulatory authorities.
4. Specific provisions or characteristics of the bonds. For example, first mortgage bonds generally carry a rating one level higher than debentures for the same firm, and debentures are often rated one level higher than subordinated debentures.

When originally issued, most bonds are awarded a rating of B or above, with the highest-quality bonds carrying an AAA/Aaa rating. Triple-A bonds are viewed by the rating agencies as having the lowest probability of default, so the issuing firms have to pay the least for debt financing. Table 16.2 indicates that between 1983 and 1992, the yield to maturity on Aaa-rated bonds was about 1.2 percent below that for Baa bonds. The differences in yields to maturity, although for bonds already outstanding, illustrate the differences in coupon rates attached to bonds in different rating groups.

Table 16.2

Yield to Maturity on Long-Term U.S. Treasury and Corporate Bonds

The differences in yields approximate the differences in coupon rates required from the issuing firm. Hence, other things being equal, firms strive for as high a rating as possible in order to reduce their interest costs.

Year	U.S. Treasury Bonds	Corporate Bonds			
		Aaa	Aa	A	Baa
1983	10.84	12.04	12.42	13.10	13.55
1984	11.99	12.71	13.31	13.74	14.19
1985	10.75	11.37	11.82	12.28	12.72
1986	8.14	9.02	9.47	9.95	10.39
1987	8.64	9.38	9.68	9.99	10.58
1988	8.98	9.71	9.94	10.24	10.83
1989	8.58	9.26	9.46	9.74	10.18
1990	8.74	9.32	9.56	9.82	10.36
1991	8.16	8.77	9.05	9.30	9.80
1992	7.52	8.14	8.46	8.62	8.98
Average yield	9.23	9.97	10.32	10.68	11.16
Average risk premium (yield − Treasury bill yield)	2.27	3.01	3.35	3.72	4.19

Source: Federal Reserve Bulletin, various issues.

Notice in Table 16.2 that all bonds, even the long-term Treasury bonds, carry a risk premium above that of short-term U.S. Treasury bills. Thus, we see that the average risk premium for long-term government bonds over this time period was 2.27 percent. As we move from long-term government bonds to corporate bonds, the yield to maturity increases due to default risk. Yield spreads between bonds also vary over time. In 1983, for example, long-term U.S. Treasury bonds had a yield to maturity of 10.84 percent, whereas corporate Baa bonds were yielding 13.55 percent, for a difference—a yield spread—of 2.71 percent (or 271 basis points). However, in 1992, the difference in yields between the same two bond categories was 1.46 percent (8.98 − 7.52). For firms entering the bond market, the going interest rate on outstanding issues of similar maturity and quality provides a good point of reference for estimating the coupon interest rate (and hence the before-tax cost) for a new bond issue.

What about the actual experience of bonds with respect to default? Do lower-quality bonds, with higher yields, actually have higher default rates? Table 16.3 presents cumulative default rates (for 1 year, 3 years, 5 years, 7 years, and 9 years after original issuance) for bonds issued during the 1971–1991 period. As the table indicates, for bonds in the top three categories (the A's) default after 9 years of issuance was 0.17 percent for AAA bonds, 1.79 percent for AA bonds, and 1.49 percent for A-rated bonds. The default experience has been low for these bonds. The default rate of BBB bonds is 4.09 percent after 9 years. Moving to the non-investment grade bonds of BB, B or C, we find that default rates for bonds issued in the 1971–1991 time period are fairly high—from 14 percent after 9 years for BB-rated bonds, to over 35 percent of B-rated bonds. Finally, for C-rated bonds, we see that over 35 percent of them defaulted within 5 years and almost 40 percent defaulted within 7 years from the date they were issued. Based on this information we see that bond ratings at the time of original issue do a good job of differentiating low-risk from high-risk bonds.

Table 16.3

Mortality Rates by Original Bond Rating, 1971–1991

The default rates indicate the cumulative percentage of bonds that have defaulted 1, 3, 5, 7 and 9 years after they were originally issued.

Original Rating	Years After Original Issuance				
	1	3	5	7	9
AAA	0.00%	0.00%	0.00%	0.17%	0.17%
AA	0.00	1.09	1.52	1.71	1.79
A	0.00	0.45	0.93	1.08	1.49
BBB	0.10	1.51	2.72	3.96	4.09
BB	0.00	4.53	8.97	14.02	14.02
B	1.72	14.90	25.00	30.09	35.54
C	1.55	26.01	35.40	38.85	na

Source: Adapted from Exhibit 10 in Edward I. Altman, "Revisiting the High-Yield Bond Market," *Financial Management* 21 (Summer 1992): 78–92.

MEDIUM-TERM NOTE FINANCING

In recent years, due primarily to the shelf registration procedure implemented in 1982, firms have turned to using medium-term notes as another source of financing. Medium-term notes have a maturity of 1 to 10 years and traditionally are noncallable, senior, unsecured, fixed-rate instruments.[3] As of the end of 1990, U.S. corporate securities outstanding were as follows (in billions of dollars):

Security	Amount	Percentage of Total
Long-term bonds and notes	$791.1	37.4%
International bonds	131.1	6.2
Medium-term notes	97.6	4.6
Bank loans to non-financial firms	546.0	25.8
Asset-backed securities	68.1	3.2
Commercial paper	482.5	22.8
Total	$2,116.4	100.0%

The commercial paper is entirely short-term in nature (with a maturity of 270 days or less), and some of the bank loans and asset-backed securities are also short-term in nature. Once these short-term securities are excluded, the amount of financing provided by medium-term notes was over 6 percent of total debt financing in 1990. Only firms that are of investment grade (with bond ratings of BBB/Baa or above) have been able to secure financing using medium-term notes. Although the effective cost of medium-term notes has been slightly more than that for comparable maturity bonds, medium-term notes are more flexible and can be tailored to meet any maturity needs of the issuing firm. They also can be quickly and easily issued.

TERM LOANS

As an alternative to a bond issue or using medium-term notes, firms—especially smaller ones—also rely on bank borrowings. The mechanics of these borrowings often take the form of **term,** or amortized, **loans.** The purpose of the amortization is to see that principal and interest are paid off on some predetermined schedule. Firms that borrow from banks may be smaller than firms that raise funds through a public bond issue, and the maturity (or length) of financing is typically 5 to 10 years.

To illustrate, suppose Clark's Products borrowed $55,000 on a 3-year loan to be repaid in three equal annual installments. The nominal rate of interest is 12 percent on the declining principal balance of the loan. The annual payments, which include both

---

[3] This discussion draws heavily on Crabbe (1992).

Table 16.4

Principal and Interest Amortized over Three Annual Installments at 12 Percent

Typical of many term (or installment) loans, the last payment differs from the earlier ones

Year	Payment	Interest*	Principal Repayment	Remaining Balance
1	$22,899.00	$6,600.00	$16,299.00	$38,701.00
2	22,899.00	4,644.12	18,254.88	20,446.12
3	20,899.65[†]	2,453.53	20,446.12	0

* First-year interest is $(0.12)(\$55,000)$; for year 2 it is $(0.12)(\$38,701.00)$; and for year 3 it is $(0.12)(\$20,446.12)$.
[†] This last payment is the sum of the remaining balance of $20,446.12 and the interest of $2,453.53.

principal and interest, are just an annuity. Thus, the size of each payment is

$$PMT = PV_0 / \left[\frac{1}{k} - \frac{1}{k(1+k)^n} \right]$$

$$PMT = \$55,000 / \left[\frac{1}{0.12} - \frac{1}{0.12(1+0.12)^3} \right] \approx \$22,899$$

Hence, Clark's makes three equal annual payments of approximately $22,899 to repay the loan.[4] The **amortization schedule,** which breaks down the payments between principal and interest, is presented in Table 16.4. Note that more of the payment goes to pay back the principal as the years go by. Also, the last payment, as shown in Table 16.4, is often slightly different from the earlier payments. Home mortgage or car loans typically employ exactly the same approach.

DEBT FINANCING AND THE VALUE OF THE FIRM

In Chapter 15 we saw that firms issuing new equity experience a decrease in the value of their outstanding common stock. Does this same pattern hold for firms that issue bonds or take out bank loans? That is, does the value of a firm's common stock fall when it issues bonds or takes out a term loan? Table 16.5 indicates the valuation effect of various types of security sales and bank loans. Just as the value of a firm's common stock falls when it issues new equity offerings, likewise, as shown in Table 16.5, the issuance of convertible debt (which has characteristics of both debt and equity) results in a drop in value. Issuing straight (i.e., nonconvertible) debt, on the other hand, has little if any negative impact on the value of the firm.

[4] Most loans of this type are actually payable monthly or quarterly.

Table 16.5

Impact of Securities Offerings and Bank Borrowing on the Value of the Firm's Common Stock

As firms sell securities or borrow from banks, shareholders revise their expectations, and common stock returns drop for unfavorable events and increase for favorable events.

Type of Security Offering	2-Day Abnormal Return		
	Smith[c]	James[b]	Lummer and McConnell[c]
Common stock	−3.14%		
Convertible preferred stock	−1.44		
Preferred stock	−0.19		
Convertible bonds	−2.07		
Public straight bonds	−0.26	−0.11%	
Private placement of debt		−0.91	
Bank loan agreement		1.93	
New bank credit agreements			0.61%
Revised bank agreement-favorable			−0.01
Revised bank agreement-unfavorable			3.98
			−3.86

[a] Clifford Smith, "Investment Banking and the Capital Acquisition Process," *Journal of Financial Economics* 15 (January/February 1986): 3–29.
[b] Christopher James, "Some Evidence on the Uniqueness of Bank Loans," *Journal of Financial Economics* 19 (December 1987): 217–35.
[c] Scott L. Lummer and John J. McConnell, "Further Evidence on the Bank Lending Process and the Capital-Market Response to Bank Loan Agreements," *Journal of Financial Economics* 25 (November 1989): 99–122.

Finally, in line with Fama (1985), we see from Table 16.5 that the bank loan review and renewal process plays an important role. Whereas bank loan agreements in total have a positive impact on the value of the firm, it is important to distinguish between new bank loan agreements and revisions of existing loan agreements. New loan agreements, as shown in Table 16.5, have no impact on the value of the firm. In revised loan agreements, the revision can be either favorable or unfavorable. A favorable loan revision involves either lengthening the maturity of the loan, reducing the interest rate, increasing the size of the loan, or making the protective covenants less restrictive. Favorable revisions in bank loan agreements result in almost a 4 percent increase in the value of the firm's stock. On the other hand, an unfavorable revision is associated with a loss in value of almost 4 percent. Through their review process, banks provide access to information about the firm that is not otherwise available to the capital markets.

Concept Review Questions

- Are most bonds currently issued in bearer form or fully registered form? Why?
- What are some factors that influence a bond's rating?
- Describe the effects on a firm's stock price of issuing convertible debt, issuing straight debt, and obtaining a term loan.

FINANCING IN THE 1990S

Because of dramatic shifts in inflation over time, innovations in the financial markets, and the development of worldwide capital markets, the degree of sophistication required for raising long-term capital has increased greatly. Firms now use many different forms of debt financing.

ZERO-COUPON BONDS

In 1981 Martin Marietta sold $175 million of 30-year bonds with a 7 percent coupon rate at 54 percent of par, for an effective yield to maturity of 13.25 percent. These securities were one of the first **deep discount bonds.** Subsequently, many firms have issued **zero-coupon bonds.** These bonds, like U.S. Treasury bills, are issued at a discount; that is, the interest is the difference between their original issue price and the maturity value. Why would any firm issue zero-coupon bonds? The answer is that these bonds have a yield (or cost) to maturity of approximately 1 percent less than similar-quality coupon bonds sold at par. The cost to the firm is lower primarily because these bonds are callable only at a substantial premium. From the purchaser's standpoint there are two advantages to a zero-coupon bond. First, because there are no periodic interest payments to be received, there is no reinvestment rate risk. That is, the purchaser can lock in the expected compound return irrespective of what happens to interest rates over the life of the bond.[5] Second, purchasers are much surer of not having the bond called by the issuing firm. Because of these characteristics, purchasers are willing to accept a lower return than on a coupon-paying bond.

Zero-coupon bonds have some unusual characteristics that differentiate them from the coupon-bearing bonds we valued in Chapter 3. To illustrate, assume that Anderson Products is planning a $100 million par value, 10-year, 12 percent zero-coupon issue. Assuming (for simplicity) that interest is compounded annually, the net proceeds, B_0, from the bond (ignoring flotation costs) are equal to

$$B_0(\text{zero-coupon}) = \frac{\text{par}}{(1 + k_b)^n} \qquad (16.1)$$

$$= \frac{\$100,000,000}{(1 + 0.12)^{10}} = \$32,197,324$$

Anderson will receive approximately $32 million from the bond issue, and in 10 years it will repay $100 million to the purchasers of the bonds. Although annual cash interest payments are not made, the Internal Revenue Service has ruled that *both the firm issuing the bonds and investors purchasing them* must impute and report interest

---

[5] As discussed in Chapter 7 there is a reinvestment rate assumption built into any IRR (or yield to maturity) calculation. If you purchase a 15-year, 9.4 percent coupon bond at par that pays interest annually, your expected return is the bond's yield to maturity, which is 9.4 percent. However, *you will realize the 9.4 percent only if you can reinvest each of the nine annual interest payments* (received at time $t = 1$ through $t = 9$) *at 9.4 percent.*

Table 16.6

Present Value and Interest per Year for a 12 Percent, $1,000 Par, Zero-Coupon Bond

The interest on zero-coupon bonds is determined using the present value techniques discussed in Chapter 2.

Year	Present Value (12%) at End of Year (1)	Present Value (12%) at Beginning of Year (2)	Interest (1) − (2) (3)
1	$ 360.61†	$321.97††	$ 38.64
2	403.88	360.61	43.27
3	452.35	403.88	48.47
4	506.63	452.35	54.28
5	567.43	506.63	60.80
6	635.52	567.43	68.09
7	711.78	635.52	76.26
8	797.19	711.78	85.41
9	892.86	797.19	95.67
10	1,000.00	892.86	107.14
			$678.03

† For year 1, $321.97(1.12) = $360.61; for year 2, $360.61(1.12) = $403.88. The rest were computed in a similar manner.
†† The original selling price is simply the present value of $1,000 discounted at 12 percent for 10 years.

(for tax purposes) just as if cash had changed hands. The actual amount of interest declared, as shown in Table 16.6, increases each year due to the compounding involved. Notice in the table that the total amount of interest (per $1,000 par value bond) of $678.03 is just equal to the difference between the par (or maturity) value of the bond and its original price of $321.97 per $1,000 bond. If market interest rates remain constant over the entire 10-year period, the values given in column 1 of Table 16.6 show the market value at time $t = 1$, $t = 2$, and so forth.

So far, so good. Zero-coupon bonds seem simple and straightforward. Now let's compare them with a similar coupon (or interest-bearing) bond. We will see that when market interest rates change, the *percentage* price change on a zero-coupon bond is greater than that on a coupon bond. This makes perfect sense: With the zero-coupon bond nothing is received (or paid) until maturity, whereas with a coupon bond the current market value is a function of both the periodic coupon interest payments and the bond's par value.

Consider Figure 16.2, which shows the percentage change from the original price for the Anderson Products 12 percent zero-coupon bond and a similar 12 percent interest-bearing 10-year bond. If the market interest rate on the bonds is 12 percent, then the coupon bond will sell at its par value of $1,000 (par bond), while the zero-

Figure 16.2

Percentage Price Fluctuations for Zero-Coupon Versus Coupon Bonds

This figure is based on 10-year, 12 percent bonds selling at their original price. However, the general relationships hold for all similar zero-coupon and coupon interest-bearing bonds.

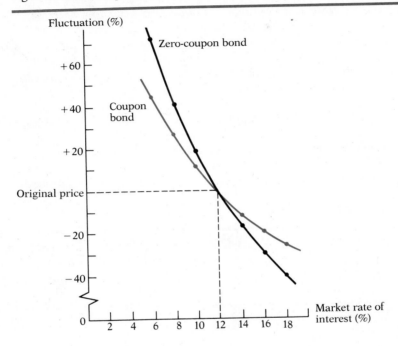

coupon bond will sell at $322 per bond. Assume you are an investor who has an equal dollar amount to invest in either bond. For simplicity, assume this amount is $322,000. With that you can buy 1,000 ($322,000/$322) zero-coupon bonds or 322 ($322,000/$1,000) coupon interest-bearing bonds. If market interest rates increase from 12 to 16 percent, which choice exposes you to more interest rate risk? To see, let's calculate the new market price for both bonds.

For the 322 12 percent coupon bonds, each with a par value of $1,000, their value is

$$B_0 = \$322,000(0.12)\left[\frac{1}{0.16} - \frac{1}{0.16\,(1 + 0.16)^{10}}\right] + \frac{\$322,000}{(1 + 0.16)^{10}}$$

$$= \$186,756 + \$72,992 = \$259,748$$

The 4 percent increase in interest rates led to a decrease in value of $62,252 (i.e., $322,000 − $259,748), or a decrease of about 19.33 percent.

From Equation 16.1, for the 1,000 zero-coupon bonds with a total par value in 10 years of $1,000,000, we have

$$B_0(\text{zero-coupon}) = \frac{\$1,000,000}{(1 + 0.16)^{10}} = \$226,684$$

Now the same 4 percent rise in interest rates leads to a decrease in value of $95,316 (i.e., $322,000 − $226,684), or a 29.60 percent decrease. These figures, when calculated for a number of other market interest rates and plotted (as in Figure 16.2), demonstrate the increased price volatility or interest rate risk that investors experience with zero-coupon as opposed to coupon bonds. By buying zero-coupon bonds, investors expose themselves to greater price fluctuations as market interest rates change.

So far we have considered a zero-coupon bond with 10 years to maturity. What happens to the interest rate risk (as evidenced by its price volatility) as the maturity is shortened? As Figure 16.3 shows, the shorter the maturity, the lower the interest rate risk. This is due to the reduced impact of discounting with short- versus long-maturity bonds. From the issuing firm's standpoint, the primary attraction of zeros is their

---

Figure 16.3

Relationship of a Zero-Coupon Bond's Price Fluctuation, the Current Market Rate of Interest, and Bond Maturity

This relationship for zero-coupon bonds is exactly the same as that shown in Figure 3.3 for coupon (interest-bearing) bonds.

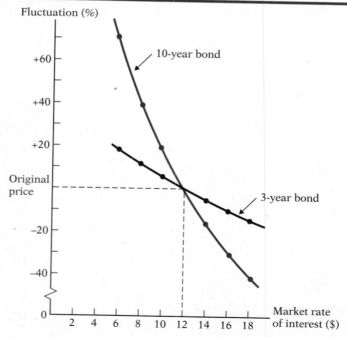

reduced cost vis-à-vis similar coupon bonds. For investors, their primary advantage when compared to coupon-bearing bonds is that they lock in the return.

JUNK BONDS

Junk bonds, or high-yield bonds, are those rated BB/Ba and below. During the 1980s, Michael Milken, of the investment banking firm of Drexel Burnham Lambert, helped create a massive new bond market centered around these bonds. Table 16.7 indicates that over the 1982–1991 time period, junk bonds accounted for 15.5 percent of the total financing secured from publicly issued bonds. Because of their lower priority relative to other debt in the event of financial distress, junk bonds have elements of both debt and equity securities.

Junk bonds are issued by firms with low credit ratings that are willing to pay anywhere from $1\frac{1}{2}$ to 3 or 4 percent more than a triple A-rated firm to raise long-term debt. These were often growing firms that would rather borrow from the public than from banks or other financial institutions. Toward the middle and latter parts of the 1980s, junk bonds became widely used to finance mergers and in leveraged buyouts. The high levels of borrowing forced firms to be more competitive. But in late 1988, Michael Milken was forced to leave Drexel after he was indicted for securities fraud. Without Milken, confidence in the junk bond market fell. More importantly, some

Table 16.7

Total Publicly Issued Bonds and Junk (or High-Yield) Bonds, 1982–1991 (in $ millions)

Junk bond financing increased significantly in the 1980s before falling off. In 1991 and beyond the amount of junk bond financing has again increased somewhat.

Year	Total Straight Debt (1)	Total Junk Bonds (2)	Junk to Total (3) (2)/(1)
1982	$ 47,798	$ 2,798	5.8%
1983	46,903	7,417	15.8
1984	99,416	14,952	15.0
1985	101,098	14,670	14.5
1986	155,672	34,177	22.0
1987	126,541	30,680	24.2
1988	113,840	26,380	23.2
1989	152,145	27,661	18.2
1990	92,105	1,297	1.4
1991	156,663	9,901	6.3
Total	$1,092,181	$169,933	15.6

Source: Adapted from Exhibit 1 in Edward I. Altman, "Revisiting the High-Yield Bond Market," *Financial Management* 21 (Summer 1992): 78–92.

firms that had issued junk bonds, such as Integrated Resources, Hillsborough Holdings, and Campeau, got into severe financial difficulties. Finally, by February 1990 Drexel itself was in such severe financial difficulty that it filed for bankruptcy.

An era had come to an end. However, the junk bond market has since stabilized. Although we will not see the growth in junk bonds in the 1990s that existed in the 1980s, the junk bond market still has a viable and important role to play. Excesses occurred in the 1980s, but in many cases the firms using junk bonds were simply securing financing by a public cash offering instead of through the institutional investors who traditionally supplied their long-term debt financing. Junk bonds will continue to fill an important but more traditional role as a source of financing in the future.

VARIABLE RATES

The majority of loans made by commercial banks are now variable rate loans. That is, the interest rate may vary over the 5- to 10-year life of the loan. Often the rate is expressed as some fixed percentage over the prime interest rate.[6] For example, the loan agreement may specify that the rate will be "2 percentage points over prime." This means that if the current **prime rate** charged by the bank to its best customers is 13 percent, the interest rate on the loan will be 15 percent. Because interest is typically changed every time the prime rate changes, the bank in effect varies the total payment required each period to pay the principal and interest on the loan. In addition to bank loans that carry adjustable rates, there are also floating rate (or adjustable rate) notes that are issued directly by firms via cash offerings to the public or through private placements.

HYBRIDS, ASSET-BACKED SECURITIES AND OTHER INNOVATIONS

During the last 15 years the types of securities available for corporate use have expanded dramatically. Many of the new securities combine elements of debt, equity, options, variable interest rates, and the like into new securities. Although we have examined a few of the innovations, like medium-term notes, zero-coupon bonds, and variable rate loans and securities, many other innovations have been forthcoming. Some of the more successful new securities have been the following:

1. DUAL CURRENCY BONDS   These bonds pay interest in U.S. dollars, but the repayment of principal is in a currency other than the dollar.
2. EXTENDABLE NOTES   An extendable note has an interest rate that adjusts every 2 or 3 years; the noteholder has the right at that time to "put" the notes back to the issuing firm.
3. PUTTABLE BONDS   These bonds can be redeemed at the option of the bondholder, or if a certain "event" occurs.

---

[6] As noted in Chapter 22, prime is an artificial (or administered) rate.

4. STANDARD & POOR'S INDEX NOTES   These are zero-coupon notes whose principal repayment is linked to the value of the S&P Index, providing that the index is above a certain value.
5. LIQUID YIELD OPTION NOTES   These are a zero-coupon convertible debt issue.
6. PUTTABLE CONVERTIBLE BONDS   These are convertible bonds that can be redeemed prior to maturity at the option of the bondholder, on certain specified dates or at prespecified prices.

During this same period there has been another innovation—the increased use of asset-backed securities; this process is often referred to as *securitization*. Mortgage-backed securities, including collateralized mortgage obligations (CMOs), have been around for some time. But firms have also turned to other assets as collateral for financing. Thus, in late 1992 Citibank offered a $2.2 billion floating rate note backed by credit card receivables. Likewise, in 1992 GPA Group, an aircraft leasing firm based in Ireland, sold a $521 million Eurobond that was securitized by aircraft lease receivables. While developments in the next 15 years may not be as rapid as in the past 15, innovative investment banking firms will continue to come up with new ways to help firms raise capital.

Concept Review Questions

- Describe some different forms of debt financing that firms have recently adopted.
- What are some advantages to a firm of issuing zero-coupon bonds?
- Why have junk bonds become a viable means of financing for some firms?
- Give some examples of hybrid securities.

MANAGING LONG-TERM DEBT

Until recently, liability management consisted simply of deciding what securities to issue. Debt was left to mature, then was retired—perhaps with the proceeds from a new bond issue. High and volatile interest rates, the growth of international financial markets, and innovative investment banking firms have changed all that, and the management of long-term liabilities has taken a dramatic turn. Let's consider some of the techniques now available.

REFUNDING

A few years ago, when interest rates were high, many firms issued long-term debt. What happened when market rates fell? Astute managers saw the fall in rates as an opportunity to replace (or refund) the older, high interest rate bond with a similar bond offering a lower coupon rate. In a bond **refunding,** the firm calls all the old bonds at a fixed price and simultaneously issues new, lower coupon rate bonds. The bond owners have no choice; when a bond is called it must be surrendered, for the firm stops paying interest on it. This process is discussed in Appendix 16A. The decision to refund depends on the net amount required to call the existing bond and the present value of the future incremental cash flows. It is thus just another use of the net present value, NPV, framework.

However, two complications can arise. First, how does the firm decide on the best time to refund? The answer depends primarily on the relationship of current market interest rates to forecasted interest rates next month, in 3 months, and so forth. The firm may benefit from a refunding today, but it must also consider whether it would be better off waiting, in the hope that interest rates will fall further.

To protect investors, many bonds now carry a provision that prohibits them from being called for refunding for a period of 5 to 10 years. This brings us to the second complexity. What can the firm do if it wants to refund a bond issue but is prohibited by some provision in the bond indenture?

ALTERNATIVES TO REFUNDING

Three alternatives are available when a firm is prohibited from refunding a bond issue.[7]

1. One alternative is a public **tender offer.** This is an offer to the current bondholders to sell their bonds back to the firm at a predetermined price. This offer may not result in the retirement of the entire issue, but it can substantially reduce the size of the issue in question.
2. An alternative to the public tender offer is a **private market purchase.** Here the firm approaches one or several institutional investors who own a large amount of the firm's bonds and offers to buy them back. Another alternative sometimes employed is to swap debt for some of the firm's common stock.
3. The nonrefundable provision that has appeared in recent years appears to limit an issuing firm's flexibility to retire debt when interest rates fall. Recently, however, Wall Street has come up with a strategy that firms can use to circumvent the nonrefundable provision. Firms have always been able to call bonds through a *cash call,* with money raised by selling additional equity, selling assets, or from internally generated funds. But if interest rates have fallen and the issuing firm wants to retire debt without using a cash call, it might employ a "simultaneous tender and call" approach. The essence of this approach is to offer to buy back the bonds (through a tender offer) at a slight premium to the call price; at the same time the firm (or its investment banker) threatens to call the bonds using a cash call. In late 1992 bondholders filed a lawsuit against May Department Stores and Morgan Stanley (its investment banking firm), alleging breach of contract, violation of the

---

[7] A fourth approach is a tactic called **defeasance,** which means to "render null and void." To do this a firm enters into an arrangement with a trustee, usually a bank. The obligation for the bond is passed on to the trustee along with a portfolio of securities, typically U.S. Treasury bonds. The deal is structured so that the interest and principal proceeds from the portfolio of Treasury bonds will exceed those required to service the bond issue in question. Hence, for all intents and purposes the debt has been retired—and removed from the firm's balance sheet—without actually calling the bond issue before it was due. The problem with defeasance is that it is very costly; due to the lower interest rate on Treasury bonds relative to corporate bonds, the firm may have to acquire, say, $105 in Treasury bonds to retire $100 of the firm's debt.

Trust Indenture Act, bad faith, and fraud after the simultaneous tender and call approach was employed on a $250 million May Department Store bond. Holders of the May bonds argue that the tender and call is coercive. The investment bankers disagree, believing "it's not coercive, it's a business proposition."

INTEREST RATE SWAPS

Interest rate swaps are also increasingly used, especially with the widespread use of floating rate (or variable rate) financing. The idea is to separate the interest payments from the principal payments for long-term financing. The firm raises funds wherever it can, as cheaply as possible—and then converts from floating to fixed rate, or vice versa, depending on the desires of the firm and expectations about the trend of future interest rates. This conversion is accomplished by agreeing to swap interest payments (but generally not the principal) with another party. Interest rate swaps are discussed in Chapter 23.

Concept Review Questions

■ Describe three alternatives to refunding a bond issue.

■ What are interest rate swaps?

PREFERRED STOCK

Preferred stock is an intermediate form of financing between debt and equity. Like debt, preferred stock generally has a par value—typically $25, $50, or $100—and also pays a fixed return. But preferred stock legally is a form of ownership; cash dividends paid on preferred stock are similar to cash dividends on common stock in that they are not a tax-deductible expense for the issuing firm.

When preferred stock is issued, the selling price is set close to par. When a $100 par value, 13 percent preferred stock is issued, it will sell close to par and pay cash dividends of $13 [i.e., ($100)(0.13)] per year. The market price on preferred stock fluctuates; if the market yield (where yield = dividend per share/market price per share) on preferred stocks goes up, the market price of outstanding preferred stocks decreases. Because preferred stock is viewed by investors as being similar to bonds, the market yield on preferred stocks tends to move in much the same manner as the yield to maturity on bonds. As market interest rates on bonds rise, the market yield on preferred stocks also rises due to the declining price of the latter.

If the firm does not have sufficient cash flow to pay dividends on its preferred stock, it can omit the payment. Unpaid dividends on preferred stock are called **arrearages.** Most preferred dividends are *cumulative:* all past or present dividends must be paid before any further cash dividends are paid on the firm's common stock. Managers view dividends on preferred stock like any other fixed obligation, and they fully intend to pay the preferred dividends on time. However, preferred stock does provide a safety valve if the firm needs it.

Like common stock, preferred stock does not have any fixed maturity date. However, many recent issues of preferred stock make a provision for periodic repayment via a sinking fund. Virtually all preferred stock is callable at the option of the issuing firm. If a firm goes out of business, the claim of preferred stockholders is junior to that of any debt, but senior to that of common stockholders.

The use of preferred stock, like the issuance of long-term debt, may result in additional restrictions being placed on the firm in the form of limitations on the payment of cash dividends for common stock, maintenance of a minimum level of common equity, or a minimum requirement for the ratio of net working capital to the total debt and preferred stock of the firm. The primary function of these restrictions is to ensure that the firm can make cash dividend payments to its preferred stockholders. Although many preferred stocks have only limited voting rights, the tendency in recent years has been toward fuller voting rights.

From the firm's standpoint, preferred stock has certain advantages:

1. Because the returns to preferred stockholders are limited, financial leverage is possible, because any extraordinary cash flows accrue only to common stockholders.
2. Nonpayment of cash dividends on preferreds does not throw the firm into default.
3. Control of the firm generally remains with the common stockholders.

The primary disadvantage of preferred stock from the firm's standpoint is that cash dividends paid to service the preferred stock are not an allowable deduction for tax purposes. Unlike debt, which preferred stock approximates in many respects, dividends on preferred stock must be paid out of after-tax earnings. This treatment makes the cost of most preferred stock much higher than the cost of debt. Preferred stock is used on a wide-scale basis in only two industries—banking and public utilities. Banks have issued preferred stock in recent years in order to increase their capital base. They found that issuing preferred stock was preferable to issuing additional common stock in order to meet requirements for additional capital. Public utility firms, on the other hand, have used preferred stock for a long time. Due to their regulated nature, they can often pass the higher costs of preferred stock on to consumers through their customer rate base. Firms that have more than one issue of preferred stock outstanding include BankAmerica, Boston Edison, Georgia Power, Illinois Power, Royal Bank of Scotland, and Wells Fargo.

In recent years, a new twist in preferred stock financing was introduced—**adjustable rate preferred stock.** Instead of paying a fixed cash dividend, the dividend rate on this type of issue is tied to a U.S. Treasury security index and adjusted quarterly. The appeal of adjustable rate preferred stock is twofold. First, it allows the issuing firm to issue preferred stock at a lower dividend rate than otherwise. Second, by doing so, the firm adds to its equity base (thereby improving the ratio of total debt to total assets) without issuing additional shares of common stock.

Concept Review Questions

- Describe the similarities of preferred stock to both debt and common equity.
- What are the advantages and disadvantages of preferred stock?

LONG-TERM FINANCING AND FINANCIAL DISTRESS

Differences and conflicts always exist between stockholders and bondholders. Stockholders want to maximize their return; as we know, higher returns and higher risks go hand-in-hand, so stockholders tend to favor higher risk. Bondholders, however, thought they purchased a much safer security; they become upset when the firm engages in activities that cause this safety to be eroded.

If the firm prospers, the common stockholders exercise their option to pay off the bondholders, and then claim everything else for themselves. Alternatively, if the firm fails, the stockholders (because of limited liability) walk away from the firm and turn it over to the bondholders. Although the stockholders may lose their initial investment, at least they aren't liable for any further losses. We can summarize the effects as follows:

If the Firm Prospers	If the Firm Fails
Bondholders are paid off	Stockholders walk away
Stockholders claim the rest	Bondholders may receive something

Of course, there are many intermediate positions. We need to examine them briefly.

A firm facing financial distress has a number of alternatives open to it, depending on the severity of the situation. The fundamental decision is whether to modify the firm or to liquidate it. Within each alternative are out-of-court and in-court procedures. These are as follows:

Out-of-Court Alternatives
1. An **extension** involves nothing more than the creditor's agreeing to delay the payments due from the firm; that is, it extends the payment schedule. The creditor and the firm both hope that with a little more time, the firm can right itself and proceed on its way.
2. A **composition** is more serious. It gives creditors only a pro rata settlement on their claims. Generally, creditors will agree to composition only when it appears that they will receive more from accepting the settlement than from forcing the firm into bankruptcy, with its legal expenses and complications.
3. A "voluntary" liquidation is called an **assignment.** It is often more efficient, can be effected faster, and provides creditors with a higher settlement than an in-court liquidation. One problem, however, is getting all creditors to agree to the assignment.

In-Court Alternatives
The in-court alternatives are covered by the Bankruptcy Reform Act of 1978. The basic alternatives for firms are as follows:

1. In a **liquidation,** the assets of the firm are sold under the direction of the courts, with the proceeds going to pay claimants in a general order of priority spelled out

2. In a **reorganization,** the firm is actually put back on its feet, typically after extensive modifications both in terms of its businesses and in terms of the claims of creditors. Former stockholders usually end up with very little ownership in the reorganized firm.

Although somewhat different in detail, the liquidation versus reorganization decision is no different conceptually than keeping or divesting assets, or divisions, of a firm, as discussed in Chapters 10. The issue is whether the parties (primarily the creditors) are better off (i.e., have a higher NPV) under liquidation or reorganization.

Concept Review Question

■ What are the out-of-court and in-court alternatives available to a firm experiencing financial distress?

KEY POINTS

1. Bonds and preferred stock take many different forms. These alternatives assist firms in raising long-term funds as cheaply as possible while providing features that appeal to investors.
2. AAA/Aaa-rated bonds have the lowest cost, or yield to maturity, of any long-term corporate bonds; they also have the lowest failure rate. As the bond rating decreases, the cost to the firm goes, up as does the probability of failure.
3. When firms issue straight debt or take out bank loans, the value of the firm is unaffected. However, when bank loan agreements are revised, common stockholders benefit if the revision is a favorable revision, and they lose if it is an unfavorable one.
4. As interest rates fluctuate, zero-coupon bonds change in market price relatively more than similar coupon (or interest-bearing) bonds.
5. In the last 15 years numerous new securities have appeared in addition to medium-term notes, zero-coupon bonds, and variable-rate securities. These new securities often incorporate elements of debt, equity, options, and the like.
6. Firms have increasingly begun to practice active liability management. Tactics include bond refundings (or buybacks) and interest rate swaps.
7. Preferred stock, while legally a form of equity, has many features that make it similar to debt.

QUESTIONS

16.1 How might the call provision, the maturity of a bond, and sinking fund provisions interact?

16.2 As corporate treasurer, how would the following conditions influence your willingness to include a sinking fund provision and the need for a call feature in a new bond issue?

a. Market interest rates are expected to fall.
b. Your firm anticipates heavy cash outflows in relation to its cash needs in the next 5 to 10 years.

c. Market interest rates are expected to fluctuate substantially, both above and below the coupon rate on the new issue.

16.3 Explain the difference between fully registered and bearer bonds. What advantages, if any, exist for the firm by issuing fully registered bonds? What are the advantages for the investor?

16.4 Explain why investment banking firms require a bond to be rated by Moody's and Standard & Poor's before it is underwritten. How specifically does the rating influence the cost to the issuing firm?

16.5 "In a loan amortization schedule, the last payment will never be equal to the prior payments." Is this statement true or false? Why?

16.6 The percentage price fluctuation of zero-coupon bonds is greater than the percentage price fluctuation of similar coupon bonds as market interest rates fluctuate; it is also greater the longer the maturity of the zero. Explain.

16.7 In recent years, when interest rates were very high, a number of large firms issued medium-term notes. These notes payed interest periodically, and the principal was repaid when the notes matured. Why do you think firms issued these notes instead of obtaining similar maturity term loans?

16.8 When might a firm want to refund a bond issue? How might it proceed if the bond indenture prohibits refunding for another 8 years?

16.9 Preferred stock often is called a hybrid security. Why? It can be said that preferred stock combines the worst features of both common stock and bonds. Explain why this might be so.

16.10 If the corporate income tax were abolished, would we expect to see more, or less, debt? More, or less, preferred stock? Why?

16.11 When a firm is in financial distress, what out-of-court and in-court alternatives exist?

CONCEPT REVIEW PROBLEMS

See Appendix A for solutions.

CR16.1 Desktop Industries has obtained a 5-year, $100,000 term loan with an interest rate of 15 percent. Interest is paid annually. Prepare a loan amortization schedule for Desktop.

CR16.2 Assume Desktop Industries' term loan in CR16.1 required monthly payments. By developing an amortization schedule for the first 5 months of the loan, show how monthly payments will affect interest and principal repayments.

CR16.3 AT&E is considering issuing either a 5-year zero-coupon bond or a 5-year coupon-bearing bond with annual payments. Both bonds will pay a 10 percent interest rate. If AT&E needs $50 million from external debt financing, how many $1,000 maturity value zero-coupon bonds will have to be issued? How many $1,000 par (or maturity) value coupon-bearing bonds will have to be issued?

CR16.4 Katharine recently purchased a $1,000 maturity value, 10 percent, 20-year, zero-coupon bond and a 10 percent, 20-year, coupon-bearing bond at par. If immediately after she purchased these bonds, overall bond rates increased by 2 percent, what was her percentage loss on each bond?

PROBLEMS

16.1 The Long Island Corporation has no short-term debt, but it does have a $10 million, 10 percent coupon rate mortgage bond outstanding with a limited open-end provision. Additional 10 percent mortgage debt can be issued as long as all the following restrictions are met:

1. Ratio of debt to equity (i.e., total debt/total stockholders' equity) remains below 0.4.
2. Interest coverage (i.e., EBIT/interest) is at least 5.
3. The depreciated value of the mortgaged assets is at least 2.5 times the mortgage debt.

The firm has a depreciated value of mortgage assets of $60 million, equity of $80 million, and earnings before interest and taxes, EBIT, of $12 million. Assuming that half the new bond issue would be used to add assets to the base of mortgaged assets, how much additional debt can Long Island issue?

16.2 Carolina Paper has a $50 million bond issue outstanding, with a 12 percent coupon rate. The current market interest rate on comparable-quality bonds is 11 percent. The bonds have 25 years to maturity but can be called with a premium equal to 1 year's interest.

a. What is the market price of the bonds?
b. How much is the call price on the bonds?
c. Should Carolina Paper call these bonds or purchase them? In explaining your answer, remember to consider any other factors that might influence purchasing the bonds.

16.3 Huron Cement has just issued $30 million of 10 year, 10 percent coupon rate bonds. A sinking fund provision requires equal payments to be made at the end of each of the next 10 years, in order to retire one-tenth of the bonds each year. Huron's tax rate is 35 percent.

a. How large must the annual sinking fund payments be to retire the bond in 10 equal installments over the life of the bond? (*Note:* The bonds will be retired at their par value.)
b. What is Huron's *annual* after-tax cash outlay to meet the interest and sinking fund obligations each year? [*Remember:* (1) Interest payments are tax-deductible, but sinking fund payments are not; and (2) no interest is paid on bonds once they are retired.]

16.4 Welker Products is taking out an 8-year, $44,000 term loan, with an interest rate of 16 percent per year. Interest is paid annually, and the firm's marginal corporate tax rate is 40 percent.

a. What is the size of the yearly payment? (*Note:* Round all figures to the nearest dollar.)
b. Determine the loan amortization schedule.
c. Determine the net cash outflow per year to service both principal and interest after taking into account the tax deductibility of interest for tax purposes. (*Note:* Round to the nearest dollar.)

16.5 A 4-year, 10 percent loan for $30,000 exists. Determine the amortization schedule if **(a)** annual discounting is employed, or **(b)** semiannual discounting is used. (*Note:* Round all figures to the nearest dollar.)

16.6 Brozik Products needs to raise approximately $10 million by issuing 20-year bonds. The following alternatives are available:

1. A public offering of $10 million of 8 percent coupon rate bonds at a price to net the firm $9,850,000.
2. A private placement of $10 million in bonds at par, with an 8.5 percent coupon rate and no flotation costs.
3. A public offering of a deep discount bond that will pay $400,000 in interest each year and have a maturity value of $25 million. The firm will net $9,800,000 from the bonds.
4. A private placement of zero-coupon bonds that will net the firm $9,900,000 and have a

maturity value of $45 million. Interest payments are annual and the principal will not be repaid until maturity.

Which bond has the cheapest percentage cost to maturity? (*Note:* To solve this, calculate the IRR for each of the four options.)

16.7 Davis Industries has two alternative $10 million bonds it can issue. If the bond carries a fixed coupon rate, the interest rate will be 11 percent. If a variable rate bond is used, the rate will be pegged 1.5 percent above prevailing rates on 1-year U.S. Treasury bills and adjusted annually. In both cases interest is paid annually. A sinking fund of $1 million per year will begin at the end of year 1 for either bond. The firm's marginal tax rate is 40 percent.

a. Determine the year-by-year after-tax cash flows Davis will incur for each bond if 1-year U.S. Treasury bill rates turn out to be as follows:

Year	Prevailing 1-Year U.S. Treasury Bill Rate
1	10.0%
2	9.5
3	9.0
4	10.0
5	10.5
6	12.0
7	13.0
8	12.0
9	11.5
10	11.0

b. Without discounting the cash flows, does it appear that one bond would be preferable if Davis knew what interest rates would be? Why?

16.8 Stephens needs $100 million in new debt financing. If the firm uses a coupon-bearing bond, the interest rate is $9\frac{1}{2}$ percent and the bond will be issued at par. If it uses a zero-coupon bond, the interest rate is 9.2 percent. Assume that interest is paid annually and either bond will have a maturity of 10 years.

a. If the coupon-bearing bond is employed, (1) what is the per year interest, and (2) what is the cash outflow (ignoring any taxes) in the tenth year?
b. If the zero-coupon bond is employed,

   (1) What is the par value of the zero-coupon bond in order to raise the $100 million needed?
   (2) What is the imputed interest in year 1? in year 2?
   (3) What is the cash outflow in the tenth year?

c. What can we say about the cash flow demands that the two securities will place on Stephens?

16.9 Maness Metals is planning to issue $100 million par value of 15-year, zero-coupon bonds at a yield of 14 percent.

a. If interest is assumed to be paid annually, (1) what is the initial value, B_0, of the bonds, and (2) what is the imputed interest for year 2?

b. What happens to your answers for (a) if interest is assumed to be paid semiannually? Why do your answers to (a) and (b) differ?

c. Recalculate (a) and (b) if the maturity of the bond issue is only 3 years. How does this change your answers to (a) and (b)? Which bond (the 15-year or the 3-year) would result in less percentage price fluctuation from the initial value as market interest rates change?

16.10 Chancey Industries needs to raise $7.8 million through an issue of preferred stock. The preferred will have a $60 per share par value and pay an 8 percent dividend. Assume that there are no flotation costs, that the preferred will be outstanding for a long time (so it can be treated as a perpetuity), and that it will be sold to yield purchasers a 9.6 percent return.

a. What price will Chancey receive per share?

b. How many shares will Chancey have to issue?

c. Why might Chancey choose preferred stock instead of debt?

16.11 Adkisson Railroad needs to raise $9.5 million for capital improvements. One possibility is a new preferred stock issue. The 8 percent dividend, $100 par value stock would be sold to investors to yield 9 percent. Flotation costs for an issue of this size amount to 5 percent of the gross proceeds. These costs will be deducted from the gross proceeds in determining the net proceeds of $9.5 million. Assume that the preferred stock will be outstanding for a long time (so it can be valued as a perpetuity).

a. At what price will the preferred be offered to investors? (Carry to three decimal places.)

b. How many shares must be issued to net $9.5 million?

16.12 Misra needs to raise $600,000. It has the following alternatives: (1) sell common stock at $50 per share; (2) sell 8 percent preferred stock at par ($100 par); or (3) sell 9 percent debentures at par ($1,000 par). Assume that there are no flotation costs. The firm expects EBIT to *increase* by 20 percent after the additional funds are secured and investments made. Partial balance and income statements for Misra are as follows:

Balance Sheet		Income Statement	
Current liabilities	$ 100,000	EBIT	$200,000
Common stock ($3 par)	300,000	Interest	20,000
Retained earnings	600,000	EBT	180,000
Total liabilities and		Taxes	63,000
stockholders' equity	$1,000,000	EAT	$117,000

a. What is the current EPS *before* the new financing is undertaken?

b. What is the estimated EPS under each of the financing plans, assuming that EBIT has increased?

16.13 Cooley Industries is a fast-growing conglomerate operating in the mid-Atlantic states. Although it has used only short-term debt previously, Cooley is in the market for long-term financing. Based on its investment banking firm's recommendation, two plans are being considered, as follows:

Plan I	Plan II
$20 million of straight debt issued at par (ignore flotation costs)	$20 million preferred stock issued at par (ignore flotation costs)
Par is $1,000 per bond	Par is $80 per share
12% coupon rate	11.5% dividend rate
Expected common stock P/E = 12 times	Expected common stock P/E = 13 times

EBIT is estimated to be $14 million; short-term interest (under either plan) is $1 million; the tax rate is 30 percent; and there are 3 million shares of common stock outstanding.

a. For plans I and II, determine the expected EPS.
b. If Cooley wants to maximize its market price per share, P_0, which plan should it choose?

16.14 Mini Case Pomona Sports is in need of $25,000,000 of new long-term financing. Because it is not experienced in seeking new financing, it has employed you to provide it with advice.

a. If Pomona seeks long-term debt financing in the form of bonds or bank loans, what alternatives are available? What are the features of each?
b. If a bond issue is decided upon, what type of features might be included in the bond indenture? What is the impact of these provisions?
c. If the term structure of interest rates is upward sloping, is a long-term bond issue necessarily best? What if the term structure is downward sloping?
d. Two different bond issues are being considered: a 25-year coupon bond that will pay interest semiannually and carry a coupon interest rate of 12 percent, or a 25-year zero-coupon bond that has a yield to maturity of 11 percent (compounded semiannually).

   (1) From the firm's standpoint, what are the advantages and disadvantages of a zero-coupon bond versus a coupon bond? What are the tax consequences?
   (2) Ignoring flotation costs, what is the size of the zero-coupon bond issue?
   (3) Assume that after either bond is issued, interest rates jump 2 percent. What is the new price of the two bonds? Which has the bigger percentage change in its value? Why?
   (4) Independent of (3), assume it is now 10 years later. What are the cash flow consequences of the two different bonds on the firm? (*Note:* Assume the firm is profitable, and its marginal tax rate is 35 percent.) Compute the year-10 net cash flows associated with the two bonds.

e. Instead of issuing debt, Pomona could issue preferred stock. The preferred stock would carry a dividend of 11 percent.

   (1) How is preferred stock similar to debt? To equity?
   (2) What are the per year cash flows if everything is the same as in (d4) above?

REFERENCES

Bonds and their provisions are examined in:

BARNEA, AMIR, ROBERT A. HAUGEN, and LEMMA W. SENBET. "A Rationale for Debt Maturity Structure and Call Provisions in the Agency Theoretic Framework." *Journal of Finance* 35 (December 1980): 1223–34.

———. "Market Imperfections, Agency Problems, and Capital Structure: A Review." *Financial Management* 10 (Summer 1981): 7–22.

BLUME, MARSHALL E., DONALD B. KEIM, and SANDEEP A. PATEL. "Returns and Volatility of Low-Grade Bonds 1977–1989." *Journal of Finance* 46 (March 1991): 49–74.

FLANNERY, MARK J. "Asymmetric Information and Risky Debt Maturity Choice." *Journal of Finance* 41 (March 1986): 18–37.

KALOTAY, ANDREW, and BRUCE TUCKMAN. "Sinking Fund Prepurchases and the Designation Option." *Financial Management* 21 (Winter 1992): 110–18.

LABER, GENE. "Bond Covenants and Forgone Opportunities: The Case of Burlington Northern Railroad Company." *Financial Management* 21 (Summer 1992): 71–77.

MITCHELL, KARLYN. "The Call, Sinking Fund, and Term-To-Maturity Features of Corporate Bonds: An Empirical Investigation." *Journal of Financial and Quantitative Analysis* 26 (June 1991): 201–22.

OGDEN, JOSEPH P. "A Rationale for the Sinking-Fund Provision in a Quasicompetitive Corporate Bond Market." *Journal of Business Research* 16 (February 1988): 197–208.

ROBBINS, EDWARD H., and JOHN D. SCHATZBERG. "Callable Bonds: A Risk-Reducing Signaling Mechanism." *Journal of Finance* 41 (September 1986): 935–49.

Bond ratings have been studied extensively. See, for example:

HAND, JOHN R. M., ROBERT W. HOLTHAUSEN, and RICHARD W. LEFTWICH. "The Effect of Bond Rating Agency Announcements on Bond and Stock Prices." *Journal of Finance* 47 (June 1992): 733–52.

PINCHES, GEORGE E., and KENT A. MINGO. "A Multivariate Analysis of Industrial Bond Ratings." *Journal of Finance* 28 (March 1973): 1–18.

PINCHES, GEORGE E., and J. CLAY SINGLETON. "The Adjustment of Stock Prices to Bond Rating Changes." *Journal of Finance* 33 (March 1978): 29–44.

SCHWENDIMAN, CARL J., and GEORGE E. PINCHES. "An Analysis of Alternative Measures of Investment Risk." *Journal of Finance* 30 (March 1975): 193–200.

Current developments in bank lending, new financing, and liability management are discussed in:

CRABBE, LELAND. "Corporate Medium-Term Notes." *Journal of Applied Corporate Finance* 4 (Winter 1992): 90–102.

FAMA, EUGENE. "What's Different about Banks?" *Journal of Monetary Economics* 15 (January 1985): 29–39.

FINNERTY, JOHN D. "An Overview of Corporate Securities Innovation." *Journal of Applied Corporate Finance* 4 (Winter 1992): 23–39.

———, ANDREW J. KALOTAY, and FRANCIS X. FARRELL, JR. *Evaluating Bond Refunding Opportunities.* Cambridge, Mass.: Ballinger, 1988.

Selected material on financial distress is contained in:

ALTMAN, EDWARD I. "A Further Empirical Investigation of the Bankruptcy Cost Question." *Journal of Finance* 39 (September 1984): 1067–89.

GILSON, STUART C. "Managing Default: Some Evidence on how Firms Choose Between Workouts and Chapter 11." *Journal of Applied Corporate Finance* 4 (Summer 1991): 62–70.

PINCHES, GEORGE E., and JAMES S. TRIESCHMANN. "The Efficiency of Alternative Models for Solvency Surveillance in the Insurance Industry." *Journal of Risk and Insurance* 41 (December 1974): 563–77.

WEISS, LAWRENCE A. "The Bankruptcy Code and Violations of Absolute Priority." *Journal of Applied Corporate Finance* 4 (Summer 1991): 71–78.

APPENDIX

16A Refunding a Bond or Preferred Stock Issue

Refunding is the issuance of new securities to replace an existing bond or preferred stock issue. A firm occasionally refunds to get rid of overly restrictive provisions associated with the existing issue, but the primary motive is to replace existing financing with new financing whose cost is substantially less. This replacement is possible if the coupon rate on a new bond issue (or dividend rate on preferred stock) is substantially lower than the coupon (or dividend) rate on the existing issue. To refund an issue, firms exercise their option to call it.

The decision to refund can be approached in essentially the same manner as the replacement capital budgeting decision. To do this, the incremental (new minus old) after-tax cash flows must be calculated and then discounted to determine the net present value, NPV, of the proposed refunding. Thus,

$$NPV = \sum_{t=1}^{n} \frac{\Delta CF_t}{(1 + k_i)^t} - \Delta CF_0 \qquad (16A.1)$$

where

ΔCF_t = the incremental after-tax cash flows resulting because of the refunding
k_i = the after-tax cost of the new bond issue
ΔCF_0 = the after-tax initial investment associated with the refunding

The decision rule is as follows:

1. If NPV is greater than zero—refund.
2. If NPV is less than zero—don't refund.
3. If NPV is equal to zero—you are indifferent.

In discounting the CFs, the current after-tax cost of the new issue is used as the discount rate because it represents the appropriate rate for the risk involved. Because one issue is simply replacing another and there is little risk involved, the use of a higher rate such as the firm's opportunity cost of capital is inappropriate.

To understand refundings, consider the example of Albany Oil, which issued a 30-year, $50 million, $11\frac{1}{4}$ percent coupon-rate bond 5 years ago at par, with flotation costs of $480,000. Because these flotation costs are being amortized over the life of the bond, $16,000 ($480,000/30) is charged off per year. Because 5 years have gone by, the remaining unamortized flotation costs are $480,000 - [(5 years)($16,000)] = $400,000. The bonds can be called at 106, so the call premium is 6 percent of $50 million. Because of a drop in long-term market interest rates, Albany can now issue $50 million of 10 percent coupon rate bonds at par, with flotation costs of $875,000. To ensure that funds will be available when needed, the new bonds will be issued 1 month before the existing bonds are retired. The net proceeds from the new issue can be invested for 1 month at the Treasury bill rate of 6 percent. Albany's marginal tax rate is 40 percent. The relevant data are as follows:

	Existing Issue		New Issue
Face value	$50 million		$50 million
Coupon interest rate	$11\frac{1}{4}$%		10%
Original life	30 years		25 years
Remaining life	25 years		25 years
Flotation costs (remaining or total)	$400,000		$875,000
Marginal tax rate		40%	
Interest overlap		1 month	
Call premium on existing bonds		6%	
Treasury bill rate		6%	

To determine the NPV, we use the following steps:

STEP 1: *Determine the incremental initial investment associated with refunding.* This step involves the call premium, the flotation costs, write-off for tax purposes of the unamortized flotation costs on the existing issue, and interest during the overlap period. First, we calculate the before-tax initial investment, as follows:

Before-Tax	
Call price on old bonds (106% of par)	$53,000,000
Additional interest paid during overlap period*	468,750
Less: Net proceeds of new issue†	49,125,000
Interest earned on new issue proceeds during overlap period‡	245,625
Before-tax initial investment	$ 4,098,125

* One month's interest on old bonds = ($50,000,000)(0.1125)(1/12) = $468,750.
† Face value less flotation costs = $50,000,000 - $875,000 = $49,125,000.
‡ One month's interest on proceeds = ($49,125,000)(0.06)(1/12) = $245,625.

Next, the tax consequences must be taken into account. This involves the following items: the call premium and unamortized flotation costs on the old bond that can be written off for tax purposes, and the additional interest during the overlap period. For Albany Oil, the tax consequences affecting the initial investment are as follows:

Tax-Deductible Expenses	
Call premium on old bond ($53,000,000 − $50,000,000)	$3,000,000
Unamortized flotation costs on old bond	400,000
Additional interest paid during overlap period	468,750
Less: Additional interest earned on new issue proceeds	245,625
Total tax-deductible expenses	$3,623,125
Tax savings ($3,623,125)(0.40)	$1,449,250

Initial Investment	
Before-tax outlay	$4,098,125
Less: Tax savings	1,449,250
Initial Investment, ΔCF_0	$2,648,875

STEP 2: *Determine the incremental cash savings resulting from the refunding.* This step involves the interest cash flows, the tax savings on them, and the tax impacts of the different amortization rates for the flotation costs of the two issues. For the old bonds, the following after-tax cash flow existed:

Interest on old bond ($50,000,000)(0.1125)		$5,625,000
Tax deductions:		
Interest	$5,625,000	
Amortization of flotation costs ($480,000/30)	16,000	
Total	$5,641,000	
Tax savings ($5,641,000)(0.40)		2,256,400
After-tax cash outflow on old bond		$3,368,600

For the new bonds Albany proposes to issue, the after-tax cash outflow is as follows:

Interest on new bond ($50,000,000)(0.10)		$5,000,000
Tax deductions:		
Interest	$5,000,000	
Amortization of flotation costs ($875,000/25)	35,000	
Total	$5,035,000	
Tax savings ($5,035,000)(0.40)		2,014,000
After-tax cash outflow on new bond		$2,986,000

The incremental cash savings that will occur for each of the next 25 years is as follows:

Cash outflow on old bond	$3,368,600
Less: Cash outflow on new bond	2,986,000
Annual cash saving, ΔCF_t	$ 382,600

STEP 3: *Calculate the net present value.* Now that the incremental initial investment and the annual cash savings are available, we can calculate the NPV of refunding, using the after-tax interest rate on the new bond issue as the discount rate. This after-tax rate is $0.10(1 - T)$, or 6 percent. With the after-tax cash flow stream as follows:

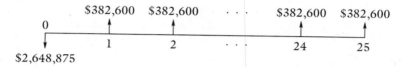

the net present value is

$$NPV = \$382,600\left[\frac{1}{0.06} - \frac{1}{0.06\ (1 + 0.06)^{25}}\right] - \$2,648,875$$

$$= \$4,890,912 - \$2,648,875 = \$2,242,037$$

Because the NPV is positive, the existing $11\frac{1}{4}$ percent bonds should be refunded.[1] If the NPV were negative, Albany would not want to refund the issue unless it wanted to remove some overly restrictive covenants imposed on the firm by the present bond issue. Refunding (or refinancing) a preferred stock issue uses the same concepts, except that the dividends on preferred stock are not tax deductible.

CONCEPT REVIEW PROBLEM

See Appendix A for solution.

CR16A.1 Five years ago, Milo Industries issued $500,000 of 15-year, 15.5 percent, coupon-bearing bonds. The bonds were issued with a call provision allowing the firm to call the bonds at an 8 percent permium above par. Flotation costs of $15,000 are being amortized over the life of the bonds. If interest rates on bonds with similar maturity and risk have dropped to

---

[1] As presented, the refunding analysis keeps the firm's debt/equity ratio the same, but changes the cash flows to the firm. It can be argued that to neutralize risk, the cash flows (or the financial strain) on the firm should be kept the same. The present value of the cash savings, which is $4,890,775.80, represents the size of a loan that could be borrowed (with principal and interest, at 10 percent, being paid over 25 years) with the same after-tax cash flow impact on the firm. If the size of this term loan, which neutralizes the cash flow risk differential, is larger than the initial investment required to refund the old bond, refunding should take place. The decision whether or not to refund remains the same if it is viewed in this manner, as opposed to the approach described in the text. This risk-neutralization approach is used for the lease versus purchase analysis considered in Chapter 18.

14 percent and flotation costs for issuing $500,000 of new bonds are $12,000, should Milo call the old bonds and refund with new 10-year bonds? The firm's tax rate is 40 percent. For simplicity, assume there is no interest overlap.

PROBLEMS

16A.1 Johnson Management is considering whether to refund a $50 million, 20-year, 12 percent coupon rate bond issue that was sold 5 years ago. It is amortizing $2 million in flotation costs on the 12 percent bonds over their 20-year life. The $50 million in new 15-year bonds would carry an annual interest rate of 10 percent. A call premium of 7 percent would be required to retire the old bonds, and flotation costs of $1.75 million would apply to the new issue. The marginal tax rate is 30 percent, and there is a 1-month overlap. The Treasury bill rate is 8 percent. Should Johnson refund the bonds?

16A.2 Micro Computers currently has $150 million of 14 percent coupon-rate bonds outstanding, with a remaining life of 25 years. They were issued 5 years ago with a flotation cost of $1.5 million; the unamortized flotation cost is now $1.25 million. Right now, $150 million of 25-year, 12.5 percent coupon-rate bonds could be issued at par to refund these bonds. Interest rates are not expected to decline further, flotation costs on the new bonds are $2.25 million, the call premium on the old bonds is 12 percent, there is a 1-month overlap, and Micro's tax rate is 36 percent. The Treasury bill rate is 9 percent. Should the firm refund the existing bonds?

16A.3 Central Florida Power & Light is considering refinancing $100 million of existing 13 percent dividend-rate preferred stock. The preferred does not have a maturity date, but it can be called at 106.5 percent of par. The $100 million new preferred issue would carry a 12 percent dividend rate and require $2 million in flotation costs; there is a 1-month overlap. The Treasury bill rate is 8 percent. Central Florida's tax rate is 40 percent. The $2 million in flotation costs are completely deductible for tax purposes in the current year. Thus, flotation costs are *not* amortized, as they are with bonds. Also, the call premium is *not* deductible for tax purposes when a preferred stock refinancing occurs. Should Central Florida refinance the preferred issue? (*Note:* Remember that dividends are an after-tax expense. This fact influences both the cash savings and the discount rate employed.)

17

Warrants and Convertibles

EXECUTIVE SUMMARY

Warrants are long-term options issued by the firm; as such their valuation follows the same procedures employed for valuing any other call option. However, there are three complications that must be considered. First, due to the longer time period before warrants expire, the effect of cash dividends, whose payment reduces the value of the underlying common stock, often has to be considered. Second, when warrants are exercised, the number of shares of common stock outstanding increases. Finally, changes in the firm's capital structure proportions, causing changes in the riskiness of the underlying common stock, must be considered.

Convertible securities are, in effect, straight debt or preferred stock that also has an option attached. There are three values that are important when valuing convertibles—the straight debt or preferred stock value, the conversion value (i.e., its common stock value), and the value of the call option that can be exercised by the owner of the convertible. The most straightforward way to value convertibles is to value the straight debt or preferred stock and then value the call option. Like warrants, the presence of cash dividends, increases in the number of shares of common stock outstanding when the securities are converted, and changes in capital structure leading to changes in risk must be considered when valuing convertibles.

Because most convertibles contain a call provision, the firm can call the security for retirement. If the conversion value is above the call price, investors should convert; otherwise they should accept the call price. From the firm's standpoint, the optimal policy to avoid wealth transfers is to call the convertible when its conversion value equals its call price. At the same time, the firm may not force conversion if the after-tax cash outflow is greater with conversion than without. Convertibles help firms and investors deal with risk, mitigate agency costs, and deal with asymmetric information and adverse financing costs.

WARRANTS

In Chapters 15 and 16 we considered the two main external sources of long-term financing for the firm—common stock and long-term debt. Now we examine two other securities employed by firms. These are warrants and convertibles, of which the most important are convertible bonds. Both of these types of securities have option-like characteristics. Hence, we employ our knowledge of options from Chapter 5 in order to understand and value warrants and convertibles.

DIFFERENCE BETWEEN WARRANTS AND CALL OPTIONS

Warrants are simply a long-term call option that allows the purchaser or holder to buy shares of stock in a firm at a specific price for a certain time period.[1] A significant amount of privately placed debt and a far smaller percentage of public offerings are packaged with warrants issued along with the debt. Warrants may also be given to investment bankers as compensation for underwriting services. Warrants are almost always detachable, which means that shortly after the package of securities is issued, the bonds and the warrants can be sold separately. Table 17.1 shows the characteristics of some warrants. The original life for most of these warrants was 5 to 8 years. The British Petroleum warrants have an exercise price of $80, whereas the exercise price for each of the other warrants is under $10. All of these warrants have a low value, but if the price of the common stock into which they are convertible rises, so will the value of the warrant.

From the preceding discussion it is clear that warrants are like call options. In fact, from the investor's standpoint, a warrant is almost exactly the same as a call option on the common stock of the issuing firm. One key difference is that options are created by investors themselves (i.e., the firm on which the option is written is *not* involved in creating options). Warrants, on the other hand, are created by the firm. Hence, the firm is directly involved in determining the number of warrants issued, the term (or expiration date) of the warrants, and the exercise price at which the firm's common stock can be purchased. Because the firm creates the warrant, when warrants are exercised the number of shares of common stock outstanding increases.[2] In contrast, when a call option is exercised, the writer of the call is responsible for having the required shares, and the number of shares of stock that the firm has outstanding does not change. As we shall see subsequently, this increase in the number of shares outstanding when warrants are exercised influences their value.

---

[1] There are a few warrants outstanding that allow the purchase of the stock of another firm or the purchase of bonds.

[2] From an accounting standpoint, using the current number of shares of common stock outstanding to calculate earnings per share, EPS, produces simple EPS. Taking account of all the shares of common stock that will be outstanding after the warrants are exercised results in fully diluted EPS. The same accounting treatment exists for shares that may be issued when convertible securities are employed. See Chapter 24.

Table 17.1

Warrant Characteristics for Selected Firms

Most warrants can be exchanged for one share of common stock. Also, as the numbers indicate, many of the publicly traded warrants have a low price, as does the common stock for which the warrants can be exchanged.

Firm	Expiration Date	Warrant Exercise Price per Share	Number of Shares per Warrant	Stock Price per Share	Lower Limit of Warrant Value*	Actual Warrant Price	Premium over Lower Limit†
American Exploration	2/1/93	$2.75	1	$ $2\frac{1}{4}$	0	$ $\frac{5}{8}$	$ $\frac{5}{8}$
Astrotech International	3/31/95	6.00	1	$9\frac{1}{8}$	$3\frac{1}{8}$	$4\frac{5}{8}$	$1\frac{1}{2}$
British Petroleum	1/31/93	80.00	1	$56\frac{5}{8}$	0	$\frac{9}{32}$	$\frac{9}{32}$
Go-Video	3/9/95	8.25	1	3	0	$1\frac{1}{2}$	$1\frac{1}{2}$
Magma Copper	11/11/95	8.50	1	11	$2\frac{1}{2}$	$4\frac{3}{4}$	$2\frac{1}{4}$
Manville	1/6/96	9.40	1	9	0	$2\frac{3}{4}$	$2\frac{3}{4}$
Wheeling-Pittsburgh	3/3/96	6.3583	1	$6\frac{3}{8}$	0	$2\frac{3}{4}$	$2\frac{3}{4}$

Source: Various financial publications as of May 11, 1992.
* Maximum of (market price of common stock − exercise price)(number of shares purchased with one warrant) or zero, as given by Equation 17.1.
† Actual warrant price − lower limit of warrant price.

VALUING WARRANTS

Option Value

To understand the valuation of warrants, let's consider FirstGenetic which has just issued some 5-year warrants with an exercise price of $40. FirstGenetic's current stock market price is $31. Based on what we learned about call options from Chapter 5, the lower limit on the value of this warrant (or option to buy a share of FirstGenetic common stock) can be depicted as in Figure 17.1. Like any call option, however, the warrant will actually trade above the lower limit of its value. The height of the actual warrant price (given by the dashed line in Figure 17.1) above the lower limit will depend on the following:

Stock price, P_0

Exercise price, X

Time to maturity, t

Risk-free rate, k_{RF}

Variability of the underlying asset, σ

These are the same factors that determine the value of any call option.

Figure 17.1

Relationship Between the Market Value of a Warrant and Its Lower Limit

Until expiration the market value of a warrant (given by the dashed line) will be greater than the lower limit (given by the solid colored line).

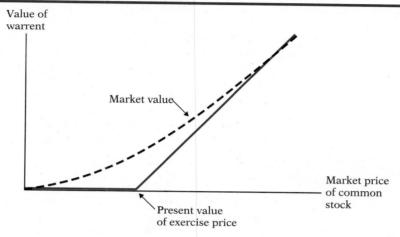

Once a warrant is designed and issued, the exercise price is known. Also, for simplicity, let's hold the stock price, P_0, constant. In this situation, the height of the actual warrant price above the lower limit depends on three factors—the risk-free rate, k_{RF}, the time to maturity, t, and the standard deviation of the underlying asset's returns, σ. Of course, as time runs out, the actual price of the warrant snuggles closer and closer to the lower limit. On the final day of its life, its price hits the lower limit. The lower limit on the value of a warrant is the maximum of (1) the market value of the common stock that it can be exercised for, minus the exercise price (for warrants that are in-the-money), or (2) zero (for warrants that are out-of-the-money). Thus,[3]

$$\begin{matrix} \text{lower} \\ \text{limit} \end{matrix} = \text{MAX} \left[\begin{pmatrix} \text{market price of} \\ \text{common stock} \\ - \text{ exercise price} \end{pmatrix} \begin{pmatrix} \text{number of shares} \\ \text{purchased with} \\ \text{one warrant} \end{pmatrix}, 0 \right] \qquad (17.1)$$

If we ignore some complications for the present, determining the value of the FirstGenetic warrants is straightforward. As a young firm with extensive research and development needs, FirstGenetic does not pay any cash dividends on its common stock. The risk-free rate is 0.08, and the volatility of the returns on FirstGenetic's common stock is estimated to be 0.40. With a maturity of 5 years, an exercise price of $40, and a current market price of FirstGenetic's common stock of $31, we can

---

[3] Later in the chapter we use the adjusted market price, P_0^*, to account for the impact of dilution which occurs when warrants are exercised. When using Equation 17.1 in such a case, we would use the adjusted market price instead of the market price indicated in the equation.

treat warrants like any other call option and use Table B.6 to value the warrant as follows:

STEP 1: Calculate the standard deviation times the square root of time:

$$\sigma(t)^{0.5} = (0.40)(5)^{0.5} = 0.8944$$

STEP 2: Calculate the market price divided by the present value of the exercise price:

$$\frac{P_0}{X/e^{k_{RF}t}} = \frac{\$31}{\$40/e^{(0.08)(5)}} = 1.1562$$

STEP 3: Multiply the tabled value by the stock price. From Table B.6, we find that the value is approximately 0.396, indicating a value of the FirstGenetic warrants of $31(0.396) = $12.28. Thus, even though FirstGenetic's current stock market price of $31 is less than the exercise price of $40, the warrant has considerable value due its risk and the long time to maturity.

Some Complications

There are some complications that we have ignored thus far. The first is that the Black-Scholes option pricing model assumes no cash dividends are paid. Thus, it will not correctly value warrants issued by a dividend-paying firm. In fact, warrantholders lose every time a cash dividend is paid, because the dividend reduces the stock price, P_0, and therefore the value of the warrant. To determine the warrant value when cash dividends are present, we can adjust the Black-Scholes model for any known cash dividends to be paid, or we can use the binomial method discussed in Chapter 5.

A second complication also exists. Remember from Chapter 5 that when a call option is exercised there is no change in either the firm's assets or the number of shares of common stock outstanding. But when warrants are exercised, the number of shares of outstanding common stock increases. To illustrate the calculation of the warrant price in the presence of **dilution**—that is, an increase in the number of shares of common stock outstanding—assume that before the warrant was issued FirstGenetic was an all-equity firm that had 100,000 shares of common stock outstanding. At the current market price of $31 per share, the value of the firm, V, was ($31)(100,000) = $3,100,000. This was also the value of the equity of the firm, S. FirstGenetic sold 20,000 warrants at $10 per warrant, for a total of $200,000 [i.e., ($10)(20,000)]. Two points should be recognized: First, the total value of FirstGenetic after the warrants are sold is $3,100,000 + $200,000 = $3,300,000. Second, the warrant purchasers appear to have received a good deal because they paid only $10 for warrants that we determined in the last section were worth $12.28. If the warrant purchasers got a good deal, then the firm did not because it sold the warrants for less than their theoretical value. In fact, the warrant purchasers did not fare as well, nor did the firm fare as poorly, once we consider the impact of dilution.

To calculate the value of a warrant, allowing for dilution, we need to determine the value of the call option, or warrant, on the firm *after allowing for the immediate* *impact* of the financing proceeds secured from the warrant financing. To do this we determine an adjusted market price per share, P_0^*, and then calculate the value of the call option on the firm, V_c, given this adjusted market price. This adjusted market price takes account of the increase in the value of the firm due to the proceeds received from the warrant financing. The value[4] of the warrant after considering dilution is

$$\text{value of warrant with dilution} = \left(\frac{1}{1+q}\right)(V_c) \tag{17.2}$$

where q is the number of new shares that may be issued per share of existing common stock outstanding. After FirstGenetic sells the warrants, the total value of the firm is $3,300,000. Dividing $3,300,000 by the number of shares outstanding before any warrants are exercised (which is 100,000), we find that the adjusted current market price, P_0^*, of FirstGenetic is $33 per share. The number of original shares of common stock was 100,000, and the number of shares that can be issued due to the warrant financing is 20,000; hence $q = 20,000/100,000 = 0.20$.

The value of the warrant, or call option, V_c, using the adjusted market price, P_0^*, of $33, is determined as follows:

STEP 1:   Calculate the standard deviation times the square root of time, which is just $(0.40)(5)^{0.5} = 0.8944$, as determined before.

STEP 2:   Calculate the market price divided by the present value of the exercise price. Using the adjusted market price of $33, it is

$$\frac{P_0^*}{X/e^{k_{RF}t}} = \frac{\$33}{\$40/e^{(0.08)(5)}} = 1.2308$$

STEP 3:   Multiply the tabled value by the stock price. From Table B.6, we find that the value is approximately 0.421, so the value of the warrant after considering the impact of the new financing is $33(0.421) = $13.89.

Now, employing Equation 17.2, we can determine the value of the warrant after adjusting for dilution as follows:

$$\text{value of warrant with dilution} = [1/(1+0.20)](\$13.89) = \$11.58$$

Previously, before we considered the impact of any potential dilution on the value of the FirstGenetic warrant, its estimated value was $12.28. After allowing for dilution, we see that the value of the warrant is $11.58. Although the value of the warrant is less than previously estimated, the warrant purchasers still bought a warrant whose value was worth more than the $10 they paid for it. The firm received only $10 for a warrant with a theoretical value of $11.58.

---

[4] Our discussion follows Galai and Schneller (1978).

Changing Capital Structure Proportions

A third complication sometimes must be considered. This complication arises when the firm issues warrants and debt as a package and the new financing results in a change in the firm's proportions of debt and equity financing. The change in the financing proportions changes the risk of the firm's equity, which in turn affects the value of the warrant. In our example, FirstGenetic it was an all-equity-financed firm before the warrants were issued. What if FirstGenetic issues a debt/warrant package? The standard deviation of the underlying assets will not necessarily change, but the change in the proportions of debt and equity employed causes the equity risk (or its standard deviation) to change. What if FirstGenetic issued the warrants along with debt and received a total of $900,000 from the financing? The warrants by themself are still worth $200,000, so the value of the debt is $700,000. The adjusted market price of the stock, P_0^*, is still $33 per share as determined before. This is now calculated as follows:

$$S = V - B = (\$3,100,000 + \$900,000) - \$700,000 = \$3,300,000$$

and

$$P_0^* = \$3,300,000/100,000 \text{ shares} = \$33$$

The new standard deviation for the common stock/warrant package may be determined as follows: First, the standard deviation of the firm's underlying assets must be equal to the average standard deviation of the firm's equity and the standard deviation of its debt. Therefore, the standard deviation of a non-levered firm's assets is

$$\begin{pmatrix} \text{standard deviation} \\ \text{of non-levered} \\ \text{firm's assets} \end{pmatrix} = \begin{pmatrix} \text{proportion in} \\ \text{common stock} \end{pmatrix}\begin{pmatrix} \text{standard deviation} \\ \text{of common stock} \end{pmatrix} \qquad (17.3)$$

$$= (\$3,100,000/\$3,100,000)(0.40) = 0.40$$

Because FirstGenetic was previously financed entirely with equity, the standard deviation of FirstGenetic's assets was exactly equal to the standard deviation of its common stock. If the standard deviation of the firm's assets is the same after the debt/warrant financing as it was before, then we can adjust the financing proportions and rearrange Equation 17.3 to solve for the new standard deviation of the firm's common stock and warrants based on the new equity to total financing ratio of $3,300,000/$4,000,000. Thus,

$$\begin{pmatrix} \text{standard deviation} \\ \text{of common stock} \\ \text{and warrants} \end{pmatrix} = \begin{pmatrix} \text{standard deviation} \\ \text{of non-levered} \\ \text{firm's assets} \end{pmatrix} / \begin{pmatrix} \text{proportion in} \\ \text{common stock} \\ \text{and warrants} \end{pmatrix}$$

$$= (0.40)/(\$3,300,000/\$4,000,000) \approx 0.48$$

We can now calculate the value of the warrant, after considering the change in the capital structure proportions and the effects of dilution.

STEP 1: Calculate the standard deviation times the square root of time. This is now $(0.48)(5)^{0.5} = 1.0733$

STEP 2: Calculate the market price divided by the present value of the exercise price. Using $P_0^* = \$33$ as before, this is 1.2308

STEP 3: Multiply the tabled value by the stock price. From Table B.6, we find that the value is approximately 0.468, so the value of the call, V_c, is $\$33(0.468) = \$15.44$.

Now, employing Equation 17.2, we can determine the value of the warrant after adjusting for both the change in the firm's debt/equity proportion and dilution, as follows:

value of warrant with dilution = $[1/(1 + 0.20)](\$15.44) = \$12.87$

We see that the value of the warrant, once debt is also employed, has increased from $11.58 to $12.87. The intuition behind this is straightforward: By employing debt, FirstGenetic has increased the risk that all equityholders face because of the prior debt claim that has to be met. This increased risk is captured by the increase in the standard deviation attributable to both the stockholders and the warrantholders. But, as risk increases, the value of any option also increases; therefore the value of the warrant has increased.

Once warrants have been issued, they require little attention from the firm. Unlike convertibles (discussed next), the conversion of warrants cannot be forced. Thus the main control the firm has comes when the expiration date is set at the outset or if a step-up in the exercise price is specified. Other than that, the firm may attempt to purchase the warrants from investors and retire them if they desire to get rid of the warrants prior to their expiration date.

Concept Review Questions

- How are warrants and call options different?
- What are some complications that are encountered when using the Black-Scholes option pricing model to price warrants?

CONVERTIBLES

Some bonds, and an even smaller percentage of preferred stock, contain another feature—convertibility. Convertible securities are bonds or preferred stock originally issued as debt or preferred stock; however they contain a provision that allows them to be exchanged for common stock of the issuing firm at the discretion of the investor.[5] There is no charge for making this exchange, and the exchange can be made whenever the investor wishes. Thus, with a convertible, investors have an option-like security.

Consider a $1,000 par convertible bond that has a stated **conversion** (or **exercise**) **price** of $50. The number of shares the bond can be converted into, called the **conversion ratio**, is the par value of the convertible security divided by the conversion price, or $1,000/$50 = 20 shares. A few other characteristics of convertible bonds are as follows: First, convertible bonds are typically debentures, and they are generally subordinated. Thus, *most convertible bonds are convertible subordinated debentures*.[6] Second, when convertible bonds are designed and issued, their stated coupon interest rate is less than that required on nonconvertible bonds of similar quality and maturity, and their conversion price is set above the current market price of the firm's common stock. The lower coupon interest rate is due to a feature of convertible debt that straight (non-convertible) debt doesn't have—the option to convert the bond into common stock.

Table 17.2 presents some characteristics of convertible bonds for selected firms. The coupon interest rates range from a high of 14 percent for Hudson Foods to a low

Table 17.2

Convertible Debt Characteristics for Selected Firms

Convertible bonds come in many shapes and sizes. Although not shown, most convertible bonds are callable and are also subordinated.

Firm	Bond or Note				Current Conversion Value*	Actual Convertible Price	Premium over Conversion Value†
	Coupon Interest Rate	Maturity	Conversion Ratio	Common Price per Share			
Anacomp	13.875	2002	57.14	4.000	228.56	1,052.50	823.94
Bank of New York	7.500	2001	25.58	43.375	1,109.53	1,250.00	140.47
Hudson Foods	14.000	2008	81.63	7.375	602.02	1,070.00	467.98
IBM	7.875	2004	6.51	93.875	611.13	1,025.00	413.87
Illinois Tool Works	zero	2005	6.51	64.125	417.45	465.00	47.55
Sterling Software	zero	2005	46.30	17.375	804.46	1,000.00	195.54
Western Digital	9.000	2014	69.20	4.250	294.10	625.00	330.90

Source: Various financial publications as of May 11, 1992.
* (Market price of common stock)(conversion ratio)
† Actual convertible price − current conversion value

[5] Similar to a few warrants, some convertibles allow for the purchase of another firm's stock or for the purchase of bonds.
[6] Generally convertible subordinated debentures carry a bond rating that is one grade lower than the other long-term debt issued by the firm. Thus, if the firm's other bonds carry a rating of BBB, its convertible subordinated debentures would carry a bond rating of BB.

of 7.50 percent for Bank of New York. In addition, two of the convertible bonds, Iilinois Tool Works and Sterling Software, are zero-coupon bonds (discussed in Chapter 16). The **conversion value** is simply the amount the bond is worth if it is immediately converted into common stock, and the dollar premium is the difference between the actual price of the convertible bond and its conversion value. In examining Table 17.2, we see that the conversion value of all but one of the bonds (that issued by Bank of New York) is less than their par value of $1,000.

In addition to domestic convertible bonds, there are also international convertible bonds. Firms such as American Brands, Bank of Tokyo, and Mitsui Bank have employed convertible Eurodebentures for financing purposes.

VALUING CONVERTIBLES

The owner of a convertible in essence owns a bond and a long-term call option on the firm's stock. This is very similar to owning a bond and a warrant, but with an important difference. To exercise the warrant, the investor keeps the bond and must pay cash to the firm as determined by the exercise price in the warrant. To claim the shares with a convertible bond the investor must surrender the bond in order to exercise the call option. In valuing convertibles there are three components that need to be considered: the straight bond value, the conversion value, and the call option value.

Straight Bond Value

The straight bond value, or price, is what the security would sell for if it were not convertible into common stock. This is nothing more than our familiar bond valuation model which, as first considered in Chapter 3, is

$$B_0 = \sum_{t=1}^{n} \frac{I}{(1 + k_b)^t} + \frac{M}{(1 + k_b)^n}$$

where B_0 is the current price, I is the interest per period, M is the maturity value of the bond, and k_b *is the market rate of interest on comparable quality and comparable maturity nonconvertible bonds.* When firms issue convertible bonds they pay less in terms of the coupon interest rate than if the bond were not convertible. This makes sense, because the firm is also providing the investor with an option that has value. Suppose Shaws Discount Stores is issuing some $1,000 par value, 7 percent coupon rate convertible bonds. The market interest rate that Shaws would pay *if the bond were not convertible is 11 percent,* and the maturity of the convertible is 10 years. The straight bond value is a minimum value, or floor, below which the value of the convertible bond will not trade. Although the convertible bond is issued at a discount from its par, or maturity, value, *when it matures* its value solely as a bond will be $1,000 per bond. This bond floor at the maturity of the bond is illustrated in Figure 17.2(a). As long as the value of the firm at the maturity of the bond is sufficient, bondholders are protected by the straight bond value floor; otherwise the firm defaults on the bond, and the bondholders claim the firm's assets.

Figure 17.2

Value of a Convertible Bond at Maturity

In (a), the conversion value is shown along with the straight bond value. If the value of the firm is low, the firm defaults on the bond; otherwise its straight bond value is the maturity value of the bond. In (b), the value of the convertible at maturity is shown to depend on the maximum of the curves in (a).

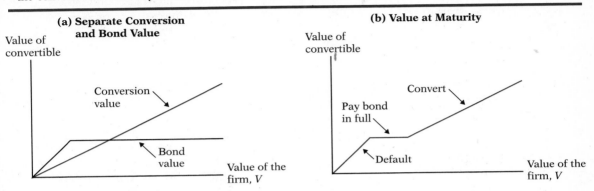

(a) Separate Conversion and Bond Value

Value of convertible

Conversion value

Bond value

Value of the firm, V

(b) Value at Maturity

Value of convertible

Convert

Pay bond in full

Default

Value of the firm, V

Conversion Value

There is another floor that also limits the downward fluctuation in the market value of any convertible; this time it is provided by how much the convertible is worth solely in terms of its common stock value. Assume the conversion price for the Shaws Discount convertible bond is $50, and the market price of Shaws common stock when the convertible is first issued is $30 per share. The conversion ratio is $1,000/$50 = 20 shares of stock, and the original conversion value[7] is

$$\text{conversion value} = (\text{conversion ratio})(\text{common stock market price}) \qquad (17.4)$$
$$= (20)(\$30) = \$600$$

At the instant when the convertible bond is sold, its conversion value—that is, how much the stock it can be converted into is worth—is $600. As the market price of the firm's stock increases or decreases, the conversion value of the convertible security will fluctuate accordingly. As also shown in Figure 17.2(a), the conversion, or common stock, value is a straight upward-sloping line. At maturity, the value of a convertible is determined by the state of the firm and the value of its common stock. As shown in Figure 17.2(b), at maturity the value of the convertible will depend on whether the firm is solvent or insolvent, and whether the conversion value is above or below the straight bond value at maturity of $1,000.

---

[7] To be entirely correct, the price per share should be that which would exist if all available shares covered by warrants and convertible securities were already issued. If the number of additional shares of common stock potentially to be issued is not too great, the error caused by employing the current stock market price is minimal.

Value Before Maturity

So far we have considered the value of a convertible security at maturity. Before maturity, the straight bond value of the convertible will be less than at maturity; that is, it will be at a discount. The reason is that all convertibles have a coupon interest rate that is lower than the market rate of interest on comparable quality and maturity nonconvertible bonds when they are issued. Therefore, the straight bond value will be less than the par, or maturity, value. With a coupon interest rate of 7 percent, and assuming nonconvertible bonds are yielding 11 percent, the straight bond value when the Shaws Discount convertible is originally issued is

$$\text{straight bond value} = \$70\left[\frac{1}{0.11} - \frac{1}{0.11(1 + 0.11)^{10}}\right] + \frac{\$1,000}{(1.11)^{10}}$$
$$= \$764$$

This is shown as a curved line in Figure 17.3(a). This straight bond value floor is not as solid as it looks; it will change as market interest rates fluctuate. Thus, if market interest rates go up, the straight bond value declines, and vice versa. Likewise, if the firm's financial condition deteriorates, the floor will also fall. The conversion value, which is the same as it is at maturity, is also shown in Figure 17.3(a).

A third element also needs to be taken into consideration when valuing convertible securities before maturity—that is the value of the option that exists. Before maturity, investors have the protection of the higher of the straight bond value floor or the conversion value floor, and they have also have an option to convert the bond into common stock. Because this option is valuable, the value of the convertible security

---

Figure 17.3

Value of a Convertible Bond Before Maturity

In (a), the conversion value is shown along with the bond value. As the value of the firm increases the bond value first increases rapidly; then as the firm value increases further, the bond value approaches the maturity value of the bond. In (b), the higher of the bond or conversion value [from (a)] determines the lower limit on the value of the convertible. Due to the straight bond floor and the option to convert, the market value of the convertible is at a premium over the lower limit of the value of the convertible.

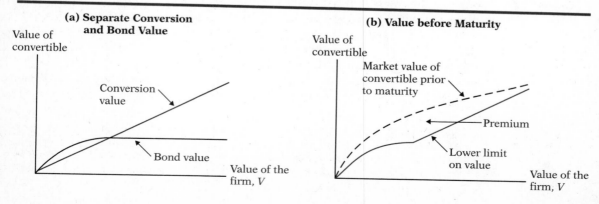

before maturity will always be greater than the lower limit on its value. The behavior of the convertible security's price before maturity is shown in Figure 17.3(b). The difference between the market price of the convertible and its lower limit is the premium, or value of the call option incorporated in the convertible bond.

To determine the worth of a convertible before maturity, the most straightforward approach is to value the straight bond and then value the call option. Valuing this call option is just like valuing warrants. Like warrants, however, the presence of cash dividends on the firm's common stock, dilution, and changes in capital structure proportions, and therefore risk, also influence the value of the option to convert. Once investors convert the bonds, the prior interest payments made on the convertible are no longer paid, the number of shares of common stock outstanding increase, and the proportions of debt and equity change.

To illustrate this valuation process, assume that Shaws Discount does not pay any cash dividends on its common stock, the proportion of equity in the capital structure with the convertible bonds outstanding is 0.60 and will increase to 0.80 if all the convertible bonds are converted, the standard deviation of the equity before conversion is 0.50, the adjusted market price, P_0^*, is $32, the risk-free rate is 7 percent, and q (which is the number of new shares of common stock that may be issued as a percentage of the existing shares) is 0.30. Employing Equation 17.3, we find that the standard deviation of the firm's assets if it was all equity financed is determined as follows:

$$\text{standard deviation of non-levered firm's assets} = (0.60)(0.50) = 0.30$$

After allowing for the conversion and retirement of the convertible bond, the new standard deviation of Shaws' equity is

$$\begin{pmatrix} \text{new standard} \\ \text{deviation} \\ \text{of equity} \end{pmatrix} = \begin{pmatrix} \text{standard deviation} \\ \text{of non-levered} \\ \text{firm's assets} \end{pmatrix} \Big/ \begin{pmatrix} \text{new} \\ \text{proportion} \\ \text{in equity} \end{pmatrix}$$
$$= 0.30/0.80 = 0.375$$

We can now calculate the value of the call, V_c, and the value of the option included in the convertible, after considering the change in the capital structure proportions and the effects of dilution.

STEP 1:   Calculate the standard deviation times the square root of time:

$$\sigma(t)^{0.5} = (0.375)(10)^{0.5} = 1.1859$$

STEP 2:   Calculate the market price divided by the present value of the exercise price:

$$\frac{P_0^*}{X/e^{k_{RF}t}} = \frac{\$32}{\$50/e^{(0.07)(10)}} = 1.2888$$

STEP 3: Multiply the tabled value by the stock price. From Table B.6, the value is approximately 0.523, so the value of the call, V_c, is $32(0.523) = \$16.74$.

Now, employing Equation 17.2, we find that the value of the option to purchase one share of common stock after adjusting for both the change in the firm's debt/equity proportions and dilution is

$$\text{value of call with dilution} = [1/(1 + 0.30)](\$16.74) = \$12.88$$

Because each convertible bond can be exchanged for 20 shares of common stock, and the option to purchase one share of stock is worth \$12.88, the value of the conversion option is about \$258 [i.e., (\$12.88)(20) = \$257.60 ≈ \$258]. Adding this to the straight bond value of \$764, determined previously, we find that the value of the convertible when it is first issued is \$1,022.

FORCING CONVERSION

Most convertibles contain a clause that allows the firm to call the security at a specific price. If the firm calls the convertible, the investor has a brief period, generally 30 days or less, to either convert the security or accept the call price. From the investor's standpoint the choice is obvious: If the conversion value is greater than the call price, convert; otherwise, accept the call price. Many firms call a convertible security only when the conversion value is greater than the call price; this situation is often referred to as a **forced conversion**. If the conversion value is less than the call price, the situation is often referred to as an **overhanging issue.** The firm cannot force conversion in the case of an overhanging issue because if they call the issue, rational investors will accept the call price.

From the firm's standpoint, there are two straightforward rationales for when the convertible should be called. The value of the firm is not affected by when the convertible is called. However, *the relative position of stockholders and bondholders is affected by the timing of the call.* The first rationale focuses on the relationship between the call price and the market value of the convertible. Consider what happens if the firm calls the security when the convertible's market value is below the call price. The firm then pays more for the bond than it is worth, thereby transferring wealth from stockholders to bondholders. Likewise, if the bond is not called when the conversion value is above the convertible's market value, bondholders are allowed to hold a valuable asset at the expense of stockholders. The optimal policy for the firm to follow based on the relationship of the call price and the market value of the convertible is *to call the bonds when their market value equals their call price.* Empirical evidence, however, suggests that most firms do not follow this policy; they typically wait until the bond's market value is substantially above the call price.[8]

---

[8] See, for example, Ingersoll (1977), Mazzero and Moore (1992), or Singh, Cowan, and Nayar (1991).

Why do firms wait before calling? A second rationale involves the cash flows to the firm.[9] As long as the firm does not call the convertible, the after-tax cash flow to service the convertible is a function of the interest rate on the convertible, the percent of the convertible outstanding, and the firm's effective tax rate. By forcing conversion, if the firm pays cash dividends, the cash flow to the firm is equal to the number of shares that will be issued by forcing conversion and the per share cash dividend rate. From a cash flow standpoint, why should the firm force conversion if the result is an increase in after-tax cash outflow?[10]

HOW AND WHEN FIRMS EMPLOY CONVERTIBLES

One often hears the comment that convertibles are used on the one hand to provide cheap debt financing or on the other hand to allow the firm to sell common stock at a higher-than-market rate. The cheap debt financing argument rests on the premise that the coupon interest rate required with a convertible is less than the coupon rate that would have been required had the firm issued straight debt. However, you should be able to see that the logic behind this argument is faulty because the investor purchases *both* a bond and an option. The cheap debt financing argument ignores the option entirely.

Likewise, the argument that the firm can sell common stock at an "above market price" rests on the knowledge that the exercise price contained in the convertible is greater than the market price of the firm's common stock. The cheap equity argument, however, ignores both the bond and the option, and simply looks at the conversion value of the convertible versus the market price of the convertible. Given the nature of convertible securities, it is not surprising that the expected return required by investors falls between that required on straight bonds and on common stock. If investors require an expected return that falls between those of bonds and stocks, what does it mean the cost to the firm has to be? You know enough finance not to be fooled by improper comparisons such as those incorporated in either the cheap debt or cheap equity financing arguments. Convertibles provide neither cheap debt nor cheap equity financing. Rather, they provide financing whose after-tax cost to the firm is between the costs of straight debt and common equity.

Firms employ convertibles when their nature provides benefits that are not generally available with other forms of financing. Let's briefly consider when and why firms use convertibles and warrants:

1. RISKY SITUATIONS Convertibles and bond/warrant combinations tend to be issued by smaller and more speculative firms, or sometimes by larger firms that have a high degree of risk. Suppose you are approached by a small firm that wants some debt financing to develop and manufacture the next generation of optical scanners. You know that if the project goes well you will get your money back.

[9] This rationale is supported by the results of Asquith and Mullins (1991).
[10] A number of other rationales have been suggested. Harris and Raviv (1985), for example, suggest that firms with favorable information will delay convertible calls to avoid depressing the firm's stock price. Other signaling or agency arguments have also been advanced. Some of the references at the end of the chapter review these other arguments.

However, if the project does not do well, you will receive nothing. Although some information on the project exists, you know that the next generation of optical scanners rests on yet-to-be-proven advances the firm is still working on. This type of project is very hard to evaluate, and even if it does prove successful, the firm may be preempted by other firms that are also racing to develop the next generation of optical scanners. One way to compensate for the additional hard-to-evaluate risk, is to provide investors with a "piece of the action." This can easily be accomplished by granting investors an option that can be exercised if the firm is successful.

2. AGENCY COSTS   Holders of the firm's straight debt are interested in the payment of principal and interest on the debt. To be more assured of receiving these payments, they favor low-risk investment projects. Stockholders, on the other hand, own a call option whose value increases when the firm undertakes high risk–high return projects. Therefore, stockholders want firms to issue debt as though it were going to be employed to finance low-risk projects, and then switch and undertake high-risk projects, thereby transferring wealth from bondholders to stockholders. To protect themselves from this possible expropriation of wealth, bondholders can require higher interest rates and more stringent bond covenants and restrictions. These actions are costly, however, and also restrict the flexibility of the firm. Using convertibles or warrants is a way to reduce these agency costs.

3. ASYMMETRIC INFORMATION AND ADVERSE FINANCING COSTS   When firms issue new equity they suffer negative price reactions. Therefore, firms will issue equity only when the investment projects under consideration are not very good; why share really good projects, and the expected increase in the value of the firm, with new equityholders? Building on the theoretical and empirical findings of negative price consequences when firms issue common stock, Stein (1992) proposes that firms may issue convertible bonds to bridge the gap between the negative price consequences associated with an equity issue and the potential for costly financial distress associated with a debt issue. When coupled with a call provision that enables early forced conversion, convertibles provide an indirect way to issue equity that entails less adverse price impacts than offering common stock.

4. INTERNATIONAL   Often when firms invest in international capital investment projects or have substantial international exposure, they are exposed to additional risks. These include possible adverse actions by foreign host governments and exposure to fluctuating exchange rates. In such cases, due to the unusual risks faced by the firm and because they are debt instead of equity, convertibles may tend to limit some of the firm's risk exposure. Whereas a country might be tempted to simply expropriate an equity investment, a debt claim may have more likelihood of being paid off—in part or full.

5. TAX CONSEQUENCES   When a firm issues debt that is convertible, or a debt/warrant package, the coupon interest rate is lower than the coupon interest rate if straight debt had been issued. Hence, the tax shield provided by the financing is reduced. This is a disadvantage if the firm is in a high tax-paying situation. Therefore, firms that have less use for the tax shields associated with interest tend to issue convertibles or bonds with warrants. Such firms generally have lower effective marginal tax rates.

Concept Review Questions

■ What are some of the characteristics of a convertible bond?

■ Define the three components that need to be considered when valuing convertible bonds.

■ Briefly explain how to price a convertible bond before maturity.

■ Why do firms issue convertible securities?

KEY POINTS

1. Warrants are simply long-term call options; hence the steps for determining their valuation proceed like those for the valuation of any other option. Cash dividends, the increase in the number of shares of common stock outstanding when they are exercised (or converted), and changing capital structure proportions must be taken into consideration when valuing warrants.

2. A convertible bond in essence is composed of a bond and a long-term option. The higher of the straight bond value and the conversion value of the security provides the floor, or minimum value, of the convertible. Due to the warrant, or long-term option part of the convertible, the convertible will trade before maturity at a premium to its minimum value.

3. Cash dividends, the increase in the number of shares of common stock outstanding when the bond is converted, and changing capital structure proportions must also be taken into account when valuing the warrant-like aspect of a convertible bond.

4. Convertibles *do not provide* either cheap debt or cheap equity financing. Their cost to the firm, and the return required by investors, is between that of straight debt and common equity.

5. Due to the call option contained in convertibles, the firm can force conversion if the market value of the convertible is greater than the call value. One rationale for forcing conversion, to minimize wealth transfers between bondholders and stockholders, applies when the market value equals the call price. However, most firms wait until the market value is substantially higher than the call price before calling convertibles. A second rationale focuses on the after-tax cash flow consequences to the firm; it shows that the firm should not force conversion if the after-tax cash outflows of the firm will increase as a result.

6. Warrants and convertibles are generally employed when the firm's risk is high, to reduce agency costs, to deal with asymmetric information and adverse financing costs, to deal with international risks, and when the firm has little use for the tax shields associated with interest.

QUESTIONS

17.1   Warrants are very similar to any other call option. How should they be valued? What complications exist that are not present with short-term call options? How do the valuation procedures have to be modified to deal with these complications?

17.2   Under what circumstances, if ever, does it make sense to exercise a warrant prior to maturity?

17.3   Sometimes firms extend the lives of warrants that are about to expire unexercised. What is the cost of doing this?

17.4 Banks, insurance companies, and other lenders often require an "equity kicker" in the form of warrants to accompany a loan. When negotiating the loan an alternative would have been to require a higher interest rate and/or additional loan restrictions. What are the advantages to the lender and to the borrower of the "equity kicker" arrangement?

17.5 How should convertibles be valued? What complications exist, and how should they be dealt with?

17.6 Consider three securities—common stock, straight bonds, and convertible bonds. In each case indicate how the security's value is affected. Which securities have their value affected the most/the least by the following?

a. The price of the firm's common stock increases.
b. Interest rates decline.
c. The firm embarks on a risky new project.
d. The firm increases its cash dividends on common stock.

17.7 One rationale for firms to follow is to call a convertible security when the conversion value equals the call price. Why is this so? In practice, firms tend to wait until the conversion value is substantially above the call price. What reasons can you suggest to explain this behavior?

17.8 Under what circumstances, if any, does it make sense for an investor voluntarily to convert a convertible bond prior to maturity?

17.9 It has been argued that convertibles have substantial advantages to the firm as a means of financing. When compared to straight debt, the argument goes, firms get cheap debt financing because they pay less than the going market interest rate for the debt. When compared with selling common stock directly, firms are able to sell common stock at a price above the current market price of the firm's common stock. Thus, the firm is in a "heads I win, tails you lose" situation. Evaluate this argument.

17.10 What reasons exist for using convertibles or bonds with warrants?

17.11 Why, if everything else is equal, might an investor prefer a bond with a warrant attached instead of a convertible bond?

CONCEPT REVIEW PROBLEMS

See Appendix A for solutions.

CR17.1 Morris International has warrants outstanding with a 3-year maturity and an exercise price of $35. The current market price for Morris's common stock is $28. If the risk-free rate is 6 percent and the volatility of Morris International's common stock is 0.30, what is the current price of the warrants? Assume the firm does not pay dividends and there are no dilution effects.

CR17.2 Applebee Computer, an all-equity firm, has a current stock price of $60 per share, with 1 million shares outstanding. As an incentive, 40,000 warrants were sold to the firm's managers at a price of $10 per warrant. The warrants have an exercise price of $70 and a maturity of 5 years.

a. Calculate the expiration value of the firm's warrants if the common stock sells at the following prices: (**1**) $60 per share, (**2**) $80 per share, (**3**) $100 per share.
b. If the risk-free rate of return is 5 percent and the standard deviation of Applebee's common stock is 0.313, what is the value of the warrants today?

CR17.3   In 1989 Sony paid $3.4 billion for Columbia Pictures. To help finance the purchase Sony sold $470 million of 4-year bonds with 4-year warrants attached. The coupon rate on the bond was amazingly low—0.3 percent. Sony was able to offer this astonishing low rate on bonds because the warrants attached to the bonds had an exercise price close to the current stock price.

a. Sony's current stock price is $42, the capital structure previous to issuing the bonds and warrants is 100 percent equity, the warrant's exercise price is $45, the risk-free rate is 5 percent, and the standard deviation of the firm's common stock is 0.20. Ignoring the effects of issuing debt and the dilution of common stock, what is the value of the warrants?

b. Now assume Sony had 24 million shares of common stock outstanding and issued 7.52 million warrants at $10.37 per warrant. Each warrant could purchase one share of stock at the exercise price. Taking into consideration dilution effects but ignoring changes in capital structure, what is the value of the warrant?

c. Now assume that Sony issues both debt and warrants and that Sony adds $470 million to its capital structure. (*Note:* The value of the warrants from (b) is included in the $470 million.) If you consider both the dilution effects and the change in capital structure, what is the value of Sony's warrants?

CR17.4   Bakers Supermarket recently issued 20-year, 12 percent, semiannual interest paying convertible debentures with a conversion price of $25 per share. Baker's common stock is trading at $10 per share.

a. What is the straight bond value if other 20-year bonds of similar quality currently pay 14 percent semiannually?

b. What is the conversion ratio and the conversion value of the bond?

c. What is the value of the convertible before maturity if its capital structure is comprised of 30 percent equity before conversion and 50 percent equity after conversion, its standard deviation of equity before conversion is 0.30, its adjusted market price is $11.30, the risk-free rate is 6 percent, and q is 0.15?

CR17.5   Ten years ago Volkman Corp. issued 20-year, 11 percent, semiannual interest paying convertible debentures with a call provision of 10 percent above par allowed 10 years after issuance. The conversion price of the debentures is $50, and the current market price of Volkman common is $65.

a. What is the conversion value of the convertible debentures?

b. Straight debentures of similar risk and maturity to Volkman's convertible debentures have a semiannual return of 7.5 percent. The new standard deviation of the equity is 0.30, the adjusted market price, P_0^*, is $68, the risk-free rate of return is 7 percent, and q is 0.20. Ignoring call risk, in other words, assuming the firm will not call the debentures and they will mature in 10 more years, what is the value of the convertible debentures?

c. Now assume Volkman calls the debentures at 10 percent above par. Is there a transfer of wealth? If so, from whom to whom?

PROBLEMS

17.1   Bryan Steel's common stock price is $34. A new warrant is being issued with an exercise price of $38, its life is $3\frac{1}{2}$ years, the risk-free rate is 0.10, and the volatility of Bryan's common stock is 0.45 per year. Ignoring any dilution that occurs when the warrants are exercised, what is the value of the warrant?

17.2   Warrants for Pleasure Industries allows its warrantholders to purchase 10 shares of common stock at the exercise price of $35. The market price of the common stock is $37.50, and the market price of a warrant is 15 percent greater than its lower limit value.

a.   What is the market price of a warrant?
b.   At what dollar premium over its lower limit value is the warrant selling?

17.3   Ross Systems, an all-equity firm that does not pay cash dividends on its common stock, wants to value some warrants it is considering issuing. The risk-free rate is 9 percent, the standard deviation of the firm's common stock is 0.50, the current price of the stock is $19, the warrants will have a 4-year life, and the exercise price will be $30.

a.   Ignoring possible dilution, what is the value of each warrant?
b.   Taking into account the impact of dilution, Ross estimates the adjusted stock price, P_0^*, will be $20 and q will be 0.14. What is the value of each warrant? How much impact does dilution have on the warrant price?
c.   What is the lower limit on the value of the warrant? How much of a premium over the lower limit is indicated by the value of the warrant in (b)?
d.   Ross plans to sell 500,000 warrants. If it anticipates selling them at a 10 percent discount from their value, how much (ignoring any flotation or issuance costs) should Ross obtain from the financing?

17.4   Healthcare Plus is a firm that currently has a total value, V, of $140 million, equity of $100 million, and debt of $40 million. There are 5,000,000 shares of common stock outstanding, and the firm does not pay any cash dividends. Healthcare Plus is in the process of issuing a $60 million bond/warrant package. The 15-year bonds will carry a coupon interest rate of 7 percent, while the rate on comparable quality and maturity nonconvertible bonds is 10 percent. The warrants will have a 6-year life, the risk-free rate is 8 percent, the exercise price is $35, and the standard deviation of the firm's current equity is 0.80. Twenty warrants will be issued along with each $1,000 par value bond.

a.   What is the value of the bonds without considering the warrants?
b.   What is the approximate value of the warrants, before dilution and the new standard deviation resulting from the changed capital structure proportions after the financing?
c.   Now determine the value of the warrant after taking account of dilution and the changing standard deviation.
d.   If the bond/warrant package sells for $1,000 per package, is it fairly valued?

17.5   Professional Developers, Ltd., pays cash dividends of $3 per share, has a dividend payout ratio of 75 percent, and a P/E ratio of 10. To raise additional funds, Professional has decided to issue a $20,000,000, 25-year convertible debenture ($1,000 par) with a coupon rate of 11 percent and a conversion price of $50. Interest is paid yearly.

a.   What is Professional's current EPS?
b.   What is the market price per share of Professional's common stock?
c.   What is the conversion value per bond?
d.   If 60 percent of the convertible debentures are ultimately converted, how many additional shares of common stock will be issued?
e.   If comparable quality nonconvertible bonds are yielding 12 percent, what is the initial straight bond value (per bond) of the convertible? What is its straight bond value in 10 years (assuming market interest rates remain constant)?

17.6   A 30-year maturity, $1,000 par convertible bond will be issued at par; it has an 8 percent coupon rate. The market rate of interest on comparable quality and maturity straight bonds is 11 percent. Interest is paid yearly.

a.   What is the straight bond value of the convertible?
b.   What is the straight bond value if **(1)** the maturity is only 10 years, and **(2)** if it is only 4 years?
c.   If the maturity is 30 years, what is the straight bond value if the market rate of interest is **(1)** 13 percent, **(2)** 9 percent, **(3)** 7 percent?
d.   What general conclusions can you reach about the stability of the straight bond value, or floor, for convertibles?

17.7   NewPark Systems is an all-equity firm that is planning a $10,000,000 convertible bond issue. NewPark's investment bankers have suggested that the 10-year bonds carry an interest rate of 7.5 percent; comparable quality and maturity bonds are presently yielding 12 percent. The investment bankers have recommended that the conversion price be $24. NewPark does not pay cash dividends on its common stock, the current stock price is $20 per share, the adjusted market price, P_0^*, is $18 per share, the risk-free rate is 8.50 percent, the standard deviation of the firm's equity is 0.40, and q is 0.25. If the convertible bonds are expected to sell at their par value, should you accept the investment bankers' recommendations?

17.8   You have been called in to help Platinum International design a convertible bond issue. Specifically, you have to provide guidance regarding the conversion price. Platinum currently has a total market value of $125 million—$110 million in equity and $15 million in debt. The firm wants to issue $50 million of convertible bonds. You believe 15-year bonds can be issued with a coupon interest rate that is $3\frac{3}{4}$ percentage points below what Platinum's existing long-term debt is yielding, which is 10 percent. There are currently 4,400,000 shares of common stock outstanding, no cash dividends are paid, the risk-free rate is 6 percent, and the standard deviation of the firm's current equity is 0.36.

a.   What is the convertibles' straight bond value?
b.   What is the approximate value of the conversion option, before considering dilution and the new standard deviation resulting from the changed capital structure proportions after the financing? To estimate the value of the option, assume you decide to try a conversion price of $40. What does your approximate option calculation tell you about the conversion price that should be included in the convertible?
c.   Now assume that you adjust the conversion price by $10—that is, based on your answer to (b) you employ a conversion value of either $30 or $50. What is the value of the option to convert after taking account of dilution and the changing standard deviation? What is your recommendation?

17.9   Jeff owns one convertible bond ($1,000 par) issued by Bellefonte Corp. He has gathered the following information:

Market price of the convertible bond	$1,280
Conversion price	20
Market price per share of common stock	25
Call price of the convertible bond	1,100

a.   If Jeff converts right now, what is the value of the common stock received? Should he voluntarily convert?
b.   Assume Bellefonte calls the convertible. At what common stock market price would Jeff be indifferent between converting and receiving the call price?

17.10 Microtonics needs to raise $35,000,000 in new financing. Due to the firm's fast growth, its investment banker thinks subordinated debt is the best bet. Two alternative plans have been proposed.

Plan I	Plan II
Straight subordinated debt issued at par (ignore flotation costs) 20-year maturity 10% coupon rate Expected common stock P/E = 8	Straight subordinated debt with warrants issued at par (ignore flotation costs) 30 warrants per $1,000 par bond; each warrant can be used to purchase one share of stock; the exercise price is $20 20-year maturity 9% coupon rate Expected common stock P/E = 8

The firm anticipates EBIT will be $16,000,000. Other interest charges are $2,000,000, the tax rate is 35 percent, and there are 2,000,000 shares of common stock outstanding.

a. Determine the straight bond value of the 9 percent subordinated debt issued in plan II. What is the implied value of the warrants?
b. Calculate the EPS and market value of the common stock for both plans. (*Note:* In calculating EPS do not worry about the common stock that would be issued if the warrants are exercised.) Which plan should be employed? Why?
c. Determine the EPS for plan II as in (b), but now assume that the warrants are exercised. If the P/E increases to 9 times after the warrants exercised, which plan should the firm choose? Does this agree with your conclusion in (b)? How much new cash will the firm receive when the warrants are exercised?

17.11 Fresno Industries needs $10,000,000 for expansion. The company expects EBIT of $8,000,000 after the expansion, there is no other interest, the tax rate is 35 percent, and a common stock P/E of 9 times is estimated. There are currently 1,000,000 shares of common stock outstanding. Two financing plans being considered are as follows:

Plan I	Plan II
Straight debt at par with warrants (ignore flotation costs) 20 warrants per $1,000 par bond; each for one share of common stock 12% coupon rate 20-year maturity Expected common stock P/E = 9 times	Convertible debt at par (ignore flotation costs) Conversion price = $20 10% coupon rate 20-year maturity Expected common stock P/E = 9 times

a. Determine the anticipated EPS under each plan and the market price per share. Which plan should Fresno take? Why?
b. To analyze further the effects of the two plans, Fresno estimates that in 4 years EBIT will be $13 million, and that (1) the warrants will all be exercised, because they expire in 4 years, or (2) it will have forced all the convertibles to be converted. Assuming full warrant exercise or full conversion, and a P/E of 10 under plan I and 11 under plan II, what is the new EPS and common stock market price for each plan? Which plan should be chosen? (*Note:* For plan II assume no interest is paid in the fourth year.)

c. Why does the result in (b) conflict with your conclusion in (a)? Is it better to maximize value now (at time $t = 0$) or in 4 years? Considering your answers to both (a) and (b), which plan do you recommend?

17.12 Mini Case Andrecomp is in the process of assessing its financing needs for the next year. Due to the high risk but growing nature of its business, Andrecomp has a need for more financing. As CFO you are responsible for providing the financing plan. In evaluating the situation, you note that 2 years ago a large common stock financing was undertaken. Since then Andrecomp's stock price has fluctuated some, but overall there has been little change in the stock price level. With that in mind, and knowing that substantial profits appear to be at least a year away, you have concluded a direct stock offering is not desirable or feasible. At the same time, you are not sure a straight bond offering can provide the needed financing. Therefore, you are considering a bond/warrant issue or a convertible bond issue.

a. Summarize when a bond/warrant package and convertibles are desirable. Can they help Andrecomp and at the same time provide benefits to investors?

b. You are evaluating two different financing packages, both of which would raise $40,000,000. Andrecomps' value, V, is $100,000,000, of which $70,000,000 is equity and $30,000,000 is debt. The risk-free rate is 7 percent, comparable quality and comparable maturity debt costs 12 percent, there are 1,000,000 shares of common stock outstanding, and the standard deviation of the firm's equity is 0.60. The two plans are as follows:

Plan I	Plan II
Straight debt at par with warrants (ignore flotation costs)	Convertible debt at par (ignore flotation costs)
3 warrants per $1,000 par bond; each for one share of common stock; 3-year expiration	Conversion price = $125
Exercise price = $90	8% coupon rate
11% coupon rate	8-year maturity
20-year bond maturity	

(1) Calculate the straight bond value of the bonds contained in the two plans.

(2) Ignoring, for the time being, the impact of the financing on the stock price and the standard deviation, calculate the approximate value of the warrant and the option contained in the convertible.

(3) Now, recalculate the value of the warrant and the call option contained in the convertible after taking into account the adjusted market price of the common stock, P_0^*, and the impact of the financing on the standard deviation.

(4) What conclusion do you arrive at about the value of the two different plans? Does one appear to be superior in terms of the value to Andrecomp?

c. Andrecomp anticipates that EBIT will be $20,000,000, its interest on existing debt is $3,000,000 per year, and its marginal tax rate is 40 percent. Taking account of the additional interest with either financing plan, what will be the earnings per share, EPS, with each financing plan? (*Note:* Ignore any additional shares of common stock from exercise or conversion.) Now, what will EPS be in 4 years if EBIT is $30,000,000, interest on the total debt for the firm is $5,500,000, T is 40 percent, and **(1)** the warrants have all been exercised and the bond called for plan I, and **(2)** the convertible bond has been fully converted? What conclusions do you draw from the impact on EPS? Does this support or conflict with what you concluded in (b4)?

REFERENCES

Some aspects of warrants are examined in the following:

CROUHY, MICHEL, and DAN GALAI. "Common Errors in the Valuation of Warrants and Options on Firms with Warrants." *Financial Analysts Journal* 47 (September/October 1991): 89–90.

GALAI, DAN, and MIER A. SCHNELLER. "Pricing of Warrants and the Value of the Firm." *Journal of Finance* 33 (December 1978): 1333–42.

HOWE, JOHN S., and PEIHWANG WEI. "The Valuation Effects of Warrant Extensions." *Journal of Finance* 48 (March 1993): 305–14.

Information on convertibles, and some of their reasons for use, is contained in:

ASQUITH, PAUL, and DAVID W. MULLINS, JR. "Convertible Debt: Corporate Call Policy and Voluntary Conversion." *Journal of Finance* 46 (September 1991): 1273–89.

HARRIS, MILTON, and ARTUR RAVIV. "A Sequential Signalling Model of Convertible Debt Call Policy." *Journal of Finance* 40 (December 1985): 1263–81.

INGERSOLL, JONATHAN. "An Examination of Corporate Call Policies on Convertible Securities." *Journal of Finance* 32 (May 1977): 463–78.

KIM, YONG CHEOL, and RENE M. STULZ. "Is There a Global Market for Convertible Bonds?" *Journal of Business* 65 (January 1992): 75–91.

McCONNELL, JOHN J., and EDUARDO S. SCHWARTZ. "The Origin of LYONs: A Case Study in Financial Innovation." *Journal of Applied Corporate Finance* 4 (Winter 1992): 40–47.

MAZZERO, MICHAEL A., and WILLIAM T. MOORE. "Liquidity Costs and Stock Price Response to Convertible Security Calls." *Journal of Business* 65 (July 1992): 353–69.

ROSENGREN, ERIC S. "Defaults of Original Issue High-Yield Convertible Bonds." *Journal of Finance* 48 (March 1993): 345–62.

SINGH, AJAI, ARNOLD R. COWAN, and NANDKUMAR NAYAR. "Underwritten Calls of Convertible Bonds." *Journal of Financial Economics* 29 (March 1991): 173–96.

STEIN, JEREMY C. "Convertible Bonds as Backdoor Equity Financing." *Journal of Financial Economics* 32 (August 1992): 3–21.

18

Leasing

EXECUTIVE SUMMARY

Leases come in many sizes, shapes, and forms, but all require periodic lease payments from the lessee (the user) to the lessor (the owner). Unless the lease is cancelable, leasing obligates firms to a series of legally enforceable payments similar to those required when debt financing is issued.

The decision to purchase or to lease an asset is a financing decision. The basis for comparison is the cash flows that occur if the asset is purchased versus those that arise if the asset is leased. This comparison is accomplished by performing an incremental analysis to determine the net present value of leasing versus purchasing. Risk is neutralized in terms of the cash flow demands on the firm by using the concept of an equivalent loan for the purchase alternative. This loan can be determined directly or the net present value can be determined using the after-tax cost of debt as the discount rate. As with other financial decisions, the analysis comes down to focusing on the proper incremental set of cash flows, their timing, and riskiness.

LEASING AND THE FIRM

Firms often enter into rental agreements that are called **leases.** The owner of the property is the **lessor,** who leases it to the user, or the **lessee.** Virtually anything that is needed by the firm—machinery, buildings, warehouses, airplanes, computers, ships, and so forth—can be leased. Our primary focus is from the standpoint of the lessee, but it is helpful to begin by understanding who provides lease financing. That is, who are the lessors?

Lease financing can be provided by manufacturers as part of their regular sales effort, or it can be provided by firms that specialize in lease financing. In the former category, GATX, a railroad car manufacturer, is the largest lessor of railcars and IBM is a major computer lessor. In the latter category, General Electric Capital, a subsidiary of General Electric, has acquired numerous small lessors to fit its specialized operations. With over $7 billion invested in leased assets, General Electric Capital is possibly the biggest lessor in the United States. In addition, lease financing is increasingly being provided by commercial banks, investment bankers, subsidiaries of other firms, and commercial finance companies.

TYPES OF LEASES

Leases come in many sizes, shapes, and forms, but in all cases the lessee (who has acquired use of the asset) is required to make periodic payments to the lessor. These payments generally are made monthly, quarterly, or semiannually, with the first payment due when the lease agreement is signed.

Service Lease

A **service lease** is a short-term lease that generally is cancelable. It is often used to finance office machines, cars, and similar relatively inexpensive assets that require periodic maintenance. These leases often are often called maintenance leases because the lessor generally is responsible for all service, as well as for any insurance or property taxes on the assets. The costs incurred by the lessor are built into the lease payments and thus passed along to the lessee. Large service leases should be subjected to financial evaluation like that discussed later in the chapter; smaller ones, or leases of short duration, are typically not subjected to an extensive financial analysis.

Financial Lease

The term **financial lease** is employed for tax purposes to identify a long-term, noncancelable contract between the lessor, who owns the asset, and the lessee, who agrees to lease the asset for some specified period of time. Financial leases are a form of long-term financing similar to borrowing. The lessee gains the use of the asset immediately but in return has entered into a binding obligation to make payments as specified in the lease contract. Entering into a lease is similar to borrowing in terms of the cash flow consequences to the lessee. For this reason, the financial analysis employed by lessees presented later in the chapter will compare the cash flow consequences of leasing versus borrowing. Most financial leases are *net* leases: the lessee agrees to provide maintenance and pay for insurance coverage and/or property taxes related to the leased asset.

Sale and Leaseback

A **sale and leaseback** occurs when the owner of an asset decides to sell it to another party and then lease it back. This type of transaction occurs frequently when a firm wants to raise capital by selling a building or factory but also wants to maintain the use of the facility for some specified period of time. The popularity of sale and leaseback agreements is growing, as many firms attempt to translate the estimated 20 percent of their total assets in real estate into more productive uses. From the lessee's standpoint, the financial analysis of selling and leasing back versus borrowing is essentially the same as for other financial leases.

Table 18.1

Characteristics of the Major Types of Leases

Service leases, often of short duration, are usually not analyzed extensively for their financial impact. Financial leases, including sale and leasebacks and leveraged leases, are all similar from the standpoint of how the lessee evaluates them.

Type of Lease	Parties Involved	Duration	Provider of Maintenance; Payment of Insurance and Taxes
Service	Lessee and lessor	Short	Lessor
Financial	Lessee and lessor	Long	Lessee
Sale and leaseback	Lessee (seller) and lessor (buyer)	Long	Lessee
Leveraged	Lessee, lessor (equity participant), and lender	Long	Lessee

Leveraged Lease

A fourth major type of leasing, and one that has also become increasingly popular in recent years, is the **leveraged lease.** This arrangement involves three parties instead of two—the lender who puts up much of the money, the lessor (or equity participant) who owns the asset, and the lessee. Leveraged leases are complicated from the standpoint of both lender and lessor, but they remain a financial lease from the standpoint of the lessee. Table 18.1 summarizes the characteristics of the basic lease types.

TAX CONSIDERATIONS

From the lessee's standpoint, the lease payments are an expense of doing business and are deductible for tax purposes. Because the lessor owns the asset, depreciation is allowed as a tax-deductible expense.

Internal Revenue Service rules about what constitutes a lease for tax purposes were substantially modified under the Economic Recovery Tax Act of 1981. These rules were further modified by the Tax Equity and Fiscal Responsibility Act of 1982. Under the present rules, a lease is created under the following conditions:

1. The property qualifies for depreciation for tax purposes.
2. The transaction has economic substance independent of the tax benefits.
3. The lease is entered into within 90 days after the property is placed in service.
4. The lessee may be allowed to purchase the asset at the end of the lease if the option price is at least 10 percent of the original cost of the property.

Except in the next section, when accounting issues are discussed, we assume the leases under discussion in the remainder of the chapter are financial leases for tax purposes.

ACCOUNTING FOR LEASES

Our primary concern is the evaluation of the financial consequences of leasing, but let's pause briefly to consider their accounting treatment. *There are vast differences in both terminology and treatment for accounting versus tax purposes.* The main terminology difference is that accountants refer to long-term leases that have to be capitalized on the firm's financial statements as **capital leases.** Any other leases are called **operating leases.**

Until 1976, all leases provided "off-balance-sheet" financing. That is, the fact that the firm had the use of the assets, as well as contractual obligations to make periodic lease payments, showed up (if at all) only as a footnote. Because lease obligations are as binding as debt, however, the reported accounting statements tended to misrepresent a firm's position if it leased long-term assets. Under FASB No. 13[1] a capital lease exists if one or more of the following conditions are met:

1. The lease transfers ownership of the property to the lessee by the end of the lease term.
2. The lease gives the lessee the option to purchase the property, and it is likely the option will be exercised.
3. The lease term is equal to 75 percent or more of the estimated economic life of the property.

If these requirements (which are a good deal different from the tax requirements) are met, then the present value of the lease payments must be entered as a liability on the right-hand side of the balance sheet. A corresponding entry must also be made on the left-hand side to record the value of the asset. (This is typically lumped with other long-term assets of the firm.) This asset is then amortized over its useful life, resulting in a reduction in reported income. Any lease that does not meet the FASB criteria is considered an operating lease for accounting purposes.

The net effect of FASB No. 13 has been for accounting statements to reflect somewhat more accurately the firm's debt-type obligations. To get around this reporting requirement, many firms are structuring long-term leases so they are technically *not* capital leases as specified by FASB No. 13. These operating leases do not have to be shown on the firm's balance sheet and show up only in the footnotes accompanying the financial statements. Although many firms are keeping substantial lease obligations off their balance sheets, the benefits from doing so are questionable unless the lease is economically justified, as discussed subsequently, and unless we assume that analysts, investors, and bankers are naive and do not adjust for this continued off-balance-sheet financing.

---

[1] *Financial Accounting Standards Board No. 13,* "Accounting for Leases" (Stamford, Conn.: FASB, 1976).

Concept Review Questions

- What are some of the similarities and differences among a service lease, a financial lease, a sale and leaseback, and a leveraged lease?
- According to the Internal Revenue Service, what are the conditions under which a lease is created?
- Describe the differences between a capital lease and an operating lease.

SETTING LEASE RATES

Although our primary interest is from the lessee's standpoint, it is helpful to understand what factors lessors consider in setting lease rates. By understanding this process, lessees will be in a better position for knowledgeable lease bargaining.

For financial leases, the lessor wants to set a rate that provides a satisfactory return. This is done by focusing first on four items,[2] as follows:

1. The lessor's after-tax required rate of return on debt-type investments, k_i[3]
2. The lessor's marginal tax rate, T
3. The cost of the leased asset, CLA_0
4. The depreciation allowed by the IRS, Dep_t

When these items have been determined, the proper lease rate for the lessor to quote is determined using the following five-step procedure:

STEP 1:   Determine the ownership benefit. The tax benefit from owning the asset is the depreciation tax shield.

STEP 2:   Calculate the present value of the ownership benefit. Employing the lessor's after-tax required rate of return on debt-type investments, we can determine the present value of the ownership benefit using Equation 18.1, as follows:

$$\begin{matrix} \text{present value} \\ \text{of benefit} \end{matrix} = \sum_{t=1}^{n} \frac{Dep_t(T)}{(1 + k_i)^t} \tag{18.1}$$

STEP 3:   Calculate the amount to be recovered from lease payments. The net amount recoverable from lease payments is equal to the cost of the leased asset minus the present value of the benefit of ownership calculated in step 2, so that:

$$\begin{matrix} \text{net amount recoverable} \\ \text{from lease payments} \end{matrix} = CLA_0 - \begin{matrix} \text{present value} \\ \text{of benefit} \end{matrix} \tag{18.2}$$

---

[2] Although resale values are important, for simplicity they are ignored. Resale values for lessors are examined in Problem 18.2.

[3] The logic behind using k_i as the lessor's minimum discount rate is similar to that discussed later in the chapter for lessees. If markets are perfect and the tax status and all other factors are similar between lessors and lessees, then the returns to lessors from leasing are exactly equal to the cost of leasing to lessees.

STEP 4: Determine the after-tax lease payment, ATL. Because lease payments are made in advance (at the beginning of each period), the after-tax lease payments are determined by solving for ATL in the following formula:

$$\text{net amount recoverable from lease payments} = \left[\sum_{t=1}^{n} \frac{ATL}{(1 + k_i)^t} \right] (1 + k_i) \qquad (18.3)$$

In Equation 18.3, ATL is an annuity due. The term $(1 + k_i)$ converts ATL from an ordinary annuity to an annuity due.

STEP 5: Determine the before-tax lease payment, L. To complete the process, the lessor adjusts the lease payment to its before-tax amount, as follows:

$$L = \frac{ATL}{(1 - T)} \qquad (18.4)$$

The lease rate L is what the lessor will quote to a prospective lessee. By doing so, the lessor will achieve the desired after-tax return on the leased asset. If any higher lease rate is quoted, the lessor's return increases accordingly.

To illustrate setting lease rates, assume that LeaseFirst has been approached to supply a 3-year lease on a $1,000,000 piece of specialized equipment. The equipment has a normal recovery period of 3 years for tax purposes; LeaseFirst's marginal tax rate is 35 percent; its before-tax required return, or cost of debt, on debt-type investments is 13.85 percent; and no resale value is assumed. Straight line depreciation will be employed, and *for simplicity the half-year convention in the IRS depreciation tax code will be ignored (for this and all problems in this chapter)*. Thus, depreciation will be one-third on the original cost each year on this 3-year asset. What lease rate will LeaseFirst quote if the yearly lease payments are made in advance?[4]

The specific steps employed by LeaseFirst are shown in Table 18.2. In the first two steps, the present value of the ownership benefit to LeaseFirst is found to be $295,318. Then in step 3 the amount to be recovered from lease payments is simply $1,000,000 − $295,318, or $704,682. In steps 4 and 5 the after- and before-tax lease payments are determined. By collecting three annual lease payments of $392,928, each payable at the beginning of the year, LeaseFirst will receive its 13.85 percent before-tax (or 9 percent after-tax) required return.

Other things being equal, the following actions will serve to increase the lease rates quoted by lessors:

1. Using straight-line rather than MACRS depreciation for tax purposes.
2. Raising the discount rate.
3. Increasing the number of payments by going to semiannual, quarterly, or monthly payments instead of yearly payments.

---

[4] The same basic procedure would be employed in determining semiannual, quarterly, or monthly lease payments.

Table 18.2

Setting a Lease Rate

Using this step-by-step procedure, we can determine the lease rates to quote for any leased asset.

Steps 1 and 2: Determine Present Value of Ownership Benefit

Depreciation = \$1,000,000/3 ≈ \$333,333 per year

$$\begin{aligned}
\text{present value} \atop \text{of benefit} &= \left(\sum_{t=1}^{n} \frac{Dep_t(T)}{(1 + k_i)^t} \right) \\
&= (\$1,000,000/3)(0.35)\left[\frac{1}{0.09} - \frac{1}{0.09(1 + 0.09)^3} \right] = \$295,318
\end{aligned}$$

Step 3: Calculate Amount to Be Recovered from Lease Payments

\$1,000,000 − \$295,318 = \$704,682

Step 4: Determine After-Tax Lease Payment, ATL

$$\$704,682 = ATL\left[\frac{1}{0.09} - \frac{1}{0.09(1 + 0.09)^3} \right](1.09)$$

$$\$704,682 = ATL(2.7591)$$
$$2.7591 ATL = \$704,682$$
$$ATL = \$704,682/2.7591 \approx \$255,403$$

Step 5: Calculate Before-Tax Lease Payment, L

$$L = \frac{\$255,403}{1 - 0.35} \approx \$392,928$$

In practice, three other factors must be considered. The first is that the lessor still owns the asset, and there will be some resale value for most assets after the lease terminates. Resale values serve to lower the quoted lease rate. Second, it is important to realize that information asymmetries generally exist between lessors and lessees. Lessors often know more about the asset than the lessee, and they may have economies of scale not enjoyed by the lessees. Finally, lessors will adjust the quoted lease rates upward to account for the transaction costs of setting up the lease agreement, and they will also factor in the costs incurred in obtaining information about potential lessees and the lessee's risk of default. Thus, lease rates are actually set in a slightly more complex environment than the model outlined in Equations 18.1 through 18.4.

Concept Review Questions

- Describe the procedure a lessor should perform when setting lease rates.
- What are some factors that would affect the lease rates set by the lessor?

To Lease or Not to Lease?

If financial markets are perfect—that is, if there are no transaction costs, financial distress costs, taxes, information asymmetries, and so forth—then debt and lease obligations are valued exactly the same by lessors and lessees. In a perfect market, the cost of debt or lease financing would be the same, and the lessee would be indifferent between leasing and borrowing. Given less-than-perfect markets, however, it is important to consider reasons for leasing. Some valid reasons exist; others often advanced are dubious, at best.

GOOD REASONS FOR LEASING

Tax Benefits

One of the most important reasons for leasing is the tax benefits associated with leasing. Lessees often benefit from leasing if they have a lower marginal tax rate than lessors. Due to the difference in tax rates, the IRS-based depreciation tax benefit may be worth more to the lessor with a higher tax bracket, resulting in savings to the lessee.

Flexibility and Convenience

A second reason for leasing is that it may increase the flexibility of the firm. It is often preferable to lease certain types of assets rather than to purchase them. In addition, the convenience of having the lessor obtain, set up, and maintain assets may be a significant advantage at times, especially with highly technical pieces of equipment. By leasing, the firm has an easily exercisable option to expand on its asset base. This option is also valuable in today's rapidly changing economic environment.

Cancellation Option

Operating leases and even some longer-term financial leases, such as those on computers, often contain an option to cancel. That is, the user or lessee may have the option of canceling the lease at its discretion. This option is valuable and enhances the desirability of leasing. However, the lessee must recognize that lessors charge a higher lease rate to compensate themselves for issuing this option. Some leases that initially appear to be expensive are fairly priced once this cancellation option is recognized and valued.

Other Factors

Three other factors also favor leasing. First, because many leases are set at a fixed rate (that is, the lease payments do not change), the lessee is not surprised by higher cash outflows as economic conditions or interest rates change. Second, lessors are increasingly providing value-added services such as maintenance, insurance, and so forth, which allow the lessees to focus their primary attention on their businesses, not on the maintenance of assets. Finally, for firms with international operations, leasing assets as opposed to buying them may provide some protection against having them expropriated by foreign governments. For all of these reasons, more and more firms are leasing instead of buying assets.

DUBIOUS REASONS FOR LEASING

Capital Conservation

One argument often advanced to justify leasing is the conservation of the firm's working capital. Those who offer this argument say that the lease provides "100 percent" financing. However, because virtually all lease agreements require the first payment in advance, even under the best of circumstances less than 100 percent financing is secured. For small firms there may be some validity in this argument, because they do not have the same access to the financial markets and therefore may have to finance the purchase with internally generated funds. Larger firms, however, can generally secure approximately the same amount of financing from the financial markets. For them, leasing does not appear to be a viable means of conserving working capital.

Increased Debt Capacity

Another argument often made is that the use of leases increases the firm's debt capacity. This is said to occur because the combination of leasing and borrowing results in more long-term financing (or debt capacity) than that achieved by borrowing alone. This argument assumes, however, that bankers, lenders, and the financial markets are naive and do not recognize that leasing places a financial obligation on the firm, just as borrowing does. If lease financing really increased borrowing capacity, lenders and the financial markets would be inefficiently assessing the risk and cash flow obligations of leases. This does not appear to be the case.

Avoidance of Restrictions

Bonds or term loans often impose restrictive covenants on the firm, potentially limiting its financial flexibility. By leasing the asset, the lessee may be able to avoid some of these restrictions. Although this argument often appears to have some justification in a technical sense, most of the time the actual restrictions on the firm due to bond or term loan covenants are substantially less than their perceived impact. This reason is not often of much importance as a reason for leasing instead of purchasing.

Concept Review Questions

- What are some good reasons and some not so good reasons to lease an asset?
- Comment on the statement: "By leasing I am able to increase my firm's debt capacity."

EVALUATION OF FINANCIAL LEASES

The evaluation of leases from the lessee's standpoint is straightforward as long as certain basic ideas are understood. These relate to (1) the interaction between the firm's capital budgeting decision and the decision to lease or purchase the asset, (2) why debt financing is the appropriate standard of comparison, and (3) the fact that an incremental analysis of the lease versus purchase cash flows is employed.

WHAT DECISION ARE WE CONCERNED WITH?

When a firm makes a capital budgeting decision concerning the possible acquisition of an asset, it calculates the net present value of the proposed project. If the capital budgeting NPV is positive, then the asset should be acquired because it assists in maximizing the value of the firm. *Capital budgeting implicitly assumes that assets to be acquired will be purchased.* If leasing is a strong possibility, however, then the basic capital budgeting decision must be supplemented by further analysis to determine whether the asset should be leased or purchased. To make this supplemental financing decision, we calculate the **net present value of leasing, NPV**$_{lease}$.[5] If the net present value from leasing is positive, then the asset should be acquired by leasing; otherwise, it should be purchased.

The basic capital budgeting decision and the lease evaluation decisions interact. If some specialized machinery needed by a firm has an NPV value of $15,000, then the

---

Figure 18.1

Interaction of Capital Budgeting and Leasing Decisions

If the capital budgeting NPV is positive, then the firm leases if NPV$_{lease}$ (i. e., the net present value from leasing versus purchasing) is positive. Even if the capital budgeting NPV is negative, especially favorable lease terms can still lead to leasing.

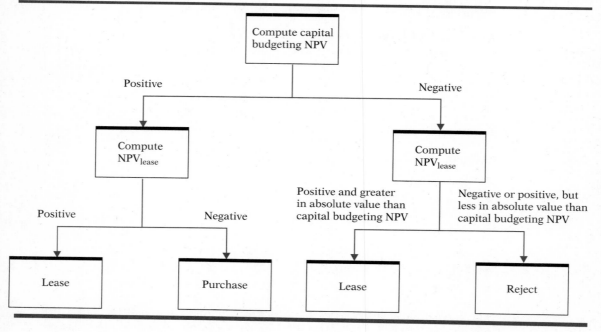

---

[5] The net present value from leasing versus purchasing is sometimes called the net advantage of leasing, NAL. The internal rate of return, IRR, could also be employed, to make the lease versus purchase decision as shown later in the chapter.

capital budgeting decision has been reached. If the machinery can be either leased or purchased, however, then a subsequent calculation (the net present value showing the advantage of leasing) must be made to determine the preferable means of financing. If this subsequent NPV_{lease} is positive, then the use of the machinery should be secured by leasing. If the NPV_{lease} is negative, then the machinery should be purchased.

One complication arises if the net present value in the original capital budgeting decision is negative. In this case, there may be instances in which the use of the assets still should be acquired if especially favorable lease terms are available. Consider a case in which the capital budgeting NPV is $-\$5,000$, but the subsequent NPV_{lease} is $\$7,000$. Because the net difference is a positive $\$2,000$, the assets should be leased. If the NPV_{lease} were negative, however, or positive but less than $\$5,000$, the assets would not be leased or purchased. All these conditions are summarized in Figure 18.1. For simplicity, we assume that the capital budgeting NPV is positive. Our concern is with the financing decision of whether the assets should be leased or purchased.

WHY COMPARE LEASING WITH BORROWING?

To evaluate whether leasing is preferable to purchasing, we need to make an assumption about the mode of financing used if the asset is purchased. Leasing imposes the same kind of financial commitment on the firm that borrowing does. Thus, the relevant standard of comparison to use when evaluating leasing is to compare it with purchasing the asset and financing the capital needs via borrowing. We are interested in neutralizing the risk between the two alternatives. The way to accomplish this is by establishing an equivalent borrowing amount that, in terms of the after-tax cash flows in each future period, is exactly the same as the after-tax lease cash flows. By doing so, the risk is neutralized.

There are two primary ways to accomplish this risk neutralization. The first (which is by far the simplest) involves using the lessee's after-tax cost of debt capital, k_i, as the relevant discount rate. This after-tax cost of debt capital is equal to $k_b(1 - T)$, where k_b is the lessee's before-tax borrowing rate and T is the firm's marginal tax rate. The second method involves determining the actual equivalent loan that neutralizes the risk. We will illustrate both these methods.

THE NET PRESENT VALUE OF LEASING VERSUS PURCHASING

A financial lease is evaluated in terms of the after-tax cash flows and opportunity costs incurred by leasing rather than purchasing the asset. The major elements of the decision are these:

1. The lease payments, L, made periodically by the lessee on an after-tax basis. In line with industry practice, we assume the first payment occurs at the time the lease is signed, time $t = 0$.
2. The depreciation tax shield, calculated by multiplying the annual IRS depreciation by the lessee's marginal tax rate. By entering into a lease, the firm incurs an opportunity cost equal to the forgone depreciation tax shield.
3. The cost of the leased asset, CLA_0.

Employing these variables in an incremental framework, we calculate the net present value of leasing as follows:

$$NPV_{\text{lease}} = CLA_0 - \left\{ \left[\sum_{t=1}^{n} \frac{L_t(1 - T)}{(1 + k_i)^t} \right](1 + k_i) + \sum_{t=1}^{n} \frac{Dep_t(T)}{(1 + k_i)^t} \right\} \tag{18.5}$$

Because the lease payments, L, are an annuity due, the term $(1 + k_i)$ converts them from an ordinary annuity to an annuity due. The NPV_{lease} simply finds the cost of leasing the asset (the part of Equation 18.5 in braces, which includes both explicit and opportunity costs) versus the cost of the asset (represented by CLA_0). As long as the cost of leasing is less than the cost of the asset, Equation 18.5 will be positive and the asset should be leased.

To illustrate lease evaluation, let's consider the example of SolarSound, which is considering whether to lease or purchase some specialized equipment. The capital budgeting analysis indicating the equipment should be secured has already been completed. The remaining question is whether to lease or purchase the equipment. The equipment has a 5-year economic and tax life, and straight line depreciation will be employed for tax purposes.[6] (The half-year convention will be ignored in determining the per year depreciation.) The equipment's resale value is zero, the marginal tax rate is 40 percent, and the firm's before-tax cost of borrowing is 12 percent. The equipment costs $40,000 if purchased, or it can be leased for 5 years at $10,000 per year. The first lease payment is payable in advance.

To determine how to finance the equipment, the first step SolarSound undertakes is to calculate its after-tax cost of debt, k_i, which is the discount rate employed in Equation 18.5. Because k_b is 12 percent and the marginal tax rate is 40 percent, $k_i = k_b(1 - T) = 12\%(1 - 0.40) = 7.20$ percent. This is the discount rate that neutralizes the risk in terms of the after-tax cash flows under the two financing methods, and it should be used in the NPV_{lease} analysis as follows:

$$NPV_{\text{lease}} = \begin{array}{c} \text{cost of} \\ \text{the asset} \end{array} - \left(\begin{array}{c} \text{present value of} \\ \text{the lease payments} \end{array} + \begin{array}{c} \text{present value of the forgone} \\ \text{depreciation tax shield} \end{array} \right)$$

$$= \$40,000 - \left(\$10,000(1 - 0.40)\left\{ \frac{1}{0.072} - \frac{1}{0.072(1 + 0.072)^5} \right\}(1 + 0.072) \right.$$

$$\left. + \$8,000(0.40)\left\{ \frac{1}{0.072} - \frac{1}{0.072(1 + 0.072)^5} \right\} \right)$$

$$NPV_{\text{lease}} = \$40,000 - (\$26,232 + \$13,051) = \$717$$

Because the net present value of leasing versus purchasing is positive, SolarSound should lease the assets.

THE EQUIVALENT LOAN METHOD

An alternative approach to the lease versus purchase decision is the **equivalent loan method**, which calculates the per period equivalent loan that is exactly equal to the

---

[6] Remember that for tax purposes all assets are depreciated to zero over their normal recovery period.

after-tax cash flows experienced with the lease. In our example the leasing cash flows for each period are as follows:

	Year					
	0	**1**	**2**	**3**	**4**	**5**
1. Cost of leased asset	40,000					
2. After-tax lease payment, $L(1 - T)$	− 6,000	−6,000	−6,000	−6,000	−6,000	
3. Lost depreciation tax shield, $Dep(T)$		−3,200	−3,200	−3,200	−3,200	−3,200
4. Net cash flow from leasing	− 34,000	−9,200	−9,200	−9,200	−9,200	−3,200

We must now determine the size of a loan that in each period produces exactly these same net cash flows. In other words, the after-tax payments on the equivalent loan will be $9,200 from $t = 1$ through $t = 4$ and $3,200 at $t = 5$. To calculate the equivalent loan, we begin at year 5. The amount borrowed at the beginning of each year is determined as follows:

amount borrowed $t = 4$ is $3,200/(1 + 0.072) = \$2,985.07$
amount borrowed $t = 3$ is ($2,985.07 + $9,200)/1.072 = \$11,366.67$
amount borrowed $t = 2$ is ($11,366.67 + $9,200)/1.072 = \$19,185.33$
amount borrowed $t = 1$ is ($19,185.33 + $9,200)/1.072 = \$26,478.85$
amount borrowed $t = 0$ is ($26,478.85 + $9,200)/1.072 = \$33,282.51$

The cash flows from the loan for years 1 through 5 that make them equivalent to the cash flows from borrowing are then calculated as shown in Table 18.3. To do this, we compute the exact after-tax interest cash outflows along with the principal repayments. As the table shows, the equivalent loan has exactly the same cash outflows in years 1 through 5 as the lease payments calculated above. Now all that is necessary is to show the difference in the two sets of cash flows—the cash flows from leasing minus those from the equivalent loan:

	Year					
	0	**1**	**2**	**3**	**4**	**5**
1. Net cash flow from leasing	34,000.00	−9,200	−9,200	−9,200	−9,200	−3,200
2. Net cash flow from borrowing	33,282.51	−9,200	−9,200	−9,200	−9,200	−3,200
3. NPV (row 1 − row 2)	717.49	0	0	0	0	0

Table 18.3

The Net Cash Flows from the Equivalent Loan

The principal repayments in row 4 are determined by $33,282.51 − $26,478.85 = $6,803.66, and so forth. The calculations to determine the cash flows with the equivalent loan are analogous to what was done in Chapter 14 when the adjusted present value and flows-to-equity were computed.

	Year					
	0	1	2	3	4	5
1. Amount borrowed at beginning of the year	33,282.51	26,478.85	19,185.33	11,366.67	2,985.07	
2. Interest at 12 percent (lagged one year)		−3,993.90	−3,177.46	−2,302.24	−1,364.00	− 358.21
3. After-tax interest (row 2) × 0.60		−2,396.34	−1,906.48	−1,381.34	− 818.40	− 214.93
4. Principal repaid: difference in successive amounts from (row 1) above		−6,803.66	−7,293.52	−7,818.66	−8,381.60	−2,985.07
5. Net cash flow from borrowing: (row 1) for year 0; (row 3) + (row 4) for years 1 to 5	+33,282.51	−9,200.00	−9,200.00	−9,200.00	−9,200.00	−3,200.00

Because the cash flows are equal in years 1 through 5, we are left with the difference between the net cash flow from leasing at $t = 0$ and the equivalent borrowing, also at time $t = 0$. This net present value of $717.49 ≈ $717 is the same as we calculated previously with the NPV_{lease} approach using the after-tax discount rate of 7.20 percent.

In general, calculating the NPV_{lease} using the after-tax discount rate is easier than the equivalent loan method. However, if the firm is in a temporary non-tax-paying position, the equivalent loan method may be more appropriate, because the tax rate can more easily be adjusted upward once the firm becomes profitable again.

SOME COMPLICATIONS

With either the NPV_{lease} or the equivalent loan procedure, evaluating the leasing decision is straightforward. In addition, the methods are practical to employ and theoretically correct, because they focus on which means of financing is more consistent with the firm's goal. With either of these approaches, complications often encountered can be readily incorporated into the analysis. To illustrate these complications we use the NPV_{lease} approach, but the equivalent loan could also be employed.

Two primary complications often occur—incremental operating costs, O_t, if an asset is purchased, and the estimated resale value, RV_n, if the asset is purchased. With these complications the NPV_{lease} equation becomes

$$NPV_{\text{lease}} = CLA_0 - \left\{ \left[\sum_{t=1}^{n} \frac{L_t(1-T)}{(1+k_i)^t} \right] (1+k_i) \right.$$
$$\left. + \sum_{t=1}^{n} \frac{Dep_t(T)}{(1+k_i)^t} - \sum_{t=1}^{n} \frac{O_t(1-T)}{(1+k)^t} + \frac{RV_n(1-T)}{(1+k)^n} \right\} \tag{18.6}$$

The appropriate opportunity cost of capital for the asset in question, k, is employed for discounting the incremental operating expenses and resale value, because risk neutralization does not extend to these items. If the asset's risk is equal to the average firm risk, then k is the firm's opportunity cost of capital.[7]

FINDING THE PERCENTAGE COST OF A LEASE

Instead of solving for the NPV_{lease} or equivalent loan, it is also possible to determine the percentage annual cost of the lease. This step involves solving for the internal rate of return, rather than the net present value. To solve for the cost of the lease, we can rearrange Equation 18.5 as follows:

$$CLA_0 - L_0(1-T) = \sum_{t=1}^{n} \frac{L_t(1-T)}{(1+IRR)^t} + \sum_{t=1}^{n} \frac{Dep_t(T)}{(1+IRR)^t} \tag{18.7}$$

Note that because the lease payments are payable in advance, the after-tax outlay associated with the initial payment, L_0, is subtracted from the cost of the leased asset, CLA_0. We then solve for the unknown percentage rate, IRR. This is the after-tax cost of the lease. The decision rule is as follows:

1. If cost of leasing, IRR, is less than cost of debt, k_i, accept.
2. If cost of leasing is greater than cost of debt, reject.
3. If cost of leasing is equal to cost of debt, you are indifferent.

Note that this relationship is exactly *opposite* that used in making capital budgeting decisions. The reason is that we are comparing cash outflows instead of cash inflows. Here, if the IRR is less than the specified rate, we accept; previously, it was just the reverse.

To illustrate this calculation, consider the lease for SolarSound. The left-hand side of Equation 18.7 is

$$CLA_0 - L_0(1-T) = \$40,000 - \$6,000 = \$34,000$$

[7] These topics are examined in Problems 18.10, 18.13, and 18.15.

The cash flows for the right-hand side are $9,200 for years 1 through 4 and $3,200 for year 5. Solving for the internal rate of return, which is the effective after-tax percentage cost of the lease, we get 6.32 percent. Because this cost is less than SolarSound's after-tax cost of debt of 7.20 percent, we make the same decision as before: lease the asset.

Concept Review Questions

- What are two primary ways to accomplish risk neutralization of cash flows between leasing and borrowing?
- In what situation would the equivalent loan method be more appropriate than the after-tax discount rate method when calculating the NPV of a lease?
- Describe how to calculate the annual percentage cost of a lease.

KEY POINTS

1. Leasing is a major source of long-term financing. Tax implications and options to expand and cancel, along with value-added services, explain why leasing is increasingly popular.
2. Leasing places a financial obligation on the firm similar to debt.
3. Financial leases are evaluated by lessees based on the net present value of leasing versus purchasing the assets, using the after-tax cost of debt capital as the discount rate. This framework separates the capital budgeting (or investment) decision from the financing decision. Alternatively, the equivalent loan method or internal rate of return provide the same decision as the NPV_{lease} decision criterion.
4. Incremental operating expenses for a purchased asset make leasing more attractive, whereas purchasing becomes more attractive if assets are expected to have some resale value at the end of the lease. A higher discount rate, which reflects the risk of the asset, should be employed when evaluating the effects of estimated resale values or incremental operating expenses.

QUESTIONS

18.1   How does FASB No. 13, "Accounting for Leases," reduce the ability of firms to employ off-balance-sheet financing? Should a firm benefit by this financing?

18.2   What factors (both those discussed in the model covered by Equations 18.1 through 18.4 and others) affect the lease rates quoted by lessors? In which direction—an increase or a decrease in the quoted rate—does each affect lease rates?

18.3   Explain some of the valid and some of the dubious reasons for leasing.

18.4   How do capital budgeting and financing decisions, to lease or buy, interact? Be sure to discuss the case in which the capital budgeting NPV is negative while the NPV_{lease} is positive.

18.5   Explain why it is important to neutralize risk in terms of the cash flow obligations of the firm when conducting a lease or buy analysis. How does the after-tax cost of debt, k_i, relate to this issue?

18.6   The NPV_{lease} equation is

$$NPV_{lease} = CLA_0 - \left\{ \left[\sum_{t=1}^{n} \frac{L_t(1-T)}{(1+k_i)^t} \right](1+k_i) + \sum_{t=1}^{n} \frac{Dep_t(T)}{(1+k_i)^t} \right\}$$

Explain what each of the terms represents.

18.7   Explain the calculations needed to determine the equivalent loan, and why the equivalent loan method leads to the some decision reached with NPV_{lease} and the percentage cost of leasing methods.

CONCEPT REVIEW PROBLEMS

See Appendix A for solutions.

CR18.1   Medical Equipment Rental is leasing ultrasound machines to physical therapy departments across the country. The firm has asked you to recommend an appropriate advance *monthly* rental fee. The cost of a machine is $32,000, it will be depreciated using straight line over 5 years, and it has no expected resale value. (*Note:* Ignore the half-year convention when calculating depreciation.) If the tax rate is 40 percent and the before-tax cost of debt 9 percent, what is the monthly rental fee?

CR18.2   Employee Temp is considering purchasing or leasing laptop computers and portable printers for their employees. The computers and printers cost $50,000, have an economic life of 5 years, will be depreciated using straight line depreciation, and have zero resale value. (*Note:* Ignore the half-year convention when calculating depreciation.) The firm's cost of debt is 12 percent, and its tax rate is 35 percent. If the lease payments are $11,000 per year in advance, what is the net present value of leasing the equipment?

CR18.3   Torbort Products is planning to replace its fleet of sales reps' cars. The firm can borrow funds at a rate of 12 percent and purchase the fleet for $200,000, or rent the fleet for $70,000 per year payable in advance. The economic life of the cars is 3 years, they will be depreciated using straight line depreciation, and their resale value is zero. (*Note:* Ignore the half-year convention when calculating depreciation.) The firm's tax rate is 36 percent. Using the equivalent loan method, find the net present value of leasing the fleet.

CR18.4   BCI needs a crane that costs $100,000. The firm could borrow funds to purchase the crane at a before-tax cost of 14 percent or could rent the crane for $25,000 per year with the first payment made at $t = 0$. The crane has an economic life of 5 years with a resale value of $40,000 at $t = 5$, and it will be depreciated using straight line depreciation. (*Note:* Ignore the half-year convention when calculating depreciation.) If the crane is purchased, annual property taxes of $4,000 will be assessed to BCI. The firm's opportunity cost of capital is 18 percent, and its tax rate is 30 percent. Should BCI lease the crane?

CR18.5   Markel Partnerships owns several professional office complexes. Recognizing the trend for office complexes to have both small trees and large planter greenery, Markel's is analyzing an offer from a local greenhouse. Lease payments would be $6,000 per year payable in advance. The trees and plants could be purchased for $25,000 with an expected life of 5 years and no resale value. Straight line depreciation is used. (*Note:* Ignore the half-year convention when calculating depreciation.) Markel's tax rate is 40 percent. What is the percentage cost of leasing? If Markel's after-tax cost of debt is 8 percent, should Markel purchase or lease the plants?

PROBLEMS

18.1   Coyne Financial is setting lease rates for two pieces of equipment:

	Loader	Digger
CLA_0	$600,000	$900,000
Normal recovery period	5 years	3 years

Depreciation is straight line over the normal recovery period. (*Note:* Ignore the half-year convention when calculating depreciation.) If the lease payments are made at the beginning of each period (that is, $t = 0$, $t = 1$, etc.), Coyne's marginal tax rate is 35 percent, and its-before-tax return on debt-type investments is 16.92 percent, what lease rate, L, should be quoted on each piece of equipment?

18.2   TFX Leasing is assessing the impact of a number of different factors on the lease rates it quotes. Assume that the asset costs $350,000 and that it will be depreciated over its 5-year normal recovery period via straight-line. (*Note:* Ignore the half-year convention when calculating depreciation.) If TFX's marginal tax rate is 40 percent, determine the lease rate in each case below. (*Note:* Assume each part is independent of the other parts.)

a.   TFX's required *after-tax* return on debt-type investments is 8 percent.
b.   TFX's required after-tax return on debt-type investments is 10 percent.
c.   TFX's required after-tax rate of return on debt-type investments is 8 percent, and the estimated before-tax resale value is $50,000. {*Note:* In calculating the present value of the resale value, use $RV_n(1 - T)\left[\dfrac{1}{k} - \dfrac{1}{k(1 + k)^n}\right]$ where $RV_n = $50,000$ and the opportunity cost of capital, k, is 14 percent. The present value of the resale value, along with the present value of the depreciation, is subtracted from CLA_0 in Equation 18.2 to determine the net amount recoverable from lease payments.}

18.3   Vermont Capital is setting lease rates for a $600,000 asset with a 3-year normal recovery period using straight line depreciation. (*Note:* Ignore the half-year convention when calculating depreciation.) Vermont's tax rate is 40 percent and its before-tax required rate of return on debt-type investments is 10 percent. Determine the lease rate under the following conditions:

a.   The annual lease payments are payable in advance. (*Note:* The payments occur at $t = 0$, $t = 1$, and $t = 2$, respectively.)
b.   The lease payments are semiannual and made in advance. (*Note:* Continue to use annual depreciation.)

18.4   Norton Industries needs three trucks that cost $100,000 in total. Saveway Leasing has offered to lease the trucks to Norton for a total of $25,000 per year for each of 5 years, with the lease payments payable in advance. Norton will depreciate the trucks via straight line depreciation over their 5-year normal recovery period, the firm's marginal tax rate is 30 percent, and Norton's before-tax cost of debt is 10 percent. (*Note:* Ignore the half-year convention when calculating depreciation.) Should Norton lease or purchase the trucks? (Assume that the capital budgeting decision has already been made and the acquisition of the trucks is desirable.)

18.5   Central Trust Bank has just completed a capital budgeting analysis on some automatic teller units. The conclusion was that the bank should acquire the units. They cost $250,000 and have a 3-year economic and tax life; straight line depreciation will be employed if they are purchased. (*Note:* Ignore the half-year convention when calculating depreciation.) Central Trust Bank has a 35 percent marginal tax rate, and its before-tax borrowing cost is 13.85 percent. Consider whether Central Trust Bank should purchase or lease the automatic tellers in each case below.

a.   The lease payment is $100,000 for each of 3 years, payable in advance. (*Note:* The payments occur at $t = 0$, $t = 1$, and $t = 2$.)

b.   The lease payment is $100,000 for each of 3 years, payable at the end of each year. (*Note:* The payment occurs at $t = 1$, $t = 2$, and $t = 3$.)

c.   The lease rate is $90,000 for each of 3 years, payable at the beginning of each year ($t = 0$ through $t = 2$).

18.6   After completing a capital budgeting analysis, Great Pacific Railroad recently purchased some railroad cars for $10 million. The cars will be depreciated over their 10-year normal recovery period employing straight line depreciation. (*Note:* Ignore the half-year convention when calculating depreciation.) Rebecca, one of the firm's directors, suggested that Great Pacific investigate a sale and leaseback agreement for the railroad cars, as many other railroads are doing. Upon checking, you find the railroad cars can be sold for $10 million and then leased back for 10 years at $1.6 million per year, with the lease payments being made in advance. Great Pacific's marginal tax rate is 40 percent and its before-tax cost of borrowing is 16.67 percent.

a.   Should Great Pacific enter into the sale and leaseback agreement?

b.   What is the maximum lease payment Great Pacific should be willing to pay?

18.7   Union Mutual is thinking about buying or leasing a piece of used equipment. It is still in good shape and can be used for another 5 years. The equipment will be depreciated over its 5-year normal recovery period via straight line depreciation, the firm's tax rate is 30 percent, and the before-tax cost of borrowing is 14.30 percent. (*Note:* Ignore the half-year convention when calculating depreciation.) The equipment will cost $2 million, but it can be leased for $540,000 per year, payable at the beginning of each of the 5 years.

a.   If the capital budgeting NPV is positive, should Union Mutual lease or purchase the equipment?

b.   Rework (a) if 10 semiannual lease payments of $270,000 each (payable at the beginning of each 6-month period) are made. (*Note:* Continue to use annual depreciation.)

18.8   A piece of equipment costs $300,000 and has a 5-year normal recovery period. For capital budgeting purposes the after-tax cash flows, CF, are estimated to be $98,000 per year, the firm's marginal tax rate is 40 percent, and the opportunity cost of capital is 16 percent. Straight line depreciation will be employed, the lease rate, L, is $90,000 each year (at the beginning of the year) for 5 years, and the after-tax cost of borrowing, k_i, is 9 percent. (*Note:* Ignore the half-year convention when calculating depreciation.)

a.   Should the use of the equipment be acquired?

b.   After answering (a), determine if it should be leased or purchased.

18.9 John Evans Labs is investigating whether new laboratory equipment is needed. The equipment, which requires an initial investment of $550,000, has a 3-year normal recovery period and will be depreciated via straight line depreciation. (*Note:* Ignore the half-year convention when calculating depreciation.) The net cash flows before taxes, CFBT, are $285,000 for each of 3 years. The firm's tax rate is 40 percent, and the appropriate discount rate is 14 percent.

a. Should John Evans acquire the new laboratory equipment?
b. After deciding the equipment should be acquired, John Evans is now considering whether to lease or purchase it. The lease would be $215,000 for each of 3 years, payable in advance. John Evans estimates its before-tax cost of borrowing is 15 percent. Should John Evans lease or purchase the equipment? [*Note:* Because the discount rate changes, the present value of the depreciation tax shield in (b) is different from that determined in (a).]
c. What decision should John Evans make in (b) if the capital budgeting net present value determined in (a) was −$15,000? Discuss the logic behind this decision.

18.10 Guaranteed Benefit is evaluating whether to lease or purchase an asset that has a positive capital budgeting NPV. The following basic conditions exist: CLA_0 is $210,000, n is 3, depreciation is straight line, T is 35 percent, L is $82,000, k_i is 11 percent, lease payments are made annually in advance, and k is 15 percent. (*Note:* Ignore the half-year convention when calculating depreciation.)

a. Determine the base case NPV_{lease}.
b. Determine the effect of the following conditions on the lease versus purchase decision for Guaranteed Benefit. (*Note:* Each part is independent of the other parts.)
   (1) If the asset is purchased, Guaranteed will incur incremental operating costs of $5,000 (before taxes) per year.
   (2) If the asset is purchased, Guaranteed estimates the before-tax resale value will be $40,000.

c. Independent of (a) and (b), suppose CLA_0 is $325,000, L is $90,000, n is 5, depreciation is straight line, k_i is 13 percent, and k is 16 percent. (*Note:* Ignore the half-year convention when calculating depreciation.) If the asset is purchased, Guaranteed will incur incremental operating costs of $10,000 (before taxes) per year. Finally, Guaranteed estimates the before-tax resale value will be $75,000. Should Guaranteed lease or purchase the asset?

18.11 Quality Leasing needs to set a lease rate on the following equipment: CLA is $200,000, n is 5 years, depreciation is straight line, T is 40 percent, k_b is 15 percent, and lease payments are made at the beginning of the year. (*Note:* Ignore the half-year convention when calculating depreciation.)

a. Determine the lease rate Quality Leasing will quote. (*Note:* Carry the lease rate to two decimal places.)
b. Parkland Distributors needs to lease the equipment. Determine the NPV_{lease} if everything is the same as for Quality, and L is as determined in (a).

18.12 Atlanta Trucking is evaluating the lease or purchase of some over-the-road rigs. The rigs cost $12 million, and the lease is $4 million for each of 4 years on an annual basis, payable in advance. Atlanta's before-tax cost of borrowing is 14 percent, and the marginal tax rate is 40 percent. For simplicity, assume the rigs can be depreciated to zero for tax purposes using straight line depreciation over 4 years and there is no half-year convention.

a. Should the rigs be leased or purchased (assuming that the capital budgeting decision has been made and is positive)?

b. Now employ the equivalent loan method and show that you get the same answer as in (a).

18.13 Marsh Distributors is considering a lease arrangement as a means of acquiring the use of some new equipment. The equipment costs $150,000 and has a 3-year normal recovery period, and straight line depreciation will be employed. (*Note:* Ignore the half-year convention when calculating depreciation.) If purchased, the *after-tax* resale value will be $10,000. The marginal tax rate is 30 percent, the appropriate opportunity cost of capital, k, is 14 percent, and the before-tax cost of debt is 11.43 percent. If the three lease payments are made in advance, what is the maximum lease payment Marsh can make and still lease the asset? Assume the NPV is positive.

18.14 LTI has decided to acquire a new computer which the capital budgeting analysis indicates is economically justified. The cost of the computer is $500,000, and it can be leased at $120,000 per year with the five annual payments made in advance. LTI's before-tax cost of debt is 10 percent, the marginal tax rate is 30 percent, and the computer will be depreciated over 5 years via straight line. (*Note:* Ignore the half-year convention when calculating depreciation.)

a. By computing the percentage cost of the lease, determine whether LTI should lease or purchase the computer.

b. Without calculating it, is the NPV_{lease} positive or negative? Why?

c. What is LTI's percentage cost of the lease if it does not expect to be profitable for the next 5 years? Should it lease or buy the asset? (*Note:* Assume that there is no carryback or carryforward and that the capital budgeting NPV is still positive.)

18.15 **Mini Case** Cantronics Systems is a medium-sized firm that specializes in energy- and cost-effective waste management systems. It has traditionally purchased equipment but is now considering leasing a new Systemease. Your job is to advise Cantronics on how to proceed.

a. The head of the accounting department is concerned about the impact of leasing on the firm's balance sheet. Briefly, how will the lease be treated? Explain why it is the tax treatment and not the accounting treatment that is important.

b. From the lessor's standpoint, what factors determine the lease rate quoted?

c. From the lessee's standpoint, why might Cantronics lease Systemease, instead of purchasing it?

d. The following information has been estimated for Systemease: The initial investment will be $1,400,000, and training expenses of $150,000 are required, which will be deductible for tax purposes. The normal recovery period is 7 years, and straight line depreciation will be employed. (*Note:* Ignore the half-year convention when calculating depreciation.) The net cash flows before taxes are $500,000 each year, the firm's marginal tax rate is 35 percent, and the appropriate opportunity cost of capital is 17 percent. Cantronics' before-tax cost of borrowing is 18.46 percent, and Systemease can be leased for $315,000 per year payable in advance.

(1) Should Cantronics acquire Systemease?

(2) Should it lease or purchase Systemease? (*Note:* Ignore the training expenses when calculating the NPV_{lease} because they have to be paid by the firm with either leasing or purchasing.)

(3) Instead of the NPV_{lease} as in (2), what is the percentage cost of leasing?

e. Assume everything is the same as in (d) except now you find out there is a resale value at the end of the life of Systemease of $100,000, and additional maintenance charges of $30,000 per year before taxes will be required if Cantronics purchases Systemease. What decisions should now be made (in terms of acquiring or not acquiring the system, and leasing versus purchasing)? [*Note:* The additional maintenance should be included in both the capital budgeting and the lease versus purchase calculations.]

REFERENCES

For an examination of different types of leases, see:

COPELAND, THOMAS E., and J. FRED WESTON. "A Note on the Evaluation of Cancelable Operating Leases." *Financial Management* 11 (Summer 1982): 60–67.

GRIMLUND, RICHARD D., and ROBERT CAPETTINI. "A Note on the Evaluation of Leveraged Leases and Other Investments." *Financial Management* 11 (Summer 1982): 68–72.

SLOVIN, MYRON B., MARIE E. SUSHKA, and JOHN A. POLONCHEK. "Corporate Sale-and-Leasebacks and Shareholder Wealth." *Journal of Finance* 45 (March 1990): 289–99.

For theoretical, empirical, and practical aspects of leasing, see:

FINUCANE, THOMAS J. "Some Empirical Evidence on the Use of Financial Leases." *Journal of Financial Research* 11 (Winter 1988): 321–33.

FRANKS, JULIAN R., and STEWART D. HODGES. "Lease Valuation When Taxable Earnings Are a Scarce Resource." *Journal of Finance* 42 (September 1987): 987–1005.

LEASE, RONALD C., JOHN J. McCONNELL, and JAMES S. SCHALLHEIM. "Realized Returns and the Default and Prepayment Experience of Financial Leasing Contracts." *Financial Management* 19 (Summer 1990): 11–20.

LEWIS, CRAIG M., and JAMES S. SCHALLHEIM. "Are Debt and Leases Substitutes?" *Journal of Financial and Quantitative Analysis* 27 (December 1992): 497–511.

MUKHERJEE, TARUN K. "A Survey of Corporate Leasing Analysis." *Financial Management* 20 (Autumn 1991): 96–107.

SCHALLHEIM, JAMES S., RAMON E. JOHNSON, RONALD C. LEASE, and JOHN J. McCONNELL. "The Determinants of Yields on Financial Leasing Contracts." *Journal of Financial Economics* 19 (September 1987): 45–67.

Short-Term Financial Management

EXECUTIVE INTERVIEW

William J. Sinkula
Executive Vice President
and Chief Financial Officer
The Kroger Co.

The Kroger Co. owns grocery and convenience stores as well as manufacturing plants that produce private-label goods for its stores. We asked Mr. Sinkula to tell us how working capital is managed in the food merchandising industry.

Short-term, or working, capital management differs from company to company. For some, receivables management is the key; for others, it's inventory management. In food merchandising, managing cash and accounts payable are the most important aspects of working capital management.

The Kroger Co.'s working capital management changed considerably after 1988, when both Kohlberg, Kravis, and Roberts (KKR) and the Dart Group tried to take us over. As a takeover defense, we borrowed $4 billion and paid it out as a dividend to our shareholders. This action served as a successful defense against the raiders but made us a very highly leveraged company.

As a result, working capital management became more important to us. Before 1988, we managed the company from the income statement; we were pretty passive about working capital management. Since then, we manage from the balance sheet and cash flow statement, and debt ratios and working capital management now have a higher profile in the company.

Working Capital Policies at Kroger

For both our merchandising and manufacturing operations, the emphasis is the same—to operate with a minimum amount of net working capital. We focus first on accounts payable; cash ranks second; accounts receivable is third. Kroger has good purchasing power and can generally get favorable credit terms. Although we prefer a cash discount to extended payment terms, we analyze our options and choose the better alternative from a cash flow standpoint.

In our industry, managing inventories involves not just reducing the dollar investment but also allocating shelf space to products customers want. The customer is the driving force governing inventory levels. We also use a technique called forward-buying to prepurchase inventory. Manufacturers that sell to our industry run frequent price promotions, at well below list price. We invest as much as $150 million in forward-buy inventories. The key is to buy enough product to last until the next promotion. Although we have to store the inventory, quite often in outside facilities at extra cost, promotion prices are so deep that we can still earn a very good return.

Cash Management

It's extremely important for us to manage our cash efficiently; our cash position can change by $70 million to $100 million in a couple of days. When weekends or holidays tie up cash in the stores, we have incredible swings in cash levels. So we have a working capital agreement with more than forty major domestic and international banks to cover any shortfalls until we can clear the receipts. Then we transfer those funds from a bank in the same geographic area as the store to the main collection account at our primary bank. To speed the clearing process we now encode checks right in the stores. Knowing the level of expected shortfalls and surpluses is critical. As a highly leveraged company, we don't want to borrow money and then find out we have excess funds to invest overnight at a low rate like 2 1/2 percent.

In terms of managing float, we focus on collection float, because we receive large numbers of checks. Three days' of receipts tied up in the stores that aren't yet useful funds is a lot of money. We no longer use a disbursing bank in a remote location to increase float, but we have four different disbursement banks. The check-clearing pattern on each of those banks is fairly predictable, which allows us to know what's going to clear on a particular day and to plan for short-term financing if required.

Because we are in a cash-oriented business, accounts receivable are not a dominant factor for Kroger. Most of our receivables are due from the same people to whom we owe money—our suppliers—for promotional allowances and vendor coupons. We collect billions of vendor coupons in our stores, send them to be counted, and then get the money back. To reduce our receivables, we use accounts receivable and payable software that offsets the receivables against the payables.

Short-Term Financing and Banking Relationships

Our primary short-term financing arrangement, an $850 million working capital line, is part of a bank revolving credit and term loan agreement from a syndicate of banks. All of our assets are pledged on our bank credit agreement.

We negotiated three special features into the working capital portion. First, we can issue unrated commercial paper, up to the whole $850 million. Instead of borrowing from the banks under the interest rate formula, we can borrow at commercial paper rates and typically save 40 or 50 basis points. The unrated commercial paper markets tend to be very short-term, primarily overnight, but we have been able get 60- and 90-day maturities when necessary.

We also negotiated a competitive bid agreement with our bank syndicate. Banks have the option of bidding the rate at which they would lend us money for 1 to 30 days. We accept bids up to the highest rate we're willing to pay. All banks receive the highest rate we accept (much like the auction process for Treasury bills). Last year, we had about $200 million outstanding under the competitive bid agreement, in addition to our commercial paper borrowings.

Another feature that's been a marvelous help is the step-down provision: as our coverage of interest payments improves, our spread over the base (prime) rate or the Eurodollar rate (LIBOR) decreases. For example, when our cash interest coverage ratio is below 1.75:1, the margin over base rate is 3/4 of 1 percent and 1 3/4 percent over LIBOR. Right now we're paying 1 percent over LIBOR, because our coverage ratio is above 2.50:1.

As a company, we work very hard to keep our banks informed. We invite our bankers to the annual shareholders' meeting, host a dinner for them with the board of directors, have a full informational meeting, and take them to visit stores. Sometimes we talk about finance, other times, about operations. The better the bankers understand our business, the more responsive they'll be to our needs.

Decisions in three crucial areas directly affect the value of the firm—its investment decisions, its financing decisions, and its short-term (or day-to-day) financial management decisions. In Chapter 19 we examine the primary factors that are at play when a firm determines its short-term financial management policy. Then in Chapter 20 we look at cash and marketable securities, followed by accounts receivable and inventory in Chapter 21. Chapter 22 shifts to the sources of short-term financing, and then in Chapter 23 we examine the steps firms can and are taking to hedge themselves against changes in interest rates.

19 Short-Term Financial Management Policy

EXECUTIVE SUMMARY

Effective management of current assets and current liabilities is at the core of financial management. Firms that are efficient devote much time and attention to short-term financial management. By doing so they are able to manage this portion of the firm's assets and liabilities in a manner that contributes to the overall goal of maximizing the value of the firm. Although there is much less theory to drive the firm's short-term financial management decisions than in the areas of capital budgeting, capital structure, and the like, the same forces of incremental cash flows, risks, and opportunity costs are at play when a firm's short-term financial management decisions are made.

To understand short-term financial management policy, it is important to understand the firm's cash cycle. Both the asset and the liability sides may be managed in an aggressive or a conservative manner. One guideline is the matching principle, whereby temporary assets are financed with temporary financing, and permanent current and long-term assets are financed with permanent financing. Other things being equal, aggressive asset management lowers costs, whereas aggressive liability management lowers cash outflows related to interest. Both have the effect of increasing the returns, but they also increase the risk exposure of the firm.

Short-term financial management is not a one-time decision. The best strategy may vary, depending on the season of the year, the level of interest rates, or the stage of the business cycle. It is a dynamic area; the firm must be responsive to ongoing needs and goals, the state of the economy, trends in marketing and production, and the risks involved. As these factors change, the firm's short-term financial management policies must also change.

MANAGING SHORT-TERM ASSETS AND LIABILITIES

A firm's assets are normally classified as either current or long-term. Current assets are those expected to be converted into cash within 1 year. They are cash and marketable securities, accounts receivable, inventory, and other current assets such as prepaid expenses. Liabilities also are split between current and long-term, with current liabilities those expected to be paid within 1 year. Current liabilities include short-term debt, accounts payable, and other current liabilities such as accruals and the current portion of long-term debt. Sometimes the term **working capital** is used to refer to both current assets and current liabilities. Thus, short-term financial management, or working capital management, focuses on the coordinated control of the firm's current assets and current liabilities.

SHORT-TERM FINANCIAL MANAGEMENT DECISIONS

To gain some understanding of the types of decisions required in short-term financial management, consider Figure 19.1, which depicts the flow of cash through a firm. On the right-hand side of the figure are those long-term financial management areas that include capital investments, raising capital, and the related areas of determining the firm's opportunity cost of capital, capital structure, and dividend policy. The other aspect of financial management, which focuses on the short-term day-to-day activities of the firm, is depicted on the left-hand side of Figure 19.1. The basic short-term financial management decisions facing a firm include the following:

1. COLLECTIONS AND DISBURSEMENTS   One of the primary responsibilities of a firm is to manage the collection of funds from customers and to pay suppliers, employees, marketing costs, taxes, and so forth. This frequently includes the implementation of some type of cash and check collection system and the development of various systems for cost effectively making cash disbursements.
2. CASH CONCENTRATION   Managers also have the responsibility for designing and implementing a system to gather funds from many banks so they can be concentrated for effective management and investment purposes.
3. LIQUIDITY MANAGEMENT   The firm's liquidity—both on the asset side and the liability side—must also be managed. Liquidity management includes decisions regarding the synchronization of cash inflows and outflows, and determination of the expected surpluses or deficits of cash (via cash budgets as discussed in Chapter 25). Liquidity management also includes managing the firm's portfolio of short-term marketable securities and choosing the type and maturity structure of the firm's short-term borrowings.
4. BANK RELATIONS   Another responsibility is designing the firm's banking network and managing its banking relationships. This category includes determining which banks to deal with and the services that will be secured from each.

Figure 19.1

Flow of Cash Through a Firm

Both short-term and long-term financial management are important for achieving the goal of maximizing the value of the firm. Short-term financial management is more operationally focused and less theoretical than long-term financial management.

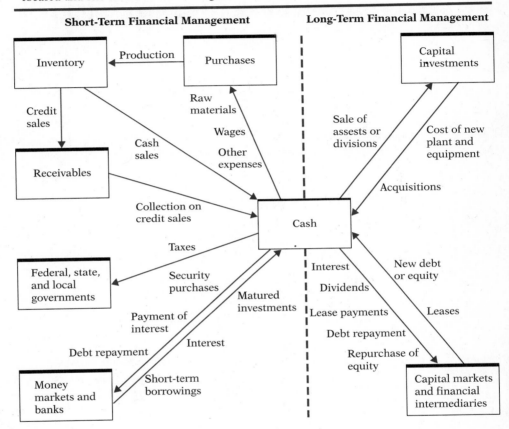

5. RECEIVABLES Management of the firm's credit policy and the resulting collection procedures is also important. Although basic credit terms and customers must be determined in conjunction with marketing personnel, the ultimate responsibility for implementation and maintenance falls in the short-term financial management area.

6. INVENTORY Inventory is the responsibility of many individuals within the firm. The major activities we are concerned with include determining how much investment in inventory is needed and how to finance it.

7. HEDGING Sophisticated firms increasingly manage, or hedge, some of their interest rate risk exposure through the use of financial instruments such as forward contracts, futures, interest rate swaps, and options.

We will examine each of these areas in Chapters 20 to 23. Before doing so, it is important to understand more about short-term financial management in general, why it is needed, and how firms can proceed with estimating how much in the way of current assets and current liabilities they need.

WHY DO FIRMS HAVE SHORT-TERM ASSETS AND LIABILITIES?

In a world of perfect markets where there are no transactions costs, no time delays in the production, marketing, and check-clearing system, and no financial distress costs, the value of the firm would be independent of its current asset and current liability decisions. If that were true, there would be no need to study short-term financial management.

But markets are not perfect. Imperfect markets, and delays and/or costs, are what create the need for a firm to concern itself with short-term financial management. Let's briefly consider some of the reasons why firms need current assets and current liabilities.

1. TRANSACTION COSTS   Transaction costs consist of (1) the service fees for buying and selling securities or (2) the potential loss in value when a "fire sale" must be made at a price below what could be received if more time was available. Because of transactions costs, firms hold cash or marketable securities with a major emphasis on liquidity—that is, the ability to be quickly and cheaply available as cash in order to meet short-term needs.
2. TIME DELAYS   Time delays arise in the production, marketing, and cash collection aspects of a firm's business. Because transactions do not happen instantaneously, many activities affect current asset and liability needs. These include (1) maintaining inventory (raw materials, work in process, or finished goods), (2) offering credit policies to help sell the product, (3) providing cash discounts for early payment, and (4) reducing the float when customers pay their bills. All these steps involve some costs that must be weighed against the benefits involved.
3. FINANCIAL DISTRESS COSTS   Financial distress costs include legal and other direct and indirect costs such as managerial time associated with reorganization, bankruptcy, or fending off financial difficulties. Because of the high cost most managers equate with financial distress, they tend to keep a significant amount of liquid balances, even though they generally earn less on these balances than on the firm's long-term asset investments. Alternatively, firms may incur costs to have access to credit markets, although they do not anticipate actually having to take advantage of this additional borrowing capacity.

Other items could be mentioned, but the point should be clear: In theory, short-term assets and liabilities are not needed; in practice, they become one of the most important topics managers must deal with. In this and the next four chapters, we'll see the importance of effective short-term financial management decisions in maximizing the value of the firm.

THE IMPORTANCE OF SHORT-TERM ASSETS AND LIABILITIES

Short-term assets and liabilities typically comprise a large part of a firm's total assets and liabilities. Consider the percentage breakdown of current assets and current liabilities (both compared to total assets) for manufacturing firms in 1986, 1989, and 1992[1]:

	1986	1989	1992
Current Assets			
Cash and marketable securities	6.2%	4.9%	4.8%
Accounts receivable	14.8	15.0	13.7
Inventory	16.3	15.4	13.7
Other	3.0	3.2	3.3
Total current assets	40.3%	38.5%	35.5%
Current Liabilities			
Short-term debt	3.9%	4.2%	4.3%
Accounts payable	7.9	7.8	7.5
Income tax payable	1.3	1.2	0.7
Current portion of long-term debt	1.4	1.8	2.1
Other	11.2	10.6	10.5
Total current liabilities	25.7%	25.6%	25.1%

Current assets account for about 40 percent of the total assets for manufacturing firms, whereas current liabilities comprise about 25 percent. Among current assets, the largest investment is in inventory and the second largest is in receivables. For current liabilities, the largest percentages are in the "other" category (which includes accruals) and in accounts payable. Comparing the 3 years, we see that investment in current assets decreased, while the amount of current liabilities remained relatively constant.

Some of the more significant reasons why short-term financial management is important are as follows:

1. The size and volatility of current assets and current liabilities make them a major managerial concern. Managers spend much of their time on the day-to-day activities that revolve around short-term financial management.
2. The relationship between sales growth, or growth opportunities, and short-term assets and liabilities is both close and direct. As sales increase, firms must increase inventory and accounts payable. Increased sales generate a higher level of accounts receivable. So current assets and liabilities must be managed as firms increase or decrease their scale of operations and sales. At the same time, some of the current liabilities—especially accounts payable—tend to increase and decrease sponta-

[1] Bureau of the Census, *Quarterly Financial Report for Manufacturing, Mining and Trade Corporations,* Second Quarter 1986, 1989, and 1992.

neously as inventory and accounts receivable increase and decrease. This **spontaneous short-term financing** (due to the use of trade credit as discussed in Chapter 20) must be kept in mind as we consider both the current assets and their financing (by both current and long-term sources).

3. Financial problems show up first in a firm's current assets and liability accounts, especially its level of accounts receivable, inventory, and the flow of cash into and out of the firm. Firms that are doing well maintain control of their accounts receivable and inventory and ensure the continual flow of cash.

4. Short-term assets and liabilities are especially important for smaller firms, because these firms often carry a higher percentage of both than do larger firms. Their survival is much more dependent on effective short-term financial management than that of larger firms.

Concept Review Questions

■ Explain the terms *current assets*, *current liabilities*, and *working capital*.

■ Why is short-term financial management important and necessary?

■ Give some examples of short-term financial management decisions a firm must make.

LIQUIDITY AND THE CASH CYCLE

Liquidity is an important factor in determining a firm's short-term financial management policies. It is a function of current asset and liability levels and composition, and the ability to raise cash when needed. The variability in current asset and liability levels is also important; however, for many firms the ongoing level of current assets and liabilities is fairly steady. Accordingly, we focus our primary attention on the level, not the variability, of the firm's current assets and current liabilities. Marketable securities, which are short-term investments for excess cash, are highly liquid. Accounts receivable, which arise from the sale of the firm's goods or services, are less liquid than marketable securities. Inventory is a current asset but is often less liquid than accounts receivable.

Liquidity has two major aspects—ongoing liquidity and protective liquidity. **Ongoing liquidity** refers to the inflows and outflows of cash through the firm as the product acquisition, production, sales, payment, and collection process takes place over time. **Protective liquidity** refers to the ability to adjust rapidly to unforeseen cash demands and to have backup means available to raise cash. We begin by addressing ongoing liquidity and defer a discussion of protective liquidity until later in the chapter.

The firm's ongoing liquidity is a function of its cash cycle. (The cash cycle is shown in the upper left part of Figure 19.1.) As raw materials are purchased, the firm's current liabilities increase through accounts payable. Subsequently, the firm pays for these purchases. During the same time, the raw materials are converted into finished goods through the production process. After reaching the finished goods inventory, they can be sold—for cash or on credit. In the latter case, accounts receivable are created.

Figure 19.2

Cash Conversion Cycle for a Typical Firm

By integrating both current assets and current liabilities, the cash conversion cycle emphasizes the firm's ongoing liquidity.

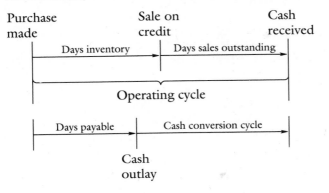

Finally, the accounts receivable are collected, resulting in cash. Ongoing liquidity is influenced by all aspects of the cash cycle, because increases in purchases, inventory, or receivables will decrease liquidity. A decrease in any of the three, other things being equal, will increase ongoing liquidity.

A helpful way to look at the cash flow for the firm is to analyze the firm's cash conversion cycle. A **cash conversion cycle** reflects the net time interval in days between actual cash expenditures of the firm on productive resources and the ultimate recovery of cash. As shown in Figure 19.2, once the purchase of the raw materials is made, the **days inventory** determines the average number of days it takes to produce and sell the product. The **days sales outstanding** determines the average number of days it takes to collect credit sales. The **operating cycle,** which is

$$\text{operating cycle} = \text{days sales outstanding} + \text{days inventory} \qquad (19.1)$$

measures the total number of days from purchase to the time when cash is received. Because the raw materials typically are not paid for immediately, we must also determine how long the firm defers its payments. The difference between the operating cycle and the **days payable** is the cash conversion cycle:

$$\text{cash conversion cycle} = \text{operating cycle} - \text{days payable} \qquad (19.2)$$

As the cash conversion cycle lengthens, the firm's ongoing liquidity worsens; as the cycle is shortened, the firm's ongoing liquidity improves.

To determine a cash conversion cycle, we employ the following steps:

STEP 1:   Calculate the **receivables turnover,** which is:

$$\text{receivables turnover} = \frac{\text{sales}}{\text{accounts receivable}} \tag{19.3}$$

STEP 2:   Calculate the **inventory turnover:**

$$\text{inventory turnover} = \frac{\text{cost of goods sold}}{\text{inventory}} \tag{19.4}$$

STEP 3:   Determine the **payables turnover:**

$$\text{payables turnover} = \frac{\text{cost of goods sold} + \text{general, selling, and administrative expenses}}{\text{accounts payable} + \text{salaries, benefits, and payroll taxes payable}} \tag{19.5}$$

STEP 4:   Divide the three turnover ratios into 365 days to calculate the days sales outstanding, days inventory, and days payable, respectively.

days sales outstanding = 365/receivables turnover   (19.6)

days inventory = 365/inventory turnover   (19.7)

days payable = 365/payables turnover   (19.8)

STEP 5:   Using Equations 19.1 and 19.2, and the values determined in step 4 above, calculate the cash conversion cycle.

These steps are shown in Table 19.1 for Anacomp Inc., for 1990, 1991, and 1992. An examination of various liquidity measures (current ratio, quick ratio, and net working capital) in Table 19.1 indicates that the firm's liquidity appears to have deteriorated somewhat over this period. By calculating the cash conversion cycle, however, we see that its ongoing liquidity has improved since 1990. The cash conversion cycle is a quick and convenient way to analyze the ongoing liquidity of the firm over time. Although it does not show how risky the cash flows are, it does focus on our main concern—cash flows.

Table 19.1

Cash Conversion Cycle for Anacomp, Inc.

Although traditional liquidity measures indicate Anacomp's liquidity has deteriorated somewhat, its cash conversion cycle has actually improved during this time period.

	1990	**1991**	**1992**
Liquidity Measures			
Current ratio (current assets/current liabilities)	1.36	1.17	1.21
Quick ratio [(current assets – inventory)/current liabilities)]	0.94	0.85	0.86
Net working capital (current assets – current liabilities; in millions of dollars)	$67.90	$34.96	$42.34
Turnover Ratios			
Receivables turnover	5.22	5.17	5.30
Inventory turnover	5.44	6.43	6.09
Payables turnover	6.12	7.77	6.08
Cash Conversion Cycle			
Days sales outstanding	69.84 days	70.59 days	68.83 days
Days inventory	67.10	56.76	59.93
Operating cycle	136.94	127.35	128.76
Less: Days payable	59.64	46.98	60.03
Cash conversion cycle	77.30 days	80.37 days	68.73 days

Concept Review Questions

■ How *is on-going liquidity* different from *protective liquidity?*

■ Explain how to calculate a firm's cash conversion cycle.

STRATEGY FOR CURRENT ASSET AND CURRENT LIABILITY MANAGEMENT

Essential elements that must be considered in establishing a firm's short-term financial management policies are cash flows, liquidity, risk, and the level of returns that are necessary to compensate for the risk. We begin by analyzing first the strategy for current asset management and then that for current liabilities.

CURRENT ASSETS

The major current assets are cash, marketable securities, accounts receivable, and inventory. We will examine these assets in some detail in Chapters 20 and 21. Here, it is helpful to consider the factors that influence a firm's investment in current assets.

Current Asset Levels

Many factors influence the general level of current assets; four of the most important are:

1. NATURE OF THE FIRM'S BUSINESS   The specific activities pursued by the firm often have an important influence on the level of the firm's current assets. Retail firms have much larger inventories than manufacturing firms, leading to a larger percentage of current assets. On the other hand, fast-food chains, such as McDonald's and Wendy's, always have more current liabilities than current assets; due to the nature of the business, they operate—very successfully, we might add—with very few current assets.

2. SIZE OF THE FIRM   As shown below, smaller firms have a much higher percentage of current assets (and current liabilities) than larger firms.[2]

	Manufacturing Firms	
	Assets of $1,000 Million or Greater	Assets Under $25 Million
Assets		
Cash and marketable securities	3.4%	11.6%
Accounts receivable	10.8	26.5
Inventory	11.0	23.9
Other	3.4	3.7
Total	28.6%	65.7%
Current Liabilities		
Short-term debt	3.7%	7.7%
Accounts payable	7.9	13.6
Income tax payable	0.9	0.5
Current portion of long-term debt	1.7	3.4
Other	9.4	7.2
Total	23.6%	32.4%

The primary reasons for the differences between current asset levels of small and large firms are that: (a) large firms can devote the resources and attention necessary to manage their current assets; (b) larger firms may have some economies of scale in current asset or current liability management, or they may have more predictable cash flows; (c) larger firms have more access to the capital market than smaller firms; and (d) as firms get larger, they become more capital intensive. By capital intensive we mean they tend to use more machines and equipment in the production and distribution process.

[2] Bureau of the Census, *Quarterly Financial Report for Manufacturing, Mining, and Trade Corporations,* Third Quarter 1992.

Table 19.2

Working Capital for Crown Products

Although there have been year-to-year fluctuations, the relationships among working capital components are stable enough for planning purposes.

Year	Current Assets (in thousands)	Current Liabilities (in thousands)	Net Working Capital (in thousands)	Sales (in thousands)	Current Assets/ Sales	Current Liabilities/ Sales	Net Working Capital/ Sales
1	$ 74	$20	$54	$250	29.6%	8.0%	21.6%
2	77	21	56	284	27.1	7.4	19.7
3	90	26	64	275	32.7	9.5	23.3
4	92	25	67	298	30.9	8.4	22.5
5	98	23	75	315	31.1	7.3	23.8
6	110	30	80	375	29.3	8.0	21.3
Average					30.1%	8.1%	22.0%

3. RATE OF INCREASE (OR DECREASE) IN SALES   As sales increase, generally both accounts receivable and inventory also increase, along with a spontaneous increase in accounts payable. Consider Crown Products, which has been analyzing its current assets and liabilities in relation to sales, as shown in Table 19.2. Current assets have averaged about 30 percent of sales, and current liabilities have been about 8 percent of sales. Note that as sales have increased, current assets have increased by roughly the same proportion. Likewise, current liabilities have tended to increase due to the spontaneous change in accounts payable as inventory expands.

4. STABILITY OF THE FIRM'S SALES   The more stable the sales, the lower the level of current assets. On the other hand, firms with highly volatile sales must have more current assets, particularly cash and inventory.

Aggressive Versus Conservative Management

In examining the firm's current asset policies, we will concentrate on the composition of the firm's balance sheet. We will examine the effect that changes in the firm's policies have on its asset composition, and thus on its cash conversion cycle, expense levels, and risk and the returns required by the firm. For the time being, we are not concerned with how the firm finances its current assets; *our concern is solely with the composition of these assets.* A firm can manage its current assets conservatively or aggressively. To see this, consider Figure 19.3, which illustrates both conservative (with higher current asset levels) and aggressive (with lower current asset levels) approaches.

Because current assets never drop to zero, we can think of the firm as having a need for some **permanent current assets** on an ongoing basis. At the same time, virtually

Figure 19.3

Aggressive Versus Conservative Asset Management for Crown Products

Aggressive management leads to higher risk and higher returns; conservative management provides lower risk exposure and lower returns.

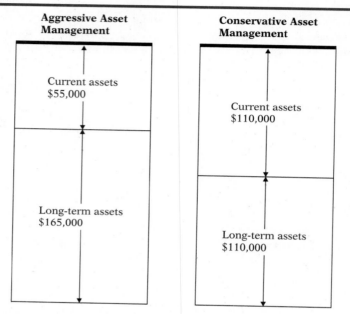

Aggressive Asset Management

Current assets $55,000

Long-term assets $165,000

Conservative Asset Management

Current assets $110,000

Long-term assets $110,000

Characteristics of Aggressive Asset Management
1. Low levels of current assets, but effectively and aggressively managed.
2. Short cash conversion cycle.
3. Lower expenses and higher revenue leading to higher EBIT.
4. High risk–high return strategy.

Characteristics of Conservative Asset Management
1. High levels of current assets.
2. Long cash conversion cycle.
3. Higher expenses and lower revenue leading to lower EBIT.
4. Low risk–low return strategy.

all firms have a need for **seasonal (or temporary) current assets** that fluctuate over the year (or business cycle). The size of both the permanent and temporary current assets is determined, in part, by how aggressive a firm is toward the level of current assets it maintains.

Other things being equal, an aggressive asset management policy leads to lower current assets, a shorter cash conversion cycle, lower expenses, and higher risk and higher required returns to compensate for the increased risk. Conservative asset management practices have just the opposite effects.

The Level of Current Assets. Aggressive asset management generally means lower levels of all current assets. The firm keeps only a minimal level of cash and marketable securities on hand and relies on effective management and the possibility of short-term borrowing to meet any unexpected cash needs. Likewise, aggressive accounts receivable and inventory management will generally lead to lower levels of both.[3]

Cash Conversion Cycle. More aggressive management shortens the cash conversion cycle. Remember from Equation 19.1 that the operating cycle is determined by adding the days inventory to the days sales outstanding. Aggressive asset management increases turnover, by lowering the average level of both receivables and inventory. So, an aggressive policy shortens the firm's operating cycle, which leads to a shorter cash conversion cycle. This shorter cash conversion cycle increases a firm's ongoing liquidity, because it does not have as large a proportion of its assets tied up in accounts receivable and inventory.

Expense and Revenue Levels. Aggressive current asset management will have the effect of reducing expenses. Fewer accounts receivable will be carried, so there will be lower carrying costs. In addition, fewer receivables will have to be written off as uncollectible. Likewise, by keeping inventory to a minimum, the firm avoids the carrying cost associated with inventory, as well as the possibility for loss due to obsolescence, theft, and so forth. This, in turn, leads to higher earnings before interest and taxes, EBIT, and ultimately to higher cash flows, as compared with the results of a conservative asset management policy.

A further effect of aggressive asset management may be to increase expected revenues, which could also lead to a higher EBIT level. This can occur in two ways: First, if returns from investing in long-term assets are higher than on short-term assets, which they typically are, then total cash inflows should increase. Second, the firm could attempt to increase total cash inflows by tailoring its credit-granting policy to encourage sales. These more lenient credit terms, however, would be granted only if they were expected to lead to a higher level of EBIT than without them.[4]

Risk and Return. Finally, let's consider what happens to the risk and returns required by the firm. In Chapter 4 we developed the idea of the capital asset pricing model, CAPM, and nondiversifiable risk (beta) as a means of quantifying risk. Some of these ideas can be employed here, but it is easier to think of risk in terms of the variability in currents assets, a scarcity of cash, or other adverse consequences. We can still maintain the conceptual framework that the higher the risk, the higher the return, and vice versa. Likewise, in Chapter 5 we introduced the idea of options, and we saw that the common stock of a firm is just a call option. Other things being equal, we

---

[3] In some circumstances, an aggressive accounts receivable or inventory policy could result in a high level of one or both. This is an exception to the general idea that the more aggressive the current asset policy, the lower their level. As noted in Chapter 21, a net present value approach is employed to determine the proper level of accounts receivable and inventory to maintain.

[4] Based on accepting positive NPV projects, the tendency would be for higher, rather than lower, accounts receivable. They would still be aggressively and effectively managed, however, so that they do not get out of control.

know that more risk, as evidenced by an increase in the standard deviation of the firm's assets, benefits common stockholders at the expense of bondholders.

The risks associated with an aggressive asset position include the possibility of running out of cash or being otherwise so strapped for funds that effective management of the firm is impeded. Likewise, the firm might keep inventory so low that sales are lost when stockouts occur. The risk associated with an aggressive accounts receivable policy could also result in lost sales if too low a level is kept.

To see the effect of aggressive versus conservative asset management policies, while holding other risks constant, consider Crown Products. It can adopt an aggressive or a conservative asset management position, with anticipated effects as follows[5]:

	Aggressive	**Conservative**
Sales	$375,000	$375,000
All expenses	325,000	335,000
EBIT	$ 50,000	$ 40,000

As shown previously in Figure 19.3, the aggressive approach has only $55,000 in current assets, whereas the more conservative approach has $110,000. The impact of fewer current assets and therefore lower expenses shows up in an anticipated EBIT of $50,000 for the aggressive plan, as opposed to only $40,000 with the conservative plan. Thus, by employing a more aggressive approach that exposes the firm to more risk, the firm has increased its anticipated EBIT, and ultimately its cash inflows.

CURRENT LIABILITIES

Now that we have considered current assets, let's consider the financing needed to support these assets. There are two fundamental decisions the firm must make with regard to financing: First, how much will it secure from short-term versus long-term debt (or liability) sources? Second, how much should the firm borrow in relation to what is put up by its owners? The first of these, the short-term versus the long-term question, is considered here. As we will see, the matching principle is widely employed to address this question. The second part, how much debt relative to equity should be employed, is discussed in Chapters 11 and 12. Here, we ignore this aspect of the problem and confine our attention to short-term financing.

Current Liability Levels

Retail firms carry more current assets than do manufacturing firms. This is primarily because retail firms have to carry more inventory. Because most merchandise for inventory is bought on credit, however, what would you expect the level of a typical retail firm's accounts payable to be, compared to that of a typical manufacturing firm? It will be larger, simply because larger inventories lead spontaneously to larger ac-

---

[5] For simplicity, we assume total assets and revenues are constant.

counts payable. So, a major factor influencing the firm's level of current liabilities is its level of inventory and other current assets. Other things being equal, businesses that require high levels of current assets will have a tendency for fairly high levels of current liabilities.

A second element influencing the level of current liabilities is the amount of flexibility desired by the firm. If a firm has a low level of current liabilities it has flexibility, because short-term borrowing can generally be easily employed. Also, accounts payable can be built up in an emergency without endangering the firm. If the firm already has a high level of current liabilities, however, then little flexibility is left. The more flexibility the firm wants, the less it will finance with current liabilities.

Aggressive Versus Conservative Management

Other things being equal, the lower the current liabilities, the more conservative the firm's liability management policies. As shown in Figure 19.4, the higher the level of current liabilities, the more aggressive the policy. This is exactly opposite the effects of an aggressive versus a conservative asset policy. In what follows in this section, *we focus on the liabilities, holding assets constant.* Then, in the next section, we will consider assets and liabilities together. An aggressive liability management policy results in higher current liabilities, a shorter cash conversion cycle, lower interest costs (if short-term rates are less than long-term rates), and higher risk and higher returns required. Conservative policies have just the opposite effect.

The Level of Current Liabilities.   Current liabilities consist of accounts payable, short-term loans or notes payable, various accrued expenses, and the current principal portion of long-term debt due.[6] An aggressive management approach increases the firm's reliance on short-term liabilities. Accounts payable will be used to the greatest extent possible—and payments on them will be made as late as possible without incurring a bad credit reputation. Short-term borrowing will also be used extensively.

Cash Conversion Cycle.   By employing more accounts payable and accruals, aggressive liability management shortens the cash conversion cycle. Larger payables and accruals lead to a shorter payables turnover. This leads to a longer days payable and a shorter cash conversion cycle. Aggressive liability management tends to increase the ongoing liquidity of the firm by shortening the cash conversion cycle—but it also provides less future flexibility.

Interest Costs.   To understand fully the impact of aggressive versus conservative liability management on a firm's interest costs, we need to consider the term structure of interest rates discussed in Appendix 3A. The yield curve plots the term to maturity versus the yield to maturity for borrowings that are equally risky but that differ in terms of length to maturity. Yield curves are generally upward-sloping—which means that long-term debt financing is more expensive than short-term debt financing. An expected benefit of an aggressive liability management program is the ability to borrow funds at a cheaper rate, meaning less cash outflows, than the firm would pay for long-term debt financing.

---

[6] The management of current liabilities is discussed in Chapter 22.

Figure 19.4

Aggressive Versus Conservative Liability Management for Crown Products

Aggressive liability management is a high risk–high return strategy, whereas a conservative approach produces lower risks and lower returns.

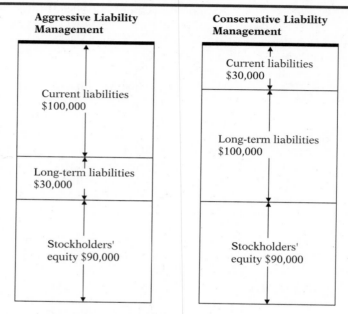

Characteristics of Aggressive Liability Management
1. High levels of current liabilities.
2. Short cash conversion cycle.
3. Lower interest costs if short-term rates are lower than long-term rates.
4. High risk–high return strategy.

Characteristics of Conservative Liability Management
1. Low levels of current liabilities.
2. Long cash conversion cycle.
3. Higher interest costs if long-term rates are higher than short-term rates.
4. Low risk–low return strategy.

To see the expected benefits of an aggressive versus a conservative policy, consider again the example of Crown Products. Figure 19.4 presented two different liability strategies. The aggressive one employs $100,000 in current liabilities and only $30,000 in long-term liabilities. The conservative policy employs $30,000 in current liabilities and $100,000 in long-term liabilities. If short-term interest rates are 10 percent and long-term rates are 14 percent, then the total before-tax interest cash outflow is $14,200 [i.e., $(0.10)($100,000) + (0.14)($30,000)$] for the aggressive policy, and $17,000 [i.e., $(0.10)($30,000) + (0.14)($100,000)$] for the conservative one. As long as long-term rates are higher than short-term rates, cash outflows associated with interest are reduced, leading to higher cash flows and earnings for the firm.

Risk and Return.   The main risk of an aggressive liability policy comes from general economic conditions and the continual need to refinance current liabilities. This is especially true if a firm is using extensive short-term financing through borrowing. Although the firm may be able to secure the financing, it is exposed to interest cost fluctuations. These fluctuating interest costs, and the continual need to refinance, increase the firm's risk exposure. An additional risk arises from reduced flexibility when the current liability level is high. Other things being equal, there are substantial risks associated with an aggressive liability policy that relies on large amounts of short-term debt. Greater returns are expected, however, by (1) reducing the cash conversion cycle, and (2) financing at interest rates that are generally (but not always) lower than long-term rates.

Concept Review Questions

- What factors affect a firm's level of current assets?
- Contrast an aggressive current asset management policy with a conservative current asset management policy.
- What are the effects on a firm of an aggressive current liability management policy and a conservative current liability management policy?

PUTTING IT ALL TOGETHER

We have considered separately both current assets and current liabilities. Now it is time to put them together and discuss the management of the firm's working capital in total. The three basic strategies a firm could follow, as illustrated in Figure 19.5, are

---

Figure 19.5

Alternative Short-Term Financial Management Policies

By altering both its asset and its liability structure, the firm can vary its short-term financial management policies considerably.

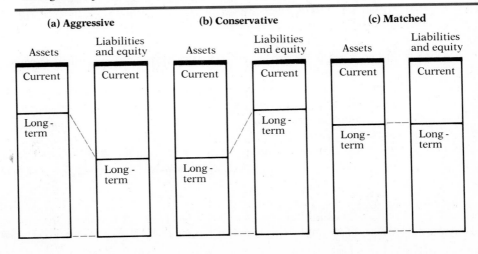

aggressive, conservative, or matched. The matched strategy, which is often cited as a guideline employed for short-term financial management, is embodied in the matching principle, or the idea of self-liquidating debt.

THE MATCHING PRINCIPLE

The **matching principle** can be stated as follows: Permanent investments in assets (both long-term and current) should be financed with permanent sources of financing, and temporary assets should be financed with temporary financing sources. The idea behind the matching principle is to match, or counterbalance, the cash-flow-generating characteristics of the assets with the maturity of the financing. A temporary buildup in current assets should be financed with current liabilities, which can be liquidated as the investment in current assets is reduced. A buildup in permanent current and long-term assets will take longer to convert to cash; thus, long-term financing will be needed.[7]

The matching principle can be applied to our previous discussion of aggressive versus conservative asset and liability policies. From Figure 19.5, we see that an aggressive asset policy calls for a low level of current assets, and a conservative policy calls for a high level. Likewise, an aggressive liability policy calls for a high level of current liabilities, and a conservative policy calls for a low level. To match them, the following rules apply:

1. If a firm has an aggressive current asset position (with a low level of current assets), then it should counterbalance its risks by employing a conservative liability position (with a low level of current liabilities).
2. If a firm has a conservative current asset position (employing a high level of current assets), then it should counterbalance its risks by employing an aggressive liability position (with a low level of current liabilities).
3. If a firm has a moderate current asset position, then it should counterbalance its risks by employing a moderate liability position.

The implication of the matching principle is that the firm should establish some *target* for its net working capital position that takes into account risks, the returns required, and the appropriate current asset and current liability positions.

To see this, let's reconsider Crown Products. With an aggressive asset approach it employs fewer current assets, so expenses are reduced and anticipated EBIT and cash inflows increase, compared to a conservative approach. Likewise, an aggressive liability approach employs more current liabilities and results in lower total cash outflows for interest than a more conservative liability policy. As shown in Table 19.3, the following combinations exist for Crown Products: (1) a high risk–high return policy employing both aggressive asset and aggressive liability strategies; (2) two intermediate matching strategies employing either an aggressive asset–conservative liability or a conservative asset–aggressive liability strategy[8]; and (3) a low risk–low return policy

---

[7] Matching can be accomplished by matching on the basis of maturity, cash flows, or duration. Duration matching is discussed in Chapter 23.
[8] An alternative matching strategy would be a more moderate position in both current assets and current liabilities. Matching ideas can also be employed when hedging interest rate risk, as discussed in Chapter 23.

Table 19.3

Impact of Alternative Current Asset and Current Liability Strategies on the Earnings of Crown Products

A high-risk strategy employs low current assets and high current liabilities, whereas a low-risk strategy is just the opposite. The matching principle, which attempts to match temporary current assets and current liabilities, results in a trade-off between risk and return.

	Asset and Liability Management Strategy				
	Aggressive Asset– Aggressive Liability	Aggressive Asset– Conservative Liability	Conservative Asset– Aggressive Liability	Conservative Asset– Conservative Liability	
Sales	$375,000	$375,000	$375,000	$375,000	Impact of asset
Expenses	325,000	325,000	335,000	335,000	← strategy
EBIT	50,000	50,000	40,000	40,000	
Interest	14,200	17,000	14,200	17,000	← Impact of liability
EBT	35,800	33,000	25,800	23,000	strategy
Taxes (35%)	12,530	11,550	9,030	8,050	
EAT	$ 23,270	$ 21,450	$ 16,770	$ 14,950	
	High-risk, high-return strategy	Intermediate positions more in line with matching principle		Low-risk, low-return strategy	

employing both conservative asset and conservative liability policies. Note that the two intermediate strategies embody the matching principle. In line with the risks involved, the aggressive strategy has anticipated earnings of $23,270, whereas the conservative strategy has anticipated earnings of only $14,950.

Which strategy should Crown select? As we know, it is not earnings that are important; it is the cash flows and market value of the firm. Assume that Crown Products has 10,000 shares of stock outstanding. The anticipated earnings per share of the four strategies will be as follows:

	Anticipated EAT	÷	Number of Shares	=	Anticipated EPS
Aggressive asset–aggressive liability	$23,270		10,000		$2.327
Aggressive asset–conservative liability	21,450		10,000		2.145
Conservative asset–aggressive liability	16,770		10,000		1.677
Conservative asset–conservative liability	14,950		10,000		1.495

To determine the per share market value, we know that $P_0 = (EPS)(P/E)$, where P/E is the firm's price/earnings ratio. Because aggressive asset or liability policies are viewed as being more risky by stockholders, other things being equal, they should have a lower P/E ratio than more conservative policies. Crown Products needs to estimate the potential impact of the various current asset and current liability strategies on its expected market value. One way is to forecast P/E's for various risk-return strategies. For our example, assume these estimates are as follows:

	Anticipated EPS	×	Anticipated P/E	=	Anticipated P_0
Aggressive asset–aggressive liability	$2.327		9		$20.94
Aggressive asset–conservative liability	2.145		10		21.45
Conservative asset–aggressive liability	1.677		11		18.45
Conservative asset–conservative liability	1.495		12		17.94

Based on these expected market values, Crown should implement one of the matching strategies (aggressive asset–conservative liability), because it results in the highest anticipated market value.

RECOGNIZING AND DEALING WITH LIQUIDITY PROBLEMS

The firm's short-term financial management policies should consider many factors. No matter how much planning is done, however, the firm must be able to recognize signs of declining liquidity and know how to deal with the situation. Some of the most important signs of deteriorating liquidity are these:

1. An unexpected buildup in inventory (an increase in the days inventory).
2. An increase in the firm's level of outstanding accounts receivable (an increase in the days sales outstanding).
3. A decline in the firm's daily or weekly cash inflows.
4. Increased costs that the firm is unable to pass on to its customers.
5. A decline in the firm's net working capital, or an increase in its debt ratio.

These and similar occurrences indicate the firm has (or will have) a liquidity problem.
  There are many different approaches for dealing with liquidity problems, depending on the source of the problem, its severity, and its expected length. Managers often take some of the following steps to deal with liquidity problems:

1. Control and reduce investment in inventory.
2. Reexamine and tighten up on credit and reduce the firm's level of accounts receivable.
3. Increase short-term or long-term debt, or issue equity.
4. Control overhead and increase awareness of the need for effective asset management.
5. Lay off employees.
6. Reduce planned long-term (capital) expenditures.
7. Reduce or eliminate cash dividends.

If these measures are not sufficient, more drastic steps will be necessary. The important point is that firms must plan for meeting ongoing liquidity problems as part of their short-term financial management policies.

PROTECTIVE LIQUIDITY

Until now we have been talking about the firm's ongoing liquidity. There is, however, another aspect of liquidity, sometimes called protective liquidity, or financial slack, which is the ability to have liquid resources to meet unexpected cash demands. These demands may arise when, due to unforeseen circumstances, larger cash outflows (or smaller cash inflows) than expected occur. In some cases cash is needed to take advantage of unexpected opportunities. As we discussed earlier, firms with high growth opportunities, or growth options, have more desire for financial slack then those with a low level of growth opportunities.

Planning the firm's short-term financial management policies and liquidity needs involves uncertainty. Some of this uncertainty can be eliminated by effective cash budgeting (discussed in Chapter 25), but uncertainty still remains. Effective managers, whether they follow a conservative, aggressive, or matched short-term financial management policy, always maintain some protective liquidity. This may be in the form of one or more **lines of credit,** which are short-term borrowing agreements the firm has negotiated with a bank. At the firm's discretion, it may borrow or pay back on the line of credit.

Another strategy is to maintain a fairly large marketable securities portfolio or to have a bond or stock issue ready. Other firms establish bank relations and keep the bank regularly informed about possible borrowing needs. An alternative approach, to be discussed in Chapter 22, is to factor (or sell) the firm's accounts receivable. Increasingly firms also hedge (as discussed in Chapter 23 for interest rate risk and in Chapter 28 for foreign exchange rate risk), to insulate themselves against severe adverse shifts in rates or prices. Effective short-term financial management involves a continual trade-off between risk and return. To deal with the risk of running short on cash at a crucial point in time, firms establish various means of ensuring protective liquidity as they formulate their short-term financial management policies.

Concept Review Questions

- Explain the matching principle.
- What are some important signs of deteriorating liquidity?
- Describe some strategies of protective liquidity management.

KEY POINTS

1. The goal of short-term financial management is to assist in maximizing the value of the firm. Short-term financial management focuses on the magnitude and timing of the cash flows and on the risks and returns involved. Although more operational in nature and based less on theory than is long-term financial management, effective short-term financial management is of vital importance to firms.

2. The cash conversion cycle, by taking account of the turnover of receivables, inventory, and payables, provides information about ongoing liquidity.
3. Both current assets and current liabilities may be managed conservatively or aggressively. A coordinated short-term financial management policy focuses on both asset and liability management.
4. To finance current assets, many firms follow the matching principle: Temporary assets are financed with temporary funds, permanent assets with long-term sources of funds.
5. Firms are also concerned about protective liquidity, or financial slack, as they formulate their short-term financial management policies.

QUESTIONS

19.1   In a world of perfect markets, firms should not have current assets and current liabilities. What accounts for the sizable levels of current assets and current liabilities we observe in practice?

19.2   Determine the impact of the following actions on a firm's cash conversion cycle:

a. The firm loosens its credit terms, leading to increased sales and accounts receivable. Sales increase more than receivables, on a percentage basis.
b. Payments on accounts owed are stretched from a 20-day average to a 35-day average.
c. The firm borrows on a short-term note instead of stretching payables, as in (b).
d. By introducing new control procedures, the firm reduces its inventory.

19.3   Explain why the basic nature of the firm's business and its size influence the amount of current assets required. Do the same factors also influence current liabilities?

19.4   Consider how an aggressive (versus a conservative) asset management position influences (a) the level of current assets, (b) the cash conversion cycle, (c) expense levels, and (d) risk and returns required.

19.5   Consider how an aggressive (versus a conservative) liability management position influences (a) the level of current liabilities, (b) the cash conversion cycle, (c) interest costs, and (d) risk and returns required.

19.6   At certain times the term structure of interest rates may be such that short-term rates are higher than long-term rates. Does it follow that the firm should finance entirely with long-term debt during such periods? Explain.

19.7   The firm faces two primary decisions with respect to its financing: the percentage of short- or long-term financing to employ, and the amount of borrowing to use relative to the owners' contribution. Discuss both decisions and how they might affect each other.

19.8   What is the matching principle? How does its use relate to the firm's cash conversion cycle, and its risk and returns?

CONCEPT REVIEW PROBLEMS

See Appendix A for solutions.

CR19.1   Russell Corp. has a receivable turnover of 6.75, an inventory turnover of 9.54, and a payables turnover of 9.13.

a. What is Russell's operating cycle?
b. Its cash conversion cycle?

CR19.2 Two companies—MaxIncome and SafetyFirst—-producing similar products have completely different short-term financial management policies. Income statements and balance sheets for each of the companies are:

Balance Sheet

	MaxIncome	SafetyFirst
Cash and marketable securities	$ 6,598	$ 17,855
Accounts receivable	15,125	25,632
Inventory	18,365	46,123
Net long-term assets	48,306	48,306
Total assets	$ 88,394	$137,916
Short-term bank loans	$ 18,232	$ 5,362
Accounts payable	18,185	11,565
Long-term debt	4,930	77,816
Common stock	33,562	33,562
Retained earnings	13,485	9,611
Total liabilities and stockholders' equity	$ 88,394	$137,916
Income Statement		
Sales	$265,233	$302,555
Cost of goods sold	162,900	177,930
General, selling, and administrative expenses	87,716	118,617
Taxes	5,847	2,403
Net income, EAT	$ 8,770	$ 3,605

What are the current ratio (current assets/current liabilities), quick ratio [(current assets − inventory)/current liabilities], net working capital (current assets − current liabilities), and cash conversion cycle for each firm?

CR19.3 Kyle, controller of Masters Golf, is investigating different working capital policies. Two different pro forma (or projected) balance sheets have been developed as follows:

	Aggressive	Conservative
Cash and marketable securities	$ 6,873	$ 8,856
Accounts receivable	18,462	29,357
Inventory	22,300	46,659
Net long-term assets	16,180	16,180
Total assets	$63,815	$101,052
Short-term bank loans	$ 8,000	$ 3,000
Accounts payable	15,543	5,000
Long-term debt	0	57,440
Common stock	23,269	23,269
Retained earnings	17,003	12,343
Total liabilities and stockholders' equity	$63,815	$101,052

Kyle also estimated that sales under an aggressive policy will be $166,658, with cost of goods sold of $86,534 and general, selling, and administrative expenses of $57,689. A conservative policy would result in sales of $185,732, cost of goods sold of $92,344, and general, selling, and administrative expenses of $75,554. (*Note:* These figures do not include interest expenses for Masters Golf.)

a. If the interest rate is 10 percent on long-term debt, 6 percent on short-term debt, and the tax rate is 40 percent, what are Masters Golf's current ratio (current assets/current liabilities), cash conversion cycle, net profit margin (net income/sales), and return on equity (net income/stockholders' equity) under each policy?

b. Assume Masters Golf has 5,000 shares of common stock. If the aggressive policy results in a P/E ratio of 8, while the conservative policy results in a P/E ratio of 12, what is the stock price under the two policies?

CR19.4   International Travel is considering adopting one of three short-term financial management policies, an aggressive policy, a matched policy, or a conservative policy. Ann, the CFO, projects sales for each policy under three different economic scenarios: a robust economy, a standard economy, and a poor economy.

Sales	Aggressive	Matched	Conservative
Robust	$1,400	$1,200	$900
Standard	1,200	1,000	800
Poor	900	700	500

In each case all expenses *except* interest are expected to be 50 percent of sales

a. Ann estimates interest costs will be $36 for the aggressive policy, $50 for the matched policy, and $66 for a conservative policy, no matter what the economic condition. If the firm's tax rate is 40 percent, the number of shares of common shares is 100, and there is an equal probability for each economic state, what are the expected earnings per share and the standard deviation of earnings per share for each policy?

b. If investors assign a P/E ratio of 10 for the aggressive policy, 11 for the matched policy, and 12 for the conservative policy, which policy should International Travel adopt?

PROBLEMS

19.1   Malott, Inc., is planning to make a $10 million investment in long-term assets and is attempting to estimate how much additional net working capital will be needed to support this expansion. The long-term asset turnover ratio (sales/long-term assets) on the new investment is estimated to be 2. From past experience, Malott estimates its total asset turnover ratio (sales/total assets) is 1. Also, for every dollar increase in current assets the firm experiences, about 60 percent of the increase can be financed through spontaneous increases in current liabilities. Determine the increase in net working capital (current assets − current liabilities) that should accompany the anticipated increase in long-term assets.

19.2   San Francisco Systems has the following turnover ratios: receivables turnover, 6.0; inventory turnover, 4.0; payables turnover, 3.75.

a. Find San Francisco Systems' cash conversion cycle.
b. Now find its cash conversion cycle if receivables turnover improves to 7.0 and inventory turnover increases to 5.5.
c. Now assume the inventory conversion period is as determined in (b) and the payables turnover increases to 5.3. If the firm then wants a cash conversion cycle of no more than 35 days, what must the receivables turnover be?

19.3 Lee Corporation specializes in the design, manufacture, and marketing of products for the transmission and control of power. For 2 recent years, information is as follows:

	Year −1 (in thousands)	Year 0 (in thousands)
Sales	$2,524	$2,711
Cost of goods sold	2,106	2,224
Cost of goods sold plus general, selling, and administrative expenses	2,353	2,497
Accounts receivable	377	382
Inventory	619	602
Accounts payable plus accrued wages and employee benefits	223	245

Fresno Paper produces and markets a variety of paper products through its five divisions. Information for the same 2 years is as follows:

	Year −1 (in thousands)	Year 0 (in thousands)
Sales	$1,233	$1,403
Cost of goods sold	1,021	1,173
Cost of goods sold plus general, selling, and administrative expenses	1,123	1,286
Accounts receivable	138	136
Inventory	138	153
Accounts payable plus accrued wages and employee benefits	78	82

a. Calculate the cash conversion cycle for both firms for both years.
b. What trends, if any, are evident between year −1 and year 0?
c. Do you think part of these differences are caused by the industries they operate in? Why or why not?

19.4 Wood Management Group is attempting to determine its optimal level of current assets. It is considering three alternative policies, as follows:

	Aggressive	Average	Conservative
Current assets	$ 500	$ 700	$ 900
Long-term assets	1,000	800	600
Total	$1,500	$1,500	$1,500

In any case, the firm will employ the following financing: current liabilities of $700, long-term debt of $200, and common equity of $600. Sales are expected to be $2,500. Because of lower costs with the more aggressive policies, the anticipated ratio of EBIT to sales is 13 percent with the aggressive policy; whereas it is 12 percent with the average risk policy and 11 percent with the conservative policy. Interest is $65, and the tax rate is 30 percent.

a. Determine anticipated net income under the three different plans.
b. In this problem, we assumed that both total assets and sales are the same with any of the policies. Are these typically valid assumptions?
c. How, specifically, does the risk vary under the three plans? As part of your analysis, calculate the current ratio (current assets/current liabilities) and net working capital (current assets − current liabilities).

19.5 LeCompte Software keeps a large inventory, in order not to lose sales. Its new vice-president for finance has recommended that the firm's inventory be cut. Doing so would reduce the inventory level by $150,000 and allow the firm to forgo renewing a $150,000 note payable with a 12 percent interest rate that matures soon. An abbreviated income statement for LeCompte is as follows:

EBIT	$1,000,000
Interest	140,000
EBT	860,000
Taxes (35%)	301,000
Net income, EAT	$ 559,000

With 100,000 shares of stock outstanding and a P/E ratio of 10 times earnings, LeCompte's current stock price is $55.90.

a. Scenario 1: If the anticipated EBIT and P/E ratio are unaffected by the reduction in inventory and notes payable, what would the new market price be? (*Note:* Carry to three decimal places for EPS.)
b. Scenario 2: The marketing manager for LeCompte believes the inventory reduction will result in lower sales, and thus EBIT may decrease to $950,000. What would the anticipated market price be if this happens?
c. If there is a 60 percent chance that EBIT will stay at $1,000,000, and a 40 percent chance it will drop to $950,000, what action should LeCompte Software take?
d. What are your answers to (a) through (c) if the marginal tax rate is only 20 percent?

19.6 Three companies—Aggressive, Average, and Conservative—follow different working capital policies, as their names imply.

	Aggressive	Average	Conservative
Current assets	$ 300	$ 400	$ 600
Long-term assets	700	600	400
Total	$1,000	$1,000	$1,000
Current liabilities	$ 500	$ 350	$ 200
Long-term debt	100	250	400
Common equity	400	400	400
Total	$1,000	$1,000	$1,000

Selected income and balance sheet data are as follows:

	Aggressive	Average	Conservative
Sales	$1,800	$1,800	$1,800
Cost of goods sold	1,260	1,280	1,300
Cost of goods sold plus general, selling, and administrative expenses	1,560	1,580	1,600
Accounts receivable	120	160	240
Inventory	150	200	300
Accruals and accounts payable	250	200	100
Short-term borrowing	200	150	100

The interest rate on short-term debt is 10 percent, and on long-term debt it is 12 percent. The tax rate is 30 percent.

a. Determine the net income for each firm.
b. Calculate the cash conversion cycle for each firm.
c. What is the current ratio (current assets/current liabilities) and the net working capital (current assets − current liabilities) for each firm?
d. Are there other factors that would have to be taken into account in practice? What are the major ones?

19.7 Salomon & Morgan is considering whether to adopt plan I or plan II for its current assets and liabilities. Adopting one plan versus the other is expected to affect sales, expenses, and interest. As a result, taxes and anticipated earnings after tax, EAT, will also vary. Based on a 50 percent probability of a good or bad year, Salomon & Morgan's finance department has made the following projections:

	Plan I		Plan II	
	Good Year	**Bad Year**	**Good Year**	**Bad Year**
Probability	0.50	0.50	0.50	0.50
Sales	$900,000	$800,000	$850,000	$760,000
All expenses except interest and taxes	750,000	710,000	730,000	680,000
EBIT	150,000	90,000	120,000	80,000
Interest	20,000	17,000	18,000	15,000
EBT	130,000	73,000	102,000	65,000
Taxes (40%)	52,000	29,200	40,800	26,000
EAT	$ 78,000	$ 43,800	$ 61,200	$ 39,000

Salomon & Morgan has 10,000 shares of common stock outstanding. Risk will be measured by the coefficient of variation of earnings per share.

a. Calculate the mean EPS, standard deviation of EPS, and coefficient of variation of EPS for both plans.
b. If plan I carries an anticipated P/E ratio of 11 times earnings and plan II has an anticipated P/E of 10 times, which plan should Salomon & Morgan choose?

19.8   Williams has the following balance sheet and income statement:

Balance Sheet		Income Statement	
Cash and marketable		Sales	$1,800
securities	$ 50	Cost of goods sold	
Accounts receivable	100	(70% of sales)	1,260
Inventory	100	General, selling, and	
Long-term assets	600	administrative expenses	190
Total assets	$850	EBIT	350
		Interest	25
		EBT	325
Short-term debt	$ 50	Taxes (36%)	117
Accounts payable	70	Net income, EAT	$ 208
Salaries, benefits, and			
payroll taxes payable	40		
Other current liabilities	40		
Long-term debt	150		
Stockholders' equity			
(100 shares)	500		
Total liabilities and			
stockholders' equity	$850		

a. Determine Williams' current liquidity position by calculating its current ratio (current assets/current liabilities), net working capital (current assets − current liabilities), ratio of current assets to total assets, ratio of current liabilities to total assets, and cash conversion cycle.

b. If its current P/E ratio is 8 times earnings, what is Williams' present market price per share?

c. The marketing vice-president believes significant sales are being lost because of not offering enough credit to customers and lack of inventory. Working with the chief financial officer, she has prepared the following plan:

■ $250 will be raised: $100 will be additional short-term debt with a 12 percent interest rate, and the other $150 will be additional long-term debt with a 14 percent interest rate.

■ Cash will increase by a total of $50 (this includes the additional cash raised with the new financing), accounts receivable by $115, and inventory by $115. Because of the increase in inventory, accounts payable will increase $30. (*Note:* Current assets increase by $30 more than the $250, due to the $30 of spontaneous short-term financing provided by the increase in accounts payable.)

■ Sales are expected to be $2,200, cost of goods sold will remain 70 percent of sales, and general, selling, and administrative expenses will increase by $30.

■ All other accounts remain the same.

Because investors are expected to view the new plan as being more risky, the new P/E ratio is estimated to be 7 times earnings.

(1) Calculating the same information as in (a), what is Williams' new liquidity position?

(2) Calculate the new income statement. What is the new anticipated market price per share?

(3) Should Williams proceed with the plan?

19.9 Pittsburgh Distributors has the following balance sheet and income statement:

Balance Sheet		Income Statement	
Cash	$ 25,000	Sales	$900,000
Accounts receivable	60,000	Cost of goods sold	400,000
Inventory	65,000	General, selling, and	
Long-term assets	350,000	administrative expenses	100,000
Total assets	$500,000	All other expenses	250,000
		Net income, EAT	$150,000
Accounts payable plus			
salaries, benefits, and			
payroll taxes payable	$ 80,000		
Other current liabilities	20,000		
Long-term debt	100,000		
Stockholders' equity			
(50,000 shares)	300,000		
Total liabilities and			
stockholders' equity	$500,000		

a. Determine Pittsburgh Distributors' liquidity situation by calculating the current ratio (current assets/current liabilities), net working capital (current assets − current liabilities), the ratio of current assets to total assets, the ratio of current liabilities to total assets, and the cash conversion cycle.

b. What is the current market price per share of Pittsburgh's stock if its P/E ratio is 8 times earnings?

c. David, Pittsburgh's chief financial officer, is very conservative and believes that the current ratio needs to be raised to 2.0. To accomplish this, he proposes to sell 2,500 shares of common stock to net the firm $20 per share. The proceeds will be added to the firm's cash account. Assuming that everything else remains the same, determine the following:

   (1) Pittsburgh's new liquidity position, as in (a).
   (2) Its new anticipated market price per share.
   (3) Whether or not Pittsburgh should issue the stock.

19.10 Nashville Manufacturing is preparing a 2-year plan for its asset investments, as given in the following schedule. (For simplicity, long-term assets are assumed to be constant at $40 million, as is stockholders' equity. Thus, you have to concern yourself only with current assets, current liabilities, and long-term debt.)

	Date	Total Current Assets per Period (in millions)
Year 1	3/31	$30
	6/30	36
	9/30	42
	12/31	39
Year 2	3/31	33
	6/30	39
	9/30	45
	12/31	42

a. Current liabilities tend to equal one-third of Nashville's current assets. If Nashville has a total of $15 million in long-term debt every quarter, determine the amount of short-term borrowing required per quarter to complete the financing of the firm's current assets.

b. Instead of (a), assume that no long-term debt exists. How much short-term debt will be needed per quarter to match, or counterbalance, current assets?

c. If short-term interest rates are 9 percent and long-term rates are 11 percent, how much interest does Nashville save over the 2 years by matching its current assets?

19.11 Mini Case DJ Fashions is an aggressive, young firm that has grown dramatically during the last few years. Until now it has fared well, but lately it has been experiencing continuing working capital problems. You have been called in to evaluate DJ's operations and suggest changes in funding in order to meet the continuing working capital problems.

a. What do we mean by the term "short-term financial management"? What are the primary short-term financial management decisions faced by firms? How are they related to each other?

b. DJ Fashions' balance sheet and income statement are as follows:

Balance Sheet		Income Statement	
Cash and marketable		Sales	$7,000
securities	$ 125	Cost of goods sold	3,150
Accounts receivable	750	General, selling, and	
Inventory	300	administrative expenses	3,500
Long-term assets	1,625	EBIT	350
Total assets	$2,800	Interest	115
		EBT	235
Short-term debt	$ 800	Taxes (40%)	94
Accounts payable	800	Net income, EAT	$ 141
Salaries, benefits, and			
payroll taxes payable	400		
Other current liabilities	300		
Long-term debt	100		
Stockholders' equity	400		
Total liabilities and			
stockholders' equity	$2,800		

Determine DJ's current liability position by calculating its current ratio (current assets/current liabilities), ratio of current assets to total assets, ratio of current liabilities to total assets, and cash conversion cycle. In assessing DJ's liquidity position, focus on the figures calculated above and other information that can be gleaned from the balance sheet and income statement. What conclusions do you reach?

c. In order to improve its liquidity ratios, one alternative open to DJ is to increase the short-term debt by $1,000 and add the same amount to the cash position. While this is just a cosmetic change, it does affect the figures calculated in (b). What are the new figures if everything else remains as in (b)?

d. Explain in detail what an aggressive versus a conservative liquidity management system entails. In addition to the levels of current assets and current liabilities, are there other factors that should be considered?

e. Does DJ have a liquidity problem? If so, what are the causes of the problem?

REFERENCES

Recent books on short-term financial management include:

HILL, NED C., and WILLIAM L. SARTORIS. *Short-Term Financial Management*. New York: Macmillan, 1988.

KALLBERG, JARL G., and KENNETH L. PARKINSON. *Corporate Liquidity: Management and Measurement*. Homewood, IL.: Irwin, 1993.

SCHERR, FREDERICK C. *Modern Working Capital Management*. Englewood Cliffs, N.J.: Prentice-Hall, 1989.

Two articles attempting to show theoretically that firms should have current assets and current liabilities are:

COHN, RICHARD A., and JOHN J. PRINGLE. "Steps Toward an Integration of Corporate Financial Theory." In *Readings on the Management of Working Capital*. Edited by Keith V. Smith. St. Paul, Minn.: West, 1980. Pp. 35–41.

MORRIS, JAMES R. "The Role of Cash Balances in Firm Valuation." *Journal of Financial and Quantitative Analysis* 18 (December 1983): 533–45.

The cash conversion cycle is discussed in:

GENTRY, JAMES A., R. VAIDYANATHAN, and HEI WAI LEE. "A Weighted Cash Conversion Cycle." *Financial Management* 19 (Spring 1990): 90–99.

RICHARDS, VERLYN D., and EUGENE J. LAUGHLIN. "A Cash Conversion Cycle Approach to Liquidity Analysis." *Financial Management* 9 (Spring 1980): 32–38.

20 Cash and Marketable Securities

EXECUTIVE SUMMARY

Effective management of the firm's cash and marketable securities requires that we understand techniques for cash gathering and disbursing, how the firm's cash balance can be minimized, and the basic instruments and techniques of marketable securities portfolio management. Adequate cash is needed for ordinary operating purposes. However, because demand deposits provide lower returns than marketable securities, the firm wants to minimize its cash balance while maintaining sufficient liquid reserves.

Because of mail, processing, and transit floats, special techniques are employed to speed the gathering of cash coming into the firm. For managing disbursements, firms can benefit from using controlled disbursing systems and zero balance accounts. In evaluating the effectiveness of these systems, the incremental costs must be compared with the incremental benefits in a net present value framework.

In determining the minimum cash balance to maintain, the firm's expected cash inflows and outflows can be modeled or broken down on a daily basis. By doing so, the firm can identify projected purchase or sale dates for marketable securities. The funds in the marketable securities portfolio must be invested for the highest possible return commensurate with the risk-return posture of the firm and the liquidity needs dictated by the projected inflows and outflows of cash.

THE CASH MANAGEMENT FUNCTION

Cash refers to currency on hand plus the demand deposits held in checking accounts at various commercial banks. **Marketable securities** are the short-term investments the firm may temporarily hold that can be quickly converted into cash. Together, cash and marketable securities form the **liquid assets** of the firm. Three main questions

665

relate to liquid asset management:

1. How should the firm design its cash-gathering and cash-disbursing systems?
2. How should the investment in liquid assets be split between cash and marketable securities?
3. How should the marketable securities portfolio be managed?

Before discussing these, however, we need to consider some general aspects of the cash management function. Because liquid assets generally provide lower returns than long-term assets, we need to understand why firms hold liquid assets. Then we will discuss the general risk-return aspects of liquid assets.

REASONS FOR HOLDING CASH

Firms hold cash for four basic reasons:

1. TRANSACTIONS PURPOSES In the everyday course of business, firms need a certain minimum amount of cash on hand to meet cash outflow requirements. These include routine items such as paying the monthly bills, making payments to suppliers, and the like. In addition, cash is needed for major items such as tax payments, dividends, salaries, and paying interest and/or principal related to debt.
2. HEDGE AGAINST UNCERTAINTY A second reason for holding liquid assets is as a hedge against uncertain future events. These funds often are held in the form of marketable securities. An alternative to holding liquid assets to hedge against uncertainty is to obtain a line of credit. With a line of credit from a bank, the firm can borrow up to a specified maximum amount over some time period. Lines of credit generally require a commitment fee, whether they are used or not. Thus, protective liquidity is the second reason for holding cash.
3. FLEXIBILITY Many firms hold substantial amounts of liquid assets in anticipation of taking advantage of unforeseen opportunities and having the capability of funding growth options, or opportunities, quickly and easily. Likewise, during periods of economic downturn, firms postpone capital expenditures and attempt to hoard liquid assets to "weather the storm."
4. COMPENSATING BALANCE REQUIREMENT Banks perform many services for firms, including the collection and disbursement of funds, handling interbank transfers, providing lines of credit, and making loans. The compensation received by the bank comes from two sources—direct fees and **compensating balances.** A compensating balance is a specified amount the firm agrees to leave on deposit in its checking account. Typically this amount is set at some level related to the size of the loan or the amount of services provided.

RISK AND RETURN

The fundamental risk involved in holding too little cash relates to an inability to operate in the normal manner. If cash inflow is a problem, paying bills may have to be deferred, capital expenditures curtailed, short-term financing obtained, and assets sold. Growth options, or opportunities, that present themselves will have to be by-passed. In an extreme case, the firm may have to file for protection under the bankruptcy code or be forced into liquidation. The risk-return tradeoff for liquid assets involves the following:

1. Having enough cash and liquid reserves (or protective liquidity, in the form of marketable securities and/or lines of credit) to meet all the firm's obligations and take advantage of growth opportunities.
2. Not holding excess liquid reserves, because investment in long-term assets gener-ally provides higher returns than short-term investments.
3. Maintaining a minimum cash balance while actively managing the firm's portfolio of marketable securities to ensure as high a return as possible commensurate with the risk involved.

These tradeoffs will guide our discussion as firms make liquid asset decisions consistent with maximizing the value of the firm.

Concept Review Questions
- Why do firms hold cash?
- What are some of the risks of holding too much cash? Of holding too little cash?

CASH MANAGEMENT TECHNIQUES

The flow of cash into and out of the firm is continual. Although the level of cash at any point in time is a function of many factors, certain cash management ideas are fundamental to any firm, whatever its size, industry, or the state of the economy. Two major aspects of cash management involve speeding the inflows through a cash-gathering system and controlling the outflows via a cash-disbursing system. Before discussing these, however, we need to understand payment systems.

PAPER BASED VERSUS ELECTRONIC PAYMENT SYSTEMS

In the United States, Canada, and a relatively few other countries the major means of making non-cash payments is through checks. Although electronic payment is becom-ing more widespread in the United States, particularly for larger transactions between firms, we will start our discussion assuming a paper based system. A paper based system is in contrast to **giro systems,** which are employed in most European and many other countries for smaller transactions. These giro systems, often run by the postal service, operate on the basis of direct debits and credits. In a giro system, a seller sends an invoice to the buyer. The invoice includes a giro payment stub (called a giro accep-tance) encoded with the seller's bank and account number. The buyer signs the stub, takes it to the local post office, transmits the information through the girobank, with the result being a debit to the buyer's account and a credit to seller's account.

We will discuss large transaction size electronic payment systems shortly; however, first we will consider cash-gathering and cash-disbursing in a paper based system.

SPEEDING THE INFLOWS

The complexity of the cash-gathering system depends on the size of the firm and the scope of its operations. Small local firms have very simple systems; large national or multinational firms have very extensive systems. In the cash-gathering system, the concept of float is vital.

Float

Float is the length of time between when a check is written and when the recipient receives the funds and can draw upon them (when it has "good funds"). The **average collection float** is found by multiplying the number of days of float times the average daily dollar amount that is in the collection system. The sources of cash-gathering float, as shown in Figure 20.1, are:

1. MAIL FLOAT   The time that elapses between when a customer places the check in the mail and when the selling firm receives it and begins to process it is the **mail float.**
2. PROCESSING FLOAT   The time it takes the selling firm to deposit the check in its bank after receiving the check is the **processing float.**
3. TRANSIT FLOAT   The time required for the check to clear through the banking system until the recipient can draw upon it (i.e., has "good funds") is the **transit float.**

There are three primary ways that checks can be cleared between banks. The first is when banks located near one another meet on a daily basis, either individually or through a local clearing house, to swap checks drawn on each other. The second way is based on the Federal Reserve check clearing system. The Fed maintains 12 district banks, 25 branches, and 47 regional check processing centers that facilitate the check clearing process. The third way is through a **direct send.** The process with a direct send is somewhat like that employed with a local clearing house, except the banks are not located geographically close to one another.

The Federal Reserve System has established a schedule specifying when funds will be available, no matter where the check is deposited for collection. The float within the banking system has steadily declined due to requirements imposed on the Federal Reserve system by both the Depository Institutions Deregulation and Monetary Control Act of 1980 and the use of more sophisticated clearing mechanisms.

A firm should focus first on the processing float. That is, the firm must establish an efficient internal system to minimize the delay between receipt of the customer's check (if it comes directly to the firm) and when it is deposited in the bank. After this has been accomplished, other techniques for reducing float can be considered.

Decentralized Collections

Mail float can be minimized by having decentralized collection points located in parts of the country where the firm has many customers. Two basic devices used for this purpose are local offices and lockboxes.

Local Offices.   If the firm has local offices in the major regions in which it operates, it can have collections directed to these offices. Once the checks are received, they can

Figure 20.1

Typical Payment System and Resulting Float

All three types of float are important and should be minimized as the firm strives to shorten its cash collection cycle.

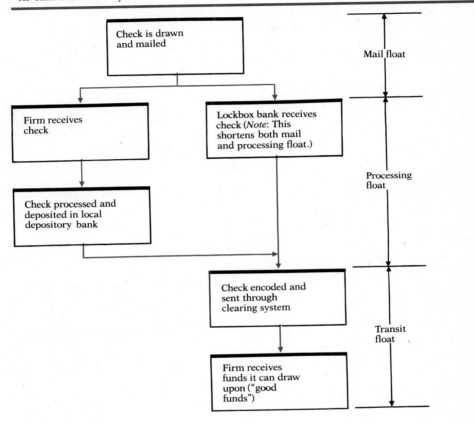

be deposited in a local depository bank, which is tied into the firm's overall banking network.

Lockboxes.   If the firm does not have local offices, or if it wants to keep collections out of the local offices, a widely used alternative is to establish lockboxes. With a **lockbox,** the customer is directed to send the payment to a post office box in a specified city.[1] A bank picks up the mail several times a day and begins the clearing process while notifying the firm, via electronic means, that the checks have been received. At the conclusion of the day, all check photocopies, invoices, deposit slips, and related materials are sent to the firm. To determine where to set up lockboxes, the

---

[1] Lockboxes are often classified in two categories: wholesale lockboxes, which are designed for low-volume but high-dollar value per item transactions, and retail lockboxes, which provide for efficient processing of high-volume, low-dollar value checks.

firm can engage the services of banks or other cash management consulting services. Typically a national firm will establish lockboxes in various parts of the country depending on its customer base and the regional efficiency of the postal service.

The purpose of both local office and lockbox collection points is to keep mail float to a minimum. Lockboxes also reduce the processing float. The benefits gained from the reduced float, however, must be compared to the cost involved. With a local office arrangement, the costs involve personnel, equipment, and space. With a lockbox arrangement, the cost is the fee charged by the bank either directly or through a compensating balance requirement.

Banking Network

Large firms employ more than one bank for their gathering and disbursing systems. A typical "tiered" banking arrangement suitable for a large national firm is shown in Figure 20.2. Using a local office system, customers mail their checks to local offices that process and then forward them to local depository banks. The deposits are transferred to regional concentration banks and finally to the firm's main account at

---

Figure 20.2

Typical Banking and Cash Movement System for a Large Firm

If the firm uses lockboxes, most of the deposits go directly to the regional concentration banks, speeding up the cash-gathering system.

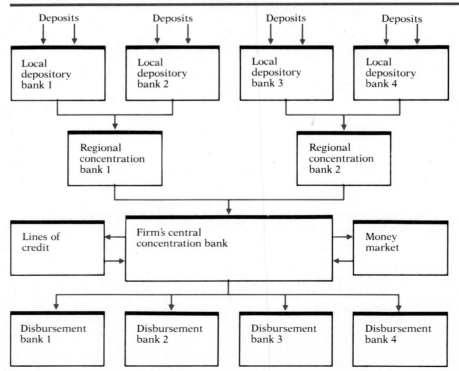

its central concentration bank. The rationale for a tiered system is that the greatest check clearing efficiency is often obtained by organizing the cash-gathering system in this manner.

If lockboxes are employed, they are generally set up at the regional concentration banks, and the local depository banks are bypassed. The regional concentration bank maintains the lockbox, forwards the funds to the firm's central concentration bank, and sends the supporting documents to the firm. Concentration banks typically are located in a Federal Reserve city, in order to speed up the clearing process. In addition, the lockbox should be close to the customers to be served so that mail float is kept to a minimum.

Once the funds are at the firm's central concentration bank, they can be used to meet the cash outflows of the firm, and any extra funds can be quickly invested in marketable securities. If the firm is short of cash, it can draw on its lines of credit. (The typical firm's banking network will also include various disbursement accounts at one or more banks.)

Other Approaches

Some other approaches that could be employed to improve the efficiency of the collection process include the following:

1. SPECIAL HANDLING   To provide special handling of large amounts, a courier might be dispatched to collect a check directly, in order to reduce mail and/or transit time.
2. PREAUTHORIZED CHECKS   A **preauthorized check** system might be created when the firm receives a large volume of payments in fixed amounts from the same customers. With the preauthorized procedure, the customer authorizes the firm to draw checks directly on the customer's demand deposit account. This method reduces mail and processing float and increases the regularity and certainty of cash inflows to the firm.
3. RECEIPT OF PAYMENT REQUIRED   A third alternative is for the firm to demand that the payment be received (not just mailed) by a certain date. This system can be used if a customer is going to take advantage of a cash discount. The receipt of payment approach eliminates mail float.
4. PAYMENT BY WIRE TRANSFER   A fourth alternative would be for the firm to demand payment by a wire transfer. This also eliminates float.

Because all these approaches have costs and benefits related to reducing the float, they must be considered when determining the most effective means of structuring the firm's cash-gathering system.

Analysis of Cash-Gathering Techniques

A basic model that can be employed to assess the cost effectiveness of various cash-gathering techniques compares the incremental costs with the incremental benefits:

ΔC = after-tax costs

ΔB = after-tax benefits = $(\Delta t)(TS)(I)(1 - T)$ 　　　　　　　　　　(20.1)

where

ΔC = the incremental after-tax costs of a new method compared to an existing method

ΔB = the incremental after-tax benefits associated with a new method compared to an existing method

Δt = the time (in days) that float is changed

TS = the size of the transaction

$I/365$ = the daily interest rate

T = the firm's marginal tax rate

With this method, the following decisions will be made:

1. If ΔC is greater than ΔB, stay with the present method.
2. If ΔC is less than ΔB, switch to the proposed method.
3. If ΔC is equal to ΔB, you are indifferent.

Note that $\Delta B - \Delta C$ is simply the net present value, NPV. The only difference from other NPVs is that discounting is not employed, due to the short time periods involved.

This approach is extremely flexible. It can be conducted on a per unit or total basis, and on a daily or yearly basis. To illustrate its use, we first consider a lockbox example and then alternative transfer mechanisms.

Lockbox Example.   Suppose that your firm now has all collections sent to the home office. To increase efficiency and reduce float, a lockbox operation is being considered. You estimate that the reduction in float (both mail and processing) will be 3 days, the average check size is $440, the yearly rate of interest is 10 percent, and the firm's marginal tax rate is 30 percent. Employing Equation 20.1, we can find the approximate *per unit* benefits of the lockbox, as follows:

$$\Delta B = (\Delta t)(TS)(I)(1 - T) = (3)(\$440)(0.10/365 \text{ days})(0.70) = \$0.253$$

On a per unit basis, the benefits are $0.253 per check processed. If the after-tax costs charged for the lockbox are less than this amount, the lockbox operation should be established, because the incremental benefits will be greater than the incremental costs. In addition, any employee time freed would be another benefit that also should be taken into account.

Instead of determining the benefits on a per unit basis, we could calculate them on a daily basis. If there are 300 checks per day, then the average daily volume of checks processed through the lockbox is $132,000 [i.e., (300)($440)]. The incremental benefits *per day* are then

$$\Delta B = (3)(\$132,000)(0.10/365 \text{ days})(0.70) = \$75.95$$

Thus, if the bank charged less than $75.95 per day after tax (on a 365-day year), then the firm should implement the lockbox arrangement.

Finally, we can also use Equation 20.1 to determine the incremental benefits *per year*. To do this, *either the daily volume, TS, must be converted to a yearly basis, or the daily interest rate, I/365, must be converted to a yearly interest rate.* The incremental after-tax benefits per year from the lockboxes are thus:

$$\Delta B = (3)[(365 \text{ days})(\$132,000)](0.10/365 \text{ days})(0.70) = \$27,720$$

or

$$\Delta B = (3)(\$132,000)(0.10)(0.70) = \$27,720$$

Again, we would make our decision by comparing the incremental costs versus the incremental benefits. This time, however, we do it on a yearly basis, instead of on the per unit or per day basis determined previously.

Transfer Mechanism Example.   In the example above, we did not know the costs. We can also start out, however, by knowing what the incremental costs, ΔC, are, and then determine what the reduction in the float time, Δt, the average size, TS, or the interest rate, I, would have to be for us to be indifferent between the two methods. Suppose that your firm is in the 40 percent tax bracket and is investigating whether one of two methods should be employed to move funds between two banks. The first method costs $5 per unit, and the alternative costs $1, so that $\Delta C = (\$5 - \$1)(1 - 0.40) = \$2.40$. The reduction in float time, Δt, is 2 days, and the yearly interest rate, I, is 10 percent. Setting ΔC equal to ΔB, we have

$$\Delta C = \Delta B$$
$$\$2.40 = (2)(TS)(0.10/365 \text{ days})(1 - 0.40)$$
$$TS = \frac{\$2.40}{(2)(0.10/365)(0.60)} = \$7,300 \text{ on a per unit basis}$$

If the average size of the check transferred between the two banks is at least $7,300, it pays to use the first method. If the reduction in float time were only 1 day, the size of the average transfer would have to be $14,600 for the first method to be justified.

In practice, the models become more complex, because there are additional considerations, such as having numerous locations and the service credits earned by having compensating balances at the banks. Nevertheless, the basic analytical concept of comparing the incremental costs versus the incremental benefits remains the same.

CONTROLLING THE OUTFLOWS

In the design of the firm's cash-disbursement system, the emphasis is on controlling and slowing down the outflow of cash as long as possible without incurring the ill will of the firm's suppliers. The place to begin is with payment procedures. They should be designed so the firm pays *just before* the due date. Paying earlier simply reduces the time that cash is available to the firm for investment.

Controlled Disbursing

Transit float is a function of the processing inefficiencies of various banks, their location, and the Federal Reserve system. To take advantage of transit float, firms may establish a **controlled disbursing** system. The idea is to locate the firm's disbursing banks so that payments to the firm's suppliers will remain outstanding as long as possible. The specific location of the controlled disbursing banks depends on the location and amount of billings by the firm, delays in transit time, and the costs involved. Generally the bank is located in a small or medium-sized city and receives only one delivery of checks from the Fed per day.

The cost analysis of alternative cash-disbursing systems is similar to that employed for cash-gathering systems. Suppose that a New Jersey–based firm in the 35 percent tax bracket is considering the establishment of two disbursing banks, one in northern California and the other in South Dakota. It expects that transit float will be increased by 2 days, the size of the average check is $5,000, and the yearly interest rate is 8 percent. Using Equation 20.1, we find that the incremental benefits are

$$\Delta B = (2)(\$5,000)(0.08/365 \text{ days})(1 - 0.35) = \$1.425$$

As long as the two banks charge less than $1.425 per check, the firm should go ahead. For example, if the firm writes 800 checks per month, it can afford to pay up to $1,140 [i.e., (800)($1.425)] after-tax per month to establish the controlled disbursing system. By maximizing transit float, the firm can increase its cash level and employ the excess cash in other ways. The system does mean, however, that suppliers will be without payment for an additional number of days. The ill will created among

---

Figure 20.3

Zero Balance Account System

Instead of divisional accounts, separate zero balance accounts could be kept for payroll, suppliers, cash dividends, and so forth.

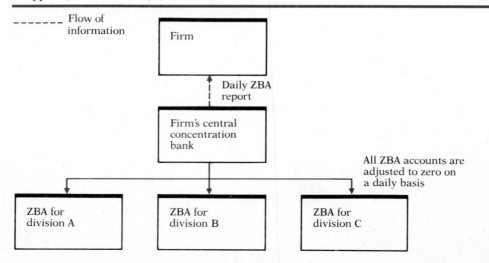

suppliers must be taken into account when a controlled disbursing system is being established.

Zero Balance Accounts

When a large firm is organized on a divisional basis, invoices from suppliers often go to divisional finance offices for payment. If each division has its own disbursing bank, excess cash balances may build up, reducing the efficiency of the firm's cash-disbursing system. To prevent this buildup, the firm may establish a **zero balance account** system at its central concentration bank (see Figure 20.3). Each division continues to write its own checks, which are all drawn on individual disbursing accounts at the concentration bank. Although these accounts are like individual demand deposit accounts, they contain no funds. Thus their name—"zero balance."

Each day the checks written on the individual disbursing accounts presented for payment are paid by the concentration bank. As they are paid, a negative balance builds up in the individual accounts. At the end of the day, the negative balances are restored to zero by means of a credit from the firm's master account at the central concentration bank. Each day, the firm receives a report summarizing the activity of the various accounts, so that marketable securities can be bought or sold as needed, depending on the balance in the firm's master account. Zero balance accounts allow much more control, while maintaining divisional autonomy for payments. They are often an effective means of controlling the cash-disbursement system.

Other Approaches

Various other approaches for controlling cash disbursements include the following:

1. CENTRALIZED PAYABLES   When a firm has many divisions, it could have the invoices received and verified at the divisional level but actually paid at the firm's headquarters. In this instance, all invoices must be forwarded to the central office for payment. Control can be maintained, and the disbursement cycle may be slowed by this procedure.
2. TIMING CHECK ISSUANCES   By issuing checks at certain times during the week, the firm may increase its float. Thus, if average mail float is 1.5 days, by issuing checks on Wednesday or Thursday the firm may gain an extra 2 days (over the weekend) of float. Likewise, issuing a payroll on Friday also means that not all the checks can clear the banking system before Monday or Tuesday of the next week.

    The benefits and costs of all the cash-disbursing techniques must be analyzed. The basic framework to employ is the same as that presented earlier. In the disbursing situation, the benefit arises from the additional length of time the firm will have the funds available. This benefit has to be weighed against the additional costs incurred to gain better control of the disbursement of cash.

INTERACTIONS

Until now we have examined a number of techniques that could be used to improve the efficiency of the firm's cash-gathering system or to control the cash-disbursing system. In medium- to large-size firms, with various plants and offices, gathering and disbursing problems quickly become complex. In addition, there are obvious interactions between the two that must be taken into account. If the firm decides to employ lockboxes and/or have collections made by local offices, numerous banks will be involved. Using controlled disbursing also will lead to creating accounts at still other banks. In the end the two decisions, gathering and disbursing, cannot be made in isolation. Rather, their joint effects, costs, and benefits must be considered in order to create an efficient cash management system that balances the risks and returns involved.

Concept Review Questions

- Describe several approaches firms employ to decrease the cost of float.
- What are some ways a firm can employ to increase its transit float?
- Describe how a zero balance account system can be used to control the cash-dispersing system of a firm.

ADVANCES IN PAYMENT AND INFORMATION SYSTEMS

Up to this point we have concentrated primarily on a paper based check system. During the last 20 years or so there have been extensive discussions and projections about moving to a checkless and paperless society. Substantial progress has been made during that period of time.

ELECTRONIC PAYMENT SYSTEMS

Although checks are still widely employed in the United States, there has been slow but steady movement toward the use of electronic payment systems, often referred to as **electronic funds transfer, EFT.** Electronic funds transfer involves the replacement of paper checks with an electronic payment system. The electronic systems fall into two basic groups: The first is automated clearing houses, ACHs, whose primary orientation is to provide service to consumers and handle smaller payments. The second is various wire transfer systems.

To implement the movement of funds electronically between financial institutions, the **Automated Clearing House, ACH,** system has been developed.[2] Today, there are 42 ACH associations; most are owned by groups of banks and other financial institutions. The majority of the ACHs are operated by the Federal Reserve system under contract with the ACH. Over 20,000 financial institutions participate in the ACH network. The ACH system is a batch process, store-and-forward system. To reduce costs, many items are sent at once. In recent years, many changes have occurred in the ACH system, and the Federal Reserve system has initiated procedures for

---

[2] Formally, depository transfer checks, DTCs, were widely used to move funds between banks via the mail. These are being replaced with electronic DTCs. Once the electronic DTC is initiated, it is actually processed as an ACH transfer.

reducing risks associated with ACH transactions. Some common uses of the ACH system by firms include (1) direct deposit of payroll, (2) payment of cash dividends to shareholders, (3) payment of taxes, insurance premiums, and the like, and (4) payment of suppliers. Among the largest users of the ACH system are the federal and state governments.

The second form of electronic payment is via **wire transfer.** This system is used by firms for large dollar transfers. The **Fedwire** is a bank-to-bank payment system operated by the Federal Reserve system. Firms can initiate transfers by calling their bank or using a terminal hooked up to the bank's network. The **Clearing House Interbank Payment System, CHIPS,** is a payment settlement system operated by the New York Clearing House Association. CHIPS is used to settle most international transactions.[3] With wire transfer, the funds are transferred on a same-day basis, and transit float is eliminated. Wire transfers cost a good bit more, however, than using the ACH system. Recently it was estimated that approximately $1.3 trillion changes hands daily via wire transfers. Of this total, about half was via Fedwire, and the other half occurred via CHIPS. The average transfer on Fedwire was about $3 million, whereas on CHIPS it approached $5 million per transaction.

ELECTRONIC DATA INTERCHANGE

At the same time that electronic payment systems have been growing, other advances in automation are affecting the whole ordering and payment system employed by firms. Increasingly, firms are using **electronic data interchange, EDI**, which affects everything from the ordering and manufacturing cycle to the flow of documents related to shipment and payment. Electronic data interchange refers to the exchange of all transaction-related information between two firms in computer-readable form. Thus, its implications are important in all aspects of a firm—both financial and nonfinancial. Interfacing EDI with EFT enables firms to move from a paper based system to a non-paper based system. Although there are obvious benefits to such a move, there are also costs. That is one of the reasons that moving to an integrated EDI/EFT system has been much slower than anticipated. At the same time there is increasing evidence that progress has and is still being made in implementing effective, cost efficient EDI/EFT systems.

THE EDI EXPERIENCE AT NEWELL

Newell is a manufacturer of hardware, housewares, and office products that serves firms such as K mart, Wal-Mart, Target, Ace Hardware, and Canadian Tire. To streamline their whole operations, manage inventory, and reduce stockouts at their

---

[3] The equivalent of CHIPS in the United Kingdom is CHAPS. S.W.I.F.T., the Society for Worldwide Interbank Financial Communication, should also be mentioned. While not a payment system, S.W.I.F.T. provides for the exchange of information between banks. The settlement of the financial transactions then takes place through CHIPS, CHAPS, or some other mechanism.

customers' sites, Newell has designed the following program:

1. A retail store, such as K mart, captures sales data at the point of sale when the UPC (universal price code) bars are scanned by laser at the check-out counter.
2. Sales data from various stores and warehouses are consolidated at the customer's headquarters daily and transmitted electronically to Newell.
3. When inventory falls to a predetermined level, a replenishment order is generated, and shipping documents are transmitted electronically to the appropriate Newell division.
4. Once an order has been shipped, the shipping data are transmitted electronically from the division to Newell headquarters.
5. An advance shipping notice and invoice are transmitted electronically to the customer's headquarters. The advanced shipping data are then retransmitted to individual stores by the customer's headquarters.
6. Newell is linked electronically to most of its common carriers, allowing it to monitor carrier performance and order progress from the time it is shipped until it arrives at the customer's warehouse or retail outlet.

Through EDI, Newell transmits the following items: point of sale data, forecasts, inventory data, purchase orders, advance shipping notices, invoices, electronic funds transfer, and information about shipping status. Although checks are still used, more and more firms like Newell are turning to EDI/EFT.

Concept Review Questions
- Describe how automatic clearing can benefit a firm.
- How does the electronic data interchange system at Newell work?

DETERMINING THE DAILY CASH BALANCE

Now that we have examined cash gathering and disbursing, the second question raised at the beginning of the chapter can be addressed: How should the investment in liquid assets be split between cash and marketable securities? The approach we examine is based on the idea that firms will attempt to keep as little cash in demand deposits as possible. We assume that the firm has a marketable securities portfolio of a sufficient size that funds can be transferred from it to the demand deposit account as needed. Because marketable securities typically earn higher returns than demand deposits held by firms (which typically earn no interest), there is an incentive to leave excess funds in the marketable securities portfolio.

GENERAL PROCEDURE

The following five-step procedure can be employed to determine the firm's daily cash balance. It involves estimating the major inflows and outflows and then modeling the routine cash flows.

STEP 1:   Prepare cash budgets on a monthly basis. Updates will be made, often weekly, as needed.

STEP 2:   Break major cash inflows and outflows out of the cash budget. Major items would include such items as taxes, dividends, lease payments, debt service obligations, wages, and the like.

STEP 3:   Identify the timing of the major inflows and outflows expected to occur during the month. From this information, we can estimate approximate times when daily transfers into or out of the marketable securities portfolio may be needed.

STEP 4:   Model the remaining, or routine, cash inflows and outflows[4] to determine when (based on historical patterns) we would expect their inflow and outflow to occur during the month. In this process it is important to consider seasonal influences, day-of-the-month effects, day-of-the-week effects, vacations, and the like. The output of this modeling process provides an estimate of the net daily inflow or outflow from routine items. Based on this information, and the timing of the major inflows and outflows from step 3, the planned times for adding to or selling marketable securities can be estimated. This step specifies the firm's estimated daily cash balance for each day of the month.

STEP 5:   As the month progresses, compare the actual routine cash inflows and outflows with the projected ones. Also, the exact timing of major cash inflows and outflows is known, or can be more accurately estimated. Other developments can be added as they occur. The actual dates and amounts of marketable security purchases and sales will be adjusted from those estimated in step 4 as the month progresses.

This approach to estimating the intramonth (or daily) cash balance is shown in Figure 20.4. The goal is to maintain the actual cash balance at some predetermined level. Obviously, this level depends on the charges or credits the bank passes on to the firm. However, by breaking out the major items and then modeling the routine ones, the firm's monthly cash budget can easily be broken down into a day-by-day estimate of the necessary cash balance.

Transfers to and from the marketable securities portfolio use the same balancing of incremental costs and benefits discussed earlier. Therefore, it may not be profitable to switch funds to and from the marketable securities portfolio every day. If it costs $50 to move funds in or out of the marketable securities portfolio, the incremental interest, ΔI, from having funds in marketable securities is 4 percent, and the marginal tax rate is 40 percent, we can proceed as follows:

$$\Delta C = \Delta B$$
$$\Delta C = (\Delta t)(TS)(\Delta I)(1 - T)$$
$$\$50(1 - 0.40) = (1)(TS)(0.04/365 \text{ days})(1 - 0.40)$$

where Δt is specified as 1 day's gain in interest. Solving for TS, the amount of cash

---

[4] See references list at end of chapter.

Figure 20.4

Model for Estimating and Controlling the Firm's Cash Balance

In practice, other factors need to be addressed. These will cause the model to increase in complexity, but the basic concepts will remain the same.

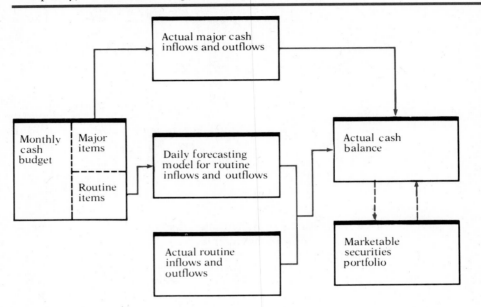

transferred, we have

$$TS = \frac{\$50(0.60)}{(0.04/365)(0.60)} = \$456{,}250$$

Therefore, there should be $456,250 that can be left in marketable securities for at least 1 day before the transfer is made. If we estimate, based on our daily cash balance model, that funds can be transferred from cash to marketable securities and left for 5 days, then

$$\$30 = (5)(TS)(0.04/365 \text{ days})(0.60)$$

$$TS = \frac{\$30}{5(0.04/365)(0.60)} = \$91{,}250$$

In this case the transfer should be made if there is more than $91,250 in excess funds in the firm's cash account. Similar calculations can be made if the differential interest rates change, or if the cost of the transaction increases or decreases. The point, however, is that the same basic benefit-cost framework can be used to determine when to transfer funds into and out of the marketable securities portfolio.

MODELS FOR DETERMINING THE TARGET CASH BALANCE

More formal models exist to help a firm determine its target cash balance, against which its actual cash balance can be compared. We will examine two: the Miller-Orr model and Stone's look-ahead model.

The Miller-Orr Model

The Miller-Orr model assumes cash inflows and outflows are uncertain and fluctuate randomly day-to-day. That is, the distribution of the daily net cash flow is described by a normal distribution. Figure 20.5 shows how the Miller-Orr model works. The model sets upper and lower control limits and a target cash balance. When the firm's cash balance reaches the upper control limit, H, the firm buys enough marketable securities to reduce its cash balance back to the target cash balance, Z. Similarly, if the cash balance drops to the lower control limit, L, then the firm sells enough marketable securities to again return its cash balance to the target. The lower cash balance is set by management, depending on how much cash shortfall risk the firm is willing to accept.

Figure 20.5

The Miller-Orr Model for Cash Balance Management

With the Miller-Orr model, the firm sells marketable securities or transfers funds from the cash account to marketable securities as needed. Note that the average cash balance is greater than the target cash balance. If the lower control limit is set at zero, then the upper control limit and the target cash balance would shift down accordingly.

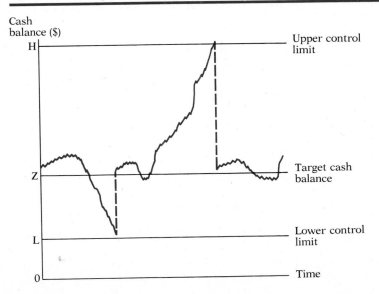

The Miller-Orr model depends on both opportunity and transactions costs.[5] The following variables are needed for the Miller-Orr model:

Z = the target cash balance
H = the upper control limit
L = the lower control limit
F = the fixed cost of buying or selling securities
k_{daily} = the opportunity cost of holding cash
σ^2 = the variance of the net daily cash flows

Then,

$$\text{target cash balance} = Z = \left[\frac{3F\sigma^2}{4k_{daily}}\right]^{1/3} + L \qquad (20.2)$$

and

$$\text{upper control limit} = H = 3Z - 2L \qquad (20.3)$$

The average daily cash balance is different from the target cash balance and equals

$$\text{average cash balance} = (4Z - L)/3$$

To illustrate the Miller-Orr model, suppose that L (the lower control limit) = zero, F = \$300, k = 10% = 0.10 per year, and the standard deviation, σ, of the daily cash flows is \$4,000. The daily compound opportunity cost is

$$(1 + k_{daily})^{365} - 1 = 0.10$$
$$(1 + k_{daily})^{365} = 1.10$$
$$1 + k_{daily} = (1.10)^{1/365}$$
$$1 + k_{daily} = 1.000261$$
$$k_{daily} = 0.000261$$

and the variance, σ^2, of the net daily cash flows is ($\$4,000)^2$ = 16,000,000. Then the

---

[5] An earlier model, developed by Baumol (1951) was based on the economic order quantity inventory model.

target cash balance, Z, is

$$Z = \left[\frac{3(\$300)(16{,}000{,}000)}{4(0.000261)}\right]^{1/3} + 0 \approx \$23{,}982 + 0 = \$23{,}982$$

The upper control limit, H, is

$$H = 3(\$23{,}982) - 2(0) = \$71{,}946$$

and the average cash balance is given by

$$\text{average cash balance} = [4(\$23{,}982) - 0]/3 = \$31{,}976$$

What occurs if everything is the same as before, except that the firm sets a lower control limit of $10,000? Then,

target cash balance = $23,982 + $10,000 = $33,982
upper control limit = $3(\$33{,}982) - 2(\$10{,}000) = \$81{,}946$
average cash balance = $[4(\$33{,}982) - \$10{,}000]/3 = \$41{,}976$

Thus, increasing or decreasing the lower control limit simply increases or decreases all of the levels by the amount of the change in the lower limit.

In examining the Miller-Orr model, note that the target cash balance is *not* midway between the upper and lower control limits. Therefore, the cash balance will, on average, hit the lower limit more often than the upper limit. This placement tends to limit the opportunity costs incurred.

When tested by firms, the Miller-Orr model does a reasonably good job if the distribution of net daily cash flows is approximately normal, the cash flows are random from day-to-day, and only one source of investment is available.

The Stone Model

The Stone model is similar in spirit to the Miller-Orr model, except that it places more attention on managing cash balances than on determining the optimal transaction size. Although upper and lower control limits are used, they do not automatically signal an investment or disinvestment decision. Rather, the action required depends upon the cash flows that are expected over the next few days. Figure 20.6 depicts the Stone model. The outer control limits function like those in the Miller-Orr model. With the Stone model, however, once a firm hits or exceeds the outer control limits, it "looks ahead" a few days to determine whether within that time frame its anticipated cash balance will move to *within* the inner control limits. If the balance moves back inside the appropriate inner control limit *sometime* in the "look ahead" period, no action is taken. If the cash balance is not anticipated to move within the inner control limit sometime in the look-ahead period, then a purchase or sale of marketable securities is triggered.

684 Part Five: Short-Term Financial Management

Figure 20.6

The Stone Model for Cash Balance Management

With the Stone model, two upper and lower control limits are employed. When the firm hits (or exceeds) an outer control limit, it "looks ahead" a few days to determine if it will move back inside the inner control limit. If it will, then no action is taken. Otherwise, securities are bought or sold as needed.

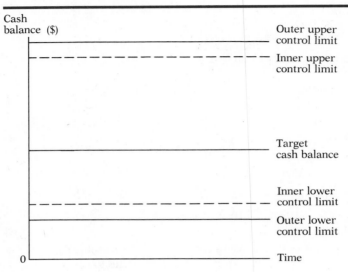

To illustrate Stone's model, assume that we have the following set of net cash flows (for simplicity we assume actual and expected cash flows are the same):

Day	Net Cash Flow
1	$20,000
2	−15,000
3	−45,000
4	15,000
5	10,000
6	20,000
7	−40,000
8	−10,000
9	−5,000
10	15,000

The initial cash balance is $60,000; the outer lower control limit is $25,000, and the inner lower limit is $35,000. As shown in Figure 20.7, on day 3 the outer lower control limit is breached (i.e., $60,000 + $20,000 − $15,000 − $45,000 = $20,000). Accordingly, the firm looks ahead a few days at anticipated net cash flows.

Figure 20.7

The Stone Model in Action

At day 3 a possible sell signal is given. However, by looking ahead, the firm finds no action is required. On day 7 another sell signal is given. This time, by looking ahead, the firm finds that cash balances won't be sufficient without the sale of marketable securities.

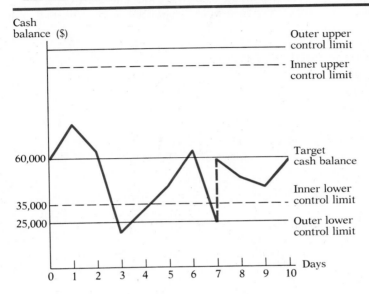

Assume a 3-day look-ahead policy is followed. We see that in days 4, 5, and 6 the cash balance increases and is at least as high as the inner lower control limit (as required by Stone's model). Thus, no transaction is made. On day 7, the outer lower control limit of $25,000 is again reached. The firm then looks ahead 3 days, as follows:

Day	Net Cash Balance
7	$25,000
8	25,000 − 10,000 = $15,000
9	15,000 − 5,000 = 10,000
10	10,000 + 15,000 = 25,000

Because at no time during the next three days will the cash balance return to the inner lower control limit of $35,000, a transaction is triggered. The firm sells $35,000 worth of securities on day 7 to bring its cash balance back up to the target of $60,000. This is also shown in Figure 20.7.

Unlike the Miller-Orr model, the Stone model does not provide an indication of how the outer upper and lower control limits are set. The Miller-Orr model, however, could be employed to determine both the target cash balance and the control limits, while the forecast (or look-ahead) period is set judgmentally. In contrast to the

Miller-Orr model, the Stone model requires no assumptions except that transfers to/from marketable securities are instantaneous. The price paid for this lack of assumptions is recognizing that the Stone model is an ad-hoc model that relies solely on judgment and the firm's past experience. While it is easy to adjust for seasonal or cyclical factors, there is no expectation that this model will lead to an optimal policy. Using the Stone model along with past experience and sensitivity analysis, however, provides the intuition of how firms set policies to control their cash balances.

Concept Review Questions

- Detail the five-step procedure employed to determine the firm's daily cash balance.
- Describe how to use the Miller-Orr model and the Stone model to determine target cash balances.

MANAGEMENT OF THE MARKETABLE SECURITIES PORTFOLIO

Excess cash above what is needed to meet the firm's cash balance requirement will be invested in marketable securities. Because of the need for liquidity and stability of principal, long-term bonds or common stock generally are not appropriate investments for temporary excess cash, unless some type of hedge is employed to counteract any potential loss of principal.

INVESTMENT ALTERNATIVES

Managers have a choice of many different marketable securities for short-term investments. These are shown in Table 20.1. U.S. Treasury bills are direct obligations of the U.S. government. They are typically considered the safest marketable security. The yield on Treasury bills is often used as a proxy for the risk-free rate, k_{RF}. All other marketable securities are viewed as being more risky, because they are not issued or backed directly by the U.S. government. Money market mutual funds are a pool of short-term marketable securities managed by an investment adviser. **Dutch auction preferred stock** may also be employed. This is a short-term security that is resold every 49 days. The advantage is that the dividends received on a dutch auction preferred stock are, like any other cash dividends received by one firm from another, partially exempt from corporate income taxes.

In addition, in recent years numerous other investment alternatives have become available. Many firms that pay the full amount of corporate taxes find that investing in tax-exempt securities provides higher after-tax returns.[6] Mortgage backed and other asset backed securities have also become more popular. Other firms have invested heavily in Eurodollar or LIBOR denominated investments. Still others have bought long-term bonds and then entered into interest rate swaps (swaps are discussed in

---

[6] Firms that purchase tax-exempt securities limit their purchases to no more than 2 percent of their assets. To limit tax arbitrage gains, an IRS provision limits the amount of interest corporations can deduct if they invest more than 2 percent of their assets in tax-exempt securities.

Chapter 23) to achieve a variable LIBOR rate return on their investment. Although these and many other innovations have occurred, we will focus on the basics of managing the marketable securities portfolio.

SELECTION CRITERIA

In assessing the selection of alternative marketable securities, we look at the risk, liquidity, maturity, and yield aspects of the alternative investments.

Risk

As general economic conditions change from boom to recession, market rates of interest change. In addition, monetary and fiscal policies can also influence market interest rates. As market interest rates go up, the market price of outstanding debt instruments decreases. As market interest rates go down, the market price of outstanding debt increases.

Figuring the Yield on Treasury Bills.   To examine the risks as economic conditions change, let's consider one specific money market security—Treasury bills. U.S. Treasury bills are non-interest-bearing discount securities that are sold through regular weekly and monthly auctions; 91- and 182-day maturity bills are sold weekly, and 365-day maturity bills are sold monthly. Because they are redeemed at full face value at maturity, the interest earned is the difference between the face value (if held to maturity) and the discounted price. Two interest rates are quoted for Treasury bills—the bank discount yield, k_{BD}, and the bond equivalent yield, k_{BE}.

The **bank discount yield** expresses the investor's expected return on a Treasury bill as a percent of the face value of the security, so that

$$k_{BD} = \left(\frac{P_M - P_0}{P_M}\right)\left(\frac{360 \text{ days}}{n}\right) \qquad (20.4)$$

where

k_{BD} = the bank discount yield
P_M = the maturity value of the Treasury bill
P_0 = the discounted price
n = the number of days until maturity

Note that the bank discount yield is based on 360 days.[7]

To illustrate, suppose that you purchase a 182-day Treasury bill with a face value of $10,000 at a price of $9,500. What is your bank discount yield? Employing Equation 20.4, we have

$$k_{BD} = \left(\frac{\$10,000 - \$9,500}{\$10,000}\right)\left(\frac{360}{182}\right) = \frac{\$180,000}{\$1,820,000} = 9.89\%$$

---

[7] Neither the bank discount nor the bond equivalent yield is calculated employing compound interest. Our presentation is in line with their use in practice.

Table 20.1

Characteristics of Marketable Securities

Given the wide variety of securities, maturities, and denominations, firms can tailor a marketable securities portfolio to meet their needs.

Instrument	Description	Maturity	Interest Basis	Marketability	Denomination
Treasury bills	Direct obligation of the U.S. government; exempt from state and local income tax	91 days to 1 year	Discount	Excellent secondary market	$10,000 and up
Federal agency issues	Notes issued by agencies created by the U.S. government; not explicitly backed by the government	5 days to several years; over half less than 1 year	Typically interest bearing, but may be discount	Good to excellent secondary market	$5,000 and up
Repurchase agreements (repos or buy-backs)	Sale of government securities by a bank or securities dealer with a simultaneous agreement to repurchase	1 day to 3 months	Repurchase price set higher than selling price, paid at maturity	Limited	$500,000
Short-term tax exempts	Notes issued by states, municipalities, local housing agencies, and urban renewal agencies; exempt from federal income tax	2 months to 1 year	Interest bearing, paid at maturity, or discount	Good secondary market	$1,000
Finance paper	Unsecured notes issued by large finance companies or bank holding companies	3 to 270 days	Either discount or interest bearing, paid at maturity	Limited secondary market, but firm will usually redeem early	$100,000

Table 20.1

Characteristics of Marketable Securities (*Continued*)

Instrument	Description	Maturity	Interest Basis	Marketability	Denomination
Commercial paper	Unsecured notes issued by smaller finance companies or industrial firms; increasingly used by non-U.S.-based firms	30 to 270 days	Discount	Limited secondary market, but dealer may arrange buy-back	$100,000
Negotiable certificates of deposit, CDs	Receipts for time deposits at commercial banks; very active market for overseas branches of U.S.-based banks	30 to 91 days or longer	Interest bearing, paid at maturity	Good secondary market	$1,000,000
Banker's acceptances	Time draft (or order to pay) issued by a business firm (usually an importer) that has been accepted by a bank	30 to 180 days	Discount	Good secondary market	$100,000
Eurodollars	Dollar-denominated time deposits at overseas banks	1 day to 1 year	Interest bearing, paid at maturity	Limited secondary market	$1,000,000
Money market mutual funds	Pool of short-term money market instruments	Shares may be sold any time	Credited to account monthly	Good; provided by fund itself	$500
Dutch auction preferred stock	Specially designed preferred stock	Resold every 7 weeks	Dividend paying, at maturity	Limited secondary market	$100,000

Alternatively, if someone told you that the bank discount yield on a 182-day $10,000 Treasury bill was 9.89 percent, and you wanted to find out how much you would pay for the security, we could rearrange Equation 20.4 and solve for P_0 as follows:

$$P_0 = P_M \left[1 - \frac{(k_{BD})(n)}{360 \text{ days}} \right] \quad\quad\quad (20.5)$$

$$= \$10,000 \left[1 - \frac{(0.0989)(182)}{360} \right]$$

$$= \$10,000 \, (1 - 0.05) = \$9,500$$

Because the bank discount yield is based on 360 days, and most interest rates are for 365 days, the **bond equivalent yield** for a Treasury bill is generally calculated. It is as follows:[8]

$$k_{BE} = \frac{(365 \text{ days})(k_{BD})}{360 \text{ days} - (k_{BD})(n)} \quad\quad\quad (20.6)$$

For our example, the bond equivalent yield is

$$k_{BE} = \frac{(365)(0.0989)}{360 - (0.0989)(182)} \approx 10.56\%$$

Because of the difference between the 360- and 365-day years, the bond equivalent yield is always higher than the bank discount yield.

To illustrate the risks that may exist with Treasury bills, let's continue with our example. If we buy the 182-day Treasury bill for $9,500 and hold it until maturity, then our bond equivalent yield is 10.56 percent. But what happens if we have to sell before it matures and interest rates on Treasury bills have increased from the time we purchased the Treasury bill? Suppose that we were forced to sell in 60 days, and the bank discount yield at that time was 11.00 percent.

To see the effect of having to sell when interest rates have moved higher, we first determine the price of the Treasury bill with 122 (i.e., $182 - 60$) days to maturity as follows using Equation 20.5:

$$P_0 \text{ selling price} = \$10,000 \left[1 - \frac{(0.11)(122)}{360} \right]$$

$$= \$10,000(1 - 0.037278) = \$9,627.22$$

Then the actual bond equivalent yield over the 60 days the Treasury bill was owned

---

[8] This formula applies only to Treasury bills with 182 days or less to maturity; another formula is used for longer-maturity bills. For simplicity, we employ Equation 20.6 even when the maturity exceeds 182 days. It should be noted that the bond equivalent yield is *not an effective interest rate* based on compound interest, only an approximation.

can be determined using Equation 20.7:

$$k_{BE} = \frac{(\text{selling price} - \text{purchase price})(365)}{(\text{purchase price})(\text{days owned})} \tag{20.7}$$

$$= \frac{(\$9,627.22 - \$9,500)(365)}{(\$9,500)(60)} \approx 8.15\%$$

Because of changes in market rates of interest, which adversely affected the price of the Treasury bill when we sold prematurely, our actual return was only 8.15 percent instead of our anticipated return of 10.56 percent.

U.S. Treasury bills are issued and backed by the U.S. government. Many other marketable securities are issued by individual firms or banks. **Commercial paper,** which is simply short-term unsecured borrowing, is issued by consumer finance companies or by industrial, retail, or even public utility firms. Likewise, many different banks issue negotiable **certificates of deposit,** which are short-term unsecured borrowings. The specific firm or issuer of the marketable security in these cases is responsible for payment. Managers must consider the ability of the firm issuing the marketable security to pay interest and principal on time.

Liquidity

Most marketable securities have excellent or good secondary markets. For commercial paper, however, it may be necessary to see if the issuing firm will redeem the security early if needed. Likewise, there is a limited secondary market for Eurodollars and **repurchase agreements.** Because firms use their marketable securities portfolio as a source of ready cash, the liquidity aspect of the investment also requires careful consideration.

Maturity

The maturity of the marketable securities is also of prime importance. Most large firms keep some cash invested overnight in repurchase agreements and other shorter-maturity securities. Then they follow a layered approach of matching longer cash availability with investments in longer term marketable securities.

Yield

The final selection criterion is the yield on the marketable securities. Table 20.2 presents the yields on various securities during the 1986–1992 period. We see that yields went up and then fell between 1986 and 1992. Also notice that Eurodollar deposits always provide more returns than any other marketable security, whereas Treasury bills, being the least risky, provide the lowest returns.

THE MARKETABLE SECURITIES PORTFOLIO

The basic considerations for designing the firm's marketable securities portfolio are presented in Figure 20.8. The interaction of risk, liquidity, and maturity determines the returns. The firm's risk-return posture then determines the specific composition of

Table 20.2

Yields on 3-Month Money Market Instruments

Treasury bills, being the least risky, provide the lowest returns. Eurodollars, being more risky and less liquid, provide the highest returns.

Instrument	Year						
	1986	1987	1988	1989	1990	1991	1992
Treasury bills	5.97%	5.78%	6.67%	8.11%	7.51%	5.40%	3.44%
Finance paper— directly placed	6.38	6.54	7.38	8.72	7.87	5.71	3.63
Commercial paper	6.49	6.82	7.66	8.99	80.6	5.87	3.75
Certificates of deposit	6.51	6.87	7.73	9.09	8.15	5.83	3.68
Banker's acceptances	6.38	6.75	7.56	8.87	7.93	5.70	3.62
Eurodollars	6.71	7.07	7.85	9.16	8.16	5.86	3.70

Source: Federal Reserve Bulletin, various issues.

the marketable securities portfolio. Very risk-averse firms might have a marketable securities portfolio composed almost entirely of U.S. Treasury bills. More aggressive firms will opt for a large portion in higher-yielding Eurodollars or certificates of deposit issued by overseas branches of U.S.-based banks. The impact of the returns on a big marketable securities portfolio, particularly when short-term interest rates are high, can be significant.

Concept Review Questions

- What are some marketable securities used by firms for short-term investments?
- How do risk, liquidity, maturity, and yield affect the composition of a firm's marketable securities portfolio?

Figure 20.8

Considerations Influencing the Composition of the Marketable Securities Portfolio

The risk-return posture of the firm plays a pivotal role in determining the final composition of its portfolio of marketable securities.

Considerations	Influence	Depends on	Decision
Risk Liquidity Maturity	→ Yields →	Firm's risk-return posture →	Marketable securities portfolio mix

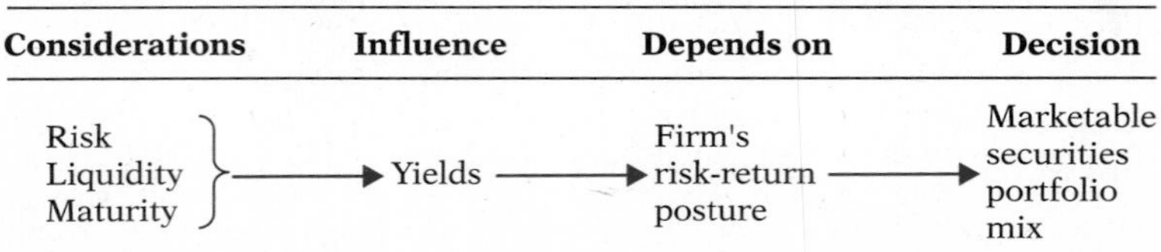

KEY POINTS

1. Management of the firm's liquid asset focuses on cash inflows and outflows, the trade-off between holding cash versus investing in marketable securities, and how to structure the marketable securities portfolio.

2. Because of float, firms attempt to speed the cash gathering process while controlling (or slowing) disbursements. The primary means for speeding collections are lockboxes and an efficient banking arrangement. Disbursements are managed by using controlled disbursing, zero balance accounts, and similar arrangements.

3. When comparing cash management alternatives, the incremental costs and benefits are analyzed in a NPV framework.

4. Determining the amount to hold in a firm's demand deposit account versus the amount to invest in marketable securities depends on forecasting and the incremental interest to be earned in marketable securities. The Miller-Orr and Stone models provide insight on how firms control their cash balances.

5. Risk, liquidity, maturity, and yield (or return) concerns determine how the firm's marketable securities portfolio is structured.

QUESTIONS

20.1 The objective of the firm is to maximize the value of the firm. Because the return on real assets typically exceeds the return on marketable securities, explain why firms generally keep 5 to 10 percent of their assets in cash and marketable securities.

20.2 Explain the different types of float and how they affect the firm's cash-gathering system. Do these same types of float apply to the firm's cash-disbursing system?

20.3 How can the firm speed up the cash-gathering process? Which float does each attempt to shorten?

20.4 Identify procedures the firm can employ to control the disbursement of cash. How does each serve to (a) increase float or (b) lower the firm's cash balance needs?

20.5 What impact would the following have on the firm's average cash balance?

a. Interest rates on marketable securities decrease.
b. Cost of trading marketable securities increases.
c. The firm's concentration bank raises its compensating balance requirement.
d. A zero balance account procedure is implemented.
e. New billing procedures allow a better correspondence between cash inflows and cash outflows.

20.6 Analyze the specific assumptions incorporated in the Miller-Orr and Stone models for determining the firm's target cash balance. What similarities and differences exist between the models?

20.7 Discuss the criteria that influence the firm's marketable securities selection procedure.

20.8 Treasury bills are widely employed by firms as an investment for temporary excess cash. Because they have the lowest yield of any marketable security, why are Treasury bills chosen?

20.9 During the last 25 years or so, many retail firms and others that issue credit cards have shifted from billing all customers on the last day of the month to "cycle billing." With cycle billing, customers are billed (often in alphabetical order) throughout the month. From the standpoint of the credit card issuer, what effect does cycle billing have on cash flows and average cash balances? Does it also have an impact on accounts receivable? Explain.

CONCEPT REVIEW PROBLEMS

See Appendix A for solutions.

CR20.1   It takes Casablanca Company 6 days to receive and deposit checks from customers. Management of Casablanca is considering a lockbox system to decrease float time to 4 days. Average daily collections are $20,000, and the cost of funds is 6 percent.

a. What will be the reduction in outstanding cash balances as a result of implementing the lockbox system?

b. If the firm's tax rate is 36 percent, what is the maximum daily charge that Casablanca can afford to pay for the lockbox system?

CR20.2   The Tucker Corporation disperses $500,000,000 in checks per year and they take an average of 2.84 days to clear. Tucker estimates it could increase the float to 4.15 days by opening a checking account in a small Mississippi bank. If $T = 40$ percent and $I = 8.7$ percent, what are the annual benefits from opening a checking account in Mississippi?

CR20.3   Kathy, assistant controller of KT Gear, is analyzing the firm's management of cash and marketable securities. Brokerage fees are $100 per transfer, the firm's tax rate is 40 percent, and incremental interest from having funds invested in marketable securities is 5 percent. If fund transfers occur every 7 days, what is the minimum amount that should be transferred? (*Note:* Assume a 365-day year.)

CR20.4   Kathy, from CR20.3, would like to use the Miller-Orr model to analyze KT Gear's cash balance policy. The standard deviation of the net daily cash flow is $10,000. To meet compensating balance requirements the firm keeps a minimum of $500,000 in the bank. What are KT Gear's recommended target cash balance, upper control limit, and average cash balance?

CR20.5   Now assume KT Gear has an actual cash balance of $588,000 on day $t = 0$ and has the following actual cash flows thereafter:

Day	Net Cash Flow
1	+40,000
2	−30,000

Using the Miller-Orr model to establish the outer upper control limit, Kathy employed the Stone model with an inner upper limit of $604,000.

a. Based on discussions with the firm's sales department and on past experience, Kathy expected the following cash flows over the next 4 days: +$10,000, +$10,000, −$10,000 and −$5,000. Using the Stone model with a 2-day look-ahead period, should Kathy transfer funds out of the firm's account?

b. Now assume the expected cash flows for the next 4 days are +$30,000, +$5,000, zero, and +$5,000 instead of those expected in (a). Should Kathy transfer funds? If so, how much should be transferred?

CR20.6   Tony, cash manager for KJI Inc., is considering the purchase of a Treasury bill for $9,900 that will mature in 50 days.

a. What is the bank discount yield on the Treasury bill?

b. What is the bond equivalent yield on the Treasury bill?

c. After 10 days, the bank discount yield on 40-day Treasury bills increased to 7.5%, and at that time Tony was forced to sell the Treasury bill and move funds into the firm's cash account. What was the bond equivalent return on the Treasury bill?

PROBLEMS

20.1 Melton & Sons projects its sales will be $120 million next year. All sales are for credit, but the credit policies are in good shape because there are very few bad debts and payments are mailed on time. Melton is concerned, however, about the cost of float time. Its marginal tax rate is 30 percent.

a. If funds could be invested to earn 7 percent, what is the incremental daily benefit of a 1-day reduction in float time using a 365-day year?
b. What is the daily benefit of a 1.5 day reduction in float if the funds could earn 8 percent?

20.2 New Hampshire Healthcare currently has all incoming checks sent directly to its headquarters. The average mail time is 4 days, processing time is 2 days, and transit time is 1.5 days. The average cash inflow is $2 million per calendar day.

a. What is the average collection float in dollars?
b. Although internal processing time is 2 days, New Hampshire is actually able to record the incoming checks for accounting purposes on its accounting records in 1 day. How much in dollars does New Hampshire have recorded on its accounting records that are not actually "good funds" in its bank account? (*Note:* Don't forget the 1.5 days of transit time.)
c. By modifying its system, New Hampshire Healthcare can reduce total float time *by* 2.25 days. The proposed system will cost $350,000 before taxes per year to operate, the interest rate is 12 percent, a 365-day year is assumed, and the marginal tax rate is 40 percent. Should New Hampshire implement the modified cash collection system? (*Note:* Solve for the yearly $\Delta B - \Delta C$.)

20.3 Mead-Tampa currently has a centralized cash-receiving system located in Tampa, Florida. Its average float time on collections is 5.7 days. A North Carolina bank has approached Mead-Tampa, offering to establish a lockbox system that should reduce the float time to 2.9 days. (So the net reduction is 5.7 − 2.9, or 2.8 days.) Mead's daily collections are $600,000, and excess funds can be invested at 10 percent. If there are 800 checks per day, how much is the maximum Mead-Tampa can afford to pay *per check* for the lockbox operation? Assume a 365-day year and a tax rate of 30 percent.

20.4 Harcourt Supply presently uses a 2-lockbox system that has a total average daily transaction balance of $1 million (based on a 365-day year). The banks do not charge a direct fee, but they require Harcourt to keep a total of $2 million in compensating balances on which no interest is paid.

Fred, a recent finance graduate, has recommended that Harcourt switch to a new lockbox system. The savings in float time would be 1.2 days, the average check size is $500, the interest rate is 9 percent, and the firm's marginal tax rate is 34 percent. As compensation to the banks, Harcourt would have its compensating balance requirement reduced to $1.8 million (still no interest paid), pay $0.05 per check processed, and pay additional fixed fees of $50,000 to the banks each year. Based on the yearly incremental costs and benefits, should Harcourt make the switch recommended by Fred? (*Note:* Don't forget that interest can be earned on the freed compensating balances.)

20.5   Presently, Reuss Industries is using a lockbox arrangement. Reuss believes, however, that it can save money by eliminating the lockbox system and handling the process internally. The lockbox costs $5 per day and $0.50 per check processed. Currently, 400 checks per day are being processed. If Reuss eliminates the lockbox, total costs will be $40,000 per year before taxes, and float time will increase by 2 days. Assume the average transaction size is $500 per check, the yearly interest rate is 11 percent, a 365-day year is employed, and the tax rate is 40 percent.

a.   Should Reuss eliminate the lockbox system? (*Note:* Compute the yearly incremental costs and benefits.)

b.   At what incremental float time would Reuss be indifferent between the two approaches?

20.6   Delaware Industries receives a periodic deposit of $20,000 at its San Juan, Puerto Rico, office. A mail process that costs $1 and takes 3 days is presently used to transfer the funds to its concentration bank in Cleveland. Alternatively, a wire transfer system costing $9 that makes the funds immediately available could be employed. Assume a 365-day year and a tax rate of 35 percent.

a.   If Delaware earns 12 percent on excess funds once they reach the concentration bank, which transfer method should be employed?

b.   What is the lowest dollar amount that should be transferred via wire transfer?

20.7   ElectroSystems has been growing so fast it has not examined its cash-gathering system. Presently, all cash comes into its corporate office. A downturn in the economy, however, has affected both sales and profitability. Now appears to be an appropriate time to review the cash-gathering system. A consulting firm, for a fee of $100,000, has just presented the following information to ElectroSystems:

Present	Proposed
Home office collection system costing $75,000 per year.	Five lockboxes; the cost per check processed is $0.30.
Average daily volume is $900,000, with an average check size of $1,500, based on receipts for 270 days per year.	Twice-daily transfer of funds from *each* lockbox via wire transfer at a cost of $8 each.
	Reduction in float time, 2.6 days.
	Home office expenses of $50,000 per year.

a.   If ElectroSystems can earn 9 percent on the excess funds and it is in the 40 percent marginal tax bracket, what are the yearly incremental after-tax costs and benefits of moving to the new system (ignoring the consultant's one-time fee of $100,000)? Should the switch be made? (*Note:* When calculating ΔC, assume that checks are processed only 270 days a year. When calculating ΔB, assume the $900,000 is available for all 365 days.)

b.   Was the consultant's report worthwhile?

20.8   Andy of Hudson Valley Tire needs to know how much money would be saved by a controlled disbursing system. The average daily payables are $200,000, the controlled disbursing will add 1.5 days to the float, and the excess funds can be invested at 13 percent. Based on a 365-day year and a marginal tax rate of 30 percent, what are the yearly incremental benefits associated with the controlled disbursing system?

20.9   Sequoia Marine Supplies has set up a controlled disbursing system with two out-of-town banks. The net benefit $(\Delta B - \Delta C)$ of the system to Sequoia is $28,700 per year. If Sequoia writes 200 checks per day with an average amount of $400, how many days of additional float will Sequoia obtain if the interest rate is 7 percent and the banks charge $0.10 per check cleared? Assume a 365-day year and that Sequoia is operating at a loss so that taxes are not relevant.

20.10   Ketcham International maintains a number of checking accounts in various banks to allow its divisions to pay suppliers. The total average daily cash balance (over all the banks) is $480,000, on which no interest is earned. To control disbursements better, Ketcham is investigating whether to set up a series of zero balance accounts at the Second National Bank. The bank will provide the service for a direct fee of $10,000 a year before taxes, plus a daily average compensating balance of $400,000. By implementing the new arrangement, Ketcham would free up $80,000 per day. No interest is earned on funds left with the bank in the $400,000 compensating balance arrangement.

Ketcham expects the float time to increase by 0.75 days with the zero balance account system. The average daily payables are $300,000, the excess funds can be invested at 12 percent, a 365-day year is assumed, and the marginal tax rate is 40 percent.

a.   What is the yearly (before-tax) interest earned on the $80,000 freed?
b.   What are the total yearly after-tax incremental costs and benefits of the zero balance accounts?

20.11   Southeast Imports has determined its daily standard deviation of cash flows is $50,000. The opportunity cost of holding cash is 9.5 percent per year, the cost of buying or selling marketable securities is $150, and the firm has established a minimum cash level of $150,000. What is Southeast Imports' target cash balance, its upper and lower control limits, and its average cash balance? (*Note:* Assume a 365-day year.)

20.12   The variance of the daily cash flow for a firm is $9,000,000, the opportunity cost of holding cash is 11 percent per year, and the cost of buying or selling marketable securities is $200 per transaction.

a.   What is the target cash balance, the upper control limit, and the average cash balance? (*Note:* Assume a 365-day year.)
b.   What happens to your answers in (a) if the cost of holding funds drops by 25 percent, to 8.25 percent per year?
c.   Independent of (b), what happens to your answers in (a) if the cost of buying or selling marketable securities increases by 25 percent, to $250 per transaction?

20.13   After trying the Miller-Orr model, Tracy Production has decided to employ the Stone model. It has established a target cash balance and control limits as follows:

Outer upper control limit	$100,000
Inner upper control limit	90,000
Target cash balance	50,000
Inner lower control limit	30,000
Outer lower control limit	20,000

Tracy's present cash balance is $70,000. If its cash flows (actual and expected) are as follows and it employs a 2-day look-ahead period, what action is required? (*Note:* If it has to buy or sell securities, buy or sell enough to bring it back to its target cash balance.)

Day	Net Cash Flow
1	$40,000
2	5,000
3	−10,000
4	−30,000
5	− 5,000
6	25,000
7	−15,000
8	−10,000
9	5,000
10	−10,000

20.14   A 91-day Treasury bill with a $10,000 maturity value was purchased at 97.40 (as a percent of its maturity value).

a.   What is the bank discount yield on the Treasury bill?
b.   What is its bond equivalent yield?
c.   Why is the bond equivalent yield always higher than the bank discount yield?

20.15   Sam's Supers had excess cash that it used to purchase a $1 million (maturity value) 182-day Treasury bill when the bank discount yield was 7.9 percent.

a.   What market price (ignoring transactions costs) did Sam's pay? (*Note:* Round all answers to the nearest dollar.)
b.   After 80 days, Sam's had to sell the Treasury bill. Due to heavy government financing, the bank discount rate had climbed to 8.40 percent when Sam's sold the bill. What was the actual bond equivalent yield on the Treasury bill?
c.   If Sam's sells the Treasury bill after 120 days, how do the answers in (a) and (b) change?

20.16   Spivey Energy has the following schedule of excess cash available and cash needs over the next 6 months:

Time	Cash Availability/Needs
Now	$2 million excess cash
In 2 months	An additional $2 million excess cash
In 4 months	$2 million cash needed
In 6 months	An additional $2 million cash needed

The structure of short-term interest rates is as follows:

Now		Expected in 2 Months	
Maturity Period	Yield (Annual)	Maturity Period	Yield (Annual)
2 months	7.3%	2 months	8.0%
4 months	7.4	4 months	8.1
6 months	7.5		

Assume that once marketable securities are purchased, they are held to maturity. If it costs $100 every time marketable securities are purchased, which securities should be purchased to maximize the before-tax income from the added investment? [*Hint:* Remember the yields are on an annual basis. To convert to monthly, just divide the yearly figure by 12. For simplicity, (1) do *not* compound your results, and (2) take the transactions costs at the end of the time period.]

20.17 Mini Case You have just been hired by Worldwide Toys as their cash manager. On your first day on the job you find that the cash management system is in disarray. Consequently, it must be overhauled, and in the process you must educate your employees and the firm's management.

a. As a first step you find that the three basic issues relating to cash (or liquid asset) management are not clearly understood. Explain these issues.

b. There has been a lot of confusion concerning the issue of float. Explain what float is, how it exists for both cash inflows and cash outflows, what parts can be controlled (and how), and how the issue of "good funds" relates to float. The firm's accounting manager has typically provided estimates of "good funds" by examining the firm's day-by-day cash account as recorded by the firm's accounting system. Is this a good policy? Explain.

c. Three alternatives to the present cash flow system have been presented to you. What decisions should be made in each case?

(1) Lockbox: Average collection float is presently 6.3 days. By going to a lockbox system, the firm can reduce the float to 2.8 days. The daily collections are $1,500,000, excess funds can be invested at an incremental rate of 8 percent, and there are 2,500 checks per day. The bank will charge $200 per day plus 20 cents per check processed. Worldwide's effective tax rate is 40 percent. (*Note:* Assume a 365-day year throughout, and calculate the daily benefits and costs.)

(2) Controlled disbursing: The firm's average daily payables are $800,000, consisting of 1,000 checks, and the present payable float is 1.5 days. The new payables float will be 3.4 days. The bank will charge $400 per day plus 8 cents per check. The tax rate is still 40 percent, and the interest rate is 8 percent.

(3) Wire transfer: Worldwide currently employs ACH transactions to move funds between various banks and its concentration bank. Switching to wire transfers would reduce float by 1 day. The ACH transactions cost $1.78 per transfer, whereas wire transfers cost $4.45 per transfer. The number of transfers per day is 30, and the average size is $2,000. The tax rate is 40 percent, and the interest rate is 8 percent.

d. To determine the firm's target cash balance, you decide to implement the Miller-Orr model. By sampling over the last year the daily standard deviation of the cash flows has been estimated to be $800,000. Given the uncertainty involved, the minimum cash level has been set at $1,000,000. The opportunity cost of holding cash is 8 percent per year, and the cost of buying or selling marketable securities is $300. Assuming a 365-day year, what are the target cash balance, the upper and lower control limits, and the average cash balance?

e. Excess funds will be invested in marketable securities. Summarize the different types of marketable securities available. Also, indicate what risks must be considered when constructing the firm's marketable securities portfolio.

f. Two different Treasury bills exist as follows:

$10,000 maturity value, 90-day bill with P_0 of $9,780

$10,000 maturity value, 245-day bill with P_0 of $9,390

(1) Which Treasury bill has the higher bond equivalent yield?
(2) Now assume that the Treasury bill has to be sold by Worldwide Toys in 70 days. The bond discount yield on the shorter maturity bill is 8.70 percent, whereas it is 8.90 percent on the longer-maturity bill. What would the actual yield on the two Treasury bills be over this time period?

REFERENCES

For some recent developments, see:

CUDJOE, JAMES, and GREG FLIGHT. "Implementing an International EDI/EFT Program—General Electric's Experience." *Journal of Cash Management* 12 (May/June 1992): 19–22.

FIX, JOHN N., and JOHN R. RANDELLI. "Treasury Management in 1992: The Shape of the Industry." *Journal of Cash Management* 12 (November/December 1992): 18–22.

KAHN, RANDY, and ROBERT ROSDORFF. "Practical Applications of Financial EDI." *Journal of Cash Management* 12 (January/February 1992): 20–23.

For more on cash gathering and disbursing, see:

BATTIN, CARL ALAN, and SUSAN HINKO. "A Game Theoretic Approach to Cash Management." *Journal of Business* 55 (July 1982): 367–81.

MAIER, STEVEN F., and JAMES H. VANDER WEIDE. "What Lockbox and Disbursement Models Really Do." *Journal of Finance* 38 (May 1983): 361–71.

For more on cash flow forecasting and models, see:

BAUMOL, WILLIAM J. "The Transactions Demand for Cash: An Inventory Theoretic Approach." *Quarterly Journal of Economics* 66 (November 1952): 545–56.

HEIKKI, RINNE, ROBERT A. WOOD, and NED C. HILL. "Reducing Cash Concentration Costs by Anticipatory Forecasting." *Journal of Cash Management* 6 (March–April 1986): 44–50.

MILLER, MERTON H., and DANIEL ORR. "A Model of the Demand for Money by Firms." *Quarterly Journal of Economics* 80 (August 1966): 413–35.

STONE, BERNELL K. "The Use of Forecasts and Smoothing in Control-Limit Models for Cash Management." *Financial Management* 1 (Spring 1972): 72–84.

———, and TOM W. MILLER. "Daily Cash Forecasting and Seasonal Resolution: Alternative Models and Techniques for Using the Distribution Approach." *Journal of Financial and Quantitative Analysis* 20 (September 1985): 335–51.

Marketable securities, and their management, are discussed in:

ALDERSON, MICHAEL J., KEITH C. BROWN, and SCOTT L. LUMMER. "Dutch Auction Rate Preferred Stock." *Financial Management* 16 (Summer 1987): 68–73.

FRANKLE, ALAN W., and J. MARKHAM COLLINS. "Investment Practices of the Domestic Cash Manager." *Journal of Cash Management* 7 (May–June 1987): 50–53.

21
Accounts Receivable and Inventory

EXECUTIVE SUMMARY

Accounts receivable represents a sizable percentage of most firms' assets. The primary determinants of the receivables level are the industry, the level of total sales, and the firm's credit and collection policies. Firms cannot discriminate on price; however, they may offer different conditions of sale. Therefore, the most important credit-granting decisions are (1) who will receive credit, and (2) what the conditions of the sale will be.

The actual credit decision involves an analysis of the size and timing of the cash flows involved and of the risks in a present value framework. Those credit opportunities with positive NPVs should be accepted, and those with negative NPVs should be rejected. The receivables pattern approach to managing collections focuses on the payment and receivables pattern relative to the month the sale occurred. As such, it is not influenced by the level of sales.

Like accounts receivable, inventory also represents a sizable percentage of most firms' assets. The basic costs associated with inventory are carrying costs, ordering costs, and costs associated with running short. The ABC method, the economic order quantity model, material requirements planning, and just-in-time are all models employed to manage a firm's inventory. NPV techniques are employed to make inventory decisions because, like accounts receivables, the basic decisions are similar to those found in any other investment the firm makes.

RECEIVABLES, INVENTORY, AND THE FIRM

To complete our analysis of the firm's current assets, we turn our attention to accounts receivable and inventory. Firms typically sell goods and services on both a cash and a credit basis. In the former, cash is received immediately; in the latter, the extension of

trade credit leads to the establishment of accounts receivable. Receivables represent credit sales that have not been collected. Over time, as the customers pay these accounts, the firm receives the cash associated with the original sale. If the customer does not pay an account, a **bad debt** loss is incurred. To make sales, most firms carry various types of inventory. Firms carry inventory to ensure a smooth production cycle and to assist in the marketing effort. Without both receivables and inventory, most firms would cease to operate or would be much less efficient.

The investment in accounts receivable and inventory is similar to the long-term, or capital budgeting, decision discussed in Chapters 7–10, so many of the techniques used in this chapter are similar to those used in making capital budgeting decisions. Throughout, the emphasis is on the magnitude, timing, and riskiness of the cash flows, and the opportunity costs associated with a firm's investment in receivables and inventory. In managing these the goal remains to maximize the overall value, V, of the firm.

IMPORTANCE OF RECEIVABLES AND INVENTORY

The financial goals of the firm must be coordinated with its marketing and production efforts. There is always a trade-off between risk and return, and different departments often want different policies. Nowhere is this more evident than in determining and maintaining proper levels of receivables and inventory. The marketing department may want lenient credit terms and collection policies in order to increase sales; the marketing effort also benefits from high inventory levels. With high inventory levels, the firm can promise immediate delivery, knowing that it will not lose sales because of stock outages. Higher inventory levels help the production department as well, enabling it to purchase in larger quantities, use longer production runs, and suffer less down time or unanticipated adjustments in the production schedule. These varying desires often conflict, however, with the objectives of the chief financial officer. Other things being equal, the CFO wants to minimize the firm's accounts receivable and inventory levels. Lower levels have two important financial benefits: First, less financing has to be secured, because the firm has less investment in receivables and inventory. Second, profits should be higher relative to sales or assets, because long-term investments are expected to generate higher returns than short-term assets.

The result must be a trade-off between risk and return. On the one hand, there is the risk of not granting enough credit or having enough inventory, thereby suffering sales losses. On the other hand, too high a level of receivables and inventory has a cost that may offset any sales or production benefits. A coordinated effort, involving marketing, production, and finance, is required to balance the risks and the returns. Most firms have substantial investments in receivables and inventory. Large manufacturing firms may have "only" 30 percent of total assets invested in receivables and inventory. But over 50 percent of the total assets of most retail and smaller manufacturing firms is invested in receivables and inventory, and that figure increases to over 60 percent for wholesale firms.

The investment in both receivables and inventory is influenced by many factors. One primary determinant is the industry in which the firm operates. The industry effect is caused by competition, the characteristics of the product, the production process, and so forth. Recent surveys of credit policies have indicated that the actions of competitors are the major factor governing the credit terms granted. At the same time, trade credit is more likely to be extended if the seller has a cost advantage over competing suppliers or lenders or has (or can achieve) greater market power.[1] Likewise, a firm's investment in inventory is largely influenced by production processes and the requirements imposed by competition. The importance of the industry effect cannot be minimized when examining a firm's investment in both receivables and inventory. Inventory management techniques are examined later in the chapter. For now, let's concentrate on receivables.

SIZE OF ACCOUNTS RECEIVABLE

The size of the investment in accounts receivable is influenced by factors in addition to industry effect, cost advantage, and market power effect. First, as shown in Figure 21.1, is total sales. Certain credit policies, such as liberal payment periods, encourage more sales. The state of the economy, the aggressiveness of the firm's marketing efforts, and other like factors also influence sales. As total sales increase, the level of credit sales and the investment in receivables usually increases. Second, the firm's credit and collection policies also influence the size of the investment in receivables.

Figure 21.1

Factors Affecting the Investment in Accounts Receivable

The level of sales, percentage of credit sales, and credit and collection policies determine the level of the firm's accounts receivable. Likewise, the credit management operation directly influences the flow of funds to the firm's cash account.

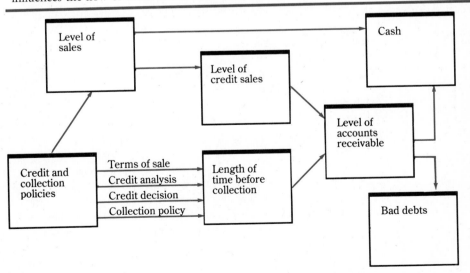

---

[1] For a discussion of these and other issues see Mian and Smith (1992).

These policies can be broken down into four distinct aspects:

1. Terms and conditions of credit sales.
2. Credit analysis.
3. Credit decision.
4. Collection policy.

The decisions in these areas largely determine the length of time between the granting of credit and the receipt of cash. As the length of time before collection increases, the firm's investment in receivables increases. Shortening the days sales outstanding reduces the firm's investment in receivables. The level of investment in accounts receivable is a function of the firm's industry, its total sales, and its credit and collection policies.

Concept Review Questions

- What are the benefits and the risks of minimizing the firm's accounts receivable and inventory levels?
- Describe factors that affect the size of a firm's accounts receivable.

CREDIT AND COLLECTION MANAGEMENT

In this section, we will explore in more detail the four main aspects of credit and collection policies. In doing so, we want to see how they are established and the effect they can have on the value of the firm.

TERMS AND CONDITIONS OF SALE

Although most firms and industries grant trade credit, there are substantial variations. If the goods are produced to the customer's specifications, the selling firm may ask for cash before delivery. If the deliveries are irregular or if some risk is involved, the seller may require **cash on delivery, COD.** If ordinary trade credit is granted, goods are on an open account, with payment due in some prespecified length of time, such as 30 or 60 days. As an inducement to encourage early payment, firms often offer a cash discount. If a firm sells on a 2/10, net 30 basis, customers who pay within 10 days receive a 2 percent discount; in any case, full payment is due within 30 days. In an open account agreement, the seller delivers the goods and provides an invoice, which constitutes the customer's bill and contains the terms of the arrangement. Likewise, in some industries **seasonal dating** is employed, with payment being timed to coincide with the buyer's anticipated cash inflows.

If the goods are large in size, or if the seller is unsure about the payment ability of the customer, other devices may be employed. The most common is the use of a draft, which is just a written order to pay a specified amount of money at a specified point in time to a given person (or to the bearer). The selling firm might agree to sell the goods only if the sale is made through a draft. If a **sight draft** is employed, before receiving title to the goods, the customer would have to pay when the draft is presented. Alternatively, the draft could be a **time draft,** which states that payment will be made a certain number of days after presentation to the customer. A time draft can be accepted by the customer or the customer's bank. If the customer accepts the draft, he or she acknowledges acceptance in writing on the back of the draft. This then becomes a **trade acceptance.** If the draft is accepted by the customer's bank, it becomes a **banker's acceptance.** The bank substitutes its creditworthiness for the customer's. As noted in Chapter 20, banker's acceptances are a major short-term marketable security; most of them arise from international trade.

The wide variety of terms and conditions have some logic to them, but tradition within an industry also plays a part. Sellers will demand early payment if the customers are in a high-risk class, if the accounts are small, or if the goods are perishable.

CREDIT ANALYSIS

To conduct a credit analysis, information is needed on the creditworthiness and paying potential of the customer. Among the numerous sources that exist for securing this information are these:

1. ACCOUNTING STATEMENTS   Based on accounting statements provided by the potential customer, a credit-granting firm may judge the stability and cash-generating ability of the customer.
2. CREDIT RATINGS AND REPORTS   Dun & Bradstreet is probably the best known and most comprehensive credit agency. Its regular *Reference Book* provides credit ratings on about 2 million firms, both domestic and foreign. In addition, the National Association of Credit Management enlisted TRW, Inc., to develop a computer-based credit retrieval system. A typical credit report includes the following information:
    a. Summary of recent accounting statement(s).
    b. Key ratios and trends over time.
    c. Information from the firm's suppliers indicating the firm's payment pattern.
    d. Description of the firm's physical condition and unusual circumstances related to the firm or its owners.
    e. A credit rating indicating the agency's assessment of the creditworthiness of the potential customer.
3. BANKS   Most banks maintain credit departments and may provide credit information on behalf of their customers.
4. TRADE ASSOCIATIONS   Many trade associations provide reliable means of obtaining credit information.
5. COMPANY'S OWN EXPERIENCES   Past experiences of the firm may have lead to some formal guidelines to look for when gathering credit information and "sizing up" the creditworthiness of a potential customer.

CREDIT DECISION

Once the information is collected, a credit decision has to be made. That is, should credit be granted (and under what terms of sale) or not? To do this, many firms employ an approach based on classifying potential customers into risk classes. With such a system, a firm might form a number of risk classes, as follows:

Risk Class	Estimated Percentage of Uncollectible Sales	Percentage of Customers in This Class
1	0–1%	35%
2	$1-2\frac{1}{2}$	30
3	$2\frac{1}{2}-4$	20
4	4–6	10
5	More than 6	5

Customers in class 1 might be extended credit automatically and their status reviewed only once a year. Those in class 2 might receive credit within specific limits, with their status checked semiannually. Similar decisions could be made on the other categories. To protect against the possibility of loss, customers in class 5 might have to accept goods on a COD basis. This requirement for group 5 is perfectly legal, because it is the terms of the sale, *not* the sale price or cash discount (if any), that are affected. Some objective basis must exist, however, for placing a customer in one risk class as opposed to another.

To make the risk class judgment, many firms use **credit scoring models.** A typical model is as follows:

Variable	Weight	Credit Score*	Risk Class
Fixed charges coverage	4	Greater than 47	1
Quick ratio	11	40–47	2
Years in business		32–39	3
(maximum of 15)	1	24–31	4
		Less than 24	5

*Credit score = 4(fixed charges coverage) + 11(quick ratio) + 1(years in business).

Based on either statistical or some other method of analysis, firms determine the relevant variables that are reliable indicators of their customers' creditworthiness. In this example three variables and their weights have been determined. The three variables are fixed charges coverage [(EBIT + lease expenses)/(interest + lease expenses)]; quick ratio [(current assets − inventory)/current liabilities]; and years in business. Suppose that a new customer with the following conditions applies for credit:

Fixed charges coverage	3.5
Quick ratio	0.8
Years in business	11

The customer's credit score would be $4(3.5) + 11(0.8) + 1(11) = 33.8$, and it would be placed in risk category 3.

This type of approach is being supplemented by rapid advances in computer-based information systems in larger firms, to limit risk exposure to credit losses. Smaller firms often employ time-sharing computer facilities to achieve many of the same benefits. For example, through Dun & Bradstreet a firm could designate a set of accounts to be monitored periodically for significant changes in the information in the D&B data base. If and when changes occur, that information can be electronically transmitted to the firm granting trade credit so that it can take action by reducing or eliminating credit granting to the firm in question.

Many complexities can be introduced in making credit decisions, but let's start out with the basics. To make the decision, firms compare the costs of granting credit with the benefits to be derived from granting credit, taking into account risk and the magnitude and timing of the cash flows.

The Basic Model

To make the credit decision, the firm needs the following information:

> cash inflows = the cash benefits expected to arise from the sale of goods on credit
> cash outflows = the cash outflows associated with the goods to be sold. (Note that any fixed costs are not relevant, because they will be incurred by the firm whether or not credit is granted.)
> T = the firm's marginal tax rate

The after-tax cash flow, CF_t, received by a firm from a credit sale can be summarized by[2]

$$CF_t = (CFBT_t)(1 - T) \tag{21.1}$$

where $CFBT_t$ (cash flow before taxes) equals cash inflows minus cash outflows in time period t.

To determine whether to grant credit, we compare the present value of the benefits with the cost of granting credit, given the risks involved. The net present value, NPV,

---

[2] This is the same as Equation 8.3, except no depreciation is shown. The focus is on the variable cash flows associated with production and selling, assuming the firm already has the necessary long-term assets in place. Depreciation is not relevant. If the credit decision requires a sizable investment in new equipment, however, depreciation must be included.

for the credit-granting decision is

$$NPV = \frac{CF_t}{k} - CF_0 \tag{21.2}$$

where[3]

CF_t = the after-tax cash flows in each time period

k = the after-tax opportunity cost of capital reflecting the risk class of the potential customer

CF_0 = the investment the firm makes in its accounts receivable

The decision rule for the net present value when making the credit-granting decision is as follows:

1. If NPV is greater than zero, grant credit.
2. If NPV is less than zero, do not grant credit.
3. If NPV is equal to zero, you are indifferent.

Making the Credit Decision

To use Equation 21.2, the granting firm's investment in accounts receivable, CF_0, and the net cash flows expected from granting credit,[4] CF_t, must be determined. These are:

$$CF_0 = (VC)(S)(DSO/365 \text{ days}) \tag{21.3}$$

and

$$CF_t = [S(1 - VC) - S(BD) - CD](1 - T) \tag{21.4}$$

where

VC = the variable cash outflow of producing and selling the goods as a percentage of cash inflows

S = the cash inflows (sales) expected each period

DSO = days sales outstanding

BD = bad debts as a percentage of cash inflows from sales

CD = the dollar amount of additional credit department cash outflow for administering or collecting the accounts receivable

T = the firm's marginal tax rate

To illustrate this approach to the credit-granting decision, consider Empire Electronics, which groups firms into risk categories. Two of these risk classes, X and Y, are

---

[3] Equation 21.2 is the perpetuity form for the net present value. If the benefits are not expected to continue until infinity, then NPV techniques for limited-life projects should be employed.
[4] For simplicity, we ignore cash discounts in Equation 21.4.

shown below:

Risk Class	Opportunity Cost of Capital (k)	Days Sales Outstanding (DSO)	Sales (S)	Bad Debts as a Percentage of Sales (BD)	Additional Collection Department Cash Outflows (CD)
X	18%	55 days	$200,000	9%	$10,000
Y	22	60	250,000	11	13,000

At present, Empire does not grant credit to firms in either class. The question is, should Empire modify its terms and now extend credit to firms in either or both risk classes? In addition to the data given above, Empire's variable cash outflows are 82 percent of sales, and its tax rate is 35 percent.

To make the decision, let's first consider class X. We can find the additional initial investment (at cost) in accounts receivable using Equation 21.3, as follows:

$$CF_0 = (VC)(S)(DSO/365 \text{ days})$$
$$= (0.82)(\$200,000)(55/365) = \$24,712$$

The additional expected cash inflows, CF_t, are found using Equation 21.4, as follows:

$$CF_t = [S(1 - VC) - S(BD) - CD](1 - T)$$
$$= [\$200,000(1 - 0.82) - \$200,000(0.09) - \$10,000](1 - 0.35)$$
$$= (\$36,000 - \$18,000 - \$10,000)(0.65) = (\$8,000)(0.65) = \$5,200$$

Thus, if Empire grants credit to firms in risk class X, it benefits by receiving incremental expected after-tax cash inflows of $5,200 per period. To obtain these additional CFs, Empire must make an additional investment of $24,712 in accounts receivable. Employing a time line, the cash flows are as follows:

The net present value, which is the benefit to the firm from granting credit to firms in risk class X, employing Equation 21.2, is

$$NPV = \frac{CF_t}{k} - CF_0 = \frac{\$5,200}{0.18} - \$24,712 = \$28,889 - \$24,712 = \$4,177$$

Because the net present value is positive, Empire should grant credit to potential customers in risk class X. By doing so, it is making a decision that increases the value of the firm.

The same calculations can be carried out for firms in risk class Y:

$$CF_0 = (0.82)(\$250,000)(60/365) = \$33,699$$

and

$$CF_t = [\$250,000(1 - 0.82) - \$250,000(0.11) - \$13,000](1 - 0.35)$$
$$= (\$45,000 - \$27,500 - \$13,000)(0.65) = (\$4,500)(0.65) = \$2,925$$

The net present value is then

$$NPV = \frac{\$2,925}{0.22} - \$33,699 = \$13,295 - \$33,699 = -\$20,404$$

Because the net present value is negative, Empire would not grant credit to firms in risk class Y.

In the first case, the additional investment in accounts receivable was less than the present value of the expected cash inflows arising from granting credit.[5] In the second case, the investment was greater. Thus, credit should be granted to customers in risk class X, but not to those in risk class Y.

COLLECTION POLICY

Once the granting decision has been made, we cannot ignore the final step—namely, following up to ensure the collection of these receivables. The rate at which receivables are converted into cash measures the efficiency of the collection policy. To ensure collections, we establish a collections department that is responsible for monitoring and following up on receivables. We first consider some techniques for monitoring accounts receivable; then we consider how to analyze changes in collection policies.

Managing Collections

Two basic techniques for monitoring the receivables investment are the days sales outstanding and the receivables pattern approach.

Days Sales Outstanding.   The days sales outstanding is calculated by dividing the firm's accounts receivable by average daily sales:

$$\text{days sales outstanding} = \frac{\text{accounts receivable}}{\text{sales}/365 \text{ days}} \tag{21.5}$$

---

[5] In addition to the standard credit decision just discussed, the same basic approach can be employed to analyze the size of the cash discount offered or the terms of sale. Although these are also important issues, both the cash discount offered and the terms of sale are influenced by competition and are subject to infrequent change.

If a firm's receivables are $1,800,000 and its sales for the year are $14,600,000, its days sales outstanding, DSO, is

$$DSO = \frac{\$1,800,000}{\$14,600,000/365} = \frac{\$1,800,000}{\$40,000} = 45 \text{ days}$$

The DSO is easy to calculate, but it is not very effective for internal use in monitoring a firm's collections. It is an aggregate measure and tends to hide many individual differences among customers in terms of payments. In addition, the DSO is influenced by changes in the level of receivables or changes in sales. If receivables increase to $2,000,000, the days sales outstanding goes to 50 days in our example [$2,000,000 ÷ ($14,600,000/365)]. If receivables stay at the original level of $1,800,000, the DSO can also increase to 50 days if sales drop to $13,140,000 [$1,800,000 ÷ ($13,140,000/365)]. From a control standpoint, the increase in the level of receivables to $2,000,000 might require different actions by the collection department from those needed if sales decreased to $13,140,000.

A Receivables Pattern Approach.   Instead of using the days sales outstanding or some other aggregate measure of accounts receivable, it is better to take a management-by-exception approach, using receivables pattern data for the firm's receivables. The **receivables pattern** is that percentage of credit sales remaining unpaid in the month of the sale and in subsequent months. The key to understanding receivables patterns is to remember that *each* month's credit sales are kept separate, as well as the collections received on these credit sales. Consider a firm that has credit sales of $100,000 in January. Collections on the $100,000 are as follows:

Month	Collections from January Sales	Payment Pattern	Receivables from January Sales Outstanding at End of Month	Receivables Pattern
January	$10,000	10%	$90,000	90%
February	30,000	30	60,000	60
March	30,000	30	30,000	30
April	30,000	30	0	0

In January, 10 percent of the credit sales are paid, followed by 30 percent each in February, March, and April.[6] The receivables pattern, which is simply 100 percent minus the cumulative percentage payments, declines from 90 percent in January to zero in April. This information is graphed in Figure 21.2.

Because the receivables pattern approach relates uncollected accounts receivable to the months in which they arise, it has two significant advantages from a management standpoint: First, it disaggregates the receivables into their collection pattern relative

---

[6] For simplicity, we ignore bad debts.

Figure 21.2

Graph of Payment and Receivables Pattern for January Credit Sales

The receivables pattern in (b) is derived from the payment pattern in (a). By focusing on the receivables pattern, the firm can easily determine whether payments are being made in the manner expected.

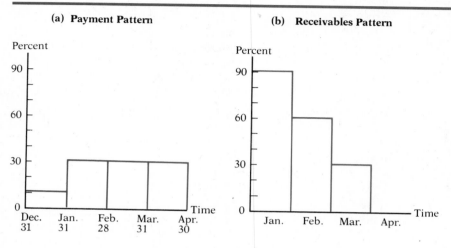

(a) Payment Pattern   **(b) Receivables Pattern**

to the month in which they occur. Second, because accounts receivable are related to sales in the month of origin, they are not sales-dependent. No matter what the sales pattern, any changes in payment behavior can be recognized immediately.

To see how we might exercise control, consider Table 21.1, which provides both budgeted and actual receivables patterns over a 6-month period. Note that the budgeted receivables pattern was 91, 61, and 20 percent for January sales, whereas the

Table 21.2

Budgeted Versus Actual Accounts Receivable Patterns

Looking across the bottom two rows, we see that since November, the actual receivables still outstanding both 1 and 2 months after the sales are greater than the budgeted receivables. The slow collection is not unique to the January credit sales.

	October	November	December	January	February	March
Budgeted						
Percent of same month sales	90%	91%	93%	91%	91%	90%
Percent of 1 month before	65	64	62	61	61	62
Percent of 2 months before	36	26	24	22	20	20
Actual						
Percent of same month sales	91%	93%	96%	90%	88%	89%
Percent of 1 month before	70	68	69	66	65	65
Percent of 2 months before	34	32	30	30	28	30

actual receivables are 90, 65, and 30, respectively. In both the first and second months after the credit sales, the collections came in slower than expected. Further examination of Table 21.1 indicates this same pattern has been occurring since November. By focusing on the exceptions, or the deviations of the actual from the projected pattern, management is in a good position to change the collection policy or modify the classes of customers who are eligible to receive credit.

Analysis of Changes in Collection Policy

Now that we have some idea of how to analyze and control collections, we can evaluate other important questions. Should we change our existing credit granting or collection policies? To evaluate changing policies and, possibly, curtailing credit previously granted, we simply employ the NPV approach discussed previously. A second decision is to tighten or loosen collection procedures related to existing customers. Consider the following, which shows the existing collection experience and proposed effects of improving the firm's collection procedures:

Situation	Opportunity Cost of Capital (k)	Days Sales Outstanding (DSO)	Sales (S)	Bad Debts as a Percentage of Sales (BD)	Collection Department Cash Outflows (CD)
Old	15%	60 days	$1,000,000	10%	$50,000
New	15	55	1,000,000	7	90,000

Under the existing procedures, the days sales outstanding is 60 days, sales are $1,000,000, bad debts are 10 percent of sales, and collection department cash outflows are $50,000. By expanding our collections department, we would be able to reduce the days sales outstanding to 55 days, and bad debts would drop to only 7 percent. Our collection department cash outflows, however, would increase from $50,000 to $90,000. The question is this: Will the firm benefit from increasing its collection efforts?

To answer, we begin by calculating the incremental initial investment and incremental cash flows after taxes that are associated with the revised procedures. Then we can employ Equation 21.2 to determine whether the change adds to the profitability of the firm. The incremental investment, ΔCF_0, is equal to

$$\text{incremental investment, } \Delta CF_0 = \frac{\text{investment, new } (N)}{} - \frac{\text{investment, old } (O)}{} \tag{21.6}$$

$$= (VC_N)(S_N)(DSO_N/365) - (VC_O)(S_O)(DSO_O/365)$$

If the variable cash outflows are 80 percent of sales in either case, then using the data given above, the incremental investment is

$$\Delta CF_0 = (0.80)(\$1,000,000)(55/365) - (0.80)(\$1,000,000)(60/365)$$

$$= \$120,548 - \$131,507 = -\$10,959$$

By reducing the days sales outstanding from 60 to 55 days, the new collection plan frees $10,959 that can be used elsewhere in the firm.

The incremental cash flow after-tax, ΔCF_t, due to the change in the collection policy is

$$\begin{array}{l} \text{incremental after-tax} \\ \text{cash flow, } \Delta CF_t \end{array} = \begin{array}{l} \text{after-tax cash} \\ \text{flow, new } (N) \end{array} - \begin{array}{l} \text{after-tax cash} \\ \text{flow, old } (O) \end{array} \qquad (21.7)$$

$$= [S_N(1 - VC_N) - S_N(BD_N) - CD_N](1 - T)$$
$$- [S_0(1 - VC_0) - S_0(BD_0) - CD_0](1 - T)$$

If the tax rate is 40 percent, then the incremental after-tax cash flow due to implementing the new collection policy is

$$CF_t = [\$1,000,000(1 - 0.80) - \$1,000,000(0.07) - \$90,000](1 - 0.40)$$
$$- [\$1,000,000(1 - 0.80) - \$1,000,000(0.10) - \$50,000](1 - 0.40)$$
$$= (\$200,000 - \$70,000 - \$90,000)(0.60) - (\$200,000$$
$$- \$100,000 - \$50,000)(0.60)$$
$$= (\$40,000)(0.60) - (\$50,000)(0.60) = \$24,000 - \$30,000 = -\$6,000$$

Implementing the tighter policy reduces cash inflows by $6,000 per period. To determine if the firm should implement the proposed change, we calculate the NPV as follows:

$$\text{net present value} = \frac{-\$6,000}{0.15} - (-\$10,959)$$
$$= -\$40,000 + \$10,959 = -\$29,041$$

Because the net present value is negative, the firm is worse off with the new policy.

To carry this idea a little further, consider what would happen if everything were the same as in the preceding example, except that the days sales outstanding decreases to 40 days if we undertake the new collection policy. The incremental after-tax cash flows are still $-\$6,000$ as before, but the firm is able to reduce its investment in receivables even more than before. With a 40-day average DSO, the incremental investment is

$$\Delta CF_0 = (0.80)(\$1,000,000)(40/365) - (0.80)(\$1,000,000)(60/365)$$
$$= \$87,671 - \$131,507 = -\$43,836$$

The NPV if the days sales outstanding drops to 40 days is

$$NPV = \frac{-\$6,000}{0.15} - (-\$43,836) = -\$40,000 + \$43,836 = \$3,836$$

Because the NPV is positive, the firm would now proceed to implement the proposed change in collection policy.

Still other things might happen if the firm implements a new collection policy. One possibility is for the tighter collection policy to reduce sales. Any changes of this type can be investigated employing the approach just described. By focusing on the cash flows, risks, and opportunity costs, we can determine whether a change in the firm's credit granting or collection policies will benefit the firm (those with positive NPVs) or not (those with negative NPVs). By making credit and collection management decisions that increase the value of the firm, we can assist in achieving our goal of maximizing the value of the firm. Policies should be based on maximizing net cash inflows, spending time on large or risky accounts, and looking beyond the immediate future. Then, the maximum benefits can be secured at the least possible cost.

Concept Review Questions

- What does a typical credit report contain?
- Describe how a credit scoring model can help a firm assign customers to risk classes.
- Describe two basic techniques for monitoring a firm's account receivables.

INVENTORY MANAGEMENT

Inventory, like receivables, represents a sizable investment and must be managed effectively. Although the formal responsibility for the control of inventory lies with operating divisions, financial managers are also concerned about their management. The more efficiently the firm manages its inventory, the lower the investment required—which, other things being equal, will increase the value of the firm.

TYPES OF INVENTORY

Firms have different types of inventories. The three most common are raw materials, work-in-process, and finished goods. *Raw materials* consist of goods that are used to manufacture a product. *Work-in-process inventory* consists of partially completed goods requiring additional work before they become finished goods. *Finished goods* are those goods on which production has been completed and that are ready for sale.

For manufacturing firms, the purpose of holding inventory is to uncouple the acquisition of the goods, the stages of production, and selling activities. Without inventory, particularly work-in-process inventory, each stage of production would be dependent on the preceding stage's finishing its operation. As a result, there would be delays and considerable idle time at certain stages of production. Likewise, the raw materials and finished goods inventory uncouple the purchasing and selling functions from the production function. Manufacturing firms hold all three types of inventory. Wholesale and retail firms typically hold only a finished goods inventory. Service firms may have no inventory except for a few supplies related to their activities.

BENEFITS FROM INVENTORY INVESTMENT

In addition to uncoupling the firm's operations, a number of other benefits may be associated with the investment a firm makes in its inventory:

1. TAKING ADVANTAGE OF QUANTITY DISCOUNTS   Often suppliers will offer customers quantity discounts if they purchase a certain number of items at the same time. To take advantage of such discounts, firms need to hold inventory.
2. AVOIDING STOCK OUTAGES   When a firm runs out of inventory, it has a stock outage. If this occurs in the production process, it may disrupt the production cycle and even cause it to stop. If finished goods are not on hand, sales may be lost and the firm's reliability as a supplier comes into question.
3. MARKETING BENEFITS   Often there are distinct marketing benefits in terms of increased sales associated with having a full and complete line of merchandise. Also, developing the reputation for always being able to supply the needed items may be part of the firm's marketing strategy.
4. INVENTORY SPECULATION   In times of inflation, or if other factors are causing prices to increase, firms can benefit by increasing inventory. Other things being equal, this will increase the profitability of the firm.

COSTS OF INVENTORY INVESTMENT

The cost of a firm's investment in inventory consists of three main elements—carrying costs, ordering costs, and costs of running short.

1. CARRYING COSTS   Carrying costs include the direct investment the firm has in its inventory, including storage, insurance, property tax, and spoilage and deterioration. In addition, there is an opportunity cost associated with having funds tied up in nonproductive or excess inventory. Thus, if it keeps $5 million in inventory when only $2 million is needed, the firm has $3 million tied up that could be used elsewhere.
2. ORDERING COSTS   The primary costs associated with ordering inventory include the clerical costs of placing the order, plus transportation and shipping costs.
3. COSTS OF RUNNING SHORT   The main costs associated with running short (stock outages) include lost sales, loss of customer goodwill, and disruption of the firm's production process.

To avoid these costs, firms attempt to control their inventory levels.

ALTERNATIVE APPROACHES FOR MANAGING INVENTORY

Many different approaches exist for managing inventory. Four important ones are the ABC method, the economic order quantity approach, material requirements planning, and the just-in-time method.

The ABC Method

One inventory management approach is the **ABC method.** To illustrate, consider a firm that has thousands of inventory items, ranging from very expensive to very inexpensive. The A items require a high investment. For example, 10 percent of the items may account for 50 percent of the dollar inventory investment. Category B items might constitute 30 percent of the items and 35 percent of the dollar value, while the C items contribute 60 percent of the items but only 15 percent of the dollar investment. By separating the inventory into different groups, firms can concentrate on items for which effective inventory control is most important. A formal system involving extensive and frequent monitoring is likely for category A items. Items in group B will be reviewed and adjusted less frequently—perhaps quarterly—and C items may be reviewed only annually. The ABC method has two advantages: It focuses attention where it will do the most good, and it makes the financial management of inventory paramount. That is, other considerations (marketing, production, purchasing) are met, and then financial considerations are employed to control the firm's inventory investment.

The EOQ Model

A slightly more complex model for managing inventory is the **economic order quantity, EOQ,** model. The primary purpose of the economic order quantity model is to determine how often and what quantity to order, and the average inventory to have on hand. The traditional EOQ model assumes constant demand, constant carrying costs, and constant ordering costs. However, by adding safety stocks to the model and modifying the basic EOQ model, more realism can be brought into the EOQ approach to inventory management.

MRP and Just-in-Time Methods

Under **material requirements planning, MRP,** computers are used to schedule the deliveries of material and parts close to the time they are needed. MRP is a top-down system that starts with an annual sales forecast.

At the other end in terms of sophistication and computer technology is the **just-in-time** approach. With this system the firm contracts with suppliers for both the goods *and* the time when they will be received. Because the firm wants to maintain almost zero inventory, the suppliers must be located nearby in order to make delivery on a daily or even hourly basis. From the firm's standpoint, the method requires a totally different approach to the production and management process. That is why it often takes new or completely redesigned plants and labor contracts to achieve the anticipated benefits of the just-in-time approach to controlling investment in inventory.

Effective management of the firm's inventory involves a balancing of the costs and benefits associated with the investment in inventory. Investment in inventory is really just like any other investment a firm makes. So the NPV framework can also be employed to assist in deciding whether to increase or decrease inventory investment.

ANALYSIS OF INVESTMENT IN INVENTORY

Often when a firm is considering an investment in some new long-term assets, such as building a new plant, streamlining storage facilities, and the like, part of that problem involves investment in current assets. As we saw in Chapter 8, any changes in net working capital (current assets minus current liabilities) must be analyzed as part of this larger problem.

However, some investments in inventory may not relate to the acquisition of long-term assets by the firm. Consider, for example, Thrifty Stores. After an extensive study by its marketing and finance departments, the firm concluded that sales could be increased significantly if the firm increased its level of finished goods inventory. The increased sales would result from carrying a more complete line, resulting in multiple sales and increased customer traffic. In support of this plan, it has data from a pilot study in its Birmingham store. The firm's inventory would have to be increased by $4 million, and the increased after-tax cash flows, CF_t, are estimated to be $600,000 per year. Assuming the cash flows are expected to last for a long time, the time line for the cash flows is as follows:

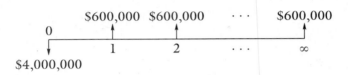

The question is this: Should the additional investment in the inventory be made?

After further evaluation, the firm has concluded that a 12 percent discount rate is appropriate. Employing Equation 21.2, we find that the net present value of this inventory buildup is

$$NPV = \frac{\$600,000}{0.12} - \$4,000,000 = \$5,000,000 - \$4,000,000 = \$1,000,000$$

Because the net present value is positive, the increased inventory investment should be made.

What happens, however, if Thrifty estimates that there will be increased expenses (storage, losses, and so forth) resulting from the increased inventory level carried? These expenses are expected to reduce cash inflows by $70,000 per year. In addition, the senior vice-president believes that $80,000 of the estimated cash flows are extremely unlikely to come in. The additional investment is still $4 million, but the expected cash inflows are now $450,000 (i.e., $600,000 − $70,000 − $80,000) per year, which produces the following projected cash flow stream:

$450,000 $450,000   · · · $450,000

0

1   2   · · ·   ∞

$4,000,000

The net present value is now

$$NPV = \frac{\$450,000}{0.12} - \$4,000,000 = \$3,750,000 - \$4,000,000 = -\$250,000$$

Obviously, based on this set of expected cash flows and the 12 percent opportunity cost of capital, Thrifty should not increase its inventory investment.

Three items must be stressed about making inventory decisions: First, the emphasis has to be on cash flows. Second, because various types of inventory are held by firms, close attention should be devoted to the most important items. A management-by-exception framework can be used to control investment in all other items. Finally, the risks and returns must be considered. For many firms, inventory is the most important single investment.

INTERACTION OF ACCOUNTS RECEIVABLE AND INVENTORY DECISIONS

Until now we have considered separately the management of receivables and the management of inventory. In practice, there are interactions between the firm's accounts receivable and its inventory. This interaction is often hard to see or to achieve, however, because the functions of inventory management and receivables management are typically separate areas of responsibility within the firm. To the extent possible, inventory and receivables policies should be developed and evaluated on a joint basis, because there are trade-offs between them. The investment includes those cash outflows required for the incremental investment in receivables given by Equation 21.3 plus the incremental investment in inventory. Likewise, the benefits are the incremental cash inflows from the joint receivables/inventory decision. Combinations of tighter inventory control with relaxed credit, looser inventory policy and tighter credit, and varying mixes between these two can be evaluated in terms of the cash flow consequences to the firm. By viewing the investment in these two current assets in an integrated manner, the firm is in a better position to maximize its value.

Concept Review Questions
- Describe the costs and benefits of holding inventory.
- Describe different approaches a firm may employ to manage its inventory.
- How does the material requirements planning method defer from the just-in-time approach?

KEY POINTS

1. Accounts receivable and inventory represent a significant investment. Funds tied up in these uses are as costly as those employed elsewhere in the firm.
2. Management of account receivables involves the following areas: terms and conditions of credit sales, credit analysis, credit decision, and the collection policy.
3. Decisions on granting credit, changing credit or collection policies, and the investment in inventory involve an analysis of the magnitude and timing of the cash flows, risks, returns, and opportunity costs. This analysis is accomplished by calculating the net present value, NPV, of the proposed change in the firm's credit, collection, or inventory policies. For simplicity, the perpetuity form of the net present value decision criteria is employed.
4. Days sales outstanding is influenced by the level of sales; however, the receivables pattern approach is not affected by changes in sales.
5. The primary costs to consider in making inventory decisions are carrying costs, ordering costs, and the costs of running short.

QUESTIONS

21.1 Explain how the four parts of the firm's credit and collection policies interact.

21.2 What would be the effect of changes in the following on the level of accounts receivable?

a. The economy improves, and interest rates decline.
b. The credit manager tightens up on past due accounts.
c. The credit terms are changed from 3/10, net 30, to 2/10, net 30.
d. The firm's selling and production expenses decline relative to other firms.

21.3 Gail, the credit manager, is being criticized for the deterioration in her performance because the days sales outstanding has increased, as have bad debts. Under what circumstances is this criticism unjustified?

21.4 Why is the receivables pattern approach superior to the days sales outstanding in monitoring collections?

21.5 Compare the benefits and costs of investing in inventory.

21.6 What would be the effect of the following on the level of inventory held by the firm?

a. Inflation increases.
b. The firm's suppliers switch from truck to air freight delivery.
c. Competition increases in the firm's sales market.
d. The firm's production cycle becomes shorter.

CONCEPT REVIEW PROBLEMS

See Appendix A for solutions.

CR21.1 Markus & Associates uses the following model to determine customer trade credit: credit score = 5(current ratio) + 7(times interest earned) − 9(debt to net worth). Three of Markus & Associates' customers have the following ratios:

	A	B	C
Current ratio	2.2	2	2.5
Times interest earned	6	5	4
Debt to net worth	2	4	3

What is each customer's credit score?

CR21.2 In addition to the credit scores from CR21.1, Markus has determined that the following apply to each risk class:

	Credit Score		
	Greater than 25	10–25	Less than 10
Risk class	1	2	3
Opportunity cost of capital	12%	14%	17%
Days sales outstanding	35	55	85
Sales	$300,000	$400,000	$200,000
Bad debts as a percentage of sales	4%	10%	15%
Additional collection department cash outflows	$ 8,000	$ 18,000	$ 16,000

Markus' variable cash outflows are 75 percent of sales, and the tax rate is 40 percent. Should trade credit be offered to any of the firms? (*Note:* Use a 365-day year.)

CR21.3   Stetson Brothers has the following sales and receivables patterns for the months June through December:

Month	Sales	Collections from Current Month	Receivables from 1-Month Prior Sales	Receivables from 2-Month Prior Sales
Aug.	$30,000	$2,700	$24,000	$12,000
Sept.	20,000	1,600	15,000	12,000
Oct.	10,000	700	8,000	12,300
Nov.	20,000	1,400	3,000	10,400
Dec.	30,000	2,100	5,000	6,300

Using the receivables pattern approach for months August, September, and October, comment on Stetson's collection of accounts receivable.

CR21.4   Brad is unhappy with his firm's collection of accounts receivable. The firm currently has annual sales of $20 million, 15 percent bad debts, and days sales outstanding of 65. Brad wants to decrease both the percentage of bad debts and the days sales outstanding by doubling the size of the firm's collection department budget from $250,000 to $500,000. It is estimated that bad debts would decline to 12 percent and days sales outstanding would decrease to 55. However, Hillary, the marketing director, pointed out that sales would also decrease, to an estimated $17 million. If variable costs are 70 percent of sales, the tax rate is 35 percent, and the opportunity cost of capital is 14 percent, should the collection department budget be increased?

CR21.5   Specht Enterprises believes the firm's after-tax cash flows could be increased by $200,000 per year if it increased its inventory by $1.5 million. If the firm's opportunity cost of capital is 15 percent, what is the net present value of increasing the firm's inventory?

PROBLEMS

21.1   Deschamps Industries offers credit terms of 3/10, net 45. Twenty percent of its customers pay on the discount date, 40 percent pay on the net date, and the other 40 percent pay in 60 days. If Deschamps' average investment in accounts receivables is $500,000 and variable costs are 80 percent of sales, what is Deschamps' annual sales? Assume a 365-day year. (*Note:* Carry to five decimal places.)

21.2   River City Recreation has decided to offer credit during its fall bicycle sale. Sales are expected to be 500 units at $450 each, and River City's cost is $315 per bike. The firm estimates that 94 percent of the customers will make their payments, and the others will have to be written off as bad debts. To eliminate the bad debts, NeverFail Credit will supply customer credit reports for a one-time fee of $1,500, plus $7.50 per report. Should River City obtain the credit information? (*Note:* Do not worry about taxes.)

21.3   Cincinnati Iron Works is in the process of evaluating its credit standards. Two potential classes of new customers exist, as follows:

Risk Class	Opportunity Cost of Capital (k)	Days Sales Outstanding (DSO)	Sales (S)	Bad Debts as a Peracentage of Sales (BD)	Additional Collection Department Cash Outflows (CD)
4	16%	45 days	$511,000	8%	$15,000
5	20	55	438,000	12	25,000

The variable cash outflows as a percentage of sales are 80 percent, and the tax rate is 30 percent. Should Cincinnati extend credit to potential customers in risk class 4? In risk class 5? (Assume a 365-day year.)

21.4   Madison Group makes all sales on a credit basis. It is evaluating the creditworthiness of its customers. The results of the analysis are as follows:

Risk Class	Opportunity Cost of Capital (k)	Days Sales Outstanding (DSO)	Sales (S)	Bad Debts as a Percentage of Sales (BD)	Collection Department Cash Outflows (CD)
A	12%	20 days	$3 million	3%	$50,000
B	14	40	4	5	50,000
C	16	60	6	10	60,000
D	18	80	8	15	80,000

Variable cash outflows are 81 percent of sales, and taxes are 40 percent.

a.   Analyze each of the present classes of customers. Should Madison continue to grant credit to all four risk classes? (Assume a 365-day year.)

b.   What happens to the level of sales if Madison follows your recommendation in (a)? How would you proceed to convince Madison to follow your recommendation?

21.5 Mark's is evaluating whether to grant credit to a risky class of potential customers. Variable cash outflows are 82 percent of sales, the days sales outstanding is 65 days, sales per year (based on a 365-day year) are $10,950,000, bad debts are 12 percent of sales, additional collection department cash outflows are $300,000 per year, and the opportunity cost of capital is 12 percent. At what marginal tax rate is Mark's indifferent between granting and not granting credit to this new class of customers?

21.6 Butcher Products is a new firm. All sales are on credit, and the sales and payments for the first 6 months are as follows:

	March	April	May	June	July	August
Credit sales	$1,500	$2,000	$2,400	$2,800	$3,700	$4,900
Payments—same month	200	400	500	600	700	800
Payments—1 month later		600	800	1,000	1,250	1,500
Payments—2 months later			500	700	800	850

After 2 months the uncollected sales are written off as bad debts. Calculate the receivables pattern for Butcher. Is it becoming more or less effective? What is happening to its bad debts? Are there any indications of change occurring in July and August?

21.7 Mutual Worldwide employs the days sales outstanding (based on a 365-day year) to monitor its receivables. The sales and receivables pattern for the 4 months of February through May are as follows:

	February	March	April	May	June	July
Credit sales	$150,000	$200,000	$300,000	$300,000		
Receivables— same month sales	120,000	160,000	237,000	234,000		
Receivables—1 month before		60,000	80,000	114,000	108,000	
Receivables—2 months before			0	0	0	0 0

Total sales for the year are $2,555,000.

a. Calculate the days sales outstanding (using the total yearly sales) for each of 3 months— March, April, and May.
b. What do your results from (a) suggest about the effectiveness of Mutual's collection policies?
c. Now calculate the receivables pattern for Mutual. Is its collection policy less effective in May than in March or April?
d. Explain why you got conflicting results from the days sales outstanding versus the receivables pattern approach.

21.8 Perry Air Conditioning has annual credit sales of $1.6 million. Current collection department cash outflows are $35,000, bad debts are 1.5 percent of sales, and the days sales outstanding is 30 days. Perry is considering easing its collection efforts so that collection department outflows will be reduced to $22,000 per year. The change is expected to increase bad debts to 2.5 percent of sales and to increase the days sales outstanding to 45 days. In addition, sales are expected to increase to $1.75 million. If the discount rate is 16 percent, variable cash outflows are 75 percent of sales, and the marginal tax rate is 35 percent, should Perry make the change?

21.9   Big Rock Data believes its collection policy may be out of hand. Currently, the firm has sales of $6 million and days sales outstanding of 55 days, bad debts are 6 percent of sales, and yearly collection department cash outflows are $100,000. Its existing variable cash outflows are 80 percent of sales. If it tightens the collection policy significantly, it anticipates sales will drop to $5 million, the days sales outstanding will become 25 days, bad debts will be 3 percent of sales, and collection department cash outflows will be $75,000 per year. At this level of sales, variable cash outflows will be 83 percent of sales. Assume the corporate tax rate is 30 percent, and use a 365-day year.

a.   If the opportunity cost of capital is 14 percent, should it tighten the collection policy?

b.   What if the opportunity cost is 20 percent?

21.10   Gupta Sales has $500,000 in overdue receivables that it is considering writing off as worthless. It has been approached by a collection agency. The agency will charge $75,000 plus 50 percent of the first $200,000 collected by the agency and 25 percent of the rest collected. Gupta estimates there is a 60 percent probability that a total of $150,000 will be collected, a 30 percent probability that a total of $300,000 will be collected, and a 10 percent probability that a total of $450,000 will be collected.

a.   Should Gupta employ the collection agency?

b.   If the collection agency's fixed charge is $125,000, instead of $75,000, should Gupta employ the agency?

21.11   LaSalle Street Stores is considering three different mutually exclusive proposals for increasing its inventory level. The initial investments and after-tax cash flows are as follows:

Inventory Level	Initial Investment (CF_0)	Opportunity Cost of Capital (k)	After-Tax Cash Flow (CF_t)
A	$300,000	12%	$ 50,000
B	600,000	15	110,000
C	900,000	18	175,000

Which, if any, of the new inventory levels should LaSalle Street Stores adopt?

21.12   The Mukherjee Group presently carries an average inventory valued at $5 million. New management has proposed to reduce the inventory to $3.5 million. The expected loss in after-tax cash flows due to increased stock outages will be $200,000 per year if inventory is reduced, but losses due to theft and spoilage should decrease by $20,000 (after taxes). If the appropriate cost of capital is 16 percent, should the inventory be reduced?

21.13 Gordon Showrooms sells to its customers on a credit basis. It is considering loosening its credit granting standards to two additional risk classes, P and Q.

Risk Class	Opportunity Cost of Capital (k)	Days Sales Outstanding (DSO)	Sales (S)	Bad Debts as a Percentage of Sales (BD)	Additional Collection Department Cash Outflows (CD)
P	15%	50 days	$ 800,000	6%	$200,000
Q	20	60	1,300,000	10	60,000

Variable costs are 75 percent of sales, a 365-day year is used, and Gordon's tax rate is 40 percent. In addition, granting credit to customers in risk class P would require an investment of an additional $60,000 in inventory. Extending credit to risk class Q would require an additional $150,000 investment in inventory beyond that required for class P.

a. Should Gordon grant credit to customers in risk class P?

b. Assuming Gordon has already decided to grant credit to class P, should it also grant credit to customers in risk class Q?

21.14 NeverDry is considering changing to a seasonal dating policy under which it will produce and ship goods now but bill for the goods at a later date. The firm anticipates that this will increase sales by $800,000, the days sales outstanding will be 120 days, and the variable costs will be 0.85 of sales. Inventory will be reduced by $50,000, bad debts will be 8 percent, and additional collection department expenses will be $20,000. NeverDry's tax rate is 35 percent (assume a 365-day year).

a. If the opportunity cost of capital is 16 percent, should NeverDry change to seasonal dating?

b. If everything remains as in (a), how much more reduction in inventory would have to occur before NeverDry can profitably switch to seasonal dating?

21.15 Mini Case Aerovac Industries has grown so rapidly it has not had time to examine carefully its accounts receivables and inventory policies. Now, during the present slowdown in economic activity, the decision has been made to undertake a careful analysis of these important functions. As the senior analyst in the finance department, you have been assigned the responsibility for undertaking this analysis and for making sure Aerovac's policies are appropriate.

a. Your boss keeps saying that the investment in receivables and inventory is just as important as the investment in long-term assets, and that the analysis of this investment must take the same approach as any other investment made by the firm. Why is this so?

b. Explain, in some detail, what the major credit and collections policies are.

c. Aerovac is investigating changing its credit scoring model in order to tighten up its credit granting policy. The present model is 5(interest coverage) + 6(current ratio), + 0.9(years in business). The proposed model is 4(interest coverage) + 4(quick ratio) + 1.5(years in business). [*Note:* Interest coverage = EBIT/ interest; current ratio = current assets/current liabilities; and quick ratio = (current assets − inventory)/current liabilities.] Two firms have data as follows:

	Firm A	Firm B
EBIT	$600,000	$800,000
Interest	100,000	90,000
Current assets	100,000	80,000
Inventory	30,000	45,000
Current liabilities	50,000	60,000
Years in business	8	12

What are the credit scores under the existing and the proposed models?

d. Instead of changing the credit scoring model, Aerovac believes the opportunity cost of capital employed may be too low and that it also needs to increase its collection department expenditures to enable it to follow up more promptly. The existing and proposed policies for two classes of customers are as follows:

Risk Class	Opportunity Cost of Capital (k)	Days Sales Outstanding (DSO)	Sales (S)	Bad Debts as a Percent of Sales (BD)	Collection Department Cash Outflows (CD)
Existing					
1	14%	40 days	$15,000,000	4%	$250,000
2	16	60	$30,000,000	8	600,000
Proposed					
1	16%	30 days	$13,000,000	1%	$300,000
2	17	35	$25,000,000	2	700,000

Variable costs remain at 70 percent of sales in either case, and the firm's marginal tax rate is 35 percent. For which risk class, if either, should the proposed change be made? [*Note:* Calculate the NPV for risk class 1 under the existing policy, and then under the proposed policy. Then take the difference in the two NPVs to determine whether to stay with the existing policy (i.e., if NPV$_{old}$ is greater than NPV$_{new}$) or switch to the new policy (i.e., if NPV$_{new}$ is greater than NPV$_{old}$). Do the same for risk class 2.]

e. Aerovac uses days sales outstanding to measure the performance of its collections manager. Is this appropriate? Why or why not?

f. Briefly explain the interrelationship between a firm's receivables and inventory decisions.

REFERENCES

For information on receivables and inventory see:

GALLINGER, GEORGE W., and P. BASIL HEALEY. *Liquidity Analysis and Management.* Reading, Mass.: Addison-Wesley, 1987.

KALLBERG, JARL G., and KENNETH L. PARKINSON. *Corporate Liquidity: Management and Measurement.* Homewood, Il.: Irwin, 1993.

For more on credit and receivables management, see:

BERANEK, WILLIAM, and FREDERICK C. SCHERR. "On the Significance of Trade Credit Limits." *Financial Practice and Education* 1 (Fall/Winter 1991): 39–44.

EMERY, GARY W. "A Pure Financial Explanation for Trade Credit." *Journal of Financial and Quantitative Analysis* 19 (September 1984): 271–85.

MIAN, SHEHZAD, and CLIFFORD W. SMITH, JR. "Accounts Receivable Management and Policy: Theory and Evidence." *Journal of Finance* 47 (March 1992): 169–200.

SMITH, JANET K. "Trade Credit and Information Asymmetry." *Journal of Finance* 42 (September 1987): 863–72.

WALIA, T. S. "How Much Cash Is Tied Up in Your Accounts Receivable?" *Journal of Cash Management* 10 (July/August 1990): 48–50.

22 *Short-Term Financing*

EXECUTIVE SUMMARY

Firms make extensive use of short-term financing. For some, it provides the major source of financing. The use of short-term financing is a function of both the nature of the firm's business and how aggressive it wants to become in matching (or financing) its temporary assets with temporary liabilities. Firms that are aggressive in their use of short-term financing employ substantially larger amounts of such financing than firms that adopt a conservative position.

Trade credit financing is readily available in most industries. It is costless if cash discounts are taken. Bank loans can be obtained through single transaction loans, a line of credit, or secured financing involving either receivables or inventory. Many finance companies also provide short-term loans to firms, especially when accounts receivable or inventory are involved. Larger firms have access to commercial paper. Although the direct costs of all these sources are available, this is only one item that requires attention. For this reason, effective managers assess both the risks and returns associated with alternative sources of short-term financing as they make decisions to maximize the value of the firm.

SOURCES AND IMPORTANCE OF SHORT-TERM FINANCING

Among numerous sources of short-term financing are trade credit and short-term borrowing by the firm. Trade credit arises when one firm purchases goods from another firm and does not pay cash immediately. This creates an account payable for the purchasing firm. Trade credit often is called *spontaneous short-term financing* because it tends to expand automatically as firms purchase more goods and build up inventory. There are also **negotiated short-term financing** sources. To secure short-term borrowed funds from these sources, the firm must enter into negotiations with commercial banks, finance companies, and the like.

Aside from the matching principle discussed in Chapter 19, firms use short-term financing for two other reasons: The first is to meet seasonal needs. As firms enter into that part of the year where accounts receivable and inventory expand, they employ short-term financing. Later, when cash inflows increase, they pay down the short-term financing. The second reason is to "roll" it into longer-term financing. Many firms use short-term financing until the total amount of financing needed becomes large enough to justify long-term debt (or equity) financing.

SIZE OF SHORT-TERM FINANCING

To see the importance of short-term financing, consider that small manufacturing firms (with assets of less than $25 million), retail firms, and wholesale firms usually have current liabilities that are 35 percent or more of total assets. For larger manufacturing firms, the current liabilities drop to about 25 percent. The large size of current liabilities for small manufacturing firms, retail firms, and wholesale firms is due to the fact that these firms have large amounts of current assets. Under the matching principle, we expect such firms to have large amounts of current liabilities, which they do. The majority of these current liabilities are in the form of accounts payable and short-term borrowings—the focus of this chapter. The other short-term liabilities include various accrued items, such as wages and taxes, and current maturities of long-term debt or lease obligations. The amount of current liabilities varies both among industries and among firms in the same industry.

Short-term financing is more important than ever because of a firm's size, the varying nature of a firm's needs over the course of the year, changes in business conditions and interest rates, and changes in the money market and financing alternatives. Securing funds at the most cost-effective rate is vitally important. At the same time, the firm must ensure the availability of funds, no matter what the time of year or economic conditions. In this chapter we focus on the nature of short-term financing available, how to determine its effective annual cost, and the typical conditions surrounding alternative sources of short-term financing.

COST OF SHORT-TERM FINANCING

In determining the cost of alternative sources of short-term financing, three important ideas must be kept in mind:

1. For the purpose of comparison, we express the costs in the same units over the same period of time. If one source costs $800 for a month's financing, and

another charges a monthly rate of interest of 1.5 percent for the same amount of funds, it is not immediately obvious which is more expensive. To deal with this difference, all costs are expressed in the same units over the same time period. Because of simplicity and tradition, we convert all costs to an effective annual rate (or cost) stated in percentage terms.

2. The ultimate cost to the firm is influenced by the tax rate of the firm. The after-tax cost to the firm is

$$\text{after-tax cost} = (\text{before-tax cost})(1 - \text{the tax rate})$$

$$k_i = k_b(1 - T) \qquad (22.1)$$

where k_i is the after-tax cost, k_b is the before-tax annual cost, and T is the firm's marginal tax rate. Although a firm can employ either the before- or after-tax cost for decision-making purposes, its ultimate cost is the after-tax cost given by Equation 22.1.

3. The basic equation to calculate the before-tax effective annual interest rate, or k_b, for any short-term financing is:

$$k_b = \left(1 + \frac{\text{costs} - \text{benefits}}{\text{net amount of financing}}\right)^m - 1 \qquad (22.2)$$

where m is the number of compounding periods per year.

To see these ideas in practice, consider the cost of a $100,000 loan on which the bank will charge interest of $3,500, which will be paid in 90 days when the loan is repaid. The before-tax effective annual cost of this loan, employing Equation 22.2 and a 365-day year, is

$$k_b = \left(1 + \frac{\$3,500}{\$100,000}\right)^{365/90} - 1 = \left(1 + \frac{\$3,500}{\$100,000}\right)^{4.055556} - 1$$

$$= 1.1497 - 1 = 14.97\%$$

The after-tax cost, if the firm is in the 35 percent marginal tax bracket, is

$$k_i = (14.97\%)(1 - 0.35) = 9.73\%$$

Thus, the firm's after-tax annual cost is 9.73 percent.

Consider what would happen to the same firm if its tax bracket was either 20 percent or 0 percent. With a 20 percent tax bracket, the after-tax cost is

$$k_i \text{ with 20 percent tax bracket} = (14.97\%)(1 - 0.20) = 11.98\%$$

If the firm's tax bracket is zero, then the after-tax cost is the same as the before-tax cost, so

k_i with zero tax bracket = $(14.97\%)(1 - 0) = 14.97\%$

This example shows the importance of the firm's tax bracket for the cost of borrowing. As the tax bracket increases, other things being equal, the firm's after-tax cost of borrowing decreases.[1]

While we will employ Equation 22.2 and assume either a 365-day year (or occasionally 12 equal months) throughout most of this chapter, there are two other complications that arise when determining the effective annual rate. The first involves nominal versus effective annual rates; the second is the number of days assumed in a year. Before examining how to determine the effective interest rate for a number of different types of short-term financing, let's pause and examine these two issues.

Effective Annual Versus Nominal Interest Rate

The annual rate at which many loans and financial instruments are quoted is the stated or nominal interest rate. Thus, you may make an investment that pays interest at a nominal annual rate of 8 percent. The effective annual rate adjusts the nominal rate based on the frequency of compounding employed and the number of days assumed in a year. When a nominal rate is given, the effective annual rate can be determined as follows:

$$k_b = \left(1 + \frac{k_{\text{nom}}}{m}\right)^m - 1 \tag{22.3}$$

where

k_b = the effective annual rate of interest
k_{nom} = the nominal annual rate of interest
m = the number of compounding intervals per year

As long as there is only one compounding interval per year ($m = 1$), the effective annual rate is equal to the nominal rate. But as the compounding interval decreases, the effective annual rate increases. To see this relationship, consider the impact of the

---

[1] If compounding is not employed, the simple interest cost is given by

$$k_b = \left(\frac{\text{costs} - \text{benefits}}{\text{net amount of financing}}\right)\left(\frac{365 \text{ days}}{\text{total number of days funds borrowed}}\right)$$

$$= \left(\frac{\$3,500}{\$100,000}\right)\left(\frac{365}{90}\right) = 14.19\%$$

Simple interest always understates the effective annual interest rate.

compounding period on a 12 percent annual nominal rate:

Compounding Interval	Effective Annual Rate $k_b = \left(1 + \dfrac{0.12}{m}\right)^m - 1$
Annually ($m = 1$)	12.000%
Semiannually ($m = 2$)	12.360
Quarterly ($m = 4$)	12.551
Monthly ($m = 12$)	12.683
Daily ($m = 365$)	12.747
Continuously[2]	12.750

Often, the interest rate that banks and other lenders quote are effective annual rates. But for most other instruments—including bonds, mortgage loans, and commercial loans—only the nominal rate may be stated.[3]

Assume, for example, that your firm wants to borrow money for a period of 1 year. Essex National Bank quotes a nominal annual rate of 12.5 percent compounded quarterly. Southern Bank quotes a nominal annual rate of 12.2 percent compounded daily. Which way is your firm better off in terms of the lower before-tax cost?

Employing Equation 22.3, from Essex National Bank the effective annual cost is

$$k_b = \left(1 + \frac{0.125}{4}\right)^4 - 1 = 13.098\%$$

From Southern, the effective annual cost is

$$k_b = \left(1 + \frac{0.122}{365}\right)^{365} - 1 = 12.973\%$$

After adjusting for the difference in the compounding intervals, we see that the before-tax cost of the loan from Southern Bank is 12.97 percent, whereas it is 13.10 percent from Essex National. Other things being equal, we want the cheapest financing available. Therefore, you would recommend that the loan be obtained from Southern Bank.

---

[2] For the continuous case, the effective annual rate is

$$k_b = e^{k_{nom}} - 1 = e^{0.12} - 1 = 12.750\%.$$

[3] In 1968 the Truth-in-Lending Act specified the annual percentage rate, APR. Although many might think the APR is the effective annual rate stated in percent terms, the way it is employed is as a nominal annual rate per year, but compounded monthly. Thus, it is not an effective annual rate.

Number of Days Assumed in a Year

In the preceding example, we saw that the compounding interval had an important impact on the effective cost or yield. It was assumed that the nominal interest was earned, or charged, over 365 days. Another approach used by many banks and for some money market instruments is based on a 360-day year. This assumption increases the cost to a borrower, or the yield to a saver.

Consider a 1-year $1,000 loan at a nominal annual interest rate of 11 percent. Using a 365-day year, the borrower pays interest of $110 after 365 days. Under the 360-day method, the borrower pays interest of $110 after just 360 days. To borrow for the extra 5 days (6 days in a leap year) at 11 percent costs the borrower additional interest of ($1,000)(0.11)(5/360) = $1.53. Thus, the total interest paid over the 365 days is actually $111.53. This increases the cost of the 360-day method over the 365-day method.

When calculating an effective annual rate or cost, two steps are required: First, the 360-day nominal rate must be converted to a 365-day nominal rate. Second, the 365-day nominal rate is converted to an annual effective rate. To adjust to a 365-day nominal rate, where $k_{360\ nom}$ is a 360-day nominal interest rate, we have

$$k_{nom} = k_{360\ nom}(365 \text{ days}/360 \text{ days}) \tag{22.4}$$

In this example, an 11 percent nominal rate with a 360-day year produces a 365-day nominal rate of $0.11(365/360) = 11.153$ percent. To determine the effective annual rate, we use Equation 22.3 again. Assuming daily compounding, k_b, the effective yearly rate, is

$$k_b = \left(1 + \frac{0.11153}{365}\right)^{365} - 1 = 11.797\%$$

From the standpoint of a borrower, the use of a 360-day year raises the effective cost of a loan.

Concept Review Questions

■ Describe some alternative sources of short-term financing.

■ What important ideas must be considered when determining the effective annual cost of alternative sources of short-term financing?

ACCOUNTS PAYABLE, OR TRADE CREDIT

Most firms make purchases from other firms on credit. This transaction shows up on the purchaser's accounting records as an account payable. Trade credit is a spontaneous source of financing. If a firm typically makes purchases of $3,000 per day and pays its bills in 30 days, then the average accounts payable outstanding are $90,000.

What happens, however, if as the busy season of the year draws near, purchases increase to $5,000 per day? While the firm still pays in 30 days, the accounts payable have increased to $150,000. This difference of $60,000 ($150,000 − $90,000) in accounts payable occurred spontaneously as the firm geared up for its busy season. The firm generated $60,000 in additional financing just by increasing its purchases and taking advantage of the trade credit offered by its suppliers.

COST OF TRADE CREDIT

Instead of being concerned about granting credit, as in Chapter 21, let's assume that you are now the recipient of trade credit. Trade credit terms typically are expressed, as, for example, 1/10, net 30, which means that a 1 percent **cash discount** applies if the account is paid within 10 days. If not, the account should be paid in full within 30 days. If the firm takes advantage of the 1 percent discount, there is no cost associated with the trade credit. That is, 10 days of credit is available at no cost to the purchaser. If the firm does not take the cash discount, there is a direct cost to the firm. This annual cost is

$$k_b = \left(1 + \frac{\text{discount percent}}{100\% - \text{discount percent}}\right)^{365/(\text{date paid} - \text{discount date})} - 1 \qquad (22.5)$$

The direct before-tax annual cost of not taking a 1 percent discount by paying in 10 days is

$$k_b = \left(1 + \frac{1}{100 - 1}\right)^{365/(30-10)} - 1 = 20.13\%$$

Note in Equation 22.5 that the discount not taken is related to the number of additional days for which credit is obtained. With terms of 1/10, net 30, the 1 percent cash discount is the interest cost for an additional 20 days of credit. This assumes the purchaser pays on the 30th day if the cash discount is not taken. Often firms "stretch" their payables by not paying on the net date. What happens to the direct annual cost if the firm stretches its payables by paying them later—say, 50 days after the invoice date? The cost is

$$k_b = \left(1 + \frac{1}{100 - 1}\right)^{365/(50-10)} - 1 = 9.60\%$$

This is lower than before, because 40 (instead of 20) days of credit were obtained. As shown below, the effect of **stretching payables** is to reduce the direct cost of trade credit.

Credit Terms	If Paid on Net Date	If Paid 10 Days Past Net Date	If Paid 20 Days Past Net Date	If Paid 30 Days Past Net Date
$\frac{1}{2}$/10, net 30	9.58%	6.39%	4.68%	3.73%
1/10, net 30	20.13	13.01	9.60	7.61
2/10, net 30	44.59	27.86	20.24	15.89
2/10, net 60	15.89	13.08	11.11	9.66
3/10, net 60	24.90	20.36	17.21	14.91
4/10, net 60	34.72	28.19	23.72	20.47

Firms that pass up cash discounts can reduce the direct cost by stretching their payables. The effect of this practice, however, is to incur an opportunity cost. This is the loss of supplier good will resulting in possible curtailment of trade credit. Equally important, a firm that continually stretches its payables will suffer lower credit ratings, thereby raising the future cost of funds. Firms should always take advantage of the free credit period (10 days in our example). Nevertheless, in assessing the desirability of stretching payables (if the cash discount is not taken), both direct and opportunity costs must be considered.

ADVANTAGES OF TRADE CREDIT

Trade credit has a number of advantages as a source of short-term financing. First, it is readily available and can be conveniently obtained as a normal part of the firm's everyday activities. Second, it is free (and actually results in a reduction in the purchase price) if the discount is taken. Third, it is flexible and can expand or contract as purchases expand or contract. Finally, there are no restrictive terms (or formal agreements). For these reasons, all efficiently managed firms take advantage of trade credit. Not to do so would increase the financial burden on the firm, resulting in lower returns.

Concept Review Questions

- Explain what a spontaneous source of financing is and give an example of such a source.
- What are the advantages and costs to a firm offering trade credit?

UNSECURED LOANS

Unsecured loans[4] occur in two forms—bank loans and commercial paper. Bank loans are short-term borrowings obtained from banks or finance companies; commercial paper is a short-term security sold in the money market to investors. Firms must

---

[4] Some of these loans and even commercial paper may actually be backed by specific assets of the firm. This type of credit enhancement has gained popularity in recent years, as firms have moved to provide collateral to reduce the cost of financing. For simplicity we refer to all loans in this section as unsecured loans.

negotiate a bank loan or issue commercial paper—as opposed to obtaining trade credit, which occurs spontaneously.

BANK LOANS

Most bank loans have maturities of 1 year or less and often have a variable interest rate—that is, one that fluctuates over the life of the loan as interest rates change. The basic interest rate charged by banks is called the prime rate.[5] It is defined as the rate at which their best customers can borrow.[6] Rates on loans are generally tied to prime, so the borrower pays prime plus half a percent, prime plus 1 percent, and so on. With a prime rate loan, as the bank's prime rate changes, so will the interest rate charged the borrowing firm.

Types of Bank Loans

A bank loan may be a single (transaction) loan or a line of credit. A **transaction loan** is made by the bank for a specific purpose. To obtain a transaction loan, the parties sign a promissory note. The note specifies the amount borrowed, the interest rate on the loan, the maturity date and repayment schedule, collateral (if any) involved, and any other conditions agreed upon by the two parties. When the note is signed, the borrower receives the loan.

A line of credit is another type of agreement between a bank and a firm. A line of credit agreement means the firm can borrow up to some maximum amount over a specified time period. For example, the agreement may be that the firm can borrow, or "draw down," a $500,000 line of credit over the next year. This amount, or any portion of it, may be borrowed during this time period. Repayment can be made as desired, but by the end of the agreement all borrowings must be paid off.[7] Although lines of credit can be informal agreements in which the lender has no legal obligation to make the loan, often they are formal agreements for which the firm pays a **commitment fee** to the bank, whether or not it draws on the line of credit.[8]

---

[5] Each bank sets its own prime rate, but competition forces them to be similar. Generally, the major banks set prime a certain number of percentage points (typically 1 to 2 percent) above the rate on negotiable certificates of deposit issued by banks. Other banks typically follow suit; however, prime may vary slightly, depending on the size and location of the bank. Some banks also use other rates, such as the U.S. Treasury bill rate or the London Interbank Offered Rate, LIBOR, in addition to prime.

[6] Although prime is the rate banks supposedly charge their best customers, they also loan below prime to very important and financially strong firms. These firms have the option of issuing commercial paper which typically has a yield below the prime rate. Because of this competitive factor, banks may occasionally "split the difference" between the prime rate and the commercial paper rate for loans to very sound major firms. From the firm's standpoint bank loans may provide more flexibility than issuing commercial paper. Also, with relationship banking, firms may occasionally pay a little more interest simply to maintain and strengthen relationships with their (main) bank.

[7] Many lines of credit have a provision that sometime during the time the line is in effect, perhaps for a minimum 30-day period, the firm has to have zero borrowings from the line.

[8] The commitment fee may be 1/4 to 3/4 of 1 percent per year. Thus, on a $5 million line of credit, the commitment fee could be $12,500 to $37,500 annually, whether or not the line was used.

The Monitoring Role of Banks

Firms can obtain funds from the money and capital markets or from banks (and other financial institutions). Because of their role as an "inside" provider of funds, banks have access to information about the firm and its actions that is not available to the public. Thus, there is less information asymmetry (and less of a moral hazard problem) between the firm and the provider of funds when the firm borrows from a bank instead of going directly to the money or capital markets. The direct benefits to the firm are two-fold: First, the increased monitoring improves the likelihood of the firm fulfilling its payment obligation to the bank, and therefore reduces the cost of financial distress. Second, the increased monitoring reduces the direct cost to the firm of obtaining financing. This reduced cost to the firm of obtaining financing still results in the bank obtaining a higher return than from its other investment alternatives. The unique role of banks has received substantial empirical and theoretical attention in recent years. These advances provide far greater understanding of the important role played by banks as providers of funds to firms.[9]

Cost of Bank Loans

The cost of bank loans depends on the conditions attached to the agreement. We illustrate three different types—regular interest, discount interest, and installment interest. The effects of variable interest rates, compensating balance requirements, and interest for lines of credit are also considered.

Regular Interest.   The cost of a loan with regular interest can be solved employing Equation 22.2. Assume that there is a $10,000 loan, the bank will charge prime plus 1 percent, prime is 9 percent per year, and the loan is for 73 days. The two-step process to solve for the annual before-tax cost is as follows:

STEP 1:   Determine the interest paid:

$$\begin{array}{c}\text{interest}\\\text{paid}\end{array} = \left(\begin{array}{c}\text{amount}\\\text{borrowed}\end{array}\right)\left(\begin{array}{c}\text{annual}\\\text{interest rate}\end{array}\right)\left(\begin{array}{c}\text{portion of year}\\\text{borrowed for}\end{array}\right)$$
$$= (\$10{,}000)(0.10)(73/365) = \$200$$

STEP 2:   Employing Equation 22.2, determine k_b, which is

$$k_b = \left(1 + \frac{\$200}{\$10{,}000}\right)^{365/73} - 1 = 10.41\%$$

Note that even though the stated rate is 10 percent, the annual effective rate is 10.41 percent.

---

[9] See the references at the end of the chapter.

Discount Interest.   Under **discount interest,** the bank deducts the interest at the beginning of the loan. In such a case, the borrower in our example receives $9,800 ($10,000 − $200). From step 1 above, the interest is still $200. In step 2, $9,800 (the amount actually secured) replaces the $10,000 previously employed. The effective annual cost of a discounted loan employing Equation 22.2 is

$$k_b = \left(1 + \frac{\$200}{\$9,800}\right)^{365/73} - 1 = 10.63\%$$

Because the bank does not lend the full amount, the cost of a discounted loan is higher than a loan with regular interest.

Installment Interest.   Instead of paying the loan off in a lump sum, banks and many other financial institutions charge **installment interest,** with payments made monthly. In this case the total amount of interest is calculated and added to the original face value of the note. Then the monthly installment represents a payment of both principal and interest. Let's assume that we borrow $10,000 for 1 year, that we agree to pay interest at a 13 percent annual stated rate, and that 12 monthly payments will be made. The note will be for the principal of $10,000 plus the interest of $1,300 [i.e., ($10,000)(0.13)] for a total of $11,300. The monthly payment is $941.67 ($11,300/12).

   To solve for the cost of an installment loan, we employ present value techniques for an annuity. Thus,

$$PV_0 = PMT\left[\frac{1}{k_b} - \frac{1}{k_b\,(1 + k_b)^n}\right]$$

where *PV* is the present value, *PMT* is the per period payment, k_b is the effective before-tax cost per period, and *n* is the number of periods. Thus,

$$\$10,000 = \$941.67\left[\frac{1}{k_b} - \frac{1}{k_b\,(1 + k_b)^n}\right]$$

By financial calculator, k_b is 1.9323 percent per month, or between 23 and 24 percent per year. The cost of an installment loan is always slightly less than twice the stated nominal rate.

Variable Rate Loans.   Now that we know how interest is calculated, we can consider some additional complications. The first is a **variable rate** loan. What if a firm needed to borrow $10,000 for 150 days and was going to pay prime plus 1 percent? Interest will be figured employing the regular method. If prime was 12 percent annually for the first 73 days, $13\frac{3}{4}$ percent for the next 30 days, and $14\frac{1}{2}$ percent for the remaining 47 days, what is the cost to the firm? To solve this problem, the two-step procedure described above can be used.

STEP 1:   Determine the interest paid:

Prime Rate	Prime Plus 1 Percent	Number of Days	Interest Cost in Dollars
12%	13%	73	($10,000)(0.13)(73/365) = $260.00
$13\frac{3}{4}$	$14\frac{3}{4}$	30	($10,000)(0.1475)(30/365) = 121.23
$14\frac{1}{2}$	$15\frac{1}{2}$	47	($10,000)(0.1550)(47/365) = 199.59
			Total interest = $580.82

STEP 2:   Employing Equation 22.2, determine the before-tax effective annual cost, which is

$$k_b = \left(1 + \frac{\$580.82}{\$10,000}\right)^{365/150} - 1 = 14.73\%$$

Compensating Balance.   A compensating balance is an amount banks may require corporate customers to maintain in their demand deposit account if a loan is taken out. The compensating balance may be an average over some period, such as a month, or a minimum figure below which the account cannot drop. Average compensating balances are typical for firms. Two situations can be identified: The first is one in which the compensating balance requirement is less than the amount the firm typically keeps in the bank. In this case, the requirement does not change the cost to the firm. The second case is one in which the compensating balance requirement is above the amount the firm keeps in its demand deposit account. To illustrate this, let's use the same $10,000, 10 percent loan for 73 days that we used when computing the cost of both regular and discount interest.

Assume that the bank imposes a $2,000 compensating balance requirement, when the firm typically does not keep any money on deposit at the bank. The effect of the requirement is to reduce the proceeds of the loan by $2,000. If the loan is not discounted, the before-tax cost is

$$k_b = \left(1 + \frac{\$200}{\$10,000 - \$2,000}\right)^{365/73} - 1 = 13.14\%$$

If the loan is discounted and a $2,000 compensating balance is required, then the before-tax effective annual cost becomes:

$$k_b = \left(1 + \frac{\$200}{\$10,000 - \$2,000 - \$200}\right)^{365/73} - 1 = 13.50\%$$

Line of Credit.   Finally, let's consider a more complicated situation, in which a line of credit is involved. Suppose a firm negotiates a 91-day, $1,000,000 bank line of credit that has a one-half of 1 percent annual commitment fee on the unused portion of the line, and an interest rate of prime plus 1 percent. Assume, for simplicity, that there is no compensating balance requirement and that during the entire 91-day period the prime rate is 10 percent. For the first 30 days the firm borrows $100,000 on the line of credit. For the remaining 61 days, an additional $300,000 is borrowed, so that $400,000 in total short-term financing is obtained. What is the cost of the loan? To answer this, we can still use our two-step procedure. There are, however, a few other complications.

STEP 1: Determine the commitment fee and interest per period.

commitment fee = (unused portion)(annual commitment fee)(portion of year)

Using the equation, we obtain

first 30 days	($1,000,000 − $100,000)(0.005)(30/365) = $369.86
next 61 days	($1,000,000 − $400,000)(0.005)(61/365) = 501.37

Then the interest is determined as follows:

first 30 days	($100,000)(0.11)(30/365) = $ 904.11
next 61 days	($400,000)(0.11)(61/365) = 7,353.42

STEP 2: Employing a modification of Equation 22.2, we can determine the annual cost of the line of credit. This modification is necessary because the total costs and the average amount borrowed must be calculated and then annualized as follows:

$$k_b = \left(1 + \frac{\text{total commitment free} + \text{interest}}{\text{average net amount of financing}}\right)^{365/\text{total number of days}} - 1 \qquad (22.6)$$

The total of the commitment fees and interest is $369.86 + $501.37 + $904.11 + $7,353.42 = $9,128.76. The average net amount of financing is determined as follows:

$$\begin{array}{l}\text{average net amount} \\ \text{of financing}\end{array} = (\$100,000)\left(\frac{30}{91}\right) + (\$400,000)\left(\frac{61}{91}\right)$$

$$= \$32,967.03 + \$268,131.87 = \$301,098.90$$

The before-tax percentage cost of the credit line is

$$k_b = \left(1 + \frac{\$9,128.76}{\$301,098.90}\right)^{365/91} - 1 = 12.73\%$$

If the bank imposes a 5 percent compensating balance on the total line of credit, the calculations will have to be redone if this change reduces the net amount of financing obtained. Suppose that the firm presently keeps no compensating balance in the bank. The effect of the 5 percent requirement is to reduce the net funds obtained by $50,000 [i.e., ($1,000,000)(0.05)]. Therefore, with the compensating balance requirement, the before-tax cost increases as follows:

$$k_b = \left(1 + \frac{\$9,128.76}{\$301,098.90 - \$50,000}\right)^{365/91} - 1 = 15.40\%$$

COMMERCIAL PAPER

Another important source of short-term borrowing is from commercial paper, a short-term promissory note sold by large firms to obtain financing. In recent years the market for commercial paper has grown rapidly. Because it is an alternative to short-term bank loans, the presence of a large commercial paper market tends to exert a downward pressure on borrowing costs for larger firms.

Nature and Use of Commercial Paper

The principal issuers of commercial paper include finance companies, bank holding companies, and large industrial firms. The issue size is commonly in multiples of $100,000. All commercial paper has a maturity of 270 days or less.[10] The paper is sold through dealers or via direct placement. Dealers, who generally charge one-eighth of 1 percent commission, typically are used by firms that infrequently issue commercial paper. Larger firms, such as consumer finance companies, which obtain part of their permanent financing from commercial paper generally market commercial paper directly.

Commercial paper is rated as to its quality. These ratings are as follows:[11]

Moody's		Standard & Poor's	
P-1	Superior capacity for repayment	A-1	Greatest capacity for timely repayment
P-2	Strong capacity	A-2	Strong capacity
P-3	Acceptable capacity	A-3	Satisfactory capacity
NP	Not prime	B	Adequate capacity
		C	Doubtful capacity
		D	In default or expected to be in default

The purpose of the ratings is to provide the commercial paper buyer some indication of the riskiness of the investment. From the issuing firm's standpoint, ratings are

[10] The reason for the maximum is that if the maturity exceeds 270 days, then the issue will have to be registered with the Securities and Exchange Commission.
[11] From *Moody's Bond Record* and *Standard & Poor's Creditweek*.

important because they influence the cost of financing. Other things being equal, the higher the rating, the lower the cost to the firm.

Cost of Commercial Paper

The rate (or yield) on commercial paper tends to be 1 to 2 percentage points below the prime rate. This differential fluctuates as both general economic conditions and the level of interest rates change. Like U.S. Treasury bills, commercial paper is sold at a discount from its par value. At maturity, the difference between the selling price and the par value is the interest earned by the investor. Consider a $100,000, 180-day issue of commercial paper sold at $95,000. When it matures in 180 days, the firm will pay the holder $100,000. Employing Equation 22.2, we find that the before-tax annual cost to the firm is

$$k_b = \left(1 + \frac{\$5,000}{\$100,000 - \$5,000}\right)^{365/180} - 1 = 10.96\%$$

This rate typically will be lower than the cost of a bank loan, due to the lower cost (or yield) on commercial paper than the prime rate charged by banks.

Other costs also enter into the picture. In most cases, issuers must back their commercial paper 100 percent with lines of credit from commercial banks. This line of credit may cost the firm from one-fourth to three-fourths of 1 percent annual interest. Another common procedure is for the commercial paper issuer to have a compensating balance at a bank. In addition, there is a relatively small fee ($10,000 to $25,000) to have the commercial paper rated. Because of these additional costs, the savings from issuing commercial paper may not be as great as a firm originally thought. Suppose that the commercial paper issue just analyzed was backed by a line of credit that had a commitment fee of one-half of 1 percent a year. The total fee would be

$$(\$100,000)(0.005)(180/365) = \$246.58$$

Adding this fee to the interest of $5,000 results in a total cost of $5,246.58. Employing Equation 22.2, we find that the before-tax annual cost of the commercial paper is now[12]

$$k_b = \left(1 + \frac{\$5,246.58}{\$95,000}\right)^{365/180} - 1 = 11.52\%$$

---

[12] Note that the commitment fee is *not* deducted from the financing received in the denominator. This approach treats the commitment fee as an ongoing cost that is paid over time and is *not* a lump-sum deduction at the outset. If the commitment fee is deducted at the outset, the net proceeds are $94,753.42 (i.e., $95,000 − $246.58), and the before-tax cost is

$$k_b = \left(1 + \frac{\$5,246.58}{\$94,753.42}\right)^{365/180} - 1 = 11.55\%$$

This same approach is employed for the processing costs, factoring commissions, and warehousing fees discussed subsequently.

Although commercial paper may be an attractive form of short-term financing, it is available only to relatively large firms. Also, the commercial paper market may dry up occasionally, forcing firms to use bank loans. Firms that make extensive use of commercial paper also keep their lines of communication open with banks and typically borrow from banks in addition to using the commercial paper market.

Concept Review Questions

- Describe different types of short-term bank loans.
- What is a compensating balance?
- If commercial paper is typically a cheaper source of financing than borrowing from financial institutions, explain why all firms do not finance their short-term borrowings using commercial paper.

SECURED LOANS

Because the lender requires it, or to obtain cheaper financing, firms often use receivables or inventory to obtain short-term financing. Every state except Louisiana operates under the Uniform Commercial Code. Under the code, a security agreement or standardized document is provided to list the assets pledged as collateral. Procedures for short-term financing are described below.

FINANCING WITH ACCOUNTS RECEIVABLE

Financing with accounts receivable involves pledging receivables or factoring them. The **pledging** of receivables involves the specific use of receivables as collateral for the loan. If the borrower defaults on the loan, the funds provided when the receivables are collected will go to repay the loan. **Factoring** involves the sale of accounts receivable. The factoring firm is responsible both for credit checking and for collection of the receivables. Many banks engage in making accounts receivable loans or in purchasing receivables. Commercial finance companies and other specialized factoring firms also provide accounts receivable financing to firms. In addition, in recent years many firms have issued securities in the money or capital markets that are secured with accounts receivables. This security ranges from short-term receivables to longer-term receivables such as home mortgages and automobile loans.

Pledging Accounts Receivable

Under a pledging agreement, the borrower uses the accounts receivable as collateral for the loan. The specific agreement between the borrower and the lending institution spells out the details of the transaction. The amount of the loan is stated as a percentage of the receivables pledged. In addition, the borrower typically pays a processing fee, which often is 1 percent of the total receivables pledged. This processing fee compensates the lending institution for the time involved in reviewing the pledged receivables.

If the loan agreement is based on all the firm's receivables, then the lender has no control over the quality of the receivables pledged. An alternative procedure is for the lender to review specific invoices to decide which ones it will lend against. This method is somewhat more expensive to the lender, because the lender must review each invoice and the creditworthiness of the customer, before deciding whether to lend against it. If the lender accepts all receivables, it may be willing to grant a loan for only 60 to 70 percent of the face value of the receivables. When it "screens" invoices, the loan agreement typically increases to 85 to 90 percent of the face value of the receivables.

The cost of accounts receivable financing is a function of both the processing fee and the annual interest rate charged. Because of the basic creditworthiness of the borrower, loans secured by receivables often have a stated interest rate of 2 to 4 percent above prime. To illustrate the cost, consider Hammond Associates, which sells merchandise on a net 45 days basis. Its average credit sales are $9,000 per day, and the days sales outstanding is 60 days, resulting in accounts receivable averaging $540,000. All the receivables are pledged to the bank, which will lend 75 percent of the amount pledged at 2.5 percent over prime. The loan will be for $405,000 [i.e., ($540,000) (0.75)] for 60 days. There also is a three-quarters of 1 percent processing fee on all receivables pledged. If prime currently is 7.8 percent per year, the cost of this loan can be found by employing the same two-step approach described earlier.

STEP 1:   Determine the interest paid and other costs:

$$
\begin{aligned}
\text{processing fee} &= (0.0075)(\$9{,}000)(60 \text{ days}) = \$\ 4{,}050 \\
\text{interest} &= (0.103)(\$405{,}000)(60/365) = \underline{6{,}857} \\
\text{total processing fee and interest} &= \$10{,}907
\end{aligned}
$$

STEP 2:   Employing Equation 22.2, we find that the effective annual before-tax cost is

$$
k_b = \left(1 + \frac{\$10{,}907}{\$405{,}000}\right)^{365/60} - 1 = 17.55\%
$$

The processing fee increases the cost of the loan substantially above the nominal interest charge of 10.3 percent the bank levies for the loan.[13]

Factoring Accounts Receivable

Instead of pledging its receivables, an alternative procedure employed in industries such as finished apparel, textiles, and home furnishings is to sell (or factor) them. Through factoring, a firm sells its accounts receivable to a bank or other firm engaged in factoring. The receivables may be sold "without recourse"; in such a case the factor

---

[13] Instead of using accounts receivable as collateral, some firms set up "captive finance companies" to provide ongoing accounts receivable financing. Mian and Smith (1992) argue that secured debt, in the form of accounts receivable financing, and captive finance companies serve as a means of segregating the accounts receivable cash flows from the firm's operating cash flows. By doing so they assist in controlling underinvestment problems. Mian and Smith observe that larger, more creditworthy firms establish captive finance companies, whereas smaller, more risky firms, employ debt secured by accounts receivable.

makes the credit-granting decision and incurs any losses from nonpayment by the firm's customers. Alternatively, recourse factoring can be employed. Under recourse factoring, the granting firm typically makes the credit-granting decision and, therefore, bears the consequences of any nonpayment by the customers.

Factoring operates in two basic ways. The first is **maturity factoring,** in which the factor purchases all receivables and once a month pays the seller for the receivables. The typical maturity factoring procedure is shown in Figure 22.1. Firms that employ maturity factoring are primarily interested in avoiding credit analysis and collection expenses, and in the regularity of the cash flow. The charge for maturity factoring is the commission, which is between three-fourths of 1 percent and 2 percent of the total receivables factored.

To illustrate this type of factoring, consider Gandy Wholesale. To avoid setting up a credit and collection department, it factors all its receivables. At the end of the month, the factor provides full payment on the average due date of the receivables. If the average month has $200,000 in receivables and the factoring commission is 1.5 percent per month, then Gandy pays $3,000 per month [i.e., ($200,000)(0.015)], or $36,000 per year [($3,000)(12)], to the factor. For this amount, the factor assumes all bookkeeping and collection expenses. If this procedure allows Gandy to reduce these expenses by $1,400 per month, then the net additional cost is $1,600 per month. The effective annual cost is then

$$k_b = \left(1 + \frac{\$1,600}{\$200,000}\right)^{12/1} - 1 = 10.03\%$$

The second factoring method is **advance factoring,** in which the factor provides a loan against the receivables. Thus, on the first of the month, a firm could borrow against the receivables it is selling. If the average due date is the 20th of the month,

---

Figure 22.1

Maturity Factoring Procedure

Under maturity factoring, the firm turns almost all of its credit and receivables management functions over to the factor.

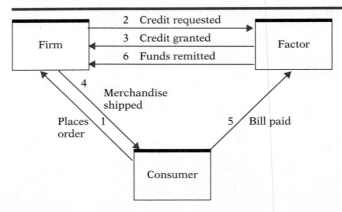

the factor will charge interest from the 1st to the 20th. This interest typically is 2 to 4 percent more than the annual prime rate. In addition, the factor still charges a factoring commission.

With advance factoring, the cost consists of both the factoring commission and the interest. To illustrate, Gandy Wholesale is now considering advance instead of maturity factoring. The receivables to be sold total $400,000, and they have an average due date of 1 month. The factoring commission is one-half of 1 percent, the annual prime rate is 9 percent, and the loan is for 1 month at 2 percent over prime. The factor will loan an amount equal to 70 percent of the face value of the receivables, or $280,000 [i.e., ($400,000)(0.70)], and the savings to Gandy will be $1,000 per month. Employing the two-step procedure, we proceed as follows:

STEP 1:   Determine the interest paid and all other costs:

$$
\begin{aligned}
\text{factoring commission} &= (0.005)(\$400,000) = \$2,000 \\
\text{interest} &= (0.11)(\$280,000)(1/12) = \underline{2,567} \\
\text{total commission and interest} &= 4,567 \\
\text{Less: Reduced cash outflows} &= \underline{1,000} \\
&\ \ \$3,567
\end{aligned}
$$

STEP 2:   Using Equation 22.2, the before-tax annual cost is

$$ k_b = \left(1 + \frac{\$3,567}{\$280,000}\right)^{12/1} - 1 = 16.41\% $$

As we saw with selling receivables, the cost increases when a fee is charged in addition to the basic interest rate.

The advantages of factoring from the firm's standpoint can be fourfold: First, the entire credit and collection operation can be shifted to the factor. This can result in a sizable savings to the selling firm. Second, more effective and timely cash management can be obtained. Third, if advance factoring is employed, then firms also may secure accelerated short-term financing from the factoring procedures. Finally, factors will often be willing to borrow money from the firm during periods when the firm has excess cash. For these reasons, factoring is continuing to become more common as an ongoing part of many firms' short-term financing strategy. Factoring is often a continuous process. Once the cycle is established, the firm automatically sends the receivables to the factor. Under continuous factoring, accounts receivable financing becomes a spontaneous source of short-term financing.

FINANCING WITH INVENTORY

A firm's inventory provides a second source of security for short-term loans. Because of the large size of the inventory for many firms and the associated carrying costs, firms often use part or all of their inventory to obtain short-term financing. The procedures are much like those discussed when receivables are employed. That is, the bank determines the percentage of the inventory value for which it will provide a loan. There are alternative methods, however, by which inventory can be secured.

Under the Uniform Commercial Code, the borrower can pledge all of its inventory under a blanket lien. This is simple, but because the borrower is free to sell the inventory, the bank has the least protection. Because of this weakness, some types of inventory are secured through the use of a trust receipt. This type of lending agreement, also known as *floor planning*, is used by automobile dealers, equipment dealers, and others who deal in "large ticket" items. With a trust receipt, an automobile dealer might reach an agreement with a bank to finance the inventory. When cars are shipped to the dealer, they are paid for in large part with funds borrowed from the bank. The trust receipt specifies that the goods are held in trust for the lender. When the cars are sold, the dealer obtains a release from the bank and then applies the proceeds to pay the loan. Under a trust receipt agreement, the bank periodically inspects the automobile dealer's inventory of cars to ensure that the pledged security is still on hand.

Another method is warehouse financing. Under a public (or terminal) warehouse agreement, the inventory is stored on the premises of a third party. The third party releases the inventory to the borrower only when authorized to do so by the lender. The lender can then maintain strict control over the collateral. Sometimes the warehouse is set up as a field warehouse. This is accomplished by establishing a separate building or area directly on the borrower's premises. To provide inventory control, the bank employs a third party to run the field warehouse. A warehouse receipt is issued by the warehouse company when it receives additional inventory. This receipt goes to the bank, and inventory cannot be released without the bank's permission.

The basic cost of inventory loans typically consists of two parts: The first is the processing fee if a blanket lien is employed, or the cost of storing the inventory if a public or field warehouse agreement is employed. Second, there is the interest cost, which is typically 2 to 4 percentage points above the prime rate. Consider a firm that employs a field warehouse agreement. The inventory loan is for 90 days, the amount of the inventory is $500,000, and the bank will lend 70 percent of the value of the collateral. The amount of the loan is $350,000 [i.e., ($500,000)(0.70)]. The field warehouse fee is $40 per day, the interest rate is 2 percent over prime, and prime is 11 percent. The annual before-tax cost is computed as follows:

STEP 1: Determine the interest paid and all other costs:

$$
\begin{aligned}
\text{field warehousing fee} &= (\$40)(90) = \$\ 3,600 \\
\text{interest} &= (0.13)(\$350,000)(90/365) = \underline{\ \ 11,219} \\
\text{total warehousing fee and interest} &= \$14,819
\end{aligned}
$$

STEP 2: The effective annual before-tax cost is determined using Equation 22.2, so that:

$$
k_b = \left(1 + \frac{\$14,819}{\$350,000}\right)^{365/90} - 1 = 18.31\%
$$

Firms often enter into continuous agreements to finance their inventory through the use of field or terminal warehouse procedures. Like the use of factoring with accounts receivable, the continual use of these forms of inventory financing creates a spontaneous form of short-term financing.

Concept Review Questions

- Describe the difference between pledging receivables and factoring receivables when securing short-term financing.
- What are the advantages of factoring accounts receivables?
- Differentiate between a *blanket lien,* a *trust receipt,* and *warehouse financing.*

CHOOSING AMONG SHORT-TERM FINANCING SOURCES

In this chapter we have stressed the cost of alternative sources of short-term financing. Some of these sources, such as trade credit and factoring or field warehouse loans, are spontaneous. That is, they tend to expand or contract automatically as the firm's accounts receivable and inventory expand or contract. Other sources of short-term financing are negotiated between the borrower and the lender.

To determine what sources of short-term financing to employ, firms should consider four specific items: matching, cost, availability, and flexibility. By matching, we mean the firm must decide how much risk it is willing to incur in financing temporary assets with temporary liabilities. As discussed in Chapter 19, a more aggressive posture will require the firm to employ more sources and amounts of short-term financing than a conservative posture.

The second important item that influences the short-term financing selection is its cost. Employing the concepts developed in this chapter, we can determine the direct cost of alternative short-term financing sources. This is an important consideration, but there is more than the direct cost of the sources. Opportunity costs must also be considered. If firms anticipate the continued need to borrow from banks, good banking relations need to be maintained even if the bank charges a higher direct cost than some other source. Trade credit (if stretched) may be less costly than an inventory loan, but if stretching occurs continually, the firm may suffer from reduced credit ratings in the future. Thus, opportunity costs must be considered along with the direct costs when considering the total cost of alternative sources of short-term financing.

The availability of credit is the third item to be considered when evaluating financing sources. If a firm cannot borrow through an unsecured loan or commercial paper offering, then some type of secured means will have to be employed. Also, over the course of the business cycle, certain sources of funds may be more or less available. Availability refers to both the amount and the conditions attached to the short-term financing. Only by examining both features will managers be in a position to consider the firm's short-term financing sources over time.

Finally, there is the issue of flexibility. Flexibility refers to the ability of the firm to pay off a loan and still retain the ability to renew or increase it. With factoring, bank loans, and lines of credit, the firm can pay off the loan when it has surplus funds. Flexibility also refers to how easily the firm can secure or increase the financing on short notice. A line of credit can be increased quickly and easily, but a negotiated short-term loan may take longer to secure. Trade credit, factoring of receivables, and field warehousing provide spontaneous sources of short-term financing that increase the firm's flexibility.

All of these items must be considered when a firm looks at its sources of short-term financing. Although the direct cost is a key element, it does not always provide the final answer. This arises because of opportunity costs relating to matching, availability, and flexibility. Because of the difficulty of quantifying opportunity costs, a practical approach is to rank sources according to their direct costs, and then consider these other factors. If the opportunity costs are significant, the ranking of the desirability of one source of short-term financing compared with another will change. Finally, because the firm's financing needs change over time, multiple sources of short-term financing must be considered, even if some of them are not being employed presently.

Concept Review Question

■ What are four specific items that should be considered when determining the source of short-term financing?

KEY POINTS

1. In order to compare the cost of alternative short-term financing arrangements, an effective annual rate, or cost, is determined. The procedure involves finding the nominal yearly cost and then converting it to an effective yearly rate of interest.
2. The effective annual interest rate provides the before-tax cost of alternative financing sources. Other dollar costs in addition to interest (or sometimes benefits) often need to be considered in order to find the cost of financing.
3. Trade credit, continuous factoring of accounts receivable, and field warehousing provide spontaneous short-term financing. Bank loans and commercial paper are negotiated short-term financing sources.
4. Although some short-term financing is unsecured, in recent years credit enhancement had become very popular. Thus, secured short-term financing has become more common. Accounts receivable may be used to secure bank loans or to obtain direct financing from the money and capital markets; an alternative is to factor accounts receivable. Inventory financing is also widely employed.
5. The specific short-term financing a firm employs depends on matching considerations, cost, availability, and flexibility.

QUESTIONS

22.1 The equation for calculating the before-tax effective annual interest rate, or cost of short-term financing, is

$$k_b = \left(1 + \frac{\text{costs} - \text{benefits}}{\text{net amount of financing}}\right)^m - 1$$

Discuss why this approach must be employed.

22.2   The effective annual rate is a function of the compounding interval and the number of days assumed in the year. Explain how both influence the effective rate.

22.3   Discuss the advantages and costs of trade credit.

22.4   Why is the rate on commercial paper typically below the prime rate? Are there other factors that tend to increase the cost of commercial paper, to undo some of its interest rate advantages?

22.5   Other things being equal, how would changes in the following conditions affect a firm's after-tax cost of funds?

a.   The prime rate increases.
b.   The bank changes from discount interest to regular interest.
c.   The bank's compensating balance requirement decreases.
d.   Tax rates increase (assume the firm is profitable).

22.6   With discount interest, the interest is deducted at the beginning of the loan, thereby reducing the net amount of financing obtained.

a.   Discuss the effect of discount interest on the effective annual cost of the loan.
b.   What if a compensating balance requirement exists? Or what if commitment fees or loan processing (origination) fees are deducted at the start of the loan? Is the effect on the cost of the loan the same as with discount interest?

22.7   Differentiate completely between maturity factoring and advance factoring.

22.8   For many of the short-term financing sources, the direct cost is made up of the interest plus some other charge (or requirement). Explain this other charge for the following:

a.   Line of credit.
b.   Discount interest.
c.   Installment interest.
d.   Compensating balance.
e.   Commercial paper.
f.   Pledging accounts receivable.
g.   Advance factoring.
h.   Inventory loans.

CONCEPT REVIEW PROBLEMS

See Appendix A for solutions.

CR22.1   Billings Corporation wants to borrow money for a period of 365 days. First National quotes a nominal annual rate of 10 percent compounded monthly, based on a 360-day year. (*Note:* Assume 12 equal-length months.) Commerce National Bank quotes a 10.2 percent nominal annual rate compounded semiannually, based on a 360-day year. What is the effective annual cost to Billings of each loan?

CR22.2   Ricardo's TV & Appliance is evaluating the cost of trade credit with terms of 1/15, net 30.

a.   What is the effective annual cost of the trade credit? (*Note:* Use a 365-day year.)
b.   What is the cost if Ricardo's can stretch its payables from 30 days to 60 days?

CR22.3   National Book Company needs a short-term loan of $500,000 for 275 days. Frontier Bank & Trust has offered three different types of loans: a regular interest loan with a stated rate of 12 percent, an 8 percent discount loan, and a 7 percent installment loan with 9 equal payments. What is the effective annual cost of each type of loan? (*Note:* Use a 365-day year.)

CR22.4   Regale borrowed $20,000 for a 60-day period to finance the increased sales and activities around the Christmas holidays. The rate on the bank loan remained at 10 percent for 20 days, then increased to 12 percent for 20 days, and then dropped to 8 percent for the remainder of the lending period. What was the effective annual cost to Regale? (*Note:* Use a 365-day year.)

CR22.5   Margo Industries has obtained a line of credit of $500,000 for the next 180 days with a commitment fee of 1 percent on the unused portion and an interest rate of 15 percent. In the first 60 days the firm borrowed $200,000 on the line of credit, then increased the borrowing to $400,000 for another 100 days. The firm then paid off the line of credit and maintained a balance of zero for the remaining 20 days. Based on a 365-day year, what was the effective annual cost of the line of credit?

CR22.6   South Florida Imports is issuing $1 million in commercial paper with a maturity of 60 days. A line of credit for 100 percent of the face value of the commercial paper was established with a financial institution: the commitment fee is $\frac{1}{2}$ of 1 percent of the line of credit, and the financial institution requires a compensating balance of 1 percent of the line of credit. Assume South Florida does not presently keep any funds at the financial institution, and use a 365-day year. What is the effective annual cost of the commercial paper if it is sold to investors for $985,000?

CR22.7   Minnesota Industries has decided to borrow against its receivables, which average $80,000 per month. The firm's bank will lend against 80 percent of the receivables, at 12 percent with a $\frac{1}{2}$ of 1 percent processing fee of the amount borrowed. The receivables can also be factored: the factor will accept 80 percent of the monthly receivables for a factoring fee of 2 percent per month. If factoring is selected a collection expense will decrease by $200 per month. What is the effective annual cost of each financing option (assuming 12 equal months)?

CR22.8   A third option available to Minnesota Industries in CR22.7 is advance factoring. Terms of the advance factoring agreement are a monthly factor fee of 1 percent, a loan cost of 12 percent, with a loan amount equal to 80 percent of the receivables. Minnesota Industries would experience reduced cash outflows of $300 per month. What is the effective annual cost of advance factoring?

CR22.9   Classic Motors has obtained a blanket lien for its inventory of automobiles. The average time an auto sits in inventory is 80 days. Classic has an average inventory of $800,000. Classic's bank charges a processing fee of 1 percent, will loan up to 60 percent of the face value of the inventory, and charges 15 percent interest rate for the inventory loan. Based on a 365-day year, what is the effective annual cost of the loan?

PROBLEMS

22.1   First Bank offers a nominal rate of 10 percent per year, compounds interest daily, and uses a 360-day year. Mahoney Bank offers a nominal rate of 10.25 percent per year, compounds interest monthly, and uses a 365-day year. By calculating the effective annual rate of interest for both banks, determine where you should place your money. (*Note:* Assume it is not a leap year.)

22.2   What is the effective annual rate on an account paying 7 percent compounded continuously? What if it is compounded quarterly? Yearly?

22.3 A financial institution uses continuous compounding and claims that a dollar deposited today will be worth $2.7183 after 20 years. What is the nominal rate of interest?

22.4 Gardner National Bank has decided to offer a $10 gift certificate to any depositor who puts at least $400 into a new or existing savings account.

a. Suppose you open a 7 percent savings account with a deposit of $500 and immediately cash the $10 gift certificate so that the bank receives a net amount of $490 from your deposit. If interest is compounded daily based on a 365-day year and the funds stay in the bank for exactly half a year, what is the effective annual cost of the funds to the bank?

b. To entice even larger depositors, the bank offers a $30 certificate for deposits of $1,000 or more. What would the new effective annual cost of the funds to the bank be if you deposited $1,000, instead of $500?

22.5 A firm receives trade credit terms of 2/15, net 45. Based on a 365-day year, what is the before-tax effective annual cost if payment is made **(a)** by the 15th day, **(b)** on the 45th day, **(c)** by stretching to 60 days past the invoice date, **(d)** 90 days past the invoice date? What other costs or considerations should be considered in addition to this direct cost?

22.6 DeVito Industries has four choices for a $50,000, 1-year loan from a bank. Which one of the following has the lowest before-tax effective annual interest rate?

(1) A 14 percent annual interest rate with no compensating balance requirement. Interest is paid at the end of the year.

(2) A 13 percent annual interest rate discounted, with no compensating balance requirement.

(3) A 9 percent annual stated interest rate with installment interest, paid in 12 equal installments.

(4) An 11 percent annual interest rate discounted, with a 10 percent compensating balance requirement. DeVito does not typically keep any funds in this bank.

22.7 Key Computers has just received a *net* amount (after interest and any compensating balance requirement) of financing of $450,000 for 146 days. Its bank loaned the money at a 15 percent annual rate, employing discount interest. The loan requires a $50,000 compensating balance, and Key keeps an average of $30,000 on deposit in the bank. If the tax rate is 40 percent, what is the after-tax effective annual interest rate on the loan? Assume a 365-day year.

22.8 Sewards has negotiated a line of credit as follows: 120-day, $2,000,000 line that has a 0.60 of 1 percent annual rate commitment fee on the unused portion of the line and an interest rate of prime plus 2 percent. Sewards anticipates borrowing $750,000 during the first 75 days, and an additional $900,000 (for a total of $1,650,000) over the last 45 days.

a. If prime is expected to be 11 percent, what is the expected before-tax annual interest rate, or cost, to Sewards? (Assume a 365-day year.)

b. What is the expected before-tax interest rate if Sewards borrows the maximum each of the 120 days?

c. How do you explain the difference in the answers between (a) and (b)?

22.9 Memphis Wholesalers has a 6-month, $1 million line of credit agreement with the Third National Bank. There is a one-half of 1 percent per year commitment fee charged on the unused portion of the line. The prime rate is 14 percent per year, and the interest rate on the line of credit is 1 percent over prime. Over the next 6 months, Memphis Wholesalers anticipates drawing on the line of credit as follows:

Month	Additional Borrowed (Repaid) per Month	Total Borrowed per Month
April	$100,000	$ 100,000
May	300,000	400,000
June	400,000	800,000
July	200,000	1,000,000
August	−300,000	700,000
September	−400,000	300,000

By October 1, the line is paid off in full.

a. What is the expected before-tax effective annual interest rate to Memphis Wholesalers? (*Note:* Do not worry about a 365-day year; simply treat each month as one-twelfth of the total.)

b. If Memphis Wholesalers decides to borrow its full line of credit every month ($1,000,000 per month), what would its expected before-tax annual interest rate be? What if Memphis borrows nothing during the 6 months?

c. Now suppose that the prime rate decreased to 12 percent. What is the expected before-tax effective annual interest rate if the borrowing is as in (a)?

22.10   Datatech is planning a $2 million issue of 270-day commercial paper. The interest rate is $11\frac{1}{2}$ percent per year, and Datatech will incur $15,000 in other issue-related expenses. Interest is to be discounted, and a 365-day year is to be used.

a. What is the before-tax effective annual interest rate for the commercial paper issue?

b. What is the after-tax cost if Datatech's marginal tax rate is 35 percent? If it is 25 percent?

c. What are some other factors Datatech would need to consider in addition to the direct cost?

22.11   Danley Transportation is going to issue $1,000,000 of commercial paper at a price of $940,822. If the issue is for 180 days and Danley's marginal tax rate is 30 percent, what is the effective annual after-tax interest rate of the commercial paper? (Assume a 365-day year.)

22.12   Barnes & Field presently uses maturity factoring at a before-tax effective annual cost of 18 percent. Under advance factoring, which is being considered, Barnes & Field would sell $1,200,000 of receivables with an average due date of 20 days. The factoring commission is one-fourth of 1 percent, the prime rate is 8 percent, and the factor will make the loan for 20 days at 3 percent over prime. The factor will loan 50 percent of the face value of the receivables. (Assume a 365-day year.)

a. By calculating the before-tax effective annual interest rate, determine if Barnes & Field should switch to advance factoring.

b. What decision would be made if everything is the same as in (a) except the loan is at 2 percent over prime and the factor will loan (or advance) $1,000,000?

22.13   Delta Industries has employed factoring for a number of years. Its sales average $1 million dollars every 30 days, with 80 percent being credit sales. The days sales outstanding, DSO, is 30 days, so the length of the loan is 30 days. The factor charges a 1 percent factoring commission on the total receivables. In addition, any loan, which may be up to 75 percent of credit sales, carries an interest rate of 11 percent per year. The factor employs a 365-day year.

Delta Industries estimates that the factoring agreement results in two savings: (1) a $1,000 reduction in credit and collection expenses for every 30-day period, and (2) a reduction in bad debts equal to one-half of 1 percent of the credit sales.

Recently, a finance company approached Delta about a loan involving the pledging of receivables. The loan could be up to 75 percent of receivables. The costs would be interest at 9 percent per year plus a three-fourths of 1 percent processing fee on the size of the loan. [So, the total processing fee on the receivables loan is $(0.0075)($600,000) = $4,500.$]

a.   By computing the effective annual interest rate, determine which plan is preferable.
b.   If Delta Industries borrows only $200,000 per 30 days on average, which plan is preferable? (*Note:* If Delta factors the receivables, it still receives the $1,000 reduction in credit and collection expenses, plus the benefit of the one-half of 1 percent reduction in bad debts on the total receivables of $800,000, because it continues selling all the remaining receivables to the factor on a maturity factor basis.)

22.14   Charter United has to build up its inventory for a 4-month period each year to meet future sales demands. It is considering a bank loan with a field warehouse security agreement. The inventory during this 4-month period averages $500,000 per month. The bank will loan a maximum of 70 percent of the average inventory at prime plus 1 percent. Prime is 9 percent per year. The field warehousing agreement costs $2,400 per month. (*Note:* Use 12 months, not 365 days.)

a.   If Charter United borrows $250,000, what is the before-tax effective annual interest rate on the loan?
b.   If Charter United borrows the maximum, what is the rate on the loan?

22.15   Denver Press has experienced a severe cash squeeze and needs $300,000 for the next 75 days. The most likely source is to borrow against its inventory. Determine the better financing alternative of the two that are available. Use a 365-day year and calculate the before-tax effective annual interest rate.

a.   The Rocky Mountain Bank will lend the $300,000 at a rate of 12 percent per year. It requires, however, that a field warehouse security agreement be employed. The field warehousing costs are $30 per day. Finally, Denver Press believes that because of lower efficiency, before-tax cash flows will be reduced by $2,500 during this 75-day time period.
b.   Bishop Finance will loan Denver Press the $300,000 at a rate of 18 percent per year under a blanket lien agreement. There are no other charges associated with this loan.

22.16   Green's Wholesalers presently uses a 90-day public warehouse agreement to finance most of its inventory. The average amount of inventory is $2,000,000, the bank lends Green's 75 percent of the value of the inventory, and the public warehousing fee is $200 per day. Total transportation costs for the 90-day period make up 1 percent of the average value of the inventory [that is, $(0.01)($2,000,000)$], the prime rate is 8 percent, and the bank will loan at 2 percent over prime. Green's is considering establishing a field warehouse on its premises, which would eliminate transportation costs but would cost $450 per day. The interest rate is 1 percent over prime, and the loan amount remains the same. (Assume a 365-day year.)

a.   What is the before-tax effective annual interest rate for the public warehouse financing agreement?
b.   Does the effective annual rate on the loan increase or decrease under the field warehousing agreement? By how much?

22.17   The Clark Corporation has a need for $300,000 in short-term financing for the next 30 days. Based on the following four options, which source should Clark select to minimize its costs? (Calculate the before-tax effective annual interest rate.)

(1)   A 91-day line of credit with a bank in the amount of $500,000. There is a 1 percent per year commitment fee on the unused portion, and the rate of interest on borrowed funds is 14 percent per year.

(2)   Forgo cash discounts on $300,000 of payables. The terms are 2/10, net 40.

(3)   Issue commercial paper with a 30-day maturity. To borrow the entire $300,000, the maturity value of the issue will be $305,000. The firm incurs $1,000 additional expenses.

(4)   Obtain a 30-day loan against $400,000 worth of receivables. The factor will loan an amount equal to 75 percent of the receivables. The factoring commission is one-half of 1 percent, and the interest rate is 15 percent per year.

22.18   Mini Case   Mielke Products, a New Jersey-based firm, manufactures and distributes legal and financial services and products directly to consumers. The firm has grown rapidly, causing a need for short-term financing. Part of its sales are for cash, but a majority are for credit. The credit sales are financed with short-term borrowings. As the CFO you have decided the whole short-term financing strategy needs to be reevaluated.

a.   What is the difference between spontaneous and negotiated short-term financing? Would you expect Mielke to be more likely to use spontaneous or negotiated short-term financing?

b.   How does the size of the firm, in general, influence its use of short-term financing? Its industry? Its aggressiveness versus conservatism?

c.   Previously, the firm has not costed out various short-term financing alternatives. Explain how, by using the effective annual interest rate, the firm can capture the relevant costs and benefits of alternative financing alternatives.

d.   Mielke can borrow from two banks as follows: Bank A will lend at a nominal rate of 16.85 percent with interest compounded monthly, and bank B will lend at a nominal rate of 16.60 percent compounded daily based on a 360-day year. If all else is equal, with which one is Mielke better off?

e.   Presently Mielke has two bank loans. The first is a 6-month loan for $1,000,000 based on discount interest that carries an interest rate of 16 percent. The loan has a compensating balance requirement of $100,000; typically Mielke would have only $15,000 in the bank. The second is a 180-day, $2,500,000 line of credit that has an annual commitment fee of 2 percent on the unused portion of the line. Over the last 180 days the interest rates and usage have been as follows:

	First 75 Days	Second 75 Days	Last 30 Days
Interest rate	14.50%	15.75%	16%
Total	$1,250,000	$1,000,000	$1,900,000

What is the effective annual interest rate on both? (*Note:* Use a 365-day year for the line of credit.)

f.   Mielke presently pays all of its accounts payable as soon as they are received. Why is this a good (or bad) policy? What about adopting a policy of paying all accounts 30 days past the due date?

g.   Instead of the bank loans, Mielke is investigating pledging and/or factoring its receivables. Two alternatives are as follows:

Pledging Receivables	Factoring Receivables
Loan is for 6 months	The agreement is for 6 months
Total receivables are $3,000,000; of which the loan is for 70 percent	The loan is for 70 percent of the receivables, which are $3,000,000
The processing fee is 1 percent of the receivables pledged every 6 months	The factoring commission is 0.80 of 1 percent of the total receivables, per every 6 months
The interest rate is 15 percent	The interest rate is 16 percent

What is the effective annual interest rate, or cost, for both? Should either of these be employed instead of the present bank loan and/or line of credit?

h. What other factors need to be considered in deciding between alternative short-term sources of financing?

REFERENCES

For general discussion, see:

MacPhee, William A. *Short-Term Business Borrowing: Sources, Terms and Techniques.* Homewood, Ill.: Dow Jones Irwin, 1984.

Moskowitz, L. A. *Modern Factoring and Commercial Finance.* New York: Thomas Y. Crowell, 1977.

For more on the role of banks see, for example:

Besanko, David, and George Kanatas. "Credit Market Equilibrium with Bank Monitoring and Moral Hazard." *Review of Financial Studies* 6 (No. 1, 1993): 213–32.

James, Christopher. "Some Evidence on the Uniqueness of Bank Loans." *Journal of Financial Economics* 19 (December 1987): 217–35.

Lummer, Scott L., and John J. McConnell. "Further Evidence on the Bank Lending Process and the Capital-Market Response to Bank Loan Agreements." *Journal of Financial Economics* 25 (November 1989): 99–122.

Rajan, Raghuram G. "Insiders and Outsiders: The Choice Between Informed and Arm's-Length Debt." *Journal of Finance* 47 (September 1992): 1367–1400.

For more on lines of credit, see:

Hawkins, Gregory. "An Analysis of Revolving Credit Agreements." *Journal of Financial Economics* 10 (March 1982): 59–81.

Hill, Ned C., William L. Sartoris, and Sue L. Visscher. "The Components of Credit Line Borrowing Costs." *Journal of Cash Management* 3 (October-November 1983): 47–56.

Secured lending and factoring is discussed in:

Farragher, Edward J. "Factoring Accounts Receivable." *Journal of Cash Management* 6 (March-April 1986): 38–42.

Mian, Shehzad, and Clifford W. Smith, Jr. "Accounts Receivable Management and Policy: Theory and Evidence." *Journal of Finance* 47 (March 1992): 169–200.

Rosenthal, James A., and Juan M. Ocampo. "Analyzing the Economic Benefits of Securitized Credit." *Journal of Applied Corporate Finance* 1 (Fall 1988): 32–44.

23 *Hedging Interest Rate Risk*

EXECUTIVE SUMMARY

Effective financial managers are concerned about controlling, or hedging, some of the risks faced by the firm. One of the primary risks that can be hedged arises from fluctuations in interest rates. The primary tools available to assist in risk management include matching assets and liabilities, forward contracts, futures, swaps, and options. In order to be able to employ these tools the firm must understand how the value of the firm is affected by changes in interest rates.

To hedge, the firm needs to determine a counter-action or counter-security whose value moves in the opposite direction to that of the asset or liability to be hedged. The hedge ratio determines how much should be purchased or sold to create the hedge. Knowing the duration of the interest-sensitive item to be hedged is often important, because it allows an estimation to be made of the change in value as interest rates change.

The widespread availability of financial forwards and futures has greatly increased the ability to hedge interest rate risk. Commercial banks and investment bankers increasingly provide both simple and very complex hedging schemes. Forward contracts can be tailored to meet the exact needs of the firm. Thus, a perfect hedge can be put in place. Using financial futures generally reduces the direct costs of the hedge but results in only a partial hedge. When futures are employed to hedge, basis risk is substituted for price (or interest rate) risk. With such risk, it is extremely important to monitor and manage the hedge over time.

In recent years interest rate swaps have become a popular means of adjusting interest rate risk exposure. With a "plain vanilla" swap, one firm raises fixed rate financing while another raises floating rate financing, and then they exchange interest payment streams. The advantage comes from each firm raising funds at its cheapest rate, and then switching from fixed to floating, or vice versa. Options may also be employed to help firms deal with interest rate risk.

Financial managers can either plan for interest rate risk or simply adjust to it. Increasingly, they are using a variety of products, loosely called "derivatives," to manage some of their interest rate risk.

RISK MANAGEMENT

Throughout the book we have emphasized the relationship between risk and required returns. Many risks the firm faces cannot be avoided. But, increasingly, firms are able to offset, or hedge, some kinds of risks. The rationale for hedging risk in an efficient market, as discussed in Chapter 28, is that by hedging the firm expects to increase its value and/or reduce taxes, financial distress costs, or agency costs. The tools for offsetting risk lie primarily in the widespread availability of new financial instruments—forward contracts, futures, swaps, and options. Before we consider the hedging of interest rate risk, let's examine the basic ideas behind risk management.

INTEREST RATES, FOREIGN EXCHANGE RATES, AND COMMODITY PRICES

To understand the principles behind risk management, consider Figure 23.1. This figure depicts the impact on the value of a firm, V, as one of three hedgeable factors—interest rates, foreign exchange rates or commodity prices—changes. In the figure, the value of the firm is depicted on the vertical axis, and the level of interest rates, foreign

Figure 23.1

Sensitivity of Firm Value to Changes in Hedgeable Factors

The risk profile line indicates the impact on the firm as rates or prices of hedgeable factors change. The steeper the slope, the greater the change in V as interest rates, foreign exchange rates, or commodity prices change.

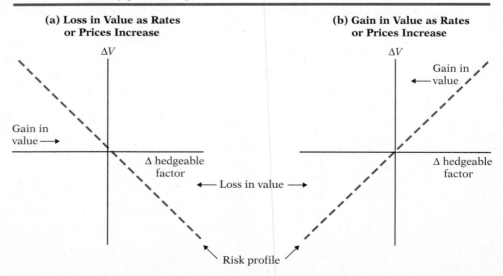

exchange rates, or commodity prices is on the horizontal axis. If the value of the firm does not change as rates (for interest and foreign exchange) or prices (for commodities) change, then the dashed **risk profile** line would be horizontal. The steeper the risk profile line, the more the value of the firm is directly affected by changes in interest rates, foreign exchange rates, or commodity prices. In Figure 23.1(a), the value of the firm is adversely affected by increases in interest rates, foreign exchange rates, or commodity prices, as shown by the dashed risk profile line that slopes downward to the right. On the other hand, if the firm benefits by increases in any of the three factors, then as shown in Figure 23.1(b), the risk profile line slopes upward to the right.

Suppose, for example, a firm employs 60 percent variable rate debt financing in its capital structure. If interest rates increase and are expected to stay higher for some period of time, the value of the firm may be negatively affected unless it can pass these higher financing costs on to customers. Likewise, if a firm does a lot of business overseas or competes against firms that do, as exchanges rates rise or fall, these changing rates will have a direct impact on the value of the firm. As a final example, consider what happens to the market value of commercial airlines, such as American Airlines, Air France, or Japan Air, as the price of aviation fuel increases. The direct consequence is an increase in the airline's costs, resulting in lower profitability, unless the increased costs can be passed on through higher ticket prices. Knowing the impact of changes in interest rates, foreign exchange rates, and commodity prices on the value of the firm is a vital part of effective financial management. Only if their impact is known and understood can the firm effectively consider how to plan for, or hedge against, the risks involved.

HEDGE RATIOS

To hedge risks arising from fluctuations in interest rates, foreign exchange rates, or commodity prices, the idea is to find two investments that are perfectly correlated. Then you buy one and sell the other so the net change in the value of the firm is zero. This is depicted in Figure 23.2, where the losses (gains) shown by the dashed blue risk profile line are exactly offset by the gains (losses) for the hedge, as shown by the black dashed hedge profile line. In practice, factors such as imperfect correlation and the cost of hedging impede the ability of the firm to completely hedge. For the time being, we ignore these complications.

Let's see in more detail how a hedge works. Assume you have a liability A to be hedged; to accomplish the hedge, you purchase an asset B. The size of the investment in B depends on how the values of A and B are related. Suppose the percentage changes in the value of A are related to percentage changes in the value of B as follows:

$$\begin{matrix} \text{expected change} \\ \text{in value of A} \end{matrix} = \delta \begin{pmatrix} \text{change in} \\ \text{value of B} \end{pmatrix} \qquad (23.1)$$

Delta, δ, measures the sensitivity of change in the value of A to changes in the value of B. Delta is the hedge ratio;[1] that is, it tells us the number of units of B that should

[1] This hedge ratio serves the same function that hedge ratios in option pricing theory (Chapter 5) serve.

Figure 23.2 .

Risk and Payoff Profiles

As depicted, the losses (gains), as shown by the risk profile, are completely offset by gains (losses) in the hedge. Thus, in this case the value of the firm is independent of any changes in the rate or price of hedgeable factors.

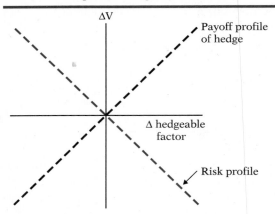

be purchased to hedge the liability A. If the value of A changes so that your liability increases, by hedging you want to experience offsetting movements in the value of B, with the net result that the firm neither gains nor loses value.

It is important to recognize that with efficient markets and costless trading, hedging transactions are zero-NPV events. Once transactions costs and other inefficiencies creep in, hedging should be looked at like insurance—it is never free, or costless. If the firm knew which direction interest rates, foreign exchange rates, or commodity prices would move, there might be little reason to hedge. If interest rates, foreign exchange rates, or commodity prices move in one direction, the firm benefits because the hedge offsets the loss in value that would have occurred otherwise. But if they move in the opposite direction, the firm suffers some "regret" by hedging. This regret can be viewed as an opportunity cost reflecting the benefits that could have accrued to the firm in terms of a higher value, V, by not hedging, less the actual value of the firm due to hedging.

Concept Review Questions

- Describe how a change in interest rates, foreign exchange rates, or commodity prices could affect the value of a firm.
- What is the net present value from a perfectly established hedge transaction with efficient markets and costless trading?

INTEREST RATE RISK

In this chapter we consider how firms can and do hedge some of their exposure to fluctuations in firm value caused by changes in interest rates. In Chapter 28 we will examine how they deal with foreign exchange exposure and other risks they face.

DURATION AND INTEREST RATE RISK

In order to examine the interest rate sensitivity of various financial instruments, it is helpful to understand the concept of duration. **Duration** is the weighted average maturity of the cash flow stream of any financial asset or liability, where the timing of each cash flow is weighted by its present value relative to the total present value of the cash flow stream. Thus, *duration is a time- and value-weighted measure* of the cash flows that are associated with an asset or liability. For concreteness, consider calculating the duration of a bond. The duration, D, of a bond paying annual interest is:[2]

$$D = (1)\left[\frac{I_1/(1 + YTM)^1}{B_0}\right] + (2)\left[\frac{I_2/(1 + YTM)^2}{B_0}\right]$$
$$+ \cdots + (n)\left[\frac{(I_n + M)/(1 + YTM)^n}{B_0}\right] \tag{23.2}$$

where

$$D = \text{the duration of the bond}$$
$$I_1, \ldots, I_n = \text{the interest payments}$$
$$YTM = \text{the bond's yield to maturity}$$
$$B_0 = \text{the bond's current price or value}$$
$$M = \text{the maturity (or par) value of the bond}$$
$$n = \text{the number of periods to maturity}$$

Assume a 4-year, $1,000 par bond has a 10 percent coupon interest rate and a current market value of $900. Using annual interest, the yield to maturity of this bond is 13.39 percent. The duration for the bond is then determined as follows:

Year (1)	Interest and Maturity Value (2)	Present Value of (2) at 13.39% (3)	Proportion of Total Value (3)/B_0 (4)	Proportion of Total Value times Year (1)(4) (5)
1	$ 100	$ 88.19	0.10	0.10
2	100	77.78	0.09	0.18
3	100	68.59	0.07	0.21
4	1,100	665.42	0.74	2.96
		$B_0 \approx \$900.00$	1.00	Duration = 3.45

The duration is 3.45 years, which is less than the bond's maturity of 4 years.[3]

---

[2] A number of duration measures exist; this one follows Macaulay. For a discussion of this and others, see, for example, Kaufman, Bierwag and Toevs (1983).
[3] For bonds paying interest semiannually, the interest in Equation 23.2 is the semiannual interest, n is the total number of periods until maturity (i.e., number of years times 2), and the yield to maturity is the rate per semiannual period.

Instead of using Equation 23.2, an easier equation to employ (although it doesn't look easier) is

$$D = \frac{I\left[\dfrac{(1 + YTM)^{(n+1)} - (1 + YTM) - (YTM)(n)}{(YTM)^2(1 + YTM)^n}\right] + \dfrac{M(n)}{(1 + YTM)^n}}{B_0} \qquad (23.3)$$

where the symbols are defined as before.[4] Using Equation 23.3, we find that duration for this 4-year bond is

$$D = \frac{\$100\left[\dfrac{(1 + 0.1339)^5 - (1 + 0.1339) - (0.1339)(4)}{(0.1339)^2(1 + 0.1339)^4}\right] + \dfrac{\$1,000(4)}{(1 + 0.1339)^4}}{\$900}$$

$D = 3.45$ years

For *all financial assets and liabilities except zero-coupon and bullet securities* that have only a single lump sum cash flow which occurs at the end of their life, *their duration is always less than their maturity.* Treasury bills and zero-coupon bonds, for example, have a duration equal to their maturity. Thus, a one-year Treasury bill has a duration of 1.00, and a 10-year zero-coupon bond has a duration of 10.00.

Why should we be interested in determining the duration of a bond, or any other financial instrument whose value is influenced by interest rates? The reason is that changes in duration are closely linked to changes in the market value of the financial instrument. Duration allows us to determine how the value, in this case the value of a bond, changes as market interest rates change. This relationship is

$$\text{duration} \approx -\frac{\text{percentage change in market value}}{\text{percentage change in } (1 + YTM)} \qquad (23.4)$$

Therefore, *for small changes* in the yield to maturity, the percent that the bond's value will change as market interest rates change is given by

$$\text{percentage market volatility} \approx \frac{-\text{duration}}{1 + YTM} \qquad (23.5)$$

$$\approx \frac{-3.45}{1.1339} \approx -3.04$$

For example, if the yield to maturity of this bond changes by 1 percent, the market value of the bond will move in the opposite direction by approximately 3.04 percent of its original market price of $900. A 1 percent increase in interest rates will therefore cause the value of the bond to decrease by approximately $(0.0304)(\$900) = \$27.36$,

---

[4] See Chua (1984). If the bond pays interest semiannually, the interest in Equation 23.3 is the semiannual interest, n is the total number of periods until maturity, the yield to maturity is the rate per semiannual period, and B_0 is determined based on semiannual discounting.

whereas a 1 percent decrease in rates will cause the bond's value to increase by about $27.36.[5]

Very short-term debt instruments have durations that are essentially zero. Thus, an overnight money market instrument earning the overnight repo rate, which is re-lent every day at that day's overnight repo rate, has a duration that is essentially zero. A medium-term debt instrument, on the other hand, has a larger duration, and its value fluctuates somewhat more as interest rates change. Finally, a long-term debt instrument has an even larger duration, and its value fluctuates even more as interest rates change. The risk profiles of these three instruments are depicted in Figure 23.3.

Notice that the short-maturity debt instrument has a risk profile with no slope—firms or individuals who hold that security experience no interest rate risk. The medium-term debt instrument has a steeper risk profile line, indicating its value fluctuates somewhat more as interest rates change. Finally, the longer-maturity debt instrument has an even steeper risk profile line—its value is very sensitive to changes in interest rates. Duration is important in helping to determine how much interest rate risk exists.[6] As such, it provides the same information that the risk profile line does and indicates the extent of interest rate risk exposure.[7]

Figure 23.3

Duration, Interest Rate Risk, and the Value of the Firm

The higher the duration of the debt, the greater the firm's interest rate sensitivity. These results hold for zero-coupon bonds as well as for interest-bearing debt instruments.

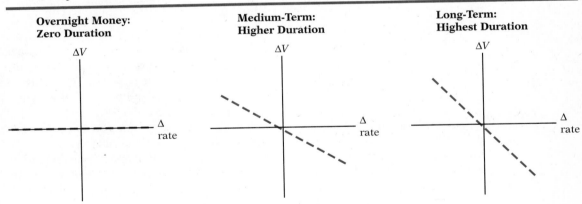

[5] This relationship is curvilinear, not linear, and holds only for small changes in interest rates. For larger changes in the yield to maturity, the price adjustment is not symmetrical.

[6] Duration helps explain some of our earlier analysis. In Chapter 3, Figure 3.3, we showed that the value of longer-maturity bonds fluctuates more than the value of shorter-maturity bonds as interest rates change. Because longer-maturity bonds have larger durations than shorter-maturity bonds, as depicted in Figure 23.3 their value must fluctuate more. Likewise, in Chapter 16 (Figure 16.2) the value of zero-coupon bonds was shown to fluctuate more than the value of interest-bearing bonds as interest rates change. Zero-coupon bonds have a duration that equals their maturity; an interest-bearing bond always has a duration that is less than its maturity.

[7] For more on assessing a firm's risk exposure see, for example, Kapner and Marshall (1990) or Smith, Smithson, and Wilford (1990).

There is one other feature of duration that makes it useful: Durations for more than one cash flow stream can be added together by taking the weighted average of the individual durations. Suppose we have a portfolio of three bonds as follows:

Bond Value	Proportion of Total	Duration
$ 3,000,000	0.15	4.16 years
8,000,000	0.40	1.09
9,000,000	0.45	6.30
$20,000,000	1.00	

The duration of this portfolio is simply $(0.15)(4.16) + (0.40)(1.09) + (0.45)(6.30) = 3.90$ years. That information for a group of assets or liabilities is extremely useful as firms construct hedges that protect them from interest rate risk.

INTEREST RATE RISK EXPOSURE

Now that we understand the basic concept of interest rate risk exposure, we need to consider the extent to which it exists and alternative strategies, from simple to complex, for dealing with it. All financial institutions, such as banks, savings and loan associations, and insurance companies, are exposed to a high level of interest rate risk. In the late 1970s and early 1980s savings and loan associations experienced the impact of interest rate risk exposure. To understand their risks, think about the "typical" savings and loan association at that point in time: It accepted deposits that were generally short-term in nature (from a few days, to months, to a few years for longer term certificates of deposit). It then employed the funds to make long-term, generally fixed-rate mortgages to help individuals finance the purchase of houses. If the S&L's borrowing costs were, for example, 5 percent, it added enough to cover its expenses and make a profit, and then lent the funds at, say, 8 percent to individuals to finance the purchase of homes. That was fine as long as interest rates remained fairly constant. But in the early 1980s, short-term interest rates increased dramatically, to a high of 18 to 20 percent. The S&Ls were still accepting short-term deposits that were now paying high interest rates, while their returns on mortgages made previously were still at, say, 8 percent. The net result was massive failures in the savings and loan industry which the federal government, and all taxpayers, paid for. Although not always as dramatic as what happened to many S&Ls, all financial institutions face interest rate risk; many of their activities are directed towards effectively dealing with this risk.

Although interest rate risk may be most apparent for financial institutions, the interest rate risk problem is widespread and affects many types of firms. The following are a few examples:

1. Many firms finance their short-term and even part of their longer-term needs for funds with financial arrangements or instruments whose cost "floats" and is tied to short-term interest rates. As interest rates rise or fall, the cash outflows required to meet these financing costs fluctuate accordingly.

2. Firms that produce or sell durable goods on credit, such as furniture and automobiles, have a portfolio of consumer loans whose market value fluctuates daily as interest rates change.
3. Firms borrow funds and often enter obligations to repay the funds via periodic repayments. This is often done through sinking fund payments for long-term debt. The cost to the firm fluctuates directly as interest rates change. If interest rates increase, the firm can reduce its cash outflow by repurchasing the bonds in the open market. If interest rates fall, they can call the bonds and retire them.

In these and many other situations the future variability and level of interest rates can either help or hurt. Firms can either plan for this interest rate risk, or they can attempt to react to it. Most firms employ one or more strategies to deal with some of their interest rate risk exposure.

MATCHING

The most straightforward approach to hedging interest rate risk is to match, or offset, the outflows and inflows. Consider Yarmouth Leasing which recently purchased some equipment and agreed to lease it out for a single payment of $3 million at the end of 2 years. At 9 percent the present value of the lease income is $3 million$/(1.09)^2 =$ $2,525,040. Because the lease income comes in all at one time at the end of 2 years, the duration of the lease income is 2.00. How could Yarmouth finance the asset so that it had no interest rate risk?[8] The answer is to issue a 9 percent, 2-year, zero-coupon bond that has a maturity value of $3 million. The zero-coupon bond has a duration that is also 2 years. Therefore, the duration of the asset and the liability have been matched. No matter what happens to interest rates, Yarmouth has hedged, or *immunized*, itself against any change in interest rates.

To introduce more complication, what if Yarmouth has also purchased another piece of equipment that it will lease out for $1.5 million for each of 5 years, with the lease payments made at the end of each of the 5 years? At 9 percent the present value of this income stream is

$$\text{present value} = \$1,500,000\left[\frac{1}{0.09} - \frac{1}{(0.09)(1 + 0.09)^5}\right] = \$5,834,477$$

and the duration of the income stream, using Equation 23.3,[9] is

$$D = \frac{\$1,500,000\left[\frac{(1 + 0.09)^6 - (1 + 0.09) - (0.09)(5)}{(0.09)^2(1 + 0.09)^5}\right]}{\$5,834,477}$$

$D = 2.83$ years

[8] There is also credit risk in that the lessee may not make the $3 million payment. In this example we ignore credit risk and other complications, as well as how profitable the lease is.
[9] Note that the last term in Equation 23.3 is zero when the loan is amortized in equal payments over time.

To hedge, or immunize, this income stream Yarmouth needs to finance the purchase with a bond or loan that has a duration of 2.83 years. The easiest way to accomplish this is to take out a 9 percent loan with principal and interest due once a year in the amount of $1.5 million. This loan has a duration of 2.83 years; thus, Yarmouth has again immunized itself against any change in interest rates.

ADJUSTING THE HEDGE RATIO

In the two examples of Yarmouth Leasing so far, the hedge ratio (as given by Equation 23.1) ended up being 1.00. That is, Yarmouth obtained financing in exactly the amount of the lease payments, with exactly the same payment stream, as the income stream on the lease. What if that was not possible, and Yarmouth could secure only a loan in the second case that had a duration of 3.90 years? Can Yarmouth still hedge its interest rate risk? The answer is "yes." The only change that has to be made is to adjust the hedge ratio, which is the ratio of the durations of the lease and the financing streams, as follows:

$$\text{hedge ratio} = \delta = \frac{\text{duration of lease}}{\text{duration of loan}} = \frac{2.83}{3.90} \approx 0.73$$

Yarmouth could hedge against changes in interest rates simply by issuing (0.73)(present value of lease) = (0.73)($5,834,477) = $4,259,168 in debt. To create a hedge that has a zero NPV, the firm would also have to issue short-term debt with a duration of essentially zero in the amount of $5,834,477 − $4,259,168 = $1,575,309. Now, if interest rates change, the change in the present value of the lease payments will be equal to the change in the value of the debt.

The above examples illustrate several points. First, the most straightforward means of hedging is to offset exactly the asset or liability by creating a hedge instrument that exactly matches it in terms of the timing and amount of the cash flows. *This matching strategy is effective if it can be achieved.* The trouble is that often it may be impossible or very costly to create an offsetting set of cash flows. In addition, in practice Yarmouth will be purchasing and leasing many assets. When this happens the financial manager's job never ends, because new financing in exactly the correct amounts and timing must be arranged for each new asset.

Second, the strategy works well if a zero-coupon security is employed. However, if any other type of financing is employed, problems may develop because this approach hedges against only across-the-board changes in interest rates. Because short- and long-term rates do not move exactly together, complications arise.

Third, durations change. Over time as the assets or liabilities under examination move closer to maturity, or as market interest rates change, duration changes. For example, holding everything else constant, *as a bond moves closer to maturity its duration becomes less and less, until at maturity its duration is zero.* As duration changes so does the percentage market volatility of the asset or liability. Hence, even if everything else remains the same, over time virtually any hedge must be adjusted to reflect the changed circumstances. Thus, if anything other than a zero-coupon or an exactly matched debt security is employed, the durations of the assets and liabilities will diverge. To ensure the proper hedge, firm must buy or sell securities to maintain the correct hedge ratio.

Firms often employ matching or duration-based procedures to hedge some of their interest rate risks. However, they also employ many other financial instruments and techniques. To understand these, we have to understand forward contracts and futures.

Concept Review Questions

- Describe, or define, *duration* and its use when hedging interest rate risk.
- What kinds of firms or industries have a high degree of interest rate risk?
- Describe how to hedge a portfolio against interest rate risk.

FORWARDS AND FUTURES

With the exception of options, most of the securities we have examined in the book assumed that the purchase or sale of the asset and delivery occurred today, at the **spot price** (today's price). However, it is also possible to place an order for later delivery at an agreed-upon **forward price.** The same assets can be bought or sold; the only difference is that delivery and payment occur some time in the future as agreed upon by the parties involved. Forward and futures contracts allow us to place orders now for later delivery.

FORWARD CONTRACTS

Forward contracts have existed for a long time, but their use for hedging risk has expanded greatly in the last few years, as commercial banks and investment banking firms have become major participants in creating forward contracts. A **forward contract** is an agreement *that obligates the owner* to buy a given asset at a specified price (the "exercise price") on a specified date, as indicated by the contract. At maturity, if the actual price of the asset is greater than the exercise price, the owner profits; if the actual price is less, the owner suffers a loss. Likewise, the seller of the contract is obligated to sell the given asset at the exercise price on the maturity date. In an efficient market, at origination, the forward contract is a zero-NPV security; in reality there is a spread that provides the seller a profit incentive to engage in selling a zero-NPV agreement.

There are at least three other points that need to be understood about forward contracts: First, although there may be an origination fee paid to the bank or investment banker helping to originate the contract, no money changes hands between the buyer and the seller until the maturity date specified in the forward contract. Second, there is credit (or default) risk, because one party (ignoring transactions costs) always gains, while the other loses, unless the market price at the maturity date exactly equals the exercise price. The credit risk arises because one party may suffer financial loss and if the loss is severe enough, could default on the forward contract. Because there is credit risk, the market for forward contracts is limited to large institutions, corporations, and governments that have lines of credit to back up the agreements. Third, providing a seller can be found, the specific asset and terms covered by a forward contract can be negotiated to meet the exact requirements of the buyer. This ability to tailor-make the forward contract is important. In recent years the market for forward contracts has grown, as many financial intermediaries have become active participants in arranging forward contracts for firms.

FINANCIAL FUTURES

In addition to forward contracts, a second important financial instrument for hedging risk is futures contracts. Futures have been in existence since at least the 1840s, but they have become much more important in the last 20 years, since the introduction of the first financial futures contract in 1975. The basic form of a **futures contract** is exactly like a forward contract: it obligates its owner to purchase a specified asset at the exercise price on the contract maturity date. Thus, the risk-hedging potential of a futures contract is exactly like that of a forward contract. While the two instruments are similar, (1) the size and maturity date of the futures contract are fixed and (2) futures are traded on organized exchanges, so that individual negotiations are not necessary to create a futures contract. This reduces the cost of dealing in futures relative to forwards, but it also means the futures contract is not constructed specifically to fit the needs of the buyer or seller. Hence the ability to obtain a 100 percent effective hedge is virtually nonexistent with futures.

Futures were originally developed for commodities such as grain, metals, and so forth. Now they exist on numerous commodities, on foreign exchange rates (as discussed in Chapter 28), and on interest rates and stock market indices. Actively traded financial futures contracts are shown in Table 23.1. The volume of financial futures traded in the United States now far surpasses that for commodities or metals. Futures exchanges also exist around the world in Toronto, London, Amsterdam, Paris, Kuala Lampur (Malaysia), Singapore, Manila, Hong Kong, Sydney, Auckland, and Tokyo. Futures have developed into a truly global financial instrument.

To understand more about interest rate futures, consider Table 23.2 which provides one day's data on three important futures—U.S. Treasury bonds, U.S. Treasury bills, and Eurodollars. Let's start with Treasury bond futures. As noted at the top of the Treasury bond quotes, they are traded on the Chicago Board of Trade, CBT, the contract size is $100,000, and they are quoted in 1/32s of 100 percent. The first column shows that eight Treasury bond futures existed which mature in June, September, December, and March. For each contract, the opening, high, low, and settlement prices are given, followed by the change in price. A 1/32 change in price means that the futures contract changed by $31.25. [This is calculated by taking ($100,000)(0.01), because they are quoted in hundredths of a percent (1/32) = $31.25]. With a change of $-13/32$, the June contract lost $406.25 [i.e., (13)($31.25)] on that day. Then the yield to maturity is given, followed by the open interest, or number of contracts outstanding.

Each contract represents both a *long* (or buyer's) and a *short* (or seller's) position and counts as one contract of "open interest." This same information is given for all the months; the dots for the last two months indicate no contracts were traded that

Table 23.1

Interest Rate and Index Futures Contracts Listed in *The Wall Street Journal* of June 10, 1992

There are many other futures listed in the *Journal* as well as some options and futures options that can also be employed in constructing hedges.

Contract	Contract Size	Exchange
Treasury bonds	$100,000	Chicago Board of Trade, CBT
Treasury bonds	$50,000	MidAmerica Commodity Exchange, MCE
Treasury bonds	$100,000	London International Financial Futures Exchange, LIFFE
German Gov't. bonds	250,000 marks	LIFFE
Treasury notes	$100,000	CBT
5-year Treasury notes	$100,000	CBT
2-year Treasury notes	$200,000	CBT
30-day interest rate	$5,000,000	CBT
Treasury bills	$1,000,000	International Monetary Market, IMM, at Chicago Mercantile Exchange
LIBOR-1 month	$3,000,000	IMM
Muni bond index	$1,000 times Bond Buyer MBI*	CBT
Eurodollar	$1,000,000	IMM
Eurodollar	$1,000,000	LIFFE
Sterling	£500,000	LIFFE
Long gilt[†]	£50,000	LIFFE
S&P 500 index	500 times index	Chicago Mercantile Exchange, CME
Nikkei 225 index	$5 times NSA[‡]	CME
NYSE composite index	500 times index	New York Futures Exchange, NYFE
Major Market index	$500 times index	CBT

* MBI stands for Municipal Bond Index.
[†] British sterling-denominated long-term bonds.
[‡] NSA stands for Nikkei Stock Index.

day. Finally, at the bottom of the Treasury bond futures quotes we see the estimated volume was 235,000 contracts, the volume the day before was 92,939, and the *open interest,* which is the total number of contracts outstanding, was 342,951, a decrease of 10,494 contracts from the day before.

The final trading and settlement (or delivery) dates are known beforehand.[10] At settlement there is great latitude in the Treasury bonds that can be delivered; the specific mechanics of delivery are guided by rules drawn up by the Chicago Board of

[10] For many futures contracts, the final trading day is the third Friday of the month. For Treasury bonds, it is the business day immediately prior to the last seven days of the month. For Treasury bond futures, the delivery, or settlement, can first occur on or after the first business day of the contract expiration month.

Table 23.2

Three Interest Rate Futures Listed in *The Wall Street Journal* of June 10, 1992

As noted in Table 23.1, there are many other interest rate futures also listed. In addition, there are interest rate futures that trade in other parts of the world.

Treasury bonds (CBT)—$100,000; pts. 32nds of 100%

	Open	High	Low	Settle	Chg	Yield Settle	Chg	Open Interest
June	100–26	100–31	100–12	100–13	−13	7.959	+.041	64,323
Sept	99–24	99–29	99–08	99–09	−14	8.073	+.045	258,725
Dec	98–20	98–25	98–05	98–05	−14	8.189	+.045	14,615
Mr93	97–19	97–23	97–05	97–05	−14	8.294	+.046	3,619
June	96–20	96–23	96–07	96–07	−14	8.393	+.046	1,131
Sp93	95–27	95–27	95–12	95–12	−14	8.484	+.047	242
Dec	. . . .	. . . .	. . . .	94–19	−14	8.570	+.048	116
Sp94	. . . .	. . . .	. . . .	93–28	−14	8.649	+.048	100

Est vol 235,000; vol Mon 92,939; open int 342,951, −10,494.

Treasury Bills (IMM)—$1 million; pts. of 100%

	Open	High	Low	Settle	Chg	Discount Settle	Chg	Open Interest
June	96.30	96.32	96.29	96.29	. . . .	3.71	. . . .	14,021
Sept	96.15	96.17	96.14	96.14	. . . .	3.86	. . . .	19,842
Dec	95.73	95.75	95.71	95.71 +.01		4.29	−.01	6,233
Mr93	. . . .	. . . .	. . . .	95.57 +.01		4.43	−.01	1,671

Est vol 4,060; vol Mon 3,743; open int 41,767, +294.

Eurodollar (IMM)—$1 million; pts. of 100%

	Open	High	Low	Settle	Chg	Yield Settle	Chg	Open Interest
June	96.03	96.03	96.00	96.00	−.01	4.00	+.01	191,781
Sept	95.75	95.77	95.74	95.74	. . . .	4.26	. . . .	299,817
Dec	95.12	95.15	95.09	95.11	. . . .	4.89	. . . .	268,008
Mr93	94.98	95.02	94.98	94.98	. . . .	5.02	. . . .	174,710
June	94.53	94.57	94.53	94.53	. . . .	5.47	. . . .	116,646
Sept	94.10	94.13	94.10	94.10	. . . .	5.90	. . . .	83,613
Dec	93.55	93.59	93.55	93.55	. . . .	6.45	. . . .	61,977
Mr94	93.41	93.45	93.41	93.41	. . . .	6.59	. . . .	58,257
June	93.13	93.16	93.12	93.12	. . . .	6.88	. . . .	36,921
Sept	92.89	92.92	92.87	92.87	−.01	7.13	+.01	30,711
Dec	92.53	92.56	92.51	92.51	−.01	7.49	+.01	29,534
Mr95	92.50	92.53	92.47	92.48	−.01	7.52	+.01	26,686
June	92.31	92.34	92.27	92.29	−.01	7.71	+.01	17,971
Sept	92.18	91.20	92.13	92.15	−.02	7.85	+.02	15,007
Dec	91.93	91.95	91.89	91.90	−.02	7.10	+.02	20,384
Mr96	91.97	91.98	91.92	91.93	−.02	7.07	+.02	13,898

Est vol 140,433; vol Mon 162,538; open int 1,440,121, −9,828.

Trade. Most positions are closed out (or "unwound") by a process called **offsetting,** which involves buying or selling the same contract to offset the original position. Thus, if a futures contract had been purchased to create a long position, most longs close out early by selling exactly the same contract they previously purchased to offset (or unwind) the position.

Looking at the second financial futures contract listed on Table 23.2, we see that 90-day U.S. Treasury bill futures are traded on the International Monetary Market, IMM (at the Chicago Mercantile Exchange), are for $1,000,000, and are traded in points of 100 percent. A 1-basis-point (or 1/100th of 1 percent) change represents a $25 change in the price of the Treasury bill contract. The information for Treasury bill futures is similar to what is presented for Treasury bond futures, except (as discussed in Chapter 21) Treasury bills are quoted on a discount as opposed to a yield basis. We see that only four Treasury bill futures contracts were available.

Finally, information on Eurodollar futures is also presented in Table 23.2. **Eurodollars** are dollars that are deposited in foreign banks or foreign branches of U.S. banks. The Eurodollar futures contract is based on the 3-month **London Interbank Offered Rate, LIBOR.** (LIBOR is the rate that banks in different countries trade at.) These are also traded on the IMM and are quoted in 1/100ths of 100 percent. Like Treasury bill futures, a change of 1 basis point means the price of the Eurodollars contract changes by $25. One feature of the Eurodollar contract that is different from the Treasury bond or Treasury bill contract is that the settlement is for cash, not securities. Also, note that Eurodollar futures are quoted at 100 minus the interest rate. For the first June future, the yield is 4.00 percent, and the settle price of 96.00 is equal to $100 - 4.00 = 96.00$. In looking at the information about Eurodollar futures in Table 23.2, we see that a full 4 years of these futures exists and that the open interest for them is much larger than for U.S. Treasury bond or bill futures. This larger open interest has important implications for firms using futures to hedge: Contracts with more open interest have more liquidity, and with longer contract availability they provide the opportunity to more easily hedge longer-term interest rates than do financial futures with only a few contracts available. For this reason Eurodollar futures are widely employed to hedge interest rate risk.

We should note one other factor before leaving Table 23.2. As we go further out in time with the Treasury bond and Eurodollar data, the price drops and the yield (to maturity) increases. This makes sense because, as we know, prices and yields are inversely related, and at this point in time the yield curve (or term structure of interest rates) was upward-sloping. The only way yields can be higher for more distant contracts is for their price to be lower.

Now that we understand something of how futures are reported in the financial press, we need to consider some of their other features. Due to (1) daily settlement, (2) margin requirements, and (3) a clearinghouse, the default (or credit) risk associated with futures contracts is far less than for forward contracts. By daily settlement, we mean they are **marked-to-market** each day, so that any change in the price of the contract is settled up immediately, instead of waiting until the maturity date of the contract. In addition, to buy or sell futures the participants must post both an initial margin and a maintenance margin. The margin is posted either in cash or with Treasury bills. The amount in the margin account is adjusted daily as the futures contracts are marked-to-market. Thus, if the settle price at the close of a day's trading is higher than the previous day's settle price, the dollar amount is credited to the account of those who previously purchased, or hold, long positions. Likewise, those holding short positions would have their margin accounts reduced. If insufficient funds are in a margin account, additional margin will have to be provided. Finally, there is a clearinghouse that interposes itself between the parties in a futures contract. Its function is to provide a bonding mechanism that ensures the contract will be performed.

Concept Review Questions

- Differentiate between *spot price* and *forward price*.
- What is the difference between a forward contract and a futures contract?
- What is meant by the term *marked-to-market*?

HEDGING USING FORWARDS AND FUTURES

USING FORWARD RATE AGREEMENTS

Forward contracts on interest rates are called **forward rate agreements, FRAs**. The market for forward rate agreements exists in a number of currencies, the principal two being the U.S. dollar and the British pound sterling. To understand how to hedge a firm's interest rate risk, let's look at Glacier International's new $100 million, 6-month floating rate loan. The interest rate is already set for the first 3 months and then will be reset based on the then-existing LIBOR rate. For simplicity, assume interest is paid only twice—once in 3 months at today's known rate, and again in 6 months based on what LIBOR is in 3 months. There are no tax considerations, nor any transactions costs. The interest due in 3 months is already known, therefore, it cannot be hedged. But the interest for the second 3-month period can be hedged. Assume the 3-month LIBOR rate today (based on futures prices or other sources) is 11 percent. To hedge, Glacier enters into a forward rate agreement as follows: Glacier will purchase a $100 million, 3-month forward contract which specifies that if 3-month LIBOR at the end of this initial 3-month period is greater than 11 percent, Glacier receives the difference. Likewise, if 3-month LIBOR is less than 11 percent, Glacier will pay.

Let's see what happens at the maturity date of the forward contract. If 3-month LIBOR at that time is exactly 11 percent, the buyer neither receives nor pays. What happens, however, if the 3-month LIBOR has gone to 12 percent? Glacier, as the buyer (with a long position) will receive, and the bank as seller (with a short position) will pay. The question is, how much? The amount of the forward contract is $100 million, the interest rate differential is 1 percent (i.e., 12% − 11%), and the period for any 3-month forward rate contract, assuming a 365-day year, is approximately 92 days. The interest to be received is ($100,000,000)(0.01)(92/365) = $252,055. This is the value at the *end of the 3-month period* covered by the Eurodollar contract, but it must be discounted back to the settlement day at the 3-month LIBOR rate in effect at the settlement date. That rate is 12 percent, so $252,055/{1 + [0.12(92/365)]} = $244,655. The bank will pay Glacier $244,655 at settlement.[11] You may wonder why we are discounting back to the settlement date of the contract. The reason is that the $252,055 is the value of holding another 3 months at the *then-specified* 3-month LIBOR rate. But, because payment is made at the settlement date, the $252,055 must be discounted at the then in effect 3-month LIBOR rate.

To see graphically the impact of this hedge, consider Figure 23.4(a). Ignoring transaction costs and taxes, the impact of a 1 percent change in interest rates changes the value of Glacier, ΔV, by $244,655. But, due to the forward rate agreement, the gain (loss) in the value of the firm is offset dollar-for-dollar. This is an example of a **perfect hedge** which resulted in the firm neither gaining nor losing as interest rates changed. (Again, we are ignoring transactions costs.) Finally, what would have happened if interest rates had fallen to 10 percent instead of increasing to 12 percent? With a decrease in interest rates, Glacier would suffer an opportunity loss because it could have saved $244,655 by not hedging.

Many times firms do not attempt to hedge all of their risk; instead they create only a **partial hedge.** The reasons for a partial hedge involve a reduction in transaction costs, a willingness to assume some interest rate risk, and the desire to benefit if interest rates fall. To see the effect of a partial hedge, let's consider what would happen if

---

[11] This is exactly the same amount that would be paid if the British Bankers Association (BBA) terms, which have become the industry standard, are employed. Their formula, if the settlement LIBOR rate is higher than the rate in the forward contract, is

$$\frac{(L - R)(D)(A)}{(B)(100) + (L)(D)}$$

where

L = LIBOR settlement rate
R = contract rate
D = days in contract, i.e., 92 for the 3-month period covered by a LIBOR forward rate agreement when a 365-day year is employed
A = contract amount
B = 360 or 365 days

Substituting in, we have

$$\frac{(12.00 - 11.00)(92)(\$100,000,000)}{(365)(100) + (12.00)(92)} = \frac{\$9,200,000,000}{37,604} = \$244,655$$

which is the same as we got before. If at settlement the contract rate is higher than the LIBOR settlement rate, the first term in the numerator becomes $(R - L)$ and the rest of the calculations are the same.

Figure 23.4

Perfect and Partial Hedges

With a perfect hedge, and ignoring transactions costs, the value of the firm, V, does not change as interest rates change. With a partial hedge, some impact on firm value remains as interest rates rise or fall.

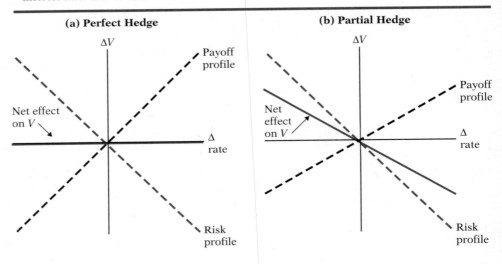

(a) Perfect Hedge   **(b) Partial Hedge**

Glacier takes out a forward rate agreement for only $50 million. The interest to be received with a 1 percent change in LIBOR is ($50,000,000)(0.01)(92/365) = $126,027, which when discounted is $126,027/{[1 + 0.12(92/365)]} = $122,327, or half of the previous amount. As shown in Figure 23.3(b), with a partial hedge the firm suffers some reduction in value as interest rates rise and benefits some as interest rates fall. In practice, partial hedges are commonplace activities that financial managers deal with as they hedge some of their firm's interest rate risk.

USING FINANCIAL FUTURES

In theory the use of financial futures to hedge interest rate risk is like using a forward contract. In practice, however, it tends to be more complex—and that complexity is heightened by the use of terms and concepts that are unique to the world of futures.

To start, consider another situation that Glacier faces. Due to seasonal fluctuations, Glacier knows it will require a $60 million, 3-month loan commencing on the termination day of the December Eurodollar futures contract.[12] The contractual rate on the loan has been negotiated to be 3-month LIBOR plus $1\frac{1}{2}$ percent, and it is now May. If interest rates go up between now and December, Glacier pays more interest. At the

---

[12] The last trading day for the Eurodollar futures contract is the second London business day before the third Wednesday of the month.

same time that interest rates change, so does the value of the Eurodollar futures contract. For every basis point change, or 1/100th of a percent, the price of a Eurodollar futures contract changes by $25—or $2,500 per one percent change in interest rates. For $60 million, a 1-percent change in interest rates produces a ($60,000,000/$1,000,000)($2,500) = $150,000 change in the price of the futures contract.

To hedge a possible increase in interest rates Glacier will *sell* 60 December 3-month Eurodollar futures contracts. We need to stop and explain why the interest rate futures contract is sold, instead of bought like a forward contract. The reason is because of the different way the two contracts are structured. *With a forward rate agreement, the process is conducted in terms of interest rates.* This is as we discussed in the last section. But, *with a futures contract the transaction is based on buying or selling in terms of the price of the contract.* As we know, if the yield (or interest rate) for a debt security increases, its price decreases. To profit from an increase in interest rates with futures, we sell at the current price and then profit when the price is lower at the settlement date. Let's see how it works.

Looking back at Table 23.2, we see that the yield on the next December Eurodollar futures contract is 4.89 percent. Ignoring transaction costs and taxes, Glacier sells 60 contracts at 95.11 (i.e., 100 − 4.89) each. The firm has now locked in an interest rate on the loan of 4.89 percent, plus $1\frac{1}{2}$ percent, or 6.39 percent on the loan which will be taken out in December. No matter if interest rates increase or decrease, the cost will be the same. Suppose in December the 3-month LIBOR rate has increased from 4.89 percent to 5.40 percent. This 51-basis point increase means Glacier will have to pay ($60,000,000)(0.0051)(1/4 of a year) = $76,500 more in interest for the 3-month loan. But, the increase in interest rates means Glacier made money on the futures position which can be used to offset the increased interest costs. The futures price in December is 100 − 5.40 = 94.60. Because Glacier sold 60 contracts, it receives (95.11 − 94.60)($2,500 per contract)(60 contracts) = $76,500. Combining the increased interest costs with the profit made on the futures contract of $76,500, the net change in costs for the loan (ignoring transactions costs and taxes) is zero. By hedging, Glacier locked in the interest rate specified in the December contract of 4.89 percent, plus the $1\frac{1}{2}$ percent premium.

Some Complications

The above example was straightforward and resulted in a perfect hedge because the deliverable asset for the futures contract was the same as what the firm wanted to hedge (i.e., 3-month LIBOR), and the timing of the loan *exactly* coincided with the termination date of the futures contract. In addition, we ignored any interim fluctuations that arose as the futures contract was marked-to-market each day. In practice things are not quite so simple.

Basis Risk

The **basis** for a futures contract is simply the difference between the futures price and the spot price, or

$$\text{basis} = \text{futures price} - \text{spot price} \tag{23.6}$$

An alternative way to think about this is based on the notion of **cost of carry,** where

$$\text{futures price} = \text{spot price} + \text{cost of carry} \qquad (23.7)$$

The cost of carry (or basis) is the difference between the opportunity cost of holding the asset and the yield earned on holding the asset. For 90-day Treasury bill futures, the cost of carry represents the net difference between the interest earned on a cash investment in Treasury bills and the initial money needed to pay for the asset (often represented by the interest rate on repurchase agreements). Other things being equal, as interest rates increase, the opportunity cost to the holder of the asset increases, so the cost of carry, and therefore the basis, also increase.

Two important predictable movements exist when considering futures and spot prices: First, the futures price should converge to the price implied by the cost of carry relation specified by Equation 23.7. The second predictable relation is depicted in Figure 23.5. At the maturity date of the contract the spot and future prices will be

Figure 23.5

Convergence to the Spot Price

The basis will not always be this "regular"; if the futures price moves above the spot price, the basis will be reversed. At the expiration date the spot and futures prices are the same.

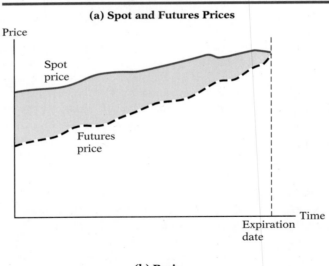

(a) Spot and Futures Prices

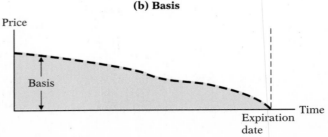

(b) Basis

equal, so the basis narrows, or converges, over time. One reason the basis is important is that convergence determines the behavior of the margin account. In Figure 23.5 as the futures price increases over time, there is a gradual flow of margin, as the positions are marked-to-market each day, from the account of the selling party to the account of the buying party.

A second reason basis is important is that if the futures position is unwound (or offset, by buying or selling the counter-contract) prior to maturity, the return on the futures position differs from the return on the underlying asset position *due to basis risk*. Or, equally likely, what if the timing of the asset agreement and the futures contract don't exactly match? The net effect is the same—there is basis risk due to timing differences between when action is required in the cash market and in the futures market.

Consider a slightly different situation faced by Glacier International. Assume now that the $60 million, 3-month loan is commencing on December 1st, instead of on the date the December Eurodollar futures contract expires, which is 2 to 3 weeks later. To hedge, Glacier sold 60 December Eurodollar contracts. Also, let's assume that on December 1 the 3-month LIBOR rate has again risen to 5.40 percent. Now, however, because the expiration date is still 2 to 3 weeks away, there is no guarantee the spot and future prices will be equal to each other. If they are not, and the futures price has fallen to only 94.75, for example, the profit on the futures contract is $(95.11 - 94.75)(\$2,500 \text{ per 1-percent move})(60 \text{ contracts}) = \$54,000$ instead of the $76,500 profit that would have been received with a perfect hedge. Combining Glacier's profit of $54,000 on the futures, with the increased interest cost of $76,500, the net increase in interest expense is $76,500 - \$54,000 = \$22,500$, instead of zero. While not a perfect hedge, Glacier is still better off than if it had not hedged at all.

Strip and Rolling Hedges

So far we have examined only a single interest rate exposure. However, many firms have continuing exposures that must be hedged. Consider now Perth Products which faces uncertainty in future borrowing costs and uses LIBOR to hedge these risks. It is now January and Perth anticipates borrowing over the year as follows:

March	$20 million
June	30 million
September	50 million
December	5 million

To hedge this interest rate exposure, in January Perth sells a **strip hedge** of Eurodollar futures as follows: 20 March futures, 30 June futures, 50 September futures, and 5 December futures.

In March Perth closes out the March futures by buying (or offsetting) 20 March futures. This same procedure is followed in June, September, and December as Perth closes out its position. The effectiveness of the hedge depends on the closeness of the futures price and the spot price (i.e., the basis) on the dates the positions are closed out.

The same procedure could be employed with longer time periods, providing that sufficient liquidity exists in the more distant futures contracts. If more distant futures contracts are not available, or if sufficient liquidity does not exist, a **rolling hedge** can be employed. Continuing with the previous example of Perth Products, a rolling hedge could be structured as follows:

January	Sell 105 March Eurodollar futures contracts (the 105 is determined by adding together the number of March, June, September, and December futures contracts from the previous example)
March	Buy 105 March Eurodollar futures contracts; sell 85 June Eurodollar futures contracts
June	Buy 85 June Eurodollar futures contracts; sell 55 September Eurodollar futures contracts
September	Buy 55 September Eurodollar futures contracts; sell 5 December futures contracts
December	Buy 5 December Eurodollar futures contracts

By stacking futures contracts in this manner, more distant interest rate exposure can be hedged. But as the hedge is rolled forward, there are transaction costs. Also, the uncertainty of the price for futures contracts is an additional source of risk. Finally, additional basis risk may be present when the positions are closed out.[13]

Cross-Hedging

Until now we have assumed a futures contract exists for the underlying asset (or interest rate) to be hedged. But often that is not the case. If Perth plans to issue commercial paper, it has a more complicated problem because there is not a commercial paper futures contract.[14] To hedge it must employ a **cross-hedge**. A cross-hedge exists every time the underlying asset is of one form (or tied to one interest rate), but the futures contract is of another form (or tied to another rate). The best procedure to use when a cross-hedge is required is to find the financial futures contract that is most highly correlated with the interest rate to be hedged. To hedge the commercial paper interest rate, Perth would probably use the Treasury bill futures contract or the Eurodollar futures contract, because the correlation of either of these futures contracts with commercial paper interest rates is generally at least 0.90.

One other point should be mentioned about cross-hedges. What if the firm wants to hedge an interest rate exposure in which the interest rate is tied to the prime rate? In this case *no good hedge is possible because the prime rate is an administered rate, not*

---

[13] There are a number of other aspects of hedging interest rate risk that are beyond our treatment. For example, we have ignored the shape of the term structure of interest rates, and whether the expectations theory of interest (as discussed in Appendix 3A) fully captures the relationship between interest rates and the term to maturity.

[14] There used to be a commercial paper contract, but due to low volume and because other highly acceptable short-term contracts, such as those on Treasury bills and Eurodollars, are available, the commercial paper contract was discontinued.

a market-determined rate. The problem with attempting to hedge the prime rate is that it may not change at all for long periods of time, even though short-term interest rates fluctuate. Thus, the correlation between the prime rate and the Treasury bill or LIBOR rates is low. If firms want to hedge an interest rate exposure, they negotiate to have the rate to be hedged tied to a rate for which there are futures contracts. Given the large and deep market for Eurodollar futures, we see why many firms negotiate to have any floating-rate borrowing tied to LIBOR. Then their interest rate exposure can be hedged by using Eurodollar futures.

Managing the Futures Hedge

Once financial futures are employed to place a hedge, the hedge must be monitored. The most important reason is due to changes in the basis. Because basis risk has been substituted for price risk, the resulting hedge is not free of risk. The basis must continually be monitored, and the hedge will occasionally need to be rebalanced as the basis changes. In addition to changes in the basis, the margin account must be monitored. Failure to do so can result in too little in the margin account, resulting in an unexpected demand for additional cash (or Treasury bills) in the account, or too much in the margin account that could be more productively employed elsewhere in the firm. Clearly, it is unwise to place a hedge and then fail to monitor it.

Concept Review Questions

■ Why is the consideration of basis risk important when attempting to hedge interest rate risk using futures contracts?

■ Describe how rolling hedges and cross-hedging are used to offset interest rate risk.

INTEREST RATE SWAPS

The first major interest rate swap occurred in August 1981 when the World Bank issued $290 million in Eurobonds and entered into a swap with IBM. Since then one of the largest growth markets in financial management has occurred in the use of swap contracts. The market for swaps is worldwide in nature, especially because firms more and more are raising funds wherever they are cheapest, and then worrying about whether the financing is in the specific form or currency desired. In its simplest form, a swap is simply an agreement between two firms to exchange cash flows. In this section we consider interest rate swaps; in Chapter 28 currency swaps will be examined.

Our discussion will focus on "plain vanilla" interest rate swaps. In a plain vanilla swap, the currency is the same for both parties, and one party is looking to exchange fixed rate debt financing for floating rate financing, while the other party is looking to exchange floating rate financing for fixed rate financing.[15] Although there may be many reasons why firms want to switch from floating to fixed or vice versa, typically they are attempting to match their financing to their assets or to protect themselves

---

[15] The parties involved in any swap are often referred to as the "counterparties."

from some type of interest rate risk. In a plain vanilla swap the principal amount, or "notational principal," is the same for both parties, and the floating rate employed is typically the 6-month LIBOR rate.[16] Therefore, only the interest cash flows are of importance. Because the interest cash flows are actually netted against one another, only the *difference in the two interest streams* is sent from one party to the other party in a plain vanilla swap.

Suppose firm A needs $5,000,000 for 5 years and can borrow at a fixed rate of 10 percent, or it can borrow at a floating rate of LIBOR plus 1.5 percent. Also, firm B needs $5,000,000 for 5 years, and it can borrow at a fixed rate of 12.50 percent or a floating rate of LIBOR plus 3.00 percent. The key to understanding why plain vanilla interest rate swaps exist is to focus on the comparative advantage that each of the firms has in terms of raising funds. This can be summarized as follows:

Party	Fixed Rate	Floating Rate
Firm B	12.50%	LIBOR + 3.00%
Firm A	10.00	LIBOR + 1.50
Difference = 2.50%		1.50%

Note that firm A has an absolute advantage relative to firm B because it can borrow at a cheaper rate whether it employs fixed rate or floating rate financing. But, on a comparative basis, firm A can borrow more cheaply at the fixed rate, and firm B has an advantage over firm A in floating rate borrowing. This can be seen by noting the 1.50 percent difference over LIBOR for floating rate financing for firm B versus the 2.50 percent difference when fixed rate borrowing is employed. As long as the differences between the fixed and floating rate financing costs are not equal (i.e., both 2.50 percent or both 1.50 percent, in this example), the incentive exists for an interest rate swap. The spread differential of 2.50% − 1.50% = 1.00%, or 100 basis points, can be shared between the two parties and allows both of them to reduce their interest rate costs. Let's see how it is done.

First, firm A borrows from a lender or the financial markets at a fixed rate of 10 percent because that is where its comparative financing advantage exists. Likewise, firm B borrows at a floating rate of LIBOR + 3.00 percent because that's where its comparative financing advantage exists. Now the two firms will enter into a swap. For simplicity, we assume they will share the spread differential of 1.00 percent equally between the two firms. To do so, firm B will agree to pay firm A a fixed rate of 12.50% − 0.50% = 12.00 percent on the $5,000,000 in financing. Firm A turns around and pays LIBOR + 3.00% to firm B to cover the floating rate financing costs incurred by firm B. This sequence of cash flows is shown in Figure 23.6.

---

[16] In the absence of barriers to capital flows, there would be no advantage to either party participating in plain vanilla interest rate swaps. A number of possible explanations have been advanced for why plain vanilla swaps are beneficial, including desires to change duration, underpriced credit risk, risk shifting, and information asymmetries. A swap contract can also be thought of and analyzed as a series of forward contracts. See Kapner and Marshall (1990) or Smith, Smithson, and Wilford (1990).

Figure 23.6

Interest Cash Flows for a Plain Vanilla Interest Rate Swap

Only the net period-by-period difference between LIBOR + 3.00% and 12% will be sent from one firm to the other.

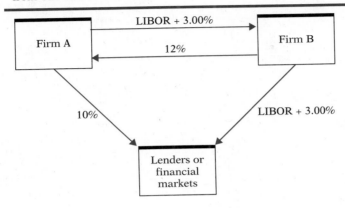

Firm A has achieved a 50-basis-point reduction in its borrowing rate as follows: It pays a fixed rate of 10 percent for its financing and also receives 12 percent fixed from firm B. This provides firm A with a 2 percent interest rate gain. Then firm A turns around and pays firm B LIBOR + 3.00 percent. Subtracting the 2.00 percent net gain, firm A's final cost is LIBOR + 1.00%, which is 50 basis points less than the cheapest floating rate financing it could have obtained directly (which was LIBOR + 1.50%). Firm B also gains. It pays LIBOR + 3.00% for its financing, but it has received this same amount from firm A. Then firm B pays a fixed rate of 12.00 percent to firm A, which is 50 basis points less than the cheapest fixed rate financing of 12.50 percent it could have received directly. The final costs of borrowing for the two firms are summarized in Table 23.3. In this example, both firms were better off by exactly half of the spread differential of 1.00 percent. However, the gains do not have to be split equally between the parties.

Firms have a number of objectives when they enter into an interest rate swap. The primary ones are to reduce their financing costs and to hedge interest rate risks. Documentation of swaps is guided by standards which have been developed by the New York-based International Swap Dealer's Association and/or the British Bankers' Association. Swaps now come in many forms in addition to the plain vanilla interest rate swap. They include zero-coupon for floating rate swaps, floating for floating (or basis) swaps, callable swaps, puttable swaps, extendable swaps, forward (or deferred) swaps, and delayed rate setting swaps, among others.

To understand more about swaps let's look at one that Hewlett-Packard entered into in 1992. The firm wanted to raise $100 million worth of Canadian dollars for 3 years and pay a floating interest rate. To accomplish this it entered into a swap with Société Générale Securities Corp., SocGen, the New York investment banking arm of the big French bank. The swap, like many recent ones, is much different from the plain vanilla swap discussed previously. Hewlett-Packard ended up paying about a tenth of a point, or $100,000, less than they would have paid on a regular floating rate issue.

Table 23.3

Borrowing Costs with an Interest Rate Swap

In this plain vanilla swap the interest rate savings are shared equally between the two parties, and no transactions costs are considered. In practice, the financial institution arranging the swap typically claims some of the interest rate savings as its commission.

Firm	Transaction	Interest Rate
A	Pays fixed rate to third party	+ 10.00%
	Pays floating rate to firm B	+ LIBOR + 3.00
	Receives fixed rate from firm B	− 12.00
	Net cost to firm A	LIBOR + 1.00%

Net savings = LIBOR + 1.50% − (LIBOR + 1.00%) = 0.50% = 50 basis points

Firm	Transaction	Interest Rate
B	Pays floating rate to third party	+ LIBOR + 3.00%
	Pays fixed rate to firm A	+ 12.00
	Receives floating rate from firm A	− (LIBOR + 3.00)
	Net cost to firm B	12.00%

Net savings = 12.50% − 12.00% = 0.50% = 50 basis points

SocGen ended up marketing an equity-linked zero-coupon note, giving investors a return that depends on the future performance of Hewlett-Packard stock. At maturity the investors who purchased the equity-linked zero-coupon note will receive between $90 and $143.60 for each $100 invested. Hewlett-Packard got the floating rate financing desired in Canadian dollars. SocGen secured the agreement and also the opportunity to earn underwriting fees and generate commissions from trading in Hewlett-Packard's stock and options. The interest rate swap provided benefits for all concerned.

Concept Review Questions

- Describe a "plain vanilla" interest rate swap.
- Why do firms use interest rate swaps?

USING OPTIONS TO MANAGE INTEREST RATE RISK

Options, like those originally discussed in Chapter 5, can also be employed to help firms deal with interest rate risk. Options on interest rates are available both on organized exchanges and over-the-counter from commercial banks and other financial institutions. In addition, options on interest rate futures, called **futures options**, are widely available on the same basic financial instruments that were listed previously on Table 23.2. *The Wall Street Journal* carries information on futures options on Treasury bonds, notes, and bills, and on Eurodollars, LIBOR, and the municipal bond index. Table 23.4 shows the available futures options on Treasury bonds and notes for

Table 23.4

Options on Two Interest Rate Futures Listed in The *Wall Street Journal* of June 10, 1992

Similar to any other option, a futures option provides the opportunity, but not the obligation, to buy or sell at a specified price in the future.

Treasury Bond (CBT)
$100,000; points and 64th of 100%

Strike Price	Calls-Settle			Puts-Settle		
	Jly	Sep	Dec	Jly	Sep	Dec
96	3–18	3–44	3–88	0–01	0–11	1–26
98	1–27	2–17	2–26	0–08	0–28	2–14
100	0–17	1–11	1–32	0–60	0–62	3–18
102	0–01	0–34	0–57	2–47	1–53	4–41
104	0–01	0–13	0–33	. . . .	3–14	6–15
106	0–01	0–05	0–18	. . . .	4–57	7–62

Est. Vol. 60,000;
Mon vol. 13,124 calls; 16,893 puts;
Op. Int. Mon 267,177 calls; 181,145 puts

Treasury Notes (CBT)
$100,000; points and 64th of 100%

Strike Price	Calls-Settle			Puts-Settle		
	Jly	Sep	Dec	Jly	Sep	Dec
100	. . . .	3–07	. . . .	0–01	0–16	1–03
101	1–55	2–20	. . . .	0–01	0–31	1–27
102	0–62	1–39	. . . .	0–08	0–50	. . . .
103	0–22	1–04	1–11	0–32	2–33	. . . .
104	0–05	0–41	0–55	. . . .	3–21	. . . .
105	0–01	0–24	. . . .	. . . .	. . . .	. . . .

Est. Vol. 25,000;
Mon vol. 384 calls; 655 puts;
Op. Int. Mon 37,345 calls; 29,589 puts

one day. Like other options, the first column indicates the available exercise prices. The next three columns provide quotes on the options available. For the December Treasury bond futures contract, for example, a strike (or exercise) price of 98 is almost at the money. (From Table 23.2 the settle price for the December Treasury bond futures contract was $98\frac{5}{32}$.) The price of the call option on the December futures contract is 2–26, that is $2\frac{26}{64}$ percent. Because the bond option contract is denominated in units of $100,000, the price of the December option on the Treasury bond futures contract on that day was $(0.0240625)(\$100,000) = \$2,406.25$.

Many uses are made of options or option-like features to reduce or manage interest rate risk. Consider a firm that is arranging a long-term financing arrangement at a floating rate with a financial institution. The reason for doing so may be that floating interest rates are currently substantially lower than the firm could obtain if it employed fixed rate financing. But, the firm is concerned about its possible interest rate risk exposure if rates increase dramatically. One solution is to arrange with the financial institution to put an **interest rate cap** on the financing. An interest rate cap is nothing more than an option on the interest rate. It sets an upper bound on how high the floating interest rate can go. For example, the firm might arrange financing that will never go above 12 percent during the life of the agreement, no matter what happens to short-term interest rates.

Similarly, the firm may cut the cost of floating rate financing by agreeing to put an **interest rate floor** on how low the interest rate may fall. This is just another option that can be incorporated into the financing agreement. Thus, the firm could agree that the interest rate on the loan would never fall below 7 percent, no matter how low short-term interest rates fall. If both a cap and a floor exist, the firm has entered into an **interest rate collar,** which constrains both how much and how little the floating rate financing will cost the firm.

Other uses of options to hedge interest rate risk exist. A "participating cap" is structured for the user who needs a cap but is unwilling or unable to pay the up-front cost of the cap. Another is the "caption," which is simply a call option on a cap. Finally, there is the "swaption," which is an option on a swap. These and many other techniques have been developed in recent years as firms, and financial institutions providing them, figure out new ways to control some of the interest rate risk exposure.

As with any other type of hedge, the use of options to hedge interest rate risk is not costless. Firms have to continually evaluate their risk exposure, determine how much the value of the firm will be adversely affected as interest rates change, and determine if the benefits of hedging outweigh the costs. In the last few years firms have become much more financially sophisticated in terms of planning for and hedging some of their interest rate risks. While many techniques beyond those examined in this chapter exist, you should now understand the basic issues involved in interest rate risk management.

Concept Review Question

■ How can an option be used to reduce interest rate risk?

GROWTH AND REGULATION OF THE DERIVATIVES MARKETS

Forwards, futures, swaps, caps, collars, options, and scores of related products are known collectively as **derivatives**. Their development in the last 15 years has revolutionized how firms and financial institutions manage their risks. The reasons for their growth stem from at least three reasons: First, derivatives are cheaper to trade than the bonds, currencies, equities, and commodities from which they are derived. Second, they have become much more familiar to both financial institutions and firms using them in recent years. Third, many countries have revised and eased the legal, fiscal, and regulatory restrictions on the use of derivatives.

A recent study by the Bank for International Settlements estimates that commercial banks had outstanding exchange-traded derivatives of $3.5 trillion at the end of 1991, up from $583 billion five years earlier. The total swaps market is estimated to be in excess of $5 trillion in contracts outstanding worldwide, which eclipses the value of all shares of stock listed on the New York and Tokyo stock exchanges combined. Another estimate is that the total derivatives market is as much as $10 trillion. Although the market has grown tremendously, there are also concerns that neither the commercial banks, investment bankers, traders, or users of derivatives fully understand the risks well enough to price them properly. Some worry that a derivatives disaster could overwhelm the world's financial system.

In response to these concerns the Bank for International Settlements and the International Organization of Securities Commissions have both prepared new sets of international capital regulations that will apply to commercial banks and investment bankers. Likewise, the Financial Accounting Standards Board, FASB, in 1992 issued rules that require banks and securities firms to record transactions in derivatives on their balance sheets. These requirements, which are effective at the end of 1993, will swell the assets and liabilities of firms with large off-balance-sheet derivative portfolios. Bankers Trust of New York, a big derivatives dealer, indicated that the requirement could cause its reported assets and liabilities to increase by 25 percent, or roughly $16 billion. Whereas derivatives were virtually unknown to financial managers 15 years ago, now financial managers have to understand derivatives and how they can be employed by the firm to reduce costs and insulate the firm from some of the financing and operating risks to which they are exposed.

Concept Review Question
- Why have derivative financial products become popular with firms in the past few years?

KEY POINTS

1. Firms can manage (or hedge) their exposure to risks caused by changes in interest rates, foreign exchange rates, or commodity prices. Analysis of the firm's risk profile line can assist in determining the potential impact on the value of the firm of changes in the rates or prices of these hedgeable factors.
2. Hedging involves both benefits and costs. Effective hedging of interest rates requires an understanding of duration and of new securities and concepts that have been developed in the last 15 to 20 years. Financial managers must know and understand these products and concepts.
3. In addition to matching assets and liabilities, financial forward contracts, financial futures, interest rate swaps, options, and many other related products, loosely referred to as derivatives, are employed to hedge interest rate risks.
4. Forwards and futures obligate the parties to act at the expiration of the contract. Forward rate agreements can provide perfect hedges; with financial futures a perfect hedge can never be achieved.
5. The prime rate, which is an administered rate, cannot be effectively hedged.
6. In a plain vanilla interest rate swap, the parties retain their principal and simply swap interest payments. Options can also be employed to hedge interest rate risk.
7. The derivatives market has grown very rapidly. At present it is estimated to be as much as $10 trillion.

Questions

23.1   Explain, in terms of the risk profile and hedge profile lines, what firms are attempting to accomplish when they hedge interest rates, foreign exchange rates, or commodities prices.

23.2   Duration is a measure of the rate of change (or elasticity) in the present value of a set of cash flows as interest rates change. Explain duration in simple terms. Why is it useful? When would a hedge ratio of 1.00 be employed versus a hedge ratio greater than or less than 1.00?

23.3   How are forward contracts and futures similar? How are they different?

23.4   Explain, step-by-step, the action a firm would take in order to hedge its interest rate risk from a floating rate loan using a forward contract. When does the firm benefit? When does it suffer regret? How could the firm employ a partial hedge instead of a perfect hedge? What is the effect of using a partial versus a perfect hedge?

23.5   Why are perfect hedges never attainable in practice when financial futures are employed to hedge interest rate risk? What is basis, and how does it relate to the remaining, or basis, risk that exists after a firm hedges?

23.6   Hedgers want futures contracts to be correctly priced, whereas speculators want them to be priced incorrectly. Why is this so?

23.7   Semone, the CEO of Regal Flavors, wants to hedge the interest rate risk associated with the firm's short-term borrowing. The Jersey Bank has offered terms of prime + 1.25 percent. Should Regal enter into the loan agreement with Jersey Bank? What issues are important in this hedging operation?

23.8   Who are the parties in a plain vanilla interest rate swap? What condition has to exist for them to enter into a transaction? Why might each want to participate in the swap?

23.9   Explain some of the ways in which options can be used to hedge, or limit, a firm's interest rate risk exposure.

Concept Review Problems

See Appendix A for solutions.

CR23.1   Bob recently purchased a 3-year zero-coupon bond for $750 and a 5-year Government National Mortgage Association bond, GNMA, bond for $750. The zero-coupon bond makes no cash interest payments and pays $1,000 upon maturity. The GNMA makes both interest and principal payments each year of $198 and matures in 5 years.

a.   What is the duration of each bond?
b.   If interest rates increase by 1 percent, what would be the approximate percent change in the market value of both investments?
c.   What is the duration of Bob's total portfolio?

CR23.2   National Bottlers Incorporated, NBI, is constructing a new bottling facility for BubbleUp, one of its distributors. NBI will be paid $1 million in 1 year and $1.8 million in 2 years.

a.   If NBI can borrow at 15 percent, what is the duration of the cash flows?
b.   Assuming NBI could secure a loan with a duration equal to 3 years, determine the hedge ratio and loan amount to immunize the firm's future cash flows.

CR23.3   Torbert International issued $5 million in 1-year variable rate bonds. The firm will make two interest payments on the bonds, one in 6 months and the other at the end of the year.

The interest rate paid on the bonds is 4 percent above the 1-year Treasury bill rate and is adjusted after 6 months. The current Treasury bill rate is 5 percent. To hedge against an increase in interest rates over the next six months, Torbert purchased a $5 million, 6-month Treasury bill forward contract with a contract rate of 5 percent.

a. If the 6-month Treasury bill rate increased to 6 percent after 6 months, what is the gain or loss from the forward contract?
b. If Torbert set up a partial hedge by purchasing a $3 million, 6-month Treasury bill forward contract with a contract rate of 5 percent, what would be the profit or loss from the forward contract and the bonds if everything else is the same as (a).

CR23.4   In 3 months Bellevue Bank will be rolling over $50 million in 90-day loans. The loan rates are tied to the 90-day Eurodollar futures rate, which is yielding 5.25 percent.

a. Should Bellevue buy or sell 50 Eurodollar contracts?
b. Assume that after the 90-day period rates decreased to 5 percent. What amount of interest will Bellevue lose on the 180-day loans? What profit will Bellevue receive from the Eurodollar futures contract if we assume they mature exactly when the loans are reset? (*Note:* For simplicity assume a 360-day year.)

CR23.5   Gonzales Electric can finance a $25 million expansion project for 2 years at a fixed rate of 12 percent or at a floating rate of LIBOR plus 2 percent. Reed Production also needs to borrow $25 million for 2 years and can finance the expansion at a fixed rate of 14 percent or a variable rate at LIBOR plus 5 percent. Establish an interest rate swap between the two, with each firm sharing equally in the benefits.

PROBLEMS

23.1   What is the duration for a 5-year, $1,000 par value bond that pays interest annually, has a coupon interest rate of 11.25 percent, and is selling for $980? Why is this duration less than the maturity of the bond?

23.2   Consider three bonds as follows: a zero-coupon bond selling at $805 that matures in 3 years at $1,000; a $1,000 par value, 9 percent coupon rate 6-year bond that pays interest annually selling at $1,050; and a $1,000 par value, 8.8 percent coupon rate 3-year bond that pays interest semiannually and is selling for $1,030.

a. Determine the yield to maturity for each of the bonds.
b. What is each bond's duration?
c. What (approximate) change in the dollar value of each bond would occur if interest rates suddenly dropped by 1 percent?

23.3   KeyIndustries just made a $2,800,000 investment in securities that promises to provide $800,000 in annual cash flows at the end of each of the next 5 years.

a. What is the duration of this set of cash inflows?
b. How could KeyIndustries finance this purchase to immunize itself from fluctuations in interest rates? (*Note:* Assume that an appropriate security is available.)
c. How would KeyIndustries have to adjust the hedge ratio if the only security available had a duration of 3.35 years? What else would the firm have to do in order to construct a zero-NPV hedge?

23.4 The market-value-based balance sheet for Community National Bank is as follows:

	Market Value	Duration
Assets		
Federal funds deposits	$100 million	0
Short-term loans	300 million	3 months
Long-term loans	600 million	4 years
Mortgages	200 million	6 years
Liabilities		
Checking and savings deposits	$500 million	1 month
Certificates of deposit	300 million	1 year
Long-term debt financing	200 million	8 years
Equity	200 million	—

a. Determine the duration of Community National Bank's assets and liabilities. (*Note:* The duration of equity, although it could be determined, is ignored. In determining the duration of the liabilities, simply employ the market value of the debt-type liabilities and use that as the "total.")
b. Has Community National hedged (that is, is it immune from) interest rate risk?
c. If not, how might the liabilities be adjusted to make the bank immune? Could the same type of action be taken with the bank's assets?

23.5 Your firm is concerned about the level of the 3-month LIBOR rate that will exist 100 days from now. As of today the 3-month forward rate is 8.60 percent. To hedge, you enter into a $40 million forward rate agreement with a bank, in which you will be paid if the 3-month LIBOR rate in 100 days is greater than 8.60 percent. (Assume a 365-day year.)

a. What happens in 100 days if the then-existing 3-month LIBOR rate is 8.60 percent?
b. What if it is 9.50 percent?

23.6 Willis Products has decided to hedge the 3-month LIBOR rate that will be in existence 145 days from now. The current 3-month rate is 10.10 percent, and the principal amount is $50 million. The agreement with Securities National Bank calls for Willis to receive if the 3-month LIBOR rate in 145 days is greater than 10.10 percent, but to pay if it is less. (Assume a 365-day year.)

a. What occurs if in 145 days 3-month LIBOR increases to 10.25 percent?
b. What if it drops to 8.70 percent?

23.7 West Bay Industries is concerned about movements in the 3-month LIBOR rate for $30 million with a settlement in 75 days. The current 3-month rate is 9 percent. The forward rate agreement calls for West Bay to receive if in 75 days the 3-month LIBOR rate is greater than 9 percent. (Assume a 365-day year.)

a. What occurs if in 75 days the 3-month LIBOR is 9.75 percent?
b. What size of contract would West Bay enter into if it wanted to hedge only 50 percent of its risk exposure? What occurs if in 75 days the 3-month LIBOR rate is 9.40 percent?

23.8   Partial quotes on Eurodollar futures for a given day are as follows:

Eurodollar (IMM)—$1 million; pts of 100%						Yield		Open
	Open	High	Low	Settle	Chg	Settle	Chg	Interest
Dec	92.56	92.61	92.48	92.49	−.04	7.51	+.04	95,920
Mar	92.44	92.50	92.40	92.40	+.02	7.60	−.02	105,637
June	92.07	92.11	92.03	92.03	+.01	7.97	−.01	48,996
Sept	91.73	91.74	91.66	91.68	+.01	8.32	−.01	24,918
Dec	91.43	91.43	91.36	91.39	+.01	8.61	−.01	17,647
Mar	91.17	91.17	91.12	91.14	+.01	8.86	−.01	14,688
⋮	⋮	⋮	⋮	⋮	⋮	⋮	⋮	⋮
Sept	90.24	90.26	90.23	90.24	+.01	9.76	−0.01	3,398

Est vol 55,658; vol Tue 51,641; open int 349,424, −1,526.

a.   What interest rate are Eurodollar futures contracts tied to?
b.   On what market are they traded?
c.   How are price and yield related? What happens, for example, when the price moves down 3 basis points?
d.   What is the open interest? Why are open interest and the number of contracts of different maturities important?
e.   What happened to the yields on this day?
f.   What can you say about the shape of the term structure of interest rates at this point in time?

23.9   Soda Beverages has seasonal fluctuations in its business. It knows that in 4 months it will have to obtain a $5 million, 3-month loan; the rate on the loan will be LIBOR plus $1\frac{1}{4}$ percent.

a.   If we assume a Eurodollar futures contract settles on the day the loan is required, how can Soda establish a perfect hedge if the present 3-month LIBOR rate is 8.00 percent?
b.   In 4 months, when the futures contract settles, the 3-month LIBOR rate has risen to 9.30 percent. What is the impact on Soda?

23.10   We anticipate receiving $30 million in 2 months that can be invested for 3 months at LIBOR. To lock in the current LIBOR rate, we can *buy* Eurodollar futures. Assume the current 3-month LIBOR rate is 8.20 percent, and there is a LIBOR futures contract that expires at the time the money is expected to be received.

a.   By hedging, how can you lock in the rate of 8.20 percent?
b.   What is the effect if the 3-month LIBOR rate at the end of 2 months is 7.9 percent?
c.   What is the effect if LIBOR increases to 8.75 percent in 2 months?

23.11   A firm was concerned about increases in 3-month LIBOR rates that are currently at 10.60 percent. Therefore, it sells 40 Eurodollar futures contracts to cover a $40 million, 3-month loan to be taken out in 5 months. The loan is at LIBOR plus 0.75 percent. In 5 months, at settlement of the contract (when it matures and when the loan is taken out), 3-month LIBOR has decreased to 8.70 percent. What is the size of the regret the firm suffered?

23.12 PowerSystems needs a 3-month loan commencing on December 1st. Assume the loan is at LIBOR plus 1 percent. The closest 3-month Eurodollar futures contract expires later that month. The size of the loan is $25 million, and the current 3-month LIBOR rate is 10.10 percent. On December 1st the 3-month LIBOR rate is 10.70 percent.

a. What is the effect if the futures price in December is actually 89.10?
b. If it is 89.70?

23.13 Mini Case You have just been hired as the new CFO of Interco. Upon examining the state of Interco's risk management knowledge and practices, you determine they have very little idea about their exposure to fluctuations in interest rates. One of your first jobs is to establish an interest rate risk management program.

a. Prepare a brief explanation of the basic issues in risk management for the firm's president and CEO. Be sure to cover the costs, both direct and opportunity.
b. One of the investments Interco made with excess funds was to invest in long-term interest-bearing bonds. Is this an appropriate investment for idle working capital funds? Use duration to explain why or why not.
c. Interco owns some assets it leases out. The expected cash flow from the leases is $700,000 to be received at the end of each of the next 5 years, and the return expected is 14 percent. Determine the duration of the lease cash flow stream. How can financing be arranged to immunize the firm from interest rate risk on the cash flows? What would the hedge look like if the only financing available had a duration of 4.1 years?
d. The president and CEO does not understand the similarities and differences between forwards and futures. Explain the differences.
e. Interco needs some floating rate financing that can be tied to either prime or LIBOR.

  (1) Explain why LIBOR is preferred to prime.
  (2) The amount of the financing is $100 million, settlement is in 60 days, and the present 3-month LIBOR rate is 8.50 percent. A forward rate agreement can be employed with an exercise price of 8.65 percent. What occurs in 60 days if the 3-month LIBOR is 8.65 percent? If it is 8.45 percent? If the firm hedges only 60 percent of the amount and in 60 days 3-month LIBOR is 8.80 percent? (Assume a 365-day year.)

f. Instead of employing a forward rate agreement as in (e), Interco could employ financial futures. If the maturity of the LIBOR financial futures contract coincides with the financing needs in 60 days, could Interco have used futures to obtain the same result as in (e)? What if the expiration date of the futures was in 50 days?

REFERENCES

For some articles and books that examine duration and hedging interest rate risk, see:

CHUA, JESS H. "A Closed-Form Formula for Calculating Bond Duration." *Financial Analysts Journal* 40 (May/June 1984): 76–78.

KAUFMAN, GEORGE G., G. O. BIERWAG, and ALDEN TOEVS. eds. *Innovations in Bond Portfolio Management: Duration Analysis and Immunization.* Greenwich, Conn.: JAI Press, 1983.

SMITH, CLIFFORD W., JR., CHARLES W. SMITHSON, and D. SYKES WILFORD. *Managing Financial Risk.* New York: Harper & Row, 1990.

For more on swaps see:

COOPER, IAN A., and ANTONIO S. MELLO. "The Default Risk of Swaps." *Journal of Finance* 46 (June 1991): 597–620.

GOODMAN, LAURIE S. "The Use of Interest Rate Swaps in Managing Corporate Liabilities." *Journal of Applied Corporate Finance* 2 (Winter 1990): 35–47.

KAPNER, KENNETH R., and JOHN F. MARSHALL. *The Swaps Handbook: Swaps and Related Risk Management Instruments.* New York: New York Institute of Finance, 1990.

TITMAN, SHERIDAN. "Interest Rate Swaps and Corporate Financing Choices." *Journal of Finance* 47 (September 1992): 1503–16.

Financial Analysis and Planning

EXECUTIVE INTERVIEW

Geoffrey Holczer
Vice President, Chief
Financial Officer, and
Treasurer
Designs, Inc.

Designs, Inc., is a Levi's-only merchandiser and the leading retailer of Levi Strauss & Co. products east of the Mississippi. We asked Mr. Holczer to discuss Designs' financial analysis and planning process.

For a company that has grown rapidly, as ours has, financial planning is critical. Our fundamental strategy is to concentrate on what we know—mall developers and customers in the eastern half of the country. Our operations are basically centralized; planning and direction come from headquarters.

We budget on an accrual basis and prepare a cash flow projection from the accrual budget. We don't have a lot of receivables or payables, since customers pay us with cash, checks, or credit cards. The credit card receivables are collected every 2 or 3 days; the payables are primarily to Levi Strauss & Co. and are due the 10th of the following month. So there really isn't that much difference between accrual basis and cash basis in our case.

Our company-wide financial planning statements include both a detailed annual budget and a less detailed 3-year plan. Essentially we have 112 planning units—each store plus corporate headquarters, plus any new stores we want to open. Personal computers streamline the process; combining them into one cohesive whole would be pretty time-consuming otherwise.

Developing the Plans

The first step is to determine how many and what type of new stores to open. For each proposed store, we prepare 2- and 5-year pro forma statements, using the general demographics of the area, standard payroll rates, and rental information. With those three factors, we can forecast the store's expected performance. Once we are confident that the required sales volume is attainable and the store's projected return exceeds an internal hurdle rate on a discounted cash flow basis, we include it in our plans.

To develop the basic inputs for our financial plans for existing stores, we monitor their performance based on profitability. The annual increase in actual profit—a combination of sales growth, margin, rent, and payroll—is the major determinant of the store's success. Sales can be up, but if you have lower prices you won't necessarily be making much profit. One store might make a lot of money at a $1 million sales level, whereas another store that does $1.2 million might have difficulty because of higher rent or payroll.

We start with forecasts of sales revenue. The first step is to look at macro issues—external factors such as whether the economy is growing or shrinking in a particular region. To estimate overall trends, we look at Levi & Strauss Co.'s market share, their corporate advertising program, and new products. Then we determine what each store is likely to achieve based on the trends. Also, the theory of large numbers works to our advantage. We're forecasting for 111 units; if we are accurate for 70 or 80, underestimate 15, and overestimate 15, the net result will be approximately equal to the forecast.

After the sales forecast, we look at the projected gross margin. Rent is basically a fixed cost. To estimate payroll expenses, we have formulas based on sales levels: how many payroll hours we need to serve customers at a given sales volume. Understanding the elasticity in demand as prices increase is not as easy. A pair of jeans might sell for $35, and the price can probably go to $39.99. When you get to $40, the question is: Will the customer still buy? If we believe we can't increase prices, we must either reduce margins or not carry the merchandise. So we evaluate each product and its price, or at least groups of items, to determine the *overall* gross margin for a store or type of store. If the margin is thin in one department or for one type of item, then we look for ways to increase margins on other items.

In our business, the rest of the expenses—supplies, bags, and similar items—are really not material. We generally group them into one category and carry forward the prior year's percent of sales. We don't waste our time trying to cut the cost of something like register tape that really doesn't affect our profitability much. We focus on a few larger items and try to understand the *relationships* among the numbers: which costs really are fixed and which ones are variable, and whether variable costs vary totally with sales or with something else. In our case, we get a much higher level of accuracy by focusing on only four or five parts of the income statement.

Someone joining Designs from another business might be astounded that we don't look closely at certain costs. But understanding our business keeps us from wasting time on nonessential analysis. For example, everyone is very concerned these days about health care costs. Our health care costs are probably $600,000 a year. If they went up by 50 percent, that would be $300,000, or about a penny a share. For us, it's much more important to figure out if sales are going to go up 1 percent or 2 percent, because then you're talking about $3 million or $4 million worth of sales—and that would have a major effect on the bottom line. We know health care costs will rise, so we factor in a standard percentage increase.

Uncertainty is a given in any business, and we use various techniques, including sensitivity analysis, probability, and decision trees, to account for uncertainty when preparing our plans. We calculate weighted averages and arrive at a pretty close sales estimate. Generally we use conservative estimates—lower sales and higher expenses—and our forecasts have been fairly accurate.

It's easy to get bogged down in numbers, particularly with computers making it so easy to run lots of scenarios. Financial managers need to understand the major revenue and cost factors that have the greatest impact on their particular company and concentrate on those. All financial plans have some guesswork in them. We feel it's better to be about 95 percent accurate on the important things than to spend a lot of time on things that represent only 5 percent.

Although it is important to understand accounting ideas, we must be careful not to confuse maximizing accounting numbers with maximizing the market value of the firm. Chapter 24 focuses on accounting-based ideas, and Chapter 25 emphasizes the primary importance that cash flow, *not* net income, plays in financial forecasting and planning.

24

Analyzing Accounting Statements

EXECUTIVE SUMMARY

Accounting statements are derived from a historical, cost-based accrual system employing generally accepted accounting principles. The two primary accounting statements are the income statement and the balance sheet. By converting these statements to common-size statements and employing ratios, we can perform an accounting analysis of a firm. It is important to remember that the analysis should be done over a number of years, that industry data should be employed, and that the analysis may raise additional questions that require further probing.

The primary point to remember about analysis of accounting statements is that its purpose is to provide clues to the magnitude, timing, and riskiness of expected cash flows. Analysis of accounting statements is useful only if it provides additional information regarding these variables, which largely determine the expected future value and riskiness of the firm.

DIFFERENT STATEMENTS FOR DIFFERENT PURPOSES

Different types of accounting statements focus on different financial activities of the firm. The three types of statements used by most firms are:

1. Financial accounting statements prepared according to generally accepted accounting principles, GAAP. These data are presented in various publications and reported to the firm's stockholders in the **annual report.**
2. Tax reporting statements. Because of differences between what is allowed for tax reporting (Internal Revenue Service regulations) and what is required for GAAP purposes, separate tax statements are prepared. Tax consequences are of vital concern because the payment of taxes is a direct cash outflow for the firm.

3. Reports for internal management. Firms often develop their own internal reporting requirements, which are based on divisions, cost centers, or some other unit. Included are such items as direct costing, contribution margin analysis, standard costs and variances, and transfer pricing.

Our interest in this chapter is in analyzing accounting statements, but we must specify *which* statements. The statements we focus on are those in category 1—the financial accounting statements prepared for external use and based on generally accepted accounting principles, GAAP. (For purposes of our discussion, we'll call them simply accounting statements, although more specifically they are *financial* accounting statements.) The objective of the generally accepted accounting principles on which accounting statements are based is to provide a consistent and objective account of the firm's status based on historical costs, where revenues and expenses are matched over the appropriate time periods. There are two reasons for focusing on GAAP statements: First, because these are prepared for the public, it is by analyzing GAAP statements that investors, creditors, and others gauge the performance of the firm. Second, unless we are employed by the firm, the GAAP statements are all we have; neither tax nor internal management statements are made public.

Concept Review Question

- Describe the different types of accounting statements prepared by a firm.

THE BASIC ACCOUNTING STATEMENTS

The annual report that a firm issues to stockholders contains important information. The primary accounting statements it contains are the income statement and the balance sheet. The income statement records the flow of revenue and related expenses through the firm over some period of time, typically a year. The balance sheet is a snapshot of the firm's assets, liabilities, and owner's claims as of a specific point in time—the end of its fiscal year. These two statements, along with the statement of cash flows (discussed in the next chapter) and the discussion accompanying the statements, provide an accounting picture of the firm. Typically, an annual report provides statements for 2 or 3 years, along with summary information for several more years.

Accounting statements report what happened to the firm in terms of sales, assets, liabilities, earnings, dividends, and so forth, over time. This information is one of the inputs investors and the general investment community use to form expectations about the required returns and riskiness of the firm. As investors form or revise their expectations about the magnitude, timing, or riskiness of the firm's returns, the market value of the firm will be affected. Understanding accounting statements is therefore important for investors, creditors, and the firm's management.

The analysis we will make here is based on General Mills, a major consumer food firm.[1] Its primary operations consist of processed dairy products, dry grocery products, and cereals.

---

[1] The information on General Mills came from its 1992 annual report. Some minor adjustments have been made to simplify the presentation and to improve consistency. In addition to the annual report, information can be obtained from the firm's 10-K report, which must be filed annually with the Securities and Exchange Commission. Annual reports and 10-Ks can be obtained by writing to most companies; many libraries have them—often on microfilm or microfiche.

INCOME STATEMENT

The income statement presents a summary of revenues and expenses for the firm during the last year. Table 24.1 presents the last 3 years' income statements for General Mills. Here are some highlights of the income statement:

1. Sales minus cost of goods sold equals **gross margin.** The gross margin indicates what the firm sells goods for in relation to the cost of the goods.
2. **Operating profit** measures the earnings of the firm after all expenses, except interest and taxes and before any adjustments.
3. Adjustments for General Mills include interest income, income from its subsidiaries, and nonrecurring items.
4. The net operating income, or earnings before interest and taxes, EBIT, reflects the firm's earnings before the costs of financing and income taxes.[2]
5. Subtracting interest expenses results in earnings before taxes, EBT. By then subtracting income taxes, we arrive at net income, or earnings after tax, EAT. Note that if the firm has preferred stock outstanding, cash dividends on it have to be subtracted from net income to arrive at the **earnings available for common stockholders, EAC.**
6. Because GAAP statements are prepared on an accrual, not a cash, basis, the $496 million in net income in 1992 does not mean that General Mills earned $496 million in cash. In Table 24.1, we see that General Mills' net sales and net income have increased over these 3 years.

One item of interest is the earnings per share, EPS. By putting earnings on a per share basis, the effects of changes in the number of shares of common stock outstanding can be held constant. Earnings per share is calculated as follows:

$$EPS = \frac{\text{earnings available for common stockholders}}{\text{number of shares of common stock}} = \frac{\text{net income} - \text{cash dividends on preferred stock (if any)}}{\text{number of shares of common stock outstanding}} \qquad (24.1)$$

For General Mills in 1992, EPS was $496/165.5 = $3.00.[3] During 1991 it was $2.86, and in 1990 it was $2.33. After adjusting for differences in the number of shares of common stock outstanding, General Mills' earnings per share increased over the 3-year period.

There are actually three EPS figures that could be reported, depending on whether any complex securities, such as convertible securities, warrants, or stock options, are employed by a firm:

1. SIMPLE EPS   The first is simple EPS as calculated using Equation 24.1.
2. PRIMARY EPS   Another is primary EPS, in which the earnings available for common stockholders are divided by the number of shares that would have been outstanding if all "likely to be converted" securities were converted.

---

[2] For our purposes, it is important to present the income statement in a slightly different manner than that used by accountants. Because interest is a cost of financing and we are concerned about various financing alternatives, interest is broken out separately.

[3] There were 165.5 million shares of stock outstanding at the end of 1992, 165.1 million at the end of 1991, and 163.2 million at the end of 1990. These figures differ slightly from those reported by General Mills.

Table 24.1

Income Statement for General Mills (in millions)

The format of this statement differs from that reported in the General Mills annual report, primarily due to breaking out interest as a separate item. General Mills' fiscal year ends on the last Sunday in May.

	For Fiscal Year		
	1990	1991	1992
Sales	$6,448	$7,153	$7,778
Cost of goods sold*	3,665	3,941	4,371
Gross margin	2,783	3,212	3,407
Selling, general, and administrative expenses	2,138	2,386	2,504
Operating profit	645	826	903
Adjustment: Income from subsidiaries and nonrecurring items	+56	+47	+14
Earnings before interest and taxes, EBIT	701	873	917
Interest	76	94	89
Earnings before taxes, EBT	625	779	828
Income taxes	244	307	332
Net income	$ 381	$ 472	$ 496

*Includes $247, $218, and $180 in GAAP depreciation expense in 1992, 1991, and 1990, respectively; and $60, $50, and $43 in lease expense, respectively.

3. FULLY DILUTED EPS   Finally, there is fully diluted EPS, in which the earnings available for common shareholders are divided by the total number of shares of common stock that would be outstanding after total conversion of the issue. Because our interest is in financial management, not accounting, we focus primarily on "simple EPS," or just EPS.

BALANCE SHEET

The balance sheet provides a record of the firm—its assets, liabilities, and resulting stockholders' equity—as of the end of its fiscal year. In looking at a balance sheet (Table 24.2), it is important to recognize that the figures are presented in terms of historical costs; they do not reflect market values, the effects of inflation, or other current information. A balance sheet thus provides, at best, only a very rough idea of the value of the firm.[4] Some key aspects of the balance sheet are:

1. The assets are divided into current (less than or equal to 1 year) and long-term

[4] A figure often reported is book value per share, which is calculated as:

$$\text{book value per share} = \frac{\text{stockholder's equity}}{\text{number of shares of common stock outstanding}}$$

For General Mills in 1992, this was $1,372/165.5 = $8.29. In 1991, it was $6.75; in 1990, it was $4.96. Book value per share is not be a meaningful figure because it does not represent the market value, the replacement value, or the liquidating value of the firm.

Table 24.2

Balance Sheet for General Mills (in millions)

The balance sheet lists assets, liabilities, and resulting stockholders' equity, or net worth, of the firm at a specific point in time. Because it is based on historical cost, it does not indicate the market value of the firm.

	1990	1991	1992
Assets			
Current assets			
Cash and marketable securities	$ 71	$ 40	$ 1
Accounts receivable	259	306	292
Inventory	394	494	487
Prepaid expenses	186	243	255
Total current assets	910	1,083	1,035
Long-term assets			
Gross property and equipment	2,883	3,337	3,909
Less: Accumulated depreciation	949	1,096	1,261
Net property and equipment	1,934	2,241	2,648
Other	445	578	622
Total long-term assets	2,379	2,819	3,270
Total assets	$3,289	$3,902	$4,305
Liabilities and Stockholders' Equity			
Current liabilities			
Accounts payable	$ 518	$ 579	$ 632
Short-term debt*	184	152	202
Accruals and other	471	541	537
Total current liabilities	1,173	1,272	1,371
Long-term liabilities			
Long-term debt	689	879	921
Deferred taxes	428	455	434
Other	190	182	207
Total long-term liabilities	1,307	1,516	1,562
Stockholders' equity			
Common stock: 204.2 shares issued	297	320	344
Less: Treasury stock	−813	−777	−803
Retained earnings	1,531	1,796	2,049
Less: Unearned ESOP and restricted stock compensation	−165	−178	−172
Less: Cumulative foreign currency adjustment	−41	−47	−46
Total stockholders' equity	809	1,114	1,372
Total liabilities and stockholders' equity	$3,289	$3,902	$4,305

*Includes current maturities of long-term debt.

(more than 1 year). Note that property and equipment is presented on both a gross basis and a net basis. The net basis reflects accumulated GAAP depreciation charged over the years as an expense in order to match expenses with associated revenues.

2. For simplicity, we have included "other" as long-term assets. Sometimes it is preferable to use another category for intangible assets.

3. Liabilities are also divided into current and long-term. Although not shown directly on the balance sheet, lease obligations for General Mills are recorded as part of its long-term debt. The present value of long-term capital lease commitments is recorded as a long-term liability, and a corresponding dollar amount is included in the property and equipment account to show the use of assets acquired by long-term capital leases. **Deferred taxes** represent the difference in the taxes actually paid to the Internal Revenue Service (discussed in Chapter 8) and those reported for GAAP purposes.

4. General Mills has only common stock outstanding; this is shown in the stockholders' equity section. General Mills also has, as part of its retirement plans, an **employee stock ownership plan, ESOP.** Note that General Mills, like most firms that are worldwide in nature, has an equity account that reflects foreign currency adjustments.

5. Retained earnings is an account that reflects the sum of the firm's net income over its life, less all cash dividends paid and any other adjustments. In a sense, it is a balancing account that (a) ties together the income statement and the balance sheet, and (b) allows assets to equal liabilities and stockholders' equity. It is important to recognize that *retained earnings is a claim on assets,* not an asset account. The retained earnings account *does not contain any cash;* the only cash is in the current asset account entitled "cash and marketable securities."

Table 24.2 shows that General Mills has increased both its current and long-term assets over the 3-year period. On the other side, the current liabilities increased, as did long-term liabilities and stockholder's equity over this same period.

Although it is not reported directly on its accounting statements, General Mills paid total cash dividends on its common stock of $245.2 million in 1992. Using the total cash dividend figure and knowing the number of shares of common stock outstanding, we can calculate the dividends per share—the dollar amount of cash dividends paid to investors during the year:

$$\text{dividend per share} = \frac{\substack{\text{total cash dividends paid} \\ \text{to common stockholders}}}{\substack{\text{number of shares of common} \\ \text{stock outstanding}}} \qquad (24.2)$$

For 1992, the dividend per share figure was $245.2/165.2 = $1.48 per share. This compares with $1.28 in 1991 and $1.10 in 1990. General Mills thus substantially increased its cash dividends.

Concept Review Questions

- Describe the items that are presented in an income statement.
- What are the three kinds of earnings per share?
- Describe the key aspects of the balance sheet.

ANALYSIS OF ACCOUNTING STATEMENTS

A firm's balance sheet reports its assets, liabilities, and stockholders' equity at a point in time; the income statement reports operations over the period of a year. Careful analysis of these statements can provide some clues about future cash flows. The point of this analysis is to help diagnose trends that indicate the magnitude, timing, or riskiness of the firm's future cash flows.

When conducting an analysis, we need to keep four ideas in mind:

1. It is necessary to look at trends; generally 3 to 5 years' worth of data are necessary to ascertain how the firm's performance is changing over time.
2. It is helpful to compare the firm's performance to that of the industry (or industries) in which it operates.[5] Although industry averages may not indicate where a firm wants to be, because of different markets, management philosophy, or whatever, the comparison is helpful in analyzing trends.
3. *The importance of carefully reading and analyzing the annual report—including the discussion accompanying the statements—cannot be overemphasized.* Often these will point to other factors—such as contractual obligations, past and future financing policies, plans for further expansion or restructuring, or the sale of part of the firm's assets—that significantly affect the entire analysis.
4. The analysis may raise further questions for which additional information is needed. The important point is not to view the analysis as an end in itself.

COMMON-SIZE STATEMENTS

Income Statement

One of the simplest and most direct ways to analyze changes over time is to calculate a **common-size statement.** A common-size income statement is constructed by dividing the various components of the income statement by *net sales.* Thus, net sales equals 100 percent, and everything else is presented as a percentage of net sales. General Mills' common-size income statement is presented in Table 24.3. Note that two ratios, the **gross profit margin** and the **net profit margin,** are listed as items (a) and (b) in the table. Comparing General Mills and the consumer foods industry, we see that General Mills has about the same relative cost of goods sold and expenses, with the consequence that net income has fluctuated close to that of the industry.

Balance Sheet

A common-size balance sheet can be calculated in the same manner, except that all the statement components are divided by *total assets* to put them on a common percentage basis. General Mills' common-size balance sheet is presented in Table 24.4. An analysis of this statement indicates that General Mills' current assets remained relatively

---

[5] It is often difficult to find comparable industry data. If good industry data are unavailable, it is generally best to use one or more similar firms for comparison. We used Quaker Oats and Heinz to generate "industry" data.

Table 24.3

Common-Size Income Statement for General Mills and the Consumer Foods Industry

A common-size income statement is calculated by dividing the various components by net sales; thus, net sales equals 100 percent.

	General Mills			Industry		
	1990	**1991**	**1992**	**1990**	**1991**	**1992**
Net sales	100.0%	100.0%	100.0%	100.0%	100.0%	100.0%
Cost of goods sold	56.8	55.1	56.2	57.3	56.4	56.4
(a) Gross margin (gross profit margin)	43.2	44.9	43.8	42.7	43.6	43.6
Selling, general, and administrative expenses and adjustments	32.3	32.7	32.0	31.2	31.6	30.6
Earnings before interest and taxes, EBIT	10.9	12.2	11.8	11.5	12.0	13.0
Interest	1.2	1.3	1.2	2.0	1.9	1.8
Earnings before tax, EBT	9.7	10.9	10.6	9.5	10.1	11.2
Income tax	3.8	4.3	4.3	3.6	3.9	4.1
(b) Net income (net profit margin)	5.9%	6.6%	6.3%	5.9%	6.2%	7.1%

constant for 1990 and 1991, before declining in 1992. Compared to others in the consumer foods industry, General Mills carries substantially less accounts receivable and inventory. Examining the investment in long-term assets, we see that General Mills is well above the industry in property and equipment but has less in "other" assets.

An analysis of the liabilities indicates that General Mills has more accounts payable but less short-term debt than the industry. General Mills has increased its reliance on long-term debt in recent years. The total of deferred taxes and other liabilities is much higher for General Mills than for the consumer foods industry. Overall, General Mills exhibits some substantial differences from the industry in terms of the composition of its assets, liabilities and stockholders' equity.

RATIO ANALYSIS

Another useful approach is to compute ratios. These ratios compare accounting variables and draw from both the income statement and the balance sheet. Although many different ratios can be calculated, we will focus on a basic set. The ratios are grouped

Table 24.4

Common-Size Balance Sheet for General Mills and the Consumer Foods Industry

All assets, liabilities, and stockholders' equity accounts are expressed as a percentage of total assets. The use of a common-size statement highlights relative percentages in accounts receivable, inventory, long-term assets, and short-term liabilities

	General Mills			Industry		
	1990	1991	1992	1990	1991	1992
Assets						
Current						
Cash and marketable securities	2.1%	1.0%	0.0%	3.7%	4.4%	3.8%
Accounts receivable	7.9	7.9	6.8	15.6	17.6	16.4
Inventory	12.0	12.7	11.3	18.1	16.7	15.9
Other	5.7	6.2	5.9	7.7	4.0	3.7
Total current	27.7	27.8	24.0	45.1	42.7	39.8
Long-term						
Property and equipment	58.8	57.4	61.5	34.6	37.6	37.1
Other	13.5	14.8	14.5	20.3	19.7	23.1
Total assets	100%	100%	100%	100%	100%	100%
Liabilities and Stockholders' Equity						
Current						
Accounts payable	15.8%	14.8%	14.7%	11.1%	11.7%	11.2%
Short-term debt	5.6	3.9	4.7	9.9	7.0	16.5
Accruals and other	14.3	13.9	12.5	10.9	11.6	13.6
Total current	35.7	32.6	31.9	31.9	30.3	41.3
Long-term						
Long-term debt and leases	20.9	22.6	21.4	20.7	18.7	12.9
Deferred taxes and other	18.8	16.3	14.9	11.3	13.1	11.9
Stockholders' equity	24.6	28.5	31.8	36.1	37.9	33.9
Total liabilities and stockholders' equity	100%	100%	100%	100%	100%	100%

into five categories, as follows:[6]

1. Liquidity ratios, which indicate the firm's ability to meet its short-run obligations.
2. Asset management ratios, which indicate how efficiently the firm is using its assets.
3. Debt management ratios, which deal with the amount of debt in the firm's capital structure and its ability to service (or meet) its legal obligations.
4. Profitability ratios, which relate net income to sales, assets, or stockholders' equity.

[6] These five groups are convenience groupings which indicate that analysts might use them in combination to examine some aspect of the firm's operations. The ratios presented are general-purpose ratios applicable to most manufacturing and retail firms. However, some are not very useful or relevant in the financial, public utility, transportation, and service industries.

5.   Market ratios, which indicate what is happening to the firm's relative market price, earnings, and cash dividends.

Liquidity Ratios

Liquidity ratios measure the firm's ability to fulfill its short-term commitments out of current or liquid assets. These ratios focus on current assets and liabilities and are often of lesser importance than other ratios when considering the long-run viability and profitability of the firm. The two primary liquidity ratios are the current ratio and the quick ratio.

The **current ratio** measures the ability of the firm to meet obligations due within 1 year with short-term assets in the form of cash, marketable securities, accounts receivable, and inventory. It is calculated as follows

$$\text{current ratio} = \frac{\text{current assets}}{\text{current liabilities}} = \frac{\$1,035}{\$1,371} = 0.8 \qquad (24.3)$$

The current ratio assumes a regular cash flow and that both accounts receivable and inventory can be readily converted into cash. A current ratio of 2.0 is sometimes employed as a standard of comparison. Current ratios of 1.0 and less are sometimes considered low and indicative of financial difficulties. Very high ratios suggest excess current assets that probably are having an adverse effect on the long-run profitability of the firm.[7]

By subtracting out inventory, which often is not highly liquid, we can calculate the **quick ratio,** which measures the firm's ability to meet its short-term obligations with cash, marketable securities, and accounts receivable:

$$\text{quick ratio} = \frac{\text{current assets} - \text{inventory}}{\text{current liabilities}} = \frac{\$1,035 - \$487}{\$1,371} = 0.4 \qquad (24.4)$$

Also called the *acid test ratio,* this ratio measures the near-term ability of the firm to meet its current liabilities without using its inventory. Quick ratios of less than 1.0 are not alarming in and of themselves. Very high quick ratios suggest excess cash, a credit policy that needs revamping, or a change needed in the composition of current versus long-term assets.

Asset Management Ratios

Asset management ratios are sometimes called activity ratios. They look at the amount of various types of assets and attempt to determine if they are too high or too low with regard to current operating levels. If too many funds are tied up in certain types of assets that could be more productively employed elsewhere, the firm is not as profitable as it should be. Four basic asset management ratios are the days sales outstanding,[8] inventory turnover, long-term asset turnover, and total asset turnover.

---

[7] Any interpretation of ratios is relative—either to the firm itself over time, or to the industry in which the firm operates. Also, knowledge of management's intent may be necessary. Consequently, what is "high" or "low," or "satisfactory" or "unsatisfactory" can be determined only in the context of a specific detailed analysis. Notice that too high a ratio may be just as indicative of a problem as too low a ratio. However, the action required is often far different.

[8] Days sales outstanding is sometimes called the average collection period.

The days sales outstanding ratio estimates how many days it takes on average to collect the sales of the firm. By dividing sales (in the denominator) by 365, we determine average sales per day. Then, when receivables are divided by average sales, we can determine how many days it will take to collect the receivables:

$$\text{days sales outstanding} = \frac{\text{accounts receivable}}{\text{sales}/365} = \frac{\$292}{\$7,778/365} = 13.7 \text{ days} \qquad (24.5)$$

This ratio provides an indication of how effective the credit-granting and management activities of the firm are. It can also be calculated using average accounts receivable for the year. If credit sales are available, then it would be preferable to employ that figure rather than total sales. A very high days sales outstanding probably indicates many uncollectible receivables. A low ratio may indicate that credit-granting policies are overly restrictive, thus hurting sales.

The second asset management ratio is the inventory turnover ratio:

$$\text{inventory turnover} = \frac{\text{costs of goods sold}}{\text{inventory}} = \frac{\$4,371}{\$487} = 9.0 \qquad (24.6)$$

This ratio can also be calculated using an average of the year's beginning and ending inventories. The higher the inventory turnover ratio, the more times a year the firm is "moving," or turning over, its inventory. Other things being equal, and assuming that sales are progressing smoothly, a higher inventory turnover ratio suggests efficient inventory management. Low inventory turnover figures often indicate obsolete inventory or lack of effective inventory management.

The **long-term asset turnover** ratio provides an indication of the firm's ability to generate sales based on its long-term asset base. For some industries, this figure is important; in others, like banking and many service industries, it is of questionable value. It is calculated as follows:

$$\text{long-term asset turnover} = \frac{\text{sales}}{\text{long-term assets}} = \frac{\$7,778}{\$3,270} = 2.4 \qquad (24.7)$$

By comparing long-term assets (primarily property and equipment) to sales, this ratio provides an indication of how effective the firm is in using these assets. The higher the ratio, other things being equal, the more effective the utilization. A low ratio may indicate that the firm's marketing effort or basic area of business requires attention.

Total asset turnover provides an indication of the firm's ability to generate sales in relation to its total asset base. For General Mills, it is

$$\text{total asset turnover} = \frac{\text{sales}}{\text{total assets}} = \frac{\$7,778}{\$4,305} = 1.8 \qquad (24.8)$$

A high total asset turnover normally reflects good management, whereas a low ratio suggests the need to reassess the firm's overall strategy, marketing effort, and capital expenditure program.

Debt Management Ratios

Debt management ratios focus on the liabilities and stockholders' equity from the balance sheet and on the income statement.[9] Three primary ratios in this category are total debt to total assets, times interest earned, and fixed charges coverage.

The **total debt to total assets** ratio is calculated as follows:

$$\text{total debt to total assets} = \frac{\text{total debt}}{\text{total assets}} = \frac{\$1,371 + \$1,562}{\$4,305} = 0.68 \qquad (24.9)$$

This ratio attempts to measure how much of the total funds are being supplied by creditors. Total debt includes all current debt plus long-term debt, lease obligations, and so forth. A high ratio indicates the use of financial leverage to magnify earnings, whereas a low ratio indicates relatively low use of creditor funds. General Mills has 68 percent of its *book-value-based* capital structure in debt-type instruments.

The second debt management ratio, **times interest earned,** is

$$\text{times interest earned} = \frac{\text{earnings before interest and taxes, } EBIT}{\text{interest}} = \frac{\$917}{\$89} = 10.3 \qquad (24.10)$$

The ability of the firm to meet its interest payments (on both short- and long-term debt) is measured by this ratio. It shows how far EBIT can decline before the firm probably will have trouble servicing its interest obligations. A high ratio indicates a "safe situation," but that perhaps not enough financial leverage is being used. A low ratio may call for immediate action.

The **fixed charges coverage** ratio provides a more comprehensive picture of the firm's ability to meet its legal financing requirements. While variations of this ratio exist, the one we calculate is

$$\frac{\text{fixed charges}}{\text{coverage}} = \frac{EBIT + \text{lease expenses}}{\text{interest} + \text{lease expenses}} = \frac{\$917 + \$60}{\$89 + \$60} = 6.6 \qquad (24.11)$$

This is a more comprehensive ratio than times interest earned and includes lease expenses,[10] which are also a fixed legal obligation. Leasing is essentially like debt in

[9] An important ratio for creditors is **days purchases outstanding:**

$$\text{days purchases outstanding} = \frac{\text{accounts payable}}{\text{credit purchases}/365}$$

which provides an idea of how promptly the firm pays its bills. Accounts payable can be obtained for virtually all firms. (For General Mills, it was necessary to refer to the discussion in the annual report to separate accounts payable from accruals, which General Mills reported together.) The problem comes with credit purchases, which are virtually never reported in accounting statements. If total purchases are available, they are often used instead. Otherwise, some annual reports provide sufficient information so that a percentage of the cost of goods sold, such as 60 percent, may be employed as an estimate of purchases. For General Mills, a thorough analysis of its annual report fails to provide any information on purchases—credit or otherwise.

[10] *Lease expenses is an income statement account that is often found only in the discussion accompanying a firm's accounting statements.* Do not confuse it with "lease obligations" or "capitalized lease obligations" accounts that are reported either on the balance sheet or in the discussion accompanying the accounting statements.

that it results in a fixed cost to the firm[11] and uses up some of the firm's debt capacity. By debt capacity, we mean the amount of fixed-cost financing the firm can effectively employ in order to maximize its value. To be even more complete, the denominator may also include sinking fund payments on long-term debt, and/or preferred dividends multiplied by $[1/(1 - \text{tax rate})]$. A high fixed charges ratio is more desirable than a low one, other things being equal. However, the question of financial leverage still needs to be considered.

Profitability Ratios

Three profitability ratios, which focus on the profit-generating ability of the firm, are net profit margin, return on total assets, and return on equity. The net profit margin, as discussed when we calculated a common-size income statement, is

$$\text{net profit margin} = \frac{\text{net income}}{\text{sales}} = \frac{\$496}{\$7,778} = 6.4\% \tag{24.12}$$

A low net profit margin indicates that (1) the firm is not generating enough sales relative to its expenses, (2) expenses are out of control, or (3) both. It is a widely used ratio of the efficiency of management. Net profit margins vary considerably by industry, with, for example, jewelry stores having much higher profit margins than grocery stores.

The second profitability ratio, **return on total assets,** indicates the ability of the firm to earn a satisfactory return on all the assets it employs. It is calculated as follows:

$$\text{return on total assets} = \frac{\text{net income}}{\text{total assets}} = \frac{\$496}{\$4,305} = 11.5\% \tag{24.13}$$

Also known as *return on investment, ROI,* this ratio tells us how effective the firm is in terms of generating income, given its asset base. It is an important measure of the efficiency of management. The higher the ratio the better, because this provides some indication of future growth prospects.

The last profitability ratio is **return on equity,** which is

$$\text{return on equity} = \frac{\text{net income}}{\text{stockholders' equity}} = \frac{\$496}{\$1,372} = 36.2\% \tag{24.14}$$

This ratio, often abbreviated to ROE, provides an accounting-based indication of the effectiveness of the firm and its management. It is directly affected by the return on total assets and the amount of financial leverage employed. However, this ratio, although helpful, does not focus on the actual returns to the firms' owners in terms of cash dividends and/or market appreciation. For this reason, *return on equity is not a reliable measure of returns.*

---

[11] Many leases have a required payment and then a contingent payment based on sales. In addition, much of the debt being issued by firms is not strictly fixed but may "float" as general interest rates change. However, both of these are still fixed-cost types of financing because they have a legal claim on income and do not share in the final distribution of earnings, as do common stockholders.

Market Ratios

The last set of ratios is somewhat different, because they focus more on the investors' viewpoint. These ratios are the price/earnings ratio, dividend yield, and dividend payout. The price/earnings, P/E, ratio indicates how much investors are willing to pay for the firm's current earnings. It is

$$\text{price/earnings} = \frac{\text{market price per share}}{\text{earnings per share}} = \frac{\$63.50}{\$3.00} = 21.2 \text{ times} \qquad (24.15)$$

In Chapter 3 we discussed two possible causes of high P/E ratios—little or no earnings or high expected growth. For General Mills it looks as if we can rule out the possibility of little or no expected earnings. Thus, the P/E ratio indicates how investors view the future prospects of General Mills. Because P/E ratios fluctuate over time, it is helpful to look at trends for both the company and the stock market in general.

The second market ratio is the dividend yield. For General Mills it is

$$\text{dividend yield} = \frac{\text{dividends per share}}{\text{market price per share}} = \frac{\$1.48}{\$63.50} = 2.3\% \qquad (24.16)$$

Because returns from investing in stocks come from cash dividends and from appreciation or loss in market price, these sources of return are part of the total return expected by investors. Generally, firms with high growth prospects have relatively low cash dividends and a relatively high market price, meaning they have a low dividend yield. Conversely, firms with low growth prospects typically have higher dividend yields.

Finally, the dividend payout ratio provides an indication of how the firm is splitting its earnings between returning them to common stockholders and reinvesting them in the firm. It is calculated as follows:

$$\text{dividend payout} = \frac{\text{dividends per share}}{\text{earnings per share}} = \frac{\$1.48}{\$3.00} = 49.3\% \qquad (24.17)$$

High-growth firms typically reinvest most of their earnings instead of paying them out, resulting in low payout ratios. Slow-growth firms in stable industries typically pay out a much higher percentage of their earnings. Dividend payout ratios are an important part of the cash dividend policy decision.

The ratios for General Mills and for the consumer foods industry are presented in Table 24.5.

The du Pont System

In an attempt to improve its financial analysis, du Pont introduced an information system that highlights relationships which might otherwise be missed. As Figure 24.1

Table 24.5

Ratios for General Mills and the Consumer Foods Industry

By comparing General Mills with the industry over time, we can spot trends that may not be evident when only a single year is examined.

Ratio	Calculation	General Mills			Industry		
		1990	1991	1992	1990	1991	1992
Liquidity							
Current	$\dfrac{\text{current assets}}{\text{current liabilities}}$	0.8	0.9	0.8	1.5	1.4	1.0
Quick	$\dfrac{\text{current assets} - \text{inventory}}{\text{current liabilities}}$	0.4	0.5	0.4	0.8	0.8	0.6
Asset Management							
Days sales outstanding	$\dfrac{\text{accounts receivable}}{\text{sales}/365}$	14.6 days	15.6 days	13.7 days	40.1 days	40.4 days	41.8 days
Inventory turnover	$\dfrac{\text{costs of goods sold}}{\text{inventory}}$	9.3	8.0	9.0	4.7	5.4	5.2
Long-term asset turnover	$\dfrac{\text{sales}}{\text{long-term assets}}$	2.7	2.5	2.4	2.6	2.8	2.5
Total asset turnover	$\dfrac{\text{sales}}{\text{total assets}}$	2.0	1.8	1.8	1.4	1.6	1.4
Debt Management							
Total debt to total assets	$\dfrac{\text{total debt}}{\text{total assets}}$	0.8	0.7	0.7	0.6	0.6	0.6
Times interest earned	$\dfrac{EBIT}{\text{interest}}$	9.2	9.3	10.3	6.0	6.2	7.4
Fixed charges coverage	$\dfrac{EBIT + \text{lease expenses}}{\text{interest} + \text{lease expenses}}$	6.3	6.4	6.6	4.3	4.5	5.1
Profitability							
Net profit margin	$\dfrac{\text{net income}}{\text{sales}}$	5.9%	6.6%	6.4%	5.5%	6.3%	7.1%
Return on total assets	$\dfrac{\text{net income}}{\text{total assets}}$	11.6%	12.1%	11.5%	7.5%	8.5%	9.4%
Return on equity	$\dfrac{\text{net income}}{\text{stockholders' equity}}$	47.1%	42.4%	36.2%	21.8%	22.5%	28.0%
Market							
Price/earnings	$\dfrac{\text{market price per share}}{\text{earnings per share}}$	16.6 times	20.3 times	21.2 times	9.4 times	11.3 times	10.2 times
Dividend yield	$\dfrac{\text{dividends per share}}{\text{market price per share}}$	2.8%	2.2%	2.3%	3.1%	2.6%	2.9%
Dividend payout	$\dfrac{\text{dividends per share}}{\text{earnings per share}}$	47.0%	44.8%	49.3%	29.9%	30.6%	29.9%

Figure 24.1

Determinants of Return on Equity for General Mills

The du Pont system of analysis provides a framework for seeing how the firm's activities interrelate to affect its performance. Anything that changes net profit margin, total asset turnover, or total debt to total assets will affect return on equity.

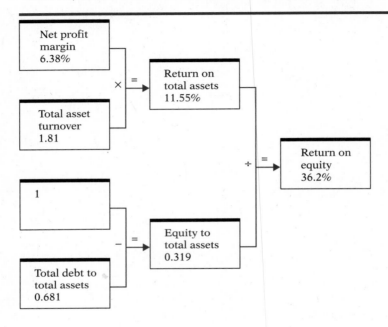

shows, the **du Pont system** ties together three ratios—net profit margin, total asset turnover, and total debt to total assets. The return on total assets is thus seen to be

$$\begin{array}{c}\text{return on}\\\text{total assets}\end{array} = \left(\begin{array}{c}\text{net}\\\text{profit}\\\text{margin}\end{array}\right)\left(\begin{array}{c}\text{total}\\\text{asset}\\\text{turnover}\end{array}\right) = (6.38\%)(1.81) = 11.5\% \qquad (24.18)$$

The importance of breaking out the net profit margin and total asset turnover as components of the return on total assets, instead of calculating return on total assets directly, is that it focuses attention on the separate ideas of profitability and asset utilization. General Mills' profitability as measured by net profit margin is acceptable; its asset utilization is better than the consumer foods industry, leading to a higher return on total assets.

The bottom part of Figure 24.1 focuses on the capital structure, or financial leverage, employed by the firm. General Mills is using 68.1 percent debt (in book value terms) in its capital structure. Instead of calculating it directly, as we did earlier, return on equity can also be calculated as :

$$\text{return on equity} = \frac{\text{return on}}{\text{total assets}} \bigg/ \left(1 - \frac{\text{total debt}}{\text{total assets}}\right) \tag{24.19}$$

$$= 11.5\%/(1 - 0.68) = 36\%$$

Using this approach, we see that return on equity is influenced by (1) net profit margin and total asset turnover, which jointly affect the return on total assets; and (2) the financial leverage employed. In order to improve return on equity, a firm has three choices: increase the profit margin, increase total asset turnover, or use more debt. Correspondingly, reductions in the net profit margin, total asset turnover, or using less debt will lower the firm's return on equity.

CONCLUSIONS FROM THE GENERAL MILLS ANALYSIS

Based on the common-size statements, the ratios, and the du Pont system, we can make the following observations:

1. General Mills' liquidity has remained constant in the last 3 years, but it is lower than that of the industry as a whole. This suggests General Mills has adopted a more aggressive working capital policy position than the consumer foods industry.
2. Its receivables and inventory are far below the industry average. Thus, it manages them very well compared to the industry.
3. General Mills' long-term and total asset turnovers have both remained fairly steady in recent years. In comparison to the consumer foods industry, however, General Mills is generating more sales from its total assets.
4. Although General Mills' debt is higher than that of the industry, its coverage ratios are better than those of the consumer foods industry.
5. Comparing General Mills' net profit margin with that of the industry, we see that it was about at the industry average until 1992, when it fell below the industry. However, due to using more debt than the industry, its return on equity is much higher than that of the industry.
6. Finally, General Mills' P/E ratio is higher than that of the industry, suggesting that the firm is regarded as having brighter growth prospects. At the same time General Mills is paying out a greater percentage of its earnings in the form of cash dividends.

Our analysis suggests that General Mills has a comparable profit margin, but a higher return on equity than the industry. The higher return on equity results from the fact that General Mills has a higher total asset turnover and has increased its reliance on debt. General Mills has lower receivables and less inventory than the industry, is generating higher revenue per dollar of assets, and appears very capable of servicing its higher level of debt.

LIMITATIONS

Our in-depth analysis of General Mills provided many insights into the firm's financial condition. But any analysis of accounting statements is subject to the following limitations:

1. The basic data arise from the accounting process and are therefore based on historical costs. Because one of the main purposes of financial accounting is to match revenues and expenses in the appropriate period, there may be little or no *direct* relationship to the firm's cash flows, especially in the short run.
2. The accounting process allows for alternative treatment of numerous transactions. Thus, two identical firms may report substantially different accounting data by employing alternative GAAP treatments.
3. "Window dressing" may appear in accounting statements. For example, by taking out a long-term loan before the end of its fiscal year and holding the proceeds as cash, a firm could significantly improve its current and quick ratios. Once the fiscal year has ended, the firm could turn around and pay back the loan—but the transaction has already served its purpose.
4. For the many firms that are multidivisional, sufficient data are generally not reported so that outsiders can examine the performance of the various divisions. Also, it is often difficult to find comparable industry data for multidivisional firms.
5. Inflation can have material effects on the firm that are not fully reflected in accounting statements. This is especially true for inventory and long-term assets, which may be seriously understated when inflation is present. The comparability of data within a firm over time, and also between firms, is therefore limited.
6. For firms with substantial international operations, other reporting problems exist in addition to those faced by domestic firms.
7. Industry averages are generally *not* where the successful firm wants to operate; rather, it wants to be at the top end of the performance ladder. Also, finding an appropriate industry for comparison is often not as simple as it sounds.

In addition to the data contained in accounting statements, many other sources of financial data exist. Some of these are listed in Table 24.6.

Concept Review Questions

- What four key ideas should be considered when conducting an analysis of the balance sheet and income statement?
- On what basis is a common-size income statement prepared? A common-size balance sheet?
- How is a firm's return on equity related to the firm's return on assets? To net profit margin? To total asset turnover?
- Describe some of the problems and limitations of any analysis using accounting statements.

Table 24.6

Sources of Financial Data

There are a great many sources of financial data. When in doubt about the availability of these or other sources, check with the reference librarian at your library.

Publication	Type of Information
Annual reports of companies	Individual company data
Bank and Quotation Record	Prices and yields of securities
Barron's	Security markets, individual securities, and analysis of individual companies
Business Week	General coverage, current and individual company trends
Cash Flow	General coverage of cash and working capital trends
Commercial and Financial Chronicle	Prices and yields of securities
Dun's Business Month	General coverage, current trends
Dun & Bradstreet's Key Business Ratios	Industry ratios
The Economist	General coverage of international developments
Federal Reserve Bulletin	Aggregate financial data
Forbes	General coverage, analysis of individual companies
Fortune	General coverage, size rankings of firms
Inc.	General coverage, especially of smaller firms
Institutional Investor	General coverage of financing trends and corporate security issues
Leo Troy's *Almanac of Business and Industrial Financial Ratios*	Industry ratios
Mergers & Acquisitions	General coverage of mergers, foreign involvement, and divestitures
Moody's Bank & Finance, Industrial, OTC Industrial, OTC Unlisted, International, and *Transportation* Manuals	Individual company data
Robert Morris Associates' *Annual Statement Studies*	Industry ratios
Standard & Poor's *Corporation Records*	Individual company data
Standard & Poor's *Industry Surveys*	Industry data
Statistical Bulletin of the Securities and Exchange Commission	Stock market activity and corporate security issues
Survey of Current Business	Aggregate financial data
Value Line Investment Survey	Individual company data
Various trade associations	Industry accounting data
The Wall Street Journal	General coverage, prices, and yields of securities

KEY POINTS

1. It is very important not to become overly enamored with analyzing and/or maximizing accounting numbers. Accounting numbers are only a means to an end; the purpose of the firm is to produce and sell quality products or services and make financial decisions that lead to the maximization of the value of the firm.
2. An income statement is presented over a period of time (typically a year), whereas a balance sheet is presented as of an instant in time.
3. Ratios can be grouped into common-type categories; five common groupings are liquidity, asset management, debt management, profitability, and market.
4. Common-size accounting statements and ratios should be analyzed over time and compared to the industry. They should also form the basis for asking further questions about the firm.
5. Limitations of accounting statements include their use of historical cost basis, alternative generally accepted treatments available, window dressing at the end of the year, sometimes-incomplete divisional data, lack of inflation adjustment, and difficulties in reflecting the financial consequences of international operations.

QUESTIONS

24.1 Accounting statements may be prepared under generally accepted accounting principles, for tax purposes, or for internal management purposes. Explain why we focus on those prepared under GAAP, and what the strengths and/or weaknesses of GAAP statements are.

24.2 If preferred stock is outstanding, the numerator of the earnings per share calculation is earnings available to common stockholders (net income − cash dividends on preferred stock), whereas it is simply net income if there is no preferred stock outstanding. Explain why this adjustment is necessary.

24.3 Book value per share, which is often referred to when someone is "touting" a common stock investment, is calculated by dividing stockholders' equity by the number of shares of common stock outstanding.

a. Based on your knowledge of the accounting process, why do you think that book value per share is generally not indicative of the value of the common stock?
b. Can you think of some specific situations when book value may provide a reasonable estimate of value?

24.4 Explain in detail why:

a. net income does not reflect cash.
b. retained earnings do not include any cash.

24.5 Explain why common-size statements may focus attention on items often overlooked when examining the firm's accounting statements directly.

24.6 Anna has been asked to conduct a complete analysis of the ability of Westbrook Enterprises to service its long-term financing obligations. In doing so, she determined that the firm has the following fixed-charge obligations over the next few years:

1. Interest of $2 million per year for each of the next 3 years.
2. Sinking fund payments of $1 million per year for each of the next 3 years. (A sinking fund is a required obligation often present when bonds are issued in order to retire some of the bonds before maturity.)
3. Lease payments of $1.5 million per year for each of the next 3 years.
4. Cash dividends on preferred stock of $1 million per year for each of the next 3 years. (The tax rate is 30 percent.)

How would you advise Anna to proceed with the analysis? Should any new ratios be calculated?

24.7   Financial leverage arises from the use of financing sources that require a fixed-cost type of financing. By employing financial leverage, the firm may be able to magnify gains (and losses) to common stockholders. Which one of these situations has the most (least) financial leverage? Why?

	A	B	C	D	E	F
Short-term debt	$ 0	$ 0	$ 0	$ 20	$ 20	$ 0
Long-term debt	0	0	50	0	30	20
Leases	0	0	0	20	0	30
Preferred stock	0	50	0	10	0	0
Common stock	150	100	100	100	100	100

24.8   The du Pont system has been widely employed to provide a framework for the analysis of ratios. Comment on its usefulness; list its strengths and weaknesses.

CONCEPT REVIEW PROBLEMS

See Appendix A for solutions.

CR24.1   Durango Shoes has operating profit, or EBIT, of $700,000. Interest expense for the year was $100,000, preferred dividends paid were $50,000, common dividends were $200,000, and taxes were $70,000. The firm has 30,000 shares of common stock outstanding and 10,000 warrants with a conversion privilege of one warrant for one share of stock. The probability of the warrants' conversion is 50 percent; therefore, there is likelihood of 5,000 warrants being converted.

a. Calculate the simple earnings per share, the primary earnings per share, and the fully diluted earnings per share.
b. What was the increase in retained earnings?

CR24.2   Terrylia Inc. has a current stock price of $20 per share, with 50,000 shares outstanding. The firm recently paid a dividend of $1.00 per share. Use the accounting statements for Terrylia to construct a common-size balance sheet and income statement and then calculate the ratios found in the chapter.

Balance Sheet

Assets
Cash	$ 70,000
Accounts receivable	200,000
Inventory	250,000
Long-term investment	30,000
Plant and equipment	700,000
Less: Accumulated depreciation	(280,000)
Total assets	$ 970,000

Liabilities and Stockholders' Equity
Accounts payable	$ 100,000
Notes payable	150,000
Accrued taxes	20,000
Bond payable	300,000
Preferred stock, $50 par value, 8% dividend	50,000
Common stock, $1 par value	50,000
Capital paid in excess of par	100,000
Retained earnings	200,000
Total liabilities and stockholders' equity	$ 970,000

Income Statement
Sales (on credit)	$2,000,000
Cost of goods sold	1,500,000
Gross margin	500,000
Selling and administrative expenses	200,000*
EBIT	300,000
Interest expense	50,000
EBT	250,000
Taxes	75,000
Net income	$ 175,000

*Includes $10,000 in lease payments

CR24.3 MTM has a net profit margin of 5 percent, total asset turnover of 2.5, and a total debt to total asset ratio of 0.40. What is the firm's return on equity?

CR24.4 The following information concerns two competitors, Jarvus and Barkell.

Balance Sheet

Assets	Jarvus	Barkell
Cash & marketable securities	$ 72,345	$138,722
Accounts receivable	41,343	73,848
Inventory	193,827	43,024
Net long-term assets	12,290	22,290
Total assets	$319,805	$277,884

Liabilities and Stockholders' Equity

Short-term bank loans	$ 54,678	$ 20,400
Accounts payable	55,705	22,556
Accruals	35,480	18,776
Long-term debt	22,116	43,555
Common stock	93,076	95,408
Retained earnings	58,750	77,189
Total liabilities & equity	$319,805	$277,884

Income Statement

Sales	$701,092	$757,098
Cost of goods sold	564,504	622,020
Gross margin	136,588	135,078
Selling and administrative expenses	51,160	61,380
Depreciation	6,376	6,632
Miscellaneous expenses	8,108	14,228
EBIT	70,944	52,838
Interest on short-term debt	5,468	2,040
Interest on long-term debt	2,677	4,016
EBT	62,799	46,782
Taxes	25,119	18,632
Net income	$ 37,680	$ 28,150

Calculate the accounting ratios for both firms.

a. To which firm would you as a credit manager or short-term lender be most likely to approve the extension of short-term trade credit or grant a short-term loan?
b. To which one would you as a banker be most likely to extend long-term credit?
c. In which firm would you as an investor be most likely to buy stock?

PROBLEMS

24.1 The PCG Company is a diversified manufacturing and retailing firm. From the list of items that follows, prepare its balance sheet and income statement.

Accounts and notes payable	$ 65,377
Accounts receivable	63,836
Accumulated depreciation	69,467
Accrued expenses	81,797
Cash	17,542

Common stock	22,776
Cost of goods sold	875,727
Deferred taxes (long-term)	11,372
Interest expense	14,122
Inventory	156,230
Long-term debt and leases	108,962
Other current assets	13,675
Property, plant, and equipment (gross)	188,900
Retained earnings	?
Sales	1,093,611
Selling, general, and administrative expenses	170,505
Taxes	15,230

24.2   Complete the balance sheet, sales, and net income information below, given the following data:

Long-term asset turnover	4.0
Total asset turnover	2.4
Total debt to total assets	0.6
Current ratio	2.0
Quick ratio	1.0
Net profit margin	5.0%
Days sales outstanding (365-day year)	15.208

Cash	$_____	Current liabilities	$	_____
Accounts receivable	_____	Long-term debt		_____
Inventory	_____	Common stock		100
Net plant and equipment	600	Retained earnings		_____
Total assets	$=====	Total liabilities and		
		stockholders' equity	$	=====
Sales	$_____	Net income	$	=====

24.3   Hibbard & Associates has the following data:

$$\text{long-term asset turnover} = 3.5$$
$$\text{total asset turnover} = 2.0$$

What percentage of total assets are current assets?

24.4   Wiebe Industries has a gross profit margin (gross margin/sales) of 25 percent on sales of $500,000 (all credit). Cash and marketable securities are $10,000, accounts receivable are $40,000, inventory is $50,000, and the current ratio is 2.0.

a.   What are Wiebe's days sales outstanding (use a 365-day year), inventory turnover, and quick ratio?

b.   How much should inventory be if management wants the inventory turnover to increase to 10 times a year?

c. What would the accounts receivable be if management wants the days sales outstanding to be 21.9 days?

24.5 Wallace Systems is applying for a bank loan. It has given the bank the following data:

Balance Sheet			
Cash	$ 40,000	Accounts Payable	$ 5,000
Accounts receivable	40,000	Notes payable	20,000
Inventory	70,000	Long-term debt	75,000
Net plant and equipment	225,000	6% preferred stock	25,000
Total assets	$375,000	Common stock ($5 par)	150,000
		Retained earnings	100,000
		Total liabilities and	
		stockholders' equity	$375,000
Sales		$390,000	
Net income		$61,500	
Dividends per share on common stock		$0.80	
Market price per share of common stock		$60	

As part of your analysis of the firm's request for a loan, you have decided to calculate the following items: (1) the number of shares of common stock outstanding, (2) earnings per share of common stock, (3) dividend payout, (4) return on total assets, (5) return on equity, (6) current ratio, and (7) quick ratio.

a. What are the calculated amounts for the seven items?
b. What can you conclude about the past profitability of Wallace Systems based on this data? Lacking any other information, would you recommend approving or disapproving the loan request?

24.6 The following data are taken from the annual report of Delux Drug Stores. In addition, relevant industry data are provided.

a. Compute the ratios for Delux corresponding to the industry ratios.
b. What are its strengths (weaknesses) compared to the retail drug industry?

Delux Drug Stores Balance Sheet as of January 31 (thousands of dollars)			
Cash	$ 8,143	Accounts payable	$ 54,449
Receivables	5,596	Notes payable	7,711
Inventory	148,554	Accrued expenses	28,823
Other current	11,608	Deferred income taxes	20,347
Net long-term assets	132,609	Long-term debt and leases	103,662
Total	$306,510	Stockholders' equity	91,518
		Total	$306,510

Delux Drug Stores Income Statement for Year Ended January 31
(thousands of dollars)

Sales		$761,734
Cost of goods sold		550,930
Gross profit		210,804
Selling, general, and administrative expenses	$156,070	
Depreciation	10,784	166,854
EBIT		43,950
Interest		15,245
EBT		28,705
Taxes		12,056
Net income		$ 16,649

Retail Drug Industry Ratios

Current	2.00	Total asset turnover	3.20
Quick	0.50	Total debt to total assets	0.43
Days sales outstanding	12 days	Times interest earned	3.00
(365-day year)		Net profit margin	3.33%
Inventory turnover	4.00	Return on total assets	10.60%
Long-term asset turnover	8.00	Return on equity	18.40%

24.7 Hickory Mills has applied to your firm for credit for future purchases it wants to make. As a first step, you calculated the following information:

	Year −1	Year 0
Current ratio	2.00	2.00
Quick ratio	1.25	1.34
Cash/total assets	10.00%	15.45%
Accounts receivable/total assets	15.00%	15.00%
Inventory/total assets	15.00%	15.00%

a. *Based on just this information,* do you believe credit should be granted to Hickory Mills? Why or why not?

b. Upon further analysis, you gather the relevant data for the 2 years, which is

	Year −1	Year 0
Cash	$ 100	$ 170
Accounts receivable	150	165
Inventory	150	165
Total assets	1,000	1,100
Accounts payable	100	200
Notes payable	100	50
Sales	3,000	2,000
Cost of goods sold	1,800	1,500
Credit purchases	1,300	1,200

Calculate the following: (1) days sales outstanding, (2) inventory turnover, and (3) days purchases outstanding. [*Note:* As given in footnote 9, days purchases outstanding equals accounts payable/(credit purchases/365).] Based on this further analysis, what conclusion do you reach now?

24.8 Indicate the impact of the following transactions on the current ratio, total debt to total assets, and return on total assets. Use a plus sign (+) to indicate an increase, a minus sign (−) to indicate a decrease, and a zero (0) to indicate either no effect or an indeterminant effect. Assume that the initial current ratio was greater than 1.0.

	Current Ratio	Total Debt to Total Assets	Return on Assets
a. Cash acquired through a short-term bank loan	___	___	___
b. Accounts receivable are collected	___	___	___
c. Payment made to creditors for previous purchases	___	___	___
d. Cash acquired through issuance of additional common stock	___	___	___
e. Cash dividend declared and paid (the dividend has not been shown as an accrual)	___	___	___

24.9 The following are the balance sheet and income statement for Decca Components:

Balance Sheet

Cash and marketable securities	$ 100,000	Accounts payable	$ 50,000
Accounts receivable	650,000	Notes payable	350,000
Inventory	1,050,000	Long-term debt	2,000,000
Property, plant, and equipment	6,000,000	Common stock	1,000,000
Less: Accumulated depreciation	(2,000,000)	Retained earnings	2,400,000
Total assets	$5,800,000	Total liabilities and stockholders' equity	$5,800,000

Income Statement

Sales	$16,000,000
Cost of goods sold	10,000,000
Gross margin	6,000,000
Other expenses	3,000,000
EBIT	3,000,000
Interest	300,000
EBT	2,700,000
Income taxes	1,080,000
Net income	$ 1,620,000

a. Calculate the following ratios: (1) current, (2) quick, (3) total debt to total assets, (4) net profit margin, and (5) total asset turnover.
b. Using the du Pont formula, calculate return on equity.
c. Now suppose that Decca Components has decided to reduce its risk of running out of cash. To accomplish this, it will issue $1,000,000 in long-term debt and add the same amount to its cash and marketable securities account. This debt will be financed at a 10 percent yearly rate. What is the impact of this transaction on the ratios calculated in (a) and (b) above?

24.10   The following data apply to Stern Products:

Sales	$1,000,000
Cost of goods sold	800,000
Net income	50,000
Total debt	250,000
Preferred stock	100,000
Common stock	100,000
Retained earnings	50,000
Days sales outstanding (365-day year)	36.5 days
Inventory turnover	5

a. Determine (1) total asset turnover, (2) net profit margin, (3) return on total assets, and (4) return on equity.
b. If sales and cost of goods sold are constant and all the following events occur *simultaneously*, what are the new net income, total debt, and return on equity?

1. Inventory turnover increases to 10.
2. Days sales outstanding decreases to 18.25 days.
3. Return on assets increases to 15 percent.
4. There are no changes in long-term assets; any reduction in assets causes an equal dollar-for-dollar reduction in the firm's debt.

24.11

Total assets	$800
Current liabilities	$ 50
Long-term debt	150
Common stock ($1 par)	100
Retained earnings	500
Total liabilities and stockholders' equity	$800

a. If return on equity equals 10 percent, find net income and return on total assets.
b. What is the firm's earnings per share?
c. If it pays out one-quarter of its current earnings as cash dividends, what are the dividends per share?
d. If the market price of the firm's common stock is $9 per share, what is the price/earnings ratio and the dividend yield?

24.12   Drake Motors has the following balance sheet and income statement:

Balance Sheet

Total assets	$2,500,000	Total debt	$1,000,000
		Stockholders' equity	1,500,000
		Total liabilities and stockholders' equity	$2,500,000

Income Statement

Sales	$5,000,000
Cost of goods sold	3,500,000
Gross margin	1,500,000
Operating expenses	900,000
EBIT	600,000
Interest	100,000
EBT	500,000
Income taxes (35%)	175,000
Net income	$ 325,000

a. If Drake has 50,000 shares of common stock outstanding, determine its present (1) total debt to total assets, (2) return on total assets, (3) return on equity, and (4) earnings per share.

b. Drake Motors is considering whether to renovate one of its existing plants by making an additional $1 million investment in total assets. The renovation will reduce the cost of goods sold by $300,000 per year, whichever plan is adopted. Two possible plans have been considered for financing the renovation. Plan I keeps the existing ratio of total debt to total assets and requires 20,000 additional shares of common stock to be issued; the new level of *total* interest paid is $150,000 per year. Plan II employs all debt financing, no common stock is issued, and the new level of *total* interest is $225,000 per year.

(1) Determine total debt to total assets, return on total assets, return on equity, and earnings per share under plans I and II.

(2) Based on your analysis, do you think Drake Motors should renovate the plant? If yes, should plan I or plan II be used?

24.13 Mini Case Accounting information for Corning Inc. for 3 recent years is as follows:

Income Statement (in millions)

	For Fiscal Year		
	−2	−1	0
Sales	$2,301.5	$2,575.9	$3,049.6
Cost of goods sold	1,405.2	1,600.9	1,925.7
Selling, general, and administrative expenses	438.6	491.8	581.8
Research and development	95.2	109.6	124.5
Other expense (−) or income (+)	−7.6	+48.8	+64.5
Interest	41.0	44.5	54.0
Taxes	103.2	116.9	136.1
Net income	$ 210.7	$ 261.0	$ 292.0

Balance Sheet (in millions)			
	−2	−1	0
Assets			
Current assets			
Cash and marketable securities	$ 156.5	$ 352.8	$ 133.0
Accounts receivable	397.5	452.4	527.2
Inventory	254.0	238.5	314.5
Other	121.8	125.6	123.2
Total current assets	929.8	1,169.3	1,097.9
Long-term assets			
Net property, plant, and equipment	991.5	1,160.6	1,351.8
Investments	818.3	826.0	804.5
Other	158.3	204.8	257.8
Total long-term assets	1,968.1	2,191.4	2,414.1
Total assets	$2,897.9	$3,360.7	$3,512.0
Liabilities and Stockholders' Equity			
Current liabilities			
Accounts payable	$ 125.1	$ 158.6	$ 191.5
Short-term debt	18.5	40.4	52.8
Other	365.1	483.0	395.2
Total current liabilities	508.7	682.0	639.5
Long-term liabilities			
Long-term debt	499.0	624.5	611.2
Deferred taxes	71.0	53.1	72.8
Other	258.5	258.3	307.5
Total long-term liabilities	828.5	935.9	991.5
Stockholders' equity			
Convertible preferred stock	0	31.6	30.7
Common stock	233.8	255.5	139.6
Retained earnings	1,275.5	1,436.4	1,640.6
Currency translation adjustment	51.4	19.3	70.1
Total stockholders' equity	1,560.7	1,742.8	1,881.0
Total liabilities and stockholders' equity	$2,897.9	$3,360.7	$3,512.0
Other Information			
Shares of common stock (in millions)	88.86	94.22	91.85
Dividends paid on common stock in (millions)	86.0	99.7	85.3
Common stock price range	$34\frac{7}{8} - 22\frac{1}{2}$	$49\frac{3}{8} - 32$	$51\frac{3}{4} - 34\frac{7}{8}$

a. Accounting statements are prepared based on a set of generally accepted accounting principles, GAAP. What are some of the key ideas underlying GAAP that influence all accounting statements? What is the significance of these assumptions for an analyst examining a firm's accounting statements?

b. Prepare common-size income statements and balance sheets for Corning for the last 3 years.

c. Now calculate ratios for the firm. (*Note:* Because lease expenses are not available, do not calculate fixed charges coverage. Also, for the market ratios, take an average of the high and low stock prices for the per share market price.)

d. What trends are evident from the analysis?

e. What additional information would be helpful in completing the analysis?

f. What limitations exist with any analysis of this type?

REFERENCES

Some useful books on the analysis of financial statements include:

FOSTER, GEORGE. *Financial Statement Analysis,* 2nd ed. Englewood Cliffs, N.J.: Prentice-Hall, 1986.

HELFERT, ERICH A. *Techniques of Financial Analysis,* 7th ed. Homewood, Ill.: Irwin, 1991.

Financial ratio patterns and their usefulness are examined in:

GOMBOLA, MICHAEL J., and J. EDWARD KETZ. "Financial Ratio Patterns in Retail and Manufacturing Organizations." *Financial Management* 12 (Summer 1983): 45–56.

PINCHES, GEORGE E., KENT A. MINGO, and J. KENT CARUTHERS. "The Stability of Financial Patterns in Industrial Organizations." *Journal of Finance* 28 (May 1973): 389–96.

Some additional topics of interest are discussed in:

BALL, BEN C., JR. "The Mysterious Disappearance of Retained Earnings." *Harvard Business Review* 65 (July-August 1987): 56–63.

DEBERG, CURTIS L., and BROCK MURDOCH. "The Immateriality of Primary EPS: What the Data Reveal." *Financial Analysts Journal* 47 (September/October 1991): 91–95.

KAPLAN, ROBERT S., and DAVID P. NORTON. "The Balanced Scorecard—Measures that Drive Performance." *Harvard Business Review* 70 (January–February 1992): 71–79.

WARFIELD, TERRY D., and JOHN J. WILD. "Accounting Recognition and the Relevance of Earnings as an Explanatory Variable for Return." *Accounting Review* 67 (October 1992): 821–42.

25 *Financial Planning and Forecasting*

EXECUTIVE SUMMARY

The primary means of forecasting cash flows relies on the cash budget, which includes all operating, investment, and financing cash inflows and outflows. The cash budget may be supplemented by pro forma statements. The usefulness of cash forecasts depends on accurate sales forecasts. Yet the future is inherently uncertain. Cash forecasting must therefore include the ability to ask alternative questions. Accurate, yet flexible, forecasts are a valuable tool in financial management.

There is no model or theory that leads directly to the optimum financial and strategic plan. Consequently, the process involves trial and error. In the short run, the emphasis is primarily on the acquisition or investment of short-term funds. In the longer run the emphasis is on the long-term investment, financing, and strategy of the firm. Inherent in the financial planning process is the consideration and evaluation of various options (to expand, shut down, secure different kinds of financing, and so forth) that are available to the firm.

CASH FLOW ANALYSIS

Although accounting statements, as examined in Chapter 24, are prepared at least yearly for all firms, they don't directly tell us about the firm's past or expected cash flows, or about what actions should be taken to maximize the market value of the firm. Figure 25.1 shows that a firm's cash inflows arise from its operations (sales and collection of receivables), its investments in securities or subsidiaries, and its financing through bonds and stock or taking out loans. The firm's outflows, also shown in Figure 25.1, go to its operations (materials, wages and salaries, rent, taxes, and so forth), to meeting its working capital and long-term investment needs, and to its financing needs through the payment of interest and dividends, and the repayment of loans and bonds.

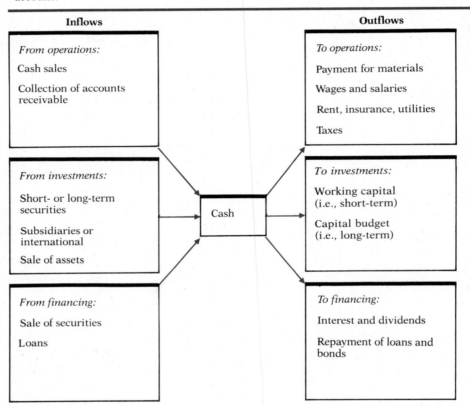

Figure 25.1

Sources of Cash Inflows and Outflows

Inflows will not equal outflows over any period of time except by chance. The excess of inflows (outflows) over outflows (inflows) results in an increase (decrease) in the firm's cash account.

STATEMENT OF CASH FLOWS

In recognition of the importance of cash flows, a **statement of cash flows**[1] now must be reported along with a firm's balance sheet and income statement. The cash flow statement replaces the former statement of changes in financial position. The statement of cash flows for General Mills is shown in Table 25.1. Note two items: (1) The statement is broken into three basic categories—operating activities, investing activities, and financing activities; and (2) due to how most firms present their statement of cash flows, the specific accounts shown in Table 25.1 do not directly correspond to the

[1] *Statement of Financial Accounting Standards No. 95*, "Statement of Cash Flows" (Stamford, Conn.: FASB, 1987).

Table 25.1

Statement of Cash Flows for General Mills (in millions)

General Mills uses the indirect approach for estimating cash flows from operating activities. Many other firms also use this approach, even though the direct approach provides more useful cash flow information

	For the Year		
	1990	1991	1992
Operating Activities			
Net income	$381	$472	$496
Deferred taxes	13	1	14
Depreciation and amortization	180	219	247
Nonrecurring items			
Change in cash from:			
Receivables	(2)	(47)	2
Inventories	(22)	(110)	1
Accounts Payable	79	63	54
Other assets and liabilities	58	(3)	(37)
Others, net	(59)	(51)	(5)
Net cash provided by operating activities	628	544	772
Investing Activities			
Capital expenditures	(540)	(555)	(695)
Proceeds from disposal of land, buildings and equipment	12	10	8
Other investments (dispositions)	(2)	(11)	39
Net cash used by investing activities	(530)	(556)	(648)
Financing Activities			
Increase (decrease) in short-term debt	(24)	(80)	150
Issuance of long-term debt	142	373	189
Payment of long-term debt	(61)	(132)	(248)
Common stock issued (retired)	169	42	39
Purchases of common stock for treasury	(150)	—	(40)
Dividends paid	(181)	(211)	(245)
Cash flows from tax leases and increase (decrease) in marketable investments	(3)	59	(8)
Net cash provided (used) by financing activities	(108)	51	(163)
Net increase (decrease) in cash and short-term investments	$(10)	$39	$(39)

inflows and outflows shown in Figure 25.1. We see that General Mills generated $772 million in cash from operations in 1992, used $648 million for investing activities, and used $163 million for financing activities. The net result was a $39 million drop in the cash and marketable securities account.

Advantages of the Statement of Cash Flows

The statement of cash flows is helpful for the following reasons:

1. The specific focus on the three separate activities of operations, investments, and financing is beneficial. This is especially so given that these are the three main functions of all firms.
2. The statement removes the effect of accruals, and it restates such items as collectibles or salaries to a cash basis.
3. The statement breaks out gross, as opposed to net, figures for such items as long-term debt transactions.

Disadvantages of the Statement of Cash Flows

At the same time, the statement does not fully convert all items to cash flows, and it introduces some additional confusion in other areas. The statement's main problems are:

1. The operating activities part of the statement of cash flows can be presented in one of two ways—the direct approach, or the indirect approach. Under the direct approach the operating activities portion of the statement might be presented as:

Operating activities	
Collections from customers	$ 600,000
Payments to suppliers	(300,000)
Payments to employees for salaries	(180,000)
Payments to creditors for interest	(15,000)
Miscellaneous payments	(10,000)
Payments for taxes	(20,000)
Net cash flow provided by operating activities	$ 75,000

The indirect approach starts from the firm's net income and then makes adjustments as needed. Comparing the direct approach (above) for determining the cash flow from operating activities with the indirect approach used by General Mills and shown in Table 25.1, we see that the direct approach provides much more useful information in terms of determining the source and use of cash from operations. Although FAS No. 95 strongly recommends the direct method, most firms have adopted the indirect method. This choice reduces the usability of the statement of cash flows.

2. The statement of cash flows does not reconcile the differences between taxes as reported on the firm's income statement with what was actually paid. In the supplemental information for General Mills, the taxes actually paid in 1992 are recorded as $326 million. Comparing this amount with the firm's income statement (Table 24.1), we see the following figures (in millions) for taxes paid:

	1990	1991	1992
Per income statement	$244	$307	$332
Per supplemental data to cash flow statement	231	258	326

The taxes reported as paid on the income statement are very similar to what General Mills actually paid, as shown on the cash flow statement; however, for some firms the differences between the actual outflow for taxes and what is reported on the income statement may be substantial.

3. The statement permits but does not require separate disclosure of the cash flows associated with discontinued operations and extraordinary items.

4. Noncash investing and financing activities (such as capital leases, debt/equity swaps, and asset exchanges) are not included on the statement. They are simply reported in a supplemental statement or in narrative form.

5. Interest or dividends received by the firm, as well as interest paid, are treated as operating activities; however, dividends paid by the firm are treated as a financing activity. This inconsistency in treatment is, at best, misleading.

The statement of cash flows is a step in the right direction. Even ignoring some of its deficiencies, however, it has one other disadvantage—it simply reports what has happened in the past. Although firms can simply react to whatever cash flows occur, most plan for the future by estimating inflows and outflows. To do this, firms use cash budgets and pro forma statements.

CASH BUDGETS

An important part of the forecasting process is the development of the firm's **cash budget,** which is just a detailed statement of the expected inflows and outflows. Cash budgets can be estimated for any period of time—often a month, a quarter, or a year. These budgets serve two purposes: First, they alert the firm to future cash needs or surpluses. Second, they provide a standard against which subsequent performance can be judged.

In preparing a cash budget, it is necessary to include all inflows and outflows expected by the firm. To do this, a detailed analysis of past cash flows is needed. Although the future cannot be expected to be exactly like the past, a thorough examination of past cash flow trends is the first step in effective cash flow forecasting by means of cash budgets.

The major items to be considered when estimating a cash budget are the following:

Cash Inflows	Cash Outflows
Cash sales	Cash purchases
Collection of accounts receivable	Payment of accounts payable
Income from investments	Wages and salaries
Income from subsidiaries	Rent, insurance, and utilities
Dividends from international ventures	Advertising, selling, and other related cash expenses
Sale of assets	Taxes (local, state, federal, and international)
Sale of securities	Capital investments
Loans	Interest and dividends
	Repayment of loans

A six-step procedure can be used to develop a cash budget:

1. Develop a scenario with an explicit set of assumptions.
2. Estimate sales.
3. Determine the cash inflows expected from operations.
4. Calculate the cash outflows expected to arise from operations.
5. Estimate any other expected cash inflows and outflows.
6. Determine the expected financing needed or surplus available.

Developing Different Scenarios

The first step in developing a cash budget is to determine the assumed conditions, or the scenario the cash budget is to cover. Because we are dealing with the future, which is uncertain, this is an important step. Assumptions concerning the state of the economy, competitor actions, conditions in the financial markets, and similar factors need to be spelled out in detail to set the stage for the rest of the analysis. Then another set of assumptions can be specified and the analysis redone to see the impact on the firm's cash flow position. This process is often called *scenario analysis*. Its purpose is to see how sensitive cash flows are to changes in the input data (or assumptions).

It is far better to allow for a range of outcomes rather than to rely on a single estimate. A firm that develops only a single estimate is likely to be caught short if there is a large deviation from the expected outcome. Likewise, managers can determine which estimates have the most impact on the firm's expected cash flows; then they can spend more time and money, if necessary, trying to improve these estimates. Finally, the longer the planning period, the more important the analysis of a number of sets of assumptions becomes. By doing these analyses, managers can gain an understanding of the possible consequences different events could have on the firm's cash inflows and outflows.

Forecasting Sales

The key element in developing an accurate cash budget is the sales forecast, which provides the basis for determining the size and timing of many of the forecasted cash inflows and outflows. The sales forecast can be based on an internal or an external analysis. The following are some forecasting techniques and their strengths and weaknesses:

Method	Time Period (Short, Medium, Long)	Accuracy	Reflects Changing Conditions?
Internal			
Linear regression	S, M	Depends	No
Sales force composite	S, M	Depends	Yes
Time series	S, M, L	Often highly accurate	Yes, but often slow
External			
Market survey	M, L	Depends	Yes
Multivariate regression	S, M, L	Depends	Yes, if built in

Three popular internal methods are linear regression, sales force composite, and time series analysis. Linear regression takes past sales and projects them into the future without any adjustment. The sales force composite method bases expected sales on estimates provided by sales personnel and the firm's marketing department. Consistency of forecasts is a major concern when the sales force composite method is employed. Forecasted sales might be the sum of separate forecasts made by managers of many of the firm's units. Left to their own, these managers will make different assumptions about inflation, growth in the economy, growth in market share, and so forth. Therefore, some method of maintaining consistent assumptions is crucial for the accuracy of the sales force composite method. Finally, time series models are available for forecasting expected sales based on past sales. These methods require more statistical expertise, but they are often best for generating accurate forecasts based on past data.

An external sales forecast, on the other hand, starts with factors outside the firm. This could be done by contracting with a firm to do a marketing research study or contacting other firms like Data Resources or Chase Econometrics, which specialize in preparing macroeconomic and industry forecasts. A statistical model that relates the firm's past sales to the projected level of gross national product, automobile sales, or whatever is most relevant might also be developed. Most firms use a variety of methods for forecasting sales. Whatever method is used, firms often start the forecast on a divisional basis in order to obtain better accuracy. Once the divisional forecasts are made, they are combined into an overall forecast of expected sales.

Linear Regression and Forecasting

Assume that in order to forecast sales we use linear regression plus information obtained from a sales force composite approach. Bartley Instruments, a robot components firm, begins with an analysis of its past sales (see Figure 25.2). Simple linear regression techniques can be used to forecast sales naively simply by extrapolating the past trend in sales. Sales is the dependent variable (indicated by Y), and time is the independent variable (designated by X). The regression model to be estimated, ignoring the residual error term, is

$$Y_t = \alpha + \beta X_t \tag{25.1}$$

where

Y_t = the forecasted sales in time period t
α = alpha, the intercept of the fitted regression equation
β = beta, the slope of the fitted regression equation
X_t = the time period

This method is easy to employ. Let's use the data from Figure 25.2 and forecast Bartley's 19X9 sales. The historical sales are as follows:

Year	Sales (Y_t) (in millions)	Period (X_t)
19X3	$2.10	1
19X4	1.85	2
19X5	3.00	3
19X6	2.90	4
19X7	4.05	5
19X8	4.15	6

The time periods are converted to 1 for the first year through 6 for 19X8. The exact procedure, the formulas employed, and the calculations are shown in Table 25.2. Based on this, the estimated regression equation is

$$Y_t = \$1.332 + \$0.479 X_t$$

Because we want to forecast sales for 19X9, which is period 7, we substitute as follows:

$$19X9 \text{ forecasted sales} = \$1.332 + \$0.479(7)$$
$$= \$1.332 + \$3.353 = \$4.685 \text{ million}$$

If we wanted to forecast the subsequent year's sales, the same procedure would be employed, except the time period would be 8, resulting in forecasted sales of $5.164 million.

This approach is simple and inexpensive to implement. For a firm (or divisions of a firm) in a stable environment, it may provide a reasonable degree of accuracy.

Figure 25.2

Projected Sales for Bartley Instruments

Bartley has experienced slow but reasonably steady growth since 19X4. The 19X9 projection assumes an "average" rate of growth—slightly higher than last year, but lower than the year before that.

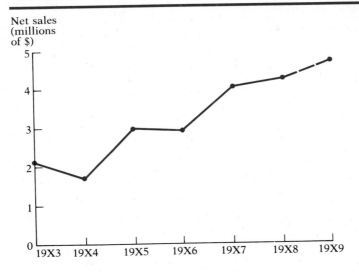

Because it ignores any factor *not* captured by a simple linear extrapolation of past sales, however, it can be misleading. Thus, influences caused by how the sales of the firm respond to changes in the business cycle are ignored. This is why other forecasting techniques and management expertise are needed when forecasting sales.

Based on simple linear regression, Bartley's 19X9 estimated sales are $4.685 million. This information is supplemented by the sales force composite forecast, along with what Bartley knows about the actions of the competition and the estimated performance of the economy in the next year. Based on this analysis, Bartley arrives at an estimate of sales of $4.5 million.

Bartley is interested in both the expected level and the potential variability of sales. If the expected variability is small, then Bartley will have more confidence in its forecast. In that event, its operating plans can be relatively simple. If the sales forecasts are not so solid, then Bartley will want to build a lot of flexibility into its plans and to monitor trends closely.

Cash Inflow from Operations

Once sales have been estimated, we can determine expected cash inflows. Because most firms sell (at least in part) on credit, the pattern of collections must be examined. First, Bartley "distributes" its estimated sales over the months of the year. This may be done by using a historical percentage of the sales that occur each month. For example, assume that February has historically accounted for 4.4 percent of total yearly sales. The estimated February sales are then (0.044)($4.5 million) ≈ $200,000. The estimated monthly sales for February through August are shown in Table 25.3.

Table 25.2

Estimated Regression Equation to Forecast Sales of Bartley Instruments

Linear regression provides a simple means of projecting sales; however, because it is based solely on past sales, it ignores any other factors (such as the state of the economy) that may influence actual sales.

Sales (Y_t) (1)	Period (X_t) (2)	$Y_t X_t$ (1)(2) (3)	X_t^2 (2)^2 (4)
2.10	1	2.10	1
1.85	2	3.70	4
3.00	3	9.00	9
2.90	4	11.60	16
4.05	5	20.25	25
4.15	6	24.90	36
Totals 18.05	21	71.55	91

Means

$\bar{Y} = \Sigma Y_t/n = 18.05/6 = 3.008$

$\bar{X} = \Sigma X_t/n = 21/6 = 3.50$

Calculation of β (slope)

$$\beta = \frac{\Sigma Y_t X_t - (n)(\bar{Y})(\bar{X})}{\Sigma X_t^2 - (n)(\bar{X}^2)}$$

$$= \frac{71.550 - (6)(3.008)(3.50)}{91 - (6)(3.50^2)} = \frac{71.550 - 63.168}{91 - 73.500} = 0.479$$

Calculation of α (intercept)

$\alpha = \bar{Y} - \beta\bar{X} = 3.008 - (0.479)(3.50) = 1.332$

$Y_t = \$1.332 + \$0.479 X_t$

Bartley knows that 30 percent of its sales are cash sales, and the remaining are credit sales. The collection of sales made on credit is estimated to occur as follows: 42 percent of total sales are credit sales that will be collected in the month following the sale; the remaining 28 percent are credit sales that will be collected 2 months after the sales are made. For simplicity, we assume that there are no bad debts. In April, Bartley's sales are $430,000, of which $129,000 are for cash. In addition, Bartley expects to collect 28 percent of the sales made 2 months ago ($56,000), and 42 percent of last month's sales, for another $126,000. The operating cash inflows are estimated to be $311,000, which is substantially less than April's expected sales of $430,000. This difference is due to the delayed receipt of cash because of credit sales.

Table 25.3

Estimated Cash Inflows from Operations for Bartley Instruments (in thousands)

With a lag in the collection of accounts receivable, the cash inflow from sales ends up being less volatile than the sales pattern.

	February	March	April	May	June	July	August
1. Total sales	$200.00	$300.00	$430.00	$500.00	$440.00	$400.00	$300.00
2. Collections—1-month lag (42% of total sales)		84.00	126.00	180.60	210.00	184.80	168.00
3. Collections—2-month lag (28% of total sales)			56.00	84.00	120.40	140.00	123.20
4. Total collections (row 2 + row 3)			182.00	264.60	330.40	324.80	291.20
5. Cash sales (30% of total sales)			129.00	150.00	132.00	120.00	90.00
6. Total operating cash inflows			$311.00	$414.60	$462.40	$444.80	$381.20

Cash Outflow from Operations

Next comes the forecast of expected cash outflows from operations. This begins with an estimate of the materials and related supplies needed in the production process. For Bartley, this figure is estimated to be 40 percent of expected sales, with the purchases made 2 months ahead of the anticipated sale. Of these purchases, Bartley pays cash for 20 percent, and the other 80 percent becomes an account payable. Bartley has a policy of paying all accounts payable in the month after they arise. In April, Bartley has total purchases of $176,000 (0.40 times June's expected sales of $440,000), of which $35,200 are for cash (see Table 25.4). In addition, $160,000 in accounts payable from the preceding month must be paid. Bartley also has other cash outflows related to operations. For simplicity, these can be broken into three categories: The first is wages, rent, selling, and other cash outflows. The other two are interest and taxes. The reason for breaking out the last two separately is that they may vary from month to month. Income taxes are payable on the 15th of April, June, September, and December, whereas payroll and other taxes are payable monthly. Total expected cash outflows related to operations are $389,500 in April.

Other Cash Inflows or Outflows

Once all cash flows from operations are determined, we can turn our attention to other possible inflows or outflows. Bartley has two other expected inflows and three other expected outflows. The inflows are from the sale of assets and cash dividends received from a small foreign subsidiary. The outflows arise from the payment of cash dividends, repayment of a loan, and from capital investments. After all these other inflows

Table 25.4

Estimated Cash Outflows from Operations for Bartley Instruments (in thousands)

Many different classifications of cash outflows from operations can be employed. Which specific ones are most appropriate depends on the firm making the cash forecast.

	March	April	May	June	July	August
1. Total purchases (40% of expected sales; purchased 2 months ahead)	$200.00	$176.00	$160.00	$120.00	$100.00	$ 80.00
2. Credit purchases (80% of total purchases)	160.00	140.80	128.00	96.00	80.00	64.00
3. Payment of credit purchases (1-month lag)		160.00	140.80	128.00	96.00	80.00
4. Cash purchases (20% of current month's total purchases)		35.20	32.00	24.00	20.00	16.00
5. Wages, rent, selling, and other cash expenses*		146.30	186.00	188.80	168.00	145.50
6. Interest*		8.00	32.00	8.00	8.00	32.00
7. Taxes*		40.00	5.00	30.00	5.00	5.00
8. Total operating cash outflow (row 3 + row 4 + row 5 + row 6 + row 7)		$389.50	$395.80	$378.80	$297.00	$278.50

* As estimated by the firm based on past and expected trends.

and outflows are estimated, they are netted to produce the following monthly figures (in thousands):

	April	May	June	July	August
Net other inflow (+) or outflow (−)	−$45.00	−$98.00	−$55.00	−$95.00	$52.00

THE CASH BUDGET

Once we know all anticipated cash inflows and outflows, we can determine the expected net cash inflow or outflow each month to see if additional financing will be needed. As shown in the top part of Table 25.5, Bartley is projecting that total cash outflows will exceed total cash inflows by $123,500 in April. The bottom part of the table shows that Bartley has $70,000 cash on hand on April 1 and a minimum cash balance of $20,000 that it needs to maintain. This results in an estimated final cash position of −$73,500 at the end of April.

Table 25.5

Net Cash Flow and Financing Needed or Surplus Available for Bartley Instruments (in thousands)

Note that row 1 in the bottom part of the table, cash and marketable securities at the start of period, is carried over as the previous month's end-of-period cash figure from row 3.

	April	May	June	July	August
Calculating Net Cash Inflow or Outflow					
1. Total operating cash inflow	$311.00	$414.60	$462.40	$444.80	$381.20
2. Total operating cash outflow	− 389.50	− 395.80	− 378.80	− 297.00	− 278.50
3. Other net inflow (+) or outflow (−)	− 45.00	− 98.00	− 55.00	− 95.00	+ 52.00
4. Net cash inflow (+) or outflow (−) (row 1 + row 2 + row 3)	−$123.50	−$ 79.20	$ 28.60	$ 52.80	$154.70
Calculating Short-Term Financing Needed					
1. Cash and marketable securities at start of period	$ 70.00	−$ 53.50	−$132.70	−$104.10	−$ 51.30
2. Change in cash balance (net cash inflow or outflow)	− 123.50	79.20	28.60	52.80	154.70
3. Cash at end of period (row 1 + row 2)	− 53.50	− 132.70	− 104.10	− 51.30	103.40
4. Minimum cash balance required	− 20.00	− 20.00	− 20.00	− 20.00	− 20.00
5. Cumulative short-term financing needed (−) or surplus (+) (row 3 + row 4)	−$ 73.50	−$152.70	−$124.10	−$ 71.30	$ 83.40

In Table 25.5, we see that Bartley has a negative cumulative expected cash position for the months of April, May, June, and July. In August the expected cash position is positive. The worst month is May, when the cash position is estimated to be −$152,700. Obviously, Bartley must do something—cut production, reduce other expenses, increase collections, or secure short- or long-term financing to cover the expected shortfall. Armed with the information obtained from the cash budget, Bartley can plan for the future. If borrowing is planned, the lender can be notified and appropriate plans made. When excess cash is available, its investment can be planned. But the basis for borrowing or investment decisions is the firm's expected cash position as estimated by its cash budget.

Concept Review Questions

- Explain why the statement of cash flows is broken down into three basic categories.
- Discuss the procedures used to develop a firm's cash budget.
- Describe and explain different methods a firm may employ to forecast sales.

FORECASTING IN PRACTICE

SCENARIO ANALYSIS

Although forecasting techniques can be implemented by hand, most firms, large and small, are turning to computerized approaches, often employing spreadsheets like Lotus 1-2-3® or Excel. This forecasting process might involve the firm, and its divisions, preparing three different forecasts, or scenarios—a best case, a most likely (or normal) case, and a worst case.

Assume that the forecast and cash budget for Bartley Instruments that we developed in the last two sections was for the normal case. Then we need to develop a best-case scenario, along with a worst-case scenario. In forecasting the best-case scenario, we need to be aware of the problems caused by high growth. As firms grow, their sales increase. Because most firms sell on credit, at least in part, the firm will need to finance a larger amount of accounts receivable. Likewise, larger inventory levels will be necessary. As growth continues, the firm will need to expand its plant and facilities, requiring additional investment in long-term assets. The funding for some of these increased needs can be provided by increased accounts payable, which will also grow

---

Figure 25.3

Quarterly Sales for 12 Quarters

Visual examination of quarterly sales indicates an upward trend in sales and also suggests a seasonal pattern.

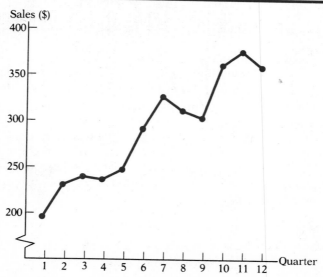

with the firm. The rest, however, has to come from two main sources—internally generated funds that are not paid out to the stockholders, and new external financing.

High rates of growth may put a firm in a cash bind. This occurs because it cannot finance the rapid cash needs with internally generated funds. As one step, most high-growth firms have low or zero cash dividend payouts. In addition, they build financial slack into the planning process. The ultimate solution to the cash needs of a growing firm is to acquire additional financing in the form of long-term debt, or additional common stock financing. However, many firms follow a "pecking order" approach to financing (see Chapters 12 and 13) and have a strong aversion to issuing additional common stock. In such a case, the growth of the firm may be constrained, or it may have to adopt a higher than desired debt/equity ratio. Thus, although growth is generally desirable, it places a strain on the cash needs of the firm that must be planned for. Failure to do so is one of the primary shortcomings of many growing firms.

Likewise, problems may arise if the worst-case scenario arises. In the worst case, both sales and cash inflows fall, but often cash outflows do not fall as fast. This is especially true if the firm has many fixed cash outflows (as opposed to variable cash outflows) that do not fall as sales and cash inflows fall. The net result may be that in the very short run problems are not too bad, but they get worse and worse unless the firm takes drastic actions to cut fixed cash outflows. Realistic forecasting of both the best- and worst-case scenarios may expose potential cash flow problems, but the causes and remedies are very different in the two cases.

SEASONALITY

One problem that often arises in practice is how to forecast for periods that are less than yearly intervals, during which the firm experiences seasonal patterns in its cash flows. Let's assume we have 12 quarters of past sales data as follows:

	1	2	3	4
Year −3	$X_1 = 193$	228	237	234
Year −2	245	289	324	309
Year −1	301	358	373	$X_{12} = 356$

(Note that the sales figure for the first quarter of year −3 is labeled X_1, and so on.) Our problem is to use the data from the 3 years to forecast the next 8 quarterly sales figures. We begin by plotting the data as in Figure 25.3. In looking at it, we see a definite upward trend in the sales data, and it appears there is some seasonality also.

First we employ linear regression to forecast sales for each of the next 8 quarters. The data are as follows:

Sales (Y_t)	Period (X_t)
$193	1
228	2
237	3
234	4
245	5
289	6
324	7
309	8
301	9
358	10
373	11
356	12

Employing the same approach discussed previously, we find that the resulting linear regression equation is

$$\text{sales} = \alpha + \beta X_t$$
$$= \$184.816 + \$15.759 X_t$$

Because we have 12 periods of data for estimating the regression equation, the forecasted sales, quarter-by-quarter for the next 8 periods (or 2 years), are:

Period	Forecasted Sales		
13	$184.816 +	$15.759(13) =	$390
14	184.816 +	15.759(14) =	405
15	184.816 +	15.759(15) =	421
16	184.816 +	15.759(16) =	437
17	184.816 +	15.759(17) =	453
18	184.816 +	15.759(18) =	468
19	184.816 +	15.759(19) =	484
20	184.816 +	15.759(20) =	500

Now we have obtained an estimate of future sales, but we have ignored seasonality. If we assume that past seasonal patterns are likely to continue, we can determine quarterly seasonal adjustment factors as follows:

STEP 1:   Determine a 4-quarter moving average for the first 4 actual observations. Note that because the number of observations is even, the average is for 2.5 quarters (halfway between quarter 2 and quarter 3).

STEP 2:   Move down one observation and determine a second 4-quarter moving average. That is, drop the first observation and pick up the fifth observation. This second 4-quarter moving average is centered halfway between quarters 3 and 4.

STEP 3:   Average the two consecutive 4-quarter moving averages from steps 1 and 2. This centered moving average is now correctly positioned at quarter 3.

STEP 4:   Repeat steps 1 through 3, moving down 1 observation at a time.

The resulting calculations for the 12 quarters are as follows:

Period	Actual Value (1)	4-Quarter Moving Average (2)	Centered 4-Quarter Moving Average (3)	Ratio of Actual to Centered 4-Quarter Moving Average (1)/(3) (4)
1	$193			
2	228			
		223.00		
3	237		229.500	1.033
		236.00		
4	234		243.625	0.960
		251.25		
5	245		262.125	0.935
		273.00		
6	289		282.375	1.023
		291.75		
7	324		298.750	1.085
		305.75		
8	309		314.375	0.983
		323.00		
9	301		329.125	0.915
		335.25		
10	358		341.125	1.049
		347.00		
11	373			
12	356			

Note that because we are using a 4-quarter moving average, it is impossible to calculate any seasonal indices (i.e., column 4 above) for the first 2 or the last 2 quarters.

The next step is to assign the seasonal indices to their respective quarters:

	\multicolumn{4}{c}{Quarter}				
	1	2	3	4	Total
Year −3			1.033	0.960	
Year −2	0.935	1.023	1.085	0.983	
Year −1	0.915	1.049			
Total	1.850	2.072	2.118	1.943	
Average	0.925	1.036	1.059	0.972	3.992

If we had more observations—at least five for each quarter—it would be helpful to drop the high and the low values (per quarter) at this point. Because we have only two, however, we will keep all the data. The sum of the average seasonal coefficients should total 4.000 because there are 4 quarters; instead, in this example it sums to only 3.992. To determine an adjusted quarterly seasonal index we proceed as follows:

	Adjusted Seasonal Index
Quarter 1:	$(0.925)(4.000/3.992) = 0.927$
Quarter 2:	$(1.036)(4.000/3.992) = 1.038$
Quarter 3:	$(1.059)(4.000/3.992) = 1.061$
Quarter 4:	$(0.972)(4.000/3.992) = 0.974$
Total	4.000

Using the adjusted seasonal indexes is easy: All we do is multiply the adjusted seasonal indexes times the previously estimated forecasts. The original and seasonally adjusted forecasted sales are as follows:

Period	Forecasted Sales Based on Linear Regression (1)	Season Adjustment Factor (2)	Seasonally Adjusted Forecasted Sales (1)(2) (3)
13	$390	0.927	$362
14	405	1.038	420
15	421	1.061	447
16	437	0.974	426
17	453	0.927	420
18	468	1.038	486
19	484	1.061	514
20	500	0.974	487

Figure 25.4

Fitted Regression Equation and Forecasted Quarterly Sales, With and Without Seasonal Adjustment

Adjusting for seasonality can materially increase or decrease per quarter sales as compared to a forecast based on simple linear regression.

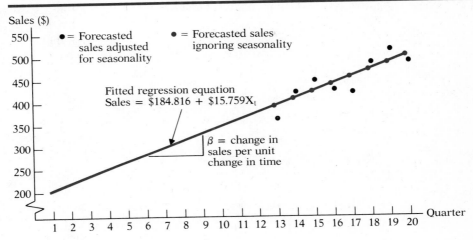

Because sales are seasonally higher in the second and third quarters, seasonally adjusting the simple linear regression forecasts results in substantially higher forecasted sales in those quarters, with lower forecasted sales in the first and fourth quarters. Both the unadjusted and seasonally adjusted forecasts are shown in Figure 25.4. Seasonally adjusting is very important in practice and improves many forecasts, provided there is some fairly consistent seasonal pattern to the firm's sales.[2]

INFLATION

Inflation can have a profound impact on the cash flows of the firm. The whole forecasting process must be reexamined in times of rapid changes in the inflation rate. Very different strategies may be necessary during periods of rapid inflation, because the firm may not be able (or want) to pass on the effects of inflation to its customers. The presence of inflation also causes suppliers of funds to change strategies to protect themselves from its effect. They may provide only variable rate financing, in which the interest rate charged on a bond or loan is adjusted over time. Many banks lend primarily on a variable rate basis. All these factors, and many more, make the cash flow estimation process more difficult. The consequence is to reduce the reliability of the

[2] The same basic procedures would be employed with monthly data, except 12-month moving averages are employed.

forecast, which makes close monitoring and evaluation of various scenarios even more important.

Effective management is enhanced by the development of cash budgets, which help managers plan and control. Once the cash budget is determined, many firms employ a **rolling forecast** that is updated every week, month, or quarter. But some care is in order. First, cash budgets were based on a set of specific assumptions—from the sales forecast on. Because events will differ in the future, the ability to do scenario analysis is essential. Second, cash needs may fluctuate *within* the budgeting period. Even though there may be plenty of cash on hand by the end of the period, different inflow and outflow patterns may leave the firm short of cash within the period.

Concept Review Questions

- Describe how to incorporate seasonal patterns in a firm's forecasted sales.
- What is the impact of inflation on a firm's forecasted sales?

PRO FORMA ACCOUNTING STATEMENTS

Pro forma statements project the firm's expected revenues, expenses, and position at the end of a forecast period.[3] Although less detailed than cash budgets, these forecasts are often required by current and prospective lenders. There are two basic approaches to developing pro forma statements:

1. One approach takes as its input the projections arising from the cash budget. These projections are then modified to account for differences between the firm's cash flows and its GAAP accounting data.

2. The second is the **percentage of sales method,** which starts with the historical relationship of sales to various income statement and balance sheet items. Pro forma statements and financing needs or surpluses are then estimated. This procedure may be naive if it assumes that all the firm's costs are variable and vary directly with sales. In practice, some costs are fixed; therefore, judgment is employed when estimating how some expenses are expected to change.

We use the percentage of sales method to estimate financing needs based on pro forma statements. Note that because pro forma statements start with accounting data, this method is not as precise as a cash budgeting approach to projecting cash flows and financing needs. However, its simplicity and its focus on the impact on reported accounting statements may make it a supplement to the more elaborate cash budgeting process. Also, banks often require pro forma statements as part of a loan agreement. We will use Smith Products, a manufacturer of specialty tools, to illustrate the use of pro forma statements. Smith begins by making its best estimate of next year's sales, which is $22 million. If sales are substantially higher or lower than the estimate, the pro forma statements will be off.

---

[3] Pro forma statements can also be constructed for some past time period. Comparison with actual past performance may best show the effect of some planned major event, such as a proposed merger or restructuring.

PRO FORMA INCOME STATEMENT

The next step is to estimate the historical relationship of expenses to sales for Smith. This is done by dividing Smith's income statement categories—cost of goods sold; selling, general, and administrative expenses; interest expenses; taxes; and cash dividends—by sales. If we use this information directly in a naive manner, Smith Products' estimated, or pro forma, income statement is as shown in Table 25.6. Based on this approach, Smith Products would expect net income to be $924,000; with projected cash dividends of $330,000, $594,000 would be shown as a transfer from the income statement to retained earnings on the firm's balance sheet.[4] The new retained earnings amount is equal to the previous years' retained earnings plus the amount transferred from the pro forma income statement.

After further analysis, Smith Products decides that all expenses and outflows will *not* vary directly with sales. Specifically, the firm estimates that the cost of goods sold will

Table 25.6

Present and Pro Forma Income Statement for Smith Products If Expenses Are Projected Naively Using a Strict Percentage of Sales Approach (in thousands)

This naive approach ignores fixed costs and often produces an estimate of net income that is biased low.

	Actual for Last Year	Basis of Projection	Pro Forma for Next Year
Sales	$20,000		$22,000
Cost of goods sold	13,500	Percentage of sales	14,850*
Gross margin	6,500		7,150
Selling, general, and administrative expenses	4,500	Percentage of sales	4,950
EBIT	2,000		2,200
Interest	600	Percentage of sales	660
EBT	1,400		1,540
Taxes (40%)	560	Historical tax rate	616
Net income	840		924
Cash dividends	300	Percentage of sales	330
Transferred to retained earnings	$ 540		$ 594

* $14,850 = ($22,000/$20,000)($13,500). The other percentage of sales estimates were calculated in the same manner.

[4] Because the naive approach assumes that all costs are variable, it generally produces an estimate of net income that is *biased low*. This results from ignoring the presence of fixed operating costs that are spread over more sales dollars as sales increase. However, if sales are decreasing and fixed operating costs are actually present, then the naive percentage of sales method produces an estimate of net income that is too high.

Table 25.7

Revised Pro Forma Income Statement for Smith Products Based on a Modified Percentage of Sales Method and Judgment (in thousands)

By taking account of fixed costs, Smith Products obtains a more realistic estimate of its expected net income.

	Basis of Projection	Pro Forma for Next Year
Sales		$22,000
Cost of goods sold	Judgment: 66% of sales	14,520
Gross margin		7,480
Selling, general, and administrative expreses	Judgment: 23% of sales	5,060
EBIT		2,420
Interest	Percentage of sales	660
EBT		1,760
Taxes (40%)	Historical tax rate	704
Net income		1,056
Cash dividends	Management forecast	350
Transferred to retained earnings		$ 706

be 66 percent of sales, that selling, general, and administrative expenses will be 23 percent of sales, and that cash dividends will be $350,000. The same interest of $660,000 and 40 percent tax rate will be assumed. Smith Products' revised pro forma income statement is shown in Table 25.7. This analysis shows that net income is expected to be $1.056 million, and the estimated amount transferred to retained earnings will be $706,000. With these estimates, we can now proceed to estimate the balance sheet and obtain a rough approximation of the financing needed to support this expected increase in sales.

PRO FORMA BALANCE SHEET AND FINANCING NEEDED

Smith's present balance sheet is given in Table 25.8, along with the projected asset and liability accounts, assuming most of them maintain their historical relationship to sales. Net long-term assets are projected based on the firm's current capital investment plan. Note that three items are not projected: Notes payable, long-term debt and lease obligations, and common stock are negotiated items that do not change as sales fluctuate. All other balance sheet items, except for net long-term assets and retained earnings, are assumed to change proportionally as sales change. Based on this procedure, Smith Products can obtain a rough estimate of its financing needs of $984,000.

This is calculated as follows:

Total assets	$16,000,000
Less: Total liabilities and stockholders' equity	15,016,000
Additional financing needed (or surplus available)	$ 984,000

Table 25.8

Forecast of Changes in Balance Sheet Items for Smith Products (in thousands)

In this example, judgment was used to estimate the long-term assets, and the naive percentage of sales method was used to forecast the other items.

	Actual for Last Year	Basis of Projection	Pro Forma for Next Year
Assets			
Cash	$ 400	Percentage of sales	$ 440*
Accounts receivable	2,100	Percentage of sales	2,310
Inventory	3,000	Percentage of sales	3,300
Total current	5,500		6,050
Net long-term assets	8,500	Judgment	9,950
Total assets	$14,000		$16,000
Liabilities and Stockholders' Equity			
Accounts payable	$ 1,300	Percentage of sales	$ 1,430
Notes payable	900	n.a.†	900
Accrued wages and taxes	1,200	Percentage of sales	1,320
Total current	3,400		3,650
Long-term debt and lease obligations	3,800	n.a.	3,800
Deferred taxes	600	Percentage of sales	660
Total long-term liabilities	4,400		4,460
Common stock and additional paid-in capital	3,000	n.a.	3,000
Retained earnings	3,200	Pro forma income statement	3,906‡
Total stockholders' equity	6,200		6,906
Total liabilities and stockholders' equity	$14,000	Total	15,016
		Additional needed	984
		Total to balance	$16,000

*$440 = ($400/$20,000)($22,000). The other percentage of sales estimates were calculated in the same manner.
† Not applicable.
‡ $3,200 from last year plus transfer to retained earnings of $706 from Table 25.7.

This figure, of course, assumes that the estimated increase in retained earnings is exactly equal to Smith's internally generated funds. In addition, it is based on maintaining the cash account at its forecasted level of $440,000.

A slight modification can be made if a firm plans to draw down its cash account to meet part of its needs. To illustrate, assume that Smith plans to draw its cash account down by $240,000. In that case, the financing needed is

Total assets	$16,000,000
Less: Total liabilities and stockholders' equity	15,016,000
Additional financing needed	984,000
Less: Cash drawn down	240,000
External financing needed	$ 744,000

Now, of course, Smith Products must decide how to finance the needed expansion. To illustrate the basic elements, assume that Smith decides to finance the total $984,000 by issuing $1 million in additional long-term debt.[5] As shown in the revised balance sheet in Table 25.9, this results in Smith's long-term debt and lease obligations account increasing by $1 million to $4.8 million, and the difference between the $984,000 needed and the $1 million obtained (i.e., $16,000) is added to the firm's

Table 25.9

Revised Pro Forma Balance Sheet for Smith Products (in thousands)

By increasing its ratio of total debt to total assets from 55.7 percent (Table 25.8) to 56.9 percent, Smith can meet the proposed increase without additional common equity financing.

Assets		Liabilities and Stockholders' Equity	
Cash	$ 456	Accounts payable	$ 1,430
Accounts receivable	2,310	Notes payable	900
Inventory	3,300	Accrued wages and taxes	1,320
Total current	6,066	Total current	3,650
Net long-term assets	9,950	Long-term debt and lease	
Total assets	$16,016	obligations	4,800
		Deferred taxes	660
		Total long-term liabilities	5,460
		Common stock and additional	
		paid-in capital	3,000
		Retained earnings	3,906
		Total stockholders' equity	6,906
		Total liabilities and	
		stockholders' equity	$16,016

[5] It issues $1 million instead of $984,000 due simply to rounding the financing off to the nearest million dollars.

cash account.[6] Obviously, other plans and many factors have to be considered when firms plan for the future.

Concept Review Questions

- What are two basic approaches to developing pro forma statements?
- Describe how to develop a pro forma income statement and balance sheet using the percentage of sales method.

FINANCIAL AND STRATEGIC PLANNING

The essence of planning is to ensure that the firm is following a dynamic policy that emphasizes the creation of value and avoids options that destroy value. Financial and strategic planning processes and models come in many sizes and shapes. In any model, however, there is an important relationship between the short- and long-run aspects. Consider Figure 25.5, which shows the relationships between a firm's short- and long-term cash flows. The firm is experiencing cash inflows and outflows during the current period. At the end of this period, the net inflow or outflow, plus the beginning cash balance, determines how much cash is available at the start of period 1. To emphasize the longer term aspects, firms may start with short-term cash budgets (e.g., monthly or quarterly) and then move to yearly cash budgets.

Figure 25.5

Relationship Between Short- and Long-Term Financial and Strategic Planning

In the short term, the emphasis is on quarterly cash flows. In the longer term, the emphasis is on the cumulative cash inflows or outflows and the financial and strategic aspects.

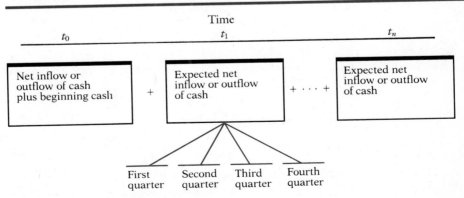

---

[6] Actually, the income statement should be reestimated to take into account additional interest above the existing $660,000 due to Smith's increasing its debt by $1 million. This would affect the size of the transfer to retained earnings. For simplicity, these secondary effects are ignored.

Long-term planning, in a sense, is just a continuation of the ideas discussed earlier for short-term planning. But there are some differences in emphasis. Consider Figure 25.6, which depicts the firm's long-term needs. Note that the long-term requirements depend on the amount of spontaneous short-term financing secured, along with the amount of short-term borrowing employed. Firms that adopt an aggressive short-term financial management strategy (as discussed in Chapter 19) will, other things being equal, need less long-term financing. Also, in the long run the firm's strategic plan, its ability to forecast accurately, and the need for flexibility all become more important than in the short run, although the basic emphasis remains the same.

The long-term approach begins by continuing what was done in the short term. Obviously, the further in the future, the less detail in the cash budget. Likewise, the further in the future, the more uncertainty concerning the projected cash flows. The longer-term cash budgets should reflect any anticipated expansion, replacement, or restructuring of the firm's assets. Then the sources of financing need to be evaluated. During the planning process the firm should consider various alternative plans and their possible consequences. An important part of the planning process involves consideration of the various options (to expand, delay or defer, abandon, and so forth) faced by the firm. Whatever the final plan adopted, the important point to remember is that financial planning forces the firm to consider its goals and needs in advance. By doing so, firms can consider all of the options available to them, ensure their flexibility, and keep attention focused on the goal of maximizing the market value of the firm.

Figure 25.6

How Short- and Long-Term Financing Meet a Firm's Needs

Spontaneous short-term financing (through accounts payable, factoring of receivables, and continuous inventory loans) meets part of the firm's cumulative financing needs (as represented by the solid wavy line). The rest are met by short-term borrowings and long-term financing.

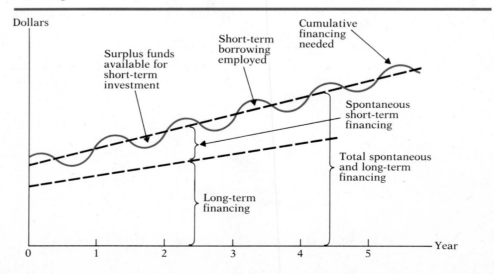

Concept Review Questions

■ How are short-term and long-term financial planning models related?

■ What is the main goal of establishing a financial and strategic planning model?

KEY POINTS

1. The statement of cash flows, which is required to be presented along with an income statement and balance sheet, records the firm's past flow of cash. Due to the use of the indirect approach to presenting the statement of cash flows, which is employed by most firms, the information is not as useful as it could be.

2. Cash budgeting, perhaps supplemented by pro forma analysis, is the main method of forecasting cash flows and financing needs or excesses. Accurate forecasting of sales is most important when making any kind of financial projections.

3. In practice, firms employ scenario analysis, find ways to deal with seasonality, and deal with inflation when making cash forecasts.

4. Financial and strategic planning is a trial-and-error activity that does not attempt to minimize risk. Rather, it is the process of deciding which risks to take and which are not worth taking. Throughout the planning process all of the options available to the firm must be continually considered, or employed as the frame of reference, in order to make effective financial management decisions.

QUESTIONS

25.1 Explain both the advantages and disadvantages of the statement of cash flows in terms of providing useful cash flow information.

25.2 Explain the various components of a firm's cash budget. How can sales be estimated? Why may a cash budget not be sufficient for planning *within* a given period?

25.3 What are the strengths and weaknesses of and the differences between the cash budget and the percentage of sales method of forecasting future cash flows?

25.4 Gates Electronics is considering making the following policy changes. In each case, indicate whether *in the next period* the move will provide more cash inflows and/or reduce outflows (+), provide more outflows and/or reduce inflows (−), or have an indeterminate or no effect (0).

a. The firm becomes more socially responsible.   _____
b. Increased competition is leading to price cutting and increased promotional
   expenses.   _____
c. The firm decides to sell only for cash; previously some sales had been on credit. _____
d. By shifting to more debt, the firm expects its return on equity to increase.   _____
e. The firm decides to change its inventory method from one GAAP method to
   another GAAP method.   _____
f. The firm's dividend payout ratio is reduced.   _____
g. Congress changes the tax laws, resulting in longer depreciation lives for tax
   purposes.   _____

25.5 What are the differences between short-run and long-run financial and strategic planning?

25.6 Explain how the firm's decision about financing temporary assets with temporary liabilities relates to planning.

25.7 How would you go about distinguishing *after the fact* between good and bad financial and strategic planning versus good or bad luck?

CONCEPT REVIEW PROBLEMS

See Appendix A for solutions.

CR25.1 Samson is attempting to predict sales for the next 3 years using linear regression. What are the expected sales in the next 3 years?

Year	Sales (Y_t) (millions)
−4	$10.0
−3	10.0
−2	10.5
−1	11.5
0	13.0

CR25.2 After reviewing your predicted sales for the next 3 years from CR25.1, the CFO decided it is important to incorporate seasonality effects into the sales estimates. Quarterly sales for Samson for the past 3 years are given below. Based on these 3 years of data estimate quarterly sales for the next 8 quarters.

Year	Quarterly Sales (in millions)			
	1	2	3	4
−2	$2.35	$2.50	$2.90	$2.75
−1	2.60	2.75	3.15	3.00
0	2.85	3.15	3.65	3.35

CR25.3 Bluestar Electronics has sales for November and December of $165,000 and $175,000, respectively. Estimated sales are:

January	$220,000	May	$200,000
February	275,000	June	175,000
March	250,000	July	150,000
April	230,000	August	150,000

The firm makes 20 percent of its sales for cash, 50 percent are on credit and collected 1 month after the sale, and 30 percent are on credit and collected 2 months after the sale (assume there are no bad debts). Material costs are 20 percent of projected sales 2 months hence, and labor is 50 percent of next months estimated sales. Bluestar typically pays for 25 percent of the materials 2 months prior to the sale and for 75 percent of the materials 1 month prior to the sale. Labor costs are paid 1 month prior to the sale. The estimated administrative expenses are $25,000 per month. The firm anticipates paying $50,000 in taxes in the months of March and June and will pay $30,000 in interest in both January and April. It will have a $150,000 cash outflow in May for new equipment. The minimum desired cash balance is $70,000; that is the beginning balance in January. Prepare a cash budget for the months of January through June and indicate the per month cumulative short-term financing needed (−) or surplus (+).

CR25.4   Boston Manufacturing has the following balance sheet and income statement. The firm estimates sales will increase by 10 percent next year. All income statement and balance sheet items are assumed to be a function of sales except long-term assets, short- and long-term debt, common stock, and dividends paid. These entries will remain constant, except for long-term assets which will increase to $40, and taxes which will be $8. Using the percentage of sales method, develop a pro forma income statement and a balance sheet for Boston Manufacturing. Will the firm need outside financing to support the 10 percent growth?

Balance Sheet
(in millions)

Assets

Cash and marketable securities	$ 5
Accounts receivable	20
Inventory	18
Long-term assets	27
Total assets	$70

Liabilities and Stockholders' Equity

Short-term bank loan	$ 9
Accounts payable	11
Accruals	10
Long-term debt	15
Common stock	10
Retained earnings	15
Total liabilities and stockholders' equity	$70

Income Statement
(in millions)

Net sales	$40
Cost of goods sold	10
Gross margin	30
Selling and administrative expenses	10
EBIT	20
Interest	2
EBT	18
Taxes	7
Net income	11
Cash dividends	3
Transferred to retained earnings	$ 8

PROBLEMS

25.1 The statement of cash flows for Amoco Corp. for 3 recent years was as follows (in millions):

	-2	-1	0
Cash Flows from Operating Activities			
Net income	$1,953	$ 747	$1,360
Depreciation, depletion, amortization, and			
retirements and abandonments	2,059	2,418	2,295
Decrease (increase) in receivables	(73)	672	(197)
Decrease (increase) in inventories	17	75	(34)
Increase (decrease) in payables and accrued liabilities	159	(1,367)	331
Deferred taxes and other items	603	297	257
Net cash provided by operating activities	$4,718	$2,842	$4,012
Cash Flows from Investing Activities			
Capital expenditures	(3,881)	(2,256)	(2,332)
Proceeds from distribution of property	185	97	129
Distribution of cash of Cyprus Minerals Co.	(23)	–	–
New investments and advances	(42)	(192)	(42)
Proceeds from sale of investments	25	131	119
Other	(11)	(32)	141
Net cash used in investing activities	$(3,747)	$(2,252)	$(1,985)
Cash Flows from Financing Activities			
New long-term obligations	334	1,153	3
Repayment of long-term obligations	(375)	(979)	(259)
Cash dividends paid	(872)	(849)	(847)
Issuances of common stock	127	161	603
Acquisitions of common stock	(937)	(363)	(443)
Increase (decrease) in short-term obligations	324	(263)	(9)
Net cash used in financing activities	$(1,399)	$(1,140)	$(952)
Increase (decrease) in cash and marketable securities	(428)	(55)	1,075
Cash and marketable securities—beginning of year	1,419	991	441
Cash and marketable securities—end of year	$ 991	$ 441	$1,516

Supplemental Cash Flow Information
The effect of foreign currency exchange fluctuations on total cash and marketable securities balances was not significant. Net cash provided by operating activities reflects cash payments for interest and income taxes as follows:

	-2	-1	0
Interest paid	$ 459	$408	$398
Income taxes paid	1,368	877	861

a. Analyze the firm's financial performance for the 3 years and comment on the primary sources of cash, the primary uses of cash, and any apparent trends. How else (in terms of a general approach) could the operating section of the statement be constructed?

b. What else would you like to know that is not reflected or apparent on Amoco's statement of cash flows?

25.2 Sales data for the last 7 years are as follows:

Year	Sales
1	$ 470
2	800
3	1,080
4	1,350
5	1,535
6	1,705
7	1,831

a. Calculate the slope, β, and intercept, α, and then predict sales for years 8, 9, and 10.
b. Plot (using graph paper) your estimated regression equation and the forecasted values for years 8, 9, and 10. Then plot the actual sales data for years 1 through 7. What conclusions can you draw about the growth in past sales and the estimated sales for years 8, 9, and 10?

25.3 J. C. Penney's revenue (in millions) for 5 recent years are shown below:

1	$11,353	4	$12,078
2	11,860	5	13,451
3	11,414		

a. Based on linear regression, forecast revenue for year 6.
b. How close is this to actual year 6 revenue of $14,146?
c. Based on actual revenue for years 1 through 6, plus actual revenue for years 7, 8, and 9 of $15,151, $15,747, and $15,296, respectively, forecast year 10 revenue.
d. How close is this to actual year 10 revenue of $16,405? What does this suggest about the use of linear regression for forecasting Penney's revenue for this time period?

25.4 Richmond Products has forecast its cash flows for the next 2 months as follows:

	First Month	Second Month
Total operating cash inflow	$210 million	$150 million
Total operating cash outflow	− 140 million	− 135 million
Other net inflow (+) or outflow (−)	− 30 million	− 90 million

Richmond's beginning cash balance is $15 million, and its minimum cash balance is $10 million. Determine Richmond's cumulative financing needed (−) or surplus (+) for both months.

25.5 Sydney & Sons is in the process of developing its cash budget for the months of January, February, March, and April. Twenty percent of sales are for cash; 50 percent of total sales are for credit and collected the next month. The remaining 30 percent are for credit and collected in 2 months. There are no bad debts.

Purchases of raw materials are made in the month prior to the expected sale and average 45 percent of expected sales. They are paid for in the month following their purchase. Wages, rent, and selling expenses are $300,000 in January and will increase by $50,000 per month. Interest of $25,000 is payable every month. Taxes of $75,000 are payable in January, and $150,000 is due in April. Cash dividends of $100,000 are payable in February. Finally, capital expenditures of $200,000 are forecast for January, and another $50,000 are expected in April.

Actual sales for November and December and forecasted sales for the next 5 months are as follows:

November	$1,000,000	March	$1,800,000
December	900,000	April	2,300,000
January	1,000,000	May	2,500,000
February	1,400,000		

Cash on hand on January 1 is $100,000, and a $50,000 minimum cash balance is required each month.

a. Prepare a cash budget for January, February, March, and April.
b. What is the maximum level of short-term financing required?
c. Suppose that sales receipts come in uniformly over the month, but all outflows are paid by the 10th of the month. Discuss the effect this would have on the cash budget. Would the cash budget just completed be valid? If not, what could be done to adjust the budget?
d. Now suppose Sydney & Sons reestimates its forecasted sales as follows:

January	$ 800,000	April	$1,900,000
February	1,100,000	May	2,200,000
March	1,500,000		

What is the effect of this on Sydney & Sons' cash budget in (a)? What is the maximum level of short-term financing now required?

25.6 The Shapiro Company is preparing plans for the next 6 months. The firm's special concern is a $2.5 million note that comes due in September. Sales (actual for May and June, and forecast for the rest) are as follows:

May	$3,400,000	October	$1,800,000
June	3,500,000	November	1,500,000
July	4,000,000	December	1,400,000
August	2,500,000	January	1,500,000
September	2,000,000		

Sales are 10 percent for cash, 75 percent credit collected in the next month, and 15 percent credit collected in 2 months. There are no bad debts. Purchases of raw materials are made as follows: 20 percent of sales 2 months ahead, paid in the month following the purchase; and 30 percent of sales expected 1 month ahead, paid in the month following the purchase. Wages, selling, and administrative expenses are estimated to be as follows:

July	$1,000,000	October	$700,000
August	900,000	November	700,000
September	800,000	December	700,000

In addition, there are lease payments of $100,000 per month. Interest payments on long-term borrowing of $300,000 in both August and November are required. Taxes of $325,000 are payable in September and December. Finally, there is the short-term note of $2,500,000 payable in September. There are no cash dividends or other inflows or outflows. Shapiro's beginning cash balance is $430,000 on July 1, and its required minimum balance is $400,000.

a. Prepare a monthly cash budget for the last 6 months of the year.
b. Will Shapiro be able to pay off the $2,500,000 note in full and on time?
c. Suppose that due to a recession sales fall off, but production does not decline as rapidly. Also, customers take longer to pay their bills. What effect might these changes have on Shapiro's ability to repay the note?

25.7 Columbia Precision Products has forecast its cash flows for the next year as follows:

	First Quarter	Second Quarter	Third Quarter	Fourth Quarter
Total operating cash inflow	$175	$195	$220	$200
Total operating cash outflow	− 140	− 180	− 120	− 120
Other net inflow or outflow	− 50	− 90	− 60	− 30

a. Determine Columbia's net cash inflow or outflow per quarter and its cumulative short-term financing needs by quarter, if its beginning cash balance is $25 and its minimum cash balance is $15.
b. What is the maximum amount of short-term financing needed? In what quarter does it occur?
c. Ignoring any costs of short-term financing, is Columbia as well off at the end of the year as at the beginning?
d. The effective before-tax costs of alternative short-term financing sources are given below. Which one would be chosen? Is there any reason why the cheapest source might not be chosen?

Bank line of credit	16%	Accounts receivable loan	13%
Inventory loan	15	Factoring receivables	18
Stretching payables	20	Commercial paper (six months)	12

25.8   North Bay Limited has quarterly sales data for the past 3 years as follows:

	Quarter			
	1	2	3	4
Year −3	300	275	295	370
Year −2	325	285	320	405
Year −1	365	325	360	440

a.   Estimate a regression equation based on these 12 quarters of data.
b.   Using the regression estimates calculated in (a), forecast the next 8 quarters (ignoring any potential seasonality).
c.   Based on the 4-quarter moving average approach, determine adjusted quarterly seasonal indexes.
d.   Using the forecasted sales from (b) and the adjusted seasonal indexes from (c), determine the seasonally adjusted forecasted sales for the next 8 quarters. How much, on average, does adjusting for seasonality increase or decrease sales for the first quarter, second quarter, third quarter, and fourth quarter?

25.9   Blakeslee's condensed income statement as of December 31 is:

	(in millions)
Sales	$4,841.4
Operating expenses	4,333.5
Income from operations	507.9
+ Other income	37.9
EBIT	545.8
Interest	180.7
EBT	365.1
Taxes	83.5
Net income	$ 281.6

a.   If we had perfect foresight and knew next year's sales were going to be $5,432.2 million, estimate next year's income statement employing the percentage of sales method.
b.   What differences exist between your pro forma income statement and Blakeslee's actual income statement for the year, listed below?

	(in millions)
Sales	$5,432.2
Operating expenses	4,823.7
Income from operations	608.5
+ Other income	70.0
EBIT	678.5
Interest	185.9
EBT	492.6
Taxes	124.9
Net income	$ 367.7

c.   Do you believe some of these differences could be anticipated to obtain a more accurate pro forma income statement? Why or why not?

25.10   Franklin Company's estimated sales for next year are $30 million. The percentage of sales for items that vary directly with sales for Franklin is given below:

Cash	5%	Accounts payable	15%
Accounts receivable	25	Accruals	10
Inventory	30	Net profit margin	5

Its net long-term assets are $6 million, notes payable are $2 million, long-term debt is $2 million, and common stock is $5 million. Franklin's present retained earnings are $5.1 million, and its dividend payout ratio is 40 percent.

a.   Prepare a pro forma balance sheet and indicate the estimated amount of additional financing needed. Assume that long-term debt will be used to finance any shortfall.

b.   What happens if Franklin's sales are $40 million and its long-term assets increase to $8 million? If long-term debt is used, how does the ratio of total debt to total assets in (b) compare with the same ratio for (a)?

25.11   El Rancho has decided to embark on a rapid expansion. Its most recent income statement and balance sheet are as follows:

Income Statement
(in millions)

Sales	$30.0
Cost of goods sold	15.0
Selling, general, and administrative expenses	6.0
EBIT	9.0
Interest	1.0
EBT	8.0
Taxes (30%)	2.4
Net income	5.6
Cash dividends	3.0
Transferred to retained earnings	$ 2.6

Balance Sheet
(in millions)

Current assets	$ 6.0	Accounts payable	$ 2.0
Long-term assets	14.0	Note payable	2.0
Total assets	$20.0	Long-term debt	6.0
		Common stock	3.0
		Retained earnings	7.0
		Total liabilities and stockholders' equity	$20.0

In attempting to determine its financial condition and needs, El Rancho believes the following will happen:

Sales	$40.0
Cost of goods sold	Same percent of sales as current year
Selling, general, and administrative expenses	$ 9.0
Interest	$ 1.0 (initially, before additional financing)
Taxes	Same percent of EBT as current year
Cash dividends	$ 3.0 (initially)
Current assets	$ 7.0
Long-term assets	$23.0
Accounts payable	$ 3.0
Notes payable	$ 2.0
Long-term debt	$ 6.0 (initially)
Common stock	$ 3.0

a. Based on these estimates, prepare a pro forma income statement and balance sheet for El Rancho. How much additional financing (regardless of where it comes from) do you estimate the firm needs?

b. What happens if El Rancho acquires sufficient additional long-term debt financing to keep its ratio of total debt to total assets at its original level? Assume interest expenses increase by $500,000.

c. By cutting its cash dividends in addition to the step taken in (b), can El Rancho finance all its cash needs? What do you think will happen to the market price of El Rancho's common stock if it cuts cash dividends? Do you see any alternative means of raising the needed funds?

25.12   Jamaica Minerals is planning to meet its long-term needs. To arrive at its needs, it has come up with the following estimates:

			Year		
	1	2	3	4	5
Net cash inflow (+) or outflow (−) before short-term financing cash flows	$20	−$15	−$30	−$60	−$10
Short-term financing cash flows	− 3	− 4	− 4	− 6	− 2
Total cash inflow (+) or outflow (−)	$17	−$19	−$34	−$66	−$12

Jamaica's beginning cash balance is $30. The minimum cash balance is $15 in years 1 and 2, $20 in year 3, and $25 in years 4 and 5. Prepare a year-by-year statement to show the maximum amount of long-term financing Jamaica will need.

25.13   Tate Systems is completing its long-run planning process. As a part of this, it has estimated the following needs for long-term funds and the amount it expects to provide out of internally generated equity funds:

			Year		
	1	2	3	4	5
Long-term financing needed per period	$5	$20	$15	$30	$43
To be provided by internally generated equity funds per period	− 6	− 7	− 7	− 8	− 10
To be raised externally (+) or surplus (−) per period	−$1	$13	$ 8	$22	$33

Tate's present capital structure contains $40 in debt and $60 in common equity. A primary goal when raising long-term capital is to remain as close as possible to this percentage target capital structure. Either long-term debt or common stock can be issued in amounts of $15 each. (*Note:* It is okay if Tate raises too much long-term capital in any period and those funds are carried forward to the next year, but it cannot have a shortfall. That is, Tate cannot borrow on a short-term basis to cover any shortfall in long-term capital.)

a.   Determine in which years Tate needs to secure additional long-term financing.
b.   Indicate, by year, whether long-term debt or common stock should be issued. (Remember that the additional internally generated funds each year are added to the firm's equity base.)
c.   What is the resulting capital structure at the end of year 5 and the ratio of total debt to total assets?

25.14   Mini Case   You have been on the job for a month as an analyst in the finance department of Playmore Enterprises. Every 3 months the firm plans for the next year and also assesses the firm's long-run financial strategy. The current planning process has been assigned to you to complete, after which it will be reviewed, and modified as needed, by the divisional vice president and other senior management.

a.   As a first step you have gathered the last 3 years' statements of cash flows. In brief, they are as follows:

	Year		
	−2	**−1**	**0**
Operating Activities			
Net income	$200	$245	$240
Depreciation	45	65	75
Other	(100)	50	180
	145	360	495
Investing Activities	(90)	(175)	(160)
Financing Activities			
Net change in debt	150	(200)	(50)
Dividends paid	(50)	(60)	(70)
	100	(260)	(120)
Net increase (decrease) in cash and marketable securities	155	(75)	215
Cash and marketable securities at beginning of the year	80	235	160
Cash and marketable securities at the end of the year	$235	$160	$375

What is the purpose of the statement of cash flows? In what format does Playmore Enterprises present its statement? What can we determine about Playmore from its statement of cash flows?

b. In order to develop a 4-quarter cash budget, you decide to estimate sales based on linear regression. Sales for the past 8 quarters are as follows:

Quarter	Sales
−7	$500
−6	525
−5	520
−4	580
−3	580
−2	560
−1	590
0	610

Based on linear regression, what are estimated sales for the next 4 quarters? Are there other factors that need to be taken into consideration when forecasting sales? Also, without actually doing it, how would you adjust for seasonality?

c. In order to develop its cash budget, Playmore has made the following estimates: Forty percent of sales are for cash, 40 percent are credit and collected in the following quarter, and 20 percent are credit and collected in 2 quarters. There are no bad debts. Purchases are made in the quarter prior to the expected sales and average 35 percent of expected sales. They are paid in the quarter following their purchase. The other estimates have been made as follows:

	Year			
	1	2	3	4
Salaries	$100	$105	$105	$115
Selling, general, and administrative expenses	125	130	125	130
Interest	60	40	40	30
Taxes	20	20	20	20
Capital expenditures	50	130	80	70
Repay debt	100	−	100	20
Dividends	30	30	35	35

The present level of cash on hand should be taken from part (a), above, and past and projected sales are given in (b). The minimum cash balance is $80. Develop the firm's cash budget for the next 4 quarters. What does your analysis indicate?

d. In addition to the projected cash budget, you are considering preparing pro forma financial statements. What is the basic procedure employed in preparing pro forma statements? What are their strengths? Their weaknesses?

e. In preparing your report, what still remains?

REFERENCES

Cash flow, and its usefulness, is discussed in:

AZIZ, ABDUL, and GERALD H. LAWSON. "Cash Flow Reporting and Financial Distress Models: Testing of Hypotheses." *Financial Management* 18 (Spring 1989): 55–63.

DRTINA, RALPH E., and JAMES A. LARGAY. "Pitfalls in Calculating Cash Flow from Operations." *Accounting Review* 60 (April 1985): 314–26.

GENTRY, JAMES A., PAUL NEWBOLD, and DAVID T. WHITFORD. "Profiles of Cash Flow Components." *Financial Analysts Journal* 46 (July-August 1990): 41–48.

For some information on economic and sales forecasts, see:

BERNSTEIN, PETER L., and THEODORE H. SILBERT. "Are Economic Forecasters Worth Listening To?" *Harvard Business Review* 62 (September-October 1984): 32–40.

GEORGOFF, DAVID M., and ROBERT G. MURDICK. "Manager's Guide to Forecasting." *Harvard Business Review* 64 (January-February 1986): 110–20.

For some examples of the effects of alternative financial strategies, see:

COOPER, KERRY, and R. MALCOLM RICHARDS. "Investing the Alaskan Project Cash Flows: The Sohio Experience." *Financial Management* 17 (Summer 1988): 58–70.

CORNELL, BRADFORD, and ALAN C. SHAPIRO. "Financing Corporate Growth." *Journal of Applied Corporate Finance* 1 (Summer 1988): 6–22.

DONALDSON, GORDON. "Financial Goals and Strategic Consequences." *Harvard Business Review* 63 (May-June 1985): 56–66.

MICHEL, ALLEN, and ISRAEL SHAKED. "Airline Performance Under Deregulation: The Shareholders' Perspective." *Financial Management* 13 (Summer 1984): 5–14.

Additional Financial Management Decisions

EXECUTIVE INTERVIEW

David Ellis
Assistant Treasurer
Sara Lee Corporation

Best known for frozen baked goods, Sara Lee Corporation also markets brand-name apparel. We asked Mr. Ellis to explain Sara Lee's strategies for expansion through acquisitions.

Our mission at Sara Lee is to be a premier consumer packaged goods company with globally recognized brands. To achieve our mission, we emphasize two major corporate strategies: margin improvement through profitable growth, and global expansion.

Sara Lee has been in the acquisition mode almost since our predecessor company was formed in 1940, and over the years, we've owned companies in diverse industries. Our current Chairman and CEO, John Bryan, recognized the need to focus on several core groups. We started to sell businesses that didn't fit. With branded consumer packaged goods as the unifying element, we concentrated on two major areas: packaged foods and branded apparel. Most of our apparel lines are frequently purchased, basic-needs items.

Acquisitions at Sara Lee	For example, we became a leader in the hosiery market with the acquisition of Hanes in 1979; since then we have increased our worldwide market share with the purchase of several foreign hosiery brands. We have also applied a "mega-branding" strategy to Hanes, using the Hanes brand name for related product lines such as activewear.

If a proposed acquisition fits our strategic focus, we look at it from a financial viewpoint. If there is an economic justification and some operating synergy—being able to use our distribution network, for example—then we perform a discounted cash flow analysis. Good assumptions are critical to this analysis, which is basically another type of capital budgeting decision. Once we develop a base case, we use sensitivity analysis to look at other scenarios.

International Acquisitions and Planning	Sara Lee has had an international presence since about 1962, when we acquired Jonker Fris (a Dutch food processor), and we continue to expand our global operations, primarily through acquisitions. Europe is our first priority because of the market size. We are also expanding our presence in Asia and Latin America, two markets with excellent growth potential. Our goal is to move into newly developing markets, where consumers are eager to buy the brand-name products we sell. For example, we were among the first companies to move into Central Europe. In general, we're not afraid to be trailblazers in situations like this—it's part of our corporate culture—and we take advantage of market opportunities as they arise.

We build our presence in a country by acquiring leading local brands that consumers already like and then expanding them. We find that works better than trying to bring in a new brand. Our strategy is to maintain the acquired brand's identity and increase the manufacturing, distribution, and marketing resources available to it.

Our acquisition analysis for international and for U.S. companies is similar. After we complete the basic financial analysis of an overseas acquisition, we also consider funds remitted to the United States. Each country has different laws governing how funds may be taken out of the country, and we may not be allowed to repatriate all of the desired funds. However, for decision-making purposes, we assume that we will bring the cash back into the United States. We also take into account the various taxes that might have to be paid on those dividends.

We look at cash flow in local currencies, using local inflation rates. Then we convert the cash flow into dollars, based on a differential between the countries' inflation rates. We compare the resulting return in U.S. dollars to a U.S. hurdle rate based on a current cost of capital; both figures include estimates of U.S. inflation. We use the same cost of capital for both domestic and international acquisitions; if we did not, we would have methodological problems in determining hurdle rates for different countries.

We adjust expected cash flows to take into account the riskiness of international acquisitions. Here we must use our best judgment to estimate whether we will achieve certain levels of cash flow. If there were a chance of expropriation or political turmoil, we probably wouldn't look at the project in the first place.

A primary concern for any company with major international operations is managing its foreign currency exposure risk. Fluctuations in foreign exchange rates can significantly affect earnings and stock price. If you accept the view that the market dislikes downward surprises and may overly penalize you for them, then it makes sense for a company to reduce that source of earnings variability by hedging at least some of the foreign income. We don't hedge all currencies because some of them aren't worth the cost. We look at each one on a case-by-case basis, depending on the costs of hedging as well as on the importance of that currency to our total income stream. Management must decide whether to accept the risk of currency fluctuations or to pay the cost, which can be high, to reduce volatility.

We use several hedging techniques, including forward exchange contracts and currency swaps. We focus mostly on European currencies. For example, we have used swaps to convert U.S. dollar- and Swiss franc-denominated debt into Dutch guilder-denominated debt. In all cases you have to look at the economic ramifications, the accounting ramifications, and the tax ramifications. You can't look just at the economics. Companies may choose not to take certain actions because the accounting consequences are a lot worse than the perceived economic insurance.

Other areas of financial management are affected by operating multinationally. Just as with international acquisitions, we evaluate capital expenditures based on strategic fit and discounted cash flow of the remitted funds. Working capital management is pretty similar for international and domestic operations, in terms of what we want to accomplish: to maximize payables and minimize receivables. However, the payment terms will be different, and in most countries the financial systems are less efficient than in the United States. In terms of financing overseas operations, the decision to use some local debt depends entirely on the particular country and the markets at the time. Most everything involved in international operations has to be done on a case-by-case basis, which makes the decisions particularly challenging.

*I*nstead of focusing on the firm's micro, or area-by-area, decisions, in this part we shift the emphasis to macro decisions, which affect the firm as a whole. Three important aspects of financial management are examined—mergers and corporate restructuring (Chapter 26), international financial management (Chapter 27), and managing foreign exchange risk (Chapter 28).

26

Mergers and Corporate Restructuring

EXECUTIVE SUMMARY

Firms both acquire and dispose of assets and take other actions that revolve around the control of assets. This area is often referred to as the market for corporate control. In addition to acquiring assets internally through their capital investment decisions, firms also acquire assets externally via mergers and acquisitions. Although many reasons are advanced to justify a merger, there are two primary benefits to be derived: The first and most important is the expected economies, or synergism. A second is that in some cases there may be tax advantages that make merging desirable.

A merger is another capital budgeting problem. To assess its economic desirability, managers must estimate the incremental expected cash inflows and outflows related to the merger. These projected net cash inflows are then discounted at the appropriate opportunity cost of capital and added to the current market value of the target firm. Then the cost, which differs depending on whether cash or stock is used, is determined. Once the costs are subtracted from the benefits, the NPV of the acquisition has been determined.

Numerous complexities exist in practice. Through it all, it is important to remember that mergers are simply one way, and not necessarily the most effective way, to contribute to the goal of maximizing the value of the firm.

Many defensive tactics can be employed by potential target firms. These consist of both preoffer and postoffer defenses. All have the goal of keeping the firm independent, or, if the firm is acquired, making sure the target's shareholders maximize their value.

Corporate restructurings are based on a two-pronged emphasis—recognition of corporate "fit" and maximizing NPV. Some typical restructuring activities involve leveraging up, using leveraged buyouts to go private, limited partnerships, voluntary restructuring, spinoffs, and divestitures. All focus on value creation and a better alignment of the interests of management with those of the firm's stockholders.

871

THE MARKET FOR CORPORATE CONTROL

Over time, firms can grow or shrink. Corporate restructuring is one of the most controversial and widely analyzed areas in financial management today. As depicted in Figure 26.1, it includes the acquisition of other firms (or portions of firms), defensive tactics that are designed to maximize the value of the firm, and restructuring the assets or liabilities of the firm. In recent years, this area has become known as the **market for corporate control,** in which various management teams vie for the right to acquire and manage corporate assets and activities. The whole practice of financial management has undergone a dramatic shift in emphasis. Managers are more concerned now than ever before with maximizing the market value of the firm. Critics contend that all this emphasis on value creation has wasted management time and effort by drawing it away from the main operating activities of the firm. They also argue that it has eroded the competitive position (and research and development emphasis) of affected businesses. Supporters are quick to point out that the developments in the market for corporate control have increased the efficiency of the resource allocation process by reducing waste and the misuse of corporate free cash flows and assets.

To better understand the issues, we focus first on acquisitions by examining sources of potential gains and how to value them, along with some procedural issues. Our focus is from the standpoint of the **bidding firm.** The company it seeks to acquire is the **target firm.** Even though there are different legal means of accomplishing an

Figure 26.1

Market for Corporate Control

The market for corporate control involves widely divergent activities including expansion via a merger or tender offer, defensive tactics of many types, and restructuring via leveraging up, going private and leveraged buyouts, limited partnerships, voluntary restructuring, spinoffs, and even the divestiture of part of the firm's assets.

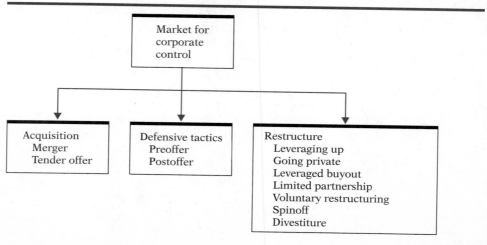

acquisition, we will refer to any acquisition of another firm, or the division of another firm, as a **merger.** It's important to keep in mind, however, that many acquisitions are accomplished via *tender offers.* In a tender offer, cash is often offered by the bidding firm directly to the shareholders of the target firm. Often the management of the target firm is not consulted before the tender offer is made.

The level of corporate restructuring activity in the United States is not constant over time; instead, there are fluctuations in activity that are generally related to stock prices and economic activity. Table 26.1 shows the level of corporate restructuring activity for the 1982–1992 period. During this period, activity rose until 1986, after which it declined somewhat. The data indicate that foreign firms were fairly active in acquiring U.S. firms or assets (9.3% of all transactions) and that U.S.-based firms also were acquiring foreign firms or assets (6.5% of all transactions). The data also indicate that almost 39 percent of the transactions involved one firm divesting some of its assets while another firm acquired the divested assets. Thus, although one often hears the term "merger" employed, it is important to recognize that entire firms are not always acquired; often it is only parts of firms. Table 26.1 also indicates that almost 9 percent of the corporate restructuring during this time period involved firms going private through a leveraged buyout.

Table 26.1

Number of Mergers Involving U.S. Firms, 1982–1992

All acquisitions of at least $5 million in size, including the acquisition of 5 percent or more of a firm if the value was at least $100 million, are shown.

Year	U.S. Firm Acquiring Another U.S. Firm	Non-U.S. Firm Acquiring U.S. Firm	U.S. Firm Acquiring Non-U.S. Firm	Total	Number (of total) That Are	
					Divestitures	Leveraged Buyouts
1982	1,409	126	82	1,617	508	148
1983	1,630	80	102	1,812	600	210
1984	2,156	130	130	2,416	753	237
1985	2,451	160	162	2,773	1,000	238
1986	3,356	281	166	3,803	1,414	330
1987	2,695	274	181	3,150	1,228	270
1988	2,721	432	157	3,310	1,260	378
1989	2,343	473	245	3,061	1,260	371
1990	2,445	446	263	3,154	1,306	241
1991	1,710	218	189	2,117	1,007	112
1992	1,838	132	229	2,199	1,021	96
Total	24,754	2,752	1,906	29,412	11,357	2,631
% of total	84.2%	9.3%	6.5%	100%	38.6%	8.9%

Source: Mergers & Acquisitions, various issues.

The trends can be seen more directly by examining the largest corporate restructuring transactions that occurred during 1992:

Bidding Firm	Target Firm	Value (in billions)
BankAmerica	Security Pacific	$5.5
Bell Atlantic	Metro Mobil CTS	2.4
Northeast Utilities	Public Service of New Hampshire	2.3
Time Warner	18% of American Television & Communications	1.6
American Re	American Re-Insurance	1.5
Society Corp.	Ameritrust	1.4
Emerson Electric	Fisher Controls	1.3
S. C. Johnson & Son	Drackett	1.1
Pennzoil	Chevron PBC	1.1
Comcast	Philadelphia cellular operations of Metromedia	1.1

The transactions by BankAmerica, Bell Atlantic, Northeast Utilities, Society Corp., and Emerson Electric were mergers in which one firm acquired all of the assets of another firm. Another four of the transactions involved one firm acquiring part of the assets of another firm. These were Time Warner's purchase of 18 percent of American Television & Communications, S. C. Johnson's purchase of Drackett from Bristol-Myers Squibb, Pennzoil's acquisition of Chevron PBC from Chevron, and Comcast's acquisition of the Philadelphia cellular operations of Metromedia. Finally, the transaction involving American Re was a leveraged buyout. These examples from just a single year make clear that there are many diverse transactions in the market for corporate control. We will focus our attention first on mergers; then later in the chapter we will consider other parts of the market for corporate control.

Concept Review Questions

- What is meant by the term *market for corporate control?*
- Describe some tactics that management teams may use to acquire and manage other corporate activities or assets.

REASONS FOR MERGING

Attempting to grow by merging is an important part of corporate strategy for many firms. So, it is important for managers to understand the potential benefits arising from a merger, as well as the danger signals in a deal. Let's look at some of the reasons, both sensible and dubious, for merging.

SENSIBLE REASONS

Any reasonable motive for merging has to provide economic gains. These gains occur when the value of the combined bidder/target firm (BT) is more than the sum of the two separate firms (B, T) before the merger, so that

$$\text{value}_{BT} > \text{value}_B + \text{value}_T$$

Two sensible reasons relate to increased economies and tax considerations.

Increased Economies

A merger should improve economic performance. This improvement may come from economies of scale: the combined firm may be of sufficient size to be able to drive down production costs, distribution expenses, research and development costs, or whatever. The attempt to secure economies of scale is a primary reason why many mergers are undertaken. A separate but somewhat related motive is to seek economies by integrating vertically. *Vertical integration* refers to ensuring a continuous flow from acquisition of raw materials, through the various stages of production, to distribution and ultimate sale. A chemical firm that uses petroleum as a key raw material may decide to acquire an oil firm to achieve better vertical integration. By doing so, the chemical firm is attempting simultaneously to ensure adequate supplies of raw materials and to become more efficient by cutting the cost of raw materials acquisition.

Another possible economic benefit could come by merging two firms having overlapping expertise that may not be utilized when both are separate. For example, merging an electronics firm and a medical research firm may produce technology that neither firm operating independently could produce. Another benefit, market protection, may be achieved by acquiring competitors in order to increase market share, revenues, and profit margins. Although there may be some antitrust considerations, increased international competition is resulting in less likelihood of the merger being challenged by the Justice Department or the Federal Trade Commission. The higher profits resulting from such a merger will, however, tend to attract more competition in the future. Consequently, the market protection may be temporary.

Finally, a merger may create increased economies by removing inefficient management and taking a fresh (and unbiased) look at the utilization of the firm's cash flows and other resources. Bidding firms are often more open to an in-depth analysis of the economic consequences of alternative uses of the firm's assets, or even selling off part of the assets, than is a firm's current management.

All attempts to secure increased economies relate to **synergism.** Synergism, or the "2 + 2 = 5 effect," refers to the idea that the sum of two parts, or firms, is worth more than the two firms are worth apart. Synergistic benefits are the primary objective of sensible mergers. It is easy (and very tempting), however, to overestimate the anticipated benefits and to underestimate the costs and problems involved. For this reason, managers must take special care to ensure that the difficulties of integrating two firms into a smoothly flowing operation are recognized at the time the merger is considered. Also, it is important to ask whether the anticipated benefits of the acquisition accrue only to your firm, or to all firms. If they are expected to accrue only to your firm, be sure to ask "Why?"

Tax Considerations

The other sensible reason for merging is to obtain tax benefits. If either the bidding or the target firm has incurred losses for tax purposes in the past, those losses can be carried back and then forward to offset the firm's tax liability. Sometimes, however, the losses are so severe that even after carrying them back or forward they are still not used up. The firm will lose these benefits unless it merges with another firm.

A second tax benefit may be due to the write-up of assets to a new tax basis; if this occurs, the combined firm will be allowed to write off more depreciation for tax purposes, thereby lowering its cash outflows for taxes.

A third, and controversial, tax effect relates to the possible increase in debt, due to the unused debt capacity of the target firm. If the target firm does not have too much debt, the bidding firm may be able to finance a large portion of the merger via issuing debt. Because interest is a tax-deductible expense, the combined firm can reduce taxes. An alternative, and non-tax, benefit of using debt financing is that it provides additional incentives for management to create operating efficiencies so that the debt can be repaid.

DUBIOUS REASONS

In addition to the sensible reasons for merging, many dubious reasons are often given. Among the more commonly heard are these:

1. DIVERSIFICATION   It is often argued that the risk of the firm can be lowered by diversifying into two or more industries. Although such a move can reduce total risk, there is no evidence that the bidding firm gains. The reason is that in an efficient market, such as the financial markets in the United States, western Europe, and other developed countries, it is easier and cheaper for individual investors to obtain diversification directly, instead of having the firm do it. In effect, the combined firm performs a redundant service that is not valued by investors. In addition, any benefits secured by either the bidding or target firm's bondholders through a coinsurance-type effect may be the result of a simple transfer of value from the firm's stockholders.

2. GROWTH FOR GROWTH'S SAKE   Firms often attempt to justify an acquisition by suggesting that it will enable the firm to keep growing in overall size (and presumably earnings), and that therefore the firm and its employees, managers, and stockholders will gain. But such growth does not produce anything of value unless it is accompanied by anticipated economies or tax benefits.

3. EARNINGS PER SHARE EFFECT   By acquiring another company, a firm often can achieve an immediate increase in EPS. This occurs because of the procedure accountants use to record the transaction—but it is, in fact, an illusion. This **EPS illusion,** unless it is accompanied by economic or tax benefits, does not serve the goal of maximizing the value of the firm. The accounting treatment of mergers is examined later.

Concept Review Questions

■ What are two viable reasons that would contribute to a financially sound merger between firms?

■ What are some dubious reasons for mergers—ones that will not result in a financially sound decision?

DECIDING WHETHER TO MERGE

In Chapter 7 we discussed the steps, or phases, in the capital budgeting process. The process for assessing whether to purchases assets via a merger is similar, but it has some additional considerations. The basic steps are:

1. Search and identification of growth opportunities
2. Estimation of the magnitude, timing, and riskiness of the incremental cash flows
3. Financial evaluation of the proposed merger
4. Negotiation
5. Implementation and integration

The first three steps are essentially identical to those discussed in Chapter 7 for any other capital investment decision. Where the merger evaluation process differs is in steps 4 and 5. Normally the bidder has to negotiate with the target; this process may require extensive time and effort. Finally, after an agreement has been reached, the merger has to be implemented, and over time the new operations have to be integrated into those of the successful bidding firm. Although all of the steps are important, we focus primarily on the financial aspects involved in evaluating whether the merger is worthwhile.

ANOTHER NPV PROBLEM

From the bidding firm's standpoint, a merger is another capital budgeting problem. To make the decision whether to merge, the bidding firm estimates the benefits in terms of the firm acquired and the incremental cash flows resulting from the acquisition, the costs in terms of the cash or securities to be offered, and the opportunity cost of capital that reflects the risk and forgone opportunities. Thus, the basic framework is

$$NPV = \text{benefits} - \text{costs} \tag{26.1}$$

where

benefits $= \Delta\text{value} + \text{value}_T$
    costs $=$ the price paid, in cash or stock

The Δvalue represents the present value of the incremental economic and/or tax benefits expected to arise due to the merger. Value$_T$ is the current (or pre-offer) market value of the target firm. Note that in an efficient market and with no incremental benefits, the NPV would be zero because the bidding firm would not be willing to pay more than the current market value for the target firm. *For a positive NPV to exist, the bidding firm must be able to realize economic or tax benefits not available to the target firm.*

Benefits

For a publicly traded target, its current value (value$_T$) is simply the market price of its outstanding securities. The incremental benefits, Δvalue, can be determined via

$$\Delta\text{value} = \sum_{t=1}^{n} \frac{\Delta CF_t}{(1 + k)^t} \tag{26.2}$$

where ΔCF_t is the incremental after-tax cash flows resulting from the acquisition of the target by the bidder, and k is the opportunity cost of capital appropriate for the incremental cash flows.[1]

The incremental after-tax cash flows, ΔCF_t, are made up of the following items:

1. Incremental cash operating inflows, incremental operating cash outflows, and the incremental depreciation. Therefore (as we did in Chapter 8 for a replacement capital budgeting decision), we have

$$\Delta\text{after-tax cash flows, } \Delta CF_t = \Delta CFBT_t(1 - T) + \Delta Dep_t(T)$$

where

$$\Delta CFBT_t = \text{the incremental cash inflows in time period } t$$
$$T = \text{the firm's marginal tax rate}$$
$$\Delta Dep_t = \text{the incremental depreciation in time period } t$$

2. Any additional outlays for new equipment (including required increases in net working capital).
3. Finally, consideration of the sale of any of the target firm's assets, when the after-tax proceeds of the sale are anticipated to be greater or less than their going concern value (which is already reflected in the market value of the target firm).

The total ΔCF_t from the merger is the net incremental benefits, where for any year t,

$$\Delta CFBT_t(1 - T) + \Delta Dep_t(T) - \begin{matrix}\Delta\text{investment in long-} \\ \text{term assets and} \\ \text{net working capital}\end{matrix} \pm \begin{matrix}\text{gain or loss on the disposition} \\ \text{of some of the target firm's} \\ \text{assets (when above or below} \\ \text{their going concern value)}\end{matrix} \tag{26.3}$$

---

[1] The approach presented here follows the net present value rule, based on using an opportunity cost, k, that incorporates the costs of both debt and equity. In Chapter 14 this approach was referred to as the adjusted discount rate NPV approach. Alternatively, the adjusted present value or flows-to-equity approaches discussed in Chapter 14 could also be used in making this decision.

Most firms project incremental cash flows for 5 to 10 years and then assume they revert to a no-growth situation thereafter. Similar to any other capital budgeting decision, sensitivity analysis can be used to assess the importance of the different input factors that go into determining the incremental value of the target.

Costs

The cost of the acquisition to the bidder is the value of the cash or securities (i.e., the offer price) the bidder will give to stockholders of the target firm. Cash is easier to consider than stock, so we will start by examining how the cost is determined when the bidder uses cash to effect the acquisition.

Cash.   If cash is employed, then the cost of the acquisition is simply the amount of cash itself. For example, assume that the bidder and target are both publicly traded all-equity firms that have market values of $250,000 and $150,000, respectively. To determine the incremental value, Δvalue, the bidder has estimated the incremental cash flows before tax, incremental depreciation, and incremental investment (some of which occurs in the future) as shown in Table 26.2. (For simplicity, no incremental benefits are estimated beyond 5 years in this example.) Using the bidder's tax rate of 40 percent, and a discount rate of 15 percent, we find the incremental value of the

Table 26.2

Estimated Incremental Value of Proposed Acquisition

In order to achieve all the benefits, the bidder estimates that it will have to invest an additional $30,000 in year 1 and $40,000 more in year 2.

Incremental Benefits and Investments

Year	$\Delta CFBT$	ΔDep^*	$\Delta Investment$
1	$30,000	$10,000	$30,000
2	60,000	20,000	40,000
3	70,000	15,000	0
4	50,000	10,000	0
5	40,000	10,000	0

Calculation of Δvalue

Year	$\Delta CFBT(1-T)$	$+$ $\Delta Dep(T)$	$-$ $\Delta Investment$	$=$	ΔCF	$/(1+k)^n$	Present Value
1	$18,000	$4,000	30,000		$-\$\ 8,000$	$(1.15)^1$	$-\$\ 6,957$
2	36,000	8,000	40,000		4,000	$(1.15)^2$	3,025
3	42,000	6,000	0		48,000	$(1.15)^3$	31,561
4	30,000	4,000	0		34,000	$(1.15)^4$	19,440
5	24,000	4,000	0		28,000	$(1.15)^5$	13,921
						Δvalue $=$	$60,990

*Δdepreciation is for the Δinvestment in the column immediately to the right.

target to be $60,990. The total benefits of the merger are the incremental value plus the present going-concern value of the target, or

$$\text{benefits} = \Delta\text{value} + \text{value}_T$$
$$= \$60,990 + \$150,000 = \$210,990$$

The bidder has to offer more than the current market value of the target, which is $150,000. With 10,000 shares of stock outstanding, the market price per share of the target before the merger is $15 (i.e., $150,000/10,000). Suppose that the bidder decides to offer $18.50 per share, or a total of $185,000, to the stockholders of the target firm. The net present value if the offer is financed with cash is

$$NPV = \text{benefits} - \text{costs}$$
$$= \$210,990 - \$185,000 = \$25,990$$

The postmerger value of the combined firm will be the sum of the premerger value of the bidder of $250,000 plus the $25,990 NPV from the merger, or $275,990. Note that the bidder suffers an outflow of cash of $185,000 in order to effect the merger.

Suppose that there are 5,000 shares of stock of the bidding firm. Before the merger the stock was worth $50.00 (i.e., $250,000/5,000) per share. After the merger the per share value is approximately $55.20 (i.e., $275,990/5,000). Because cash was employed, and the target's former stockholders sold their stock to the bidder for cash, all of the net benefits (i.e., the NPV) from the merger go to the bidder's stockholders.[2]

Stock.   What if common stock is used to finance the merger? In this case, the benefits of the merger are shared, because the target's stockholders end up owning part of the combined firm. Let's see what happens to the cost and the NPV when stock is employed.

Suppose that the same offer of $185,000 is made to the target's stockholders, but this time stock is employed. The premerger price of the bidding firm's stock is $50, so 3,700 (i.e., $185,000/$50) shares will be issued to acquire the target. With stock being employed, the stockholders of the target share in the fortunes (and costs) of the combined firm. The percent of the combined firm owned by the target's stockholders, as represented by W, is determined as follows:

$$W = \frac{\text{shares held by the target firm's former stockholders}}{\text{total shares outstanding after the merger}} \tag{26.4}$$
$$= \frac{3,700}{5,000 + 3,700} = 0.425$$

In the combined firm, the target's former stockholders own 42.5 percent of the total firm.

To determine the cost of the merger when stock is employed, we use a slightly

[2] Sometimes mergers also involve the transfer of wealth from stockholders to bondholders, or vice versa. For example, if the cash employed to finance the deal was raised by issuing new debt, there is a transfer of wealth from bondholders to stockholders, along with the benefits of the merger itself.

different procedure than before. The total value of the combined firm is given by

$$\begin{matrix}\text{total value of combined} \\ \text{firm when stock is} \\ \text{employed, value}_{BT}\end{matrix} = \text{value}_B + \text{benefit} \qquad (26.5)$$

$$= \$250,000 + \$210,990 = \$460,990$$

The cost when stock is employed is a function of the percent of the total value of the combined firm given up by the bidder's original stockholders, so

$$\text{cost with stock} = W(\text{value}_{BT}) \qquad (26.6)$$

$$= 0.425(\$460,990) = \$195,921$$

Note that this cost is higher than when cash was employed. The NPV, using Equation 26.1, is

$$NPV = \$210,990 - \$195,921 = \$15,069$$

Although the merger is still beneficial, the NPV is lower when stock is employed than when cash was used. This is always true if the same dollar value of cash or stock (the offer price of $185,000) is employed to finance the merger.

The use of cash or stock to finance the acquisition can be summarized as follows:

	Before Acquisition		After Acquisition	
	Bidder	**Target**	**Cash**	**Stock**
Market value	$250,000	$150,000	$275,990	$460,990
Number of shares	5,000	10,000	5,000	8,700
Price per share, P_0	$50	$15	$55.20	$52.99

When the same offer price is used for either cash or stock, we see that the total value of the combined firm is greater for the stock-financed acquisition. Due to sharing of the costs between the stockholders of the bidder and the target, the market value per share is $55.20 when cash is used versus $52.99 when stock is used. If all else is equal (i.e., if the offer price is the same in either case), then the bidder's existing stockholders are better off with a cash-financed acquisition.

This distinction between cash and stock financing is important. If cash is used, then the cost of the acquisition does not depend on the acquisition benefits. But, if common stock is employed, the cost is a function of how the ownership is shared between the stockholders of the two firms. In recent years, more and more use of cash has been made for financing acquisitions. The general steps for the evaluation of a proposed acquisition are shown in Figure 26.2.

Often the term **exchange ratio** is used in discussing merger terms. It is

$$\text{exchange ratio} = \frac{\text{market value of cash and/or securities offered by bidding firm}}{\text{market value of target firm's stock}} \qquad (26.7)$$

Figure 26.2

Steps in Merger Valuation

The basic steps are the same whether cash or stock is employed. Due to cost differences, however, a slightly different approach is required to determine the cost for a stock-financed merger.

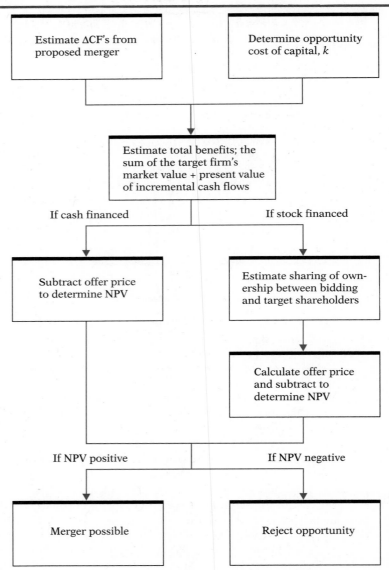

In our example the exchange ratio, with either cash or stock, is $185,000/$150,000 = 1.23. A higher exchange ratio is often required when cash is employed. This occurs because the target firm's shareholders give up ownership if cash is employed and because immediate income tax consequences (as discussed shortly) will result when cash, instead of stock, is employed.

TRYING TO AVOID MISTAKES

In any proposed merger numerous mistakes can be made. Perhaps this is why so many mergers that look good before completion turn out so poorly. Some of the ways to avoid mistakes are as follows:

1. RELY ON MARKET VALUES   It is often difficult to determine all of the value to be created using a present value approach. Although conceptually a merger is just a capital budgeting problem, and we could attempt to value the entire firm to be acquired, it is sounder to rely on the established market value for the target firm. In reasonably efficient markets the best estimate of the going-concern value of any firm, given the current use of its cash flows and assets, is given by its present market value.

2. ESTIMATE INCREMENTAL CASH FLOWS   Only the incremental cash flows resulting from the proposed acquisition should be estimated. This simplifies the problem, but it is still easy to forget some of the incremental flows, or to overestimate inflows and underestimate outflows. Remember to ask, *"How will my use of the cash flows and assets be different from—and better than—their present use?"*

3. USE THE RIGHT OPPORTUNITY COST OF CAPITAL   The proper opportunity cost to employ relates to the incremental use of the cash flows and assets. If the incremental cash flows and assets are more risky than your firm's present cash flows and assets, then a higher opportunity cost of capital is necessary.

4. DON'T FORGET TRANSACTIONS COSTS   The costs incurred by lawyers, accountants, and investment bankers often run into the millions of dollars. These costs cannot be ignored in the evaluation process.

5. BE CRITICAL   Often it is tempting to get carried away with a proposed acquisition. Surveys indicate a number of problems that firms run into when evaluating acquisitions. These include (1) underestimating the subsequent capital expenditures and additional investment in working capital required, (2) inability to reduce the target's ongoing cash outflows by as much as anticipated, after it is acquired, (3) longer transition periods and more transition-related cash outflows than anticipated, and (4) incorrect risk assessments. All of these problems serve to reduce the benefits of the merger from those anticipated.

   Another place to be critical is when a bidding war breaks out in which more than one firm wants to acquire the target firm. In most bidding wars the bidder's shareholders will actually be better off if the bidding firm loses; the "winner's curse" of overpaying often accompanies the firm that is "successful" in making the winning bid.

6. CONSIDER THE FORM OF THE FINANCING   The cash-versus-stock issue, and the amount of leverage the combined firm will have, are crucial decisions. Although this seems obvious, firms often wake up a year or two later wondering if they should have structured the deal differently. Numerous empirical and theoretical studies have examined the use of cash versus stock. These findings indicate that, other things being equal, both bidders and targets are better off if cash is employed instead of stock to finance an acquisition.

WHO BENEFITS FROM MERGERS?

Although there has been a lot of merger activity in recent years, it is doubtful that everyone has gained. Here is what we do know about mergers:

1. Stockholders of the target companies almost always gain, because most mergers involve a premium being paid over the target firm's premerger market value. Premiums average 30 to 40 percent above the premerger market value, and sometimes go as high as 100 percent. Thus, substantial benefits accrue to the targets.
2. Numerous studies concerning the postmerger value of the bidding firms indicate little or no increase in market value. Thus, studies have found no positive impact on the market value of bidding firms after a merger. In a recent study, Agrawal, Jaffe, and Mandelker (1992) examined the postmerger performance of successful bidding firms for 5 years after the merger completion date. Their findings indicate a loss in value of about 10 percent over this 5-year period when stock was employed to finance the transaction; but, if cash was employed, there was no loss in value for the bidders. On the other hand, for 50 large mergers Healy, Palepu, and Ruback (1992) find improved performance in terms of postmerger operating cash flow and asset productivity for successful bidding firms. Whether mergers lead to benefits from the standpoint of successful bidding firms is still a hotly debated issue—and one that will continue to be vigorously explored in the future.
3. Investment bankers, lawyers, and accountants providing consulting and services to merger participants have benefitted from the many mergers in recent years.

FREE CASH FLOW AND MERGERS

In 1986 Jensen presented the free cash flow hypothesis of mergers. He argued that managers with surplus, or free, cash flow over and above that needed for operating the firm will invest cash in negative net present value projects rather than pay it out to shareholders. The essence of the free cash flow hypothesis is that the presence of excess cash flow increases the agency costs of firms with poor investment opportunities. The hypothesis assumes that management values investments in operations more than investments in financial assets. This may come about because management perquisites increase with the investment in operations, even when these investments have a negative NPV. Therefore, once management has exhausted positive-NPV projects, it proceeds to invest in negative-NPV projects rather than pay these funds out to shareholders. In an empirical test of this hypothesis, Lang, Stulz, and Walking (1991) found that firms with high free cash flow and poor investment prospects actually decreased their shareholder wealth by merging; however, firms with better investment prospects did not diminish the wealth of their stockholders when making an acquisition. They interpret these findings to provide support for the free cash flow hypothesis.

Concept Review Questions

- What are the basic steps for evaluating a proposed merger?
- For a positive NPV to exist, what must the bidding firm be able to realize?
- Describe some mistakes that can be made in a merger and how the mistakes can be avoided.
- Why would corporate managers of firms with excess free cash flow invest in negative net present value projects?

MECHANICS OF A MERGER

Buying another firm is much more complicated than most other business transactions. The details and the various options and factors affecting the merger can expand rapidly.

FORM OF THE ACQUISITION

Until now, we have used the term merger to refer to any acquisition or combination of companies. A merger, however, may take various forms:

1. A *consolidation* occurs when two or more firms combine to form a completely new firm. A new legal entity is formed.
2. A merger can be accomplished through the acquisition of the stock of the target firm. The essential feature is that the bidding firm acquires both the target's assets and its liabilities by exchanging stock, cash, or other securities for the target firm's stock.
3. A merger can also be accomplished by acquiring just the assets of the target firm. If the target sells all its assets to the bidder, the proceeds from the sale (after paying off any liabilities) can be distributed to the target firm's stockholders, and the firm can be dissolved.
4. A *holding company* is another way to acquire control over another firm, although complete ownership may not be held. A firm may acquire 40 to 50 percent ownership in another firm. Though it does not control all, or even a majority of, shares, it can exercise effective control over the other firm.

TAX IMPLICATIONS

An acquisition can be taxable or tax-free for the target firm's stockholders. If it is a taxable transaction, the target's stockholders must treat the transaction as a sale for tax purposes and report any gains or losses. For example, if you purchased stock originally for $10 per share and sold out through a merger at $50 per share, your gain is $40 per share. You would pay taxes during the current period on this $40 gain. If the merger is tax-free, you retain your original $10 cost in the shares of the new firm. Only when you subsequently sell the new stock at some later date will any gain or loss in value have to be reported.

To qualify as tax-free, the transaction must meet the following conditions:

1. In a consolidation, three conditions hold: First, the acquisition must be for business purposes and not just for tax reasons. Second, there must be some continuity of the organization. Third, the stockholders of the target firm must receive a continuing interest in the new firm. The IRS has interpreted this to mean that at least 50 percent of the purchase price must be in the form of common stock.
2. In an acquisition of stock, the requirement is that only voting stock be employed and that the bidding firm must purchase at least 80 percent of the target's total voting stock.
3. In an acquisition of assets, the bidding firm must acquire at least 80 percent of the assets of the target in exchange for voting stock.

The key requirement for a merger to be tax-free is that the target firm's stockholders must receive common stock of the bidding firm.

ACCOUNTING TREATMENT

There are two basic accounting treatments for mergers: (1) pooling of interests and (2) purchase. Which method is employed can have a significant impact on the balance sheet and the profits reported for accounting purposes.

For a merger to be a **pooling of interests,** the following conditions must hold:[3]

1. Both the bidding and the target firms must have been autonomous for the 2 years preceding the merger. No more than 10 percent of the stock of the target could have been held by the bidding firm, or vice versa.
2. The merger must be effected in a single transaction or in accordance with a specific plan within 1 year after the plan is initiated. No contingent payments are permitted.
3. The bidding firm must issue voting common stock for substantially all the voting common stock of the target firm. "Substantially" means 90 percent or more.
4. The bidding firm must not dispose of a significant portion of the assets of the combined firm for 2 years after the merger.

If common stock is used, and if all other conditions are met, then the merger is treated as a pooling of interests; otherwise, it is accounted for as a **purchase.**

---

[3] "Business Combinations," APB No. 16 (New York: American Institute of Certified Public Accountants, 1970).

Balance Sheet Effects

In a pooling of interests, the consolidated balance sheet is constructed by simply adding together the two preexisting balance sheets. In a purchase, the assets acquired must be revalued to indicate the actual purchase price paid for the target firm. If a price greater than the book value of the assets is paid for the target company, the purchased assets must be revalued to reflect their fair market value. If the purchase price is more than the total fair *market value* of the assets acquired—due to trade names, marketing, or managerial expertise, and the like—then goodwill is created.

To see the difference, consider two firms—A, the bidding firm, and B, the target firm. Their premerger balance sheets are shown in Table 26.3. Firm A's assets are recorded at $1,000; B's are recorded at $200. Because B has some assets not reflected by its GAAP-based balance sheet, however, A actually paid $500 for B. Column 3 of Table 26.3 shows the postmerger combined balance sheet if the merger is concluded through the exchange of stock and if the other requirements for a pooling of interests are met. All that has happened is that the two premerger balance sheets have been added together. If cash or debt is used to finance the merger, then the $500 paid for firm B has to be recorded as the purchase price. With the purchase method, long-term assets are written up to reflect their fair market value. Goodwill is also recorded. The postmerger combined balance sheet under the purchase method is as shown in column

Table 26.3

Impact of Pooling of Interests Versus Purchase Accounting on the Postmerger Balance Sheet

As long as the price paid is more than the target's accounting book value, then the purchase method results in an increased postmerger book value for the combined firm.

| | Premerger Balance Sheets | | Postmerger Combined Balance Sheet | |
	Bidder (1)	Target (2)	Pooling of Interests (1) + (2) (3)	Purchase* (4)
Current assets	$ 300	$100	$ 400	$ 400
Long-term assets	700	100	800	1,000
Goodwill	0	0	0	100
Total	$1,000	$200	$1,200	$1,500
Debt	$ 400	$ 80	$ 480	$ 480
Stockholders' equity	600	120	720	1,020
Total	$1,000	$200	$1,200	$1,500

*Purchase price of the target firm is $500, versus its book value of $200. The long-term assets are revalued to their fair market value of $300 (representing a $200 upward revaluation from their book value of $100). The other $100 is shown as goodwill.

4. The combined assets are recorded at $1,200 with the pooling of interest treatment; they are valued at $1,500 if accounted for as a purchase.

Income Statement Effects

The two different methods of accounting for a merger can also have an impact on the earnings reported by the combined firm. This occurs because under pooling of interests, assets are brought over at their current depreciated book value. Under the purchase method, assets are revalued to reflect the value of the merger. In our previous example, if the merger was accounted for as a purchase, then the target's long-term assets were revalued upward to $300. This means that more depreciation will be

| Table 26.4 |

Impact of Pooling of Interests Versus Purchase Accounting on the Postmerger Income Statement

If the purchase price paid is more than the target firm's book value, then reported net income and earnings per share will be less with purchase accounting than with pooling of interests.

| | Premerger Income Statement | | Postmerger Combined Income Statement | |
| | | | Pooling of Interests | |
	Bidder (1)	Target (2)	(1) + (2) (3)	Purchase* (4)
Sales	$3,000.00	$600.00	$3,600.00	$3,600.00
Cash expenses	1,800.00	360.00	2,160.00	2,160.00
Depreciation	600.00	120.00	720.00	740.00
EBIT	600.00	120.00	720.00	700.00
Interest	40.00	8.00	48.00	48.00
EBT	560.00	112.00	672.00	652.00
Taxes (35%)	196.00	39.20	235.20	228.20
EAT	364.00	72.80	436.80	423.80
Writeoff of goodwill	0	0	0	10.00[†]
Net income	$ 364.00	$ 72.80	$ 436.80	$ 413.80
Number of shares of common stock	100	20	120	120[‡]
EPS	$ 3.64	$ 3.64	$ 3.64	$ 3.45

* The additional $200 in long-term assets is assumed to be written off over 10 years with straight-line depreciation. The $100 in goodwill is also written off over 10 years via the straight-line method.
[†] Goodwill is not a tax-deductible item and therefore is written off after EAT.
[‡] For consistency, we assume that common stock was employed to finance the merger, even though purchase accounting is employed.

charged off in future years than under pooling of interests. Goodwill was also created, and it must be written off over a period not to exceed 40 years.[4]

To show the effect on reported net income, the previous example is continued in Table 26.4. For simplicity, there is no impact on earnings per share if the pooling of interests method is employed: EPS is $3.64 both before and after the merger. If the purchase method is used, then an additional $200 in depreciation must be charged off, and the $100 in goodwill must also be written off. Assuming that both are done on a straight-line basis over 10 years, the resulting postmerger EPS is only $3.45 with the purchase method, versus $3.64 with pooling of interests. This accounting effect is part of the EPS illusion that mergers can have. So we see that earnings per share is subject to changes unrelated to the economic benefits of a merger.

Concept Review Questions

- What conditions must be met for an acquisition to be tax-free for the target firm's stockholders?
- What is the difference in a firm's balance sheet between the pooling of interest and purchase methods of accounting for mergers?

DEFENSIVE TACTICS

Firms have attempted to fend off unwanted takeovers through a number of actions. These basically fall into two main classifications—preoffer and postoffer defenses.

PREOFFER DEFENSES

In the preoffer group, defenses can be broken into three categories: general, shark-repellent charter amendments (that is, amendments in the company charter that are intended to repel unwanted bidders), and other repellents.

GENERAL DEFENSES
1. PRIVATE COMPANY   The best defense of all may be to be a privately owned company, such as Hallmark Cards.
2. BLOCKING STAKES   Companies with 50 percent or more of their stock owned by one individual or a tight-knit group can be all but invulnerable. Thus, 70 percent of the voting control of Hershey Foods is in the hands of a foundation.

---

[4] "Intangible Assets," APB No. 17 (New York: American Institute of Certified Public Accountants, 1970). One other technical point is important: Under pooling of interests, the income of the target firm for the entire year in which it was acquired is included in the combined firm's income. Under purchase accounting, only the appropriate pro rata income for the target firm is included. For simplicity, we include the entire year's income in any examples and problems.

3. ESOP   In recent years many firms have instituted or enlarged employee stock ownership plans, ESOPs, in order to boost the percentage of the firm owned by employees. This is another approach to placing a sizable amount of stock in the hands of a group who should be less willing to sell the firm.

4. SIZE AND POLITICS   For a very few firms, such as IBM and Exxon, size alone may still be a valid defense. Likewise, certain companies, such as AT&T or defense-oriented high-tech firms may be immune to takeover due to potential political ramifications.

5. STRONG STOCK PRICE   One of the best defenses is a strong stock price, which signifies that the investment community already believes in the firm, its management, and growth prospects. Although this is no barrier to a determined bidder who wants the company at any cost, it will still fend off many suitors.

SHARK-REPELLENT CHARTER AMENDMENTS

6. STAGGERED BOARD   Under this tactic the board of directors is classified into three groups, with only one of the three groups elected every year. Though a bidder can acquire majority ownership via a tender offer, it cannot obtain complete control of the board and the firm immediately.

7. SUPERMAJORITY   Instead of needing only one vote over 50 percent to approve a merger, many firms have asked their stockholders to change the bylaws and redefine the majority required to approve a merger. This **supermajority** is typically between two-thirds and 80 percent.

8. FAIR PRICE AMENDMENT   The supermajority provision may often be waived if the bidder pays all stockholders the same price. This amendment prevents "two-tiered bids" in which the first 80 percent of the shares tendered receive one price, and the last 20 percent receive a lower price for their stock.

OTHER DEFENSES

9. DUAL CLASS RECAPITALIZATION   Many firms, such as Ford, have a class of supervoting stock that keeps control among the descendants of the founder or the builders of the business.

10. POISON PILLS   The term **poison pill** describes a family of shareholder rights agreements. When triggered by a tender offer or the accumulation of a certain percentage of the target's shares, it provides target shareholders with the right to purchase additional shares or to sell shares to the target at very attractive prices. Poison pills raise the potential cost of an acquisition to two or three times what it would otherwise be.

POSTOFFER DEFENSES

If all of the preoffer defenses fail to work, then the target still has some postoffer defenses it can call into play. These include the following:

1. LITIGATION   Many firms file suits to protect some of their defenses that have been challenged by a bidder, or they accuse the bidding firm of violating antitrust or securities laws.

2. ASSET RESTRUCTURING   Some firms purchase assets, or make another quick merger, to acquire assets the bidder does not want or that will create an antitrust problem. An alternative is for the firm to sell its "crown jewels," that is, the assets most desired by the bidder.

3. LIABILITY RESTRUCTURING   The targeted firm sells some shares to a friendly third party, called a **white squire,** or leverages up by issuing debt and/or buying back equity.

4. STANDSTILL AGREEMENT   Under a standstill agreement, the target gets the bidder to agree during the term of the agreement not to increase its stock holdings in the target firm above a specified percentage and, in many cases, to support the management of the target firm.

These cover the majority of the defensive tactics used by firms fending off takeover bids, but new ones are always being devised. Two other items should be mentioned: The first is **greenmail** (or targeted repurchases), which occurs when an unfriendly bidder has purchased a significant stake in a target firm. Often to get rid of the unwanted suitor, the target firm buys back the common stock at a premium over its current market value. As part of the deal, the suitor agrees not to purchase any new shares in the target for some specific period in time. The second item is golden parachutes. A **golden parachute** is a supplemental compensation agreement for senior management that provides substantial additional compensation in case of a takeover and the resignation (forced or voluntary) of the covered executives. In 1984 the amount of the compensation was restricted by federal law to no more than three times the executive's annual compensation. Also, a special 20 percent excise tax was placed on the executive when he or she claimed the parachute.

Finally, if all else fails, target firms often try to find a "friendly" firm—a **white knight**—to merge with. This strategy also involves risk however, because some white knights have turned out to be less chivalrous after the merger than the target anticipated.

The use of various kinds of takeover defenses has increased in recent years. The top 1,000 firms in the United States (in terms of total stock market value) had the following antitakeover defenses in place in 1990 and 1993:

	1990	1993
Staggered board of directors	550	594
Unequal voting rights	67	92
Poison pills	495	643
Golden parachutes	441	535

Over this time period large firms were putting more antitakeover defenses in place. This suggests that in the future it will be harder, or more expensive, to take over United States-based firms.

THE TARGET'S RESPONSE AND AGENCY PROBLEMS

The management of the target firm has the responsibility to represent the interest of its owners, the stockholders. However, because of potential differences in orientation or focus, a serious agency problem might develop. Although selling out for cash or stock at a substantial premium might be in the best interests of the firm's shareholders, it might also result in the loss of jobs for many of the top management of the target firm. Because of differences in self-interests, what is best for one party may not always be best for the other. One argument made in favor of golden parachutes is to assist in overcoming agency problems of this kind. However, if the golden parachutes are too large, they may provide the wrong kind of incentive to management—which might result in selling the firm on terms that do not provide stockholders as much benefit as possible.

Concept Review Questions
- Describe some tactics a firm may employ to fend off unwanted takeovers.
- What kind of agency problem may the target's management face?

CORPORATE RESTRUCTURING

Much of the recent merger activity in this country has involved mature firms. Because of limited growth opportunities in their core businesses, many firms are rethinking how they use the cash flows generated by the firm. Instead of simply plowing the funds back into the same kinds of activities, or diversifying into areas in which they have no expertise, the motivation now—more than ever—is toward maximizing the value of the firm. There are two main points behind this emphasis on creating value: First, there is the recognition that corporate "fit" is very important; that is, firms are streamlining their operations and refocusing more on their core business. Second, maximizing NPV, and therefore the market value of the firm, is more important than ever. This recognizes the increased attention that needs to be given to the questions of *"When and how should I get into positive-NPV projects where my unique strengths provide the best opportunity to create value?"* and *"When and how should I get out of certain projects that no longer offer unique value-creating NPV opportunities?"*

LEVERAGING UP

To increase efficiency and impose the discipline created by additional debt, as well as to make themselves less attractive takeover candidates, some firms in recent years "leveraged up." This trend reached its peak in the late 1980s and has since receded somewhat. In a **leveraging up** operation, the firm dramatically shrinks the number of shares of common stock outstanding (through stock repurchases) and increases the amount of debt financing employed. These moves often result in the company shifting from a 20 to 30 percent debt to total asset ratio up to 60 or even 70 percent. The two activities can be combined in a leveraged repurchase, in which the firm issues substantial amounts of debt and uses the proceeds to buy back some of its common stock. Leveraging up forces a firm to become even more conscious of its cash flows than it was previously, and it imposes a discipline on the ongoing operations of the firm that is often missing without the additional debt. While debt has disadvantages, it is a way to impose market discipline and encourage firms to become more efficient and productive. At the same time, there is an additional benefit to the transaction. That is, the firm becomes a less tempting takeover candidate because there is no "unused debt capacity" for a bidder to take advantage of.

GOING PRIVATE AND LEVERAGED BUYOUTS

Some firms in the 1980s ended up **going private**—that is, going from a publicly owned firm with common stock actively traded on a stock exchange or in the over-the-counter market, to a privately held one controlled by a small group of owners. One of the reasons for going private is to avoid being acquired by another firm. Often the act of going private involves a management buyout. In a **management buyout** the top management of the firm usually bands together, often with an outside partner, to take all or part of the business and turn it into a private company. Usually management buyouts are highly leveraged deals that are known as **leveraged buyouts, LBOs.** In a leveraged buyout, a firm is acquired in a transaction that is financed largely by borrowing—often provided by institutional investors. The LBO debt can either be privately placed or be supplied by the use of junk (or high-yield) bonds. Other leveraged buyouts may not involve the management of the firm but may in fact be triggered by outside investors. Although leveraged buyouts and management buyouts can be one and the same, it is possible for either one to occur separately.

The largest leveraged buyout of all time involved RJR Nabisco. In 1988, F. Ross Johnson, Chief Executive Officer of RJR Nabisco, led a management-initiated proposal to take RJR private. That move touched off a bidding war that was ultimately won by the firm of Kohlberg Kravis Roberts & Co. (KKR). The final bid was a record $25 billion, which amounted to $109 per share of RJR's stock. Seventy-four percent, or $81 per share, was paid in cash; the rest was in new preferred stock and convertible debentures. These additional securities, often called *payment-in-kind* (or PIK), represented $28 per share of the package.

To finance the deal, KKR needed to raise $18.9 billion in cash. The money was raised as follows: Two billion dollars, the smallest part of the financing, came from KKR's equity investors and represented ownership in RJR Nabisco after the deal was completed. The second chunk, $11.9 billion in bank loans, came from 45 U.S., Japanese, European, and Canadian banks. Finally, the last chunk, $5 billion, was raised by selling notes to other investors.

Financing the deal was only part of the problem, because the bigger issue was how to manage RJR Nabisco effectively, sell off certain assets, and squeeze additional cash flow out of the existing operations. Efficient management of the firm was essential to pay the interest, pay debt, and make sure the whole deal didn't sink. By 1991 RJR Nabisco had made significant progress and even sold some of its stock to the public. But 1992 and 1993 were not as kind to RJR Nabisco. While the food portion of their business was doing fairly well, there was concern about the tobacco side. Continued liability suits from cancer victims, fear of a large tax increase in cigarettes, the EPA report on the dangers of second-hand tabacco smoke, and the move by a major competitor (Philip Morris) to reduce the selling price of its main cigarette brand caused RJR Nabisco's stock price in 1993 to be 25 percent less than when it went public in 1991. In response, RJR Nabisco considered splitting into two separate arms—one food and the other tobacco, each having a separate class of common stock. The hope was that with two ownerships, the market value of the entire firm would not be brought down due to problems related to the tobacco arm of the firm. After much thought RJR Nabisco shelved the proposal to split into two separate firms.

Another tactic often used in conjunction with the act of going private is an employee stock ownership, ESOP. An ESOP is essentially an employee trust fund to which a firm may contribute stock or cash at no direct cost to the employee. Under a typical ESOP-based deal for taking a company private, the firm tenders for its own stock using a bank loan. The firm then repays the loan by the ESOP, channeling periodic cash contributions to it through which the loan is paid. The result is that both principal and interest is repaid with money that is fully tax-deductible—as long as the firm's contribution to the ESOP does not exceed 25 percent of its annual payroll.

LIMITED PARTNERSHIPS

Sometimes corporate restructuring involves a fundamental change in the legal structure of the business. Some firms, for example, have reorganized themselves as *limited partnerships*. In this case the shareholders are replaced by partners and the firm's revenues and expenses are credited directly to the individual partners' accounts. These partnerships are generally known as master limited partnerships. A number of limited partnerships exist in the oil and gas industry, where producing properties have actually been spun off to partnerships. These partnership interests are then taken out of the firm itself and distributed to the firm's stockholders.

Typically, the management of a limited partnership is directly involved in how the firm is financed and where the cash flows go. This involvement creates additional incentives to make sound use of the cash flows generated. Finally, there is a tax advantage to a limited partnership. Stockholders really pay taxes twice—once at the corporate level when the corporation pays taxes, and again at the personal level. Under a limited partnership the proceeds are taxed only once, when it appears on the partners' personal income tax forms.

VOLUNTARY RESTRUCTURING

In the wake of subpar performance, or outright losses, firms often conclude that they need to restructure to become more competitive. This trend toward voluntary restructuring has gained momentum in recent years, as institutional investors have increased their ownership in firms and, more than ever, stockholders are demanding change and better performance from firms in which they own substantial stakes. Large institutional investors, such as pension funds, banks, insurance firms, and mutual funds, along with shareholder activist groups such as United Shareholders Association and

Institutional Shareholders Partners, are demanding change and better performance. This increased activity has been assisted by two changes by the Securities and Exchange Commission. The first is a requirement that firms provide fuller disclosure of executive compensation packages; this has put managers on the defensive. The second change in the SEC regulations makes it easier for shareholders to communicate with each other and with managers. This new activism by shareholders is credited, in part, with leading to the removal of the chief executive officers of General Motors, IBM, American Express, and Westinghouse in 1992 or 1993.

In the face of needed change, firms take many actions. Some of them include selling assets and laying off employees.[5] Also, there is evidence that firms decrease the number of segments in which they operate and cut the costs of production. Other trends when firms undergo voluntary restructuring include cutting R & D, increasing capital investment, reducing the amount of debt, and also reducing cash dividends. With the increased emphasis on performance, firms will increasingly be involved in voluntary restructuring.

SPINOFFS

One way for a firm to relinquish control of assets is to spin them off to shareholders. Sometimes this is done by simply distributing shares in the spinoff portion of the firm to the firm's present shareholders. Another approach is to sell part or all of the spinoff to new investors, thereby getting rid of assets and raising cash at the same time. Recently, Sears spun off 20 percent of Dean Witter Reynolds and used the proceeds to reduce debt. By the end of 1993 Sears planned to divest itself of the other 80 percent of Dean Witter Reynolds.

DIVESTITURES

As we discussed when reviewing Table 26.1, about 40 percent of all restructuring transactions in recent years have involved firms selling off part of their assets through divestitures. These are often accomplished by entering into an agreement to sell them directly to another firm. A divestiture can be thought of as reaping the benefits of prior capital investment decisions. The question, as discussed in Chapter 10, is whether the value of the firm is maximized by holding on to the assets or by selling them. As firms have streamlined their operations and focused more on corporate fit and maximizing the value of the firm, divestitures have become more commonplace. Their frequency should not decrease in the foreseeable future.

Concept Review Questions
- Describe how a firm's leveraging up may increase its market value.
- What is a leveraged buyout, and how was one used in the purchase of RJR Nabisco?
- Describe how limited partnerships, voluntary restructuring, spinoffs, and divestitures may affect a firm's market value.

---

[5] See John, Lang, and Netter (1992).

KEY POINTS

1. Mergers are only one part of the market for corporate control; related activities involve defenses, leveraging up, going private and leveraged buyouts, limited partnerships, voluntary restructuring, spinoffs, and divestitures.
2. Mergers should be undertaken only if they are expected to produce economic benefits in the form of increased economies or tax savings. Merger analysis is another net present value, NPV, problem. The costs differ depending on whether cash or stock is employed.
3. To increase the reliability of the merger analysis, firms need to do the following:
   a. Rely on market values to the greatest extent possible.
   b. Consider the unique attributes of both the target and the bidder as the incremental cash flows are estimated.
   c. Focus on the risk and returns of the target in estimating the opportunity cost of capital.
   d. Include in their analysis the transaction costs to investment bankers, lawyers, accountants, and so forth.
   e. Become very critical of all facets of the analysis, and avoid falling into the trap of overestimating the expected inflows or underestimating the magnitude of the additional outflows required and the time needed to reap the benefits of the acquisition.
   f. Remember that cash financing benefits both the target and the bidder more than stock financing.
4. Target shareholders benefit from acquisitions, but the evidence is that the bidder's shareholders either break even or lose value when firms merge.
5. Defensive tactics can be broken into preoffer and postoffer. In recent years antitakeover provisions put in place by firms have increased.
6. Corporate restructuring focuses on value creation and maximizing net present value. Focusing on these ideas and the options available to enhance the value of the firm must continually be at the forefront when considering the acquisition or divestiture of assets, taking defensive measures, and considering the size, financing mix, or structure of the firm.

QUESTIONS

26.1   There are both sensible and dubious reasons for merging. What are they? What distinguishes them?

26.2   Two firms, X and Y, are in unrelated fields and are planning to merge. No synergy is expected, but the standard deviation of the combined companies' returns will be lower than the standard deviation of either firm's separate returns. Is this a valid reason for merging? Why or why not?

26.3   A merger is another NPV problem. Explain:

a. What Δvalue is, and what cash flows must be included.
b. Why we don't use a discounted cash flow analysis to estimate the total benefits from the proposed acquisition.
c. Why the costs are different if stock is employed instead of cash.

26.4   What are some of the typical mistakes made in evaluating proposed mergers?

26.5   Who benefits from a merger? Do you think anyone loses?

26.6   Identify the different legal forms for acquiring another firm.

26.7   A merger can be taxable or tax-free to the target firm's stockholders. Why is this important? How does a merger qualify to be tax-free?

26.8 Clyde's acquired Zebra Pictures for $750 million, when Zebra's book value was only $185 million. From the standpoint of reported EPS, would Clyde's rather report this merger as a purchase or as a pooling of interests? Why?

26.9 Identify the defensive tactics a firm may employ. Are greenmail and golden parachutes also defensive tactics in the same sense as the others?

26.10 What are the two prongs (or points) behind value creation via corporate restructuring? How do the various forms of restructuring relate to this two-pronged emphasis?

CONCEPT REVIEW PROBLEMS

See Appendix A for solutions.

CR26.1 Marshall's is investigating the acquisition of Newman, an all equity firm. Marshall's tax rate is 40 percent, and the appropriate opportunity cost of capital is 15 percent. Estimates of the incremental cash flows are:

Year	ΔCFBT	ΔDep*	ΔInvestments
1	$250		$100
2	350	$20	120
3	400	40	—
4	450	40	—
5	500	40	—

$^*\Delta$depreciation is for the Δinvestment in the column immediately to the right.

Newman's current price per share is $10, with 100 shares of stock outstanding. If Marshall's pays $12 in cash per share to obtain control of Newman, what is the NPV of the proposed acquisition?

CR26.2 Goodtimes R' Here is planning to purchase WaterWilly for $100 per share. Water-Willy's market value is $800,000, and it has 10,000 shares of common stock outstanding. Goodtimes' market value is $1,500,000, and it has 75,000 shares of common stock outstanding. Goodtimes' estimates the incremental value after purchasing WaterWilly is $400,000.

a. If cash is used, what will be the price per share of Goodtimes both before and after the merger?

b. If stock is used, what will be the stock price of Goodtimes after the merger?

CR26.3 The following is premerger information on Barrett Partnerships and Exon Corporation.

	Barret	Exon
Total earnings	$50,000	$75,000
Shares outstanding	10,000	20,000
Price per share	$40	$35

a. If Barrett exchanges one share of common stock for each share of Exon, what will be the price of the new firm if the P/E ratio remains at Barrett's current P/E ratio?

b. What is the new price per share and P/E if the P/E ratio simply reflects the combined total market value and combined total earnings of the firms?

CR26.4   Burger Barn recently acquired Kosher Hot Dog. Their balance sheets and income statements are listed below.

Balance Sheets		
	Burger Barn	**Kosher Hot Dog**
Current assets	$ 50	$ 25
Long-term assets	350	200
Goodwill	0	0
Total	$400	$225
Debt	$200	$ 0
Equity	200	225
Total	$400	$225

Income Statements		
	Burger Barn	**Kosher Hot Dog**
Sales	$500	$250
Cost of goods sold	250	100
Depreciation	100	50
Interest	50	20
Taxes (40%)	40	32
Net income	$ 60	$ 48

Burger Barn paid $300,000 in cash for Kosher Hot Dog. Long-term assets of Kosher were revalued to $250. Any additions to long-term assets and goodwill will be depreciated or amortized using straight-line over 5 years. Develop a postmerger combined balance sheet and income statement under both the pooling of interests and purchase accounting methods.

PROBLEMS

26.1   Dellva Printing is analyzing the possible acquisition of Big Sky Electric. Dellva's market value is $3,000,000, and its market price per share is $40. Big Sky's market value is $800,000; Dellva estimates the incremental value, Δvalue, is $250,000, and the total purchase price would be $1,000,000.

a.   If cash is used, what is the NPV of the proposed acquisition?
b.   What is the NPV if stock is employed?
c.   Why is the NPV for a cash-financed merger greater than if stock is employed? How much more cash could be offered if the NPV for a cash-financed deal just equaled the NPV for the stock-financed deal?

26.2   West Virginia Foods is investigating a possible acquisition financed with cash. It estimates the incremental benefits and investment as follows:

Year	ΔCFBT	ΔDep*	Δ Investment
	$ 0	$ 0	$300,000
1	40,000	60,000	—
2	50,000	96,000	—
3	60,000	57,000	—
4	100,000	45,000	—
5	100,000	42,000	—
6	70,000	0	—
7	20,000	0	—

*Δdepreciation is for the Δinvestment in the column immediately to the right.

Without the incremental investment, West Virginia Foods estimates there will be very few benefits from the acquisition. Should it proceed with plans for the acquisition if the marginal tax rate is 35 percent and the appropriate opportunity cost of capital is 18 percent?

26.3   The estimated incremental benefits and investments for a proposed acquisition are:

Year	ΔCFBT	ΔDep*	ΔInvestment
0	$ 0	$ 0	$ 100,000
1	200,000	400,000	1,200,000
2	400,000	500,000	300,000
3	500,000	200,000	200,000
4 to ∞	800,000	50,000	200,000

*Δdepreciation is for the Δinvestment in the column immediately to the right.

The tax rate is 0.35, and the opportunity cost of capital is 20 percent. The present market value of the target is $1,000,000, and the bidder's market value is $4,500,000. What is the NPV if the target firm's shareholders will control 25 percent of the combined firm's shares after the acquisition? Should the proposed acquisition be completed?

26.4   Bill's Sporting Goods is examining the possible acquisition of Malatesta Industries. Bill's has estimated the following anticipated incremental benefits and investments:

Year	ΔCFBT	ΔDep*	ΔInvestment
0	$ 0	$ 0	$ 50,000
1	80,000	30,000	100,000
2	150,000	60,000	25,000
3	150,000	60,000	—
4	150,000	25,000	—
5	60,000	—	—

*Δdepreciation is for the Δinvestment in the column immediately to the right.

a. If Bill's tax rate is 0.30, calculate the incremental after-tax cash flows, ΔCF, expected from Malatesta.

b. The market value of Bill's before the merger is $900,000, and Malatesta Industries' pre-merger market value is $400,000. The market price per share of Bill's stock is $100, and the appropriate opportunity rate is 12 percent. Calculate the NPV for both a cash-financed and a stock-financed merger if Bill's pays a premium of 25 percent above Malatesta's current market value.

26.5 Longfellow has agreed to acquire Sherman Brothers. The following information is for the two firms prior to the merger:

	Longfellow	Sherman Brothers
Earnings	$600,000	$900,000
Shares of common stock outstanding	400,000	250,000
EPS	$1.50	$3.60
P/E ratio	21	21

The merger terms provide that two shares of Longfellow will be issued for every share of Sherman Brothers common stock. (*Note:* This is not an NPV problem.)

a. Josh owns 100 shares of Longfellow stock. If the P/E of the combined firm is estimated to be 19, will he gain or lose from the transaction?

b. Are synergistic benefits evident?

c. How do you reconcile the answers to (a) and (b), which appear to conflict with each other?

26.6 Lamoureux Engine is evaluating four possible targets, which have the following financial data:

	P	Q	R	U
Benefits	$2,800,000	$3,900,000	$3,100,000	$4,500,000
Shares of common stock outstanding	200,000	300,000	100,000	400,000
Stock price per share	$10	$18	$30	$7
Expected earnings	$400,000	$600,000	$700,000	$600,000

Lamoureux presently has 800,000 shares of stock outstanding, its stock price is $14, and its expected earnings are $1.6 million without any merger. Assume that the target firms have no debt, no premium is paid, and cash is used to finance the mergers.

a. Calculate the NPV of the four proposed mergers. Are any of the mergers infeasible?

b. Calculate the postmerger EPS for the feasible merger candidates.

c. If only one merger can be undertaken, which one is it? Why?

26.7 The Jones Company is in the process of acquiring Imperial Valley Industries. Prior to the merger, the following information existed:

	Jones	Imperial Valley
Total earnings	$3,000,000	$1,000,000
Shares of common stock outstanding	1,000,000	500,000
P/E ratio	15 times	10 times

a. Find the premerger EPS, market price per share, and total market value for both firms. (*Note:* This is not an NPV problem.)

b. If Jones exchanges one share of common stock for every two shares of Imperial Valley, how many shares of stock will be issued? What is the postmerger EPS for the combined firms? What percentage premium did Jones pay over Imperial Valley's premerger market value?

c. If the P/E stays at 15 times, what is the total value of the combined firm? At 14 times? Is any evidence of synergism indicated by the resulting market values?

26.8   Biller Textile is considering the acquisition of Omega Industries. Biller has estimated the following anticipated incremental benefits and investments:

Year	ΔCFBT	ΔDep*	ΔInvestment	ΔNet WorkingCapital
0	$ 0	$ 0	$ 70,000	$ 0
1	200,000	30,000	200,000	30,000
2	200,000	90,000	100,000	10,000
3	300,000	90,000	—	10,000
4	300,000	90,000	—.	10,000
5	200,000	70,000	—	—
6	100,000	0	—	—

*Δdepreciation is for the Δinvestment in the column immediately to the right.

Omega's present market value is $600,000, and Biller's is $2,000,000. The marginal tax rate is 30 percent, the discount rate is 15 percent, and Biller has 80,000 shares of stock outstanding.

a. If the exchange ratio is 1.4, what is the NPV if cash is used? If stock is employed?

b. What is the NPV for both a cash-financed and a stock-financed merger if *all of the following conditions occur simultaneously* [while everything else remains as in (a)]?

1. CFBT for years 7–10 becomes $100,000 each.
2. Omega's present market value is $1,000,000.
3. The marginal tax rate is 40 percent.
4. The discount rate is 18 percent.
5. The exchange ratio is 1.3.

26.9   Two firms, Ralston (R) and Sizemore (S), are going to merge. Ralston's market value is $11.75 million and its beta is 1.40; Sizemore has a market value of $25.50 million and a beta of 1.05. Both firms are all-equity financed, no premium or synergism is involved, and the new firm will be all-equity financed. After merging, a new project with a NPV of $6.50 million and a beta of 1.50 will be undertaken. What will be the market value of firm RS, and what will be its beta? (*Note:* There are no transactions costs, and the new project is not reflected in the existing market values or betas.)

26.10 Louisburg has just announced a tender offer for Davis Industries at a price of $100 per share. Six months ago Davis's market price per share was $50. During the last 6 months, the market portfolio, k_M, has risen from 1,000 to 1,200.

a. What is the *percentage increase* in the market portfolio during the last 6 months?
b. If the market is efficient and Davis's beta is 1.3, what is the dollar premium per share being offered for Davis?
c. If the actual market price of Davis's stock was $70 at the time of the offer, does this necessarily mean the market is inefficient?

26.11 Buffalo Enterprises has agreed to merge into Gerard. To accomplish the merger, two shares of Gerard will be exchanged for every share of Buffalo. Before the merger, the firms were as follows:

	Gerard	Buffalo
Earnings	$1,000,000	$1,000,000
Shares of common stock outstanding	500,000	500,000
EPS	$2	$3
P/E ratio	10	8

a. Calculate the postmerger EPS.
b. How much of the value of the combined firm can be attributed to synergistic effects?
c. Did the stockholders of Buffalo Enterprises gain? How about Gerard's stockholders?

26.12 Carol started her own company many years ago. She owns all 80,000 shares of stock in the firm, and her cost basis for individual income tax purposes is $1 per share. She recently received an offer to sell out at $50 per share—in stock or in cash. If she elects stock, she will receive one share of stock with a market value of $50 per share for each share of her stock.

a. If we assume Carol is in the 28 percent tax bracket for ordinary income and does not need any of the proceeds to live on, which form of payment should she favor?
b. What are her net after-tax proceeds if she accepts cash?
c. Are there any other factors she should consider?

26.13 Long Beach Laboratories is acquiring Omaha Drug. The premerger balance sheets and income statements for both firms are as follows:

Balance Sheets		
	Long Beach Laboratories	Omaha Drug
Current assets	$ 300,000	$20,000
Long-term assets	700,000	70,000
Total	$1,000,000	$90,000
Debt	$ 400,000	$10,000
Equity	600,000	80,000
Total	$1,000,000	$90,000

Income Statements		
	Long Beach Laboratories	Omaha Drug
Sales	$4,000,000	$900,000
Cash expenses	3,000,000	688,700
Depreciation	100,000	20,000
EBIT	900,000	191,300
Interest	56,000	1,400
EBT	844,000	189,900
Taxes (40%)	337,600	75,960
EAT	$ 506,400	$113,940
Shares of common stock outstanding	506,400	113,940

Long Beach will pay $450,000 in stock for Omaha, and no matter which accounting treatment is employed, the number of shares of common stock outstanding after the merger will be the sum of the two premerger share amounts. If purchase accounting is employed, then current assets for Omaha will be $20,000, long-term assets will be $230,000, and goodwill will be $200,000. Debt will be $10,000, and equity will be $440,000. The additional depreciation and goodwill is written off via the straight-line method over 5 years.

a. Determine the postmerger combined balance sheet under both the purchase and pooling of interests treatments.
b. Determine the postmerger combined income statement under both purchase and pooling of interests. Then calculate EPS for both.
c. Why does EPS decrease with the purchase method of accounting, but not when pooling of interests is employed?

26.14 Mini Case Sonny's is a rapidly growing firm that has just decided to have its stock listed on the New York Stock Exchange. To keep growing, it plans to make a few selected acquisitions during the next few years. At the same time, Sonny's has become more concerned about maximizing the value of the firm, and remaining independent.

a. Sonny's is concerned about issues that deal with the "market for corporate control." What is meant by that term?
b. What sensible reasons exist for merging? What dubious reasons?
c. Sonny's is considering acquiring Gilfords West. The following incremental benefits and investments have been estimated (in millions):

Year	ΔCFBT	ΔDep*	ΔInvestment
1	$10	$3	$ 8
2	15	4	10
3	18	3	5
4	20	2	3
5	25	1	2
6	15		2
7	10		2

*Δdepreciation is for the Δinvestment in the column immediately to the right.

If cash is employed, the current market value of Gilfords is $50 million, the opportunity cost of capital is 18 percent, and Sonny's marginal tax rate is 35 percent. What is the most Sonny's can pay for Gilfords and still proceed with the acquisition?

d. Now assume that stock will be employed. The market value of Sonny's is $400 million, and the number of shares of stock for Sonny's is 5 million. If Sonny's current shareholders will end up with at least 90 percent of the total number of shares outstanding in the combined firm, is a merger feasible? How many total shares will be outstanding after the merger?

e. Explain what the primary differences are to both the bidder and the target if cash is used instead of stock.

f. Many mistakes can occur that result in firms making inappropriate (i.e., non-wealth-maximizing) acquisitions. What are some of these mistakes?

g. If Sonny's wants to make itself a more difficult target, what kinds of steps can be taken? Which ones, in your opinion, are likely to be most effective? Can Sonny's completely protect itself from being taken over?

h. Discuss alternative corporate restructuring approaches.

REFERENCES

Three recent books that cover a wide range of topics in this area are:

AUERBACH, ALAN J. (ed.) *Corporate Takeovers: Causes and Consequences.* Chicago: University of Chicago Press, 1988.

COFFEE, JOHN C., JR., LOUIS LOWENSTEIN, and SUSAN ROSE-ACKERMAN (eds.). *Knights, Raiders, and Targets: The Impact of the Hostile Takeover.* New York: Oxford University Press, 1988.

STERN, JOEL M., G. BENNETT STEWART III, and DONALD H. CHEW (eds.) *Corporate Restructuring and Executive Compensation.* Cambridge, Mass.: Ballinger, 1989.

Some recent articles on mergers and corporate restructuring are:

AGRAWAL, ANUP, JEFFREY F. JAFFE, and GERSHON N. MANDELKER. "The Post-Merger Performance of Acquiring Firms: A Re-Examination of an Anomaly." *Journal of Finance* 47 (September 1992): 1605–21.

DATTA, DEEPAK K., GEORGE E. PINCHES, and V. K. NARAYANAN. "Factors Influencing Wealth Creation from Mergers and Acquisitions: A Meta-Analysis." *Strategic Management Journal* 13 (January 1992): 67–84.

DONALDSON, GORDON. "Voluntary Restructuring: The Case of General Mills." *Journal of Applied Corporate Finance* 4 (Fall 1991): 6–19.

HEALY, PAUL M., KRISHNA G. PALEPU, and RICHARD S. RUBACK. "Does Corporate Performance Improve After Mergers?" *Journal of Financial Economics* 31 (April 1992): 135–75.

INSELBAG, ISIK, and HOWARD KAUFOLD. "How to Value Recapitalizations and Leveraged Buyouts." *Journal of Applied Corporate Finance* 2 (Summer 1989): 87–96.

JENSEN, MICHAEL C. "Agency Costs of Free Cash Flow, Corporate Finance, and the Market for Takeovers." *American Economic Review* 76 (May 1986): 323–29.

JOHN, KOSE, LARRY H. P. LANG, and JEFFREY NETTER. "The Voluntary Restructuring of Large Firms in Response to Performance Decline." *Journal of Finance* 47 (July 1992): 891–917.

KAPLAN, STEVEN N. "The Staying Power of Leveraged Buyouts." *Journal of Financial Economics* 29 (October 1991): 287–313.

LANG, LARRY H. P., RENE STULZ, and RALPH A. WALKING. "A Test of the Free Cash Flow Hypothesis: The Case of Bidder Returns." *Journal of Financial Economics* 29 (October 1991): 315–35.

MICHEL, ALLEN, and ISRAEL SHAKED. "RJR Nabisco: A Case Study of a Complex Leveraged Buyout" *Financial Analysts Journal* 47 (September/October 1991): 15–27.

MOHAN, NANCY, M. FALL AININA, DANIEL KAUFMAN, and BERNARD J. WINGER. "Acquisition/Divestiture Valuation Practices in Major U.S. Firms." *Financial Practice and Education* 1 (Spring 1991): 73–81.

WRUCK, KAREN H. "What Really Went Wrong at Revco?" *Journal of Applied Corporate Finance* 4 (Summer 1991): 79–92.

27 *International Financial Management*

EXECUTIVE SUMMARY

The fundamental difference between domestic and international financial management is the introduction of more than one currency. Foreign exchange affects many of the firm's financial management decisions; therefore, an understanding of foreign exchange rates is essential.

The expectations theory of forward exchange rates, purchasing power parity, the international Fisher effect, and interest rate parity establish the expected relationships between product prices, interest rates, and spot and forward exchange rates. In the short run these relationships do not always hold as expected; this is often due to government intervention, transactions costs, and other imperfections. In the longer run the relationships usually conform closer to those predicted by the four parity conditions cited above.

In making investment decisions in a multinational context, the first issue is to determine the appropriate opportunity cost of capital. It may be above or below the firm's domestic rate. Cash flows are typically converted into the currency of the parent company's country before the decisions are made. Capital structure and dividend decisions must also be made considering the overall objective of the multinational firm.

In financing projects overseas, there are three choices of where to raise funds: in the U.S., in the host country, or in another country where costs are lower. The actual choice depends on the specifics of the situation. Raising funds, whether by borrowing or leasing, is truly international in scope.

Numerous specific considerations also come into play when short-term financial management, accounting, and tax aspects of multinational firms are examined. Throughout, the focus of financial management remains the same—that is, to maximize the market value of the firm—but additional complexities arise when the financial management of multinational firms is considered.

FINANCIAL MANAGEMENT IN AN INTERNATIONAL CONTEXT

Until now we have focused on doing business in the United States, but, increasingly, firms derive substantial portions of their sales outside of their home country. In 1990 some of the largest firms who had substantially more foreign than domestic sales included:

Firm	Home Country	Foreign Sales as a Percent of Total Sales
Nestle	Switzerland	98%
Roche Holding	Switzerland	96
Philips Electronics	Holland	93
Exxon	United States	86
Asea Brown Boveri	Switzerland/Sweden	85
Bayer	Germany	84
British Petroleum	Britain	79
News Corp.	Australia	78
Mobil	United States	77
Alcatel Alsthom	France	67

While many firms sell goods or services in foreign markets, they also actively work to place production and other operations internationally. Although many reasons exist for placing production facilities in various countries, there appear to be two primary reasons—and both of them relate to market imperfections. The first kind of imperfection can be thought of as *structural imperfections*, which include natural ones (transportation costs, for example) or man-made ones. Examples of man-made structural imperfections include government restrictions on investment or imports, taxes, and subsidies. The second type of imperfection includes those that are inherent in the transactions or markets themselves. Some of these imperfections include uncertainty that a supplier will deliver an item, difficulties customers face in evaluating unfamiliar products, the cost of negotiating deals, economies of scale in production, purchasing or distribution that provides advantages to local firms and imposes barriers to newcomers, uncertainty about competitor actions, and the like. The challenge faced by firms in a multinational context is far broader than simply selling or producing goods or providing services outside of the home country.

When discussing international financial management, it is important to realize that although we might initially think about firms having a global orientation, in reality most of them attempt to implement their global strategy in narrower confines. Thus, firms in the European Common Market tend to invest primarily in Western Europe and now in Eastern Europe as well. The equivalent for American firms is to invest principally in Canada, Mexico, and South America. For Japanese firms the equivalent is to invest primarily in South Korea, greater China, and Southeast Asia. The basic investment clusters that firms in the world's three main economic blocks invest in are shown in Figure 27.1. After the home region is developed, firms often invest in other

Figure 27.1

Regional Investment Clusters

While firms may "think globally," investment patterns are more regional in nature, and expansion is based on regional proximity, historical ties, and moving into another part of the triangle.

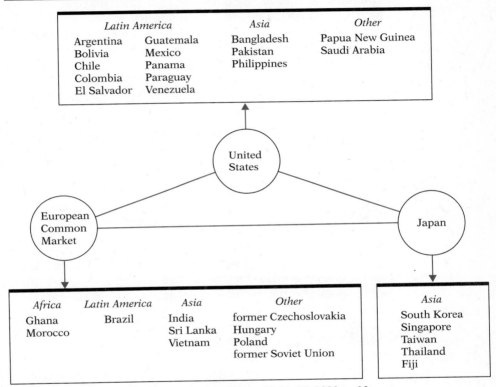

Latin America		Asia	Other
Argentina	Guatemala	Bangladesh	Papua New Guinea
Bolivia	Mexico	Pakistan	Saudi Arabia
Chile	Panama	Philippines	
Colombia	Paraguay		
El Salvador	Venezuela		

United States

European Common Market

Japan

Africa	Latin America	Asia	Other
Ghana	Brazil	India	former Czechoslovakia
Morocco		Sri Lanka	Hungary
		Vietnam	Poland
			former Soviet Union

Asia
South Korea
Singapore
Taiwan
Thailand
Fiji

Source: Adapted from "Multinationals," *The Economist,* March 27, 1993; p. 12.

regions, especially in the other parts of the triangle of the European Common Market, the United States, or Japan. For example, we see automobile manufacturers from both Japan and Germany investing in plants in the United States. Multinational firms buy, produce, employ, distribute, and thus compete in many different countries at the same time. But the primary way of doing this is through regional clusters around their home country and, more weakly, in regional clusters elsewhere. However, one important aspect of international finance is not confined to any regional cluster—this is the raising of capital. Large firms, whether international or not, raise capital around the world wherever it is cheapest.

The essential goal of international financial management is exactly as we have discussed for U.S.-based firms: to maximize the value of the firm by focusing on the after-tax cash flows, the risks, and the opportunity costs. Thus, we come back to the basic concerns of financial management—this time by focusing attention on those activities outside of the home country.

One of the most important features of international financial management is that we need to deal with more than one currency. Therefore, we need to look at how foreign exchange markets operate and why exchange rates change. Next we consider the topic of making investment decisions in an international context. That is, how do multinational companies make their capital budgeting decisions? Then we will examine international capital structure and dividend decisions, financing decisions, short-term financial management decisions, and accounting and tax issues. We will see that the basic concepts of financial management are still relevant, with some additional pitfalls to watch out for. In the next chapter we examine how multinational firms use forwards, futures, swaps, and options to hedge foreign exchange risk.

Concept Review Questions

■ What are two primary reasons why firms may place a production facility in a foreign country?

■ How are domestic financial decisions and international financial decisions similar? How are they different?

FOREIGN EXCHANGE RATES

A fundamental difference between domestic and international financial management is that international transactions are conducted in more than one currency. For example, the dollar is used in the United States, the franc in France, the rupee in India, the yen in Japan, the mark in Germany, and the peso in Mexico.

SPOT AND FORWARD RATES

Foreign exchange rates are the conversion rates between currencies. They depend on the relative supply and demand for two currencies, inflation in the countries, and other factors. The **spot rate of exchange** is the exchange rate between two currencies on any given day. The spot rate between the U.S. dollar and several other currencies, for immediate delivery on a given day, is shown in Table 27.1.

Until the early 1970s, the world was on a fixed exchange rate system. Since 1973, it has operated on a "managed" floating system. Major world currencies move—float—somewhat freely with market forces. Nevertheless, the central banks of countries intervene by buying or selling in the foreign exchange market to smooth out some of the fluctuations. Each central bank also attempts to keep its exchange rates within prescribed government limits to help the country's export or import situation. Floating exchange rates are a fact of life with which all managers must be prepared to cope.

In practice, foreign currencies are generally quoted as the number of units of the foreign currency per dollar. An exception to this is the pound sterling, which is generally quoted in dollars per pound sterling. We will begin by concentrating on

Table 27.1

Selected Foreign Exchange Rates Listed in a Recent Issue of *The Wall Street Journal*

Exchange rates can be stated two different ways; however, conversion from one to the other is straightforward. Exchange rates may change on a daily basis as conditions change in either of the countries, or as events throughout the world influence the rates.

Country	Currency	U.S. Dollars Required to Buy One Unit (1)	Number of Units of Foreign Currency per U.S. Dollar* (2)
Austria	Schilling	0.09005	11.10
Britain	Pound	1.5743	0.6352
Canada	Dollar	0.7855	1.2731
France	Franc	0.18788	5.3225
Germany	Mark	0.6335	1.5785
Hong Kong	Dollar	0.12937	7.7295
India	Rupee	0.03214	31.11
Japan	Yen	0.009003	111.07
Saudi Arabia	Riyal	0.26702	3.7450
Venezuela	Bolivar	0.01181	84.66

*Column 2 equals 1.0 divided by column 1.

understanding foreign exchange rates as units of foreign currency per dollar. Thus, if the current, or spot, rate of exchange between Germany and the United States is 1.500, that means M/$1 = 1.500, which indicates that 1.500 marks equal $1, or that the dollar price of a single mark is $0.667 (i.e., 1/1.500).

In addition to the spot rate of exchange, there are also **forward rates of exchange** that, quoted as of today, indicate the future rate of exchange for some period, such as the 30-day forward rate, the 60-day forward rate, and the 180-day forward rate. Thus, the current 180-day forward rate of exchange between the mark and the dollar may be 1.478. This simply says that the current rate of exchange for delivery 180 days from now is 1.478 M/$ (that is, 1.478 marks for every dollar).

SOME FUNDAMENTAL RELATIONSHIPS

Assuming away transactions costs, intervention by governments, and other imperfections, we can state some fundamental relationships that apply to product prices, interest rates, and spot and forward exchange rates between two countries. To generalize, assume country 1 is the domestic country and country 2 is the foreign country.

Let's define the following

where

$F_{2/1}$ = forward rate in units of country 2's currency to one unit of country 1's currency

$S_{2/1}$ = spot rate in units of country 2's currency to one unit of country 1's currency

k_{RF2} = risk-free interest rate in country 2 for the appropriate forward period

k_{RF1} = risk-free interest rate in country 1 for the appropriate forward period

i_2 = rate of inflation in country 2 for the appropriate forward period

i_1 = rate of inflation in country 1 for the appropriate forward period

In this simple world the relationship between forward and spot exchange rates, inflation rates, and interest rates is shown in Figure 27.2.

To understand these relationships, we will begin at the top left of Figure 27.2. The first relationship, based on the **expectations theory of forward exchange rates,** says that the percentage difference between the forward rate and today's spot rate is equal to the expected change in the spot rate, or

$$\frac{F_{2/1}}{S_{2/1}} = \frac{E(S_{2/1})}{S_{2/1}} \tag{27.1}$$

where E signifies the expected future spot rate of exchange of country 2's currency relative to country 1's currency. Thus, in the absence of other interventions and

Figure 27.2

The Relationship Between Spot Exchange Rates, Forward Exchange Rates, Inflation, and Interest

While imperfections, transactions costs, and government central bank intervention affect these relationships, over longer periods of time the relationships appear to hold.

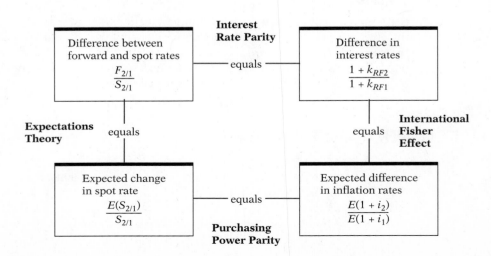

occurrences, the expectations theory of foreign exchange rates say that the best estimation of the future spot rate is the current forward rate of exchange.[1]

The second link is between the expected change in the spot rate of exchange and the inflation rate differential between the two countries. **Purchasing power parity** explains that the relationship between today's spot rate of exchange and the spot rate of exchange in the future is determined by expected differential rates of inflation between the two countries, so

$$\frac{E(S_{2/1})}{S_{2/1}} = \frac{E(1 + i_2)}{E(1 + i_1)} \tag{27.2}$$

An alternative way to think about purchasing power parity is that it implies that a unit of the domestic currency should have the same purchasing power anywhere in the world. One example of purchasing power parity is provided in Table 27.2, in which the price of a Big Mac is compared in different countries. For example, in Russia it takes 780 roubles to buy as many Big Macs as with 2.28 U.S. dollars. The rate of exchange implied by Big Macs is 780 roubles = $2.28, or $1 = 342 roubles. The actual rate of exchange was 686 roubles per dollar. Thus, prices were about twice as expensive in Russia as implied by purchasing power parity.

The third link is between expected differences in inflation rates and differences in interest rates. The **international Fisher effect,** which is based on the Fisher effect mentioned in Chapter 3, says that countries with high rates of inflation should have higher interest rates than countries with lower rates of inflation, so that

$$\frac{E(1 + i_2)}{E(1 + i_1)} = \frac{1 + k_{RF2}}{1 + k_{RF1}} \tag{27.3}$$

Thus, in addition to the real rate of interest, which is assumed to be essentially the same in all countries, the international Fisher effect indicates that differences in expected rates of inflation will be reflected by differences in risk-free interest rates between two countries.

Finally, we can complete the loop specified in Figure 27.2 by examining the **interest rate parity** relationship. It says that differences in interest rates between two countries will affect the relationship between spot and forward rates of exchange, so that

$$\frac{1 + k_{RF2}}{1 + k_{RF1}} = \frac{F_{2/1}}{S_{2/1}} \tag{27.4}$$

Thus, interest rate differentials between two countries will have to be offset by differences in the forward rate of exchange and the spot rate of exchange between the countries.

In practice, things are not quite so simple. Trade barriers exist between countries; government actions through their central banks impact inflation, interest rates, and

[1] The notion of the expectations theory employed here is similar to that employed in Appendix 3A when discussing the expectations theory of interest rate, except that now we are referring to exchange rates.

Table 27.2

Big Mac Prices in Different Countries

Although it is meant to be a little "tongue in cheek," the Big Mac index has been found to provide estimates that are strikingly similar to those provided by more sophisticated calculations.

	Price in Local Currency	Big Mac Exchange Rate	Actual Exchange Rate	Percent Local Currency Is Under (−) or Over (+) Valued %
United States	**$2.28**	---	---	---
Argentina	Peso3.60	1.58	1.00	+58
Australia	A$2.45	1.07	1.39	−23
Belgium	BFr109	47.81	32.45	+47
Brazil	Cr77,000	33,772	27,521	+23
Britain	£1.79	1.27	1.56	+23
Canada	C$2.76	1.21	1.26	−4
China	Yuan8.50	3.73	5.68	−34
Denmark	DKr25.75	11.29	6.06	+86
France	FFr18.50	8.11	5.34	+52
Germany	M4.60	2.02	1.58	+28
Holland	F15.45	2.39	1.77	+35
Hong Kong	HK$9.00	3.95	7.73	−49
Hungary	Forint157	68.86	88.18	−22
Ireland	£1.48	1.54	1.54	0
Italy	Lire4,500	1,974	1,523	+30
Japan	¥391	171	113	+51
Malaysia	Ringgit3.35	1.47	2.58	−43
Mexico	Peso7.09	3.11	3.10	0
Russia	Rouble780	342	686	−50
S. Korea	Won2,300	1,009	796	+27
Spain	Ptas325	143	114	+25
Sweden	SKr25.50	11.18	7.43	+50
Switzerland	SwFr5.70	2.50	1.45	+72
Thailand	Baht48	21.05	25.16	−16

Source: "Big Mac Currencies," *The Economist* (April 17, 1993): 79.

foreign exchange rates; and other imperfections exist. Numerous empirical tests have been conducted on portions of the relationships discussed above. In general, over longer periods of time, the relationships tend to hold up fairly well. Although violations do occur, and may last for some period of time, the relationships provide a means of estimating the relationship between spot and future exchange rates, using data supplied by the financial markets.

INTEREST RATES, SPOT RATES, AND FORWARD RATES

Using the interest rate parity relationship, at any point in time the relationship between spot and forward rates of exchange of the number of units of country 2's currency per country 1's currency unit is given by

$$F_{2/1} = \frac{S_{2/1}(1 + k_{RF2})}{1 + k_{RF1}} \qquad (27.5)$$

Let's use an example to see this relationship. For the 180-day forward rate of German marks per U.S. dollar of 1.478 M/$, mentioned previously, we have

$$F_{M/\$} = \frac{S_{M/\$}(1 + k_{RFM})}{1 + k_{RF\$}}$$

where

$F_{M/\$}$ = the current 180-day forward exchange rate in marks per dollar
$S_{M/\$}$ = the current spot exchange rate in marks per dollar
k_{RFM} = risk-free interest rate on 180-day German securities, expressed in terms of a 180-day return
$k_{RF\$}$ = risk-free interest rate on 180-day U.S. securities, expressed in terms of a 180-day return

Assume that the risk-free rate in Germany is 4 percent and that the risk-free rate in the United States is 7 percent. Then, for simplicity, assuming a 360-day year, the 180-day rates are 2 percent and 3.5 percent, respectively. With a current spot rate of 1.500 M/$, the forward rate of exchange is

$$F_{M/\$} = \frac{1.500(1.02)}{1.035} = 1.478$$

If we enter into a contract today, in 180 days we would deliver (or receive, depending on the contract) 1.478 marks per dollar.

Let us summarize and clarify this by spelling out what the relationship means. If k_{RF2} is *greater than* k_{RF1}, then

1. The forward rate, $F_{2/1}$, is greater than the spot rate, $S_{2/1}$.
2. Country 2's currency is selling at a discount.
3. Country 2's currency is weakening, relative to country 1's currency.

Alternatively, if k_{RF2} is *less than* k_{RF1}, then

1. The forward rate, $F_{2/1}$, is less than the spot rate, $S_{2/1}$.
2. Country 2's currency is selling at a premium.
3. Country 2's currency is strengthening, relative to country 1's currency.

Assuming country 2 is Germany and country 1 is the United States, then

$$
\text{if the M strengthens} \rightarrow \text{price of M} \uparrow \text{ so} \begin{cases} \text{M/\$}\downarrow, & \text{you get fewer M/\$} \\ \text{\$/M}\uparrow, & \text{it takes more \$ to buy a M} \end{cases}
$$

This relationship also implies that future interest rates and inflation in Germany are expected to be *lower* than in the United States. Alternatively,

$$
\text{if the M weakens} \rightarrow \text{price of M} \downarrow \text{ so} \begin{cases} \text{M/\$}\uparrow, & \text{you get fewer M/\$} \\ \text{\$/M}\downarrow, & \text{it takes fewer \$ to buy a M} \end{cases}
$$

This relationship implies that future interest rates and inflation in Germany are expected to be *higher* than in the United States.

Keeping these ideas and terms straight is important as we proceed. We will need this understanding in the rest of this chapter and also in Chapter 28.

Concept Review Questions

- What are the spot rate of exchange and the forward rate of exchange?
- Briefly describe the relationship between the spot and forward rates of exchange based on the expectations theory of forward exchange rates, purchasing power parity, the international Fisher effect, and interest rate parity.

CAPITAL BUDGETING IN AN INTERNATIONAL CONTEXT

We have examined how capital budgeting decisions are made for firms within a country. When investments are made outside the multinational firm's home country, the basic steps are the same; that is, we determine the opportunity cost of capital, identify the relevant incremental cash flows, and accept all projects with positive net present values. However, though the steps are the same, there are some additional complications to consider.

THE OPPORTUNITY COST OF CAPITAL

When discussing capital budgeting decisions for domestic firms we indicated the "stand-alone principle" should apply. That is, the project should stand alone in terms of cash flows, and the opportunity cost of capital used to apply to those cash flows should signify the amount of risk related to the cash flows. An important question for multinational firms is whether the opportunity cost of capital, k, for foreign projects should be different from that for similar-risk domestic projects. The answer to that question depends on two items: First, what is the systematic risk for multinational firms? Second, what are the expropriation and creditor risks?

Systematic Risk and Portfolio Concerns

Based on the capital asset pricing model, we know it is the nondiversifiable risk (measured by beta, β_j) that is important in determining the opportunity cost of equity capital. By operating in a number of countries, multinational firms expose themselves to economic cycles that are not perfectly in phase with one another. That is, while the world economy generally moves somewhat together, there are often important differences in demand among countries. For example, demand in the United States will differ from demand in either Japan or Egypt. By having a significant portion of their operations and cash flows diversified over a number of countries, multinational firms may lessen the variability of their cash flows. This is true whether the nations they have diversified into are industrialized (such as the European Common Market and Japan), newly industrializing (such as Korea or Taiwan), or less developed (such as Honduras, Pakistan, or Zaire).

The important implication is that the nondiversifiable risk for a multinational firm may be less than if the firm had not diversified geographically. This means that the opportunity cost of equity capital will be lower and, other things being equal, the returns demanded will be lower.

Expropriation and Creditor Risks

The potential advantage from geographic diversification may be offset because of the increased possibility of expropriation of part or all of the firm's investment in a foreign subsidiary. We view expropriation broadly, to include not only pure nationalization but also lesser forms such as increased ownership by the host country.[2] In either case, the multinational loses part or all of its investment or claim on cash flows from its subsidiary. Expropriation may be gradual, with an increase in demand for participation by locals or the host government in the ownership of the business. Initially, it may take the form of a high tax or the right to buy the equity of the firm at some price. Often this price is extremely low relative to the market-determined worth of the subsidiary. A more dramatic form of expropriation was that suffered a number of years ago by some multinational firms with investments in Iran.

Multinational firms can use various strategies in attempting to minimize the risk of expropriation. Generally, these fall into two categories: The first involves positive approaches, such as joint ventures, local participation, prior agreements for sale, and the like. All are designed to foster a positive, long-term relationship. The second involves limiting the investment of the parent, or controlling the raw material, production, or sales process so the subsidiaries' success is fully dependent on the parent.

It should also be noted that default risk is often more serious in foreign countries than in the United States. Because bankruptcy laws similar to those in the United States often do not exist, creditors have little recourse to recoup losses. This factor must also be considered when multinational firms make capital budgeting and marketing decisions.

If increased expropriation or creditor risk is present, it would offset, in part or total, any reduced opportunity cost from investing overseas. The net result is that the

---

[2] Instances of "pure" expropriation by countries has decreased significantly over the last 15 to 20 years.

opportunity cost of capital may be the same, lower, or higher, for an international capital budgeting project. It all depends on the project itself and the country where the investment is made.

MAXIMIZE NET PRESENT VALUE

Assume that a firm's export business has risen to the point that it is worth establishing a subsidiary in Germany. Ignoring certain complications for a minute, there are two basic ways to calculate the net present value, NPV, of its German venture:

1. The project's NPV can be evaluated entirely in terms of the German mark. Then this figure can be converted into dollars at the current exchange rate.
2. The per year cash flows can be estimated in German marks and then converted into dollars at the expected exchange rate. These dollar cash flows can then be discounted at a dollar-based opportunity cost of capital to give the investment's NPV in dollars.

Under certain conditions these approaches both provide the same result; however, the second is most often employed in practice. We will use the second method in order to illustrate the primary issues involved in making capital budgeting decisions internationally. Assume the cash flows, CFs, in marks are as follows:

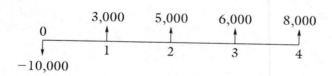

The appropriate U.S. opportunity cost of capital, k, is 18 percent and the risk-free rate, k_{RF}, is 7 percent. The 7 percent is obtained simply by looking in the newspaper for the rate on U.S. Treasury bills. Likewise, assume the risk-free rate in Germany is 4 percent.

Before discounting, we must convert the cash flows in German marks into U.S. dollars. To do this we need to forecast what the exchange rates will be in the future. Rather than attempting to predict future exchange rates directly, it is preferable to recognize, as we have throughout, that markets are reasonably efficient. Therefore, based on the international Fisher effect, we know the current difference between the U.S. and German interest rates provides the best estimate of the difference in future inflation rates. With the U.S. risk-free rate at 7 percent and the German risk-free rate at 4 percent, we see there is a 3 percent difference in nominal interest rates. That means that *expected* inflation is approximately 7 percent in the United States, and it is approximately 4 percent in Germany.[3]

---

[3] For simplicity, it is assumed that the real rate of interest is approximately zero.

We said the current spot rate was 1.5 German marks to the dollar. But because expected inflation rate in Germany is somewhat lower than in the United States, interest rate parity tells us the mark is expected to appreciate against the dollar as follows:

$$\begin{pmatrix} \text{expected spot rate} \\ \text{at end of year} \end{pmatrix} = \begin{pmatrix} \text{spot rate at} \\ \text{start of year} \end{pmatrix} \begin{pmatrix} \text{inflation rate} \\ \text{differential} \end{pmatrix} \qquad (27.6)$$

$$= (1.50)\left(\frac{1.04}{1.07}\right) = 1.458 \text{ marks per dollar}$$

At the end of year 2 the expected rate of exchange would be:

$$= (1.50)\left(\frac{1.04^2}{1.07^2}\right) = 1.417$$

The expected rates of exchange for years 3 and 4 are calculated in a similar manner. The forecasted cash flows and expected exchange rates are then:

		Year			
	0	1	2	3	4
1. Cash flow in marks, CF	−10,000	3,000	5,000	6,000	8,000
2. Forecasted spot exchange rate	1.500	1.458	1.417	1.377	1.339
3. Cash flow in dollars, CF (row 1/row 2)	−6,667	2,058	3,529	4,357	5,975

Because we have converted these cash flows into dollars, we use the dollar-denominated opportunity cost of capital of 18 percent to calculate the net present value as follows:

$$NPV = \$2,058/(1 + 0.18)^1 + \$3,529/(1 + 0.18)^2 + \$4,357/(1 + 0.18)^3$$
$$+ \$5,975/(1 + 0.18)^4 - \$6,667$$
$$= \$1,744 + \$2,534 + \$2,652 + \$3,082 - \$6,667 = \$3,345$$

With a positive NPV, we would accept the project.

UNREMITTED FUNDS

So far we have assumed all cash flows can be remitted (or brought) back to the parent company. The ability to remit funds is not as easy as we have assumed. A foreign subsidiary can remit funds to a parent in many ways including the following: dividends, management fees, interest and principal payments on debt, and royalties on the use of trade names and patents. This topic quickly becomes messy, and many complexities occur in different countries. Multinational firms must pay special attention to remittance for two reasons: First, there may be current and/or future exchange controls. Many governments are sensitive to the charge of being exploited by foreign firms. They have therefore attempted to limit the ability of multinational firms to take funds out of the host country. The second reason is taxes. Not only do taxes have to be paid in the foreign country, but the amount of taxes paid on funds remitted to the United States depends on whether the payment is a management fee, a royalty, a dividend, or simply the payment of interest or principal.

To illustrate some of the complexity, assume that Germany has a corporate tax rate of 30 percent and that it also withholds taxes at 5 percent on funds transferred out of the country. The withholding tax is not really "withheld" because it is never returned to the payer. In Table 27.3 we show the same initial cash flows in German marks as before, but *this time we assume they are before taxes.* Taking into account the German corporate taxes and the taxes withheld on remitted funds, row 5 provides the remitted cash flows in German marks. Then row 8 shows the impact of U.S. taxes, followed in row 9 by the credit for taxes paid in Germany. Finally, in row 10 the after-tax flows, CFs, in dollars are shown. The NPV is then

$$NPV = \$1,510/(1 + 0.18)^1 + \$2,590/(1 + 0.18)^2 + \$3,199/(1 + 0.18)^3$$
$$+ \$4,385/(1 + 0.18)^4 - \$6,667$$
$$= \$1,280 + \$1,860 + \$1,947 + \$2,262 - \$6,667 = \$682$$

Because the NPV is positive, the project would still be accepted.

This example illustrates some of the issues involved in determining the proper after-tax cash flows that multinationals must consider when making capital investment decisions. In practice, the issue becomes even more complex depending on taxes and how the funds can be brought out of the host country in order to channel them to the parent. These complications make the determination of the after-tax cash flow stream for international capital budgeting decisions even more challenging than for domestic capital budgeting projects.

EVALUATING ACQUISITIONS OUTSIDE THE BIDDER'S HOME COUNTRY

An acquisition of part or all of another firm is simply a big capital investment decision. The general procedures to employ in evaluating proposed acquisitions outside of the bidder's home country follow those discussed in Chapter 26. One complicating factor for merger evaluation of assets outside of the home country revolves around the impact of exchange rates on the process. The approach favored by most firms is to make the analysis in the currency of the proposed target. Thus, if an acquisition is being contemplated in Mexico, the analysis would be done in terms of the Mexican peso. The one requirement of this approach is that there be a well-developed capital market in the country of the proposed target so that a good estimate of the opportunity cost of capital can be obtained. Once the net present value is determined in the foreign currency, it can be converted into units of the home country's currency at the present rate of exchange. If the capital market in the target's home country is not well-developed, firms generally convert the incremental year-by-year cash flows back

Table 27.3

After-Tax Cash Flows to the Parent After German and U.S. Taxes

Because of restrictions on how funds are brought out of the host country and on taxes, cash flows in the parent country's currency are required in order to make effective capital budgeting decisions.

	Year				
	0	1	2	3	4
1. Cash flow before taxes, in marks	−10,000	3,000	5,000	6,000	8,000
2. German corporate tax at 30% (row 1 × 0.30)		900	1,500	1,800	2,400
3. Cash flow available for remittance to parent (row 1 − row 2)		2,100	3,500	4,200	5,600
4. Tax withheld at 5% (row 3 × 0.05)		105	175	210	280
5. Remittance after German taxes, in marks (row 3 − row 4)		1,995	3,325	3,990	5,320
6. Forecasted spot exchange rate	1.500	1.458	1.417	1.377	1.339
7. Remittance received by parent, in dollars (row 5/row 6)	−6,667	1,368	2,347	2,898	3,973
8. U.S. corporate tax at 40% (row 7 × 0.40)		547	939	1,159	1,589
9. Foreign tax credit [(row 2 + row 4)/row 6]		+689	+1,182	+1,460	+2,001
10. Cash flow in dollars, CF (row 7 − row 8 + row 9)	−6,667	1,510	2,590	3,199	4,385

to the currency of the home country and then proceed as discussed previously for any capital investment decision.

INTERNATIONAL INVESTMENT STRATEGY

Increasingly, the world is being viewed as one big market by the most aggressive and successful firms, whatever their home country. These firms are global firms that must compete effectively in many parts of the world to cover their enormous fixed investment, research and development costs, or both. The key is to develop the skills and corporate vision so that worldwide opportunities can be capitalized on while risks are dealt with effectively.

What does it take to develop an international investment strategy that will be effective in maximizing the value of the multinational firm? Some of the elements include:

1. An ability to understand and capitalize on those factors that have led to successful NPV projects and strategies for the domestic firm. Then, these opportunities must be transferred to other countries while maintaining the competitive advantage that led to the firm's success in the first place. Advantages gained by patents that

are about to run out or by trade restrictions, for instance, probably won't transfer into high-NPV projects if implemented abroad.

2. An international approach requires a solid understanding of the best mechanisms for gaining successful and profitable entry into foreign countries. Must large capital investments for production facilities be made in the country, or can goods be imported effectively? What kinds of foreign ownership, licensing arrangements, and so forth, are required? These and other related questions must be addressed, and investment and expansion decisions made based on the answers. At the same time, successful multinational firms often simultaneously bring out products on a worldwide basis by using universal parts, no matter where the product is produced or sold. This is another of the keys to a successful global investment strategy.

3. The continual monitoring of the investment and its potential for the future is essential. Given the rapidly changing world, assessing whether to increase the investment in a country, maintain it on a status quo level, or even reduce or abandon it is essential. Successful multinational firms take advantage of changes in the investment and political climates to shift production, research and development, and other components of a global strategy from country to country based on the economic opportunities presented.

4. Finally, successful multinational firms have made a commitment to consider the international dimension of all investment decisions. One way to do so is to have a management structure that stresses local management while providing key executives with international experience. For example, Dow Chemical recently met this need by seeing to it that 20 of the top 25 executives had extensive international experience.

The multinational firm's primary objective remains the same as a domestic firm's objective—to maximize the value of the firm by undertaking positive-NPV projects. In doing so it builds upon the underlying financial management concepts presented throughout the book.

Concept Review Questions

- What are some major concerns when estimating the opportunity cost of capital for a multinational firm?

- Describe two different methods of calculating the net present value of a foreign project for a multinational firm.

- Why should firms be concerned about how foreign subsidiary profits are remitted back to the parent company?

- What are some of the elements of a successful international investment strategy?

CAPITAL STRUCTURE AND DIVIDEND ISSUES

When investments are made on an international basis, they are often accomplished through the use of subsidiaries set up in various countries. In these situations, the capital structure and dividend issues become more complex because of the numerous subsidiaries and the multiplicity of different laws, tax considerations, and government regulations. But the primary point to remember is that the *multinational firm's worldwide capital structure and dividend policy should not be just the residual* of the decisions made in individual country-based subsidiaries. Rather, worldwide issues need to be considered in order to maximize the value of the firm.

CAPITAL STRUCTURE CONSIDERATIONS

At the foreign subsidiary level, a number of important points go into determining its capital structure. First and foremost, it is important to recognize that unless the parent is willing to let the subsidiary fail and default on its debt, there is *no independent risk for the subsidiary's debt*. Rather, its debt is—explicitly or implicitly—guaranteed by the multinational parent. Given this, it is really the parent's overall capital structure, not the subsidiary's, that is of primary concern.

Once this point is understood, then the objective is to acquire funds in the most cost-effective manner at each subsidiary level. For example, a subsidiary that has low debt financing costs might have a capital structure of almost 100 percent debt. Yet another subsidiary with a much higher cost of debt could have a capital structure with much less debt. The objective of the multinational parent is to raise capital as cheaply as possible on a worldwide basis and make suitable adjustments at the overall firm level to achieve its target worldwide capital structure.

Finally, multinational firms often classify (and structure) their investment in a subsidiary as debt, rather than equity. This is due to exchange controls and tax effects. From the standpoint of repatriating funds to the parent, a firm typically has wider latitude with interest and loan payments than with cash dividends or other reductions in equity. Also, by structuring the investment as debt, the parent generally can reduce its taxes.

Although some latitude exists, multinationals do not have complete freedom in choosing debt/equity ratios for foreign subsidiaries. If they have too little equity, they may run into restrictions placed on them by the host countries. But to the extent possible, the goal is to set up the foreign subsidiary's capital structure to minimize capital costs, subject to the requirement that the multinational parent be viewed as responsible by the host country. Then the multinational manages its capital structure on a global basis to maximize the value of the firm.

DIVIDEND POLICY

For firms with foreign subsidiaries, cash dividends are the most important means of transferring funds to the parent firm. Dividends often account for over 50 percent of such remittances. In setting the dividend policy for subsidiaries, two important considerations are exchange controls and financing requirements.

Multinational firms often set the dividend requirements for subsidiaries at the same or a greater dividend payout ratio than that of the parent. Thus, if the parent firm has a 50 percent dividend payout ratio, then the foreign subsidiary is expected to contribute 50 percent of its earnings to the parent. By setting a dividend requirement, multinationals attempt to establish a worldwide cash dividend policy for their subsidiaries. This has two benefits: First, the subsidiaries are contributing their appropriate part to the parent's cash dividend policy. Second, and often more important, this worldwide policy provides the multinational firm with a rationale for dealing with the exchange or currency controls of different nations. Because many nations limit dividend remittances, either in absolute terms or as a percentage of either earnings or capital, multinational parents find it is important for subsidiaries to establish and meet a constant dividend requirement. Dividends are then paid each year to demonstrate a continuing policy to the local government where the subsidiary is located.

In addition to the need to remit funds in the form of dividends, subsidiaries have continuing financing needs. In high-growth situations, multinationals may need to reinvest more funds in the subsidiaries, while in low-growth areas the need for funds is lower. This difference in demand, other things being equal, suggests differing cash dividend policies between subsidiaries located in different countries. One way some multinationals deal with differing needs, while still establishing a stable dividend remittance policy, is to have high-need subsidiaries declare the dividend even though it isn't remitted. By doing so, they establish the principle that dividends are a necessary cash flow associated with doing business. With a constant policy of paying (or at least declaring) dividends, multinational firms attempt to partially meet financing needs while maintaining the requirement for dividends to be remitted to the parent.

Concept Review Question

- What are the important links between a multinational's capital structure and dividend policies, and the capital structure and dividend policies of its foreign subsidiaries?

INTERNATIONAL FINANCING ISSUES

Raising capital used to be restricted to what was available within the home country. But, in today's international economy, raising capital is an international activity. This is true for both domestic and multinational firms.

LONG-TERM INTERNATIONAL FINANCING

Both domestic U.S. and multinational firms, along with their foreign subsidiaries, raise funds in various international markets. However, considerable differences exist in these markets compared to those in the United States. One of the biggest is the much broader role played by banks in the international market. Commercial banks in Europe, the Middle East, and Asia have more flexibility and often combine commercial banking, investment banking, and direct investment. In addition, the banks often work closely with the country's government and may even be partially government-owned. In the United States, commercial banks were required to divest their investment banking operations by the Banking Act of 1933.

The Eurodollar system that operates in the international capital markets was developed in the 1950s as banks located outside the United States began to accept interest-bearing deposits in U.S. dollars. Although most of the early activity was centered in Europe, the system, often called the **Eurocurrency system,** is now worldwide and includes many different currencies. Eurodollar loans are typically made in multiples of $1 million and have maturities lasting from a few days to 15 years or more. Generally these loans are unsecured, but they may contain certain restrictive provisions on the borrowing firm's activities. Large loans may be syndicated, with many banks participating; the lead bank coordinates the syndicate, structures the loan, and provides servicing when needed.

The model for such loans is the U.S. domestic multibank floating-rate term loan. The interest rate is usually stated as some fixed percentage above the London Interbank Offered Rate, LIBOR, with adjustments at predetermined intervals. Because LIBOR reflects the rate on liquid funds that move among the developed nations' money markets, it dampens borrowing based on interest rate speculation. Rates on Eurodollar loans typically are comparable to those in the United States, although sometimes U.S. firms have been able to obtain cheaper financing overseas.

When long-term debt is needed, both domestic and multinational firms borrow internationally. An **international bond** issue is one sold outside the country of the borrower; it can be a Eurobond or a foreign bond. A **Eurobond** is one underwritten by an international syndicate and sold primarily in countries other than the country in which the issue is denominated. Thus, a Eurobond could be denominated in the U.S. dollar, the German mark, or some other currency, but it would be sold mainly outside the country in which it was denominated. Although centered in Europe, the Eurobond market is truly international in scope and includes the Middle East and Asia. A **foreign bond** is one issued by a foreign borrower, but underwritten, sold, and denominated in one country. For example, a domestic U.S. firm might float a foreign bond in Switzerland, underwritten by a Swiss syndicate, and denominated in Swiss francs.

The Eurobond market has a number of distinguishing features:

1. Most bonds pay interest only once a year instead of semiannually.
2. Because of investor desire for anonymity, virtually all bonds are issued in bearer form, as opposed to the registered form prevalent in the United States.
3. Almost all Eurodollar issues are listed on one or more recognized securities exchanges—generally in London, Luxembourg, Frankfurt, or Switzerland.

In addition to the possibility of lower interest rates, firms employing the Eurobond market avoid registration with the U.S. Securities and Exchange Commission. In recent years, many more U.S.-based firms have been turning to foreign capital markets to secure funds. The new private placement regulation, Rule 144a (discussed in Chapter 15), may change this trend.

FINANCING DECISIONS

In raising capital and undertaking capital investment projects, multinational companies typically invest a relatively modest amount in equity capital and then raise the rest of the funds in some other manner. Three methods basically available for securing the majority of the funds are to raise them at home and export them, to raise cash by borrowing in a foreign country, or to borrow wherever interest rates are cheapest.

If a domestic firm raises cash by borrowing in its home country and then invests the funds in a subsidiary in a foreign country, it incurs an exchange rate risk. This risk has to be taken into account. An alternative is to borrow in the country where the foreign project is located. Doing so, the multinational receives a direct hedge against exchange rate fluctuations because they are borrowing in the same currency in which the investment has been made. The final alternative is to finance where interest rates are cheapest. Again, the firm has to look at exchange rate risk between where the financing is done and the home currency.

Each decision must take into account the specifics of the country, current and prospective international conditions, the length of financing needed, and the particular project. Experienced multinational firms find it is often best to use some combination of funds raised in the host country along with some provided from the domestic marketplace.

LEASING

Leasing can be employed both domestically and, especially, internationally to gain flexibility, defer or avoid taxes, and safeguard assets. For these reasons, leasing is an important part of the financing strategy for many multinational firms.

Consider what happened in the airline industry a few years ago. With deregulation and greater opportunities for carriers to operate in many countries, airlines needed more planes suited to their specific requirements. But, the back orders on aircraft were up to 7 years in some cases. To have the flexibility to take advantage of opportunities, many airlines leased planes from lessors who owned the planes through operating leases. Lessors had taken the standard operating lease and adopted it to the commercial airplane industry. Demand for operating leases was brisk because it provided airlines the flexibility to commit to new routes or increased service within a much shorter time frame.

Leasing in the international arena also may provide a substantial tax advantage through "double dipping." Through the different leasing rules of the lessor's and lessee's countries, a lease that is set up to double dip lets *both* parties be treated as the owner of the asset. Thus, both the lessor and the lessee are entitled to the depreciation tax benefits. This results in higher returns for lessors and lower effective lease rates for lessees.

Double dipping is often achieved when the lessees are based in countries that examine the economic reality of the arrangement (such as Germany, Japan, and the United States) and the lessors are located in countries that simply look at the legal ownership of the lease (such as France, Great Britain, or Switzerland). The key is what is considered an operating lease versus what is considered a financial lease. By structuring the lease to take advantage of intercountry differences, savings result that benefit both the lessor and the lessee.

Leasing can also be used in order to limit the ownership of assets by subsidiaries in unstable countries. In the event of nationalization, the multinational parent often has more chance of recovering or receiving some compensation for assets taken over if they are not owned by the local subsidiary. Also, lease payments are sometimes treated differently from dividends, interest, or royalty payments. In these cases leasing also helps deal with the exchange controls that would make other means of bringing funds out of the host country unsatisfactory.

Concept Review Questions

- Describe how a multinational firm may obtain debt in a foreign country.
- What are Eurobonds and foreign bonds? How do they differ?
- What are some advantages of leasing for a multinational firm?

SHORT-TERM FINANCIAL MANAGEMENT IN AN INTERNATIONAL CONTEXT

Multinational firms must also pay particular attention to numerous short-term financial management issues that arise due to dealing in different currencies, the large number of cross-border transactions, and differences that exist in numerous operating procedures.

CASH MANAGEMENT

Multinational firms pay particular attention to the effective management of their international cash flows. One important difference that occurs in many countries relates to the structure of the banking system. In many countries banks operate on a nationwide basis. This change from the still somewhat segmented banking structure in the United States has immediate implications. Instead of having to deal with a host of banks, as is generally the case in the United States, multinationals often need to deal with no more than one or two banks in other countries, even if they have substantial operations and sales in that country.

A second difference is the payment system in many countries. Although the payment system in the United States is largely check-driven, that is often not the case elsewhere. In many countries giro systems or other direct debit and credit mechanisms exist, and are much more widely used than checks.

Some of the major issues in international money movement are as follows:

1. CONCENTRATION BANKING   To control the flow of funds internationally, multinational firms concentrate their cash at a single bank within a country or on a regional level. Often European-wide systems are established at a bank in London or Amsterdam, and Asian systems are located in Tokyo or Singapore. Once cash is concentrated, funds can be controlled and invested, and a zero-balance-type procedure can be implemented.

2. DEBIT TRANSFER   For disbursements, most European banks charge the customer's account immediately, so the bank, not the firm, gains the advantage of float. Also, on international transactions, European banks generally take funds out of a customer's account 2 days before the foreign funds are made available.

3. INTERNATIONAL LOCKBOX   This technique involves establishing one or more lockbox s in a country so that payments can be settled in the country in

which the currency is legal tender. With this system, cross-border check clearing is avoided, thus increasing the efficiency of the multinational's cash system.

4. INTRACOMPANY NETTING   Many multinational firms have large sums of money tied up in intracompany transactions. With these transactions, one subsidiary's payables are another subsidiary's receivables. To avoid the physical transfer of funds, many multinationals "net" the funds flowing between subsidiaries once a month.

INTERNATIONAL PURCHASES OR SALES

Although most domestic trade is on an open account basis, this is not true for firms involved in international purchases or sales. Due to lack of credit knowledge, communications difficulties, and the like, the process becomes more complex. Most international trade requires three main documents: (1) an order to pay, or draft, (2) a bill of lading, and (3) a letter of credit. A draft, as discussed in Chapter 21, is simply an order to pay on demand or at a specific point in time. Now let's briefly consider use of bills of lading and letters of credit.

A **bill of lading** is a shipping document that has a number of functions. Primary among these are to serve as a contract to order the shipment of goods from one party (the seller) to another (the customer) and to provide title to the goods. The bill of lading and the draft proceed together. Their use is recognized in international law, and banks or other financial institutions in virtually all countries handle these documents. By using the draft and bill of lading, a seller can sell the goods and still obtain protection, because title is not released until the draft has been accepted.

The letter of credit is the third document. A **letter of credit** is a written statement made by the customer's bank that it will pay out money (honor a draft drawn on it), provided the bill of lading and other details are in order. Before the seller ships the goods, a letter of credit must be supplied. This letter is often irrevocable and confirmed by a bank in the seller's country. By obtaining the letter of credit, the seller ascertains before shipping the goods the creditworthiness and certainty of payment from the customer. Once the goods are shipped, they are covered by the bill of lading and accompanied by a draft (typically a time draft) that must be accepted by the customer's bank. The general sequence of events is illustrated in Figure 27.3. This process may seem complicated, but it is routine in international trade.

EXPORT CREDIT INSURANCE

Practically all countries provide *export credit insurance* for their exporters. This insurance protects exporters against the risk of nonpayment by the purchasers. In the United States, export credit insurance is administered by the Foreign Credit Insurance Association, FCIA, which is a cooperative effort of the Export-Import Bank and a group of approximately 50 insurance companies. The insurance companies provide protection from commercial risks, while the Export-Import Bank covers political risks. Instead of selling insurance on a case-by-case basis, the FCIA approves limits for each exporter within which they are provided coverage.

Figure 27.3

Letter of Credit Transaction

The general sequence of transactions, in simplified form, is illustrated with those labeled (1) occurring before those labeled (2). Finally, as indicated by (3), payment is made and title to the goods passes to the buyer.

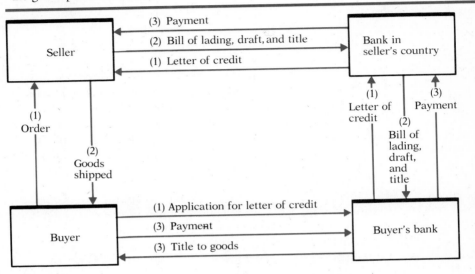

EURO- AND UNIVERSAL COMMERCIAL PAPER

Euro-commercial paper is a short-term note issued by firms, in this case by firms outside the United States, and usually denominated in dollars. Typically, Euro-commercial paper has a longer maturity than commercial paper issued in the United States, and an active secondary market for it exists.

Universal commercial paper also exists to help U.S.-based firms raise short-term funds. Universal commercial paper is issued by U.S. firms but denominated and paid in specified foreign currencies. Although it sells in the United States, universal commercial paper provides a short-term liquid security whose interest rates are tied to various foreign markets. This proves beneficial when firms have dealings in currencies other than the U.S. dollar.

Concept Review Questions

- What are some basic differences of cash management between a domestic firm and a multinational firm?
- What are the three main documents required in international purchases or sales?
- Describe export credit insurance and how it benefits a multinational firm.

International Accounting and Tax Issues

There are at least two other important issues that multinational firms must consider. These relate to accounting reporting requirements and tax considerations within and between countries.

ACCOUNTING CONSIDERATIONS

When the result of foreign operations must be reported, the financial analysis of firms with international operations presents additional problems beyond those faced within the United States. Under FAS No. 52,[4] U.S.-based firms must use the **functional currency**—that is, the primary currency in which a foreign subsidiary operates—as the basis for computing and translating adjustments. All balance sheet items of the subsidiary are translated at the exchange rate prevailing on the final day of the parent's fiscal period, and any resulting gain or loss is reported both as an asset and in a special equity account on the parent's balance sheet.

To see the impact of this procedure, consider an example in which a German subsidiary of a U.S. firm purchases equipment for 100 marks (M) when 1 M = $0.50. If the functional currency is the mark, the historical cost of the equipment is 100M. If the functional currency of the subsidiary is the U.S. dollar, the historical cost of the equipment is $50. Assume that at a later date the exchange rate is 1 M = $0.80. If the functional currency is the mark, the historical cost is still 100M, but the translated amount is now $80. This $80 will be reported on the parent's balance sheet as an asset and in a special equity account recording the foreign currency translation adjustment. If the dollar is the functional currency, the historical cost is $50 regardless of any changes in the exchange ratio. Thus, only $50 would be reported on the parent's balance sheet.

From the standpoint of analysis, this reporting guideline affects the parent firm in several ways: (1) the U.S.-based firm's assets and equity change every year, depending on exchange rates; (2) firms facing similar situations may report different results, depending on the functional currency employed; and (3) firms are not required to provide information in the annual report concerning the functional currency employed. These and similar problems make the analysis of accounting statements for a multinational firm even more difficult and challenging than for a firm doing all its business within the United States.

TAX CONSIDERATIONS

The domestic tax system is important for domestic firms operating solely within the United States. As complicated as domestic tax planning can be, the planning for multinational firms is even more complex. Effective integration of domestic and

[4] *Statement of Financial Accounting Standard No. 52,* "Foreign Currency Translation" (Stamford, Conn.: FASB, 1981).

international tax planning requires adjusting to different laws, customs, and currencies. The starting point is that the U.S. government taxes U.S.-based multinationals on their worldwide income. Using the idea of domestic tax neutrality, the government attempts to tax a dollar earned domestically at the same rate as a dollar equivalent earned abroad. In addition, to prevent double taxation, the United States and most other countries grant tax credits for income taxes paid in various countries. For U.S. multinationals, the foreign income often is not taxed until it is actually remitted as a dividend to the parent firm. The advantage, of course, is that the tax is deferred until the U.S. parent firm actually receives the income.

Because of these complications, many multinationals attempt to reinvest the earnings of a foreign subsidiary in the country where the earnings were generated. In addition, there are often tax advantages if the subsidiary pays licensing fees or other "expenses" to the parent firm, instead of repatriating funds in the form of cash dividends. Unlike dividends from a domestic U.S. corporation, which are partially exempt from taxes, dividends received by a U.S. firm from a foreign subsidiary are fully taxable. These and many other considerations make the tax aspects of multinational operations a challenging and important topic for managers.

Concept Review Questions

- What is functional currency, and how does it affect a multinational firm's balance sheet?
- What are some difficulties encountered by multinational firms when attempting to manage their international taxes?

KEY POINTS

1. The spot rate of exchange is for settlement today, whereas the forward rate of exchange is determined today but with settlement set for some specified time in the future.
2. The expected relationship between product prices, interest rates, and spot and forward exchange rates can be specified using the expectations theory of forward exchange rates, purchasing power parity, the international Fisher effect, and interest rate parity. In practice, government intervention, transactions costs, and other imperfections cause these relationships to hold more in the long run than in the short run.
3. Key considerations when making international capital expenditure decisions include, in addition to items discussed for domestic decisions, forecasted exchange rates, taxes, and questions of how the funds are to be brought back to the home country.
4. Capital structure, dividend policy, and other decisions must be made keeping the view of the parent firm in mind.
5. Short-term international financial management decisions have many of the same complexities as domestic decisions, but differences in the financial systems and markets, exchange rates, and steps to minimize cross-border transactions must be considered.
6. Although some differences exist, including some in the areas of accounting and taxation, multinational firms apply all of the fundamental concepts and decision rules of financial management. The goal remains the same: to maximize the value of the firm by focusing on the magnitude and timing of cash flows, the risks incurred, and the opportunity costs.

QUESTIONS

27.1   Explain the difference between spot and forward exchange rates.

27.2   The average exchange rate (in terms of the number of units of the foreign currency per U.S. dollar) in year −1 and year 0 for three countries was

	Year −1	Year 0
Mexico (peso)	22.727	41.429
Singapore (dollar)	0.971	0.752
Belgium (franc)	1.678	2.032

What can you conclude about the worth of the U.S. dollar vis-a-vis the currencies of these other countries in year −1 and in year 0? What about the expected rate of inflation in these countries compared to the expected rate of inflation in the United States?

27.3   What factors influence the opportunity cost of capital used when international capital budgeting decisions are made? What conclusions can be reached?

27.4   What two general methods are available for determining the NPV for an international capital budgeting project?

27.5   How can we estimate future exchange rates by using presently available data and assuming the market is efficient?

27.6   Explain how foreign exchange risk, repatriation of funds, expropriation risk, and credit risk all influence international capital budgeting decisions.

27.7   What are the main factors to consider when determining a multinational firm's capital structure?

27.8   Summarize the important aspects of a multinational firm's dividend policy.

27.9   Many firms issue zero-coupon bonds in the Eurobond market. Explain the motivation for issuing zero-coupon bonds in general and also why a firm might choose to do it through the Eurobond market instead of in the domestic bond market.

27.10   What are the primary differences between the Eurobond market and the bond market in the United States?

27.11   Explain "double dipping" and other international aspects of leasing.

27.12   Explain the impact of FAS No. 52 on a U.S.-based multinational's accounting statements. Does this rule pose any additional problem for analyst's?

CONCEPT REVIEW PROBLEMS

See Appendix A for solutions.

CR27.1   Use Table 27.1 to answer the following questions:

a.   If a Honda Accord costs $20,000 in the United States, what will it cost in yen in Japan?

b.   If a BMW costs 47,356 marks in Germany, what will that BMW cost in dollars in the United States?

c.   If a British MG costs $15,000 in the United States, how many pounds will it cost in Britain?

CR27.2   Assume inflation *over the next 6 months* is expected to be 3 percent in the United States and 6 percent in France. Using Table 27.1, what is the 6-month forward rate of exchange between the franc and the dollar?

CR27.3   Your firm is evaluating a proposed expansion of its textile subsidiary in India. The cost of the expansion will be 900,000 rupees, with expected cash flows in year 1 of 300,000 rupees, in year 2 of 500,000 rupees, and in year 3 of 500,000 rupees. The current spot exchange rate is 30 rupees per U.S. dollar, the risk-free rate in India is 10 percent, and the risk-free rate in the U.S. is 5 percent. Ignoring taxes and remittance fees, what is the net present value of the project if the opportunity cost of capital is 15 percent?

CR27.4   The United States Bottling Company is considering opening a plant in Canada. The cost of the plant will be $800,000 Canadian dollars. Cash flows from the plant will be $200,000 Canadian dollars in year 1, $500,000 Canadian dollars in year 2, $300,000 Canadian dollars in year 3, and $400,000 Canadian dollars in year 4. The corporate tax rate for Canada is 40 percent, while the U.S. corporate tax rate is 35 percent. Canada has a remittance fee of 3 percent for foreign companies. The current spot rate for a Canadian dollar per U.S. dollar is 1.25, the risk-free rate in Canada is 4 percent, and in the United States the risk-free rate is 6 percent. If the opportunity cost of capital is 10 percent, what is the net present value of the plant?

CR27.5   An American company's Japanese subsidiary purchased a computer for ¥440,000, when the spot exchange rate was 1¥ per $0.009 U.S. dollars.

a.   If the functional currency of the subsidiary is the Japanese yen, what is the historical cost of the computer?
b.   If the functional currency of the subsidiary is the U.S. dollar, what is the historical cost of the computer?
c.   Now assume the exchange rate changed to 1¥ = $0.01. What is the cost reported on the firm's balance sheet if the functional currency is the Japanese yen?

PROBLEMS

27.1   Spot and forward rates for Canada and France relative to the U.S. dollar are:

	Units of Foreign Currency per U.S. Dollar	
Rate	Canadian Dollar	French Franc
Spot	1.192	6.253
30-day forward	1.198	6.247
90-day forward	1.205	6.241
180-day forward	1.213	6.232

a.   What can we say about the expected rate of inflation in both countries relative to the expected rate of inflation in the United States?
b.   What about the expected rate of inflation in Canada relative to the expected rate of inflation in France?

27.2   If the British pound has a spot rate of 1.771 U.S. dollars per pound while the German mark has a spot rate of 0.544 dollars per German mark, what is the spot rate of exchange between the pound and the mark?

27.3   The current spot rate for the Israeli shekel is 1.817 shekels to the U.S. dollar, while it is 7.15 Chinese yuan to the U.S. dollar. What is the spot rate of exchange between the shekel and the yuan?

27.4   Assume that the current rate of exchange is 1,250 Italian lire per dollar. If the current yearly nominal risk-free interest rate in Italy is 14 percent per year and it is 6 percent in the United States, what is the implied 6-month forward rate between the lira and the dollar? (*Note:* For simplicity, assume a 360-day year and 30-day months.)

27.5   Given a spot rate of 0.159 Swedish krona per dollar and expected rates of inflation of 9 percent in Sweden and 5 percent in the United States, what is the expected spot rate of exchange in 1 year, 3 years, and 6 years?

27.6   Douglas Communications is exploring whether to make an investment in Malta. The expected cash flows, in lira, are:

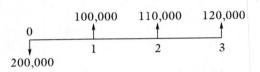

The spot rate is 0.300 lira per U.S. dollar, and the opportunity cost of capital, k, in U.S. dollars is 25 percent. The U.S. risk-free rate, k_{RF}, is 5 percent, and it is 10 percent in Malta. Should the investment be made?

27.7   The expected cash flows in pounds from an investment in Britain are as follows:

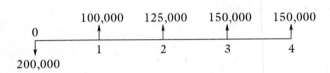

Taxes in Britain have already been taken into account. The U.S. opportunity cost, k, is 16 percent, the U.S. corporate tax rate is 35 percent, and the current spot rate is 0.560 pounds to the dollar. The U.S. risk-free rate is 6 percent and 9 percent in Britain.

a.   Determine the expected spot rate of exchange for the next 4 years between the pound and the dollar.
b.   What are the after-tax cash flows in dollars? (*Note:* Ignore any foreign tax credits.)
c.   Should the project be undertaken?

27.8   Lytle Productions is evaluating whether to invest in a project in the Netherlands. The expected cash flows, in guilders, are as follows:

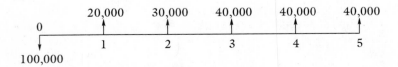

The spot rate is 2.086 guilders per U.S. dollar. The discount rate, k, is 20 percent. The U.S. risk-free rate, k_{RF}, is 8 percent, while it is 6 percent in the Netherlands. Should the investment be made?

27.9   The before-tax cash flows in Austrian schillings and the forecasted spot exchange rates between the schilling and the dollar are as follows:

	0	1	2	3
Cash flow before taxes, in schillings	−40,000	20,000	40,000	50,000
Forecasted spot exchange rate	0.600	0.658	0.724	0.800

The corporate tax rate in Austria is 20 percent, and the tax rate for funds withheld is 6 percent; the U.S. corporate tax rate is 35 percent. The U.S. grants a full tax credit for both foreign corporate taxes and taxes withheld.

a.   Calculate the after-tax cash flows in U.S. dollars.
b.   If the opportunity cost of capital, k, in U.S. dollars is 15 percent, should the project be undertaken?
c.   Independent of (a) and (b), now assume that everything remains the same except that the United States allows a tax credit for only 40 percent of the foreign corporate income taxes and taxes withheld. Should the project now be undertaken?

27.10   Austin Petroleum is considering an investment in Jordan. The expected before-tax cash flows in the Jordan dinar are as follows:

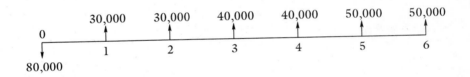

The opportunity cost of capital, k, in U.S. dollars is 14 percent, the spot rate is 0.700 dinar per U.S. dollars, the risk-free rate, k_{RF}, is 6 percent in the United States and 11 percent in Jordan. Jordan's corporate tax rate is 25 percent, and it has a 5 percent withholding tax. The U.S. corporate tax rate is 40 percent.

a.   Calculate the expected spot rates of exchange for years 1 through 6.
b.   What are the expected after-tax cash flows in U.S. dollars?
c.   Should the project be accepted?
d.   Independent of (a) through (c), and everything remaining the same, Austin fears the project may be expropriated after 4 years, resulting in little or no compensation. What is the project's NPV?

27.11   Kramer Industries is based in the United States and has one plant in France. The firm has net income of $500, U.S. assets of $4,000, and U.S. equity of $1,000. The French subsidiary just started this year and bought equipment worth 10,000 francs when the exchange rate was 1 franc = $0.15. Thus, the cost of the purchase in U.S. dollars was $1,500 [i.e., (10,000)($0.15)]. At the end of the firm's fiscal year, the rate of exchange was 1 franc = $0.30. In reporting the results of its operations, Kramer must report the subsidiary's assets along with its U.S. assets. These results appear both as assets and as a part of the firm's equity.

a. If the functional currency of the subsidiary is the dollar, what are Kramer's total assets and its stockholders' equity? Its return on equity?
b. If the functional currency is the franc, what are Kramer's total assets and its stockholders' equity? Its return on equity?
c. What will happen next year if the functional currency is the franc and everything remains the same except that the exchange rate changes?

27.12 Mini Case Answer the following questions that all deal with international financial management:

a. If the spot rate of exchange is 3 francs per dollar and the risk-free rate in the United States is 9 percent, while it is 6 percent in Switzerland, what are the implied 180-day and 360-day forward rates of exchange? (*Note:* Assume a 360-day year.) Is Switzerland's currency strengthening or weakening relative to the U.S. dollar?
b. What is interest rate parity? What does it imply about forward rates and inflation?
c. What major factors need to be considered when determining the opportunity cost of capital for international projects?
d. A firm is evaluating two possible mutually exclusive investments as follows:

	Investment A		Investment B	
	Year	CF	Year	CF
Cash flows, in units	0	−50,000	0	−50,000
of the foreign currency	1	20,000	1	35,000
	2	40,000	2	55,000
	3	80,000	3	70,000
	4	60,000	4	80,000
			5	80,000
			6	60,000
Spot rate of exchange	2.00		5.00	
k_{RF} home currency	10%		10%	
k_{RF} foreign currency	13%		8%	

The opportunity cost is 16 percent for both projects. Which should be undertaken?
e. The remittance of funds causes problems when making international capital investment decisions. What are some of the key issues in terms of remitting funds?
f. What are important differences in making capital structure and dividend decisions for domestic firms versus multinational firms?
g. Describe how firms raise funds internationally. Then indicate the differences in short-term financial management for a domestic firm located in the United States, versus a multinational firm.

REFERENCES

International financial management covers many topics; for more extensive coverage see, for example:

EITEMAN, DAVID K., and ARTHUR I. STONEHILL. *Multinational Business Finance,* 5th ed. Reading, Mass.: Addison-Wesley, 1989.

SHAPIRO, ALAN C. *International Corporate Finance,* 2nd ed. Cambridge, Mass.: Ballinger, 1988.

For more on purchasing power and interest rate parity see, for example:

ABUAF, NISO, and PHILIPPE JORION. "Purchasing Power Parity in the Long Run." *Journal of Finance* 45 (March 1990): 157–74.

HUANG, ROGER D. "Risk and Parity in Purchasing Power." *Journal of Money, Credit & Banking* 22 (August 1992): 338–56.

WHEATLEY, SIMON. "Some Tests of International Equity Integration." *Journal of Financial Economics* 21 (September 1988): 177–212.

Numerous articles cover aspects of international financial management, including:

CHOI, FREDERICK D. S., and RICHARD LIVICH. "International Accounting Diversity: Does it Affect Market Participants." *Financial Analysts Journal* 47 (July/August 1991): 73–82.

HODDER, JAMES E., and LEMMA W. SENBET. "International Capital Structure Equilibrium." *Journal of Finance* 45 (December 1990): 1495–1516.

JOHN, KOSE, LEMMA W. SENBET, and ANANT K. SUNDARAM. "Cross-Border Liability of Multinational Enterprises, Border Taxes, and Capital Structure." *Financial Management* 20 (Winter 1991): 54–67.

LESSARD, DONALD R. "Global Competition and Corporate Finance in the 1990s." *Journal of Applied Corporate Finance* 3 (Winter 1991): 59–72.

MAHAJAN, ARVIND. "Pricing Expropriation Risk." *Financial Management* 19 (Winter 1990): 77–86.

PORTER, MICHAEL E. "Capital Disadvantage: America's Failing Investment System." *Harvard Business Review* 70 (September/October 1992): 65–82.

PROWSE, STEPHEN D. "Institutional Investment Patterns and Corporate Financial Behavior in the United States and Japan." *Journal of Financial Economics* 27 (September 1990): 43–66.

———. "The Structure of Corporate Ownership in Japan." *Journal of Finance* 47 (July 1992): 1121–40.

28

Managing Foreign Exchange Risk

EXECUTIVE SUMMARY

Virtually all firms, whether wholly domestic or multinational, face economic risks as foreign exchange rates change. In addition, firms that engage in any business in which funds flow across borders face exchange rate risk. As the world has moved from fixed to floating exchange rates, foreign exchange rates have become more volatile. And, increasingly, firms market and produce all over the world. Hedging some of a firm's foreign exchange exposure is now more important than ever.

The primary issues with hedging are twofold: first, to determine the degree of the firm's economic or transactions exposure; second, to determine whether the expected benefits from actively hedging the firm's exchange rate exposure are more than the expected costs. As such, the decision is another net present value problem.

Some hedging can be done by invoicing in the home currency, leading and lagging, establishing a reinvoicing center, shifting production to countries where the sales will be made, or raising funds in the countries where they will be used. Although most firms use some or all of these approaches, increasingly they deal with much of their foreign exchange risk through the use of financial derivatives. Depending on the nature of the foreign exchange exposure, firms can purchase (go long in) forward contracts, futures, swaps and options, or they can sell (go short in) the same financial derivatives. Each has its own unique characteristics, costs, and benefits that must be considered as firms develop, monitor, and modify their foreign exchange risk exposure programs.

RISK MANAGEMENT

Since all firms face a variety of risks, risk is one of the fundamental items that financial managers must worry about. We've looked at some of these risks in other chapters. Now we turn to the risk caused by fluctuations in exchange rates.

STRATEGIES FOR DEALING WITH RISK

In our increasingly global business environment, firms face another risk that we have ignored—the change in the rate of exchange of one currency for another currency. Consider the following example: A major department store chain purchases over 40 percent of its inventory overseas. Typical of most firms purchasing abroad or selling overseas, there is a delay between when the goods are received and when payment is made. During that period of time the firm is exposed to exchange rate risk. If the home currency weakens before payment on the inventory is made, the department store chain suffers a larger-than-planned cash outflow. In the face of such a situation the firm has three choices:

1. Do nothing, in terms of either hedging or passing the higher costs on to the firm's customers in the form of higher retail prices. With a do-nothing strategy, the cash flows and profits of the department store chain suffer.
2. Raise retail prices enough to pass the higher costs on to the firm's customers. This strategy may retain profit and cash flow margins but may result in lost sales if demand for the products is price sensitive.
3. Hedge part or all of the exchange rate exposure, in order to minimize the losses (if the domestic currency weakens) or gains (if the domestic currency strengthens) due to exchange rate fluctuations.

Although this is only one example, it highlights the general strategies for dealing with exchange rate risk: ignore it, price it (that is, see that sufficient returns are expected to compensate for the risk exposure), or hedge it. Increasingly, firms recognize that many of the financial risks they face can be hedged. As discussed in Chapter 23, the main financial price risk factors that can be hedged arise from fluctuations in interest rates, foreign exchange rates, and commodity prices.

SHOULD RISK EXPOSURE BE HEDGED?

Simply being exposed to financial price risk is not a sufficient condition for a firm to decide to manage, or hedge, its risk exposure. Firms should manage their risk exposure only if the risk management strategy is expected to increase the value of the firm. The value of the firm can be increased if the risk management strategy reduces the taxes paid by the firm, reduces the probability and costs associated with financial distress, or reduces agency costs.[1]

Reduced Taxes

The corporate tax code in many countries, including the United States, is progressive—that is, it taxes higher income at higher rates. Under a progressive tax code, firms in the progressive region of the tax schedule have a greater tax-based incentive to hedge. In addition to the progressive nature of the tax code, tax preference items (such

---

[1] See Smith and Stulz (1985); Bessembinder (1991); or Nance, Smith, and Smithson (1993) in the end-of-chapter references.

as tax loss carry forwards, foreign tax credits, and investment tax credits) also provide tax-based incentives to hedge.

Reduced Financial Distress Costs

In Chapter 11 we identified two components of the costs of financial distress—the direct costs involving actual outlays for lawyers and so forth, and indirect costs, such as the contracting costs with customers, employees, and suppliers. By hedging exchange rate risk, firms can reduce the variance of the expected cash flows, thereby lowering the probability of default or of triggering some borrowing covenant restriction. In addition to the direct cost of bankruptcy, firms that hedge reduce the indirect cost of financial distress. Thus, firms that have less volatile cash flows will be more likely to be able to satisfy their customers, employees, and suppliers—thereby lowering the contracting costs associated with serving these stakeholders of the firm.

Reduced Agency Costs

Hedging can also reduce agency costs. First, underinvestment problems exist because if the firm's value is too low or too volatile, shareholders will opt to bypass growth options that result from positive net present value projects, because the gains accrue primarily to the bondholders. Second, we know that the stock of a firm is simply a call option on the value of the firm. Wealth transfers can occur if the firm takes more risky positive-NPV opportunities or issues more fixed-claim securities. By reducing the volatility of the expected cash flows, hedging can also control shifts in wealth.

In a strict Modigliani and Miller world (discussed in Chapter 11), no financial policy or contract, including those arising from hedging, can alter the value of the firm. However, once we consider the impacts of taxes, financial distress costs, and agency costs, firms may benefit from hedging. In this chapter we focus on the basic issues and approaches to managing the firm's exchange rate risk exposure. While the primary focus is on identifying and managing foreign exchange exposure, other kinds of exposure are also relevant in today's competitive environment. Another part of the risk exposure is interest rate risk exposure, which we discussed in Chapter 23.[2] A final type of risk exposure, to changes in commodity prices, we leave to others.

Concept Review Questions

- What responses are available for a multinational firm when faced with exchange rate risk?
- What benefits may result because of a firm hedges its exchange rate risk exposure?

IDENTIFYING THE FIRM'S FINANCIAL RISK EXPOSURE

Before we can deal with managing a firm's foreign exchange risk exposure, we need to understand at least two important items: first, what kind of exposure we should be concerned with, and second, how firms identify financial risk exposure.

---

[2] Reviewing Chapter 23, especially the features of forward contracts, futures, and swaps, may prove beneficial before reading the latter part of this chapter.

WHAT DO WE MEAN BY "FOREIGN EXCHANGE EXPOSURE"?

Foreign exchange exposure can be broken down into three types: translation exposure, transaction exposure, and economic exposure. Figure 28.1 provides a convenient way to think about the three types of exposure.

Translation exposure is the easiest to deal with because it refers to the accounting treatment arising from fluctuations in exchange rates. Although not an inconsequential issue, translation exposure does not affect the economic value of the firm in the marketplace; consequently, we would like to ignore translation exposure completely. In practice, however, translation exposure is important since it affects the firm's GAAP income statement. Many of the protective covenants incorporated in debt securities or borrowings from banks contain provisions that are based on the firm's GAAP earnings. CFOs we have talked to indicate that the primary impact of changes in exchange rates is in terms of the firm's cash flow; however, because of how some financing agreements are structured, translation exposure occasionally enters into the picture.

Transaction exposure refers to the impact of exchanging one currency for another when the rate of exchange between the currencies changes from the time the transaction occurs until it is settled. Often transaction exposure is relatively short-term in nature. Many of the techniques discussed later in the chapter deal with how firms can protect themselves, at a cost, against adverse movements in exchange rates that would result in loss of value due to transaction exposure.

Figure 28.1

Translation, Transaction and Economic Foreign Exchange Exposure

Translation exposure does not directly impact the firm's cash flows; however, some changes in exchange-induced accounting reported figures, especially earnings, may trigger protective covenants in loan agreements. Firms primarily hedge translation and economic exchange rate exposure.

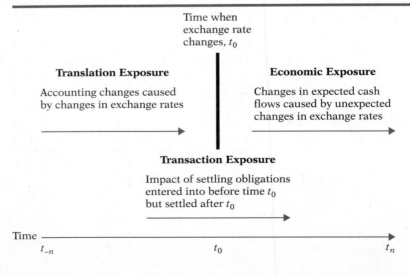

Economic exposure refers to the impact of foreign exchange exposure that directly affects the cash flows and, thus, the long-run value of the firm. Whereas the effects of both translation and transaction exposure typically show up directly in a firm's GAAP accounting statements, the impact of economic exposure is not readily dealt with in the conventional accounting statements employed today.

Foreign exchange exposure is more important today than it was 30 years ago because of the increasing globalization of firms and the movement from fixed to floating exchange rates that has been accompanied by much greater volatility in exchange rates. At the same time, firms are more aware of how to hedge some or all of these risks.

IDENTIFYING AND MEASURING FINANCIAL RISK EXPOSURE

To illustrate the approach firms are taking to identify and measure financial risk exposure, it is helpful to examine the efforts of two firms in this regard—Eastman Kodak and Merck. Eastman Kodak illustrates the dramatic impact that competition, in conjunction with currency exposure, can have on a firm. Thus, Eastman Kodak illustrates economic exposure. Merck, on the other hand, illustrates how firms can identify and deal with transaction exposure.

The Eastman Kodak Experience

Eastman Kodak's primary businesses include photography, chemicals, information systems, and health care products.[3] During the early 1980s the economic performance of Eastman's photography sector was coming under increasing pressure from competitors. In particular, Fuji Photo of Japan had become a major worldwide competitor of Eastman Kodak. Fuji was benefiting from the quality of its product and its marketing efforts. In addition, it was benefiting from the weak yen/dollar exchange rate. With a weak yen, Fuji's largely yen-denominated cost of production was less than Kodak's dollar-denominated cost of production. The effect was to make Kodak film less competitive with Fuji film both in Japan and in other parts of the world, and to make Fuji more competitive in Kodak's domestic market—the United States. The currency exposure of the firms, which arose from the denomination of Kodak's costs primarily in dollars and the denomination of Fuji's costs primarily in yen, was having a direct bearing on Kodak's sales and cash flow generation. The basic impact on Kodak is illustrated in Figure 28.2.

In response to this and other developments, Kodak implemented a plan to identify major competitors in all of its primary markets, their sourcing and pricing strategies, and how sensitive Kodak's market share might be to changes in currency exchange rates. At the same time, Kodak moved further into currency hedging programs that would deal not only with shorter-term transaction exposures but also with their longer-term competitive exposures. Kodak's objective from this plan was to hedge against adverse movements in exchange rates as well as to add value to the firm.

---

[3] This example is taken primarily from Ahn and Falloon (1991).

Figure 28.2

Impact of Yen/Dollar Exchange Rate on Eastman Kodak

As the value of the yen weakened, the value of Eastman Kodak was adversely affected. Likwise, if the value of the yen strengthened, Eastman Kodak's value would be positively affected.

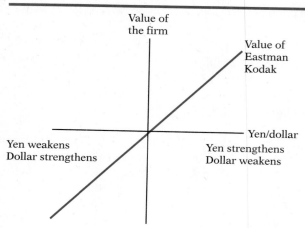

Merck's Transaction Risk Exposure

Merck is a worldwide leader in pharmaceuticals.[4] Slightly over 50 percent of its sales are overseas, and about 40 percent of Merck's assets are also located overseas. The typical structure in the drug industry is to establish subsidiaries in many overseas markets. These subsidiaries, of which Merck had approximately 70, are typically importers of the product at some stage of manufacture and are responsible for finishing, marketing, and distributing within the country. Sales are denominated in the local currency, and costs are a combination of local currency (for finishing, marketing, distribution, administration, and taxes) and the currency of the country where the basic manufacturing and research are conducted—U.S. dollars for Merck.

With a large percent of its sales occurring in foreign currencies, in the early 1980s Merck began assessing its exposure to changes in currency exchange rates. With this type of global exposure, Merck first determined the extent to which cash inflows and outflows were matched in the individual currencies. Merck quickly found they were not well matched in many currencies—the firm had an exchange rate mismatch. One possible approach to the problem involved redeploying resources by shifting manufacturing sites, research centers, and employees to other countries to better match resources, sales, and costs. Merck quickly decided that approach was not an effective means of dealing with the problem; even after reallocation the firm would continue to have a large global foreign exchange exposure.

Merck's foreign exchange exposure is primarily of the transactions variety. Its goal became to reduce the potential impact of exchange volatility on future cash flows. By

[4] This example is taken from Lewent and Kearney (1990).

reducing the volatility of the future cash flows, Merck felt it would be in a better position to undertake future growth option investments in research and development, which are *the* source of Merck's future growth opportunities. In order to hedge the transaction exposure Merck considered options and forward/futures/swaps. (Forwards, futures, and swaps are grouped together because they have the same basic effect on the firm—that is, they put the firm under an *obligation* to act.)

To illustrate Merck's analysis, consider Figure 28.3(a) which demonstrates the potential impact as the dollar strengthens or weakens against a foreign currency. If the dollar strengthens, Merck gains; but, if the dollar weakens, Merck suffers a loss in value. Figure 28.3(b) illustrates the impact of using forward/futures/swaps to hedge. Except for the cost of the transaction, Merck is fully hedged against all changes in exchange rates. Whether exchange rates move for or against Merck, the firm is hedged. Figure 28.3(c) illustrates the impact of using options to hedge Merck's exchange rate risk. With the use of options, Merck benefits if the dollar strengthens, and it does not lose if the dollar weakens. Given potential exchange rate movements in either direction, Merck was unwilling to forgo the potential gains if the dollar weakened. Therefore, Merck decided options were the preferred means of hedging for the firm.[5] Merck also concluded that a certain level of cash outflow in the form of option costs could be justified as the price of an insurance policy designed to preserve the ability of the firm to carry out its research and development plan.

Figure 28.3

Hedging Merck's Transaction Exchange Exposure

In (a) the unhedged value of Merck is shown. In (b) the effect of using forwards/futures/swaps to hedge is shown, while the impact of using options is shown in (c). Merck decided to employ options, instead of forwards/futures/swaps to hedge, because of the opportunity cost if the foreign currency strengthens and Merck had employed forwards/futures/swaps.

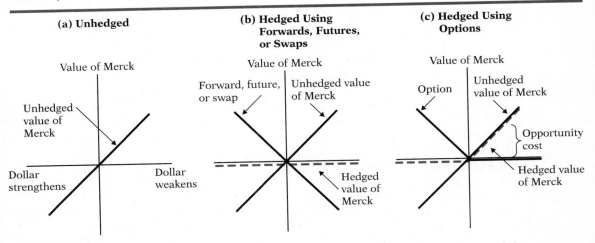

---

[5] This *does not* mean options are the preferred means of hedging for other firms or in other situations.

"I Don't Need to Hedge"

Sometimes firms get the mistaken impression they have no need to hedge. An example might be if the firm produces and sells entirely within one country. The firm's logic might be as follows: "Because all of my production and sales are confined to one currency, and all of my financing is also done in the same currency, there is no need to hedge." Nothing could be further from the truth! As long as the firm has *competition from outside the currency in question,* it has a potential foreign exchange problem. Witness what happened to the U.S. automobile industry in the 1980s. Although quality and style were also issues, an important part of the problem was that the weakness of the yen made Japanese cars much more affordable in the United States than many of their American-made competitors.

Another example is the French automobile manufacturer, Renault. The firm believes its geographic diversification provides sufficient protection. "We deal in the Deutschemark, the British pound, the Italian lira, the Spanish peseta, and other . . . [European currencies]." Due to this diversity, Renault feels that "so many currencies gives us a natural hedge, that the balance of countries is a hedge in itself. Clearly, there are times when currency movements are going to hurt you, but overall, we think our policy is sound." This may be, but in the fall of 1992 Renault suffered a $108 million quarterly loss when Britain and Italy sharply devalued their currencies.

The key issues are threefold: First, the firm must actively determine the extent to which it is subject to transaction and economic exposure risk. Second, it must investigate alternative means by which any exchange rate exposure might be hedged. Some of these strategies for dealing with exchange rate risk involve the operating, investment, and financing decisions of the firm. Another strategy for dealing with exchange rate risk depends on financial markets and derivatives, such as forward contracts, futures, swaps, and options. Third, the firm must determine whether the benefits from hedging outweigh the costs. At that point, the decision to hedge is simply another net present value problem. If the expected benefits of hedging are greater that the costs, the firm should hedge; if not, the firm should continue with its unhedged exchange rate exposure.

Concept Review Questions

- Describe the three types of foreign exchange exposure discussed in this section.
- Describe how Eastman Kodak and Merck approached the problem of exchange rate risks.
- What are the key issues when determining if a firm should hedge its exchange rate risk?

OPERATING, INVESTMENT, AND FINANCING APPROACHES TO HEDGING EXCHANGE RATE RISK

Numerous approaches exist for hedging the firm's transaction or economic exposure. No one approach provides the best solution all of the time, and since the approaches are not mutually exclusive, firms normally employ a number of different approaches for dealing with part, or all, of their transaction or economic exchange rate risk exposure.

INVOICE IN THE HOME CURRENCY

Firms that sell products to foreign customers can mitigate any transaction-based foreign exchange problem by invoicing in the home currency. Thus, if a Mexican firm is exporting to the United States, it could require payment in pesos. Although this idea sounds great, the U.S. purchasers will recognize that they bear all of the foreign exchange risk in this transaction, and consequently will seek to negotiate a lower purchase price to account for the additional risk they bear. If the firm invoicing in the home currency is not careful, it will lower its cash flows by more than it would cost to go unhedged and bear any exchange rate losses, or, alternatively, to hedge the exchange rate exposure itself.

LEADING AND LAGGING

Transaction exposure can also be reduced by accelerating or delaying the timing of payments that are made or received in foreign currencies. To **lead** is to collect (or pay) early. A firm or subsidiary collecting a weak currency would like to collect early. To **lag** is to collect (or pay) later. Thus, a firm collecting a strong currency would like to collect later. Leading and lagging also applies to paying. Thus, a firm in a country with a weak currency, and having debts to a firm in a strong-currency country will lead; that is, it will pay early. Likewise, a firm in a strong-currency country with debts to a firm in a weak-currency country will lag, or pay later.

Leading and lagging can be done with other independent firms or with subsidiaries. When done with other independent firms, constraints exist because it is impossible to force them to pay early or late in most cases. The best that can be done when dealing with independent firms is to time the cash outflows from the paying firm.

Between a parent firm and its subsidiaries, or between two subsidiaries, leading and lagging can be implemented on a much wider basis. Such items as receivables, payables, lease payments, royalties, management fees, interest or principal, dividends, and the like can all be led or lagged. Because leading and lagging have important implications for minimizing foreign exchange exposure, some countries have imposed restrictions on the practice. A sample of some of these restrictions is provided in Table 28.1.

REINVOICING CENTER

Another means of dealing with transaction exposure is to set up a **reinvoicing center,** which is a separate subsidiary responsible for all interfirm transfers. With a reinvoicing center, the firm's various subsidiaries sell goods to other subsidiaries by going through the reinvoicing center. Title passes to the center and all transaction exposure (for transactions *within* the firm) lies with the center. The center then imposes a small

Table 28.1

Lead and Lag Restrictions for Selected Countries

These are a sample of some lead and lag guidelines established by various countries.

Country	Export Lead	Export Lag	Import Lead	Import Lag
Australia	Allowed—no limit	Allowed—no limit	Allowed—no limit	Allowed—no limit
Chile	90 days	90 days	Not allowed	120 days
Germany	Allowed—no limit	Allowed—no limit	Allowed—no limit	Allowed—no limit
Japan	360 days	360 days	360 days	360 days
Korea	Allowed—no limit	180 days	Not allowed	120 days
Spain	Allowed—no limit	30 days	90 days	90 days
United Kingdom	Allowed—no limit	Allowed—no limit	Allowed—no limit	Allowed—no limit
United States	Allowed—no limit	Allowed—no limit	Allowed—no limit	Allowed—no limit
Venezuela	Not allowed	Not allowed	Not allowed	Not allowed

charge for its services and resells the goods to another subsidiary or the parent. The benefits of a reinvoicing center are that all transaction exposure for transfers within the firm is centrally located, expertise can be developed, and leading and lagging can be coordinated. The primary disadvantage is the cost associated with setting up and maintaining the center.

LOCATE INVESTMENT WHERE SALES OCCUR

Another way to deal with some exchange rate risks is to locate subsidiaries in the countries where the final goods or services are to be sold. Thus, the decisions by two German auto makers, BMW and Mercedes-Benz, to build plants in the southeastern United States will insulate them from many exchange rate fluctuations between the German mark and the U.S. dollar, providing they sell the cars in the United States and they purchase all (or virtually all) of the component parts in the U.S. as well.

ACQUIRE FINANCING IN THE COUNTRY WHERE IT WILL BE USED

Another strategy to protect firms against some exchange rate risks is to acquire the financing where it will be employed. For example, if a firm needs financing in Thailand and has a plant there that will produce cash flows that can be used to pay the financing costs, the firm can insulate itself from certain exchange rate risks. In a coordinated policy, where investments, sales, financing, and repayment are all located within a county, firms can reduce some of their exchange rate exposure. Of course, when funds have to flow back to the parent, or to a subsidiary in another country, exchange rate risk still remains.

In addition to the operating, investing, and financing approaches for dealing with foreign exchange risk, over the last decade firms have made more and more use of forwards, futures, swaps, and options to hedge exchange rate risks. In the remainder of the chapter, we will consider these various alternatives.

Concept Review Question

■ Explain how a firm could decrease exchange rate risk by invoicing in the home currency, by leading or lagging, by using a reinvoicing center, and by investing or obtaining financing in the foreign country.

HEDGING USING FORWARD CONTRACTS

A foreign exchange forward contract is an agreement drawn up for a given maturity or settlement day to deliver (or receive) units of one currency relative to the other currency based on the relationship of the then-existing spot price and the exercise price stated in the contract. Forwards are traded in many currencies for 1, 2, 3, 6, 9, and 12 months. For the major currencies—the dollar, sterling, yen, and mark—quotes are also available for 4 months, 5 months, and so forth. This over-the-counter market, through commercial and investment bankers, can provide almost any kind of coverage using foreign exchange forward contracts.

To hedge an exchange rate exposure we need to take an offsetting position with a foreign exchange forward contract. If we stand to lose as a foreign currency *weakens* relative to the home currency, we would *sell* a foreign exchange forward contract to offset the expected loss in value. Likewise, if we stand to lose as the foreign currency *strengthens* relative to the home currency, we would *buy* a foreign exchange forward contract. By taking such an offsetting position we are "covered" or "square" because no exchange rate risk exposure exists.

SELLING A FORWARD

Let us examine how a foreign exchange forward contract can be used to hedge against a possible loss as a foreign currency weakens. Assume we are selling goods to a Swiss firm with payment due in 90 days. The agreed-upon price is 2,000,000 Swiss francs, SF; the current spot rate of exchange is 1.15 SF/$; and the 3-month forward rate of exchange is 1.25 SF/$. Because the forward rate is above the spot rate, the Swiss franc is expected to weaken against the dollar—that is, in the future it will take more francs to buy a dollar.

First, let us see what might happen when we receive payment in 3 months under three different scenarios:

1. If in 3 months the then-existing spot rate of exchange is 1.25 SF/$, then the amount received, in dollars, is 2,000,000/1.25 = $1,600,000.

2. If in 3 months the Swiss franc weakens more quickly than now expected, and the spot rate then existing is 1.60 SF/$, then we receive 2,000,000/1.60 = $1,250,000, for a loss of $350,000 (i.e., $1,600,000 − $1,250,000).
3. If in 3 months the franc strengthens so the spot rate is 1.00 SF/$, then we receive 2,000,000/1.00 = $2,000,000, for a gain of $400,000 (i.e., $2,000,000 − $1,600,000).

Obviously, we are not indifferent among these outcomes.

To remove the uncertainty associated with what may happen with foreign exchange rates, we can hedge by *selling* a forward contract for 2,000,000 francs for delivery in 90 days with an exercise price at the existing 3-month forward rate of 1.25 SF/$. This way we lock in $1,600,000. If the franc weakens faster than now expected, we gain by hedging; if the franc strengthens, then we have an opportunity loss by hedging. That is, if we hedge and the spot rate in 3 months is 1.00 SF/$, we lost $400,000 because the 2,000,000 Swiss francs could have been converted to $2,000,000 when they were received. Thus, any gain or loss from the hedge exactly offsets the loss or gain from the foreign exchange exposure.

Ignoring the cost of the forward contract, we can depict what happens by selling (or going short) with the foreign exchange contract as follows:

Time Period	Event	
t_0	Sell 2,000,000 francs forward for 90 days at an exercise price of 1.25 SF/$	
	2	**1**
	←	←
t_{90}	Deliver 2,000,000 francs as promised under the forward contract	Receive 2,000,00 francs from the Swiss purchaser
	→	
	Receive $1,600,000 from the buyer of the forward contract	

This is an example of taking a short position with a foreign exchange forward contract. Belief that the forward rate is an unbiased estimate of the expected future spot rate does not preclude hedging to protect against unexpected changes in the future spot rate.

BUYING A FORWARD

Firms may also need to take long positions with foreign exchange forward contracts. To understand this, assume that we are importing goods from Great Britain. The agreement is for the goods to cost 187,500 pounds, or £187,500. Payment will be made in 4 months in pounds. The current spot rate is 1.67 $/£. (Remember, with pounds the "normal" procedure is for the exchange rate to be quoted in dollars per pound.) The 4-month forward rate is 1.60 $/£. In examining the forward and spot rates, we see that the pound is expected to weaken relative to the dollar. However, the U.S. purchaser is concerned that this trend may be reversed and wants to hedge against an increase in the pound. To do this, the importer takes a long position by *purchasing* a 4-month foreign exchange forward contract with the exercise price set at the existing 4-month forward rate of 1.60. By doing so the importer is assured the cost will be (£187,500)(1.60) = $300,000. No matter what occurs the price of $300,000 is locked in. Again, ignoring the cost of the forward contract, we can depict what happens by buying (or going long) with the foreign exchange forward contract as follows:

Time Period	Event
t_0	Purchase £187,500 forward for 4 months at an exercise price of 1.60 $/£
t_4	1 Pay seller of forward contract $300,000
	2 3 Receive £187,500 under the the forward contract Pay British firm £187,500

OTHER CONSIDERATIONS WHEN USING FORWARD CONTRACTS

Now that we understand more about the use of forward contracts to hedge foreign exchange risk, a few other points should be mentioned. First, with any forward contract there is credit risk—one of the parties may default on the contract. Because of this possibility, the use of forwards is restricted to institutions, corporations, and governments with easy access to sufficient lines of credit to back them up. Second, the use of partial hedges is relevant for hedging part (instead of all) of the foreign exchange risk.[6] Finally, in addition to the foreign exchange forwards discussed previously, there are also *forward* foreign exchange agreements. Whereas the traditional foreign exchange forward contract sets a rate in the future for the spot exchange of currencies, it is also possible to enter into forward contracts that at maturity fix the forward rate at that time. These and other developments are constantly occurring in the dynamic area of devising ways to assist firms in managing their foreign exchange risk.

---

[6] Partial hedges, and some of the other specifics of forward contracts and futures (considered next), are dealt with in more detail in Chapter 23.

Concept Review Questions

- When attempting to hedge exchange rate exposure, when should a multinational firm sell a foreign exchange forward contract, and when should it buy a foreign exchange forward contract?

- Describe what would happen to a short hedge if the spot rate of exchange is as expected, less than expected, and greater than expected.

HEDGING USING FUTURES CONTRACTS

In addition to forward contracts, there are also foreign exchange futures contracts. The basic form of a futures contract is just like a forward contract; it obligates its owner to purchase a specified asset at the exercise price on the contract maturity date. But, unlike forward contracts, futures are of a fixed size and maturity date. Table 28.2 indicates the major foreign exchange futures listed in a recent *Wall Street Journal*. We see that futures were available for the yen, mark, Canadian dollar, pound, Swiss franc, Australian dollar, and the U.S. Dollar Index, USDX. The USDX is a measure of the U.S. dollar's composite value against several foreign currencies.

In examining the data for the yen, we see that the futures contract is traded on the International Monetary Market, IMM, which is located at the Chicago Mercantile Exchange. The contract size is 12.5 million yen, and the price is in dollars per thousand yen. Two contracts were available for the yen; and the open, high, low, settle, and change prices are given, along with the contract's lifetime high and low as well as the open interest. At the bottom of the quotes for the yen we see that the volume on the day's activity was 19,011 contracts, the previous day's volume was 21,742, and the open interest was 62,631 contracts—a decrease of 3,250.

In all cases except the USDX, delivery at the termination of the contract is physical; that is, a specific number of units of foreign currency have to be delivered, unless the contract is closed out first. Also, the minimum movement of a futures price is $12.50 for the yen, mark, Canadian dollar, pound, and Swiss franc; it is $10 for the Australian dollar and $5 for the USDX.

SELLING A FUTURE

To understand the use of a futures contract (instead of a forward contract) to hedge foreign exchange risk, let us reconsider the two examples used previously. First, consider the U.S. firm selling to a Swiss firm with payment due in 90 days. The price was 2,000,000 Swiss francs, the current spot rate of exchange was 1.15 SF/$, and the 3-month forward rate of exchange was 1.25 SF/$. *If the payment is due on the same date that the futures contract expires,* then a perfect hedge can be created to lock in the 3-month forward rate of exchange of 1.25 by selling (or going short) 16 contracts. The 16 is determined by dividing the 2,000,000 francs by the number of francs per contract, which is 125,000 as shown in Table 28.2. In 3 months, on the delivery date, the U.S. firm receives 2,000,000 francs from the Swiss purchaser, delivers the

Table 28.2

Major Foreign Exchange Futures Listed in a Recent Issue of *The Wall Street Journal*

There are other futures, futures options, and options listed.

	Open	High	Low	Settle	Change	Lifetime High	Lifetime Low	Open Interest
Japanese Yen (IMM)—12.5 million yen: $ per yen (.00)								
Mar	.6920	.6925	.6907	.6914	−.0025	.8357	.6780	59,352
June	.6942	.6942	.6927	.6932	−.0025	.7530	.6850	3,225
Est vol 19,011; vol Wed 21,742; open int 62,631, −3,250.								
German Mark (IMM)—125,000 marks; $ per mark								
Mar	.5947	.5972	.5936	.5970	+.0031	.6012	.5000	58,357
June	.5949	.5967	.5937	.5968	+.0030	.6007	.5057	4,214
Sept	—	—	—	.5966	+.0030	.5980	.5410	241
Mr	—	—	—	.5968	+.0032	.5975	.5915	375
Est vol 36,349; vol Wed 49,872; open int 63,208, +61.								
Canadian Dollar (IMM)—$100,000 dlrs; $ per Can $								
Mar	.8381	.8390	.8357	.8376	—	.8595	.7890	25,204
June	.8325	.8315	.8294	.8304	—	.8522	.8107	3,419
Sept	.8245	.8250	.8240	.8242	—	.8468	.8100	225
Dec	.8225	.8225	.8225	.8210	+.0010	.8420	.8120	176
Est vol 2,580; vol Wed 5,045; open int 28,934, −384.								
British Pound (IMM)—62,500 pds; $ per pound								
Mar	1.6700	1.6734	1.6668	1.6704	+.0044	1.6734	1.4600	24,461
June	1.6440	1.6476	1.6416	1.6448	+.0042	1.6950	1.4400	2,183
Est vol 8,432; vol Wed 7,491; open int 26,473, +349.								
Swiss Franc (IMM)—125,000 francs; $ per franc								
Mar	.6670	.6697	.6641	.6695	+.0040	.6744	.5740	36,880
June	.6645	.6680	.6620	.6676	+.0040	.6725	.5850	1,320
Mr	—	—	—	.6670	+.0040	.6725	.6540	785
Est vol 20,472; vol Wed 27,463; open int 39,066, +325.								
Australian Dollar (IMM)—100,000 dlrs; $ per A $								
Mar	.7605	.7645	.7599	.7627	−.0001	.7854	.7055	3,256
Est vol 388; vol Wed 515; open int 3,313, +650.								
U.S. Dollar Index (FINEX)—500 times USDX								
Mar	92.75	92.95	92.45	92.464	−.36	105.65	92.25	4,770
June	93.42	93.42	93.25	93.10	−.37	100.43	92.80	273
Est vol 3,250; vol Wed 3,385; open int 5,045, +288.								
The Index: High 92.49; Low 92.16; Close 92.16, −.25.								

2,000,000 francs as promised when the 16 futures contracts were sold, and receives $1,600,000 (i.e., 2,000,000/1.25 = $1,600,000) under the futures contract. Again, the cost of the contract will have to be taken into consideration.

BUYING A FUTURE

The same basic ideas apply to the use of a futures hedge in the case of our other example, the U.S. firm importing goods from England that will cost £187,500. With a 4-month forward rate of 1.60 $/£, and *assuming a futures contract exists that settles at the same time the payment is due,* the firm can lock in its cost of $300,000 [i.e., (£187,500)(1.60 $/£) = $300,000] by purchasing (or going long in) the futures contract. The futures contract size is £62,500, as shown in Table 28.1, so the number of contracts needed is 187,500/62,500 = 3. When delivery occurs, the U.S. firm settles the futures contract by paying $300,000 and receiving £187,500, which it then uses to pay the British firm. In so doing the firm has reduced its risk exposure so that no matter what the actual rate of exchange is at settlement, the cost is $300,000 (plus the cost of the futures contracts).

OTHER CONSIDERATIONS WHEN USING FUTURES CONTRACTS

In practice, the size of the futures contract and its maturity rarely matches the firm's needs exactly. In that case perfect hedges are not possible. (In Chapter 23 we explored the implications of less than perfect hedges.) Also, it often happens that the currency needed to be hedged against does not have a traded futures contract. This is a case in which cross hedging is required. When a cross hedge is needed, the typical approach is to find which futures contract most closely tracks the currency to be hedged. Suppose a U.S. firm sold some goods to an importer in Finland. There is no futures contract on the Finnish markka. The way to proceed is to determine the futures contract whose movements are most highly correlated with movements in the *spot* rate on the markka. To do that we might gather data on the spot rate for the markka, along with data on the futures prices of three different futures contracts—the British pound, Swiss Francs, and German marks. Then we would calculate the *day-to-day changes* in all four series.

If the data for the spot rate on the markka and the German mark futures prices for 4 days are as follows, the first step is to determine the changes, or:

Day	Spot Rate Markka/$	ΔMarkka/$	Futures Mark/$	ΔMark/$
1	5.413		0.6301	
2	5.418	0.005	0.6303	0.0002
3	5.414	−0.004	0.6303	0.0000
4	5.407	−0.007	0.6294	−0.0009

Assuming we had sufficient data (in practice this means at least 50 observations)[7] then we run the following regression:

$$\Delta\text{spot} = \alpha + \beta\Delta\text{futures}$$

where

Δspot is the change in the spot price, markka/$
Δfutures is the change in the futures price, mark/$

We would do the same for the other two futures contracts. Typically the one with the highest explanatory power, or R^2, would be chosen to hedge the exposure because that contract's futures price is most highly correlated with movements in the spot rate. Other items discussed in Chapter 23, including rolling and strip hedges, also apply to hedging longer-term foreign exchange exposure using foreign exchange options.

Concept Review Questions

- How are foreign exchange futures contracts and foreign exchange forward contracts similar? How are they different?
- Explain how to use a futures contract to offset exchange rate risk.
- Define cross-hedging, and explain when it can be used to hedge exchange rate risk.

HEDGING USING SWAPS

In Chapter 23 we discussed interest rate swaps. Currency swaps also exist. In a plain vanilla currency swap, the transaction involves the exchange of principal denominated in one currency for principal denominated in another currency at the beginning of the swap, *and*

1. Fixed interest payments in one currency into fixed interest payments in another currency, or
2. Fixed interest payments in one currency into floating interest payments in another currency, or
3. Floating interest payments in one currency into floating interest payments in another currency, *and*

reexchange of the original principal at the end of the swap.

PARALLEL LOANS

To illustrate a currency swap, let's start with a **parallel (or back-to-back) loan.** A parallel loan involves two firms in separate countries arranging to borrow in each

---

[7] While we used "days" in the example, more often the data employed is weekly or monthly.

other's currency for a specific period of time, exchanging principal and interest payments, and at the agreed termination date returning the principal. For example, assume the current spot exchange rate between the Japanese yen and the U.S. dollar is 110 yen per dollar, ¥110/$1. A U.S. firm with a subsidiary in Japan wants to expand its operations in Japan and needs ¥550 million to do so. At the same time, a Japanese firm wants to expand its operations in the United States and needs to invest $5 million in its U.S. subsidiary. Both firms want to hedge any exchange rate risk exposure.

A straightforward way to accomplish this, which firms often used in the past, is a parallel loan. The structure of a typical parallel loan is shown in Figure 28.4. At the current rate of exchange of ¥110/$1, ¥550,000,000/110 = $5,000,000. To set up the parallel loan, the U.S. parent borrows in the U.S. and then lends the funds to the Japanese subsidiary in the U.S., while the Japanese parent borrows in Japan and then lends the funds to the U.S. subsidiary in Japan. The two loans are for the same amount, at the current spot rate of exchange, and for a specified maturity of, say, 6 years. At the end of 6 years the loans are repaid to the original parent firm (and then the original lenders). Let's assume the fixed interest rate was 10 percent in the United States and 8 percent in Japan. During the life of the loan, the U.S. subsidiary would pay interest of (¥550,000,000)(0.08) = ¥44,000,000 per year to the Japanese parent. At the same time the Japanese subsidiary would pay the U.S. parent interest of ($5,000,000)(0.10) = $500,000 per year.

Default risk can be protected through a right of offset or through a third-party guarantee. A further agreement can provide for maintenance of the principal parity in case the spot rate of exchange between the two currency changes. For example, if the U.S. dollar weakened against the yen by 5 percent for a period of 30 days, the U.S. parent might have to advance additional dollars to the Japanese subsidiary to bring the principal value of the two loans back into agreement. A similar provision would apply if the yen weakened against the dollar.

Figure 28.4

Structure of a Parallel, or Back-to-Back, Loan

With a parallel loan firms can set the financing up so they loan/repay in the currency desired. Before swaps were introduced in 1981, parallel loans provided the same result; sometimes they are still employed to get around currency controls imposed in various countries.

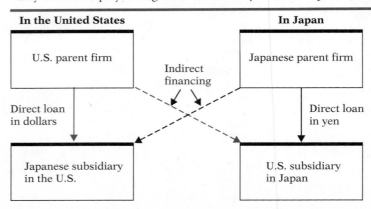

CURRENCY SWAPS

Although the parallel loan is straightforward, in practice one of the big difficulties is to find the counter-firm that has exactly the offsetting need. To avoid this problem, currency swaps have been developed. In the above example, a currency swap would involve the U.S. parent raising the $5 million in the U.S., while the Japanese firm raises ¥55 million in Japan. Then the firms agree to swap the initial principal, interest payments for 6 years, and then reswap the principal at the end of the 6 years. This sequence is depicted in Figure 28.5. Thus, the swap accomplishes everything, in a far easier manner, than the parallel loan.

Default risk has been reduced because now there is one combined agreement, the currency swap. In practice only the net amount, or difference, is transferred between the parties. Also, while both loans could be fixed rate loans, it is more typical for at least one of the loans to be a floating rate loan. Finally, with the growth of the swap market, intermediaries (such as Chemical Bank, Citicorp, and J.P. Morgan) actually provide the services needed by a party (such as the U.S. parent) and then they seek to offset, or cover, their position. Hence, the role of the intermediary is *not* that of bringing the

Figure 28.5

Structure of a Currency Swap

With this plain vanilla currency swap, the firms borrow where it is cheapest, swap principal and interest payments, and at the termination of the agreement reswap the initial principal. Many other variations of currency swaps also exist.

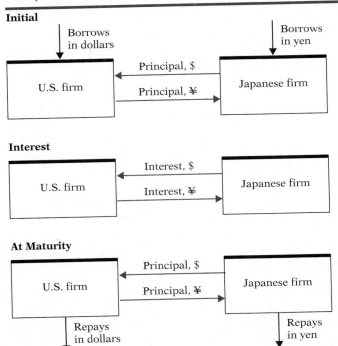

two parties together; rather, it is to provide the services needed, for a fee, and then hedge the resulting risk exposure. With the number of banks who have developed large swap operations, the cost to the firm is less now than it was in the early days of the swap market. Also, more sophisticated types of currency swaps can be arranged; but the preceding discussion indicates the function of swaps as a means of dealing with exchange rate risk.

Concept Review Questions

- Describe how multinational firms use parallel loans to offset exchange rate risk exposure.
- What is one difficulty with a parallel loan and how does a currency swap correct for this difficulty?

HEDGING USING CURRENCY OPTIONS

The currency options market operates in a manner similar to the foreign exchange futures market, except it allows the firm the choice of exercising the option or letting it expire. Table 28.3 presents some recent quotes on foreign exchange options listed on the Philadelphia Exchange for the British pound and the Swiss franc.

To illustrate options, let's use the British pound as an example. The contract is for 31,250 British pounds. The last spot price of the pound, quoted in cents per pound, was 156.58, or $1.5658 per pound. The first column in Table 28.3 indicates the various exercise (or strike) prices available—they range from 155 (or $1.55) to 170 ($1.70). The second column lists the month in which the option expires. These range from May to September. The next two columns indicate the volume and last price for call options on the British pound. As we see, there are calls available for strike prices from 155 to 170. For the June call with a strike price of $157\frac{1}{2}$, the volume was 20 and the price was 2.32 cents per pound. The last two columns provide the same information for puts.

Exchange-traded options are also available on the Philadelphia Exchange for the U.S. dollar versus the Australian dollar, Canadian dollar, German mark, and the Japanese yen. They are also available between the pound and the mark and between the mark and the yen. In addition to the Philadelphia Exchange, foreign exchange options are also available on the International Monetary Exchange, IMM, at the Chicago Mercantile Exchange, and on exchanges in London, Holland and Singapore. Over-the-counter options can be obtained from commercial or investment banks against a number of other currencies, and for different amounts. Employing the basic ideas developed for valuing options using the Black-Scholes model, foreign currency options can be valued.[8] We will leave this issue to others and, instead, focus on using options to hedge a firm's foreign exchange risk exposure.

---

[8] The pricing of foreign exchange options is more complicated than discussed in Chapter 5. The share price, P_0, becomes the exchange rate. Then, instead of one interest rate, there are two—one for the domestic currency and one for the foreign currency. Finally, because the foreign interest rate is like a cash dividend, that complication also has to be taken into consideration. See, for example, Garman and Kohlhagen (1983).

Table 28.3

Some of the Foreign Exchange Options Listed in a Recent Issue of *The Wall Street Journal*

These options are listed on the Philadelphia Exchange. There are also options on the Australian dollar, the Canadian dollar, French franc, German mark, Japanese yen, and Swiss franc listed on the Philadelphia Exchange.

		Calls		Puts	
		Vol.	Last	Vol.	Last
British Pound					**156.58**
31,250 British Pounds-cents per unit					
155	May	21	2.12	110	0.60
155	Jun	2	3.55	4	2.00
155	Sep	8	5.20	—	—
$157\frac{1}{2}$	Jun	20	2.32	—	—
$157\frac{1}{2}$	Sep	80	3.97	—	—
160	May	10	0.40	—	—
160	Jun	2	1.35	—	—
165	Jun	10	0.42	—	—
$167\frac{1}{2}$	Jun	30	0.26	—	—
170	Jun	10	0.12	—	—
Swiss Franc					**70.55**
62,500 Swiss Francs-cents per unit					
68	Sep	—	—	5	1.27
$69\frac{1}{2}$	May	44	1.40	—	—
70	May	10	1.02	5	0.39
70	Jun	10	1.45	—	—
70	Sep	2	2.34	9	2.10
$70\frac{1}{2}$	May	—	—	3	0.52
71	May	107	0.42	100	0.74
71	Jun	13	1.01	—	—
72	Sep	10	1.50	—	—
73	Jun	38	0.42	—	—
75	Jun	2	0.14	—	—

BUYING A CALL

Assume we have a U.S. firm that has purchased goods from a British manufacturer, with payment in the amount of £4,000,000 to be made in June. At the current spot rate of $1.5658 (from Table 28.3), the amount due *if settlement were today* is

(4,000,000)(1.5658) = $6,263,200. What might happen when payment is made if the firm does not hedge? Assume the spot rate at settlement is

1.53	The outflow is (4,000,000)(1.53) = $6,120,000. The firm does not want to hedge.
1.59	The outflow is (4,000,000)(1.59) = $6,360,000. The firm wants to hedge.

The firm is concerned about the dollar weakening against the pound, which would make the actual spot price more than $1.5658 when payment is due. The size of the option is 31,250 British pounds per contract, so in order to hedge the firm could purchase 4,000,000/31,250 = 128 June call options with a strike price of $157\frac{1}{2}$ (or $1.575). The cost of the option (from Table 28.3) is 2.32 cents per pound, so the cost per option is (31,250)($0.0232) = $725. With 128 options required, the total cost of the hedge is (128)($750) = $96,000. If the dollar weakens just a little against the pound, stays the same, or strengthens, the firm will let the hedge expire; the cost to the firm is simply the cost of the hedge, or $96,000.

What happens when payment is due if the dollar has weakened and is now trading at 1.64? The cash outflow to the firm if they had not hedged would be (4,000,000)(1.64) = $6,560,000, which is $296,800 (i.e., $6,560,000 − $6,263,200) greater than indicated by the spot rate of exchange when the purchase was made. But, by buying the call, the firm can lock in the cost of the £4,000,000 at $1.57\frac{1}{2}$, for an outlay of $6,300,000. The net cost to the firm, compared with no change in the spot rate of exchange, is $6,300,000 − $6,263,200 = $36,800 plus the cost of the option of $96,000, for a total of $132,800. While the firm did not fully offset the weakness in the dollar, at least it cut its loss from $296,000 if they had gone unhedged to $132,800. To obtain a "better" outcome, the firm could have purchased a call with a lower strike price; but in order to do so the cost of the call would have increased substantially.

BUYING A PUT

Instead of having to pay funds in another currency, our firm might be selling goods to a British firm, with the payment to be made in pounds. Say the amount of the sale was £3,400,000. At the current spot rate of exchange of 1.5658, the dollar amount to be received is $5,323,720. What might happen when payment is received if the firm does not hedge? Assume the spot rate at settlement is, again,

1.53	The inflow is (3,400,000)(1.53) = $5,202,000. The firm wants to hedge.
1.59	The inflow is (3,400,000)(1.59) = $5,406,000. The firm does not want to hedge.

To hedge, the firm could purchase 3,400,000/31,250 = 108.8 ≈ 109 June put options with an exercise price of 155. Note that because the number of contracts does not come out be an even number, even under the best of circumstances a perfect hedge is not possible. The cost per option (from Table 28.3) is 2 cents per pound, so the total cost is $(31,250)(\$0.02)(109) = \$68,125$. If on settlement day the spot rate of exchange is 155.5, or 1.555 cents per pound, the firm throws the option away; they are out the price of the option. However, if the dollar had weakened, the firm would have benefitted by being hedged.

OTHER CONSIDERATIONS WHEN USING CURRENCY OPTIONS

Currency options are similar to insurance against adverse movements in exchange rates. They can hedge part or all of the risk involved and at the same time allow the firm to benefit if exchange rates move in the firm's direction. Thus, one advantage currency options have over forward contracts, futures or swaps, is that the firm has not locked in a specific exchange rate irrespective of the movement in exchange rates. This is why firms, such as Eastman Kodak and Merck discussed earlier in the chapter, sometimes prefer options over other forms of hedging instruments.

In addition to currency options, there are also futures options. With a futures option, the owner of the futures option, upon exercise, merely acquires a long or short futures position with the futures price equal to the exercise price of the option. All of these, and other, techniques are employed by firms to protect themselves against the effects of exchange rate risk.

Concept Review Questions

- What are some advantages of using currency options for hedging?
- Describe when and how a multinational firm will employ a currency call option to hedge exchange rate risk.
- When would a multinational firm use a put option to hedge against exchange rate risk?

KEY POINTS

1. Virtually all firms, whether purely domestic or multinationals, may face economic exposure that makes them more or less vulnerable as exchange rates change.
2. Reasons for hedging include reduced taxes, reduced costs of financial distress, and reduced agency costs. Hedging is just another net present value problem; it make sense to hedge only if the expected benefits are greater than the expected costs.
3. Types of exchange risk exposure include translation, transaction, and economic. Translation exposure is accounting oriented; although it does not affect the firm's cash flows, it is sometimes important due to financial loan covenants. Transaction and economic exposure has direct cash flow implications. Firms employ a variety of approaches to hedge transaction and economic exposure.
4. Techniques employed to hedge some of the firm's translation and economic exposure include invoicing in the home currency, leading and lagging, using reinvoicing centers, locating investment where the sales occur, and raising financing where it will be used.

5. Forward contracts, exchange rate futures and currency swaps can be employed to lock in a specific rate of exchange; by using one of them the firm does not worry whether exchange rates move for or against it. Exchange rate options, on the other hand, provide the opportunity, but not the requirement, to lock in a specific rate of exchange.

6. The derivative market has expanded rapidly; many other features can be built into hedging instruments. Throughout, the emphasis must be on assessing the risk exposure of the firm, determining how much of it the firm wants to hedge, and examining the benefits and costs of hedging. If the firm does not hedge exchange rate risk it can either ignore it, or price it—that is, pass the costs of not hedging on to others.

QUESTIONS

28.1 "If there are no taxes, if there are no transactions costs, and if the investment policy of the firm is fixed, then the financial policies of the firm are irrelevant." Since the management of financial risk is one of the firm's financial policies, this statement implies firms should never concern themselves with hedging financial price risk. Why, then, do firms hedge financial price risk?

28.2 "Because of the relationships specified by the expectations theory of forward exchange rates, by purchasing power parity, by the international Fisher effect, and by interest rate parity, hedging exchange rate risk is not necessary." Discuss this statement.

28.3 Distinguish among translation, transaction, and economic foreign exchange exposure. Why, with few exceptions, should firms not be concerned with translation risk?

28.4 "All firms have a foreign exchange problem." Do you agree or disagree with this statement? Why?

28.5 Operating, investment, and financing strategies exist for hedging foreign exchange risk. Although these seem very adequate, firms have increasingly moved to using financial derivatives to assist them in hedging exchange rate risk. What deficiencies exist with operating, investing, or financing approaches to dealing with exchange rate risk?

28.6 What alternative derivatives are available for hedging exchange rate risk? How are they similar? How are they different?

28.7 Under what conditions would a U.S. firm go long in a forward or futures contract rather than go short?

28.8 Parallel loans existed long before currency swaps. What advantages and disadvantages exist with currency swaps compared with parallel loans?

28.9 In order to use an option to hedge foreign exchange risk, a premium must be paid to purchase the option. Assume the forward rate of exchange is 2.10 foreign to 1 domestic and you purchase a call with a strike price equal to the current forward rate. The premium paid reduces the *effective* strike price to 1.95 foreign/1 domestic. Taking into account the premium paid, there is substantially less than a 50 percent probability you will ever exercise the option. Why would you ever want to purchase an exchange rate option?

CONCEPT REVIEW PROBLEMS

See Appendix A for solutions.

CR28.1 A U.S.-based firm sold 200,000 bushels of grain to an Australian company for 500,000 Australian dollars. Payment for the grain will be received in 6 months. The current spot rate of exchange is A$1.25 per U.S. dollar and the 6-month forward rate of exchange is A$1.15 per U.S. dollar.

a. Is the Australian dollar expected to strengthen or weaken relative to the U.S. dollar?
b. If the spot rate does not change, what amount in American dollars will the U.S. firm receive for the grain? If the spot rate does drop, as predicted by the forward rate, what amount will the U.S. firm receive?
c. Establish a hedge using forward contracts to offset the exchange rate risk. Demonstrate the effectiveness of the hedge by showing the profit and loss if the spot price in 6 months is A$1.35 per U.S. dollar.

CR28.2   Assume the 200,000 bushels of grain sold in CR28.1 is being imported from Canada. The cost of the grain is Can$300,000. The current spot rate is Can$1.20 per U.S. dollar, and the forward contract rate is Can$1.10 per U.S. dollar. The U.S.-based firm has the option of paying for the grain now or in 3 months when delivery is made. (*Note:* Assume 4 equal-length quarters per year.) If the opportunity cost of capital is 10 percent, should payment be made today?

CR28.3   Best Eastern has agreed to purchase equipment from an Italian firm in 3 months for 600,000,000 Italian lira. The current spot price is Lira 1,200 per U.S. dollar, and the 3-month forward rate is Lira 1,150 per U.S. dollar.

a. If Best Eastern paid for the equipment today in U.S. dollars, what is the outlay?
b. What is the cost, in U.S. dollars, if Best Eastern waits and pays in 3 months and the spot rate at that time is equal to today's 3-month forward rate?
c. Assuming futures contracts exist for the size and maturity needed, should Best Eastern buy or sell a futures contract to hedge the exchange rate exposure? What are the results if the spot rate in 3 months is Lira 1,100 per U.S. dollar?

CR28.4   San Antonio General needs 300,000 British pounds to expand its British plant, and a British firm needs $600,000 to expand its American subsidiary. The spot rate is £0.50 per U.S. dollar. The prime rate is 10 percent in the United States and 15 percent in Britain. Both firms need funds for 5 years and can borrow at the prime rate.

a. If a parallel loan were established between the two firms, what would the interest payments be?
b. Now assume San Antonio General borrows $600,000 at the U.S. prime rate and converts it to British pounds. Immediately after the funds are converted the British pound weakens to a spot rate of £0.60 per U.S. dollar. If San Antonio General planned to pay the loan using U.S. dollars converted to British pounds, what is the annual percentage cost of the funds?

CR28.5   Imports, Inc. just purchased furniture worth 3,000,000 francs from a Swiss company. Payment for the shipment is due in May. Use the information in Table 28.3 to answer the following questions:

a. If the shipped furniture were paid today in U.S. dollars, what would it cost?
b. Is Imports, Inc. concerned with the Swiss franc strengthening or weakening in relation to the U.S. dollar?
c. If Imports, Inc. attempts to use options to hedge its exposure, how many and what kind of options will the firm need to purchase?
d. What is the total cost of the hedge if options with a strike price of $0.70 and a maturity of May is used?
e. Assume the Swiss franc strengthens in relationship to the U.S. dollar to $0.80 per Swiss franc. What is the loss if Imports Inc. had not purchased the options? If Imports Inc. purchased the options, what is the total cash flow to the firm?

PROBLEMS

28.1 You are exporting goods from the United States to Mexico. The agreed-upon price is 8 billion pesos, the current spot rate is 2,750 pesos/$, and the 3-month forward rate is 2,800 pesos/$.

a. How can you lock in your proceeds using a forward contract? What amount will you receive?

b. If in 3 months the actual spot rate of exchange is 2,900 pesos/$, did you benefit or lose by hedging? By how much?

28.2 Hunt Industries has just made a major sale to a Japanese firm. The payment will be ¥100 million. The payment will be made in 180 days, and the 180-day forward rate is ¥123.24/$.

a. How can Hunt lock in the dollar amount it will receive? What is the amount in dollars?

b. Assume Hunt does not hedge and the actual spot rate of exchange in 180 days is ¥125.80/$. How much would Hunt gain or lose by going unhedged? Now assume the spot rate in 180 days is ¥121.20/$. How much is Hunt's gain or loss by going unhedged?

28.3 Bergstrom's Systems has just agreed to sell some goods to a Malaysian firm. The agreed-upon price is 12 million ringgits, payment will be made in 90 days, and the current spot rate of exchange is 2.712 ringgits/$. Bergstrom's decides to hedge this against a possible weakening in the Malaysian ringgit by selling a 90-day forward contract with an exercise price of 2.900 ringgits/$.

a. What sequence of transactions takes place (both today and in 90 days)?

b. If the actual spot rate of exchange in 90 days is 3.150 ringgits/$, is Bergstrom's better or worse off by engaging in the forward contract? By how much?

28.4 We are importing goods from Spain, with the payment to be made in Spanish pesetas in 2 months. The agreed-upon price is 450 million pesetas, the spot rate of exchange is 109.95 pesetas/$, and the exercise price in the 60-day forward contract is 115.38.

a. What sequence of transactions takes place (both today and in 60 days)?

b. If the actual spot rate of exchange in 60 days is 118.35 pesetas/$, are we better or worse off by engaging in the forward contract? By how much?

28.5 LBG is selling to a British firm with the agreed-upon price at payment of £312,500. Payment is due on the same day the British pound futures contract expires, so a perfect hedge can be created. The current spot rate is $1.46/£, and the forward rate of exchange when the futures contract expires is currently $1.42/£.

a. If LBG wants to lock in its proceeds, what should it do? How many contracts are involved?

b. If at the receipt date (which is also the futures contract expiration date) the spot rate is $1.50/£ , did LBG benefit or lose by hedging? By how much?

c. What if the agreed-upon price was £330,000? Could a perfect hedge have been formed?

d. What if the date the payment was to be received did not coincide with the date the futures contract expires? Could a perfect hedge have been formed?

28.6   You are importing goods from Canada that will cost $875,000 in Canadian dollars in 3 months. The payment is due on the last day of the month 3 months from now. The 3-month Canadian futures contract expires 1 to 2 weeks before payment is due, and the 3-month forward rate is 1.221 C$/US$.

a.   Is a perfect hedge available? Why or why not?
b.   In order to lock in your costs, what hedge (even if not perfect) should be placed?
c.   If when you pay the bill the spot rate of exchange is C$1.150/US$, did you gain or lose on the transaction? (*Note:* A precise dollar answer may not be feasible, but you can make calculations to determine the basic impact.)

28.7   Lander Productions deals with firms in Spain, Italy, and Greece on a regular basis. Lander would like to hedge some of its foreign exchange rate risk, but there are no futures contracts on the Spanish peseta, the Italian lira, or the Greek drachma. Recent weekly data was gathered from *The Wall Street Journal* for the futures prices on the British pound and the Swiss franc versus the U.S. dollar, along with spot exchange rate for the U.S. dollar versus the peseta, the lira, and the drachma, as follows:

	Futures		Spot		
Week	$/£	$/Franc	Peseta/$	Lira/$	Drachma/$
1	1.5114	0.6632	116.81	1509.30	219.75
2	1.5158	0.6670	115.82	1500.85	218.75
3	1.5046	0.6705	112.63	1463.91	212.55
4	1.5010	0.6782	114.53	1492.25	215.70
5	1.4292	0.6493	117.67	1532.00	221.75
6	1.4060	0.6470	118.43	1544.45	221.90
7	1.4334	0.6583	117.58	1569.83	220.30
8	1.4170	0.6591	117.71	1591.85	221.70
9	1.4434	0.6537	119.08	1594.26	225.40
10	1.4238	0.6535	118.78	1609.09	225.00
11	1.4774	0.6599	116.98	1577.41	222.40

a.   Determine the 10 week-to-week differences for the five difference currencies.
b.   Which is the best futures contract to hedge the spot peseta/$ exchange rate? The lira/$ exchange rate? The drachma/$ exchange rate? How good a hedge do you think can be made using either of the futures contracts? If you do not think a good hedge is available with any of the futures contracts, what alternatives exist to hedge the exchange rate risk?

28.8   A U.S.-domiciled firm has a subsidiary in the Netherlands that needs a 45 million guilder loan; at the same time a Netherlands-domiciled firm has a subsidiary in the United States that needs a $25 million loan. Assume the current exchange rate is 1.80 guilders/$. A 4-year parallel loan is going to be set up; the interest rate is fixed for each loan, and it is 7 percent in the Netherlands and 10 percent in the United States.

a.   Determine the structure of the parallel loan and the cash flows that are expected to be made from one firm to the other throughout the loan.
b.   To protect against changes in exchange rates, the principal amount of the loan will be adjusted once each year. The firm whose home currency is weakening will have to increase

its principal in the loan. Assume the interest rate parity relationship holds and that the two interest rates are the risk-free rates for the respective countries. What are the expected spot rates at time $t = 1$, $t = 2$, and $t = 3$? (*Note:* Carry to three decimal places.) By how much will the U.S.- or Netherlands-domiciled firm have to increase the principal of the loan at times $t = 1, 2$, and 3? What will the new interest amount be for the three time periods for the new principal?

c. Instead of changing the principal, what other way could the change in interest rates be accomplished?

28.9 Wise Enterprises, of Princeton, New Jersey, just purchased merchandise worth 1 million French francs, with payment due in francs in 90 days. The spot rate of exchange today is FFr5.32/$. A 3-month over-the-counter call option (from a bank) is available with the following characteristics:

Size of option	FFr250,000
Strike price	FFr5.30/$
Option premium, per option	$400

Assume Wise went ahead with purchasing the call options to hedge the exchange rate exposure. Today the options mature, and the current spot exchange rate is FFr5.22/$.

a. Should Wise exercise the options?
b. At what spot exchange rate today would Wise be indifferent between exercising the options and letting them expire?

28.10 Toys-for-You just sold one of its subsidiaries to Kyoto Miniatures for 100 million yen, with payment to be received in yen in 40 days. The spot rate of exchange between the yen and the dollar is ¥110.25/$, or $0.009070/¥. Toys is concerned about changes in exchange rates, so it is considering hedging using put options traded on the Philadelphia Exchange. The options are for 6,250,000 yen each. The 88 option (that is, with an exercise exchange ratio of $0.0088/Y) costs 0.0036 cents per yen, the 89 option costs 0.0063 cents per yen, the $90\frac{1}{2}$ option costs 0.0116 cents per yen, and the 91 option costs 0.014 cents per yen.

a. What would it cost Toys if it uses the 88 option to hedge? The 89 option? The $90\frac{1}{2}$ option? The 91 option? (*Note:* The cost of the option on the yen is quoted in *fractions* of a cent; it is necessary to convert to dollars.)
b. Assume that Toy-for-You went ahead and purchased the 91 options. Today the options mature, and the current spot rate of exchange is $0.00915/¥. What should Toys do? What did the hedge cost Toys?
c. What should Toys do if the current spot rate of exchange is $0.00905/¥? What is the total cost to Toys?

28.11 Mini Case Malibou Sports has just hired you to be its hedge manager. Up until now the firm has not systematically considered the financial price risk it is exposed to, but with Malibou's rapid growth and its large amount of foreign transactions more systematic attention to risk management is required.

a. The board of directors has asked to be briefed on the following issues:

(1) Given that there are always costs involved, why should Malibou Sports consider hedging? (As one of the directors noted, "We are in the sports merchandising business, not in the business of speculating.")

(2) Why, given that Malibou imports about as much as it exports, should Malibou consider hedging its foreign exchange risk? (As another director noted, "Over the long run exchange rates work things out, and, therefore, hedging is not needed.")

(3) How can Malibou employ operating, investing, and financing strategies for dealing with exchange rate exposure? What are the strengths and weaknesses of each, and why may these strategies not "solve" all of Malibou's exchange rate risk problems?

Prepare your report.

b. Your report in (a) was so persuasive that the directors will meet again next week. They want a report on the use of derivatives for dealing with exchange rate risk. In particular they need a clear, but simple, explanation of the techniques available, their strengths and weaknesses, and your recommendations about the strategy Malibou needs to employ in hedging exchange rate risk. You need to prepare this report also.

c. As part of your report in (b), the board of directors is concerned about how to go about hedging some of its exchange rate exposure in lesser developed countries. As another board member notes, "For many of the countries there are no futures contracts traded." How are you going to respond to this concern?

d. Malibou has just placed an order for shoes manufactured in the Philippines. Malibou owes 8 million Philippine pesos in 4 months. The present spot rate is 26.20 pesos/$ and the current 4-month forward rate is 26.75 pesos/$. Malibou is considering three alternatives: going unhedged, hedging using a forward contract, and hedging using an over-the-counter call option from a bank. The forward contract would be at the current forward rate and would cost $6,000. The option would carry an exercise price of 26.30 pesos/$ and cost $2,500.

(1) Compare the alternative ways that Malibou can hedge. What do you recommend?

(2) Assume 4 months have passed and the settlement day on the purchase has arrived. The actual spot rate is 27.15 pesos/$. Evaluate the results under the three alternatives.

(3) Instead of an actual spot rate of 27.15 pesos/$ in (b), assume the actual spot rate turned out to be 26.00 pesos/$. Now evaluate the results of the three alternatives.

e. Because of the success of the Malibou name in Germany, a big order was just received from a German sporting chain. Payment of the 2.5 million marks will be in 90 days. The spot rate of exchange is 1.58M/$ (or $0.6320/M) while the 90-day forward rate is 1.60M/$ ($0.625/M). Four alternatives are being considered: going unhedged, hedging using a forward contract, hedging using futures contracts, and hedging using a put option. The forward contract would have an exercise price of 1.61M/$ and cost $23,000. The futures contracts are for 62,500 marks each, with a strike price of 1.61M/$, and will cost $485 per contract. The options are also for 62,500 marks each, with an exercise price of 1.61M/$, and will cost 0.53 cents per mark. [*Note:* The cost of an option on the German mark is quoted in cents per mark; it is *not* necessary, as in problem 28.10 (a), to convert to dollars.]

(1) Compare the alternative ways Malibou can hedge. What do you recommend?

(2) Assume 4 months have passed and the settlement day on the sale has arrived. The actual spot rate is 1.63M/$. Evaluate the results under the four alternatives.

(3) Instead of an actual spot rate of 1.63M/$ in (b), assume the actual spot rate turned out to be 1.58M/$. Now evaluate the results of the four alternatives.

REFERENCES

For more on the strategic aspects of hedging in general and of foreign exchange risk, see, for example:

AHN, MARK J., and WILLIAM D. FALLOON. *Strategic Risk Management: How Global Corporations Manage Financial Risk for Competitive Advantage.* Chicago: Probus Publishing, 1991.

BESSEMBINDER, HENDRIK. "Forward Contracts and Firm Value: Investment Incentive and Contracting Effects." *Journal of Financial and Quantitative Analysis* 26 (December 1991): 519–32.

JORION, PHILLIPPE. "The Exchange-Rate Exposure of U. S. Multinationals." *Journal of Business* 63 (July 1990): 331–45.

LEWENT, JUDY C., and A. JOHN KEARNEY. "Identifying, Measuring and Hedging Currency Risk at Merck." *Journal of Applied Corporate Finance* 2 (Winter 1990): 19–28.

NANCE, DEANA R., CLIFFORD W. SMITH, JR., and CHARLES W. SMITHSON. "On the Determinants of Corporate Hedging." *Journal of Finance* 48 (March 1993): 267–84.

SMITH, CLIFFORD W., JR., CHARLES W. SMITHSON, and D. SYKES WILFORD. *Managing Financial Risk.* New York: Harper & Row, 1990.

SMITH, CLIFFORD W., and RENE M. STULZ. "The Determinants of Firms' Hedging Policies." *Journal of Financial and Quantitative Analysis* 20 (December 1985): 391–405.

Specifics on forwards, futures, swaps, options, and exchange rate management are covered in:

BRIYS, ERIC, and MICHEL CROUHY. "Creating and Pricing Hybrid Foreign Currency Options." *Financial Management* 17 (Winter 1988): 59–65.

DUBOFSKY, DAVID A. *Options and Financial Futures.* New York: McGraw-Hill, 1992.

GARMAN, MARK B., and STEVEN W. KOHLHAGEN. "Foreign Currency Option Values." *Journal of International Money and Finance* 2 (March 1983): 231–37.

HULL, JOHN. *Options, Futures, and Other Derivative Securities.* 2nd ed. Englewood Cliffs, N.J.: Prentice-Hall, 1993.

KHOURY, SARKIS J., and K. HUNG CHAN. "Hedging Foreign Exchange Risk: Selecting the Optimal Tool." *Midland Corporate Finance Journal* 5 (Winter 1988): 40–52.

STOLL, HANS R., and ROBERT E. WHALEY. *Futures and Options.* Cincinnati: South-Western, 1993.

Solutions to Concept Review Problems

Chapter 1

CR1.1

Sales	$700,000
Cost of goods sold	100,000
Administrative expenses	300,000
Depreciation	50,000
Earnings before interest and taxes, EBIT	250,000
Interest	60,000
Earnings before taxes, EBT	190,000
Taxes (40%)	76,000
Earnings after tax, EAT (Net income)	$114,000

CR1.2

  a. net cash flow = $64,000

  b. net cash flow = −$216,000

CR1.3

Cash Inflows		Cash Outflows	
Sales for cash	$26,000	Cash expenses	$12,000
Cash on hand	500	Interest	6,000
Total	$26,500	Taxes	3,040
		Cash dividend	500
		Short-term debt	1,500
		Total	$23,040

net cash flow = $3,460

CR1.4

  a. projected return $= \dfrac{\$11,000}{\$10,000} - 1 = 10\%$

  b. $NPV = \dfrac{\$11,000}{1.15} - \$10,000 = -\$435$

CR1.5

Their calculations were correct, and yes, it is possible to have a negative net income and a positive net cash flow.

Chapter 2

CR2.1   a. $NPV = \$26,316$

b. $\dfrac{\$600,000}{1 + IRR} = \$500,000$

$\$600,000 = \$500,000 + \$500,000 IRR$

$IRR = (\$600,000 - \$500,000)/\$500,000 = 20\%$

CR2.2   a. $FV_{10} = \$6,000(1.10)^{10} = \$15,562$

b. $FV_5 = \$8,000(1.05)^5 = \$10,210$

c. $FV_7 = \$857$

d. $FV_3 = \$11,910$

CR2.3   a. $PV_0 = \$6,000/(1.10)^{10} = \$2,313$

b. $PV_0 = \$8,000/(1.05)^5 = \$6,268$

c. $PV_0 = \$292$

d. $PV_0 = \$8,396$

CR2.4   a. $PV_0 = \$800$

b. $PV_0 = \dfrac{\$80}{0.10 - 0.04} = \$1,333$

c. $PV_0 = \left(\dfrac{\$80}{0.10}\right)\left[\dfrac{1}{(1.10)^3}\right] = \$601$

CR2.5 $FV_3 = \$25,000\left(1 + \dfrac{0.08}{1}\right)^{3(1)} = \$31,493$

$FV_7 = \$31,493\left(1 + \dfrac{0.10}{2}\right)^{4(2)} = \$46,530$

CR2.6   a. $PV_0 = \dfrac{\$5,000}{\left(1 + \dfrac{0.10}{12}\right)^{3(12)}} = \$3,709$

b. $k_{\text{effective annual}} = \left(1 + \dfrac{0.10}{12}\right)^{12} - 1 = 10.47\%$

CR2.7   a. $\$1,000,000/20 = \$50,000$ per year

$PV_0 = \$50,000\left[\dfrac{1}{0.08} - \dfrac{1}{0.08(1.08)^{20}}\right] = \$490,907$

b. $PV_0 = \$530,180$

CR2.8   a. $FV_5 = \$500\left[\dfrac{(1.10)^5 - 1}{0.10}\right] = \$3,053$

b. $FV_5 = (\$3,053)(1.10) = \$3,358$

c. $k_{\text{effective annual}} = \left(1 + \dfrac{0.08}{4}\right)^4 - 1 = 8.243\%$

$FV_5 = \$500\left[\dfrac{(1.08243)^5 - 1}{0.08243}\right] = \$2,948$

CR2.9   **a.** $NPV = \dfrac{\$140,000}{(1.12)^1} + \dfrac{\$200,000}{(1.12)^2} + \dfrac{\$250,000}{(1.12)^3} - \$500,000 = -\$37,616$

b. $\dfrac{\$140,000}{(1 + IRR)^1} + \dfrac{\$200,000}{(1 + IRR)^2} + \dfrac{\$250,000}{(1 + IRR)^3} - \$500,000 = 0$

$IRR = 7.96\%$

CR2.10   If the 2.9% financing is taken, the payment is:

$\$20,000 = PMT \left\{ \dfrac{1}{0.029/12} - \dfrac{1}{(0.029/12)[1 + (0.029/12)]^{2(12)}} \right\}$

$PMT = \$858.74$

If the rebate is taken and the remainder financed at 8 percent by the bank, the payment is:

$\$18,000 = PMT \left\{ \dfrac{1}{0.08/12} - \dfrac{1}{(0.08/12)[1 + (0.08/12)]^{2(12)}} \right\}$

The $PMT = \$814.09$; take the rebate.

Chapter 3

CR3.1   **a.** $B_0 = \$50 \left[\dfrac{1}{0.04} - \dfrac{1}{0.04(1.04)^{30}} \right] + \dfrac{\$1,000}{(1.04)^{30}} = \$865 + \$308 = \$1,173$

b. $B_0 = \$1,149$

CR3.2   The interest per semiannual period is $(0.06)(\$1,000)/2 = \$30$, and the number of periods is $(2)(20) = 40$.

$\$945 = \displaystyle\sum_{t=1}^{40} \dfrac{\$30}{(1 + k_b)^t} + \dfrac{\$1,000}{(1 + k_b)^{40}}$

The yield to maturity, or k_b, is 3.25 percent for half a year, so the YTM on an annual basis is 6.50 percent.

CR3.3   **a.** $k_p = \dfrac{\$6.50}{\$70} = 9.29\%$

b. $P_0 = \dfrac{\$6.50}{0.10} = \$65$ per share

CR3.4 $P_0 = \dfrac{\$1.65(1.06)}{0.14 - 0.06} = \dfrac{\$1.749}{0.08} = \$21.86$

CR3.5 $P_0 = \dfrac{\$1.980}{(1.14)^1} + \dfrac{\$2.376}{(1.14)^2} + \dfrac{\$2.851}{(1.14)^3} + \dfrac{\$3.421}{(1.14)^4} + \dfrac{\$45.328}{(1.14)^4}$

$= \$1.74 + \$1.83 + \$1.92 + \$2.03 + \$26.84 = \$34.36$

CR3.6   At first glance this problem may appear to be extremely complicated and time-consuming; however, by combining the future value equations in the numerator for the dividend payments with the present value of the required rate of return, the equation becomes a simple annuity with a lump sum value for the stock price in year 20. To find the current value of the stock, each of the future dividend payments can be represented as follows:

$P_0 = \dfrac{\$1.65(1.20)^1}{(1.14)^1} + \dfrac{\$1.65(1.20)^2}{(1.14)^2} + \cdots + \dfrac{\$1.65(1.20)^{20}}{(1.14)^{20}} + \dfrac{P_{20}}{(1.14)^{20}}$

Dividing both the numerator and the denominator by 1 plus the growth rate, we can fix the numerator to a single value of \$1.65. Thus, the dividend payments from year 1 through year 20 can be modeled as an annuity with constant payments of \$1.65 and discounted back at negative 5 percent. To find the price of the stock in year 20, the dividend valuation model is used with an estimated dividend in year 20.

$$P_0 = \frac{\$1.65(1.20)^1/(1.20)^1}{(1.14)^1/(1.20)^1} + \frac{\$1.65(1.20)^2/(1.20)^2}{(1.14)^2/(1.20)^2} + \cdots + \frac{\$1.65(1.20)^{20}/(1.20)^{20}}{(1.14)^{20}/(1.20)^{20}}$$

$$P_0 = \frac{\$1.65}{(0.95)^1} + \frac{\$1.65}{(0.95)^2} + \cdots + \frac{\$1.65}{(0.95)^{20}} + \frac{P_{20}}{(1.14)^{20}}$$

$$P_0 = \frac{\$1.65}{[1 - 0.05)]^1} + \frac{\$1.65}{(1 - 0.05)]^2} + \cdots + \frac{\$1.65}{(1 - 0.05)]^{20}} + \frac{P_{20}}{(1.14)^{20}}$$

$$D_{20} = \$1.65(1.20)^{20} = \$63.257, \text{ so } P_{20} = \frac{\$63.27(1.06)}{0.14 - 0.06} = \$838.16$$

$$P_0 = \$1.65\left[\frac{1}{-0.05} - \frac{1}{-0.05(1 - 0.05)^{20}}\right] + \frac{\$838.16}{(1.14)^{20}} = \$59.05 + \$60.99 = \$120.04$$

CR3.7 $$P_0 = \frac{\$2.00(1 - 0.15)}{0.20 - (-0.15)} = \frac{\$1.70}{0.35} = \$4.86$$

CR3.8 $$\text{return} = \frac{\$2.50(1.06) + [\$35(1.06) - \$35]}{\$35} = 13.57\%$$

Chapter 4

CR4.1 $\bar{k}_{\text{IBM}} = 10\%$, $\bar{k}_{\text{DC}} = 9.6\%$, and $\bar{k}_{\text{market}} = 9.4\%$

CR4.2 $\sigma_{\text{IBM}} = [0.2(-15 - 10)^2 + 0.6(10 - 10)^2 + 0.2(35 - 10)^2]^{0.5} = (250)^{0.5}$

$\qquad\quad = 15.81\%$; $\sigma_{\text{DC}} = 22.96\%$, and $\sigma_{\text{market}} = 10.46\%$

$$CV_{\text{IBM}} = \frac{15.81\%}{10\%} = 1.58$$

$$CV_{\text{DC}} = \frac{22.96\%}{9.6\%} = 2.39$$

CR4.3 $\bar{K}_{\text{p+IBM}} = 0.8(9.4\%) + 0.2(10\%) = 9.52\%$

$\qquad\quad \bar{K}_{\text{p+DC}} = 9.44\%$

CR4.4 $$\beta_{\text{Bram}} = \frac{10.56\%(0.45)}{8.67\%} = 0.55$$

$$\beta_{\text{Itel}} = \frac{12.15\%(0.85)}{8.67\%} = 1.19$$

CR4.5 $k_{\text{Bram}} = 6.0\% + 0.55(11.0\% - 6.0\%) = 8.75\%$

$\qquad\quad k_{\text{Itel}} = 11.95\%$

CR4.6 $k_{\text{Bram}} = 8.0\% + 0.55(13.0\% - 8.0\%) = 10.75\%$

$\qquad\quad k_{\text{Itel}} = 13.95\%$

CR4.7   **a.** $P_{0Bram} = \dfrac{\$2.00(1.03)}{0.0875 - 0.03} = \$35.83$

$P_{0Itel} = \dfrac{\$4.00(1.06)}{0.1195 - 0.06} = \$71.26$

b. $P_{0Bram} = \$26.58$ and $P_{0Itel} = \$53.33$

Chapter 5

CR5.1 $V_c = \text{Max}(0, \$54 - \$55)(100) = \$0$
$V_p = \text{Max}(0, \$60 - \$49)(100) = \$1,100$
$\text{profit} = \$0 + \$1,100 - \$300 - \$200 = \$600$

CR5.2   If the call is purchased, the payoff is:

	Stock Price = $90	Stock Price = $50
Buy a call	$100(\$90 - \$60) = \$3,000$	0

If a loan for $5,000/1.08 = $4,629.63 is taken out and stock is purchased, the payoff is:

	Stock Price = $90	Stock Price = $50
Buy stock	$ 9,000	$ 5,000
Repay loan	−5,000	−5,000
Total payoff	$ 4,000	$ 0

The payoff from buying stock with the loan is $\$4,000/\$3,000 = 1\frac{1}{3}$ as much as from buying the option. Therefore,

$\text{value of } 1\frac{1}{3} \text{ calls} = \$6,000 - \$4,629.63 = \$1,370.37$

$\text{value of 1 call for 100 shares} = (\$1,370.37)(3/4) = \$1,028$

CR5.3 $\text{return from upward movement} = \dfrac{\$90}{\$60} - 1 = 50\%$

$\text{return from downward movement} = \dfrac{\$50}{\$60} - 1 = -16.67\%$

The probability of an upward movement is:

$8\% = (W)(50\%) + (1 - W)(-16.67\%)$; so $W = 0.37$.

$V_c = \dfrac{\$1,110}{1.08} = \$1,028$

CR5.4 $d_1 = 0.083$ and $d_2 = -0.177$; from Table B.5, $N(d_1) \approx 0.532$, while $N(d_2) \approx 0.429$, so $V_c = \$8.31$.

CR5.5 $V_p = \$9.35$

CR5.6   **a.** $N(d_1) \approx 0.957$ and $N(d_2) \approx 0.719$; $S = \$15.263$ million.

b. $B = \$4.737$ million

c. default option = $0.655 million

CR5.7   The proceeds from the new issue is $\$32,000,000/(1.10)^{15} \approx \$7.661$ million, while it costs $\$12,000,000/(1.10)^{10} \approx \$4.627$ million to retire the existing bonds. The approximately $3 million remaining after refinancing is employed to retire stock, so the total value of the firm remains at $20 million. $N(d_1)$ is ≈ 0.889 and $N(d_2)$ is ≈ 0.433, so $S = \$13.607$ million and $B = \$6.393$ million.

Chapter 6

CR6.1

$$\$1,198 = \sum_{t=1}^{40} \frac{\$50}{(1 + k_b/2)^t} + \frac{\$1,000}{(1 + k_b/2)^{40}}$$

$k_b = 4\%$ semiannually, or 8 percent annually

$k_i = 8\%(1 - 0.35) = 5.20\%$

CR6.2

$k_{ps} = 9.14\%$

CR6.3

k_s(dividend valuation approach) $= \dfrac{\$7.20(1 - 0.50)}{\$40} + 0.04 = 13\%$

k_s(capital asset pricing model) $= 6\% + 1.5(14\% - 6\%) = 18\%$

k_s(bond yield + risk premium) $= 8\% + 6\% = 14\%$

The average cost of equity capital is 15%.

CR6.4

opportunity cost of capital = 12.45%

CR6.5

Component		W
Short-term debt	$ 10,000,000	0.074
Long-term debt	38,280,000	0.283
Preferred stock	12,000,000	0.089
Equity	75,000,000	0.554
Total market value	$135,280,000	1.000

CR6.6

$k_{\text{short-term}} = 6\%(1 - 0.35) = 3.90\%$; $k_{\text{long-term}} = 9\%(1 - 0.35) = 5.85\%$; $k_{ps} = 10\%$; and the average $k_s = (16.67\% + 16.80\% + 15\%)/3 = 16.16\%$.

CR6.7

opportunity cost of capital = 11.79%

CR6.8

The new $k_s = 17.76\%$, so the opportunity cost of capital is 12.68%.

CR6.9

$$\beta_U = \frac{1.5}{1 + (1 - 0.40)(0.50)} = 1.15$$

$\beta_{\text{levered division}} = (1.15)[1 + (1 - 0.35)(20\%/80\%)] = 1.34$

$k_{\text{divisional}} = 18.06\%$, so the divisional opportunity cost of capital = 15.62%.

Chapter 7

CR7.1

payback period$_A$ = 2.33 years while payback period$_B$ = 1.20 years.

CR7.2

$$NPV_A = \frac{\$200}{(1.10)^1} + \frac{\$200}{(1.10)^2} + \frac{\$300}{(1.10)^3} - \$500 = \$73$$

$NPV_B = -\$474$

CR7.3

$$\$500,000 = \frac{\$350,000}{(1 + IRR)^1} + \frac{\$250,000}{(1 + IRR)^2} + \frac{\$80,000}{(1 + IRR)^3}$$

$IRR_A = 21.82\%$

$IRR_B = 16.96\%$

CR7.4 $NPV_A = \$84,899$, while $NPV_B = \$101,052$.

CR7.5 $$\$500,000 = \frac{\$8,000,000}{(1 + IRR)^1} + \frac{\$8,000,000}{(1 + IRR)^2} + \frac{-\$20,000,000}{(1 + IRR)^3}$$

By trial-and-error, $IRR \approx 19\%$ and $\approx 1581\%$. The $NPV = -\$1,641,998$. Do not accept C.

CR7.6 $FV_A = \$350,000(1.10)^2 + \$250,000(1.10)^1 + \$80,000 = \$778,500$. $MIRR_A = 15.90\%$ and $MIRR_B = 16.96\%$.

CR7.7   For Select Seed $NPV = \$985$, $IRR = 28.86\%$, and $MIRR = 20.52\%$. For Cheap Seed $NPV = \$524$, $IRR = 48.30\%$, and $MIRR = 31.64\%$. Plant the Select Seed.

CR7.8 $$\$3,160 = \frac{\$2,370}{(1 + \Delta IRR)^1} + \frac{\$1,370}{(1 + \Delta IRR)^2} + \frac{\$580}{(1 + \Delta IRR)^3}$$

$\Delta IRR = 22.58\%$

CR7.9 $$NPV_{A \text{ over 3 years}} = \frac{\$25,000}{(1.15)^1} + \frac{\$25,000}{(1.15)^2} + \frac{\$25,000}{(1.15)^3} - \$40,000 = \$17,080.63$$

$$NPV_{A \text{ over 9 years}} = \$17,080.63 + \frac{\$17,080.63}{(1.15)^3} + \frac{\$17,080.63}{(1.15)^6} = \$35,696$$

$NPV_B = \$22,985$; accept A.

CR7.10   The equivalent annual $NPV_A = \$7,481$ while equivalent annual $NPV_B = \$4,817$.

Chapter 8

CR8.1   a.

Year	MACRS Factor	Depreciation
1	0.1429	$35,725
2	0.2449	61,225
3	0.1749	43,725
4	0.1249	31,225
5	0.0893	22,325
6	0.0893	22,325
7	0.0893	22,325
8	0.0445	11,125

b. No, the Internal Revenue Service assumes all assets are purchased half way through the year.

CR8.2   a. Depreciation per year is $3,600, $5,760, $3,456, $2,073.60, $2,073.60, and $1,036.80 for years 1 through 6, respectively.

b. The remaining undepreciated value is $5,184, and the selling price is $9,000. The net cash proceeds are $7,855.20.

c. The selling price is $4,500 and the net cash proceeds are $4,705.20.

CR8.3   The $500,000 is a sunk cost and should be ignored.
$CF_0 = \$200,000 + \$100,000 + \$40,000 = \$340,000$.

CR8.4   The operating cash flows for the 6 years are $183,500, $196,100, $182,660, $174,596, $174,596, and $168,548, respectively.

CR8.5

Estimated resale value	$10,000
Less: Tax on sale ($10,000)(0.35)	− 3,500
Recovery of net working capital	40,000
Net terminal cash inflow	$46,500

CR8.6 $NPV = \$387,175$; expand.

CR8.7   The initial investment, depreciation tax shield, and terminal cash flows remain the same. The operating cash flows decrease by $(\$125,000)(1 - 0.35) = \$81,250$ per year. The new NPV is $\$71,221$. Still expand.

CR8.8   The incremental initial cash flows are:

Cost of new ovens	$ 335,000
Tax on sale of old ovens	
($100,000 − $80,000)(0.40)	8,000
Less: Sale of old ovens	−100,000
Incremental initial investment	$ 243,000

ΔCF:

	Year			
	1	2	3	4
Δrevenues	$58,500	$67,240	$76,240	$85,500
Δcosts	6,000	12,176	18,544	25,102
ΔCFBT	52,500	55,064	57,696	60,398
ΔDep	35,833	91,667	91,667	35,833
ΔCF	45,833	69,705	71,285	50,572

The incremental terminal cash flows are:

After-tax proceeds of selling new ovens ($50,000)(1 − 0.40)	$ 30,000
After-tax proceeds of selling old ovens ($20,000)(1 − 0.40)	−12,000
Incremental terminal cash flow	$ 18,000

The $NPV = -\$52,191$; do not replace.

CR8.9

Project	NPV
A	$21
B	41
C	0
D	27
E	36
F	18

Take A, D, E, and F, with a total NPV of $102.

Chapter 9

CR9.1   a.   risk premium = $1.4(12\% - 6\%) = 8.4\%$

   $k_{\text{project}} = 6\% + 8.4\% = 14.4\%$

   b. $NPV = \$13,570$; accept the project.

CR9.2 $NPV_{10\text{ year}} = \$2,037,537$, while $NPV_{5\text{ year}} = -\$1,295,690$. The expected net present value $= \$370,924$.

CR9.3   a.   The after-tax operating cash flows $= \$21,600$ per year and $NPV = \$8,469$.

b.

Percent Change	Arrangements Sold per Year	NPV
−30%	420	−$12,072
−20	480	− 5,225
−10	540	1,622
0	600	8,469
+10	660	15,316
+20	720	22,163
+30	780	29,010

CR9.4 The financial break-even point in dollars is $18,928; in units the break-even point is $\approx$ 526 units.

CR9.5 **a.** The NPVs are −$14,354 for the downturn, $8,469 for the base case, and $35,857 for the improved economy.

  b. The expected NPV is $9,838 and the standard deviation about the expected NPV is $19,479.

Chapter 10

CR10.1 **a.** $NPV = \$1,416$; keep the mowers.

  b. $NPV = \sum_{t=1}^{3} \dfrac{(\$7,000)}{(1.15)^t} - (\$10,000 + \$3,000) = \$2,983$

Purchase the conversion kits.

CR10.2 The value of the division if kept is:

$$NPV = \frac{\$3,000,000}{(1.14)^1} + \frac{\$3,500,000}{(1.14)^2} + \frac{\$3,500,000}{(1.14)^3} + \frac{\$4,000,000 + \$41,600,000}{(1.14)^4}$$

$$= \$34,685,976$$

The divestiture proceeds of $45 million − $6 million = $39 million is greater than the division's NPV; sell the division.

CR10.3 **a.** $NPV = -\$24,343,098$; do not expand.

  b. The present value of the inflows at $t = 3$ is $50 million + $40 million = $90 million. From Table B.6 the value is $\approx$ 0.474, so the value of the option to expand is ($57.387 million)(0.474) = $27,201,438. The strategic NPV is −$24,343,098 + $27,201,438 = $2,858,340.

CR10.4 $\sigma(t)^{0.5} = 0.953$

$$\frac{P_0}{x/e^{K_{RF}t}} = \frac{\$60}{\$45/e^{(0.07)(3)}} = 1.645$$

From Table B.7, the factor is $\approx$ 0.116, so the option to abandon = ($60 million)(0.116) = $6,960,000. The strategic $NPV = \$2,858,340 + \$6,960,000 = \$9,818,340$.

CR10.5 present value of forecasted cash flow$_1$ = $\$15,000/e^{(0.18)(1)} = \$12,529$
present value of forecasted cash flow$_2$ = $\$25,000/e^{(0.18)(2)} = \$17,442$

The two tabled values from Table B.7 are $\approx$ 0.058 and 0.033; the value of the guarantee is ($12,529)(0.058) + ($17,442)(0.033) = $1,302.

Chapter 11

CR11.1   a. $V_U = \dfrac{\$4.5 \text{ million}}{0.15} = \$30 \text{ million}$

b. $k_s{}^L = 0.15 + (0.15 - 0.10)(\$15/\$15) = 20\%$

opportunity cost of capital $= (0.10)(\$15/\$30) + (0.20)(\$15/\$30) = 15\%$

$V_L = S_L + B = \$30 \text{ million}$

No.

CR11.2   a. $V_U = \dfrac{\$4.5 \text{ million}(1 - 0.40)}{0.15} = \$18 \text{ million}$

$k_s{}^U = 0.15 + (0.15 - 0.10)(1 - 0.40)(0/\$18) = 15\%$

opportunity cost of capital $= 15\%$

b. $V_L = \$18 \text{ million} + 0.40(\$15 \text{ million}) = \$24 \text{ million}$

$k_s{}^L = 0.15 + (0.15 - 0.10)(1 - 0.40)(\$15/\$9) = 20\%$

opportunity cost of capital $= (10\%)(\$15/\$24)(1 - 0.40) + (20\%)(\$9/\$24) = 11.25\%$

CR11.3   a. $V_U = \$170 \text{ million}$

$V_L = \$170 \text{ million} + \left[1 - \dfrac{(1 - 0.32)(1 - 0.20)}{(1 - 0.28)}\right]\$60 \text{ million}$

$= \$184.7 \text{ million}$

The gain from leverage is \$14.7 million.

b. $V_U = \$175$ million and $V_L = \$193$ million. With $T_{PS} = T_{PB}$, the gain to leverage is $TB = \$18$ million.

CR11.4   a.   For Project I \$104,000 and \$48,000; for Project II \$120,000 and \$10,000.

b. $NPV_I = \dfrac{\$104,000}{1.15} - \$100,000 = -\$9,565$

$NPV_{II} = \$4,348$

c.   A stockholder would prefer I, whereas a bondholder would prefer II.

CR11.5 $V_U = \dfrac{\$10 \text{ million}(1 - 0.40)}{0.15} = \$40 \text{ million}$

Debt	Without Financial Distress $V_L = V_U + TB$	With Financial Distress Costs $V_L = V_U + TB -$ financial distress
\$ 0	\$40	\$40.0
20	48	47.5
25	50	49.0
30	52	50.5
35	54	51.0
40	56	50.0
45	58	49.0

With no financial distress, use \$45 million debt. When financial distress is considered, employ \$35 million of debt.

Chapter 12

CR12.1

a. $S_L = \dfrac{[\$500,000 - (0.08)(\$1,000,000)](1 - 0.30)}{0.12} = \$2,450,000$

$V = S_L + B = \$2,450,000 + \$1,000,000 = \$3,450,000$

b. $\dfrac{\text{opportunity cost}}{\text{of capital}} = 8\%(1 - 0.30)\left(\dfrac{\$1,000,000}{\$3,450,000}\right) + 12\%\left(\dfrac{\$2,450,000}{\$3,450,000}\right)$

$\approx 10.15\%$

c. $S_L = \$1,750,000$ and $V = \$3,250,000$. Do not restructure.

CR12.2

a. $S_U = V_U = \dfrac{\$400,000(1 - 0.40)}{0.15} = \$1,600,000$

$S_L = \dfrac{[\$400,000 - (0.10)(\$800,000)](1 - 0.40)}{0.17} = \$1,129,412$

$V_L = S_L + B = \$1,929,412$

b. $\$800,000/\$16 = 50,000$ shares of common stock will be retired.

$P_0 = \dfrac{\$1,129,412}{50,000} = \$22.59$

c. $P_0 = \dfrac{\$1,129,412}{60,000} = \$18.82$

CR12.3

a. $EPS_{\text{all equity}} = \dfrac{\$500,000(1 - 0.40)}{100,000} = \$3.00$

$EPS_{\text{levered}} = \dfrac{[\$500,000 - (0.12)(\$400,000)](1 - 0.40)}{50,000} = \$5.42$

b. $P_{0 \text{ all equity}} = 12(\$3.00) = \$36.00$
$P_{0 \text{ levered}} = \$43.36$

CR12.4

a. With equity financing, EAT is \$1,888,000; shares of common stock are 540,000, and EPS is \$3.50. With debt financing, EAT is \$1,836,800, and EPS is \$3.67.

b. $EBIT^* = \$1,880,000$

CR12.5

a. $EPS = \$2.50$ and $P_0 = \$37.50$

b. $NPV = (\$800,000/0.10) - \$6,000,000 = \$2,000,000$

c. $EPS = \dfrac{[\$3,000,000 - (0.10)(\$26,000,000)](1 - 0.40) + \$800,000}{288,000} = \$3.61$

$P_0 = 13(\$3.61) = \$46.93$; accept the project.

Chapter 13

CR13.1

net income $= \$50,000,000(1 - 0.35) = \$32,500,000$
equity financing needed $= \$25,000,000(0.40) = \$10,000,000$
dividends $= \$32,500,000 - \$10,000,000 = \$22,500,000$
dividend payout ratio $= \$22,500,000/\$32,500,000 = 69.23\%$

CR13.2   a.
Common stock ($1 par value)	$ 1,100
Additional paid-in capital	32,900
Retained earnings	47,000
Total equity	$81,000

b.
Common stock ($0.25 par value)	$ 1,000
Additional paid-in capital	30,000
Retained earnings	50,000
Total equity	$81,000

CR13.3   Before the ex-dividend date $P_0 = \$100,000,000/5,000,000 = \$20$ and $P/E = \$20/\$4 = 5$ times. The dividends paid are $(5,000,000)(\$1) = \$5,000,000$, so after the ex-dividend date the market value of equity is $\$100,000,000 - \$5,000,000 = \$95,000,000$, $P_0 = \$95,000,000/5,000,000 = \$19$ and $P/E = \$19/\$4 = 4.75$ times.

CR13.4   The shares repurchased $= \$5,000,000/\$20 = 250,000$; number of common shares outstanding $= 5,000,000 - 250,000 = 4,750,000$; so the market value of equity $= \$95,000,000$, $P_0 = \$95,000,000/4,750,000 = \$20$, the new EPS is $[(\$4)(5,000,000)]/4,750,000 = \$4.21$, and $P/E = \$20/\$4.21 = 4.75$ times.

CR13.5   a.   New debt $= \$900,000(2/1) = \$1,800,000$, so total capital expenditures $= \$2,700,000$.

b.   dividends $= \$900,000 - \$700,000 = \$200,000$
$DPS = \$200,000/100,000 = \$2$

$$P_0 = \frac{\$2(1 + 0.05)}{0.16 - 0.05} = \$19.09$$

c. $P_0 = \$22.97$.

Chapter 14

CR14.1   a. $NPV = -\$51,816$

b. $\beta_S^U = 1.3\left(\frac{0.70}{1.00}\right) = 0.91$

$k_S^U = 3\% + 0.91(7\% - 3\%) = 6.64\%$

base case $NPV = \displaystyle\sum_{t=1}^{10} \frac{\$135,000}{(1.0664)^t} - 1,000,000 = -\$35,835$

interest tax shield $= (\$800,000)(0.06)(0.25) = \$12,000$ per year

$PV_{\text{tax shield}} = \displaystyle\sum_{t=1}^{4} \frac{\$12,000}{(1.0664)^t} = \$40,979$

$APV = -\$35,835 + \$40,979 = \$5,144$

CR14.2   The loan payment is $\$230,873$ per year, and the interest tax shield is $\$12,000$, $\$9,257$, $\$6,349$, and $\$3,267$ per year.

$$PV_{\text{tax shield}} = \frac{\$12,000}{(1.0664)} + \frac{\$9,257}{(1.0664)^2} + \frac{\$6,349}{(1.0664)^3} + \frac{\$3,267}{(1.0664)^4} = \$27,154$$

$APV = -\$35,835 + \$27,154 = -\$8,681$

CR14.3   a. $\beta_S^U = 1.2\left(\frac{0.65}{1.00}\right) = 0.78$

$k_S^U = 8\% + 0.78(15\% - 8\%) = 13.46\%$

base case $NPV = \$7.57$ million

interest tax shield $= \$200(0.10)(0.40) = \$8$ million per year

$PV_{\text{tax shield}} = \$42.62$ million

APV (for both locations) $= \$7.57 + \$42.62 = \$50.19$ million

b. First, determine the financing benefits. The interest tax shield is $(\$200)(0.05)(0.40) = \$4$ million per year and the present value of the interest tax shield is $\$21.31$ million. The savings in cash outflows due to the subsidized loan, with a discount rate of $(10\%)(1 - 0.40) = 6\%$, is:

$$PV_{\text{debt financing}} = \sum_{t=1}^{10} \frac{\$4}{(1 + 0.06)^t} + \frac{\$200}{(1 + 0.06)^{10}} = \$141.12 \text{ million}$$

The savings from the subsidized loan is $\$200 - \$141.12 = \$58.88$ million. $APV = \$7.57 + \$21.31 + \$58.88 = \$87.76$ million.

CR14.4 The tax benefit from interest deductions is for the 7 years from $t = 4$ to $t = 10$.

$$PV_{\text{tax shield}} = \frac{\left[\sum_{t=1}^{7} \dfrac{\$4}{(1.1346)^t}\right]}{(1.1346)^3} = \$11.94 \text{ million}$$

$APV = \$7.57 + \$11.94 + \$58.88 = \$78.39$ million

CR14.5

	Year			
	0	1	2	3
Cash flow to stockholders	$-\$100,000$	$\$20,400$	$\$20,400$	$\$145,400$

$$FTE = \frac{\$20,400}{(1.20)^1} + \frac{\$20,400}{(1.20)^2} + \frac{\$145,400}{(1.20)^3} - \$100,000 = \$15,310$$

Chapter 15

CR15.1 The issue offering is $x(1 - 0.15) = \$500,000$, so the flotation costs are $\$88,235$.

CR15.2 net proceeds per share $= \$32(1 - 0.05) = \$30.40$
number of shares $= \$10,000,000/\$30.40 = 328,947$

CR15.3 **a.** number of shares $= \dfrac{(550,000)(4)}{10 + 1} + 1 = 200,001$

b. number of directors $= \dfrac{(130,000 - 1)(10 + 1)}{550,000} = 2.60 = 2$

c. number of directors $= \dfrac{(130,000 - 1)(5 + 1)}{550,000} = 1.42 = 1$ No.

CR15.4 **a.** $EPS = \$700,000/700,000 = \$1$ per share
dividend $= (\$1)(0.70) = \$0.70$

$$P_0 = \frac{D_1}{k_s - g} = \frac{\$0.70(1.08)}{0.12 - 0.08} = \$18.90$$

b. $P_0 = (18)(\$1) = \$18$

CR15.5

Cash	$\$250,000$	Liabilities	$\$400,000$
Other	$750,000$	Common stock ($1 par)	$60,000$
Total assets	$\$1,000,000$	Additional paid-in capital	$390,000$
		Retained earnings	$150,000$
		Total liabilities and stockholders' equity	$\$1,000,000$

Chapter 16

CR16.1

Year	Payment	Interest	Principal Repayment	Remaining Balance
1	$29,832	$15,000	$14,832	$85,168
2	29,832	12,775	17,057	68,111
3	29,832	10,217	19,615	48,496
4	29,832	7,274	22,558	25,938
5	29,829	3,891	25,938	0

CR16.2

Month	Payment	Interest	Principal Repayment	Remaining Balance
1	$2,379	$1,250	$1,129	$98,871
2	2,379	1,236	1,143	97,728
3	2,379	1,222	1,157	96,571
4	2,379	1,207	1,172	95,399
5	2,379	1,192	1,187	94,212

CR16.3

B_0(zero-coupon) $= \$1,000/(1.10)^5 = \$620.92$
number of zero-coupon bonds $= \$50,000,000/\$620.92 = 80,526$
number of coupon-bearing bonds $= \$50,000,000/\$1,000 = 50,000$

CR16.4

The bond prices before the increase were zero-coupon bond $= \$1,000/(1.10)^{20} = \$148.64$, and coupon-bearing bond $= \$1,000$. After the increase B_0 (zero-coupon) $= \$103.67$ and B_0 (coupon-bearing) $= \$850.61$. The percentage loss was -30.25% for the zero-coupon bond and -14.94% for the coupon-bearing bond.

CR16A.1

$\Delta CF_0 = \$32,000$ and $\Delta CT_t = \$4,850$. The $NPV = -\$1,815$.

Chapter 17

CR17.1

$(0.30)(3)^{0.5} = 0.5196$

$$\frac{\$28}{\$35/e^{(0.06)(3)}} = 0.9578$$

price $= \$28(0.181) = \$5.07$

CR17.2

a. (1) $V_W = \text{MAX} (\$60 - \$70, 0) = 0$
   (2) $V_W = \text{MAX} (\$80 - \$70, 0) = \$10$
   (3) $V_W = \text{MAX} (\$100 - \$70, 0) = \$30$

b. $P_0^* = \dfrac{\$60,400,000}{1,000,000} = \$60.40$

$q = \dfrac{40,000}{1,000,000} = 0.04$

$(0.313)(5)^{0.5} = 0.7000$

$\dfrac{\$60.40}{\$70/e^{(0.05)(5)}} = 1.1079$

$V_w = \$60.40(0.309) = \$18.66$

$V_w(\text{with dilution}) = \left(\dfrac{1}{1 + 0.04}\right)(\$18.66) = \$17.94$

CR17.3

a. $(0.20)(4)^{0.5} = 0.4000$

$$\frac{\$42}{\$45/e^{(0.05)(4)}} = 1.1400$$

$V_w = (\$42)(0.218) = \$9.16$

b. $V_{(\text{before})} = (\$42)(24{,}000{,}000) = \$1{,}008$ million

$V_{\text{after}} = \$1{,}008 + (\$10.37)(7.52) = \$1{,}085.98$ million

$$P_0^* = \frac{\$1085.98\ \text{million}}{24\ \text{million}} = \$45.25$$

$$q = \left(\frac{7.52\ \text{million}}{24\ \text{million}}\right) = 0.313$$

$(0.20)(4)^{0.5} = 0.4000$

$$\frac{\$45.25}{\$45/e^{(0.05)(4)}} = 1.2282$$

$V_w = \$45.25(0.264) = \$11.946$

$$V_{w(\text{with dilution})} = \left(\frac{1}{1+0.313}\right)\$11.946 = \$9.10$$

c. $\sigma_{\text{common stock and warrants}} = (0.20)/\left(\frac{\$1{,}085.98}{\$1{,}478}\right) = 0.27$

$(0.27)(4)^{0.5} = 0.5400$

$$\frac{\$45.25}{\$45/e^{(0.05)(4)}} = 1.2282$$

$V_w = (\$45.25)(0.310) = \$14.028$

$$V_{w\ (\text{with dilution})} = \left(\frac{1}{1.313}\right)(\$14.028) = \$10.68$$

CR17.4

a. $B_0 = \sum_{t=1}^{2\times20} \frac{\$60}{(1.07)^t} + \frac{\$1{,}000}{(1.07)^{2\times20}} = \$867$

b. conversion ratio $= \$1{,}000/\$25 = 40$
conversion value $= (40)(\$10) = \$400$

c. $\sigma_{(\text{non-levered firm})} = (0.30)(0.30) = 0.09$

$\sigma_{(\text{after conversion})} = 0.09/0.50 = 0.18$

$$V_{c\ (\text{with dilution})} = \left(\frac{1}{1.15}\right)(\$5.153) = \$4.48$$

value of convertible $= \$867 + \$179 = \$1{,}046$

CR17.5

a. conversion value $= (20)(\$65) = \$1{,}300$

b. $B_0 = \$796$
value of conversion option $= (20)(\$38.31) = \$766$
value of convertible $= \$796 + \$766 = \$1{,}562$

c. The call price $= \$1{,}100$ and the transfer from bondholders to stockholders is $\$1{,}562 - \$1{,}100 = \$462$.

Chapter 18

CR18.1

$$\text{present value of ownership benefit} = \sum_{t=1}^{5} \frac{(\$6,400)(0.40)}{(1.054)^t} = \$10,962$$

amount recovered from lease = $32,000 - $10,962 = $21,038

$$\$21,038 = ATL\left[\frac{1}{0.0045} - \frac{1}{0.0045(1.0045)^{60}}\right](1.0045)$$

$ATL = \$399$ and $L = \$665$

CR18.2 $NPV_{\text{lease}} = \$50,000 - (\$30,938 + \$14,048) = \$5,014$; lease the asset.

CR18.3

	Year			
	0	1	2	3
Net cash flow from leasing	$155,200	-$68,800	-$68,800	-$24,000
Amount borrowed	142,451	84,592	22,288	

$NPV_{\text{lease}} = \$142,451 - \$155,200 = -\$12,749$

CR18.4 $NPV_{\text{lease}} = \$100,000 - (\$73,214 + \$22,861 - \$8,756 + \$12,239) = \$442.$

CR18.5

$$\$25,000 - \$6,000(1 - 0.40) = \sum_{t=1}^{4} \frac{\$6,000(1 - 0.40)}{(1 + IRR)^t} + \sum_{t=1}^{5} \frac{(\$25,000/5)(0.40)}{(1 + IRR)^t}$$

$IRR = 5.05\%$

Purchase.

Chapter 19

CR19.1

a. 92.33

b. 52.35

CR19.2

Ratio	MaxIncome	SafetyFirst
current ratio	1.10	5.29
quick ratio	0.60	2.57
net working capital	$3,671	$72,683
receivables turnover	17.54	11.80
inventory turnover	8.87	3.86
payables turnover	13.78	25.64
cash conversion cycle	35.47	111.26

CR19.3

a.

	Aggressive	Conservative
net income	$13,173	$7,146
current ratio	2.02	10.61
receivables turnover	9.03	6.33
inventory turnover	3.88	1.98
payables turnover	9.28	33.58
cash conversion cycle	95.16	231.13
net profit margin	7.90%	3.85%
return on equity	32.71%	20.01%

b. $P_{0\,\text{aggressive}}$ is $21.04 and $P_{0\,\text{conservative}}$ is $17.16.

CR19.4   **a.**

	Aggressive	Matched	Conservative
Earnings per share			
Robust economy	$3.98	$3.30	$2.30
Standard economy	3.38	2.70	2.00
Poor economy	2.48	1.80	1.25
Expected EPS	$3.28	$2.60	$1.85
Standard deviation	$0.62	$0.62	$0.44

b. $P_{0\,(\text{aggressive})} = (10)(\$3.28) = \$32.80$
$P_{0\,(\text{matched})} = \$28.60$
$P_{0\,(\text{conservative})} = \$22.20$

Adopt the aggressive policy.

Chapter 20

CR20.1   **a.** $(6 - 4)(\$20,000) = \$40,000$

b. $\Delta B = (\$40,000)(2)(0.06/365)(1 - 0.36) = \$8.42$

CR20.2 $\Delta B = (4.15 - 2.84)(\$500,000,000)(0.087/365)(1 - 0.40) = \$93,674$

CR20.3 $\$100(1 - 0.40) = (7)(TS)(0.05/365)(1 - 0.40)$
$TS = \$104,286$

CR20.4   The daily compounded opportunity cost is:

$(1 + k_{\text{daily}})^{365} - 1 = 0.05$
$$k = 0.000134$$

$$Z = \left[\frac{3(\$100)(\$10,000)^2}{4(0.000134)}\right]^{1/3} + \$500,000 = \$538,252$$

The upper control limit is $614,756, and the average cash balance is $551,003.

CR20.5   **a.** The outer upper control limit is $614,756, and the inner upper control limit is $604,000.

	t_0	t_1	t_2	t_3	t_4
Actual	$588,000	$628,000	$598,000		
Expected	588,000	598,000	608,000	$598,000	$593,000

The outer upper limit is breached at $t = 1$. Looking ahead to $t = 3$, the expected cash balance is inside the inner upper control limit. Take no action.

b. The outer upper control limit is still breached on day $t = 1$. Looking ahead to $t = 3$, the expected cash level of $623,000 is above both the inner and outer upper control limits; therefore, transfer funds. The size of the transfer is $623,000 − $538,252 = $84,748.

CR20.6   **a.** $k_{\text{BD}} = \left(\dfrac{\$10,000 - \$9,900}{\$10,000}\right)\left(\dfrac{360}{50}\right) = 7.20\%$

b. $k_{\text{BE}} = \dfrac{(365)(0.072)}{360 - (0.072)(50)} = 7.37\%$

c. $P_0 = \$10,000\left[1 - \dfrac{(0.075)(40)}{360}\right] = \$9,917$

$k_{\text{BE}} = \dfrac{(\$9,917 - \$9,900)(365)}{(\$9,900)(10)} = 6.27\%$

Chapter 21

CR21.1   credit score$_A$ = 5(2.2) + 7(6) − 9(2) = 35
credit score$_B$ = 9
credit score$_C$ = 13.5

CR21.2 $NPV_A = \dfrac{\$33,000}{0.12} - \$21,575 = \$253,425$

$NPV_B = \dfrac{\$2,400}{0.17} - \$34,932 = -\$20,814$

$NPV_C = \dfrac{\$25,200}{0.14} - \$45,205 = \$134,795$

CR21.3

	August	September	October	November	December
Percent of same month's sales	91%	92%	93%	93%	
Percent of 1 month before		41	52	63	68
Percent of 2 months before			0	0	0

CR21.4 $NPV = \dfrac{-\$123,500}{0.14} - (-\$700,000) = -\$182,143$

CR21.5 $NPV = -\$166,667$

Chapter 22

CR22.1   First National: $k_{\text{nom}} = 0.10(365/360) = 0.10139$

$$k_b = \left(1 + \frac{0.10139}{12}\right)^{12} - 1 = 10.62\%$$

Commerce National Bank: $k_{\text{nom}} = 0.102(365/360) = 0.10342$

$$k_b = \left(1 + \frac{0.10342}{2}\right)^{2} - 1 = 10.61\%$$

CR22.2   a. $k_b = \left(1 + \dfrac{0.01}{1 - 0.01}\right)^{365/(30 - 15)} - 1 = 27.71\%$

b. $k_b = 8.49\%$

CR22.3 $k_{b\,\text{regular interest}} = \left(1 + \dfrac{\$45,205}{\$500,000}\right)^{365/275} - 1 = 12.17\%$

$k_{b\,\text{discount loan}} = \left(1 + \dfrac{\$30,137}{\$469,863}\right)^{365/275} - 1 = 8.60\%$

Installment interest:

monthly payment $= \dfrac{\$500,000 + \$26,370}{9} = \$58,486$

$k_b = 1.0406\%$ per month, or 12.49% per year

CR22.4 $k_b = \left(1 + \dfrac{\$328.77}{\$20,000}\right)^{365/60} - 1 = 10.43\%$

CR22.5 $k_b = \left(1 + \dfrac{\$1,041.09 + \$21,369.87}{\$288,888.89}\right)^{365/180} - 1 = 16.36\%$

CR22.6 $k_b = \left(1 + \dfrac{\$15,000 + \$821.92}{\$985,000 - \$10,000}\right)^{365/60} - 1 = 10.29\%$

CR22.7 $k_{b\,\text{bank}} = \left(1 + \dfrac{\$320 + \$640}{\$64,000}\right)^{12/1} - 1 = 19.56\%$

$k_{b\,\text{factoring}} = 22.24\%$

CR22.8 $k_b = \left(1 + \dfrac{\$800 + \$640 - \$300}{\$64,000}\right)^{12/1} - 1 = 23.60\%$

CR22.9 $k_b = \left(1 + \dfrac{\$4,800 + \$15,780.82}{\$480,000}\right)^{365/80} - 1 = 21.11\%$

Chapter 23

CR23.1

a. The YTM for the zero-coupon bond is 10.06%, while its duration is 3. The duration of the GNMA bond is:

$$\$750 = \sum_{t=1}^{5} \frac{\$198}{(1 + YTM)^t} \quad \therefore\ YTM_{GNMA} = 10.03\%$$

$$D_{GNMA} = \frac{\$198\left[\dfrac{(1.1003)^{5+1} - (1.1003) - (0.1003)(5)}{(0.1003)^2(1.1003)^5}\right]}{\$750} = 2.81$$

b. Δ market value of zero-coupon $\approx \dfrac{-3}{1.1006} \approx -2.73\%$

Δ market value of $GNMA \approx \dfrac{-2.81}{1.1003} \approx -2.55\%$

c. $D_{\text{portfolio}} = \left(\dfrac{\$750}{\$1,500}\right)(3) + \left(\dfrac{\$750}{\$1,500}\right)(2.81) = 2.905$

CR23.2

a. $PV_0 = \dfrac{\$1,000,000}{(1.15)^1} + \dfrac{\$1,800,000}{(1.15)^2} = \$2,230,624$

$$D = (1)\left[\frac{\dfrac{\$1,000,000}{(1.15)^1}}{\$2,230,624}\right] + (2)\left[\frac{\dfrac{\$1,800,000}{(1.15)^2}}{\$2,230,624}\right] = 1.61$$

b. $\delta = \dfrac{1.61}{3} = 0.537$

The loan amount is $(0.537)(\$2,230,624) = \$1,197,845$, while a zero-duration loan of $\$2,230,624 - \$1,197,845 = \$1,032,779$ is also required.

CR23.3   a. interest = ($5,000,000)(0.01)(1/2) = $25,000

$$\text{gain} = \frac{\$25,000}{1 + \dfrac{0.06}{2}} = \$24,272$$

b. interest = ($3,000,000)(0.01)(1/2) = $15,000

$$\text{gain} = \frac{\$15,000}{1.03} = \$14,563$$

The net increase in interest (due to the partial hedge) = $24,272 − $14,563 = $9,709.

CR23.4   a. Buy, or go long.

b. lost interest on loan = ($50,000,000)(0.0025)(90/360) = $31,250
    profit on futures contract = (0.25)($2,500)(50) = $31,250

CR23.5   Gonzales should borrow at the floating rate, while Reed borrows at the fixed rate.

Gonzales	Pays floating rate to third party	LIBOR + 2.00%
	Pays fixed rate to Reed	11.50
	Receives floating rate from Reed	−(LIBOR + 2.00)
	Net cost to Gonzales	11.50%
Reed	Pays fixed rate to third party	14.00%
	Pays floating rate to Gonzales	LIBOR + 2.00
	Receives fixed rate from Gonzales	−11.50
	Net cost to Reed	LIBOR + 4.50%

Chapter 24

CR24.1   a. $$\text{simple } EPS = \frac{\$480,000}{30,000} = \$16.00$$

$$\text{primary } EPS = \frac{\$480,000}{35,000} = \$13.71$$

$$\text{fully diluted } EPS = \frac{\$480,000}{40,000} = \$12.00$$

b. $480,000 − $200,000 = $280,000

CR24.2

Cash	7.2%
Accounts receivable	20.6
Inventory	25.8
Long-term investment	3.1
Plant and equipment (net)	43.3
Total assets	100.0%

Accounts payable	10.3%
Notes payable	15.5
Accrued taxes	2.1
Bond payable	30.9
Preferred stock	5.2
Common stock	5.2
Capital paid in excess of par	10.3
Retained earnings	20.6
Total liabilities and stockholders' equity	≈ 100.0%

Sales	100.0%
Cost of goods sold	75.0
Gross margin	25.0
Selling & administrative expenses	10.0
EBIT	15.0
Interest expense	2.5
EBT	12.5
Taxes	3.8
Net income	8.7%

current ratio = \$520,000/\$270,000 = 1.9
quick ratio = \$270,000/\$270,000 = 1.0
days sales outstanding = \$200,000/(\$2,000,000/365) = 36.5 days
inventory turnover = \$1,500,000/\$250,000 = 6.0
long-term asset turnover = \$2,000,000/\$450,000 = 4.4
total asset turnover = \$2,000,000/\$970,000 = 2.1
total debt to total assets = \$570,000/\$970,000 = 58.8%
times interest earned = \$300,000/\$50,000 = 6.0
fixed charge coverage = \$310,000/\$60,000 = 5.2
net profit margin = \$175,000/\$2,000,000 = 8.8%
return on total assets = \$175,000/\$970,000 = 18.0%
return on equity = \$175,000/\$400,000 = 43.8%
earnings per share = (\$175,000 − \$4,000)/50,000 = \$3.42
price/earnings = \$20/\$3.42 = 5.8
dividend yield = \$1.00/\$20 = 5.0%
dividend payout = \$1.00/\$3.42 = 29.2%

CR24.3   return on equity = 12.5%/(1 − 0.40) = 20.8%

CR24.4

	Jarvus	Barkell
current ratio	2.1	4.1
quick ratio	0.8	3.4
days sales outstanding	21.5	35.6
inventory turnover	2.9	14.5
long-term asset turnover	57.0	34.0
total asset turnover	2.2	2.7
total debt to total assets	0.5	0.4
times interest earned	8.7	8.7
net profit margin	5.4%	3.7%
return on total assets	11.8%	10.1%
return on equity	24.8%	16.3%

a. Both suppliers and short-term lenders are concerned with liquidity ratios; they would favor Barkell.

b. Jarvus has more debt but the same times interest earned as Barkell. Jarvus is more profitable; a slight nod to Jarvus.

c. Stockholders are particularly concerned with profitability ratios; another slight nod to Jarvus.

Chapter 25

CR25.1 $Y_t = \$8.75 + \$0.75X_t$
The predicted sales for the next 3 years are $13.25 million, $14.00 million, and $14.75 million.

CR25.2 $Y_t = \$2.344 + \$0.088X_t$
Adjusted seasonal indices are 0.928, 0.975, 1.089, and 1.008 for quarters 1, 2, 3, and 4, respectively.

Quarter	Predicted, without adjustment	Predicted, with adjustment
Year 1		
1	3.49	3.24
2	3.58	3.49
3	3.66	3.99
4	3.75	3.78
Year 2		
1	3.84	3.56
2	3.93	3.83
3	4.02	4.38
4	4.10	4.13

CR25.3   Cumulative short-term financing needed $(-)$ or surplus $(+)$ per month is $-\$65,250$, $-\$46,750$, $-\$27,750$, $+\$32,250$, $-\$34,000$, and $-\$10,000$.

CR25.4   The transfer to retained earnings is $9.0 million, total assets are $87.3 million, and total liabilities and stockholders' equity is $81.1 million. The firm needs $6.2 million in outside financing.

Chapter 26

CR26.1 $NPV = \$1,607 - \$1,200 = \$407$

CR26.2   a. $NPV = \$200,000$

$$P_{0\,\text{before}} = \frac{\$1,500,000}{75,000} = \$20$$

$$P_{0\,\text{after}} = \frac{\$1,500,000 + \$200,000}{75,000} = \$22.67$$

b. $NPV = \$1,200,000 - \$1,080,000 = \$120,000$

$$P_{0\,\text{after}} = \frac{\$1,500,000 + \$1,200,000}{125,000} = \$21.60$$

CR26.3   a.   Barrett Partnerships premerger $EPS = \$50,000/10,000 = \$5$, while its premerger $P/E = \$40/5 = 8$.

$$EPS_{new} = \frac{\$50,000 + \$75,000}{10,000 + 20,000} = \$4.17$$

$$P_{0\,new} = (\$4.17)(8) = \$33.36$$

b. $V = (\$40)(10,000) + (\$35)(20,000) = \$1,100,000$

$$P_{0\,new} = \frac{\$1,100,000}{30,000} = \$36.67$$

$$P/E_{new} = \frac{\$36.67}{\$4.17} = 8.79 \text{ times}$$

CR26.4

	Pooling of Interests	Purchase
Current assets	$ 75	$ 75
Long-term assets	550	600
Goodwill	0	25
Total	$625	$700
Debt	$200	$200
Equity	425	500
Total	$625	$700

	Pooling of Interests	Purchase
Sales	$750	$750
Cost of goods sold	350	350
Depreciation	150	160
Interest	70	70
Taxes (40%)	72	68
Writeoff of goodwill	0	5
Net income	$108	$ 97

Chapter 27

CR27.1   a.   ¥2,221,400

b. $30,000

c.   £9,528

CR27.2 $E(S_{2/1}) = \text{FFr } 5.4775$

CR27.3 $NPV = -\$687$

CR27.4   The cash flow in dollars for years 0 through 4 are $-\$640,000$, $\$129,479$, $\$331,792$, $\$202,449$, and $\$274,587$. $NPV = \$91,566$.

CR27.5   a.   ¥440,000   b. $3,960   c. $4,400

Chapter 28

CR28.1

    a.   Strengthen.

    b. $400,000 and $434,783.

    c.   In 6 months receive A$500,000; at A$1.35/$1 this is $370,370. The loss of $64,413 (i.e., $434,783 − $370,370) is made up by the gain on the forward contract. The U.S. firm receives $434,783.

CR28.2

The expected cost of the grain is Can$300,000/1.10 = $272,727; discounted back the *PV* of the cost of the grain is:

$$\frac{\$272,727}{1 + \dfrac{0.10}{4}} = \$266,075$$

If payment is made today, the amount is Can$300,000/1.20 = $250,000. The gain to paying today is $266,075 − $250,000 = $16,075.

CR28.3

    a. $500,000

    b. $521,739

    c.   Buy, and lock in the price of $521,739.

CR28.4

    a.   U.S. subsidiary would pay (£300,000)(0.15) = £45,000 to the British firm. The British firm's subsidiary would pay ($600,000)(0.10) = $60,000 to the U.S. firm.

    b.   Annual interest in dollars is ($600,000)(0.10) = $60,000. In pounds it is ($60,000)(0.60) = £36,000. The cost of funds, including the currency exchange risk, is:

$$£300,000 = \sum_{t=1}^{5} \frac{£36,000}{(1 + k)^t} + \frac{£300,000}{(1 + k)^5}$$

$$k = 12\%$$

CR28.5

    a. $2,116,500

    b.   Strengthening.

    c.   48 call options

    d.   (48)(62,500)($0.0102) = $30,600

    e.   cost = ($3,000,000)(0.80) = $2,400,000
loss = $2,400,000 − $2,116,500 = $283,500

With the option, the firm locked in a price of ($3,000,000)(0.70) = $2,100,000, plus the cost of the option of $30,600, for a total cash flow of $2,130,600; the savings was $2,400,000 − $2,130,600 = $269,400.

APPENDIX

B

Financial Tables

Table B.1

Present Value Factors for $1 Discounted at k Percent for n Periods:

$$PV_{k,n} = \frac{1}{(1+k)^n}$$

Discount Rate, k

Period, n	1%	2%	3%	4%	5%	6%	7%	8%	9%	10%	11%	12%	13%	14%	15%	16%	17%	18%	19%	20%
1	0.990	0.980	0.971	0.962	0.952	0.943	0.935	0.926	0.917	0.909	0.901	0.893	0.885	0.877	0.870	0.862	0.855	0.847	0.840	0.833
2	0.980	0.961	0.943	0.925	0.907	0.890	0.873	0.857	0.842	0.826	0.812	0.797	0.783	0.769	0.756	0.743	0.731	0.718	0.706	0.694
3	0.971	0.942	0.915	0.889	0.864	0.840	0.816	0.794	0.772	0.751	0.731	0.712	0.693	0.675	0.658	0.641	0.624	0.609	0.593	0.579
4	0.961	0.924	0.888	0.855	0.823	0.792	0.763	0.735	0.708	0.683	0.659	0.636	0.613	0.592	0.572	0.552	0.534	0.516	0.499	0.482
5	0.951	0.906	0.863	0.822	0.784	0.747	0.713	0.681	0.650	0.621	0.593	0.567	0.543	0.519	0.497	0.476	0.456	0.437	0.419	0.402
6	0.942	0.888	0.837	0.790	0.746	0.705	0.666	0.630	0.596	0.564	0.535	0.507	0.480	0.456	0.432	0.410	0.390	0.370	0.352	0.335
7	0.933	0.871	0.813	0.760	0.711	0.665	0.623	0.583	0.547	0.513	0.482	0.452	0.425	0.400	0.376	0.354	0.333	0.314	0.296	0.279
8	0.923	0.853	0.789	0.731	0.677	0.627	0.582	0.540	0.502	0.467	0.434	0.404	0.376	0.351	0.327	0.305	0.285	0.266	0.249	0.233
9	0.914	0.837	0.766	0.703	0.645	0.592	0.544	0.500	0.460	0.424	0.391	0.361	0.333	0.308	0.284	0.263	0.243	0.225	0.209	0.194
10	0.905	0.820	0.744	0.676	0.614	0.558	0.508	0.463	0.422	0.386	0.352	0.322	0.295	0.270	0.247	0.227	0.208	0.191	0.176	0.162
11	0.896	0.804	0.722	0.650	0.585	0.527	0.475	0.429	0.388	0.350	0.317	0.287	0.261	0.237	0.215	0.195	0.178	0.162	0.148	0.135
12	0.887	0.788	0.701	0.625	0.557	0.497	0.444	0.397	0.356	0.319	0.286	0.257	0.231	0.208	0.187	0.168	0.152	0.137	0.124	0.112
13	0.879	0.773	0.681	0.601	0.530	0.469	0.415	0.368	0.326	0.290	0.258	0.229	0.204	0.182	0.163	0.145	0.130	0.116	0.104	0.093
14	0.870	0.758	0.661	0.577	0.505	0.442	0.388	0.340	0.299	0.263	0.232	0.205	0.181	0.160	0.141	0.125	0.111	0.099	0.088	0.078
15	0.861	0.743	0.642	0.555	0.481	0.417	0.362	0.315	0.275	0.239	0.209	0.183	0.160	0.140	0.123	0.108	0.095	0.084	0.074	0.065
16	0.853	0.728	0.623	0.534	0.458	0.394	0.339	0.292	0.252	0.218	0.188	0.163	0.141	0.123	0.107	0.093	0.081	0.071	0.062	0.054
17	0.844	0.714	0.605	0.513	0.436	0.371	0.317	0.270	0.231	0.198	0.170	0.146	0.125	0.108	0.093	0.080	0.069	0.060	0.052	0.045
18	0.836	0.700	0.587	0.494	0.416	0.350	0.296	0.250	0.212	0.180	0.153	0.130	0.111	0.095	0.081	0.069	0.059	0.051	0.044	0.038
19	0.828	0.686	0.570	0.475	0.396	0.331	0.277	0.232	0.194	0.164	0.138	0.116	0.098	0.083	0.070	0.060	0.051	0.043	0.037	0.031
20	0.820	0.673	0.554	0.456	0.377	0.312	0.258	0.215	0.178	0.149	0.124	0.104	0.087	0.073	0.061	0.051	0.043	0.037	0.031	0.026
21	0.811	0.660	0.538	0.439	0.359	0.294	0.242	0.199	0.164	0.135	0.112	0.093	0.077	0.064	0.053	0.044	0.037	0.031	0.026	0.022
22	0.803	0.647	0.522	0.422	0.342	0.278	0.226	0.184	0.150	0.123	0.101	0.083	0.068	0.056	0.046	0.038	0.032	0.026	0.022	0.018
23	0.795	0.634	0.507	0.406	0.326	0.262	0.211	0.170	0.138	0.112	0.091	0.074	0.060	0.049	0.040	0.033	0.027	0.022	0.018	0.015
24	0.788	0.622	0.492	0.390	0.310	0.247	0.197	0.158	0.126	0.102	0.082	0.066	0.053	0.043	0.035	0.028	0.023	0.019	0.015	0.013
25	0.780	0.610	0.478	0.375	0.295	0.233	0.184	0.146	0.116	0.092	0.074	0.059	0.047	0.038	0.030	0.024	0.020	0.016	0.013	0.010
26	0.772	0.598	0.464	0.361	0.281	0.220	0.172	0.135	0.106	0.084	0.066	0.053	0.042	0.033	0.026	0.021	0.017	0.014	0.011	0.009
27	0.764	0.586	0.450	0.347	0.268	0.207	0.161	0.125	0.098	0.076	0.060	0.047	0.037	0.029	0.023	0.018	0.014	0.011	0.009	0.007
28	0.757	0.574	0.437	0.333	0.255	0.196	0.150	0.116	0.090	0.069	0.054	0.042	0.033	0.026	0.020	0.016	0.012	0.010	0.008	0.006
29	0.749	0.563	0.424	0.321	0.243	0.185	0.141	0.107	0.082	0.063	0.048	0.037	0.029	0.022	0.017	0.014	0.011	0.008	0.006	0.005
30	0.742	0.552	0.412	0.308	0.231	0.174	0.131	0.099	0.075	0.057	0.044	0.033	0.026	0.020	0.015	0.012	0.009	0.007	0.005	0.004
35	0.706	0.500	0.355	0.253	0.181	0.130	0.094	0.068	0.049	0.036	0.026	0.019	0.014	0.010	0.008	0.006	0.004	0.003	0.002	0.002
40	0.672	0.453	0.307	0.208	0.142	0.097	0.067	0.046	0.032	0.022	0.015	0.011	0.008	0.005	0.004	0.003	0.002	0.001	0.001	0.001
45	0.639	0.410	0.264	0.171	0.111	0.073	0.048	0.031	0.021	0.014	0.009	0.006	0.004	0.003	0.002	0.001	0.001	0.001	*	*
50	0.608	0.372	0.228	0.141	0.087	0.054	0.034	0.021	0.013	0.009	0.005	0.003	0.002	0.001	0.001	0.001	*	*	*	*

*Value is zero to three decimal places.

Table B.1

$PV_{k,n}$ (Continued)

Period, n	21%	22%	23%	24%	25%	26%	27%	28%	29%	30%	31%	32%	33%	34%	35%	40%	45%	50%	55%	60%
1	0.826	0.820	0.813	0.806	0.800	0.794	0.787	0.781	0.775	0.769	0.763	0.758	0.752	0.746	0.741	0.714	0.690	0.667	0.645	0.625
2	0.683	0.672	0.661	0.650	0.640	0.630	0.620	0.610	0.601	0.592	0.583	0.574	0.565	0.557	0.549	0.510	0.476	0.444	0.416	0.391
3	0.564	0.551	0.537	0.524	0.512	0.500	0.488	0.477	0.466	0.455	0.445	0.435	0.425	0.416	0.406	0.364	0.328	0.296	0.269	0.244
4	0.467	0.451	0.437	0.423	0.410	0.397	0.384	0.373	0.361	0.350	0.340	0.329	0.320	0.310	0.301	0.260	0.226	0.198	0.173	0.153
5	0.386	0.370	0.355	0.341	0.328	0.315	0.303	0.291	0.280	0.269	0.259	0.250	0.240	0.231	0.223	0.186	0.156	0.132	0.112	0.095
6	0.319	0.303	0.289	0.275	0.262	0.250	0.238	0.227	0.217	0.207	0.198	0.189	0.181	0.173	0.165	0.133	0.108	0.088	0.072	0.060
7	0.263	0.249	0.235	0.222	0.210	0.198	0.188	0.178	0.168	0.159	0.151	0.143	0.136	0.129	0.122	0.095	0.074	0.059	0.047	0.037
8	0.218	0.204	0.191	0.179	0.168	0.157	0.148	0.139	0.130	0.123	0.115	0.108	0.102	0.096	0.091	0.068	0.051	0.039	0.030	0.023
9	0.180	0.167	0.155	0.144	0.134	0.125	0.116	0.108	0.101	0.094	0.088	0.082	0.077	0.072	0.067	0.048	0.035	0.026	0.019	0.015
10	0.149	0.137	0.126	0.116	0.107	0.099	0.092	0.085	0.078	0.073	0.067	0.062	0.058	0.054	0.050	0.035	0.024	0.017	0.012	0.009
11	0.123	0.112	0.103	0.094	0.086	0.079	0.072	0.066	0.061	0.056	0.051	0.047	0.043	0.040	0.037	0.025	0.017	0.012	0.008	0.006
12	0.102	0.092	0.083	0.076	0.069	0.062	0.057	0.052	0.047	0.043	0.039	0.036	0.033	0.030	0.027	0.018	0.012	0.008	0.005	0.004
13	0.084	0.075	0.068	0.061	0.055	0.050	0.045	0.040	0.037	0.033	0.030	0.027	0.025	0.022	0.020	0.013	0.008	0.005	0.003	0.002
14	0.069	0.062	0.055	0.049	0.044	0.039	0.035	0.032	0.028	0.025	0.023	0.021	0.018	0.017	0.015	0.009	0.006	0.003	0.002	0.001
15	0.057	0.051	0.045	0.040	0.035	0.031	0.028	0.025	0.022	0.020	0.017	0.016	0.014	0.012	0.011	0.006	0.004	0.002	0.001	0.001
16	0.047	0.042	0.036	0.032	0.028	0.025	0.022	0.019	0.017	0.015	0.013	0.012	0.010	0.009	0.008	0.005	0.003	0.002	0.001	0.001
17	0.039	0.034	0.030	0.026	0.023	0.020	0.017	0.015	0.013	0.012	0.010	0.009	0.008	0.007	0.006	0.003	0.002	0.001	0.001	*
18	0.032	0.028	0.024	0.021	0.018	0.016	0.014	0.012	0.010	0.009	0.008	0.007	0.006	0.005	0.005	0.002	0.001	0.001	*	*
19	0.027	0.023	0.020	0.017	0.014	0.012	0.011	0.009	0.008	0.007	0.006	0.005	0.004	0.004	0.003	0.002	0.001	*	*	*
20	0.022	0.019	0.016	0.014	0.012	0.010	0.008	0.007	0.006	0.005	0.005	0.004	0.003	0.003	0.002	0.001	0.001	*	*	*
21	0.018	0.015	0.013	0.011	0.009	0.008	0.007	0.006	0.005	0.004	0.003	0.003	0.003	0.002	0.002	0.001	0.001	*	*	*
22	0.015	0.013	0.011	0.009	0.007	0.006	0.005	0.004	0.004	0.003	0.003	0.002	0.002	0.002	0.001	0.001	*	*	*	*
23	0.012	0.010	0.009	0.007	0.006	0.005	0.004	0.003	0.003	0.002	0.002	0.002	0.001	0.001	0.001	*	*	*	*	*
24	0.010	0.008	0.007	0.006	0.005	0.004	0.003	0.003	0.002	0.002	0.002	0.001	0.001	0.001	0.001	*	*	*	*	*
25	0.009	0.007	0.006	0.005	0.004	0.003	0.003	0.002	0.002	0.001	0.001	0.001	0.001	0.001	0.001	*	*	*	*	*
26	0.007	0.006	0.005	0.004	0.003	0.002	0.002	0.002	0.001	0.001	0.001	0.001	0.001	*	*	*	*	*	*	*
27	0.006	0.005	0.004	0.003	0.002	0.002	0.002	0.001	0.001	0.001	0.001	0.001	*	*	*	*	*	*	*	*
28	0.005	0.004	0.003	0.002	0.002	0.002	0.001	0.001	0.001	0.001	0.001	*	*	*	*	*	*	*	*	*
29	0.004	0.003	0.002	0.002	0.002	0.001	0.001	0.001	0.001	*	*	*	*	*	*	*	*	*	*	*
30	0.003	0.003	0.002	0.002	0.001	0.001	0.001	0.001	*	*	*	*	*	*	*	*	*	*	*	*
35	0.001	0.001	0.001	0.001	*	*	*	*	*	*	*	*	*	*	*	*	*	*	*	*
40	*	*	*	*	*	*	*	*	*	*	*	*	*	*	*	*	*	*	*	*
45	*	*	*	*	*	*	*	*	*	*	*	*	*	*	*	*	*	*	*	*
50	*	*	*	*	*	*	*	*	*	*	*	*	*	*	*	*	*	*	*	*

*Value is zero to three decimal places.

Table B.2

Present Value Factors for an Annuity of $1 Discounted at k Percent for n Periods:

$$PVA_{k,n} = \sum_{t=1}^{n} \frac{1}{(1+k)^t} = \frac{1}{k} - \frac{1}{k(1+k)^n}$$

Period, n	Discount Rate, k																			
	1%	2%	3%	4%	5%	6%	7%	8%	9%	10%	11%	12%	13%	14%	15%	16%	17%	18%	19%	20%
1	0.990	0.980	0.971	0.962	0.952	0.943	0.935	0.926	0.917	0.909	0.901	0.893	0.885	0.877	0.870	0.862	0.855	0.847	0.840	0.833
2	1.970	1.942	1.913	1.886	1.859	1.833	1.808	1.783	1.759	1.736	1.713	1.690	1.668	1.647	1.626	1.605	1.585	1.566	1.547	1.528
3	2.941	2.884	2.829	2.775	2.723	2.673	2.624	2.577	2.531	2.487	2.444	2.402	2.361	2.322	2.283	2.246	2.210	2.174	2.140	2.106
4	3.902	3.808	3.717	3.630	3.546	3.465	3.387	3.312	3.240	3.170	3.102	3.037	2.974	2.914	2.855	2.798	2.743	2.690	2.639	2.589
5	4.853	4.713	4.580	4.452	4.329	4.212	4.100	3.993	3.890	3.791	3.696	3.605	3.517	3.433	3.352	3.274	3.199	3.127	3.058	2.991
6	5.795	5.601	5.417	5.242	5.076	4.917	4.767	4.623	4.486	4.355	4.231	4.111	3.998	3.889	3.784	3.685	3.589	3.498	3.410	3.326
7	6.728	6.472	6.230	6.002	5.786	5.582	5.389	5.206	5.033	4.868	4.712	4.564	4.423	4.288	4.160	4.039	3.922	3.812	3.706	3.605
8	7.652	7.325	7.020	6.733	6.463	6.210	5.971	5.747	5.535	5.335	5.146	4.968	4.799	4.639	4.487	4.344	4.207	4.078	3.954	3.837
9	8.566	8.162	7.786	7.435	7.108	6.802	6.515	6.247	5.995	5.759	5.537	5.328	5.132	4.946	4.772	4.607	4.451	4.303	4.163	4.031
10	9.471	8.983	8.530	8.111	7.722	7.360	7.024	6.710	6.418	6.145	5.889	5.650	5.426	5.216	5.019	4.833	4.659	4.494	4.339	4.192
11	10.368	9.787	9.253	8.760	8.306	7.887	7.499	7.139	6.805	6.495	6.207	5.938	5.687	5.453	5.234	5.029	4.836	4.656	4.486	4.327
12	11.255	10.575	9.954	9.385	8.863	8.384	7.943	7.536	7.161	6.814	6.492	6.194	5.918	5.660	5.421	5.197	4.988	4.793	4.611	4.439
13	12.134	11.348	10.635	9.986	9.394	8.853	8.358	7.904	7.487	7.103	6.750	6.424	6.122	5.842	5.583	5.342	5.118	4.910	4.715	4.533
14	13.004	12.106	11.296	10.563	9.899	9.295	8.745	8.244	7.786	7.367	6.982	6.628	6.302	6.002	5.724	5.468	5.229	5.008	4.802	4.611
15	13.865	12.849	11.938	11.118	10.380	9.712	9.108	8.559	8.061	7.606	7.191	6.811	6.462	6.142	5.847	5.575	5.324	5.092	4.876	4.675
16	14.718	13.578	12.561	11.652	10.838	10.106	9.447	8.851	8.313	7.824	7.379	6.974	6.604	6.265	5.954	5.668	5.405	5.162	4.938	4.730
17	15.562	14.292	13.166	12.166	11.274	10.477	9.763	9.122	8.544	8.022	7.549	7.120	6.729	6.373	6.047	5.749	5.475	5.222	4.990	4.775
18	16.398	14.992	13.754	12.659	11.690	10.828	10.059	9.372	8.756	8.201	7.702	7.250	6.840	6.467	6.128	5.818	5.534	5.273	5.033	4.812
19	17.226	15.678	14.324	13.134	12.085	11.158	10.336	9.604	8.950	8.365	7.839	7.366	6.938	6.550	6.198	5.877	5.584	5.316	5.070	4.843
20	18.046	16.351	14.877	13.590	12.462	11.470	10.594	9.818	9.129	8.514	7.963	7.469	7.025	6.623	6.259	5.929	5.628	5.353	5.101	4.870
21	18.857	17.011	15.415	14.029	12.821	11.764	10.836	10.017	9.292	8.649	8.075	7.562	7.102	6.687	6.312	5.973	5.665	5.384	5.127	4.891
22	19.660	17.658	15.937	14.451	13.163	12.042	11.061	10.201	9.442	8.772	8.176	7.645	7.170	6.743	6.359	6.011	5.696	5.410	5.149	4.909
23	20.456	18.292	16.444	14.857	13.489	12.303	11.272	10.371	9.580	8.883	8.266	7.718	7.230	6.792	6.399	6.044	5.723	5.432	5.167	4.925
24	21.243	18.914	16.936	15.247	13.799	12.550	11.469	10.529	9.707	8.985	8.348	7.784	7.283	6.835	6.434	6.073	5.746	5.451	5.182	4.937
25	22.023	19.523	17.413	15.622	14.094	12.783	11.654	10.675	9.823	9.077	8.422	7.843	7.330	6.873	6.464	6.097	5.766	5.467	5.195	4.948
26	22.795	20.121	17.877	15.983	14.375	13.003	11.826	10.810	9.929	9.161	8.488	7.896	7.372	6.906	6.491	6.118	5.783	5.480	5.206	4.956
27	23.560	20.707	18.327	16.330	14.643	13.211	11.987	10.935	10.027	9.237	8.548	7.943	7.409	6.935	6.514	6.136	5.798	5.492	5.215	4.964
28	24.316	21.281	18.764	16.663	14.898	13.406	12.137	11.051	10.116	9.307	8.602	7.984	7.441	6.961	6.534	6.152	5.810	5.502	5.223	4.970
29	25.066	21.844	19.188	16.984	15.141	13.591	12.278	11.158	10.198	9.370	8.650	8.022	7.470	6.983	6.551	6.166	5.820	5.510	5.229	4.975
30	25.808	22.396	19.600	17.292	15.372	13.765	12.409	11.258	10.274	9.427	8.694	8.055	7.496	7.003	6.566	6.177	5.829	5.517	5.235	4.979
35	29.409	24.999	21.487	18.665	16.374	14.498	12.948	11.655	10.567	9.644	8.855	8.176	7.586	7.070	6.617	6.215	5.858	5.539	5.251	4.992
40	32.835	27.355	23.115	19.793	17.159	15.046	13.332	11.925	10.757	9.779	8.951	8.244	7.634	7.105	6.642	6.233	5.871	5.548	5.258	4.997
45	36.095	29.490	24.519	20.720	17.774	15.456	13.606	12.108	10.881	9.863	9.008	8.283	7.661	7.123	6.654	6.242	5.877	5.552	5.261	4.999
50	39.196	31.424	25.730	21.482	18.256	15.762	13.801	12.233	10.962	9.915	9.042	8.304	7.675	7.133	6.661	6.246	5.880	5.554	5.262	4.999

Table B.2

$PVA_{k,n}$ (Continued)

Period, n	Discount Rate, k																			
	21%	22%	23%	24%	25%	26%	27%	28%	29%	30%	31%	32%	33%	34%	35%	40%	45%	50%	55%	60%
1	0.826	0.820	0.813	0.806	0.800	0.794	0.787	0.781	0.775	0.769	0.763	0.758	0.752	0.746	0.741	0.714	0.690	0.667	0.645	0.625
2	1.509	1.492	1.474	1.457	1.440	1.424	1.407	1.392	1.376	1.361	1.346	1.331	1.317	1.303	1.289	1.224	1.165	1.111	1.061	1.016
3	2.074	2.042	2.011	1.981	1.952	1.923	1.896	1.868	1.842	1.816	1.791	1.766	1.742	1.719	1.696	1.589	1.493	1.407	1.330	1.260
4	2.540	2.494	2.448	2.404	2.362	2.320	2.280	2.241	2.203	2.166	2.130	2.096	2.062	2.029	1.997	1.849	1.720	1.605	1.503	1.412
5	2.926	2.864	2.803	2.745	2.689	2.635	2.583	2.532	2.483	2.436	2.390	2.345	2.302	2.260	2.220	2.035	1.876	1.737	1.615	1.508
6	3.245	3.167	3.092	3.020	2.951	2.885	2.821	2.759	2.700	2.643	2.588	2.534	2.483	2.433	2.385	2.168	1.983	1.824	1.687	1.567
7	3.508	3.416	3.327	3.242	3.161	3.083	3.009	2.937	2.868	2.802	2.739	2.677	2.619	2.562	2.508	2.263	2.057	1.883	1.734	1.605
8	3.726	3.619	3.518	3.421	3.329	3.241	3.156	3.076	2.999	2.925	2.854	2.786	2.721	2.658	2.598	2.331	2.109	1.922	1.764	1.628
9	3.905	3.786	3.673	3.566	3.463	3.366	3.273	3.184	3.100	3.019	2.942	2.868	2.798	2.730	2.665	2.379	2.144	1.948	1.783	1.642
10	4.054	3.923	3.799	3.682	3.571	3.465	3.364	3.269	3.178	3.092	3.009	2.930	2.855	2.784	2.715	2.414	2.168	1.965	1.795	1.652
11	4.177	4.035	3.902	3.776	3.656	3.543	3.437	3.335	3.239	3.147	3.060	2.978	2.899	2.824	2.752	2.438	2.185	1.977	1.804	1.657
12	4.278	4.127	3.985	3.851	3.725	3.606	3.493	3.387	3.286	3.190	3.100	3.013	2.931	2.853	2.779	2.456	2.196	1.985	1.809	1.661
13	4.362	4.203	4.053	3.912	3.780	3.656	3.538	3.427	3.322	3.223	3.129	3.040	2.956	2.876	2.799	2.469	2.204	1.990	1.812	1.663
14	4.432	4.265	4.108	3.962	3.824	3.695	3.573	3.459	3.351	3.249	3.152	3.061	2.974	2.892	2.814	2.478	2.210	1.993	1.814	1.664
15	4.489	4.315	4.153	4.001	3.859	3.726	3.601	3.483	3.373	3.268	3.170	3.076	2.988	2.905	2.825	2.484	2.214	1.995	1.816	1.665
16	4.536	4.357	4.189	4.033	3.887	3.751	3.623	3.503	3.390	3.283	3.183	3.088	2.999	2.914	2.834	2.489	2.216	1.997	1.817	1.666
17	4.576	4.391	4.219	4.059	3.910	3.771	3.640	3.518	3.403	3.295	3.193	3.097	3.007	2.921	2.840	2.492	2.218	1.998	1.817	1.666
18	4.608	4.419	4.243	4.080	3.928	3.786	3.654	3.529	3.413	3.304	3.201	3.104	3.012	2.926	2.844	2.494	2.219	1.999	1.818	1.666
19	4.635	4.442	4.263	4.097	3.942	3.799	3.664	3.539	3.421	3.311	3.207	3.109	3.017	2.930	2.848	2.496	2.220	1.999	1.818	1.666
20	4.657	4.460	4.279	4.110	3.954	3.808	3.673	3.546	3.427	3.316	3.211	3.113	3.020	2.933	2.850	2.497	2.221	1.999	1.818	1.665
21	4.675	4.476	4.292	4.121	3.963	3.816	3.679	3.551	3.432	3.320	3.215	3.116	3.023	2.935	2.852	2.498	2.216	2.000	1.818	1.667
22	4.690	4.488	4.302	4.130	3.970	3.822	3.684	3.556	3.436	3.323	3.217	3.118	3.025	2.936	2.853	2.498	2.222	2.000	1.818	1.667
23	4.703	4.499	4.311	4.137	3.976	3.827	3.689	3.559	3.438	3.325	3.219	3.120	3.026	2.938	2.854	2.499	2.222	2.000	1.818	1.667
24	4.713	4.507	4.318	4.143	3.981	3.831	3.692	3.562	3.441	3.327	3.221	3.121	3.027	2.939	2.855	2.499	2.222	2.000	1.818	1.667
25	4.721	4.514	4.323	4.147	3.985	3.834	3.694	3.564	3.442	3.329	3.222	3.122	3.028	2.939	2.856	2.499	2.222	2.000	1.818	1.667
26	4.728	4.520	4.328	4.151	3.988	3.837	3.696	3.566	3.444	3.330	3.223	3.123	3.028	2.940	2.856	2.500	2.222	2.000	1.818	1.667
27	4.734	4.524	4.332	4.154	3.990	3.839	3.698	3.567	3.445	3.331	3.224	3.123	3.029	2.940	2.856	2.500	2.222	2.000	1.818	1.667
28	4.739	4.528	4.335	4.157	3.992	3.840	3.699	3.568	3.446	3.331	3.224	3.124	3.029	2.941	2.857	2.500	2.222	2.000	1.818	1.667
29	4.743	4.531	4.337	4.159	3.994	3.841	3.700	3.569	3.446	3.332	3.225	3.124	3.030	2.941	2.857	2.500	2.222	2.000	1.818	1.667
30	4.746	4.534	4.339	4.160	3.995	3.842	3.701	3.569	3.447	3.332	3.225	3.124	3.030	2.941	2.857	2.500	2.222	2.000	1.818	1.667
35	4.756	4.541	4.345	4.164	3.998	3.845	3.703	3.571	3.448	3.333	3.226	3.125	3.030	2.941	2.857	2.500	2.222	2.000	1.818	1.667
40	4.760	4.544	4.347	4.166	3.999	3.846	3.703	3.571	3.448	3.333	3.226	3.125	3.030	2.941	2.857	2.500	2.222	2.000	1.818	1.667
45	4.761	4.545	4.347	4.166	4.000	3.846	3.704	3.571	3.448	3.333	3.226	3.125	3.030	2.941	2.857	2.500	2.222	2.000	1.818	1.667
50	4.762	4.545	4.348	4.167	4.000	3.846	3.704	3.571	3.448	3.333	3.226	3.125	3.030	2.941	2.857	2.500	2.222	2.000	1.818	1.667

Table B.3

Future Value Factors for $1 Compounded at k Percent for n Periods:

$$FV_{k,n} = (1 + k)^n$$

Period, n	Compound Rate, k																			
	1%	2%	3%	4%	5%	6%	7%	8%	9%	10%	11%	12%	13%	14%	15%	16%	17%	18%	19%	20%
1	1.010	1.020	1.030	1.040	1.050	1.060	1.070	1.080	1.090	1.100	1.110	1.120	1.130	1.140	1.150	1.160	1.170	1.180	1.190	1.200
2	1.020	1.040	1.061	1.082	1.102	1.124	1.145	1.166	1.188	1.210	1.232	1.254	1.277	1.300	1.323	1.346	1.369	1.392	1.416	1.440
3	1.030	1.061	1.093	1.125	1.158	1.191	1.225	1.260	1.295	1.331	1.368	1.405	1.443	1.482	1.521	1.561	1.602	1.643	1.685	1.728
4	1.041	1.082	1.126	1.170	1.216	1.262	1.311	1.360	1.412	1.464	1.518	1.574	1.630	1.689	1.749	1.811	1.874	1.939	2.005	2.074
5	1.051	1.104	1.159	1.217	1.276	1.338	1.403	1.469	1.539	1.611	1.685	1.762	1.842	1.925	2.011	2.100	2.192	2.288	2.386	2.488
6	1.062	1.126	1.194	1.265	1.340	1.419	1.501	1.587	1.677	1.772	1.870	1.974	2.082	2.195	2.313	2.436	2.565	2.700	2.840	2.986
7	1.072	1.149	1.230	1.316	1.407	1.504	1.606	1.714	1.828	1.949	2.076	2.211	2.353	2.502	2.660	2.826	3.001	3.185	3.379	3.583
8	1.083	1.172	1.267	1.369	1.477	1.594	1.718	1.851	1.993	2.144	2.305	2.476	2.658	2.853	3.059	3.278	3.511	3.759	4.021	4.300
9	1.094	1.195	1.305	1.423	1.551	1.689	1.838	1.999	2.172	2.358	2.558	2.773	3.004	3.252	3.518	3.803	4.108	4.435	4.785	5.160
10	1.105	1.219	1.344	1.480	1.629	1.791	1.967	2.159	2.367	2.594	2.839	3.106	3.395	3.707	4.046	4.411	4.807	5.234	5.695	6.192
11	1.116	1.243	1.384	1.539	1.710	1.898	2.105	2.332	2.580	2.853	3.152	3.479	3.836	4.226	4.652	5.117	5.642	6.176	6.777	7.430
12	1.127	1.268	1.426	1.601	1.796	2.012	2.252	2.518	2.813	3.138	3.498	3.896	4.335	4.818	5.350	5.936	6.580	7.288	8.064	8.916
13	1.138	1.294	1.469	1.665	1.886	2.133	2.410	2.720	3.066	3.452	3.883	4.363	4.898	5.492	6.153	6.886	7.699	8.599	9.596	10.699
14	1.149	1.319	1.513	1.732	1.980	2.261	2.579	2.937	3.342	3.797	4.310	4.887	5.535	6.261	7.076	7.988	9.007	10.147	11.420	12.839
15	1.161	1.346	1.558	1.801	2.079	2.397	2.759	3.172	3.642	4.177	4.785	5.474	6.254	7.138	8.137	9.266	10.539	11.974	13.590	15.407
16	1.173	1.373	1.605	1.873	2.183	2.540	2.952	3.426	3.970	4.595	5.311	6.130	7.067	8.137	9.358	10.748	12.330	14.129	16.172	18.488
17	1.184	1.400	1.653	1.948	2.292	2.693	3.159	3.700	4.328	5.054	5.895	6.866	7.986	9.276	10.761	12.468	14.426	16.672	19.244	22.186
18	1.196	1.428	1.702	2.026	2.407	2.854	3.380	3.996	4.717	5.560	6.544	7.690	9.024	10.575	12.375	14.463	16.879	19.673	22.901	26.623
19	1.208	1.457	1.754	2.107	2.527	3.026	3.617	4.316	5.142	6.116	7.263	8.613	10.197	12.056	14.232	16.777	19.748	23.214	27.252	31.948
20	1.220	1.486	1.806	2.191	2.653	3.207	3.870	4.661	5.604	6.727	8.062	9.646	11.523	13.743	16.367	19.461	23.106	27.393	32.429	38.338
21	1.232	1.516	1.860	2.279	2.786	3.400	4.141	5.034	6.109	7.400	8.949	10.804	13.021	15.668	18.822	22.574	27.034	32.324	38.591	46.005
22	1.245	1.546	1.916	2.370	2.925	3.604	4.430	5.437	6.659	8.140	9.934	12.100	14.714	17.861	21.645	26.186	31.629	38.142	45.923	55.206
23	1.257	1.577	1.974	2.465	3.072	3.820	4.741	5.871	7.258	8.954	11.026	13.552	16.627	20.362	24.891	30.376	37.006	45.008	54.649	66.247
24	1.270	1.608	2.033	2.563	3.225	4.049	5.072	6.341	7.911	9.850	12.239	15.179	18.788	23.212	28.625	35.236	43.297	53.109	65.032	79.497
25	1.282	1.641	2.094	2.666	3.386	4.292	5.427	6.848	8.623	10.835	13.585	17.000	21.231	26.462	32.919	40.874	50.658	62.669	77.388	95.396
26	1.295	1.673	2.157	2.772	3.556	4.549	5.807	7.396	9.399	11.918	15.080	19.040	23.991	30.167	37.857	47.414	59.270	73.949	92.092	114.48
27	1.308	1.707	2.221	2.883	3.733	4.822	6.214	7.988	10.245	13.110	16.739	21.325	27.109	34.390	43.535	55.000	69.345	87.260	109.59	137.37
28	1.321	1.741	2.288	2.999	3.920	5.112	6.649	8.627	11.167	14.421	18.580	23.884	30.633	39.204	50.066	63.800	81.134	102.97	130.41	164.84
29	1.335	1.776	2.357	3.119	4.116	5.418	7.114	9.317	12.172	15.863	20.624	26.750	34.616	44.693	57.575	74.009	94.927	121.50	155.19	197.81
30	1.348	1.811	2.427	3.243	4.322	5.743	7.612	10.063	13.268	17.449	22.892	29.960	39.116	50.950	66.212	85.850	111.06	143.37	184.68	237.38
35	1.417	2.000	2.814	3.946	5.516	7.686	10.677	14.785	20.414	28.102	38.575	52.800	72.068	98.100	133.18	180.31	243.50	328.00	440.70	590.67
40	1.489	2.208	3.262	4.801	7.040	10.286	14.974	21.725	31.409	45.259	65.001	93.051	132.78	188.88	267.86	378.72	533.87	750.38	1051.7	1469.8
45	1.565	2.438	3.782	5.841	8.985	13.765	21.002	31.920	48.327	72.890	109.53	163.99	244.64	363.68	538.77	795.44	1170.5	1716.7	2509.7	3657.3
50	1.645	2.692	4.384	7.107	11.467	18.420	29.457	46.902	74.358	117.39	184.56	289.00	450.74	700.23	1083.7	1670.7	2566.2	3927.4	5988.9	9100.4

Table B.3

$FV_{k,n}$ (Continued)

Period, n	21%	22%	23%	24%	25%	26%	27%	28%	29%	30%	31%	32%	33%	34%	35%	40%	45%	50%	55%	60%
1	1.210	1.220	1.230	1.240	1.250	1.260	1.270	1.280	1.290	1.300	1.310	1.320	1.330	1.340	1.350	1.400	1.450	1.500	1.550	1.600
2	1.464	1.488	1.513	1.538	1.563	1.588	1.613	1.638	1.664	1.690	1.716	1.742	1.769	1.796	1.823	1.960	2.103	2.250	2.403	2.560
3	1.772	1.816	1.861	1.907	1.953	2.000	2.048	2.097	2.147	2.197	2.248	2.300	2.353	2.406	2.460	2.744	3.049	3.375	3.724	4.096
4	2.144	2.215	2.289	2.364	2.441	2.520	2.601	2.684	2.769	2.856	2.945	3.036	3.129	3.224	3.322	3.842	4.421	5.063	5.772	6.554
5	2.594	2.703	2.815	2.932	3.052	3.176	3.304	3.436	3.572	3.713	3.858	4.007	4.162	4.320	4.484	5.378	6.410	7.594	8.947	10.486
6	3.138	3.297	3.463	3.635	3.815	4.002	4.196	4.398	4.608	4.827	5.054	5.290	5.535	5.789	6.053	7.530	9.294	11.391	13.867	16.777
7	3.797	4.023	4.259	4.508	4.768	5.042	5.329	5.629	5.945	6.275	6.621	6.983	7.361	7.758	8.172	10.541	13.476	17.086	21.494	26.844
8	4.595	4.908	5.239	5.590	5.960	6.353	6.768	7.206	7.669	8.157	8.673	9.217	9.791	10.395	11.032	14.758	19.541	25.629	33.316	42.950
9	5.560	5.987	6.444	6.931	7.451	8.005	8.595	9.223	9.893	10.604	11.362	12.166	13.022	13.930	14.894	20.661	28.334	38.443	51.640	68.719
10	6.728	7.305	7.926	8.594	9.313	10.086	10.915	11.806	12.761	13.786	14.884	16.060	17.319	18.666	20.107	28.925	41.085	57.665	80.042	109.95
11	8.140	8.912	9.749	10.657	11.642	12.708	13.862	15.112	16.462	17.922	19.498	21.199	23.034	25.012	27.144	40.496	59.573	86.498	124.06	175.92
12	9.850	10.872	11.991	13.215	14.552	16.012	17.605	19.343	21.236	23.298	25.542	27.983	30.635	33.516	36.644	56.694	86.381	129.75	192.30	281.47
13	11.918	13.264	14.749	16.386	18.190	20.175	22.359	24.759	27.395	30.288	33.460	36.937	40.745	44.912	49.470	79.371	125.25	194.62	298.07	450.36
14	14.421	16.182	18.141	20.319	22.737	25.421	28.396	31.691	35.339	39.374	43.833	48.757	54.190	60.182	66.784	111.12	181.62	291.93	462.00	720.58
15	17.449	19.742	22.314	25.196	28.422	32.030	36.062	40.565	45.587	51.186	57.421	64.359	72.073	80.644	90.158	155.57	263.34	437.89	716.10	1152.9
16	21.114	24.086	27.446	31.243	35.527	40.358	45.799	51.923	58.808	66.542	75.221	84.954	95.858	108.06	121.71	217.80	381.85	656.84	1110.0	1844.7
17	25.548	29.384	33.759	38.741	44.409	50.851	58.165	66.461	75.862	86.504	98.540	112.14	127.49	144.80	164.31	304.91	553.68	985.26	1720.4	2951.5
18	30.913	35.849	41.523	48.039	55.511	64.072	73.870	85.071	97.862	112.46	129.09	148.02	169.56	194.04	221.82	426.88	802.83	1477.9	2666.7	4722.4
19	37.404	43.736	51.074	59.568	69.389	80.731	93.815	108.89	126.24	146.19	169.10	195.39	225.52	260.01	299.46	597.63	1164.1	2216.8	4133.4	7555.8
20	45.259	53.358	62.821	73.864	86.736	101.72	119.14	139.38	162.85	190.05	221.53	257.92	299.94	348.41	404.27	836.68	1688.0	3325.3	6406.7	12089
21	54.764	65.096	77.269	91.592	108.42	128.17	151.31	178.41	210.08	247.06	290.20	340.45	398.92	466.88	545.77	1171.4	2447.5	4987.9	9930.4	19342
22	66.264	79.418	95.041	113.57	135.53	161.49	192.17	228.36	271.00	321.18	380.16	449.39	530.56	625.61	736.79	1639.9	3548.9	7481.8	15392	30948
23	80.180	96.889	116.90	140.83	169.41	203.48	244.05	292.30	349.59	417.54	498.01	593.20	705.65	838.32	994.66	2295.9	5145.9	11222	23857	49517
24	97.017	118.21	143.79	174.63	211.76	256.39	309.95	374.14	450.98	542.80	652.40	783.02	938.51	1123.4	1342.8	3214.2	7461.6	16834	36979	79228
25	117.39	144.21	176.86	216.54	264.70	323.05	393.63	478.90	581.76	705.64	854.64	1033.6	1248.2	1505.3	1812.8	4499.9	10819	25251	57318	126765
26	142.04	175.94	217.54	268.51	330.87	407.04	499.92	613.00	750.47	917.33	1119.6	1364.3	1660.1	2017.1	2447.2	6299.8	15688	37876	88843	202824
27	171.87	214.64	267.57	332.95	413.59	512.87	634.89	784.64	968.10	1192.5	1466.6	1800.9	2208.0	2702.9	3303.8	8819.8	22747	56815	137706	324518
28	207.97	261.86	329.11	412.86	516.99	646.21	806.31	1004.3	1248.9	1550.3	1921.3	2377.2	2936.6	3621.9	4460.1	12347	32984	85222	213445	519229
29	251.64	319.47	404.81	511.95	646.23	814.23	1024.0	1285.6	1611.0	2015.4	2516.9	3137.9	3905.7	4853.3	6021.1	17286	47826	127834	330840	830767
30	304.48	389.76	497.91	634.82	807.79	1025.9	1300.5	1645.5	2078.2	2620.0	3297.2	4142.1	5194.6	6503.5	8128.6	24201	69348	191751	512803	*
35	789.75	1053.4	1401.8	1861.1	2465.2	3258.1	4296.7	5653.9	7424.0	9727.9	12720	16599	21617	28097	36448	130161	444508	*	*	*
40	2048.4	2847.0	3946.4	5455.9	7523.2	10347	14195	19426	26520	36118	49074	66520	89963	121392	163437	700037	*	*	*	*
45	5313.0	7694.7	11110	15994	22958	32860	46899	66749	94740	134106	189325	266579	374389	524464	732857	*	*	*	*	*
50	13780	20796	31279	46890	70064	104358	154948	229349	338443	497929	730406	*	*	*	*	*	*	*	*	*

*Value is greater than 999999.

Table B.4

Future Value Factors for an Annuity of $1 Compounded at k Percent for n Periods:

$$FVA_{k,n} = \sum_{t=0}^{n-1}(1+k)^t = \frac{(1+k)^n - 1}{k}$$

Period, n	1%	2%	3%	4%	5%	6%	7%	8%	9%	10%	11%	12%	13%	14%	15%	16%	17%	18%	19%	20%
1	1.000	1.000	1.000	1.000	1.000	1.000	1.000	1.000	1.000	1.000	1.000	1.000	1.000	1.000	1.000	1.000	1.000	1.000	1.000	1.000
2	2.010	2.020	2.030	2.040	2.050	2.060	2.070	2.080	2.090	2.100	2.110	2.120	2.130	2.140	2.150	2.160	2.170	2.180	2.190	2.200
3	3.030	3.060	3.091	3.122	3.152	3.184	3.215	3.246	3.278	3.310	3.342	3.374	3.407	3.440	3.473	3.506	3.539	3.572	3.606	3.640
4	4.060	4.122	4.184	4.246	4.310	4.375	4.440	4.506	4.573	4.641	4.710	4.779	4.850	4.921	4.993	5.066	5.141	5.215	5.291	5.368
5	5.101	5.204	5.309	5.416	5.526	5.637	5.751	5.867	5.985	6.105	6.228	6.353	6.480	6.610	6.742	6.877	7.014	7.154	7.297	7.442
6	6.152	6.308	6.468	6.633	6.802	6.975	7.153	7.336	7.523	7.716	7.913	8.115	8.323	8.536	8.754	8.977	9.207	9.442	9.683	9.930
7	7.214	7.434	7.662	7.898	8.142	8.394	8.654	8.923	9.200	9.487	9.783	10.089	10.405	10.730	11.067	11.414	11.772	12.142	12.523	12.916
8	8.286	8.583	8.892	9.214	9.549	9.897	10.260	10.637	11.028	11.436	11.859	12.300	12.757	13.233	13.727	14.240	14.773	15.327	15.902	16.499
9	9.369	9.755	10.159	10.583	11.027	11.491	11.978	12.488	13.021	13.579	14.164	14.776	15.416	16.085	16.786	17.519	18.285	19.086	19.923	20.799
10	10.462	10.950	11.464	12.006	12.578	13.181	13.816	14.487	15.193	15.937	16.722	17.549	18.420	19.337	20.304	21.321	22.393	23.521	24.709	25.959
11	11.567	12.169	12.808	13.486	14.207	14.972	15.784	16.645	17.560	18.531	19.561	20.655	21.814	23.045	24.349	25.733	27.200	28.755	30.404	32.150
12	12.683	13.412	14.192	15.026	15.917	16.870	17.888	18.977	20.141	21.384	22.713	24.133	25.650	27.271	29.002	30.850	32.824	34.931	37.180	39.581
13	13.809	14.680	15.618	16.627	17.713	18.882	20.141	21.495	22.953	24.523	26.212	28.029	29.985	32.089	34.352	36.786	39.404	42.219	45.244	48.497
14	14.947	15.974	17.086	18.292	19.599	21.015	22.550	24.215	26.019	27.975	30.095	32.393	34.883	37.581	40.505	43.672	47.103	50.818	54.841	59.196
15	16.097	17.293	18.599	20.024	21.579	23.276	25.129	27.152	29.361	31.772	34.405	37.280	40.417	43.842	47.580	51.660	56.110	60.965	66.261	72.035
16	17.258	18.639	20.157	21.825	23.657	25.673	27.888	30.324	33.003	35.950	39.190	42.753	46.672	50.980	55.717	60.925	66.649	72.939	79.850	87.442
17	18.430	20.012	21.762	23.698	25.840	28.213	30.840	33.750	36.974	40.545	44.501	48.884	53.739	59.118	65.075	71.673	78.979	87.068	96.022	105.93
18	19.615	21.412	23.414	25.645	28.132	30.906	33.999	37.450	41.301	45.599	50.396	55.750	61.725	68.394	75.836	84.141	93.406	103.74	115.27	128.12
19	20.811	22.841	25.117	27.671	30.539	33.760	37.379	41.446	46.018	51.159	56.939	63.440	70.749	78.969	88.212	98.603	110.28	123.41	138.17	154.74
20	22.019	24.297	26.870	29.778	33.066	36.786	40.996	45.762	51.160	57.275	64.203	72.052	80.947	91.025	102.44	115.38	130.03	146.63	165.42	186.69
21	23.239	25.783	28.676	31.969	35.719	39.993	44.865	50.423	56.765	64.002	72.265	81.699	92.470	104.77	118.81	134.84	153.14	174.02	197.85	225.03
22	24.472	27.299	30.537	34.248	38.505	43.392	49.006	55.457	62.873	71.403	81.214	92.503	105.49	120.44	137.63	157.41	180.17	206.34	236.44	271.03
23	25.716	28.845	32.453	36.618	41.430	46.996	53.436	60.893	69.532	79.543	91.148	104.60	120.20	138.30	159.28	183.60	211.80	244.49	282.36	326.24
24	26.973	30.422	34.426	39.083	44.502	50.816	58.177	66.765	76.790	88.497	102.17	118.16	136.83	158.66	184.17	213.98	248.81	289.49	337.01	392.48
25	28.243	32.030	36.459	41.646	47.727	54.865	63.249	73.106	84.701	98.347	114.41	133.33	155.62	181.87	212.79	249.21	292.10	342.60	402.04	471.98
26	29.526	33.671	38.553	44.312	51.113	59.156	68.676	79.954	93.324	109.18	128.00	150.33	176.85	208.33	245.71	290.09	342.76	405.27	479.43	567.38
27	30.821	35.344	40.710	47.084	54.669	63.706	74.484	87.351	102.72	121.10	143.08	169.37	200.84	238.50	283.57	337.50	402.03	479.22	571.52	681.85
28	32.129	37.051	42.931	49.968	58.403	68.528	80.698	95.339	112.97	134.21	159.82	190.70	227.95	272.89	327.10	392.50	471.38	566.48	681.11	819.22
29	33.450	38.792	45.219	52.966	62.323	73.640	87.347	103.97	124.14	148.63	178.40	214.58	258.58	312.09	377.17	456.30	552.51	669.45	811.52	984.07
30	34.785	40.568	47.575	56.085	66.439	79.058	94.461	113.28	136.31	164.49	199.02	241.33	293.20	356.79	434.75	530.31	647.44	790.95	966.71	1181.9
35	41.660	49.994	60.462	73.652	90.320	111.43	138.24	172.32	215.71	271.02	341.59	431.66	546.68	693.57	881.17	1120.7	1426.5	1816.7	2314.2	2948.3
40	48.886	60.402	75.401	95.026	120.80	154.76	199.64	259.06	337.88	442.59	581.83	767.09	1013.7	1342.0	1779.1	2360.8	3134.5	4163.2	5529.8	7343.9
45	56.481	71.893	92.720	121.03	159.70	212.74	285.75	386.51	525.86	718.90	986.64	1358.2	1874.2	2590.6	3585.1	4965.3	6879.3	9531.6	13203	18281
50	64.463	84.579	112.80	152.67	209.35	290.34	406.53	573.77	815.08	1163.9	1668.8	2400.0	3459.5	4994.5	7217.7	10435	15089	21813	31515	45497

Table B.4

$FVA_{k,n}$ (Continued)

Period, n Compound Rate, k

n	21%	22%	23%	24%	25%	26%	27%	28%	29%	30%	31%	32%	33%	34%	35%	40%	45%	50%	55%	60%
1	1.000	1.000	1.000	1.000	1.000	1.000	1.000	1.000	1.000	1.000	1.000	1.000	1.000	1.000	1.000	1.000	1.000	1.000	1.000	1.000
2	2.210	2.220	2.230	2.240	2.250	2.260	2.270	2.280	2.290	2.300	2.310	2.320	2.330	2.340	2.350	2.400	2.450	2.500	2.550	2.600
3	3.674	3.708	3.743	3.778	3.813	3.848	3.883	3.918	3.954	3.990	4.026	4.062	4.099	4.136	4.173	4.360	4.553	4.750	4.952	5.160
4	5.446	5.524	5.604	5.684	5.766	5.848	5.931	6.016	6.101	6.187	6.274	6.362	6.452	6.542	6.633	7.104	7.601	8.125	8.676	9.256
5	7.589	7.740	7.893	8.048	8.207	8.368	8.533	8.700	8.870	9.043	9.219	9.398	9.581	9.766	9.954	10.946	12.022	13.188	14.448	15.810
6	10.183	10.442	10.708	10.980	11.259	11.544	11.837	12.136	12.442	12.756	13.077	13.406	13.742	14.086	14.438	16.324	18.431	20.781	23.395	26.295
7	13.321	13.740	14.171	14.615	15.073	15.546	16.032	16.534	17.051	17.583	18.131	18.696	19.277	19.876	20.492	23.853	27.725	32.172	37.262	43.073
8	17.119	17.762	18.430	19.123	19.842	20.588	21.361	22.163	22.995	23.858	24.752	25.678	26.638	27.633	28.664	34.395	41.202	49.258	58.756	69.916
9	21.714	22.670	23.669	24.712	25.802	26.940	28.129	29.369	30.664	32.015	33.425	34.895	36.429	38.029	39.696	49.153	60.743	74.887	92.073	112.87
10	27.274	28.657	30.113	31.643	33.253	34.945	36.723	38.593	40.556	42.619	44.786	47.062	49.451	51.958	54.590	69.814	89.077	113.33	143.71	181.59
11	34.001	35.962	38.039	40.238	42.566	45.031	47.639	50.398	53.318	56.405	59.670	63.122	66.769	70.624	74.697	98.739	130.16	171.00	223.75	291.54
12	42.142	44.874	47.788	50.895	54.208	57.739	61.501	65.510	69.780	74.327	79.168	84.320	89.803	95.637	101.84	139.23	189.73	257.49	347.82	467.46
13	51.991	55.746	59.779	64.110	68.760	73.751	79.107	84.853	91.016	97.625	104.71	112.30	120.44	129.15	138.48	195.93	276.12	387.24	540.12	748.93
14	63.909	69.010	74.528	80.496	86.949	93.926	101.47	109.61	118.41	127.91	138.17	149.24	161.18	174.06	187.95	275.30	401.37	581.86	838.19	1199.3
15	78.330	85.192	92.669	100.82	109.69	119.35	129.86	141.30	153.75	167.29	182.00	198.00	215.37	234.25	254.74	386.42	582.98	873.79	1300.2	1919.9
16	95.780	104.93	114.98	126.01	138.11	151.38	165.92	181.87	199.34	218.47	239.42	262.36	287.45	314.89	344.90	541.99	846.32	1311.7	2016.3	3072.8
17	116.89	129.02	142.43	157.25	173.64	191.73	211.72	233.79	258.15	285.01	314.64	347.31	383.30	422.95	466.61	759.78	1228.2	1968.5	3126.2	4917.5
18	142.44	158.40	176.19	195.99	218.04	242.59	269.89	300.25	334.01	371.52	413.18	459.45	510.80	567.76	630.92	1064.7	1781.8	2953.8	4846.7	7868.9
19	173.35	194.25	217.71	244.03	273.56	306.66	343.76	385.32	431.87	483.97	542.27	607.47	680.36	761.80	852.75	1491.6	2584.7	4431.7	7513.4	12591
20	210.76	237.99	268.79	303.60	342.94	387.39	437.57	494.21	558.11	630.17	711.38	802.86	905.88	1021.8	1152.2	2089.2	3748.8	6648.5	11646	20147
21	256.02	291.35	331.61	377.46	429.68	489.11	556.72	633.59	720.96	820.22	932.90	1060.8	1205.8	1370.2	1556.5	2925.9	5436.7	9973.8	18053	32236
22	310.78	356.44	408.88	469.06	538.10	617.28	708.03	812.00	931.04	1067.3	1223.1	1401.2	1604.7	1837.1	2102.3	4097.2	7884.3	14961	27983	51579
23	377.05	435.86	503.92	582.63	673.63	778.77	900.20	1040.4	1202.0	1388.5	1603.3	1850.6	2135.3	2462.7	2839.0	5737.1	11433	22443	43375	82527
24	457.22	532.75	620.82	723.46	843.03	982.25	1144.3	1332.7	1551.6	1806.0	2101.3	2443.8	2840.9	3301.0	3833.7	8033.0	16579	33666	67233	132045
25	554.24	650.96	764.61	898.09	1054.8	1238.6	1454.2	1706.8	2002.6	2348.8	2753.7	3226.8	3779.5	4424.4	5176.5	11247	24040	50500	104213	211273
26	671.63	795.17	941.46	1114.6	1319.5	1561.7	1847.8	2185.7	2584.4	3054.4	3608.3	4260.4	5027.7	5929.7	6989.3	15747	34860	75751	161531	338038
27	813.68	971.10	1159.0	1383.1	1650.4	1968.7	2347.8	2798.7	3334.8	3971.8	4727.9	5624.8	6687.8	7946.8	9436.5	22046	50548	113628	250374	540862
28	985.55	1185.7	1426.6	1716.1	2064.0	2481.6	2982.6	3583.3	4302.9	5164.3	6194.5	7425.7	8895.8	10649	12740	30866	73295	170443	388081	865381
29	1193.5	1447.6	1755.7	2129.0	2580.9	3127.8	3789.0	4587.7	5551.8	6714.6	8115.8	9802.9	11832	14271	17200	43214	106279	255666	601527	*
30	1445.2	1767.1	2160.5	2640.9	3227.2	3942.0	4813.0	5873.2	7162.8	8730.0	10632	12940	15738	19124	23221	60501	154106	383500	932368	*
35	3755.9	4783.6	6090.3	7750.2	9856.8	12527	15909	20188	25596	32422	41029	51869	65504	82636	104136	325400	987794	*	*	*
40	9749.5	12936	17154	22728	30088	39792	52571	69377	91447	120392	158300	207874	272613	357033	466960	*	*	*	*	*
45	25295	34971	48301	66640	91831	126382	173697	238387	326688	447019	610723	833058	*	*	*	*	*	*	*	*
50	65617	94525	135992	195372	280255	401374	573877	819103	*	*	*	*	*	*	*	*	*	*	*	*

*Value is greater than 999999.

Table B.5

Cumulative Distribution Function

d	0.00	0.01	0.02	0.03	0.04	0.05	0.06	0.07	0.08	0.09
−3.00	0.001	0.001	0.001	0.001	0.001	0.001	0.001	0.001	0.001	0.001
−2.90	0.002	0.002	0.002	0.002	0.002	0.002	0.002	0.001	0.001	0.001
−2.80	0.003	0.002	0.002	0.002	0.002	0.002	0.002	0.002	0.002	0.002
−2.70	0.003	0.003	0.003	0.003	0.003	0.003	0.003	0.003	0.003	0.003
−2.60	0.005	0.005	0.004	0.004	0.004	0.004	0.004	0.004	0.004	0.004
−2.50	0.006	0.006	0.006	0.006	0.006	0.005	0.005	0.005	0.005	0.005
−2.40	0.008	0.008	0.008	0.008	0.007	0.007	0.007	0.007	0.007	0.006
−2.30	0.011	0.010	0.010	0.010	0.010	0.009	0.009	0.009	0.009	0.008
−2.20	0.014	0.014	0.013	0.013	0.013	0.012	0.012	0.012	0.011	0.011
−2.10	0.018	0.017	0.017	0.017	0.016	0.016	0.015	0.015	0.015	0.014
−2.00	0.023	0.022	0.022	0.021	0.021	0.020	0.020	0.019	0.019	0.018
−1.90	0.029	0.028	0.027	0.027	0.026	0.026	0.025	0.024	0.024	0.023
−1.80	0.036	0.035	0.034	0.034	0.033	0.032	0.031	0.031	0.030	0.029
−1.70	0.045	0.044	0.043	0.042	0.041	0.040	0.039	0.038	0.038	0.037
−1.60	0.055	0.054	0.053	0.052	0.051	0.049	0.048	0.047	0.046	0.046
−1.50	0.067	0.066	0.064	0.063	0.062	0.061	0.059	0.058	0.057	0.056
−1.40	0.081	0.079	0.078	0.076	0.075	0.074	0.072	0.071	0.069	0.068
−1.30	0.097	0.095	0.093	0.092	0.090	0.089	0.087	0.085	0.084	0.082
−1.20	0.115	0.113	0.111	0.109	0.107	0.106	0.104	0.102	0.100	0.099
−1.10	0.136	0.134	0.131	0.129	0.127	0.125	0.123	0.121	0.119	0.117
−1.00	0.159	0.156	0.154	0.152	0.149	0.147	0.145	0.142	0.140	0.138
−0.90	0.184	0.181	0.179	0.176	0.174	0.171	0.169	0.166	0.164	0.161
−0.80	0.212	0.209	0.206	0.203	0.200	0.198	0.195	0.192	0.189	0.187
−0.70	0.242	0.239	0.236	0.233	0.230	0.227	0.224	0.221	0.218	0.215
−0.60	0.274	0.271	0.268	0.264	0.261	0.258	0.255	0.251	0.248	0.245
−0.50	0.309	0.305	0.302	0.298	0.295	0.291	0.288	0.284	0.281	0.278
−0.40	0.345	0.341	0.337	0.334	0.330	0.326	0.323	0.319	0.316	0.312
−0.30	0.382	0.378	0.374	0.371	0.367	0.363	0.359	0.356	0.352	0.348
−0.20	0.421	0.417	0.413	0.409	0.405	0.401	0.397	0.394	0.390	0.386
−0.10	0.460	0.456	0.452	0.448	0.444	0.440	0.436	0.433	0.429	0.425
−0.00	0.500	0.496	0.492	0.488	0.484	0.480	0.476	0.472	0.468	0.464

Table B.5

Cumulative Distribution Function (Continued)

d	0.00	0.01	0.02	0.03	0.04	0.05	0.06	0.07	0.08	0.09
0.00	0.500	0.504	0.508	0.512	0.516	0.520	0.524	0.528	0.532	0.536
0.10	0.540	0.544	0.548	0.552	0.556	0.560	0.564	0.567	0.571	0.575
0.20	0.579	0.583	0.587	0.591	0.595	0.599	0.603	0.606	0.610	0.614
0.30	0.618	0.622	0.626	0.629	0.633	0.637	0.641	0.644	0.648	0.652
0.40	0.655	0.659	0.663	0.666	0.670	0.674	0.677	0.681	0.684	0.688
0.50	0.691	0.695	0.698	0.702	0.705	0.709	0.712	0.716	0.719	0.722
0.60	0.726	0.729	0.732	0.736	0.739	0.742	0.745	0.749	0.752	0.755
0.70	0.758	0.761	0.764	0.767	0.770	0.773	0.776	0.779	0.782	0.785
0.80	0.788	0.791	0.794	0.797	0.800	0.802	0.805	0.808	0.811	0.813
0.90	0.816	0.819	0.821	0.824	0.826	0.829	0.831	0.834	0.836	0.839
1.00	0.841	0.844	0.846	0.849	0.851	0.853	0.855	0.858	0.860	0.862
1.10	0.864	0.867	0.869	0.871	0.873	0.875	0.877	0.879	0.881	0.883
1.20	0.885	0.887	0.889	0.891	0.893	0.894	0.896	0.898	0.900	0.901
1.30	0.903	0.905	0.907	0.908	0.910	0.911	0.913	0.915	0.916	0.918
1.40	0.919	0.921	0.922	0.924	0.925	0.926	0.928	0.929	0.931	0.932
1.50	0.933	0.934	0.936	0.937	0.938	0.939	0.941	0.942	0.943	0.944
1.60	0.945	0.946	0.947	0.948	0.950	0.951	0.952	0.953	0.954	0.954
1.70	0.955	0.956	0.957	0.958	0.959	0.960	0.961	0.962	0.962	0.963
1.80	0.964	0.965	0.966	0.966	0.967	0.968	0.969	0.969	0.970	0.971
1.90	0.971	0.972	0.973	0.973	0.974	0.974	0.975	0.976	0.976	0.977
2.00	0.977	0.978	0.978	0.979	0.979	0.980	0.980	0.981	0.981	0.982
2.10	0.982	0.983	0.983	0.983	0.984	0.984	0.985	0.985	0.985	0.986
2.20	0.986	0.986	0.987	0.987	0.987	0.988	0.988	0.988	0.989	0.989
2.30	0.989	0.990	0.990	0.990	0.990	0.991	0.991	0.991	0.991	0.992
2.40	0.992	0.992	0.992	0.992	0.993	0.993	0.993	0.993	0.993	0.994
2.50	0.994	0.994	0.994	0.994	0.994	0.995	0.995	0.995	0.995	0.995
2.60	0.995	0.995	0.996	0.996	0.996	0.996	0.996	0.996	0.996	0.996
2.70	0.997	0.997	0.997	0.997	0.997	0.997	0.997	0.997	0.997	0.997
2.80	0.997	0.998	0.998	0.998	0.998	0.998	0.998	0.998	0.998	0.998
2.90	0.998	0.998	0.998	0.998	0.998	0.998	0.998	0.999	0.999	0.999
3.00	0.999	0.999	0.999	0.999	0.999	0.999	0.999	0.999	0.999	0.999

Table B.6

Call Option Value for Non-Dividend-Paying Stocks (in decimal form) Relative to Share Price

Standard Deviation Times the Square Root of Time

Share Price Divided by the Present Value of the Exercise Price

	0.05	0.10	0.15	0.20	0.25	0.30	0.35	0.40	0.45	0.50	0.55	0.60	0.65	0.70	0.75	0.80	0.85	0.90	0.95	1.00	1.05	1.10
0.40	*	*	*	*	*	*	*	0.002	0.005	0.010	0.017	0.025	0.036	0.047	0.061	0.075	0.091	0.107	0.125	0.143	0.161	0.180
0.45	*	*	*	*	*	*	0.002	0.005	0.010	0.017	0.026	0.037	0.049	0.063	0.079	0.095	0.112	0.130	0.148	0.167	0.186	0.206
0.50	*	*	*	*	*	0.001	0.004	0.009	0.017	0.026	0.038	0.051	0.065	0.081	0.098	0.115	0.133	0.152	0.171	0.191	0.210	0.230
0.55	*	*	*	*	*	0.003	0.008	0.016	0.026	0.037	0.051	0.066	0.082	0.099	0.117	0.136	0.155	0.174	0.194	0.214	0.233	0.253
0.60	*	*	*	*	0.002	0.007	0.014	0.024	0.037	0.051	0.066	0.083	0.100	0.119	0.137	0.157	0.176	0.196	0.216	0.236	0.256	0.275
0.65	*	*	*	0.001	0.005	0.012	0.023	0.035	0.050	0.066	0.083	0.101	0.119	0.138	0.158	0.177	0.197	0.217	0.237	0.257	0.277	0.296
0.70	*	*	*	0.004	0.010	0.020	0.033	0.048	0.065	0.082	0.100	0.119	0.138	0.158	0.178	0.198	0.218	0.238	0.257	0.277	0.297	0.316
0.75	*	*	0.002	0.008	0.018	0.031	0.046	0.063	0.081	0.100	0.119	0.138	0.158	0.178	0.198	0.218	0.238	0.258	0.277	0.297	0.316	0.335
0.80	*	*	0.005	0.015	0.028	0.044	0.062	0.080	0.099	0.118	0.138	0.158	0.178	0.198	0.218	0.237	0.257	0.277	0.296	0.316	0.335	0.354
0.82	*	*	0.007	0.019	0.033	0.050	0.068	0.087	0.106	0.126	0.146	0.166	0.186	0.206	0.225	0.245	0.265	0.284	0.304	0.323	0.342	0.361
0.84	*	0.002	0.010	0.023	0.039	0.057	0.075	0.094	0.114	0.134	0.154	0.174	0.193	0.213	0.233	0.253	0.272	0.292	0.311	0.330	0.349	0.367
0.86	*	0.003	0.013	0.028	0.045	0.063	0.082	0.102	0.122	0.142	0.161	0.181	0.201	0.221	0.241	0.260	0.280	0.299	0.318	0.337	0.356	0.374
0.88	*	0.005	0.017	0.034	0.052	0.070	0.090	0.110	0.129	0.149	0.169	0.189	0.209	0.229	0.248	0.268	0.287	0.306	0.325	0.344	0.362	0.381
0.90	*	0.008	0.022	0.040	0.059	0.078	0.098	0.117	0.137	0.157	0.177	0.197	0.217	0.236	0.256	0.275	0.294	0.313	0.332	0.351	0.369	0.387
0.92	0.001	0.012	0.028	0.047	0.066	0.086	0.106	0.125	0.145	0.165	0.185	0.205	0.225	0.244	0.263	0.283	0.302	0.320	0.339	0.357	0.376	0.393
0.94	0.003	0.017	0.035	0.054	0.074	0.094	0.114	0.134	0.153	0.173	0.193	0.213	0.232	0.252	0.271	0.290	0.309	0.327	0.346	0.364	0.382	0.400
0.96	0.006	0.023	0.042	0.062	0.082	0.102	0.122	0.142	0.162	0.181	0.201	0.220	0.240	0.259	0.278	0.297	0.316	0.334	0.352	0.370	0.388	0.406
0.98	0.012	0.031	0.051	0.071	0.091	0.111	0.130	0.150	0.170	0.189	0.209	0.228	0.247	0.266	0.285	0.304	0.322	0.341	0.359	0.377	0.394	0.412
1.00	0.020	0.040	0.060	0.080	0.099	0.119	0.139	0.159	0.178	0.197	0.217	0.236	0.255	0.274	0.292	0.311	0.329	0.347	0.365	0.383	0.400	0.418
1.02	0.031	0.050	0.070	0.089	0.109	0.128	0.148	0.167	0.186	0.205	0.224	0.243	0.262	0.281	0.299	0.318	0.336	0.354	0.372	0.389	0.406	0.423
1.04	0.045	0.061	0.080	0.099	0.118	0.137	0.156	0.175	0.194	0.213	0.232	0.251	0.270	0.288	0.306	0.324	0.342	0.360	0.378	0.395	0.412	0.429
1.06	0.060	0.073	0.091	0.109	0.128	0.146	0.165	0.184	0.203	0.221	0.240	0.258	0.277	0.295	0.313	0.331	0.349	0.366	0.384	0.401	0.418	0.435
1.08	0.075	0.086	0.102	0.119	0.137	0.156	0.174	0.192	0.211	0.229	0.248	0.266	0.285	0.302	0.320	0.338	0.355	0.373	0.390	0.407	0.424	0.440
1.10	0.091	0.100	0.114	0.130	0.147	0.165	0.183	0.201	0.219	0.237	0.255	0.273	0.291	0.309	0.327	0.344	0.362	0.379	0.396	0.412	0.429	0.445
1.12	0.107	0.113	0.126	0.141	0.157	0.174	0.192	0.209	0.227	0.245	0.263	0.281	0.298	0.316	0.333	0.351	0.368	0.385	0.401	0.418	0.435	0.451
1.14	0.123	0.127	0.138	0.152	0.167	0.184	0.201	0.218	0.235	0.253	0.270	0.288	0.305	0.323	0.340	0.357	0.374	0.391	0.407	0.424	0.440	0.456
1.16	0.138	0.141	0.150	0.163	0.177	0.193	0.210	0.226	0.243	0.261	0.278	0.295	0.312	0.329	0.346	0.363	0.380	0.396	0.413	0.429	0.445	0.461
1.18	0.153	0.154	0.162	0.174	0.187	0.203	0.219	0.235	0.251	0.268	0.285	0.302	0.319	0.336	0.353	0.369	0.386	0.402	0.418	0.434	0.450	0.466
1.20	0.167	0.168	0.174	0.185	0.198	0.212	0.227	0.243	0.259	0.276	0.292	0.309	0.326	0.342	0.359	0.375	0.392	0.408	0.424	0.440	0.455	0.471
1.25	0.200	0.200	0.204	0.212	0.223	0.235	0.249	0.264	0.279	0.295	0.310	0.326	0.342	0.358	0.374	0.390	0.406	0.421	0.437	0.452	0.468	0.483
1.30	0.231	0.231	0.233	0.239	0.247	0.258	0.271	0.284	0.298	0.313	0.328	0.343	0.358	0.373	0.389	0.404	0.419	0.435	0.450	0.465	0.480	0.494
1.35	0.259	0.259	0.260	0.264	0.271	0.281	0.292	0.304	0.317	0.331	0.345	0.359	0.374	0.388	0.403	0.418	0.433	0.447	0.462	0.476	0.491	0.505
1.40	0.286	0.286	0.286	0.289	0.294	0.302	0.312	0.323	0.335	0.348	0.361	0.375	0.389	0.403	0.417	0.431	0.445	0.460	0.474	0.488	0.502	0.516
1.45	0.310	0.310	0.311	0.312	0.317	0.323	0.332	0.342	0.353	0.364	0.377	0.390	0.403	0.416	0.430	0.444	0.458	0.471	0.485	0.499	0.512	0.526
1.50	0.333	0.333	0.333	0.335	0.338	0.343	0.351	0.360	0.370	0.381	0.392	0.404	0.417	0.430	0.443	0.456	0.469	0.483	0.496	0.509	0.522	0.535
1.75	0.429	0.429	0.429	0.429	0.429	0.431	0.435	0.440	0.446	0.453	0.461	0.470	0.480	0.490	0.500	0.511	0.522	0.533	0.545	0.556	0.567	0.579
2.00	0.500	0.500	0.500	0.500	0.500	0.501	0.502	0.505	0.508	0.513	0.519	0.525	0.533	0.540	0.549	0.558	0.567	0.576	0.586	0.595	0.605	0.615
2.25	0.556	0.556	0.556	0.556	0.556	0.556	0.556	0.558	0.560	0.563	0.567	0.571	0.577	0.583	0.590	0.597	0.604	0.612	0.620	0.629	0.637	0.646
2.50	0.600	0.600	0.600	0.600	0.600	0.600	0.600	0.601	0.602	0.604	0.607	0.610	0.614	0.619	0.624	0.630	0.636	0.643	0.650	0.657	0.665	0.672
2.75	0.636	0.636	0.636	0.636	0.636	0.636	0.636	0.637	0.637	0.639	0.641	0.643	0.646	0.650	0.654	0.659	0.664	0.670	0.676	0.682	0.688	0.695
3.00	0.667	0.667	0.667	0.667	0.667	0.667	0.667	0.667	0.667	0.668	0.669	0.671	0.673	0.676	0.680	0.684	0.688	0.693	0.698	0.703	0.709	0.715
3.50	0.714	0.714	0.714	0.714	0.714	0.714	0.714	0.714	0.714	0.715	0.715	0.716	0.718	0.720	0.722	0.724	0.728	0.731	0.735	0.739	0.743	0.748
4.00	0.750	0.750	0.750	0.750	0.750	0.750	0.750	0.750	0.750	0.750	0.751	0.751	0.752	0.753	0.754	0.756	0.759	0.761	0.764	0.767	0.771	0.775
4.50	0.778	0.778	0.778	0.778	0.778	0.778	0.778	0.778	0.778	0.778	0.778	0.778	0.779	0.780	0.781	0.782	0.784	0.785	0.788	0.790	0.793	0.796

*Value is zero to three decimal places

Table B.6

Call Option Value (Continued)

Standard Deviation Times the Square Root of Time

Share Price ÷ PV(Exercise Price)	5.00	4.50	4.00	3.50	3.00	2.75	2.50	2.25	2.00	1.75	1.70	1.65	1.60	1.55	1.50	1.45	1.40	1.35	1.30	1.25	1.20	1.15
0.40	0.981	0.962	0.929	0.876	0.795	0.742	0.679	0.607	0.525	0.435	0.416	0.397	0.378	0.358	0.338	0.319	0.299	0.279	0.259	0.239	0.219	0.200
0.45	0.982	0.964	0.933	0.883	0.805	0.754	0.694	0.625	0.546	0.459	0.440	0.422	0.403	0.384	0.364	0.345	0.325	0.305	0.285	0.265	0.245	0.225
0.50	0.983	0.966	0.936	0.888	0.814	0.766	0.708	0.641	0.565	0.480	0.462	0.444	0.426	0.407	0.388	0.369	0.349	0.330	0.310	0.290	0.270	0.250
0.55	0.983	0.967	0.939	0.893	0.822	0.775	0.720	0.656	0.582	0.500	0.482	0.464	0.446	0.428	0.409	0.391	0.371	0.352	0.333	0.313	0.293	0.273
0.60	0.984	0.969	0.942	0.897	0.829	0.784	0.731	0.668	0.597	0.517	0.500	0.483	0.465	0.448	0.429	0.411	0.392	0.373	0.354	0.335	0.315	0.295
0.65	0.985	0.970	0.944	0.901	0.835	0.792	0.740	0.680	0.611	0.534	0.517	0.500	0.483	0.466	0.448	0.430	0.411	0.393	0.374	0.355	0.336	0.316
0.70	0.985	0.971	0.946	0.905	0.841	0.799	0.749	0.691	0.624	0.548	0.532	0.516	0.499	0.482	0.465	0.447	0.429	0.411	0.393	0.374	0.355	0.336
0.75	0.986	0.972	0.948	0.908	0.846	0.805	0.757	0.700	0.636	0.562	0.547	0.531	0.514	0.498	0.481	0.464	0.446	0.428	0.410	0.392	0.373	0.354
0.80	0.986	0.973	0.949	0.911	0.851	0.811	0.764	0.709	0.646	0.575	0.560	0.544	0.528	0.512	0.496	0.479	0.462	0.444	0.427	0.409	0.391	0.372
0.82	0.986	0.973	0.950	0.912	0.853	0.814	0.767	0.713	0.650	0.580	0.565	0.549	0.534	0.518	0.501	0.485	0.468	0.451	0.433	0.415	0.397	0.379
0.84	0.986	0.973	0.950	0.913	0.854	0.816	0.770	0.716	0.654	0.585	0.570	0.554	0.539	0.523	0.507	0.490	0.474	0.457	0.439	0.422	0.404	0.386
0.86	0.987	0.974	0.951	0.914	0.856	0.818	0.772	0.719	0.658	0.589	0.575	0.559	0.544	0.528	0.512	0.496	0.479	0.463	0.445	0.428	0.410	0.392
0.88	0.987	0.974	0.652	0.915	0.858	0.820	0.775	0.722	0.662	0.594	0.579	0.564	0.549	0.533	0.518	0.501	0.485	0.468	0.451	0.434	0.417	0.399
0.90	0.987	0.974	0.953	0.916	0.859	0.822	0.777	0.725	0.666	0.598	0.584	0.569	0.554	0.538	0.523	0.507	0.490	0.474	0.457	0.440	0.423	0.405
0.92	0.987	0.975	0.953	0.916	0.861	0.824	0.780	0.728	0.669	0.602	0.588	0.573	0.559	0.543	0.528	0.512	0.496	0.479	0.463	0.446	0.429	0.411
0.94	0.987	0.975	0.953	0.917	0.862	0.826	0.782	0.731	0.673	0.607	0.592	0.578	0.563	0.548	0.533	0.517	0.501	0.485	0.468	0.452	0.435	0.417
0.96	0.987	0.975	0.954	0.918	0.864	0.827	0.784	0.734	0.676	0.611	0.597	0.582	0.568	0.553	0.537	0.522	0.506	0.490	0.474	0.457	0.440	0.423
0.98	0.987	0.975	0.954	0.919	0.865	0.829	0.787	0.737	0.679	0.615	0.601	0.586	0.572	0.557	0.542	0.527	0.511	0.495	0.479	0.463	0.446	0.429
1.00	0.988	0.976	0.954	0.920	0.866	0.831	0.789	0.739	0.683	0.618	0.605	0.591	0.576	0.562	0.547	0.532	0.516	0.500	0.484	0.468	0.451	0.435
1.02	0.988	0.976	0.955	0.921	0.868	0.833	0.791	0.742	0.686	0.622	0.609	0.595	0.580	0.566	0.551	0.536	0.521	0.505	0.489	0.473	0.457	0.440
1.04	0.988	0.976	0.955	0.921	0.869	0.834	0.793	0.744	0.689	0.626	0.612	0.599	0.585	0.570	0.556	0.541	0.526	0.510	0.494	0.478	0.462	0.446
1.06	0.988	0.976	0.956	0.922	0.870	0.836	0.795	0.747	0.692	0.629	0.616	0.602	0.589	0.574	0.560	0.545	0.530	0.515	0.499	0.484	0.467	0.451
1.08	0.988	0.976	0.956	0.923	0.871	0.837	0.797	0.749	0.695	0.633	0.620	0.606	0.592	0.578	0.564	0.550	0.535	0.520	0.504	0.488	0.473	0.456
1.10	0.988	0.977	0.957	0.924	0.873	0.839	0.799	0.752	0.698	0.636	0.623	0.610	0.596	0.582	0.568	0.554	0.539	0.524	0.509	0.493	0.478	0.462
1.12	0.988	0.977	0.957	0.924	0.874	0.840	0.800	0.754	0.700	0.640	0.627	0.614	0.600	0.586	0.572	0.558	0.543	0.529	0.513	0.498	0.483	0.467
1.14	0.988	0.977	0.957	0.925	0.875	0.842	0.802	0.756	0.703	0.643	0.630	0.617	0.604	0.590	0.576	0.562	0.548	0.533	0.518	0.503	0.487	0.472
1.16	0.988	0.977	0.958	0.926	0.876	0.843	0.804	0.758	0.706	0.646	0.634	0.621	0.607	0.594	0.580	0.566	0.552	0.537	0.522	0.507	0.492	0.477
1.18	0.988	0.978	0.958	0.926	0.877	0.844	0.806	0.760	0.708	0.649	0.637	0.624	0.611	0.597	0.584	0.570	0.556	0.541	0.527	0.512	0.497	0.482
1.20	0.989	0.978	0.958	0.927	0.878	0.846	0.807	0.763	0.711	0.653	0.640	0.627	0.614	0.601	0.588	0.574	0.560	0.546	0.531	0.516	0.501	0.486
1.25	0.989	0.978	0.959	0.928	0.881	0.849	0.811	0.768	0.717	0.660	0.648	0.635	0.623	0.610	0.597	0.583	0.569	0.556	0.541	0.527	0.513	0.498
1.30	0.989	0.979	0.960	0.930	0.883	0.852	0.815	0.772	0.723	0.667	0.655	0.643	0.631	0.618	0.605	0.592	0.579	0.565	0.551	0.537	0.523	0.509
1.35	0.989	0.979	0.961	0.931	0.885	0.855	0.819	0.777	0.729	0.674	0.662	0.650	0.638	0.626	0.613	0.600	0.587	0.574	0.561	0.547	0.533	0.519
1.40	0.989	0.979	0.962	0.933	0.888	0.858	0.822	0.781	0.734	0.680	0.669	0.657	0.645	0.633	0.621	0.609	0.596	0.583	0.570	0.557	0.543	0.529
1.45	0.989	0.980	0.962	0.934	0.890	0.860	0.826	0.785	0.739	0.687	0.675	0.664	0.652	0.641	0.629	0.616	0.604	0.591	0.579	0.566	0.552	0.539
1.50	0.990	0.980	0.963	0.935	0.892	0.863	0.829	0.789	0.744	0.692	0.682	0.670	0.659	0.647	0.636	0.624	0.612	0.599	0.587	0.574	0.561	0.549
1.75	0.990	0.982	0.966	0.940	0.900	0.874	0.843	0.806	0.765	0.719	0.709	0.699	0.688	0.678	0.668	0.657	0.646	0.635	0.624	0.613	0.602	0.590
2.00	0.991	0.983	0.968	0.944	0.907	0.883	0.854	0.821	0.783	0.740	0.731	0.722	0.713	0.703	0.694	0.684	0.675	0.665	0.655	0.645	0.635	0.625
2.25	0.991	0.984	0.970	0.948	0.913	0.890	0.863	0.833	0.797	0.758	0.750	0.742	0.733	0.725	0.716	0.708	0.699	0.690	0.681	0.672	0.663	0.655
2.50	0.992	0.985	0.972	0.951	0.918	0.897	0.872	0.843	0.810	0.774	0.766	0.759	0.751	0.743	0.735	0.727	0.719	0.711	0.704	0.696	0.688	0.680
2.75	0.993	0.986	0.973	0.953	0.922	0.902	0.879	0.852	0.821	0.788	0.781	0.773	0.766	0.759	0.752	0.745	0.737	0.730	0.723	0.716	0.709	0.702
3.00	0.993	0.986	0.974	0.955	0.926	0.907	0.885	0.859	0.831	0.799	0.793	0.786	0.780	0.773	0.767	0.760	0.753	0.747	0.740	0.734	0.727	0.721
3.50	0.994	0.987	0.977	0.959	0.933	0.915	0.895	0.872	0.847	0.819	0.814	0.808	0.802	0.797	0.791	0.785	0.780	0.774	0.769	0.763	0.758	0.753
4.00	0.994	0.988	0.978	0.962	0.938	0.922	0.904	0.883	0.860	0.836	0.831	0.826	0.821	0.816	0.811	0.806	0.801	0.796	0.792	0.787	0.783	0.779
4.50	0.994	0.989	0.980	0.965	0.942	0.927	0.911	0.892	0.871	0.849	0.844	0.840	0.836	0.831	0.827	0.823	0.818	0.814	0.810	0.807	0.803	0.799

Share Price Divided by the Present Value of the Exercise Price

Table B.7

Put Option Value for Non-Dividend-Paying Stocks (in decimal form) Relative to Share Price

Standard Deviation Times the Square Root of Time

	0.05	0.10	0.15	0.20	0.25	0.30	0.35	0.40	0.45	0.50	0.55	0.60	0.65	0.70	0.75	0.80	0.85	0.90	0.95	1.00	1.05	1.10
0.40	1.500	1.500	1.500	1.500	1.500	1.500	1.501	1.502	1.505	1.510	1.517	1.525	1.536	1.547	1.561	1.575	1.591	1.607	1.625	1.643	1.661	1.680
0.45	1.222	1.222	1.222	1.222	1.222	1.223	1.224	1.227	1.232	1.239	1.248	1.259	1.272	1.286	1.301	1.317	1.334	1.352	1.370	1.389	1.408	1.428
0.50	1.000	1.000	1.000	1.000	1.000	1.001	1.004	1.009	1.017	1.026	1.038	1.051	1.065	1.081	1.098	1.115	1.133	1.152	1.171	1.191	1.210	1.230
0.55	0.818	0.818	0.818	0.818	0.819	0.822	0.827	0.834	0.844	0.856	0.869	0.884	0.900	0.918	0.935	0.954	0.973	0.992	1.012	1.032	1.052	1.072
0.60	0.667	0.667	0.667	0.667	0.669	0.674	0.681	0.691	0.703	0.717	0.733	0.749	0.767	0.785	0.804	0.823	0.843	0.862	0.882	0.902	0.922	0.942
0.65	0.538	0.538	0.539	0.540	0.544	0.551	0.561	0.574	0.588	0.604	0.621	0.639	0.658	0.677	0.696	0.716	0.736	0.755	0.775	0.795	0.815	0.835
0.70	0.429	0.429	0.429	0.432	0.439	0.449	0.462	0.477	0.493	0.511	0.529	0.548	0.567	0.587	0.606	0.626	0.646	0.666	0.686	0.706	0.726	0.745
0.75	0.333	0.333	0.335	0.341	0.351	0.364	0.380	0.396	0.414	0.433	0.452	0.472	0.491	0.511	0.531	0.551	0.571	0.591	0.611	0.630	0.650	0.669
0.80	0.250	0.250	0.255	0.265	0.278	0.294	0.312	0.330	0.349	0.368	0.388	0.408	0.428	0.448	0.468	0.487	0.507	0.527	0.546	0.566	0.585	0.604
0.82	0.220	0.220	0.227	0.238	0.253	0.270	0.288	0.307	0.326	0.345	0.365	0.385	0.405	0.425	0.445	0.465	0.484	0.504	0.523	0.542	0.561	0.580
0.84	0.190	0.192	0.200	0.213	0.229	0.247	0.266	0.285	0.304	0.324	0.344	0.364	0.384	0.404	0.424	0.443	0.463	0.482	0.501	0.520	0.539	0.558
0.86	0.163	0.166	0.176	0.191	0.208	0.226	0.245	0.265	0.284	0.304	0.324	0.344	0.364	0.384	0.404	0.423	0.443	0.462	0.481	0.500	0.518	0.537
0.88	0.136	0.141	0.154	0.170	0.188	0.207	0.226	0.246	0.266	0.286	0.306	0.326	0.345	0.365	0.385	0.404	0.424	0.443	0.462	0.480	0.499	0.517
0.90	0.111	0.119	0.134	0.151	0.170	0.189	0.209	0.229	0.249	0.268	0.288	0.308	0.328	0.348	0.367	0.386	0.406	0.424	0.443	0.462	0.480	0.498
0.92	0.088	0.099	0.115	0.134	0.153	0.173	0.192	0.212	0.232	0.252	0.272	0.292	0.311	0.331	0.350	0.370	0.389	0.407	0.426	0.444	0.463	0.480
0.94	0.067	0.081	0.099	0.118	0.138	0.158	0.177	0.197	0.217	0.237	0.257	0.277	0.296	0.315	0.335	0.354	0.372	0.391	0.410	0.428	0.446	0.464
0.96	0.048	0.065	0.084	0.104	0.124	0.144	0.164	0.183	0.203	0.223	0.243	0.262	0.281	0.301	0.320	0.339	0.357	0.376	0.394	0.412	0.430	0.447
0.98	0.032	0.051	0.071	0.091	0.111	0.131	0.151	0.171	0.190	0.210	0.229	0.249	0.268	0.287	0.306	0.324	0.343	0.361	0.379	0.397	0.415	0.432
1.00	0.020	0.040	0.060	0.080	0.100	0.119	0.139	0.159	0.178	0.197	0.217	0.236	0.255	0.274	0.292	0.311	0.329	0.347	0.365	0.383	0.400	0.418
1.02	0.011	0.030	0.050	0.069	0.089	0.109	0.128	0.147	0.167	0.186	0.205	0.224	0.243	0.261	0.280	0.298	0.316	0.334	0.352	0.369	0.387	0.404
1.04	0.006	0.023	0.041	0.060	0.080	0.099	0.118	0.137	0.156	0.175	0.194	0.213	0.231	0.250	0.268	0.286	0.304	0.322	0.339	0.357	0.374	0.391
1.06	0.003	0.017	0.034	0.052	0.071	0.090	0.109	0.127	0.146	0.165	0.183	0.202	0.220	0.238	0.257	0.275	0.292	0.310	0.327	0.344	0.361	0.378
1.08	0.001	0.012	0.028	0.045	0.063	0.082	0.100	0.118	0.137	0.155	0.174	0.192	0.210	0.228	0.246	0.264	0.281	0.299	0.316	0.333	0.349	0.366
1.10	*	0.009	0.023	0.039	0.056	0.074	0.092	0.110	0.128	0.146	0.164	0.182	0.200	0.218	0.236	0.253	0.271	0.288	0.305	0.322	0.338	0.355
1.12	*	0.006	0.018	0.034	0.050	0.067	0.085	0.102	0.120	0.138	0.156	0.173	0.191	0.209	0.226	0.243	0.261	0.278	0.294	0.311	0.327	0.344
1.14	*	0.004	0.015	0.029	0.044	0.061	0.078	0.095	0.113	0.130	0.148	0.165	0.182	0.200	0.217	0.234	0.251	0.268	0.284	0.301	0.317	0.333
1.16	*	0.003	0.012	0.025	0.039	0.055	0.072	0.089	0.106	0.123	0.140	0.157	0.174	0.191	0.208	0.225	0.242	0.258	0.275	0.291	0.307	0.323
1.18	*	0.002	0.009	0.021	0.035	0.050	0.066	0.082	0.099	0.116	0.133	0.150	0.166	0.183	0.200	0.217	0.233	0.250	0.266	0.282	0.298	0.313
1.20	*	0.001	0.007	0.018	0.031	0.045	0.061	0.077	0.093	0.109	0.126	0.142	0.159	0.176	0.192	0.209	0.225	0.241	0.257	0.273	0.289	0.304
1.25	*	*	0.004	0.012	0.023	0.035	0.049	0.064	0.079	0.095	0.110	0.126	0.142	0.158	0.174	0.190	0.206	0.221	0.237	0.252	0.268	0.283
1.30	*	*	0.002	0.008	0.017	0.027	0.040	0.053	0.068	0.082	0.097	0.112	0.127	0.143	0.158	0.173	0.189	0.204	0.219	0.234	0.249	0.263
1.35	*	*	0.001	0.005	0.012	0.021	0.032	0.045	0.058	0.071	0.085	0.100	0.114	0.129	0.144	0.159	0.173	0.188	0.203	0.217	0.232	0.246
1.40	*	*	*	0.003	0.009	0.017	0.026	0.037	0.049	0.062	0.075	0.089	0.103	0.117	0.131	0.145	0.160	0.174	0.188	0.202	0.216	0.230
1.45	*	*	*	0.002	0.006	0.013	0.021	0.031	0.042	0.054	0.067	0.079	0.093	0.106	0.120	0.133	0.147	0.161	0.175	0.188	0.202	0.215
1.50	*	*	*	0.001	0.004	0.010	0.017	0.026	0.036	0.047	0.059	0.071	0.084	0.097	0.110	0.123	0.136	0.149	0.163	0.176	0.189	0.202
1.75	*	*	*	*	*	0.003	0.006	0.011	0.017	0.024	0.033	0.042	0.051	0.061	0.072	0.083	0.094	0.105	0.116	0.127	0.139	0.150
2.00	*	*	*	*	*	*	0.002	0.005	0.008	0.013	0.019	0.025	0.033	0.040	0.049	0.058	0.067	0.076	0.086	0.095	0.105	0.115
2.25	*	*	*	*	*	*	*	0.002	0.004	0.007	0.011	0.016	0.021	0.027	0.034	0.041	0.049	0.057	0.065	0.073	0.082	0.090
2.50	*	*	*	*	*	*	*	*	0.002	0.004	0.007	0.010	0.014	0.019	0.024	0.030	0.036	0.043	0.050	0.057	0.065	0.072
2.75	*	*	*	*	*	*	*	*	0.001	0.002	0.004	0.007	0.010	0.013	0.018	0.022	0.028	0.033	0.039	0.045	0.052	0.059
3.00	*	*	*	*	*	*	*	*	*	0.001	0.003	0.004	0.007	0.010	0.013	0.017	0.021	0.026	0.031	0.037	0.042	0.048
3.50	*	*	*	*	*	*	*	*	*	*	0.001	0.002	0.003	0.005	0.007	0.010	0.013	0.017	0.021	0.025	0.029	0.034
4.00	*	*	*	*	*	*	*	*	*	*	*	0.001	0.002	0.003	0.004	0.006	0.009	0.011	0.014	0.017	0.021	0.025
4.50	*	*	*	*	*	*	*	*	*	*	*	*	0.001	0.002	0.003	0.004	0.006	0.008	0.010	0.013	0.015	0.018

Share Price Divided by the Present Value of the Exercise Price

*Value is zero to three decimal places.

Put Option Value (Continued)

Standard Deviation Times the Square Root of Time

	1.15	1.20	1.25	1.30	1.35	1.40	1.45	1.50	1.55	1.60	1.65	1.70	1.75	2.00	2.25	2.50	2.75	3.00	3.50	4.00	4.50	5.00
0.40	1.700	1.719	1.739	1.759	1.779	1.799	1.819	1.838	1.858	1.878	1.897	1.916	1.935	2.025	2.107	2.179	2.242	2.295	2.376	2.429	2.462	2.481
0.45	1.448	1.468	1.487	1.507	1.527	1.547	1.567	1.586	1.606	1.625	1.644	1.663	1.681	1.769	1.847	1.917	1.977	2.028	2.105	2.155	2.186	2.204
0.50	1.250	1.270	1.290	1.310	1.330	1.349	1.369	1.388	1.407	1.426	1.444	1.462	1.480	1.565	1.641	1.708	1.766	1.814	1.888	1.936	1.966	1.983
0.55	1.091	1.111	1.131	1.151	1.170	1.190	1.209	1.228	1.246	1.265	1.283	1.300	1.318	1.400	1.474	1.538	1.593	1.640	1.711	1.757	1.785	1.802
0.60	0.962	0.982	1.001	1.021	1.040	1.059	1.078	1.096	1.114	1.132	1.150	1.167	1.184	1.264	1.335	1.397	1.451	1.496	1.564	1.608	1.635	1.651
0.65	0.865	0.874	0.893	0.912	0.931	0.950	0.968	0.986	1.004	1.021	1.039	1.055	1.072	1.150	1.219	1.279	1.330	1.374	1.440	1.482	1.508	1.523
0.70	0.764	0.784	0.802	0.821	0.840	0.858	0.876	0.893	0.911	0.928	0.945	0.961	0.977	1.052	1.119	1.178	1.227	1.270	1.333	1.374	1.399	1.414
0.75	0.688	0.707	0.725	0.744	0.762	0.779	0.797	0.814	0.831	0.848	0.864	0.880	0.896	0.969	1.034	1.090	1.139	1.180	1.241	1.281	1.305	1.319
0.80	0.622	0.641	0.659	0.677	0.694	0.712	0.729	0.746	0.762	0.778	0.794	0.810	0.825	0.896	0.959	1.014	1.061	1.101	1.161	1.199	1.223	1.236
0.82	0.599	0.617	0.635	0.653	0.670	0.687	0.704	0.721	0.737	0.753	0.769	0.784	0.799	0.870	0.932	0.987	1.033	1.072	1.131	1.169	1.193	1.206
0.84	0.576	0.594	0.612	0.630	0.647	0.664	0.681	0.697	0.714	0.729	0.745	0.760	0.775	0.845	0.907	0.960	1.006	1.045	1.103	1.141	1.164	1.177
0.86	0.555	0.573	0.591	0.608	0.625	0.642	0.659	0.675	0.691	0.707	0.722	0.727	0.752	0.821	0.882	0.935	0.981	1.019	1.076	1.114	1.136	1.149
0.88	0.535	0.553	0.570	0.588	0.605	0.621	0.638	0.654	0.670	0.685	0.701	0.716	0.730	0.798	0.859	0.911	0.956	0.994	1.051	1.088	1.110	1.123
0.90	0.516	0.534	0.551	0.568	0.585	0.602	0.618	0.634	0.650	0.665	0.680	0.695	0.709	0.777	0.837	0.889	0.933	0.970	1.027	1.063	1.085	1.098
0.92	0.498	0.516	0.533	0.550	0.566	0.583	0.599	0.615	0.630	0.645	0.660	0.675	0.689	0.756	0.815	0.867	0.911	0.948	1.003	1.040	1.061	1.074
0.94	0.481	0.498	0.515	0.532	0.549	0.565	0.581	0.597	0.612	0.627	0.642	0.656	0.670	0.737	0.795	0.847	0.889	0.926	0.981	1.017	1.039	1.051
0.96	0.465	0.482	0.499	0.515	0.532	0.548	0.564	0.579	0.594	0.609	0.624	0.638	0.652	0.718	0.776	0.826	0.869	0.905	0.960	0.995	1.017	1.029
0.98	0.449	0.466	0.483	0.500	0.516	0.532	0.547	0.563	0.578	0.592	0.607	0.621	0.635	0.700	0.757	0.807	0.850	0.885	0.939	0.974	0.996	1.008
1.00	0.435	0.451	0.468	0.484	0.500	0.516	0.532	0.547	0.562	0.576	0.591	0.605	0.618	0.683	0.739	0.789	0.831	0.866	0.920	0.954	0.976	0.988
1.02	0.421	0.437	0.454	0.470	0.486	0.501	0.517	0.532	0.546	0.561	0.575	0.589	0.603	0.666	0.722	0.771	0.813	0.848	0.901	0.935	0.956	0.968
1.04	0.407	0.424	0.440	0.456	0.472	0.487	0.502	0.517	0.532	0.546	0.560	0.574	0.587	0.650	0.706	0.754	0.796	0.831	0.883	0.917	0.938	0.949
1.06	0.395	0.411	0.427	0.443	0.458	0.474	0.489	0.503	0.518	0.532	0.546	0.560	0.573	0.635	0.690	0.738	0.779	0.814	0.866	0.899	0.920	0.931
1.08	0.382	0.399	0.414	0.430	0.445	0.461	0.475	0.490	0.504	0.518	0.532	0.546	0.559	0.621	0.675	0.723	0.763	0.797	0.849	0.882	0.902	0.914
1.10	0.371	0.387	0.402	0.418	0.433	0.448	0.463	0.477	0.492	0.505	0.519	0.532	0.546	0.607	0.661	0.708	0.748	0.782	0.833	0.866	0.886	0.897
1.12	0.360	0.375	0.391	0.406	0.421	0.436	0.451	0.465	0.479	0.493	0.506	0.520	0.533	0.593	0.647	0.693	0.733	0.767	0.817	0.850	0.870	0.881
1.14	0.349	0.365	0.380	0.395	0.410	0.425	0.439	0.453	0.467	0.481	0.494	0.507	0.520	0.580	0.633	0.679	0.719	0.752	0.802	0.835	0.854	0.866
1.16	0.339	0.354	0.369	0.384	0.399	0.414	0.428	0.442	0.456	0.469	0.483	0.496	0.508	0.568	0.620	0.666	0.705	0.738	0.788	0.820	0.839	0.851
1.18	0.329	0.344	0.359	0.374	0.389	0.403	0.417	0.431	0.445	0.458	0.471	0.484	0.497	0.556	0.608	0.653	0.692	0.725	0.774	0.806	0.825	0.836
1.20	0.320	0.335	0.350	0.364	0.379	0.393	0.407	0.421	0.434	0.448	0.461	0.473	0.486	0.544	0.596	0.641	0.679	0.712	0.760	0.792	0.811	0.822
1.25	0.298	0.313	0.327	0.341	0.356	0.369	0.383	0.397	0.410	0.423	0.435	0.448	0.460	0.517	0.568	0.611	0.649	0.681	0.728	0.759	0.778	0.789
1.30	0.278	0.292	0.307	0.321	0.334	0.348	0.361	0.374	0.387	0.400	0.412	0.424	0.436	0.492	0.542	0.585	0.621	0.652	0.699	0.729	0.748	0.758
1.35	0.260	0.274	0.288	0.302	0.315	0.328	0.341	0.354	0.367	0.379	0.391	0.403	0.415	0.469	0.518	0.560	0.596	0.626	0.672	0.702	0.720	0.730
1.40	0.244	0.257	0.271	0.284	0.297	0.310	0.323	0.335	0.348	0.360	0.372	0.383	0.395	0.448	0.495	0.537	0.572	0.602	0.647	0.676	0.694	0.704
1.45	0.229	0.242	0.255	0.268	0.281	0.294	0.306	0.318	0.330	0.342	0.354	0.365	0.376	0.429	0.475	0.515	0.550	0.579	0.623	0.652	0.669	0.679
1.50	0.215	0.228	0.241	0.254	0.266	0.278	0.290	0.302	0.314	0.326	0.337	0.348	0.359	0.410	0.456	0.495	0.530	0.558	0.602	0.630	0.647	0.657
1.75	0.162	0.173	0.184	0.195	0.206	0.217	0.228	0.239	0.249	0.260	0.270	0.280	0.290	0.336	0.378	0.414	0.445	0.472	0.511	0.537	0.553	0.562
2.00	0.125	0.135	0.145	0.155	0.165	0.175	0.184	0.194	0.203	0.213	0.222	0.231	0.240	0.283	0.321	0.354	0.383	0.407	0.444	0.468	0.483	0.491
2.25	0.099	0.108	0.117	0.125	0.134	0.143	0.152	0.161	0.169	0.178	0.186	0.195	0.203	0.242	0.277	0.308	0.335	0.357	0.392	0.415	0.428	0.436
2.50	0.080	0.088	0.096	0.104	0.111	0.119	0.127	0.135	0.143	0.151	0.159	0.166	0.174	0.210	0.243	0.272	0.297	0.318	0.351	0.372	0.385	0.392
2.75	0.065	0.072	0.079	0.087	0.094	0.101	0.108	0.116	0.123	0.130	0.137	0.144	0.151	0.185	0.215	0.242	0.266	0.286	0.317	0.337	0.349	0.356
3.00	0.054	0.061	0.067	0.073	0.080	0.087	0.093	0.100	0.107	0.113	0.120	0.126	0.133	0.164	0.193	0.218	0.240	0.260	0.289	0.308	0.320	0.326
3.50	0.039	0.044	0.049	0.054	0.060	0.065	0.071	0.077	0.082	0.088	0.094	0.099	0.105	0.133	0.158	0.181	0.201	0.218	0.245	0.262	0.273	0.279
4.00	0.029	0.033	0.037	0.042	0.046	0.051	0.056	0.061	0.066	0.071	0.076	0.081	0.086	0.110	0.133	0.154	0.172	0.188	0.212	0.228	0.238	0.244
4.50	0.022	0.025	0.029	0.033	0.037	0.041	0.045	0.049	0.053	0.058	0.062	0.067	0.071	0.093	0.114	0.133	0.150	0.164	0.187	0.202	0.211	0.217

Share Price Divided by the Present Value of the Exercise Price

APPENDIX

C

Answers to Selected Problems

(All answers are based on using formulas or a financial calculator for present and future values and the Black-Scholes formulas for option values.)

Chapter 1

1.2 $24,900.

Chapter 2

2.3   a. $73,000.
      b. $133,500.

2.10   a. $1,496.18.
      b. $1,630.84.
      c. $1,880.83.

2.17   a.   7.23%.
      b.   6.04%.
      c.   Approximately 10%.
      d.   7.23%

2.20   a. $30,000.
      b. $37,500.
      c. $24,793; $32,150.

2.21   a.   12%, 15%, and 11.05%.

Chapter 3

3.3   a.   7.02%.
     b.   11.92%.

3.6.   a.   16%.
      b.   14.71%.

3.11 $26.12.

3.13 $11.71.

3A.2   a.   6.95%, 6.91%, 7.13%, and 7.30%.

Chapter 4

4.4   a.   12.5%.
     b.   9%, 7.81%, and 4.58%.

4.10   13.49%.

4.13   28.44%.

4.17   a.   9.90%
      b.   0.99
      c.   0.20, 0.55, and 0.25.

4A3.   a.   10.5% and 10%.
      b.   26.31% and 14.84%.
      c.   10.375% and 23.08%.

Chapter 5

5.3 **a.** $15.36.
      b. $12.83.

5.6 **a.** $12.58 and $15.06.
      b. $21.82 and $5.42.

5.10 **a.** $1.49.
      b. $3.73.
      c. $0.40.

5.15 **a.** $41.91 million and $18.09 million.
      b. $4.76 million.

Chapter 6

6.5 **a.** 9%.
      b. 11.37%, 19%, and 17%.
      d. 15.79%.
      e. 13.66%.

6.7 **a.** 14.18%.
      b. 16.58%.

6.12 9.50%, 9.80%, and 10.20%.

6.15 **a.** 0.987 and 1.119.
      b. 16.25% and 17.40%.

Chapter 7

7.4 $NPV_X = \$9,986$;
      $NPV_Y = \$13,525$;
      $IRR_X = 15.78\%$; $IRR_Y = 14.19\%$.

7.9 **a.** 19% and 15%.
      b. $3,006 and $4,924.
      c. 13.98%.
      d. 16.21% and 14.09%.

7.13 **a.** $436 and $600.
      b. $201 and $192.

7.14 −$8,625, −$10,674, and −$10,903.

Chapter 8

8.5 −$23,678.

8.8 **a.** $545.
      b. −$104,973.

8.13 $8,650.

8.17 **a.** $2,112.
      b. −$492.

8.19 **a.** $26,143 and −$15,913.

Chapter 9

9.1 **a.** $2,000.

9.7 −$101,454.

9.9 **a.** $45,933.
      b. −$111,679 and −$27,375.

9.13 **a.** $476,893.

Chapter 10

10.4 $1,516.88.

10.7 $2.98, $2.44, and $12.90.

10.11 $54.

10.14 $8.

10.17 $6.38 and $6.46.

Chapter 11

11.3 **a.** $285,429.
      b. $1,110,000.

11.6 **a.** $16,000,000.
      b. $20,000,000.

11.9 **a.** $60,000.
      b. 28.57%.
      c. $10,000.

Chapter 12

12.1 a. $505.83 million.
      b. $514 million and $490 million.

12.5 a. $4.80.
      b. $290,000.
      c. $4.97 and $5.28.

12.8 a. $2.60 and $3.6725.
      b. $26.
      c. $30.60.

12A.1 0.39 and 0.22.

Chapter 13

13.1 a. $200,000.
      b. −$200,000 and $400,000.

13.5 a. $4.00.
      b. $4.00 and $3.97.

13.9 $93.75.

13.11 3-for-1.

Chapter 14

14.2 14.30%.

14.4 a. 8.00%.
      b. 6%.
      c. $47,381.

14.6 a. −$370,798.
      b. −$1,268,581.
      c. −$1,730,798.
      d. $3,485,651.

14.7 $48,932.

Chapter 15

15.1 a. $29,515,000.
      b. 1.62%.

15.5 a. 2.
      b. 3.

15.8 450,000.

15.10 95%.

Chapter 16

16.1 $14 million.

16.6 a. 8.15%.
      b. 8.5%.
      c. 7.62%.
      d. 7.86%.

16.11 a. $88.889.
       b. 112,500.

16.13 a. $29.64 and $29.51.

16A.1 $2,546,246.

Chapter 17

17.1 $13.88.

17.4 a. $771.82.
      b. $13.18.
      c. $11.71.
      d. $1,006.02.

17.9 b. $22.

17.11 a. $39.78 and $40.95.
       b. $63.92 and $61.96.

Chapter 18

18.1 $364,926.

18.5 a. −$3,172.
      b. $11,636.
      c. $14,762.

18.13 $53,685.

18.14 a. 11.51%.
       c. 10.05%.

Chapter 19

19.2 a. 54.75.
      b. 21.17.
      c. 9.73.

19.5 a. $57.07.
      b. $53.82.
      c. $55.77.
      d. $68.80, $70,24, $66.24, and $68.64.

19.10 **a.** $5, $9, $13, $11, $7,
$11, $15, and $13.
b. $20, $24, $28, $26,
$22, $26, $30, and $28.
c. $600,000.

Chapter 20 **20.3** $0.40274.

20.9 6.43.

20.12 **a.** $16,774.74, $50,324.22,
and $22,366.32.
b. $18,391.82, $55,175.46,
and $24,522.43.
c. $18,070.04, $54,210.18,
and $24,093.39.

20.14 **a.** 10.29%
b. 10.71%

Chapter 21 **21.3** $152,250 and −$17,660.

21.5 46.25%.

21.8 $61,740.

21.13 **a.** $385,808.
b. $94,726.

Chapter 22 **22.4** **a.** 11.04%
b. 13.10%.

22.7 10.51%.

22.9 **a.** 16.00%.
b. 15.56%.
c. 13.86%.

22.12 **a.** 22.16%.
b. 16.66%.

22.15 **a.** 21.31%.
b. 19.33%.

Chapter 23 **23.1** 4.08.

23.3 **a.** 2.76.
c. 0.824.

23.7 **a.** $55,352.
b. $14,773.

Chapter 24 **24.3** 42.9%.

24.4 **a.** 29.2, 7.5, and 1.0.
b. $37,500.
c. $30,000.

24.10 **a.** 2.0, 5.0%, 10.0%, and 20.0%.
b. $55,500, $120,000, and 22.2%.

Chapter 25 **25.2** **a.** $2,159.8, $2,386.5,
and $2,613.2.

25.4 $45 million and −$30 million.

25.8 **a.** $Y_t = \$275.89 + \$9.67X_t$.
b. $402, $411, $421, $431, $440,
$450, $460, and $469.
c. 1.015, 0.875, 0.945, and 1.165.
d. $408, $360, $398, $502, $447,
$394, $435, and $546.

25.10 **a.** $1.5 million.
b. $6.7 million and 64.7%.

Chapter 26   26.3 $143,881.   26.9 $43.75 million and 1.21.

26.8   a. $52,017 and $36,558.   26.10   a.   20%.
        b.   −$41,677 and −$25,261.   b. $37.

Chapter 27   27.4   1,298.544.   27.8 $736.

27.6   −$19,821.

Chapter 28   28.3   b. $328,407.   28.9   a.   Yes.
                                                    b.   5.30.
28.6   b.   9 contracts.
        c. $23,769.

Glossary

abandonment decision Capital budgeting decision where the net present value of continuing to operate is compared with the after-tax proceeds if the project is discontinued.

ABC method Inventory control procedure where items are grouped in categories by their value. Group A items require high investment and the most control.

adjustable rate preferred stock Preferred stock where the cash dividend rate is tied to a U.S. Treasury security index and is adjusted quarterly.

adjustable discount rate NPV Net present value if the discount rate is a weighted cost of equity and debt, such as the firm's opportunity cost of capital or some divisional discount rate.

adjusted present value Base-case net present value of a project if financed solely with equity plus the present value of any financing side effects.

advance factoring Short-term financing in which a lender (factor) provides a loan against a firm's receivables.

agency costs The sum of financial contracting costs, costs of monitoring, and loss of wealth when agents' pursue their own interests.

agency relationship Results when there is a principal and an agent to whom decision making authority is delegated. Agency relationships involve management, stockholders, creditors and/or other stakeholders.

American option A call or put option that can be exercised at any time up to and including its expiration date.

amortization schedule Schedule that shows how a term loan will be paid off by specifying both the principal and interest payments made per payment.

annual percentage rate, APR Legally specified nominal interest rate determined by multiplying the periodic per period rate by the number of periods in the year.

annual percentage yield, APY Legally specified compound annual effective interest rate that must be reported for all deposit accounts.

annual report Report issued to stockholders by corporations that contains basic accounting statements as well as management's opinion of the past year's operations and prospects for the future.

annuity A series of equal cash flows for a specified number of periods.

annuity due A series of equal cash flows for a specified number of periods, with each cash flow occurring at the beginning of the period.

arbitrage pricing theory Theory that specifies the required return on any asset is a function of a number of factors, not just the risk-free rate and the expected return on the market portfolio as given by the capital asset pricing model.

arrearages An overdue payment; used to describe cash dividends on cumulative preferred stock that have not been paid.

asset beta Unlevered beta that indicates the riskiness of the firm's assets, without regard for how the firm is financed. Beta for an all-equity firm or unlevered set of assets.

asset substitution Occurs when a firm invests in more risky assets than those expected by the firm's bondholders (or other creditors).

assignment An out-of-court procedure for liquidating a firm.

asymmetric information Condition when information is known to some, but not all, of the concerned parties.

automated clearing house, ACH System employed to move funds electronically based on batch processing of information.

average collection float The number of days of float times the average daily dollar amount in the collection system.

bad debt Occurs when a seller extends credit to a buyer, and the buyer fails to pay the account.

balance sheet Accounting statement that records the assets of the firm and claims against them (liabilities and equities), as of a specific moment in time.

bank discount yield How yields are figured on Treasury bills.

banker's acceptance A draft drawn on a specific bank by a seller to obtain payment for goods that have been shipped (sold) to a customer. The bank, by accepting (or endorsing), assumes the obligation of payment at the due date.

bankruptcy costs Includes legal and other direct costs associated with bankruptcy or reorganization procedures.

basis The difference between the futures price and the spot price of a futures contract.

bearer form Bonds that are not registered (or recorded) by the firm (or its agency). No owner's name appears on the bond certificate, so whoever holds it is the owner.

best efforts Procedure for selling a security issue in which an investment banking firm agrees to market the issue, but it is not underwritten and there is no guarantee the full amount of the issue will be sold.

beta, β_j A measure of an asset's non-diversifiable, or systematic, risk. Calculated by (1) regressing the returns for an asset against the returns for the market portfolio or (2) dividing the covariance between the returns on an asset and the market portfolio by the variance on the market's return.

bidding firm The firm that is buying another firm in a merger or acquisition.

bill of lading Shipping document that authorizes the shipment of goods from one party (the seller) to another (the customer).

binomial option pricing model Option pricing model in which the underlying asset can take on only two possible (discrete) values in the next time period for each possible value in the present time period.

Black-Scholes option pricing model A model for valuing European call or put options which assumes the distribution for the instantaneous rate of return on the underlying asset is normal and constant over time.

blue sky laws State laws pertaining to security market regulation.

bond A long-term (typically 10 years or more) promissory note issued by the borrower promising to pay a specified interest per year and/or maturity value.

bond equivalent yield Means of converting bank discount yield on Treasury bills to an approximate 365-day annualized yield.

bond rating Estimates supplied of the probability of repayment of principal and interest on a bond.

book value Assets minus liabilities, or stockholders' equity.

book value per share Common shareholders' equity divided by the number of shares of common stock outstanding.

break-even analysis Analysis of the level of sales at which a project's NPV is just equal to zero.

business risk Source of risk because of the basic nature of the industry in which the firm operates.

call option The right, but not the obligation, to purchase an asset at a stated price within a specified time period.

call premium The difference between a bond's or preferred stock's par value and what the firm has to pay to call it for retirement.

call provision Stipulation in a bond or preferred stock issue allowing the firm to retire the securities before maturity.

capital asset pricing model, CAPM A model of required rates of return for financial assets. The required rate of return is equal to the risk-free rate plus a risk premium based on the expected return on the market portfolio and the asset's non-diversifiable risk as measured by beta.

capital budget A statement of the firm's planned long-term investment projects, usually done annually.

capital budgeting The process by which long-term investments are generated, analyzed, and placed on the capital budget.

capital budgeting process The four capital budgeting steps are: search and identification of growth opportunities; estimating the magnitude, timing and riskiness of cash flows; selection or rejection; and control and postcompletion audit.

capital lease A lease that meets certain GAAP requirements and accordingly must be capitalized and shown as both an asset and a liability on the firm's balance sheet.

capital market Financial market where long-term (longer than 1-year) financial assets such as bonds, preferred stock, or common stock are bought or sold.

capital market line Set of all efficient portfolios consisting of various combinations of the risk-free asset and the market portfolio.

capital rationing A situation where a constraint is placed on the funds available such that some wealth-maximizing capital budgeting projects cannot be accepted.

capital structure The long-term financing of the firm, typically represented by bonds, leases, preferred stock, and common stock.

cash budget A detailed forecast of all expected cash inflows and outflows by the firm for some period of time.

cash conversion cycle The net time interval in days between actual cash expenditure by the firm on its productive resources and the ultimate recovery of cash.

cash discount A provision often included in a firm's credit terms. Payment within the discount period allows the customer to reduce the cost of the purchase.

cash dividend The distribution to investors who own common or preferred stock of some of the firm's cash.

cash flow The actual cash coming into a firm (cash inflow) or paid out by a firm (cash outflow).

cash flow after tax, CF Equals cash flow before tax minus taxes (CFBT − taxes); or cash flow before tax times 1 minus the marginal tax rate, plus depreciation for tax purposes times the marginal tax rate $[CFBT(1 - T) + Dep(T)]$.

cash flow before tax, CFBT Equals cash inflows minus cash outflows.

cash offering Primary market transaction in which a firm sells securities to the general public for cash.

cash on delivery, COD Term of sale where payment is required at the time the goods are delivered to the buyer.

certificate of deposit, CD A short-term time deposit issued by a bank.

characteristic line A line indicating the relationship between the rates of return on an asset or portfolio and the corresponding rates of return on the market portfolio.

chief financial officer, CFO The individual ultimately responsible for making and implementing financial decisions in a firm.

Clearing House Interbank Payment System, CHIPS International wire transfer system.

clientele effect The tendency of firms to attract a certain kind of stockholder, depending on the cash dividend policy maintained by the firm.

coefficient of variation, CV A measure of relative riskiness calculated by dividing the standard deviation by the mean (or expected value) of the distribution.

commercial paper Short-term nonsecured promissory note issued by commercial finance and industrial firms. The maximum maturity is 270 days.

commitment fee   A fee charged by the lender on a line of credit; generally charged on the unused portion of the line.

common-size statement   Accounting statement expressed in percentage terms.

common stock   A document that represents (residual) ownership in a corporation. The common stockholder is the last to receive any distribution of earnings or assets.

compensating balance   Money on deposit with a bank to compensate the bank for services rendered.

complementary projects   Two or more capital budgeting projects that interact positively so that the total cash flows, if all are undertaken, are more than the simple sum of their individual cash flows.

composition   Out-of-court agreement between a firm and its creditors whereby the creditors receive less than the total amount due them in full settlement of their claim.

compound rate   Rate applicable when interest is earned not only on the initial principal, but also on the accumulated interest from previous periods.

consol   Perpetual coupon rate bond.

constant growth model   Form of the dividend valuation model in which cash dividends are expected to grow at a constant percentage rate, g, until infinity. The price of the stock is $P_0 = D_1/(k_s - g)$.

controlled disbursing   System in which the firm directs checks to be drawn on a bank that is in a small- or medium-size city to maximize the amount of transit float before the check is finally deducted from the firm's demand deposit account.

controller (comptroller)   The individual in a firm who normally is responsible for preparing financial statements, for cost accounting, for internal auditing, for budgeting, and for the tax department.

conversion price   The effective price paid for common stock by converting a convertible security into common stock.

conversion ratio   The number of shares of common stock received for converting a convertible security; equals the par value of the convertible divided by the conversion price.

conversion value   The value of a convertible security in terms of the common stock into which it can be converted. It equals the conversion ratio times the market price per share of common stock.

convertible security   Bond or preferred stock that, at the option of the owner, may be exchanged for a predetermined number of shares of common stock.

corporation   A legal entity formed to conduct business and given the power to act as an individual and limited liability.

correlation   A statistical measure of the degree of linear relationship between two random variables. It can vary from +1.0 (perfect positive correlation), to 0.0 (no relationship), to −1.0 (perfect negative correlation).

coupon interest rate   The stated percentage rate of interest on a bond relative to its par value.

covariance   A statistical measure of the degree of linear relationship between two random variables. Similar to correlation except the covariance is not bounded by plus and minus one.

credit scoring model   Point-based system used to determine the creditworthiness of customers based on key financial and credit characteristics.

creditors   Persons or firms to which money is owed. The firm's creditors include those that have fixed-type financial claims on the firm arising from short- or long-term debt.

cross-hedge   Hedge required where no futures contract exists in the underlying asset or commodity being hedged.

cumulative   Provision in many preferred stocks and income bonds which requires that all past cash dividends or interest be paid in full before any additional dividend or interest is paid.

cumulative voting   System of electing the board of directors whereby each share is entitled to 1 vote. By voting more than once for a single director, cumulative voting encourages minority representation on the board of directors.

current ratio   Current assets divided by current liabilities.

days inventory   The number of days of the year, 365 divided by the inventory turnover.

days payable The number of days in the year, 365, divided by payables turnover.

days purchases outstanding Accounts payable divided by credit purchases per day.

days sales outstanding Accounts receivable divided by the average sales per day (sales/365 days).

debenture Unsecured long-term borrowing by a firm backed only by its full faith and credit.

debt capacity The amount of debt or debt-type securities (like leases and preferred stock) a firm can service.

deep discount bond Bond whose coupon interest rate is set substantially below the prevailing market interest rate at the time of issue. Accordingly, the bond must be sold at a discount from its par (maturity) value.

default premium Additional return required to compensate an investor for the risk that the bond issuer will not be able to make interest payments or repay the principal amount on schedule, or that the firm issuing stock will fail.

defeasance To "render null and void." Procedure whereby a firm, through a trustee, sets aside enough Treasury securities to meet the interest and principal payments on some of the firm's outstanding debt.

deferred taxes A liability account on the balance sheet that represents the additional income tax due in the future arising because the firm has claimed larger expenses (primarily depreciation) for tax purposes than for GAAP accounting purposes.

depreciable life An asset's normal recovery period specified by the Internal Revenue Service for tax purposes.

depreciation For tax purposes, depreciable lives and amounts are provided by the Internal Revenue Service. (For accounting purposes, an annual charge against current income to record the wear and tear of assets.)

derivatives Futures, options, swaps and other custom-tailored financial instruments whose value is tied to fluctuations in other securities or markets.

dilution Reduction in the percentage ownership and income to which each share of common stock is entitled.

direct placement Sale of securities from the firm to the ultimate purchaser, without the services of an investment banking firm.

direct send When the depositing bank sends a check to another bank or clearing system (thereby eliminating the local Federal Reserve bank) to speed the check clearing process.

discount (on a bond) Difference between the current market price on a bond selling below its par value and its par value.

discount interest Process whereby a lender deducts the interest at the start of the loan.

discount rate The rate used to calculate the present value of future cash flows.

diversifiable risk That part of an asset's total risk that can be eliminated in a diversified portfolio; also called company-specific or unsystematic risk.

diversifying Investing in more than one asset where the assets do not move proportionally in the same direction at the same time.

divestiture Decision by a firm to sell off some of its assets.

dividend extra Practice of paying an extra or special cash dividend in addition to the regular dividend.

dividend payout ratio Dividends per share divided by earnings per share, or total cash dividends divided by net income.

dividend per share Calculated by dividing total cash dividends to common stockholders by the number of shares of common stock outstanding. Reflects how much in cash dividends the investor will receive for owning one share of stock.

dividend reinvestment plan Plan in which stockholders can elect to have their cash dividends reinvested in order to purchase additional shares of common stock.

dividend valuation model Model that says the current market price of common stock is equal to the present value of all expected cash dividends discounted at the investor's required rate of return.

dividend yield Dividend per share divided by market price per share.

divisional opportunity cost of capital Cost of capital for a specific division of a firm, or for a set of projects that have been grouped together; the minimum required return for projects as risky as those faced by the division.

du Pont system   An accounting-based system of analysis that focuses on profitability, asset utilization, and financial leverage.

duration   The weighted average maturity of the cash flow stream for any financial asset or liability.

dutch auction preferred stock   Marketable security that is resold every 49 days. Firms bid (in terms of the lowest return they are willing to accept) for the security.

earnings after tax, EAT   Calculated by subtracting cost of goods sold; general, selling, and administrative expenses; depreciation; interest; and taxes from sales. Also called net income.

earnings available for common stockholders, EAC   Equals net income minus cash dividends on preferred stock.

earnings before interest and taxes, EBIT   Earnings before interest on debt and income taxes are deducted; also called net operating income.

earnings before tax, EBT   Earnings before income taxes are deducted.

earnings per share, EPS   Calculated by taking net income minus any cash dividends on preferred stock, and then dividing by the number of shares of common stock outstanding.

economic exposure   Extent to which the value of a firm will change due to an adjustment in exchange rates.

economic life   The length of time an asset will be economically useful.

economic order quantity, EOQ   The optimal inventory order size that minimizes total cost, which is the sum of the ordering plus the carrying costs.

effective annual interest rate   Actual interest rate earned (paid) after adjusting the nominal or stated interest rate for the frequency of compounding employed and the number of days assumed in a year, and then annualized.

effective interest rate   The per period rate of interest taking account of both the frequency of compounding and the nominal rate of interest.

efficient frontier   Set of portfolios that have the highest expected return at level of risk, and the lowest risk at each level of expected return.

efficient market   Market in which security prices adjust rapidly to the announcement of new information so that current market prices fully reflect all available information, including risk.

efficient market hypothesis   Proposition that states in an efficient market prices react quickly and unambiguously to new information.

efficient portfolio   A portfolio that provides the highest expected return for a given amount of risk, and the lowest risk for a given expected return.

electronic data interchange, EDI   Electronic transmission of virtually all of a firm's business correspondence.

electronic funds transfer   Payment electronically instead of using a paper-based check.

employee stockownership plan, ESOP   Employee trust fund to which a firm may contribute stock or cash at no direct cost to the firm.

EPS-EBIT analysis   A technique used when examining the effect of alternative capital structures on a firm's earnings per share.

EPS illusion   The increase in earnings per share that can result solely from a merger.

equilibrium   When the expected return equals the required rate of return, assets are neither overpriced nor underpriced.

equipment trust certificate   Form of security in which the trustee holds title to the assets until the security is paid off in full by the firm employing the financing.

equivalent annual cost   The net present value of the cost of a capital budgeting project divided by the present value of an annuity over the project's life.

equivalent annual NPV   The net present value of a capital budgeting project divided by the present value of an annuity over the project's life. This produces a yearly equivalent NPV that allows mutually exclusive projects with unequal lives to be compared.

equivalent loan method   Approach for evaluating leases by determining the amount of the loan which makes leasing equivalent to purchasing and financing with debt; makes the period-by-period after-tax cash flows the same from purchasing and financing with debt and from leasing.

Eurobond Bond underwritten by an international syndicate and sold primarily in countries other than the country in which the issue is denominated.

Eurocurrency system The worldwide system in which one country's currency is on deposit in another country.

Eurodollar U.S. dollars deposited in a U.S. branch bank located outside the United States or in a foreign bank.

European option A call or put option that can be exercised only at its expiration date.

event risk Risk caused by a drastic, unanticipated increase in a firm's debt or circumstances that causes the market price of its outstanding bonds to fall.

ex ante **(expected or required) rate of return** The return required or expected before the fact from investing in stocks, bonds, or real assets.

ex-dividend date The date set by the securities industry to determine who is entitled to receive a cash dividend, stock dividend, or stock split; four business days (Monday through Friday) before the record date.

ex post **(realized) rate of return** The return realized after the fact from investing in stocks, bonds, or real assets.

exchange ratio The relationship of the market value of the cash and securities offered by the bidding firm divided by the market value of the target firm in a proposed merger.

exercise (strike) price Price at which the owner of an option can buy (a call option) or sell (a put option) the underlying asset.

expansion project Capital budgeting project designed to improve the firm's ability to produce or market its goods by expanding its scale of operations.

expectations theory Theory that (implied) forward interest rates are unbiased estimates of expected future interest rates.

expectations theory of forward exchange rates Theory that the expected future spot rate of exchange at time t equals the current t-period forward exchange rate.

expected NPV The mean or average net present value obtained from a probability distribution of possible NPVs.

expected return on a portfolio, $\overline{K}_p$ The average of the expected returns for a group of assets weighted by the proportion of the portfolio devoted to each asset.

extension An out-of-court procedure by which creditors grant a debtor additional time before paying the full amount of past-due obligations.

factoring The sale of a firm's accounts receivables as a means of speeding up the inflow of funds, or to obtain a loan.

feasible set The set of all possible portfolios.

Fedwire Wire transfer system operated by the Federal Reserve Bank.

finance The money resources available to governments, firms, or individuals, and the management of these monies.

financial distress Situation in which a firm is having difficulty meeting its financial obligations.

financial distress costs The sum of the direct and indirect costs associated with bankruptcy and financial difficulties.

financial intermediaries Financial institutions such as banks, savings and loan associations, insurance companies, pension funds, and investment companies that assist in the transfer of funds from suppliers to demanders of funds.

financial lease Long-term lease that meets certain criteria as set by the Internal Revenue Service.

financial leverage The use of securities bearing a fixed charge to finance a portion of the firm's capital needs. Arises from using bonds, preferred stock, or leases.

financial management The acquisition, management, and financing of resources for firms by means of money, with due regard for prices in external economic markets.

financial manager Anyone directly engaged in making or implementing financial decisions.

financial markets Markets which deal with cash flows over time that facilitate bringing together the suppliers of funds and the demanders of funds.

financial risk A source of risk arising if the firm uses financing sources that have a fixed but prior claim relative to common stock.

firm commitment offering Primary market transaction where an investment banking firm guarantees the issuing firm a fixed price for the securities sold.

Fisher effect The nominal, or observed, risk-free interest rate is approximately equal to the real rate of interest plus expected inflation.

fixed charges coverage Earnings before interest and taxes plus lease expenses, divided by the sum of interest charges plus lease expenses.

float The length of time between when a check is written and when the recipient receives the funds and can draw upon them (has "good funds").

flotation cost Cost of issuing new stock or bonds. The difference between what the securities are sold to the public for and what the firm receives, plus any other costs such as accounting and legal fees.

flows-to-equity Present value of the after-tax and financing cost cash flows that accrue to equity investors discounted at their levered required rate of return, minus the net after-tax outlay made by the equity investors.

forced conversion Situation that can arise if the conversion value of a convertible security is greater than the call price; the issuer can force investors to convert by calling the security.

foreign bond Bond issued by a foreign borrower, but underwritten, sold, and denominated in one country.

foreign exchange rate The price of a unit of a country's currency relative to the price of a unit of another country's currency.

forward contract An arrangement to buy or sell a specified amount of a given asset on a specified future date, at a price set when the contract is entered into.

forward interest rate The rate of interest sometime in the future.

forward price Price agreed upon today for delivering or receiving an asset in the future.

forward rate of exchange The rate of exchange between two currencies as set today, but with the transaction to occur at some specified future date.

forward rate agreement, FRA An interest rate forward contract.

free cash flow theory Free cash flow is the cash flow above that needed to fund all positive NPV projects. Theory that a firm's stock price will increase with unexpected increases in payout to claimholders and decrease with unexpected decreases in the demand for funds via new issues.

fully registered Process whereby bonds are registered with respect to principal and interest. The registration agent keeps a list and mails out interest checks to the bondholders.

functional currency Primary currency in which a foreign subsidiary operates. The functional currency is used when accounting for the results of foreign operations.

future value The amount to which a lump sum, or series of cash flows, will grow by a given future date when compounded at a given interest rate.

future value factor, $FV_{k,n}$ Set of factors that for different rates, k, and periods, n, converts a present value into a larger future value.

future value factor for an annuity, $FVA_{k,n}$ Set of factors that for different rates, k, and periods, n, converts an annuity into a single future value.

futures contract Standardized contract to buy or sell a specified amount of a given asset on a specified future date.

futures options An option on a futures contract.

generally accepted accounting principles, GAAP Reporting requirements established by the Financial Accounting Standards Board that determine the rules by which firms produce accounting statements.

giro system Electronic payment system employed in many countries (often run through the postal system). Provides direct transfer from the payor to the payee.

going private Process by which a publicly owned firm whose common stock is actively traded becomes a privately held firm.

golden parachute Special employment contract granted to key executives in case of termination when a firm is acquired in a merger.

greenmail Practice whereby a stake in a target firm is purchased, and then sold back to the firm at some price above its current market value.

gross margin Net sales minus cost of goods sold.

gross profit margin Gross margin divided by net sales.

growth option An option to make an additional capital investment in the future that can only exist if some proposed or current project is funded.

growth rate, *g* Compound percentage growth rate (often, but not always, in cash dividends).

hard capital rationing Situation where positive net present value cannot be accepted due to the inability to raise external funds.

hedge ratio (delta) The number of units of an asset that are needed to hedge one unit of a liability.

hurdle rate The minimum acceptable return. It is the rate against which a project's internal rate of return is compared.

income bond Bond that will pay interest only to the extent it has the earnings to do so.

income statement Accounting statement that records the results of the firm's operations over some period of time, typically a year; shows revenues, expenses, and resulting net income (or loss).

incremental cash flows The cash flows form a new project or venture minus the cash flows on an existing project or venture.

incremental IRR approach Method used to evaluate mutually exclusive projects to ensure the same ranking is obtained using the internal rate of return, IRR, as with net present value, NPV.

indenture Legal agreement between the issuing firm and the bondholders. Provides the specific terms of the bond.

independent projects Capital budgeting projects whose cash flows are unrelated. Acceptance of one has no bearing on whether another project is accepted or rejected.

inflation A condition in which the price level increases; reflects changes in purchasing power.

initial investment The net after-tax cash outflow associated with a capital budgeting project to get it started. This outflow typically occurs immediately (at time t_0), but for large projects may be spread out over a number of time periods.

initial public offering, IPO The original sale of a firm's securities to the public. A primary market transaction.

installment interest A method of computing interest on the total principal for the total life of the loan; then, using annuities, a fixed payment per period is made, with part of it going to principal and part to interest.

interest The rate paid on money that is borrowed, or received on money lent; usually stated as a percentage rate per year.

interest rate cap Option, or contract, that places an upper limit on the interest rate in a floating rate financing instrument.

interest rate collar Option, or contract, that places both an upper and lower limit on the interest rate in a floating rate financing instrument.

interest rate floor Option, or contract, that places a lower limit on the interest rate in a floating rate financing instrument.

interest rate line Line that shows the relationship between dollars today and dollars in the next period. The slope is the per period rate of interest.

interest rate parity Theory that the interest rate differential between two countries is equal to the difference between the forward exchange rate and the spot exchange rate.

interest rate risk Change in market price of a bond as general interest rates change. Long-term bonds have more interest rate risk than short-term bonds, thereby leading to a maturity premium on long-term bonds.

interest rate swap Agreement between two parties to swap interest, but not principal, payments.

internal rate of return, IRR The discount rate that equates the present value of a series of cash inflows with the initial investment at time $t = 0$.

internally generated funds Those cash flows generated by the firm's operations that can be paid out to stockholders or reinvested in the business.

international bond   A bond sold outside the country of the borrower.

international Fisher effect   Theory that differential rates of inflation between two countries are reflected by differences in their respective risk-free rates.

interrelated projects   Capital budgeting projects in which the cash flows are intertwined so they cannot be examined separately.

in-the-money   Option that has value and is worth converting at the asset's current market price. A call option is in-the-money when the market price is above the exercise price; a put option is in-the-money when the current market price is less than the exercise price.

inventory turnover   Cost of goods sold dividend by inventory.

investment banking firm   A firm that serves as an intermediary between the financial markets and the demanders of capital. The investment banker specializes in underwriting and selling new securities, and advising corporate clients.

investment opportunities line   Line or schedule that shows possible capital investments ranked in order by their internal rate of return.

junk bond   Bond rated BB/Ba or below.

just-in-time   Inventory (and production) system where inventory is minimized by contracting with suppliers so deliveries are made, often daily or hourly, as needed for production.

lag   To collect (pay) late due to a strong (weak) domestic currency relative to a foreign currency.

lead   To collect (pay) early to take advantage of a weak (strong) domestic currency relative to a foreign currency.

lease   A rental agreement whereby the lessee obtains the use of an asset in exchange for an agreement to make payments to the lessor.

lessee   The user of a leased asset.

lessor   The owner of an asset that is leased to someone else.

letter of credit   An agreement sent by one party (generally a bank) to another, concern-

ing funds that will be made available. Usually a buyer supplies a letter of credit to the seller when they are unknown to each other.

leveraged buyout, LBO   Transaction in which a publicly owned firm is acquired by someone else (or a group), financed largely by borrowing.

leveraged lease   A lease in which the lessor generally supplies 20 to 30 percent of the funds and borrows the rest from a lender.

leveraging up   When a firm dramatically increases its amount of debt and at the same time shrinks the number of shares of common stock outstanding.

limited liability   Under the law, stockholders can lose no more than they have invested in a firm; they are not personally liable for the firm's debts.

line of credit   Agreement between a firm and a bank whereby the firm can borrow up to a maximum amount.

liquid assets   A firm's cash and marketable securities.

liquidation   The process of dissolving the firm by selling its assets.

liquidity preference theory   Theory that interest rates reflect both expectations about future interest rates and a maturity premium that compensates longer-term investors for greater risk.

liquidity premium   Additional return to compensate investors for additional transactions costs that arise due to investing in less liquid stocks or bonds.

lockbox   An arrangement whereby a firm has its customers make payments to a post office box. A local bank makes collections from the box, processes the checks, and forwards the money to the firm's central bank.

London Interbank Offered Rate, LIBOR   Interest rate that banks in different countries trade at.

long   Taking an ownership position in a financial or real asset.

long-term asset turnover   Sales divided by long-term (fixed) assets.

mail float   The time that elapses between when a customer places a check in the mail, and when the selling firm receives it and begins to process it.

majority voting   A system of electing the

board of directors whereby a simple majority is required to elect each director.

management buyout   Top management, usually with the assistance of an outside partner, takes all or part of a firm and turns it into a private firm.

marked-to-market   Daily settlement required with futures contracts where any gain or loss is immediately realized.

market for corporate control   Market where various management teams vie for the right to acquire and manage corporate activities and assets.

market portfolio   The portfolio of all risky assets. For the stock market, the New York Stock Exchange, NYSE, or Standard & Poor's 500 stock indices are often used as a proxy for the market portfolio.

market price of risk   The slope of the capital market line; the equilibrium expected reward per unit of risk.

market rate of interest   Current interest rate, or yield to maturity, on bonds based on the current market prices of bonds.

market segmentation theory   Theory that interest rates reflect different supply and demand conditions for bonds of various maturities.

marketable security   Short-term debt security that can be quickly converted into cash with little or no loss of principal.

matching principle   A guideline for working capital management that holds that temporary assets should be financed by temporary financing and permanent assets should be financed by permanent sources of financing.

material requirements planning, MRP   Centralized inventory and production system to coordinate orders and inventory with production needs.

maturity   The length (or term) to maturity for a bond expressed in years. At maturity, the borrower must redeem the bond at its par value.

maturity factoring   Short-term financing in which the factor purchases all of a firm's receivables and pays for them once a month.

maturity premium   Additional return required on longer-term bonds to compensate the investor for the grater price fluctuation as market interest rates change.

mean (expected value)   The weighted average of all possible outcomes, where the weights are the probabilities assigned to the expected outcomes.

merger   The acquisition of a firm, a division of a firm, or part or all of its assets by another firm.

modified accelerated cost recovery system, MACRS   Depreciation system set up by the Economic Recovery Tax Act of 1981 and modified by the Tax Reform Act of 1986.

modified internal rate of return, MIRR   The discount rate that equates the initial investment at time $t = 0$ with a project's terminal value, where the terminal value is the future value of the cash inflows, compounded at some required rate of return, k.

money market   Financial market in which funds are borrowed or lent for short periods of time (up to 1 year).

moral hazard   When asymmetric information exists so that information available to the firm's managers is superior to that available to outside investors. Managers can take unobservable self-interested actions that are detrimental to the principles.

mortgage bond   Bond secured by a lien on real property of the firm, such as buildings or equipment.

multiple internal rates of return   Condition that may arise when calculating the internal rate of return, IRR, if there are non-simple cash flows.

mutually exclusive projects   Capital budgeting alternatives of which only one need be selected.

negotiated short-term financing   Short-term financing such as bank loans or loans secured by accounts receivable or inventory that are negotiated and have a specific length.

net present value, NPV   The present value of the future cash flows, discounted at the opportunity cost of capital, or required rate of return, minus the initial investment.

net present value of leasing, NPV$_{lease}$ Method to decide whether an asset should be leased or purchased. The NPV equals the cost of the asset minus the present value of the after-tax lease payments and forgone IRS depreciation tax shield, where the after-tax cost of borrowing is used as the discount rate.

net profit margin   Net income divided by sales.

net working capital   current assets minus current liabilities.

no growth model   Form of the dividend valuation model in which no growth in future cash dividends is expected. Therefore, $P_0 = D_1/k_2$.

nominal interest rate   Stated or observed interest rate per year.

nondiversifiable risk   That part of an asset's total risk that cannot be eliminated in a diversified portfolio, also called systematic or market risk. Measured by beta.

nonsimple cash flow   A set of cash flows whose sign changes from positive to negative (or vice versa) more than once. For every change in sign, there may be one internal rate of return.

normal recovery period   Lives for tax purposes established under the modified accelerated cost recovery system, MACRS, of depreciation.

offsetting   Procedure for closing out a futures contract by buying of selling the same contract to offset the original position.

ongoing liquidity   A function of the expected inflows and outflows of cash through the firm over time.

operating cash flows   Cash flows after tax, expected to occur over the economic life of a capital investment project.

operating cycle   Part of the cash conversion cycle; equal to the days inventory plus the days sales outstanding.

operating lease   Term used in accounting to describe any lease that does not meet the criteria established for capital leases.

operating leverage   The use of assets which require fixed operating costs no matter what the level of sales.

operating profit   Net sales minus all expenses except interest and taxes, but before any adjustments. If there are no adjustments, operating profit equals earnings before interest and tax.

opportunity cost   The cost associated with an alternative or forgone opportunity bypassed.

opportunity cost of capital   Required return that is forgone by investing in real assets rather than in a similar risk investment, such as securities.

option   The right, but not the obligation, to buy or sell an underlying asset or undertake some financial opportunity at a fixed price during a specified time period.

ordinary annuity   A series of equal cash flows for a specified number of periods, with each cash flow occurring at the end of the period.

organized security exchange   Formal organizations that have a physical location and exist to bring together buyers and sellers of securities in the secondary market.

out-of-the-money   Option that does not have value at the asset's current market price. A call option is out-of-the-money when the market price is below the exercise price; a put option is out-of-the-money when the current price is higher than the exercise price.

overhanging issue   Convertible security whose conversion value is less than its call price, so that conversion cannot be forced.

over-the-counter, OTC, market   A market for securities based on telecommunications facilities that bring together buyers and sellers of securities. Many stocks and most bonds trade in the OTC market.

overpriced   Situation where the expected return is less than the required rate of return.

parallel (back-to-back) loans   Parent domestic firm loans to the domestic subsidary of a foreign parent firm, while the foreign parent firm loans to the foreign subsidary of the parent domestic firm. Accomplishes the same result as a swap of currencies.

par value (of common stock)   An arbitrary value employed for accounting purposes; has no economic significance except in rare circumstances.

par (maturity) value   The stated or face value of a bond, typically $1,000 per bond.

partial hedge   Position where the full amount of the risk exposure is not hedged; only a portion of the risk exposure is hedged

partnership   An unincorporated business owned by two or more individuals.

payables turnover   Cost of goods sold + general, selling and administrative expenses/accounts payable + salaries, benefits and payroll taxes payable.

payback period   The amount of time T (in years) for the expected cash inflows from a capital budgeting project to just equal the initial investment at time $t = 0$.

payment date   The date set by a firm when a cash dividend, stock split, or stock dividend will be paid.

pecking order theory   Capital structure and financing theory that suggests firms value the flexibility associated with financial slack; internally generated funds will be used first, then debt, and finally new common stock.

perfect hedge   Hedge in which any fluctuations in the underlying asset (or liability) can be completely offset by taking the opposite position in another liability (or asset).

percentage of sales method   Method of developing pro forma statements where historical percentages of items to sales or assets are used for projection purposes.

permanent current assets   The minimum current assets the firm always needs to have on hand to maintain its operations.

perpetuity   A stream of equal cash flows expected to continue forever; an infinite annuity.

pledging   Short-term borrowing where the loan is secured by the borrower's accounts receivable.

poison pill   Tactic used to make a merger more difficult. When triggered by a tender offer or the accumulation of a certain percent of ownership, target shareholders have the right to purchase additional shares, or to sell shares to the target at very attractive prices.

pooling of interests   An accounting method employed when firms merge. The assets of the two firms are added together on an account-by-account basis to form the combined firm's postmerger balance sheet.

portfolio   A combination of various assets, or securities, owned for investment.

portfolio beta   A weighted average of the betas for the assets in the portfolio, where the weights are determined by the proportion devoted to each asset.

preauthorized check   A check that does not require the signature of the person on whose account it is drawn.

preemptive right   A provision that allows current common stockholders to purchase additional shares offered by the firm before they are offered to outsiders.

preferred stock   Stock that has a prior but limited claim on assets and income before common stock, but after debt.

premium (on a bond)   Difference between the current market price of a bond selling above its par value and its par value.

present value   The value today of a given future lump sum, or series of cash flows, when discounted at a given discount rate.

present value factor, $PV_{k,n}$ Set of factors that for different rates, k, and periods, n, converts an annuity into its present value.

present value factor for an annuity, $PVA_{k,n}$ Set of factors that for different rates, k, and periods, n, converts an annuity into its present value.

present value of growth opportunities, PVGO   Value created by the presence of profitable future investment opportunities that are expected to return more than the required rate of return.

present value profile   A graph that plots the relationship between a project's net present value and the discount rate employed.

price/earnings ratio, P/E   Market price per share of common stock divided by earnings per share.

primary market   Market in which financial assets are originally sold, with the proceeds going to the issuing firm (or government).

prime rate   An administered interest rate the bank's best customers are supposedly charged. Most customers will pay more than prime, such as "prime plus 2 percent."

private market purchase   Purchase by a firm of its own bonds (or stock) directly from an institutional investor.

private placement   Financing directly between a demander of funds and a supplier of funds that bypasses the public.

pro forma statements   Forecasted accounting statements; typically an income statement and a balance sheet.

probability The chance of a single event's occurrence. A probability distribution is a listing of all possible outcomes and their chances of occurrence.

probability of success Likelihood that the net present value will be positive when simulation is employed.

processing float The length of time it takes a firm to process and deposit a customer's check after receiving it.

profitability index The present value of future cash flows, discounted at the required rate of return divided by the initial investment for the project.

project debt capacity Incremental contribution that a capital investment makes to the firm's ability to borrow. As firms add more profitable opportunities, they generate more future cash inflows leading to the ability to service more debt.

project financing Capital investment which is often financed largely with debt; the claim of the providers of capital is against the cash flows of the project rather than against the firm as a whole.

proprietorship An unincorporated business owned by one individual.

protective covenants Provisions written into bonds or loan agreements.

protective liquidity The ability to adjust rapidly to unforeseen cash demands, and to have backup sources of cash available.

proxy fight An attempt by an outside group to obtain control of the firm's board of directors. This is done by soliciting proxies, which are authorizations given by a stockholder that lets someone else exercise the stockholder's voting rights at a stockholder meeting.

public offering Sale of securities to the general public by a firm; can be either a general cash offer or a rights offering.

purchase An accounting method employed when firms merge. The assets of the target firm are revalued to their fair market value, and any remaining difference between the purchase price and the revalued assets is recorded as goodwill.

purchasing power parity Theory that the expected differential rate of inflation for two countries is equal to the expected spot rate of exchange t-periods in the future divided by the current spot rate of exchange.

pure play firm Firm in the same line of business with the same operating risk as a division of a firm.

put option The right, but not the obligation, to sell an asset at a stated price within a specified time period.

quick ratio Current assets minus inventory divided by current liabilities.

receivables pattern Method for analyzing a firm's receivables calculated by determining the percentage of credit sales still outstanding in the month of the sale and in subsequent months.

receivables turnover Sales/accounts receivable.

record date The date determined by a firm when the stockholder books are closed to determine who the current stockholders are.

red herring Preliminary registration statement that can be distributed when a proposed security offering is being reviewed by the Securities and Exchange Commission.

refunding Process of replacing an old bond issue with a new one; often done if market interest rates have dropped so that the firm can save on interest costs.

registration statement Statement filed with the Securities and Exchange Commission when a firm plans to issue securities to the public.

regulatory project Capital budgeting project that is required for which no measurable cash inflows are expected to occur.

reinvestment rate risk Risk that arises when a bond is called or matures and investors have to reinvest in a lower coupon interest rate bond.

reinvoicing center Center set up through which all intrafirm transfers involving more than one currency flow. Allows firms to net out transfers, thereby helping to deal with exchange rate exposure.

reorganization An in-court procedure under Chapter 11 of the Bankruptcy Reform Act of 1978 during which the firm is revitalized.

replacement chain By finding the common life this procedure allows the net present values for mutually exclusive projects with unequal lives to be compared.

replacement project Capital budgeting project that replaces existing assets that are physically or economically obsolete.

replicating portfolio Process of valuing an option by taking a levered position in the underlying asset.

repurchase agreement Sale of government securities by a bank or a government securities dealer with a simultaneous agreement to repurchase them in a certain number of days at a specified price.

required (rate of) return The minimum return necessary to attract a firm or investor to make an investment.

residual theory of dividends A theory that specifies firms should first make all their capital budgeting decisions. After the necessary financing has been secured any remaining internally generated funds would be paid out as cash dividends.

retained earnings An equity account on the balance sheet that reflects the sum of the firm's net income (losses) over its life, less all cash dividends paid.

return For any period, the sum of cash dividends, interest, and so forth, and any capital appreciation or loss (the difference between the beginning and ending market values).

return on equity Net income divided by stockholders' equity; or return on total assets divided by 1 minus the total debt to total asset ratio.

return on total assets Net income divided by total assets; or net profit margin times total asset turnover.

reverse split An action to decrease the number of shares or common stock outstanding and simultaneously increase their par value.

rights offering Means of selling common stock whereby current stockholders have the first opportunity of buying the issue.

risk The degree of uncertainty associated with something happening, or a situation in which there is exposure to possible loss. Frequently used interchangeably with the term uncertainty.

risk-free rate, k_{RF} The interest rate on assets that are viewed as being free of any risk premium. In nominal terms, the risk-free rate equals the real rate of interest plus an inflation premium.

risk-neutral Approach employed for valuing options; in a risk-free world the return on the option is equal to the risk-free rate.

risk premium The difference between the required rate of return on an asset and the risk-free rate.

risk profile Line that indicates how the market value of a firm is influenced by changes in interest rates, foreign exchange rates or commodities prices.

rolling forecast Process in which cash budgets are updated by dropping the most recent period and adding another period in the future.

rolling hedge Long term hedge using futures contracts that involves moving the hedge forward as near-term contracts expire and reinvesting in longer term contracts.

sale and leaseback An arrangement arising when a firm sells an asset to another and simultaneously agrees to lease the property back for a specified period of time.

scenario analysis The process of simultaneously changing a number of input variables to see what the effect is on the outcome.

seasonal (temporary) current assets The difference between the firm's total current assets and its permanent current assets.

seasonal dating Credit arrangement where goods are shipped, but payment is not due until the time the goods have been sold.

secondary market Market for financial assets that have already been issued. This market includes both the organized security exchanges and the over-the-counter market.

security market line, SML Graphic representation of the capital asset pricing model, CAPM. Shows the relationship between nondiversifiable risk (beta) and required rates of return for individual assets or portfolios of assets.

sensitivity analysis An analysis of the effect of changing one of the input variables (or assumptions) at a time to ascertain how much the result is affected.

separation theorem The choice of investments is independent of consumption preferences. All investors accept or reject the same projects based on net present value.

sequential analysis   Method of analyzing capital budgeting projects when risk, and therefore the opportunity cost, varies over the life of the project.

serial bonds   Bonds issued at the same time, but with different years to maturity. Typically, the coupon interest rate may vary depending on the maturity.

service lease   A short-term lease that can be canceled at any time after proper notice has been given to the lessor.

shelf registration   Process whereby large firms can gain prior approval from the Securities and Exchange Commission for public offerings of securities to be issued over the next 2 years.

short   The mirror image of owning, or being long in an asset. Selling, or promising to deliver an asset in the future.

sight draft   An order to pay on sight.

signaling   Process of conveying information through a firm's actions.

simple cash flow   A sequence of cash flows where there is only one change in sign (from positive to negative, or vice versa). There will be no more than one internal rate of return.

simple interest   Interest is received only on the initial principal; it is not compounded.

simulation   Method of calculating the probability distribution of possible outcomes from a project.

sinking fund   Required payments to retire part of a bond or preferred stock issue before maturity.

smoothed residual dividend policy   Cash dividend policy whereby the firm sets a long-run target dividend payout ratio and ties it to a specific dividend per share, while fluctuating around its target capital structure.

soft capital rationing   Situation where positive net present value projects are not accepted due to managerial imposed internal constraints.

spontaneous short-term financing   Short-term financing that tends to expand (contract) as the firm's current assets expand (contract).

spot interest rate   Interest rate today.

spot price   Price agreed upon for delivering or receiving an asset today.

spot rate of exchange   The current rate of exchange between two currencies for immediate delivery.

spreadsheet program   Computer program that allows data to be manipulated.

stakeholder   Parties in addition to stockholders, management and creditors that have in interest in the firm. Includes employees, customers, suppliers, and the community at large.

stand-alone principle   A capital budgeting project should be evaluated by comparing it with the return that could be secured by investing in a similar risk project.

standard deviation, σ   A statistical measure of the spread of a distribution from its mean or expected value. The square root of the variance.

statement of cash flows   Accounting statement that reports the flow of cash into and out of the firm during the year.

stock dividend   A means of issuing additional shares of common stock. From an accounting standpoint, it involves a transfer from retained earnings to the common stock and additional paid-in capital accounts.

stock split   An action to increase the number of shares of common stock outstanding and simultaneously reduce their par value.

stockholder wealth maximization   An objective of the firm that helps maximize the total market value of the firm. To maximize the value of stockholder claims on the firm by maximizing the market value of the firm, S, or per share price, P_0

strategic NPV   Value of the original NPV plus the follow-on call or put option.

stretching payables   Practice of not paying an account by its net date, but taking longer to pay the bill.

strip hedge   Hedging over time by taking an offsetting position in each of the future periods in which the hedge is required.

subordinated debenture   Unsecured long-term borrowing of the firm that has a lower claim than other unsecured claims.

substitute projects   Two or more capital budgeting projects where the acceptance of all of them results in total cash flows less than the sum of the individual cash flows.

sunk cost   Cost that has already occurred and cannot be altered; accordingly, it does not influence subsequent decisions.

supermajority   Provision requiring more than 50 percent (often two-thirds or even 80 percent) approval when a merger is approved.

syndicate   A group of investment banking firms that have agreed to cooperate in purchasing and then reselling a security issue.

synergism   The idea that the value of two firms is greater than the sum of their separate values; the "2 + 2 = 5 effect."

systemwide project   Capital budgeting projects where all of them have to be accepted or rejected as a package, because they are 100 percent complementary projects.

target capital structure   The planned-for capital structure, or the debt ÷ market value of equity ratio, around which the firm attempts to fluctuate.

target firm   A firm that is being pursued or is bought out in a merger.

taxes   A fee levied on individuals or firms by a federal, state or local government unit.

tender offer   An offer by a firm or group directly to stock- or bondholders to purchase their stock or bonds at a certain price.

term loan   Loans with maturities of 1 to 10 years that are paid off by periodic payments over the life of the loan. The payment is fixed at a given dollar amount per period, with more going to pay interest in the early payments and more to pay principal in the later payments.

term structure   The relationship between the yield to maturity and the length to maturity for bonds that are equally risky.

terminal cash flow   The net after-tax cash inflow or outflow that occurs when a capital budgeting project is terminated.

time draft   A draft that must be paid at a stated future date.

times interest earned   Earnings before interest and taxes divided by interest charges.

total asset turnover   Sales divided by total assets.

total debt to total assets   A ratio that indicates how much of the firm's funds are being supplied by its creditors.

total risk   For a security or portfolio, total risk is measured by its standard deviation.

trade acceptance   Time draft drawn upon and accepted by a firm.

trade credit   Interfirm credit that arises when one firm sells to another through a credit sale. It appears as an account receivable on the seller's books and as an account payable on the buyer's records.

transaction exposure   Extent to which a given exchange rate change will impact the value of foreign exchange transactions into which the firm has already entered.

transaction loan   Bank loan made for a specific purpose for a predetermined length of time.

transactions costs   Any explicit or implicit cost connected with making a transaction. It could be a commission associated with buying or selling assets (explicit), or the time spent reading and interpreting information (implicit).

transit float   The length of time it takes for a check to clear through the banking system until the recipient can draw upon it (have "good funds").

translation exposure   The accounting exposure when exchange rates change.

treasurer   The individual in a firm who is normally responsible for seeing that funds are obtained as needed, for making sure cash is collected and invested, for maintaining relations with banks and other financial institutions, and for seeing that bills are paid on time.

Treasury bill   Short-term security issued by the U.S. government. Issued weekly, T-bills mature in 1 year or less and are often used as a proxy for risk-free rate.

uncertainty   A situation in which the probabilities can be ascertained only subjectively. In finance, the terms risk and uncertainty are often used interchangeably.

underinvestment   Occurs when a firm fails to take all growth opportunities (i.e., all positive net present value opportunities) because they primarily benefit the firm's bondholders (or other creditors), not the firm's stockholders.

underpriced   Situation where the expected return is greater than the required rate of return.

underpricing   Issuance of securities below their fair market value.

underwritten The process whereby an investment banking firm purchases securities from an issuing firm and then immediately resells them.

variable rate (loan) Loan on which the interest rate is not fixed, but fluctuates based on the prime rate, LIBOR, or some other rate.

variance, σ^2 A statistical measure of the spread of a distribution from its mean or expected value.

venture capital Early stage high-risk financing for smaller, or start-up, firms.

warrant A long-lived call option to purchase a fixed number of shares of common stock at a predetermined price during some specified time period.

weighted average cost of capital The cost of the last dollar of additional funds secured; the firm's opportunity cost of capital or required return for projects of average risk.

white knight The friendly third firm in a situation in which one firm (the potential bidding firm) is attempting to take over a target firm.

white squire Friendly firm where a large percentage of another firm's common stock is placed to ward off any potential takeover by a third firm.

wire transfer Means of transferring money between banks using the Federal Reserve's wire system or a commercial bank wire system.

working capital The firm's current assets and current liabilities.

yield curve A plot of the relationship between yield to maturity and length (or term) to maturity for equally risky bonds.

yield to call, YTC The compound return earned on a bond purchased at a given price and held until it is called.

yield to maturity, YTM The compound return earned on a bond if it is purchased at a given price and held to maturity. The rate of return that equates the present value of the anticipated interest payments and principal to its current market value.

zero balance account System whereby the bank and the firm create a demand deposit account that contains no funds. Each day the bank transfers enough funds into the account to meet all checks presented for payment.

zero-coupon bond Long-term bond issued at a discount from its par value, for which interest each period is simply the difference in the market value at the beginning and end of the period.

Index

Boldface page numbers indicate definitions. Page numbers followed by n indicate footnotes.

Capital Budgeting (7–10)

The *after-tax operating cash flow,* where $CFBT$ is the cash flow before-tax in any period t, T is the firm's marginal tax rate, and Dep is the depreciation in period t, is

$$CF_t = CFBT_t - \text{taxes}_t = CFBT_t(1 - T) + Dep_t(T)$$

When cash flows for periods through n are discounted at the opportunity cost k, and CF_0 is the initial cash outlay, the *net present value* is

$$NPV = \sum_{t=1}^{n} \frac{CF_t}{(1 + k)^t} - CF_0$$

The unknown rate, or *internal rate of return,* given cash flows at $t = 0$ through n, is

$$\sum_{t=1}^{n} \frac{CF_t}{(1 + IRR)^t} = CF_0$$

The *strategic, or total, net present value,* of a proposed project is

strategic NPV = original NPV + value of follow-on opportunity

Capital Structure (11)

In the absence of taxes *Modigliani-Miller's Proposition I* says that the value of the firm is determined by capitalizing its (economic) earnings before interest and taxes, $EBIT$, by the required return on equity, k_s^U, so that

$$V_L = S_L + B = \frac{EBIT}{k_s^U} = V_U$$

With no taxes *Modigliani-Miller's Proposition II* says that the return demanded by levered equity owners depends on the required return on the unlevered equity plus a risk premium based on the difference in the return on unlevered stock, k_s^U, and bonds, k_b, adjusted for the amount of debt employed, so that

$$k_s^L = k_s^U + (k_s^U - k_b)(B/S_L)$$

The *Modigliani-Miller value of a levered firm with taxes* is equal to the value of an unlevered firm plus a debt tax shield, or

$$V_L = V_U + TB$$

Once *Modigliani-Miller's Proposition II is modified for corporate taxes,* the cost of equity capital becomes

$$k_s^L = k_s^U + (k_s^U - k_b)(1 - T)(B/S_L)$$

When *Modigliani-Miller's Proposition I is modified for corporate taxes* the value of the levered common stock is

$$S_L = \frac{(EBIT - k_b B)(1 - T)}{k_s^L}$$

(continued on next page)

Miller's model, including corporate taxes and personal taxes on stock, T_{ps}, and on debt, T_{pb}, specifies the value of the levered firm as

$$V_L = V_U + \left[1 - \frac{(1 - T)(1 - T_{ps})}{(1 - T_{pb})} \right] B$$

The *value of the levered firm with financial distress and agency costs* is

$$V_L' = V_U + \begin{array}{c} \text{present value} \\ \text{of tax} \\ \text{savings} \end{array} - \left(\begin{array}{c} \text{present value} \\ \text{of financial} \\ \text{distress costs} \end{array} + \begin{array}{c} \text{present value} \\ \text{of agency} \\ \text{costs} \end{array} \right)$$

Adjusted Present Value and Flows-to-Equity (14)
The *adjusted present value* differs from net present value in that it discounts the operating cash flows at the unlevered cost of equity capital and then considers the benefits of financing as a separate step, so that

$$APV = \text{base-case } NPV \text{ of project's operating cash flow discounted at } k_s^U$$
$$+ \text{ present value of financing benefits}$$

The *flows-to-equity* approach deals with the after-operating-and-financing cash flows discounted at the levered cost of equity capital, where

$$FTE = \text{present value of after-tax cash flow accruing to the stockholders discounted at } k_s^L$$
$$- \text{ net outlay by stockholders}$$

Debt Financing (16)
The *payment under an amortized loan* of *PMT* per period, where the loan is of size PV_0, when the per period rate is k and there are n periods, is

$$PMT = PV_0 \left/ \left[\frac{1}{k} - \frac{1}{k(1 + k)^n} \right] \right.$$

The *value of a zero-coupon bond* with a maturity value of par, with n periods to maturity, when the discount rate is k_b, is

$$B_0 = \text{par}/(1 + k_b)^n$$

Leasing (18)
Ignoring incremental operating expenses and any resale value, the *net present value of leasing* relative to purchasing, where the cost of the leased asset is *CLA*, the per period lease rate is L for n periods with the first payment made today, the tax rate is T, the after-tax cost of debt is k_i, and the per period depreciation is *Dep*, is

$$NPV_{\text{lease}} = CLA_0 - \left\{ \left[\sum_{t=1}^{n} \frac{L_t(1 - T)}{(1 + k_i)^t} \right] (1 + k_i) + \sum_{t=1}^{n} \frac{Dep_t(T)}{(1 + k_i)^t} \right\}$$

Short-Term (20–22)
The *benefits for making cash and marketable security decisions* depend on the change in time, Δt, the transaction size, *TS*, the interest rate, *I*, and the tax rate T, so that

$$\Delta B = (\Delta t)(TS)(I)(1 - T)$$